한국성경주석총서

고 린 도 후 서

강 창 희 지음

도서출판 횃불

Korea Bible Commentary Series

The Second Epistle to the Corinthians

Chang Hee Kang Ph.D.

Torch Press

이 책을 나를 신앙으로 길러 주시고
기도로 도와주신 나의 어머니
신동일(申東日, 1922년 -) 권사님께 드립니다.

편집인 서문

한국복음주의신학회는 한국교회의 복음주의신학을 발전시키는데 크게 공헌한 바 있다. 특히 한국복음주의신학회가 계획하고 진행시키고 있는 한국성경주석총서는 현재뿐만 아니라 미래의 한국교회를 위해서 나침반 역할을 할 귀한 복음주의 신학의 자료가 될 것이다.

금번에 한국성경주석총서의 한 부분으로 강창희 박사의 고린도후서 주석이 출간된 것을 진심으로 기쁘게 생각한다. 강박사는 고린도후서에 관한 여러 가지 이론들을 학문적으로 제시하고 그 중에서 가장 올바른 입장으로 독자들을 안내한다. 그리고 강박사는 본문을 주석할 때 성경의 정확무오성을 근거로 많은 자료들을 활용하여 본문의 내용을 알기 쉽게 주석하였다. 원래 한국성경주석총서는 성경본문의 원뜻을 잘 밝혀서 현대인들이 알기 쉽게 읽을 수 있도록 계획된 주석서이다. 본 주석은 앞으로 고린도후서를 더 심층적으로 연구하기를 원하는 학자들과 신학도들, 그리고 성도들에게 귀한 안내서가 될 것이다.

본서의 출판을 위해 여러 가지 역경이 있었음에도 불구하고 큰 뜻을 가지고 계속 수고해 주신 기독교 선교횃불재단의 이형자 원장님과 여러 임직원들에게 깊은 감사의 마음을 드린다. 본서가 그 원래의 계획대로 하나님의 뜻을 더 많은 사람들에게 나타내는 역할을 하며 이로 인해 한국교회가 하나님의 말씀 위에 더 든든히 서 갈 수 있게 되기를 기도한다.

신약 편집인 박형용

간 행 사

선교 21세기를 맞이한 한국교회가 하나님의 축복 가운데 놀라운 성장을 이루었지만 우리 손으로 복음주의 입장에서 성경을 해석하는 주석총서를 내지 못한 안타까움을 감출 수 없었습니다. 그리하여 복음주의 신학과 신앙을 같이하는 믿음의 동역자들이 뜻을 모아 한국성경주석총서를 발간하기로 결의하고 집필자와 편집위원들을 선정해 놓았지만 강의와 연구 등에 분주한 나머지 별다른 진전 없이 여러 해를 보내고 말았습니다.

그간 편집위원도 바뀌고 한국복음주의신학회 임원진도 여러 번 교체되었으나 성경주석을 발간해야 하겠다는 결의는 변함없었습니다. 한국교회뿐 아니라 복음적인 세계교회가 함께 지향해야 할 방향을 제시할 필요를 느꼈고 올바른 성경 해석과 적용을 통해 성도들과 교회가 더욱 건실하게 성장하도록 돕기 위하여 성경주석 발간 작업을 계속해 왔습니다. 집필자는 물론 편집위원들의 노고에 감사를 드리며 이익 추구의 차원을 떠나 선교적 사명에 동참하는 뜻으로 본 주석총서의 출판을 맡아주신 횃불측에 깊은 감사를 드립니다.

복음주의 신학의 최근 동향을 고찰하면서 학문적 연구와 자료를 수집하고 비판하면서 복음주의 계통의 교인과 신학생 그리고 목회자들이 마음놓고 펴 들 수 있는 성경주석을 발간하게 된 데 대하여 하나님께 감사를 드립니다.

목회자들과 신학생은 물론 평신도들까지도 이해할 수 있도록 배려한 본 총서가 한국교회 강단을 기름지게 하고 개인의 삶에 부요함을 가져오는 복된 총서가 되리라 기대합니다. 귀한 성경주석총서가 계속되어 출간될 수 있도록 성도 여러분의 기도와 성원을 부탁합니다. 감사합니다.

한국복음주의신학회한국복음주의신학회

차 례

고린도후서 개 론

고린도후서 주석 (내용 분해)

약 어

AB	Anchor Bible
ABD	*The Anchor Bible Dictionary*, ed. D. N. Freedman (6 vols.; New York: Doubleday, 1992)
ABR	*Australian Biblical Review*
AGJU	*Arbeiten zur Geschichte des antiken Judentums und des Urchristentums*
ANF	The Ante-Nicene Fathers
ANRW	*Aufstieg und Niedergang der römischen Welt. Geschichte und Kultur Roms im Spiegel der neueren Foschung. ed. H. Temporitni and W. Haase, Berlin and New York, 1972 -.*
ASV	American Standard Version
ATANT	Abhandlungen zur Theologie des Alten und Neuen Testaments
AUS	*Andrew University Seminary Studies*
ASV	American Standard Version(1901)
AV	Authorized Version
BAGD	W. Bauer, A Greek-English Lexicon of the New Testament and Other Early Christian Literature, ed. W. F. Arndt, F. W. Gingrich, and F. W. Danker (Chicago: University of Chicago, 1979)
BBB	Bonner Biblische Beiträge
BEThL	Bibliotheca Ephemeridum Theologicarum Lovaniensium

BHT	Beiträge zur historischen Theologie
Bib	*Biblica*
BJRL	*Bulletin of the John Rylands University Library of Manchester*
BZ	*Biblische Zeitschrift*
BZNW	Beihefte zur *ZNW*
CBQ	*Catholic Biblical Quarterly*
ConB	Coniectanea biblica
ConNT	*Coniectanea neotestamentica*
CTR	*Criswell Theological Review*
ÉBib	Études Bibliques
ESV	English Standard Version
ETr	English Translation
EvT	*Evangelische Theologie*
FRLANT	Forschungen zur Religion und Literatur des Alten und Neuen Testaments
FS	Festschrift
GNB	Good News Bible
HNT	Handbuch zum Neuen Testament
HTR	*Harvard Theological Review*
IB	*Interpreter's Bible*
ICC	International Critical Commentary
JAARSup	*Journal of the American Academy of Rligion Supplement*
JB	The Jerusalem Bible
JBL	*Journal of Biblical Literature*
JETS	*Journal of the Evangelical Theological Society*

JJS	*Journal of Jewish Studies*
JSNT	*Journal for the Study of the New Testament*
JSOT	*Journal for the Study of the New Testament*
JTS	*Journal of Theological Studies*
KJV	King James Version
MNTC	Moffatt NT Commentary
NANF	The Nicene and Ante-Nicene Fathers
NAG	*Nachrichten von der Akademie der Wissenschaften in Göttingen*
NCB	New Century Bible
NEB	The New English Bible
NICNT	New International Commentary on the New Testament
NIV	New International Version
NPNF	The Nicene and Post-Nicene Fathers
NovT	*Novum Testamentum*
NovTSup	Novum Testamentum, Suplement
NTS	*New Testament Studies*
OPT	*Old Testament Pseudepigrapha*
REB	The Revised English Bible, 1989
PG	*Patrologia Graeca*, ed, J. -P Migne (Paris: Migne, 1857-66)
RB	*Revue biblique*
RsPhTh	*Revue des sciences philosophiques et théologuiques*
RSR	*Recherches de sciences religieuse*
RSV	Revised Standard Version
RV	Revised Version, 1881-1885
RTR	*The Reformed Theological Review*

SANT Studien zum Alten und Neuen Testament

SBL Society of Biblical Literature Symposium Series

SBLDS SBL Dissertation Series

SBLSBS SBL Sources for Biblical Study

SBT *Studies in Biblical Theology*

ScEs *Science et esprit*

SE *Studia Evangelica*

SJT *Scottish Journal of Theology*

SNTSMS Society for New Testament Studies Monograph Series

SO *Symbolae osloeness*

ST *Studia Theologica*

StBibT *Studia Biblica et Theologica*

Str-B H. Strack and P. Billerbeck, *Kommentar zum Neuen Testament*

TBü Theologische Bücherei

TDNT G. Kittel and G. Friedrich eds. *Theological Dictionary of the New Testament*

TEV Today's English Version

TSK *Theologische Studien und Kritiken*

TNTC Tyndale New Testament Commentary

TynB Tyndale Bulletin

TZ *Theologische Zeitschrift*

WBC Word Biblical Commentary

WMANT Wissenschaftliche Monographien zum Alten und Neuen Testament

WUNT Wissenschaftliche Untersuchungen zum Alten und Neuen

	Testasment
ZNW	*Zeitschrift für die neutestamentliche Wissenschaft*
ZTK	*Zeitschrift für Theologie und Kirche*

사본 약어는 Nestle-Aland의 약어를 따르고 있다. 잘 알려진 서적, 영어 번역 성경, 그리고 저널(journal=정기간행물)은 일반적으로 쓰는 약자를 그대로 썼고, 잘 알려지지 않은 저널은 원래의 저널 명칭을 그대로 썼다. 혹 명시되지 않은 약어들은 마틴이나 트롤의 주석, 그리고 *TDNT* I, xvii-xl 에 나타난 약어를 따라 썼으므로 이를 참고하기를 바란다.

참고문헌

Alexander, W. M. "St. Paul' s Infirmity," *The Expository Times* 10 (1904) 469-73, 545-48.

Allo, E. B. *Saint Paul: premiere épître aux Corinthians*. ÉBid. Paris: Gabalda, 1925.

_______. B. *Saint Paul: seconde épître aux Corinthians*. ÉBid. Paris: Gabalda, 1936, 1956.

Ashcraft, Morris. "Paul' s Understanding of Apostleship" *Review and Expositor* 55 (1958) 400-412.

Aune, D. E. "Magic in Early Christianity," in *Aufstieg und Niedergang der roemischen Welt*, 2/26.2, ed. H. Temporini and W. Haase. Berlin & New York: Walter de Gruyter, 1981, 1507-57.

Avram, Wes. "2 Corinthians 4:1-18," *Interpretation* 55 (2001) 70-73.

Babel, Henry. *The Reformation: Many Men with One Idea*. Geneva: Foundation of Les Clefs de Saint-Pirre, 1985.

Bachmann, P. *Der zweite Brief des Paulus an die Korinther*. Kommentar zum Neuen Testament VIII. Leipzig: Verlagsbuchhandlung Werner Scholl, 1918.

Bammel, E. "Herkunft und Funktion der Traditionselemente in 1 Kor 15:1-11," *ThZ* 11 (1955), 401-19.

Barclary, W. *The Letters to the Corinthians*. Philadelphia: Westminster Press, 1975.

Barnett, P. *The Second Epistle to the Corinthians.* Grand Rapids: Wm. B. Eerdmans Publishing Company, 1997.

Barré, M. L. "Qumran and the 'Weakness' of Paul," *CBQ* 42 (1980) 216-27.

Barrett, C. K. *Essays on Paul.* Philadelphia: Westminster/London: SPCK, 1982.

______. *A Commentary on the First Epistle to the Corinthians.* Harper' s NT Commentaries. New York: Harper & Row, Publishers, 1968.

______. *A Commentary on the Second Epistle to the Corinthians.* Harper' s NT Commentaries. New York: Harper & Row, Publishers, 1973.

______. *The Signs of an Apostle.* Philadelphia: Fortress, 1972.

______. "New Testament Eschatology I: Jewish and Pauline Eschatology," *SJT* 6 (1953) 136-55.

______. "Cephas and Corinth," in *Essayns on Paul.* Philadelphia: Westminster/London: SPCK, 1982.

______. "Paul' s Opponents in II Corinthians", *NTS* 17 (1970-71) 233-254.

______. "shaliaḥ and Apostle," *Donum Gentilicium: New Testament Essays in Honour of David Daube*, ed. C. K. Barrett, E. Bammel, and W. D. Davies. Oxford: Clarendon Press, 1978.

______. "Titus," *Essayns on Paul.* Philadelphia: Westminster/London: SPCK, 1982.

______. "*ΨΕΥΔΑΠΟΕΤΟΛΟΙ* (2 Cor 11,13)" in *Mélanges Bibliques en Hommage au R. P. Béda Rigaux*, ed. A. Descamps and A. de Halleux. Gembloux: Duculot, 1970, 377-96; reprinted in *Essays on Paul.* London: SPCK 1982, 87-107.

______. "Christianity at Corinth," *BJRL* 46 (1964) 269-97. Reprinted in *Essays on Paul.* London: SPCK, 1982, 1-27.

Bates, W. H. "The Integrity of 2 Corinthians," *NTS* 12 (1965-66) 50-69.

Batey, R. "Paul' s Interaction with the Corinthians," *JBL* 84 (1965) 139-46.

________. *New Testament Nuptial Imagery.* Leiden: Brill, 1971.

Bauckham, R. J. "The Worship of Jesus in Apocalyptic Christianity," *NTS* 27 (1980-81) 322-41.

Baumert, N. *Täglich Sterben und Auferstehen: Der Literalsinn von 2 Kor 4,12-5,10.* SANT 34. München: Kösel-Verlag, 1973.

Baumgarten, J. *Paulus und die Apokalyptik. Die Auslegund apokalyptischer Überlieferung in den echten Paulusbriefen.* WMANT 44. Neukirchen-Vluyn: Neukirchener Verlag, 1975.

Baur, F. C. *Paul: the Apostle of Jesus Christ.* ETr. Zeller, E. London: Williams & Norgate, 1876.

Beale, G. K. "The Old Testament Background of Reconciliation in 2 Corinthians 5-7 and its Bearing on the Literary Problem of 2 Corinthians 6:14-7:1" , *NTS* 35 (1989-90) 550-81.

Behm, J. "*καρδία*," in *TDNT* 3:609-916.

Beker, J. Christiaan. *Paul the Apostle: The Triumph of God in Life and Thought.* Philadelphia: Fortress Press, 1980.

Belser, J. E. *Der zweite Brief des Apostels Paulus an die Korinther.* Freiburg: J. C. B. Mohr, 1910.

Bengel, J. A. *Gnomon of the New Testament III: Romans, I and II Corinthians*, ETr. Edingburgh: T. & T. Clark, 1863.

Bernard, J. H. "The Second Epistle to the Corinthians," *The Expositor' s Greek Testament*, ed. Nicoll, W. R. London: Hodder & Stoughton,

1882.

Betz, O (ed.). *Abraham unser Vater: Festschrift für O. Michel,* Leiden: Brill, 1963.

Betz, H. D. "2 Cor. 6:14-7:1: An Anti-Pauline Fragment?" *JBL* 92 (1973) 88-108.

______. "Eine Christus-Aretalogie bei Paulus (2 Kor 12,7-10)," *ZTK* 66 (1969) 288-305.

______. "Apostle," in *ABD*, ed. D. N. Freedman. New York: Doubleday, 1992, 1:309-11.

______. *2 Corinthians 8 and 9: A Commentary on Two Administrative Letters of the Apostle Paul.* Ed. MacRae, G. W. Philadelphia: Fortress Press, 1985.

______. *Der Apostel Paulus und die sokratische Tradition. Eine exegetische Untersuchung zu seiner "Apologie" 2 Korinther 10-13.* BHT 45. Tübingen: J. C. B. Mohr, 1972.

______. "The Literary Composition and Function of Paul' s Letter to the Galatians," *NTS* 21 (1975) 353-80.

Bieder, W. "Paulus und seine Gegner in Korinth," *TZ* 17 (1961), 319-33.

Bieringer, R. "Teilungshypothesen zum 2. Korintherbrief: Ein Forschungsüberblick," in R. Bieringer and Lambrecht, eds., *Studies on 2 Corinthians*, BEThL 112. Leuven: Leuven University Press, 1994.

Billerbeck, P. and Strack, H. *Kommentar zum Neuen Testament aus Talmud und Midrasch.* München: Beck, 1924 .

Black, D. A. "The Weak in Thessalonica: A Study in Pauline Lexicography,"

JETS 25 (1982) 307-21.

________. *Paul, Apostle of Weakness. Astheneia and Its Cognates in the Pauline Literature.* New York: Lang, 1984.

Blomberg, C. L. "The Structure of 2 Corinthians 1-7," *CTR* 4 (1989) 3-20.

Boers, Hendrikus "2 Corinthians 5:14-6:2: A Fragment of Pauline Christology," *CBQ* 64 (2002) 539-46.

Bonhöffer, A. *Epiktet und das Neue Testament.* Giessen: Töpelmann, 1911; 1964 reprint.

Bonneau, G. "La vie, à la mort. Le conflit à Corinthe et ses enjeux théologuiques en 2 Co 2,14-7,4," *ScEs* 51 (1999) 351-66.

Bonsirven, J. *Exégèse rabbinique et exégèse paulinienne.* Paris: Beauchesne et ses fils, 1939.

Boobyer, G. H. "*Thanksgiving" and the "Glory of God" in Paul.* Borna-Leipzig: Noske, 1929.

Bornkamm, G. "The History of the Origin of the So-called Second Letter to the Corinthians," in *The Authority and Integrity of the New Testament.* By K. Aland, et al. London: SPCK, 1965, 73-81 (from *NTS* 8 [1962] 258-64).

_______. *Jesus of Nazareth,* ETr. Irene and Fraser with Robinson, Kames M. Minneapolis: Fortress Press, 1995.

______. *Paul,* ETr. Stalker, D. M. G. New York: Harper & Row, 1971.

_______. *The Authority and Integrity of the New Testament* (London: SPCK, 1965).

Bousset, W. "Der zweite Brief and die Korinther," in *Die Schriften des Neuen Testaments,* II. Ed. Weiss, J. Göttingen: Vandenhoeck &

Ruprechet, 1907, 141-90.

_______. *Kyrios Christos: A History of the Belief in Christ from the Beginnings of Christianity to Irenaeus.* Etr. Steely, J. E. Nashville and New York: Abingdon, 1970.

Bowker, J. W. " 'Merkabah' Visions and the Visions of Paul,' *Journal of Semitic Studies* 16 (1971) 157-73.

Bradshaw, P. F. *Daily Prayer in the Early Church.* London: SPCK, 1981.

Bruce, F. F. *1 and 2 Corinthians*, NCB. Grand Rapids: Eerdmans/London: Marshall, Morgan & Scott, 1971.

Buck, Jr., C. H. "The Collection for the Saints," *HTR* 43 (1950) 1-29.

Buck, Jr., C. H. and Taylor, G. *Saint Paul: A Study of the Development of His Thought.* New York: Scribner, 1969.

Bujard, W. *Stilanalystische Untersuchungen zum Kolosserbrief*, SUNT 11. Göttingen: Vandenhoeck & Ruprecht, 1973.

Bultmann, R. *The Second Letter to the Corinthians.* ETr. Minneapolis: Ausburg, 1985.

_______. "The Primitive Christian Kerygma and the Historical Jesus," in *The Historical Jesus and the Kerygmatic Christ: Essays on the New Quest of the Historical Jesus*, ed. & ETr. Braaten, C. E. and Harrisville, R. A. New York: Abingdon Press, 1964.

_______. *Der Stil der paulinischen Predigt und die kynisch-stoische Diatribe,* FRLANT 13. Göttingen: Vandenhoech & Ruprecht, 1910.

_______. *Der zweite Brief an die Korinther.* Göttingen: Vandenhoeck & Ruprecht, 1987.

_______. *Exegetische Probleme des zweiten Korintherbriefes.* Darmstadt:

Wissenschaftliche Buchgesellschaft, 1963.

______. *Glauben und Verstehen,* I. Tübingen: Mohr, 1933.

______. "*καυχάομαι, χαύχημα, καύχησις, ἐγκαυχάομαι, κατακαυχάομαι,*" *TDNT* 3: 646-54.

______. *The Second Letter to the Corinthians.* ETr. Harrisville, Roy A. Minneapolis, MN: Augsburg, 1985.

______. *Theology of the New Testament 1*, ETr. Grobel, K. London: SCM Press, 1952.

Burton, Ernst de W. *A Critical and Exegetical Commentary on the Epistle to the Galatians.* ICC. Edinburgh: T. & T. Clark, 1921.

Byrnes, Michael. *Conformation to the Death of Christ and the Hope of Resurrection: An Exegetico-Theological Study of 2 Corinthians4, 7-15 and Philippians 3, 7-11.* Roma: Editrice Pontificia Universita Gregoriana, 2003.

Calvin, J. *The Second Epistle of Paul the Apostle to the Corinthians and the Epistles to Timothy, Titus, and Philemon.* ETr. Calvin' s New Testament Commentaries 10. Grand Rapids: Eerdmans/Edinburgh: Oliver and Boyd, 1964(=1547).

Carrez, M. "Le 'nous' en 2 Corinthians," *NTS* 26 (1979-80) 474-86.

Carson, D. A. and et al, *An Introduction to the New Testament.* Grand Rapids: Zondervan Publishing House, 1992.

______. *From Triumphalism to Maturity: An Exposition of 2 Corinthians 10-13.* Grand Rapids: Baker, 1984.

Chadwick, Henry. " 'All Things to All Men,' (1 Cor.9:22)," *NTS* 1 (1954-55) 261-75.

Champion, L. G. *Benedictions and Doxologies in the Epistle of Paul.* Oxford: Published Privately, 1934.

Charlesworth (ed.), J. H. *The Old Testament Pseudepigrapha*, 2 vols. London: Darton, Longman and Todd/New York: Doubleday, 1983.

Chavasse, C. *The Bride of Christ.* London: Religious Book Club, 1930.

Chrysostom, John. *Patrologia Graeca*, ed, Migne, J. P. Paris: Migne, 1857-66. ETr. "Homiles of St. John Chrysostom on the Second Epistle of St. Paul, the Apostle to the Corinthians," *The Nicene and Post-Nicene Fathers(NPNF)*, vol. XII. Grand Rapids: Eerdmans, 1979.

Clarke, W. K. L. *New Testament Problems.* London: SPCK, 1929.

Clavier, H. "La santé de l' apôtre Paul," in *Studia Paulina in honorem Johannis de Zwaan.* Haarlem: 1953.

Cohn-Sherbok, D. "Paul and Rabbinic Exegesis", *SJT* 35 (1982) 117-32.

Collange, J. -F. *Énigmes de la deuxième éptîre de Paul aux Corinthiens*, SNTSMS 18. Cambridge: University Press, 1972.

Collins, J. N. "Georgi's 'Envoys' in 2 Cor 11:23," *JBL* 93 (1974) 88-96.

Conzelmann, H. "Korinthian und die Madichen der Aphrodite. Zur Religionsgeschichte der Stadt Korinth," *Nachrichten von der Akademie der Wissenschaften in Göttingen* 8 (1967) 247-61.

Cousar, C. B. *Theology of the Cross.* Minnneapolis: Augusburg Fortress, 1990.

Cullmann, O. *Christology of the New Testament.* ETr. Guthrie, Shirley C. and Charles Hall, A. M. Philadelphia: Westminster, 1959.

Danker, F. W. "Paul' s Debt to the *De Corona* to Demosthenes: A Study of

Rhetorical Techniques in Second Corinthians," in Watswon, D. F. ed., *Persuasive Artistry* Sheffield: JSOT Press, 1991.

Daube, David. "Participle and Imperative in 1 Peter" in E. G. Selwyn, *The First Epistle of St. Peter.* London: Macmillan & Co. Ltd, 1946.

Dautzenberg, G. "Der zweite Korintherbrief als Briefsammlung: Zur Frage der literarischen Einheitlichkeit und des theologischen Gefuges von 2 Kor 1-8," *ANRW* II.25.4, 3045-66.

Davies, W. D. *Paul and Rabbinic Judaism: Some Rabbinic Elements in Pauline Theology.* London: SPCK, 1948.

______. *The Gospel and the Land: Early Christianity and the Jewish Territorial Doctrine.* Berkeley: University of California, 1974.

de Wette, W. M. L. *Kurze Eklärung der Briefe an die Corinther.* Leipyig: Hirzel, 1855[3].

Deissmann, G. A. *Bible Studies,* ETr. Grieve, A. Edinburgh: T. & T. Clark, 1903.

______. *Light from the Ancient East: The New Testament Illustrated by Recently Discovered Texts of the Greco-Roman World.* London: Hodder and Stoughton, 1910.

Delco, M. "The Courts of the Church of Corinth and the Courts of Qumran," in *Paul and Qumran*, ed. Murphy-O' Connor, J. London: Chapman, 1968.

Delling, G. on "*σκόλοψ*," in *TDNT* 7:409-13.

______. "*πλεονέκτης κτλ.*," in *TDNT* 6:266-74.

______. *τρεῖς*, in *TDNT* VIII, 216-25.

Denney, J. *The Second Epistle to the Corinthians.* The Expositor' s Bible.

London: Hodder/New York: Armstrong, 1894. Reprint Grand Rapids: Eerdmans, 1943.

Derrett, J. D. M. "2 Cor 6,14ff. a Midrash on Dt 22,10," *Bib* 59 (1978) 231-50.

deSilva, D. A. "Recasting the Moment of Decision: 2 Corinthians 6:14-7:1 in Its Literary Context," *AUS* 31 (1993) 3-16.

Dibelius, Martin. *A Fresh Approach to the NT and Early Christian Literature.* London: Ivor Nicholson and Watson, 1936.

DiCicco, M. M. *Paul' s Use of Ethos, Pathos and Logos in 2 Corinthians 10-13,* Mellen Biblical Press Series 31. Lewiston: Mellen Biblical Press, 1995.

Dillard, Raymond B. *2 Chronicles.* Waco, TX.: Word Book Publishers, 1987.

Dinkler, E. *Signum Crucis. Aufsätze zum Neuen Testament und zur christlichen Archäologie.* Tübingen: Mohr, 1967.

Dodd, C. H. *New Testament Studies.* Manchester: Manchester University Press, 1953.

Doty, W. G. *Letters in Primitive Christianity.* Philadelphia: Fortress, 1973.

Drescher, R. "Der zweite Korinterbrief und die Vorgaenge in Korinth seit Abfassung des ersten Korientherbriefs," *TSK* 70 (1897) 43-111.

Dumbrell, W. J. "The Newness of the New Covenant: The Logic of the Argument in 2 Corinthians 3," *RTR* vol. 61 (2002) 61-84.

Dunn, J. D. G. "Paul' s Understanding of the Death of Jesus," in *Reconciliation and Hope*, ed. Banks, Robert. Grand Rapids: Eerdmans, 1974, 125-41.

______. *Unity and Diversity in the New Testament.* London: SCM Press, 1977.

______. "The Incident at Antioch," *JSNT* 18 (1983) 3-57.

______. *Christology in the Making: A New Testament Inquiry into the Origins of the Doctrine of Incarnation.* London: SCM Press, 1980.

______. *Jesus and the Spirit.* London: SCM Press/Philadelphia: Westminster, 1975.

______. *The Theology of Paul the Apostle.* Grand Rapids: Eerdmans, 1998.

Dupon, J. *Gnosis: la connaissance religieuse dans les épîtres de Saint Paul.* Louvain: E. Nauwlaerts/Paris: Gabalda, 1949.

Ebner, M. *Leidenslisten und Apostelbrief. Untersuchungen zu Form, Motivik und Funktion der Peristasenkataloge bei Paulus*, FB 66. Würzburg: Echter Verlag, 1991.

Ewald, H. *Die Sendschreiben des Apostels Paulus.* Güttingen, 1857.

Ellis, E. E. "II Corinthians v. 1-10 in Pauline Eschatology", *NTS* 6 (1959-60) 211-24.

______. "Paul and his Co-workers," *NTS* 17 (1971) 437-52.

______. *Prophecy and Hermeneutics in Early Christianity.* Grand Rapids: Eerdmans, 1978.

______. "How The New Testament Uses the Old" in *New Testament Interpretation,* ed. Marshall, I. H. Exter: Paternoster Press, 1977, 199-219.

______. *Paul' s Use of the Old Testament.* Edinburgh: Oliver and Boyd, 1957.

______. *Wisdom and Prophecy and Hermeneutic in Early Christianity: New Testament Essays.* Grand Rapids: Wm. B. Eerdmans, 1978.

Estius, G. *Omnes Divi Pauli Apostoli epistolas commentariorum Tomus Prior.* Douaci: Balthagar Bellerus, 1614.

Fallon, F. T. *2 Corinthians*, New Testament Message 11. Wilmington, Del.:

M. Glazier/Dublin: Veritas, 1980.

Fee, G. D. "II Corinthians vi.14-vii.1 and Food Offered to Idols," *NTS* 23 (1977) 140-61.

______. "χάρις in II Corinthians I.15," *NTS* 24 (1977-78) 533-38.

Feuillet, A. "La demeure céleste et la destinée des chretiens: Exégèse de 2 Cor 5,1-10 et contribution à l' étude des fondements de l' eschatologie paulinienne," *RSR* 44 (1956) 161-92, 360-402.

Filson, F. V. "The Second Epistle to the Corinthians," *IB* 10. New York: Abingdon Press, 1953, 265-425.

Fitzgerald, J. T. *Cracks in an Earthen Vessel: An Examination of the Catalogues of Hardships in the Corinthian Correspondence*, SBLDS 99. Atlanta, Ga.: Scholars Press, 1988.

Fitzmeyer, J. A. *Essays on the Semitic Background of the New Testament.* London: Chapman, 1971.

_______. "Glory Reflected on the Face of Christ (2 Cor. 3:7-4:6) and a Palestinian Jewish Motif," *NTS* 42 (1981) 630-44.

_______. "Some Notes on Aramaic Epistolography," *JBL* 93 (1974) 214-16.

_______. "Qumrân and the Interpolated Paragraph in 2 Cor. 6:14-7:1," *CBQ* 23 (1961) 271-80.

Flew, R. N. *Jesus and His Church.* London: Epworth, 1938.

Foerster, "σατανᾶς" in *TDNT,* vii, 151-163.

Forbes, C. "Comparison, Self-Praise and Irony: Paul's Boasting and the Conventions of Hellenistic Rhetoric", *NTS* 32 (1986) 1-30.

Ford, David F. *Meaning and Truth in 2 Corinthians.* London: SPCK, 1987.

France, R. T. "The Worship of Jesus" in *Christ the Lord*, FS. Guthrie, D. ed.,

Rowdon, H. H. Leicester: IVP, 1982, 17-36.

Francis, D. P. "The Holy Spirit. A Statistical Inquiry," *Exp Tim* 96 (1985) 136-37.

Fraser, J. W. "Paul' s Knowledge of Jesus: 2 Corinthians 5.16 once more" *NTS* 17 (1970-71) 293-313.

Fridrichsen, A. "Peristasenkatalog und res gestae: Nachtrag zu 2 Cor. 11, 23ff." *SO* 8 (1929) 78-82.

______. "Zum Stil des paulinschen Peristansenkatalogs. 2 Cor 11,23ff." *SO* 7 (1928) 25-29.

Friedrich, G. "Die Gegner des Paulus im 2. Korintherbrief," in Michel *FS* 181-215.

______. "Lohmeyer's Theses über das paulinische Briefpräskript kritisch beleuchtet," *ZNW* 46 (1955) 273-74.

______. *Amt und Lebensführung: Eine Auslegung von 2 Kor. 6:1-10.* Neukirchen-Vluyn: Neukirchener Verlag, 1963.

Funk, Robert Walter. "The Apostolic Parousia: Form and Significance" in *Christian History and Interpretation: Studies Presented to John Knox*, ed. Farmer, W. R. Moule, C. F. D. and Niebuhr, R. R. Cambridge: At the University, 1967.

Furnish, V. P. *II Corinthians*, AB 32A. Garden City, N.Y.: Doubleday, 1984.

______. *Theology and Ethics of Paul.* New York: Abingdon.

George, A. R. *Communion with God in the New Testament.* London: Epworth Press, 1953.

Georgi, D. *Die Gegner des Paulus im 2 Korintherbrief*, WMANT 11. Neukirche-Vluyn: Neukirchner Verlag, 1964.

_______. *Die Geschichte der Kollekte des Paulus für Jerusalem*, TF 38. Mamburg-Bergstedt: H. Reich. Evangelischer Verlag, 1965.

_______. *The Opponents of Paul in Second Corinthians.* ETr. Philadelphia: Fortress 1986.

_______. *Remembering the Poor: The History of Paul' s Collection for Jerusalem* ETr. Nashville: Abingdon Press, 1992.

Gilchrist, J. M. "Paul and the Corinthians-The Sequence of Letters and Visits," *JSNT* 34 (1988) 47-69.

Glombitza, O. "Mit Furcht und Zittern. Zum Verstaendnis von Phil. 2:12," *NovT* 3 (1959) 100-06.

Gnilka, J. "2 Cor. 6:14-7:1 in the Light of the Qumran Texts and in the Testaments of the Twelve Patriarchs," in *Paul and Qumran: Studies in New Testament Exegesis,* ed. Murphy-O' Connor, J. London: Chapman, 1968, 48-68.

Godet, F. *Commentary on St. Paul' s First to the Corinthians.* vol. 1. ETr. Edinburgh: Clark, 1893.

Göttsberger, J. "Die Hülle des Moses nach Ex 34 und Kor 3." *BZ* 16(1922) 1-17.

Goguel, M. *Introduction au nouveau Testament, IV/2: les epitres pauliniennes.* Paris: Leroux, 1926.

Goudge, H. L. *The Second Epistle to the Corinthians*, Westminster Commentary. London: Methuen & Co., 1927.

Grosheide, F. W. *Commentary on the First Epistle to the Corinthians,* NICNT. Grand Rapids: Wm. B. Eerdmans Publishing Company, 1955.

Günther, J. J. *St. Paul' s Opponents and their Background: A Study of*

Apocalyptic Jewish Sectarian Teachings. Leiden: Brill, 1973.

Guthrie, D. *New Testament Introduction*. Chicago: Inter-Varsity Press, 1970.

Güttgemannes, E. *Der leidende Apostel und sein Herr*. Göttingen: Vandenhoeck & Ruprecht, 1966.

_______. *Der leidende Apostel und sein Herr. Studien zur paulinischen Christologie*. FRLANT 90. Göttingen: Vandenhoeck und Ruprecht, 1966.

Hafemann, S. J. *Sufferring and Ministry, in the Spirit: Paul' s Defense of Hid Ministry in 2 Corinthians 2:41-3:3*. Grand Rapids: Eerdmans, 1990.

Hagner, D. A. "Paul in Modern Jewish Thought," in *Pauline Studies: Essays Presented to F. F. Bruce*. Exeter: Paternoster Press, 1980, 143-65.

_______. *The Use of the Old and New Testaments in Clement of Rome*, Supplementary volumes to *Novum Testamentum*. Leiden: Brill, 1973.

Hainz, J. "Koinonia: Kirche als Geneischaft bei Paulus," *Biblische Untersuchungen* 16 (1972), 47-51.

_______. *Ekklesia: Strukturen paulinischer Gemeinde-Theologie und Gemeinde-Ordnung*. Regensburg: Verlag Friedrich Pustet, 1972.

Hall, B. "All Things to All People: A Study of 1 Corinthians 9.19-23," in Fortna and Gaventa, *The Conversation Continues* (1990) 137-57.

Hall, David R. *The Unity of the Corinthian Correspondence*. London/New York: T & T Clark International, 2003.

Hanhart, K. *The Intermediate State in the New Testament*. Groningen: Druk. V. R. B. Kleine, 1966.

Hansen, R. P. C. 2Corinthians, *Torch Bible Commentaries*. London:SCM,

1967.

Hanson, A. T. "The Midrash in II Corinthians 3: A Reconsideration," *JSNT* 9 (1980) 2-23.

_______. *Studies in Paul' s Techniqü and Theology.* Grand Rapids: Eerdmans, 1974.

_______. *The Paradox of the Cross in the Thought of St Paul,* JSNTSS 17. Sheffield: JSOT, 1987.

Hanson, R. P. C. *The Second Epistle to the Corinthians.* London: SCM Press, 1954.

_______. *2 Corinthians,* Torch Bible Commentaries. London: SCM, 1967.

Harris, M. J. "2 Cor 5:1-10: A Watershed in Paul' s Eschatology?" *TynB* 22 (1971) 32-57.

_______. "2 Corinthians," *The Expositor' s Bible Commentary,* ed. Gaebelein, F. E. Grand Rapids: Zondervan, 1976, 299-406.

_______. "Prepositions and Theology in the Greek New Testament," *The New International Dictionary of New Testament Theology,* ed. Brown, C. vol. 3. Grand Rapids: Zondervan Publishing House, 1978, 1171-1215.

_______. *The Second Epistle to the Corinthians.* Grand Rapids: Eerdmans, 2005.

Harvey, Van A. *A Handbook of Theological Terms* New York: Macmillan, 1964.

Hauck, "κοινωνός" in *TDNT* 3:797-809.

Hausrath, Adolf. *Der Vier-Capitelbrief des Paulus an die Korinther.* Heidelberg: Bassermann, 1870.

Hays, H. Richard. *The Faith of Jesus Christ.* Chico, CA.: Scholars Press, 1983.

Heckel, U. *Kraft in Schwachheit. Untersuchungen zu 2. Kor10-13*, WUNT 2, Reihe 56. Tübingen: Mohr, 1993.

Heinrici, C. F. G. *Das zweite Sendschreiben des Apostel Paulus an die Korinther.* Berlin: de Gruyter, 1887.

Hengel, M. *Acts and the History of Earliest Christianity.* ETr. Bowden, J. London: SCM Press, 1979.

______. *Crucifixion*, ET. London: SCM, 1977.

______. *Between Jesus and Paul.* ETr. Bowden, J. Philadelphia: Fortress, 1983.

Héring, J. *The Second Epistle of Saint Paul to the Corinthians.* London: Epworth, 1967.

Hettlinger, R. F. "2 Corinthians 5:1-10," *SJT* 10 (1957) 174-94.

Hippolutus, *Apostolic Tradition*, esc. 21.

Hock, Ronald F. *The Social Context of Paul's Ministry: Tentmaking and Apostleship.* Philadelphia: Fortress Press, 1980.

Hodge, C. *An Exposition of the Second Epistle to the Corinthians.* New York: A. C. Armstrong & Sons, 1891, reprint, Edinburgh: Banner of Truth, 1959.

Höistad, R. "Eine hellenistische Parallele zu 2 Kor 6, 3ff." Coniectanea Neotestamentica IX (1944) 22-27.

Holl, Karl "Der Kirchenbegriff des Paulus in seinem Verhaeltnis zu dem der Urgemeinde," *Gesammelte Aufsaetze zur Kirchengeschichte, II: Der Osten.* Tübingen: J. C. B. Mohr, 1928, 44-67.

Holladay, C. H. *Theios Aner in Hellenistic Judaism: A Critiqü of the Use of This Category in New Testament Christology.* SBLDS 40. Missoula:

Scholars Press, 1977.

Holmberg, B. *Paul and Power. The Structure of Authority in the Primitive Church as Reflected in the Pauline Epistles.* ConB 11. Lund: Gleerup, 1978.

Holtz, T. "Die Bedeutung des Apostelkonzils für Paulus," *NTS* 16 (1974) 110-48.

Holtzmann, H. J. *Lehrbuch der historisch-kritischen Einleitung in das Neuen Testament.* Freiburg: J. C. B. Mohr, 1886.

Horsely, G. H. R. *New Documents Illustrating Early Christianity* I. North Ryde: Macquarie University, 1981.

Howe, E. M. "Interpretations of Paul in the Acts of Paul and Thelka," *Pauline Studies*, FS., Bruce, F. F. ed. Hagner, D. A. and Harris, M. J. Grand Rapids: Eerdmans/Exeter: Paternoster, 1980, 33-49.

Hughes, Frank. W. "The Rhetoric of Reconciliation: 2 Corinthians1.1-2.13 and 7.5-8.24," 246-61 in Watson, D. F. ed., *Persuasive Artistry.* Sheffield: JSOT Press, 1991.

Hughes, P. E. *Paul's Second Letter to the Corinthians.* Grand Rapids: Eerdmans, 1962.

Huppenbaur, H. W. "Belial in den Qumrantexten," *TZ* 15 (1959) 81-89.

Hurd, Jr., J. C. *The Origin of 1 Corinthians.* Macon, Ga: Mercer Press, 1983.

Hydahl, N. "Die Frage nach der literarischen Einheit des Zweiten Korinthierbriefes," *ZNW* 64 (1973) 289-306.

Jeremias, J. "*ἄνθρωπος*" TDNT I, 366

______. *Abba. Studien zur neutestamentlichen Theologie und Zeitgeschichte.* Göttingen: Vandenhoeck und Ruprecht, 1966.

______. *Jerusalem in the Time of Jesus*, ETr. Cave, F. H. and C. H. London: SCM Press, 1969.

______. *Jerusalem zur Zeit Jesu*. Göttingen: Vandenhoeck & Ruprecht, 1958.

______. "*παράδεισος*" in *TDNT*, 5:765-73.

______. " *Ἀβραάμ*" in *TDNT*, I:8-9.

Jervell, J. "Der schwache Charismatiker," in *Rechtfertigung*, FS Käsemann, E. ed. J. Friedrich, W. Poehlmann and Stuhlmacher, P. Tûbingen/Göttingen: Mohr/Vandenhoeck & Ruprecht, 1976, 185-98.

______. *Imago Dei, Gen. 1:26f. im Spätjudentum, in der Gnosis und in den paulinischen Briefen*. FRLANT 76. Göttingen: Vandenhoeck & Ruprecht, 1960.

______. *The Unknown Paul*, Chap. 5: "The Signs of an Apostle," ETr. Harrisville, R. A. Minneapolis: Augsburg, 1984.

Jewett, R. *Paul's Anthropological Terms: A Study of Their Use in Conflict Settings*. *AGJU* 10. Lieden: Brill, 1972.

______. "The Agitators and the Galatian Congregation," *NTS* 17 (1970-71) 198-212.

______. "The Reaction of 1 Corinthians and the Trajectory of the Pauline School," *JAARSup* 44 (1978) 389-444.

Johnson, L. T. *The Writings of the New Testament*. Philadelphia: Fortress, 1986.

Jonas, H. *Gnosis und die spaetantiker Geist*. Gtötingen: Vandenhoeck & Ruprecht, 1954.

Jones, P. R. "The Apostle Paul: A Second Moses according to II Corinthians

2:14-4:7," Unpublished Ph. D. dissertation, Princeton Theological Seminary, 1973.

Judge, E. A. "Paul' s Boasting in Relation to Contemporary Professional Practice," *ABR* 16 (1968) 37-50.

________. "The Conflict of Educational Aims in New Testament Thought", *Journal of Christian Education* 9 (1966) 32-45.

Jülicher, A. *Einleitung in das Neuen Testament.* Tübingen: J. C. B. Mohr, 1931.

Kamlah, E. "Wie beurteilt Paulus sein Leiden? Ein Beitrag zur Untersuchung seiner Denkstruktur," *ZNW* 54 (1964) 217-32.

Käsemann, E. *The Perspectives on Paul.* ETr. Kohl, M. Philadelphia: Fortress Press, 1971.

_______. *Die Legitimität des Apostels. Eine Untersuchung zu II Korinther 10-13.* Darmstadt: Wissenschaftliche Buchgesellschaft, 1956, originally in *ZNW* 41 (1942) 33-71.

Keck, L. E. "The Poor among the Saints in the New Testament," *ZNW* 56 (1965) 100-29.

Kelly, J. N. D. *Early Christian Creeds.* London: Longman, 1960.

______. *Early Christian Doctrines.* London: A & C. Black, 1958.

______. *The Epistle of Peter and Jude.* New York: Harper & Row, Publishers, 1969.

Kennedy, G. A. *Classical Rhetoric and Rhetorical Criticism.* Chapel Hill: University of North Carolina Press, 1984.

Kennedy, J. H. *The Second and Third Epistles of St Paul to the Corinthians.* London: MacMillan, 1900.

Ker, R. E. "Fear or Love? A Textual Note," *The Expository Times* 72 (1960-61) 195-96.

Keyes, C. W. "The Greek Letter of Introduction," *American Journal of Philosophy* 56 (1935) 28-44.

Kierkegaard, Soeren Aabye. "Of the Difference between a genius and An Apostle," in *The Present Age and Two Minor Ethico-Religious Treatises.* New York: Oxford University, 1940.

Kim, C. H. *Form and Structure of the Familiar Greek Letter of Recommendation.* SBLDS 4. Missoula: Scholars, 1972.

Kim, Seyoon. *The Origins of Paul' s Gospel.* Grand Rapids: Eerdmans, 1981.

Kirk, J. A. "Apostleship since Rengstorf," *NTS* 21 (1974/75) 249-64.

Kittel, G. "αὐτάρκεια" in *TDNT,* 1:466-67.

______. "εἶδος" in *TDNT,* 2:373-75.

______. "δόξα" in *TDNT,* 2:233-37.

Kleinknecht, K. T. *Der leiden Gerechtfertigte.* WUNT 2nd ser. 13. Tübingen: Mohr, 1984.

Kloepper, A. *Kommentar über das zweite Sendschreiben des Apostles Paulus an die Gemeinde zu Korinth.* Berlin: de Gruyter/G. Reimar, 1874.

Knox, J. *Chapters in the Life of Paul.* New York: Abingdon Press, 1950.

Knox, R. A. *A New Testament Commentary for English Readers, vol. II: The Acts of the Apostles, St. Paul' s Letters to the Churches.* London: Burns, Oates, and Washbourne, 1954.

Knox, W. L. "Abraham and the Quest for God" *HTR* 28 (1935) 50-56.

________. *St. Paul and the Church of Gentiles.* Cambridge: University Press, 1939.

Koester, H. *Introduction to the New Testament.* II. Philadelphia: Fortress, 1982.

______. "ὑποστάσις" in *TDNT*, 8:572-589.

______. "σπλάγχνον κτλ." in *TDNT*, 7:548-59.

Kohlenberger III, John R. and Swanson, James A. *The Hebrew English Concordance to the Old Testament with the New International Version.* Grand Rapids: Zondervan Publishing House, 1998.

Kraftchick, S. J. Ethos and Pathos Appeals in Galatians Five and Six, and T. H. Lobricht and J. L. Sumney, eds., *Paul and Pathos,* SBLSymS 16. Atlanta: Society of Biblical Literature, 2001.

______. "Death in us, Life in you: The Apostolic Medium," in Lovering, Jr, E. H. ed., *SBL 1991 Seminar Papers.* Atlanta: Scholars Press, 1991, 618-37.

Kremer, J. *2. Korintherbrief.* Stuttgart: Verlag Katholisches Bibelwerk, 1990.

Krenkel, M. *Beiträge zur Aufhellung der Geschichte und der Brief des Apostels Paulus*, 2nd ed. Barunschweig: Schwetschke, 1895.

Kuhn, K. G. "Die Schriftrollen vom Toten Meer", *EvT* 11 (1951) 72-75,

Kümmel, W. G. *The Theology of the New Testament according to Its Major Witnesses.* ETr. Steely, John E. Nashville: Abingdon Press, 1973.

______. *Introduction to the New Testament*, ed. Kee, Howard Clark. London: SCM, 1975.

Ladd, G. E. *A Theology of the New Testament.* Grand Rapids: Wm. B. Eerdmans Publising Company, 1974.

Lake, K. *The Earlier Epistles of St. Paul.* London: Livingston's, 1927.

Lampe, G. W. H. "Church Discipline and the Interpretation of the Epistles to the Corinthians," in *Christina History and Interpretation*, Studies presented to John Knox, ed. Farmer, W. R. et al. Cambrdige: University Press, 1967.

Lang, F. G. *Die Briefe an die Korinther.* Göttingen: Vandenhoek & Ruprecht, 1986.

_______. *2 Korinthers 5, 1-10 in der neuren Forschung.* BGBE 10. Tübingen: Mohr, 1973.

Lapide, Cornelius a. "Commentarius in Secundam Epistolam ad Corinthos," in *Commentaria in Scripturam Sanctam* XVIII. Paris: L. Vives, 1866. (van den Steen, C. *Commentaria in omnes Divi Pauli Epistolas.* Antverpiae: apud Henricum et Cornelium Verdussen, 1705.

Liddel, Henry G. and Scott, Robert. *A Greek-English Lexicon.* Oxford: Clarendon, 1996.

Lietzmann, H. *An die Korinther 1/2.* HNT 9. Tübingen: J. C. B. Mohr, 1949.

_______. *Mass and Lord's Supper.* ETr. Reeve, D. H. G. Leiden: Brill, 1979.

Lightfoot, J. B. *The Epistle of St. Paul to the Galatians.* London: Macmillan, 1865; reprint, Grand Rapids: Zondervan, 1962.

Lincoln, A. T. "Paul the Visionary: the Setting and Significance of the Rapture to Paradise in 2 Corinthians 12:1-10," *NTS* 25 (1979) 204-20.

_______. *Paradise Now and Not Yet: Studies in the Role of the Heavenly Dimension in Paul's Thought with Special Reference to his Eschatology.* SNTSMS 43. Cambridge: University Press, 1981.

Lohmeyer, E. " Probleme paulnischer Theologie I. Briefliche Grussüberschriften," ZNW 26 (1927) 158-73.

Long, Fredrick J. *Ancient Rhetoric and Paul's Apology: The Compositional*

Unity of 2 Corinthians. Cambridge: Cambridge University Press, 2005.

Lohse, Eduard *Umwelt des Neuen Testaments*. Göttingen: Vandenhoeck & Ruprecht, 1971. 『신약성서배경사』. 박창건 역. 서울: 대한기독교출판사, 1971.

Lüdemann, G. *Paul, Apostle to the Gentiles*, ETr. Jones, F. S. Philadelphia: Fortress, 1984.

Lütgert, W. *Freheitspredigt und Schwarmgeister in Korinth; ein Beitrag zur Charqkteristik der Christuspartei*. Gütersloh: Verlag Mohn 1908.

MacRae, G. W. "Whom Heaven Must Receive until the Time: Reflection on thre Christology of Acts," in *Interpretation* 26 (1972) 151-165.

Malherbe, A. J. *The Cynic Epistles*. SBLSBS 12. Missoula: Scholars Press, 1977.

________. *Paul and the Popular Philosophers*. Minneapolis: Fortress Press, 1989.

________. *Social Aspects of Early Christianity*. Barton Rouge: Louisiana State University, 1977.

Manson, T. W. *Studies in the Gospels and Epistles*. Manchester: Manchester University Press, 1962.

______. "2 Cor 2:14-17: Suggestions Toward an Exegesis," in *Studia Paulina* (de Zwaan FS), ed. Sevenster, J. and van Unnik, W. C. Haarlem: Erven F. Bohn, 1953, 155-62.

Marshall, I. H. "Meaning of 'Reconciliation'", in *Unity and Diversity in New Testament Theology*, ed. Guelich, R. A. Grand Rapids: Eerdmans, 1978, 119-120.

Marshall, P. "Hybris, Not Gnostics in Corinth," in *SBL, 1984 Seminar Papers*, ed., Richards, K. H. Chico: Scholars, 1984, 275-87.

_______. *Enmity in Corinth: Social Convention in Paul' s Relations with the Corinthians.* WUNT 2/23. Tübingen: Mohr, 1987.

Martin, R. P. *Carmen Christi: Philippians ii.5-11 in Recent Interpretation and in the Setting of Early Christian Worship.* Cambridge: Cambridge University Press, 1967.

_______. "Gospel," *International Standard Bible Encyclopedia*, ed. Bromiley, G. W et al. Grand Rapids: Eerdmans, 1982, 2:529.

_______. "Writing and Materials," "Papyrus," in *Dictionary of the Bible and Religion*, ed. Gentz, W. Nashville: Abingdon Press, 1986.

______. *Colossians and Philemon.* NCB. 1981.

______. *New Testament Foundations* 2. Grand Rapids: Eerdmans, 1978.

______. *Philippians.* NCB. Grand Rapids: Eerdmans, 1976.

______. *Reconciliation: A Study of Paul' s Theology.* London: Marshall, Morgan & Scott/ Atlanta: John Knox, 1981.

______. *2 Corinthians.* Word Biblical Commentary. vol. 40. Waco, TX.: Word Books Publisher, 1986.

_______. *The Spirit and Congregation: Studies in 1 Corinthians 12-15.* Grand Rapids: Eerdmans/Exeter: Paternoster Press, 1984.

Marxen, W. *Introduction to the New Testament: An Approach to its Problems*, ETr. Buswell, G. Philadelphia: Fortress, 1968.

Maurer, C. "*σκεῦος*" *TDNT* VII, 360.

McCant, J. W. "Paul' s Thorn of Rejected Apostleship," *NTS* 34 (1987-88) 550-72.

______. *2 Corinthians.* Sheffield: Sheffield Academic Press, 1999.

McCray, L. D. "Paul's Opponents in Corinth: An Examination of Walter Schmithals' Thesis on Gnosticism in Corinth," Ph.D. dissertation. Southern Baptist Theological Seminary, 1985.

McDermott, J. M. "The Biblical Doctrine of KOINONIA," *BZ* 19 (1975) 64-77, 219-33.

McNamara, Martin *The New Testament and the Palestinian Targum to the Pentateuch*. Rome: Pontifical Biblical Institute, 1966.

_______. *Targum and Testament. Aramaic Paraphrases of the Hebrew Bible: A Light on the New Testament*. Grand Rapids: Wm. B. Eerdmans, 1972.

McQuilkin, J. Robertson. *Understanding and Applying the Bible*. Chicago: Moody Press, 1983. 『성경의 해석과 적용』, 송용조 역. 서울:서울성경학교출판부, 1992.

Mealand, D. L. "'As Having Nothing and yet Possessing Everything', 2 Cor 6:10c," *ZNW* 67 (1976) 277-79.

Meeks, W. A. *The First Urban Christians: The Social World of the Apostle Paul*. New Haven: Yale University Press, 1983.

Meinardus, Otto F. A. *St. Paul in Greece*. Athen: Lycabettus Press, 1972.

Mell. U. *Neue Schöpfung. Eine traditionsgeschichtliche und exegetische Studie zu einem soteriologischen Grundsatz paulinischer Theologie*. BZNW 56. Berlin and New York: Tpöelmann/De Gruyter, 1989.

Menoud, P. H. "L'écharde det l'age satanique (2 Cor 12,7)," in *Studia Paulina*, FS. de Zwaan, ed. Sevenster, J. N. and van Unnik, W. C. Haarlem: Erven F. Bohn, 1953, 163-64.

Menzies, A. *The Second Epistle of the Apostle Paul to the Corinthians.* London: Macmillan & Co., 1912.

Metzger, B. M. *A Textual Commentary on the Greek New Testament.* New York/London: United Bible Societies, 1971.

________. *The Text of the New Testament: its transmission, corruption, and restoration.* New York: Oxford University Press, 1992.

Meyer, H. A. W. *Critical and Exegetical Handbook to the Epistles to the Corinthians II.* ETr. Dickson, W. P. Edinburgh: T. & T. Clark, 1879.

Michael, J. H. "Work out Your Own Salvation," *Expositor* 9 (1924) 439-50.

Milik, J. T. *Ten Years of Discovery in the Wilderness of Judea,* SBT 26. London: SCM, 1959.

Mitton, C. L. *The Formation of the Pauline Corpus of Letters.* London: Epworth Press, 1955.

Moffatt, J. *First Epistle to the Corinthians.* London: Hodder & Stoughton, 1938.

_______. *Grace in the New Testament.* London: Hodder & Stoughton, 1931.

_______. *An Introduction to the Literature of the New Testament.* Edinburgh: Clark, 1918[3].

Mommsen, T. "Die Rechtsverhaeltnisse des Apostels Paulus," *ZNW* 2 (1901) 81-96.

Morray-Jones, C. R. A. "Paradise Revisited (2 Cor 12:1-12): The Jewish Mystical Backgrounbd of Paul' s Apostolate. Part 1: the Jewish Sources: Part 2: Paul' s Heavenly Ascent and its Significance, " *HTR* 86, (1993) 177-217, 265-92.

Moule, C. F. D. "A Reconstruction of the Context of Maranatha Invocation and Jude 14, 15(I Enoch 1:9)," in *Christ and Spirit in the New Testament.* FS Moule, C. F. D. ed. Londars, B. and Smalley, S. S. Cambridge: University Press, 1973.

________. *Essays in New Testament Interpretation.* Cambridge: University Presss, 1982.

______. "St Paul and Dualism: the Pauline Conception of Resurrection." *NTS* 12 (1965-66) 106-23.

_______. *An Idiom Book of New Testament Greek.* Cambridge: University Press, 1979.

______. *The Phenomenon of the New Testament*, SBT 2d ser. 1. Naperville: Allenson, 1967.

Moulton, J. H. A *Grammar of New Testament Greek I: Prolegomena.* Edinburgh: Clark, 1908[3].

Mullins, T. Y. "Benedictions as a New Testament Form," *AUS* 15 (1977) 59-64.

______. "Paul' s Thorn in the Flesh," *JBL* 76 (1957) 299-303.

Munck, J. "Paul, The Apostles, and the Twelve," *ST* III (1949) 96-110.

________. *Paul and the Salvation of Mankind*, ETr. Clarke, Frank. London: SCM, 1954, 1959.

Muraoka, T. "The Use of WS in the Greek Bible," *NovT* 7 (1964) 51-72.

Murphy-O' Connor, J. "Philo and 2 Cor 6:14-7:1," *RB* 95 (1988) 55-69. Reprinted in Lorenzi (ed.), *The Diakonia of the Spirit (2Co 4:7-7:4).* Biblical-Ecumenical Section 10. Rome: Abbaye de S. Paul, 1989, 133-46.

______. "Another Jesus(2 Cor 11:4)," *Revue Biblique* 97 (1990) 238-51.

_______. *The Theology of the Second Letter to the Corinthians*. Cambridge: Cambridge University Press, 1991.

_______. "Paul and Macedonia: The Connection between 2 Conrinthians 2.13 and 2.14," *JSNT* 25 (1985) 99-103.

_______. (ed.), *Paul and Qumran: Studies in New Testament Exegesis*. Chicago/London: Priory/ Chapman, 1968.

_______. *Paul: A Critical Life*. Oxford: University Press, 1996.

_______. *St. Paul's Corinth: Texts and Archaeology*. Good News Studies 6. Wilmington: Glazier, 1983.

_______. *The Theology of the Second Letter to the Corinthians*. Cambridge: Cambridge University Press, 1991.

Nickle, K. F. *The Collection*. SBT 48. London: SCM Press, 1966.

Nietzsche, F. "The First Christians," in *The Dawn of Day*. New York: Macmillan Co., 1903.

_______. "The Antichrist: An Attempted Criticism of Christianity," in *The Complete Works of Friedrich Nietzsche*, ed. Levy, O. vol. 16. New York: Macmillan Co., 1910-27.

Noh, Jae Young. "An Exegesis of 2 Corinthians 5:16-21 and Its Contribution to Pauline Theology." Ph.D. diss. Trinity Evangelical Divinity School, 1997.

O'Collins, G. G. "Power Made Perfect in Weakness: 2 Cor 12:9-10," *CBQ* 33 (1971) 528-37.

Oepke, A. "δύω" *TDNT* II 319.

Olivier, F. "Συναποθνήσκω, D' un article de lexique à Saint Paul, II Corinthiens, vii, 3," *RsThPh* 17(1929) 103-33.

Ollrog, W. H. *Paulus und seine Mitarbeiter.* WMANT 50. Neukirchen-Vluyn: Neukirchener Verla, 1979.

Oostendorp, D. W. *Another Jesus: A Gospel of Jewish Christian Superiority in II Corinthians.* Kampen: Kok, 1967.

Osborne, R. E. "Paul' s Silent Years," *JBL* 84 (1965) 59-65.

Osiander, J. E. *Commentar über den zweiten Brief Pauli an die Korinther.* Stuttgart: Calwer Verlag, 1858.

Park, D. M. "Paul' s sko,loy th/| sarki,: Thorn or Stake?(2 Cor. xii 7)," *NovT* 22 (1980) 179-83.

Pate, C. M. *Adam Christology as the Exegetical & Theological Substructure of 2 Corinthians 4:7-5:21.* Lanham and New York: University Press of America, 1991.

Patte, D. *Early Jewish Hermeneutics in Palestine. SBL* series 22. Missoula: Scholars Press, 1975.

Pearson, B. A. "The Pneumatikos-Psychikos Terminology in 1 Corinthians: A Study in the Theology of of the Corinthian Opponents of Paul and Its Relation to Gnosticism," *SBLDS* 12. Missoula, Mont.: SP. 1973, 51-81.

Peel, M. L. "Gnostic Eschatology and the New Testament," *NovT* 12 (1970) 141-65.

Pherigo, L. P. "Paul and the Corinthian Church," *JBL* 68 (1949) 341-50.

Pierce, C. A. *Conscience in the New Testament.* SBT 15. London: SCM Press, 1955.

Plummer, A. *A Critical and Exegetical Commentary on the Second Epistle of the St. Paul to the Corinthians.* ICC 47. Edinburgh: T. & T. Clark, 1915.

Powell, C. H. *The Biblical Concept of Power.* London: Epworth Press, 1963.

Price, J. L. *Interpreting the New Testament.* New York: Holt, 1961.

Prümm, K. *Diakonia Pneumatos I: Theologische Auslegung des zweiten Korintherbriefs.* Rome/Freiburg/Wien: Herder, 1967.

Ramsay, W. M. "Historical Commentary on the Epistles to the Corinthians," *Expositor* 6th series 3 (1901) 220-40, 343-60.

________. *St. Paul and the Traveller and Roman Citizen.* London: Hodder & Stoughton, 1935.

Reicke, "*πᾶς*" in *TDNT* 5:886-90, 892-96.

Reitzenstein, R. *Hellenistic Mystery-Religions*, ETr. Steely, J. E. Pittsburgh: Pickwick Press, 1978.

Rensberger, D. "2 Corinthians 6:14-7:1-A Fresh Examination," *StBibT* 8 (1978) 25-49.

Renstorf, Karl. "*ἀποστολός*" in *TDNT* 1:407-47.

______. "*στέλλω*" in *TDNT* 7:588-99.

Reumann, J. *Righteousness in the New Testament.* Philadelphia: Fortrress Press, 1982.

Richards, E. R. *The Secretary in the Letters of Paul.* WUNT 2/42. Tübingen: Mohr, 1991.

Richardson, R. "The Thunderbolt in Q and the Wise Man in Corinth," in *From Jesus to Paul.* FS. Beare, F. W. Waterloo, Ont.: Laurier University Press, 1984, 91-111.

Riesner, Rainer. *Die Frühzeit des Apostels Paulus: studien zur Chronologie, Missionsstrategie und Theologie.* Tübingen: J. C. B. Mohr, 1994.

Rigaux, B. *The Letters of St. Paul*, ed. and ETr. Yonich, S. Chicago:

Franciscan Herald Press, 1968.

Rissi, M. *Studien zum zweiten Korinterbrief.* ATANT 56. Zurich: Zwingli Verlag, 1969.

Robertson, A. T. *A Grammar of the Greek New Testament in the light of Historical Research.* Nashville: Broadman Press, 1934.

Robinson, J. A. T. *Redating the New Testament.* London: SCM Press, 1976.

______. *The Body, A Study in Pauline Theology.* SBT 5. London: SCM Press, 1952.

Robinson, J. M. *A New Quest of the Historical Jesus.* Philadelphia: Fortress Press, 1983.

Roetzel, Calvin. *Paul: The Man and the Myth.* Minneapolice: Fortress Press, 1999.

Roloff, J. *Apostolat-Verkündigung-Kirche.* Gütersloh: G. Mohn, 1965.

Rowland, C. *The Open Heaven: A Study of Apocalyptic in Judaism and Early Christianity.* London: SPCK, 1982.

Rückert, L. J. *Der zweite Brief Pauli an die Korinther.* Leipzig: K. F. Koehler, 1837.

Saake, H. "Paulus als Ekstatiker. Pneumatologische Beobachtungen zu 2 Kor 12, 1-10," *Biblica* 53(1972) 404-10. (Also in *NovT* 15 [1973] 153-60).

Sampley, J. P. *"And the Two Shall Become One Flesh": A Study of the Traditions in Ephesians.* SNTSMS 16. Cambridge: University Press, 1971, 34-51.

Sanders, E. P. "Paul on the Law, His Opponents, and the Jewish People in Philppians 3 and 2 Corinthians 11," in *Anti-Judaism in Early Christianity vol. I: Paul and the Gospels.* ed. Richardson, Peter and

Granskou, David. *Studies in Christianity and Judaism* 2. Waterloo/ Ontario: Wilfrid Laurier University Press, 1986.

________. *Paul and Judaism: A Comparison of Patterns of Religion.* Philadelphia: Fortress, 1977.

Saulnier, C. "Hérode Antipas et Jean le Baptiste. Quelques remarques sur les confusions chronologiques de Flavius Josèphe," *Revue Biblique* 91 (1984) 362-76.

Savage, T. B. *Power through Weakness: Paul' s Understanding of the Christian Ministry in 2 Corinthians.* SNTSMS 86. Cambridge: University Press, 1996.

Schäfer, P. "New Testament and Hekhalot Literature: The Journey into Heaven in Paul and Merkavah Mysticism," *JJS* 35 (1984) 19-35.

Schlatter, A. *Paulus, der Bote Jesu. Eine Deutung seiner Briefe an die Korinther.* Stuttgart: Clawer Verlag, 1969.

Schlicher, H. *Der Brief an die Epheser.* Düsseldorf: Patmos Verlag, 1968.

Schmidt, K. L. "Luzifer als gefallene Engelsmacht," *TZ* 7 (1951) 261-79.

______. "κολαφίζω," in *TDNT* 3:818-21.

Schmiedel, P. W. *Die Briefe an die Thessaloniker und an die Korinther.* Hand-Commentar zum Neuen Testament, vol. 2. Freiburg: J. C. B. Mohr, 1892.

Schmithals, W. "Die Korintherbriefe als Briefsammlung," *ZNW* 64 (1973) 263-88.

______. *Gnosticism in Corinth: An Investigation of the Letters to the Corinthians.* ETr. Nashville/New York: Abingdon Press, 1971.

______. *The Office of Apostle in the Early Church,* ETr. Steely, John E.

Nashville: Abingdon Press, 1969.

Schnackenburg, R. "Apostles before and during Paul' s Time," in *Apostlolic History and the Gospel.* ed. Gasque, W. W. and Martin, R. P. Grand Rapids: Eerdmans, 1970.

Schopes, H. J. *Theologie und Geschichte des Judenchristentums.* Tübingen: J. C. B. Mohr, 1964.

Schrenk, G. "*βάρος, βαρέω*," in *TDNT* I:551-9.

______. "*γράφω*," in *TDNT* I:742-49.

Schulz, S. "Die Decke des Moses. Unterschungen zu einer vorpaulinischen überlieferung in II Cor 3:7-18," *ZNW* 48 (1958) 1-30.

Schürer, E. *The History of the Jewish People in the Age of Jesus Christ*, ed. Vermes, G. and Millar, F. vol. II. Edinburgh: T. & T. Clark, 1973.

Schütz, J. H. *Paul and Anatomy of Apostolic Authority.* SNTSMS 26. Cambridge: University Press, 1975.

Schweitzer, "*πνεῦμα*," in *TDNT* 6:389-52.

Scott, C. A. Anderson *Christianity according to St Paul.* Cambridge: Cambrdige University Press, 1961.

Seesemann, H. *Der Begriff KOINONIA im Neuen Testament.* BZNW 14. Giessen: Töpelmann, 1933.

Segalla, "Coerenza linguistica ed inita letteraria della 2 Corinzi," *Teologia* 13 (1988) 149-66.

Sellin, G. "Hauptprobleme des Ersten Korintherbriefes," *ANRW* 25.4. Berlin: de Gruyter, 1987, 2940-3044.

Semler, J. S. *Paraphrasis II. Epistolae ad Corinthos.* Halle: Carl Hermann Hemmerde, 1776.

Shaw, G.v. *The Cost of Authority: Manipulation and Freedom in the New Testament*. London: SCM, 1983.

Sherwin-White, A. N. *Roman Society and Roman Law in the New Testament*. Oxford: Clarendon, 1963.

Singer, S. *Authorized Daily Prayer Book*. London: Eyre and Spottiswoode, 1925.

Souček, J. B. "Wir erkennen Christus nich mehr nach dem Fleisch", *EvT* 19 (1959) 300-14.

Souter, A. "A Suggested Relationship between Titus and Luke," *The Expository Times* 18 (1906-7) 280.

Spicq, C. "L'image sportive de 2 Corinthiens 4, 7-9." *Ephemerides theologicae lovanienses* 13 (1937) 202-29.

______. "*ΥΠ*ΟΜΟΝΗ, patientia,' " *RsPhTh* (1930) 83-106.

Spittler, R. P. "The Limits of Ecstasy: An Exegesis of 2 Corinthians 12:1-10," in *Current Issues in Biblical and Patristic Interpretation: Studies in honor of Merril C. Tenney*, ed. Hawthorne, G. F. Grand Rapids: Eerdmans, 1975, 259-66.

Stählin, G. "*φιλέω*," in *TDNT* IX:119-24.

______. " 'Um mitzusterben und mitzuleben.' Bemerkungen zu 2 Kor 7,3," *Neues Testament und christliche Existenz*. FS Herbert Braun. ed. Betz, H. D. and Schottroff, L. Tübingen: J. C. B. Mohr, 1973, 503-21.

Stange, E. "Diktierpausen in den Paulusbriefen," *ZNW* 18 (1917-18) 109-17.

Stanley, C. D. *Paul and the Language of Scripture: Citation Technique in the Pauline Epistles and Contemporary Literature*. SNTSMS 74. Cambridge: University Press, 1992.

Stanton, G. N. "Matthew 11:28-30," *Expository Times* 94 (1982) 3-9.

Stegman, Thomas. *The Character of Jesus: The Linchpin to Paul's Argument in 2 Corinthians.* Analecta Biblica 158. Roma: Editrice Pontificio Istituto Biblico, 2005.

Stephenson, A. M. G. "A Defence of the Integrity of 2 Corinthians," *The Authorship and Integrity of the New Testament* by Aland, K. et al. SPCK Theological Collections 4. London: SPCK, 1965, 82-97.

Stockhausen, C. K. "2 Corinthians 3 and the Principles of Pauline Exegesis," in Evans, C. A. and Sanders, J. A. eds., *Paul and the Scriptures of Israel.* JSNTSS 83. Sheffield: JSOT, 1993, 143-64.

Stowers, S. K. "Peri men gar and the Integrity of 2 Corinthians 8 and 9," *NovT* 32 (1980) 340-48.

Strachan, R. H. *The Second Epistle of Paul to the Corinthians.* London: Hodder & Stoughton, 1935.

Strack, H.L. and Billerbeck, P. Kommentar zum Neven Testament aus Talmud und Midrasch. vol.3 Münich:Beck, 1992.

Strathmann, H. "λειτουργία" in *TDNT* IV:226-231.

Strelan, J. G. "Burden-Bearing and the Law of Christ: A Re-Examination of Galatians 6:2," *JBL* 94 (1975) 266-76.

Stuhlmacher, P. "Das paulinische Evangelium," in *Das Evangelium und die Evangelien.* WUNT 28. Tübingen: Mohr, 1983.

_______. "Erwägungen zum ontologische Charakter der καινὴ κτίσις bei Paulus," *EvT* 27 (1967) 1-35.

Suhl, A. *Paulus und seiner Briefe.* Gütersloh: Mohr, 1975.

Sumney, Jerry L. "Paul' s 'Weakness' : An Integral Part of His Conception of

Apostleship," *JSNT* 52 (1993) 71-91.

Sundermann, H. G. *Der schwache Apostel und die Kraft der Rede: Eine rhetorische Analyse von 2 Kor 10-13.* Europäische Hoschschulschriften XXIII 575. Frankfurt: P. Lang, 1966.

Swete, H. B. *The Holy Spirit.* London: Macmillan, 1910.

______. *The Life of the World to Come.* London: Macmillan, 1917.

Tabor, J. D. *Things Unutterable; Paul's Ascent to Paradise in its Greco-Roman, Judaic, and Early Christian Contexts.* Studies in Judaism. Lanham and London: University Press of America, 1986.

Tachau, P. *"Einst" und "Jezt" im Neuen Testament.* FRLANT 105. Göttingen: Vandenhoeck & Ruprecht, 1972.

Talbert, C. H. *Reading Corinthians.* New York: Crossroad, 1987.

Tannehill, R. C. *Dying and Rising with Christ: A Study in Pauline Theology.* BZNW 32. Berlin: Töpelmann, 1967.

Tasker, R. V. G. *The Second Epistle to the Corinthians.* TNTC 8. Grand Rapids: Eerdmans, 1958.

Taylor, J. "The Ethnarch of King Aretas at Damascus: A Note on 2 Cor 11.32-33," *Revue Biblique* 99 (1992) 719-28.

Taylor, N. H. "The Composition and Chronology of Second Corinthians," *JSNT* 44 (1991) 67-87.

______. *Paul, Antioch and Jerusalem: A Study in Relationships and Authority in Earliest Christianity.* JSNTSS 66. Sheffield: Sheffield Academic Press, 1992.

Theissen, Gerd. *The Social Setting of Pauline Christianity: Essays on Corinth,* ETr. and ed. Schütz, J. H. Philadelphia: Fortress Press, 1982.

Theolbald, M. *Die überstroemende Gnade. Studien zu einem paulinischen Motivefeld.* Wurzburg: Echter, 1982.

Thierry, J. J. "Der Dorn im Fleische," *NovT* 5 (1962) 301-10.

Thiessen, H. C. *Introduction to the New Testament.* Grand Rapids: Eerdmans, 1979.

Thiselton, A. C. "Realized Eschatology at Corinth," *NTS* 24 (1977-78) 510-26.

Thrall, M. E. "A Second Thanksgiving Period in II Corinthians," *JSNT* 16 (1982) 118-25.

________. " 'Putting on' or 'stripping off' in 2 Corinthians 5:3," *New Testament Textual Criticism, Its Significance for Exegesis*, ed. Epp, E. J. and Fee, G. D. Oxford: Clarendon Press/New York: Oxford University Press, 1981, 221-37.

________. "The Pauline Use of *ΕΥΝΕΙΔΗΣΙΣ*," *NTS* 14 (1967-68) 118-25.

________. "The Problem of II Cor. VI.14-VII.1 in Some Recent Discussion," *NTS* 24 (1978) 132-48,

________. *The Second Epistle to the Corinthians*, ICC. Edinburgh: T&T Clark, 1994.

________. *A Critical and Exegetical Commentary on the Second Epistle to the Corinthians.* vol II. Edinburgh: T & T Clark, 2000.

Thyen, H. *Der Stil der jüdisch-hellenistischen Homilie*, FRLANT 65. Göttingen: Vandenhoeck & Ruprecht, 1955.

Trakatellis, D. "Power in Weakness: Exegesis of 2 Corinthians 12, 1-13" in *Verteidigung und Begründung des Apostolischen Amtes(2Kor 10-13)*, ed., Lohse, Eduard. Monographische Reihe von Benedictina. Roma: Abtei St. Paul vor den Maurn, 1992.

Travis, S. H. "Paul' s Boasting in 2 Corinthians 10-12," *Texte Untersuchgen* 112 (1973) 527-32.

Turner, N. *Grammatical Insights into the New Testament.* Edinburgh: T. & T. Clark, 1965.

van Unnik, W. C. "Die Decke des Moses, Untersuchungen zu einer vorpaulinischen Uberlieferung in II Cor. 3.7-18," *ZNW* 49 (1958) 1-31.

______. "The Christian' s Freedom of Speech," *BJRL* 44 (1961-62) 466-88.

______. "Reisepläne und Amen-Sagen. Zusammenhang und Gedankenfolge in 2 Korinther 1:15-24," in *The Collected Essays of W. C. van Unnik,* NovTSup, Part One, 29. Leiden: Brill, 1973, 215-34.

______. "With Unveiled Face: An Exegesis of 2 Corinthians iii. 12-18," *NovT* 6 (1963) 153-69.

Verbrugge, V. D. *Paul' s Style of Church Leadership Illustrated by his Instructions to the Corinthians on the Collection: To Command or not to Command.* San Francisco: Mellen Research University Press/Lewiston, NY.: Edwin Mellen Press, 1992.

Vielhaur, P. "Oikodome. Das Bild vom Bau in der christlichen Literatur vom Neuen Testament bis Clemens Alexandrinus," 1-168 in *Oikodome Aufsaetze zum Neuen Testament,* 1. ed. Klein, G. TBü 65. Munich: Kaiser, 1979.

______. *Geschichte der urchristlichen Literatur.* Berlin: de Gruyter, 1975.

Vliet, H. van *No Single Testimony. A Study on the Adoption of the Law of Deut. 19:15 par. into the New Testament,* Studia Theologica Rheno-Traiectina 4. Utrecht: Kemink & Zoon, 1958.

von Dobschütz, E. *Christian Life in the Primitive Church,* ETr. Bremmer, George London: G. P. Putnam' s Sons, 1904.

_______. "Zwei-und dreiliedrige Formeln. Ein Beitrag zur Vorgeschichte der Trinitätsformel," *JBL* 50 (1931) 117-47.

von Hofmann, J. C. K. *Der zwei Brief Pauli an die Korinther.* Die heilige Schrift des Neuen Testaments II 3. Nördlingen: C. H. Beck, 1866.

von Rad, "*δόξα*," in *TDNT* 2:228-42.

Vos, G. *The Pauline Eschatology.* Grand Rapids: Eerdmans, 1979.

Wan, S. *Power and Weakness: The Second Letter of Paul to the Corinthians.* Harrisburg, Pa.: Trinity Press International, 2000.

Watson, F. B. "2 Cor. X-XIII and Paul' s Painful Letter to the Corinthians," *JTS* 35 (1984) 324-46.

Weber, H. R. *The Cross: Tradition and Interpretation.* ETr. Jessett, E. Grand Rapids: Eerdmans/London: SPCK, 1978.

Weber, Max. *The Protestant Ethic and the Spirit of Capitalism.* London: Unwin Papberbacks, 1985.

Weima, J. A. D. *Neglected Endings: The Significance of the Pauline Letter Closings.* JSNTSS 101. Sheffield: Sheffield University, 1994.

Weiss, J. *Earliest Christianity.* ETr. New York: Harper, 1959.

______. *Paul and Jesus.* ETr. London/New York: Harper & Brothers, 1909.

______. *The History of Primitive Christianity,* vol. 1, ed. Grant, F. C. London: MacMillan, 1937.

Wendland, H. D. *Die Briefe an die Korinther*, NTD 7 Göttingen: Vandenhoeck & Ruprecht, 1964, 1972.

Wettstein, J. J. 177-215 in *Novum Testamentum Graecum* II. Amsterdam,

1752.

Whitely, D. E. H. *The Theology of St. Paul.* Philadelphia: Fortress, 1966.

Wilckens, U. *Weisheit und Torheit.* Tübingen: J. C. B. Mohr, 1959.

Wiles, G. P. *Paul' s Intercessory Prayers.* SNTSMS 24. Cambridge: University Press, 1974.

Wilson, R. McL. "Gnosis at Corinth," in *Paul and Paulism: Essays in Honor of C. K. Barrett,* ed. Hooker, M. D. & Wilson, S. G. London: SPCK, 1982, 102-14.

Windisch, H. *Der zweite Korintherbrief.* Göttingen: Vandenhoeck & Ruprecht, 1924.

______. "καπηλεύω," in *TDNT* 3:603-06.

Winter, B. W. *Philo and Paul among the Sophists.* SNTSMS 96. Cambridge: University Press, 1997.

Witherington III, B. *Conflict and Community in Corinth: A Socio-Rhetorical Commentary on 1 and 2 Corinthians.* Grand Rapids: Eerdmans/Carlisle: Paternoster, 1995.

______. *The Paul Quest: The Renewed Search for the Jew of Tarsus.* Illinois: IVP, 1998.

Wolff, C. *Der zweite Brief des Paulus an die Korinther.* THKNT 8. Berlin: Evangelische Verlagsanstalt, 1989.

Yamauchi, Edwin M. "Pre-Christian Gnosticism, The New Testament and Nag Hammadi?in Recent Debate," *Themelios* 10 (1984) 22-27.

Young, F. and Ford, D. F. *Meaning and Truth in 2 Corinthians.* Grand Rapids: Eerdmans, 1988.

Zerwick, M. and Grosvenor, M. *A Grammatical Analysis of the Greek New*

Testament, II. Rome: Biblical Institute Press, 1979.

Ziegler, K. L. *Theologische Abhandlungen* 2. Güttingen: Die Terich, 1804.

Ziesler, J. A. *Pauline Christianity*. Oxford: Oxford University Press, 1983.

_______. *The Meaning of Righteousness in Paul: A Linguistic and Theological Enquiry*. SNTSMS 20. Cambridge: University Press, 1972.

Zmijewski, J. *Der Stil der paulinischen 'Narrenrede': Analyse der Sprachgestaltung in 2 Kor 11, 1-12, 10 als Beitrag zur Methodik von Stiluntersuchungen neutestamentlicher Texte*. BBB 52. Bonn/Koeln: Hanstein, 1978.

Zuntz, G. *The Text of the Epistles*. London: Oxford University Press, 1953.

강창희. 『복음서의 지명과 복음서의 역사성』. 서울: 솔로몬, 2001.

박윤선. 『고린도전후서』. 서울: 영음사, 1981.

이상근. 『고린도전후서』. 대구: 성등사, 1969.

정규남 『고린도후서강해』 서울:엠마오, 1994.

한철하 『21세기 인류의 살 길』 서울:아세아연합신학대학교출판부, 2003.

고대 작가들

Augustine(A.D. 354-430).

De Haer.

Clement of Alexandria(A.D. 150-215).

The Stromata in *ANF* vol 1.

The First Epistle of Clement to the Corinthians

The Letter of Clemments to the Corinthians

Chrysostom, John(A.D. 344-401).

Homilies on the Epistles of Paul to the Corinthians.

Cicero(106-43 B.C.)

Ad Familieares

In Verrem

Diogenes(240-152 B.C.)

Laertius

Dionysius(A.D. 200-265)

Hal.

Epictetus(A.D. 50-130)

The Discouses

Epiphanius(A.D. 298-403)

Haereses

Euripides(484-406 B.C.)

Hippolytus.

Orestes.

Irenaeus(A.D. 130?-202).

Against Heresies

Epideixis

Justin(A.D. 100-165)

1 Apology

Origen(A.D. 185-254)

De Principiis

Against Celsus

Philostratus(A.D. 170-245)

Vit. Apollonius(Life of Apollonius)

Plato(427-347 B.C.)

Phaedo

Phaedrus.

Protagoras.

Republic.

Plutarch(A.D. 46?-119?)

Moralia

Polybius(200?-118 B.C.)

Refutatio

Seneca(A.D. 4-65)

Ep.

Letters

Xenophon(431-350 B.C.)

Anabasis

Cyropaedia

Tertullian(A.D. 160-220)

Against the Valentinians

trinitas

De Pudicitia

De Resur. Carnis

구약외경과 위경 그리고 다른 유대 문서들

Josephus(A.D. 37?-100?)

Antiquities of the Jews

The Jewish War

Jubilees

Testaments of the Twelve Patriarchs

Philo(A.D. 10?-50?)

De Post. Caini

On Special laws

On the Change of Names

On the Confusion of Tongues

On the Embassy to Gaius

On the Migration of Abraham.

Phaedrus

Quod Det. Pot.

Rev. Div. Her.

Vit. Moses.

다른 기독교 문서들

Acts of Paul and Thecla

Ascension of Isaiah

Epistle to Diognetus

Joseph and Aseneth

서 언

필자의 은사이신 마틴(Ralph P. Martin)박사는 풀러 신학교에 재직 중이시던 80년대 초반부터 풀러 신학교수들이 주축이 된 세계성경주석(WBC) 시리즈의 신약부분 주필로 일해 오셨다. 마틴 박사 자신도 고린도후서를 맡아 매우 광범위한 여러 학자들의 연구를 망라하는 학구적이고도 복음주의적인 주석책을 펴내셨다.[1] 마틴 박사는 재직중 수년 동안 고린도후서 강의를 해오셨고, 나도 그의 강의를 들었다. 그의 제자 된 나는 졸작을 내느니 차라리 그분의 책을 번역하여 독자들에게 소개하는 것이 실제적으로 독자들에게 도움이 된다고 생각했다. 그러나 고린도후서를 연구하면서 나름대로 고린도후서의 주석을 써야겠다는 생각이 들었다. 고린도후서에 대해 나름대로 생각하는 부분들과 더 강조하고 싶은 부분도 생겨나게 된 것이다. 더구나 고린도 교회의 분쟁에 대한 바울의 자세와 교훈이 오늘날 한국교회 목회자들과, 믿는 사람들이 처한 온갖 분쟁의 해결에 대해 성경적인 지침이 된다는 생각을 하고 부족하나마 고린도후서 주석을 써서 그들에게 도움을 주는 것이 좋겠다는 생각이 들었다.

마틴 박사는 1997년에 출간된 바넷(Paul Barnett)의 고린도후서 주석을 추천하는 글에서 고린도후서에 대해서 다음과 같이 요약하고 있다. "고린도후서는 많은 역사적, 문서적, 해석적 문제를 안

---

1) Ralph P. Martin, *2 Corinthians, Word Biblical Commentary*, vol. 40 (Waco, TX.: Word Books Publisher, 1986).

고 있는 서신이다. 특별히 현대인들, 그 중에서도 설교 본문으로 고린도후서를 택하는 이들에게 어려운 책이다. 그러나 고린도후서는 복음진리의 풍부한 광산과 같으며, 설교, 목회사역, 그리스도인의 삶에 대해 바울의 설교를 이해하기 위해서 매우 귀중한 자원이 된다"라고 말했다.[2] 이 말은 바레트(C. K. Barrett)가 고린도후서에 대해서 한 말과 유사하다. "고린도후서는 바울이 생각하는 사도직에 대한 가장 충분하고 열정적인 자료이다."[3] 마틴 박사는 그의 고린도후서 강의에서 바울 사도의 사도로서의 개인적 성품과 그의 목회 신학적 특징을 강조하였다. 마틴 박사는 그의 강의나 책에서 바울 사도가 그리스도의 십자가의 고뇌와 희생을 그의 목회적 삶에 직결하는 것을 놓쳐서는 안 된다고 자주 언급 하였다. 바울 사도는 고린도 교회에서 많은 비난을 받는 가운데 자신을 "고난 받는 사도"로 이해한다.[4] 그리스도의 죽음이 부활을 가져 왔듯이, 그의 사도적 고난과 약함이 고린도 교회에서의 그의 사도적 권위의 회복과 승리를 궁극적으로 가져오리라고 확신한다(고후 12:9, 13:4). 이런 사상은 복음서에서 예수님께서 제자들에게 말씀하신 제자도와 일치된다. "아무든지 나를 따라 오려거든 자기를 부인하고 자기 십자가를 지고 나를 좇을 것이니라"(마 16:24; 병행구: 마 10:38; 막 8:34; 눅 9:23; 14:27). 그러나 이런 십자가의 능력이 인간에게 있는 것이 아니라 하나님 자신의 능력임을 분명히 밝힌다(고후 1:9; 12:9, 10; 13:4).

주석가들은 고린도후서가 가장 해석하기 힘든 서신이라고 말

2) Paul Barnett, *The Second Epistle to the Corinthians* (Grand Rapids: Eerdmans, 1997).

3) Martin, x, 재인용.

4) Martin, lviii-lxi.

한다.[5] 고린도후서의 복잡한 배경과 정황 이해를 확실히 알 수 없고 추측만 하므로 본문 이해를 분명히 할 수 없다는 것이다. 그러나 고린도후서가 바울의 서신 가운데 바울의 깊은 개인적 내면성을 가장 잘 들어내는 서신이라고 말한다.[6] 그는 사도로서, 목회자로서 사역의 고뇌를 겪으면서 그리스도의 제자로서의 길을 걸어간다(4:7-15; 6:3-13). 그는 십자가의 고통을 받고 그 사랑을 교인들에게 나타내는 것이 하나님의 화해의 사자의 임무라는 것을 안다(5:20; 12:14-15).

흔히 고린도후서의 서술 목적을 바울의 훼손된 사도권 확립이라고 말하나 그 목표보다 상위 목표는 그의 사역에서 그리스도를 존귀하게 하는 것이다. 사도권 확립은 이 궁극적 목표를 위한 수단이다. 고린도 교회에서 거짓 사도들의 잘못된 가르침을 버리고, 바울의 바른 가르침을 따름으로 그리스도의 왕권이 확립되게 하는 것이 바울의 궁극적 관심이다. 이점이 고린도후서에서 분명히 언급되지는 않았으나 암시된 곳은 많다(2:14; 4:4-5; 5:15; 10:5-6, 8; 11:2; 12:9; 13:3, 10). "우리가 우리를 전파하는 것이 아니라 오직

5) Martin, x.

6) M. Hengel, *Between Jesus and Paul,* Etr. J. Bowden (Philadelphia: Fortress, 1983); R. H. Strachan, *The Second Epistle of Paul to the Corinthians,* Moffatt *New Tetstament commentary 7/2,* (London: Hodder & Stoughton, 1935), xxix; Martin, lxii; 이상근, 『고린도전후서』(대구: 성등사, 1969), 250; C. K. Barrett, *The Second Epistle to the Corinthians, Harper's NT Commentaries* (New York: Harper & Row, Publishers, 1973), 32, 34; A. Jülicher, *Einleitung in das Neuen Testament* (Tübingen: J. C. B. Mohr, 1931), 87; R. Bultmann, *Der zweite Brief an die Korinther* (Göttingen: Vandenhoeck & Ruprecht, 1987), 21; Friedrich Lang, *Die Briefe an die Korinther* (Göttingen und Zürich: Vandenhoeck & Ruprecht, 1986), 10; H. C. Thiessen, *Introduction to the New Testament* (Grand Rapids: Eerdmans, 1979), 206.

그리스도 예수의 주되신 것과 또 예수를 위하여 우리가 너희의 종 된 것을 전파함이니라"(4:5). 또 "모든 이론을 파하여 하나님 아는 것을 대적하여 높아진 것을 다 파하고 모든 생각을 사로잡아 그리스도께 복종케 하나니"라고 말한다(10:5). 계속해서 "주께서 주신 권세는 너희를 파하려고 하신 것이 아니요 세우려고 하신 것이니 내가 이에 대하여 지나치게 자랑하여도 부끄럽지 아니하리라"고 말한다(10:7; 참조 13:10). 그러나 바울은 자신이 부족하지만 그리스도의 사도임을 확신하기 때문에 자신과의 화해는 곧 그리스도와의 화해임을 확신한다(5:19-7:2). 그러므로 고린도 교인들이 자신과 화해할 것을 자주 권면한다(5:18-21; 6:11-13; 7:1).[7]

이렇게 해서 바울이 고린도 교인들과 어느 정도 화해에 성공하였는지는 알 수 없다. 그러나 분명한 사실은 바울이 고린도후서에서 기독 교회의 내분은 물론 모든 그리스도인들의 가정이나 다른 인간 관계의 불화에 대한 기독교적 화해 방법을 위한 지침을 제공하고 있다는 것이다.[8] 특별히 교회 분쟁을 겪는 교역자들에게 사역자로서 신뢰 회복을 위해 취해야 할 목회자의 바른 자세가 무엇인지 가르쳐 준다. 그것은 십자가에서 나타난 그리스도의 겸손함과 희생적이면서도 뜨거운 사랑이다(2:4; 4:7-15; 5:14, 15; 6:4-10; 12:14, 15). 교역자들은 자신들의 권세를 주장하기 전에 먼저 바울처럼 정직하고 의롭고 그리스도의 정신을 따라 바르게 살아야 한다(7:2; 12:11, 15). 그렇게 살면 불신과 오해가 생기지 않는다는 말이 아니라 문제가 생겨도 바울처럼 담대하게 자신을 변명할 수 있다.[9] 과

---

7) Martin x, lvii.

8) Martin x, xi.

9) Martin x, lxii.

연 우리 중에 바울처럼 온전하여 자신을 변명할 수 있는 사람들이 얼마나 되는가? 바울은 자신의 사도직에 대한 변명을 하면서, 또 고린도 교인들을 책망하면서도, 그리스도의 사랑과 인내의 모본을 따라서 궁극적으로는 화해를 위해 애쓰는 모습을 놓쳐서는 안 된다(4:7-15; 6:11-13; 7:2; 11:11; 12:15; 13:7, 10). 그래서 아래에서 우리가 제안하는 바와 같이 고린도후서의 주제는 화해라고 할 수 있다.

이 책은 한국복음주의신학회에서 요청한대로 신학생, 목회자, 평신도들을 위한 주석책으로서 순수하게 학문적이면서도 실제적 신앙 향상과 설교의 재료로 쓰이는 데 필요하도록 만들었다. 그러나 우리의 신앙이 과학적이고 이성적 근거 없이는 맹목적이 되고 설득력을 잃게 되므로, 선배들의 학문적 연구와 노력의 도움과 자신의 연구를 토대로 하여 썼다. 그러므로 어떤 논쟁적인 문제가 있는 본문 뒤에는 그 논쟁점을 정리하고 나름대로의 의견을 제시하였다.

끝으로 본서를 처음부터 끝까지 읽으며 교정을 위해 애써주신 제자 안성덕 목사님(경건신학연구소 상임연구원)께 심심한 사의를 표한다.

이제 이 부족한 사람이 이 주석을 쓸 때 성령님의 조명이 있어서 본문의 의미를 보다 분명히 나타낼 수 있게 되기를 기원하며, 또 이 책을 읽는 독자들에게도 같은 성령의 비췸이 있기를 기원하는 바이다.

2006년 여름

파사데나, Fuller 신학교, 도서관에서

강 창 희

고린도후서 개론

1. 주제와 중심 교훈

고린도후서는 고린도전서에 비해 독자들의 관심을 받지 못했다.[10] 아마 그 이유는 후서가 전서에 비해서 구체적인 여러 문제를 나누어 다루는 것도 아니고 또 그 짜임새가 복잡하고 뚜렷한 주제를 직접 언급하고 있지 않기 때문이다. 주제와 관련하여 우선 고린도후서가 바울의 변명인가, 또는 고린도 교인들을 위한 교훈인가라는 문제가 있다. 대부분의 주석가들은 12장 19절에서 바울이 자신의 말을 "변명"이라는 말로 나타내고, 또 전체 내용이 이와 부합된다고 보아서 고린도후서의 주제를 바울의 사도직 변명이라고 본다. 바울이 고린도 교회를 떠난 후에 고린도 교회에 들어 온 전도자들이 바울과 그의 교훈을 반대하면서 그들의 사역을 정당한 것으로 가르쳤다. 이에 맞서서 바울은 자신의 사도직과 사역의 정당성을 주장하게 된 것이다(11:2이하). 사실 고린도후서 전체에서 바울은 그의 반대자들을 공격하면서, 그가 진정한 그리스도의 사도임을 증거하는 말을 자주 하고 있다. 그러나 12장 19절에서 바울은 자신이 지금까지 한 말을 자신을 위한 사사로운 변명으로 생각하지 말라고 한다. 오히려 바울은 그가 한 모든 말의 목적은 고린도 교인들의 덕을 세우기 위함이라고 한다. 그러나 이

10) 고린도후서 연구논문은 고린도전서 연구의 30% 정도이다(*Religious Periodicals*를 보라).

말을 공평하게 생각하면, 변명도 되고 교훈도 된다는 말이다. 바울이 자신의 한 말이 변명이라는 것을 실제로 부인한다고 보기보다는 바울이 독자들과 상관없는 바울 자신의 변명이라고만 생각하지 말고 그 변명을 통해서 독자들에게 가르치는 교훈이 있다는 것이다. 그러므로 우리는 바울이 자신의 사도적 진정성을 논하는 변명들은 곧 고린도 교인들이 어떻게 진정한 그리스도인으로서 살아가야 하는가에 대한 교훈으로 인정해야 할 것이다. 즉 아래에서 밝히듯이 고린도후서의 주제는 바울과 고린도 교회의 상호 화해의 주제인데, 화해란 그 성격상 일방적일 수 없고 상호 간의 이해와 자세의 변화를 전제로 하기 때문이다. 바울은 자신의 변명을 통하여 고린도 교인들의 자세가 변화되기를 원하는 것이다.

주제를 파악하기가 어려운 다른 이유는 고린도후서에서 바울의 어조가 일정하지 않기 때문이다. 그의 어조는 때로는 온건하게, 때로는 강경하게 교차적으로 나타난다. 고린도후서에는 바울의 사도로서의 사랑과 위엄이 교차되어 나타나고 있다. 그는 고린도 교인들의 순종적이고 신앙적 자세를 칭찬하면서도 그들의 불신앙적 자세를 엄하게 꾸짖는다. 이런 이중적 특징이 대체로 앞부분(1-9)과 뒷부분(10-13)으로 양분되어 있으나, 더 자세히 보면, 앞부분의 중심 부분인 3장부터 6장에서 바울이 자신의 사도직을 변명하는 부분에서도 바울의 적들을 염두에 두고 말하는 듯한 비판적인 내용들이 있는가 하면, 뒷부분(10-13)에서도 고린도 교회에 대한 바울의 애절한 사랑의 표현들이 발견된다(10:1b; 11:11; 12:15; 13:7, 9). 이런 이중적 특징 때문에 서신의 내용이 연결이 잘되지 않는 듯이 보이고 이해하기 어려운 부분들이 있다. 때로는 바울이 형편상 암시적 의도를 가지고 쓴 곳도 있다. 당시 형편을 잘 아는 독자들은 이해 할 수 있는 부분들이었겠지만 우리들은 잘 알지 못하는 복잡한 상황들이 있었을 것이다. 이렇게 고린도후서의 난이함은 일반적인 언어적, 문화적, 시대적 차이뿐만 아니라 고린도 교회의 복잡한 사정과 바울자신의 자유로운 필체에서 비롯된 것이다.

바울이 고린도 교회를 떠난 후에(A.D. 52년; 행 18:18 이하) 들어 온 거짓 사도들이 바울을 비난하면서 자신들의 잘못된 복음을 가르쳤다(10:10; 11:4). 바울은 내심 고린도 교인들이 바울을 위해 일어나서 그를 변명해주기를 원했으나 다수의 고린도 교인들은 오히려 거짓 사도들을 따른 것으로 보인다(12:11; 13:2). 바울은 이런 상황에서 자신의 사도직을 스스로 방어하고 자신이 참된 그리스도의 사도임을 스스로 변명할 수밖에 없게 되었다(11:18; 12:1, 11). 그는 고린도 교회를 세운 사도로서 고린도 교회가 비복음적이고 비사도적인 교회로 전락하는 것을 좌시할 수 없었다(12:14, 15). 그의 고린도 교회를 향한 지극한 사랑과 사도로서의 책임이 고린도 교회를 그에게 다시 돌아오게 하기 위해 그들의 자세 변화를 매우 간곡하게 호소하기도 하고(1:23; 2:4; 4:12; 6:11-13; 7:2-3; 12:14, 15; 13:5, 7, 9), 또 엄하게 경책하기도 하는 것이다(11:2-3, 7-33; 12:14, 15, 16-13:2). 고린도후서 전반부는 주로 위로와 화해의 어조이지만 후반부는 오히려 매우 강경한 어조이다. 그러나 전반부에서도 목회적 위기를 나타내는 어귀들이 나온다. 고린도후서를 쓰기 전에 바울은 고린도 교회의 사역에 있어서 긴박한 위기에 직면하고 있었다. 바울을 반대하는 세력이 일어나서 그를 괴롭혔던 것이다(2:1 이하; 3:1; 7:5). 바울은 자기가 애써 세운 고린도 교회의 교인들이 자신을 떠나서 다른 거짓 사도를 따르는 것을 안타까워했다(7:2, 5; 10:12-18; 11:4-22; 12:16-18, 21; 13:2). 그리고 자신이 진심으로 고린도 교인들을 사랑하고 있음을 자주 말하고, 또한 그들도 자신을 그렇게 진심으로 사랑하기를 원한다(1:23; 2:4; 5:14; 6:6; 7:11; 11:11; 29; 12:15; 19; 참조, 2:4, 8; 8:7, 8, 24; 참조, 고전 4:14, 15; 16:24). 바울은 자신의 진실한 사랑을 그리스도의 희생적 사랑을 따라 사역하는 자신의 모습에서 증명하려고 한다. 자신이 복음의 내용이나 삶에서 그리스도와 가장 가까운 사도임을 증명하려고 애쓴다(2:14; 4:7-15; 5:14-15; 6:3-10; 11:2-33; 12:5-10; 13:4). 특별히 그가 복음의 본질인 그리스도의 약함을 따라서 고난을 가장 많이 겪고 약함의 정신을 목회에 적용해 온 진정한 그리스도의 사도임을 도처에서 강조한다(4:7-15; 6:4-10; 11:23-33; 12:9, 10; 15; 13:4). 반면에 바울의 반대자들은 거짓 사도들이다. 그들은 복음의 본질이 아닌 "육체적인 것"이나 외양을 자랑하는 가장한 사도들이다. 그들은 그리스도를 "육체를 따라" 가르치는 거짓 사도들이다(5:12, 16; 10:2-12; 11:8). 여기서 "육체"라는 말은 "영"과는 대조적인 개념으로서 하나님의 계시가 아닌, 인간 경험이나 오관(五觀)에 의해 인식되는 세상적인 외적 판단 기준이다.[11] 바울은 고린도 교인들을 위해 희생하는 사도이지만(4:7-15; 12:15; 13:7), 그들은 고린도 교인들을 종으로 삼고 허세를 부리는 거짓 사도들이다(11:13-15, 20). 문제는 고린도 교인들이 진정한 사도에 대한 바른 판단을 하지 못하고 오히려 세속적 인위적 권위를 휘두르는 거짓 사도들의 권세를 진정한 사도적 권세로 잘못 보고, 약

11) Bultmann, *The Second Letter to the Corinthians* (Minneapolis, MN.: Augsburg, 1985), 154.

함 가운데 사역하는 바울의 사도직을 의심하는 것이다(13:3). 그러나 바울은 그의 안타까움과 배신감을 개인적 감정이나 이기심에서가 아니라, 죄인들을 위해 죽으신 그리스도를 본받는 사도로서 고린도 교인들을 사랑하는 부모로서, 그들이 거짓된 교리로 말미암아 멸망당하는 것을 도저히 방관할 수 없어서 그와 화해할 것을 설득하고 있다(4:7-15; 5:14, 18-21; 6:11-13; 7:2; 11:29; 12:14-15). 그리고 사도적 강한 책임감을 가지고 고린도 교회가 진정한 사도적 교회가 되도록 바른 믿음과 선을 행하도록 끈질기게 종용한다(11:4-5; 12:19; 13:7, 10).

그래서 바울은 디도를 통해서 고린도 교인들을 꾸짖는 소위 "눈물의 편지"(The Tearful Letter)를 이왕에 보냈다(2:4; 7:8). 그러나 편지의 반응을 가져오기로 한 디도가 제때 오지 않아 애태웠다(2:13). 오래 기다린 후 드디어 디도가 좋은 소식을 가지고 왔다(7:6). 즉 대다수의 교인들이 바울에게로 되돌아 왔다는 것이다(7:9). 그래서 고린도후서 전반부에서 바울은 주로 위로와 기쁨을 나타내고 있다. 그러나 바울은 아직도 그를 따르지 않는 무리들이 남아 있음을 알고 이들에게 확고하게 경고할 필요를 느꼈다. 그래서 후반부에서는 고린도 교인들의 잘못을 책망하며 그들의 배신에 대해 안타까워하며 우려를 나타내고 있다(10:1; 12:20-13:2).[12] 이런 안도와 우려의 이중적 집필 동기로 보아서 전체의 주제가 곧 바울과 고린도 교인 사이의 관계 회복, 즉 화해임을 알 수 있다. 중

12) 10-13장에 대해서 2:4의 "눈물의 편지," 또는 "혹독한 편지"의 일부가 추가 편집된 것이라고 보는 견해도 있고, 또는 9장까지 쓴 후에 고린도 교회의 상황이 다시 악화되었다는 소식을 듣고서 이에 대응하기 위해 썼다는 견해도 있다. 이에 대해서는 통일성 문제를 다룰 때에 더 검토하게 될 것이다.

요한 것은 이 화해라는 주제 자체가 아니라 어떤 화해를 어떻게 이루는가이다. 바울은 그의 화해의 성격과 방법을 그리스도의 십자가식 화해로 규정짓고 있다(고후 6:11; 13:4). 이런 화해의 성격과 방법은 바울의 십자가의 신학(*a theologia crucis*)에 기초하고 있다.[13] 그의 적들은 반대 사상을 갖고 있었다. 즉 오도된 영광의 신학(*a theologia gloriae*) 이었다. 고난 없는 영광은 참된 하나님의 영광이 아니다(고후 4:7-18). 고난 가운데 하나님의 능력과 영광이 온전히 나타날 수 있기 때문이다. 그렇지 않은 하나님의 영광이란 것은 참된 영광이 아니라 가장된 것이다(고후 12:9). 바울은 고린도후서에서 분쟁을 종식시키기 위해서 어떤 인위적인 방법도 쓰지 않는다. 바울이 13장에 걸쳐서 화해를 위해서 여러 말을 하고 있으나 그 중심적 화해 원칙은 하나이다. 곧 우리 각자가 그리스도의 십자가의 죽으심을 중심으로 믿고 본받아 행하여야 진정한 그리스도인의 화해가 이루어 질 수 있다는 것이다. 십자가에서 보는 대로 그리스도께서 자신을 낮추시고 겸손할 때 하나님의 구원의 역사가 일어났다. 하나님의 화해의 역사를 보기 위해서는 우리 모두 용서 받은 죄인이라는 것을 깊이 인식하는 데 있다. "너희가 믿음에 있는가 너희 자신을 시험하고 너희 자신을 확증하라. 예수 그리스도께서 너희 안에 계신 줄을 너희가 스스로 알지 못하느냐? 그렇지 않으면 너희가 버리운 자니라"(고후13:5). 그리스도인들의 개인적 문제나, 교회의 문제의 해결은 다름 아닌 모두가 그리스도를 통한 하나님의 용서와 구원하심을 믿는 믿음에 서있

---

13) J. Calvin, *The Second Epistle of Paul the Apostle to the Corinthians and the Epistles to Timothy, Titus, and Philemon*. ETr. Calvin' s New Testament Commentaries 10. (Grand Rapids: Eerdmans/Edinburgh: Oliver and Boyd, 1964[=1547]), 25-29.

을 때 가능하다. 바울은 예수 믿는 신앙을 가지면 갈등이 안 생긴다거나 모든 갈등이 다 해결된다는 것이 아니라, 예수 믿는 진리는 갈등을 예방하고, 갈등을 극복하기 위한 유일한 효과적인 처방이며, 예수 믿는 이들은 이 진리에 입각하여 갈등 해소를 위해 부단히 힘써야 한다는 것이다(고후 5:9-10, 13-15). 그것은 예수 믿는 진리만이 그리스도인과 교회의 존재 근거이며 존재 이유이기 때문이다. 그러므로 고린도후서의 주제는 외적으로는 전체 고린도 교인들과 바울 사도와의 화해이지만, 내적으로는 모두 참된 신앙 즉 예수 믿고 죄 사함 받아 구원 얻는 중심 진리를 따라 살자는 것이다.[14] (이런 점에서 바울의 화해는 바울의 대적자들을 제외한 화해이다; 11:13-15). 이렇게 우리는 사도직 변명이라는 들어난 주제를 이끌어 가는 바울의 근본적인 신앙적 신학적 주제를 역시 바울의 중심 신학인 기독론적 화해라고 보는 것이다(5:18-21; 6:11-13; 7:2; 롬 3:25; 5:1, 10, 11; 고전 7:15; 14:33; 엡 2:14, 15; 골 1:20).

10장부터 시작되는 후반부에서 바울은 화해나 위로의 메시지 대신에 거의 경계와 책망으로 일관된 글을 쓰고 있으나, 그것도 고린도 교회를 다시 방문하기 전에 관계회복을 촉구하는 것이 목적이므로 넓은 시각에서 화해의 범주에 들어 있다고 할 수 있다. 주로 엄격한 책망으로 이루어진 이 부분에서도 바울은 화해를 위한 진술들을 잊지 않는다(11:11; 12:14, 15). 특히 처음과 나중부분을 화해적 진술들로 마무리 짓는다(10:1; 13:7, 9-13). 반대자들에 대한 강력한 정죄를 제외하고는 일반 교인들을 위한 경계의 권면

---

14) Barrett, 323, V. P. Furnish, *II Corinthians*, AB 32A (Garden City, N.Y.: Doubleday, 1984), 564, Martin, 440, Thrall, 844. M. E. Thrall, *A Critical and Exegetical Commentary on the Second Epistle to the Corinthians*, vol. II (Edinburgh: T & T Clark, 2000), 844.

들이 대부분이다. 이 부분에서 바울은 반대자들에 의해 훼손된 바울의 사도로서의 리더십 회복을 위해 자신의 사역과 생애가 오로지 그리스도의 십자가의 희생을 통한 구원 사건에 중심을 두고 있음을 강조하면서 그의 반대자들은 그렇지 못하다는 것을 역설한다(11:23-33; 12:9-10; 13:4). 그러나 서신의 마지막 13장 7, 9, 10절에서 바울은 문제가 되는 고린도 교인들에 대한 사도권 사용(징계) 보다는 고린도 교인들이 스스로 회개하여 3차 방문이 화해의 방문이 되기를 바라고 있다. 이와 같은 화해와 견책의 교차가 전반부에도 간간히 비치고 있다(4:7-15; 5:14-21; 6:10-7:3). 그러므로 후반부에 집중되어 있는 공격적 메시지도 복음의 근본적 화해의 주제 안에 있다고 봐야 한다. 바울은 복음의 사도로서 훼손된 사도적 리더십을 고린도 교회에서 다시 회복함으로써 그리스도의 왕권이 확립되고 하나님의 구원 사역이 성공적으로 계속되기를 원하는 것이다. 바울의 지도력 회복 시도가 결코 이기적인 생각에서가 아니라, 고린도 교인들을 잘못된 거짓 사도들의 가르침에서부터 구원해야 한다는 사도적 책임과 자식을 사랑하는 "부모"의 순수한 심정에서 나온 것임을 강조하고 있다(2:4; 7:3; 11:4, 29; 12:14-15, 19; 고전 4:14,15). 그것은 결국 죄인을 위해 죽으시고 화해의 큰 사역을 이루신 그리스도의 심정이다(4:7-15; 5:14). 그러므로 이런 그리스도의 심정의 평가 기준에서 볼 때, 바울의 사도직은 정당한 것이며, 거짓 사도들의 사도직은 정당치 못하다는 논리다. 고린도 교인들이 이런 바울의 순수한 심정을 알고 화해하기를 촉구하고 있다: "고린도인들이여 너희를 향하여 우리의 입이 열리고 우리의 마음이 넓었으니, 너희가 우리 안에서 좁아진 것이 아니라 오직 너희 심정에서 좁아진 것이라. 내가 자녀에게 말하듯하노니 보답하는 양으로 너희도 마음을 넓히라" (고후6:11-13).

그러나 이런 화해의 주제가 분별없는 일변도식 화해를 지향하는 것은 아니다. 바울은 고린도 교인들이 그리스도를 진정으로 따르지 않으면 결국 하나님께 정죄 받을 것임을 고린도후서 후반부에서 뿐만 아니라 전반부에서도 분명히 말하고 있다(2:6; 6:14-7:1; 11:3). 그리고 거짓 사도들을 하나님과 대립된 사단의 일꾼들로 정죄하고 있다(11:15). 복음은 믿는 자들에게는 기쁜 소식이지만, 거절하는 자들에게는 심판과 저주가 된다는 진리가 여전히 인정되고 있다(2:15-16). 인간들의 진정한 화해는 그리스도를 통한 하나님과의 화해의 모델을 따를 때 가능한 것이다.

이런 화해는 결국 고린도 교인들이 바울이 진정한 그리스도의 사도임을 인식할 때 가능하므로 고린도후서, 특히 후반부에는, 바울의 사도권 확립과 관련된 내용들이 많다. 그래서 고린도후서의 전체 주제를 바울의 사도권을 위한 변명이라고 보는 것이다. 그러나 바울의 사도권 회복의 주제는 그리스도의 왕권 또는 그리스도의 몸된 교회를 세우는 일과 상호 긴밀히 연결되어 있다(4:5; 10:5-6, 8; 13:4, 10). 바울은 자신의 고린도 교회에서의 사도권 회복이 곧 고린도 교회에서의 그리스도의 왕권 회복으로 보았다(4:5; 5:11, 20; 10:5-6, 8; 11:4; 13:10).[15] "주께서 주신 권세는 너희를 파하려고 하신 것이 아니요 세우려고 하신 것이니 내가 이에 대하여 지나치게 자랑하여도 부끄럽지 아니하리라" (10:8). 이 두 가지 주제가 서로 얽혀 있는 것은 바울 자신이 진정한 그리스도의 사도로서 매사에 결코 실수함이 없이 온전하다는 굳은 확신을 갖고 있기

15) Thrall, 844.

때문이다. 바울이 자신이 진정한 그리스도의 사도라는 확신을 분명히 갖고서 그의 생각하고 하는 것은 거의 모두 그리스도의 위탁과 인정을 받은 것으로 믿기 때문이다(고전7:25, 40; 고후4:6; 5:20; 10:8; 11:10; 17; 13:10). 반면에 그를 반대하는 이들은 거짓 사도들이요 사단의 일꾼들이다(11:13, 15). 그러나 고린도후서에서 사도권 회복이나 방어보다 더 궁극적인 바울의 관심은 예수의 주되심과 그의 왕권을 회복하는 일이다. 이를 위해 필요한 것이 바울 사도와 고린도 교회가 화해하는 것이다. 화해를 통해서만이 그리스도의 교회를 굳건하게 세울 수 있기 때문이다. 그러나 고린도 교회 회중의 이중성 때문에 화해에 대한 바울의 어조가 달리 나타나는 것이다. 즉 전반부에서는 지지하는 다수를 향해서 온화하게 나타나고, 후반부에서는 반대하는 다수를 향해서 강경하게 나타나는 것이다. 전반부에서는 주로 고린도 교인 전체에 대하여 화해를 위해 필요한 설득을 계속하지만, 후반부에서는 주로 화해를 방해하는 반대 세력을 단호히 정죄하고 배척한다(11:13-15; 12:19-13:2).

그러므로 고린도후서의 외적인 주제는 사도직 변명이라고 할 수 있으나, 내적인 주제는 고린도 교인들과 바울 사도와의 화해이고, 암시적인 궁극적 주제는 그리스도의 왕권 회복이라고 할 수 있다. 한마디로 전체 주제를 말한다면 사도권 방어를 통한 화해라고 할 수 있다. 바울은 그의 반대자들을 물리치고 다수의 고린도 교인들에 대하여 예수 믿어 죄 사함 받아 구원 얻는 중심 진리를 따라 같은 하나님의 나라 백성으로서 서로 용서하며 사랑하는 공동체를 만들자는 것이다. 고린도후서 전반부는 물론 후반부에서도 바울은 고린도 교회에 대한 그의 지극한 사랑을 자주 언급하는 것을 보면, 이런 화해의 주제가 결코 피상적인 주제는 아니다(1:23; 2:4; 4:12; 5:14; 6:6; 7:1, 3; 10:1; 11:11; 12:15; 13:7, 10). 고린도후서 전체에서 화해를 위한 분명한 기독론적 설명들이 고르게 나타나지만(1:19; 2:17; 4:4, 7-15; 6:4-10; 8:9; 10:5; 11:2; 12:10; 13:4), 바울의 복음의 정통성(2:17-4:6; 참조, 11:4), 바울의 도덕성(1:12, 23; 3:4-6; 4:2; 5:11; 6:3-13; 7:2; 10:13-18; 11:6, 10; 12:14), 교회 설립자로서 바울의 사도적 위상 같은(10:8; 11:5; 12:, 11, 14; 13:10; 고전 4:15) 사도직 변명과 관련된 다른 설명들도 있다. 이런 설명들도 결국 바울의 진정성을 변호하는 내용으로서 고린도 교인들과의 진실한 관계 회복을 위한 것들이다. 그러나 그리스도의 고난을 통한 죄인과의 화해를 위한 사랑이 중심적 설명이며, 다른 설명들은 이 기독론적 설명(주제, 교훈)에 근거한 작은 설명들이다. "약한 가운데 강해지는 그리스도의 능력"도 결국 기독론적 주제와 관련된 중요한 주제로 볼 수 있다(4:7-15; 12:9, 10; 13:4, 9). 바울의 기독론 중심 사상은 아래("통일성"과 "바울의 사도직 이해")에서 더 자세히 다루게 될 것이다.

2. 저 자

고린도후서가 바울의 저서임은 다음 세 가지 증거로 확실하다.

첫째, 1장 1절에서 저자가 바울임을 분명히 밝히고 있다.

둘째, 고린도후서 전체가 바울의 용어, 문체, 사상으로 일관되어 있다. 예로 "우리가 … 저와 같은 형상으로 화하여"(τὴν αὐτὴν εἰκόνα, 고후 3:18)라는 말씀은 로마서 2장 29절과 같다.

"그리스도는 하나님의 형상(εἰκὼν τοῦ θεοῦ) 이니라"(고후 4:4) 라는 말씀은 골로새서 1장 15절, 로마서 8장 29절, 고린도전서 11장 7절과 유사하다. 고린도후서 5장16-17절과 갈라디아서 6장 13-15절에는 육체를 따라 자랑하는 것과 새로운 피조물의 대조가 나타난다. 고린도후서 12장 18절에 "성령으로 행함"이란 말씀은 갈라디아서 5장 16절과 같다. 고린도후서 12장 12절의 "사도의 표된 것은 … 표적과 기사와 능력을 행함이라"는 말씀은 로마서 15장 18절과 유사하다. 고린도후서 12장 14절에서 바울은 자신과 고린도 교인들과의 관계를 부모와 어린 자식과의 관계로 설명하는데 고린도전서 3장 1, 2절에 같은 관계 묘사가 나온다. 고린도후서 12장 20절은 갈라디아서 5장 20절과 흡사하다. 무엇보다 십자가와 그리스도의 희생과 사랑을 그의 사역에 적용시키는 것은 바울의 목회신학의 특징이다.[16)]

셋째, 교회의 전승이 일치되어 바울의 저작을 지지한다. 폴리캅, 터툴리안, 알렉산드리아의 클레멘트, 이레네우스가 본서를 인용하였고, 말시온과 무라토리 정경 목록에 본서가 기록되어 있다.[17)]

---

16) 갈 6:17; 빌 1:24; 2:17; 골 1:24; 딤후 4:6; 고후 6:3-10; 11:24-29.

17) H. C. Thiessen, 207; C. K. Barrett, 46-47; 이상근, 243-44; 크레멘트1서(1 Clement, A.D. 95, 96)가 고린도후서를 알고 있었는가에 대한 논쟁이 있다. D. A. Hagner, *The Use of the Old and New Testaments in Clement of Rome*, NovTSup 34 (Leiden: Brill, 1973), 213: "클레멘트가 고린도후서를 알았음을 암시하는 강력한 가능성이 남아 있다"라고 말한다. 그러나 이에 대해서 회의 적인 M. J. Harris, *The Second Epistle to the Corinthians* (Grand Rapids: Eerdmans, 2005), 2, 주, 3, 4를 보라.

3. 수신자

서두에서 바울은 수신자를 고린도교회 교인들로 밝히고 있다. 고린도 교인들은 바울을 따르는 다수와 그를 반대하는 소수로 나눠져 있었다고 본다. 이런 파벌에 대한 경고가 고린도전서에서부터 있었고(고전 1장; 12:25이하) 후서 전체에서도 이런 분쟁에 대해 논하고 있다. 특히 10장부터 13장은 그를 반대하는 이들에 대한 경고라고 본다. 9장 1절에 고린도 교회가 속한 아가야 지방에 대한 언급이 있으므로 9장은 같은 헌금 주제를 논하는 8장과 달리 아가야 지방의 다른 교회들에게 쓴 것이라는 주장도 있으나 거의 모든 학자들이 9장이 원래부터 고린도후서에 있는 내용이라고 본다.[18)]

4. 역사적 배경과 고린도 교회 문제

바울은 50년 말에 고린도에 와서 고린도 교회를 세운 뒤에 52년에 떠났다(행 18:18 이하). 그 후 55년 초에 고린도 교회의 문제를 전해 듣고 나서(고전 1:11) 고린도전서를 써 보냈다. 같은 해에 바울이 고린도 교회를 방문했으나 반대자들로 말미암아 매우 어려

18) H. D. Betz, *2 Corinthians 8 and 9* (Philadelphia: Fortress Press, 1985), 92-3; Martin, 250, 281.

운 고통의 방문이었다(고후 2:1). 56년 초에 디도 편에 "눈물의 편지"를 보내어 그들을 책망하였다(고후 2:6-11). 그 후 56년 여름에 디도를 통해서 고린도 교회가 다시 안정되었다는 기쁜 소식을 듣고 고린도후서를 썼다(그러나 어떤 학자들은 1-9장을 쓴 후에 다시 고린도 교회가 어려워 졌다는 소식을 듣고서 10-13장을 이어서 썼다고 본다).[19] 고린도후서는 마게도냐의 빌립보, 데살로니가, 또는 베뢰아 등에서 썼을 가능성이 크다(2:13; 7:5; 8:1; 9:2-4; 빌 4:15).[20] 그 후 바울이 3차 방문 시에 고린도에서 로마서를 썼다.[21]

1세기 고린도는 이스머스(Isthmus) 지방의 발달된 상업 도시였다. 고린도의 발전은 좋은 지리적 위치 때문이다. 뒤로는 전쟁 시 요새로 삼는 아프로디테 신전이 있는 작은 산(아크로포리스, 557m), 앞으로는 에게해를 바라보는 항구 도시로서 아테네 서쪽 90km에 가까이 위치하여 아테네의 발달된 문화와 접촉할 수 있었을 뿐만 아니라(실제로 아테네와 가장 가까운 도시 였다) 지중해의 발달된 해안 도시들을 잇는 교통의 요지였다. 남북 방향으로는

19) W. M. Ramsay, "Historical Commentary on the Epistles to the Corinthians," *Expositor* 6th series, 3 (1901), 220; E. B. Allo, *Saint Paul: seconde épître aux Corinthiens*, Ebib (Paris: Gabalda, 1934), 223; J. L. Price, Interpreting the New Testament (New York: Holt, 1961), 385; Martin, lxvi; Thrall,77; Harris, 50, 105.

20) Harris, 65.

21) 로마서 16:23의 "이 성의 재무 에라스도와 … 문안하노라"라는 말은 필자가 1994년 5월 초 고린도 유적지에서 바다로 나가는 중심 도로 한 가운데 ERASTUS라는 이름이 어른 손바닥 정도의 크기의 글자로 가로로 새겨진 것을 본 것을 상기시킨다. 아마 롬 16:23의 에라스도와 동일인으로서 길을 건설한 후에 건설자로서 그의 이름을 새겨 놓은 것으로 짐작된다.

마게도냐 지방[22]의 남단(지금의 그리스의 발칸 반도의 남단)과 펠로포네 반도(아가야 지방)[23]의 북단을 잇고 있는 남북의 길목에 위치한 반면, 동서 방향으로는 로마가 있는 서쪽 지중해(이오니아 바다)와 소아시아(지금의 터키)쪽 동쪽 지중해(에게해)를 잇는 지점에 위치한 육상과 해상교통의 중심지였다. 그러나 그 위치상, 양 반도를 잇는 이점이 있으나 로마와 소아시아 간의 해상교통을 막아 버려서 배들이 페로포네 반도를 따라 남쪽으로 돌아서 소아시아 지방으로나 북 그리스 연안으로 올라가야 하는 불편을 주었다. 그래서 네로황제는 고린도에 운하를 파서 로마쪽 지중해바다와 에게해를 연결하려 하였으나 중지하였다. 1893년에야 이 운하가 완성되었다. 고린도는 이 운하의 남쪽 페로포네 반도 북동쪽에 위치하고 있다.[24] 이 도시는 양쪽 바다에 있는 위치상 두 항구가 있었다. 서쪽 바다, 즉 로마쪽으로 향해서 3km 지점에는 레케움(Lechaeum) 항구가 있었고, 동쪽바다, 즉 소아시아 지방을 향해서 14km지점에는 겐그리아(Cenchraea) 항구가 위치하고 있었다. 한 마디로 고린도는 두 바다를 잇는 도시이며 두 반도를 잇는 요충적인 헬라 도시였다.

기원전 146년 로마의 루키우스 뭄미우스(Lucius Mummius)가 고린도를 파괴해버렸는데 1세기가 지난 기원전 44년에 줄리어스

22) 마게도냐는 고린도의 북쪽 지방으로서 빌립보, 데살로니가, 베뢰아 등, 바울의 중심 사역지 중의 하나였다. 행 16:9, 10, 12, 18:5; 19:21, 22; 롬 15:26; 고전 16:5; 고후 1:16; 2:13; 7:5; 8:1; 9:2, 4, 11:9; 빌 4:15; 살전 1:7, 8; 4:10; 딤전 1:3 등.

23) 고린도는 아가야 지방의 중심도시였다. 18:12, 27; 19:21; 롬 15:26; 고전 16:15; 고후 1:1; 9:2; 11:10; 살전 1:7, 8.

24) Barrett, 1.

시저가 다시 복구하여 번창하였다.[25] 현재의 고린도 유적지는 아볼로 신전 외에는 거의 로마 시대에 재건된 고린도이다. 물론 바울이 전도할 당시의 모습을 엿볼 수 있다. 유대교 회당이라는 글자가 발견되었고,[26] 또 회당의 대리석 기둥의 주두(柱頭)부분이 고린도 박물관 근처에 남아 있는 것을 필자는 보았다(행 18:4). 또 로마 도시에서 흔히 발견되는 여러 개의 신전, 반원형 극장, 공중 목욕시설, 재판소, 저자거리 등의 유적이 아직 남아 있는 것을 보았다. 고린도 시는 매우 부유하고 음란한 도시였다고 고대 기록들은 전한다. "고린도"란 희랍어 동사(κορινθιαζέσθαι, 고린디아제스다이)의 뜻이 "행음한다"는 뜻으로서 고린도는 행음하는 도시로 고대 희랍인들에게 이름난 곳이다.[27] 기원전 4세기 작가 필레테루스(Philetaerus)는 고린디아스테스(κορινθιαζέστες)라는 연극을 썼는데, 그 말은 곧 "창녀"란 뜻이다(아데네우스, *Deiphnoso-pistae* 7:313c; 13:559a). 고린도의 주신(主神)은 아프로디테(Aphrodite)였는데 이 여신 신전에는 천 명의 신전 창녀들이 예배와 관련된 음행을 하였다.[28] 플라톤은 고린디안 코레(κορίνθιαν κόρη)라는 말을 "창녀"라는 뜻으로 썼다.

이런 고린도와 같은 항구 도시들의 부패에 대해서 1 세기 키케

25) Martin, xxviii.

26) Martin, 2.

27) Martin, 2.

28) H. Conzelmann, "Korinthian und die Madichen der Aphrodite. Zur Religionsgeschichte der Stadt Korinth," *Nachrichten von der Akademie der Wissenschaften in Göttingen* 8 (1967), 247-61; Murphy-O'Connor, *St. Paul's Corinth: Texts and Archaeology*, Good News Studies 6 (Wilmington: Glazier, 1983), 126, 127.

로(Cicero)는 다음과 같이 말했다: "항구 도시들은 도덕적 부패를 보여 준다. 이런 도시들은 외국 언어와 풍습을 절제 없이 받아 들이고 외국 상품은 물론 외국풍습까지 받아들인다. 그 결과 그 도시들의 전통적 체제 중에서 변하지 않는 것은 하나도 없게 된다."[29] 한편 고린도는 문화와 지적 수준도 매우 높은 곳이어서 "고린도 말"이라면 수준 높고 교양 있는 언어로 인식되었다.[30] 또 일찍이 호머도 "부유한 고린도"라고 그 부유함을 인정하였다(*Illiad*, 2:570). 이런 고린도 시에 하나님의 은혜와 그의 종 바울의 사역으로 교회가 세워졌다. 교회의 대다수는 이방인들이었을 것이다. 그들은 다양한 삶의 배경과 풍습을 가졌을 것이다. 그들은 유대인의 회당을 통해서 유대교의 가르침에 접한 이들도 있었을 것이다(행 18:4). 그러나 대부분 부패한 이방 사회의 영향을 받은 이들이었을 것이다. 따라서 이런 사람들을 위하여 도덕과 행위 문제가 자연히 중요한 문제로 떠오르게 된 것이다(고전 5:1; 고후 6:14-18; 롬 1:26 이하).

고린도 교회의 일부는 유대인 디아스포라(이방지역에 사는 유대인)이었을 것이다. 알렉산드리아의 유대인 철학자 필로는 고린도시에 유대인들이 살고 있다고 쓰고 있다(*On the Embassy to Gaius*, 281-82). 사도행전 18장 4절에 바울은 고린도의 유대인 회당에서 유대인들과 헬라인들에게 권면하였다고 했다. 그러나 이 교회의 대다수는 이방인이었을 것이다.

---

29) 어떤 학자들은 고린도가 다른 항구 보다 특히 부패했다는 말을 부인한다. Barrett, 23; Conzelmann, 12.

30) Martin, *2 Corinthians*, xxx,

바울은 제 2 차 전도여행 시에 일 년 반 혹은 그 이상을 고린도 교회 설립을 위해 보냈다(행 18:11, 18). 사도행전 18장 12절에 언급된 고린도가 속한 아가야 지방의 총독, 갈리오의 부임 날짜가 51년 7월 1일이므로, 바울은 그 직전 겨울(50년 말과 51년 초 사이)에 고린도에서 사역을 시작하였을 것이다.[31] 바울은 이 때 신실한 브리스길라와 아굴라를 만나 함께 천막을 만드는 일을 하면서 사역을 했다(행 18:2-3). 그들은 유대인 부부로서 로마에서 살다가 49년 로마 황제 글라우디오(Claudius)의 유대인 추방령에 따라 고린도로 이주해 왔던 것이다. 고린도후서 5 장 1 절의 "땅 위에 있는 우리의 장막집" 에 대한 표현은 고린도 교회교인들에게 천막을 만들면서 자비량 사역을 하던 사도 바울을 보다 생생하게 기억하게 하였을 것이다.

그러나 바울이 회당에서의 설교 사역을 시작할 때 유대인들의 반대가 일어났다. 그래서 유스도라는 사람의 집으로 옮겨 복음 사역을 계속했다(행 18:4-7). 바울은 환상 중에 "이 성 중에 내 백성이 많으니 두려워 말고 복음을 전하라. 내가 너와 함께 하리라"는 하나님의 말씀을 들었다(행 18:8-10). 그러나 1년 6개월 쯤 지나서 갈리오 총독이 부임해왔을 때 유대인들이 바울을 고소하고 회당장 소스데네를 매질하면서 극렬한 반대 투쟁을 벌였다(행 18:12). 이에 바울은 브리스길라와 아굴라와 함께 에베소를 거쳐 안디옥으로 떠났다(행 18:18-22). 이렇게 바울의 고린도 교회 설립은 끝났으나 바울은 그 후에도 고린도 교회에서 일어나는 여러 문제를

31) 바울의 고린도 사역을 시작한 해에 대해서 조금 다른 견해들이 있다. Martin, 서론 30-31에 있는 참고문헌을 보라.

직접 해결하고 관여함으로 실제로는 고린도 교회의 사역을 계속하였다. 그러나 심각한 문제들은 바울이 고린도 교회를 떠나면서부터 일어났다.[32)]

첫째, 성도들의 도덕적 해이, 혹은 이에 대한 관용적 태도(고전 5:1 이하; 참고: 고후2:5)가 문제가 되었다. 이방인들로서 세상의 관습을 좇거나 흔히 보아왔던 고린도 교인들은 도덕적 기준이 분명치 않았던 것 같다. 이에 대해서 바울은 고린도전서에서 구체적인 크리스챤 윤리적 규범을 제시하고 있다. 즉 음행금지(5 장), 성도 상호간 세상 법정에 고소하는 문제(6 장), 혼인문제(7 장), 우상의 제물문제(8장, 10장), 우상숭배문제(10장) 등에 대해서 바울은 원칙적 기독교 윤리(6:12; 10:23, 24)에 기초한 구체적인 기독교 윤리를 제공하고 있다. 원칙적 기독교 윤리란 첫째, 기독교인의 신앙 양심이다. 기독교인이라면 할 일과 하지 않아야 할 일들을 자신의 개인적 양심에 따라서 판단해야 한다. 대부분의 경우 윤리적 책임은 논란의 여지없이 자명하므로 그대로 지키면 된다. 그러나 상황에 따라, 개인적 양심에 따라서 판단해야 될 때가 있음을 바울은 인정한다. 둘째, 이 보다 더 큰 원칙으로서 개인적으로는 거리낌이 없는 윤리적 행위라 할지라도 다른 사람에게 거리낌이 되는 행위라면 삼가해야한다. 윤리란 인간관계를 질서 있게 유지해가는 것이 그 목적이기 때문이다. 특히 성도와의 관계를 중시해야 한다. 세상 사람과의 인간관계 유지를 위한 나의 윤리적 행동이 교회 구성원인 어떤 성도에게 거리낌을 주어서는 안 된다.

---

32) 더 자세한 고린도 교회관련 바울의 사역 연대기를 아래의 "저작 동기, 목적, 인간 바울" 에서 보라.

나와 성도와의 바른 관계가 교회의 일치와 결속을 위해 필요한 것이다. 우선 순위는 세상 사람과의 관계가 아니라 성도와의 관계에 있다. 세상 사람들과의 교제는 적극적인 것은 아니더라도 수동적인 교제는 가능하다. 세상 사람들에게 초대받으면 갈 것이고 차린 음식은 먹을 것이다(10:27; 5:10). 그러나 자신의 양심에 거리끼지 않는 일이라도 어떤 성도들에게 거리낌이 된다면 피해야 하는 것이 더 큰 원칙이다.

둘째, 성도들의 바른 교회생활이 문제가 되었다. 즉 예배 시에 여자들이 수건 쓰는 문제(11장), 성만찬의 공정한 분배 문제(11장), 성령의 은사의 적절한 사용문제(12장-14장), 부활의 확실성 문제(15장) 등이다.

셋째, 교회 내의 파벌의 형성과 분쟁이었다(고전 1:11-13; 참조, 고후 12:20-13:2). 바울은 고린도전서에서 이미 고린도 교회가 4개의 분파로 나뉘어져 있었음을 말하고 있다 (고전 1:12). 뿐만 아니라 교인 각자가 받은 성령의 은사를 서로 자랑하면서 '내 것이 네 것보다 낫다' 고 서로 자랑하며 분쟁 하였다. 그리스도의 교회에서 가르치고 지켜야 하는 영적이며 신앙적인 문제 자체가 분쟁의 원인이 되었으니 아이러니칼한 것이다. 이런 싸움 가운데 신학적인 분쟁도 있었다. 그들은 그들의 "지혜" 와 "자유" 를 소유하고 있음을 자랑하였다. 이런 지혜와 자유는 당시에 유행하던 영지주의사상(靈知主義思想, 노스티시즘, Gnosticism: 구원에 대한 비밀스런 영적 지식을 깨달아서 구원 얻는다는 1세기부터 4세기경 로마시대에 유행한 이방 종교사상)의 용어였으므로 고린도교회가 영지주의사상에 영향 받은 기독교 이단자들에 의해서 혼란이 가중되었다고 보는 이들이 많다.[33] 그러나 우리는 영지주의가 이 때((1세기 중엽)에 완전히 체계를 갖춘 종교사상으로 유행했다고 보지 않고 헬레니즘의 신비주의적 영향을 받아 태동하고 있었다고 본다.[34] 여하튼 이런 초보적인 영지주의적 사고가 고린도 교회의 신앙에 큰 파장을 불러 일으켰다고 볼 수 있다. 모든 근본적 신앙을 왜곡시키고 바울이 놓은 신학적 근거를 흔들었다고 볼 수 있다. 바울은 이에 대해서 자신의 복음은 세상의 지혜가 아니라 십자가에 나타난 역설적인 하나님의 지혜라고 역설한다(고전 1-2장). 그리고 아마도 영지주의적 신비한 지식과 관련하여 발생했을 성령의 은사와 관련한 영적 능력을 자랑함으로써 생긴 갈등 문제에 대해서 보다 더 좋은 은사는 아가페적 사랑이라고 하면서 그리스도의 희생적 사랑을 통한 그리스도의 몸 된 교회의 일치를 강조하고 있다(고전 12장-13장; 고후 5:18-21).

고린도후서의 갈등 문제는 헬라적 영지주의적 영향이 문제가 아니라 바울이 떠난 후 예루살렘 교회에서 온 거짓 유대인 사도들이 문제였다(3장, 11:12-13, 23).[35] 그들은 바울이 세운 고린도 교회에 나중에 들어 와서 세력을 확장시켰다. 따라서 그들은 바울의

---

33) Walter Schmithals, *Gnosticism in Corinth*, ETr. John E. Steely, (Nashville: Abingdon, 1971), 102-114; Willi Marxen, *Introduction to the New Testament: An Approach to its Problems*, ETr. G. Buswell, (Philadelphia: Fortress, 1968), 75.

34) Martin, xxxii; F. F. Bruce, *1 and 2 Corinthians, NCB* (Grand Rapids: Eerdmans, 1971), 21.

35) Thrall, 926-945, 특히 927. Thrall은 한 동안 고린도 교회의 문제가 영지주의자들에 의한 것이라는 의견이 지배적이었으나, 지금은 주로 유대인 기독교인들에 의한 것으로 보는 경향을 지적한다. 한편, M. J. Harris는 반대자들의 주류는 예루살렘에서 온 12제자들과 관련된 유대주의적인 선교사들이며, 이들이 기존의 영지주의자들과 결탁하여 바울을 대항하는 것으로 본다(67-87).

사상이나 교훈, 그리고 그의 인격까지도 공격하여 바울의 모든 잔재를 고린도 교회에서 아예 없애려 한 듯이 보인다. 그들이 바울을 비난한 내용은 고린도후서에 직접적으로나 암시적으로 나타나고 있다. 그들의 비난은 다음과 같다: 바울의 외양이 볼 품이 없다(10:10); 그의 언변이 신통치 않다(10:10); 순수한 히브리인이 아니다(이방 영향을 받았다; 11:22); 영적 체험이 부족하다(12:1-4); 신령한 경험이 부족하다(12:7), 자기 몸의 병도 못 고치는 무능한 사도이다 (7-10, 12); 예루살렘 교회로부터 받은 추천장이 없고, 바울의 복음은 모세의 율법전통을 훼손하고 있다(3:1-15); 바울은 신뢰성이 없이 방문 약속도 지키지 않았다(1:15-24); 바울은 고린도 교회를 떠나서 사역함으로 고린도 교회에 대해 관심도 없고 사랑도 없다(2:4; 6:11-13; 7:3; 10:8; 11:7-11; 13:10); 금전 문제가 있다(7:2; 11:7-10, 12:16). 이외에도 아마 바울의 복음의 정통성을 문제 삼았을 수도 있다(11:4, 23; 13:3).[36] 이런 바울의 "약점들"을 가지고 바울의 사도로서의 부족함을 공격한 것이다.[37]

바울은 이에 대해서 적극적으로 자신의 사도직을 변명한다. 자신이 말은 잘하지 못하나 지식에 있어서 못할 것이 없다(11:6); 자신도 순수한 히브리 사람이다(11:22); 자신에게도 영적 체험이 있다(12:1-4); 몸의 병은 하나님께서 자신을 자고하지 못하도록 주신 것이며, 오히려 몸의 약함을 통해서 하나님의 능력이 나타난다. 그리스도의 십자가의 고난에 동참케 하고 그 능력을 나타내는 하나님의 뜻이다(12:7-10); 자신은 추천장이 필요 없다. 자신의 사역

36) Harris, 69-70.

37) 아래 "저작 동기 목적 그리고 인간 바울"과 "고린도후서의 특징들"에서 구체적 약점들을 찾아보라.

으로 인한 고린도 교회 교인들의 영적 심령의 변화와 구원 받음 자체가 오히려 가장 확실한 추천장이다(3:1-3); 나는 다른 사도보다 그리스도를 위해 많은 사역에 힘썼고 또 수반된 고난을 받은 사도이다. 과거에도 그리스도의 고난에 동참하였을 뿐만 아니라 지금 현재도 이런 고난을 받고 있지 않는가? 즉 자신이 고린도 교회 문제로 인해 받는 심적 고통과 몸의 병이다(4:7-15; 6:4-10; 11:23-27; 12:7); 고린도 교회 방문 약속을 취소한 것은 고린도 교회 형편이 방문 여건을 갖추지 않았으므로 취소한 것이다. 그러므로 방문약속 취소는 고린도 교회를 위한 것이지 자신의 이익을 위해 부린 변덕이 아니다(3:11-23); 자신은 재정적으로 의존하지 않는 사역을 하며(11:7-11), 결코 사욕으로 돈을 취한 적이 없다(12:14-18); 자신은 고린도 교인들을 진심으로 사랑하며, 그의 희생적 사역이 이를 증명한다(1:12, 23; 2:4; 4:7-15; 5:14; 6:4-10; 7:2; 8:8; 11:2, 11; 23-28; 12:15); 바울의 복음의 정통성은 그리스도 중심적 사역의 특징인 고난과 승리에서 나타난다(2:17; 3:1-3, 18; 4:1-15; 5:14, 15; 6:4-10; 11:23-12:12; 13:4).

한편 바울의 자신의 약함에 대한 깊은 인식은 고린도 교회의 그의 대적자들의 공격에 의한 것만이 아니라는 견해도 있다. 마틴은 보다 넓게 바울과 바울의 대적자들을 지원하는 예루살렘 교회 기둥 사도들과의 근본적인 불화가 바울의 자신의 약함에 대한 깊은 인식의 기저에 있다고 본다.[38)] 그 불화는 주로 예루살렘 사도들의 할례 같은 유대교의 율법주의를 완전히 벗어나지 못한 유대교적 복음과 믿음으로 의롭게 되는 바울의 복음과의 갈등이라고 본다

38) Martin, liii-lxi.

(행 15:1, 2). 사도행전 15장 1-19절에서 보도하는 A.D. 50년의 예루살렘 사도회의는 바로 이런 갈등을 해소하기 위한 모임이었다. 베드로는 고넬료의 경험을 가지고 이방인에게 율법을 요구하지 않는 복음이 가능함을 말했고, 바울도 그의 이방인 선교여행을 통해서 이방인에게 복음의 능력이 나타남을 보고했다. 야고보의 제안은 이방인들에게 간략한 유대교의 율법을 준수케 하자는 제안이었으나 이방인 신자들에게는 결국 어느 정도 유대교적 율법을 지워주는 제안이었던 것으로 볼 수 있다. 그러나 이런 제안에 대해서 바울이 얼마나 동의하고 그 결의에 참여했는지는 알 수 없다. 실제로 바울은 이 결정에 아무런 참여를 하지 못한 것으로 보인다. 사도행전 21장에서 바울이 마지막으로 예루살렘에 왔을 때, 야고보는 사도행전 15장의 이방인 신자들을 위한 율법 준수 결정을 자신을 포함한 "우리들"이 써서 각 이방 교회에 보낸 것으로 말하는데, 바울은 이를 잘 알지 못했던 것으로 보인다(21:25). 이런 중요한 결정에 바울이 제외되고 예루살렘 사도들의 일방적인 권위에 의해서 이방교회를 위한 복음 선교 정책이 결정되었던 것으로 보인다. 고린도전서 8장 1-10절의 제물에 대한 바울의 가르침도 예루살렘 공문과는 별 상관이 없이 바울 스스로가 가르치는 것으로 보인다. 또 갈라디아서 2장 12절에 언급된 안디옥 교회에서 베드로와 바나바가 이방인 신자들과 함께 식사하다가 야고보로부터 온 어떤 이들이 이르기 전에 저희들을 두려워하여 떠났다는 사실과 이에 대한 바울의 비판도 이런 갈등을 보여주고 있다. 마틴은 이 일 후에 바울은 예루살렘 교회와 관계를 중시하는 안디

---

39) Martin, lvi.

옥 교회의 지원을 더 이상 받지 못하게 되었다고 한다.[39] 더구나 안디옥 교회 출신 바나바와 마가 문제로 바울이 다투고 결별한 것도 안디옥 교회와의 협력 관계가 끊어지게 된 중요한 원인이라고 볼 수 있다(행 15:39). 아마 그 결과 경제적으로 어렵게 된 바울은 50년 초 고린도 교회 사역을 시작할 때 천막을 만들며 자비량선교를 시작하였을 것이다(행 18:3). 이때 바울은 자비량 선교를 그의 선교정책으로 작정하였던 것 같다. 바울의 재정 독립적 선교 문제가 특별히 고린도 사역에서 거론되는 것이 결코 우연이 아닐 것이다(고전 9:7-18; 고후 7:2; 11:7-10).

바울은 이런 예루살렘 교회를 주축으로 하는 율법주의적 복음이 이방 선교에 방해가 된다고 보았을 뿐만이 아니라 복음 진리 자체에 방해가 된 것으로 보는 것이 분명하다(갈 2:16). 그의 서신 아무데서도 유대교와 관련된 어떤 구체적 율법을 지킬 것을 가르치지 않는다. 대신 근본적인 하나님의 신앙과 성령의 열매와 거룩한 삶을 강조할 뿐이다. 고린도후서 3장 1-18절, 갈라디아서 3장 28, 29절, 로마서 3장 27-31절을 쓴 바울이 유대교의 율법적 관습을 결코 이방인에게 가르칠 수가 없었을 것이다.

문제는 바울의 일관된 이신득의 주장이 예루살렘 기둥 사도들과의 대립을 점차 심화시켰을 것이라는 점이다.[40] 그 결과 바울은 예루살렘 사도들과 점점 멀어지고 소외되었을 것이라고 보는 것이다. 이런 바울의 소외로 인한 불안은 바울이 로마서를 쓸 때에도 나타난다. 바울은 로마서를 고린도후서를 보내고 3차 고린도 교회 방문 시 예루살렘 방문을 앞두고 고린도에서 썼다. 바울은

---

40) Martin, liii.

로마 교인들에게 다음과 같은 특별한 기도를 부탁한다. "나로 유대에 순종치 아니하는 자들에게서 구원 받게 하고 또 예루살렘에 대한 나의 섬기는 일을 성도들이 받음직 하게하고"(롬15:31). "유대에 순종치 아니하는 자들"이란 말 가운데 바울의 복음을 반대하는 유대교 유대인들뿐만 아니라 기독교인들이 포함되어 있을 수도 있다. 더구나 이런 의구심은 이 말 다음에 나오는 "예루살렘에 대한 나의 섬기는 일을 성도들이 받음직 하게하고"라는 말에서 입증된다. 이 말은 분명히 예루살렘의 믿는 성도들 가운데서도 바울의 복음에 반대하는 이들이 있어서 바울의 헌금조차 거절할 수 있음을 바울이 심각하게 걱정하고 있는 것을 보여준다. 이렇게 예루살렘 사도들과의 갈등이 고린도 교회에서부터 생긴 것이 아니라 예루살렘 사도회의 이후에 점차 증폭되었다고 볼 수 있다. 안디옥에서 쓰인 마태복음이 세계선교적 비전과 함께 유대교 전통의 보존에 대해 강조하는 것도 특히 베드로의 우월성과 교회의 수장으로서의 인정을 언급한 것도 예사로운 것이 아닌 것이다(마 5:17-20; 7:21; 10:5, 6; 15:24; 16:16; 23:2; 28:19-20). 예루살렘과 안디옥의 반 바울 여파가 고린도 교회까지 미쳤고, 고린도 교회에 들어온 예루살렘에서 온 선교사들에 의해서 더욱 심화되었을 것이 거의 분명하다. 그 반대자들을 그들 나름대로 복음의 정통성을 주장하며, 특히 그들의 역사적 예수와의 연계성과 예루살렘 사도들의 인준을 내세웠을 것이다(3:1-15; 5:12, 16). 그리고 그들은 바울이 예루살렘 사도들에 비해서 열등하다는 여러 증거들을 제시하여 다수의 고린도 교인들을 자기들의 사람들로 만들었을 것이다. 이에 대해서 바울은 외롭게 자신의 사도직을 변명할 수밖에 없는 처지에 놓이게 된 것이다(5:12; 11:5, 23; 12:11, 19). 만일 고린도 교회의 거짓 사도들에게 밀리기 시작하면 연쇄적으로 그의 다른 사역지까지 반 바울파의 세력이 미쳐서 그의 지금까지의 복음 사역이 크게 위태롭게 위축될 것을 예측하고, 바울은 절대 절명의 위기의식을 가지고 이들을 단호하게 대처하기로 결단한 것이다(10:12-18; 11:2, 4, 13-15).

이런 바울의 사도직의 변명과 논쟁의 중심 축은 두 가지다. 첫째는 자신의 도덕적 양심적 결백이고, 둘째는 그의 사도직과 복음의 신적기원과 그리스도의 죽음과 부활의 유형의 목회적 적용이다. 그는 도덕적으로 조금도 거리낌이 없다고 한다(1:12; 4:2; 7:2; 12:16-18). 또 신학적으로는 바울의 복음 사역은 하나님의 영이 주체가 되어 수행된다는 것과(3:2-18), 또 하나는 그리스도의 약함의 능력이 나타난다는 것이다(12:9; 13:4). 특히 마지막의 그리스도의 약함의 능력의 진리는 바울에게 중요한 그리스도의 사도로서의 존재와 사역의 근거를 제공해주고 있다(4:7-15; 5:14-15; 6:4-10; 12:9; 13:4). 바울은 그의 신학의 기본 원칙인 "십자가의 고난과 부활의 영광의 승리," 즉, "약함의 능력"을 그의 사도직 변명과 그의 사역의 정당성의 판단기준으로 사용한다. 자신의 부족함을 일부 수용하면서도 도리어 그 것을 "십자가의 약함"에 견주어서, 오히려 그의 약점들이 하나님의 능력이 나타나는 통로가 된다고 믿는다(11:6; 12:10, 11). 바울은 그의 소외되고 약한 처지에도 불구하고 그의 사역은 하나님의 영에 의한 것이므로 진실한 것이며, 그리스도의 능력은 언제나 약함에서 나타나므로, 자신의 약함이 문제가 되지 않고 오히려 진정한 사도의 증거라는 확신을 가지고 있다. 그러므로 바울은 이런 목회적 곤경에 처해서 취할 수 있는 두 가지의 자세, 즉 적극적으로 자신의 "잘 난 점들"을 자랑하거나,

반대로, 소극적으로 피해의식에 사로잡혀서 "하나님의 징벌"로 보면서 자신을 낮추지도 않았다. 바울은 시종여일 "복음적인 방법"으로 그의 반대자들을 대적하고 있다. 그렇게 함으로써 신학적으로나 목회적으로나 바울 자신이야 말로 그를 반대하는 적들과 달리 분명하게 진정한 복음적 사도임을 증명하려는 것이다. 바울은 이런 메시지가 거짓 사도들과 맞서 싸울 수 있는 유일한 복음적 무기임을 잘 알고 있었다(13:4). 이런 바울의 변명과 설득이 얼마나 고린도교회 거짓 사도들의 세력을 꺾고 고린도 교회 교인들을 다시 완전히 바울과 그의 복음의 편으로 오게 했는지 우리는 알 수 없다.[41] 그러나 적어도 바울이 그가 목회적 곤경에 처해서 피해의식에 사로 잡혀서 그의 어려움을 자신의 약점이나, 실수로 돌리거나, 또는 "죄"에 대한 "하나님의 징벌"로 보지 않고, 십자가의 고난에 비추어서 적극적인 이해를 하면서 탈출구를 찾고 있는 것만은 분명하다. 아무데서도 바울이 고린도 교회가 자신을 비난하는 데 대해서 자신의 잘못을 시인하거나 뉘우치지 않는다. 주의해야 할 것은 이런 바울의 적극적인 변명의 자세가 우리 목회자들이 언제나 취해야하는 모델이라고 하는 것은 무리다. 우리가 바울처럼 완벽하지 않은 한, 무턱대고 바울의 변명방식을 천편일률적으로 우리의 모든 변명방식으로 사용할 수 없다. "십자가의 승리와 고난의 논리"는 자칫하면 우리 자신에 대한 거짓된 자위적 방편이 될 수도 있다. 우리가 목회적 곤경에 처할 때 진실하고 겸손하게 자신의 죄를 회개해야할 때가 더 많을 것이다. 바울의 사

41) Harris, 53: Harris는 바울이 고린도를 방문하여 몇 달간 로마서를 쓴 것을 보면 고린도 교회가 많이 바울을 중심으로 안정되었다는 것을 보여준다고 말한다(롬 15:20-21; 23-24; 28).

역은 그리스도 중심적 사역의 특징인 고난과 승리로 점철된 사역이다(2:14-16; 4:7-17; 13:4). 그러나 바울은 이런 기독론적 증명을 외적 사역에서 뿐만 아니라 그의 마음에서 우러나는 고린도 교인들에 대한 진실한 사랑을 통해서 나타낸다. 바울이 그렇게도 사랑하는 고린도 교인들이 자신을 의심하고 무시하여도 그는 진실한 사랑을 나타내기 위해 애쓰고, 또 그들의 사랑을 받기 위해 애쓴다(1:12, 23; 2:4; 4:7-15; 5:14; 6:4-10; 7:2; 8:8, 24; 11:2, 11; 23-29; 12:15). 이런 의미에서 고린도후서는 바울 사도가 자신의 사랑을 의심하는 고린도 교인들에게 보내는 사랑의 편지이다(참조, 고전 16:24; 빌 1:8).[42] 사심이 없는 진실한 아가페 사랑이 모든 인간관계와 진정한 의미의 성공적 목회의 비결이다.

5. 저작 동기, 목적, 그리고 인간 바울

흔히 동기와 목적 또는 주제가 서로 밀접히 연결되어 있어서 구별하기 어려울 때가 있는데, 고린도후서의 경우에도 그렇다. 우선 고린도후서의 들어난 집필의 직접적인 동기는 바울이 디도가 전해온 고린도 교회의 안정된 소식을 듣고 기뻐하면서 쓴 것이다(1:3, 4; 7:6이하). 그러나 바울은 아직도 그를 반대하는 이들이 남아 있어서, 그의 3차 방문 시에 대비하여 다시 반대 운동을 준비할 것을 경계하고 이들을 확고하게 정죄하여 아예 고린도 교회에 발

42) H. G. Sundermann, *Der schwache Apostel und die Kraft der Rede: Eine rhetorische Analyse von 2 Kor 10-13*, Europäische Hoschschulschriften XXIII 575 (Frankfurt: P. Lang, 1966), 208, 211.

을 붙이지 못하게 하겠다는 단호한 의지를 가지고 10-13장을 계속 쓰게 된 것이다(10:2-6; 11:2-4, 13-15; 13:1-2). 즉 디도로부터 고린도 교회의 호전된 소식을 듣고서 자신을 지지하는 이들을 격려하는 한편 반대하는 이들을 책망하려는 동기 또는 목적을 가지고 썼다. 이런 동기가 위에서 지적한 고린도후서의 외적 주제가 바울의 사도직 변명이라는 것과도 관련되는 것이다. 그러므로 이런 피상적인 동기나 목적과 관련하여 다른 목회적 신학적 동기나 목적들을 검토해 보아야 한다. 또한 이런 동기를 검토할 때 나타나는 바울의 인간성을 살펴볼 것이다.

고린도후서의 집필 목적은 다른 바울서신의 공통적 목적을 포함한다. 즉 바울은 그가 세우고 떠난 교회가 여전히 바울의 사도로서의 권위를 인정하면서 그의 가르침을 받아 순종하여 바른 믿음을 계속 가지게 하려는 데 있다(13:5, 7). 바울의 모든 편지의 초두에 있는 "그리스도의 사도된 나 바울"이란 칭호가 이런 의도를 잘 나타내 준다. 이런 서신의 목적을 한 마디로 "사도적 현존"(apostolic presence)이라고 한다.[43] 비록 몸은 떠나 있으나 마음은 너희들과 함께 있다는 뜻이 편지를 통해 전해지고 또 실제적으로 교회 제 문제들을 직접 다룸으로써 교회를 떠나 있는 동안에 사도의 기능을 계속 수행하는 것이다. 예로, 바울은 고린도전서 5장 3절에서 고린도 교인들에게 음행한 자를 치리하도록 명한 것을 다음과 같이 말한다. "실로 몸은 떠나 있으나 영으로는 함께 있어서 거기 있는 것 같이 이 일 행한 자로 이미 판단하였느니라." 이런

43) Robert Walter Funk, "The Apostolic Parousia: Form and Significance" in *Christian History and Interpretation: Studies Presented to John Knox*, ed. W. R. Farmer, C. F. D. Moule and R. R. Niebuhr (Cambridge: At the University, 1967), 263-66.

서신의 기능은 고린도 교회와 같이 바울을 공격하는 무리가 득세하는 위태로운 교회에 절실히 필요한 것이다. 실제로 고린도후서 10장 11절에서 바울은 그의 이런 사역에 대해 비판하는 세력을 경계하는 듯이 말한다.

이런 일반적인 목적 외에 고린도후서의 숨겨진 목적은 앞서 고린도후서의 주제를 복합적으로 말했듯이, 바울을 반대하는 세력이 등장한 고린도 교회에서의 목회적 위기 상황에서 바울은 그의 사도직 변명을 통해서 사도권을 확립하려는 것이다. 그리고 더 나아가서 그리스도의 왕권을 세우려는 것이다(4:5; 10:5-6, 8; 13:10). 바울은 그를 반대하는 세력이 단순히 그를 반대하는 사람들이 아니라 "다른 예수, 다른 복음, 다른 영"(11:4)을 전하는 이단 세력으로 보기 때문에 이에 대해서 단호히 대처하고 있다. 그들은 가장된 거짓사도들이요 사단의 일꾼들이었다(11:13-15). 이런 자들에게 그의 사역을 결코 양보할 수 없었다. 이런 면에서 요즈음 흔히 보는 인간적 갈등으로 인한 목회자들 간의 경쟁이나 대립의 경우와는 구별해야 한다. 그러므로 고린도후서 주제를 단순히 바울의 사도권 방어라든가 리더십 유지라고 보는 것은 너무 피상적이다. 바울의 싸움의 목적은 사욕을 배제한 순수한 그리스도의 사도로서 복음의 방어에 있는 것이다. 고린도 교인들이 바른 믿음을 가지는 것이 최종 목적이다: "너희가 믿음에 있는가 너희 자신을 시험하고…이는 우리가 옳은 자임을 나타내고자 함이 아니라 우리는 버리운 자 같을 지라도 너희로 선을 행하게 하고자 함이라"(13:5, 7). 바른 믿음이란 그리스도의 십자가와 부활의 신앙이다(4:7-10; 6:4-10; 13:4). 바울은 고린도 교인들이 이 바른 믿음을 본받아 자신이 그리스도의 약함을 따라 사역하는 진정한 그리스도의 사도라는 것을 인정하게 하는 것이 일관된 주제이다(4:7-15; 5:14, 15; 6:4-10; 12:9, 10; 13:4, 7, 10). 바울은 그의 사도권을 방어하는 일과 그의 사도적 리더십의 특성인 종으로서의 리더십(the servant leadership)을 함께 다루고 있다. 또한 대조적으로 사욕적이고 세속적인 거짓사도들의 문제도 자주 언급된다(3:1; 5:12; 10:7, 10, 12, 16; 11:18, 20). 우리가 아래에서 바울의 사도권 방어를 논할 때 바울 자신의 개인적 유익을 위한 싸움이 아니라 고린도 교회의 유익을 위한 그리스도의 복음의 방어라는 순수한 목적이라고 바울이 거듭 강조하고 있음을 염두에 두어야 한다. 이것은 우리가 의례적으로 바울의 순수한 동기를 들어서 그를 칭찬하려는 것이 아니라 고린도후서 전체에서 바울 자신이 일관되게 주장하는 특성이기 때문이다(1:12, 23; 2:17; 3:1, 18; 4:1-6; 5:14, 15, 20; 6:1, 4-13; 7:2-4; 10:5, 8; 12, 14, 11:4, 13-15; 13:5, 7, 10).

바울의 고린도후서 집필 동기와 목적을 보다 분명히 검토하기 위해서 바울이 고린도 교회에 보낸 다른 편지들과 관련된 바울의 고린도 교회 사역 일정을 간단히 살펴 볼 필요가 있다.

바울은 고린도전서를 쓴 후에 자신의 리더십에 도전하는 고린도 교회의 문제를 알고 애를 태우며 디도를 시켜 한 통의 편지를 보냈는데 일반적으로 그 편지를 눈물의 편지(The Tearful Letter)라고 한다(2:4; 13). 고린도후서 2장 4절에 바울이 "많은 눈물"로 편지를 썼다고 했기 때문이다. 이 편지는 물론 전해지지 않는다. 또 어떤 이들은 이 편지를 "엄격한 편지"(The Stern Letter, The Severe Letter)라고도 한다. 그 내용이 엄한 질책들이었다고 보기 때문이다. 이렇게 보면 고린도 교회에 보낸 편지는 모두 3통이 된다. 그러나 고린도전서 5장 9절에 "내가 너희에게 쓴 것"이라는 말이 있다. 희랍어 본문에는 분명히 "내가 너희에게 편지로 썼다" (Ἔγραψα ὑμῖν ἐν τῇ ἐπιστολῇ)라고 편지란 말이 있으므로 고린도전서 이전에도 지금은 없어진 또 다른 한 통의 편지(The Lost Letter)가 있었다고 볼 수 있다. 이렇게 보면 모두 4통이 된다. 그러나 학자들 사이에 편지 횟수와 바울의 고린도 교회 방문 횟수에 대한 이견이 많다. 예로 고린도후서 2장 4절의 "눈물의 편지"는 다름 아닌 고린도전서라고 보기도 한다.[44] 고린도전서의 내용 중 고린도 교인들을 책망하는 말들이 있기 때문이다(4:3-21; 6:89:3; 14:37-38). 그러나 고린도전서의 책망의 강도가 약하고, 다른 많은 주제들을 다루고 있으므로 "눈물의 편지"라고 부르는 것이 어렵다. "없어진 편지"와 "눈물의 편지"가 현존하지 않는 것은 그 내용이 사사로운 문제들을 다루고 있기 때문에 아마도 바울의 명령으로 폐기했다고 본다.

우리 나름대로 편지의 횟수와 바울의 방문일정을 세워 두어야 할 필요가 있다. 다음은 마틴 박사가 제시한 바울의 고린도 교회 방문과 서신 전달 횟수를 정리한 것이다.[45] 부기된 연대에 대한 학자들의 견해에 조금 차이가 있으나 대개 이런 일정을 따르고 있다.[46]

(1) 바울의 고린도 교회 설립하고 사역하다(행18:1 이하). 50년 말-51년 초

(2) 바울이 고린도를 떠나 에베소로 가다(행18:18 이하). 52년 초

44) Hughes, 57.

45) Martin, ; xxxiv.

46) F. Lang; 14, Martin, xlvi, ; Thrall, 77, 참조.

(3) 바울이 고린도전서 5장 9절에 언급된 "잃어버린 편지"를 보내다(어떤 학자들은 고후6:14-7:1이 이 편지의 일부라고 함). 53년 혹은 54년

(4) 바울이 글로에로부터 고린도 교회에 파당이 있다는 말을 듣다(고전 1:11). 55년 초

(5) 이즈음 바울은 고린도 교회로부터 여러 가지 교회 문제와 신앙생활에 관한 질문을 받았다. 55년 초

(6) 바울은 즉시 답장으로 고린도전서를 썼다. 55년 초

(7) 디모데를 고린도 교회로 보내어 가르치게 하다(고전 4:17; 16:10). 55년 초

(8) 이즈음 고린도 교회 내에서 바울을 대적하는 한 지도자가 나타나서 바울의 신뢰성을 공격하다(고후 2:5-11; 7:8-13). 디모데는 이런 위기를 수습하지 못하고 에베소로 돌아오다. 55년 여름

(9) 디모데의 보고를 받고 바울 자신이 고린도를 방문(2번째)하였으나 결국 그는 교회 앞에서 모욕을 당하고 큰 근심 중에 에베소로 돌아오다(고후 2:1). 55년 여름

(10) 바울은 에베소로 돌아온 후 즉시 "눈물의 편지"(The Tearful Letter) 혹은 "엄격한 편지"(The Stern Letter, The Severe Letter)를 쓰다. 디도가 이 편지를 가지고 고린도로 가다 (고후 2:4; 7:8). 55년 늦여름

(11) 바울은 에베소를 떠나 드로아에서 그 편지의 결과를 기다리다가 디도를 만나지 못해서 답답해하면서 마게도냐로 건너가서 (고린도 쪽으로 더 가까운) 드디어 디도를 만나고 그 편지의 결과로 고린도 교인들의 대다수가 바울을 지지하게 되었다는 반가운 소식을 듣고 안도하면서 고린도후서를 쓰다(고후 2:12-13; 7:6-16).

55년 가을

(12) 바울은 고린도후서 전체를 일시에 썼거나, 아니면 1-9장까지 써서 보낸 후에 다시 악화된 고린도 교회 사정을 듣고 10-13장을 더 써서 보내다(이렇게 편지 쓴 때를 나누어 고린도 교회의 사정이 달라졌다고 봄으로써 1-9장과 10-13장의 다른 편지의 내용을 설명할 수 있다. 그러나 우리는 한 번에 다 썼다고 본다. 즉 위에서 말한 대로 바울은 처음부터 자신을 반대하는 무리가 여전히 있음을 알고 마지막 부분[10-13]에서 이들에게 엄중하게 경고하고 있다고 볼 수 있다).

(13) 바울은 약 일 년 후 고린도 교회를 세 번째 방문하다(행 20:2). 55년 겨울과 56년 봄 사이.

위 11항과 12항에서 보듯이 고린도후서의 집필 동기는 이중적이다. 고린도 교회가 다시 바울에게 돌아온 시점에서 1-9장을 위로의 하나님께 감사하면서 썼고, 10장부터 13장까지는 고린도 교회 전체, 혹은 그를 반대하는 일부 사람들을 질책하기 위해서 썼다. 1-9장과 10-13장의 바울의 어조가 격변하는 문제로 인해 제기된 고린도후서의 통일성 문제는 아래에서 논의하지만, 여기서 간단히 언급할 수 있다. 즉 바울이 1-7장에서는 디도를 통해서 다시 바울에게 돌아온 고린도 교회의 소식을 듣고 주로 감사와 위로의 글을 썼고, 8, 9장에서는 다시 돌아온 고린도 교인들에게 그동안 중단되었던 예루살렘 성도들을 위한 헌금을 마치도록 종용하고, 10-13장에서는 아직도 자신을 반대하는 무리들에게 마음속에 두었던 말을 다하는 것으로 보면, 목회 심리학적 측면에서, 이런 순서가 자연스럽고, 고린도후서가 원래부터 하나의 편지라는 확신을 주는 것이다.

위의 목회적 배경에서 바울은 3차 고린도 교회 방문을 앞두고서 원만한 방문이 되도록 하기 위해서는(특히 2차 방문이 매우 어려웠던 기억을 회상하면서[2:1; 12:20, 21]) 방문 전에 편지로 몇 가지 문제를 먼저 해결해야 한다고 생각했다. 고린도 교회 교인들에게 오해를 일으킨 바울의 방문 취소 경위 설명(1:15-2:3), 바울의 권면과 사도직의 진정성 확증(2:4-7장), 예루살렘 교회를 위한 헌금 권면(8-9장), 그리고 반대하는 이들에 대한 경계와 질책(10-13장) 등이다. 이런 구체적인 집필 목적들은 전체적 집필 목적을 가리키고 있는 것이다. 즉 고린도 교회에서 바울의 대적자들에 의해서 훼손된 사도로서의 리더십 회복이다. 실제로 고린도후서 전체에서 바울의 사도직 변명이 자주 나온다. 바울은 그의 사도직의 정당성을 여러 가지로 변명해야 했던 것이다. 때로는 고린도 교인들의 이성에, 때로는 감성에 호소하면서 자신이 얼마나 진실로 고린도 교인들을 사랑하는가를 애써 증명하려고 한다(1:12, 23; 2:4; 5:14; 6:6; 7:2, 3; 11:11, 23-29; 12:19).[47] 특히 바울은 자신과 그리스도와의 밀접한 관계를 증명하여 자신의 진실한 사랑을 나타내려고 한다(4:7-15; 6:4-10; 12:9). 그리스도께서 죽으신 동기가 죄인을 사랑함인 것 같이 바울도 그리스도를 따라 희생적인 사랑을 고린

47) M. M. DiCicco, *Paul's Use of Ethos, Pathos, and Logos in 2 Corinthians 10-13*, MBPS 31 (Lewiston: N.Y.: Mellen Biblical, 1995), 77-112. 바울의 변명과 의사소통문제를 논하는 다음 저서들을 보라. S. J. Kraftchick, Ethos and Pathos Appeals in Galatians Five and Six, and T. H. Lobricht and J. L. Sumney, eds., *Paul and Pathos*, SBLSymS 16 (Atlanta: Society of Biblical Literature, 2001); Thomas Stegman, *The Character of Jesus: The Linchpin to Paul's Argument in 2 Corinthians*, Analecta Biblica 158 (Roma: Editrice Pontificio Istituto Biblico, 2005).

도 교인들에게 나타낸다(4:10; 5:14, 15; 6:4-10; 7:2; 11:29; 12:15; 13:7, 9). 바울은 그가 참된 사도가 아니라는 고린도 교회의 거짓사도들에게 대항해서 그가 참된 사도인 증거는 기사와 이적 뿐만이 아니라 그리스도의 고난에 깊이 동참하였기 때문임을 입증하려고 애쓴다. 그리스도의 고난이 죄인을 사랑하기 때문인 것 같이, 바울의 고난도 궁극적으로는 고린도 교인들을 사랑하기 때문에 달게 받은 것이다(4:7-15; 6:4-10; 11:23-33; 참조, 행14:22; 20:23-24; 21:13). 그리고 그의 고난에 대한 대가는 장래의 영광에 있다. 고난은 모든 그리스도인들이 영광에 이르기 전에 겪는 과정이며, 신실하게 살아가려는 그리스도인들의 삶의 모든 국면에서 계속 경험해야 하는 필연적인 요소라고 한다. 그는 고난 중에 지친 자신의 약한 존재에 집착하여 낙심하지 않는다는 것을 거듭 강조한다(4:1, 8, 16). 그의 현재의 미약하고 적들에게 공격받는 존재("겉사람")는 일시적인 존재 형태일 뿐이며 그의 영원한 진정한 존재는 아니다. 그의 진정한 영적 존재("속사람")는 이미 그리스도 안에서 새로운 피조물로서 성장하고 있으며(4:16; 5:17) 그의 성공적인 사역으로 그 가치를 인정받고 있다. 그리고 이 세상을 떠날 때, 혹은 주님의 강림 시에 온전한 영광스런 존재로 재형성되고 인정받게 될 것이다(5:1-10; 고전 15:42-52). 이런 새로운 영적 존재로 탄생하는 소망이 있으므로 바울은 현재의 자신의 외적 모습을 보고, 더구나 반대자들에게 시련 받는 처지에서, 존재해체의 뼈아픈 경험에서도 결코 낙심하지 않는다고 한다. 그러나 부활의 소망 이전에, 현재에서도 과거의 그리스도께서 고난 받으시고 부활하신 것처럼 자신의 약함 가운데 그리스도의 능력이 나타난다고 말한다(4:7-15; 12:9, 10; 13:4). 더구나 그런 진리를 자신의 경험을 통해서가 아니라 그리스도의 계시를 통해서 직접 받았다고 한다(12:9, 10). 이런 그리스도의 약함의 능력의 신학이 바울의 목회의 거의 모든 분야에 적용되고 있는 것을 볼 수 있다(4:5, 7-15; 6:4-10; 8:9; 11:7; 11:23-33; 12:9, 10; 12:15; 13:4; 7, 9). 이런 신학적인 설명은 바울의 인간관계와도 밀접하게 연결되어 있음을 알아야한다. 즉 그리스도의 죽음과 부활은 죄인을 위한 사랑, 바울의 고린도 교인들에 대한 사랑과 연결되어있다. 이런 신학적, 인간적 사랑을 통한 사도직 변명 외에도 바울은 사역자로서의 자신의 도덕성을 극구 변명한다(1:12, 23; 2:17; 3:4-6; 4:2; 5:11; 6:3-13; 7:2; 10:13-18; 11:6, 9; 12:16-18; 13:7 등). 그의 사도직은 역설적으로 그리스도의 종으로서의 지도자이다(the servant leadership). 그리스도의 약함의 능력을 그의 사역 가운데서 증명하는 것이 바울의 사도적 사명이요 관심이라고 할 수 있다. 이와는 대조적으로 반대자들의 세속적이고 사욕적인 리더십이 언급된다(3:1; 5:12; 10:7, 10, 12, 16; 11:13-15; 18, 20). 이런 사도직의 변명의 직접적인 목적은 3차 방문이 원만하게 이루어지도록 하는 것이다(10:2; 12:14; 20, 21; 3:1).

그러나 앞서 지적한 바와 같이 더 궁극적인 집필 목적이 있다면, 그것은 그리스도의 왕권 회복이다(2:14-17; 3:3-18; 4:6; 5:17-21; 10:5-6, 8, 17; 13:4, 7). 고린도 교회와의 화해를 통해서 교회의 머리되신 그리스도의 왕권을 회복하는 것이 바울의 궁극적인 집필 목적이다(5:19-21; 10:5-6, 8; 13:7; 엡 2:14, 15; 4:15; 고전 15:24, 25). 그러나 바울 자신이 그리스도의 사도임을 굳게 믿고 있으므로 바울의 사도권 회복과 그리스도의 왕권 회복의 두 가지 목적이 상호 긴밀히 얽혀 있다(3:5; 4:5; 10:5-6, 8; 13:10). 고린도 교인들이 바울에게로 돌아오는 것이 곧 그리스도에게로 돌아오는 것이다(7:2, 7

이하; 13:4). 바울과 화해하는 것이 곧 그리스도와 화해하는 것이다(5:20-21; 6:11-13; 7:2; 13:5-6). 이 목적과 관련하여 고린도 교인들이 그리스도 중심의 바른 믿음을 갖게 하는 것을 고린도후서를 쓰는 목적이라고 말할 때도 있다(12:19; 13:5, 7, 10).

바울은 자신이 세운 고린도 교회가 자기를 떠나가려는 것을 막기 위한 목회적 목적을 가지고 자신이 진정한 그리스도의 사도임을 변명하여 다시 화해하려고 한다. 그러나 이런 목회적 목적이라도 순수하지 못한 사욕적인 동기에서 나온 것일 수도 있다. 다시 말하면 바울뿐만 아니라 바울의 대적자들도 같은 목적을 가지고 고린도 교인들을 자기편으로 만들려고 할 수 있다. 그래서 바울은 자신이 사욕을 버리고 언제나 희생적으로 사역함을 극구 주장하고 있다(2:17; 4:2, 7-15; 5:14; 6:4-10; 7:2; 11:23-12:11; 12:14; 13:4, 7). 그러므로 고린도후서의 내적 동기는 바울이 2장 4절에서 밝히는 "눈물의 편지"의 집필 동기와 같다고 할 수 있다: "오직 내가 너희를 향하여 넘치는 사랑이 있음을 너희로 알게 하려 함이라." 실제로 바울은 고린도후서 전체에서 사도직 변명의 근본 동기를 고린도 교회를 향한 자신의 진실된 사랑이라고 말한다(2:4; 5:14; 6:6; 11:11, 29; 12:15). 그리고 고린도 교인들을 향한 그의 진정한 사랑을 신학적 설명, 자신의 도덕성, 이성적 판단, 감성적 호소 등을 통해서 밝힌다. 신학적으로 자신의 사도직의 신적 기원과 사명을 확고하게 말하며(2:17; 3:4, 5; 4:6; 10:8; 11:5; 12:11; 13:10), 또한 자신과 그리스도와의 존재론적 실존론적인 밀접한 관계를 자신의 고난의 삶과 주님으로부터 직접 받은 계시 경험을 통해서 설명한다(11:23-12:10). 도덕적으로 바울은 양심적으로 진실하게 일한다고 말한다(1:12; 23; 2:17; 3:4-6; 4:2; 5:11; 6:3-13; 7:2; 11:6-10, 31;

12:19). 이성적으로 고린도 교인들이 옳고 그름을 선택하기를 바울은 촉구한다(10:5-18; 11:5, 20, 22; 12:11, 13; 13:8). 감성적으로도 호소한다(2:4; 6:11-13; 7:3; 11:29; 13:7, 9). 때로는 이 진실한 사랑을 그리스도에게로 이끄는 중매자로서의 간절함으로 나타내기도 하며(11:2), 또 자식에 대한 부모의 진실한 마음으로도 설명한다(6:13; 12:14; 고전 4:15; 갈 4:19). 이렇게 바울은 고린도 교인들이 그의 진실한 사랑을 알게 하기 위해서 온갖 의사소통 방법뿐만 아니라 패러디, 아이러니, 풍자 같은 문학적, 수사학적 방법을 자주 사용한다(11장). 바울은 이와 같은 그의 진실한 사랑의 고백에 상응하여 고린도 교인들도 진실한 사랑을 나타내도록 촉구한다: "너희를 더욱 사랑할수록 나는 덜 사랑을 받겠느냐"(12:15; 참조, 6:1, 11-13; 8:8, 24, 11:11, 29; 13:9). 이런 바울 사도의 진실한 사랑의 동기가 바울의 사도권 확립이라는 목적에만 집중해온 학자들의 주목을 받지는 못했으나, 우리는 이 동기가 고린도후서의 목적뿐만 아니라 해석과 관련하여 매우 중요한 요소라고 본다.[48]

끝으로, 이상의 바울의 외적이고 내적인 저작 동기 또는 목적과 함께 나타나는 고린도후서의 또 다른 주제는 바울의 내면적인 인간적 모습이다. 바울은 한마디로 열정적인 사랑과 온유한 겸비함, 그리고 냉철한 이지를 함께 갖춘 사람이다(2:17: 3:1, 2; 4:1-6; 5:14, 15; 6:14-7:1; 7:2; 10:5-18; 12; 11:2, 29; 12:15). 위에서 말한 바와 같이 바울은 다수의 고린도 교인들에 대하여 그의 진실한 사랑을 나타내려는 동기에서 고린도후서를 쓰고 있다. 이런 그의 열정적인

48) H. G. Sundermann, *Kraft der Rede*, 280, 211. 고린도후서는 고린도 교회에 보내는 바울의 러브레터라고 한다.

사랑이 있기 때문에 바울은 반대자들의 도전을 인내하거나 하나님의 뜻에 맡기는 유보적인 자세를 취하지 않는다. 그는 주저하지 않고 적극적으로 반대자들이나 그들의 동조자들을 공격하며 자신의 사도권을 방어한다. 이런 강경한 자세는 특히 10장 이후에 더 분명하게 나타난다. 앞부분에서는 고린도 교회가 호전되었다는 소식을 듣고(7:6 이하) 주로 유화적인 자세로 다수의 고린도 교인들을 설득하고 있으나, 10장 이후에는 그의 3차 방문을 염두에 두고서 그의 반대파에 대한 보다 분명한 자세를 보여주어서 3차 방문이 2차 방문처럼 어렵게 되지 않도록 예방해야겠다고 생각하고 매우 단호한 어조로 말한다(2:1; 12:14, 20, 21; 13:1). 이런 적극적 공격적 자세가 바울의 개인적 성격에서 기인하는 것으로도 볼 수 있고, 사도로서 그리스도의 교회를 바르게 인도해야하는 책임감에서 기인한다고도 할 수 있으나, 무엇보다 이단적 반대파로부터 고린도 교회를 구원해야겠다는 위기의식에서 기인하는 것이다. 그들은 "다른 예수, 다른 영, 다른 복음"을 가르치는 무리들이며, 거짓 사도들이요, 사단의 일꾼들이기 때문이다(11:4, 13-15). 이들을 좌시할 경우 고린도 교회뿐만 아니라 다른 교회까지 그들의 이단적 세력이 번지면, 지금까지 자신이 이룬 복음 사역의 성과에 큰 어려움이 생길 절대 절명의 위기가 올 것이라고 판단한 것이다. 그러므로 바울은 자신의 사욕이나 감정에서 반대파들을 공격하는 것이 아니라 그들의 객관적인 유해적 증거들에 대하여 그리스도의 사도로서의 책임 의식을 가지고 복음의 순수성을 보전하고 그리스도의 몸 된 교회를 반대자들의 잘못된 가르침으로부터 지켜서 사도적 교회로 보존하기 위해서 모든 희생을 무릅쓰고 반대자들을 공격하는 것이다(10:8; 12:19; 13:10).

이렇게 바울은 냉정한 합리주의적 사고와(10:5-18; 12:13-21; 13:2) 내적인 열정을 함께 가진 사람이다(2:4-11; 7:2; 11:2, 29;참조, 갈 4:17-19). 그는 그의 반대자의 잘못된 가르침을 분명히 지적하고 단호하게 거절하면서도(2:5-11; 10:5-18; 11:3, 13-15, 18), 고린도 교회에 대한 사랑과 화해의 자세를 견지하고 있다(5:19-21; 6:11-13; 7:2; 11:11, 29; 12:15; 참조, 빌 1:8). 그의 화해는 진리를 양보하지 않는 화해이며, 세상적 요구와의 단절을 전제로 한 화해이다(6:14-7:1). 그는 다른 대적자들처럼 사도로서의 외적 영적 자격을 마지못해 자랑하면서도, 자신의 약점이나 그리스도와 함께 홀로 고난 받는 것을 참된 사도의 표로 분명히 제시하였다(11:23-33, 12:5-11). 실로, 아이러니하게도, 고린도 교회의 반대자들의 핍박이나 비난이 없었더라면, 이러한 바울의 참된 사도로서의 표는 아예 알려지지도 않았을 것이다. 진정한 그리스도인의 인격의 판단 기준이나, 진정한 목회 지침을 이렇게도 분명하게 구체적으로 찾기가 어려웠을 것이다. 이런 냉정하면서도 열정적인 성격이 그의 본래의 성격일 수도 있다. 율법의 열심으로 그리스도의 교회를 핍박하고, 스데반의 죽음을 당연히 여겼던 냉정한 사람이다(행 8:1; 22:4; 26:10, 11; 빌 3:6). 그러나 그리스도 안에서 그런 열심과 냉정함이 승화되어 교인들을 열심히 사랑하고 복음을 증거하고, 한편으로 그의 대적자들을 향하여 복음을 열심히 수호하는 사람으로 변화되었을 것이다(롬 12:11, 고후 11:2, 갈 4:17, 18). 바울 스스로 그의 사랑의 근거가 그리스도의 사랑임을 밝힌다: "그리스도의 사랑이 우리를 강권하시는 도다"(5:14a). 또 그의 이성적 판단 기준의 근거가 그리스도가 주신 사도권이라고 한다(10:8; 13:7). 그러므로 바울의 사랑의 열정과 이성의 냉철함을 단순히 역설적이라는 논리적 용어로 정의하는 것은 옳지 않다. 그것은 하나님의 온전케 하시는 은혜의 결과이다(12:9; 13:9; 빌4:11, 12).

한편, 이런 열정적 사랑의 모습과는 대조적으로 인내하고 겸손하고 온유한 모습도 있다. "차라리 약한 것을 자랑하겠다"는 것도 그의 인내와 겸비를 나타낸다(11:30; 12:9, 10). 이런 성격은 그리스도를 만나기 전에는 없다가 만난 후에 얻은 새로운 성품인 것같이 보인다(빌2:1-10). 자신은 부인하고 하나님께 온전히 의지할 때 나타나는 능력을 그의 고난의 사역을 통해서 경험하고서 또 계시로 듣고서, 그는 공격적인 자세만이 아니라, 자신을 낮출 때 오히려 그리스도의 진정한 능력이 나타나서 자신을 보호하고 승리하게 한다고 확신한다(1:10, 12; 4:7-15; 6:4-10; 10:1; 11:23-33; 12:9; 12, 14, 15; 13:4, 7, 9). 그러나 바울의 이런 온유함이나 겸비 같은 약하게 보이는 자세가, 그의 나약한 인간성을 나타내는 것이 아니라, 그리스도의 수난(passion)이나 죽음과 같이, 하나님의 구원의 지혜와 능력이 나타날 때까지 모든 인간적인 생각과 욕심을 끊고 온전히 인내하며 기다리는 자세로 보아야 한다(1:12; 12:9, 12). 바울의 온유함과 겸비도 결국은 열정적 신앙의 다른 표현인 것이다. 그렇다면, 바울의 인간성은 그리스도의 사랑에 근거한 열정적인 사랑과 동시에 그리스도의 사도로서의 책임감에 근거한 냉철한 이성이 함께 조화된 것이라고 생각된다.

사실 그의 모든 "육체적 자랑"도 그가 원하는 것이 아니었다.[49]

49) 아래 "고린도후서의 특징들"에서 바울의 자랑하는 그의 강점들을 그의 약점들과 함께 찾아보라. 바울은 그의 약점들을 자랑한다고 하나 결국 그의 반대자들의 요구에 따라서(13:2), 또 기대하였던 그의 지지자들이 침묵함으로(12:11), 자신이 자신의 강점들을 자랑할 수밖에 없다고 말한다(11:16-18; 12:1).

반대파들이 외적인 사도적 조건들을 자랑하여 고린도 교인들을 미혹하는 터에 할 수 없이 한다고 거듭 밝힌다(11:1, 16-18; 12:1; 12:11). 그는 자신이 자랑하기를 원치 않았다. 오히려 고린도 교인들이 적극적으로 반대자들에 맞서서 그를 참된 사도로 방어해주기를 원했다. 그러나 고린도 교인들은 중립적이었던 것 같다. 아직 믿음이 어린 상태에서 복음 신앙이 뿌리를 내린지 얼마 되지 않았으므로 이들의 침묵은 이해할 수 있다. 그러나 바울은 분명히 이에 대해서 섭섭했다(3:1, 2; 12:11). 그래서 할 수없이 바울은 자신을 스스로 자랑할 수밖에 없었던 것이다(12:11).

바울의 인성이 이렇게 역설적인 것은 그가 주를 본받고, 주님과 교통함으로 모든 복잡한 인간관계와 모든 어려운 정황에서 이기는 "일체의 비결"을 배웠기 때문일 것이다(고전 11:1; 빌 3:17; 4:12, 13; 12:9, 10). 실제로 바울의 역설적 성격이 보다 성숙한 그리스도인의 인격으로 승화되었다고 보아야 한다. 이런 성숙한 인격이 바울의 서신의 집필 동기와 목적을 파악하는 데 도움이 된다. 이외의 바울의 인간적인 특성에 대해서는 아래의 "고린도후서의 특성"에서 더 논의 될 것이다.

6. 저작 장소 및 연대

저작 장소와 연대는 고린도후서 7장 5-6절에 의거해 볼 때, 바울이 고린도후서를 마게도냐로 가서 디도를 만난 후에 쓴 것이 분명하다. 어떤 학자들은 더 정확한 장소를 가리켜 마게도냐 지방의 첫 성이며 바울이 세운 교회가 있는 빌립보라고 한다. 실제로 어떤 사본(B2)이나 역본(시리아, 콥틱)은 빌립보에서 쓰였다고 밝히

기도 한다. 플러머는 이런 사본이나 역본이 일찍이 기록된 것이므로 신빙성이 있다고 한다.[50)]

저작 연대는 대개 55년 가을로 본다.[51)] 이 연대 측정은 고린도전서 16장 1-2절에서 바울이 고린도 교회가 예루살렘 교회를 위해 헌금하기를 원했는데, 고린도후서 8장 10절과 9장 2절에 1년 전에 헌금을 준비하였다고 하므로, 전서와 후서의 차이가 1년 이라고 본다. 또 바울이 고린도를 떠난 해가 갈리오가 아가야 지방에 부임한 51년 7월 1일 이후로 보고 (행전 18:12, 18)[52)] 그 후 바울의 활동 연한을 4년으로 보면 55년 가을로 연대가 잡힌다. 그러나 학자들마다 조금씩 연대의 차이가 있다.[53)]

7. 내용 분해

학자들마다 그들이 보는 고린도후서의 특징이나 강조점에 따라서 각기 다른 내용 분해를 하고 있다. 그러나 초두의 인사말이

---

50) Plummer, 19. *A. Plummer, A Critical and Exegetical Commentary on the Second Epistle of St. Paul to the Corinthians*, ICC 47 (Edinburgh: T. & T. Clark, 1915), xxix-xxx.

51) Martin, 66; 이상근, 249; Furnish, 55; G. Kümmel, *Introduction to the New Testament*, ed. Howard Clark Kee (London: SCM, 1975), 241.

52) Otto F. A. Meinardus, *St. Paul in Greece* (Athen: Lycabettus Press, 1972), 67; Martin, 30 (서론); 참조 Rainer Riesner, *Die Frühzeit des Apostels Paulus: studien zur Chronologie, Missionsstrategie und Theologie* (Tübingen: J. C. B. Mohr, 1994), 184. 여기서 Riesner는 Gallio가 50년 7월 1일부터 52년 6월 30일까지 아가야 총독으로 있었다고 한다.

53) 57년 여름과 가을 사이: E. B. Allo, 57-70; H. Windisch, *Der zweite Korintherbrief*, (Göttingen: Vandenhoeck & Ruprecht, 1924), 27; 50혹은 53년 여름: G. Lüdemann, *Paul, Apostle to the Gentiles*, ETr. F. S. Jones, (Philadelphia: Fortress, 1984), 162-67.

나 2-7장의 본론이나 8, 9장의 헌금 그리고 10-13장의 사도직에 대한 변명이라는 전체적 내용 윤곽에 대해서 이견이 없다. 그리고 고린도후서의 본론의 중심 주제가 사도직의 변명이라는 데에도 이견이 없다. 그러나 고린도후서의 내용이 원래 단번에 쓴 것으로 보지 않고 문서적으로 분리된 것으로 봐야한다는 논쟁이 있다. 고린도후서가 여러 가지 서신으로 이루어졌다는 가설을 믿는 이들은 그 여러 문서들 중에서 어떤 중심 주제를 찾고, 또 그 주제가 다른 주제 보다 더 중요한 바울의 관심을 가졌다고 하면서 다른 내용 분해를 제시한다. 학자들의 논쟁가운데 서신의 통일성 문제와 관련되는 부분은 (1) 헌금을 다루는 같은 내용을 바울이 8, 9장에 따로 나누어 기록하는 듯이 보임으로써 논의되는 통일성 문제; (2) 2장 14절-7장 4절의 내용이 바울의 사도직을 변명하는 내용으로서 위로를 강조하는 1장 1절-2장 13절과 그리고 7장 5-16절 사이에 삽입되어 있는 듯이 보이는 문제; (3) 6장 14절-7장 1절의 내용이 세상에서의 분리된 거룩한 생활을 강조함으로써 화해의 문맥을 강조하는 문맥 사이(6:13 이전과 7:2 이후)사이에 삽입된 것처럼 보이는 문제; (4) 10장에서 13장의 내용이 1장에서 9장의 우호적인 어조와 전혀 다르게 비판적이고 책망하는 어조로 쓰인 것 등이다. 이런 통일성 문제에 대한 설명은 바울이 고린도전서와 후서에서 언급하는 바울이 썼다는 서신들(고전 5:9; 고후 2:4)과 관련하여 논의되기도 한다. 학자들은 온갖 추정으로 통일성을 의심케 하는 부분들의 기록 연대와 순서를 추정하여 짜 맞추기를 하여 왔으나, 아무런 사본상의 문서적인 증거가 없으므로 결국 추정에 지나지 않는다. 모든 고린도후서 사본은 1장부터 13장의 내용이 그대로 있을 뿐이며 어떤 차이도 없다. 그러므로 바울이 고린도후서를 쓸 때 일정한 기간 동안 쓰면서, 고린도 교회의 문제에 대한 바울의 생각이나 관심이 추가되거나, 고린도 교회의 문제가 새롭게 바뀌면서 서신의 내용이나 어조가 달라진 것이라 것이 지배적인 가설이다.[54)]

우리는 위에서 목회 신학적 측면에서 고린도 후서의 통일성을 믿으면서 현재의 내용 그대로가 바울이 원래 쓴 한 통의 편지라고 했다. 즉 디도로부터 고린도 교인 대다수가 다시 바울에게로 돌아왔다는 소식을 듣고 안도하면서 1-7장까지를 쓴 후에, 8, 9장에서 바울 사도의 중요한 사역인 헌금 사역에 대해서 언급하고, 마지막으로는 아직도 자신을 반대하는 잔존 세력에 대해서 단호히 경계하는 것이다. 그러므로 우리의 고린도후서 내용분해는 통일된 구조를 믿는 이들의 내용 분해와 거의 유사하다. 우리는 2장 12-13절과 7장 4절의 내용이 우연히 끊어진 것이 아니라 바울이 의식적으로 나누어서 2장 14절-7장 4절에서는 하나님께서 실제적으로 그의 사역과 분명히 함께 하심을 증거하려 하였다고 본다. 즉 2장 12-13절에서 바울은 드로아에서 디도를 만나지 못하고 고린도 교회의 소식을 듣지 못해서 근심하면서 마게도냐로 갔던 기억을 되살리다가 그 말을 채 맺지 않고 하나님께서 자신의 복음 사역과 함께 하심을 감사하면서 자신의 사도직 변명을 7장 4절까지 장황하게 설명하였다. 7장 5-7절에 가서야 바울은 2장 13-14절에서 자신이 디도를 만나지 못하고 마게도냐로 근심 중에 갔던 일을 재차 언급하면서 하나님께서 함께 하심으로 마게도냐에서 디도를 만나서 고린도 교회의 좋은 소식을 듣게 되었음을 말한다. 이렇게 디

54) Bruce, xliii.

도를 만난 일을 나누어 설명함으로써 바울은 하나님께서 큰 근심 중에 있던 자신에게 큰 위로를 주셨음을 강조하는 효과를 가지려 한다. 또한, 그런 위로의 하나님을 찬양하고, 그 하나님이 바로 자신의 사역을 주도하시는 분임이 "역사적"으로 증거 되었음을 분명히 입증하는 효과를 나타내려는 것이다. 그의 사도직의 진실성에 대한 주장은 2장 14절-7장 4절의 주관적인 "신학적" 주장만은 아니라는 것이다. 그것은 객관적인 역사적 사실이라는 것이다. 즉 어려운 가운데서 디도를 만나게 해주셔서 위로해 주신 하나님의 사역으로도 그의 사도직의 진실성이 입증된 것이라는 데 바울의 관심이 있다. 이와 비슷한 사례가 1장에도 있다. 1장 3절부터 바울은 위로의 하나님을 찬양하고 있다. 1장 8-9절에서는 바울은 그가 찬양하는 위로의 하나님의 위로의 역사적 증거를 말하고 있다. 즉 바울과 그 일행이 아시아에서 죽을 뻔했으나 하나님께서 구원하셨음을 간증함으로써 위로의 하나님이 실제로 바울의 사역을 도우심을 증거하고 있는 것이다.

8장과 9장에서는 예루살렘 성도들을 위한 헌금 약속을 거론하면서 3차 방문을 앞두고 헌금을 차질 없이 완수할 것을 바란다. 고린도 교인들이 바울에게 다시 돌아 온 것을 기뻐한 후에 헌금문제를 취급하는 것은 자연스럽다. 헌금은 바울에게 대한 고린도 교인들의 충성심의 구체적 증거가 되기 때문이다(8:8, 24).

10장부터 13장까지 바울은 그를 반대하는 이들에게 매우 격렬한 말로 논쟁한다. 거의 모든 내용이 반대자들의 바울에 대한 비난에 대한 대답이다. 반대자들의 바울의 외모나, 언변(10:7, 10; 11:6), 떳떳하게 보수를 받지 않는 문제와 재정 문제에 대한 비난(11:7-10; 12:16), 이와 대조되는 그들의 자랑(10:12, 15-18; 11:18)에 대한 바울의 공격, 그리고 이들의 자랑에 현혹되어 이들을 따르는 고린도 교인들의 어리석음에 대한 바울의 질책(11:20; 13:5), 그리고 바울의 자랑(11:10; 23-12:12)과 징계의 경고(12:20-13:2) 등으로 나타난다. 그러나 여기에도 바울은 전반부에 있는 그의 온유함과 사랑의 자세를 계속 견지하는 것에 유의해야 한다(10:1; 12:14, 15; 13:7, 9-13).

고린도후서 전체에 대한 보다 자세한 내용분해는 목차에서 제시된 바를 참고하기 바란다. 거기서의 내용분해를 통해서 우리는 고린도후서가 바울의 사도직 변명(혹은 자천)이라는 주제로 겉으로 보기보다는 짜임새 있는 내용을 갖고 있음을 알 수 있다. 사도직 변명의 주제가 지배적이면서도, 위로와 권면, 헌금 종용, 반대자들에 대한 경계 같은 여러 다른 주제들이 나타난 것은 다른 서신에서도 나타나는 특성으로서, 다양한 목회적 관심을 거론해야 하는 목회적 서신의 자연스런 특징으로 보아야 한다. 오늘날의 학자들이 원하는 논문형식의 통일된 체계와 같은 통일된 체계를 찾으려는 것은 타당하지 않다.

한편, 같은 주제가 자주 반복이 된 경우가 많은 데, 이것은 강조를 위한 것이다. 이런 반복은 주제를 떠나 다른 문제를 다루다가 다시 주제로 돌아오는 주제 이탈(digression)의 문제로 볼 수도 있다. 이것은 바울의 저술에 흔히 나타나는 특징으로써 주제의 설명을 새로운 소재나, 어조로 말하는 것이다. 그러나 이런 특징을 주제이탈이라고 보기보다는 구어체에서 흔히 나타나는 주제에 대한 부가적 설명이라고 보는 것이 낫다. 특히 바울은 디도를 어렵게 만나 고린도 교회의 좋은 소식을 들은 것을 고난 중에 위로하시는 하나님께서 바울의 사역과 함께 하시는 증거로 삼고 있다. 이런 증거는 고린도 교인들에게는 물론 그를 반대하는 반대자들에게 사도 바울의 진실성을 객관적으로 입증하는 산 증거가 되기 때문이다.

8. 통일성

고린도후서의 통일성 문제는 바울 서신 중에서도 가장 큰 논쟁이다. 크게는 1-7장, 8-9장, 10-13장이 원래 다른 편지들이었는데 하나로 되었다고 주장하는 "분할론"(partition theory)이다. 18세기부터 시작된 이 논쟁은 아직도 끝나지 않았다.[55)]

이미 지적한 바와 같이 고린도후서는 3차 방문을 앞두고 이 방문이 2차 방문과 달리 원만한 방문이 되게 하기 위하여 바울의 사도직과 관련된 몇 가지 문제들을 해결하여 바울의 사도직을 변명한다는 일관된 목적이 있다(물론 이런 특별한 목적에는 고린도 교인들의 신앙 강화를 통하여 고린도 교회에서 그리스도의 왕권을 공고하게 한다는 서신을 쓰는 일반적이고 궁극적인 목적이 전제되어 있다[4:5; 10:5-6, 8; 12:19; 13:5, 7, 9, 10, 11].). 8, 9장의 헌금의 주제를 제외하면 고린도후서 전체는 자신이 그리스도의 진정한 사도임을 그를 지지하는 사람들에게나(1-7장), 그를 반대하는 사람들에게 대하여(10-13장) 적극적으로 변명하는 글이다. 사실 헌금 주제도 그가 고린도 교회를 다시 방문하기 전에 약속한 헌금을

---

55) 고린도후서 통일성 논쟁사는 다음 책들에서 찾아보라. R. Bieringer, "Teilungshypothesen zum 2. Korintherbrief: Ein Forschungsüberblick," in R. Bieringer and J. Lanbrecht, eds., *Studies on 2 Corinthians*, BEThL 112 (Leuven: Leuven University Press, 1994), 67-105; V. P. Furnish, 30-35; Martin, xl-xlv.

미리 해결하여서 바울의 사도직에 대한 저희들의 지지의 증거를 보여주기를 원한다고 보면 사도직 변명의 큰 주 주제와도 자연스럽게 연관되는 것이다. 또 앞부분과 대조되는 10-13장의 엄격한 책망도 처음부터 바울이 마음속에 하고 싶었던 말을 편지 끝에서야 한 것이라고 본다. 처음부터 좋지 않은 말로 편지를 시작하는 것은 다수의 고린도 교인들이 돌아온 지금, 화해의 분위기 형성을 위해 적절하지 못하다고 생각했을 것이다(5:20). 그러나 동시에 지속적인 화해를 위해서는 화해에 방해되는 요소를 단호히 제거해야함을 느끼고 3차 방문을 앞두고 잘못된 행위를 고치도록 엄명하는 것이다. 처음에는 위로와 감사의 말씀을 주로 쓰고(1-7장), 다음은 좀 어려운 헌금 이야기를 쓰고(8-9장), 그 다음으로는 더 어려운 책망과 책벌을 쓰고 있다(10-13장)고 보면 목회 심리학적 측면에서 매우 사려 깊게 정리된 편지라고 볼 수 있다. 이런 통일성은 당시 그리스 로마 시대의 대표적 수사학의 예라고 일컫는 기원전 4세기 디모스데네스(Demosthenes)의 *De Corona* 의 연설문에서나, 키케로(Cicero)의 연설문에서 마지막 부분에서 적들이나 청중에게 강한 어조로 말하고 있다는 사실에서도 증명된다.[56)]

---

56) F. W. Danker, "Paul's Debt to the *De Corona* to Demosthenes: A Study of Rhetorical Techniques in Second Corinthians," in D. F. Watswon, ed., *Persuasive Artistry* (Sheffield: JSOT Press, 1991), 262-80; Frank. W. Hughes, "The Rhetoric of Reconciliation: 2 Corinthians1.1-2.13 and 7.5-8.24," in D. F. Watson, ed., *Persuasive Artistry* (Sheffield: JSOT Press, 1991), 246-61. 이들이 반대하는 견해 즉 10-13장에서 책망은 1-9장의 화해와 설득을 무산시키는 것으로서 후대 편집의 증거이며, 고린도후서를 통일된 하나의 서신으로 볼 수 없는 증거라고 주장하는 견해를 다음에서 보라. Plummer, xxix-xxx; J. Murphy-O'Connor, *The Theology of the Second Letter to the Corinthians* (Cambridge: Cambridge University Press, 1991), 10-11. 이상의 논쟁

한편 고린도전서는 로마의 클레멘트, 이그나시우스, 폴리캅 같은 고대 교부들이 인용하면서도 고린도후서는 분명히 언급하지 않는다는 사실에서 고린도후서가 후기 사도 시대에 편집되었다고 추론하는 이들도 있다.[57] 그러나 초기 교회에서 여러 신약의 책들이 자유롭게 사용되는 정황에서 고린도전서의 내용이 고린도후서보다 실제적이고 일반적이기 때문에 더 넓게 유포되었을 것이다.[58] 2세기에는 고린도후서도 넓게 알려 졌다. 바울의 원래의 편지들이 여전히 남아 있는데 이것들을 따로 모아서 하나의 편지로 편집했을 가능성이 적고, 설령 원래의 몇 개의 편지가 파손되어서 편집했다하더라도 이들을 마치 한 통의 편지로 종합하여 편집하였다는 것을 증명하기 어렵다. 감히 바울의 편지를 하나의 편지 인양 편집하는 권한을 누가 가졌는가? 또한 이런 추정은 여러 사본들이 보여주는 대로 고린도후서가 한 편의 통일된 편지로 나타난다는 사실을 설명하기 어렵다.[59] 어쨌든 고린도후서가 전서 보다 늦게 유통되었다는 사실에서 고린도후서의 통일성을 의심하는 것은 타당하지 않다.

물론, 고린도후서는 로마서나 고린도전서 같이 체계적으로 쓴 편지는 아니다. 그렇게 체계적으로 써야할 경우가 아니었다. 그동안 오해로 말미암아 소원해 진 고린도 교인들에게, 바울의 진정한

을 David R. Hall, *The Unity of the Corinthian Correspondence* (London/New York: T & T Clark International, 2003) 87-91에서 보라.

57) G. Bornkamm, "The History of the Origin of the So-called Second Letter to the Corinthians," *NTS* 8(1962), 258-64.

58) Hall, 86.

59) Hall, 87.

심정을 드러내어서 어떻게 하든지 고린도 교인들을 보다 가깝게 만드는 것이 서술의 목적이기 때문이다. 그간 바울을 비난하는 반대파들과의 지속된 대립으로 말미암은 바울의 복잡한 감정이 고린도후서에서의 필체를 보다 즉흥적으로 만들었고, 그 결과로 나타난 잦은 주제 이탈로 인해서 통일성을 의심케 만드는 부분이 있다. 바울은 디도를 통해 "엄한 편지"를 고린도 교회에 보내 문제된 사람을 치리하는 등 강경한 목회적 조치를 취하고, 그 결과를 드로아에서 애타게 기다렸으나 디도를 만나지 못하고, 한 참 후 마게도냐(빌립보)에서 드디어 디도를 만났다. 바울은 그가 가져온 고린도 교회의 자신에 대한 반전된 지지의 반가운 소식을 듣고 고린도 교인들을 격려하면서 여전히 반대하는 이들을 경계하면서 편지를 쓰기 때문에, 고린도후서는 바울의 기쁜 감정(전반부)과 격한 감정(후반부)이 교차되어서 대조적인 양상으로 나타나는 것이다. 바울은 여러 가지 주제들을 연계하여 말하기 때문에, 어떤 주제는 다른 주제 사이에 들어 있는 경우도 있다. 예를 들면 디도를 통해 고린도 교회의 소식을 기다리다가 디도를 만나지 못해서 괴로웠다는 말을 2장 13절에서 한 후에 주로 자신의 사도직 변명이라고 할 수 있는 말을 7장 초두까지 하다가 7장 6절에 가서야 디도를 만나 기뻐했다는 말을 하면서 1장의 위로의 주제와 다시 연결시키며 말하는 것이다. 여러 가지 주제가 중첩되어 있음을 다음과 같이 고린도후서의 내용을 나누어 보면 알 수 있다.

1. 1장 1절에서 1장 11절까지 바울은 (디도의 편지를 받고) 환난 가운데 위로하시는 하나님을 찬양하며 기뻐한다.

2. 1장 12절에서 2장 13까지 약속대로 고린도 교회에 방문하지

않고 대신 "엄격한 편지"를 보낸 이유를 설명한다(위의 목차에서는 이 부분을 포함하여 7장 16절까지를 사도직의 진정성에 대한 변명이라는 하나의 주제로 묶었으나 여기서는 주제가 중첩되어 있음을 나타내기 위해서 달리 나눈다). 2장 13절에서 디도를 드로아에서 만나지 못해 괴로웠음을 말한다.

3. 2장 14절에서 6장 13절까지 바울은 그의 사도직의 진정성에 대해서 변명한다.

4. 6장 14절에서 7장 4절까지 바울은 불신자와 구별된 삶을 살아야 할 것을 가르친다.

5. 7:5-16 마게도냐에서 디도를 만나서 기뻤다는 1장의 주제를 다시 말하며, "혹독한 편지"에 대한 적극적 반응에 대해서 감사한다.

6. 8장과 9장은 고린도 교인들이 약속한 헌금을 자신의 방문 전에 마칠 것을 부탁한다.

7. 10장에서 13장은 그의 방문 이전에 자신을 반대하는 여러 문제들에 대해 답하고, 이런 문제로 교회를 어지럽히는 "거짓 선지자들"에 대해서 경고한다.

이렇게 여러 가지 주제가 함께 있음에도 불구하고 고린도후서는 대체로 바울의 임박한 고린도 교회 방문을 대비하여 화해라는 큰 주제 아래서 몇 가지 화해에 장애되는 문제들 - 징계 받은 사람의 징계 해제로 방문 분위기 조성(2:5-11); 바울의 복음과 사도직의 진정성 확립(2:14-7:4); 고린도 교인들의 거룩한 생활 확립(6:14-7:1); 바울의 방문 전 헌금 수거 완료(8장, 9장); 바울 사도에 대한 남은 의구심을 해소(10-13) 등을 위해 쓴 편지라고 본다.[60] 바울은 이런 문제들을 미리 해결하지 않으면 그의 고린도 교회 방문이 이전의 방문 시에 경험했던 것과 같은 어려움을 다시 경험하게 될 것을 생각한 것이다. 고린도후서에서 바울은 방문과 관련하여 그의 두려움을 나타낸다: "내가 다시 근심으로 너희에게 나아기지 않기로 결단 하였노니"(고후 2:1). 바울은 12장 끝에서 실제로 그가 이런 두려움을 가지고서 다시는 같은 경험을 하지 않겠다는 의도로 고린도후서 마지막을 썼다고 말한다. "내가 갈 때에 너희를 나의 원하는 것과 같이 보지 못하고… 거만함과 어지러움이 있을까 두려워하고, 또 내개 다시 갈 때에 내 하나님이 나를 너희 앞에서 낮추실까 두려워하고… 그 행한 바 더러움과 음란함과 호색함을 회개치 아니함을 인하여 근심할까 두려워하노라"(12:20-21). 다시 말하면 바울은 전반부에서 다수의 고린도 교인들과 원만한 관계를 유지하기 위해서 온건하게 설득하여 자신의 사도직을 변명하고 있고, 10-13장의 후반부에서는 그의 사역 가운데 "약함 가운데 강하게 하시는 하나님의 역사하심"을 증거하여 보다 강경한 어조로 그의 사도직의 진정성을 변명하고 있다. 그러나 이 부분에서조차 바울은 화해의 진술을 잊지 않으며(11:2-4, 11; 12:14, 15), 특히 첫 부분과 마지막 부분에서 화해의 말로 시작하고 마무리함으로써 바울의 중심 의도가 결국 화해를 통한 교회의 안정임을 알 수 있다(10:1; 13:7-10). 이렇게 보면 고린도후서의 다양성을 사도직의 정당성 이해를 통한 화해라는 통일된 시각에서 정리하여 볼 수 있다. (바울은 그의 진정한 목적은 고린도 교회에서 반대자들로 말미암아 훼손된 그리스도의 왕권 회복이라고 믿는다[4:5;

60) Tasker, 34; Barnett, 19.

5:20; 10:5-6, 8; 13:10]. 그러나 그 자신이 그리스도의 진실한 사도로서 진실하게 사역하고 있음을 확신하기 때문에 그의 사도권 확립이 곧 그리스도의 왕권 확립으로 믿는다[4:5; 10:5-6, 8; 13:10]). 화해라는 목회적 목적을 위해 쓴 하나의 서신이라는 견해는 보수적 학자들뿐만 아니라 비평적 학자들 에게서도 지지를 받아 왔다.[61] 그러나 통일성에 대해서 반대하는 의견도 많아서 고린도 후서의 통일성에 관한 논란은 매우 복잡한 논쟁을 일으켜 왔다.[62] Johann Salomo Semler (1725-91)가 1776에 *Paraphrasis II. Epistolae ad Corinthos, 고린도 주석*(Halle)에서 고린도후서 10장 1절-13장

61) J. H. Berdnard(1903); H. Lietzmann(1909); A. Menzies(1912); H. L. Goudge(1927); E. B. Allo(1936); R. V. G. Tasker(1958); *The Second Epistle of Paul to the Corinthians (Grand Rapids: Eerdmans, 1958); D. Guthrie(1961-1970)*; D. Guthrie(1961-1970); P. E. Hughes(1962); *Paul' s Second Letter to the Corinthians* (Grand Rapids: Eerdmans, 1962); W. G. Kümmel(1963); A. M. G. Stephenson(1965); W. H. Bates(1965); J. L. Price(1967); N. Hyldahl(1973); M. J. Harris(1976); Martin(1986); Thrall(1994); 재인용, Martin, xlii; Martin의 목록과 유사하나 보다 자세히 정리한 고린도후서 통일성에 대해 다른 의견을 가진 학자들에 대해서 Thrall, II, 48-49를 보라. 최근에 통일성을 주장하는 책은 Fredrick J. Long, *Ancient Rhetoric and Paul's Apology: The Compositional Unity of 2 Corinthians* (Cambridge: Cambridge University Press, 2004); M. J. Harris, *The Second Epistle to the Corinthians* (Grand Rapids: Eerdmans, 2005), 26-51: pp. 26-51까지 통일성에 대한 여러 이론들의 검토와 p. 51에서 고린도후서 통일성에 대한 Harris의 결론을 보라.

62) E. B. Allo, *Saint Paul: premiere épître aux Corinthians* (Paris: Gabalda, 1925); W. H. Bates, "The Integrity of II Corinthians," *NTS* 12 (1965), 56-69; N. Hydahl, "Die Frage nach der literarischen Einheit des Zweiten Korinthierbriefes," *ZNW* 64 (1973), 289-306; W. G. Kümmel, *Introduction to the New Testament*, 205-216; H. Lietzmann, *An die Korinther* (Göttingen: Vandenhoech & Ruprecht, 1965). 통일성을 반대하는 글 학자들을 Martin, xlii에서와 Thrall, II, 48-49에서 보라.

10절은 독립된 편지이며, 9장은 고린도가 아닌 다른 곳에 보낸 편지로 보았다.[63] 그 후 1870년에는 Adolf Hausrath가 *Die Viercapietelbrief des Paulus an die Korinther(고린도에 보낸 바울의 4장의 편지)*(Heidelberg: Bassermann)에서 10-13의 마지막 4장을 소위 "눈물의 편지," Tranenbrief (2:3-4:9, 7:8, 12)로 보고, 이 부분이 1-9장보다 먼저 쓰였다고 하여 이 이론의 주창자가 되었다.[64]

현대의 비평 학자들의 다양한 견해도 대개 이 두 사람의 이같은 단편설을 중심으로 전개되고 있다. 고린도후서가 여러 단편들로 이루어져 있다는 단편설은 대체로 3개로 구분된다.[65]

1. 1-9장과 10-13장으로 나누어야 한다는 주장이 있다. 이 주장도 10-13장이 1-9장보다 먼저 쓰였다고 보는 주장과, 현재의 위치대로 두어야 한다는 주장으로 나누어 진다. 이 주장의 근거는 1-9장의 바울의 부드럽고 화해적 어조가 10-13장에 와서 급격하고 공격적인 어조로 급변하였다는 데 있다. 어조가 변한 이유에 대해서 학자들은 대개 세 가지 이유를 제시한다: (a) 1-9장에서 바울은 그를 지지하는 다수의 교인들에게 좋은 말로 격려하고 나서, 10-13

63) H. D. Betz는 Semler의 가설은 그가 그의 선생 Siegmund Jacob Baumgarten(1706-57)이 쓴 고린도전서주석(*Auslegung der beiden Briefe St. Pauli an die Corinthier* [Halle: Gebaur, 1961])을 출판하면서 이 주석에 영향 받은 것으로 본다. 고린도전서이지만 고린도후서 8장, 9장을 자세히 분석한 부분이 있기 때문이라는 것이다(H. D. Betz, *2 Corinthians 8 and 9*, Hermeneia (Philadelphia: Fortress Press, 1985), 4; 참조, Martin, xli).

64) 10-13장을 바울이 고후2:4에 언급한 "눈물의 편지"라고 보는 학자들을 Plummer, xxviii과 D. Guthrie, 444, n. 2에서 보라.

65) 고린도후서가 여러 편지로 구성되었다고 보는 가설들에 대해서, Harris, 8-51을 보라.

장에서 여전히 그를 반대하는 무리들에 대해서 엄하게 말하고 있다. 우리는 이 견해를 따르고 있다; (b) 바울이 1-9장을 다 쓰고 난 뒤에 고린도 교회의 사정이 다시 악화되었으므로 이에 대해 단호하게 대처하여 썼다; (c) 10-13장은 바울이 고린도후서 2:4과 7:8에서 언급한 "눈물의 편지" (또는 "엄격한 편지")로서 편집자가 첨부시킨 것이다.[66] 이렇게 나누는 것에 대해 뒤에서 더 논의하겠다.

2. 2장 14절-7장 4절을 독립된 서신으로 보는 견해가 있다.[67] 이 부분은 바울이 드로아에서 디도를 만나지 못하여 고린도 교회 소식을 듣지 못하므로 안타까워 하였으나(2:13) 그를 마게도냐에서 만나서 고린도 교회의 좋은 소식을 듣고 안도하게 되었다(7:5-7)는 고린도후서 집필 동기를 말하는 두 구절 사이에 들어 있는 긴 부분으로서 바울의 사도직의 진실성을 변호하는 부분이다. 2장 13절과 7장 5절이 직접 연결되므로 그 사이에 있는 내용이 편집자에 의해서 삽입된 독립된 편지라는 견해이다. 그러나 이렇게 혼돈을 일으키는 삽입을 편집자가 하였다고 보기 어렵다. 바울이 디도가 가지고 온 반가운 소식을 받은 사실의 신학적 의미, 즉 그

66) F. F. Bruce, 1 and 2 Corinthians, 169-70; R. P. Martin, 2 Corinthians, xlvi.88) J. C. Hurd Jr., *The Origin of 1 Corinthians* (London: SPCK, 1965), 135-39; Jewett, 389-444; Schmithals, 265; Suhl, 208.

67) J. Weiss, *Earliest Christianity* (New York: Harper, 1959), 323-57; R. Bultmann, *The Second Letter to the Corinthians*; P. Vielhaur, *Geschichte der urchristlichen Literatur* (Berlin: de Gruyter, 1975), 153; Bornkamm, 31-32, and Suhl, *Paulus*, 261-62; Georgi, *Opponents*, 17; 다른 학자들과 자료들을 위해서, Martin, xlii; N. H. Taylor, "The Composition and Chronology of Second Corinthians," *JSNT* 44(1991), 69, 주 1, 2 보라;.

의 사역과 함께하시는 하나님을 논하다가 7장 5절에 가서 다시 디도를 만난 기쁨을 말하면서 이 대목을 끝내었다고 보는 것이 옳다.[68)]

3. 2장 14절-7장 4절(6:14-7:13 제외)과 10-13장을 "눈물의 편지"(또는 "혹독한 편지")로 보는 주장이 있다.[69)] 두 부분 모두 바울이 자신의 사도직을 변명하는 내용으로서 매우 강력한 표현들이 많기 때문이라고 한다. 뿐만 아니라 그런 표현들이 서로 일치하고 있다고 한다.[70)] 즉 10장 6절과 2장 9절, 11절 11절, 또 12장 15절과 2장 4절 그리고 13장 2, 10절과 2장 3절 등이 서로 일치된 내용을 갖고 있으므로 "눈물의 편지"의 일부라고 볼 수 있다는 것이다. 그러나 이런 일치된 내용은 고린도전서에서도 찾을 수 있고 고린도후서 1장에서도 찾을 수 있다.[71)] 그리고 10-13장은 "눈물의 편지"라기 보다는 "분노의 편지"라는 것이 옳을 것이다.[72)] 퍼니쉬는 다음과 같은 이유를 들면서 이 견해 ("눈물의 편지")를 반대한다.[73)]

1) "눈물의 편지"의 주제는 바울을 대항한 형제에 대한 것인데

---

68) Allo, 44-45.

69) J. Weiss, *Earliest Christianity* (New York: Harper, 1959), 323-57; R. Bultmann, *The Second Letter to the Corinthians*, ETr. Roy A. Harrisville, (Minneapolis, MN.: Augsburg, 1985); P. Vielhaur, *Geschichte der urchristlichen Literatur*, 153; J. H. Kennedy, *The Second and Third Epistles of St. Paul to the Corinthians* (London: MacMillan, 1900), 81-85.

70) Kennedy, 81-85. 그러나 Bruce, 167과 C. K. Barrett, *The Second Epistle to the Corinthians*, 13에서 반대의견을 보라.

71) Barrett, 168.

72) V. P. Furnish, 37.

73) Furnish, 37.

(고후2:3-11; 7:8-12), 10-13장에는 이에 대한 암시조차 없다. 이를 "눈물의 편지"의 일부이니까 그런 내용이 없을 수도 있다고 반박하는 것은 침묵으로부터의 논리, 즉 "어떤 사실이 없음은 있다는 것을 증거한다"는 식의 논리로서, 신빙성이 없다. 혹은 이를 편집자가 편집할 때 이미 해결된 고린도 교회 문제를 그 사람이 여전히 살아 있는 상황에서 다시 거론하여 문제를 일으킬 필요가 없다는 판단을 하여 그 내용을 없앴다는 것도 억지 추정일 뿐이다.[74] 편집자가 마음 대로 사도 바울의 권위 있는 편지의 내용을 함부로 잘라 버릴 수 있는 권한을 갖고 있었다고 보기 어렵다.

2) 바울은 "눈물의 편지"에서 그가 고린도 교회 방문을 취소하였음을 말하였을 것인데(고후1:15-17, 2:3-4), 10-13장에서는 이런 말이 전혀 없다.

3) "눈물의 편지"는 바울이 방문을 취소한 대신에 쓴 편지인데(1:23-2:4), 10-13장은 오히려 방문을 예상하면서 쓴 편지이다(12:14, 20, 21; 13:1).

4) 바울이 고린도후서 7장 5절에서 "눈물의 편지"의 좋은 결과에 대해 말할 때 10-13장의 주된 내용인 거짓 사도에 대한 언급이 없다.[75]

5) 이상의 "눈물의 편지"로 10-13장을 보는 주장은 자연히 이 뒷부분이 1-9장보다 먼저 쓰였다고 본다. 바울이 앞부분에서 이

---

74) G. Bornkamm, "The History of the Origin of the So-Called Second Letter to the Corinthians," in *The Authority and Integrity of the New Testament* (London: SPCK, 1965), 259.

75) M. E. Thrall, "A Second Thanksgiving Period in II Corinthians," in *JSNT* 16 (1982), 101-124, 특히 122.76) Bornkamm, 77; A. Suhl, *Paulus und seiner Briefe* (Gütersloh: Mohr, 1975), 203-62.

편지를 언급한 것으로 보기 때문이다(2:4, 7:8). 그러나 이런 주장도 아무런 사본적 근거가 없다. 모든 사본은 현재 순서대로 나타난다.

이런 주장에 대해 이상에서 제시한 우리의 반대 근거 외에도 목차에 제시한 우리의 내용 분해에서와 같이 2장 14절-7장 4절의 "고난과 승리의 사역"이라는 주제가 1:1-13과 7:5-16에 있는 "위로의 하나님이 함께 하시는 사역"과 일치된 주제이므로 1:1-13과 다른 편지라는 것은 옳지 않다.

4. 8장과 9장이 다른 편지라는 주장이 있다. 보른캄(E. Bornkamm)과 술(A. Suhl)은 8 장을 1장 1절-2장 13절과 7장 5-16절과 함께 9장과는 다른 독립된 편지로서 9장보다 보다 조금 일찍 보낸 편지라고 하였다.[76] 쥬엣(R. Jewett)과 슈미탈스(W. Schmithals)도 거의 같은 견해를 갖고 있다.[77] 벧츠(H. Betz)와 게오르기(D. Georgi)는 8장은 고린도 교회에 보낸 편지이며, 9장은 아가야 지방의 여러 교회에 보낸 편지라고 하였다.[78] 그러나 이들과 달리 불트만(R. Bultmann) 과 필하우어(P. Vielhaur)는 9장이 8장보다 앞서 보낸 편지라고 본다.[79]

---

76) Bornkamm, 77; A. Suhl, *Paulus und seiner Briefe* (Gütersloh: Mohr, 1975), 203-62.

77) R. Jewett, "The Reaction of 1 Corinthians and the Trajectory of the Pauline School," *JAARSup* 44 (1978), 389-444; W. Schmithals, "Die Korintherbriefe als Briefsammlung," *ZNW* 64 (1973), 263-88.

78) H. D. Betz, *2 Corinthians 8 and 9*, 91-95; D. Georgi, *The Opponents of Paul in Second Corinthians* (Edinburgh: T. & T. Clark, 1986), 17.

79) Bultmann, 18; Vielhaur, 153.

학자들이 8장과 9장을 분리하는 근거는 8장과 9장의 연결 (9:1의 연결 구절)부분이 어색하다는 것과 8장과 9장의 내용을 비교해 볼 때 동시에 기록되었다고 보기에 어색한 곳이 있다는 것이다.

첫째, 9장 1절의 "…에 대하여"(Περὶ μὲν γὰρ…) 라는 연결구에 대해서 봐이스(J. Weiss)는 9장 1절의 연결구는 마치 8장에서 헌금에 대하여 아무런 언급도 하지 않은 것처럼 헌금에 대해서 말을 꺼내고 있다고 하였다.[80] 이에 대해서 플러머와 브루스는 오히려 이 구절은 앞서서 말한 바를 되풀이함을 전제하고 하는 말이라고 하였다.[81] 바레드는 "…에 대하여 쓸 필요가 없나니"라는 말은 앞장에서 헌금을 이미 언급하였음을 강하게 시사 한다고 한다.[82] 희랍어 페리손 (περισσόν)이란 말은 "지나치게 많은"이란 형용사로서 "쓰는 것" (to write, γραφείν)이라는 주어를 갖고 있는데, 헌금에 대하여 "쓰는 것 (적는 것)이 내게 너무 지나치게 많다"는 뜻이 되어서 바울이 이미 헌금에 대하여 8장에서 충분히 논하였으

80) J. Weiss, *The History of Primitive Christianity*, vol. 1, ed. F. C. Grant (London: MacMillan, 1937), 353; H. D. Betz, *2 Corinthians 8 and 9*, 90.

81) F. F. Bruce, *I and II Corinthians*, 171; Plummer, 252; S. K. Stowers, "*Peri men gar* and the Integrity of 2 Corinthians 8 and 9," *NovT* 32 (1980) 340-48. Stowers는 Περὶ μὲν γὰρ(그러므로 …에 대하여)가 신약에서 행 28:22에 다시 나오나 새로운 글을 시작하는 데 쓰인 것이 아니며, 신약 외 90 개의 쓰인 경우도 모두 단순한 연결구로 쓰였다고 하여, 이 연결구가 8장과 9장이 하나의 글임을 증거한다고 주장한다. 이에 대해 Thrall은 8장과 9장이 독립된 글임을 주장하면서 γάρ는 편집적인 추가이며, Περὶ μὲν은 Demosthenes의 편지 초두에 나온다고 한다. 그러나 이런 주장은 사본상의 아무런 증거가 없다; P. Barnett, 429-430.

82) Barrett, *The Second Epistle to the Corinthians*, 233.

므로 다시 논하는 것이 필요치 않다는 뜻으로 보인다. 길크라이스트(J. M. Gilchrist)는 여기의 περί,(⋯ 대하여)라는 말이 사도행전 28장 22절에서와 같이 앞의 말과 연결하는 연결구로 쓰였다고 했다.[83] 데니(Denney)가 지적했듯이 9장 1절의 "(성도를)섬기는 일에 대하여" (Περὶ μὲν γὰρ ⋯ τῆς διακονίας)라는 어귀는 바울이 미묘한 사항을 다룰 때 쓰는 것이며, τῆς διακονίας(섬기는 일)의 관사와 "쓸 필요가 없나니" 이라는 말은 이미 언급한 헌금에 관한 논의를 다른 시각에서 다루기 위해 쓰는 "부드러운 변환구절" (a smooth transition)이라고 본다(참조, 빌 3:1).[84] 바울은 8장까지 쓴 후 얼마간 시간이 경과 한 후에 9장을 시작하면서 8장에서 자기가 쓴 내용을 다시 상기시키면서 쓴다고 보면 8장과 9장의 연결의 어색함은 별문제가 안 된다. 더구나 1절에서 바울은 자신이 같은 주제를 반복하는 것에 대해서 독자들이 지루해할 것을 이해하며 말을 시작하고 있다. 그러므로 9장 1절은 8장과 9장이 하나의 연속된 글임을 입증하는 가장 명백한 증거이다.

둘째, 헌금에 대한 언급이 9장과 8장에서 동시적이 아니라 다른 시간을 암시한다고 지적하는 이들이 있다. 9장에서는 8장에서 언급한 "헌금 위원들" 의 방문이 실현된 것으로 보이며, 고린도 교인들의 헌금에 대한 열의가 매우 고조된 것으로 나타난다고 한다.[85]그러나 9장 3절의 "(내가) 이 형제들을 보낸 것" (ἔπεμψα)이

83) J. M. Gilchrist, "Paul and the Corinthians-The Sequence of Letters and Visits," *JSNT* 34 (1988), 65, n.7.

84) Denney, 279-280.

85) G. Bornkamm, "The History of the Origin of the So-Called Second Letter to the Corinthians," *NTS* 8, (1962), 260-61.

란 말은 편지에서 흔히 나오는 서간문 과거 또는 예상과거(epistolary aorist=anticipatory aorist)로 보아야 한다.[86] 즉 편지의 수신자들이 편지를 받고 난 뒤에는 지금 편지 발송인의 동작이 과거의 동작이 되므로 발신자가 그 동작을 현재가 아닌 과거로 쓴다. 그러므로 9장 3절에서 바울이 "이 형제들을 보냈다"는 말은 지금 보내고 있다는 말로 보아야한다. 8장 18, 22절에서도 바울은 형제들을 "보냈다"(συνεπέμψαμεν)는 서간 과거형을 쓰고 있다고 본다. 바울은 9장 3절에서 같은 형제들을 지금 보내고 있다고 말하는 것이다. 그렇다면 8장과 9장은 동시적인 것이며 시간적 차이를 논할 수 없다. 8장과 9장에서 바울은 고린도 교인들의 헌금에 대한 열의가 식었음을 알고 그들의 열의를 고무시키고 있다. 특히 바울은 9장에서 지금 보내는 형제들이 마게도냐인들임을 지적하면서 바울이 마게도냐 교인들에게 고린도 교인들이 이미 1년 전부터 이 헌금을 시작하였다고 하여 마게도냐 교인들로 부터 헌금을 거두었는데(9:2) 지금 바울이 보내는 마게도냐 형제들이 고린도 교회에 가서 아직 헌금하지 않은 것을 보면 자신의 사도적 진실성과 관련하여 오해 받게 되고 고린도 교인들의 입장도 난처해질 것임을 지적하고 있다(9:3). 이런 이유로 바울은 8장에서 언급한 헌금 문제를 9장에서 다시 논해야만 했다.

그러므로 8장과 9장을 서로 독립된 편지로 나눌 필요가 없다. 무엇보다 모든 사본은 8장과 9장의 연결에 있어서 한결같다. 8장과 9장이 독립된 글이라는 아무런 사본적인 증거가 없다.[87] 연결

86) Furnish, 38.

87) Plummer, 252.

의 어색함과 중복된 내용은 하나의 편지를 쓰면서 얼마의 시간이 경과한 후에 다시 쓰기 시작하면서 지난번에 말한 것을 다시 반복한 것으로 본다면 자연스러운 것이다.

5. 6장 14절-7장 1절이 현재의 위치에 삽입되었다고 보는 견해가 있다. 이런 견해는 6장 14절-7장 1절의 세 가지 특성에 근거한다. 1) 6장 13절과 7장 2절이 서로 연결이 잘 되는데, 이 두 구절 사이에 있는 이 부분이 그 연결을 끊고 있다. 6장 13절과 7장 2절에서 바울은 고린도 교인들에게 마음을 넓혀서 화해하자고 권하는데, 6장 14절-7장 2절에서 바울은 분리된 거룩한 생활을 강조함으로써 문맥을 끊고 있다. 2) 이 부분의 내용이 이원론적 사상으로서 바울의 사상이 아니다. 3) 9개의 희귀어들(*Hapax legomena*)이 있다.

이런 본문의 특성에 근거하여 본문의 기원에 대해 대개 두 가지 비평적인 견해가 있다. 1) 본문의 내용이 엄격한 이원론 사상에 근거한 분리주의적 사상인데 바울이 고린도전서 5장 9절에 언급한 바울이 고린도 교회에 보낸 소위 "잃어버린 편지"(The Lost Letter)의 내용도 성도의 거룩한 생활을 논한 것이므로 이 편지의 내용의 일부를 편집자가 여기에 발췌하여 적었다고 한다.[88] 2) 본문의 사상이 바울의 사상과 달리 이원론적 분리주의이므로 바울의 글이 아니다라고 한다. 후자에 속한 여러 학자들은 이 부분이 쿰란 문서에서 왔다고 한다. 내용이 쿰란의 이원론적 분리주의 사상과 유사하고 특

88) J. C. Hurd Jr., *The Origin of 1 Corinthians* (London: SPCK, 1965), 135-39; Jewett, 389-444; Schmithals, 265; Suhl, 208.

히 15절에 있는 벨리알이란 말이 쿰란문서에 나오기 때문이다.[89)]

첫째, 6장 14절-7장 1절이 앞 뒤 문맥과 연결이 안 된다는 주장이 있으나, 이 부분의 내용을 전체 문맥에 비추어 보면 오히려 적절한 내용으로 문맥에 잘 들어맞음을 알 수 있다. 즉 화해를 위해서 고린도 교인들에게 있는 화해의 장애가 되는 세속적인 요소를 단호히 제거하라는 것이다. 같은 내용이 마지막 부분인 12장 19절 이하에서도 나타나므로 이런 내용을 외적인 요소로 보는 것은 잘못이다. 연결이 안 됨을 인정하면서도 바울이 가끔 주제를 이탈하므로 바울이 이곳에서도 화해의 주제를 이탈하여 분리주의적인 그리스도인의 생활에 대하여 썼다는 견해도 있다. 그러나 이 부분을 주제 이탈이라고 볼 필요가 없다. 화해의 주제에 잘 들어맞는다. 바울이 추구하는 화해는 세속적인 화해가 아니라 하나님의 거룩하심을 따르는 거룩한 화해이다(6:16) 물론 고린도후서에 주제 이탈의 예는 있다. 바울은 7장 5절에 가서 비로소 2장 13절에 언급한 마게도냐에서 디도를 만난 일을 다시 상기하면서 전반부를 마

89) Karl Georg Kuhn이 제일 먼저 쿰란 문서와의 연결을 제안하였다. K. G. Kuhn, "Die Schriftrollen vom Toten Meer," *EvT* 11 (1951) 72-5; R. Bultmann, *The Second Letter to the Corinthians*, ETr. (Minneapolis: Ausburg, 1985), 원 저서명, Der zwei Brief an die Korinther, ed. E. Dinker, (Göttingen: Vandenhoeck & Ruprecht, 1976); J. A. Fitzmyer, "Qumrân and the Interpolated Paragraph in 2 Cor. 6:14-7:1," *CBQ* 23 (1961), 271-80; D. Georgi, 12; J. Gnilka, "2 Cor. 6:14-7:1 in the Light of the Qumran Texts and in the Testaments of the Twelve Patriarchs," in *Paul and Qumran: Studies in New Testament Exegesis,* ed. J. Murphy-O'Connor, *Paul and Qumran*, 48-68; 참조, H. D. Betz, "2 Cor. 6:14-7:1: An Anti-Pauline Fragment " *JBL* 92 (1973), 88-108. 여기서 Betz는 갈라디아 교회의 바울의 반대자들의 글에서 유래하였다고 한다. 또, Bornkamm, "The Origin of the So-called Second Letter to the Corinthains," 77f. 에서 Bornkamm은 고린도 교회의 반대파의 글에서 유래하였다고 한다.

무리 짓는다.[90] 그러나 이런 예조차 결국 바울의 사도적 진실성 변명이라는 큰 주제 아래 있다고 보면 심각한 주제 이탈은 아니다. 고린도후서에서 취급하는 다른 문제들도 바울은 주로 생각이 나는 대로 언급하고 있으며, 각 문제에 대한 자신의 소견을 논다가 다른 문제를 끼워서 언급한다. "방문 취소문제," "추천서 문제," 금전 문제," 등을 취급할 때 앞의 문제와 연계시키거나, 분명한 매듭이나 시작이 없이 말한다. 이런 필체는 고린도전서에서 "…에 대하여는" 이라고 사안별로 구별하여 논하는 것과는 대조적이다. 그러나 이런 모든 문제도 결국 사도권 방어를 통한 화해를 이루기 위한 주제 아래 있다고 볼 수 있다. 이런 자유롭고 즉흥적인 필체를 고려할 때, 또 6장 14절-7장 1절이 화해의 장애가 되는 고린도 교인들의 불의한 삶의 청산을 요구하는 것이라고 볼 때, 이 부분을 이질적인 자료로 제외시킬 수 없다.

둘째, 쿰란의 용어(벨리알)와 사상(이원론)이 나온다고 이 부분이 쿰란 문서에서 왔거나 바울 자신이 인용하였다고 하는 것도 받아들이기 어렵다.[91] 벨리알이란 말이 1QM 13장 1-4절에 나오나 다른 유대 문서에도 나온다(쥬빌리서 1:20; 레위의 증언 19:1; CD 4:13; 이사야의 승천 1:8; 2:4 등). 바울이 이런 용어를 모를 리가 없고 쓰지 않을 까닭이 없다. 이원론적인 사상, 즉 육과 영의 대조(7:1)도 쿰란인들에게 익숙한 것임이 사실이다(1QS 3:8; 1QH

90) Thrall, 121.

91) Martin, 199에 벨리알과 관련된 쿰란 문서와 유대교 문서를 보라. 1QM 13:1-4: "이스라엘의 하나님을 송축할찌어다. … 그러나 사악한 궤계를 가진 벨리알에게 저주가 있을찌어다."

92) Fitzmyer, 278.

13:13, 14; 15:21, 22; 17:25; 1QM 7:5).[92] 그러나 바울 서신에서도 육과 영의 대조가 가끔 있다. 골로새서 2장 5절에서 바울은 "내가 육신으로는 떠나 있으나, 심령으로는 너희와 함께 있어…"라고 이원론적 표현을 하고 있다. 이런 표현이 신학적, 윤리적 이원론인가란 문제는 논란이 될 수 있으나 적어도 바울의 인간학적 표현(영과 육으로 구성된 인간)은 된다.[93] 또 이와 유사한 표현이 고린도후서 2장 13절과 7장 5절에 나온다.[94] 또 고린도전서 7장 34절에도 같은 대조가 있다. 이러므로 육과 영의 대조가 바울의 표현이 아니라는 증거는 없다.

머피 오코너(Murphy-O'Conner)는 쿰란 병행구가 필로의 작품 가운데 더 많이 나타나지만 아무도 이를 쿰란의 영향으로 보는 이가 없음을 지적하면서 헬레니즘과 유대교의 영향을 받은 고린도 교회의 교인들에게 바울이 충분히 이런 용어를 자유롭게 쓸 수 있다고 하였다.[95] 세상적 습관에 젖어 있는 고린도 교인들에게 이에서 벗어날 것을 권면하고 있는 것이다.[96]

끝으로, 9개의 희귀 용어들(*Hapax legomena*)이 이 부분에 나온

93) R. Jewett, "Paul's Anthropological Terms: A Study of Their Use in Conflict Settings," *AGJU* 10 (Lieden: Brill, 1971), 184, 85; Barrett, 202.

94) Jewett, "Paul's Anthropological Terms," 133; H. Lietzmann, *An die Korinther 1/2* (Tübingen: J. C. B. Mohr, 1969), 131; R. Bultmann, *Theology of the New Testament 1*, ETr. K. Grobel (London: SCM Press, 1952), 56.

95) Murphy-O'connor, *The Theology of the Second Letter to the Corinthians*, 68. Murphy-O'Connor는 이런 쿰란적 특징은 아마도 아볼로에 의해 영향 받은 것이라고 제안했다(고전16:12). 그는 고후 9:14-15과 유사한 글을 필로에게서 인용한다. "이 세상에 대한 불신은 하나님께 대한 신앙이다." (De Abraham, 269). Murphy-O'Connor의 다른 글을 참조하라. "Philo and 2 Cor. 6:14-7:1," *RB* (1988), 55-59.

96) Murphy-O'Connor, *The Second Letter*, 69.

다고 해서 이 부분이 바울에 의해서 쓰인 것이 아니라고 할 수 없다. 바울이 이런 희귀 용어를 쓴 경우가 많다. 바울은 고린도전서 4장 7-13절에서 6개의 희귀 용어들을 썼고, 고린도후서 6장 3-10절에서는 4개를 썼다. 고린도후서 안에서만 50개의 희귀 용어가 발견된다.[97] 더구나 본문의 희귀 용어들은 구약 인용의 번역이다. 또 휘(G. D. Fee)는 본문의 희귀 용어가 서로 관련된 희랍어들임을 지적하면서 그 관련된 희랍어는 자주 쓰인 말들임을 지적했다. 적어도 3개의 용어가 희귀어로 볼 수 있으나 **μετέχω-μετοχή, μολύνω-μολυσμός, ἑτεροζυγέω-ζυλός, σύζυγος**에서와 같이 이 세 개의 희귀어들이 일반어들과 연결되므로 사실상 희귀어라고 보기 어렵다.[98]

랜스버거(D. Rensberger)와 마틴은 본문의 독특성을 감안하여 바울이 어떤 외부적 문서를 직접 인용은 않지만 사용하고 있다고 보았다.[99] 그러나 이 부분이 주로 구약 인용이나 간접 인용이 있으므로 구태여 외부 문서 의존을 상상할 필요가 없다. 드레트(J. D. M. Derrett)는 이 부분을 신명기 22장 10절의 유대교적 성경 해석(Midrash)이라고 했다.[100] 4절은 신명기 22장 10절이나 레위기 19장 19절, 또 16절은 레위기 26장 11, 12절, 에스겔 11장 20절, 36

97) P. E. Hughes, *Paul's Second Epistle to the Corinthians* (Grand Rapids: Eerdmans, 1976), 242.

98) G. D. Fee, "2 Corinthians 6:14-7:1 and Food Offered to Idols," *NTS* 23 (1977), 144-47.

99) D. Rensberger, "2 Corinthians 6:14-7:1-A Fresh Examination," *StBibT* 8 (1978), 25-49; Martin, 193.

100) J. D. M. Derrett, "2 Cor. 6:14ff. a Midrash on Dt. 22:10," *Bib* 59 (1978), 231-50.

장 28절, 37장 26절, 예레미야 31장 31-34절, 그리고 17절 상반절은 이사야 52장 11절, 하반절은 에스겔 11장 17절(LXX); 20장 34, 41절(LXX), 그리고 18절은 사무엘하 7장 14절을 각기 인용하거나 반영한다. 바울이 이렇게 구약 인용을 몰아서 하는 경우가 없다고 하나 일반적으로 바울이 구약을 많이 의존하는 것은 잘 알려진 사실이다. 해리스(M. J. Harris)는 이 본문에 나타나는 바울과 관계없는 용어가 여전히 바울과 관계있는 말들임을 보여주고 있다.[101] 트롤도 4장 3-6절의 불신자들의 불신앙과 사단에 대한 언급과, 5장 21절의 "의"에 대한 교훈 등이 본문에도 나타난다고 보았다.[102]

이렇게 보아서 본문 6장 14절-7장 1절은 지금의 자리에 원래 있었다고 보아서 무리가 없다. 편집 비평적 의견들은 사본적 근거가 없을 뿐만 아니라 바울의 서신을 편집자의 의도에 따라 적당히 꾸밀 수 있거나, 외부의 문서를 삽입할 수 있다는 발상에 근거하고 있다.[103] 이런 발상은 매우 추상적이며 실제적 가능성이 희박하다. 누가 누구에게 바울의 권위 있는 서신을 함부로 변경하여 편집하도록 위임을 할 수 있는가? 무엇보다 사본 상의 아무런 증거가 없다. 모든 사본에서 고린도후서는 이 부분을 가지고 있다.

트롤은 6장 14절-7장 1절은 6장 1-2절에서 바울이 "하나님의 은

---

101) Harris, 22.

102) Thrall, 34-35.

103) C. L. Mitton, *The Formation of the Pauline Corpus of Letters* (London: Epworth Press, 1955), 26. 여기서 Mitton은 초대 교회가 바울의 서신들을 방치하고 무시하고 섞인 상태로 두었는데, 편집자들에 의해 편집되었다고 한다. 이에 대한 비판을 Murphy-O'Connor, *The Second Letter*, 68에서 보라.

혜를 헛되이 받지 말라"고 하는 경고의 말을 계속 하는 것이라고 하면서 본문의 삽입설을 반대한다.[104] 그러면서 트롤은 고난의 사역과 화해를 권면하는 6장 3-13절을 바울에게 흔한 주제 이탈의 예로 본다. 그러나 5장 18절 전후에서 이미 시작된 화해의 주제가 6장 1-2절과 11-13절에서 강화되고, 7장 2절 이하에서도 계속되므로, 6장 14절-7장 1절은 화해의 장애를 제거하라는 강한 요구로 볼 수 있다. 또 드실바(deSilva)는 이 부분에서 바울이 고린도 교인들에게 거짓 사도들과의 관계를 끊도록 권면하고 있으므로 화해의 문맥에 있어서 아무런 문제가 없다고 하였다.[105] 위에서 지적하였듯이 유사한 내용이 12장 19절 이하에서도 반복되고 있으므로 결코 외적인 요소로 볼 수 없다. 즉 바울은 화해를 권면하면서 화해에 방해되는 세상적 요소를 단절하라고 권면하는 것이다.

그러나 고린도후서의 통일성 문제 중 논쟁이 가장 치열한 부분은 위에서 처음 언급한 10-13장이 독립된 서신인가라는 문제이다. 이 부분이 독립된 서신이나, 혹은 독립된 서신 (눈물의 편지)의 일부인가 하는 논쟁의 근거는 대개 이 부분의 몇 가지 특징에 근거한 것이다. 첫째로, 이 부분이 1-9장 부분과 매우 다른 어조를 갖고 있는 점이다. 실제로 1-9장에서 바울은 고린도 교인들에게 일반적으로 매우 다정히 칭찬하고 고무하며 화해를 호소하고 있는데 반하여 10-13장에서 바울은 배우 단호한 태도로 고린도 교인들을 신랄하게 꾸짖고 있다. 이런 어조의 차이를 부인할 수 없으나 어조

104) M. E. Thrall, "The Problem of II Cor. VI.14-VII.1 in Some Recent Discussion," *NTS* 24 (1978), 132-48, 특히, 146.

105) David A. deSilva, "Recasting the Moment of Decision: 2 Corinthians 6:14-7:1 in Its Literary Context," *AUS* 31 (1993), 3-16.

의 차이가 1-9장과 10-13장이 서로 다른 서신이라는 분명한 증거라고 볼 수는 없다. 바울은 10장 1절에서 이런 어조의 변화를 스스로 인정하고 있다. 둘째로, 10-13장의 내용 가운데 1-7장의 내용을 반영하면서 그 보다 먼저 쓴 것처럼 보이는 부분이 많다는 것이다. 예를 들면 10-13장에서 바울은 고린도 교회 방문을 예정하는데 반하여 1-9장에서는 바울이 방문을 이미 한 것으로 말하고 있다는 것이다. 그러나 우리는 바울은 2장 1절에서는 이전의 "고통의 방문" ("The Painful Visit")을 말하고 있으며, 10-13장에서는 고린도후서를 쓰면서 그의 "세 번째 방문"을 말한다고 본다(12:14, 20, 21, 13:1). 셋째로, 10-13장에는 희귀 용어들이 많이 나타난다는 것이다. 그러므로 혹 이 부분이 2장 4절의 "눈물의 편지"의 일부가 아닌가 하는 추측도 하게 하였다. 그러나 앞서 말한 바와 같이 희귀 용어가 있다고 다른 서신으로 볼 수는 없다. 바울은 그의 서신 여러 곳에서 희귀 용어를 집중적으로 쓰곤 했다. 이렇게 바뀐 어조 외에 독특한 언어의 사용이나 바울의 임박한 방문에 대한 언급 등을 들어서 이 부분의 독립성을 주장하는 학자들이 많다. 어떤 이들은 10-13장을 1-9장 보다 먼저 쓰인 서신의 일부가 후에 첨부된 것이라고 하고,[106] 어떤 이들은 반대로 10-13장이 1-9장이

---

106) J. S. Semler, *Paraphrasis, II. Epistolae ad Corinthos* (Halle, 1776)-처음으로 고린도후서를 나눈 사람; C. H. Dodd, "The Mind of Paul (1)," in *New Testament Studies* (Manchester: Manchester University Press, 1953), 67-82; J. H. Kennedy, *The Second and Third Epistles of St Paul to the Corinthians* (London: MacMillan, 1900); F. Lang, *Die Briefe an die Korinther* (Göttingen: Vandenhoek & Ruprecht, 1986); A. Plummer, *A Critical and Exegetical Commentary*; C. H. Talbert, *Reading Corinthians* (New York: Crossroad, 1987); F. B. Watson, "2 Cor. X-XIII and Paul's Painful Letter to the Corinthians," *JTS* 35 (1984), 324-46; J. Héring, *The Second*

쓰여진 후 몇 달 있다가 나중에 쓰여졌다고 보고,[107] 어떤 이들은 1-9장을 더 나누어 각 편지(위에서 언급한)의 사이에 쓴 것이라고도 한다.[108]

Epistle of Saint Paul to the Corinthians (London: Epworth, 1967). K. Lake, *The Earlier Epistles of St. Paul* (London: Rivingston's, 1927); M. Goguel, *Introduction au nouveau Testament, IV/2: les epitres pauliniennes* (Paris: Leroux, 1926); R. H. Strachan, *The Second Epistle of Paul to Corinthians,* MNTC 7/2(London: Hodder & Stoughton/New York: Harper & Brothers, 1935); F. V. Filson, "The Second Epistle to the Corinthians," *IB* 10 (New York: Abingdon Press, 1953); R. P. C. Hanson, *2 Corinthians*, Torch Bible Commentaries (London: SCM, 1967); Francis Watson, "2 Cor. x-xiii and Paul's Painful Visit to the Corinthians" , *JTS* 35(1984) 324-46.

107) M. Krenkel, *Beiträge zur Aufhellung der Geschichte und der Brief des Apostels Paulus*, 2nd ed. (Barunschweig: Schwetschke, 1895); R. Drescher, "Der zweite Korinterbrief und die Vorgaenge in Korinth seit Abfassung des ersten Korientherbriefs," *TSK* 70 (1897)43-111; L. P. Pherigo, "Paul and the Corinthian Church," *JBL* 68(1949) 341-50; C. H. Buck, "The Collection for the Saints," *HTR* 43(1950) 1-29; J. Munck, *Paul and the Salvation of Mankind*, ETr. Frank Clarke, (London: SCM, 1954, 1959); F. F. Bruce, *1 and 2 Corinthians*; J. M. Gilchrist, "Paul and the Corinthians--The Sequence of Letters and Visits," *JSNT* 34(1988) 47-69; R. Batey, "Paul's Interaction with the Corinthians," *JBL* 84 (1965), 139-46; V. P. Furnish, 41; R. P. Martin, *2 Corinthians*, xlii; H. Windisch, *Der Zweite Korintherbrief.*

108) H. D. Betz, *2 Corinthians 8 and 9* ; G. Bornkamm, "The History of the Origin of the So-called Second Letter to the Corinthians" ; G. Dautzenberg, "Der zweite Korintherbrief als Briefsammlung: Zur Frage der literarischen Einheitlichkeit und des theologi-schen Gefuges von 2 Kor 1-8," *ANRW* 25.4 (Berlin: de Gruyter, 1987), 3045-66; D. Georgi, *The Opponents of Paul in Second Corinthians* (Edinburgh: T. & T. Clark, 1986), 10-17; G. Sellin, "Hauptprobleme des Ersten Korintherbriefes," *ANRW* 25.4 (Berlin: de Gruyter, 1987), 2940-3044; A. Suhl, *Paulus und seiner Briefe* (Gütersloh: Mohr, 1975), 203-62; N. H. Taylor, "The

첫째, 현재의 순서를 인정하는 이들의 견해는 다음과 같다.

1) 어떤 학자들은 바울이 1-9장을 써서 보낸 후에 고린도 교회로부터 다시 혼란이 일어 났다는 소식을 듣고 이에 대해 노하여 10-13장을 다시 보냈는데 나중에 합해져서 지금의 모양이 되었다고 한다.[109] 리차드스(R. E. Richards)는 고린도후서 10-13이 추가로 쓴 것이라는 견해를 키케로의 서신 가운데 처음 쓴 편지를 쓴 후에 새로운 소식을 듣고 계속 이어서 쓴 편지의 예를 들어서 설명한다.[110] 그러나 다른 유사한 키케로의 편지에는 새 소식을 듣고서 이미 쓴 편지에 덧 부쳐서 쓴다는 말이 있다.[111] 그러나 고린도후서의 경우 이런 말이 전혀 없다. 또한 이런 경우 보른캄이 일찍이 지적한 바와 같이 바울이 10장에서 고린도 교인들이 왜 그렇게 빨리 변하는가에 대한 질책이 있을 법한데(갈 4:14-16에서처럼) 그런 질책이 없으므로 이런 주장의 신빙성이 약화된다.[112]

2) 12장 18절에서 8장과 9장의 방문 계획을 편지 끝에서 재차

Composition and Chronology of Second Corinthians," *JSNT* 44 (1991), 67-87. 이상의 각주는 Taylor의 논문"Composition and Chronology of Second Corinthians" 의 68면의 각주에서 대부분 인용하였다.

109) Munck, 171; R. A. Knox, *A NT Commentary for English Readers,* vol. II, (London: Burns, Oates, and Washbourne, 1954), 175; F. F. Bruce, 169; R. P. Martin, 44, 487; D. A. Carson, *From Triumphalism to Maturity: An Exposition of 2 Corinthians 10-13* (Grand Rapids: Baker Book House, 1984), 75.

110) E. R. Richards, *The Secretary in the Letters of Paul,* WUNT 2, Reihe 42 (Tübingen: Mohr, 1994), 83, 179-84.

111) Richards, *The Secretary in the Letters of Paul,* 85; Cicero, *Ad Familieares,* I 9:26.

112) Bornkamm, 259; Thrall, 903-904. Thrall은 이외에도 추가 편집설을 반대하는 다른 몇 가지 견해를 설명한다.

언급하는 것이라고 보면 하나의 편지이다.[113] 10-13장을 나중에 보냈다는 이들 가운데 어떤 이들은 바울이 디도를 고린도에 파송한다는 8장 16-24절, 9장 3-5절의 말(ἔπεμψα, συνεπέμψαμεν)을 서간문 과거(epislatory aorist, 즉, 과거이지만 현재적 의미)로 보고 12장 18절의 디도의 파송 (συναπέστειλα)은 단순 과거로 보아서 10-13장은 1-9장을 보낸 후에 썼다고 한다.[114] 그러나 미리 정한 전제를 따라 서신 과거나 단순 과거로 보는 것은 반증을 위한 증거가 될 수 없다. 모두 같은 파송 사실에 대해서 언급하는 것으로 보는 것이 자연스럽다.

3) 바울이 고린도 교회의 두 그룹에 대해서 말한다고 본다. 즉 1-9장은 바울을 따르는 이들에게, 10-13장은 바울을 반대하는 그룹을 향해서 하는 말이라고 설명한다.[115] 디도에게서 고린도 교회의 대다수가 다시 바울에게로 돌아 왔다는 소식을 듣고 감사와 위로의 말로 편지를 썼으나, 아직 반대하는 무리가 있음을 알고 그들에게 경고의 메시지를 써서 다음 방문을 준비하는 것이다. 이 견해가 무리가 없는 견해라고 본다. 그러나 이 견해를 반대하는 이들은 10-13장에서 바울은 고린도 교회 교인 전체를 상대로 "너희"라고 말하고 있으며 어느 특정한 사람들을 지칭하고 있지 않다고 한다.[116] 그러나 바울이 특정한 사람들을 염두에 두고 말하면서도 전체 고린도 교인들에게 보내는 편지이므로 "너

113) W. G. Kümmel, *Introduction to the New Testament*, ed. Howard Clark Kee (London: SCM, 1975), 290.

114) Furnish, 38.

115) Hughes, 24.

116) Plummer, 35.

희"라고 말하는 것은 자연스럽다. 더구나 반대하는 자들을 가르켜 특정한 개인이나 사람들을 지칭하는 곳들도 있다. 10장 11절에서 "이런 사람"(ὁ τοιοῦτος)이라고 개인을 지칭하며, 11장 4절에서도 "누가 가서(ὁ ἐρχόμενος) 우리가 전하지 아니한 다른 예수를 전파하거나…"에서 볼 수 있듯이 단수가 나온다.[117] 11장 18절에는 "여러 사람(πολλοί)이 육체를 따라 자랑하니…"라고 복수의 사람들이 바울을 대적하는 것으로 나온다. 계속해서 11장 22에는, "저희가 히브리 사람이냐(Ἑβραῖοί εἰσιν)?"라고 한다.

둘째, 10-13장이 1-9장보다 먼저 쓰여졌다는 학자들의 견해는 다음과 같다.

1) 이 두 부분의 내용 가운데 서로 비슷한 여러 구절들을 비교하여 보면서 10-13장의 말들은 1-9장의 말들을 상기시키는 말들(과거에 한 말들)이라고 보면서 10-13장이 먼저 쓰여졌다고 한다.[118] 플러머는 다음과 같이 1-9장과 10-13장의 말들 가운데 비슷한 말들을 골라 맞추면 10-13장의 말들이 1-9장의 말들보다 앞선 것임을 알 수 있다고 한다. 그러나 10-13장의 내용들은 1-9장에서 이미 한 말들을 반복하거나 반대자들에게 경고하는 말로 보면 무리가 없다.

117) 이런 단수를 일반화 단수로 보아서 전체 반대자들을 지칭한다는 견해도 있다 (Furnish, 488; Allo, 277; Hughes, 377; Bultmann, 204; Windisch, 326; Thrall, 664). 그러나 이를 반대하는 이들은 단수를 반대자들의 대표자, 대변인으로 본다 (Plummer, 296; Barrett, 275; Martin, 335).

118) Plummer, 30-33; R. H. Strachan, *The Second Epistle of Paul to the Corinthians* (London: Hodder & Stoughton, 1935), 17-19.

고후 1-9장	고후 10-13장
1:24 "이는 너희가 믿음에 섰음이라."	13:5 "너희가 믿음에 있는가 너희 자신을 시험하고…"
7:16 "내가 너희를 인하여 범사에 담대한 고로 기뻐하노라."	12:20, 21 "내가 갈 때에 내가 원하는 것 같이 보지 못하고…회개치 아니함을 인하여 근심할까 두려워 하노라."
2:3 "나의 기쁨이 너희의 기쁨인 줄 확신하노라." 7:4 "기쁨이 넘치는 도다."	10:2 "너희와 함께 있을 때에 나로 하여금 이 담대한 태도로 대하지 않게 하기를 구하노라."
3:2 "너희가 우리의 편지라."	13:10 "…이렇게 쓰는 것은 대면할 때에…엄하지 않게 하려 함이라."
7:16 "내가 너희를 위하여 범사에 담대한 고로…" (너희를 신뢰한다, θαρρῶ ἐν ὑμῖν).	10:1 "떠나 있으면 담대한…" (너희를 불신한다, θαρρῶ εἰς ὑμᾶς).
2:9 "너희가 범사에 순종하는지…."	10:6 "너희의 복종이 온전히 될 때에 모든 복종치 않는 것을 벌하려고 예비하는 중에 있노라."
4:2 "궤휼 가운데 행하지 아니하며…"	12:16 "어떤 이의 말이 … 공교한 자가 되어 궤계로 너희를 취하였다 하니"
7:2 "우리가 … 속여 빼앗은 일이 없노라."	12:17 "내가 … 누구의 이를 취하더냐"
1:23 "다시 고린도에 가지 아니한 것 너희를 아끼려 함이라."	13:2 "내가 다시 가면 용서하지 아니 하리라."
2:3 "내가 이같이 쓴 것은 … 도리어 근심을 얻을까 염려함이요."	13:10 "엄하지 않게 하려 함이라."
3:1 "우리가 다시 자천하기를 시작하겠느냐"	10:7 "자기가 그리스도에 속한 것 우리도 그러한 줄을…." 11:5 "내가 지극히 큰 사도들 보다 부족한 것이 조금도 없는 줄 생각하노라."
5:12 "우리가 다시 너희에게 자천하는 것이 아니요."	11:18 "나도 자랑하겠노라." 11:23 "저희가 그리스도의 일꾼이냐 … 나도 더욱 그러 하도다."

예로 플러머는 10-13장의 근심이 1-9장의 기쁨보다 시간적으로 앞선다고 한다.[119] 그러나 7장에서 근심이 기쁨이 되었다고 말하나, 그렇다고 이를 위의 대조와 결부시켜서 근심의 내용이 있는 10-13장이 기쁨의 내용이 있는 1-9장보다 앞선다는 분명한 증거로 삼을 수는 없다. 바울이 고린도 교회의 안정된 소식을 듣고 기뻐하면서 편지를 썼으나(1-9장) 편지의 마지막 부분에 가서 반대자들에 대한 엄한 경고가 필요하다고 생각해서 근심 가운데 10-13장을 썼다고 보면 지금 그대로의 순서에 무리가 없다.

"속여 빼앗았다"는 비난에 대해서 10-13장의 반대자들의 비난에 대해 더 강하게 말하고(12:16-18), 1-9장의 대다수의 회중들에게는 너그럽게 말한 것이다(7:2). 3장 1절과 5장 12절에서 자천(自薦)한다는 말에 "다시"(πάλιν)라는 부사가 들어 있으므로 11장에서 바울이 자신을 자랑하는 여러 말들을 연상케 한다고 볼 수 있다. 즉 지난 편지(10-13장)에서 "나를 자천했는데 다시 자천할 필요가 있겠느냐?" 라는 의미로 볼 수 있다. 그러나 바울은 2장에서 이미 자신을 자천하고 있다. 그의 사역이 하나님께서 함께 하시는 사역임을 여러 곳에서 분명히 나타내고 있다. 2장 15절에서 이미 "우리"는 "그리스도의 향기"라고 했다. 또 2장 17절에 "우리"는 "그리스도 안"에서 말한다고 했다. 3장 1절에서는 이런 자천의 말을 한 후에, "다시 자천할 필요가 있겠는가?"라고 반문 한 것이므로 11장의 자천을 염두에 둔 것이라고 말 할 수 없다. 5장 12절의 말도 마찬가지이다. 3장과 4장에서 자신을 자천한 여러 가지 말들—의의 직분(3:9), 너희의 양심에 맡겨 천거한다(4:2), 보배

119) Plummer, 30-33.

를 담은 질그릇(4:7) 등—에 대한 말이며, 바로 5장 11절에서 "우리가 하나님 앞에 알리어졌고 또 너희의 양심에도 알리어졌기를 바라노라."는 말에 대해서 "다시" 자천할 필요가 없다고 한 것이다.[120] 휴즈(Hughes)와 알로(Allo)가 지적한대로 이상의 모든 대조된 말들의 뜻을 다른 의미로 생각 할 수 있다.[121] 휴즈는 플러머가 짝을 맞춘 구절들을 다른 의미로 해석하면서 그 자신이 만든 다른 짝들을 열거하여 10-13장의 말들이 오히려 1-9장의 말들을 전제한 것임을 설명하고 있다.[122] 그러므로 플러머의 이런 짝 맞추기식 설명으로 10-13장을 먼저 썼음을 증명하려는 시도는 확신을 주지 못한다.

2) 어떤 이들은 고린도후서 10장 16절에 "너희 지경을 넘어 복음을 전하려 함이라"는 말을 가지고 10-13장이 먼저 쓰였음을 증명하려고 한다. 즉 1-9장을 쓸 때에는 바울이 마게도냐에 있었고, 10-13장을 쓸 때는 마게도냐로 가기 전 에베소였다고 보아야 한다는 것이다. 마게도냐에서 너희 지경을 넘어 복음을 전한다면 남쪽밖에는 없는데 남쪽은 아가야지방으로 복음이 전해진 곳이고, 더 남쪽은 바다이므로, 이 말은 결국 에베소에서 한 말이라는 것이다. 그러나 대부분의 주석가들은 이 말은 마게도냐에서도 할 수 있는 말이라고 본다. 즉 로마나 스페인으로 가서 전도하리라는 말

120) R. V. G. Tasker, *The Second Epistle to the Corinthians*, TNTC 8 (Grand Rapids: Eerdmans, 1958), 34.

121) Hughes, 24-28; Allo, 56; W. H. Bates, "The Integrity of 2 Corinthians," *NTS* 12 (1965-66), 60-61.

122) Hughes, 31-33.

123) Martin, 45.

로 생각할 수 있다(롬15:24, 28),[123] 또 베이츠(W. H. Bates)가 지적한 것처럼 바울이 에베소에서 "눈물의 편지"를 썼다는 것도 증명되지 않았다.[124] (이 경우 10-13장이 "눈물의 편지"의 일부라는 주장을 전제로 한다.)

3) 10-13장을 나누는 어떤 학자들은 이 부분의 어조와 성격이 급하므로 고린도후서 2장 4절에 바울이 보냈다는 "눈물의 편지"의 일부가 첨부된 것으로 추정했다.[125]

이상에서 말하는 10-13장을 1-9장보다 먼저 썼다는 견해 에 대해 적어도 몇 가지 반박을 할 수 있다.

a) 어떻게 앞뒤로 꼭 맞는 지금과 같은 10장 1절부터 13장 10절까지의 부분이 남아서 들어 왔겠는가라는 어려운 질문을 할 수 있다. 브루스,[126] 스트라찬,[127] 보른캄[128]은 후대 편집자의 적절한 편집에 돌리지만, 타스커는 이런 안이한 설명에 만족하지 않는다: "도대체 어떤 편집자가 바울의 서신에 손을 댈 수 있는 권위를 가졌는가?"[129] 만일 편집자가 있어서 바울의 편지를 아무런 설명도 없이 짜깁기하고 바울의 말로 보이게 하는 것은 성실치 못할 뿐만 아니라 독자를 속이는 것이다. 이런 것을 초대교회가 묵인하였다

124) Bates, 62.

125) Adolf Hausrath, *Der Vier-Capitelbrief des Paulus an die Korinther* (Heidelberg: Bassermann, 1870); Kennedy, 81-85; Strachan, 16.

126) Bruce, 167.

127) Strachan, 21.

128) Bornkamm, 259.

129) Tasker, 28.

고 볼 수 없고 이런 편집자를 상상할 수도 없다. 당시 헬라시대의 편지의 편집 가운데 짜깁기식 편집이 있었으나, 바울의 편지도 그렇게 되었다는 증거는 없다.[130)]

b) "눈물의 편지"는 문제된 사람에 대한 지시가 들어 있어야 할 텐데 10-13장에는 그런 사람을 전혀 언급치 않는다.[131)] 보른캄은 편집 당시에 그 사람이 살아 있었고, 화해가 되었으므로(2:8), 그 사람에 대한 언급이 있는 부분이 제거되었다고 한다. 그러나 이런 주장은 추정에 불과하고, 편집자의 재량권을 인정하기도 어렵다.

c) 10-13장의 내용이 2장 4절의 "눈물의 편지"의 애통하는 내용과는 다르다는 점이다. 이에 대해 보른캄은 바울이 겉으로는 진노하는 마음을 가졌으나 속으로는 애통하는 마음을 가지고 썼다고 한다.[132)] 그러나 바울은 10-13장에서 주저나 망설임이 없이 담대하게 쓰고 있다(10:1). "눈물의 편지"(혹은 "엄격한 편지")는 특정 개인의 사사로운 편지였으므로 바울 스스로 파기를 지시하였을 것이다.[133)]

d) 거스리(D. Guthrie)는 10-13장의 위치가 지금대로라는 매우 설득력 있는 제안을 하였다. 그는 바울이 그의 여러 서신에서 그의 독자들을 칭찬한 후에 그를 반대하는 이들에 대한 경계를 한다고 지적 하였다. 바울 서신의 끝 부분에서 적들에 대한 경계의 말

---

130) P. Vielhaur, *Geschichte der urchristlichen Literatur*, 154-55; A. Deissmann, *Bible Studies*, ETr. A. Grieve (Edinburgh: T. & T. Clark, 1903), 236.

131) Murphy-O'Connor, *The Second Letter*, 11.

132) Bornkamm, 259.

133) Martin Dibelius, *A Fresh Approach to the NT and Early Christian Literature* (London: Ivor Nicholson and Watson, 1936), 154.

이 나온다(고전 4:14-21; 갈 6:12-17; 살후 3:6-15; 딤후 4:14-18).[134] 이런 제안은 보른캄이 지적한 바, 심판에 대한 말이 바울 서신 뿐만 아니라 대부분의 신약의 다른 책 뒤에 나온다는 지적과도 유사하나 보른캄은 이런 사실도 편집자의 편집으로 돌리기 때문에 거스리(Guthrie)의 결론과는 다르다.[135] 거스리의 제안이 다른 제안에 비해 설득력이 가장 높다. 다만 다른 곳에서는 4장이나 되는 경계의 말이 없으므로 고린도후서 10-13장의 경우는 다른 서신의 경계의 부분들과는 달리 취급되어야 하지 않는가라는 질문을 할 수도 있다. 그러나 고린도 교회의 사태가 어느 교회 사태보다 심각하였으므로 많은 경계를 필요로 하였을 것이다.

이상의 고린도후서의 통일성 문제는 다른 어떤 서신 보다 복잡한 논쟁을 갖고 있다. 그것은 고린도후서가 갖고 있는 세 가지 특징으로 말미암은 것이다. 즉 고린도후서에 연결이 매끄럽지 못한 부분이 있다는 것, 고린도 전, 후서 안에 다른 편지에 대한 언급이 있는 것(고전 5:9; 고후 2:4), 그리고 초대 교회에서 고린도후서가 비교적 늦게 사용되기 시작한 사실이다. 그러나 우리는 고린도후서의 통일성을 지지하는 근거를 아래와 같이 정리해 볼 수 있다.

여기서 바넷의 제안을 중심으로 통일성의 증거를 정리하기로 한다.[136]

첫째, 고린도후서는 구조의 통일성이 있다. 어색한 연결들은

134) D. Guthrie, *New Testament Introduction* (Chicago: Inter-Varsity Press, 1970), 446.
135) Bornkamm, 261-62.
136) Bornkamm, 17-23; 451-56.

모두 나름대로 설명할 수 있으므로 통일성에 있어서 큰 문제가 되지 않는다.

a. 10장 1절의 어색한 연결과 어조의 변화는 바울 사도가 방문에 앞서서 자신을 지지하는 이들과 반대하는 이들에 대하여 자신의 사도직을 변명하기 때문이다. 그러므로 10장 1절은 앞서 1-9장의 유화적인 어조를 전제하고서 이제는 반대자들의 비난에 대해서 강경한 어조로 바꾼다는 양보적인 진술로 이해 할 수 있다. 1-9장과 10-13장이 모두 "약함을 통해 강하게 하시는 하나님의 사역"을 말하고 있으나, 1-9장에서는 그를 지지하는 다수의 고린도 교인들을 상대로 주로 온건하게 말하고, 10-13장에서는 그를 반대하는 이들과 거짓 사도들을 염두에 두고 특히 그들의 자신에 대한 비난에 대하여 논리적으로 대처하며 강경한 어조로 말하고 있다고 본다. 바울은 임박한 그의 세 번째 고린도 교회 방문 이전에 그의 반대자들의 비난과 그로 인한 오해에 대해 분명히 해명함으로써 방문 시에 일어날 어려움의 소지를 미리 없애겠다는 목회적 취지에서 10-13장을 마지막 부분에서 쓰는 것이다.[137] 바울은 반대자들을 피해서는 안 되고 정면 대결해야 할 것을 결심했다. 그들이 분명히 신학적으로 도덕적으로 잘못된 무리이기 때문에 인내하거나 방치하면 자신을 포함하여 고린도 교회에 유해할 수밖에 없다고 단정하였다(11:4, 13-15).

b. 바울이 디도를 만난 일을 서신 중심부분(2:14-7:4)의 시작과 끝에 언급하고 있는 것은 하나님께서 고린도 교회를 위한 사도 바울의 사역을 모든 난관에도 불구하고 도와 주신다는 증거를 디도

137) Tasker, 171.

의 만남이라는 생생한 경험을 통해서 증거 하려는 것이다.

c. 중심 부분에 이어 헌금 문제를 다루어 다시 돌아온 고린도 교인들의 바울에 대한 사랑, 또는 충성심을 확증하게 하는 것이다(8:8, 24).

d. 이어서 강력한 어조로 그의 적들과 그 동조자들을 심하게 공격함으로써 아직 남아 있는 반대 세력의 기세를 꺾는다.

고린도후서의 구조적 통일성에 대한 중요한 증거는 고린도후서 1-9장과 10-13장을 비교해볼 때 나타나는 내용의 통일성이다. 전반부에서도 후반부에 나타나는 바울의 반대자들에 대한 격렬한 표현을 예상케 하는 반대자들에 대해서 경계하는 내용들이 적지 않게 나온다는 사실이다(2:11, 16; 3:1; 4:2; 5:16; 6:3-16; 7:2). 이것은 고린도후서를 쓸 때 처음부터 바울은 아직 반대자들이 적지 않게 남아 있다는 사실을 알고 썼다는 증거로 볼 수 있다. 그러나 마지막에 가서 이들에 대한 보다 단호한 질책을 하여 다음 방문 시에 다시 반대하는 일이 없도록 하기 위한 예방적 조치로 볼 수 있다. 무엇보다 후반부에서 바울 자신이 이런 의도를 스스로 밝히고 있다(10:2; 13:10).

또한 고린도후서의 순서에 대한 바울의 목회 심리적 접근을 지적할 수 있다. 처음에는 디도를 통해 전해들은 고린도 교회의 회개 소식을 듣고, 위로와 감사의 내용을 집중적으로 말하고(1-7장), 그 후에 좀 어려운 부탁인 예루살렘 성도들을 위한 헌금을 독려하고(8-9장), 끝으로 제일 어려운 권면으로서 아직도 분명히 입장을 정리하지 못한 이들과 반대자들에 대해서 질책과 경고의 말을 한 것이다(10-13). 이런 구조적 통일성은 최근에 논의되는 고린도후서가 고대 희랍 사회의 변명문과 구조적으로 일치된다는 연구로

도 지지된다.[138)]

둘째, 10-13장에서 다른 바울 서신에서는 잘 쓰지 않는 희귀어들이 나오지만 앞의 1-9장에서도 같은 희귀어들이 나온다는 사실은 하나의 편지임을 지지해준다.

a. 10장 1절의 παρακαλῶ("권면하다")과 2절의 δέομαι("간구한다")는 말이 함께 결합되어 나오는데, 다른 바울 서신에서는 볼 수 없으나, 5장 20절에 나오며, 같은 절의 τῇ πεποιθήσει("담대함", "확신")은 앞서 1장 15절, 3장 4절, 8장 22절에 나오는 데, 고린도후서 이전에는 쓰이지 않았으며, 고린도후서 이후에 쓰인 에베소서 3장 12절과 빌립보서 3장 4절에 다시 나올 뿐이다. 이런 증거들은 고린도후서의 통일성을 지지해 준다.

b. 1-9장에서 바울은 그의 사역을 "의의 사역" 이라하고 자신을 "하나님의 사신" 이라고 하는데(3:9, 4:1, 6:3, 4), 10-13장에서도 거짓사도들이 "의의 사도" 로 가장한다고 한다(11:15). 이런 "의의 사역" 이란 말은 다른 데서 나오지 않는 표현이다.

c. "자랑한다" (καυχάομαι)는 말이 고린도후서 이전의 편지에서는 나오지 않는 말인데, 고린도후서 전체에서 사용되고 있다(3:1, 4:2, 5:12, 6:4, 10:12, 18, 12:11).

d. 4장 2절과 12장 16절에서 두 개의 같은 말들이 겹쳐서 나온다. 즉 "궤휼 가운데 행하지 아니하며 하나님의 말씀을 혼잡케 아니하고" 에서 "궤휼" 과 "혼잡" 이 함께 나온다(ἐν πανουργίᾳ μηδὲ δολοῦντες). 4장 2절에서는 번역상 두 말이 붙어 있지는 않으나

138) 아래 "고린도후서의 특징들" 에서 찾아보라.

헬라어 본문에서는 붙어 나온다. 12장 16절에서는 두 말이 명사형으로 되어 붙어 있다. "공교한 자가되어 궤계로"(πανοῦργος δόλῳ). 이런 두 말이 다른 바울 서신에 함께 나타나지 않는다.

e. "우리가 그리스도 안에서 하나님 앞에 말하노라"는 말이 2장 17절과 12장 19절에 나오며 다른 바울 서신에 나오지 않는다.

f. 고린도후서에 나오는 네 개의 "고난" 관련 구절들(1:7-11; 4:7-10; 6:4-10; 11:23-12:10)들이 전체에 골고루 나오고 있다. 물론 다른 바울 서신에서도 고난 구절이 나오므로 통일성의 결정적인 근거는 되지 못하나 지지하는 근거는 된다. 그러나 고난 관련 구절 가운데 공통적 언어들이 고린도후서 전체에서 고르게 나온다. ὑπερβολή("지나친", "지극히", 1:8; 4:7; 12:7); στενοχωέω("둘러 싸이다", "고난을 당하다")/στενοχωρία("고난", 4:8; 6:4; 12:10); διάκονος("일꾼", 6:4; 11:23); ἀνάγκη("궁핍", 6:4; 12:10) πληγκή("매맞음", 6:5; 11:23), φυλακή("갇힘", 6:5; 11:23), κόπος("수고함", 6:5; 11:23) ἀγρυπνία("자지못함", 6:5; 11:27), νηστεία("굶주림", 6:5; 11:27). 이 중에서 φυλακή, κόπος, ἀγρυπνία, νηστεία는 다른 바울 서신에서는 나타나지 않는 글이다.

이러한 같은 말이 1-13장에 일관되게 나오는 현상은 10-13이 독립된 서신이 아니라 같은 편지라는 언어적 증거라고 본다.

셋째, 1-9장에서의 바울의 고린도 교인들에 대한 적극적인 자세와 기쁨은 고린도 교인들의 바울의 "엄격한 편지"를 받고 회개하고, 바울에게 충성하기로 한 것에 대한 상대적이고 부분적인 반응으로 보아야 하며, 고린도 교인들에 대한 완전하고 절대적인 반응으로 볼 수는 없다. 바울은 고린도 교인들이 아직도 많은 부분에서 고쳐야할 것들이 있다고 보고 있다(12:19-21). 그러므로 10-13장의 바뀐 어조는 당연한 것이다.[139)]

넷째, 앞서 언급했듯이 고린도후서는 바울이 그의 고린도 교회에 대한 목회적 방침들을 따라서 순서대로 썼다. 초두에서 7장까지는 디도의 도래로 말미암은 고린도 교인들의 충성을 확인하고 그들의 바울 자신에 대한 사도로서의 신뢰를 굳건케 하며, 8장과 9장에서는 디도를 통한 헌금 사역의 완수를 지시한다. 그리고 끝으로 10장에서 13장에서는 그의 세 번째 방문 이전에 반대자들에 대한 단호한 경고와 함께 아직도 고린도 교인들에게 남아있는 바울에 대한 적대적인 앙금이나 오해를 말끔히 씻기 위해서 솔직하고 분명하게 말하는 것이다.

다섯째, 바울의 고린도후서를 당시 헬라 수사학적 관행을 따라서 처음에는 부드러운 어조로 청중과의 관계를 형성하는 주제들을 가지고 시작하다가 종국에 이르러서는 점차 강한 어조로 가장 중요한 문제들을 강조함으로써 청중들에게 보다 효과적이고 극적인 감흥을 일으킬 수 있는 수사학적 형식을 취하고 있다는 견해가 있다.[140)] 예로 데모스데네스(Demosthenes, 384-322 B.C.)가 아테네 사람들에게 자신을 변명하면서 보낸 서신이 그렇다.[141)] 이런

139) Barnett, 22.

140) Barnett, 17.

141) H. D. Betz, *Der Apostel Paulus und die sokratische Tradition, Eine Exegetische Untersuchung zu seiner Apologie 2 Korinther 10-13,* BHT 45 (Tübingen: J. C. B. Mohr, 1972); G. Kennedy, *Classical Rhetoric and Rhetorical Criticism*(Chapel Hill:

견해가 고린도후서의 통일성을 지지해줄 수 있으나, 이보다 바울은 독자들을 사랑하는 목회적 온유함과 함께 독자들을 진리로 가르치려는 교사로서의 강직함을 적절히 구사하여 고린도후서를 쓰고 있다고 보는 편이 옳다. 바울은 10장에서 13장에서 뿐만 아니라 5장 20절-6장 2절, 6장 11절-7장 1절에서도 강렬한 어조를 보이고 있으며, 자세히 보면 10장에서 13장이 모두 강렬한 것만은 아니다. 바울은 12장 19절에서 그의 어조를 한결 낮추고 있고 13장 5절에서 끝까지 바울은 보다 신중한 자세를 취함으로써 7-9장과 과히 다르지 않다고 본다. 그렇다면 어조가 다르기 때문에 독립된 편지라는 주장은 약화된다. 서론에서 지적하였듯이 서신 초두에는 위로와 감사의 내용을 중심으로 쓰고(1-7장), 다음에는 조금은 어려운 문제인 헌금 당부를 하고(8-9장), 마지막으로 반대자들에 대한 질책과 경계를 쓰고 있다. 이런 순서는 바울이 목회적 입장에서 교인들의 반응을 고려하여 주제를 적절하게 정리하였음을 나타낸다.

여섯째, 고린도후서 전체에서 쓰이는 대명사를 조사해보면, 일관된 용법이 나오고, 이것은 바울이 고린도후서에서 같은 독자들을 대상으로 삼고 있다는 증거이다. 그러므로 고린도후서는 하나의 통일된 서신이다. 10-13장을 포함하여 고린도후서에서 바울이 사용하는 대명사는 일인칭 대명사, "나" 또는 "우리"와 대조하여

University of North Carolina Press, 1984); A. J. Malherbe, *Social Aspects of Early Christianity* (Barton Rouge: Louisiana State University, 1977); F. Young and D. F. Ford, *Meaning and Truth in 2 Corinthians* (Grand Rapids: Eerdmans, 1988) 46-44; Barnett은 기원전 4세기의 Demosthenes는 연대상으로 바울과 멀다고 보고, F. Young과 D. F. Ford가 제안하는 Halicarnassus의 Dionysius나 Quintilia 같은 이들의 영향을 받은 당시 대중들의 일반적 수사학적 지식수준에 근거하였다고 본다(18).

이인칭 대명사, "너희"를 쓰고 있다(11:21, 12:10에서는 "나"만 쓰고 있음). "나"와 "너"의 대명사가 함께 쓰인 것은 바울과 고린도 교인들과의 관계를 향상하기 위한 의도를 나타낸다. 삼인칭 대명사는 적게 쓰이는데, 이것의 중요성을 간과할 수 없다. 바울은 삼인칭의 사람들에 대해서 간접적으로 언급한다. 삼인칭 대명사는 세 개의 부류를 가리킨다. 문맥에 따라서 삼인칭 대명사는 때로는 예수를 믿으면서 바울을 반대하는 고린도 교인들 나타내기도 하고(10:2, 7), 때로는 교회에 나오지만 진실히 믿지 않으면서 회개치 않은 비도덕적이고 세속적인 고린도인들을 나타내기도 한다(12:21; 13:2; 참조, 6:14-7:1). 10장 12절-12장 13절에 나오는 삼인칭 대명사는 거짓 사도들로서 고린도 교회에 들어온 외부 인사들을 가리킨다(11:4, 5, 13; 참조, 12:11). 이들은 고린도 교인들에게 접근하여 바울을 비난하는 이들이다. 이렇게 나누는 것이 고린도후서를 바르게 이해하는 데 중요할 뿐만 아니라 고린도후서의 통일성을 지지하는 증거로 삼을 수도 있다. 즉 이런 삼인칭 대명사가 1-9장에서도 나온다는 사실을 중시해야 한다. 바울에 대한 비난은 1장 12-14, 17절에도 나온다. 2장 17절-3장 16절, 그리고 어쩌면 5장 11-13절에서도 유대교 전통주의자들로서 바울을 반대하는 이들이 나온다. 거룩한 생활을 가르치는 6장 14절-7장 1절의 대상은 회개치 않은 세속주의적 명목상의 고린도 교인들이다. 이렇게 같은 대상을 가리키는 삼인칭 대명사가 고린도후서 전체에서 쓰인 사실은 바울이 처음부터 3인칭으로 나타나는 그의 반대자들에 대한 공격을 준비하였다가 마지막(10-13장)에 이르러 한꺼번에 집중적으로 공격하여 그의 방문 전에 그들의 태도가 크게 변화되거나 적어도 그 기세가 약화되기를 바라는 것으로 본다. 이런 입장에서 보면, 10장 1-11절의 비판적 내용은 삼인칭의 그룹 가운데 바울을 반대하는 고린도 교인들이 디도가 전한 "엄격한 편지"를 받고서 바울에게 순종하지 아니하고 바울을 반대하여, 바울은 함께 있을 때는 아무것도 못하는 무능한 사람이고, 떠나 있으면 편지로 이래라 저래라 시켜먹기 좋아하는 사람이라고 비난하는 이들의 비난을 바울이 빗대어서 말하는 것이라고 볼 수 있다. 10장 12-18절의 대상은 고린도 교회에 들어온 거짓 사도들이다. 소위 "바보의 연설"(11:1-12:13)이 시작되는 11장부터는 고린도 교인들이 거짓사도들의 바울에게 대한 비난을 따라서 바울을 오해하는 문제들을 정면으로 돌파하고 있다. 그는 외모를 자랑하는 거짓 사도들과 자신을 비교해도 조금도 부족하지 않다고 한다. 그러면서 그가 거짓 사도들과 구별되는, 참된 사도로서의 증거가 있는데, 그 것은 그가 그리스도의 고난에 동참함으로 소유한 그리스도의 약함이라고 한다. 그리스도의 약함의 증거가 그의 사역 가운데 나타났고, 그의 육체 가운데에도 있다. 이렇게 1장부터 13장에 나타난 삼인칭 대명사들은 문맥에 따라서 단순히 바울을 반대하는 고린도 교인들과, 세속적인 고린도 교회 교인들, 그리고 예루살렘에서 온 거짓 사도들의 세 구룹을 가리킨다. 이런 고린도후서 전체에 나타나는 삼인칭 대명사의 일관된 용법이 고린도후서의 통일성을 지지하는 근거가 된다.

일곱째, 바울의 임박한 세 번째 고린도 교회 방문이 고린도후서 전체에 나타나고(2:1, 3, 9:4, 10:2, 6, 11:9, 12:14, 20, 21, 13:1, 2, 10), 각 방문과 관련된 기사에서 바울은 구체적인 문제 해결을 지시한다. 즉 문제가 된 사람의 징계해제로 그의 방문 전에 화해 분위기를 조성한다(2:1, 3); 그의 방문 전에 헌금 문제를 해결하여 방문 시에 부담을 덜게 한다(9:4); 방문 전에 바울의 사도적 자격이나 복음의 진정성에 대한 의심을 버리고 또한 세속적 관행을 버린다(10:1-12, 11:1-12:20, 21, 13:1, 2, 10).

여덟째, 12장 18절의 "내가 디도를 권하고 함께 한 형제를 보내었으니 디도가 너희의 이를 취하더냐 "(παρεκάλεσα Τίτον καὶ συναπέστειλα τὸν ἀδελφόν· μήτι ἐπλεονέκτησεν ὑμᾶς Τίτος)라는 말이 모두 과거시제로 되어있으므로 앞서 8:18, 22에서 바울이 디도와 두 형제를 보내는 것과 시제적으로 나중에 일어난 것이므로 10-13장도 나중에 쓰였다는 견해가 있다. 그러나 헌금을 위한 현재의 세 번째 방문을 가리킨다고 볼 수도 있고, 또는 8장 6절에 언급한 이전의 디도의 방문을 가리킨다고도 볼 수 있다. 현재의 방문일 경우 8장 23절에서는 분명히 형제들(두 명)이라고 말하는데, 12장 18절에서는 한 형제만을 언급하므로 맞지 않으나, 바울이 디도에게 관심을 집중하고 형제의 수에는 관심을 두지 않고 있다고 볼 수 있다. 8장 6절의 방문일 경우에도 8장 6절에는 한 형제란 말이 없으므로 맞지 않는다고 할 수 있으나, 역시 8장 6절에서도 디도 중심의 사역에 관심을 가지다보니 형제에 대한 언급을 하지 않았다고 볼 수도 있다.[142] 한편, 8장 18, 22절의 단순과거(aorist)는 서간용과거(epistolary aorist)로서 "보내노니"라고 현재로 번역하는 것이 옳으나, 12장 18절은 보통 역사적 시제로 번역한다(NIV). 그러나 12장 18절의 단순과거도 서간용과거로 볼 수

142) Martin, 448.

있다.[143] 고린도 교인들이 디도를 맞이한 후에 편지를 읽을 것을 예상하고 현재의 일을 과거시제로 썼다고 볼 수 있다. 이 경우 바울이 편지를 쓰고 있을 때를 기준으로 12장 18절의 방문은 아직 이루어지지 않은 방문이다. 그러나 "디도가 너희의 의를 취하더냐?"란 말은 이미 디도가 방문한 이후를 가리킨다고 볼 수 있다. 이 경우 12장 8절의 이 말은 8장 6절의 과거의 디도의 방문 같은 그의 과거의 행위에 대한 기억을 회상하라는 진술로 보아야 한다. 이렇게 12장 18절의 방문은 8장 6절에 언급된 과거의 방문을 가리키거나, 8장 18, 22절의 현재의 방문을 가리킬 가능성이 모두 있다. 그러므로 12장 18절의 과거시제가 10-13장이 1-9장보다 나중에 기록된 것을 가리키는 결정적인 증거라고 볼 수 없다.

아홉째, 고린도후서는 화해라는 하나의 큰 주제가 흐른다. 위에서 이미 지적한 것처럼, 고린도후서는 화해라는 하나의 큰 내적인 주제위에, 바울의 사도직 변명이라는 외적인 주제와, 그리스도의 왕권 확립이라는 궁극적 주제로 구성되어 있다고 볼 때 주제적 통일성을 갖는다. 전반부는 물론 후반부에서도 바울은 화해적인 말로 고린도 교인들을 설득한다(11:2-4, 11; 12:14, 15), 특히 후반부의 처음과 마지막 부분을 화해적인 말로 시작하고 마무리 짓는다(10:1; 13:7, 9, 10). 10-13장의 전체 어조가 1-9장과 달리 강경하지만 자세히 읽어보면 바울의 강경한 어조는 화해적 방문을 위해서 반대하는 지도자들을 향한 것이며(10:6, 10-12; 11:12-16; 13:1-2) 다수의 고린도 교인들에 대해서는 3차 방문 이전에 회개하고 원만

143) Barnett, 22.

한 방문이 되도록 준비하라는 주제를 계속 지키고 있다. 바울은 3차 방문 시에 그가 가진 사도권(즉 징계권)을 반대하는 소수에 대하여 한정적으로 사용할 뜻도 있으나 소수의 반대자들과 동조자들이 미리 회개함으로써 사도권을 사용하지 않게 되도록 전체 고린도 교인들이 협조하여 준비할 것을 계속 바라고 있다(10:2, 8; 11:11; 12:19-21; 13:5, 7, 9, 10). 또한 바울은 자신이 그리스도의 사도임을 확신하기 때문에 그의 사도권 방어는 곧 그리스도의 왕권 확립과 직결되어 있다고 믿는다(4:5; 10:5-6, 8; 13:10).[144] 바울의 사도직 방어의 근본 논리는 "그리스도의 약함의 능력" 이다(4:5, 7-15; 6:4-10; 11:10, 30; 12:9, 10; 13:5, 7). 이 진리가 바울을 인격이나 사도직에 있어서 그의 반대자들과 구별하는 가장 분명하고 일관된 증거로 고린도후서 전체에서 사용되고 있다. 이와 관련하여 바울은 그리스도의 사도로서 그리스도의 순수한 사랑을 가지고 고린도 교인들을 극진히 사랑한다는 것을 강조한다(1:23; 2:4; 4:12; 5:14; 6:6; 7:1-3; 10:1; 11:11, 29; 12:15; 13:7). 또한 바울은 그의 극진한 사랑에 상응하는 고린도 교인들의 사랑의 반응을 간청하기도 한다(6:11-13; 8:8, 24; 12:15). 이런 사랑의 주제와 함께 위에서 지적한 고린도후서에서 바울의 사도직과 관련된 작은 주제들, 즉, 바울의 복음의 정통성(2:17-4:6; 참조, 11:4), 바울의 도덕성(1:12, 23; 2:17; 3:4-6; 4:2; 5:11; 6:5-13; 7:2; 10:13-18; 11:10; 12:14), 교회 설립자로서 바울의 사도적 위상(10:8; 11:5; 12:, 11, 14; 13:10) 같은 주제들은 모두 기독론적 화해라는 큰 주제 아래에 있다고 본다(1:19; 2:17; 4:4, 7-15; 6:4-10; 8:9; 10:5; 11:2; 12:10; 13:4). 또한 이런

144) Thrall, 844.

화해는 그리스도의 왕권이 온전하게 이루어 질 때 일어나는 것이라고 볼 때 화해란 주제와 그리스도의 왕권 확립의 주제는 서로 상관되는 것이다(10:5, 6; 13:10).

한편, 바울은 사도로서 고린도 교인들과의 원만하고 진실한 관계를 원하지만, 그것은 사도와 교인이라는 형식적인 관계가 아니라 보다 내면적이고 진실한 사랑의 관계를 원한다(7:3). 그래서 그는 사도로서의 권위를 말하기도 하지만, 그보다 그의 약하고 부끄러운 모습을 솔직히 보여 준다(11:33, 12:5). 바울의 "약한 것에 대한 자랑" 도 하나님의 은혜의 경륜이 중심적인 신학을 나타내지만 동시에 바울이 사도라는 높은 위치에서 자신올 여러 약점을 가진 인간 바울로서 자신을 일부로 낮추어서 고린도 교인들과 진정한 사랑의 관계를 이루려는 의도도 나타낸다고 본다. 서로 약한 인간들임을 알고 위로하는 그런 인간적인 진실한 관계를 원했던 것이다(1:4-6). 물론 이런 바울의 인간사랑은 단순한 휴머니즘이 아니라 그리스도의 사랑에서 나온 것이다: "그리스도의 사랑이 우리를 강권하시는 도다" (5:14a). 이런 사랑과 화해의 일관된 주제가 고린도후서의 통일성을 지지한다고 할 수 있다.

열째로, 어조가 전혀 달라 보이는 고린도후서 전반부(1-9장)와 후반부(10-13)에서 유사한 어귀들이나 개념들, 작은 주제들이 나타난다. 이런 것들이 고린도후서의 전후반부가 결국 하나의 서신이라는 것을 지지해 준다: 그리스도 중심(1:5, 19, 21; 2:10, 14, 17; 3:4, 5, 14, 18; 4:4, 10, 11; 5:9-11, 14, 15, 17, 20; 6:4-10, 15; 8:9; 10:5, 8, 18; 11:2, 3, 10, 23; 12:2, 9, 10, 19; 13:3, 4, 10); 그리스도 안(1:20, 21; 2:14; 10:7, 17, 12:2, 19; 13:2); 예수와 함께 죽고 살고(4:14; 12:5); 고린도인들과 함께 죽고 함께 살고(7:3, 11:29; 참조,

5:9); 우리는 죽고 너희는 살고(4:12; 13:7); 진실한 사랑의 증거(2:4; 5:14, 15; 8:8, 24; 11:11; 12:14, 15); 진리를 나타냄(4:2; 13:8; 참조, 2:17; 11:10); 말씀(복음)을 혼잡케 하지 않음(2:17; 4:2; 11:3, 4); 세상 죄와의 단절(6:14-7:1; 12:21); 약하나 강함(4:7-15; 6:4-10; 8:2; 12:9, 10; 13:4, 9); (헌금 사역을 위해) 디도와 형제들을 보냄:(8:18-24; 9:3; 12:17, 18); 성령의 보증(1:22; 12:18; 참조, 11:4); 자랑하기(3:1; 10:12; 11:5, 18; 12:11, 12); 육체 대로(1:17; 5:16; 10:2, 3; 11:18); 외모로 자랑(5:12; 10:7); 재물 약취 혐의(7:2; 12:16); 방문과 관련한 근심, 슬픔의 감정(2:1; 12:21); 몸을 떠나 주와 함께 거하는 것(5:9; 12:2, 3); 부모와 자녀(6:13; 12:15); "사랑하는 자들아"(*ἀγαπητοί*)(7:1과 12:19); "그리스도로 말미암아 하나님을 향하여"(*διὰ τοῦ Χριστοῦ πρὸς τὸν θεόν*)라는 말이 3장 4절, 그리고 "그리스도 안에서 하나님 앞에서"(*κατέναντι θεοῦ ἐν Χριστῷ*)라는 말이 12장 19절에서 나온다.

위에서 지적했듯이 이런 1-9장과 10-13장의 공통적인 어귀들이 곧 고린도후서의 통일성을 증명하는 것은 아니다. 그런 것들은 단지 한 사람 바울이 썼다는 증거 일 뿐이다. 예로 "그리스도 안"이란 어귀는 바울 서신의 보편적인 어귀이다. 또한 바울의 맹세의 양식구가 유사한 형태로 몇 개나 나오고 있으나 로마서 9장 1절에도 나온다(1:23; 11:11; 11:31; 12:6). 또 "사랑하는 자들아"(*ἀγαπητοί*)라는 말은 자주 나오는 말은 아니지만 고린도전서 10장 14절, 15장 58절, 빌립보서 2장 12절, 4장 1절, 로마서 12장 19절에도 나타나기 때문이다. 엄밀하게 말하여 이것들은 다만 바울 한 사람이 쓴 글임을 증거 할 뿐이다. 그러나 적어도 이런 어귀나 개념들이 고린도후서의 통일성을 지지해준다고 말할 수는 있다.

열한째, 고린도후서의 편집설을 지지할 만한 사본적 증거가 없다. 모든 고린도 사본은 전체로 볼 때 같은 구조와 내용을 가지고 있다. 고린도전서 5:9에 지금은 "잃어 버린 편지"(The Lost Letter), 혹은 "이전 편지"(The Previous Letter)와 고린도후서 2장 4절의 "눈물의 편지"(The Tearful Letter), ("혹독한 편지"[The Severe Letter], 또는 "고통의 편지"[The Painful Letter])에 대한 언급이 있어서 이런 편지의 남은 부분들이 고린도후서의 어느 부분(연결이 안 된다고 보이는)과 관련이 없는가라는 견해가 있다. 그러나 우리가 본대로 이런 견해를 위한 내적 증거들이란 것들은 추론들일 뿐이며 확정적 증거는 없었다. 이와 관련된 고린도후서를 이룬다고 가정하는 다른 편지들의 존재도 마찬 가지로 불투명한 것이었다. 외적 사본적 증거가 전혀 없다. 그러므로 이런 추정에 의한 온갖 추론은 근거가 빈약하며 지금의 내용과 순서가 모두 사도 바울의 원래 쓴 대로라는 견해를 믿어도 좋다. 이런 사본적 증거 외에도 우리는 고린도후서의 통일성을 지지하는 학자들의 견해가 상당한 학문적 근거들 위에 서 있음을 지적해왔다.

끝으로, 적어도 후기 초대교회가 고린도후서를 사용한 증거가 있다. 고린도후서는 A.D. 95년 또는 96년 로마의 클레멘트가 당시 어려움에 빠진 고린도 교회에게 보낸 편지(*The First Letter of Clement to the Corinthian*)에 직접 언급되지 않고 있으나 암시적으로 언급되었다(고린도전서는 언급됨). 그러나 비평학자들은 직저접 언급이 않된 사실을 근거로 고린도후서가 이 때까지 여러 조각으로 나눠져 있다가 이후에 편집되었으리라는 추측을 한다. 2세기 중엽에 가서야 고린도후서가 널리 쓰였다는 것이다.[145] 그러나 퍼니쉬가 지적한 것처럼 클레멘트1서 5장 5-6절에 고린도후서 6장 5절과 11장 23절 이하를 반영하고 있는 듯하다.[146] 거기서 바울의 투옥, 추방, 돌로 맞음과 같은 인내를 언급하고 있다. 또 I 클레멘트 38장 2절에서는 고린도후서 9장 12절의 "부족함을 보충한다"(*προσαναπληροῦσα τὰ ὑστερήματα*)와 유사한(*ἁναπληωθη τὸ ὑστέρημα*)란 말이 나온다. 해그너(D. Hagner)는 고린도전서 16장 17절에 이 말과 더 비슷한 말(*τὸ*··· *ὑστέρημα*···*ἀναπληῶσαν*)이 나오므로 고린도후서와의 연관을 위한 증거로 사용될 수 없다고 했으나,[147] 퍼니쉬는 클레멘트와 고린도후서의 문맥이 모두 하나님께 감사하는 내용이나, 고린도전서에는 바울의 "기쁨"을 말하기 때문에 오히려 고린도후서와의 연관성이 있다고 보았다.[148] 그러나 이런 증거와는 관련 없이 해그너는 결론적으로 클레멘트가 고린도후서를 알았다는 가능성을 말했고,[149] 퍼니쉬는 오히려 이를 의심한다.[150] 그러나 이런 두 개의 병행구는 중요한 외적 증거로서 고린도후서의 편집설에 반대하는 반증이 될 수 있다.[151]

---

145) Kennedy, 158; Furnish, 29, 30, 40; Bornkamm, 263.

146) Furnish, 30.

147) Donald Hagner, *The Use of the Old and New Testaments in Clement of Rome*, Supplementary volumes to *Novum Testamentum* (Leiden: Brill, 1973), 210.

148) Furnish, 451.

149) Hagner, 213.

150) Furnish, 30; Harris, 2, 3..

151) 고린도후서의 통일성을 주장하는 학자들이 대다수이다. J. H. Bernard, "The Second Epistle to the Corinthians," *The Expositor's Greek Testament*, ed. W. R. Nicoll (London: Hodder & Stoughton, 1882); H. Lietzmann, *An die Korinther 1/2*, HNT 9 (Tübingen: J. C. B. Mohr, 1969); A. Menzies, *The Second Epistle of the*

이러한 1-9장과 10-13장의 통일성에 대한 여러 가지 증거는 결정적인 것은 아니지만 사본 상의 증거와 함께 고린도후서의 통일성을 지지해준다. 이런 증거는 1-9장과 10-13장 사이에 어떤 시간이 경과했다는 가정을 불필요하게 만든다. 또한 9장을 쓴 이후에 고린도 사태가 달라져서 10-13장을 계속 썼다는 주장도 약화시킨다.

지금은 대다수의 학자들이 고린도후서의 통일성을 지지하는 추세이다. 이런 추세의 가장 근본적인 이유는 다른 신약 편집비평의 경우에서와 같이 아무런 문서적 증거가 없다는 사실이다. 우리

Apostle Paul to the Corinthians (London: Macmillan & Co., 1912); H. L. Goudge, *The Second Epistle to the Corinthians*, Westminster Commentary (London: Methuen & Co., 1927); E. B. Allo, *Saint Paul: seconde épÎtre aux Corinthians*, ÉBid (Paris: Gabalda, 1936, 1956); R. G. B. Tasker, *The Second Epistle to the Corinthians*, TNTC 8(Grand Rapids: Eerdmans, 1958); D. Gutherie, *New Testament Introduction* (Chicago: Inter-Varsity Press/London: Tyndale Press, 1961, 1963, 1970); P. E. Hughes, *Paul's Second Epistle to the Corinthians*; W. G. Kümmel, *Introduction to the New Testament*, ETr. H. C. Kee, (Nashville: Abingdon, 1963); A. M. G. Stephenson, "A Defence of the Integrity of 2 Corinthians," *The Authorship and Integrity of the New Testament*, SPCK Theological Collections 4, 82-97, (London: SPCK, 1965); W. H. Bates, "The Integrity of 2 Corinthians," *NTS* 12(1965-66) 50-69; J. L. Price, *Interpreting the New Testament* (New York: Holt, Rinehart & Winston, 1961); N. Hyldahl, "Die Frage nach der literarischen Einheit des zweiten Korintherbriefes," *ZNW* 64 3/4(1973) 289-306; M. J. Harris, "2 Corinthians," *The Expositor's Bible Commentary*, ed. F. E. Gaebelein(Grand Rapids: Zondervan, 1976); R. P. Martin, xlv-xlvi; M. E. Thrall, *The Second Epistle to the Corinthians*, ICC (Edinburgh: T&T Clark, 1994) 5-25; Paul Barnett, *The Second Epistle to the Corinthians* (Grand Rapids: Wm. B. Eerdmans Publishing Company, 1997) 17-25.

가 가지고 있는 수많은 고린도후서 사본들은 모두 같은 순서대로 발견된다. 뿐만 아니라 큰 사도인 바울의 서신을 함부로 편집할 수 있는 권세를 가진 자가 아무도 있을 수 없다는 것이다.[152] 그러나 고린도후서에서 들어나는 차이와 대조적 구문에 대해서 학문적 의문을 가지고 연구하는 것을 탓하는 것은 옳지 않다. 우리는 확실한 지식에 이르기 위해서 가능한 노력을 다 해야 한다.

9. "고통의 방문"("The Painful Visit")과 "눈물의 편지,"("엄격한 편지"["The Tearful Letter"="The Stern Letter"])

고린도후서 2 장 4절에 언급된 "큰 환난과 애통한 마음이 있어 많은 눈물로 쓴 편지"는 바울이 고린도 교회를 두 번째 방문하여 심한 모욕을 당한 후에 에베소에 돌아와 써서 디도를 통해서 보낸 편지였다(2:1). 바울은 그 편지를 보낸 후에 고린도 교인들의 그 편지에 대한 반응을 초조히 기다렸다. 드디어 기다리던 좋은 소식을 디도를 통해서 받고 안도하며 고린도후서를 쓴 것이다(2:12, 13; 7:6-7). 사도행전 18장 18절에서 바울이 고린도 교회를 설립했을 때는 특별히 교회로 부터 받은 고통이 없었던 것 같으므로 그 후에 잠시 방문하였다가 모욕당하고 돌아왔다고 본다. 바울이 두 번째 방문 시에 모욕당했다는 근거는 2장 1절에 "내가 다시 근심으로 너희에게 나가지 않기로 스스로 결단하였노니"라는 말이다. 그러나 어떤 이들은 이런 해석을 따르지 않고 2장 1절은 바울의

152) Tasker, 28.

첫 번째 방문시의 어떤 고통의 경험을 말하고 있다고 본다.[153] 그러나 "다시"(πάλιν)란 부사가 "근심으로"(ἐν λύπῃ)라는 부사구 앞에 있어서 특히 "근심 가운데서의 방문"은 하지 않겠다는 뜻으로 보아서, 첫 번째 교회 설립 시의 방문을 묘사한다고 보기 어렵다.

2장 4절을 첫 번째 방문으로 보는 이들은 바울이 "눈물의 편지"를 따로 쓴 것이 아니고 고린도전서를 가리킨다고한다. 눈물을 머금고 고통 중에서 고린도전서를 썼다는 것이 전혀 불가능한 말은 아니다. 모팻(J. Moffatt)은 고린도전서는 이따금씩 바울의 정서적인 격앙을 보여 준다고 한다(고전 5, 6).[154] 그러나 고린도후서 2장 4절과 7장 8절을 보면 바울의 정서는 매우 격앙되어 있었고 고린도전서 한 두절에 나타나는 감정보다는 고조된 것이다. 전체 고린도전서의 크기로 보아서 이런 정도의 감정의 표현을 가지고 고린도후서 2장 4절과 7장 8절의 격앙된 표현과 비교하기는 어렵다. 또 휴즈도 2:4의 편지가 고린도전서를 가리킨다고 보면서 고린도전서의 내용을 자세히 보면 눈물로 썼을 가능성이 있는 부분들이 적지 않다고 하였다.[155]그러나 위에서 지적했듯이 고린도전서의 전체 내용이 그렇게 아픈 눈물을 흘리는 편지라고 보기에는 너무 일반적 목회 내용이 지배적이다.

어떤 이들은 이 편지가 10-13장에 일부 들어 있다고 주장한다는 것을 위에서 지적했다. 이 부분의 내용이 주로 질책이 많이 있으므로, "눈물의 편지"를 "엄격한 편지"라고 부르는 것이다. 우리

153) R. Batey, "Paul's Interaction," *JBL* 84 [1965], 139-46.

154) J. Moffatt, *Introduction to the Literature of the NT,* 119, n. 122.

155) Hughes, 57.

는 이런 제안을 사본상의 증거가 없는데도 편집을 가정하는 추정으로 보고 거절했다.

"눈물의 편지"도 사본 상의 증거는 없다. 아마 디벨리우스(M. Dibelius)가 말했듯이 사사로운 개인의 징계 문제를 다르고 있었으므로 바울의 지시에 따라 파기시켰을 것이다.[156]

10. 고린도후서의 특징들(구조, 문학, 신학)

지금까지 고린도후서의 특징들을 거의 지적하였으나 개론 부분을 마치기 전에 이미 언급한 특징들을 다시 요약하고 분명히 언급하지 않은 점들을 지적할 것이다.

첫째, 가장 뚜렷한 구조적 특징은 1-9장과 10-13장의 두 대조적 내용이 한 편지 안에 기록되었다는 것이다. 대부분의 학자들이 이를 인정한 반면 소수의 학자들은 이 대조적인 특징이 과장된 것이며 거의 전체(8, 9장 제외)가 바울의 자신의 사도직 방어라는 주제를 중심으로 실망과 질책 등으로 일관되어 있다고 한다.[157] 대조하려는 것이 바울의 의도는 아니었을 것이다. 만일 그랬다면 더욱 더 분명한 대조적인 글을 쓸 수 있었을 것이다. 그러나 10-13장에서 바울의 질책은 양적으로 길고 질적으로 강도가 매우 높다. 이 대조적 어조의 원인에 대한 여러 추측은 이미 논한 바이지만 가장 신빙성이 있는 것은 거스리(D. Guthrie)의 제안으로서 바울 자신

156) Martin Dibelius, *A Fresh Approach to the NT*, 154.

157) Tasker, 31; R. A. Knox, 175.

의 글에서 보는 대로 엄격한 말은 뒤에 두는 경향이 여기서도 반영되었다는 것이다.[158] 고린도 교회의 문제가 매우 심각했고 바울이 죽은 후에도 계속되어 A.D. 95년 또는 96년에 로마의 감독 클레멘트까지도 I 클레멘트서(*The First Letter of Celement to the Corinthians*)를 보내어 고린도 교회의 분쟁을 종식시키려고 애쓴 것을 보면 고린도후서의 마지막 4장의 엄격한 경고문은 그리 긴 것이 아닌 지도 모른다.

우리는 고린도후서의 구조가 전체적으로는 조직적이라고 본다. 디도를 만나서 고린도 교회의 기쁜 소식을 듣고 자신의 사역이 하나님이 도우시는 사역임을 믿고 증거하면서 이와 관련시커 그의 사역의 성실성을 증거하는 것이다. 헌금에 대한 부탁(8, 9장)도 고린도 교인들이 그의 사역의 성실성을 믿는 증거로서 요구되고 있다. 그렇다면 1-9장과 10-13장의 다른 어조는 같은 주제, 즉 그의 사역의 신실성에 대한, 다른 표현 방법이라고 볼 수 있다.

최근 문학비평 학자들은 고린도후서를 고대 희랍의 수사학에서 법정에서의 연설이나 변명의 형식에 비추어 분석하기도 한다.[159] 즉 (1)변명자의 신뢰성 중심의 자기소개(exordium); (2) 사건에 나타난 사실들의 전개(narratio); (3) 사실들의 진실과 거짓의

158) Guthrie, 446.

159) Harris, 107-108: Harris는 Witherington III, viii-ix, 335-36; Kennedy, *Interpretation*, 87-91; Betz, *Der Apostel Paulus und die sokratische Tradition*, 38-41, 88-90; Peterson, 75-139, 162; Sundermann, 45 등의 고린도후서의 수사학적 분석과 구성을 열거하고 있다; Fredrick J. Long, *Ancient Rhetoric and Paul's Apology: The Compositional Unity of 2 Corinthians* (Cambridge: Cambridge University Press, 2005).

증거, 반대자들의 견해와 일치와 불일치 점들 지적(propositio); (4) 변명자의 입장을 지지해주는 논증(probatio/argumentatio); (5) 고소자의 논증에 대한 반증(refutatio); (6) 사건을 마무리 짓는 말과 청중들의 동의를 일으키는 말(peroratio). 실제 사용에서는 이상의 6개 항목 중에 몇 개가 생략되기도 한다. 학자들은 아래와 같이 고린도후서 전체를 이런 요목에 대입시켜 보기도 하고 1-7장, 8-9장. 10-13장같이 한 주제로 되어 있는 부분을 나누어 대입시켜서 보기도 한다.

서신의 서두 인사(1:1-2)[160)]
감사와 소개(exordium): 1:3-7
사건 사실 확인(Narratio): 1:8-2:16
사실 검증, 평가(Propositio): 2:17
논고/변증 (Probatio/refutatio): 3:1-13:4
논쟁 I (3:1-6:13)
논쟁 II (주제이탈)(6:14-7:1)
논쟁 III (확대) (7:2-16)
논쟁 IV (8:1-9:15)
논쟁 IV (10:1-13:4)
논쟁 V (10:1-13:4)
반박 논증(Peroratio) (13:5-10)
마지막 인사(13:11-13)

160) B. Witherington III, *Conflict and Community in Corinth: A Socio-Rhetorical Commentary on 1 and 2 Corinthians* (Grand Rapids: Eerdmans/Carlisle: Paternoster, 1995), viii-ix, 335-36.

또한 어떤 이들은 고린도후서에서 히브리 문학의 대칭구문(chiasmus)을 분석하였다.[161] 물론 서신으로서의 인사말, 주제말, 호소, 축복, 등의 분석도 있다.[162]

이런 수사학적 분석에 의하면 고린도후서가 고대 희랍의 변명문의 구조와 유사한 통일성을 나타낸다는 것이다. 사실 고린도후서는 처음부터 끝까지 바울의 변명으로서 통일된 서신이라고 할 수 있다.

둘째, 바울은 많은 대조법을 쓰고 있다. 대조법은 강론의 경우에 많이 나타나며, 대조법을 통해서 바울이 진리를 보다 객관적으로 독자들에게 제시하여 독자들 가르침을 스스로 이해하고 선택하도록 도우려는 것이다. "위로"와 "환난"(1:4-7), "하나님의 거룩함과 진실함" 그리고 "하나님의 은혜"와 "육체의 지혜"(1:12), "구원 얻는 자들"과 "망하는 자들"(2:15), "생명에 이르는 냄새"와 "사망에 이르는 냄새"(2:16), "하나님의 영"과 "의문"(3:3, 6), "돌비"와 "심비"(3:3), "새 언약의 일꾼"과 "의문의 일꾼"(3:6, 7), "영의 직분"과 "정죄의 직분"(3:8, 9), "모세의 수건"과 "주의 영광"(3:13-18), "질그릇과 보배"(4:7), 예수의 죽음과 생명(4:10), "겉 사람"과 "속(사람)"(4:16), "일시적인 환난의 경한 것"과 "영원한 영

---

161) Harris, 110-113에서 여러 학자들의 대칭구조 분석을 제시한다. Segalla, "Coerenza linguistica ed inita letteraria della 2 Corinzi," *Teologia* 13 (1988) 149-66; C. L. Blomberg, "The Structure of 2 Corinthians 1-7," *CTR* 4 (1989), 15; G. Bonneau, "La vie, à la mort. Le conflit à Corinthe et ses enjeux théologuiques en 2 Co 2,14-7,4," *ScEs* 51 (1999), 351-66.

162) Furnish, 43, xi-xii; Schelke, xvii; Hafemann, 37-39, Harris, 114, 재인용.

광의 중 한 것"(4:17), "보이는 잠간 있는 것"과 "보이지 않는 영원한 것"(4:18), "땅위의 장막 집"과 "하나님이 지은 집"(5:1), "벗는 것"과 "덧입는 것"(5:4), "거 하는 것"과 "떠나는 것"(5:8, 9), "미친 것"과 "정신이 온전한 것"(5:13), "육체 따라 아는 것"와 "새로운 피조물로서 (아는 것)"(5:16-17), "영광"과 "욕", "악한 이름"과 "아름다운 이름," "속이는 자" "참된 자,"(6:8) "무명한 자"와 "유명한 자," "징계를 받는 자"와 "죽임을 당하지 않는 자"(6:9), "근심하는 자"와 "항상 기뻐하는 자," "가난한 자"와 "많은 사람을 부요하게 하는 자," "아무것도 없는 자"와 "모든 것을 가진 자," (6:10), "(부모)와 "자녀"(6:13), "(믿는 자)"와 "믿지 않는 자," "의"와 "불법" "빛"과 "어두움"(6:14) "그리스도와 벨리알"(6:15), "하나님의 성전"과 "우상"(6:16), "너희"와 "저희"(6:17), "거룩함"과 "더러움," "육"과 "영"(7:1), "함께 죽고, 함께 살고"(7:3), "하나님의 뜻대로 하는 근심"과 "세상 근심"(7:10), "불의 행한 자"와 "불의 당한 자"(7:12), "명령"과 "간절함"(8:8), "가난함"과 "부요함"(8:9), "평안"과 "곤고함"(8:13), "너희의 유여함"과 "저희의 부족함"(8:14), "많이 거둔 자"와 "적게 거둔 자"(8:15), "주 앞에서"와 "사람 앞에서"(8:21), "참 연보"와 "억지"(9:5), "적게 심는 자"와 "많이 심는 자"(9:6), "억지로 내는 것"과 "즐기며 내는 것"(9:7), "대면함"과 "떠나 있음"(10:1, 11, 13:10), "겸비함과 담대함"(10:1), "파(괴) 하려는 것"과 "세우려는 것"(10:8), "편지는 중하나, 풍모와 말은 약하다"(10:10), "분량 밖의 자랑"과 "분량의 한도내에서의 자랑"(11:13), "주 안에서의 자랑"과 "자기중심("육체를 따르는") 자랑"(10:17, 18), "깨끗함"과 "부패함"(11:3), "바울 자신"과 "큰 사도들"(11:5; 12:11), "말"과 "지식"(11:6), "너희를 높이고, 나를 낮추고"(11:7), "거짓 사도"와 "그리스도의 사도"(11:13), "사단"과 "광명의 천사"(11:14), "사단의 일꾼"과 "의의 일꾼"(11:15), "지혜로운 자"와 "어리석은 자"(12:19), "저희"와 "나"(11:22, 23), "몸 안"과 몸 밖"(12:2, 3), "약함"과 "강함"(12:10; 13:3, 4, 9), "부모"와 "어린 아이"(12:14), "그리스도"와 "우리"(12:4), "우리"와 "너희"(12:7). "악"과 "선"(13:7); "인증 받은 자(옳은 자)"와 "인증 받지 못한 자(버리운 자)"(13:5-7). 이렇게 드러난 문자적 대조 외에도 개념적인 대조나 암시적인 대조가 있다. 예로 바울과 대적자들의 신학 사상이나 특성 그리고 목회 관련 문제들이 줄곧 대조되어 나타난다.

이외에도 열거법이나(6:4-10; 12:20, 21) 점층법을 쓰고 있으나(4:8-10; 11:22-28) 대조법처럼 지배적인 특성은 아니다.

셋째, 2번에서 말하는 대조법과 함께 많은 아이러니한 역설적 표현들이 있다. 구원받는 자에게는 생명에 이르게 하는 향기, 망하는 자들에게는 죽음에 이르게 하는 향기(2:15, 16), 질그릇 속의 보배(4:7), 바울은 죽고 그 생명이 고린도 교인들에게서 나타난다(4:10), 차라리 약한 것을 자랑한다(11:31), 내 능력은 약한 가운데서 온전하게 된다(12:9), 사랑할수록 덜 사랑을 받는다(12:15) 등이다.

넷째, 주석가들은 한결같이 고린도후서는 바울의 인간적이고 심리적인 측면을 많이 보여 주는 서신이라고 한다.[163] 바울의 솔직한 감정 표현이 도처에 나타나 있다. 고린도후서에는 다른 서신에서 보지 못하는 바울의 인간적 단면들을 많이 볼 수 있다. (1) 비

163) Barrett, 32, 34.

록 바울의 적들의 편견이 있는 말이므로 신빙성 문제가 있지만, 바울의 외모나 풍채가 빈약했다(5:12; 10:10).[164] (2) 그는 설교가 약했다(10:10; 11:6). (3) 바울은 논쟁에 뛰어난 사람으로서 진리를 수호하는 데는 크게 공헌을 하였으나, 원만한 인간관계 유지는 어려웠을 것이라고 짐작 된다(여기서 논쟁은 웅변력과는 구별 되어야한다. 바울은 실제로 언변이 부족하다는 반대자들의 비판을 스스로 인정한다[11:6]). 바울은 상당한 문장력을 갖고 있어서 편지로 주는 감화력은 강했다(10:10). 고린도후서에 자주 "… 하느냐?"라는 부정을 예상케 하는 질문들과, 상대방의 논리의 취약성을 놓치지 않고 지적하는 말들이 발견된다(3:5; 5:2, 12; 6:12; 7:2-3; 10:7, 12, 17; 11:6, 14-15, 20-30; 12:7, 13, 19; 13:4 등). 또 냉소적인 반어법을 써서 독자들을 대면한다. "바울은 자신을 보배를 담고 있는 질그릇" 으로 표현한다(4:7). "우리는 구원을 얻는 자들에게나 망하는 자들에게나 하나님 앞에서 그리스도의 향기니… 누가 이것을 감당하리요?" (2:15-16). "무명한 자 같으나 유명한 자요…" (6:9). 11장 4절의 "만일 누가 가서 … 다른 복음을 받게 할 때는 너희가 잘 용납하는 구나." 12장 13절의 "너희는 나의 이 공평치 못한 것을 용서하라." 는 말과 또 12장 9절 이하의 "약한 데서 강해진다" 는 반어법(irony)으로서 고린도의 독자들의 마음을 세게 흔들 수 있는 효과적인 표현이다. 바울의 논쟁은 희랍적인 수사학의 기법과

164) 참조, Tasker,175: 바울 서신과 사도행전에서 보여주는 대로 바울의 건강은 일반적으로 매우 좋은 것으로 보인다: "바울은 특별히 강건한 체구를 가지고 매우 뛰어난 체력과 육체적 지구력을 가진 남자" 이다. 그러나 고후12:7에서 말하는 "몸의 가시" 나 갈4:13-15의 "육체의 연약함" 은 바울의 건강의 다른 측면을 보여 준다.

또한 히브리적 논쟁 기법을 함께 쓰고 있다.[165] 고린도 교회의 그의 대적자들이 헬라적 지혜를 자랑하는 이들임을 감안하여 헬라적 수사학을 썼을 것이다. 그러나 바울의 이런 수사학적 기법은 역시 기독교 복음의 죽음과 생명의 패러독스에 기초한 것이라고 생각된다(5:14, 14). 그는 그의 적들처럼 당시 수사학적 기법으로만 논쟁하는 것이 아니라 그리스도의 종으로서 죽는 자 같으나 사는 자의 원리에 기초하여 논쟁한다(4:7-12; 6:8-10). 반대로 바울은 어리석은 논쟁을 피하라고 말한다(딤후 2:23; 딛 3:9).

한편 바울의 뛰어난 논쟁실력이 때로는 그의 사역에 부정적으로 나타나기도 하였을 것이다. 바울의 논쟁적 성격이 그가 다른 사람과 함께 사역하는 데 어려움을 주지 않았는가 생각된다. 제 2 차 전도 여행 떠날 때 마가를 데리고 가는 문제로 바나바와 심히 다투고 서로 갈라 서게 된 것과(행 15:37-39), 또 베드로가 이방인과 함께 식사하다가 유대인이 나타나자 자리를 옮긴 일을 외식이라고 면책한 일(갈 2:11-14) 등에서도 이런 논쟁적 성격이 부정적으로 나타난 것이 아닌가 생각된다. (4) 그는 경솔하지는 않더라도 감정의 기복이 많은 사람이었던 것 같다. 1장과 7장에서 그렇게 기뻐하면서도, 디도를 만나지 못했을 때 매우 초조했으며(2:13), 또 그를 반대하는 이들에게 매우 엄하게 대한다(10:11, 11:4, 7, 13, 16-18, 13:2). 바울은 고통이나 역경을 잘 참을 수 있는

165) E. A. Judge, "Paul's Boasting in Relation to Contemporary Professional Practice," *ABR* 16 (1968), 37-50; H. D. Betz, *Der Apostel Paulus und die sokratische Tradition*; Christopher Forbes, "Comparison, Self-praise and Irony: Paul's Boasting and the Conventions of Hellenistic Rhetoric," *NTS* 32 (1986), 1-30. 이상은 바울의 수사학과 희랍의 수사학의 유사성을 논함. S. H. Travis, "Paul's Boasting in 2 Corinthians 10-12," *SE* 6 (1973), 527-32. Travis는 유대 수사학과의 관련을 주장함.

사람이지만 고통에 무감각한 사람은 아니었다. 그가 고린도후서에 나타낸 여러 고통과 역경에서의 초조함과 불안에 대한 표현들이 있다(2:13; 4:8, 16-17; 6:3-10; 7:5; 11:27-28). (5) 그는 관용의 사람이다. 그는 불의에 대해서 징계하여야 하나 동시에 그 불의한 사람을 사랑하여 그에게 새로운 의로운 삶의 기회를 주어야 한다고 믿는 사람으로 보인다(2:5-8). 그는 그리스도의 교회는 정죄하는 바리새적, 유대교 회당과는 달라야함을 알고 있었다. 아들을 주신 하나님의 사랑에 감복한 이들이 모인 사랑의 공동체로서의 정체성을 유지해야 함을 알고 있다(2:8; 5:14). 그가 8장에서 디도와 두 형제들을 추천하면서 매우 고조된 말로 그들을 높인다. 그들의 약점을 감추고 그들의 장점을 크게 알려서 그들을 하나님의 지도자로서 높이 세워 준다. 또 문제가 되는 고린도 교인들을 징계하기를 원하지 않고 스스로 회개하기를 바란다(13:10). (6) 바울은 하나님께서 자신의 사역과 함께 하심을 굳게 믿는 불굴의 투지의 사람이었다. 그는 그의 사역가운데 온갖 절망과 낙심과 염려와 두려움을 경험하면서도 이런 고난은 결국 하나님의 위로와 사랑과 능력을 경험하게 되는 과정임을 믿고 있었다(2:12-16; 3:9; 4:17; 7:5, 9-11; 11:23-33; 참조, 딤후 4:7, 8, 18). (7) 바울은 위 4번에서 지적한 예민한 감정을 가진 사람이었으나 결코 사사로운 감정에 빠져서 교회 문제를 처리하는 사람이 아니었다. 그가 반대자들을 사사로운 감정에서 비판하지 않고, 언제나 그리스도 중심적 신학(4:7 이하, 5:14-22, 6:3 이하)에 입각하여 그리스도의 권세를 교회에 세우는 그의 사도적 책임(5:20; 10:8, 11:2; 13:9-10)을 통감하여 객관적인 근거를 제시하면서 반대자들을 공격하거나 자신을 방어한다(10:13, 16; 11:22-12:18). (8) 바울은 정직함, 진실함 같은 높은 도덕성을 갖춘 사람이었다(1:12; 2:17; 3:4-6; 4:2; 5:11; 6:3-13; 7:2; 10:13-18; 11:6, 23-28; 12:14-18). (9) 무엇보다 바울은 깊은 사랑과 냉철한 이성을 함께 소유한 사람이다. 문제가 된 사람을 치리하도록 지시한 뒤에, 곧 사랑을 나타내어 치리 해제를 지시하는 것이 단적인 예이다(2:5-10). 자신의 반대파들에 대해서도 감정적 대응을 자제하고 이성적 논리로서 대응한다: "모든 이론을 파하며, 하나님 아는 것을 대적하여 높아진 것을 다 파하고 모든 생각을 사로잡아 그리스도에게 복종케 하니"(10:5). 물론 이런 이성적 논리도 사랑과 같이 하나님이 주시는 힘에 근거하고 있음을 유념해야 한다(10:4). 이렇게 사랑과 이성이라는 두 가지의 대조적인 성격이 고린도후서 전체에 복합적으로 나타난다. (10) 때로는 사도라는 권위 의식에서 벗어나 보통 사람으로 말한다. 아시아에서 당한 고생을 말할 때 죽음에 대한 두려움이 있었음을 솔직히 말한다(1:8, 9). 언변이 부족하다는 사실을 인정하였다(11:6). 또한 다메섹 성에서 광주리를 타고 도망한 부끄러운 일도 자신의 약함을 드러내기 위해 술회한다(11:32, 33). 자기에게 있는 "몸의 가시"도 말한다(12:7). 또 그런 가시가 없다면 바울 자신이 많은 계시로 말미암아 자만해질 수 있는 연약한 존재임을 시인한다.

다섯째, 고린도후서는 바울의 고난의 신학을 강조하고 있다. 바로 앞에서 지적한 바울의 인간적 단면들이 있으나 바울은 여전히 신학자로서 글을 쓰고 있다. 바레트는, 고린도후서가 가장 개인적 감정적인 서신이면서도, 가장 신학적인 서신이라고 말했다.[166] 바울의 고난의 신학 또는 약함의 신학이 고린도후서에만 나타나

166) Barrett, 32.

는 것은 아니나 어느 서신보다 자주 이 서신의 여러 곳에서 언급되고 있다(2:14-17; 4:7-5:21; 6:4-10; 7:5-7; 11:23-30; 12:7-10; 13:4; 참조, 고전 1:25-29; 빌 2:6-11). 바울이 고린도 교회로 말미암은 고통이 특별히 심각했다고 볼 수 있다(11:28). 그러나 이런 고난의 신학은 바울 신학의 특징이며 또 기독론을 중심으로 신약 신학 전체의 특징이다.[167] 바울의 신학은 "다른 예수," "다른 복음," "다른 영"(11:4)을 전하는 고린도 교회의 거짓 사도들의 잘못된 신학 사상 - 희생과 고난을 배제하는 신비주의적 영험주의나 무사 안일한 만사형통주의-을 경계하는 것이라고 볼 수도 있다.

여섯째, 하나님 중심 신학이다. 바울은 그의 사역의 주인은 하나님이심을 믿는다. (1) 그 자신이 하나님의 뜻으로 말미암아 사도가 되었다(1:1; 3:6; 5:18, 20). (2) 1장 초두에서 부터 예수 그리스도의 하나님, 자비의 아버지, 모든 위로의 하나님을 찬양한다(1:3, 4). (3) 하나님은 신실하시며, 그가 세우신 바울 사도도 신실하다(1:18-22). (4) 하나님께서 바울의 사역을 승리로 이끄신다(2:14-16). (5) 바울은 하나님의 말씀을 순수히 보전하여 전한다(2:17;4:2). (6) 바울의 능력은 하나님에게서 온 것이다(4:5). (7) 바울은 그의 복음은 하나님의 계시로 받았다(4:6; 12:9). (8) 바울의 사역의 진실성은 하나님께서 아실 것이다(5:11). (9) 하나님께서 바울의 사역과 함께 하신다(6:1). (10) 바울은 고난 가운데서 하나님의 위로를 받는다(1:3, 4; 7:6). (11) 근심도 하나님의 뜻대로 하는 근심은 구원에 이르고 회개하게 한다(7:10). (12) 하나님께서 마

167) J. D. G. Dunn, *Jesus and the Spirit* (London: SCM/ Philadelphia: Westminster, 1975), 334: "바울은 고난의 주를 알지 못하고 영광의 주를 알 수 없었다."

게도냐 교회에 은혜를 주셨다(8:1). (13) 하나님께서는 즐겨 내는 자를 사랑하시고(9:7), 모든 선한 일을 많이 하게 하신다(9:8). (14) 헌금은 결국 하나님께 감사한 마음을 갖게 하고, 하나님께 영광이 된다(9:13). (15) 바울의 사역 한계는 하나님이 정해 주신 것이다(10:13). (16) 바울의 열심은 하나님의 열심이다(11:2). (17) 바울의 복음은 하나님의 복음이다(11:7). (18) 하나님이 바울의 증인이시다(11:31). (19) 바울의 3층천의 체험은 하나님이 주신 것이다(12:2). (20) 바울의 진실성은 하나님이 아신다(12:19). (21) 하나님께서 바울의 진실성을 증거하실 것이다(13:4). (22) 하나님께서 고린도 교인들을 악에서 지켜 주시고 평강을 주신다(13:11).

이렇게 바울은 하나님 중심적 사역을 하기 때문에 그의 반대자들에 대한 공격이나 사도직 방어를 함에 있어서 사사로운 감정에 빠지기 쉬운 경우에 있어서도 늘 객관적이고 신학적인 토대에서 논하고 있음을 주시해야 한다. 그는 인간 바울로서의 사사로운 감정을 떠나 어디까지나 그리스도 중심적 신학적 사상에 입각하여 그리스도의 사도로서의 권위와 책임을 굳게 지킨다(4:7-15; 5:14, 15; 8:8; 10:5-8; 13:4, 5).

끝으로, 위의 다섯 번째 항목과 관련하여 바울은 그리스도의 약함을 따라서 사역하는 것을 진정한 그리스도의 사도의 표로 제시하고 있다(4:5, 7-15; 6:4-10; 8:9; 10:1; 11:23-33; 12:9, 10; 12:15; 13:4, 7, 9).[168] 고린도후서에서 바울은 그의 사도직과 관련된 여러

168) David Alan Black, *Paul, Apostle of Weakness. Astheneia and Its Cognates in the Pauline Literature* (New York: Lang, 1984), 85: 바울서신에서 약함(ἀσθένεια)이란 말이 모두 44번 나오는데, 고린도 전후서에 29번 나오고, 고린도후서에 14번 나온다. 14번 모두 10-13장에 나온다. 불랙(Black)은 바울은 이 단어의 잦은 사용으

가지 그의 "약함의 문제들"을 다루면서, 그리스도의 죽으심의 주제에 근거하여 문제를 해결해 간다. 바울의 약함은 그가 받은 비난 가운데 나타난다. (1) 일반적인 방문취소에 대하여 신뢰성 문제가 야기되었다(1:15-2:1). (2) 말씀의 목격자가 아니다(예루살렘 큰 사도들에 비교할 때 열등하다, 3:1-4:6; 5:16-17). (3) 언변이 약하다(10:10). (4) 외모가 약하다(10:10). (5) 신령한 체험이 부족하다(12:1-7). (6) 스스로 사도로서 부족함을 느끼고 다른 사도들이 다 받는 교회의 보조를 혼자 받지 않는 것이다(11:5-10). (7) 겉으로는 교회의 재정보조를 받지 않는다고 하면서도 물질을 은밀히 취한다(7:2; 12:14, 16). (8) 사도적 권위나 위엄이 부족하다(10:8; 13:2; 10; 12:12). 사도적 권능이 없으므로 고난의 사역을 한다(4:7-15; 6:4-10; 11:23-33). 바울은 이런 약함들을 오히려 그의 사도직의 진정성의 증표로 제시하면서 그리스도의 고난과 죽음과 부활에 비추어 그 의미를 설명한다(4:10-14; 5:14, 15; 6:4-10; 12:10; 13:4).[169)]

로 "약함의 신학"을 형성하였다고 한다. Martin은 불랙의 연구에서 더 나아가 바울의 예루살렘 사도회의 이후 할례 문제로 예루살렘 유대주의자들과의 소원한 관계가 되었고, 또 갈2:11-14의 이방인과 식사 문제로 선교지원을 하던 안디옥 교회와의 결별이 바울의 약함의 신학의 역사적 배경이라고 본다(B. Holmberg, *Paul and Power. The Structure of Authority in the Primitive Church as Reflected in the Pauline Epistles*. ConB 11 [Lund: Gleerup, 1978], 32-34; J. D. G. Dunn, "The Incident at Antioch," *JSNT* 18 [1983], 3-57; M. Hengel, *Acts and the History of Earliest Christianity*, tr. J. Bowden, [London: SCM Press, 1979], 123; Martin, lvi, 재인용). 고린도 교회에서 예루살렘 사도들의 추천장을 가지고 온 선교사들의 반바울 운동이 고린도후서에서 바울의 위기감을 더 고조시켰다고 본다(Martin, liii-lxi, 특히, lvi, lix).

169) 바울은 자신의 강점도 논한다. 바울의 강점은 도덕성(1:12; 4:2; 7:2; 12:14-18), 복음의 신적 권위(3:3-7; 4:6); 그의 깊은 지식(11:6; 참조, 행 26:24); 그의 사도적 "표

심지어 헌금문제를 취급할 때에도 헌금의 근거를 우리를 위해서 가난하게 되신 그리스도의 구원의 은혜에서 찾는다(8:9). 바울이 이런 기독론적 역설(逆說)을 자신의 사도직 변명을 위해 사용하고 있으나, 단순히 논쟁적인 방편에서 사용하는 것이 아니라 바울의 일관된 신앙과 신학적 입장 즉 십자가의 그리스도와 연합된 확고한 자아 인식과 특별한 계시에서 비롯된 것이라고 본다(4:5, 7-15; 5:14-15; 롬6:1이하; 빌1:21; 12:9). 바울은 실제로 이런 십자가의 능력이 그의 사역 가운데 나타나는 것을 증거한다. 즉 1장과 7장에서 고린도 교회의 어려움이 해소 되었다는 기쁜 소식을 디도로 통해서 듣고서 환난 중에서 위로하시는 하나님께 감사한다. 어려운 일의 추이를 인내로 지켜보면서 그 일이 해결될 때 하나님의 은혜로 믿고 감사하는 것이다. 또 2:14-17에서 도처에서 이김을 주시는 하나님께 감사한다는 말도 이런 맥락에서 이해할 수 있다.

11. 바울의 반대자들

고린도 교회의 바울의 반대자들의 성격 규명에 대한 갖가지 논쟁이 있어왔다. 이들의 성격을 규명하는 것이 바울과 고린도 교회와의 관계를 설명하는데 필요하다. 반대 자들의 성격은 고린도후서에서 바울이 이들에 대해 언급한 부분을 살펴봄으로써 짐작할

적과 기사와 능력"(12:1-7, 12); 고린도 교회의 설립자(3:2; 12:14; 고전 9:2; 행 18:11); 고난의 사역 등이다(한편, 고난의 사역은 약함의 증거로도 말함)(11:23-33). 바울이 그의 약함을 강조하는 것은 그리스도 중심 신학에 기초한 것이지만 고린도 교인들의 감성에 호소하려는 측면도 있다고 본다(2:4; 6:11-13; 7:1-3; 11:11; 12:15; 13:4).

수 있다.[170)]

1) 그들은 아마도 예루살렘 사도들의 추천서를 가진 것을 자랑하면서 바울이 추천서를 가지지 않았음을 약점으로 지적한 이들이다(2:17; 3:1; 5:12; 10:7, 10-12; 11:18; 12:1).

2) 그들은 하나님의 말씀을 "복잡케" 하는 이단자들이다(2:17; 11:4).

3) 그들은 자신들은 말씀의 목격자들이고 예수를 만난 것을 자랑하면서 바울은 그렇지 못한 것을 무시한다(11:21).[171)] 이에 대해서 바울은 "우리가 예수를 육체를 따라 알거나 보이는 대로 알지 아니하고 믿음으로 안다" 고 대응한다(5:7; 17).

4) 그들은 언변을 자랑하면서 바울의 언변과 외모의 부족함을 거론한다(10:10; 11:6). 이에 대해서 바울은 이것들은 "육체적 자랑" 으로 가치가 없다고 맞대응한다(10:4). 그러나 자신은 하나님의 능력을 가졌고(10:4) 또한 지식이 있음을 자랑한다(11:6).

5) 그들은 유대인의 혈통을 자랑하면서 바울의 이방적 성향을 흠 잡는다(11:21-22). 그러나 그들이 율법주의를 주장한다고 볼 수 없다. 고린도후서에는 율법이나 할례라는 말이 한 번도 나타나지 않는다(참조, 3장).

6) 그들은 영적 체험이나 능력을 자랑한다. 그러므로 바울이 자신의 약함을 자랑한다고 하면서도 (11:4, 30; 12:5, 9-10), 자신도 영적 체험과 능력이 있음을 억지로 "자랑" 하였다(11:17-18; 12:1-6, 12). 한편 그들은 바울이 자신의 "몸의 가시" 를 고치지 못함을 그의 무능함으로 지적했으라 본다. 이에 대해서 바울은 오히려 그의 "몸

170) Thrall, 926-945; Harris, 67-87(특히, 79-80).

171) Bultmann, 156.

의 가시"는 자신이 자고하지 못하도록 하나님께서 주신 것이라고 말한다. 이들의 영적 체험과 능력의 자랑은 고린도 교회 초창기에 있던 소위 "영적 체험주의자들"(the pneumatics; the spirituals)과 합세하여 반 바울 세력을 형성하였을 것으로 본다(고전 12장).[172)]

7) 반대자들은 이런 영적능력과 함께 매우 권위주의적인 자세로 고린도 교인들을 위협하고 함부로 대했다(11:20). 바울은 이에 대해서 겸비와 약함의 종으로서의 사도직을 나타낸다(1:24; 4:5; 10:1; 13:7, 9).

8) 그들은 바울이 고린도 교회를 떠난 후에 고린도 교회에 들어왔다 (10:16). 바울은 이것은 그의 선교 지경을 침입하는 행위로서 잘못된 것이라고 한다.

9) 그들은 바울의 자립형 사역을 고린도 교회의 성의를 무시하고 사랑하지 않는 처사로 비판했다(11:7-15). 또한 그들은 바울이 예루살렘 헌금을 근거로 교묘하게 교회의 재정을 축낸다고 비판했다(12:16). 그들은 바울의 자립형 사역은 예수님이 제자파송 때 지시하신 재정의존형 전도사역에 정면 배치되는 것이라고 비판했을 것이다(마 10:10-11;눅 9:4; 10:7). 바울은 이에 대해서 이미 고전 9장에서 자신도 이런 지시를 존중한다고 말했고, 여기서는 자신의 재정독립형 사역도 남에게 누를 끼치지 않는 유익이 있다고 논한다.

---

172) Harris, 78, 79; Harris는 반대파들에 대한 여러 학자들의 견해를 요약하기 전에 "영지주의자들"(Gnostics)로 보는 Schmithals와, "영적체험주의자들"(pneumatics)로 보는 E. Ellis, "초기 영지주자들"로 보는 Godet의 견해(74-79)를 소개하면서, 보다 종합적인 P. Marshall의 "잡다한 헬라파"와 유대주의자들로 규정하는 견해(263-65)에 관심을 보이고 결론에서 반대파들을 "영적 체험주의자들"과 예루살렘 배경의 유대주의자들이 합세한 것으로 말한다(87). P. Marshall, "Hybris, Not Gnostics in Corinth," in *SBL, 1984 Seminar Papers*, ed., K. H. Richards, (Chico: Scholars, 1984), 275-87.

이렇게 바울의 반대자들의 성격 규명이 대체로 나타나지만 학자들은 이들의 종교적 배경에 비추어 이들의 성향을 다음과 같이 파악하고 있다.

첫째, 반대자들은 유대인 기독교인들이다. 바우어(F. C. Baur)는 고린도 교회의 유대인들과 이방인들의 싸움이라는 가설에 기초하여 이방인들이 주축이 된 고린도 교회에 유대인들이 침투해 들어와 혼란케 하고 있다고 보았다.[173] 이런 단순한 가설로는 복잡한 고린도 교회의 정황을 제대로 설명할 수 없다고 보기 때문에 그의 의견을 그대로 수용하는 학자들은 없으나 반대자들이 유대인들이라고 주장하는 이들이 여전히 있다.[174] 그들은 팔레스틴(예루살렘)에서 온 유대인 기독교인들이다.[175] 고린도후서 11장 5, 22절에 의하면 반대자들은 유대인이며 예루살렘 사도와 관련이 있고, 이들은 아마도 사도들의 추천장을 가지고 왔을 것이다(3:1). 그러나 이들의 헬레니즘적 특징 (헬라식 수사학, 능변[10:10]; 다른 영[11:4])과 고린도 교회 같은 이방 교회에서 영향력을 행사할 수 있었음을 고려할 때(11:4), 순수한 팔레스틴 유대인이라 보기 어렵다. 더구나 이들은 할례 문제로 싸우지 않은 것 같으므로 갈라디아서의 경우와도 다르다고 할 수 있으나, 마틴이 지적한 것처럼 이들이 유대 기독교를 배경으로 가지고 있는 한 바울

173) F. C. Baur, *Tübinger Zeitschrift für Theologie*, 4.

174) E. Bammel, *ThZ* 11 (1955), 412; D. W. Oostendorp, *Another Jesus: A Gospel of Jewish Christian Superiority in II Corinthians* (Kampen: Kok, 1967), 83; G. G. O'Collins, "Power Made Perfect in Weakness: 2 Cor 12:9-10," *CBQ* 33 (1971), 531; Plummer, xxxvii; xl-xli; Plummer의 유대주의자들이라는 견해 대한 Thrall의 반대 견해를 보라(928).

175) C. K. Barrett, 56; W. G. Kümmel, 285; Plummer, 60.

의 이신득의 사상과 갈등을 일으켰을 가능성을 생각할 수 있다(고후 3장).[176)]

둘째, 반대자들은 유대인 기독교 영지주의자들이란 의견이 있다.[177)] 그러나 이런 의견은영지주의가 초대 기독교보다 일찍 생성된 것으로 가정하는 잘못이 있다.[178)] 신약 성경에 영지주의적 사상이 반영되어 나오나, 그것은 매우 초기 단계의 영지주의적 사상이 신약 시대에 움트고 있었다는 것을 보여 줄뿐 완전한 영지주의는 2세기 이후에나 발견될 수 있다는 것이 학자들의 지배적인 견해이다.[179)] 그러므로 고린도후서의 반대자들이 초기 영

---

176) Martin, 서론, lvi.

177) Windisch, 328; Bultmann, 205; W. Schmithals, *Gnosticism in Corinth,* 117-285; U. Wilckens, *Weisheit und Torheit* (Tübingen: J. C. B. Mohr, 1959); E. Güttgemanns, *Der leidende Apostel*, 168; U. Wilckens, *Weisheit*, 218, 주, 2.

178) Eduard Lohse, *Umwelt des Neuen Testaments*, (Göttingen: Vandenhoeck & Ruprecht, 1971), 『신약성서배경사』, 박창건 역 (서울: 대한기독교출판사, 1971) 219, 227: 영지주의 사상의 논문집 *Corpus Hermeticum*을 살피면서, 비록 이 문서가 기원후 1, 2세기에 기록된 것이나 그 이전의 전승은 그 이전부터 오래 동안 구전되어온 것이므로 기독교 이전부터 영지주의가 있었다고 주장한다. 그러나 그 구전 전승이 반드시 기독교 복음 이전에 형성되었다는 증거는 없다.

179) Barrett, 29; G. W. MacRae, *Interpretation* 26 (1972), 489-91; R. McL. Wilson, "Gnosis at Corinth," in *Paul and Paulism: Essays in Honor of C. K. Barrett,* ed. M. D. Hooker & S. G. Wilson (London: SPCK, 1982), 102-114; B. A. Pearson, "The Pneumatikos-Psychikos Terminology in 1 Corinthians: A Study in the Theology of of the Corinthian Opponents of Paul and Its Relation to Gnosticism," *SBLDS* 12 (Missoula, Mont.: SP. 1973), 51-81; Edwin M. Yamauchi, "Pre-Christian Gnosticism: The NT and Nag Hammadi in Recent Debate," *Themelios* 10 (1984), 22-27; L. D. McCray, "Paul 's Opponents in Corinth: An Examination of Walter Schmithals' Thesis on Gnosticism in Corinth" (Ph.D. diss., Southern Baptist Theological Seminary, 1985); Thrall, 781.

지주의적 영향 아래 있었다 해도 그들을 완전한 의미의 영지주의자라고 할 수는 없다. 더구나 이런 초기 영지주의라는 개념을 당시의 혼합주의적 헬레니즘 사상과 완전히 독립적으로 구별해 내어 정의 한다는 것도 어려운 일이다.[180] 헹엘(M. Hengel)은 "이제는 고린도 영지주의에 대해서 그만 말하자"라면서 영지주의가 기독교 이전에 나타났다고 보는 근거가 약함을 지적하였다.[181] 퍼니쉬(Furnish)는 고린도후서에서 "지식"이란 말이 영지주의적 의미로 쓰이지 않았다고 하였다(2:14;4:6; 6:6; 8:7; 10:5; 11:6).[182]

셋째, 반대자들은 일반적으로 헬라영향을 받은 유대인 기독교인들이다. 게오르기(D. Georgi)와 다른 학자들은 이 유대인들이 방랑하면서 신적 능력을 나타내던 헬라시대의 신인들(神人, δεῖοι ἄνδρες)의 유형을 따랐다고 하지만, 이에 대한 증거가 불충분하다.[183] 프리드릭(G. Friedrich)은 이 유대인들이 헬라 신인사상에 영향을 받았으며, 기사와 이적을 행하는 일단의 그룹으로서 그 기

---

180) Guthrie, 434-35.

181) M. Hengel, *Crucifixion*, ET (London: SCM, 1977) 18, n. 10.

182) Furnish, 53.

183) D. Georgi, *Die Gegner des Paulus im 2 Korintherbrief*, WMANT 11 (Neukirche-Vluyn: Neukirchner Verlag, 1964), 31-38, 254, 285; G. Bornkamm, *Paul*, tr. D. M. G. Stalker (New York: Harper & Row, 1971), 172; M. Rissi, *Studien zum zweiten Korinterbrief*, ATANT 56 (Zurich: Zwingli Verlag, 1969) 42-44; J. -F. Collange, *Énigmes de la deuxième épître de Paul aux Corinthiens*, SNTSMS 18 (Cambridge: University Press, 1972) 18-20; J. H. Schütz, *Paul and the Anatomy of Apostolic Authority*, SNTSMS 26 (Cambridge: University Press, 1975), 177-86; cf. Martin, 339; Thrall, 668.

원을 사도행전의 스데반과 빌립에서 찾았다(행6:9, 10; 8:6).[184] 그러나 홀러데이(C. H. Holladay)는 헬라시대에 신인들이 실제로 존재했다는 증거가 없다고 했다.[185] 그래서 많은 학자들은 반대자들을 유대인들이되 헬라 영향을 받은 예루살렘에서 온 선교단원들로 본다. 이들은 초대교회 스데반, 빌립처럼 헬라문화와 유대교전통에 함께 익숙하면서 기독교 신앙을 가진 선교적 열정을 가진 사람들로 추정된다. 트롤은 마태복음서 마지막의 세계 선교 대위임(마 28:19-20)을 받은 헬라문화에 영향 받은 유대인 기독교인들로 구성된 선교단체들이 고린도까지 와서 유대전통에 입각한 복음 사역을 하는 것으로 추정한다.[186] 이들은 예루살렘 사도들의 추천서를 가지고 있으며(3:1), 나아가 역사적 예수와의 교분도 있음을 가지고 자랑하였던 것으로 보인다(5:16). 마태복음이 안디옥 같은 헬라인들과 유대인들이 공존한 도시에서 기록되었으므로 이런 추정도 가능하다. 그러나 이 경우 행위 구원이나 할례, 율법을 강조했을 텐데 그런 증거가 확실하지 않은 것이 이상하다.[187] 다만 3장에서 "모세의 수건"과 "의문의 일시적 영광"을 새 언약의 일꾼이 가지는 복음 사역의 영광과 비교하며 논할 때 이들의 율법주의적 경향을 논할 수 있을 것이다. 그러나 이 경우에도 이들이

184) G. Friedrich, "Die Gegner des Paulus im 2. Korintherbrief," in FS O, Michel Abraham unser Vater, ed. O. Betz, M. Hengel, P. Schmidt, 181-215, AGJU 5 (Leide: Brill, 1963), 212.

185) C. H. Holladay, *Theios Aner in Hellenistic Judaism: A Critique of the Use of This Category in New Testament Christology*, SBLDS 40 (Missoula: Scholars Press, 1977), 237-41; C. K. Barrett, 103.

186) C. H. Holladay, 669-70.

187) Martin 338; 마 7:23; 23:23; 25:40, 45.

직접 율법주의를 표방한다는 분명한 증거는 없고 이들의 예루살렘과의 사도들과의 연결이나 역사적 예수와의 친분에 대한 자랑을 유대주의 낡은 전통에 비추어서 암시적으로 비난하는 것으로 추정할 수 있을 뿐이다(5:16).

넷째, 반대자들은 다양한 여러 그룹들이며 서로 싸우면서도 바울에게 대하여는 일치되어 대항하였다. 이 견해가 대다수 주석자들의 견해다.[188] 고린도 교회의 파당은 고린도전서 1장 10절-4장 21절에 나타나 있고 그런 추세가 고린도후서에도 이어져 왔다고 봐야 할 것이다. 물론 고린도후서의 반대자들은 외부에서 들어왔지만 내부적인 파당과 야합하였으리라는 추측을 할 수 있다. 극단적 자유주의자들과 또 전통주의자들이 서로 대립하였고, 또 이미 영적 부활에 참여하고 있다는 일종의 실현된 종말론주의자들, 또는 영지주의적 자유주의자들(Gnostic liberalists)이 바울의 가르침에 대항하였다.[189] 그들은 자신들이 영적 사람들로서 이 세상 문제들로부터 초월하였으므로 세상의 어떤 것들로부터도 자유롭다고 생각하여 도덕적 방종으로 흘렀다(12:21). 이런 여러 그룹의 대표적인 반대파는 유대인 헬라주의자들이라는 것이 위에서 말한 반대자들의 유대적이고도 헬라적인 복합적 특징들로 설명할 수 있기 때문이다. 카슨(D. A. Carson)은 보다 복합적이고 보편적인 시각에서 반대자들의 성격을 세속적 낙관적 기적주의자들이라고

---

188) Martin, 336-42; Thrall, 665-70.

189) D. A. Carson and et al, *An Introduction to the New Testament* (Grand Rapids: Zondervan Publishing House, 1992), 274-75; A. C. Thiselton, "Realized Eschatology at Corinth," *NTS* 24 (1977-78), 510-26; Furnish, 53: "헬라적 유대인 기독교 선교사들"; Guthrie, 436.

보았다.[190]

반대 그룹의 성격을 분명히 규명하기는 어려우나, 위의 네 번째 주장 즉, 바울이 지적한 반대파의 직접적 특징이나 암시적 표현들을 통해서 그들은 기사를 행하며, 예루살렘 사도들과 역사적 예수와의 친분을 강조하는 유대인 기독교인들이라는 것으로 짐작할 수 있다. 바울은 이들의 사상에 반대하여 과거의 역사적 예수보다, 기적의 예수 보다 사람과 세상을 변화시키는 내면적 영적 능력의 예수를 강조하며(5:16-17; 10:4), 영광 보다는 고난을 강조하는 사상과 갈등을 일으켰다(고전 1:22-23; 고후 4:7-14; 11:23-33; 12:9-12; 13:4). 한편, 해리스가 지적하는 대로, 유대주의적 선교사들 함께 고린도전서에 언급하는 기존의 "영적 체험주의자들"도 여전히 바울을 반대하는 세력을 형성하고 있다고 볼 수 있다(고전 12:3-10; 14:12, 13, 22, 23, 37; 12:1-12, 20-13:2).[191]

12. 고린도후서에서의 바울의 사도직 이해

다른 서신에서와 같이 고린도후서에서 바울의 사도직에 대한 이해는 여러 곳에서 신학적인 의미뿐만 아니라 수사학적, 사회학적, 그리고 목회학적 의미가 따로 나타나기도 하고 복합적으로 나타나기도 한다.[192] 바레트(C. K. Barrett)는 "고린도후서는 바울의

---

190) Carson, 기적주의(51, 63, 64, 67); 세속주의(59); 만사형통주의(67); 적극적 사고주의(67).

191) Harris, 78, 79, 87.

192) James D. G. Dunn, *The Theology of Paul the Apostle* (Grand Rapids: Eerdmans, 1998), 760, 763.

사도직에 대한 이해에 관한 가장 완전하고 열정적인 자료를 가지고 있다"고 했다.[193] 특별히 바울은 고린도후서에서 그 교회의 거짓 사도들과의 특별한 갈등의 정황에 처해 있었으므로 그의 사도직의 의미를 신학적, 도덕적, 이성적, 감성적 각도에서 설명해야 했다(13:3). 여기서 우리는 바울의 신학적 변명을 집중하여 검토하려고 한다. 바울이 보기에 반대자들은 그들의 사도직을 그리스도 중심으로 이해하지 못하고 구약적 전통을 오해하여 "하나님이 주신 영광과 능력의 직책"으로 이해하고 있었다(3:14; 4:4). 그들은 사도의 "외모"와 "육체적 조건"을 중시하는 이들이었다(5:12; 10:7). 그들은 "다른 예수, 다른 복음, 다른 영"을 전하는 이들이다 보니, 고린도 교인들은 사도직을 제대로 이해할 수가 없었다(11:4). 바울은 복음을 분명히 하나님의 계시로 받았고, 그 계시가 그리스도의 죽으심과 부활에서 구체적으로 나타났음을 알고 있다(3:5, 18; 4:4; 5:15). 다시 말하면 사도는 하나님의 사람이나, 특별히 그리스도의 종으로서 그리스도의 특성을 내면적 인격으로 함양한 사람이어야 하고 또 사역 가운데서 약함 가운데서 강하게 하시는 하나님의 능력을 실제로 증거할 수 있어야 한다(1:12; 4:7-15; 6:4-10; 12:9-12; 13:4). 그래서 바울은 고린도 교회에서 반대자들로 말미암아 훼손된 그의 사도직을 회복하기 위해서 그의 사도직의

193) Barrett, *A Commentary on the Second Epistle to the Corinthians,* 53: "this epistle contains··· the fullest and most passionate account of what Paul meant by apostleship."; *The Signs of an Apostle* (Philadelphia: Fortress, 1972), 35-46; Calvin Roetzel, *Paul: The Man and the Myth* (Minneapolice: Fortress Press, 1999), 54: "갈라디아서를 제외하고 바울의 사도직에 대한 도전이 고린도후서에서 보다 더 강한 곳이 없다."

정당성과 반대자들의 사도직의 부당성을 기독론적 판단 기준에 의해서 설명한다.[194] 즉 그리스도의 약함을 통한 구원 사역을 중심으로 해서 자신의 사역과 생애가 전개됨을 일일이 지적하면서 반대자들의 사역이 그렇지 못함을 지적하고 있다. 비울은 그의 사도직의 정당성 문제와 관련하여 고린도 교회의 대적자들의 사도직의 부당한 여러 가지 점들도 지적하고 있다. 그러나 그들의 가장 큰 문제는 복음을 막연하게 이해하고, 그리스도 중심, 특히 그의 고난을 중심으로 명확히 이해하지 못하는 것이다.

고린도 후서에서 바울은 자신을 변명하면서 자신에 대한 적극적인 표현과 부정적인 표현을 모두 사용하고 있다(1:12; 2:15; 3:6, 9; 4:1-6, 16; 5:18; 6:4; 7:2; 10:4, 8, 10; 11:2, 10, 22-12:10 등). 이런 표현들은 바울 자신의 자기이해를 나타내는 것일 수도 있고, 반대자들의 바울에 대한 비난을 나타내는 것일 수도 있다. 이런 표현들로 바울은 그의 사도직 변명 또는 사도로서의 자아 이해를 윤리적, 신학적, 행정적, 그리고 심정적 시각에서 다각도로 설명하고 있다. 첫째, 바울은 신앙양심을 따라 사역하고 있으며(1:12; 4:2), 사욕 대신, 공동체의 유익을 먼저 생각한다(1:23; 2:17; 4:12; 11:7-11; 12:14-19; 13:9). 둘째, 바울은 하나님께서 새로운 구원역사를 위해 세우신 새 언약의 일군이며, 하나님께서 주신 계시의 말씀을 그대로 순수하게 전한다(2:17-4:6; 참조, 11:4, 13-15). 셋째, 바울은 그리스도의 사도로서 기꺼이 그리스도의 고난에 동참해왔다(4:7-15; 6:4-10; 11:22-12:9, 10). 넷째, 그리스도의 권세와 자비의 균형을 이룬 목회를 하고 있다(5:12-7:3; 10:1-8; 12:9; 13:3, 10). 다섯째,

---

194) Thrall, 964.

바울은 자의적이 아니라 사도들의 협약에 따라서 고린도 교회를 세우고 사역을 시작하였으므로, 다른 사역자들이 고린도 교회에 들어와서 사역하는 것을 용납할 수 없다(10:13-18; 고전4:15). 이런 증거들이 바울이 진정한 그리스도의 사도임을 입증하고 고린도 교회에 대한 바울의 사도적 가르침과 목회적 주장을 지지하는 근거들로 제시되고 있다. 이런 증거들 중에서 그리스도 중심적 사도적 변명 또는 자아 이해가 가장 중심적인 것으로 나타난다. 학자들은 바울의 사도직과 관련된 여러 가지 동기나 의미들을 열거하였으나 어떤 이들은 그 동기와 의미들이 결국 신학적 의미와 상관된 것임을 분명히 지적하지 못하였다.[195] 우리는 바울이 다른 서신에서와 같이 고린도후서 초두에서 밝히는 "그리스도 예수의 사도"라는 바울의 자아인식을 중시해야 한다고 본다. 바울은 이런

195) 많은 문헌 중에서 다음 것들만 골라 쓴다. Morris Ashcraft, "Paul's Understanding of Apostleship" *Review and Expositor*, 55 (1958), 400-412; Barrett, *The Signs of an Apostle*; Ronald F. Hock, *The Social Context of Paul's Ministry: Tentmaking and Apostleship* (Philadelphia: Fortress Press, 1980, 62-4; Ernst Käsemann, "Die Legitimität des Apostles", *ZNW* 41 (1942), 33-71; Seyoon Kim, *The Origins of Paul's Gospel* (Grand Rapids: Eerdmans, 1981); J. A. Kirk, "Apostleship since Rengstorf," *NTS*, 21(1974/75) 249-64; Lüdemann, *Paul, Apostle to the Gentiles*; J. W. McCant, "Paul's Thorn of Rejected Apostleship," *NTS* 34 (1988), 550-72; J. Munck, *Paul and The Salvation of Mankind* ; Calvin Roetzel, *Paul: The Man and the Myth*, 48-68; W. Schmithals, *The Office of the Apostle*, ETr. J. E. Steele (Nashville: Abingdon, 1969); R. Schnackenburg, "Apostles before and during Paul's Time," in *Apostlolic History and the Gospel*, ed. W. W. Gasque and R. P. Martin (Grand Rapids: Eerdmans, 1970), 287-303; J. H. Schütz, *Paul and Anatomy of Apostolic Authority*, SNTSMS 26 (Cambridge: University Press, 1975); J. L. Sumney, "Paul's 'Weakness'," 71-91; Thrall, 964: "고린도후서는 독자들이 알고 있으리라고 보는 그리스도 사건의 주요 요소들에 대한 암시들로 차있다."

자아인식, 또는 존재인식을 중심으로 여러 논쟁의 주제들을 다루고 있다고 본다. 무엇보다 바울은 "그리스도의 사도"라는 자아인식에서부터 그의 사도직을 변명하고 있다. 나아가 사도직 변명이라는 중심 주제는 결국 바울의 신학의 중심 주제인 "그리스도를 통한 하나님의 구원" 에 근거하고 있다고 본다(5:14,15). 이것은 고린도후서에서 바울은 그의 사도직의 정당성을 그리스도의 고난, 죽음, 부활, 재림이라는 일련의 구원역사를 따라서 설명하기 때문이다. 특히 바울은 수사학적 효과(독자들의 효과적 이해를 위한)를 얻기 위해서 그리스도의 구원 사건에서 발견되는 대조적 유형, 즉, "죽음," "희생," "온유," "겸비," "약함" 등의 특성과 이에 대조되는, "부활," "영광," "강함"이라는 성격을 따라 교차적으로 설명한다. 바울은 시종일관 "그리스도 예수의 사도"라는 자아인식을 가지고 고린도 교회에서의 사도직 수행과 복음사역이 "그리스도의 겸비와 영광이라는 구원 역사의 유형"을 따라서 이루어지고 있음을 설명하고 있다.[196)]

---

196) Ernst Käsemann은 학자들이 바울의 사상의 다양성을 주장하는 나머지 바울의 한 가지 중심사상을 찾으려는 시도를 도외시하는 것은 잘못된 것이라고 하면서 바울이 비록 *Summa Theologia*를 쓰지는 않았더라도 바울의 신학적 특징은 너무나 뚜렷하다고 한다. 그는 결국 이신득의 사상이 바울의 중심사상이라고 동의한다. Ernst Käsemann, "The Spirit and the Letter," in *Perspectives on Paul* (Philadelphia: Fortress Press, 1971), 138. 그러나 "약함"이 바울 신학의 중심으로 보는 견해도 많다. 이것이 중심 신학으로 된 때에 대해서는 고린도 사역에서부터라는 견해도 있으나 대체로 바울의 사역 초기부터라고 본다. 고린도 때부터라고 보는 이들은, A. A. Black, *Paul, Apostle of Weakness: Asthenia and its Cognates in the Pauline Literature* (New York: Peter Lang, 1984), 101; and, "The Weak in Thessalonica: A Study in Pauline Lexicography," *JETS* 25(1982), 307-21, 특히 307; R. P. Martin, *2 Corinthians*, WBC, 40 (Waco, TX: Word Books, 1986), lix; 이에 반대하면서 바울

1. 그리스도의 사도

바울은 다른 서신에서와 같이 고린도후서에서 "하나님의 뜻을 따라 그리스도의 사도 된 나 바울"이라고 자신의 사도됨을 밝힌다. 고린도후서는 고린도 교회에서 일어난 사도 바울에 대한 각종 의구심과 비난에 대해서 바울이 변명하는 내용이 중심이므로 먼저 "사도"의 의미를 검토하는 것이 필요하다.

1.1 "사도"의 뜻

사도(*ἀπόστολος*)란 말의 어원은 헬라 문화와 유대교 문화에서 찾을 수 있다. 실제로 특사 또는 전달자라는 뜻의 *ἀπόστολος*라는 명사형이 헬라 문학에서 사용된 예는 극히 드물다

의 초기부터 "약함"의 신학이 있었다고 보는 견해는, J. L. Sumney, 72, 관련 참고 문헌을 주 4에서 찾으라. 보다 일반적으로 "고난"을 바울의 중심 신학으로 보는 견해를 Sumney, 82, 주 43, 55-59에서 찾으라. 특히 S. J. Kraftchick는 고린도후서에서 예수의 죽음과 부활에 대한 바울의 묵상이 "그의 사도로서의 삶과 경험을 해석하는 해석학적 열쇠"라고 한다. Steven. J. Kraftchick, "Death in us, Life in you: The Apostolic Medium," in E. H. Lovering, Jr, ed., *SBL 1991 Seminar Papers* (Atlanta: Scholars Press, 1991), 626. 이는 우리의 견해와 일치한다. 그러나 이 글은 문학적 접근방법으로서 예수의 죽음과 부활을 "생산적 암유"(generative metaphor)로 보면서 고후 4:7-15, 5:14-15, 그리고 8장과 9장(헌금)에서 그리스도의 죽음과 부활이 분명히 명시된 부분만을 취급한다. 우리는 보다 신학적이고 역사적인 시각에서 그리스도의 죽음과 부활이 바울의 신학의 중심이며 개인적 체험임을 중시하여 고린도후서 거의 전체 내용의 근간을 이루고 있다고 보는 것이다. 삼니(Sumney)는 많은 학자들이 살전 1:6-7을 그리스도의 고난 모방을 의 주제를 따라 해석한다고 한다. Sumney, 79, 80, 주 43, 50-52를 보라. 참조, 고전 9:2, 롬 8:17, 31-39, 15:37.

(*Herodotus* 1.21; Plato, *Epinomis* 7.346a). 그러나 자주 쓰이는 동사형 ἀπόστολλειν으로 부터 그 근본적 의미는 누구나 알 수 있었다고 본다(Origen, *Commentary on John* 32.17). 즉 "보내심을 받은 자"라는 수동적인 사역자의 의미가 있다. 이 말의 뜻과 가까운 구약과 유대교의 용어는 שלח(솨라흐)에서 특별한 권위를 가지고 보내심을 받은 특사란 뜻이다(LXX, 사 6:8; 렘 1:7; 스 2:3, 등; 미쉬나, *m. Berakot* 5.5; *m. Meila* 6.1-4). 바울이 생각하는 "사도"(ἀπόστολος)란 말의 뜻이 유대교의 특사라는 개념과 얼마나 관련 있는가에 대한 논쟁이 있으나 신약성경에서 쓰인 용례를 찾아 대개 아래와 같은 몇 개의 뜻으로 대별할 수 있다.[197]

(1) 좁은 의미로는 예수님께서 직접 복음 전파의 사명을 맡긴 12명(요 20:21; 행 1:21-23)과 사도 바울을 가리킨다(행 9장; 고전 4:9; 9:2; 딤전 1:12; 딤후 1:12; 딛 1:1-3).[198]

(2) 넓은 의미로는 초대 교회가 복음 전파자로 인정한 예수의 형제 야고보(행전 15:13; 12:17; 고전 15:7; 갈 1:19, 참조 약 1:1), 바나바(행 14:3, 4); 아볼로(고전 4:6, 9), 안드로니아, 유니아(롬 16:7); 실루아노, 디모데(갈 1:1, 6; 참조, 고후 1:1)를 포함한다.

---

197) H. D. Betz, "Apostle," in *Anchor Bible Dictionary*, ed. D. N. Freedman (New York: Doubleday, 1992), 1:309-11; Barrett, *The Signs of an Apostle*; Karl Renstorf, "ἀποστολός" in *Theological Dictionary of the New Testament*, ed. G. Kittel and G. Friedrich (Grand Rapids: Eerdmans, 1964), 1:407-47); J. A. Kirk, 249-64; J. Roloff, *Apostolat-Verkündigung-Kirche*, (Gütersloh: Verlag Mohn, 1965), 9-37; J. Hainz, *Ekklesia: Strukturen paulinischer Gemeinde-Theologie und Gemeinde-Ordnung* (Regensburg: Verlag Friedrich Pustet, 1972), 128-29; Thrall, 945-951.

198) Morris Ashcraft, "Paul's Understanding of Apostleship," 403-406.

(3) 사도들은 교회의 설립자들이며, 수호자들이며, 최고의 감독자들이며, 치리의 최종적 권위자였다(마 16:18; 고전 4:15; 12:28; 고후 12:14; 엡 2:20; 4:11-16; 행 5:2; 6:2-4; 15:6).[199]

(4) 사도들의 말씀은 최고의 권위를 가졌다(벧전 1:1; 벧후 1:1; 3:15-16).

그러나 이런 의미들은 사도라는 개념의 발전적 결과이며 바울은 실제적 목회 상황에서 그의 사도직과 그의 복음의 정통성에 대한 그의 반대자나 교인들의 계속되는 의구심에 대하여 자주 변명했어야 했다(고전 2:3; 4:1, 18; 고후 10:2; 13:2; 갈 1:6이하). 쉬츠(John Schütz)는 초대교회에서 사도직에 대한 일정한 판단기준이 바울 시대뿐만 아니라 그의 사후에도 정해진 바가 없었다고 한다.[200] 그러나 위에서 제시한 바와 유사한 사도직에 대한 판단 기준이 초대교회에서 일반적으로 인식되고 있었다고 본다. 그러나 사도들은 실제 목회 상황에서 반대자들의 도전에 직면하여 자신들의 사도직의 근거를 어떤 모양으로든지 제시해야 했을 것으로 추정된다. 특히 바울의 사도직의 정통성에 대한 의구심은 바울의 교회의 핍박자로서의 과거 경력보다는, 바울 자신이 팔레스틴 유

---

199) Johannes Munck, "Paul, The Apostles, and the Twelve," *ST* III(Fasc. I, 1949), 108;(=*Paul and the Salvation of Mankind*, 36-68). 여기서 뭉크는 사도행전 15장의 예루살렘의 사도회의를 언급하면서 사도들을 일종의 기독교 산헤드린 공회 회원으로 본다.

200) John Schütz, *Paul and the Anatomy of Apostolic Authority* (Cambridge: Cambridge University Press, 1975), 21. 1세기말 클레멘트(Clement of Rome)가 고린도 교회에 보낸 서신에서 사도직에 대한 판단 기준 확립을 위해 노력하고 있음을 보여준다. Clement, "The First Epistle of Clement to the Corinthians," *ANF* vol. 1, (Grand Rapids: Eerdmans, 1981), 5-21.

대인이 아닌, 디아스포라 유대인이며, 또한 그의 사역 대상이 유대인이 아닌 이방인이라는 점과, 이와 관련된 그의 복음의 특성, 즉 전통적 율법주의에 반대하는 이신득의 사상, 또한 다른 사도들과는 달리 재정적으로 교회에 의존하지 않는 그의 사역의 독특성 때문이라고 본다(고전 9:18; 고후 11:7, 9).

(5) 사도들의 권위는 그들이 그리스도와 그를 믿는 자들과의 중개자(medium)이며 그리스도의 인격, 삶, 능력을 가장 많이 닮은 이들이라는 인식에 기인한다(롬 15:8; 고전 4:1; 15; 7:40; 고후 4:5; 5:20; 11:2-33; 12:10-12; 갈 6:17).[201)]

1.2 바울의 사도직 이해

고린도후서의 주제를 "바울의 사도직에 대한 변명"이라고 할 수 있다. 바울은 고린도 교회에서 그를 반대하는 대적자들에 맞서서 자신이 진정한 그리스도의 사도인 증거들을 찾아 설명해야 했다. 그러므로 바울은 고린도후서 서두에서 밝히는 자신이 "하나님의 뜻으로 말미암아 그리스도 예수의 사도가 되었다"(1:1)라는 언급은 보다 주의 깊게 다루어져야 한다. 이와 유사한 표현이 빌립보서, 데살로니가전후서, 빌레몬서를 제외한 다른 모든 바울 서신에서 첫 구절에 나온다.[202)] 이 사실은 바울이 편지를 쓸 때 자신의 사도직의 신적 권위에 대한 인식을 분명히 갖고 있었고 또한 수신자들에게 이를 확인시키는 것이 매우 중요함을 알고 있었다는 것

201) S. J. Kraftchick, 626.

202) 적어도 4곳에서 바울은 자신이 사도임을 분명히 언급한다: 롬 11:13; 고전 9:1, 2; 16:9.

이다. 바울은 서신의 초두에서 무엇보다 그의 사도직의 신적 기원을 분명히 밝혀서 그 자신의 신분이나 그의 편지가 인간적인 요소가 아닌 신적 요소에 의해 지배받는 특별히 구별된 권위 있는 것임을 밝힌다. 그의 사도직의 권위가 신적인 요소에 의해 구별된 것임을 가리키는 판단기준들을 찾아보자.

첫째로, 바울의 사도직의 신적 기원은 다메섹 도상에서 주께서 그를 직접 부르신 역사적 사실에서 찾을 수 있다.[203] 바울은 비록 암시적 표현을 쓰고 있으나 그의 서신 여러 곳에서 자신의 회심 경험을 언급하고 있다(빌 3:4-12; 갈 1:12-17; 고전 9:1, 16; 15:8-9; 참조, 행 9:1-19; 22:4-16; 26:9-19). 고린도후서 4장 4-6절에서도 바울은 자신에게 영광의 그리스도가 나타나셔서 그를 직접 사도로 부르셨고, 또한 복음을 계시하셨음을 암시한다. "어두운 데서 빛이 비취리라 하시던 그 하나님께서 예수 그리스도의 얼굴에 있는 하나님의 영광을 아는 빛을 우리 마음에 비취셨느니라"(고후 4:6; 참조 3:18).

그러나 그의 사도로서 부르심에 대해서도 그는 어디까지나 암시적 표현을 쓰면서 직접적인 언급은 피한다. 사도행전의 기록 밖에서 바울의 회심 경험에 대한 직접적인 증언을 찾아 볼 수 없다. 그는 사도로 부르심을 받은 회심 경험에 대해서는 직접적인 표현을 아끼면서도 그의 사도직 보유 사실에 대해서는 직접적인 표현을 자주 쓴다. 사도로서의 권위에 대해서는 분명하게 언급하면서

203) Seyoon Kim, 67; Johannes Munck, 26: Munck는 갈 1:15-16에서 구약 예언자의 부르심에 비추어 하나님이 바울을 부르신 것으로 나타낸다고 한다.

도 회심 경험을 직접 언급하지는 않는다. 이 사실은 하나님께 부르심을 받은 사도라 해서 자신의 경건함을 주관적 체험에 의존하여 나타내는 것은 자칫하면 영적인 교만에 빠질 수 있다고 보았기 때문이다. 실제로 바울은 고린도후서에서 영적 체험이 흔히 이를 듣는 이들의 지나친 관심과 상상을 자극하여 필요 이상으로 진실을 과장하고 호도하거나, 영적으로 교만해 질 수 있는 위험을 경계한다(고후 12:6-7). 신적이고 영적인 체험은 다른 "육체의 자랑"과 마찬가지로 또 하나의 오만함이 될 수 있기 때문이다. 신비한 경험을 하였다는 사실에 집착한 나머지 자신이 여전히 죄인 인간이라는 사실을 잊고, 자신이 이제 마치 주님과 대등하게 되어 상통하게 되었다는 잘못된 인식을 당사자나 청중이 갖게 될 수 있기 때문이다. 그러므로 바울은 "기록된 바 자랑하는 자는 주 안에서 자랑하라 함과 같게 하려 함이라"(고전 1:31; 고후 10:17)고 한다. 여기서 "주 안에서"라는 어귀는 주님의 절대적이고 사람의 중심을 보시는 권능의 현존하심을 나타낸다. 믿는 자는 이런 주님의 권위 앞에서 겸손해야 한다. 영적 체험이라 할지라도 지나치게 자랑하는 것은 주님 보시기에 교만한 일이며 죄악된 것이므로 주의해야 한다(고후 10:17; 12:7; 롬3:27). 영적 체험을 했거나 능력을 나타냈다고 해서 그 능력이 마치 자신에게서 나온 것처럼 자신이 잘못 인식하거나 상대방에게 잘못 알릴 수가 있기 때문이다. 그 능력의 영광을 하나님에게 돌리지 않고 자기가 취하는 죄를 지을 수 있기 때문에 특별히 유의해야 한다. 더구나 고린도 교회의 바울의 적들이 영적 체험을 가지고 자신들의 사도적 권위의 증거로 삼아 자랑하고 있으나 바울은 이를 어리석은 자랑으로 보았다(고후 11:17).[204] 이런 것들은 한마디로 "육체를 따라 자랑하는 것"에 속한다. 바울은 "여러 사람이 육체를 따라 자랑하니 나도 자랑하겠노라"(11:18)라고 하면서 자신이 유대인이라는 것과 사역에서 남보다 더 많이 수고하였다는 것과 그리고 계속해서 12장에서 삼층천의 체험을 간증하면서 할 수 없이 억지로 자랑한다고 했다(12:1). 그러면서 그는 그리스도의 사도로서 그리스도의 고난과 죽음의 생애를 본받아 사역하는 것이 그리스도의 능력을 입는 길임을 알고 실제로 그의 사역 가운데 그리스도를 위한 능욕과 고난을 기쁘게 받음으로 강하게 되었다고 말한다(고후 12:9, 10). 그의 중심 사상은 어디까지나 그리스도의 십자가를 통한 구원이었으며 그의 사역은 바로 복음의 본질인 그리스도의 고난과 죽음의 사역을 그대로 따른 것임을 증거하므로써 비본질적인 것들을 외형적으로 "육체를 따라 자랑"하며, 사역하는 그의 대적자들의 사역과 구별된 진정한 그리스도의 사도로서의 사역임을 변증하고 있다.

---

204) 바울의 반대자들을 영지주의 사상에 영향 받은 이단자들이라고 보는 학자들이 많다. W. Lütgert, *Freheitspredigt und Schwarmgeister in Korinth; ein Beitrag zur Charqkteristik der Christuspartei* (Gütersloh: Verlag Mohn 1908); W. Schmithals, *Gnosticism in Corinth*, ETr. (Nashville/New York: Abingdon Press, 1971), 102-114; G. Friedrich, "Die Gegner des Paulus im 2 Korintherbrief," in *Abraham unser Vater: Festschrift für O. Michel, ed. O. Betz, etc.*, (Leiden: Brill, 1963), 181ff.; D. Georgi, *The Opponents of Paul in Second Corinthians* (Philadelphia: Fortress Press, 1986), 230-64; C. K. Barrett, "Paul's Opponents in II Corinthians", *NTS* 17 (1970-71), 233-254; J. J. Günther, *St. Paul's Opponents ad their Background* (Leiden: Brill, 1973); W. Marxen, *Introduction to the New Testament: An Approach to its Problems*, ETr. G. Buswell (Philadelphia: Fortress, 1968), 75. 그러나 바울의 대적자들을 단순히 신령한 체험을 중시하는 자들로 보는 것이 무난하다. D. Guthrie, *New Testament Introduction*, 434-35; Margaret E. Thrall, *A Critical and Exegetical Commentary on the Second Epistle to the Corinthians*, vol II (Edinburgh: T & T Clark, 2000), 926-945, 특히 927을 보라.

이런 자세는 그리스도의 희생적 목회자적 가르침과 일치한다(막 10:45; 10:11-12).

이렇게 바울은 그의 회심 사건이 그의 사도직의 신적 기원을 분명히 증거 할 수 있음에도 불구하고, 그 자고(自高)케하는 위험성 때문에 직접적인 언급을 자제한 것으로 보인다. 그러므로 바울은 사도직을 언제 어떻게 받았느냐는 것보다는 그가 현재 사도직을 가지고 있다는 사실을 주로 강변한다. 바울에게 있어서 자신이 그리스도의 사도라는 사실은 기정 진실로서 더 논쟁할 필요가 없다고 생각하는 듯하다. 그러나 고린도 교인들의 오해와 비난 때문에 억지로 변명해야하는 것이 괴로운 것이다. 무엇보다 스스로를 사도로 자천하는 것이 못마땅하였다. "우리가 다시 자천하기를 시작하겠느냐 "(고후 3:1; 5:12; 7:2; 10:5, 11:22, 23; 12:12, 19; 13:7; 참조, 고전 2-4).[205] 사도로 자천하는 것은 "육체적 자랑" 에 해당되는 것이고 바울의 반대자들이나 하는 것이었다. 그러나 다수의 고린도 교인들이 무관심한 가운데 바울은 고린도후서에서 자신이 "하나님의 뜻을 따라 그리스도의 사도가 되었다" 는 사실을 스스로 밝히지 않으면 안 될 어려운 입장에 서 있었다(11:1, 16-18, 12:11)..

둘째로, 위에서 말 한 것과 유사하게, 바울에게 있어서 그리스도의 사도의 진정한 증거는 외적 증거가 아니라 그리스도의 죽음과 부활에 근거한 내적 증거였다(10:7; 11:23, 24, 12:9, 10). "너희는 외모만 보는 도다. 만일 사람이 자기가 그리스도에게 속한 줄

205) 고린도전서에서 바울이 이미 자천하였는데 이제 "다시" 할 필요가 있겠는가라는 뜻으로 본다. F. F. Bruce, *1 and 2 Corinthians*, 189; P. E. Hughes, *Paul's Second Epistle to the Corinthians*, 85.

을 믿을 진대 자기가 그리스도에 속한 것 같이 우리도 그러한 줄을 자기 속으로 다시 생각할 것이라" (10:7). 바울의 사도직 판단기준은 다른 사도들의 것과 다르다. 다른 사도들은 유창한 언변(고후 10:10; 11:6)이나, 사역의 수고들(11:23)이나, 예루살렘 사도들과의 연관성(11:5), 유대적 기원(11:22), "표적과 기사" (12:11-12) 등을 사도직의 판단 기준으로 삼았다. 바울 자신도 이런 사도적 증거를 어느 정도 가지고 있다고 증언하지만(고후 12:12; 참조, 롬 15:18) 그 것들만으로 진정한 그리스도의 사도로 입증되는 것은 아니었다.[206] 바울은 이런 능력들만으로 그의 사도직을 정당화할 수는 없었다. 예를 들어 다른 사도들도, 심지어 거짓 사도들도 많은 기적이나 영적 능력을 행사하였다. 그런 기적은 헬레니즘 당시의 신인들(神人, δεῖοι ἄνδρες)도 행하는 것이었다(행 14:11).[207] 고린도 교회 거짓 사도들도 행하는 것으로 짐작된다(고후 12:11-12, 23). 바울은 고린도전서에서도 기적을 행하는 그의 반대자들을 경계를 하면서, 그의 복음은 기적이나 지혜 대신에 십자가에 못 박힌 그리스도를 전하므로 유대인에게는 거리낌 바가 되고 헬라인에게는 미련한 것이 된다고 하였다(고전 1:22, 23). 바울은 예수님도 이런 기적 행하는 사람들을 경계하였다는 사실을 알고 있

---

206); Roetzel, 60-62; Furnish, 556: 바울은 사도의 기적 수행 능력을 사도의 가장 근본적이고 특징적인 임무, 즉 복음선포에 종속시켰다. 10:7에서 누가 진정으로 "그리스도에 속한" (Χριστοῦ εἶναι) 사도인가 사도직 논쟁의 핵심이다. 이에 대한 여러 의견을 R. P. Martin, 308이하에서 찾아보라. 결국 그 판단 기준은 어느 사도가 그리스도를 가장 닮은 사역을 하고 있느냐라는 것이라고 바울은 암시한다. 그러면서 자신의 "약함" 에 대한 자랑과 이를 그리스도의 "약함" 과 결부시켜 자신의 진정성을 증거한다(11:30; 12:10; 13:4). 또 424를 보라.

207) Georgi, 25, n. 95; 230-64.

었을 것이다(마 7:22-23; 12:38, 39). 기적들은 참된 믿음을 가진 이들에게는 하나님의 역사의 증거가 되나 외적 증거만을 찾는 이들에게는 내적인 영적 성숙을 방해하는 요소가 될 수 있는 것이다. 그런 기준은 결국 육체를 따라 찾는 피상적 기준이므로 본질적 가치가 없다(11:18). 물론 바울 자신도 기적을 행하였음을 사도적 증거로 제시하고 있다(12:12). 그러나 바울이 내세우는 진정한 본질적인 사도의 표는 그리스도의 고난에 동참하는 것과 그의 약함이다. 이것은 단순한 역설적 변명이 아니라 약함 가운데 오히려 하나님의 능력이 나타나는 것을 그의 사역 가운데 체험하였기 때문이다. 반대자들의 문제는 비본질적인 사도의 표를 본질적인 것으로 내세우는 것이다.

바울이 제시하는 "그리스도의 사도"의 증거는 그가 그를 사도로 임명한 그리스도의 사역과 인격을 따라서 행하는 것이다. 그러므로 고린도후서 초두에서 바울은 그의 사역을 양심을 따라서 하나님의 거룩함과 진실함으로 행하였다고 한다(고후 1:12). 그러나 중반부와 후반부에서 바울은 진정한 사도직을 위한 신학적인 근거에 중점을 둔다. 즉 진정한 사도직이란 그리스도의 고난에 동참하는 것이요 인간의 연약함 가운데 나타나는 하나님의 능력을 증거 해야 한다고 한다(4:7-12; 5:14이하; 11:30; 12:9-10; 13:4; 참조, 갈 6:17). 바울은 그의 반대자들의 "육체적 자랑"에 대응하여 어쩔 수 없이 그의 개인적 경건함과 도덕적 우월성도 언급하나(1:12; 2:17; 11:8-10; 12:12, 13), 그리스도의 복음을 보배로 자신을 질그릇으로 표현함으로써 사도의 능력의 원천이 결국 자신의 경건이 아니라 하나님의 능력임을 밝힌다(4:7). 사도가 본받아야 하는 그리스도의 진정한 권위는 그의 개인적 경건이나 외적 표적과 기사에 있는 것이 아니라 고난과 대속적 죽으심에서 나타났다고 본다. 그리스도는 광야에서 하나님의 아들의 증거로 기적을 요구하는 사탄의 시험을 피하셨고, 또한 바리새인들의 기적의 요구를 거부하셨고, 대신 희생적 죽음을 통한 메시아의 길을 택하셨다(마 4:1-11; 12:37-39; 막 10:45). 그가 죽으심으로 그는 영광의 구세주로 등극하게 되었다(빌 2:9-11). 그의 진정한 권세는 대속적, 희생적 죽음을 통하여 확립 되었다. 이것이 불신자들에게는 어리석음이요 거리끼는 것이지만, 믿는 자들에게는 하나님의 구원의 능력이요, 지혜인 것이다(고전 1:23, 24; 2:6 이하). 이런 이치는 하나님의 지혜의 이치이므로 인간의 지혜로는 알 수 없다. "하나님의 미련한 것이 사람보다 지혜 있고 하나님의 약한 것이 사람보다 강하니라" (고전 1:25; 참조, 고후 12:9). 하나님은 그의 무한하신 지혜로운 경륜으로 사람의 제한된 기대나 생각을 압도함으로써 사람에게 찬양과 영광을 영원히 받으시기에 합당하신 분이다(롬 11:34-35; 빌 2:9-11). 더구나 바울은 이런 십자가의 구원의 지혜를 성령을 통해서 자신에게 계시되었다고 함으로써 자신의 사도직과 함께 사도적 가르침도 하나님으로부터 받은 것임을 확인한다(고전 2:10이하; 고후 3:9, 18, 4:6).

이렇게 바울은 지혜로우신 "하나님의 뜻으로 말미암아 그리스도 예수의 사도" 된 증거가 근본적으로 개인적 경건이나 유대적 전통, 기적이나 표적 같은 외적 증거나 인간적 자랑에 있는 것이 아니라 그리스도의 죽음과 부활의 사역에서 명확히 나타난 하나님의 구원 역사의 유형을 따라 나타나는 것임을 굳게 믿고 있다. 즉 고난을 통한 위로와 승리의 사역이다(고후1:4-11; 4:7-15). 이런 의미에서 그의 사도적 권위는 다른 거짓 사도들의 사도직과 분명히 구별되는 신적 권위를 가지고 있다. 바울은 그의 독자들이 진정한 사도직에 대한 내적 증거를 근거로 하여 바울이 당하는 현재의 고난과 어려움을 진정한 사도의 증거로서 적극적으로 판단하기를 원하는 것이다(고후 4:18). 바울은 그의 고난으로 점철된 사역이 반대자들의 사도직과 자신의 사도직을 차별화시키는 가장 분명한 증거로 삼는다(고후 11:16-33; 12:10). 반대자들은 사욕을 따르는 거짓사도이며, 자신은 교인들을 위해 희생을 마다하지 않는 진정한 그리스도의 사도이다. 실제로 바울은 반대자들과 달리 교회에 의존하지 않는 경제적 자립형 사역을 하였다(11:7-9). 이런 사역의 동기를 보다 비판적인 시각에서 보면, 바울은 자립형 사역을 통해서 반대자들의 의존형 사역과 차별화해야할 필요를 느꼈을 것이다. 반대자들과 사도권 문제로 갈등이 많은 고린도 교회에서 바울은 그가 돈을 받지 않고 희생적으로 사역하는 진정한 그리스도의 사도라는 것을 증명해서 그의 사도적 위신과 명예를 지키는 반면, 반대자들의 입지를 약화시키려 했다고 볼 수도 있다. 그러나 이런 목회적 동기는 그리스도의 희생의 본을 따르려는 신앙적 동기보다 우선적이라고 볼 수 없다. 바울은 그의 사역의 동기가 순수한 기독론적 동기임을 독자들에게 알리는 것이 그의 일관된 목적이기 때문이다(12:19). 그는 그가 복음 사역에서 받은 많은 수고와 고난이 그가 결코 이기적인 삯군 목자가 아니라 그리스도처럼 자신을 희생하는 목자임을 분명히 증거한다고 보았다(11:16-33; 참조, 막 10:45; 요10:10-12). 그 결과 고린도 교인들이 바른 믿음을 가지게 되고 고린도 교회에 그리스도의 왕권을 확립하는 것이다(4:5; 10:5-6, 8;12:19 13:10).

셋째로, 바울의 사도로서의 임무는 그리스도의 복음을 해석하는 것과 함께 "그리스도의 사신"(*ὑπὲρ Χριστοῦ οὖν πρεσβεύομεν*)으로서 복음을 전하는 것이다(5:20; 11:4; 참조, 고전 9:16; 갈1:8).[208] 대부분의 학자들은 지나치게 바울을 복음의 해석자로만 보는 경향이 있다.[209] 그러나 바울은 "예수 믿고 구원 얻는 진리"를 그대로 전하는 것을 그의 가장 중요한 사명으로 알고 있었다. 물론 그리스도의 죽음과 부활을 각 교회 형편과 그리스도인의의 개인적 경건에 적용하여 해석하는 것도 바울 서신의 중요한 부분이다. 많은 학자들은 바울이 예수의 복음을 각 교회 형편에 따라 달리 해석하였다고 한다.[210] 그러나 한 가지 중심 사

---

208) 바울의 *εὐαγγελίξω*는 고전 1:17; 9:16; 18; 15:1, 2; 고후 10:16; 11:7; 갈 1:8, 9, 11, 16, 23; 4:13; 롬 1:15; 10:15; 15:20에서, *κήρυσσω*는 고전 1:23; 9:27; 15:11, 12; 고후 1:19; 4:5; 11:4; 갈 2:2; 5:11; 빌 1:15; 살전 2:9에서, *κήρυσσω*는 고전 1:21; 2:4; 15:14; 롬 16:25에서 찾으라.

209) 예로, Roetzel, 67; H. Richard Hays, *The Faith of Jesus Christ* (Chico, CA.: Scholars Press, 1983), 64-67. 그러나 Roetzel은 바울의 해석자로서의 기능을 인정하면서도 전체적으로는 그의 전달자로서의 기능을 논한다.

210) 학자들이 바울의 중심사상을 제시한 것을 다음과 같이 열거할 수 있다. 가장 뛰어난 영지주의 사상(Richard Reitzenstein), 제의사상(William Heitmüller, Wilhelm Bousset), 케리그마-실존주의적 이해, 신앙(Bultmann), 신비주의(Heinrich Weinel, Gustav Adolf Deissmann), 믿음의 교육("*Glaubenslehe*r"), 교육계획서("*lehrplan*"), 주제들과 전망(Keck), 계약규범(E. P. Sanders, *Paul and Judaism: A Comparison of Patterns of Religion*, [Philadelphia: Fortress, 1977], 75, 236), 중심적 유형과 근본 교리들(Whitely), 이신득의(Wendland, Kümmel, Käsemann), 신비주의적 종말론(Heinrich Julius Holtzmann, Otto Pfleiderer, William Wrede, Albert Schweitzer), 그리스도 안에 있는 존재(Davies), 십자가에 달리신 메시아 예수와의 일체화(Dahl). 하나님과 죄인의 화해(R. P. Martin, *Reconciliation: A Study of Paul's Theology* [London: Marshall, Morgan & Scott/ Atlanta: John Knox, 1981], 46-47), 하나님의 승리와 창조세계의 구원(J. Christiaan Beker, *Paul the Apostle: The*

상을 가지고 각 교회의 형편과 문제를 해석한다는 견해도 많다.[211] 이런 중심 사상이 무엇이냐에 대한 일치가 없으나, 대체로 이신득의 사상이나 이와 관련된 사상이라는 결론에 이르고 있다. 이신득의 사상은 로마서와 갈라디아서의 분명한 주제이다(롬 3:24, 28; 4:5; 5:1; 10:9; 갈 2:16; 3장, 4장). 다른 바울 서신에서 이 사상이 분명히 나타나지는 않는 것은 바울은 각 교회의 당면 문제만 집중하여 논하는 경향이 있기 때문이다. 그러나 그런 서신에서도 그리스도를 통한 이신득의 사상이 중심 사상으로 전제되어 있는 증거들이 많이 있다.[212] 이신득의 사상은 복음의 해석이라기보다 복음 그 자체이며, 바울은 이를 그대로 전하는 것을 그의 중심 사역으로 알고 있었다(롬 15:19; 갈 1:12; 참조, 막 10:45; 요 3:16).

이신득의 사상이 개인주의적 구원에 집착되었다고 보고 보다 넓게 창조질서의 회복으로 구원 개념을 확장하여 보는 이들도 있으나 바울의 구원론의 초점은 역시 예수 그리스도를 통한 죄인 인간 구원이다.[213] 만물의 구원은 인간 구원의 부수적인 이차적인

Triumph of God in Life and Thought [Philadelphia: Fortress Press, 1980], 13, 14). Beker와 Martin의 주에서 위의 학자들의 주제들을 참고하였으나 필자의 견해도 있다. 거기서 관련 주제의 참고 문헌도 찾을 수 있다.

211) J. C. Beker, 1, Beker는 바울이 하나님의 승리라는 묵시론적 중심 사상을 축으로 삼아(coherence), 그의 삶의 처지에 따라 해석했다고 본다(contingency). 그러나 다른 데서는 이신득의 사상을 중심으로 썼다고도 한다(35).

212) Ernst Käsemann, 164: "바울은 하나의 고착된 주석방법이나 폐쇄적 교리적 체계를 발전시키지는 않았다. 그러나 그는 그의 전체 신학을 지배하는 한 가지 주제를 가지고 있다, 즉 이신득의 교리이다."

213) Beker, ix, 19, 351이하. 여기서 베커는 바울의 중심 사상을 하나님의 승리와 창조세계의 회복으로 본다. 이런 견해는 바울의 분명한 인간 구원론을 모호하게 만들어 버리고 결국 자연주의적 회복사상으로 곡해하는 문제가 있다.

것이며 그 반대가 될 수 없다(고전 15:27, 28; 빌 3:21; 골 1:20). 이것은 바울 서신에서 인간의 죄의 회개와 구원 문제가 집중적으로 다루어지고 있는 사실 뿐만 아니라 창세기를 비롯한 성경 전체에서 인간의 죄의 문제가 창조세계의 질서 파괴의 근본원인으로 취급되고 있기 때문이다(창 3:17; 6:5-7; 레 1:4; 수 7:1).

한편 사도는 주께로부터 받은 구원의 복음을 가감 없이 전달하는 일차적인 책임을 가지고 있다. 바울은 그의 서신 도처에서 그의 복음은 주께로부터 직접 계시로 받은 것임을 천명하고 있다(고전 7:25, 40; 고후 3:3-5, 18; 4:6). 특히 갈라디아서에서 이점을 강조하면서 그는 주께로부터 받은 복음을 그대로 가감 없이 전했음을 강조한다(갈 1:9, 12 이하). 그러므로 학자들이 바울을 복음 전승의 해석자로만 보는 것은 바울 자신의 증언에 배치된다. 바울은 그리스도의 사도로서 그리스도의 복음을 전하는 데 충실했다고 증언한다. 키엘케골(S. Kierkegaard)도 이점을 강조한다.

> 누군가 절대적으로 목적론적으로 입장이 정해진 사람이 있다면 그는 다름 아닌 사도이다. 사도에게 계시된 교리는 그 의미를 생각하라고 준 것이 아니고, 그 자신을 위해서 준 것도 아니다. 반대로, 그는 사명을 받았고, 그 교리를 전하고, 사용하는 권한을 받은 것이다. 편지를 어떤 도시에 전하도록 보냄을 받은 사람일 뿐이며, 그 내용과는 아무런 상관이 없고, 다만 그 편지를 전해야 하는 사람이다. 외국에 간 사절과도 같이 가지고 간 멧세지의 내용에 대해서는 책임이 없고 다만 그것을 바로 전하는 사명을 가진 것이다…계시는 인간의 이해를 초월하는 역설적인 성격이 있다. 그럼에도 불구하고 그것을

> 전해 듣는 사람들이 어느 정도 이해하는 것이 도처에서 증명되었다. 세상에 이 계시를 전하도록, 말씀을 선포하도록, 부르심을 받은 사람은 주님의 전달자로서 행동하고, 고통당하고, 간단없는 분주한 삶을 살아야한다.[214]

이렇게 바울은 "하나님의 뜻으로 말미암아 그리스도 예수의 사도된" 자신을 복음의 해석자보다는 전달자로 이해하면서 그의 서신들을 쓴 것이다(참조, 살전 2:4; 딤후 1:11). 바울은 복음 전파자였으며 필요한 경우에만 교회 설립에 관여했다.[215] 교회도 복음으로 말미암아 생성된 것이다(살후 2:13). 사도행전과 고린도전서에서는 사도들이란 예수의 부활의 증인들이었음을 강조한다. 바울도 이를 가장 중요한 그의 임무로 생각한다(행 17:18; 23:6; 롬 1:4, 6:5; 고전 15:13; 빌 3:11). 그의 복음전파는 그의 사도직에 대한 진술과 대개 연계되어 나타난다.[216] 그는 복음을 위하여 옥에 갇혔다(딤후 2:9; 몬 1:13). 그가 복음을 전하지 않으면 화가 미칠 것이라고 하였다(고전 9:16).

바울은 복음을 해석하는 경우에도 그의 사사로운 견해(해석)를 주님의 명령과 구별하고 있다(고전 7:12, 40). 그의 서신들은 그리스도의 사도로서 그리스도의 말씀을 전하는 공적인 서신이며 그

---

214) Soeren Aabye Kierkegaard, "Of the Difference between a genius and An Apostle," in *The Present Age and Two Minor Ethico-Religious Treatises*, (New York: Oxford University, 1940), 160ff.

215) Ernst von Dobschütz, *Christian Life in the Primitive Church*, ETr. George Bremmer (London: G. P. Putnam's Sons, 1904), 63.

216) Ernst De Witt Burton, *A Critical and Exegetical Commentary on the Epistle to the Galatians* (Edinburgh: T. & T. Clark, 1921), 378f.

리스도의 말씀과 같은 권위를 갖는다.[217] "하나님의 뜻으로 말미암아 그리스도 예수의 사도된 바울"이라는 어귀가 없는 서신의 경우는 수신자들이 자신의 사도직에 대해 의심할 여지없이 분명히 알고 있으므로 재삼 언급하는 것이 오히려 어색하다고 느껴 쓰지 않았다고 생각 된다. 바울은 그리스도의 전달자로서의 권위를 가지고 수신자들에게 권면하는 것이다. "이런 사람은 우리가 떠나 있을 때에 편지들로 말하는 자가 어떠한 자이면 함께 있을 때에 행하는 자도 그와 같은 자인 줄 알라"(고후 10:11). 펑크(Robert Funk)는 바울이 그의 서신을 통해서 그가 세운 교회에서의 사도적 현존(apostolic presence)같은 효과를 나타낸다고 했는데, 사도적 현존은 실제로 사도를 보낸 주님의 현존하심을 가리키는 것이다.[218] 실제로 바울은 고린도후서 13장 10절에서 "주께서 내게 주신 권세를 따라 엄하지 않게 하려 하노라"라고 말하고 있고 또, "명령"이란 말이나(고전 7:10, 12, 17; 14:37), "순종"이란 말을 쓰고 있다(고후 2:9; 10:6). 그리고 이미 고린도전서에서 "다른 사람들에게는 내가 사도가 아닐지라도 너희에게는 사도니 나의 사도됨을 주 안에서 인친 것이 너희라"(고전 9:2)라고 말하면서 고린도

217) 다이스만(G. A. Deissmann)이후 바울의 서신을 공한(公翰)이 아닌 사신(私信)으로 보면서 바울의 서신의 신학적 가르침의 시대적 제한성과 우연적 성격을 강조해왔다. 그러나 Dieter Betz는 갈라디아서가 1세기 당시 로마시대의 공한과 같은 구조를 가지고 주의 깊게 쓴 것임을 지적했다. Gustav Adolf Deissmann, *Light from the Ancient East:: The New Testament Illustrated by Recently Discovered Texts of the Greco-Roman World*, (London: Hodder and Stoughton, 1910); Hans Dieter Betz, "The Literary Composition and Function of Paul's Letter to the Galatians."

218) Robert Walter Funk, "The Apostolic Parousia: Form and Significance" in *Christian History and Interpretation: Studies Presented to John Knox*, ed. W. R. Farmer, C. F. D. Moule, and R. R. Niebuhr (Cambridge: At the University, 1967), 263-66.

교회의 설립자로서의 권위를 나타내고 있다. 데살로니가 전서 마지막 부분에서도 바울은 "내가 주를 힘입어 너희를 명하노니 모든 형제에게 이 편지를 읽어 돌리라"(살전 5:27)고 한다. 이런 바울의 언명들은 바울의 사도의 권위는 주님의 권위로서 절대적인 권위이며 순종만이 올바른 반응이라는 것을 분명히 하고 있다.[219]

이렇게 볼 때 복음 전파자로서의 바울의 역할은 해석자로서의 역할보다 선행한다고 볼 수 있다.[220]

넷째로, 바울은 이런 절대적 권위를 가진 사도직을 수행함에 있어서 그리스도의 사도로서 그리스도의 인격과 사역의 특성을 본받아야 함을 늘 잊지 않고 있다. 즉 절대적인 사도적 권한은 주님의 또 다른 모습, 즉 온유와 관용의 자세와 균형을 이루어 행사되어야 함을 잘 알고 있었다.

바울은 그리스도의 화목케 하는 직책을 대행하고 있다(5:19). 그는 하나님의 화해의 은혜를 사람들에게 베푸는 일의 동역자이다(6:1, 3). "너희를 대하여 대면하면 겸비하고 떠나 있으면 담대한 나 바울은 이제 그리스도의 온유와 관용으로 친히 너희를 권하고 …이 담대한 태도로 대하지 않게 하기를 구하노라"(고후 10:1, 2; 13:10; 참조, 마 11:29). "내가 명령으로 하는 말이 아니요 오직 다른 이들의 간절함을 가지고 너희의 사랑의 진실함을 증명코자 함이로라"(고후 8:8). 즉 바울은 그리스도의 권위는 그의 겸비와 상호보완적인 것으로 알고 있고, 자신의 사도직도 그렇게 이해하

219) 고전 11:17; 16:1; 골 4:10; 살전 4:11; 5:27; 살후 3:4, 6, 10, 12; 딤전 1:18; 4:11; 5:7, 21; 6:13; 딤후 2:14; 4:1; 딛1:5; 몬1:8.

220) 이에 반대하는 견해를 보라. Hays, 442-46.

고 있다. 사도의 권위는 주님의 권위와 같이 역설적으로 온유한 면이 있는 것이다.[221)]

바울이 언급하는 사도로서의 겸비함의 한 가지 이유는 그가 이전에 교회를 핍박하였던 과거 때문이다(고전 15:8-9; 딤전 1:13, 14). 이와 함께 너무 갑작스럽게 사도가 되어서 신빙성이 약한 것도 문제였다[222)] 그러나 이런 약점들을 생각할 때마다 하나님의 은혜로 말미암아 사도가 된 사실을 부각시킴으로써 그의 "약함" 의 반대효과를 일으키고 있다(고후 12:9-10). 이것이 바울의 의도된 수사학적 기술 이라기보다는 그가 늘 말하는 은혜로 말미암는 구원 사상에 근거한 자연스런 고백이라고 본다. 바울은 그리스도의 은혜로 구속함을 받은 그리스도인은 존재론적으로 그리스도와 영적으로 연합되었으므로 실제로 그리스도를 본받아 살아야 당연하다는 것을 도처에서 가르친다(롬 6:5, 13; 살전 1:6; 빌 2:1). 그러나 바울은 자주 독자들에게 자신이 그리스도를 본받는 것같이 자신을 본받으라고 가르친다(고전 4:16; 11:1; 빌 3:17, 살후 3:7, 9; 참조, 빌 3:10). 이렇게 감히 말할 수 있는 것은 바울이 그리스도의 사도로서 그리스도의 인격을 철저히 따르고 있다는 증거이다. 그는 그리스도를 본받으라는 말과 함께 그리스도를 본받은 자신을 본받으라는 말을 할 수 있는 그리스도의 진정한 사도가 되었음을 입증한다. 이런 바울의 그리스도의 사도로서의 확고한 자세를 기회주의자나 협잡꾼의 말로 악평하는 것은 고린도 교회의 바울의

---

221) R. P. Martin, *2 Corinthians*, 424.

222) Ben Witherington III, *The Paul Quest: The Renewed Search for the Jew of Tarsus* (Illinois: IVP, 1998), 157.

대적자들의 편에 서는 것과 같다.[223] 바울은 이와 유사한 고린도 교회의 대적자들의 비난에 대해서 변화된 고린도 교인들의 자세가 자신의 사도직의 진정성을 대변한다고 말한다(고후 3:2, 3). 또한 바울 사도의 인격에 대한 보다 객관적인 적극적 평가는 그의 서신의 감화력과 그의 전승에 대한 후대교회의 보전으로 강화된다.[224] 무엇보다 바울의 서신에서 보듯이 바울이 복음의 내용을 그의 사역에 실제로 적용하여 실천한 사실은 바울의 사도됨의 진정성을 입증해 준다. 바울은 복음을 전하면서 복음을 따라 살기를 힘쓴 것이다.

끝으로, 바울의 사도직의 진정성의 한 가지 중요한 판단기준은 사도적 교회의 보존과 성장이다. 바울은 고린도교회의 설립자로

223) 니체는 바울이 권위에 굶주린 거짓 천사로서 예수에게서 그의 영혼의 문제의 해결을 찾았다고 한다. Friedrich Nietzsche, "The Antichrist: An Attempted Criticism of Christianity," in *The Complete Works of Friedrich Nietzsche*, ed. O. Levy, vol. 16 (New York: Macmillan Co., 1910-27), 178-87; "The First Christians," in *The Dawn of Day* (New York: Macmillan Co., 1903), 56-61; 유사하게 G. Shaw는 바울이 보복적으로 교묘한 수단을 써서 권위를 행사하는 협잡꾼이라고 한다. G. Shaw, *The Cost of Authority: Manipulation and Freedom in the New Testament*, (London: SCM, 1983), 106, 114, 122, 125, 등에서 바울은 변덕스럽고 정치적인 술수로 그의 교인들을 다룬다고 비판하면서 "In this the Christian Paul is not perhaps so different from the persecuting Saul." (125)이라고 혹평한다, 그러나 이에 대한 반대 견해도 있다. Henry Chadwick, "'All Things to All Men,'(1 Cor.9:22)," *NTS* 1(1954-55), 261-75. 특히 75쪽에서 바울은 어려운 상황에 잘 대처하는 훌륭한 변증가요 목회자라고 한다. 무엇보다 바울의 서신이 후대를 위해 잘 보존되었다는 사실 자체가 바울의 진실성을 반증한다. 이와 관련한 논쟁을, B. Hall, "All Things to All People: A Study of 1 Corinthians 9.19-23," in Fortna and Gaventa, *The Conversation Continues* (1990), 137-57. Beker, 7과 Dunn, 576에서 찾아 보라.

서 고린도교회의 보존에 대한 독특한 권한이 있음을 나타낸다 (3:1;10:13-15; 고전 4;15). 바울은 고린도후서에서 변화된 고린도 교인들이 바로 그의 자천서라고 한다(3:2). 그의 사도로서의 임무는 고린도 교인들을 순결한 신부로 단장하여 신랑 예수에게 바치는 것이다(11:2). 다시 말하면 고린도 교회를 이단적 사도들의 영향으로부터 보호하여 순수한 사도적 교회로 세우는 것이다(11:4). 그러므로 그는 단호하게 문제 있는 사람의 치리를 명하고, 세상과 분리된 거룩한 생활을 명하면서도 한편으로는 간절한 마음으로 고린도 교인들을 권면하면서 그의 희생적 사역을 통하여 얻은 좋은 성과를 감사한다(2:6; 6:14-7:1; 1:2-14; 7:7, 11). 고린도 교인들은 고난과 회개를 통해서 하나님의 오묘하신 구원 역사를 체험하고서 예전 보다 더 성숙한 그리스도인으로 성장하게 되었다. 그러나 이런 성과는 항상 악한 세력에 의해 훼손되고 파괴되므로 사도는 이를 계속 유지하고 보존해야할 책임이 있다(10:8; 11:3, 4; 13:10; 참조, 갈 3:1; 4:19). 이는 곧 그리스도 교회의 안정과 평강의 유지를 말한다(롬 14:17; 엡 2:13-22). 이에 대해 커크(J. A. Kirk)는 "바울에게 있어서 사도직이란 절대적 주장에 의해서가 아니라, 그 사도직을 수행하는 자의 열매로 증명된다" 고했다.[225] 바울은 고린도 교회를 그리스도의 평강이 거하는 교회가 되도록 힘써왔으며 반대 세력을 누르고 어느 정도 그 목적을 이루었다.[226]

이상에서 본 바와 같이 고린도후서에서의 바울의 사도직 신분

224) Roetzel, 68.

225) Kirk, "Apostleship since Rengstorf," 261.

226) 그러나 고린도 교회의 분쟁은 1세기 말에도 종식되지 않았다. Clement, "The Letter of Clemment to the Corinthians," *ANF*, vol. 5-21.

에 대한 내용은 바울의 사도직의 평가 기준의 신적 기원, 그리스도의 죽음과 부활과의 연속성, 그리스도의 복음을 전달자와 해석자, 그리스도의 온유한 인격과 화해의 품성보유, 그리고 교인들의 성숙된 삶과 교회의 평강의 유지 등으로 대별될 수 있다고 본다.

우리는 바울의 사도직의 판단 기준들이 각기 또는 서로 균형과 조절이 되는 것을 보았다. 바울의 사도직의 신적 기원에 대한 확신은 사도직의 소명의 체험을 암시적으로 표현함으로써 애써 자제하는 듯하고, 사도로서의 도덕성이나 표적과 기사 같은 외적 증거는 그리스도의 고난과 죽음이라는 복음의 중심적 주제로 희석시키며, 복음 전달자로서의 권위는 그리스도의 겸비하심으로 제한시키며, 그의 교인들을 위한 강력한 신앙 훈련이나 요구는 그의 희생적 사역으로 대조 된다. 이런 사도직의 역설적 양면성이 고린도후서 전체의 구조에도 나타내고 있다고 본다. 바울은 고린도후서 전반부(1-9장)에서 주로 온유한 자세로 말하면서 후반부(10-13장)에서는 강경한 어조로 말하는데, 이를 두 가지 다른 편지의 합본으로 보거나, 고린도 교회의 상황의 변화에 따른 반응으로 보는 일반적인 견해를 떠나서 단순히 바울의 사도직의 양면성을 나타내는 것이라고 볼 수도 있을 것이다.[227] 그 비중에서 차이는 있으나, 전 후반 가릴 것 없이 고린도후서 전체에서 이런 양면성이 교차적으로 언급되고 있음을 알 수 있다.

한편, 바울의 그리스도 중심적 사고에 나타난 양면성은 하나님의 역사 경륜의 특성이기도 하다. 하나님은 약한 것을 들어 강하

---

227) 고린도후서의 통일성 문제는 주 46을 보라.

게 사용하심으로 그의 신실하심과 영광을 극대화시키시기 위함이다(신 7:7-9; 8:16; 삼상 2:7-8; 말 1:2-3; 눅 1:51-55; 고후 12:9, 10). 그리스도의 사역의 양면성은 바로 하나님의 사역의 양면성을 나타내는 것이다. 그러므로 바울의 그리스도 중심적 사고는 곧 하나님 중심적 사고라고 볼 수 있다. 바울의 사도직의 원천은 자신의 능력이 아니라 하나님의 능력이다. 하나님의 능력은 구체적으로 그리스도의 죽음과 부활에서 가장 명확히 증명되었다. 바울은 그리스도의 가르침을 따라서 사역하고 있다. 그러므로 바울은 진정한 그리스도의 사도이다. "하나님의 뜻으로 말미암아 그리스도의 사도 된 바울" 이라는 바울의 사도직의 양식 어귀가 이런 일치된 의미를 함축하고 있다.

2. 1장에서 9장의 바울의 겸비와 권위

위에서 살펴본 바울의 사도직의 양면성이 고린도후서 전체에서 고르게 나타나고 있다. 바울은 그의 사도직을 10장 1절에서 언급하는 그의 사도적 담대함(θαρρῶ)을 겸비함(ταπεινός)과 대조적으로 융합하여 온전한 권위로 승화시키고 있다. 이런 현상을 도덕적 중용의 자세나 원만한 인간관계를 위한 처세술, 또는 목회적 감수성으로 설명할 수도 있으나,[228] 우리는 궁극적으로 바울의 신학의 중심인 그리스도의 죽음과 부활 신앙에서 기인한다고 본다. 이런 사실은 고린도후서에 나타난 대부분의 바울의 사도직 변명이 대체적으로 그리스도의 죽음과 부활과 관련하여 설명하고 있기 때문이다. 예수 그리스도의 죽음과 부활의 양면적 유형이 고

---

228) H. Chadwick, 275; Beker, 61.

린도후서에서 바울의 인격과 사역에 역설적 특성으로 대조되고 조화되어 나타나고 있는 것이다. 우리는 고린도후서를 한번 대강 읽어 가면서 이런 사실을 확인해 볼 것이다. 이런 목적을 위해서 읽어 갈 때 나타나는 각 구절의 주석적인 문제들은 뒤에 나오는 해당되는 주석을 참고하기를 바란다.

고린도후서는 초두부터 사도직의 고난과 위로(승리)를 그리스도의 고난과 승리와 연계하여 설명한다. "그리스도의 고난이 우리에게 넘친 것 같이 우리의 위로도 그리스도로 말미암아 넘치는 도다"(1:5). 바울은 "그리스도의 사도"로서 그리스도와 연합하여 사역하므로 그리스도의 고난과 승리의 사역을 그대로 수행하는 것이라는 의미가 있다. 1장 3절부터 11절까지 바울은 자신의 사역의 고통, 특별히 "아시아에서 당한 환난"을 언급하면서 죽음의 경지에서도 "죽은 자를 다시 살리시는 하나님"(9)을 의지하여 다시 살아나게 된 경위를 설명하면서 하나님께 감사한다.

1장 12절에서 2:3절까지는 바울 사도의 권위에 해당되는 말이다. 바울 사도는 그의 내적 진실성에 대한 확신을 가지고 그가 고린도 교회 방문계획을 취소하게 된 경위를 설명한다. 바울은 하나님의 거룩함과 진실함으로서 양심을 따라서 사역한다(1:12). 그러므로 방문 취소의 이유는 바울 자신의 유익을 고려한 것이 아니라 고린도 교인들을 "아끼려 함이라"고 한다(1:23). 즉 고린도 교회 형편이 방문에 적합하지 못하였기 때문이며 결코 자신의 유익을 고려하여 변덕을 부린 것이 아니라고 한다. 그러면서 "우리가 너희 믿음을 주관하려는 것이 아니요 오직 너희 기쁨을 돕는 자가 되려함이니 이는 너희가 믿음에 섰음이라"(1:24)고 한다. 바울의 사도적 권위는 고린도 교인들의 믿음을 직접 세워주는 것이 아니라 스스로 세우도록 조력하는 것이라고 한다. 바울의 사도직은 상대방에게 유익을 주고 상대방 스스로 믿음을 갖도록 도와주는 것이지 강제로 행사하는 것이 아님을 명백히 보여 준다. 이렇게 남을 세워주고 유익하게 하는 도덕성도 바울 자신의 것이 아니라 결국 그리스도의 희생적 죽으심을 본받는 데서 기인한다(5:14).

2장 4절부터 11절까지 사도의 겸비의 주제가 나타난다. 그는 지난번에 보낸 "눈물로 쓴 편지" 의 동기에 대해서 언급하면서 그 편지를 쓰게 된 동기가 사도의 권위를 나타내기 위한 것이 아니라 오히려 사도의 사랑을 나타내기 위한 것이라고 한다. 문제된 사람을 징계하는 일로 모두 함께 고통을 당하였으나 이제는 그를 용서함으로써 사랑을 증거해야 할 때라고 하면서 징계를 해제할 것을 권한다. 그러나 이 사건에 대한 바울의 편지는 그 동기가 사랑이라고 해도 사도의 권위 행사였음이 분명하다. 다만 지금은 바울이 그 징계를 해제하도록 권하는 자세는 사랑이나 겸비에 해당한다. 이런 예는 바울의 사도직 이해의 이중적인 면을 극명하게 나타내는 예이다.[229]

2장 12절에서 끝까지 에서는 겸비와 권위의 주제가 함께 나타난다. 바울은 드로아에서 디도를 만나지 못하고 근심하면서 마게도냐로 갔다고 한다.[230] 그러나 그 근심이 결국 기쁨으로 되게 하신 하나님께 감사하면서 자신의 사역을 언제나 성공적인 것으로 인도하심을 감사한다. 그의 사역의 성공은 그의 반대자들의 실패

---

229) Martin, 2 Corinthians, 40.

230) 이때 마게도냐로 간 것은 행전 20:1의 기사와 일치한다고 본다. 대개 주후 55년 말로 본다. C. K. Barrett, "Titus," in *Essays on Paul* (London: SPCK, 1982), 123; J. A. T. Robinson, *Redating the New Testament* (London: SCM Press, 1976), 50, 55.

와 대조된다. 그의 고난의 사역의 결과는 항상 선하게 나타나서 그가 그리스도의 진정한 사도임을 증명한다.

3장에서 바울은 사도의 권위에 집중한다. 그의 사도직은 하나님께로부터 받은 것이며(3:5) 영원한 영광의 직분이다(3:8). 그를 반대하는 거짓 사도들의 직분은 일시적 영광의 직분일 뿐이다. 바울의 반대자들의 사도직을 모세의 얼굴의 일시적 영광에 비추어 언급함으로써 그들이 유대교 율법주의나 할례당으로 추정된다.[231] 바울은 이들에 대해서 그의 사도적 직분이 영적인 것이며 주의 영광을 나타내는 것이라고 하면서 그의 사도직의 권위의 우월성을 증거한다.

4장에서는 바울의 겸비, 즉 그의 사역의 점철된 고난에 집중한다. 그러나 여기서도 복음의 역설이 적용된다. 즉 과거 다메섹에서 나타난 영광의 주님으로부터 부름 받은 복음 전파 사명과 장래의 부활의 승리의 소망을 함께 간직하고 있다.[232] 즉 사도의 현재적 고난은 장래의 영광과 위로에 대한 소망과 믿음으로 극복될 수 있다(13-15). "우리의 잠시 받는 환난의 경한 것이 지극히 크고 영원한 영광의 중한 것을 우리에게 이루게 함이니 우리의 돌아보는 것은 보이는 것이 아니요 보이지 않는 것이니 보이는 것은 잠간이요 보이지 않는 것은 영원함이니라"(17). 이런 바울의 고난과 영광이 점철된 역설적 사역이야 말로 그의 사역이 그리스도의 죽음과

231) 3:7-18을 출 34:29-35의 미드라쉬(Midrash=랍비식 성경해석)로 보는 견해에 대하여 다음을 보라, J. Göttsberger, "Die Hülle des Moses nach Ex 34 und Kor 3." *BZ* 16 (1922) 1-17; H. Windisch, 112; S. Schulz, "Die Decke des Moses. Unterschungen zu einer vorpaulinischen überlieferung in II Cor 3:7-18," *ZNW* 48 (1958) 11; Georgi, 282.

232) Seyoon Kim, 67.

부활의 사역을 따른 합법적인 증거이다. 이런 고난과 영광의 대조적 증거는 단순한 예증이 아니라 진정한 사도직의 필수적인 요소이다. 고난은 사도직의 비정상적인 요소가 아니라 정상적인 요소이며, 일시적이고 부분적인 것이 아니라 전체 사역에서 나타나는 현상이다(8절의 ἐν παντί, "사방으로"]는 "모든 일에"라고 번역될 수 있다). 바울은 이미 그가 전하는 복음의 메시지를 십자가의 약함을 통해 나타나는 하나님의 능력이라고 규정하였다(고전 1:18). 그의 사역 또한 그의 복음의 내용과 일치하는 것은 당연하다. 바울의 사역의 고난 또는 반대자들이 제기하는 바울의 약점들은 오히려 그리스도의 고난의 사역에 해당하는 것으로써 바울의 사역의 정당성을 변증하고 있다.[233] 7절에서 질그릇으로 표현되는 그의 약함과 8절 이하의 그의 온갖 고난은 스토익 철학이 가르치는 것같이 인간 자신의 힘으로 극복되는 것이 아니라 예수를 죽은 자 가운데서 살리신 하나님의 능력으로 극복되는 것이다(7-14).[234] 더구나 그 고난의 사역은 현재에서도 부분적으로 나타나지만 장차 온전하게 나타날 영광의 예비적인 것이다. 그러므로 바울의 고난의 사도직은 하나님이 함께하시는 사역이며, 또 장차 영광으로 보상하실 정당한 사역이다. 이런 설명의 근저에는 바울 자신이 그리스도와 존재론적으로 일치되었다는 의식이 있다. 바울의 고난과 죽음이 곧 예수의 고난과 죽음이며, 그의 생명 또한 예수의 것이라는 확신이다(11-14). 그러므로 크래프트칙(S. J. Kraftchick)은 여기서 "예수의 생명이 바울의 존재 안으로 침투했

233) Victor Furnish, *II Corinthians* (New York: Doubleday & Co., 1984), 33.

234) Kraftchick, 630.

다. 그것은 고난을 극복함으로써 이루어진 것이 아니라 재해석함으로써 이루어진 것이었다."라고 말한다.[235] 그러나 "재해석"이란 말이 단순히 개념적인 작업을 가리킨다면 적절치 않다. 바울에게 있어서 그리스도와의 일치는 단순한 해석이 아니라 존재론적 확신 또는 신앙인 것이다. 바울이 흔히 사용하는 "ἐν Χριστῷ"("그리스도 안에서")라는 말은 이런 의미를 뒷받침한다. 이 말은 존재론적 일치를 나타내는데, 그렇다고 바울 자신이 곧 그리스도라는 개념이 아니라, 바울이 그리스도의 주권, 왕권, 능력에 의해 전적으로 지배받는 상태를 가리킨다. 바울은 질그릇으로서 복음과 구별되듯이 그리스도와도 구별된다. 바울은 그리스도의 종이 된 것이다. 그리고 그의 고난과 부활의 능력에 참예하는 것이다(고후 1:7; 4:7-15).

5장은 다시 바울의 권위와 겸비가 교차적으로 나타난다. 바울은 현재의 고난 후에 오는 장래 승리의 소망을 확인한다. 그리고 바울은 그의 사도직의 내적 진정성을 반대자들의 사도직의 외적인 요소들과 대조한다. 특히 5장 11절에서 15절까지에서 바울은 모든 사람들을 위해 죽었다가 다시 사신 그리스도의 본을 따라 그 자신도 다른 이들의 유익을 위해서 희생하면서 산다고 한다. 즉 사도직의 겸비를 나타낸다. 그리고 이 겸비는 미래적 승리를 예견케 한다. 뿐만 아니라 바울은 그리스도의 승리로 인해 이미 현재에서도 그리스도인은 새로운 존재로서 살아간다는 것을 힘써 말한다(5:16-17). "누구든지 그리스도안에 있으면 새로운 피조물이라. 옛것은 지나가고 보라 새 것이 되었도다." 여기서 바울은 그리

235) Kraftchick, 632.

스도인의 존재론적 인식과 우주론적 인식 또는 세계관을 그리스도의 죽음과 부활의 패러다임을 통해서 인식하고 있다.[236] 5장 14, 15절에서 그리스도의 죽음과 부활을 언급하였으므로 17절의 ἐν Χριστῳ("그리스도 안")는 그리스도의 죽음과 부활로 창조된 새로운 존재와 세계를 가리킨다고 봐야한다.[237] ἵνα와 ὥστε로 시작되는 15, 16, 17, 21은 그리스도의 죽음과 부활의 결과를 나타내며, 그 결과 형성된 17절의 새로운 피조물은 18, 19절에서 화해의 사역을 한다. 이렇게 바울은 이 부분에서 가장 분명하게 그리스도의 죽음과 부활의 패러다임을 그의 사도직의 합당성의 판단기준으로 제시하고 있다. 반대로 바울의 반대자들은 "육체를 따라서" 사도직을 판단하므로 그들의 사도직은 그릇된 것임을 암시하고 있다(5:16, 10:7; 11:18).

계속해서 5장 18절부터 21절까지 자신의 사도직을 하나님의 화해의 사신으로 설명하면서 6장에서는 겸비와 영광이 교차되는 자신의 사도직 사역이 그리스도의 사역과 일치됨을 묘사한다(6:1, 2). 그러면서 계속해서 화해의 주제를 가지고 고린도 교인들이 참된 그리스도의 사도로서 사역하는 자신의 사역에 동참할 것을 권면한다. 그러나 바울은 진정한 화해를 위한 선결 조건이 충족되어야 함을 지적한다. 즉 불신자들, 즉 바울의 반대자들과의 관계 단절이다(6:14-7:1). 이런 강력한 권면은 바울의 사도직의 권위를 나타내는 것으로 본다.

---

236) Kraftchick, 626-628. 아래 주 65를 보라.

237) 17절의 evn Cristw/의 여러 해석을 Margaret E. Thrall, *A Critical Commentary on the Second Epistle to the Corinthians*, vol. I (Edinburgh: T&T Clark, 1994), 424-426. 지배적인 뜻은 "믿는 자와 그리스도와의 일치" 이다.

7장 5절에서 바울은 2장에서 언급한 디도와의 반가운 상봉을 통해서 고린도 교인들의 회개의 소식을 듣고 기뻐한다. 고린도 교인들이 바울의 적들에 맞서서 바울이 보낸 디도에게 순종하였고 그의 지시를 따른 것이다(7:11-15). 고린도 교회에서의 바울의 사도권의 재확립을 확인하는 기쁨이다. 오랜 고난 후에 오는 위로를 하나님의 선물로 받게 된 것이다. 여기서 1장에서의 고난 후의 위로와 승리의 주제가 다시 나타난다. 이런 부분은 사도의 겸비를 나타내지만 또한 승리의 주제가 있으므로 권위를 나타낸다고도 볼 수 있다. 이런 중복된 부분들이 다른 데도 있다(4:7-12; 6:3-10; 11:23-30; 12:10, 등). 그것은 "약함이 곧 강함" 이라는 십자가의 역설적 성격 때문이다.

8장과 9장에서 바울은 고린도 교인들의 회개와 충성심 회복을 확인한 후에 자신이 세운 여러 교회에서 실시하고 있는 가난한 예루살렘 교인들을 위한 헌금에 계속 동참하여 다음 방문 시 까지 그 일을 마무리 지을 것을 권한다. 그러므로 이 부분은 사도의 권위에 관한 부분이다. 그러나 여기서도 바울은 결코 강요하지 않으려고 조심하면서 그들 스스로 헌금에 즐겁게 동참하도록 권면한다. "할 마음만 있으면 있는 대로 받으실 터이요 없는 것을 받지 아니하시리라" (8:12). "각각 그 마음에 정한 대로 할 것이며 인색함으로나 억지로 하지 말지니 하나님은 즐겨 내는 자를 사랑하시느니라" (9:7). 여기서도 바울은 헌금의 근본정신을 결국 그리스도의 구원 은혜에서 찾는다. 그리스도는 우리를 부요하게 하기위해서 가난하게 되셨으므로 우리가 그의 구속의 은혜에 보답하는 것이 당연하다고 가르친다(8:10). 그리스도의 구원의 은혜를 "부요" 와 "가난" 이라는 재정적인 말로 대조적으로 표현하고 있다. 또 바울은 헌금을 "자신을 주께 드리는 것"이라고 말하기도하고 (8:5), 또는 사람들을 섬기는 봉사의 직무로 표현하기도 한다(9:12, 13). 이런 표현들도 결국 기독론적 의미와 연결된다.[238] 8장, 9장의 이런 내용은 바울의 권위를 나타낸다. 그러나 온유와 겸비한 자세로 독자들을 설득하고 있다.

이와 같이 바울은 디도를 만나서 고린도 교회의 안정된 소식을 듣고 그동안 고린도 교회에 대한 염려를 다 잊고 위로와 기쁨이 충만하여 9장까지를 썼다. 그러나 우리가 본대로 바울은 간간히 그의 약함과 고난의 사도직 수행을 대조시켜 쓰고 있다. 이런 바울의 사역의 대조는 그리스도의 죽음과 부활의 대조에 근거하여 그 신학적, 목회학적 의미를 나타내고 있다. 또한 이와 같은 대조의 일치된 병행은 "그리스도의 사도"라는 바울의 사도직의 정당성을 가리키고 있다.

3. 10장에서 13장의 바울의 강함과 약함

10장 초두에서 바울은 지금까지의 온건한 어조를 바꾸어서 강경한 어조로 말하기 시작한다. 10장부터 13장은 앞의 1장부터 9장까지의 내용에 비해서 주로 엄격한 권면의 말들이 지배적이다. 사도의 권위를 나타내는 말들이 지배적이다. 그러나 이 부분에서도 바울은 권위와 겸비를 더욱 분명히 대조하고 있다. 10장 첫 절에서 바울은 "너희를 대하여 대면하면 겸비하고 떠나 있으면 담대한 나 바울은 이제 그리스도의 온유함과 관용으로 친히 너희를

---

238) Kraftchick, 635.

권하고…"라고 겸비와 관용을 처음부터 분명히 언급한다. 또한 이 부분에서 바울은 그의 육체적 약함을 그리스도의 약함에 따라 이해하며 약할 때 곧 강하게 되는 구원 진리를 계시로 받으면서 기뻐한다(12:9-10).

앞서 지적했듯이 10장부터 13장을 후대의 편집의 결과로 보는 견해가 많다.[239] 즉 바울의 엄격한 편지가 이곳에 첨부되어 편집되었다는 설명이다. 그러나 어떤 문서적 증거도 없다. 더구나 누가 감히 사도 바울의 편지를 함부로 편집할 권한을 "편집자"에게 주었단 말인가?[240] 그는 그의 편지에 "친필"로 써서 그의 편지의 진정성을 보전하였던 분이다(살후 3:17).

우리는 앞서 지적한 바와 같이 이런 어조의 변화는 1장부터 9장까지의 내용이 주로 온건한 내용임으로 마지막 부분에서 바울이 보다 엄격한 내용으로 그를 반대하는 자들에게 경계해야할 필요를 느끼고 쓰기시작 했기 때문이라고 본다. 물론 우리가 본 바와 같이 바울 특유의 강, 온의 조화는 1장부터 9장에도 나타나있다. 그러나 바울은 편지를 끝내기 전에 지금까지 쓴 내용을 다시 검토한 결과 너무 온건하고 약한 내용으로써 아직도 숨어있을 반대자들에 대한 경계가 약할 뿐만 아니라, 자신을 지지하는 사람들에게도, 사도로서의 권위가 없는 유약한 사도로 인식될 것으로 생각하여 보다 엄격한 내용을 쓴 것이라고 본다(10:4, 7. 10; 11:2; 12:12, 13:3, 5, 10). 다시 말하면 채드위크(Chadwick)가 말하는 바울 사도의 목회자로서의 놀라운 유연성과 융통성의 균형감각을 찾은 것

239) 고린도후서의 통일성에 대한 복잡한 논쟁을 잘 정리한 두 개의 주석책을 들 수 있다. R. P. Martin, *2 Corinthians*, xl-xliii; Thrall, 3-49.

240) Tasker, 28.

이었다고 볼 수 있다.[241] 실제로 바울은 그가 10장부터 강경한 자세로 말하는 것은 다음 고린도 교회 방문 시에 피차 편하게 만나기 위해서는 아예 편지로 마음에 남아 있는 할 말을 다해 버리는 것이 좋겠다는 뜻에서라고 한다(10:2). 대다수 고린도 교회 교인들이 바울에게로 돌아 왔으나(7:7, 15), 아직도 바울에 대한 비난과 오해의 앙금이 완전히 가시지 않았을 것으로 보고 다시 지난 번 방문 때와 같은 수모를 겪지 않기 위해서는 이런 문제들을 완전히 짚고 넘어 가야 한다고 보았다(10:2-6). 바울은 12장과 13장에서 이와 같은 이유를 반복하고 있다(12:20, 21; 13:2, 10). 이 문제들은 결국 바울의 사도직의 진정성에 대한 문제들이다. 즉 바울의 보잘 것 없는 외양과 언변의 부족, 복음의 정통성문제, "기사와 능력"의 부족함, 그리고 자비량 선교방식과 재정문제이다. 이 중에서도 바울이 주로 다루는 문제는 바울이 고린도 교회로부터 재정지원을 고사하고 자비량 선교를 하는 데 대한 문제(11:7-12)와 예루살렘 헌금과 관련하여 재정 관리에 대한 의문점이다(12:13-18). 8장과 9장에서 예루살렘 성도들을 위한 헌금을 독려하고 난 뒤에 다른 문제들과 함께 특히 자신의 재정문제에 대한 고린도 교인들의 의구심을 차제에 말소시켜야겠다고 결심한 듯하다.[242] 이렇게 10장은 8장, 9장의 헌금독려에 이어 바울의 재정 관리 문제에 대한

241) H. Chadwick, 275.

242) 학자들 가운데 오히려 돈의 주제가 8장 9장과 10장과의 연계에 장애가 된다고 본다. 당장 10장에 돈 문제가 언급되지 않았다고 이렇게 보는 것은 잘못이다. 11장과 12장에 돈 문제가 논의되고 있다. 헌금 독려 후에 직접 자신의 돈 관련 비리 소문에 대해서 언급하기를 피했을 것이다. A. Plummer, *A Critical and Exegetical Commentary on the Second Epistle of the St. Paul to the Corinthians*, ICC 47 (Edinburgh: T. & T. Clark, 1915), 269; J. Héring, 69.

의구심 해소를 중심으로 다른 문제들도 다루고 있다고 보면 어조상의 강, 온의 대조적 연결뿐만이 아니라 내용의 연결에도 문제가 없다. 이렇게 보면 고린도후서 전체가 하나의 통일된 편지로 보는데 어려움이 없는 것이다.

그러나 바울의 목회적 유연성을 10장이후의 강경한 어조의 변화의 직접적인 동기로 본다 해도 보다 근본적인 신학적 동기는 역시 예수의 죽음과 부활이라고 보아야한다. 10장 이후 바울의 사도직 변명의 논지는 "그리스도의 약함과 강함"의 대조로 이루어지기 때문이다. 더구나 이 대조의 근거가 예수의 죽음과 부활임을 13장 4절에서 분명히 밝히고 있다.

위에서 지적한 바와 같이 10장에서 마지막 13장까지에서 바울은 주로 강경한 어조로 "육체적 자랑"을 하는 그의 대적자들과 맞서서 자신의 육체적 자랑, 즉 강함을 열거하다가 끝에서는 자세를 바꾸어 자신은 차라리 자신의 약함을 자랑하겠다고 한다(11:18; 11:30). 왜냐하면 그의 약함이 바로 그리스도의 약함을 가리키며, 또한 바로 그 약함이 그리스도의 강함으로 변화되게 하는 전 단계이기 때문이라고 한다(12:9). 이런 약함이 그의 대적자들의 자랑거리에는 들어 있지 않음으로 자신이야말로 진정한 그리스도의 사도임을 나타낸다. 결국 약함을 통해 강해지는 것은 그리스도의 죽음과 부활의 진리이며, 바울의 사역은 이 유형을 따라 이루어지는 것이다.[243] 더구나 그리스도의 사역과 자신의 사역의 일치는 자신의 경험에 입각한 주장이 아니라 하나님의 계시로 인한 객관적인

243) Jerry L. Sumney, "Paul's 'Weakness'," 71-91:," 약함"과 "강함"으로 대변되는 바울의 사도직 변명이 고린도후서 이전(51 B.C.) 데살로니가 집필 당시(41 B.C.)부터 바울의 사도직의 중심 사상이라는 주장을 보라. 참조, 살전 1:6-7; 2:15.

진리인 것이다. "(주께서) 내게 이르시기를 내 은혜가 네게 족하도다. 이는 내 능력이 약한 데서 온전하여짐이라 하신지라" (11:9a).[244)]

10장에서 바울은 고린도 교회 반대자들이 바울이 사도로서 외양이 약하고 언변이 부족하다는 비평에 대해서 사도의 평가는 외모에 있지 않고 그가 실재적으로 그리스도에 속하였는가를 검증해야 한다고 지적한다(10:7; 참조, 5:16-17). 그리고 자신의 언변의 부족함을 시인하나 지식은 부족하지 않다고 한다(10:10; 11:6). 여기서 "말"(λόγος)은 피상적일 수 있으나 "지식"(γνώσις)은 보다 본질적인 개념을 의미한다. 바울은 그리스도를 아는 지식에 관한 한 분명히 바른 지식을 가지고 있다(6:6; 11:4, 10; 13:8; 빌 3:8).

10장 13절부터 16절에서 바울은 새로운 사도의 진정성의 증거를 제시한다. 그것은 사도는 정해진 자신의 목회나 선교 영역 한계 안에서 일하여야 한다는 것이다. 이것은 바울의 일방적 선언이 아니라 예루살렘 사도 회의에서 결정된 것이다(갈 2:9). 바울은 이를 지켰으나, 그의 대적자들은 이를 지키지 않고 바울의 영역, 즉 고린도 교회에 들어와서 바울의 영역을 침범한 것이다. 고린도전서 9장 2절에서 바울은 그가 고린도 교회의 사도임을 분명히 말한다. 던(J. Dunn)은 예루살렘 측 사도들이 바울의 교회들을 그들의

---

244) 이 말씀은 바울의 "몸의 가시"에 대한 치료의 기도에 대한 하나님의 응답이다. 그러나 이 말씀이 바울의 약함을 통한 강함이라는 사도직 변명논리의 문맥에서 언급되고 있으므로 바울이 그의 사역에 대한 하나님의 지지(支持)로써 제시하고 있다고 본다.

영향권으로 끌어 들이려는 시도에 대해서 바울이 반감을 가졌다고 한다.[245] 10장에서 바울이 그의 선교 영역을 침범한 이들을 책망한 이후에 계속해서 자기 영역에 들어와서 자기와 고린도 교인들 사이를 이간하는 이들의 배후세력을 11장 5절에서 예루살렘 사도들과 연계시켜 말하는 것으로 보기 때문이다(참조, 갈 2:9).[246] "내가 지극히 큰 사도들보다 부족한 것이 조금도 없는 줄 생각하노라." 바울은 이방의 사도로 부르심을 받았으나 자신에게 할당 된 지역의 한계를 따라 선교하는 것이 일종의 선교 윤리로 보았다(갈 2:9). 이를 어기는 것은 불의한 것이다(10:16-18). 바울은 로마서에서 로마 교인들에게 "내가 그리스도의 이름을 부르는 곳에는 복음을 전하지 않기를 힘썼노니 이는 남의 터 위에 건축하지 아니하려 함이라"(15:20)라고 말하면서 서바나(스페인)로 그들의 지원을 받아 가기를 희망하고 있다.

거짓 사도들은 남의 한계를 침범했을 뿐 아니라 이단적 복음을 가리키고 있고 고린도 교인들은 이를 분별없이 받아들였다(11:4). 뿐만 아니라 이들은 바울이 교회로부터 재정적 보조를 받지 않는다는 것을 자랑하면서도, 뒤로는 돈을 챙긴다고 비난하였던 것 같

245) Dunn, 578.

246) 고린도후서 10장 11장에서 거론하는 고린도 교회에서의 바울의 반대자들의 정체는 갈라디아 교회의 유대주의자들의 정체와 흡사하다. 이들에 대한 바울의 묘사가 흡사하다. 갈 2:4과 고후 11:2을 비교해보라. 또한 이들 모두가 유대인들인 것이 확실하다(갈 2:14; 고후 11:22). 다만 고린도전서에서 거론하는 영적 은사 문제와 고린도후서 11:4의 "다른 영" 에 대한 언급에 근거해서 영지주의적 요소가 있는 것으로 보는 견해가 있다. Walter Schmithals, *Gnosticism in Corinth: An Introduction of the Letters to the Corinthians.*

247) Roetzel, 55.

다(11:11; 12:16; 17-18).[247] 바울은 "복음을 값없이" 전함으로 교회에 재정적 부담을 주지 않는다는 선교원칙을 고수하였으나, 다른 사도들은 바울이 교회 재정적 지원을 통한 교회와의 우호적 관계를 무시하고 독선적인 사역을 한다고 비난하였던 것 같다. 학(Ronald F. Hock)은 1세기 헬레니즘 사회에서 철학자들이 자신의 사상을 따르는 후원자의 집에서 거하는 사회적 관습을 따라 고린도 교회의 바울의 적들도 고린도 교회의 어떤 부자의 가정에 들어가 살면서 교회의 재정지원을 받았을 것이라고 추정한다.[248] 이들은 바울이 천막을 만들면서 자비량 선교를 하는 것을 고린도 교인들에게 뿐만 아니라 다른 사도들에게도 비우호적인 자세로 보았다고 한다(참조, 행 18:3). 즉 고린도 교인들에게 바울은 돈을 받지 않고 순전한 봉사의 정신으로 일하는 것으로 비춰져서 존경을 받는 반면에, 다른 사도들은 돈을 받고 일함으로써 이를 탐하는 삯군 목자들로 비난 받게 한다고 바울을 비판하였다는 것이다. 고린도전서 9장에서 바울은 이런 비난을 받고 재정적 지원을 받는 것은 성경적이며 주님의 명령을 따르는 당연한 것임을 인정하면서도, 자신은 복음을 값없이 전하는 선교 방법을 계속 지키겠다고 천명한다(고전 9:18; 고후 11:7). 그렇게 하는 이유는 고린도 교인들에게 재정적인 폐를 끼치지 않기 위함이라고도 한다(고후 11:9). 바울은 12장 14, 15절에서도 같은 주제를 다시 논하면서 자신은

---

248) Hock, 62-4; 유사하게 바울의 사역을 1세기 헬레니즘 철학자들이나, 유대교 전통에 따라 보는 연구들도 있다. Jerry L. Sumney, 71-91; Gerd Theissen, *The Social Setting of Pauline Christianity: Essays on Corinth*, ETr. and ed. J. H. Schütz (Philadelphia: Fortress Press, 1982), 39; A. J. Malherbe, *Paul and the Popular Philosophers* (Minneapolis: Fortress Press, 1989), 37.

부모로서 사랑하는 자식 같은 교인들에게 재물을 쓸지언정 얻지는 않을 것이라고 재확인 한다.

그러나 한편 반대자들은 바울이 재정 지원을 받지 않는 것은 자신이 사도로서 무엇인가 부족하다고 느끼기 때문에 스스로 받지 않는 것이라고 비웃었다고 보는 견해도 있다. 이에 대해서 바울은 자신은 재정지원을 받는 다른 사도들보다 조금도 부족한 것이 아니라고 반박하면서 순수하게 남에게 폐를 끼치지 않으려는 이유에서 자비량 선교를 한다고 말한다는 것이다(11:5-10). 바울이 스스로 사도로서 부족함을 느껴서 사례를 받지 않았다는 주장은 타당성이 없다. 바울 자신이 언제나 자신의 사도직에 대해서 확고하게 말하기 때문이다.

마틴이 추정하는 바울의 사역의 역사적 배경에 의해서 보면 안디옥 교회로부터의 선교지원 단절 이후에 바울은 자신의 복음 사역이 율법적 복음을 지지하는 세력이나 고린도 교회 같이 문제가 많은 교회로부터 재정적으로 자유로워지지 않으면 언제고 다시 어려움을 겪을 것이라고 보고 이런 교회로부터의 재정 지원을 받는 것을 사양했다고 볼 수도 있다.[249)]

이외의 바울이 교회의 재정적 지원을 받지 않는 다음과 같은 이유들을 제시 할 수 있다.

첫째로, 바울은 자비량 선교가 그리스도의 희생을 전하는 복음전도의 본질에 부합하는 효과적인 복음전도 전략으로 알고 있었다. 고린도후서 11장 7절에서 바울은 "내가 너희를 높이려고 나를 낮추어 하나님의 복음을 값없이 너희에게 전함으로 죄를 지었느

---

249) Martin, 서론, liii-lvi.

냐?"고 질문한다. 고린도전서 9장 18절에서도 바울은 "값없이 복음을 전한다"는 같은 소신을 나타내고 있는데, 거기서 바울은 자신의 선교전략은 되도록 많은 사람에게 복음을 전하기 위하여 유대인에게는 유대인으로, 이방인, 즉 율법 없는 사람에게는 율법 없는 사람으로, 약한 자들에게는 약한 자로 되어 그들을 얻고자 함이라고 한다. 고린도후서 11장 7절에서는 바울은 재정적 지원을 받지 않고 스스로 천막을 만들어 자비량 선교를 하는 이유를 "자신을 낮추는 일"로 보는 듯하고, 고린도전서 9장 22a절의 "약한 자들에게는 내가 약한 자가 된 것은 약한 자들을 얻고자 함이요"라는 말도 천막을 만드는 어려운 일을 하면서 가난한 사람들의 동료가 되었음을 나타내는 듯하다. 학(Hock)도 고린도후서 11장 7절을 이와 같이 해석하면서 바울이 천막을 만드는 일은 매우 어려운 일로서 고린도 교인들 대다수에게는 존경을 받으며, 가난한 자들에게는 자신을 겸손히 낮추는 것으로 비춰었을 것이라고 한다.[250] 그렇다면 바울의 천막 만드는 일을 한 것은 자신의 경제적

250) Martin, 64. Hock은 고후 11:9에서 바울이 마게도냐의 교인들에게 지원을 받았다는 사실도 바울이 얼마나 궁핍했는가를 반증하고 있다고 한다. 즉 천막 만드는 수입이 충분하지 못했다는 것이다. 대다수의 학자들이 천막 만드는 일이 바울의 겸손의 삶을 나타낸다는 데 동의 한다. Plummer, *Second Epistle to the Corinthians*, 302; H. Windisch, *Der zweite Korintherbrief*, MeyerK 6 (Göttingen: Vandenhoeck & Ruprecht, 1924), 334; P. E. Hughes, *Paul's Second Epistle to the Corinthians*, 384. 그러나 당시 장사하는 이들과 수공업자들이 그 기술력에 따라서는 상당한 사회적 지위를 가졌다는 주장도 있다. T. B. Savage, *Power through Weakness: Paul's Understanding of the Christian Ministry in 2 Corinthians*, SNTSMS 86 (Cambridge: University Press, 1996), 84-6. 그러나 이들을 위해 일하는 노예나 하청업자들의 비천함을 무시할 수는 없을 것이다. 더구나 바울 같이 떠돌아다니면서 자신의 생활을 위해 천막을 만드는 것은 비천한 것으로 여겼을 것이다.

수단은 물론 자신을 의도적으로 겸손히 낮추어 가난한 자들의 친구가 되어 그들에게 복음을 믿게 하기 위한 복음전도 전략과 같은 것이었다고 볼 수 있다.

둘째로, 바울의 자비량 선교는 단순히 예수님의 12제자 파송 연설에서 제자들에게 명한 말씀, 즉 "너희가 거저 받았으니 거저 주어라" (마 10:8b)를 그대로 따르는 것이다. 예수님은 파송연설에서 제자들에게 전도인으로서 온전히 하나님께 의지하는 청빈한 자세를 강조하면서 최소한의 필요한 물질만을 소유하도록 하였다(마 10:9이하; 눅 10:4, 7). 바울은 회심 초기에 이런 제자도를 예루살렘 제자들로부터 배웠을 것이다(행 9:26이하).

셋째로, 유사하게, 바울이 천막을 기워 자비량 선교를 한 것은 그리스도의 겸비함과 가난함을 본받아 자신을 낮추려는 의도도 있었다고 볼 수 있다. 어쩌면 바울은 머리 둘 곳도 없이 고생하신 예수의 전승을 알고 따랐을 수도 있다(마 8:20; 눅 9:58).[251] 위에서 지적하듯이 바울은 예수님의 말씀을 따라서 복음을 값없이 전한다고 볼 수 있고, 또 실제로 고린도전서 9장 14절에서 바울은 복음 전승에서 온 주의 말씀을 상기하면서 주의 일꾼들이 재정적 지원을 받는 근거를 찾고 있다. "이와 같이 주께서도 복음 전하는 자들이 복음으로 말미암아 살리라 명하셨느니라" (참조, 눅 10:7).[252]

---

251) 바울의 가난한 생활을 예수의 전승과 관련 짓는 것을 반대하고, 1세기 헬레니즘 사회의 철학가들의 생활양식으로 보는 이들도 있다. 주 46보라. Plummer, 303; Barrett, *Second Corinthians,* 282; Windisch, 334-35; Hock, 64.

252) 이 말씀은 70인 전도 파송 연설에 있는 눅 10:7과 유사하다. "그 집에 유하며 주는 것을 먹고 마시라 일꾼이 그 삯을 얻는 것이 마땅하니라." 눅 10:7은 마 10:8b와 상충되는 말로 들리지만 전자는 복음 사역자들의 사역이 영적 사역이니 만큼 세상의 상거래와 같이 주고받는 식의 사업과는 구별하여 하나님의 은혜의 도를 따라서 물

어떤 경우든지 바울의 자비량 선교 사역은 바울이 "그리스도의 사도"로서 그리스도의 겸비함을 실천하는 한 가지 방법이라고 볼 수 있다. 그러나 이런 겸비한 생활이 그를 진정한 사도로 존경받게 하였을 것이며, 이것이 재정 지원을 받는 다른 사도들에게는 오만하고 독선적인 자세로 보여 바울을 비난하였을 것이다. 더구나 바울의 약점을 찾는 반대자들은 바울의 독특한 선교방식을 그들의 공격의 호재로 삼았을 수 있다. 즉 바울이 다른 교회의 지원은 받으면서도 고린도 교회의 지원을 거절하는 것은 성의를 무시한다거나, 관심이 없는 증거라고 비난하였을 것이다.[253)]

바울은 이렇게 자신의 사역이 교회에 재정적 부담을 주지 않는다고 말하는 것도 "육체적 자랑" 임을 시인한다(11:10). 그러나 이런 자랑은 고린도 교인들을 사랑하는 마음을 증명하기 위해서 어쩔 수 없이 한 것임을 이해 해주기를 바란다(11:11; 12:14-15). 나아가 자신을 비난하는 고린도 사도들도 자신을 비난할 것이 아니라 자신처럼 재정적으로 독립하는 것이 좋을 것이라고 권하기까지 한다(11:12). 그러나 바울은 그들이 실제로 그렇게 할 수 없음을

질을 초월하는 사역이 되어야한다는 것을 가리키는 것이고, 후자는 전도인의 기본적 생활비를 허용하는 말로 구별해야 할 것이다. 결국 복음 사역은 값없이 하되, 필요한 생활비를 지원받을 수는 있다는 상호 보완적인 가르침이 된다.

253) 바울의 선교원칙은 직접 선교를 하는 동안은 그 교회의 지원을 받지 않다가 떠난 후에는 지원을 받는 것으로 보인다. 행 20:2-3에서 바울은 석 달 동안 그리스에 머물렀다고 했는데, 아마도 고린도에 머문 것으로 보인다. 또 이때 로마서를 썼을 것이다. 롬 16:23에서 가이오를 "온 교회의 식주인(host)" 이라고 부르며 안부를 전하는 것은 로마서를 고린도에서 쓰면서 로마로 떠날 준비를 하는 동안 바울이 고린도 교회의 식주인 가이오의 보살핌을 받은 것으로 보인다(Windisch, 337; Martin, 352, Thrall, 708).

잘 알고 있다. 그들은 거짓사도들이므로 그리스도의 희생적 사랑의 사역을 따라 사역할 수 없다(11:13-14).

바울은 "이렇게 교회에 폐를 끼치지 않는 자신의 사역에 대한 자랑"이 "어리석은 자"의 부끄러운 자랑임을 거듭 자인한다(11:16-17). 그러나 이런 "어리석은 자의 자랑"을 하지 않을 수 없는 것은 거짓 사도들이 "어리석은 자"의 "육체적 자랑"으로 고린도 교인들을 호도하고 자신을 모욕하였기 때문이라고 한다(1:18-21). 바울은 지금까지 이런 모욕을 (약한 모습으로) 참아왔으나 이제는 (강한 모습으로) 이들을 정면으로 맞대응하는 것이 필요한 때라고 생각했다(11:21). 자신의 수모가 문제가 아니라 위기에 처한 고린도 교회가 그리스도의 교회로 바로 서게 하는 것이 무엇보다 중요한 그의 사도적 사명이라고 느꼈기 때문이다(10:8; 11:2-4; 13:10). 그러므로 바울은 자신도 그들이 자랑하는 바와 못지않은 여러 가지 어리석은 자의 자랑거리들이 있음을 늘어놓기 시작한다(11:22-28).[254] 바울도 그의 대적자들 처럼 유대인이며, 아브라함의 후손이다(11:22). 또 바울도 그리스도의 일꾼으로서 그들보

---

254) Hans Windisch는 푸르타크(Plutarch, 46 BC)가 소피스트들의 지적 자랑을 비판하면서도(De se ipsum, 539 D; 546 B; 547 D70; 540), 때로는 명예를 지키기 위해서 자랑할 필요가 있음을 인정했음을 지적한다(540 C; 541 B: "Using self-glorification to pass from a humbled and piteous state to an attitude of triumph and pride, strikes us not as offensive or bold, but as great and indomitable."). 약점이나 실수를 시인하는 것은 슬기롭고 예의바른 자세로 보았다(544 A). Windisch, 315-98, 특히 345; Hans Dieter Betz, *Der Apostel Paulus und die sokratische Tradition*. 74-89. 이상 Roetzel, 56-57, ns .39, 40에서 재인용함. Roetzel은 자랑에 대한 경고에 대한 예를 유대교(Philo, *Sacr. Abel*, 32)와 시 52:1, 94:3, 잠 27:1, 렘 9:23-24등에서 찾음(57-8).

다 더 많이 수고하고 고통 받았다(11:23-27). 바울은 이런 자랑으로 자신을 비난하는 이들의 자랑을 우선 막아 놓고 자신의 진정한 자랑은 오히려 약함이며, 그 가운데 나타나는 그리스도의 능력임을 말하여 반대자들의 자랑의 어리석음과 자신의 자랑의 진정성을 증명하려는 것이다.

11장 23-27절에서 바울이 열거하는 육체의 자랑은 그의 사역에서 당한 고난과 핍박으로써 그의 자랑도 되나 동시에 그의 약함을 나타내는 것도 될 수 있다. 그러나 28절의 "모든 교회들을 위한 염려"는 자신의 약함을 나타내는 것도 되고 육체적 자랑도 된다: "내가 부득불 자랑할 진대 나의 약한 것을 자랑하리라"(30). 이어서 다메섹성에서 광주리를 타고서 도망해야 했던 자신의 초라했던 과거 경험을 회상하면서 그의 사도직의 겸비한 부분을 나타낸다(32, 33; 행, 9:23-25).

그러나 바울은 곧 다시 자신의 강함, 즉 그가 받은 환상과 계시의 자랑을 한다(12:1-5a). 바울은 다른 계시를 더 말할 수도 있으나, 이런 자신과 그의 간증에 대한 독자의 "지나친 생각"을 염려하여 그만 둔다고 한다(6). 이런 영적 체험은 결국은 육체를 따르는 어리석은 자랑에 불과하다. 바울의 대적자들은 이런 영적 자랑으로 그들의 사도권을 지키지만 바울은 이런 영적 체험이 사도권의 정당성의 적절한 증거가 되지 못한다고 말하는 것이다.[255]

곧 이어 다시 바울은 자신의 약함을 자신이 가진 고질적인 "육

---

255) R. P. Spittler, "The Limits of Ecstasy: An Exegesis of 2 Corinthians 12:1-10," *Current Issues in Biblical and Patristic Interpretation*, ed. G. Hawthorne (Grand Rapids: Eerdmans, 1975), 261.

체의 가시"를 들어 말한다(7).[256] 그리고 바로 이 약함을 계속 지녀야하는 것이 주님의 뜻으로 알게 되었고 또한 이것은 자신의 영적 자고함을 막기 위한 것으로 믿게 되었다. 여기서 바울은 그의 대적자들은 영적으로 교만하다는 것을 암시한다. 또한 여기서 가장 분명히 바울 자신이 사도로서 "강함"과 "약함"을 동시에 가지는 것이 하나님의 뜻이요 은혜임을 알고 있음을 보여주고 있다. 동시에 바울은 이런 생각이 단순히 역설적 균형이라는 일반 경험이나 보편적 논리에 의한 것이 아님을 즉시 그리스도의 약함과 능력과 연결시켜 말함으로 보여준다. 하나님의 능력은 약한 데서 온전하게 되는 것이며, 이 진리는 그리스도의 죽음과 부활에서 가장 분명히 증거 되었다(9, 10). 그러므로 바울은 그리스도의 사도로써 그의 약한 것을 보다 적극적으로 자랑하게 되었다. 결국은 바울이 약한 것을 자랑하는 것은 약함 자체를 좋아하는 병적인 패배주의적 의식을 가졌기 때문이 아니다. 주안에서 그리스도인의 약함은 결국 승리로 이어지기 때문이다. 반대자들의 영적 능력의 자랑은 이런 바울의 하나님의 능력에 호소하는 논리 앞에서 무너질 수밖에 없었을 것이다.

바울은 12장 11절과 12절에서 11장에서 시작된 "어리석의 자의 육체적 자랑"에 대한 결론을 내린다. 즉 바울은 약점들이 있으나 대적자들과 비교해 볼 때 사도의 일반적 조건에 관한 한 그는 결코 다른 사도 보다 못할 것이 없는 사도이다. "사도의 표 된 것은 내가 너희 가운데서 모든 참음과 표적과 기사와 능력을 행한 것이

256) "가시"에 대한 여러 가설들을 찾으라. McCant, "Paul's Thorn of Rejected Apostleship," 550-72.

라" (12). 그리고 이런 일련의 육체적 자랑과 관련하여 자신의 자비량 선교의 정당성과 재물에 대한 자신과 그의 동역자들의 청렴하고 희생적 자세를 다시 한 번 확인한다(13-18). 고린도 교인들에게 폐를 끼치지 않는 사역은 바울의 자랑이다. 그러나 그것은 단순한 육체적 자랑은 아니다. 천한 노동을 하는 것은 그리스도의 겸비함을 본받아 그를 겸비하게 만드는 것이기 때문이다. (아마 앞서 지적했듯이 일부 고린도 교인들은 바울이 복음을 값없이 전하는 숭고한 사역을 한다고 존경하였을 것이며 이것으로 그의 대적자들의 시기와 미움을 일으켰을 것이다).

12장 마지막 부분부터 13장으로 들어와서 10장 이후의 내용 결론적 진술이 시작된다. 바울은 그의 임박한 방문을 언급하며, 고린도 교회의 대적자들과 문제 있는 사람들을 직접 지명하면서 그들의 회개를 촉구하며, 그들을 다시 공격하기 시작한다. 바울이 이들에 대한 책망과 자신의 정당성의 근거는 여전히 그리스도의 약함과 강함의 논리이다. 바울의 사도적 진정성이 대적자들에 의해서 훼손된 것은 그리스도의 약함과 같이 일시적인 것이다. 그 진정성은 그리스도의 강함을 따라서 다시 살 것이라고 한다(13:3, 4). 고린도 교인들 자신들의 구원도 그리스도를 믿는 믿음의 여부에 따라 결정된다(13:5). 그리고 그들은 그리스도를 바로 믿는 믿음으로 바울의 사도적 진정성을 알고 따라야한다(13:6).

13장 7-10절은 결론 부분의 최종적 진술이다. 바울은 지금까지의 강한 어조를 누그러뜨리며 온유한 어조로 말을 맺는다. 바울은 지금까지 자신이 한 모든 말들은 결국 고린도 교인들을 온전히 세우기 위한 것이며 고린도교회를 사랑하는 마음에서 한 것이다. 구체적으로는 다음 방문이 순조롭게 이루어지도록 하기 위해서 직접 만나서는 하기 어려운 말들을 미리 하였다는 내용이다.

이렇게 10장부터 13장에 이르도록 바울은 그 앞에서 보다 더 자주 그의 강함과 약함을 교차적으로 서술하고 있다. 그러나 그 앞의 1장부터 9장에서도 같은 현상이 있음을 보았다. 다음 구절들은 고후 전체에서 바울의 겸비(고난)와 권위(영광과 승리)가 교차된 것을 잘 보여 준다. 괄호속의 구절들은 그리스도의 죽음(고난)과 부활을 직접 언급하는 구절들이다. 1장 3-11절(고난과 승리, 1:5, 9); 1장 12절-2장 3절(권위); 2장 4-11절(겸비); 2장 12-17절(겸비와 권위, 2:14); 3장 1-18절(권위); 4장 1절-5장 10절(겸비와 권위, 4:10, 14); 5장 11-15절(권위와 겸비, 5:14, 15); 5장 16절-6장 2절(권위, 5:20, 21); 6장 3-10절(겸비와 권위); 6장 11절-7장 4절(권위); 7장 5-15절(고난과 승리, 7:10); 8장 1절-9장 15절(권위, 온유한 권면, 감사, 8:5, 9); 10장 1절(겸비와 권위); 10장 2절-11장 22절(권위); 11장 23-33절(겸비); 12장 1-4, 5a절(권위); 12장 5b-10절(권위와 겸비, 12:10); 12장 11절-13장 6절(권위와 겸비, 13:3, 4); 13장 7-10절(겸비). 이상의 구절들은 고린도후서 전체에서 바울이 겸비(고난)나 권위(승리)에 해당되는 말들을 사용하고 있음을 잘 보여준다. 특히 이 두 개념을 교차적으로 쓰이는 곳도 적지 않음을 보았다(4:7-12; 6:3-10; 11:23-30; 12:10 등). 바울은 그의 대적자들을 강경한 어조로 공격하면서도 그것이 다른 일반교인들에게 미칠 수 있는 부작용을 염려하여, 공격 즉시, 그의 약함을 나타내는 온건한 말을 써서 강한 말이 줄 수 있는 오해의 소지를 차단하고 있다. 즉 바울의 목회적 균형 감각에서 이런 수사학적 특징이 나타났다고 볼 수 있다. 그러나 거듭 말하지만 이런 목회적 감각도 바울의 중심적 사고인 그리스도의 죽음과 부활 신앙에 근거하고 있다고 보아야 할 것이다. 위의 구절에서 보듯이 각 구절 사이에서 그리스도의 죽음과 부활이 직접적 간접적으로 언급되고 있음을 볼 수 있다. 또 더 위에서 본 바와 같이 4장, 5장, 12장과 13장에서 하나님의 능력, 그리스도의 죽음과 부활, 또는 강함과 약함, 이란 핵심적 말들이 바울의 약함과 강함이란 말들과 반복적으로 병행되게 기록되어 사도직 합법성 논쟁의 근거로 제시되고 있다. 이것으로 바울이 고린도후서에서 그리스도의 죽음과 부활이라는 역설적 특성에 근거하여 자신이 "하나님의 뜻을 따라 그리스도 예수의 사도 된 것" 임을 입증하고 있다는 것을 알 수 있다.

외견상 바울의 그리스도의 죽음과 부활이 그의 모든 서신의 주제는 아니다. 이 주제는 로마서와 갈라디아서의 주제이다.[257] 만일 다른 바울의 서신들도 이를 중심으로 관련 문제들을 설명하고 있다는 것이 증명 된다면 이것이 바울의 중심 사상임을 확증할 수 있을 것이다. 여기서 Beker의 바울에 대한 진술을 인용할 만하다.

> 초대교회의 다양한 신학적 표현 가운데서 십자가에 죽으시고 다시 사신 그리스도라는 중심점에 집중할 수 있는 그의 능력은, 그 중심점을 그의 생애의 다양함과 특수성과 결합하고 적용하는 능력과 더불어 루터를 제외하고는 어느 사도나 신학자도 달성하지 못한 업적이다.[258]

우리가 고린도후서를 대강 살펴 본 바로는 바울은 기독론적 구

257) Roetzel, 52.

258) Beker, 35 ;참조. 한철하, 「21세기 인류의 살길」 서울:아세아연합신학대하교 출판부, 2003.

원론의 대조적 유형, 죽음과 부활, 겸비와 영광의 주제들을 중심으로 자신의 사역의 정당성을 고린도 교회의 대적자들의 반대에 대응하여 설명하고 있다. 다른 말로 바울은 십자가의 신학(*theologia crucis*)과 영광의 신학(*theologia gloriae*)을 거의 균형있게 조화시키고 있다고 말할 수 있다. 그러나 엄밀히 말하면 고난 쪽으로 기울어진 균형이라고 보아야 옳다. 현재의 위로나 미래의 영광은 과거의 고난의 결과이며, 지금도 고난을 받고 있으며, 종말이 오기까지 계속 받게 될 전망이다(4:10, 17). 고난은 바울의 존재 유형이다. 이것은 갈라디아서에서 바울이 십자가의 신학을 구원과 관련하여 강조하는 것과는 다르다(갈 3:1; 4:19; 5:11; 6:2, 12, 14, 17).[259)]

이런 대조적 기록은 그동안 논쟁이 계속 되어 온 고린도후서의 통일성 문제에 대해서도 새로운 접근 방법을 제시해 주었다. 즉 8장과 9장에서 헌금문제를 다룬 뒤에 바울이 그의 대적자들이 그의 재정문제에 대한 비난을 상기하고서, 지금까지의 온건한 자세를 바꾸어서 10장부터 강경한 자세로 자신의 청렴함을 강변하고 또한 다른 문제들에 대해서도 사도로서의 자신의 정당함을 강변하고 있다. 이런 대조적이고 교차적인 기록을 고린도 교인들의 감정을 고려하는 바울의 목회자적 균형 감각에서 기인한 것으로 볼 수도 있다. 그러나 그것은 근본적으로 바울의 그리스도의 죽음과 부활의 신앙과 신학에 기초하고 있다. 여러 단락에서 자주 언급되는 그리스도의 죽음과 부활에 대한 진술이 이를 가리킨다. 이것은 바울이 다른 서신에서도 그리스도인의 존재와 삶을 그리스도의

---

259) Roetzel, 54.

죽음과 부활에 비추어 이해하고 있는 것을 볼 때 매우 자연스런 것이다.[260] 특히 바울이 고린도전서에서 하나님께서 그의 지혜 가운데 전도의 미련한 것으로 믿는 자들을 구원하시기를 기뻐하셨다고 하면서 그리스도의 십자가의 죽음 외에는 아무것도 전하지 않기로 했다고 힘주어 말한 사실을 중시해야 한다(고전 1:21, 2:2; 참조 15장; 갈 6:14). 바울은 이와 같은 신학적 맥락에서 고린도후서를 쓰고 있다고 보아야한다.

그러나 바울이 고린도후서를 "예수의 죽음과 부활의 수사학적 패러다임"을 따라 집필했다는 문학적 견해는 바울의 사도직을 위한 변명 가운데 나타난 그의 점철된 고난 중에서 괴로워하면서도 그의 사역에서의 고난을 그리스도의 고난으로 달게 받으면서 장차 나타날 하나님의 영광을 사모하는 사도 바울에 대해서 좀 안이한 평가이다.[261] 바울은 문필가이기 전에 자신을 그리스도와 연합한 존재로 생각하고 그리스도의 죽음과 부활에서 나타난 하나님의 구원 능력이 하나님의 뜻으로 부르심을 받아 그리스도의 사도된 자신의 고난의 사역 가운데 나타난다고 확신하고 열심을 가지고 이를 실천하는 목회자요, 신학자요, 신앙인이다(롬 6:1; 고후 4:10; 13:4; 갈 6:17; 빌 1:21).

---

260) 롬5, 6장; 갈 2:20-21; 6:14; 엡 2장; 5:2; 빌 1:21; 2:5이하; 골 1:13-14; 2:6-7; 11-14; 3:1이하; 살전 4:14-18; etc.

261) Kraftchick, 618-637, 특히, 626-628; W. A. Meeks, *The First Urban Christians: The Social World of the Apostle Paul* (New Haven: Yale University Press, 1983), 180-81: 십자가에 달리신 메시아에 대한 바울의 믿음이 그의 "controlling paradigm of God's mode of action"(하나님의 행동 유형의 중심적 예)이라고 함. Ibid., 174: 바울의 "세계관의 근본 methapor(암시)는 그리스도의 십자가의 못 박히심과 부활"이다.

고린도후서에서(특히 후반부에서) 바울은 그의 반대자들의 공격을 받아 매우 어려운 목회적 곤경에 처해 있으면서 그의 사도권을 확립하기 위한 근거를 찾는다. 반대자들은 아직도 복음을 이해하지 못하기 때문에 사도직도 제대로 알지 못한다고 보았다. 반대자들은 복음의 핵심이 그리스도의 고난을 통해 나타난 하나님의 능력임을 알지 못하고 막연히 구약의 전통을 따라서 또는 예수의 지상 사역의 전통을 따라서 하나님의 능력을 눈에 보이는 능력이나 기적의 전파로 알고 있었던 것 같다(5:7; 12:1-4). 바울은 이런 복음을 육체적 예수에 대한 피상적 복음으로 이해했다고 본다(5:16). 바울은 예수의 십자가와 부활을 핵심으로 한 인간의 구원을 위한 복음이 진정한 복음으로 보았다(13:4, 5; 고전 2:2). 또한 십자가로 구원받은 그리스도인은 필수적으로 비복음적인 저항 세력에 의해서 고난을 겪을 수밖에 없다고 본다(롬 8:17, 31-39; 고후 1:4). 그러므로 바울은 그가 받은 고난을 그가 그리스도의 진정한 사도라는 사실을 입증하는 가장 분명한 표로 제시하고 있다(4:7-15; 6:4-10; 11:22-33). 반대자들이 그들의 사도권 확립을 "육체적 자랑"에 두는 것을 알고서 그런 자랑을 자신도 할 수 있으나, 자신의 진정한 자랑은 그리스도의 종으로서 고난을 달게 받았다는 것이다. 바울은 실제로 그가 복음 사역을 하며 여러 고통을 받은 것을 자랑하고 있다. 이것도 역시 또 하나의 "육체적 자랑"이라고 하겠으나, 그가 이해하는 고난의 진정한 의미는 자신이 고난 받은 것을 자랑하려는 이기적 목적에 있는 것이 아니라 그리스도의 죽음에서 나타나는 하나님의 구원의 놀라운 능력과 최종적 승리를 믿는 신앙의 본을 보이는 데 있음을 밝힌다(5:13-15; 12:10; 고전 15:10). 그가 고난을 받은 것은 그의 중심적 관심이 개인적 유익이 아니라 고린도 교인들을 위한 봉사와 하나님의 능력을 찬양하고 그에게 영광을 돌리는데 있다는 것이다. 그러나 반대자들이 외적 자랑을 하기 때문에 그가 고난 받은 사실을 들어 그가 진정한 그리스도의 사도임을 입증하는 외적 증거로 제시할 필요가 있었다 (5:12; 10:7; 11:23).

바울은 자신이 그리스도의 사도임을 확신하고 있다. 그래서 그는 그리스도의 죽음과 부활을 그의 사도직의 정당성을 입증하기 위한 해석학적 열쇠로 사용하고 있다. 그는 많은 오해에도 불구하고 진정한 사도임이 밝혀 질 것이며 그의 사역은 고난 중에서도 결국 승리한다. 그러나 다시 말하지만 이런 해석의 궁극적 동기는 사도직의 정당성을 변명하거나 자신의 개인적인 사도적 권위를 세우기 위한 이기적인 것이 아니라 고린도 교인들을 성숙한 그리스도인으로 세우기 위한 목회적인 것이며 궁극적으로는 그리스도의 왕권을 확립하려는 것이다(4:5; 10:5-6, 8; 11:2; 12:19; 13:10; 참조, 엡 2:20-22; 4:10-16; 빌 2:9-10). 그의 사도권 확립은 고난을 받으시고 지금은 영광중에 계신 그리스도의 왕권을 그의 몸된 교회에 세우기 위해 필요한 수단인 것이다. 그래서 그는 "우리가 우리를 전파하는 것이 아니라 오직 그리스도 예수의 주되신 것과 또 예수를 위하여 우리가 너희의 종 된 것을 전파함이라" 고하였다 (고후 4:5). 바울은 그리스도의 희생적인 죽음에서 나타난 하나님의 사랑과 영광의 부활에서 나타난 하나님의 능력이 그의 사역에서 실제로 나타나고 있다는 것을 고린도 교인들이 알고서 모든 오해를 벗어나 화해하여 그와 함께 주안에서 함께 감동받고 기뻐하기를 간절히 바라는 것이다(1:2-14; 5:18-12; 6:11-13; 7:2, 3, 13-16). 그래서 바울은 자주 자신의 고린도 교회를 향한 진실한 자세와 희생적 사랑을 언급하고 실제로 증거한다(1:12; 2:4; 17; 3:4-6; 4, 2; 7-15; 5:11, 14; 6:6; 7:2, 3; 11:11; 29; 12:14). 또한 이에 상응하는 고린도 교인들의 진실한 사랑을 요구한다(6:11-13; 8:8, 24; 12:15). 이런 화해와 사랑의 관계를 통한 그의 사역으로 고린도 교회로 하여금 하나님 나라를 대망하며, "성령 안에서의 의와 평강과 희락"을 누리기를 바라는 것이다(고후 1:2; 5:14-21; 13:11; 참조, 롬4:17). 바울은 이것이 구원과 평강의 왕이신 그리스도에게서 파송 받은 사도가 성취해야할 궁극적인 사명으로 알고 있다.

이렇게 보면 바울의 사도직 이해는 곧 바울 자신의 자아인식이다.

13. 본 주석의 서술 방식

이 책의 독자들은 다음 사항을 염두에 두고 이 책을 읽으시기를 바란다.

첫째, 이 책은 교역자나 평신도를 모두 독자로서 염두에 두고 썼다. 전문적인 지식을 요구하는 부분도 있으나 대체로 그런 부분을 지나쳐서 읽어도 누구나 이해할 수 있도록 쓰려고 노력했다. 세상에서는 전문적인 법률해석이나, 과학적 지식에 대해서는 매우 정확한 지식을 요구하면서도 교회에서 하나님의 말씀에 대해서 대강 쉽게 넘어가려는 게으른 자세는 없는가? 하나님의 말씀은 세상의 그 무엇보다 더 정확하게 해석해야 마땅하지 않는가? 더구나 주석이란 무엇보다 정확한 해석이 필수적이므로 헬라어를 자주 쓰고 있으나, 대개 한글 번역과 함께 괄호로 처리하여서 헬라어에 익숙하지 않은 분들도 내용을 이해하는 데 별 어려움이 없도록 하였다. 또한 전문적인 학자들의 견해를 참고하여 썼으나, 어려운 논쟁부분들은 되도록 풀어서 쉽게 반복적으로 설명하려 하였다. 그러므로 혹 어려운 부분들이 나오더라도 전후를 읽으면 보다 쉽게 설명한 부분들이 있으므로 전체적 의미를 이해를 하는데 어려움이 없을 것이다. 또한 주석 앞에 있는 "내용 개요"나, 주석 뒤에 있는 "주해"에서는 해당 구절들의 주제를 중심으로 썼으므로 이 부분을 읽으면 전체적인 의미를 파악할 수 있게 하였다. 특히 주해 부분은 주석의 주제를 선택하거나 요약하여, 설교나 삶에 적용하는 부분도 있다.

둘째, 이 책은 학자들의 학문적 연구를 존중하여 사용하고 있다. 학문의 선배들의 지식적 유산을 물려받아 활용하는 것이 후배의 특권이며 책임이다. 선배들의 연구를 일일이 검토하는 것은 고통이기도 하지만, 그들의 연구들을 살펴보지 않고 자신의 주장만 하는 것은 오만한 것이다. 반면에 선배들의 견해를 그대로 받아들이는 것은 게으르고 우매한 것이다. 나는 이 주석에서 앞서 연구한 이들의 견해를 참고하였다. 대체로 마틴(R. P. Martin, 1986)의 주석(WBC)과 트랄(M. E. Thrall, 2000)의 주석(ICC)을 주로 참고하였고, 휴즈(P. E. Hughes, 1962), 바레트(C. K. Barrett, 1973), 타스커(R. V. G. Tasker, 1958), 플러머(A. Plummer, 1915), 퍼니쉬(V. P. Furnish, 1984), 빈디쉬(H. Windisch, 1924), 바넷(P. Barnett, 1997), 해리스(M. J. Harris, 2005) 등의 주석을 참고하였다.[262] 이외에도 고린도후서 주석의 고전이라고 할 수 있는 크리

262) Martin, 서론, x, xi; Margaret E. Thrall, *A Critical and Exegetical Commentary on the Second Epistle to the Corinthians*, vols. Ⅰ, Ⅱ (Edinburgh: T & T Clark, 2000); P. E. Hughes, *Paul's Second Letter to the Corinthians* (Grand Rapids: Eerdmans,

소스톰(John Chrysostom, 344-401)의 주석과[263] 그리고 칼빈의 주석을 참고하였다. 이런 학자들의 서적들 외에도 여러 연구들이 있으나 대체로 이런 서적들의 연구에 의존적이거나 보조적인 경우가 많다. 마틴의 주석은 비평적 견해를 참고하면서 보수적 입장을 견지하고 있다. 트롤의 주석은 종전의 플러머의 ICC 주석의 비평적 특성을 유지하면서도 오히려 보수적 경향을 띄고 있다. 트롤의 주석은 비교적 최근까지의 학자들의 견해들을 요약 비교하면서 자신의 견해를 아울러 제시하는 형식을 취하고 있어서 다른 학자들의 견해를 참고하는 데 크게 도움이 된다. 휴즈는 보수적 경향을 띄고 있으면서도 학문적 수준을 유지하고 있다. 해리스의 주석은 최근 학자들의 의견과 헬라어 문법에 충실한 주석이다. 다만 이책을 늦게 접촉하게 되어서 충분히 검토하지 못한 아쉬움이 있다. 필자의 언어적 한계로 독일어나 불어로 쓴 주석가들을 다 보지 못하고 주로 이를 검토한 학자들의 의견에 의존한 아쉬움이 있다. 학자들은 쟁점에 대해서는 자신들의 독특한 입장을 견지하기 때문에, 결국 내 자신의 견해를 확립해야 할 때가 있다. 즉 이들의 견해를 수정하거나 반대할 때도 있다. 그들의 주장을 분석, 종합, 비판의 과정을 거쳐 이해하고 쉽게 설명하려고 노력하였다.

1962); C. K. Barrett, ibid.; R. V. G. Tasker, *The Second Epistle of Paul to the Corinthians* (Grand Rapids: Eerdmans, 1958); A. Plummer, *A Critical and Exegetical Commentary on the Second Epistle of St. Paul to the Corinthians*, ICC 47 (Edinburgh: T. & T. Clark, 1915).

263) John Chrysostom, *Patrologia Graeca*, ed, J. -P Migne (Paris: Migne, 1857-66), ETr. "Homiles of St. John Chrysostom on the Second Epistle of St. Paul, the Apostle to the Corinthians," *The Nicene and Post-Nicene Fathers(NPNF)*, vol. XII (Grand Rapids: Eerdmans, 1979), 271-420.

복음주의적 신앙을 견지하지 않는 학자들의 견해도 변증적 목적으로 소개하고 있다. 그들의 도전적인 논쟁에 맞서서 복음주의적 신앙을 확고히 세우는 것이 필요하기 때문이다. 때로는 그들의 발견이나 제안을 수정해서 복음주의적 진리를 세우는 데 도움이 될 수 있는 것들이 있기도 하다. 특히 헬라 사상이나 시대 배경연구에 있어서 이들의 연구 성과를 무시할 수 없다. 이들의 약점은 초대교회가 이방적(주로 헬라 사상) 요소를 수용했다는 전제아래서 구약이나 유대적 영향을 과소평가하고, 이방적 영향을 확대 과장하는 것이다. 더 큰 문제는 이런 배경이나 주변적 연구에 몰두하는 나머지 자주 성경 저자의 분명한 교훈을 무시하고 회의적으로 보는 것이다. 이 책은 학자들의 주석적 관심을 언급하고 논하였으나 되도록 바울이 본문에서 말하려는 의도를 찾는데 집중하려고 하였다. 그러나 학자들 사이에 논쟁이 있는 문제에 대해서는 되도록 철저히 논하였다.

이 모든 학자들의 논쟁을 보면서 또 그 논쟁에 참여하는 필자 자신을 보면서 고린도후서 저자인 바울이 오늘날 여기 있었다면 그가 당시 그의 반대자들을 가리켜 "말씀을 복잡케 하는 이들"이라고 책망한 것처럼 우리도 역시 같은 책망을 들을 수밖에 없을 것이라는 생각이 들었다(2:17; 4:2). 각 분야가 전문화되는 오늘날의 추세를 따라서 성경 연구 분야도 전문화되어서 웬만큼 성경을 연구한 사람들이라도 그 부분의 전문 연구가가 아니면 이해하기 어려운 문제들이 점점 많아지고 있다. 그 결과 많은 주석가들은 다수의 사람들에게는 오히려 성경보다 더 이해하기가 어려운 주석책을 쓰게 된다. 그러나 다른 모든 고전 분야처럼 학문적으로 깊이 성경을 연구하는 것도 필요하다. 언어적, 문화적 차이를 극복하고 저자들의 말하는 의도를 파악하여 오늘날의 사람들에게 전달하려는 노력도 필요하다. 또 실제로 성경에서 이해하기 어려운 내용도 있으므로 이런 내용들을 심도 있게 연구해야 한다. 논쟁이 되는 부분에 있어서는 되도록 여러 주석가들의 다양한 견해를 반영하기 위해 노력했다. 그러면서도 필자 자신의 견해를 밝히려고 노력했다. 그리고 되도록 문제를 이해하기 쉽게 쓸려고 했다. 그러나 독자들이 동의하지 못할 부분이나 이해할 수 없는 부분이 있다면 양해를 구한다.

셋째, 성경 해석에 있어서 해석자들이나 독자들은 결국 각자의 주관적인 시각에서 성경을 이해하고 해석할 수밖에 없다. 주관성(또는 "믿음")은 인간의 기본적인 인식 특성이다. 필자는 신구약 성경의 모든 내용이 하나님께서 인간을 구원하시기 위해 그의 사람들에게 영적 감동으로 쓰게 하신 하나님의 말씀으로 믿는다. 이 신앙은 개혁 교회의 정통 성경 교리를 그대로 따르는 것일 뿐만 아니라 하나님께서 31년 전에 내게 주신 특별한 은혜로 믿게 된 것이다. 또한 전 아세아연합대학 총장이신 한철하 박사의 영향도 크다. 따라서 이 주석책의 모든 내용은 결국 하나님께서 그의 아들 예수 그리스도를 통해서 인간을 구원하신다는 복음을 가리키고 있는 것이다.

넷째, 주석책의 사용의 특성상 우리는 어떤 주석 책을 처음부터 차례로 읽는 것 보다는 필요에 따라서 특정한 구절을 찾게 마련이다. 그래서 처음부터 읽지 않고 부분적으로 접근하는 독자들의 이해를 돕기 위해서 이미 다른데서 한 말이나 내용을 되풀이하여 쓴 곳이 적지 않다. 위의 첫 번째 항목에서 언급한 바와 같이 이해가 되지 않는 부분은 인접한 구절들의 주석을 보거나, 각 구절이 속한 "내용개요"나 "주해" 부분을 참고할 수도 있고, 서론부분에서 관련된 주제를 찾아서 이해하는 데 도움을 얻을 수 있을 것이다.

다섯째, 이 주석을 독자들이 읽어갈 때 자주 고린도 교회에서 바울을 대적하는 반대자들에 대한 설명들을 접하게 될 것이다. 독자들은 이런 설명들이 오히려 본문의 원래의 의미를 이해하는 데 방해가 된다고 느낄 수 있을 것이다. 그러나 바울이 고린도 후서에서 말하는 내용의 대부분이 겉으로는 일반적인 신학이나 신앙에 대해 말하는 것으로 보이더라도, 거의 언제나 반대자들에 대한 경계를 염두에 두고서 말하는 것으로 보아야 하므로 어쩔 수 없이 바울의 반대자들에 대한 설명을 쓸 수밖에 없었다. 다시 말하면, 고린도 후서의 대부분의 내용이 바울의 일반적인 교훈과 함께 반대자들에 대한 경계의 말이 암시되어 있다고 보아야 한다. 예로 5장 17절의 "누구든지 그리스도 안에 있으면 그리스도 안의 새로운 피조물이라"는 말은 모든 그리스도인에게 적용되는 보편적인 표현이지만, 문맥에서 반대자들에게 비난 받는 바울에게 적용되는 말로 이해해야 한다. 즉 바울은 반대자들의 여러 비난에 직면하여서 사도로서의 존재 해체의 위기에 처했으나(4:7-18; 6:4-10; 10:10; 11:7, 22-23; 12:16), 그리스도 안에서 그리스도의 능력으로 다시 일어나서 사도로서의 정체성과 존재가치를 확립한다는 것을 의미한다(5:18-21; 12:9, 10; 13:5).

이 책은 1. 본문, 2. 본문비평, 3. 내용개요, 4. 주석, 5. 주해의 순서로 쓰인다.

첫째, 본문은 개역한글판과 헬라어 본문을 대조하면서 필자의 수정을 첨가하였다. 필자가 희랍어 원문을 해석하여 첨가한 부분은 밑줄로 표시하고, 원문에는 없으나 이해를 위해 첨가된 부분은 밑줄과 함께 괄호 (…)에 넣었다. 그러나 대조를 위해서 개역한글판의 번역을 언제나 괄호(…)에 함께 적어두었다. 개역개정판은 미처 참고하지 못했으나 개역한글판과 큰 차이가 없는 줄 안다. 때로는 2001년 표준새번역 개정판을 참고하였다. 희랍어 성경 본문은 Neslte-Aland et al ed., *Novum Testamentum Graece* (Stuttgart: Deutsche Bibelgesellscht, 1979)를 사용하였다.

둘째, 본문비평은 주로 마틴의 주석의 본문을 참고하였다. 그러나 마틴 자신도 이 부분의 전문가인 메츠거의 책을 참조하고 있으므로 그의 의견을 자주 언급하고 있다(B. M. Metzger, *A Textual Commentary on the Greek New Testament* [New York/London: United Bible Societies, 1971]).

셋째, 내용개요에서는 본문의 주제와 전후 문맥과의 관련성, 그리고 전체 고린도후서에서의 역할에 대해서 논하였다.

넷째, 주석은 되도록 간략히 중점적으로 썼으나 학자들 간에 논쟁이 되는 문제들은 보다 철저히 취급하려고 했다.

다섯째, 주해에서는 분문에 대한 필자의 견해를 요약하였다. 때로는 본문의 주제와 관련된 현재 교회의 문제에 대하여 나름대로 제안하기도 하고, 목회사역이나 그리스도인의 생활에 적용하기도 하였다.

그러나 저자, 주제, 성구 등의 색인을 마련하지 못한 것이 이 책의 미흡한 부분이다.

고린도후서 주해

거의 모든 주석가들이 고린도후서가 비조직적인 책이라고 하나 나름대로 조직적인 면이 있다. 바울이 디도를 만난 일을 2장 13절에서 잠시 말한 이후에 채 마무리 짓지 않다가 7장 6절에 가서 다시 언급하므로 혼돈이 있는 것 같이 보이나, 이것도 사도 바울 자신의 사역에 하나님이 개입하여 직접 인도하신다는 것을 증거 하기 위한 바울의 의도라고 본다. 1장에서 7장까지 자신을 다시 지지하는 고린도 교인들에게 자신이 진정한 그리스도의 사도임을 재확인하고 있다. 8, 9장이 헌금에 대한 내용으로서 위로와 화해의 내용에 맞지 않는 다고 하지만, 8, 9장의 헌금 권면은 고린도 교회 교인들이 물질을 모아서 예루살렘교회 가난한 성도들을 돕자는 바울의 목회 지침에 순종함을 보임으로써 고린도 교인들의 바울에 대한 지지를 구체적으로 증명하라는 바울의 요구가 숨어 있다고 본다(8:8, 24). 그렇다면 8, 9장도 고린도후서의 전체적 주제인 "바울의 사도직 확립" 에 잘 맞는 내용이다. 그리고 10-13장은 아직도 바울을 반대하는 이들에 대하여 3차 방문 이전에 이들의 세력을 척결하려는 바울의 단호한 의지가 나타난 것이라고 본다. 그들에게 바울이 분명히 그리스도의 권세를 가지고 사도적 교회를 세우는 사도로 강하게 자신을 나타나는 것이다. 그러나 여기서도 바울은 전체 고린도 교인들에 대한 관심과 사랑을 가지고 그들에게도 직접 권면하는 말들이 자주 나타난다(10:1; 11:11;

12:14, 15; 13:5; 7-10). 이렇게 보면 고린도후서 전체는 바울의 사도직 변명이라는 한 주제로 쓰인 조직적인 서신이다.

Ⅰ. 인사 (1:1, 2)

바울의 다른 서신과 마찬 가지로 바울은 자신을 하나님의 뜻으로 말미암아 예수 그리스도의 종 된 사도임을 밝히면서 문안한다. 다른 서신과 달리 서론 부분에서 "위로의 하나님"을 찬양하는 것이 특색이다. 그 동안 바울이 고린도 교회의 일로 얼마나 염려하고 근심하였는가를 보여 준다(고후 11:28). 그러나 근심한 만큼 하나님의 위로가 커서 지금은 감사와 찬송으로 서신을 시작한다.

A. 발신인과 수신인 (1:1)

본문:

> 1. 하나님의 뜻으로 말미암아 그리스도 예수의 사도 된 바울과 및 형제 디모데는 고린도에 있는 하나님의 교회와 또 온 아가야에 있는 모든 성도에게 (씀). 2. 하나님 우리 아버지와 주 예수 그리스도를 좇아 은혜와 평강이 있기를 원하노라.

본문비평:

Χριστοῦ ᾿Ιησοῦ(그리스도 예수)는 ℵ B M P 17에 나오고 반대 순서로 적힌 Χριστοῦ ᾿Ιησοῦ (예수 그리스도)는 A D E G K L, Latt. Cop. Arm. Aeth. Goth.에 나오고, F와 f에는 아예 없다.[1] 예수가 고유명사이고 그리스도가 칭호이므로 예수 그리스도가 원래 옳은 순서라

고 본다. 그러나 그리스도란 칭호 자체가 고유 명사화 되면서 어떤 순서도 상관없게 되었다. 바울 서신에서도 혼용이 되어 있다.

주석:

1. "하나님의 뜻으로 말미암아 그리스도 예수의 사도 된 바울과 및 형제 디모데는 고린도에 있는 하나님의 교회와 또 온 아가야에 있는 모든 성도에게 (씀)" (Παῦλος ἀπόστολος Χριστοῦ Ἰησοῦ διὰ θελήματος θεοῦ καὶ Τιμόθεος ὁ ἀδελφὸς τῇ ἐκκλησίᾳ τοῦ θεοῦ τῇ οὔσῃ ἐν Κορίνθῳ σὺν τοῖς ἁγίοις πᾶσιν τοῖς οὖσιν ἐν ὅλῃ τῇ Ἀχαΐᾳ). 이 불완전한 문장은 2절과 함께 인사말로서 2절에 있는 "은혜와 평강이 있기를 원하노라"는 말로 끝난다. 여기서는 다른 바울 서신에서처럼 발신인과 수신인을 밝힌다. 발신인은 바울과 디모데이고 수신인은 고린도 교회와 부근 아가야의 다른 성도들(교회들)이다. 발신인 바울이 "예수의 사도"라는 신분으로 이하의 글을 쓴다는 것은 이 편지가 사사로운 편지가 아니라 사도의 권위를 가지고 쓴 책임 있는 편지 즉 공한(公翰, ἐπιστολή)이란 뜻이다(참조, 고후 3:1). 동시에 이에 대한 독자들의 마땅한 존경과 순종을 암시적으로 요구한다(참조, 고후 10:5).

고린도후서의 첫 줄은 고린도전서에 있는 "부르심을 입은" (κλητός)이란 말이 없는 것을 제외 하고 고린도전서의 것과 같다. "부르심을 입은"이란 말이 있든지 없든지, "하나님의 뜻으로 말미암아"란 말이 있으므로 결국 전서와 같이 "부르심을 입은"이란 의미가

---

1) B. M. Metzger, *A Textual Commentary on the Greek New Testament* (New York/London: United Bible Societies, 1971), 505.

숨어 있다. 로마서에는 고린도전서와 같이 "부르심을 입은" 이란 말이 있다. 골로새서, 에베소서, 디모데후서에는 고린도후서와 같이 이 말이 생략되어 있다. 이 말보다는 이 말의 실제적 주어가 중요한 말이므로 이 말은 안 쓸 수 있다. 이 말의 실제적 주어는 하나님이다. 바울의 사도직은 하나님에게서 온 것이다. "하나님의 뜻" 으로 말미암은 것이다. 역사적으로 바울이 사도된 것은 다메섹으로 가는 길에서 하나님의 부르심을 받은 때부터였다. 그는 사도가 되기를 원한 것이 아니라 오히려 그 반대자의 길을 가고 있었는데 하나님의 은혜와 능력으로 사도가 되었다(고전 15:10; 갈 1:13-15; 딤전 12:13). 하나님은 바울을 "그리스도 예수의 사도" 로서 부르셨다. 더구나 고린도 교회의 거짓 사도들과 그를 따르는 이들에게 대해서 자신이 바로 하나님의 뜻에 의해 부름받은 그리스도 예수에게 속한 참된 사도임을 분명히 밝힐 필요가 있었을 것이다(고후 11:23).

사도(ἀπόστολος, 아포스토로스)란 말의 뜻은 서론 부분에서 이미 논하였다("바울의 사도직 이해"). 초대 교회에서 사도의 위치가 분명한 최고의 위치였으나 바울은 자신을 그리스도의 종으로서 부르거나(빌 1:1), 그리스도를 위해 갇힌 자(몬 1:1), 또는 아무런 호칭 없이 이름만으로 서신에 표기하기도 한다(살전, 살후 1:1). 바울은 자신의 사도로서의 신분의 중요성을 인식하였으나 이런 칭호 사용에는 연연치 않은 듯하다. 그러나 자신의 사도권이 도전 받는 교회에 편지할 때는 반드시 사도라는 칭호를 사용하였다(고린도전후서, 갈라디아서).[2] 고린도후서에서 바울이 이해하는 사도의 뜻은 그리스도로부터 직접 복음 전파의 사명을 위임받아 복음 사역을 하며 그리스도의 중개자

2) Furnish, 99; Martin, 2-3.

로서 그와 함께 고난을 받아야 하고, 또 그의 능력을 나타내야 한다. 바울은 고린도 교회 거짓 사도들을 "능력"은 가졌으나, 그리스도를 위한 고난의 경험은 자신에 비해 부족한 것으로 암시한다(11:13-15, 23 이하). 바울은 양자를 다 갖고 있다(11:22-12:12). 그러므로 그는 참된 그리스도의 사도라고 암시 한다.

바울이란 이름은 파울루스(Paulus)라는 흔한 라틴어 이름을 희랍어 Παῦλος로 표기한 것이다. 사도행전 13장 9절에 사울이란 이름이 바울로 개칭되기 시작했음을 말하고 있다. 이름의 개칭의 동기에 대해서 여러 추측들이 있다.

첫째, 사도행전 13장에서 바울이 박수 엘루마의 방해를 이기고 구브로(Cyprus) 총독 서기오 바울(Paulus)을 회개시킨 일을 기념하여 이름을 바울로 부르게 되었다는 견해가있다(Jerome, *빌레몬서 주석;* Augustine, *참회록* 8장 4절).

둘째, 바울(Paulus)이라는 라틴어 이름이 원래 "작다"는 뜻이므로 바울이 자신을 "사도가운데 가장 작은 자"로 여기고(고전 15:9) 이 이름을 사용했다(어거스틴, *영(靈)과 의문(儀文)* 7장, *De Spiritu et Littera*, VII. 여기서의 어거스틴의 견해는 위의 참회록에서의 그의 견해와 다르다).

셋째, 바울의 몸이 작았으므로 이런 이름이 별명으로 붙여졌을 것이다. 바울행전(*Acts of Paul and Thecla* 1:7)에 의하면 바울은 "키가 작고, 대머리이고, 다리는 휘어졌고, 눈이 들어갔고, 구부러진 코였다. 때로 그는 사람처럼 보였고, 때로 그는 천사처럼 보였다."[3] 이 기록의 신빙성은 반반이다. 만일 이 기록이 옳은 기록이라면, 사울이라는 이름의 의미(유달리 컸던 사울 왕, 삼상 9:2)와 대조적인 뜻을 갖는

"바울"이란 이름을 그리스도를 만나 겸손해진 바울이 더 좋아했을 것이다.

넷째, 사울이란 히브리 이름을 헬라어로 쓰면 Σαῦλος인데 이 희랍어의 형용사가 "여자 같은"이란 뜻이 되므로 바울로 고쳐 썼다.[4]

다섯째, 로마 시민권을 가진 이는 누구나 로마식 이름을 취하므로 바울은 사울이라는 이름과 유사한 바울이라는 이름을 취하였다.[5] 서양 이름이 대개 그렇듯이 그 원래의 의미는 어떻든지 상관 않고 어감에 따라서 각자가 부르기 좋은 이름을 붙인다.

위의 가능성 가운데 다섯 번째가 가장 가능성이 높다고 본다. 바울은 그의 이름의 뜻자체에 연연함이 없이 자신이 사도 된 것이 하나님의 은혜라는 생각에 만족하였을 것이다. 바울은 외모에 의해 평가받는 것을 싫어했다. 고린도후서 5장 16절에 "우리가 이제부터는 아무 사람도 육체대로 알지 아니하노라"라고 했고, 10장 7절에 "너희는 외모만 보는 도다"라고 고린도 교인들을 책망하면서 10장 10절에 그의 풍채가 빈약하다는 비난을 받았음을 상기시키고 있다. 그렇다면 자신의 외모에 따라 이름을 붙이는 것을 원하지 않았을 것이다.

디모데는 바울의 사역을 도와서 일했으므로 바울 서신의 초두에 그의 이름이 자주 언급되었다(빌 1:1; 살전 1:1; 몬 1:1; 골 1:1; 살후 1:1). 물론 소스데네스(고전 1:1)와 실바누스(살전 1:1; 살후 1:1)도 언급된 적이 있다. 디모데는 특히 고린도 교회를 위해 일했다(행 18:5;

---

3) Acts of Paul and Thecla, in *The Apocryphal New Testament* (London: William Hone, 1820), 100,

4) Hughes, 2.

5) Hughes, 2.

고전 16:10-11). 고린도후서를 쓸 때 디모데가 무엇을 하였는지 알 수 없으나 그가 고린도 교회에 잘 알려진 인물임은 틀림없다. 그래서 여기서 그가 바울과 함께 문안을 묻는 것이다. 고린도후서를 쓸 때 디모데는 바울과 함께 있었던 것으로 짐작된다.[6]

디모데의 배경에 관해서는 다음과 같이 알려졌다. 1) 그의 아버지는 헬라인이었고, 어머니는 경건한 유대인이었다(행전 16:1; 딤후 1:5). 2) 그는 루스드라 태생이었다(행 16: 3). 3) 바울의 1차 전도 여행시에 기독교인이 된 듯하다(행 16:1-2; 딤후 3:11). 4) 바울의 지시를 따라, 유대인에게 오해 받지 않기 위해서 할례를 받았다(행 16:3). 5) 어떤 특별한 은사를 받았다(딤전 1:18; 4:14; 딤후 1:6). 6) 바울의 사역을 가장 많이 도왔다(살전 3:2, 6; 고전 4:17; 고후 1:19; 딤전 1:3; 빌 2:19). 7) 내성적이면서 순진한 사람 같이 보인다(딤후 1:3-6). 8) 바울의 두터운 신임을 받고 있었다(고전 14:10; 빌 2:22; 딤전 1:2-3; 딤후 3:10).

디모데는 "형제"라고 호칭되었다. 데살로니가전서 3장 2절과 골로새서 1장 1절, 빌레몬서 1장 1절에도 같은 칭호가 나온다. 바울은 때로 디모데를 "아들"로 부른다(고전 4:17; 빌 2:22; 딤전후 1:2). 여기서 형제란 말은 단순히 주 안에서 형제 되었다는 일반적인 의미 이상으로 쓰였다. 디모데가 고린도 교회의 사역자로서 바울의 뜻과 일치되게 돕고 있다는 뜻이다.[7] 이렇게 호칭함으로써 디모데의 권위를 세워주려는 의도가 있다(고전 16:10-11). 소스데네(고전 1:1), 아볼로(고후 16:12), 두기고 (엡 6:21), 구아도(롬 16:23), 에바브로디도(빌 2:25), 오네시모(골 4:9) 등도 형제로 불렸다. "형제"라는 말은 일반

6) Tasker, 39.

7) Martin, 3.

그리스도인들을 지칭할 때 흔히 쓰였다.

"고린도에 있는 하나님의 교회와 온 아가야에 있는 모든 성도에게 (씀)"(τῇ ἐκκλησίᾳ τοῦ θεοῦ τῇ οὔσῃ ἐν Κορίνθῳ σὺν τοῖς ἁγίοις πᾶσιν τοῖς οὖσιν ἐν ὅλῃ τῇ Ἀχαΐᾳ). "고린도에 있는 하나님의 교회"(τῇ ἐκκλησίᾳ τοῦ θεοῦ τῇ οὔσῃ ἐν Κορίνθῳ)란 말은 여기와 고린도전서 1장 1절에만 나오고, 특히 단수이므로 고린도 교회의 분열을 지적한 말로 지목되었다.[8] 즉 인간들에 의해서 분열되어서는 안 되는 하나의 하나님의 교회라는 뜻이 있다. 그러나 잘못된 인간들이 있는 교회라도 여전히 하나님의 교회라는 뜻도 있나.[9] 이 "하나님의 교회"는 마땅히 하나님의 뜻에 따라 부르심을 받은 사도, 즉 바울의 주관 아래 있어야 마땅하다는 의미도 있을 것이다. 또한 고린도와 같은 방탕한 도시에 자리잡은 거룩한 하나님의 교회라는 뜻이 있다. 죄악 된 세상과의 분리된 공동체로서의 뜻도 있고(고후 6:14-7:1), 또 죄악 된 세상을 향한 복음 선포의 사명과 "그리스도의 향기"를 내야 하는 사명을 가진 공동체의 뜻도 있다(고후 2:15). 슈미트(K. L. Schmidt)는 고린도에 "있는"(τῇ οὔσῃ)이란 현재 분사의 의미를 생각하면서 "고린도 교회"라는 특정 교회라기보다 "고린도에 지금 형성되어 나타나고 있는 하나님의 교회"라는 뜻이 정확한 뜻이라고 한다.[10] 그러나 바울이 현재 편지를 쓰는 교회는 많은 문제를 갖고 있는 특정한 고린도 교회이지, 장래에 나타날 교회에 대한 편지는 아니다. 더구나 다음에 나오는 "아가야에 있는 모든 성도"들은 고린도 시 근처의 아테네의

8) Plummer, 3.

9) Calvin, 31. ; 마 13:25-30; 18:15.

10) K. L. Schmidt, *TDNT* III, 356.

성도들(행 17:34)과 겐그리아의 성도들(롬 16:1)을 포함하는 더 넓은 수신자들을 말하고 있으므로, "고린도에 있는 하나님의 교회"는 바로 고린도 교회를 의미한다는 것이 타당하다. 그러나 여기서 고린도후서가 고린도 교회 뿐만 아니라 아가야 지방의 다른 교회에도 두루 읽혀져야 한다는 뜻은 분명히 있다. 그들 모두가 이 편지의 수신자로 명시되어 있기 때문이다. 뿐만 아니라 오늘날의 모든 교회도 이 편지를 읽어야 한다. 거의 모든 교회가 고린도 교회와 같은 분열과 혼돈의 위험에 늘 노출되어 있기 때문이다. 그래서 바울은 때로 그의 서신 끝에서 그 서신을 다른 교회도 돌려가면서 읽으라고 권면하고 있다(골 4:16; 살전 5:27).

"성도" (ἅγιοι)라는 말은 구약에서 온 말로 거룩하다는 히브리어 카도쉬(קדשׁ)에서 왔다. 칠십인역(LXX)이 그렇게 번역하였다. 카도쉬의 원뜻이 "분리되다" 또는 "구별하다"는 뜻인데 죄에서의 분리와 의에 대한 충성의 두 가지 뜻이 있다. 성도들은 모든 악과 악행에서부터 벗어나서 또는 의와 불의를 구별하여 의와 의로운 일에 집착해야 함을 의미한다.[11] 구약의 유대 민족도 하나님에 의해서 다른 고대 민족들로부터 선택받은 백성이었다(민 23:9; 시 147:20). 하나님의 거룩한 백성으로서 그들의 삶은 특별한 것이었다(출 19:5, 6; 레 11:44, 45; 19:1, 2; 신 7:6; 14:2). 성도는 새 이스라엘 백성이고 교회는 새 이스라엘 백성의 공동체이다(벧전 2:9, 10). 고린도 교회 성도는 일반 고린도 사람들과 달리 더 고상하고 높은 윤리적 질서 체계 안에서 하나님의 부르심에 응답해야 할 책임이 있다(6:14~7:2).

---

11) Martin, 3.

B. 문안 (1:2)

2. "하나님 우리 아버지와 주 예수 그리스도로 좇아 은혜와 평강이 있기를 원하노라"(χάρις ὑμῖν καὶ εἰρήνη ἀπὸ θεοῦ πατρὸς ἡμῶν καὶ κυρίου Ἰησοῦ Χριστοῦ). 발신인과 수신인을 밝힌 후에 수신인에게 문안 인사를 한다. 이것도 다른 바울 서신과 다를 바 없다. 단순한 문안이 아니라 축복 기도의 문안이다. 당시 로마인들은 편지 초두에 카이레인(χαίρειν), 즉 "인사하다"라는 말을 썼는데(약 1:1), 사도들은 이 말을 비슷한 어감이 있는 카리스(χάρις), 즉 "은혜"라는 말로 고쳐 쓰기 시작했다(벧전, 벧후 1:2; 요2서 3절; 계 1:5). 하나님의 은혜로 구원 받은 성도에게 어떤 인본주의적 인사도 마땅치 않으므로, 하나님의 은혜를 기원하는 문안으로 대치하게 된 것이다. 물론 신약의 다른 서신에서 다른 문안이 발견되나 "은혜"라는 말은 가장 자주 쓰인 문안의 말이다.[12] 서두의 문안이 하나님, 그리스도의 은혜와 평강으로 시작된 것과 같이 서신의 마지막도 유사한 축복으로 끝난다(13:13).

은혜라는 말에 "평강"(εἰρήνη)이라는 말이 추가 되었다(롬 1:7; 고전 1:3; 갈 1:3; 빌 1:2; 골 1:2; 살전 1: 1 ; 살후 1:2; 몬3; 엡 1:2). 이 말도 베드로전후서 1장 2절, 요한이서 3절과 유다서 2절에 나온다. 이 말은 구약의 평강의 축복 기도와 인사말에서 자연스럽게 발달된 것이다(민 6:26; 시 122:8; 삼하 20:9; 왕하 9:31 등). 주님도 제자들이 심방

12) E. Lohmeyer, "Briefliche Grussuberschriften," *ZNW* 26 (1927), 158-73; 이에 대한 비평은 G. Friedrich, "Lohmeyers Theses," *ZNW* 46 (1955), 273-74에 있음. J. Moffatt, *Grace in the New Testament* (London: Hodder & Stoughton, 1931), 19; G. D. Fee, "*χάρις* in II Corinthians I.15," *NTS* 24 (1977-78), 533-38. 이상의 참고 문헌은 Martin, 4에서 발췌했음; 다른 참고 문헌은 Plummer, 4를 보라.

할 때 이 말로 문안의 기도하기를 원했고(마 10:12), 또 부활 후 제자들에게 같은 인사를 하였다(요 21:29, 21, 26; 눅 24:36). 이 말은 모든 셈족 민족의 공통적 인사말이었다.[13]

"은혜와 평강"(χάρις ὑμῖν καὶ εἰρήνη)이란 인사 어귀는 모든 바울 서신에서 발견되는 인사 어귀이다. 또 13장 11절의 마지막 인사말에서도 같은 말들이 나타난다. 이와 비슷한 어귀로서, "자비와 평강"이란 말이 고대 근동 세계의 서신에서 발견되었다는 연구가 있었다.[14] 그리고 유대 묵시 문학에서도 많이 발견되었다.[15] 더구나 바울 자신이 갈라디아서 6장 16절에서 같은 "자비와 평강"이란 말을 쓰고 있으므로 바울은 당시 인사말을 잘 알고 있었던 것 같다. 그러나 "은혜와 평강"이란 말이 바울의 "은혜로 말미암은 구원"과 무관하지 않다고 본다면, 역시 바울 자신이 의도적으로 쓴 인사말이라 할 수 있다. 더구나 그는 하나님의 사도로서, 그리스도 예수의 종으로서 통상적 인사말이 아닌 참된 은혜와 참된 평강을 독자들에게 기원하고 있다고 보아야 한다. 하나님과 그의 아들 예수의 구원 사역에서 인간은 참된 은혜와 평강을 얻게 된다. "평강"은 히브리어 인사말의 샬롬(שלום)과 관련된 적절한 인사언어이다. 이 인사 어귀에 모든 사람들의 보편적이고 궁극적인 소망이 들어 있다. 누구보다 고난을 적극적으로 해석하는 바울도 이런 축복과 안정과 평화를 바라는 보편적이고 궁극적인 사람들의 소망을 인정한다(롬 5:3-4; 8:17; 고후 4:7-15; 6:4-10). 복음은 인간에게 궁극적인 안정과 평안을 약속한다. 그러나

---

13) J. A. Fitzmeyer, "Some Notes on Aramaic Epistolography," *JBL* 93 (1974), 214-16; Plummer, 4.

14) E. Lohmeyer, "Probleme paulnischer Theologie," 158-73; Friedrich, 346.

15) Berger, 191-207; Furnish, 107.

궁극적인 평강은 결국 하나님께서 마지막 날에 주실 것이다. 믿는 자도 믿음의 과정에서 많은 고난을 겪게 된다. 바울 자신이 얼마나 많은 고난을 겪었는가 그는 가히 고난의 사도라고 말할 수 있다(11:23-12:10). 그는 궁극적인 평화는 그리스도 안에 있음을 믿으므로, 그리스도의 복음에 장애되는 모든 세력들과 과감히 싸운다. 복음에 장애되는 요소를 좌시하거나 타협하면서 얻는 일시적 평화보다는 오히려 맞서 싸우는 쪽을 택한다(10:1; 11:2). 그러나 고난 자체를 미화시키는 고행주의적 사상은 아니다. 그 고난은 궁극적으로 그리스도의 왕권 수립을 통한 영구적인 평화 정착을 위한 것이다. 그 고난의 사역 가운데서도 역설적으로 얻는 평강이 있다. 그것은 주 안에서 거하는 평강이다. 그런 의미에서 본문의 평강은 인사치레를 위한 단순한 희망사항만은 아니고, 고난의 길이지만 옳은 길로 믿고 행하는 이들에게 은혜로 주시는 실제적인 평강이기도 하다.

여기서 하나님 우리 아버지와 주 예수 그리스도가 병행되어 기록된 것은 삼위 중 성부, 성자 하나님의 동질성을 나타낸 것이다.[16] 구약에서 "주"(κύριος)란 말은 하나님의 이름, 여호와(יהוה)를 대신한 말이었는데, 초대 교회에서 예수 그리스도를 지칭하는 말이 되었다.[17] 그러나 불트만은 이 말이 당시 헬레니즘 사회의 "신(神)들"에 대한 칭호였다고 한다. 그러나 바울을 포함한 초대 교회가 이런 이방인들의 신에 대한 칭호를 예수님을 호칭하는 데 사용하였다면, 단순히 당시 이방사회의 언어를 사용한 것이 아니라 구약에서 "주"(אדני, 아도나이)란 말을 이미 사용하였기 때문이다.

---

16) Barrett, 87.

17) Plummer, 5; Hughes, 7.

II. 바울의 사역과 함께 하시는 위로의 하나님 찬양 (1:3-11)

본 문:

3. 찬송하리로다. 그는 우리 주 예수 그리스도의 하나님이시요, 아버지
이시며, 자비의 아버지시요, 모든 위로의 하나님이시며, 4. 우리의 모든
환난 중에서 우리를 위로하사 우리로 하여금 하나님께 받는 위로로써 모
든 환난 중에 있는 자들을 능히 위로하게 하시는 이시로다. 5. 그리스도
의 고난이 우리에게 넘친 것같이 우리의 위로도 그리스도로 말미암아 넘
치는도다. 6. 우리가 환난 받는 것도 너희의 위로와 구원을 위함이요 혹
위로받는 것도 너희의 위로를 위함이니 이 위로가 너희 속에 역사하여
우리가 받는 것 같은 고난을 너희도 견디게 하느니라. 7. 너희를 위한 우
리의 소망이 견고함은 너희가 고난에 참여한 자가 된 것 같이 위로에도
그러할 줄을 앎이라. 8. 형제들아 우리가 아시아에서 당한 환난을 너희
가 알지 못하기를 원치 아니하노니, 힘에 지나도록 심한 고생을 받아 살
소망까지 끊어지고, 9. 우리 마음에 사형 선고를 받은 줄 알았으니 이는
우리로 자기를 의뢰하지 말고 오직 죽은 자를 다시 살리시는 하나님만
의뢰하게 하심이라. 10. 그가 이 같이 큰 사망에서 우리를 건지셨고 또
건지시리라. 또한 이후에라도 건지시기를 그를 의지하여 바라노라. 11.
너희도 우리를 위하여 간구함으로 도우라. 이는 우리가 많은 사람의 기
도로 얻은 은사를 인하여 많은 사람도 우리로 말미암아(우리를 위하여)
감사하게 하려 함이라.

본문비평:

1. 4절에 ἐπί대신 ἐν이 표기됨(C, Eus. Chrys.); ἡμῶν이 없음(M, Hil. Ambr.); εἰς 대신 ἵνα를 씀(F); ἡμᾶς앞에 καί를 씀(Vulg.); αὐτοί앞에 καί를 붙임(D E F G, Latt, [r제외]; ὑπό 대신 ἀπό씀(F).

2. 6절의 어순이 사본에 따라 차이가 있다. 우리 성경은 ℵ A C M P

를 따른 것이며 모든 주석가가 이를 신빙성이 있는 기록으로 본다.[1] 다른 어순은 B D E F G K L을 따르는데, "우리가 위로를 받는다면 너희의 위로와 구원을 위함이다"(εἴτε δὲ θλιβόμεθα, ὑπὲρ τῆς ὑμῶν παρακλήσεως καὶ σωτηρίας)를 더 분명한 의미를 만들기 위해서 문장 끝에 갖다 놓았다. 뜻 자체는 변하지 않는다. 또 편집자들 사이에 문장 구조에 대한 상이한 견해가 있다.[2]

3. 8절에서 ὑπὲρ τῆς(B K L M)가 περὶ τῆς(א A C D E F G P 17)보다 더 원래의 것으로 본다. περί가 보통 ἀγνοεῖν("모른다") 뒤에 오므로(고전 12:1; 살전 4:13) 이를 따라서 바꾼 것으로 본다(참조 고후 8:23; 12:8; 살후 2:1; 롬 9:27). א[3] D[2]와 D[3] E K L Syrr. Copt. 역은 γενομένης 다음에 ἡμῖν을 삽입하고 다른 역에는 없다. ὑπὲρ δύναμιν("힘에 지나도록")이 ἐβαρήθημεν("고생을 받아") 앞에 오기도 하고(א A B C M P 17), παρὰ δύναμιν이 ἐβαρήθημεν 뒤에 오기도 한다(D F G).

4. 10절에서 "큰 사망에서"를 단수(ἐκ τηλικούτου θανάτου)로 볼 것인가, 복수(ἐκ τηλικούτου θανατῶν)로 볼 것인가 p[46] 630 1739 v1 Vulg. Syrr. Orig. Jerome, Rufinus, Ambrosiaster는 복수로 읽는다. 복수는 "나는 날마다 죽노라"(고전 15:31)을 염두에 두고 고친 것 같다. 여기서 바울은 한 번의 죽음을 각오했다고 보아 단수가 옳다고

---

1) Plummer, 14; Martin, 6-7.

2) Plummer, 14.

3) 참조, G. Zuntz, *The Text of the Epistles* (London: Oxford University Press, 1953), 104.

본다.[3] 또 "또(그가) 건지시리라" (καὶ ῥύσεται)는 미래형이 ℵ B C P 17 p[46] Cop. 등에 나오는데, "또(그가) 건지신다" (καὶ ῥύεται)는 현재형이 D[3] E F G K L M Syrr(h). Vulg. Latt. Goth., Chrys. 에 나온다.[4] A D 에는 이 말이 아예 없다. B D 1739는 ὅτι를 생략했고, ℵ A 와 T R은 갖고 있다. F G는 뒤에 ὅτι를 놓는다. Goth.과 Aeth.는 καί와 ὅτι를 다 생략했다.

5. 11절에 "많은 사람(얼굴들)의" (ἐκ πολλῶν προσώπων)가 p[46] G M 에는 단수(ἐν πολλῷ προσώπῳ)로 나온다.[5] "우리를 위하여" (ὑπὲρ ἡμῶν [ℵ A C D G M 17, Vulg. Syrr. Copt. Arm. Goth.])가 "너희를 위하여" (ὑπὲρ ὑμῶν [B D[3] E F K L P, Chrys.])보다 원래의 기록으로 본다.

내용개요:

3절의 하나님 찬양은 유대교 회당 예배의 찬양의 외침인 베라카 (ברכה, "찬양하다")에서 왔다.[6] 쿰란(1 QH 3:19ff.)과 후기 기독교 기도문에서도 유사한 찬양의 외침이 나온다(I Clement 59:1; II Clement 1:4-8). 에베소서 1장 3-14절과 베드로전서 1장 3-9절에도 유사한 찬양 어귀가 나온다. 대개 이런 어귀는 하나님의 구원에 대한 찬양인데 본문에서 바울은 아시아에서 있었던 환난 중에서의 구원을 찬양하고 있다. 최근 3절의 하나님 찬양 어귀에 대한 연구가 쿰란 찬

4) Plummer, 21; Martin, 13.

5) 이에 대한 여러 논의를 Martin, 13에서 보라.

6) S. Singer, *Authorized Daily Prayer Book*, 44.

양 문서(1QH)의 찬양 어귀들과 대조하여 진행되었다.[7] 연구 결과 바울 서신도 초대 교회 예배 시에 예배문으로 읽혀졌다는 확증이 생겼다. 바울 자신이 서신을 쓸 때 그의 앞에 예배하는 회중이 모여 있다고 가정하고 서신을 쓴 것으로 생각된다. 그러므로 그의 서신에 그토록 많은 찬양 어귀들이 있다.[8] 본문에도 이런 찬양 어귀들이 많이 있다. 1) "자비의 아버지"; 2) "위로의 하나님"; 3) 5절의 대칭구("그리스도의 고난이 우리에게 넘친 것 같이 우리의 위로도 그리스도로 말미암아 넘치는 도다")등이다.[9]

대부분은 하나님께 대한 감사로 차있다. 찬양에 이어서 감사가 따르는 것은 당시의 보편적인 편시 양식이다.[10]

3-7절에서는 환난과 위로가 대조되어 나타난다. 바울은 환난 중에서 경험한 하나님의 위로를 감사하고, 8-11절에서는 하나님의 구원(아시아에서 죽을 고비에서 구원하심)을 감사한다.[11] 결국 3-11절의 서론 부분은 하나님께 대한 감사로 차 있다. 고린도 교회의 어려운 문제가 해결되고, 바울이 환난을 무사히 지난 것은 오로지 하나님의 은혜로 말미암은 것이다. 이런 위로의 하나님에 대한 신학이 1-9장까지에만 해당되고 10-13장은 진노의 신학이 지배한다고 잘라 말할 수 없다. 10-13장에도 바울은 그가 받는 비난과 공격을 위로의 하나님이 계시므로 결국 이기리라는 같은 위로의 신학이 있다. 13장 4절에서 바

7) Martin, 7.

8) L. G. Champion, *Benedictions and Doxologies in the Epistle of Paul* (Oxford: Published Privately, 1934).

9) Martin, 7-8; Kleinknecht, *Der leidende Gerechtferigte*, 243f.; Furnish, 108; Barrett, 89-90.

10) Deissmann, *Light From Ancient East*, 168; 마카비 2서 9:20.

11) Plummer, 5.

울은 부활하신 그리스도처럼 자신도 어려움을 딛고 승리할 것을 말하고 있고, 13장 11절에서 "마지막으로 말하노니 형제들아 기뻐하라. 온전케 되며, 위로를 받으며, 마음을 같이 하며, 평안할 찌어다. 또 사랑과 평강의 하나님이 너희와 함께 계시리라"고 말한다. 뿐만 아니라, 12장 10절에서 바울은 약한 것을 오히려 기뻐하는 것은 약할 때 곧 강해지기 때문이라고 했다. 그의 모든 변명이나 공격의 근거는 십자가의 신학으로서 "약하나 강하게 하시는 위로와 능력의 하나님 중심 신학"이다(13:4). "위로"라는 말이 고린도후서에서 29번(바울 서신 전체에서 59번) 나오는데(명사형과 동사형), 10-13장에도 4번 나온다.[12] 그러므로 고린도후서 전체가 "위로하시는 하나님"을 증거하고 있다고 봐야 한다. 본문에서와 같이 현실적인 위로에 대해서도 말하고(7:6), 또 궁극적이고 미래적인 위로도 언급한다(4:17). 즉 현재 계속되는 고난 가운데서 장래에 나타날 영광을 바라며 위로 받기도 하는 것이다(고후 4:17-5:10; 참조. 롬 8:18).

바울은 서론 부분에서 이런 위로의 신학을 그의 목회 사역에 실제로 적용하고 있다. 신학이 이론이 아니라, 개인적 사변이 아니라, 이제 그의 고린도 교회를 위한 목회 사역에 적용되고 있는 것이다. 위로의 하나님의 역사가 목회자 바울의 경험 속에 나타났고, 또 그의 사역 대상인 고린도 교회 교인들에게도 나타난 것이다. 이에 대한 그의 반응은 마땅히 감사와 찬송이다. 특히 고린도 교인들이 바울에 대한 오해를 청산하고 돌아왔으므로 바울은 이런 사랑의 관계를 더욱 돈독하게 하기 위해 애쓴다(7:7-11). 우리 모두가 세상에서 함께 고통당하고 함께 위로를 받는 하나님의 형제자매들이라는 것이다. 바울은 고

12) Furnish, 109.

린도 교인들과의 원만한 관계를 원하지만, 그것은 사도와 교인이라는 형식적인 관계가 아니라 내면적인 진실한 관계를 원한다. 그래서 그는 자주 자신의 고린도 교회에 대한 사랑을 고백하고 또 그들이 상응하여 자신을 사랑하여 주기를 원한다(1:23; 5:14; 8:8, 24; 11:11; 12:15). 때로는 사도로서의 권위로 엄하게 꾸짖기도 하지만, 그의 약하고 부끄러운 모습을 솔직히 보여 주기도 한다(11:33, 12:5). 11장, 12장에서 말하는 "약한 것에 대한 자랑"도 하나님의 원칙이나 경륜으로만 볼 것이 아니라 바울이 사도라는 높은 위치에서 여러 약점을 가진 인간 바울로 자신을 낮추어서 고린도 교인들과 진정한 사랑의 관계를 이루려는 의도도 담겨 있다고 본다. 서로 약한 인간들임을 알고 서로를 위로하는 인간적인 진실한 관계를 원하는 측면도 있는 것이다(1:4-6).

주석 :

A. 위로의 하나님 찬양 (1:3-7)

3. "찬송하리로다 그는 우리 주 예수 그리스도의 하나님이시요, 아버지이시며, 자비의 아버지시요, 모든 위로의 하나님이시며" (Εὐλογητὸς ὁ θεὸς καὶ πατὴρ τοῦ κυρίου ἡμῶν Ἰησοῦ Χριστοῦ, ὁ πατὴρ τῶν οἰκτιρμῶν καὶ θεὸς πάσης παρακλήσεως). "찬송하리로다"(Εὐλογητὸς)에서 찬양의 대상은 물론 다음에 나오는 하나님이다. 이 말이 유대교 예배와 구약에서 유래했다는 설이 지배적이다.[13] 칠십인역(LXX)에 히브리어 베라카(ברכה, "찬양하다")를 번역할 희랍어를 썼다(창 14:20; 왕상 5:21; 시

13) Furnish, 108.

65:20; 67:36; 에스드라1서 4:40; 마카비2서 1:17). 바레트는 희구법으로 번역하여 "찬송하리로다"라고 하기보다 직설법으로 번역하여 "찬양합니다"라고 하는 것이 좋다고 한다.[14] 로마서 1장 25절에 직설법이 있기 때문이라고 한다. 그러나 그도 지적하였듯이 로마서 9장 5절은 본문과 마찬가지 형태로서 희구법이든 직설법이든 어느 쪽도 무방하다. 어느 쪽으로 하든지 의미는 마찬가지이나, 본문의 문맥에 비추어 볼 때, 희구법에 의한 번역이 더 낫다(ἔστω나 εἴη[…지어다]가 생략 되었다고 본다). 즉 "찬양하리로다"라는 말로써 바울은 위로와 구원의 하나님께 그의 감사한 마음을 "찬양합니다"라는 직설법 보다 강력히 나타내는 것이다. 한편, 이 말은 신약에서 하나님 찬양을 위해서만 쓰인 것이 그 특징이다(고후 11:31; 롬 1:25; 9:5; 엡 1:3).

한글개역판의 "그는 우리 주 예수 그리스도의 하나님이시요 자비의 아버지시요…"는 "우리 주 예수 그리스도의 하나님이시며, 아버지이시며"라고 해야 원문에 충실한 번역이 된다.[15] 한글 개역 번역은 뒤에 나오는 "자비의 아버지시요"와 겹치게 되므로 "아버지"를 생략하였으나 원문에는 아버지란 말이 3번 나온다. 또 다른 번역도 가능하다. "하나님, 곧 그는 우리 주 예수 그리스도의 아버지시며"라는 해석도 가능하다.[16] 대개 첫 번 번역을 따른다. 그러나 두 번역 모두 같은 의미이다(고전 15:24; 엡 1:17; 계 1:6; 3:12; 막 15:34; 요 20:17). 우리의 하나님은 더 이상 과거 유대교의 하나님이 아니며, 막연한 신이 아니라, 바로 예수 그리스도의 아버지 되시는 하나님이시다. 예수 그리스

14) Barrett, 58.

15) RSV, NIV, Tasker, 40.

16) KJV, Furnish, 109.

도로 말미암아 계시된 하나님이시다. 예수 그리스도를 믿음으로 알게 되는 하나님이시다. 더 나아가 예수 그리스도의 고난에 참여한 사람에게 자비를 베푸사 위로하시는 하나님이시다(고후 1:5).

"우리의 주의"(τοῦ κυρίου ἡμῶν). 초대교회에서 우리의 주라는 말은 아람어로 마란(מרן), 혹은 마라난(מרנן)으로 흔히 불렀다(고전 16:22). 주란 말은 구약에서 하나님께 대한 칭호였고, 또 희랍 사회에서는 신들에 대한 존칭이었다. 초대 교회에서는 믿는 자들이 예수 그리스도에 대한 그들의 복종과 충성을 나타내는 말로 쓰였다.[17] 예수 그리스도는 그를 믿는 자들의 지배자이고 통치자이며, 믿는 자들은 그의 종들이다. 이 주종 관계는 절대적이고, 영원하며, 신비적으로 연합되는 종교적 의미를 갖는다(롬 6:5; 빌 1:21).

"자비의 아버지시요"(ὁ πατὴρ τών οἰκτιρμών). 유대인의 쉐마는 "자비로우신 우리 아버지여"(아브 하라하[카]밈, אב הרחמים)으로 시작된다. 또 쿰란의 기도도 같은 말로 시작된다(1 QH 10:14, 11:29). 예레미아스는 "자비로우신 아버지"란 칭호는 하나님 자신이 자비의 원천임을 의미한다고 한다.[18] 그는 자비가 흘러 나오는 아버지이시다. 자비의 창조주이시며 근원이시다.[19] 출애굽기 34장 6절, 시편 25편 6절, 68편 17절 등에서 자비의 하나님이 언급되었다. "자비들"이라고 복수로 된 것은 히브리적 표현으로서 칠십인역(LXX)에 자주 나타난다(시 112:4; 사 53:1; 마카비1서 3:44). 즉 하나님의 자비의 풍성함을

17) Plummer, 8.

18) J. Jeremias, *Abba*, 27.

19) Windisch, *Der zweite Korintherbrief*, 38.

강조하기 위해서 복수를 쓰는 것이다. 신약에서는 로마서 12장 1절에 같은 복수의 말이 나오나 골로새서 3장 12절에는 단수로 쓰였다.

자비하신 하나님께 호소하고 기도하고 의지함으로써 인간은 환난 중에서 위로 받고 사망 중에서 구원을 얻게 된다. 하나님은 단순히 기계적으로나 운명적으로 인간을 인도하지 않으신다. 하나님은 그의 풍성하신 자비와 긍휼하심으로 인간과 교제하신다. 그러므로 그는 아버지와 같은 하나님이시다. 자비하신 하나님이란 말은 단순히 절망에 빠진 인간의 하나님께 대한 희구적인 하나님의 호칭이 아니다. 하나님 자신이 그의 자비하심을 증거하셨다(출 22:27; 34:6). 특별히 그의 아들 예수 그리스도를 죄인 인간을 구원하시기 위하여 보내실 때 그의 자비로우심이 분명히 드러났다. 본문에서는 고난 당한 고린도 교인들과 바울에게 그 자비하심을 나타내시고 고난을 이기고 위로 받게 하셨다.

"모든 위로의 하나님이시며"(θεὸς πάσης παρακλήσεως)에서 위로라는 말은 동사형과 명사형으로 고린도후서에 자주 나타나는 중심 말이다(2:7, 8; 5:20; 6:1; 7:4, 6, 7, 13; 8:4, 6; 9:5; 10:1; 12:8, 18; 13:11). 바울 서신 가운데 59번 사용되었고, 그 중 고린도후서에 29번 나온다. 본문에서 바울이 고난 중 하나님의 위로를 경험하였다고 한다. 그러나 구약 이사야서의 메시아적 위로(나함[캄], נחם)와 구원의 의미가 배경을 이루고 있다. 이사야 40장 1절, 51장 3, 12, 19절, 61장 2절 등에서 하나님의 구원의 날에 메시아적 위로를 약속하고 있다. 같은 하나님의 위로가 이제는 그리스도 예수의 구원 사역으로 말미암아 확증된 것이다. 더구나 이제 바울의 고린도 교회 사역에서의 고난을 잘 이기게 하시는 하나님은 과연 위로의 하나님이시다.

위로란 말의 뜻은 동정이나 긍휼히 여김 이상이다. 적극적으로 힘을 주고 용기를 주는 것이다.[20]

4. "우리의 모든 환난 중에서 우리를 위로하사 우리로 하여금 하나님께 받는 위로로써 모든 환난 중에 있는 자들을 능히 위로하게 하시는 이시로다"(ὁ παρακαλῶν ἡμᾶς ἐπὶ πάσῃ τῇ θλίψει ἡμῶν εἰς τὸ δύνασθαι ἡμᾶς παρακαλεῖν τοὺς ἐν πάσῃ θλίψει διὰ τῆς παρακλήσεως ἧς παρακαλούμεθα αὐτοὶ ὑπὸ τοῦ θεοῦ). "우리의 모든 환난 중에서 우리를 위로하사"에서 "우리"는 바울과 그의 사역을 돕는 디모데와 다른 동역자들을 말한다. "모든 환난 중에서"(ἐπὶ πάσῃ τῇ θλίψει)는 여기서처럼 단수로 나오기도 하고, 또 복수로 나올 때도 있다(고후 6:4; 롬 5:3; 살전 3:3). "위로"라는 말과 함께 바울 서신에서 자주 나타나는 말이며 특히 고린도후서에서 가장 많이 나타난다(바울 서신에서 명사형과 동사형 모두 24번, 고후에는 12번). "환난"이란 말은 내적(빌 1:17), 외적 환난(롬 8:35; 고전 7:28)을 모두 가리킬 수 있다. 고린도후서에서는 내적, 외적 고통을 다 말하고 있다(4:8; 7:5). 퍼니쉬는 본문의 환난은 πᾶς라는 말과 관사가 사용되었으므로 구체적인 환난의 일들을 언급한다고 봐야 한다고 말한다.[21] 단순히 모든 환난이 아니라 바울이 만난 하나 하나의 모든(every) 환난을 말한다. 예를 들어 8절에서 말하는 아시아에서 당한 환난, 또 2장 13절, 7장 5절, 11장 23-33절 등에서 말하는 육체적, 정신적 환난이다. 그러나 본문에서 바울의 관심은 두가지 환난에 집중 되어있다. 즉 아시아에서 당한 환난(1:8)과, 고린도 교회 문제로 디도를 만나지 못

20) Furnish, 109.

21) Furnish, 110.

하여 괴로워 한 것이다(7:5). 그러나 이 두 환난에서 하나님은 그를 구하여 주셨다.

마틴은 "환난"이란 말이 대개 종말론적 의미를 가졌음을 지적한다. 기독 교회가 마지막 때에 당할 환난을 가리킨다고 한다.[22] 그렇다면 바울과 고린도 교회가 당한 모든 환난은 종말론적 환난의 일부분으로 봐야 옳을 것이다. 마찬가지로 "위로"도 종말론적인 그리스도인의 승리를 의미한다. 그 때까지 환난당하는 성도들을 위한 하나님의 위로는 계속될 것이다(ὁ παρακαλῶν, 현재분사형, 계속적으로 위로하시는 분, 즉 하나님).[23]

"모든 환난 중에 있는 자들을 능히 위로하게 하시는 이시로다." 문장구조상(εἰς τὸ +부정사[δύνασθαι]), 위로 받은 자가 그 받은 위로로 환난 당한 다른 이들을 위로하도록 하심이 위로의 하나님의 뜻이다. 하나님의 위로하시는 목적이 환난 당한 개인의 위로에 국한된 것이 아니라 위로 받은 개인이 다른 환난 당한 이에게 "위로의 봉사"를 하게 하는 데 있다. 위로 받은 자는 하나님의 위로의 사역을 확장시키는 사명과 능력을 부여 받는 것이다. 바울은 그런 사명과 능력을 갖고 있다. 또 고린도 교인들도 그런 사명과 능력이 있음을 알아야 할 것이다(6절). 희랍 철인들도 비슷한 생각을 갖고 있었다. "고통을 당해 본 사람이 그와 같은 처지에 있는 이들을 도울 수 있다" (Epitectus, *Diss* III. 23.8; Seneca, *On Consolation, to Polybius*).[24] 그러나 초대 교회라

---

22) Martin, 9.

23) 이상근, 258.

24) Windisch, 39.

는 믿음의 공동체의 위로의 사역은 더 절실한 종말론적 의미를 가졌다. 세상에 사는 이들이 갖는 일반적 환난 외에 복음을 반대하고 위협하는 외적 세력과 복음을 왜곡시키는 내적 세력이 교회와 성도들을 심각한 환난 가운데 빠뜨렸다. 그러나 바울은 위로의 하나님의 구원이 늘 있었고 또 앞으로도 있을 것임을 말하고 있다.

5. "그리스도의 고난이 우리에게 넘친 것 같이 우리의 위로도 그리스도로 말미암아 넘치는 도다"(ὅτι καθὼς περισσεύει τὰ παθήματα τοῦ Χριστοῦ εἰς ἡμᾶς, οὕτως διὰ τοῦ Χριστοῦ περισσεύει καὶ ἡ παράκλησις ἡμῶν). 바울은 5절에서 그리스도의 고난과 바울의 고난, 그리스도의 위로와 바울의 위로를 서로 대칭시키면서 상관 짓고 있다. "그리스도의 고난"(τὰ παθήματα τοῦ Χριστοῦ)은 희랍어로 "고난들"이라는 복수로 되어 있다. 아마 복음서에서 말하는 예수님의 여러 가지 고난들을 나타내는 말이라고 본다(벧전 1:11; 4:13; 5:1; 골 1:24; 참조, 히 2:9, 10-단수형). 한 마디로 그리스도의 고난은 예수께서 인간 구원을 위해 겪으신 온갖 고난의 총칭이다(십자가의 고난과 달리 메시아 시대의 도래 이전에 오는 메시아적 고난이라는 견해가 있다).[25]

그리스도의 고난은 부활로 극복되었다. 그러나 바울은 복음 사역자로서 고난에 동참해야한다(빌 3:10-11; 벧전 4:13). 이런 사상이 본문에도 있다. "고난"이라는 말에 고난의 동참이라는 의미가 있고, "위로"라는 말에 고난의 극복이라는 개념이 있다. 우리는 그리스도와 함께 죽고 삶으로써(롬 6:8), 그리스도와 한 몸이 되었다(부분적 존재

25) Martin, 9.

론적 의미로). 그의 운명이 나의 운명이 되고, 그의 고난이 나의 고난이 되고, 그의 생명이 나의 생명이 된 것이다(4:10; 11; 11:23-29; 빌 1:21). 이런 바울의 세례나, 부활, 교회론에 있는 믿는 자와 그리스도와의 연합 사상에 입각하여 본문의 내용을 이해할 수 있다. 그러나 바울은 본문에서 그의 아시아에서의 환난과 또 고린도 교회로 인한 그의 고통을 그의 모든 고난들 가운데 포함시켜 말하고 있다.

"우리의 위로"는 바울 스스로 만든 위로가 아니라 바울이 하나님께 받은 위로이다. 그런데 중요한 것은 이 위로가, 위에서 언급한 바와 같이, 그리스도의 고난에 동참함으로써 받게 되었다는 사실이다. 그리스도의 고난에 동참하지 않고 받는 위로는 가짜 위로이고 세상적인 위로이고, 영원한 위로(살후 2:16)가 아니다. 십자가를 통한 부활이 참된 부활이요, 참된 영광이듯이 모든 그리스도인의 위로는 그리스도의 고난의 흔적을 가져야 한다(갈 6:17).

"넘친다"(περισσεύει)는 말은 형용사와 명사형으로 복음서에 19번, 바울 서신에 13번 나온다. 어떤 물질의 양이나 행위 또는 상태의 정도가 충족하다는 뜻이다. 본문에서 바울은 그가 그리스도의 고난에 동참한 무수한 일들을 생각하고 있을 것이다(11:23-33). 그러나 아울러 하나님의 위로가 더 컸다는 것을 강조하고 있다. 고난과 위로가 함께 균형 되게 나타남을 논하는 것이 아니라, 고난은 더 큰 위로의 전제라는 의미이다. 고난이 아니라 위로에 그 강조점이 있다. 그러므로 바울은 이미 앞에서 하나님은 위로의 하나님이시라고 하고, 고난의 하나님이란 말을 하지 않았다. 그리스도의 고난도 결국 그리스도의 위로로 끝난 것이다.

그럼에도 불구하고 앞서 지적한 바, 고난 없는 위로는 그리스도의 위로가 아니다. 그리스도의 고난에 동참함이 그리스도의 위로에 동참하기 위한 전제 조건이다. 다만 바울이 고린도후서를 쓸 때는 "고난의 때"가 지나고, "위로의 때"이므로 위로의 하나님에 대한 감사와 찬양을 강조하는 것이다.

6. "우리가 환난 받는 것도 너희의 위로와 구원을 위함이요, 혹 위로 받는 것도 너희의 위로를 위함이니 이 위로가 너희 속에 역사하여 우리가 받는 것 같은 고난을 너희도 견디게 하느니라"(εἴτε δὲ θλιβόμεθα, ὑπὲρ τῆς ὑμῶν παρακλήσεως καὶ σωτηρίας· εἴτε παρακαλούμεθα, ὑπὲρ τῆς ὑμῶν παρακλήσεως τῆς ἐνεργουμένης ἐν ὑπομονῇ τῶν αὐτῶν παθημάτων ὧν καὶ ἡμεῖς πάσχομεν). 4절의 내용이 6절에서 구체적으로 바울과 고린도 교회 교인들에게 적용되었다. 즉 하나님은 우리가 환난 받은 후에 받는 위로의 경험으로 다른 환난 받는 이를 위로케 하도록 하시는 위로의 하나님이시다. 이제 같은 하나님께서 바울의 환난 중에서 받은 그 위로로써 고린도 교회 교인들을 위로 받게 하신다. 그러나 새로운 요소로서 "고난의 인내"에 대한 교훈이 도입되었다. 우리도 고난 중에서 인내하여 고난을 이기고 위로를 받았으니, 너희도 같은 고난을 이기고 같은 위로를 받으라는 뜻이 있다. 고난을 피하는 것은 그리스도인 답지 못하다. 위로의 하나님은 그리스도에게 고난을 당하게 하신 후에 부활의 위로를 주셨다. 그리스도와 연합한 우리는 그와 함께 고난을 참음으로써 하나님의 위로를 받게 된다. 우리는 이것을 알고 고난을 잘 참아 지금의 위로를 받는다. 너희도 고난을 잘 참아 위로를 받도록 하라. 하나님, 그리스도, 바울, 고린도 교회의 순서를 따라서

고난과 위로를 설명하고 있다. 1) 하나님은 위로의 하나님이시다. 2) 그리스도는 우리를 위해 고난을 맛보시고 위로를 받으셨다. 3) 나 바울도 고린도 교인들을 위해 그랬다. 4) 이제 고린도 교회 교인들도 (나를 본받아) 그렇게 해야 한다: 위로 받기 위해 고난을 참으라. 이런 질서 있는 설명에는 교회란 그리스도의 몸이라는 바울의 교회론이 비치고 있다. 또 "내가 그리스도를 본 받는 자 된 것 같이 너희는 나를 본받는 자 되라"(고전 11:1)는 잘 알려진 바울의 모본적(模本的) 교훈 방식이 나타나고 있다(고전 4:16; 빌 3:17; 살전 1:6; 살후 3:7).[26]

바울의 위로의 사역의 혜택을 받은 고린도 교인들이 하나님께로부터 위로의 사역자로서 임명 받았음을 가르친다. 그리스도의 몸된 교회의 위로의 사역은 그 지체된 이들의사역으로 확장되어 갈 것이며, 세상에서 위로 받지 못한 이들이 그리스도의 몸된 교회에서 이들의 사역을 통해서 위로 받게 될 것이다(빌 2:1; 살전 4:18). 그리고 모든 성도들은 종국적인 하나님의 위로의 날을 기다리는 것이다(눅 2:25; 계 21:4).

여기서 "인내"는 단순한 인격적 수양에 의해 얻게 되는 덕목과 구별되어야 옳다.[27] 여기의 인내는 하나님께 의지하는 복종적인 믿음으로 얻는 것이다. 하나님을 믿음으로 성령으로 말미암는 열매이다(참조, 갈 5:22).

"구원을 위함이요"에서 구원은 구속론적인 죄로부터의 구원이 아니라 일반적인 의미의 구원이다(행 27:34; 빌 2:12).[28]

---

26) J. D. G. Dunn, *Jesus and the Spirit*, 332, 449-50.

27) Furnish, 111.

28) J. H. Michael, "Work out Your Own Salvation," *Expositor* 9 (1924), 439-50; R. P. Martin, *Philippians*, NCB, 103.

7. "너희를 위한 우리의 소망이 견고함은 너희가 고난에 참예하는 자가 된 것 같이 위로에도 그러할 줄을 앎이라"(καὶ ἡ ἐλπὶς ἡμῶν βεβαία ὑπὲρ ὑμῶν εἰδότες ὅτι ὡς κοινωνοί ἐστε τῶν παθημάτων, οὕτως καὶ τῆς παρακλήσεως.). 바울은 8 절에서 그의 아시아의 고난의 경험과 하나님의 구원을 논하기 전에 고린도 교인들이 지금까지 바울의 일행과 함께 고린도 교회 문제로 같은 고난에 동참하였으니 이제 교회 문제가 해결된 만큼 바울 일행이 받는 위로에도 동참할 줄 믿는다라고 문안의 첫 부분의 끝을 맺는다.

"너희를 위한 우리의 소망이 견고함"(ἡ ἐλπὶς ἡμῶν βεβαία ὑπὲρ ὑμῶν)은 바울이 고린도 교회 교인들이 자신과 함께 위로 받으리라는 확신이 있다는 말이다. 소망(ἐλπίς)은 분명한 믿음과 같은 뜻이다.[29] 바울과 고린도 교회 교인 사이의 관계는 "참예하는 자(들)"(코이노노이, κοινωνοί)이라는 말로 표현되었다. 이 말은 여기서 교회를 환난 중에 지키는 하나님의 위로를 서로 나누는 자들이 되자는 뜻이다. 특별히 이제 바울이 고린도후서 나머지 부분에서 서술하려고 하는 그의 고난과 위로의 경험을 함께 나누면서 진정한 그리스도인의 교제를 갖기를 바란다는 것이다.

이런 바울의 소망이 실제로 이루어졌는지는 알 수 없다. 디도가 고린도후서를 가지고가서 진정 좋은 반응을 얻고 진정한 친교(코이노니아, κοινωνιά)를 가졌는지 알 수 없다. 트롤은 고린도후서를 보내고 고린도를 방문한 바울은 거기서 로마서를 썼는데, 로마서에서 예루살렘 헌금을 언급한 것을 보면 방문이 원만하게 이루어진 증거라

29) Martin, 11.

고 한다(롬 15:26).[30] 어쨌든지, 휴즈가 지적하는 대로 바울은 고린도 후서에서 아무리 외적 조건이 나쁘고 희망이 없어 보이더라도 위로의 하나님의 역사를 굳게 믿으면서 고린도 교회의 문제도 결국 은혜롭게 해결될 수 있다는 확신을 갖는다는 것이다.[31] 이와 같은 바울의 뜻이 본문에도 나타나 있다고 본다. 이것이 자비로우시며 위로하시는 하나님을 믿는 사람의 마땅한 자세이다(롬 8:28).

B. 바울을 구원하신 하나님께 감사 (1:8-10)

8. "형제들아 우리가 아시아에서 당한 환난을 너희가 알지 못하기를 원치 아니하노니 힘에 지나도록 심한 고생을 받아 살 소망까지 끊어지고" (Οὐ γὰρ θέλομεν ὑμᾶς ἀγνοεῖν, ἀδελφοί, ὑπὲρ τῆς θλίψεως ἡμῶν τῆς γενομένης ἐν τῇ Ἀσίᾳ, ὅτι καθ' ὑπερβολὴν ὑπὲρ δύναμιν ἐβαρήθημεν ὥστε ἐξαπορηθῆναι ἡμᾶς καὶ τοῦ ζῆν). "우리가 아시아에서 당한 환난"에서 "우리"에는 디모데나 다른 누군가가 포함되었을 것이나, 확실히 알 수 없다. 그러나 고린도 교회 교인들은 대강 알고 있었던 것 같다. 바울은 환난의 내용을 밝히지 않고 환난 받은 사실만을 상기 시키면서 위로의 하나님의 역사하심을 증거하려는 것이다.[32]

바울이 아시아에서 당한 환난이 무엇인지 알 수 없으나, 학자들은 몇 가지 안을 제시했다. 1) 고린도 교회가 바울에게 반역했다는 소식이 퍼져서 소아시아에 있는 교회들도 바울에게 반역하는 일들이 일

30) Thrall, 920.

31) Hughes, 15.

32) A. Schlatter, 466; Strachan, 51; 참조, Barrett, 95; Litezmann, 100.

어났다. 교회들의 반역은 바울에게 죽음과 같은 근심을 주었을 것이다.[33] 2) 고린도 교회의 반역의 소식을 들은 소아시아 교회들이 바울을 반역하는 가운데 어떤 반대자들은 바울을 죽이려고까지 했다.[34] 3) 사도행전 19장 23-41절의 데메드리오가 주동이 되어 일으킨 난동 사건을 말한다. 그러나 사도행전 본문은 바울이 살해 위험에 처했었다는 힌트를 주지 않고 있으므로 이 견해는 신빙성이 약하다.[35] 4) 아시아는 제일 큰 도시이며 바울이 적극적으로 활동한 에베소를 가리키는 것이고, 데메드리오 난동 이후에 있었던 바울을 암살하려는 음모를 가리킨다(참조, 행전 23:12). 바울은 고린도전서 16장 8-9절에서 에베소에 대적하는 자들이 많다고 했다.[36] 5) 소아시아에서 어떤 질병에 걸렸었다(고후 12:7).[37] 그러나 8절 후반부의 말들을 보면 외부적 압력을 말하는 것처럼 보인다. 바울의 질병이라면 "우리가 당한 환난"이란 말이 적당치 않다. 바울 일행이 모두 같은 질병에 걸려서 죽을 뻔 했다는 것은 상상하기 어렵다. 결국 플러머의 제4안이 제일 타당한 듯하다. 이 경우 바울의 사역의 어느 시점인지 분명히 지적할 수 없음이 약점이다. 퍼니쉬는 바울이 빌립보서를 에베소에서 썼다고 추정하면서 빌립보서에 나타나는 바울의 임박한 죽음에 대한 설명을 그 증거로 든다(빌 1:20-23).[38] 그러나 빌립보서가 로마에서 쓰였다는 설이 지배적이므로 바울이 말하는 아시아에서의 정확한 장소를

---

33) Plummer, 16.

34) Tertullian(160-220 A.D.), *De Resur. Carnis*, 48; Plummer, 16.

35) Calvin, 36-37; Lietzmann, 100.

36) Plummer, 16-17; Furnish, 123.

37) Allo, 15-19; Barrett, 96.

38) Furnish, 123.

알 수 없다.

바울은 고린도 교인들이 이미 알고 있는 자신의 고난 받은 이야기를 다시 상세히 설명하면 혹 오만하게 자신의 의로움을 부각시킬 수 있는 위험을 보고, 어디까지나 극심한 환난 중에서 하나님의 위로와 인도하심을 부각시키려 한다. 바울은 고난 받은 일을 너무 자세히 묘사하는 경우 그 사건의 진정한 의미가 퇴색될 수 있음을 알고, 그의 고생 받은 것을 자랑하기보다 고난이 하나님의 위로와 신뢰의 계기가 되었음을 간증하는 것이다.

한편 바울은 극심한 고난 가운데서 거룩한 사도로서 순교자의 정신을 가지고 묵묵히 고난을 당했다고 하지 않고 솔직하게 고난 중에서 벗어나 살기를 원했다고 술회한다. 그러나 바울은 순교를 두려워하지는 않았을 것이다(빌 1:21). 다만 극심한 고난에 대한 인간으로서의 솔직한 반응을 숨김없이 그대로 말하는 것이다. 어쩌면 그는 하나님의 위로와 구원을 강조하는 문맥에서 의도적으로 자신의 인간적 약함을 좀 과장하는 것인지도 모른다. 동시에 바울이 암시하는 바는 자신이 위기에 처했으나 하나님의 종으로서 하나님의 특별한 구원을 받았다는 것이다(참조, 렘 1:8,19).

9. "우리 마음에 사형 선고를 받은 줄 알았으니 이는 우리로 자기를 의뢰하지 말고 오직 죽은 자를 다시 살리시는 하나님만 의뢰하게 하심이라"(ἀλλὰ αὐτοὶ ἐν ἑαυτοῖς τὸ ἀπόκριμα τοῦ θανάτου ἐσχήκαμεν, ἵνα μὴ πεποιθότες ὦμεν ἐφ᾽ ἑαυτοῖς ἀλλ᾽ ἐπὶ τῷ θεῷ τῷ ἐγείροντι τοὺς νεκρούς·). 이것이 바울이 고난을 통해 얻은 깨달음이다. 바울은 고난 받는 동안 하나님의 위로가 즉시 있다고 말하지는 않는다. 위로는 나중에 온다. 하나님의 위로와 구원은 고난

이 어느 정도 진행된 후에 오는 법이다. 그러나 고난을 겪는 동안에, "마음에 사형선고를 받은 줄 알았을 때," 바울은 하나님을 더 의지하였다. 바울은 단순히 살려달라고 하나님을 의지한 것은 아닐 것이다. 하나님은 죽은 자를 살리시는 분이시니 죽어도 좋다고 믿었을 것이다. "내게 사는 것이 그리스도니 죽는 것도 유익함이니라"(빌 1:21). 죽은 그리스도를 살리신 하나님께서 그리스도 안에 있는 그를 살리시리라(13:4)고 믿었다. 또 "하나님의 능력은 약한 데서 강해진다"(12:9-10)고 확신하게 되었다. 이것이 고린도후서 전체에 흐르는 바울의 신학이다. 고통 중에서 하나님을 멀리하게 된 사람이 있다면 그는 이런 하나님의 능력을 모르는 사람이다. 그리스도 안에 속한 사람은 그리스도처럼 사나 죽으나 유익이다. 이러한 믿음은 절대적이시고 전능하신 하나님을 믿는 믿음이 전제되어야 한다. 하나님에 절대 의존하지 않는 "믿음"은 진정한 믿음이 아니다. 믿는 자는 고난 중에서 오히려 하나님을 가까이 만나고 위로받게 된다. "내가 주께 대하여 귀로 듣기만 하였삽더니, 이제는 눈으로 주를 뵈옵나이다"(욥 42:5).

10. "그가 이같이 큰 사망에서 우리를 건지셨고 또 건지시리라. 또한 이후에라도 건지시기를 그를 의지하여 바라노라"(ὃς ἐκ τηλικούτου θανάτου ἐρρύσατο ἡμᾶς καὶ ῥύσεται, εἰς ὃν ἠλπίκαμεν [ὅτι] καὶ ἔτι ῥύσεται,). "큰 사망"이란 말은 8절, 9절에서 말한 바울과 그 일행이 아시아에서 당한 고난을 말한다.[39] 그러나 여기서는 고난이 중심적 관심이 아니고 고난으로부터 우리를

39) 사망을 단수(*θανάτου*)로 번역 하느냐(ℵ, A B, C, D, 소문자 사본, 기타 고대 번역본, RSV, NIV), 복수(*θανάτων*)로 번역하느냐(p[46] Old Latin mss.)하는 논쟁은 대체로 전자 쪽으로 기울어진 듯하다(Furnish, 114; Metzger, 574).

구원하시는 하나님이 중심적 관심이다. 과거에 우리를 구원하신 하나님께서 미래에도 우리를 구원하실 것이다. 칼빈이 말한 대로, 이 소망은 단순히 바울이 원하는 소망이 아니라 하나님이 그를 믿는 자 모두가 갖기를 원하시는 소망이다.[40] 그러므로 여기서 "우리"라는 말 가운데는 바울과 그 일행뿐 아니라 하나님을 믿는 모든 자들을 포함하고 있다고 보아야 한다.[41]

플러머는 우리는 고난으로부터 세 가지 교훈을 배운다고 한다.[42] 첫째는 우리와 같은 고난을 당한 이들을 동정하고 위로하게 한다(4절). 둘째는 우리는 고난을 겪은 후에 위로를 체험할 수 있다(5절). 셋째는 우리는 고난 중에 구원에 대한 소망을 갖는다(10절). 이외에 바로 9절에서 바울이 말한 것처럼 고난은 우리로 하여금 하나님을 의지하게 한다(9절). 또한 인내와 연단으로 성숙한 인격을 가지게 된다(롬 5:4). 나아가 인간의 궁극적인 존재 이유, 가치, 목적을 일시적인 이 현상세계의 가치에 두지 않고 영원한 자아(속사람)의 성숙과 천국의 영광에 두게 된다(4:16-5:10; 롬 8:18).

바울은 다른 사도 보다 더 많은 고난을 받았다고 술회한다(고전 15:10; 고후 11:23). 또 바울은 언제나 고난을 믿음과 소망을 가지고 적극적으로 해석하지만, 고난 받은 것을 자랑하는 것도 아니며, 고난을 행복의 수단으로 보는 고행주의자는 더욱 아니다. 그는 사역에서의

---

40) Calvin, 39.

41) 고린도후서의 "우리"에 대해서는 Christian Wolff, *Der zweite Brief des Paulus an die Korinther*, 10-11을 보라.

42) Plummer, 19.

고난을 그리스도를 위한 고난으로 달게 받지만(롬 8:17), 고난을 의도적으로 받기를 원하는 것은 아니다. 그가 다른 사도들보다 더 많은 고난을 받았으므로 그리스도를 더 가까이 따랐다고 의도적으로 자랑하는 것도 아니라고 본다. 그가 고난 받은 것이 그리스도의 고난에 동참하는 일이라면 그것은 오로지 하나님의 은혜이며 자신의 자랑거리가 될 수 없음을 잘 알고 있다(고전 15:10). 바울은 고린도후서 마지막 부분에서 자신이 받은 고난을 나열하면서 고린도 교인들에게 자신이 진정한 그리스도의 사도라는 것을 증명하면서도 결코 자신이 원해서가 아니라 그의 반대자들의 "육체적 자랑"에 맞서기 위해서 주저하면서 이런 자랑을 한다고 거듭 양해를 구한다(11:15-33; 12:9-11). 고난을 통해서 힘주시고 구원하시는 하나님을 찬양하지만(12:9-10), 그렇다고 고난 자체를 원하는 것은 아니다. 이런 점에서 바울은 우리와 성정을 같이하는 보통 사람이다. 그는 고난을 이긴 위대한 그리스도의 사도이지만 그렇다고 고난에 무감각한 초인(超人)처럼 행세하지는 않는다. 바울은 그의 사역을 위해서 고난과 죽음을 담담히 받을 준비가 되어 있었으나(빌 1:21), 자초하려고 하지는 않았다. 사실 되도록 피해서 그의 사역을 계속하기를 원했다. 그가 진정 원하는 것은 위로와 평강이다. 그는 죽음이 아니라 살아 있는 동안 주님의 재림을 맞아 산 채로 부활하는 것을 원했다(고전 15:51-52; 고후 5:4). 죽음은 인간의 최후의 적이다(고전 15:26; 53-56). 현실 삶에서 베푸시는 하나님의 여러 가지 구원은 인간의 궁극적인 죽음으로부터의 구원의 예표와 같은 것이다. 그러므로 바울은 그를 고난에서 구원하신 하나님께 감사하며, 장래의 고난에서도 하나님께서 자신을 구원하실 것을 믿는다. 바울은 사도로서 고린도 교인들과의 원만하고 진실한 관계를 원하지만, 그것은 사도와 교인이라는 형식적인 관계가 아니라 보다 내면적이고 진실한 사랑의 관계를 원한다(7:3). 그래서 그는 사도로서의 권위를 말하기도 하지만, 그보다 그의 약하고 부끄러운 모습을 솔직히 보여 준다(11:33, 12:5). 여기서도 자신이 죽을 뻔한 경험과 두려움을 솔직히 그대로 나타냄으로서 그의 약한 모습을 보여준다. 11장, 12장에서의 "약한 것들에 대한 자랑"도 하나님의 은혜와 능력의 경륜을 나타내는 것으로만 볼 것이 아니라 바울이 사도라는 높은 위치에서 자신을 여러 약점을 가진 인간 바울로서 자신을 일부로 낮추어서 고린도 교인들과 진정한 사랑의 관계를 이루려는 의도도 담겨 있다고 본다. 피차 약한 인간들임을 알고 위로하는 그런 인간적인 진실한 관계를 원했던 것이다(1:4-6).

한편, 여기서 하나님께서 바울을 어려움에서 구원하신 것 자체가 바울이 하나님이 부르시고 쓰시는 진정한 종이라는 암시가 있다.

C. 바울의 사역에의 동참 호소 (1:11)

11. "너희도 우리를 위하여 간구함으로 도우라. 이는 우리가 많은 사람의 기도로 얻은 은사를 인하여 많은 사람도 우리로 말미암아(우리를 위하여) 감사하게 하려 함이라" (**συνυπουργούντων καὶ ὑμῶν ὑπὲρ ἡμῶν τῇ δεήσει, ἵνα ἐκ πολλῶν προσώπων τὸ εἰς ἡμᾶς χάρισμα διὰ πολλῶν εὐχαριστηθῇ ὑπὲρ ἡμῶν,**). 여기서 "우리"는 분명히 바울과 디모데(1:1)를 가리킨다. "많은 사람" (**πολλῶν προσώπων**)은 문자적으로는 "많은 얼굴들"인데, 상징적 표현으로 보아서 "많은 사람들"로 번역함이 옳다고 본다.[43] 플러머는

43) Hughes, 23; Tasker, 44.

이 말 앞에 있는 ἐκ가 사람들과 연결되는 것을 받아들이기 어려우므로 "많은 얼굴들"로 해석해야 한다고 하나,[44] 휴즈가 지적한 대로 고린도후서 안에 ἐκ가 인칭과 관련되어 쓰인 경우가 많음으로 "많은 사람들"로 해석하는 것이 좋다(고후 2:17; 3:1, 5; 4:7; 5:1, 18: 7:9: 8:7; 11:26; 12:6).[45]

기도가 하나님의 뜻을 이루는 데 보조적인 힘이 있다는 것은 이교도적 생각이다. 기도는 하나님의 절대적 주권을 인정한 인간의 호소일 뿐이다. 기도는 하나님의 능력에 의지하고 인간의 무능함을 인정하는 것이다.[46] 칼빈은 "사도가 자기 형제들의 도움(기도)을 청하는 것은 결코 신앙적 의존이 아니다. 모든 인간적인 도움을 받지 못한다 하더라도 하나님께서 자신의 안전을 돌보실 것을 확신하고 있었지만 그래도 그는 자신이 교회의 기도의 도움을 받는 것이 하나님의 뜻이라는 점을 인정하고 있다"라고 말한다.[47] 휴즈는 기도는 하나님의 구원하심에 대하여 인간 편에서 마땅히 해야 할 일이라고 한다.[48]

바울의 중보기도의 요청은 자신의 구원이나 성공적 복음 전도 사역의 수행 뿐만이 아니라, 고린도 교회 교인들의 유익을 고려하고 있다. 즉 바울을 위한 그들의 중보 기도의 응답이 이루어졌을 때 바울뿐만 아니라 기도해준 고린도 교인들 모두가 감사할 것이다(고후 9:14; 롬 10:1; 빌 1:4).

"은사"(χάρισμα)는 단수형으로 나왔다. 어떤 은사인가 앞서 말한

44) Plummer, 21.

45) Hughes, 22-23.

46) Hughes, 23.

47) Calvin, 40.

48) Hughes, 22.

아시아에서의 죽을 상황에서의 구원인가 [49] 아니면 현재와 장래의 구원인가 [50] 퍼니쉬는 후자를 지지하면서 11절 상반절에서 바울이 기도로 도우라고 이미 부탁하였으므로 기도의 결과인 은사는 현재를 포함하는 미래적 은사라고 말한다.[51] 그러나 이 은사는 현재와 장래의 구원 뿐만 아니라 아시아에서 죽음에서의 구원도 포함하고 있다고 봐야한다. 고린도 교인들이 바울의 고난을 이미 듣고서 어느 정도 알고 있다면(8 절), 또 그들이 바울의 고난으로부터 구원받기를 기도했다면, 이제 그들은 그 구원으로 인하여 감사하고 있을 것이 분명하다. 여기서 바울은 고린도 교인들이 그런 중보 기도를 계속하기를 원하고 있다고 볼 수 있다.

주해(1:3-11):

3-11에서 바울은 고린도 교회의 어려운 사역과 그의 아세아 복음 사역에서 자신을 건져주신 하나님께 감사하며, 앞으로도 하나님께서 어려움 가운데 자신을 건져주실 것을 기도하도록 고린도 교인들에게 중보기도를 부탁한다. 이 부분을 위로의 하나님과 성도들의 기도로 나누어 요약 해본다.

1. 위로의 하나님

바울은 위로의 하나님을 찬양함으로 이 서신을 시작하고 있다(3

49) Plummer, 21; Windisch, 49; J. D. G. Dunn, 206.

50) Bultmann, 35; Furnish, 115.

51) Furnish, 115.

절). 하나님은 고난 중에 있는 우리를 구원하시고 위로하신다. 그러나 우리는 가끔 다음과 같은 불신앙적인질문을 접할 때가 있다. 즉 결국 하나님의 위로란, 병을 준 후에 약을 주는 격이 아닌가? 위로의 하나님은 결국 고난을 준 장본인이 아닌가? 그런 하나님을 찬양한다는 것은 어리석은 일이 아닌가? 그러나 이런 질문 자체가 하나님의 선하심에 대한 불신을 전제하고 있기 때문에 타당하지 않은 질문이다(롬 3:5). 하나님의 선하심을 믿는 사람은 이런 질문을 하지 않는다. 믿는 자는 고난을 징계로 보고 회개하거나 믿음의 훈련의 과정으로 본다.

어떤 이는 하나님은 고난을 주시지 않는다고 하나 이것은 비성서적인 대답이다. 하나님께서 아브라함에게 이삭을 바치라는 시험을 하셨다(창 22:1). 야곱에게도 많은 고난을 주셨다. 그의 고난이 흔히 생각 하는 대로 그의 간교한 짓들에 대한 벌이라는 증거는 없다. 오히려 하나님의 축복의 약속에 대한 도전적 일들이 야곱의 생애 가운데 전개되었고 하나님은 그런 도전들을 능히 이기시고 그의 약속을 지키시는 것으로 나타나고 있다. 이런 도전적 일들도 결국 하나님의 섭리 가운데 일어난 것은 사실이다. 하나님은 그런 도전적 사건을 발생시켜서 권능을 나타내시고 약속을 지키시는 신실하신 하나님으로 사람에게 찬양받으시고 영광을 받으심으로써 우리의 믿음을 돈독하게 하시고 우리와 더 가깝게 되시기를 원하시는 것이다.

그러나 또한 성경은 때로 고난이 사탄에 의한 것임을 말한다. 욥의 고통은 사탄에 의해 시작된 것이지 하나님에 의해서 시작된 것은 아니다. 하나님은 고통을 허락하였을 뿐이며, 욥에게 고난을 주자고 제의한 것은 사탄이며, 고난을 준 자도 사탄이다(욥 1:12). 또 바울도 하나님께서 자신에게 "몸의 가시"를 주셨는데, 이를 "사단의 사자"라고 부른다(고후 12:7).

그러므로 고난은 하나님이 직접 주실 수도 있고 사단을 통하여 간접으로 주실 수도 있다. 유일하시고 전능하신 하나님의 허락하심이 전제되어 있다. 그러나 이 모든 경우에 하나님은 위로자와 구원자로 나타난다. 후자의 경우는 말할 필요도 없지만, 전자의 경우도 마찬가지다. 하나님이 고난을 주시는 것은 하나님께서 고난을 통해 훈련하시거나 고난 가운데 구원하심으로써 고난 받는 자와 더 가까운 관계를 가지시고 그의 능력을 나타내어 영광 받으시기 위함이다(고후 1:9).

과연 하나님께서는 때로는 그의 권능과 영광을 보이시기 위해 재난을 주시기도 한다. 출애굽 때 바로의 고집은 하나님께서 허락하신 것이다. 그러므로 하나님은 10가지 재앙을 내리는 하나님의 권능을 나타냈다(출 10:1). 하나님은 이스라엘 백성에게는 재앙이 임하지 않게 하심으로써 그의 사랑과 구원의 능력과 영광을 나타내는 계기로 삼았다(출 10:2, 9: 26).

물론 고난을 죄의 대가로 받기도 한다. 그러나 이것도 결국 하나님이 죄로 멀어진 우리와 더 가까이 하시려는 것이므로 역시 훈련의 성격이 있다.

그러므로 하나님이 주시는 고난을 하나님의 불의하심으로 보는 것은 불신의 증거이다. 믿는 자는 하나님은 선하시고 의로우시고 자비로우신 분이심을 늘 믿어야 한다. 선하신 하나님께서 우리에게 고난을 주시는 것은 우리의 믿음을 더 강하게 하려 하심이다. 우리가 믿기 어려운 지경에서 하나님은 그의 능력과 사랑을 보여주심으로써 우리와 더 가까이 하시기를 원하신다. 그러므로 주님은 바울에게 "내 능력이 약한 데서 온전하여짐이라(고후 12:9)" 고 말씀하셨다.

우리를 올무에 빠뜨리기 위한 시험은 마귀가 하는 것이다. 그러므로 야고보서 기자가 "하나님은 … 친히 아무도 시험하지 아니하시느니라"(약 1:13)라고 말한 것은 마귀의 시험과 하나님의 시험의 성격이 다름을 가리킨 것이다. 하나님은 자신이 그의 사랑하는 백성에게 주시는 고난 혹은 시험 가운데서도 그의 능력을 그의 백성에게 나타내시기를 원하시며, 우리가 그 고난을 참고 이기도록 도우신다. "하나님은 미쁘사 너희가 감당치 못할 시험 당함을 허락지 아니하시고 시험당할 즈음에 또한 피할 길을 내사 너희로 능히 감당하게 하시느니라"(고전 10:13).

우리가 당하는 고난이 하나님이 주시는 고난인지 마귀가 주는 고난인지를 우리는 다알 수 없다. 다만 우리는 고난을 받으면 우선 안전하게 우리의 지은 죄를 회개하고, 하나님께 의지하는 겸손한 자세를 가져야 한다. 나아가 나의 죄로 인한 고난이라 할지라도 회개하면 나를 다시 구원하시는 사랑하시는 하나님이시라는 적극적 믿음을 가져야 한다. 본문에서 바울은 그의 고난이 마귀에 의한 것이라거나, 하나님이 주신 것이라는 등의 "신학적 사변"을 하지 않았다. 그는 단순히 "고난"이라고만 말한다. 그리고 그 고난에서 구원하신 하나님을 위로의 하나님, 자비의 아버지로 찬양하는 데 관심을 집중시키고 있다. 이렇게 고난에 대한 온갖 사변을 피하고 고난 중에서 구원하신 하나님을 찬양하는 데만 집중하는 바울을 보면서, 우리 자신이 매우 진지하게 보이는 신학적 논쟁이나 진리를 찾는 듯한 회의적 사색을 하다가 결국은 사변적 미궁에 빠져서 구원의 하나님을 잊게 됨을 주의해야 한다(요 9:2, 3). 이것은 믿는 자들이 흔히 무의식 중에 빠지는 하나의 위장된 불신앙이다. 믿음이 없는 사변은 우리를 논리적 미궁에 빠뜨리고 결국 우리를 하나님으로부터 멀게 만든다. 우리는 고난 중에 믿음을 약화시키는 온갖 사변을 버리고 죄를 회개하면서 겸손하면서도 우리를 구원하시는 하나님을 찬양하는 일에 전념하자(욥 1:22; 딤전 1:4; 딛 3:9). 우리의 모든 고난 중에서 십자가의 고난을 부활의 승리로 바꾸시는 전능하신 구원의 하나님을 믿자(13:4). 바울이 고린도후서에서 가르치는 한 가지 큰 교훈은 바로 많은 고난으로 말미암아 약한 가운데서 오히려 강하게 하시는 그리스도의 능력이다(1:4-10; 2:14-17; 4:7-15; 6:4-10; 7:5-6; 11:23-12:10; 13:4).

2. 기도

바울은 11절에 고린도 교회에 중보의 기도를 부탁한다. 흔히 "우리는 아버지 하나님께서 다 알아서 하시는 데 우리가 기도해서 무얼하나?"라는 생각이 들 때가 있다. 이런 생각(마 6:8)은 결국 우리를 기도 못하게 함으로써 우리와 하나님과의 관계가 멀어지게 만드는 불신앙적인 생각이다. 기도의 원칙은 내 뜻이 아닌 하나님의 뜻을 찾는 것이지만, 기도를 할 때 하나님의 뜻을 움직이게 하려는 것을 우리의 "인본주의적" 요소로 나쁘게 보아서는 안 된다(눅 18:1). 이것은 하나님이 오히려 원하시는 선한 일이다. 물론 우리의 기도가 없어도 하나님은 그가 원하시는 일을 하신다. 그럼에도 불구하고 하나님은 그의 백성이 기도로서 그와 교제하는 것을 기뻐하신다. 왜냐하면 기도의 근본적 성격이 우리 인간의 무능함과 하나님의 전능하심에 대한 고백이기 때문이다. 그러나 전체적으로 말해서 기도는 하나님의 예정과 주권을 믿으면서도 우리의 원하는 바를 자유롭게 아뢰는 역설적인 성격을 가졌다(마 26:39).

한편 중보의 기도는 바울이 그의 서신의 수신자들에게 가끔 부탁한 기도이다(롬 10:1; 고후 9:14; 살전 5:25; 빌 1:4, 19). 또 바울 자신이 그의 수신자들을 위해서 기도한다(골 1:3, 9; 살전 1:2; 살후 1:11; 3:1;

엡 1:16; 딤전 2:1; 몬 1:22). 예수님도 베드로를 위해 기도하시겠다고 하셨고(눅 22:32), 성도들을 위해 간구하시고 계시다(롬 8:34). 십자가 위에서 조롱하는 자들을 위해 기도하셨다(눅 23:34). 성령도 우리를 위해 간구하고 계시다(롬 8:27). 본문에서 바울은 우리가 중보 기도를 해야 할 이유를 말한다. 즉 우리가 한 중보 기도의 응답이 이루어졌을 때 중보 기도한 우리는 감사할 수 있게 된다. 이것은 바울의 교회론에 비추어 생각할 때 더욱 분명해진다. 우리는 그리스도의 몸(교회)의 지체로서 서로 연락하고 서로 돕는 기능을 가져야 한다(엡 4:16; 롬 12:5). 교인들은 특히 어려움에 처한 형제들을 기도로 도와야 한다(약 5:16). 또 본문에서 바울을 위해 고린도 교인들이 기도해야 하듯, 모든 교회는 교역자를 위해 기도해야 한다. 중보의 기도는 그리스도 안에 있는 사람들의 가장 진정한 교제의 모습이다.

III. 바울의 사도직의 진실성 변명(방어) (1:12-7:16)

바울은 고린도후서 전체에서 자신의 사도직에 대한 변명을 하지만, 전반부에서는 디도로부터 고린도 교회 전반이 바울에 대한 지지로 선회한 것을 전해 듣고 고무되어 글을 쓰기 때문에 자신에 대한 비난과 관련된 어떤 문제를 집중적으로 거론하지 않고, 단편적으로 또는 암시적으로 언급하면서 오히려 바울이 평소에 갖고 있는 신앙적 소신이나 신학적 소견을 주로 말한다. 그러므로 고린도후서는 고린도전서에서 "…에 대하여는" 이란 어귀로 어떤 문제를 분명하게 언급하면서 그 문제에 대해 집중적으로 거론하는 것과는 사뭇 다른 필체를 보이고 있다(고전 7:1; 8:1; 12:1; 참조, 고후 9:1).

바울은 1장 12절-7장 4절에서 자신의 사도직의 진실성과 관련된 몇 가지 문제에 대하여 해명한다. 즉, 일방적인 방문 취소 문제와 치리 문제(1:15-2:11), 추천서가 없는 문제(3:1-4:2), 바울의 "약함" 문제, 또는 사도적 권능 문제(4:7-15; 5:12-17; 6:4-10; 참조, 11:23-12:10; 13:3-10), 역사적 예수와의 관련성 문제(5:16-17; 참조, 11:22), 그리고 재물 착복 여부 문제이다(7:2; 참조, 12:16-18). 바울은 편지의 전반부에서 이런 자신에 대한 비난거리들에 대해서 공격적인 반응을 자제하고 주로 방어적으로 해명하고 설득한다. 공격적인 반응을 보이는 10장 이전에는 대다수의 교인들과 화목한 분위기를 조성하기 위해 애쓰고 있다. 바울은 그의 사도직을 거짓 사도들의 사도직과 비교하여 그 진실성을 증거하기도 하고, 자신과 고린도 교회와의 관계에 있었던 오해나 의문점들을 풀고 새로운 화해의 관계를 모색하기도 한다.

A. 바울의 고린도 교회 방문 계획 변경 경위 해명 (1:12-2:13)

바울은 그의 사도적 진실성을 본격적으로 해명하기 전에 최근 그의 고린도 교회 방문 취소로 인한 그와 고린도 교인들 사이의 언짢은 관계를 해소하려고 한다. 그 일로 인해 그의 신뢰성이 고린도 교회에서 거론되었기 때문일 것이다. 바울은 그의 진실성을 하나님의 진실성에서 기원하는 것으로 설명하면서 고린도 교인들이 이를 믿어 주기를 바란다.

1. 바울의 진실성 천명 (1:12–14)

본문:

> 12. 우리가 세상에서, 특별히 너희에게 대하여 하나님의 순수함(거룩함)과 진실함으로써 하되 육체의 지혜로 하지 아니하고 하나님의 은혜로 행함은 우리 양심의 증거하는 바니 이것이 우리의 자랑이라. 13. 오직 너희가 읽고 아는 것 외에 우리가 다른 것을 쓰지 아니하노니 너희가 끝까지 알기를 바라는 것은 14. 너희가 대강 우리를 아는 것 같이, 우리 주 예수의 날에 너희가 우리의 자랑이 되고 우리가 너희의 자랑이 되는 것이라.

본문비평:

1. 12절에서 희랍어 γάρ는 당시 서신에서 본론을 시작할 때 흔히 쓰던 말이며 별 뜻이 없으므로 해석할 필요가 없다.[1)] 우리나라 말의 "자, 이제" 에 해당될 수 있겠다.

2. 12절에서 ἁγιότητι(거룩함)로 p^{46} a A B C K (Nestle, RSV,

1) Furnish, 126.

NIV)에 나오는데, ἁπλότητι("솔직함," "순수함")로 a² D F G 고대 라틴어역, 시리아역 (AV, Aland, Vulgate)에 나온다. 전자는 실제로 성경에서 쓰인 적이 없고, 후자가 13절에서 말하는 바울의 진실성에 부합하는 말로써 문맥상 적합하다고 본다.[2] 비슷한 앞의 자음의 모양 때문에 필사자가 혼동한 듯하다. 그러나 트롤은 바울이 그의 "궤휼"을 공격받고 있는 터라(4:2; 12:16) "거룩함"이 될 수도 있다고 한다. 그러나 그는 "순수함"의 가능성도 받아들인다.[3]

3. 12절의 "우리의 자랑이라"에서 자랑(καύχησις)은 문자적 번역이나, "확신"이라고 번역할 수도 있다. "우리의 확신이라"는 말은 어느 서신보다 고린도후서에 제일 많이 나오며(29번), 고후를 이해하는 데 중요한 개념이다.[4] 그러나 자랑이라고 번역하여 반대자들의 자랑에 맞서는 것으로 이해할 수도 있다.

4. 13절의 ἕως τέλους(끝까지)의 문자적 번역은 "완전히, 충분히"로 번역함이 좋다(고전13:12).[5] 이 말에 종말론적 의미가 있음을 주장하는 학자들도 있다.[6] 14절에 종말론적 의미가 나오나 이 말이 쓰인 13절에서는 단순한 의미로 쓰였다고 보는 것이 좋다.

---

2) Martin, 18; Furnish, 127; Metzger, 575.

3) Thrall, 130.

4) R. Bultmann, *TDNT* 3: 646-54.

5) Martin, 19.

6) Plummer, 27; Windisch, 58; Barrett, 73.

내용개요:

이 부분은 문안과 위로의 하나님께 감사한 이후 본론의 시작 부분으로서 바울이 15절에서 24절까지 그의 고린도 방문 계획 취소에 대한 변명을 하기에 앞서서 그가 하나님 앞에서 양심대로 일해 왔음을 먼저 밝히면서 그리스도의 사도로서 자신의 진실함을 믿어줄 것을 말한다. 문학적 양식은 변명(apologia)의 양식을 취하고 있다.[7]

주석:

12절 "우리가 세상에서, 특별히 너희에게 대하여, 하나님의 순수함(거룩함)과 진실함으로 하되 육체의 지혜로 하지 아니하고 하나님의 은혜로 행함은 우리 양심의 증거하는 바니 이것이 우리의 자랑이라" (Ἡ γὰρ καύχησις ἡμῶν αὕτη ἐστίν, τὸ μαρτύριον τῆς συνειδήσεως ἡμῶν, ὅτι ἐν ἁπλότητι καὶ εἰλικρινείᾳ τοῦ θεοῦ, [καὶ] οὐκ ἐν σοφίᾳ σαρκικῇ ἀλλ᾽ ἐν χάριτι θεοῦ, ἀνεστράφημεν ἐν τῷ κόσμῳ, περισσοτέρως δὲ πρὸς ὑμᾶς). 이 구절은 고린도후서에서의 바울의 사도직 변명의 근본적인 자세가 무엇인지를 한마디로 잘 요약해 주고 있다. 바울은 그리스도의 사도로서 세상의 지혜나 판단 기준을 따라서 사람에게 보이려고 사역하지 않고 하나님 앞에서 진실하게 사역한다는 것이다. 그러므로 받는 사람들의 오해나 세상의 저항을 견디며 온갖 고난을 받으면서도 꿋꿋이 양심대로 바르게 사역한다는 것이다. 이런 바울의 사역 자세가 고린도후서 전체의 중요한 주제이다(4:2). 이런 바른 도덕적 자세를 고린도 교인들에게 알려

7) Martin, 7.

서 그들로 바울을 따르게 하려는 것이 고린도후서의 일관된 목적이다.

바울이 하나님의 순수함(ἁπλότης)과 진실함(εἰλικρινεία)을 자신의 사역의 기준으로 삼았음을 밝히는 것은(13:8), 거짓 사도들은 이런 기준이 아닌 피상적인 신학과 거짓과 가장된 인간적 유인 수단을 사역의 지침으로 삼기 때문이다(고후 11:3-4, 13-14). 하나님의 사람의 가장 근본적 속성은 정직함과 진실성이어야 한다. 왜냐하면 이것이 하나님 자신의 속성이기 때문이며(삼상 15:29; 신 32:4), 하나님은 거짓된 자를 미워하시기 때문이다(출 20:16; 레 19:11; 시 24:4; 잠 12:22 등).

"세상에서"(ἐν τῷ κο,σμωl)란 말은 고린도 교인들이 모르는 바울의 일반적인 삶을 가리킨다. 바울은 언제나 진실 되게 행하였으나 특히 고린도인들에게 진실히 대했다.

"하되"란 동사는 ἀναστρέφω로서 "행하다"란 뜻이다. 희랍어 성경에는 한 번 나오나 우리말성경에는 번역상 세 번 나온다(12절).

"육체의 지혜로 하지 아니하고 하나님의 은혜로 행함은"에서 "육체의 지혜"(σοφίᾳ σαρκικῇ)란 말과 "하나님의 은혜"(χάριτι θεοῦ)란 말이 대조되어 고린도전서 1장 12절-2장 16절을 상기시킨다. 다른 말로 하면 인간의 지혜와 하나님의 지혜의 대조이다. 여기서 하나님의 지혜라고 직접적 대조를 피한 것은 은혜란 말이 더 분명히 하나님께 의지하는 바울의 자세를 보여 주기 때문이다. 이 말은 또한 고린도후서 12장 9절의 "내 은혜가 네게 족하도다"란 말과도 일치된다. 바울의 사역은 하나님의 은혜와 지혜로 말미암은 것임을 강조하고 있다. 하나님은 오히려 바울의 약한 것들을 통해서 그를 강하게 만드신다. 반면에 거짓 사도들은 인간의 지혜와 궤휼을 사용함을 암시한다. 그들은 육체를 따라 자랑하면서 바울을 공격하지만(11:8) 바울은 오히려 육체의 연약함을 자랑한다(11:23-33; 12:7-10). 육체란 말은 바울 서신에서 대체로 하나님에 대항하는 인간의 반항적 자세를 표현한다. 바울은 자신을 버리고 항상 하나님께 의지하고, 하나님의 은혜와 지혜로 말미암아 힘을 얻어서 그의 사역을 수행한다(4:7-15; 6:5-10). 이것은 바울의 사역의 독특한 경험이지만, 복음의 능력의 특징이기도 하다(1:23-25).

"우리의 양심의 증거하는 바니 이것이 우리의 자랑이라." 희랍어 성경에서는 이 말이 본문에서 가장 먼저 나온 말이다. 바울은 일종의 "양심선언"을 하는 양으로 그의 변명을 시작한다. 누군가 바울에게, "무엇으로 당신이 하나님의 순수함과 진실함으로 행한다는 것을 증명하오?"라고 물을 때 바울은 "나의 하나님이 아시느니라"(11:11)라고 대답하거나 또는 "나의 양심이요"라고 대답할 것이다(4:2). 양심(συνείδησις)이란 말은 바울 서신에서 대체로 "인간의 순수한 자아 비평 능력"의 뜻으로 쓰인다(고전 8:7-13; 10:25-29; 고후 4:2; 5:11; 롬 2:15; 9:1; 13:5). 바울은 양심이란 말을 14절의 종말론적 심판과 관련시켜 말함으로써 그의 말이나 행동의 신뢰성을 더욱 분명히 하고 있다(롬 2:15-16; 9:1). 양심이란 말의 의미와 적용이 개인에 따라 다르므로 이것이 어떤 공통된 윤리 행동의 기준이 될 수 있는가란 질문에 대해서 바울은 "나의 양심의 진위(眞僞) 여부는 장차 주님의 심판대 앞에서 증거될 것"임을 첨언할 필요가 있었다(5:10). 이로써 바울은 양심이란 말의 남용을

스스로 제한하고 있다.[8)]

"이것이 우리의 자랑이라"는 말은 위에서 지적하였듯이 "우리의 확신이라"라고 번역 할 수도 있다. 그러나 이 말은 12절이 바울이 10-12장에서 반대자들의 "육체를 따라하는 자랑"(11:18)에 맞서서 자신의 약한 것들을 자랑한다는 것과 일치함을 가리키는 말로 보아 "자랑한다"라고 번역하는 것이 좋다(11:30; 12:9, 10). 바울의 사역은 십자가의 약함을 통해 나타나는 하나님의 지혜와 능력에 근거하고 있다. 그러나 반대자들은 세상이 좋아하는 온갖 육체적 자랑을 가지고 하나님의 능력을 나타낸다. 그러나 바울은 "순수함과 진실함"으로 사역하기 때문에 세상에서 고난을 받는다. 그러나 바울이 결국은 약한 데서 강하게 하시는 하나님의 은혜와 지혜로 말미암아 승리하게 된다는 뜻이 있다(2:14-17; 12:9; 13:4).

13. "오직 너희가 읽고 아는 것 외에 우리가 다른 것을 쓰지 아니하노니 너희가 끝까지 알기를 바라는 것은…"(οὐ γὰρ ἄλλα γράφομεν ὑμῖν ἀλλ᾽ ἢ ἃ ἀναγινώσκετε ἢ καὶ ἐπιγινώσκετε· ἐλπίζω δὲ ὅτι ἕως τέλους ἐπιγνώσεσθε,). "오직 너희가 읽고 아는 것 외에…"라는 말은 바울의 편지가 무슨 다른 의중을 가지고 고린도 교인들을 속이려는 의도로 쓴 것이 아

8) C. A. Pierce, "Concience in the NT," *SBT* 15 (London: SCM Press, 1955), 60-65; R. Jewett, Paul's "Anthropological Terms: A Study of Their Use in Conflict Settings," *AGJU* 10 (Leiden: Bill, 1971), 436; M. E. Thrall, "The Pauline Use of *ΣΥΝΕΙΔΣΙΣ*," *NTS* 14, (1967-68), 118-25.

니라는 말이다. 바울을 반대하는 이들 가운데 바울의 편지 내용을 가지고 폄하하는 이들이 있었던 것 같다(10:9-10). "내가 바라는 바는 너희가 지금까지 우리를 부분적으로 알았지만 완전히 아는 것이다"라는 뜻이다. 고린도 교인들은 바울의 진실성에 대해서 어느 정도 알고 있었으나 반대자들의 비난으로 말미암아 바울의 진실성을 완전히 믿지는 못했다. 바울은 이제 자신의 진실성을 더 확실히 믿어주기를 바라는 것이다. 이것이 고린도후서 집필의 목적이기도 하다.

14. 너희가 대강 우리를 아는 것 같이, 우리 주 예수의 날에 너희가 우리의 자랑이 되고 우리가 너희의 자랑이 되는 것이라 (**καθὼς καὶ ἐπέγνωτε ἡμᾶς ἀπὸ μέρους, ὅτι καύχημα ὑμῶν ἐσμεν καθάπερ καὶ ὑμεῖς ἡμῶν ἐν τῇ ἡμέρᾳ τοῦ κυρίου [ἡμῶν] Ἰησοῦ**). 바울의 진실성의 진위는 결국 마지막 날에 밝혀질 것이다. 또 그를 비난한 이들의 비양심적 거짓됨도 나타나게 될 것이다. 바울은 자신의 진실성을 주님의 최후의 심판에 맡긴다(5:10). 그 때 그가 고린도 교인들에게 양심적으로 행했음이 밝혀지고 또 바울의 진실성을 신뢰한 고린도 교인들도 그들의 판단이 옳았음을 확인하게 될 것이다. 이 말은 바울이 모든 것을 하나님과 사람 앞에서 부끄러움이 없이 양심대로 정직하게 행하고 있다는 뜻이다(4:2). 바울의 "눈물의 편지"를 통해서 고린도 교인들이 바울을 진정한 사도로 알게 되었다는 뜻도 되고,[9] 또 그 편지 받기 이전이라도 바울의 진정성을 아는 사람들은 이미 안다는 양

9) Harris, 189.

보적 뜻도 된다. "자랑" 이란 말은 12절에서와 거의 같은 의미로서 "확신" 이나 "신뢰" 라고 번역할 수도 있다. 반대자들이 그들의 "외모" (즉, 히브리인, 팔레스틴 배경, 추천서, 웅변술, 등, 3:1; 5:12; 10:7; 11:22)를 자랑하나, 바울은 최후의 날에 주님께 자신의 진실성을 인정받기를 원한다(5:10).

주해(1:12–14):

바울은 12-14절에서 자신의 도덕성을 자신의 양심과 종말론적 신앙에 입각하여 문제가 없음을 설명한다. 아마도 고린도 교회는 방문 취소에 대해서 바울이 이기적이고 변덕스러운 사람으로서 믿을 수 없는 사람이라는 비난이 있었던 것 같다. 23절에서의 방문 취소의 이유를 말하기 전에 먼저 자신의 인간성에 문제가 없음을 밝히는 것이다. 바울이 다른 구체적 변명을 하기 전에 자신이 하나님의 부르심을 받은 사도로서 진실한 사람으로 사역하고 있다는 것은 마치 재판소에서 재판을 받을 때 심각하게 자신을 위해 변론하는 것과 같다.[10] 그러므로 바울은 자신의 사역에서 발생하는 오해가 있더라도 자신은 하나님의 사도로서 언제나 진실하게 사역하고 있다는 것을 먼저 믿어 달라고 말하는 것이다.

1. 그리스도인의 진실성

바울은 그가 세상에서나 고린도 교인들에게나 하나님의 정직함과 진실함, 그리고 하나님의 은혜에 의지하여서 행하였고 육체의 지혜를 따라 행치 아니하였다고 한다(4:2). 우리 그리스도인은 하

10) Harris, 106. 고린도후서를 헬라 시대의 재판의 변론으로 보는 견해들을 보라.

나님의 백성으로서 진실해야 한다. 진실이란 이중적 기준을 가지고 상황에 따라 자기 유익에 따라 움직이는 것이 아니고 일치된 판단 기준을 따르며, 겉과 속이 다르게 말하고 행동하는 것이 아니고 언제나 일치된 자세로 신뢰할 수 있는 것을 말한다. 진실성은 말 뿐 아니라 행동으로 나타나야 한다. 그러므로 바울은 "행했다" 고했다. 진실성이 없으면 신뢰성이 없어지므로 어떤 관계(하나님과 인간, 인간과 인간)도 지속될 수 없다. 더구나 그리스도인의 존재가 하나님 앞에(coram Deo) 있음을 자각할 때 진실성은 그리스도인의 본질적 요소이다.

교회의 일에 "정치"가 필요하다는 말을 듣는다. 교회의 일이 단순한 인간관계 차원이 아닌 복잡한 차원이므로 정치가 필요하다는 것이란 말일 것이다. 교회 정치란 말이 "상황에 따른 전체 교회의 유익을 위한 적절한 대처"라고 해도, 교회의 "정치"는 세상의 정치와 구별되어야 한다. 교회 정치의 기준은 눈에 보이는 유익이 아니라 의와 진실성이어야 한다. 물론 이런 진실성은 그리스도인의 진실한 인격 형성에서부터 시작되는 것이다.

2. 양심적 삶

양심이란 우리 인간에게 공통적으로 있는 선하고 진실한 판단 기준이다. 종교개혁자들도 흔히 양심을 앞세워 자신들의 진실성을 변호했다. 루터는 1520년 여름 높은 사람들이 모인 보름스 회의에서 "내 양심은 하나님의 말씀으로 매여 있다" 고 단호히 말하여 자신의 개혁의지의 진실성을 표현했다. 항가리의 칼빈주의 종교 개혁자 스티븐 보크스케이(1556-1606)는 당시 루돌프 왕의 반종교개혁적 조치에 대항하여 일어나 그를 무찌른 뒤에 주재한 회의에서, "우리의 신앙, 우리의 양심과, 우리의 전통적 법의 자유는 우리에게 금보다 귀하다" 고 했다. 카톨릭과 개신교의 진실성에 대한 논쟁은 결국 개인의 양심의 자유를 주장한 개신교에게 유리하게 전개되었다.[11] 개혁자들의 양심에 대해 호소한 것은 바울이 유대인들과 싸울 때 양심에 호소한 것과 유사하다(행 23:1; 24:16; 참조, 고전 10:25, 27-29).

한편, 양심이란 말의 사용이 진실성을 판가름하는 중요한 기준이 될 수 있을지언정, 확실한 판단 기준이 될 수 없는 것은 그 말이 매우 남용되었기 때문이다. 뿐만 아니라 개인적 양심의 자유를 인정할 때, 양심이란 매우 모호한 판단 기준이 되어버린다. 여러 복잡한 가치 판단 기준을 배운 개인들이 말하는 양심이 어떤 일반적이고 공통된 가치 기준을 표방한다고 보기 어렵다. 바울도 깨끗한 양심(딤전 1:5, 19; 3:9; 딤후 1:3)을 더러운 양심(딛 1:15), 혹은 화인 맞은 양심(딤전 4:2)과 구별하고 있다.

그러나 인간 양심의 불완전성에도 불구하고 개인의 양심은 여전히 인간성이나 도덕성의 판단 기준으로 어느 정도 존중되어야 한다. 우리는 전체 사회나 교회의 부패함과 거짓이 개인의 양심에 의해서 지적되는 것을 여전히 본다. 인간의 전적 타락에도 불구하고, 하나님께서 주신 선한 성향이 훼손된 채로 아직 죄인 인간의 마음 한 구석에 남아 있고, 또 그 선함은 그 모호성에도 불구하고, 어느 시대에서나 어느 사회에서나 공통적인 성격을 갖고 있다는 증거도 있다(롬 2:10-15).

---

11) Henry Babel, *The Reformation: Many Men with One Idea* (Geneva: Foundation of Les Clefs de Saint-Pirre, 1985), 7, 33, 35.

2. 바울의 고린도 교회 방문 변경 해명 (1:15-2:13)

이 부분에서 바울은 구체적으로 고린도 교회와 자신 사이를 막고 있는 한 가지 문제 즉, 고린도 교회 방문 취소의 사유를 설명하고 있다. 바울은 고린도 교회를 설립하고 (50-51 A.D.) 고린도를 떠났다(행 18:18). 그 후에 고린도전서를 쓸 때, 방문하겠다고 하였고, 실제로 방문하였는데 그 방문을 "고통의 방문"(The Painful Visit)이라고 추정한다(고전 16:5-8; 고후 2:1). 바울은 그의 반대자들의 공격을 받고 황망히 떠났던 것 같다. 고린도후서 2장 1절에서 그 곤란했던 방문의 기억을 회상하고 있다. 바울은 그 때 떠나오면서 다시 방문한다고 하였으나 고린도 교회의 사정이 호전되지 않아서 방문을 미루고 있었던 것이다. 바울을 반대하는 이들은 바울이 방문약속을 갑자기 번복한 사실을 바울의 사도직 공격을 위한 호재로 삼아서 바울의 진실성이나 신뢰성 문제를 거론하였던 것 같다. 방문 약속 취소를 그의 사도로서의 인격적 결핍으로 보고 사도직에 대한 비난을 강화시켰을 것이다. 그는 본문에서 방문약속을 번복한 이유를 변명하면서 "고린도 교인들을 아끼려 함"이었고 비난자들이 말하듯이 그의 변덕스런 성격 때문은 아니라고 한다. 또 한 가지 (바울을 반대하는) 문제가 된 사람의 치리 문제가 방문에 걸림이 된 것임을 말한다. 즉 방문여건이 조성되어 있지 않은 상태인데 다시 방문해봐야 피차 어려움만 생길 것이라고 보고 여건이 조성될 때까지 기다렸던 것 같다. 그러나 이제 디도가 전한 바울의 편지(2:4)에서 바울이 지시한 대로 고린도 교회가 문제된 사람을 치리하여 방문 여건을 조성한 만큼 바울은 고린도후서를 쓰면서 다시 방문할 것을 약속한다(9:3-4; 12:20-13:1,

10). 이런 의미에서 고린도후서는 바울의 3차 고린도 방문이 원만하게 되도록 고린도 교인들을 준비시키는 목회서신이라고 볼 수 있다.

a. 초기 방문 계획 설명(1:15-16)

본문:

> 15 내가 이 확신을 가지고 너희로 두 번 은혜를 얻게 하기 위하여 먼저 너희에게 이르렀다가 16 너희를 지나 마게도냐에 갔다가 다시 마게도냐에서 너희에게 가서 너희가 보내줌으로 유대에 가기를 계획(경영)하였으니.

본문비평:

15절의 **χάριν**(은혜)이란 말 대신 **χάραν**(기쁨)이란 말로 ℵ (c) B L P 콥틱역 등에 나타난다. 의도적이든 실수든 문장의 의미에 큰 차이는 없다 바울의 방문이 고린도인들에게 은혜이기도하고 기쁨이기도 하다 그러나 사본상의 상이한 문구를 선정할 때 더 어려운 문구를 원래의 문구로 본다는 원칙(*lectio difficilior potior*, 어려운 문구를 후대 복사자가 쉬운 말로 고쳤을 가능성이 있다는 본문 비평 원칙)을 존중하여 은혜란 말을 그대로 쓴다.

주석:

15. "내가 이 확신을 가지고 너희로 두 번 은혜를 얻게 하기 위하여 먼저 너희에게 이르렀다가"(**Καὶ ταύτῃ τῇ πεποιθήσει ἐβουλόμην πρότερον πρὸς ὑμᾶς ἐλθεῖν, ἵνα δευτέραν χάριν σχῆτε,**). 바울은 14절에서 밝혔듯이 고린도 교인들도 반드

시 자신의 진실성을 알게 될 날(최후의 심판의 날)이 있음을 확신하기 때문에, 거리낌 없이 고린도 교회를 방문하고자 하였다. 그것도 한 번이 아닌 두 번씩이나 가려고 하였던 것이다. 고린도를 거쳐서 마게도냐(데살로니가, 빌립보)로 올라갔다가 다시 내려와서 고린도에 들렀다가 예루살렘으로 갈 작정이었다. 바울은 방문의 기회를 은혜란 말로 나타내고 있다. 어떤 번역자들은 기쁨이나 유익으로 번역한다. 그러나 은혜란 말이 바울이 잘 쓰는 말이며 그대로 번역해도 의미가 통하므로 달리 번역할 필요가 없다. "먼저" (πρότερον)란 말을 "계획(경영)하였으니" (ἐβουλόμην)에 붙여서 "먼저(애당초) 계획하였다" 라는 번역도 있으나 대부분의 번역은 "먼저 너희에게 이르렀다가" 라고 번역한다.

바울의 첫 번째 방문은 계획대로 시행되었다. 그 방문은 "고통의 방문" (2:1)이었다. 이 첫 번째 방문에서 매우 곤혹스런 경험을 한 바울은 "두 번째 은혜" 즉 방문 계획을 취소하였던 것이다. 문제는 바울이 언제 두 번씩 방문키로 약속하였는가이다. 리츠만은 "두 번 은혜" 를 "두 번째의 방문" 으로 해석한다. 고린도 교회를 세울 때의 방문이 첫째이고, 2장 1절의 방문이 "두 번째의 방문" 이라는 것이다.[12] 이와 달리 불트만과 플러머는 2장 1절의 "고통의 방문" 이전에 계획했다가 취소된 바울의 "두 번째 방문 계획" 이라고 본다.[13] 휴즈는 2장 1절의 방문 시에 계획하였거나, 고린도전서 5장 9절의 잃어버린 편지에서 약속하였다고 가정한다.[14] 퍼니쉬는 2장 1절의 방문 직후에 결정하였다고 한다.[15] 그러나 마틴은

12) Lietzmann, 102.

13) Bultmann, 38; Plummer, 32; Barth, 75.

14) Hughes, 32; 박윤선, 288.

"두 번씩 방문하려는 계획"의 첫 번째 방문은 실현되었고(2:1), 두 번째 방문 계획이 성사되지 못한 것으로 본다.[16] 마이어(Meyer)는 고린도전서 16장 5절에서 바울은 이미 이전에 약속한 두 번 방문을 변경하여 한 번으로 고치고 있다고 보았다.[17] 그러나 고린도전서 16장 5절이 원래 계획의 변경이라면 변경에 대한 설명이 있음직 한데 아무런 변명이 없다.

두 번씩 방문키로 한 약속은 2장 1절의 방문 이전에 한 것으로 보아야 한다. 바울은 고린도전서 16장 5절 이하에서 고린도 교회를 방문할 것을 약속했다. 그 후 바울은 그 약속을 확대하여서 "두 번씩 방문"할 것을 약속하였다. 두 번씩이나 방문하려는 계획은 필경 바울과고린도 교회와 사이가 좋았을 때에 세울 수 있기 때문이다. 그러다가 고린도 교회 문제가 악화되었을 때(55년 봄) 바울은 황급히 고린도 교회를 방문하였다("고통의 방문," 고후 2:1). 이때 바울이 처음 약속대로 방문 약속을 지키지 않았음을 공격하는 이들이 있었다고 본다. 또 디도가 바울에게 고린도 교회의 안정된 소식을 가져왔을 때에도 여전히 바울이 방문 약속을 지키지 않고 고린도 교회에 무관심함을 비난하는 소리가 있었음을 디도를 통해서 바울이 알았을 것이다. 이에 바울이 고린도후서 초두에서 애초에 계획한 "두 번씩 방문 계획"의 취소 경위를 설명해야 했었고, 대신 13장 1절에서 세 번째 방문 계획을 약속한 것이다.

16. "너희를 지나 마게도냐에 갔다가 다시 마게도냐에서 너희

---

15) Furnish, 143.

16) Martin, 25.

17) Meyer, 427.

에게 가서 너희가 보내줌으로 유대에 가기를 계획(경영)하였으니"(καὶ δι᾽ ὑμῶν διελθεῖν εἰς Μακεδονίαν καὶ πάλιν ἀπὸ Μακεδονίας ἐλθεῖν πρὸς ὑμᾶς καὶ ὑφ᾽ ὑμῶν προπεμφθῆναι εἰς τὴν Ἰουδαίαν). 바울의 애초의 계획은 분명히 고린도를 방문하는 계획이었음을 구체적 일정을 말함으로서 밝히고 있다. 바울은 원래 아가야 지방(고린도가 속해 있는)에서 예루살렘 성도들을 위한 헌금을 거두어서 예루살렘으로 갈 계획이었다(고전 16:3, 4; 롬 15:26). 그러나 고린도 교회 사태가 바울의 방문을 막았다. 사도행전 20장 2-4절에 나타나는 바와 같이 마게도냐를 떠나 드로아로 갈 때 바울과 함께한 사람들 중에 고린도 사람들이 포함되지 않았다. 이것은 고린도 교회의 문제가 해결되지 않았기 때문에 바울이 이때 고린도 교회를 방문하지 않았다는 추가적 증거로 보인다(1:23; 2:1).[18] 이때 바울의 출발지는 고린도전서를 쓰고 있던 에베소이다.[19]

바울의 여행 계획을 정리하면, 바울의 애초의 고린도 여행 계획은, 고린도전서 16장 2-8절에 있는 대로, 에베소-마게도냐-고린도-예루살렘 순이었다. 고린도후서 1장 15-16절의 수정된 계획은, 에베소-고린도-마게도냐-고린도-유대(예루살렘)로 나타난다. 바울의 실제 여행은, 에베소-고린도("고통의 방문", 2:1)-에베소(데메드리오의 난동, 행 19:23-41)-마게도냐(고린도후서를 씀: 고후 2:13; 7:5; 행 20:1b-2a)-고린도(로마서를 씀: 행 20:2b-3a)로 보인다.[20]

18) Martin, 25.

19) Harris, 194.

20) Harris, 194, 195.

b. 바울 자신은 변덕스런 사람이 아니라 미쁘신 하나님의 사역자로서 성실한 사람이다 (1:17-22).

본문:

17. 이렇게 계획(경영)할 때에 어찌 경홀히 하였으리요 혹 계획(경영)하기를 육체를 좇아 계획(경영)하여(일구이언하여) "예, 예 하고 아니, 아니라 하는 일"이 내게 있었겠느냐 18. 하나님은 미쁘시니라. 우리가 너희에게 전한 말씀(한말)은(일구이언하여)"예 하고 아니라 함"이 없노라. 19. 우리 곧 나와 실루아노와 디모데로 말미암아 너희 가운데 전파된 하나님의 아들 예수 그리스도는 (일구이언하여) "예 하고 아니라 함"이 되지 아니하였으니, 저에게는(늘)"예"만 되었느니라. 20. 하나님의 약속은 얼마든지 그리스도 안에서 "예"가 되니 그런즉 그로 말미암아 우리가 하나님께 아멘하여 하나님께 영광을 돌리게 되느니라. 21. 우리를 너희와 함께 그리스도 안에서 견고하게 하시고 우리에게 기름을 부으신 이는 하나님이시니, 22. 저가 또한 우리에게 인치시고 보증으로 성령을 우리 마음에 주셨느니라.

본문비평:

17절의 P[46] 424c Vulgate Pelagius에서 **τὸ ναὶ ναὶ καὶ τὸ οὒ οὔ**가("예, 예 하고 아니, 아니라 하는 일") 18, 19절의 단순한 형식 **τὸ ναὶ ναὶ καὶ τὸ οὒ** ("예 하고 아니라 함")로 나타난다. 어떤 이들은 단순한 형식이 원래의 것이라고 하면서 이중적인 것은 바울의 말을 마태복음 5장 37절의 말과 조화시키려는 의도에서 고쳐 쓴 것이라고 한다. 그러나 에녹2서 49장 1절의 맹세법에도 꼭 같은 이중적 대답 형식(예, 예/ 아니, 아니)이 나오므로 바울이 당시 랍비들이 흔히 쓰던 맹세 형식을 따라서 썼다고 본다. 그러므로 위 사본들의 단순한 형식은 18, 19절을 따라서 고쳐 쓴 것이고 원래의 것은 이중적 형식이다.

내용 개요:

17-22에서 바울은 자신의 일방적 방문 취소로 말미암아 야기된 고린도 교인들의 바울에 대한 불신 문제에 대하여 해명한다. 바울은 23절에서 자신들이 반대자들이 비난하듯이 변덕스럽고 이기적인 취지에서 방문을 취소한 것이 아니라 고린도 교회가 아직 바울의 방문을 받을 만한 상태가 되지 못하였기 때문이라고 말한다. 그러나 이런 이유를 밝히기 전에 바울은 그의 사도적 진정성 자체에 대한 의구심으로 말미암아 이런 불신이 야기된 것이라고 보고 자신과 동역자들(디모데, 실루아노)의 신뢰성 회복을 위하여 바울과 그의 동역자들은 하나님의 신실하신 약속, 그리스도의 주권, 성령의 보증 등으로 삼위일체 하나님에게 인정받은 사람들이라는 것을 밝히고 있다.

주석:

17. "이렇게 계획(경영)할 때에 어찌 경홀히 하였으리요 혹 계획(경영)하기를 육체를 좇아 계획(경영)하여(일구이언하여) "예, 예 하고 아니, 아니라 하는 일" 이 내게 있었겠느냐 "(**τοῦτο οὖν βουλόμενος μήτι ἄρα τῇ ἐλαφρίᾳ ἐχρησάμην; ἢ ἃ βουλεύομαι κατὰ σάρκα βουλεύομαι, ἵνα ᾖ παρ᾽ ἐμοὶ τὸ ναὶ ναὶ καὶ τὸ οὒ οὔ;**). 17절의 경홀히(**ἐλαφρίᾳ**)는 여기서만 나오는 말이나 형용사 "경홀한" (**ἐλαφρός**)은 마태복음 11장 30절과 고린도후서 4장 17절에서 나온다. 여기서 이 말이 여격 명사로서 수단을 나타내므로, 실제로는 부사로서 "경홀히" 로 번역해야 한다. 본문에서 이 말은 경망스런 성격을 나타낸다.

μήτι란 말은 부정의 답을 예상하는 의문 부사이다. 즉 "내가 경망스럽게 계획하였다고 너희가 말하지는 않겠지?"라는 뜻이다. 바울이 생각 없이 방문을 계획하였다가 취소해버린 것이 아니라는 말은 또 다른 말로 이어진다. 바울은 그의 방문을 "육체를 좇아"(κατὰ σάρκα) 계획한 것도 아니라고 말한다. 같은 말이 5장 16절, 10장 2, 3절, 11장 18절에도 나온다. "육체"는 여기서 하나님의 뜻과 배치되는 인간의 욕심을 가리킨다. 바울은 아래 22절에서 성령의 인침을 받았다고 한다. 22절의 문맥에서 바울은 성령의 인도를 받는다는 뜻을 나타낸다. 12장 18절에도 바울과 그 동역자들이 동일한 성령으로 행한다고 말한다. 이 문맥에서도 바울은 "육체"의 소욕을 따라 방문을 취소하지 않았다고 해명하는 것이다.[21] 한편 "육체를 따라"라는 말이 앞의 "경홀히"와 병행한다고 보면, "사욕을 따라 움직이는 기회주의적 자세"라는 의미로 생각할 수도 있다.[22] 고린도의 반대자들이 바울을 이런 말로 비난했을 수 있고, 바울은 이런 비난을 듣고 여기서 해명하는 것으로 볼 수 있다.

랍비들은 여러 맹세문 형식을 가지고서 사람들과 거래하고 상종할 때 쓰도록 했다. 예수님은 그런 맹세문을 사용하는 것이 거짓된 양심에서 나오는 것이라고 비난하셨다 (마 5:34-39; 23:18-22). 그러시면서 가장 단순한 맹세 형식을 인정하셨다. 그것은 당시에 실제로 쓰이던 가장 기본적 맹세 형식으로서 "예, 예" 혹은 "아니, 아니"라는 것이다(에녹2서 49:1). 사람과의 약속을 자신의 이익을 챙기기 위해서 상황의 추이에 따라서 변개할 필요가 있으

21) Héring, 9.

22) Furnish, 132, Harris, 197, 재인용.

므로, 약속의 확실성에 따라서 여러 가지 맹세문을 사용했던 것이다. 예수님은 이런 행위를 악으로 보셨다. 신실치 못한 모든 인간 관계는 "하나님의 신실하심"에 배치되는 죄악이다. 그런 불성실함을 감추고 모면하기 위한 종교적, 신학적 용어의 구사는 악한인간 속성의 표현일 뿐이다(마 5:39).

바울은 세속적 욕심을 가지고 되는 대로 살아가는 이기적 인간이 결코 아니라고 말한다. 반대로 그는 성령의 인치심을 받은 신실한 사도이다(22).

18. "하나님은 미쁘시니라. 우리가 너희에게 전한 말씀(한말)은 (일구이언하여) 예 하고 아니라 함이 없노라" (**πιστὸς δὲ ὁ θεὸς ὅτι ὁ λόγος ἡμῶν ὁ πρὸς ὑμᾶς οὐκ ἔστιν ναὶ καὶ οὔ**). 18절은 바울의 신뢰성의 근거를 바울이 전한 하나님과 복음의 신뢰성에서 찾는다. 바울의 고린도 교회에 전한 복음(**ὁ λόγος**)은 "예"하고 "아니라" 함이 없는 신실하신 하나님의 약속인 것이다. 바울과 그의 동역자들은 변치 않는 신실하신 하나님의 말씀을 전하는 사람들이다. 그런 사람들로서 어떻게 육체를 따라(즉, 사욕을 따라서) 변덕스럽게 행동할 수 있겠는가 마틴은 데니(Denney)가 "말씀"(**ὁ λόγος**)라는 말은 바울의 여행 변경에 대한 변명과 복음을 다 포함하는 말이라고 했음을 매우 지혜로운 주석이라고 찬사한다.[23] 바울이 비록 방문 계획을 취소했다고 해도 그것은 결코 인간의 사욕적인 의도에서 나온 취소가 아니고 신실하신 하나님의 사람의 결정으로서 긍정적으로 믿는 것이 옳다. 하나님은 그를 믿

23) Martin, 27; Denney, 38.

는 자들을 위하여 모든 것이 합력하여 선을 이루게 하시는 하나님이시다. 하나님의 신실하심을 믿으면 그의 "아니"도 결국 "예"가 될 수 있음을 믿는 것이다. 문제는 고린도 교인들이 바울과 그의 동역자들이 이렇게 신실하신 하나님의 사람들임을 불신하는 것이 문제이다. 바울의 방문 변경을 단순히 세속적 인간들의 변덕스런 취소로 생각하는 것이 문제다. 그러므로 바울은 고린도 교인들이 그가 전한 복음의 진실성과 하나님의 신실하심, 그리스도의 능력, 성령의 보증 등 성삼위 하나님의 신실하심과 역사하심을 믿는 것같이 이 진실한 복음을 전한 자신의 진실성도 믿어 줄 것을 바란다.

19. "우리 곧 나와 실루아노와 디모데로 말미암아 너희 가운데 전파된 하나님의 아들 예수 그리스도는(일구이언하여) 예 하고 아니라 함이 되지 아니하였으니, 저에게는 (늘) "예" 만 되었느니라" (**ὁ τοῦ θεοῦ γὰρ υἱὸς Ἰησοῦς Χριστὸς ὁ ἐν ὑμῖν δι᾽ ἡμῶν κηρυχθείς, δι᾽ ἐμοῦ καὶ Σιλουανοῦ καὶ Τιμοθέου, οὐκ ἐγένετο ναὶ καὶ οὒ ἀλλὰ ναὶ ἐν αὐτῷ γέγονεν**). 19절은 바울과 그의 동역자들이 언제나 그의 약속을 지키시고 이루시는 신실하신 하나님의 아들 그리스도의 사람들인 것을 밝힌다. 고린도 교인들이 그리스도의 복음을 받아서 그리스도인이 된 것은 바로 바울과 그의 동역자들로 말미암은 것이다. 18절의 "말씀" (**ὁ λόγος**)을 하나님의 아들 예수 그리스도로 명기한다. "너희 가운데 전파된 하나님의 아들 예수 그리스도는 예하고 아니라함이 되지 아니하였으니 저에게는 예만 되었느니라." "저에게는" (**ἐν αὐτῷ**)은 문자적으로뿐만 아니라 의미상으로 "그 안에서" 라고 해야 더 분명한 뜻이 된다. "그 분 안에서는(그리스도 안에서) 언제나 '예' (약

속)가(이) 이루어졌다."[24] 이 말은 20절을 읽으면 더 분명해진다. "그 분 안에서 하나님의 구원의 약속이 긍정적으로 이루어졌다"는 뜻이 된다. 또 죽음에서 부활하신 그리스도의 능력이 모든 그리스도 안에 있는 모든 사람들의 어려운 처지와 문제들을 능력으로 해결하여 주시고 승리하게 하신다는 의미가 있다. 2장 14-17절에서의 그리스도의 향기로서 언제나 승리하게 하시는 하나님의 역사와 12장 9, 10절에서의 "약한 데서 강해지는 그리스도의 능력"이 하나님의 사람들인 바울과 그의 동역자들에게 내재하여 결국 만사형통하게 된다는 말들을 여기서 예측하게 한다. 고린도 교인들의 바울의 변덕스러움이나 무관심에 대한 오해는 바울이 전한 그리스도의 신실하심을 믿을 때, 그의 죽으심의 능력을 믿을 때, 결국 풀리게 된다고 보는 것이다(13:3-5).

20. "하나님의 약속은 얼마든지 그리스도 안에서 예가 되니 그런즉 그로 말미암아 우리가 하나님께 아멘하여 하나님께 영광을 돌리게 되느니라"(ὅσαι γὰρ ἐπαγγελίαι θεοῦ, ἐν αὐτῷ τὸ ναί· διὸ καὶ δι᾽ αὐτοῦ τὸ ἀμὴν τῷ θεῷ πρὸς δόξαν δι᾽ ἡμῶν). 20절은 하나님의 모든 약속들은 그리스도 안에서 최종적으로 성취되었다고 한다(롬 1:2, 3; 9:5, 10; 10:4; 갈 3:16). 신실하신 하나님은 구원의 약속을 변개치 않으시고 그리스도의 죽으심과 부활을 통해 구원의 약속을 온전히 이루셨다. 이런 신실하신 하나님께 대하여 "아멘"("진실하시도다," 혹은 "확실하시도다")으로 화답하여 영광을 돌리는 것이 믿는 자의 마땅한 자세이다. 바레트

24) Martin, 26.

는 "우리로 말미암아 아멘" 한다고 번역하면서 "우리"란 죽음으로 죄인을 구원하신 그리스도를 예배하는 그리스도인의 공동체라고 하였다.[25] 20절에서와 같이 "그리스도 안"이란 말은 그리스도인이 그리스도의 구원 능력과 권위에 온전히 복종하고 믿는 것을 나타낸다(2:14, 17; 10:7, 17, 12:2, 19; 13:2). 믿는 자는 그리스도께서 그의 죽으심을 통해 죄인을 구원하셨음을 믿는다. 또한 믿는 자는 하나님께서 온갖 오해와 어려움 가운데서도 능히 그의 구원 사역을 이루어 가시는 신실하신 분이심을 믿는다. 바울도 하나님의 사역자로서 온갖 오해에도 불구하고 하나님의 구원 사역을 이루는 신실한 하나님의 사역자이다. 그러므로 고린도 교인들도 바울의 신실함을 믿는 것이 마땅하다고 권면하는 것이다.

21. "우리를 너희와 함께 그리스도 안에서 견고하게 하시고 우리에게 기름을 부으신 이는 하나님이시니"(ὁ δὲ βεβαιῶν ἡμᾶς σὺν ὑμῖν εἰς Χριστὸν καὶ χρίσας ἡμᾶς θεός,). 21절에서 바울은 그의 사도직이 하나님께로부터 온 것임을 밝힌다(2:17; 3:1-18; 4:2-6). 아마 이런 진술을 하는 이유는 바울의 반대자들이 바울을 신뢰할 수 없는 떠돌이 거짓 사도로 비난하였기 때문이라고 볼 수 있다(10:11-16; 11:5, 13-15; 12:11, 12; 13:3). 이에 대해서 바울은 21절과 22절에서 신실하신 하나님과 그리스도, 그리고 성령의 삼위일체 하나님께서 그를 사도로 세우셨음을 밝힌다. 그의 사도직이 하나님에게서 온 사실을 21절과 22절에서 특별히 4개의 동사

25) Barrett, 78. 20절이 초대 교회에서 사용하던 세례식 찬양이나 예식 어귀와 관련이 있는 지를 찾는 이들이 있다. 이를 지지하는 이들과 반대하는 이들의 견해를 Furnish, 148에서 보라. Martin, 27; Bultmann, 41을 참조하라.

로 나타내고 있다. 첫째로, 하나님은 "우리를 너희와 함께 그리스도 안에서 견고케 하셨다." 여기서 "견고하다"(βεβαιόω)라는 동사는 원래 법률적 용어로서, 물건의 구매를 법적으로 인준한다는 뜻이다.[26] 바울은 여기서 고린도전서 1장 6절 이하에서와 같이 이 말을 "견고하게 한다"는 뜻으로 쓰였다.[27] 바울의 그리스도에 대한 증거가 고린도 교인들에게 견고케 되었다는 것이다. 하나님은 복음을 전파하는 자와 듣는 자에게 그 복음의 약속을 이루어 주심으로써(롬15:8) 복음을 증거하고 견고케 하신다.[28] 나아가서 하나님은 그의 계심과 신실하심을 믿는 이들을 그리스도의 것으로 보증하신다. 그리스도인들은 그리스도의 것으로서 존재론적 연합을 이룬다.[29] 그렇다면 하나님께서 바울을 그의 말씀을 전하는 신실한 종으로서 신임하셨고 고린도 교인들은 그의 말씀을 들음으로 함께 그리스도 안에서 견고한 연합을 이루게 되었다.

둘째로, 하나님은 우리들에게 기름을 부으셨다(χρίσας). "우리"란 말이 바울과 그 일행과 함께 고린도 교인들도 포함한다고 볼 수도 있다.[30] 요한일서 2장 20절의 "너희는 거룩하신 자에게서

---

26) W. C. van Unnik, "Reisepläae und Amen-Sagen. Zusammenhang und Gedankenfolge in 2 Korinther 1:15-24," in *The Collected Essays of W. C. van Unnik,* NovTSup, Part One, 29 (Leiden: Brill, 1973), 144-59. 여기서 van Unnik은 "견고케 한다" 동사가 히브리어 "아멘"과 관련이 있음을 주장한다. Barrett는 히브리어 보다 희랍 사회에서 상업적, 법률적으로 매우 흔히 쓰인 점을 들어서 희랍적인 배경과 의미가 있다고 본다(Barrett, 78-79). Bultmann도 Barrett와 같은 견해를 갖고 있다(Bultmann, 42). Deissmann, *Bible Studies,* 104를 참조하라.

27) Bultmann, 42.

28) Barrett, 79.

29) Barrett, 79.

30) Barrett, 79.

기름 부음을 받고 모든 것을 아느니라"는 말씀에서 "기름부음을 받았다"는 말이 모든 믿는 자를 포함하는 말이다. 그러나 이 말씀은 모든 이들이 하나님의 일을 하도록 세움을 받았다는 뜻이 아니라 하나님의 은혜로 그리스도를 아는 지식을 갖게 되었다는 뜻이다. 그러나 본문에서 이 말이 바울과 그 일행만을 포함한다고 보는 것이 두 가지 이유로 타당해 보인다. 1) 본문의 주제가 바울의 사도직 임명임을 고려해야 한다.[31] "하나님이 나사렛 예수에게 성령과 능력을 기름 붓듯 하셨으매……" (행 10:38). 하나님께서 나사렛 예수를 성령과 능력으로 기름 부으심으로 하나님의 아들로 증거 하셨다. 같은 하나님이 바울을 기름 부으심으로 그의 사도로 삼으셨다. 그리스도의 기름 부으심과 사도직의 기름부음을 관련시키는 것은 본문의 Χριστὸν καὶ χρίσας ἡμᾶς라는 구절에서 "그리스도," 즉 "기름부음 받은 사람"이란 말을 "기름부음 받은 우리"와 연결시켜서 서로 관련된 의미를 나타내려는 증거가 있기 때문이다.[32] 또한 구약에 사사, 왕, 선지자들을 기름 부어 세움이 이런 표현의 배경임이 분명하다. 2) "견고케 한다"는 말에는 고린도인들을 포함시켰으므로 "기름부음 받는다"(χρίσας)라는 말을 의도적으로 사도직과 관련시켜 썼다고 보는 것이 옳다.[33]

하나님은 사도 바울과 그 일행을 그의 복음 사역을 위해 세우셨다. 사도직을 사사, 왕, 선지자의 직책과 같은 선 위에 놓고 그 권위가 사람에게서 온 것이 아니라 하나님에게서 온 것임을 의미하고 있음을 유의해야 한다(갈 1:1).

---

31) Denney, 50

32) Denney, 50, 주1; Barrett, 79.

33) Denney, 50.

22. "저가 또한 우리에게 인치시고 보증으로 성령을 우리 마음에 주셨느니라"(ὁ καὶ σφραγισάμενος ἡμᾶς καὶ δοὺς τὸν ἀρραβῶνα τοῦ πνεύματος ἐν ταῖς καρδίαις ἡμῶν). 21절에 이어서, 하나님께서 바울과 그 일행의 신뢰성을 보증하신다고 밝힌다. 즉, 셋째로, 하나님께서 바울과 그 일행을 인치셨다. "인친다"(σφραγίζω)라는 말도 법률 용어로서 "소유권자의 소유권"의 뜻이 있다. "이것은 내 것이다"라는 증표를 만드는 것을 뜻한다.[34] 하나님께서 바울과 그의 일행을 그의 종들로 삼으셨다. 그들은 하나님의 소유이다. 그러므로 아무도 이 소유권을 뺏을 수도 없고 부인할 수도 없다.

넷째로, 하나님이 바울과 그의 동역자들에게 "성령의 보증을 주셨다"(δοὺς τὸν ἀρραβῶνα τοῦ πνεύματος). 휴즈는 앞의 두 가지 동사, 즉 기름 부으심, 인치심 모두가 성령의 사역이라고 한다.[35] 기름 부음은 성령의 선물 주심을 나타내기도 한다(사 61:1-3; 눅 4:18; 행 4:27; 10:38). 인치심도 성령의 사역이다(엡 1:13). 그러나 본문의 4개의 동사(분사)들의 주어는 성부 하나님이다. 이 네 번째 동사(δίδωμι, "주다")의 주어도 역시 성부 하나님이다. 하나님이 성령을 보증(ἀρραβῶν)으로 주셔서 바울이 사도임을 증거한다. "나도 또한 하나님의영을 받은 줄로 생각하노라"(고전 7:40). 그의 동역자들도 그와 같은 영으로 행한다(고후 12:18). 그의 사역 가운데 나타난 표적과 기사와 능력이 성령의 능

34) Deissmann, 238.

35) Hughes, 43.

력이다(고후 12:12; 롬 15:18). “성령의 보증” 이란 말은 고린도후서 5장 5절에서도 같은 의미로 쓰였다. 성도들에게 나타나는 성령의 현존하심과 그의 사역은 성도들이 누릴 장래의 완전한 영광의 보증이 되는 것이다. “보증” (ἀρραβῶν, עֵרָבוֹן)이란 말은 원래 “보증금” 이란 말이다(창 38:18; 엡 1:14). 보증금을 지불하는 것은 나머지 금액을 일정한 기간 내에 납부한다는 약속이다. 그와 같이 현재의 성령의 사역은 장차 나타날 큰 하나님의 영광을 예측케 하는 것이다. 바울은 고린도후서의 마지막 부분인 12장 18절에서도 여기서와 같이 바울과 그의 동역자들이 성령으로 행하고 동일한 보조를 취한다고 하면서 사도직의 진정성을 변호한다.

한편 이 네 개의 동사(견고케함, 기름부음, 인치심, 성령의 보증을 주심)를 세례의 결과와 관련시켜 설명하기도 한다.[36] 딩클러는 “견고케 한다” 는 말은 세례의 일반적인 효과를 말하며, “기름부음” 은 세례식 때에 물을 붓는 것을 나타내고, “인치심은” 십자가로 구원받음을 의미하며, 성령의 선물은 기름부음과 인치심의 결과라고 한다.[37] 즉 바울이 이런 동사들을 세례와 관련하여 사용하고 있다는 것이다. 휴즈는 중생한 그리스도인의 삶과 관련시켜 생각한다. “기름부음” 은 우리를 부르시고 임직을 주신 것을 말하고, “인치심” 은 주신 직책을 받아서 수행하는 것을 말하고, 성령의 보증을 주심은 우리의 임무 수행에 따른 장래의 보상에 대한 약속의 현재의 증표라고 보았다.[38] 세례와의 관련성을 전혀 부인할 수도 없고, 또 일반 그리스도인의 봉사와 관련시켜 생각할 수도 있으

36) Martin, 28: 세례와 관련하여 다른 학자들의 견해를 보라.

37) E. Dinkler, 190.

38) Hughes, 43.

나, 여기서 이 4개의 동사는 어디까지나 바울의 사도직의 신적 기원을 증거함에 그 목적이 있다. 바울은 그의 사도직을 의심하는 고린도 교인들과 거짓 사도들에게 자신의 사도직의 신적 기원을 분명히 밝히는 것이다. 자신은 확실히 하나님의 부르심을 받아서 구별되게 세우심을 받은 하나님의 사도이다. "사람이 마땅히 우리를 그리스도의 일군이요 하나님의 비밀을 맡은 자로 여길 지어다" (고전 4:1). 자신이 사역의 일정을 바꾸었다고 해서 그 사정도 알아보지도 않고 이내 그를 변덕스럽다고 하거나 속물근성을 가진 단순한 세상인으로 보는 것은 옳지 않다. 문제는 바울의 신뢰성이 아니라, 사도 바울을 의심하는 고린도 교인들의 신뢰성이 문제이다. 그들의 믿음이 진실한 믿음인가를 돌이켜 보도록 질문하는 것이다. 고린도 교인들이 자신들을 그리스도인이 되도록 복음을 전한 바울을 믿지 못한다면 복음의 핵심인 하나님과, 그리스도와 성령의 사역을 어떻게 믿을 것인가라는 근본적인 문제를 제기하는 것이다. 유사하게 바울은 고린도후서 마지막에서도 다음과 같이 고린도 교인들에게 질문 하고 있다: "너희가 믿음에 있는가 너희 자신을 시험하고 너희 자신을 확증하라. 예수 그리스도께서 너희 안에 계신 줄을 너희가 스스로 알지 못하느냐 그렇지 않으면 너희가 버리운 자니라" (13:5).

주해(1:17-22):

바울은 17-22절에서 고린도 교인들에게 자신이 고린도 교회 방문을 취소하게 된 연유를 설명하기 시작한다. 실제 연유는 23절 이하에서 나온다. 즉 바울은 결코 사욕적으로("육체를 좇아") 방문을 취소한 것이 아니었다고 한다. 오히려 고린도 교인들이 방문을 받을 만한 상태가 되지 못했다고 보았기 때문이다. 2장 1절에서 지난번의 쓰라린 방문 경험을 회상하면서 다시는 그런 방문을 하지 않겠다고 하고, 12장 20, 21절에서도 바울은 3차 방문을 위해 고린도 교인들이 그들의 여러 가지 죄를 회개하면서 대비하기를 촉구한다. 그렇지 않을 경우 화해와 기쁨의 방문 대신 책벌과 근심의 방문이 되기 때문이다(2:2-3; 13:10).

본문에서는 이런 구체적인 연유를 말하기에 앞서서 바울에 대한 고린도 교인들의 불신의 근본적인 문제가 고린도 교인들의 복음에 대한 믿음이 부족한 탓이라고 보고 고린도 교인들의 신앙회복을 촉구한다(참조, 13:4). 바울이 전한 복음은 신실하신 하나님의 그리스도를 통한 구원의 약속이며, 그리고 보증으로 성령을 주셨고 마지막 날에 큰 영광의 구원이 이루어질 것을 믿고 살도록 가르치는 것이다. 고린도 교인들이 그가 전한 이 복음을 믿고 구원을 얻었으며 그리스도 안에서 모든 것이 형통하게 역사함을 믿는다. 그런데 이 신실한 복음을 전한 바울 사도를 불신하는 것은 결과적으로 바울이 전한 복음의 주이신 성삼위 하나님의 신실하심과 역사하심을 부인하게 되는 심각한 문제가 될 수 있다. 그러므로 바울은 고린도 교인들에게 바울의 신뢰성을 의심하지 말고 오히려 고린도 교인들이 자신들의 믿음이 신실하신 하나님과, 그리스도, 그리고 성령의 역사와 능력을 믿는 바른 믿음인지를 살피도록 권면하는 것이다. 고린도 교인들이 바른 믿음을 가지면 바울에 대한 그들의 신뢰성도 회복될 수 있다고 믿기 때문이다(13:5).

c. 고린도 교회가 방문할 형편이 되지 않았다(1:23-2:2); 그래서 바울은 "눈물의 편지"를 대신 썼다 (2:3-4).

본문:

23. 내가 내 영혼을 두고 하나님을 불러 증거하시게 하노니 다시 고린도에 가지 아니한 것은 너희를 아끼려 함이라. 24. 우리가 너희 믿음을 주관하려는 것이 아니요 오직 너희 기쁨을 돕는 자가 되려 함이니 이는 너희가 믿음에 섰음이라. 2:1. 내가 다시는(다시) 근심으로 너희에게 나아가지 않기로 스스로 결단 하였노니, 2. 내가 너희를 근심하게 하면, 나의 근심하게 한 자 밖에 나를 기쁘게 하는 자가 누구냐 (내가 너희를 슬프게 하면 누가 나를 기쁘게 할 것인가 나를 기쁘게 할 사람들은 너희들 뿐인데, 너희들을 슬프게 만들고서야 내가 누구에게서 기쁨을 얻는다는 말인가) 3. 내가 지금 이 글을 쓰는 것도 (내가 이같이 쓴 것은) 내가 갈 때에 마땅히 나를 기쁘게 할 너희들(자)로부터 도리어 근심을 얻을까 염려함이요, 또 너희 무리를 향한(대하여) 나의 기쁨이 (바로) 너희 무리의 기쁨인 줄 확신함이로라. 4. (지난 번 보낸 편지에서) 내가 큰 환난과 애통한 마음이 있어 많은 눈물로 너희에게 썼노니 이는 너희로 근심하게하려 한 것이 아니요, 오직 내가 너희를 향하여 넘치는 사랑이 있음을 너희로 알게 하려함이라.

본문비평:

1. 23절은 사본에 따라서 δε,(a A G Syrp, Byzantine), γάρ(p^{46}, B 69 Syrh), τε(D)로 시작된다. γάρ인 경우에는 2장 1절이 1장 23절의 방문 취소 이유를 보충하는 이유절이 된다. δέ인 경우는 2장 1절이 1장 24절과 대조를 이루는 절이 된다.[39)]

---

39) Plummer, 46.

2. 24절의 "너희 믿음"이 ὑμῶν τῆς πίστεως(a A B C K L O P)와 τῆς πίστεως ὑμῶν(D E F G)로 어순이 바뀌어 나온다. 어떤 의미의 차이도 없다.[40]

3. 2장 2절의 εἰ μή는 여기서와 같이 보통 "이외에"라는 전치사적 의미로 되나, 쉼표를 붙이면 강한 부정의 부사적 의미가 되어, "결코 … 아닌"이라고 번역된다.[41]

5. 3절의 λύπην(근심)이란 말을 λύπην ἐπὶ λύπην("근심 위에 근심", 참조, 빌 2:27)으로 확대한 사본들이 있다: D G 1739 Latin, Syrh.

6. 4절의 "넘치는"(περισσοτέρως)은 문자적으로 "더 넘치도록"이란 뜻이다. 이 말이 앞의 동사 "가진다"(ἔχω, "있음")를 수식하는지, 또는 뒤에 있는 εἰς ὑμᾶς를 수식하여 "특별히 너희를 위하여"라고 해야 하는 지가 논쟁이 될 수 있다.[42] 고린도후서 1장 12절에서 "특별히"로 번역해야 하는 용법이 있다. 그러나 다른 경우도 있다(고전 12:23; 고후 7:13; 11:23).

내용개요:

1장 17-22절에서 바울은 그의 방문 취소의 동기나 이유를 아직 밝히지 않았다. 오히려 그의 사도로서의 진실성을 삼위 하나님의

40) Plummer, 46.

41) Héring, 14.

42) Barrett, 88.

신실하신 구원 사역과 관련하여 증거한다. 고린도 교인들이 자신의 사도직의 진정성을 의심하는 것은 자신이 전한 하나님과 하나님의 말씀의 신실성을 의심하는 것과 같으므로 그들 스스로가 자신들이 믿는 복음과 하나님의 신실하심에 대한 믿음을 새롭게 해야 할 것임을 암시면서, 자신의 사도직은 성삼위하나님으로부터 인준받은 것임을 밝힌다. 방문 취소의 구체적인 실제 이유는 23절부터 나온다. 23절에서 바울은 고린도 교회가 아직 그의 방문을 받아들일 수 있는 온전한 상태가 되지 못했기 때문에 상태가 호전될 때까지 방문을 연기하는 것이 고린도 교인들을 아끼는 것이 되기 때문이라고 생각하여 가지 않았다고 한다. 2장 1절에서 바울은 자신의 최근의 고린도 교회 방문 ("고통의 방문")을 상기하면서 다시는 그러한 모욕적이고 상호 관계를 악화시키는 방문은 하지 않겠다고 결심하였다고 한다. 고린도 교인들은 바울의 변덕스러움을 비난하고 신뢰성을 의심 하였으나, 바울은 오히려 자신에 대한 고린도 교인들의 그런 잘못된 자세(2:9), 특히 "근심하게 한 자"의 훼방 때문에(2:5) 방문할 수 없었음을 암시하고 있다. 방문 취소의 근본적인 이유는 고린도 교회 편에서 (바울을 반대하는) 문제가 된 사람을 치리하지 못하고 방문 여건을 조성하지 못했기 때문이다. 그러나 이제 바울이 편지("눈물의 편지," 또는 "혹독한 편지")에서 지시한대로 고린도 교회가 문제가 된 사람을 치리하였으므로 방문 여건을 조성하였음을 칭찬한다. 그러나 바울이 이제 다시 3차 방문을 하기 위해서는 문제가 된 사람의 치리를 풀어 주어 화목한 분위기를 조성할 필요가 있으므로 그의 치리해제를 지시하고 있는 것이다(5:20; 6:1; 7:2; 13:1). 그러지 않을 경우 또 다시 어려운 방문이 될 가능성이 있기 때문이다(2:1; 11; 12:20, 21).

주석:

23. "내가 내 영혼을 두고 하나님을 불러 증거하시게 하노니 다시 고린도에 가지 아니한 것은 너희를 아끼려 함이라"(Ἐγὼ δὲ μάρτυρα τὸν θεὸν ἐπικαλοῦμαι ἐπὶ τὴν ἐμὴν ψυχήν, ὅτι φειδόμενος ὑμῶν οὐκέτι ἦλθον εἰς Κόρινθον). 23절에서 바울은 이런 신실하신 하나님이 맡기신 사도직을 가진 사람으로서 그가 고린도 교회 방문을 취소하게 된 이유를 맹세문 형식으로 밝힌다. "내 영혼을 두고 하나님을 불러 증거하시게 하노니"라는 매우 강력한 맹세문으로써 그의 진실성을 강변하고 있다.[43] 바울이 고린도에 간다고 했다가 가지 않은 것은 자신의 유익 때문이 아니라 고린도 교인들의 유익을 위함이었다. 바울은 위에서 하나님의 신실하심을 그의 아들 예수 그리스도를 통한 구원 약속의 성취와 그리고 성령의 사역을 통해 입증하였다. 휴즈가 지적한바와 같이 바울은 22, 23절에서 삼위일체 하나님의 구원 사역을 모두 언급하고 있다.[44] 신실하신 삼위 하나님이 바울의 진실성을 증거하고 계신다. 바울은 고린도교인들을 아끼려고 그의 방문을 취소한 것이지 바울 자신의 유익을 위한 것이 결코 아니었다. "내 영혼을 두고"(ἐπὶ τὴν ἐμὴν ψυχήν)란 말은 맹세문 형식으로서, 만일 내 말이 거짓이면 내 육체적 생명의 근원인 내 영혼이 벌을 받게 된다는 뜻이다.[45] 맹세문 형식을 사용한 것은 그만큼 바울의 진술이 진실하다는 것이다.[46] 바울은 자신의 신뢰성을 확고하게 하기 위

43) Hughes, 46.

44) Hughes, 45.

45) Plummer, 43.; Tasker, 491; Calvin, 25; 정규남, 「고린도후서 강해」(서울:엠마오, 1994), 25.

46) Plummer, 43.

해서 맹세문의 형식을 취하는 것이다. 바울은 고린도후서에서 이외에도 유사한 맹세문 양식을 사용한다: "주 예수의 아버지 영원히 찬송할 하나님이 나의 거짓말 아니하는 줄을 아시느니라" (11:11, 31; 12:6, 19; 참조, 롬 9:1). 이런 잇단 맹세문구 자체가 고린도 교인들의 바울에 대한 불신의 골이 상당히 깊었던 것임을 보여준다.

24. "우리가 너희 믿음을 주관하려는 것이 아니요 오직 너희 기쁨을 돕는 자가 되려 함이니 이는 너희가 믿음에 섰음이라"(**οὐχ ὅτι κυριεύομεν ὑμῶν τῆς πίστεως ἀλλὰ συνεργοί ἐσμεν τῆς χαρᾶς ὑμῶν· τῇ γὰρ πίστει ἑστήκατε**). 24절에서 바울은 고린도 교인들의 성숙한 믿음을 인정하면서 그런 성숙한 믿음을 가진 고린도 교인들이 이러한 바울의 진실된 변명을 잘 이해할 수 있음을 믿는다고 한다. 퍼니쉬는 바울이 23절에서 "너희를 아끼려 함이라"는 말을 혹 고린도 교인들 가운데 오해하여 "자기가 무엇이라고 우리를 아끼고 좌지우지 하겠다는 말인가 "라고 반발할 수 있음을 감지하고서 즉시, 24절에서 "우리가 너희 믿음을 주관하려는 것이 아니요, 오직 너희 기쁨을 돕는 자가 되게 하려 함이니" 라고 매우 민주적인 지도자로서의 발언을 하고 있다고 한다.[47] 바울의 사역의 목적은 자신의 사도적 권위를 행사하여 자신의 입장을 확장하려는 데 있지 않고, 오히려 고린도 교인들의 기쁨을 확장하려는 데 있다. 다른 곳에서도 바울은 고린도 교인들의 불순한 성향을 잘 알고서 자칫 오해할 수 있는 말을 한 후에는, 오해의 소

47) Furnish, 151-52.

지를 불식시키기 위한 말을 조심스럽게 하는 경우가 있다(고전 4:14-21; 7:35; 고후 8:8; 10:2, 8, 13:10). 그러나 바울은 우선 상대방의 기분을 맞춰 주고 보자는 세속적 제스처로서 이런 말을 하는 것은 아니라고 본다. 앞에서 바울은 "우리는 육체를 따라 계획(경영)하지 않는다"라고 하였다(1:17). 또 고린도후서 5장 16절에도 비슷한 말이 있다. 그는 거짓 선지자들의 간교함을 질타하고 있다(11:3). 그는 목회자로서 진정 고린도 교인들을 사랑하는 마음을 가지고 그들이 그의 말을 잘못 듣지 않고 바로 듣기를 원하고 있다. 그는 고린도 교인들이 바울의 진정한 의도를 알아 오해를 풀고 그를 사도로 신뢰하면서 화해하기를 원하고 있다(5:18-21).

"이는 너희가 믿음에 섰음이라." 이 말이 13장 5절의 "너희가 믿음에 있는가 너희 자신을 시험하고…"와는 반대되는 뜻이라고 하여 1-9장과 10-13장을 다른 편지로 보는 이들이 있음을 개론 부분에서 지적하였다. 두 진술이 조화되지 않음을 부인할 수 없으나, 본문에서는 고린도 교인들 다수가 바울에게 다시 돌아와서 바울을 신뢰하는 이들이었으므로 본문에서 바울이 그들이 믿음에 섰다고 말할 수 있고, 10-13장에서는 바울을 반대하는 고린도 교인들을 꾸짖고 있으므로 여기와는 다른 말을 할 수 밖에 없다. 다시 말하면 이 두 구절의 내용이 다른 것은 바울이 말하는 대상이 다르기 때문이라고 볼 수 있다. 바울은 서신 초두에서 디도가 가져온 기쁜 소식으로 말미암아 고무된 감정을 우선 기쁨과 위로의 말로 나타내고, 엄중한 말은 따로 뒤에 가서 할 것이라고 편지를 처음 쓸 때부터 계획한 것으로 본다.

그러나 고린도 교회 내에 상이한 두 그룹이 있었다고 보지 않고, 변덕스런 고린도 회중 전체를 대상으로 말한다고 볼 수도 있다. 즉 말하는 대상이 하나이지만, 그 대상의 믿음이 견고하지 못하고 흔들리는 집단임을 고려하여 적절히 대응하는 것이다. 이 경우 그들이 믿음에 섰다는 말은 사실을 나타내는 말이 아니라 단순히 상대방을 고무시키는 말이거나 최근에 바울에게 다시 돌아온 사실을 가리키는 말로 보아야 할 것이다.

2:1. "내가 다시는(다시) 근심으로 너희에게 나아가지 않기로 스스로 결단 하였노니"(Ἔκρινα γὰρ ἐμαυτῷ τοῦτο τὸ μὴ πάλιν ἐν λύπῃ πρὸς ὑμᾶς ἐλθεῖν). 2장 1절에서 바울은 매우 단호하게 "내가 다시는 근심으로 너희에게 가지 않기로 결심하였다"고 말한다. 1장 23절에서는 방문 취소의 이유를 "고린도 교회를 아끼려함"이었다고 말하였으나, 2장 1절에서 더 직접적인 이유는 근심이 있었기 때문이었다고 한다. 물론 이 근심은 고린도 교인들로 말미암은 근심이다(2:5; 11:28). 더 구체적으로 바울이 2장 1절이 암시하는 "고통의 방문" 때에 겪은 수치와 모욕 때문이었을 것이다. 2장 1절에 "다시는 아니"(μὴ πάλιν)란 말에서 바울이 이전에 방문한 경험이 있었다는 것을 알 수 있고, 그 방문은 50-52년 사이의 고린도 교회 창설 시기를 말하는 것은 아니고 55년 봄, 고린도 후서를 쓰기 3-4개월 전에 고린도 교회 어려움을 듣고 잠시 방문한 것을 가리킨다.[48] 이 방문에서 바울은 어떤 큰 모욕을 당했다. 2장 5절에서 바울을 반대하는 세력을 이끄는 인물은 "근심하는 자"로 나온다. 7장 12절에서는 같은 인물이 "불의를 행

48) 이와 다른 견해를 Plummer, 47에서 보라.

한 자"로 나온다. 이후에 바울은 다시는 근심을 가지고 고린도 교회를 방문하지 않겠다고 굳게 결심하였다. 이에 따라서 "두 번씩 방문하려는 계획"을 취소하여 가지 않았던 것이다. 그런데도 고린도 교회에서 반대자들은 아마 여행 취소 문제를 들어서 바울을 인신 공격하여 사도로서의 신뢰성이 결여 되었다고 비난하였을 것이다. 바울은 이에 대해서 "나는 그런 사람이 아니다. 오히려 너희들에게 문제가 있다"고 말하고 있다. 바울이 본문에서 유화적인 자세로 고린도 교인들을 부드럽게 대하는 이면에, 이런 단호한 입장도 숨어 있다고 보아야 한다.

2 "내가 너희를 근심하게 하면, 나의 근심하게 한 자 밖에 나를 기쁘게 하는 자가 누구냐"(εἰ γὰρ ἐγὼ λυπῶ ὑμᾶς, καὶ τίς ὁ εὐφραίνων με εἰ μὴ ὁ λυπούμενος ἐξ ἐμοῦ;). 2절은 간단한 문장이고 뜻은 분명하나 문자적 번역을 할 때 이해하기 어려울 수 있다. 전체의 뜻은, "내가 근심을 가진 채로 방문하게 되면 피차가 즐기는 방문이 될 수 없다고 생각하여 방문할 수 없었다"는 뜻이다. "내가 근심하게 한 자 밖에 나를 기쁘게 하는 자가 누구냐 "란 말이 얼른 이해하기 어려운 번역이나 틀린 번역은 아니다. 이 말을 알기 쉽게 풀면 "내가 근심을 가진 채로 가서 너희들을 근심케 하면, 내가 근심하게 한, 바로 너희가 또 나를 기쁘게 해야 할 사람들이 아니겠느냐? 그러니 이런 아이러니하고 어색한 정황에서 어찌 참된 교제가 이루어 질 수 있겠는가? 피차에 무슨 유익이 있겠는가? 그래서 아예 방문 하지 않기로 했다"는 말이다. 1장 23절에서 고린도 교인들을 아끼려고 가지 않았다고 했고, 24절에서는 고린도 교인들의 기쁨을 위해서, 고린도 교인들의 유익만을 위해 방

문을 취소하였다고 하나, 2장 2절에서는 바울의 유익, 즉 고린도 교인들에게서 받는 "기쁨"을 얻을 수 없다는 사실도 방문 취소의 이유가 되었음을 솔직히 밝힌다. 그러나 반대자들이 비난할 수 있듯이 바울이 순전히 이기적인 생각에서 방문을 취소했다는 것은 타당하지 않다. 바울이 느끼는 기쁨이란 서로 주고 나누는 상호주의적 관계에서 형성되는 것이기 때문이다. 바울은 자신의 기쁨만이 아니라 상대방의 기쁨도 함께 생각한다. 즉 바울이 고린도 교인들을 슬프게 하면 그는 기쁠 수가 없다. 그를 기쁘게 할 사람들은 고린도 교인들 뿐인데, 그들을 슬프게 만들고서야 바울은 아무에게서도 기쁨을 얻을 수가 없다. 그러므로 바울이 순전히 이기적 생각에서 방문을 취소했다는 말은 타당하지 않다. 바울은 진정으로 고린도 교인들과 함께 희로애락하고 동고동락하기를 원한다 (7:3). 이런 의미가 다음 절에서 더 분명히 나타난다.

3. "내가 지금 이 글을 쓰는 것도(내가 이같이 쓴 것은) 내가 갈 때에 마땅히 나를 기쁘게 할 너희들(자)로부터 도리어 근심을 얻을까 염려함이요, 또 너희 무리를 향한(대하여) 나의 기쁨이 (바로) 너희 무리의 기쁨인 줄 확신함이로라" (**καὶ ἔγραψα τοῦτο αὐτό, ἵνα μὴ ἐλθὼν λύπην σχῶ ἀφ᾽ ὧν ἔδει με χαίρειν, πεποιθὼς ἐπὶ πάντας ὑμᾶς ὅτι ἡ ἐμὴ χαρὰ πάντων ὑμῶν ἐστιν**). 여기서 바울은 괴로웠던 지난 일(즉 방문 취소)에 대해서 다시 쓰는 것은 제 3차 방문(13:1)을 지난 번 2차 방문처럼 고통의 방문이 되지 않도록 피차 기쁨을 나누는 방문이 되도록 하기 위한 것이라고 한다.

"내가 이같이 쓴 것은" (**ἔγραψα τοῦτο αὐτο**)에 대한 번역이 4

개로 나뉜다. 즉 1) τοῦτο αὐτὸ를 부사절로 보아서, 내가 바로 이 이유 때문에 썼다. 즉 "내가 갈 때에 마땅히 나를 기쁘게 할 자로부터 도리어 근심을 얻지 않기 위해서……."라는 말이다. 2) τοῦτο αὐτὸ를 ἔγραψα("내가 썼다")의 목적어로 생각해서, 내가 이것을 썼다. 이것이란 4절의 소위 "눈물의 편지"에서 발췌한 인용으로서 1장 23절이나 2장 1절이 될 것이다. 즉 "너희를 아끼려고 가지 않았다"라든가 "다시는 근심으로 너희에게 가지 않겠다"라는 말을 "눈물의 편지"에서 쓴 이유는 다음에 만날 때 피차 기쁨으로 만나기 위한 것이었다. 3) τοῦτο αὐτό는 고린도후서의 전체 내용을 말한다. 이 경우 고린도후서를 쓰는 것은 다음의 방문이 기쁨의 방문이 되게 하기 위함이다.[49] 4) τοῦτο αὐτό는 바울이 1장 15절 이후에서 말하고 있는 방문 취소에 대한 설명 전체를 말한다고 본다. 이렇게 과거의 일에 대해서 누누이 설명하는 것은 방문 취소와 관련하여 바울에 대한 고린도 교인들의 오해를 풀고 다음 방문은 좋은 교제가 이루어지는 화해의 방문이 되기를 원하여 쓰는 것이다. 이 마지막 해석이 문맥상 무리가 없다. 더구나 다음 절(4절)에서 "눈물의 편지"를 쓸 때에 고통의 심정으로 썼음을 피력하고 있음을 보아 그렇다. "눈물의 편지"도 고통으로 썼는데, 이제 다시 좋지 않은 지난 이야기를 꺼내는 것은 너희들이 싫어할지 모르지만 다음 방문이 좋은 방문이 되기 위해 먼저 오해를 없애는 것이 필요하다는 것이다.

3절에 "기쁨"(χαρά)이란 명사와 "기뻐한다"(χαίρειν)는 동사

---

49) Barrett, 87.

가 함께 나온다. 1장 24절에도 같은 명사형이 나왔다. 2절에서도 εὐφραίνω라는 비슷한 동사가 나온다. 바울에게서 "기쁨"은 그리스도인의 중요한 특권이요 표징이다. 기쁨은 성령의 열매이며(갈 5:22), 하나님의 주권적 통치(하나님 나라)의 특징이며(롬 14:17), 믿음(24, 롬 15:13; 빌 1:25), 소망(롬 12:12)과 자주 관련되어 나타난다. 이 기쁨은 세상의 고난 가운데서도 오히려 살아나는 특이한 기쁨이다(고후 6:10; 7:4; 살전 1:6). 이 기쁨이 그리스도인의 교제의 결과이다. 바울과 그의 교인들은 기쁨으로 교제한다. 기쁨은 우리의 신앙의 계기(計器)와 같은 것이다. 그래서 바울은 "항상 기뻐하라"(살전 5:16)고 권면한다. 바울은 우리의 신앙이 "정상적"인 신앙 상태를 유지하고 있는지 아닌지를 점검하는 쉬운 방법을 제시하고 있다. 즉 우리에게 기쁨이 있는지 없는지를 살피는 것이다. 우리는 기쁨이라는 하나님의 귀한 선물을 늘 보존하고 확대해야 할 책임이 있다는 것이다.

그러므로 바울은 고린도 교회의 사역이 어려운 중에서도 그와 고린도 교회 교인들과의 교제에서 기쁨을 살리는 것을 그의 사역의 중요한 목적으로 간주하면서 조심스럽게 말하는 것이다. 이런 점에서 방문 취소의 궁극적 이유는 그리스도 안에서 기쁨 대신 근심을 일으킬 위험을 막기 위한 것이었다.

그러나 여기서 바울은 고린도 교인들의 한 가지 타당한 질문을 예상한 듯하다. "당신이 그렇게 우리를 근심하게 하지 않고 기쁨을 주려고 애썼다면 지난 번 보낸 편지의 내용에서 우리를 꾸짖어 근심케 한 것은 무슨 까닭이요?" 이런 질문에 대해서 바울은 그런 근심은 하나님의 뜻대로 하는 근심이라고 7장 9절에서 대답한다. 결국은 고린도 교인들에게 유익과 기쁨을 주기 위한 편지라고 한다. 그러나 바울은 당장 이런 대답을 하지 않고 자신의 사랑하는 마음이 강렬함을 먼저 말한다. 너희를 근심케 한 편지도 사실은 너희를 사랑하는 마음에서 쓴 사랑의 편지라고 한다(1:24).

4. "(지난 번 보낸 편지에서) 내가 큰 환난과 애통한 마음이 있어 많은 눈물로 너희에게 썼노니 이는 너희로 근심하게하려 한 것이 아니요, 오직 내가 너희를 향하여 넘치는 사랑이 있음을 너희로 알게 하려함이라" (**ἐκ γὰρ πολλῆς θλίψεως καὶ συνοχῆς καρδίας ἔγραψα ὑμῖν διὰ πολλῶν δακρύων, οὐχ ἵνα λυπηθῆτε ἀλλὰ τὴν ἀγάπην ἵνα γνῶτε ἣν ἔχω περισσοτέρως εἰς ὑμᾶς**). 4절에서 바울은 2장 1절에서 암시한 "고통의 방문" 후에 이어서 쓴 "눈물의 편지"를 쓴 그의 심정을 고백하고 있다. 그 편지의 성격과 내용을 다 알 수는 없으나, 본문에서 대강 짐작할 수는 있다. 그 편지에서 바울은 주로 바울을 반대하며 교회를 어지럽히는 "근심하게 한 자"를 치리하도록 엄히 명령하였음이 분명하다(2:5, 6, 9). 그런 명령을 할 때 바울은 아마 고린도 교인들에게 다른 혹독한 권고의 말도 하였을 것이다. "고통의 방문"을 할 때 바울이 받은 여러 가지 모욕에 대해서도 꾸짖었을 것이다. 그러나 그는 이 편지를 "많은 눈물"로 썼다. 고린도 교인들에 대한 "넘치는 사랑"으로 썼다. 고린도후서도 같은 넘치는 사랑으로 쓴 것이 분명하다(5:14; 11:11; 12:15). 사랑이란 말이 직접 언급되지 않은 그리스도의 고난과 희생의 사역을 나타내는 진술에도 같은 사랑의 정신이 들어 있다(4:7-15; 6:4-10; 13:7).

그러므로 바울은 위에서 말해온 자신의 목회의 방침, 즉 기쁨을 주는 사역에 입각해서 소위 "눈물의 편지"도 썼다고 말하고 있다.

"이는 너희로 근심하게 하려는 것이 아니요 오직 내가 너희를 향하여 넘치는 사랑이 있음을 알게 하려 함이라." "너희를 향해 넘치는 사랑"은 "기쁨을 주는 사역"의 필수 조건이다. 바울은 여기서 사랑을 아가페(ἀγάπη)란 말로 쓰고 있다. "희생적인 신적 사랑"이야 말로 그리스도의 사랑이며 그리스도를 예배하는 그리스도인의 교제의 필수적 요소이다. 바울은 궤사로 인간들을 모으지 않는다. 그것은 거짓 사도들이 하는 짓이다(11:3, 13). 진정한 그리스도의 교회는 십자가의 희생적 사랑과 헌신의 정신으로만 이루어질 수 있다. 진정한 기쁨은 이런 교회에서 얻게 된다. 바울은 고린도 교회가 이런 교회가 되게 하기 위해서 애쓰고 있다.

주해(1:23-2:4):

이 부분에서 바울은 그의 목회 모본을 보여 준다. 그것은 모든 목회자의 외적 권세나 유익을 내세우지 않고, 회중들을 위하여 사랑하고 아끼며 희생하는 자세이다. 흔히 목회자들은 요한복음 21장 15-19절을 인용하여 목회자의 말씀을 가르치는 권위와 치리권을 논한다. 목회자가 목회를 위해서 이런 권위를 반드시 가져야함을 부인할 수 없으나 그런 권위의 내적인 요건을 망각하고 외적 권위만을 주장하면 진정한 목회자의 권위를 가질 수 없다. 목회자의 권위의 내적 요건은 무엇인가 요한복음 10장 11절의 양을 위해 목숨을 버리는 자세가 양을 치는 자세보다 우선적임을 명심해야 한다. 이런 정신이 약함으로 죽으신 그리스도의 정신이기 때문이다(13:4). 바울은 고린도후서에서 이런 약함의 능력을 그의 모든 사역에 적용하여 말하고 있다(4:7-15; 6:4-10; 8:9; 12:15; 13:7, 9). 그는 이것을 외모와 육적인 것을 자랑하는 거짓 사도들과 구별된 진정한 그리스도의 사도된 표로 제시하고 있다(3:1; 5:12; 10:7, 10, 12, 16; 11:18).

1. 복음을 집중적으로 선포하자.

바울은 자신의 사도직을 변명하면서 언제나 복음 진리나 그리스도의 사역과 관련 시켜서 설명한다(1:19-22; 2:17; 4:2-16; 6:4-10; 10:8, 18; 11:2-4, 10; 12:2; 13:4, 8). 복음 종교는 단순히 도덕 종교가 아니라, 구원 능력의 종교이다. 무엇보다 자신이 나를 구원하신 예수를 믿고 사랑하는 사람이 되어야 하고 또 남도 그렇게 되게 해야 한다. 또 잘못된 복음을 경계하고 잘못된 사람들을 담대히 경계해야 한다. 본문에서 바울이 고린도 교인들의 믿음을 주관하지 않는다는 것은 아무런 믿음을 가져도 상관치 않는다는 뜻이 아니다(2:24). 바울이 본문에서 그들이 믿음에 섰다고 하는 것은 그들이 바울에게로 돌아온 사실을 가리키는 것으로 보고, 고린도 교인들의 잘못된 믿음과 신앙생활에 대해서 깊은 관심을 가지고 권면하거나 책망한다(고전 5:1, 2; 고후 6:14-7:1; 10:7; 11:2, 4, 20, 12:16, 20, 21; 13:5; 갈 3:1).

2. 자신보다 교인들을 아끼는 사랑의 정신을 가지자(1:12, 23; 2:4; 11:2, 7; 12:15; 고전 7:35).

바울은 방문 취소를 결코 자신의 유익을 따라 결정하지 않았다. 당시 고린도 교회 형편상 자신의 방문으로 고린도 교인들이 아무런 유익을 얻을 수 없음을 알고 방문을 취소했다고 한다. 예수님도 선한 목자는 양들을 위하여 목숨을 버린다고 하였다(요 10:11). 그 자신이 몸소 이를 실천하여 구속의 사역을 이루셨다. 바울의 섬기는 사역의 정신은 바로 예수님의 구속 사역의 희생정신이다. 고린도후서 전체에서 바울은 고린도 교인들을 향한 넘치는 사랑이 있음을 나타낸다. 그 사랑은 지극한 열정과 철저한 희생의 아가페 사랑의 본보기이다(2:4; 4:7-15; 5:14, 15; 6:4-10; 7:3; 11:11; 12:14, 15; 13:7). 바울은 고린도 교인들을 진정한 아가페적 사랑을 가지고 사랑하였다.[50)]

3. 교인들을 섬기는 자세를 가지자 (1:24).

바울은 사도로서 대단한 권위를 가지고 고린도 교인들을 대한 것도 사실이다(2:9; 13:2; 고전 2:12; 4;1). 그러나 그런 권세를 주로 복음 증거를 위해서 매우 강력히 주장하나, 다른 문제를 논할 때는 오히려 보통 사람이 되어 보통사람처럼 말한다(고전 7:6, 7, 12, 26, 40: 고후 11:17, 33). 그는 어려운 일을 만날 때 초인처럼 가식적으로 말하지 않고 솔직하게 두려움을 나타내기도 하고, 또 하나님의 구원을 바라기도 한다(1:8-10; 참조, 12:8, 9, 10). 그는 "몸의 가시"도 있고, 그에 대한 기도가 즉시 응답되지 않기도 했다(12:8). 또 자신이 많은 계시로 자만에 빠질 가능성이 있는 연약한 사람이란 것

---

50) Van A. Harvey, *A Handbook of Theological Terms* (New York: Macmillan, 1964), 14. Anders Nygren이 희생적 아가페의 사랑과 이기적 에로스의 사랑을 대조하였으나, Paul Tillich는 지나친 대조를 반대하면서 이 두 사랑이 상호 관련성이 있다고 말하였다. 희생적 아가페의 사랑도 이기적인 면도 있고, 이기적인 에로스의 사랑에도 희생적인 면이 있다는 것이다. 그러나 이런 상호관련적 성격에도 불구하고 두 사랑의 고유한 특성은 충분히 강조되어야 한다.

을 인정한다(12:7). 사도라는 권위 의식을 버리고 상대방이 자신의 기분이나 감정을 고려해 가면서 말한다(고전 4:14; 고후 1:24; 7:4; 11:1, 11, 16-18; 12:1; 13:10). 이런 자세가 민주적인 자세이므로 오늘날 목회적 자세에 적당하다는 것이 아니다. 민주주의 사상이나 관습이 복음의 성격과 일치하는 점들도 있으나 일치하지 않는 점들도 있다. 우리는 다만 복음적인 성격에 충실하려고 해야 한다. 복음의 중심적 메시지에 대해서는 우리는 양보할 수 없다. 복음 자체가 예수님 외에 구원의 길이 없다고 가르치기 때문이다. 그러나 기타 우리의 인간 관계나 인격이나 일반적인 문제를 논하고 집행할 때 우리는 매우 조심스럽게 남의 의견을 존중하고 감정을 고려해야 한다. 온유하고 겸손함이 그리스도의 인격이요(마 11:29), 바울의 인격이며(고전 2:16; 4:21; 10;1; 빌 2:1), 또 그리스도의 복음을 가르치는 목회자의 지배적인 인격이어야 한다(엡 4:2). 나아가서 바울은 종의 자세로 고린도 교인들을 섬긴다고 했다(4:5). 소위 말하는 종으로서의 지도자(the servant leadership)의 본을 보이고 있다. 이것은 물론 그리스도의 모본의 결과이다(빌 2:6-8).

4. 교인들에게 기쁨을 주라(1:24; 2:2-3)

바울은 고린도후서에서 "기쁘다"(χαίρω·εὐφραίνω)는 말을 10번 이상 쓰고 "기쁨"(χαρά)이란 말을 5번 쓴다. 기뻐한다는 말이 제일 많이 나온다는 빌립보서가 같은 기쁘다는 동사를 10번 쓰고, 명사를 5번 쓴다는 사실에 비추어 보면 대단한 것이다. 바울이 어려운 목회 환경 가운데서도 오히려 기쁨을 가지는 좋은 믿음의 본을 가지고 있다는 증거이다. 바울은 디도를 만나서 기뻐하는 전반부에서 뿐만 아니라 고린도인들을 질책하는 후반부의 끝에서도 스스로 희생하는 것을 기뻐한다는 말과 함께 기뻐하라고 격려하는 말로 마치고 있다(13:9, 11). 복음을 전하는 사람들의 기본 동작은 기쁨이다. 기독교 복음은 하나님의 구원의 기쁜 소식이기 때문이다. 목회의 목적은 복음을 믿는 이들이 모여 기쁨의 교제를 통해서 구원의 하나님께 영광을 돌리는 데 있다. 모든 목회 프로그램이 교인들에게 기쁨을 주기 위한 것임을 잊지 말아야 한다. 형식적이고 인위적인 교제는 진정한 교제도 아니고 오래 갈 수도 없다. 교회에 온 사람들이 예배나 교육이나 기도회를 통해서 기쁨을 맛보면 반드시 다시 오게 된다. 바울은 그의 목회 방침을 기쁨을 주는 목회로 정하였다.

중요한 것은 교인들의 유익을 위해서 나의 기쁨을 희생할 수 있어야 한다는 점이다. 이런 경우 고통이 필연적이다. 바울도 본문에서 고린도 교인들의 유익을 위해서 언제나 희생하기를 기뻐했다(12:15; 13:9). 그런데 목회자나 성숙한 그리스도인은 이런 희생을 기쁨으로 느낄 수 있어야 한다(골 1:11). 부모가 자녀의 기쁨을 위해서 자신의 유익을 고려하지 않고 희생할 때가 많은데, 이때 부모는 고통 받으면서도 기뻐한다. 바울도 같은 부모의 심정을 가지고 고린도 교인들을 위해 희생하기를 기뻐한다고 했다(12:15). 우리가 이런 희생적 기쁨을 즐길 수 있을 때 진정한 그리스도인이 되는 것이다. 또 그 이웃이란 대상이 넓어져서 원수까지 포함하면 우리는 진정한 그리스도인의 삶에 이르는 것이다. 이런 삶이 우리 주 그리스도의 삶이었고, 이런 삶이 아니고서는 이 세상에서 진정한 기쁨을 발견할 수 없다. 왜냐하면 이 세상의 만인 대 만인의 경쟁과 투쟁하는 정신으로는 인간은 결국 지치게 되고 죽음에 이르게 될 것이기 때문이다.

그러나 그리스도인의 기쁨은 세상의 저속한 기쁨과 구별되는 거룩한 기쁨이 되어야 한다. 그리스도인의 유머는 모든 복음의 신앙과 신학에 기초되어야 하며, 저속한 말이나 농담은 오히려 실망과 재난을 초래할 수 있으므로 삼가야 한다(엡 5:4). 저속한 기쁨은 인간의 영혼을 쇠약하게 만들고, 거룩한 기쁨은 인간의 영혼을 강건하게 한다.

d. 그 편지의 결과는 매우 좋았다(2:5-11;참조, 7:6-16).

본문:

> 5. 근심하게 한 자가 있었을지라도, 그가 나를 근심하게 한 것이 아니요 어느 정도 너희 무리를 근심하게 한 것이니, 어느 정도라 함은 내가 너무 심하게 (말)하지 아니하려 함이라 6. 이러한 사람이 많은 사람에게서 벌 받은 것이 족하도다. 7. 그런즉 너희는 차라리 저를 용서하고 위로할 것이니 저가 너무 많은 근심에 잠길까 두려워하노라. 8. 그러므로 너희를 권하노니 사랑을 저(저희)에게 나타내라. 9. 너희가 범사에 순종하는지 그 증거를 알고자 하여 내가 이것을 너희에게 썼노라. 10. 너희가 무슨 일이든지 뉘게 용서하면 나도 그리하고, 내가 만일 용서한 일이 있으면 용서한 그것은 너희를 위하여 그리스도 앞에서 한 것이니 11. 이는 우리로 사단에게 속지 않게 하려 함이라. 우리가 그의 (그) 궤계를 알지 못하는 바가 아니로라.

본문비평:

1. 7절의 μᾶλλον(차라리)이 ὑμᾶς(너희들) 앞에 오는 경우(א C K L O P, 시리아역, 벌게이트, 콥틱역, 아람어역, 크리소스톰, 암부로시우스), 뒤에 오는 경우(D E F G 17, 고딕, 터툴리안), 아예 없는 경우(A B 시리아역, 어거스틴)가 있으나 이 말의 순서와 유무가 전체 뜻에 영향을 주지 않는다.

2. 9절의 A B 17은 ἐι 대신 관계대명사 ἡ(여성 단수 여격)를 가진다. 선행사는 앞에 있는 δοκιμήν(증거)으로서, "너희가 범사에 순종하는 증거"라고 번역된다.[51)]

내용개요:

바울은 4절의 "눈물의 편지"에서 징계를 지시한 "근심케 한자"를 고린도 교회가 징계한 것은 잘한 것이라고 칭찬한다. 바울은 자신의 지시에 따라서 순종한 것을 기뻐한다(2:6, 9). 즉 그것은 고린도 교인들이 바울의 사도권을 인정하는 증거이기 때문이다. 그러나 바울은 이제는 징계 해제를 지시한다. 고린도 교회가 바울에게 순종하고 돌아온 이상, 또 3차 방문을 앞두고(12:4; 13:1), 징계를 해제하여 화해의 분위기를 만드는 것이 필요하다고 볼 수도 있으나, 바울이 본문에서 말하는 이유는 그가 마귀의 궤계를 알기 때문이라고 한다. 바울이 아는 마귀의 궤계란 무엇인가? 바울은 고린도후서에서 자신이 그리스도의 약함을 따라서 사역하는 것을 그리스도의 사도된 증거로 제시한다(4:5, 7-15; 6:4-10; 11:23-33; 12:9, 10; 13:4; 7, 9). 이것은 그의 반대자들이 인위적 세속적 자랑을 하면서 권위주의적으로 사역하는 것과 대조 된다(5:12; 10:12, 16, 11:18, 20). 고린도 교회가 진정한 그리스도의 교회, 온전한 사도적 교회가 되기 위해서는 이 약함의 능력의 진리에 선 교회가 되어야 하는데 징계가 계속되는 경우 사랑이 없는 율법적 권위와 세속적 힘이 지배하는 교회로 전락될 수도 있음을 바울이 알고서 이제는 징계를 해제하라는 것이다.

---

51) Plummer, 61; Martin은 이를 반대한다. Martin, 31.

주석:

5. "근심하게 한 자가 있었을지라도, 그가 나를 근심하게 한 것이 아니요 어느 정도 너희 무리를 근심하게 한 것이니, 어느 정도라 함은 내가 너무 심하게 (말)하지 아니하려 함이라"(Εἰ δέ τις λελύπηκεν, οὐκ ἐμὲ λελύπηκεν, ἀλλὰ ἀπὸ μέρους, ἵνα μὴ ἐπιβαρῶ, πάντας ὑμᾶς). 5절의 "근심하게 한 자"(τις λελύπηκεν)에 대한 이견이 있다. 1) 고린도전서5장 1-5절의 계모와 결혼한 사람을 가리킨다.[52] 이런 해석이 터툴리안 시대(218년)에 유행하였다. 터툴리안은 이런 해석에 반대하여 바울이 근친상간한 사람을 이미 사탄에게 내어주라고 권면한 것(고전 5:5)은 영구적 정죄라고 보아야 하므로, 같은 사람을 다시 용서하라고 할 수 없다고 했다(*De pudicitia*, 13-15). 2) 바울을 반대해 왔던 사람이다.[53] 첫 번째 의견을 반대하는 이들의 주장이다. 반대하는 근거는 다음과 같다. a) 위에서 터툴리안이 지적한 것 처럼 근친상간의 죄는 매우 심각한 죄이므로 바울이 다시 용서하라고 했다고 보기 어렵다. b) 출교라는 치리를 지시하였다가(고전 5:5), 다시 번복할 경우 바울이 경홀한 사람이라는 비난을 듣게 될 것이다(고후 1:17). c) 근친상간이라는 죄는 공동체에 대한 죄는 될지언정 바울 개인에 대한 죄는 아니다. 본문에서는 바울을 반대한 죄와 공동체를 문란하게 한 죄가 동시에 언급되고 있으므로 근친상간한 사람과는 다른, 바울을 반대한 자로 보아야 한다.[54] 3) 고린도 교회의

52) Denney, 3 73; Hughes, 59-65.

53) Bruce, 185; Bultmann, 48; Barrett, 89; Martin, 37; 참조, Barnett, 124.

54) Bultmann, 45.

재정을 유용한 사람이다.[55] 이 경우 바울이 재정문제로 피해를 보았다는 등 설명이 석연치 않은 부분이 있다. 바울이 그 돈을 잠시 맡아 있었다는 추측이나 피해자가 제3의 인물이라는 설명은 모두 지나친 추측이다. 4) 바울을 반대하는 자로 고린도전서 5장 5절의 근친상간 문제와 간접적으로 관련되어 있고 또 우상을 섬기는 일과 관련된 사람으로 본다(6:14-7:1).[56] 음란한 죄와 우상숭배가 서로 관련되어있기 때문이라고 하나, 근친상간을 일반적 음란죄와 관련시키는 것이 문제다. 또 6장 14절-7장 1절은 어느 개인을 지목하여 우상숭배를 금지하였다고 보기 어렵다.

바울이 이 사람의 이름을 밝히지 않는 것은 어쩌면 당시 희랍시대의 수사학적 영향을 받아서, 상대방을 무시할 때 아예 그 이름을 언급치 않았던 데서 기인한다고 볼 수 있다. 적어도 고린도후서에서는 이런 주장이 타당하다고 볼 수도 있으나 다른 바울서신에서는 반대자들의 이름이 직접 언급된 경우도 있으므로 이런 주장의 타당성은 제한적이다. 분명한 것은 본문에서 말하는 대로 이 사람이 바울을 직접 괴롭혀 왔고, 또 고린도 교회와 바울과의 관계를 어렵게 만든 장본인이다.[57] 더 정확히 말해서 고린도 교회에서 바울을 반대하는 그룹의 우두머리이다.

한편 핀들레이(G. G. Findlay)는 이 사람이 바울을 직접 괴롭히지 않았고 바울의 동역자인 디모데를 괴롭혔다고 생각한다.[58] 그는 고린도전서 4장 17-21절, 16장 10, 11절에서 디모데가 고린도

55) Thrall, 68-69, 171-72.

56) Barnett, 124.

57) Héring, 15.

58) Hughes, 60, 재인용.

교회에 간다고 했는데, 디모데가 갔을 때 큰 모욕을 받고 왔다고 가정한다. 또 1-7장의 여러 변명 가운데 "우리"란 말이 있고, 1장 1절에 디모데가 바울과 함께 발신인으로 기록된 사실이 이를 지지한다고 한다. 그러나 1장 1절의 인사와 1장 17절에서 디모데가 간단히 언급된 것 이외에 디모데에 대한 구체적 언급이 없으므로 이 주장은 근거가 약하다.[59]

"그가 나를 근심하게 한 것이 아니요 어느 정도 너희 무리를 근심하게 한 것이니, 어느 정도라 함은 내가 너무 심하게 (말)하지 아니하려 함이라(내가 너무 지나치게 말하지 않으려고, 어느 정도라고 하나, 그가 나를 근심케 한 것이 아니고 너희 모두를 근심케 하였다)." 이 말에는 번역상의 어려움이 있다. "너무 심하게 하지 아니하려 함이라"(ἵνα μὴ ἐπιβαρῶ)라는 말은 문자적으로 "너무 무게를 두지 않기 위해서," 또는 "너무 지나치게 말하지 않으려고"라는 삽입구이다. 표준새번역 개정판(2001년)은 "과장하지 않고 말해서"라고 번역했다. 문제는 "어느 정도"(ἀπὸ μέρους)라는 말이 "근심하게 하였다"(λελύπηκεν)란 말과 관련되는지,[60] 아니면 "너희 모두"를 꾸며서 "너희들의 일부"란 뜻인지가 논란이 된다.[61] 개역한글성경은 전자와 같은 뜻으로 번역되었다. 즉 동사와 관련시켜 근심의 정도를 나타낸다. "어느 정도 … 근심하게 한 것이니." 후자로 번역하면 소수와 다수, 또는 바울 지지파와 반대파로 나뉜 교회의 양분된 상태를 나타내게 된다. 즉 바울을 반대하

59) Hughes, 60-61.

60) Windisch, 85; Barrett, 89; Martin, 37, RSV, NEB, NIV, 개역한글판.

61) Lietzmann, 106; Bultmann, 48; Hughes, 65, n. 8.

는 이 사람이 그를 따르는 이들을 근심케 하지 않았다.[62] 또는 이 사람이 고린도 교인들의 일부를 근심케 하였으나 그 결과 전체를 근심케 하였다.[63] "어느 정도"가 근심의 정도를 나타낼 수도 있고 근심하는 사람의 수를 제한한다고 볼 수도 있다. 두 가지 해석이 다 가능하나, 여기서는 대다수의 번역과 같이 "근심하다"는 동사와 관련시켜서 근심의 정도를 가리킨다고 본다.

고린도후서에 나타나는 바울의 근심의 배경에 본문의 인물이 있음을 알 수 있다(2:6, 7, 10; 7:8-12; 13:2).[64] 바울을 반대하는 수장으로서 큰 영향력이 있는 인물로 추정된다. 본문에서 바울은 이 사람이 "나를 근심케 한 것이 아니요"라고 말하나 그것은 고린도 교인 전체를 근심케 하였음을 강조하기 위해 자신에게 미친 근심을 상대적으로 약화시키는 표현이다. 실제로는 이 사람이 자신을 근심하게 했으나 자신뿐만 아니라 모두를 근심하게 하였다는 뜻이다(NIV). 바울은 언제나 자신이 다수의 고린도 교인들과 함께 동고동락(同苦同樂)하는 것으로 말한다(1:6; 4:5, 7-15; 6:11-13; 7:3, 8; 11:11; 12:14, 15; 13:7, 9).

6 "이러한 사람이 많은 사람에게서 벌 받은 것이 족하도다. 7 그런즉 너희는 차라리 저를 용서하고 위로할 것이니 저가 너무 많은 근심에 잠길까 두려워하노라" (**6 ἱκανὸν τῷ τοιούτῳ ἡ ἐπιτιμία αὕτη ἡ ὑπὸ τῶν πλειόνων, 7 ὥστε τουναντίον μᾶλλον ὑμᾶς χαρίσασθαι καὶ παρακαλέσαι, μή πως τῇ**

62) Hughes, 65.

63) Bultmann, 48.

64) Héring, 15.

περισσοτέρᾳ λύπῃ καταποθῇ ὁ τοιοῦτος). 6-7절에서 바울은 고린도 교회의 다수가 그의 지시를 따라서 이 반대자를 치리한 것으로 족하다고 하면서 이제는 그를 용서할 것을 부탁한다(7:11, 12). 바울은 고린도 교인 다수가 자신에게로 돌아 온 것을 알고 이 반대자의 징계를 해제하여 되도록 화해의 분위기를 만들어 가기를 원하는 것이다(5:19-21; 6:11-13). 더구나 3차 방문을 앞두고 이런 화해의 분위기 조성이 필요하다고 느낀 것으로 보인다. 9절에 의하면 바울이 이 반대자의 치리를 "눈물의 편지"에서 명하였다. 어떤 벌이었는지는 알 수 없다. 성찬을 못 받게 하는 벌(수찬 금지)일 가능성이 높다(고전 11;17-22; 행 2:44-46; 벧후 2:12; 디다케 10:6). 7절에서 바울이 그 반대자를 용서할 것을 권한다. "용서하고 위로할 것이니 저가 너무 많은 근심에 잠길까 두려워하노라." 여기서 그 반대자가 근심에 잠겨 있다는 사실은 그가 회개하였다는 것을 암시한다. 아마 디도를 통해서 반대자의 이런 회개 소식을 들었을 것이다. 바울은 1장과 7장에서 위로의 하나님을 찬양하고 있다. 그 자신이 위로의 하나님의 사도임이 이러한 위로의 사역을 통해서 입증되고 있다. 위로는 기쁨을 주기 위한 것이다. 그가 "너무 많은 근심"에 잠기면 그 자신 뿐만 아니라 고린도 교회라는 전체 그리스도의 공동체가 근심에 잠겨서 기뻐할 수 없다. 더구나 회개한 지체에 대하여 그리스도의 몸 된 교회는 마땅히 기뻐해야 한다. "죄인 하나가 회개하면 하나님의 사자들 앞에 기쁨이 된다"(눅 15:10).

8 "그러므로 너희를 권하노니 사랑을 저(저희)에게 나타내라" (διὸ παρακαλῶ ὑμᾶς κυρῶσαι εἰς αὐτὸν ἀγάπην·). 8절에

서 바울은 보다 적극적인 행동을 권한다. 용서, 위로, 다음에는 사랑이다. "저에게 사랑을 나타내라." "저희"라는 한글 개역성경 번역은 단수를 복수로 잘못 번역하였다. 단수 대명사, "저" 또는 "그"(αὐτόν)는 벌 받은 사람 개인을 가리킨다. "나타내라"(κυρῶσαι)는 원래는 "확인하라"는 말이다. "저에게 (너희의) 사랑을 확인하라"는 뜻이다. 또 이 말은 부정사로서 παρακαλῶ("권한다")라는 말의 목적어이다. 그러므로 이 말은 명령이 아니고 권면이다. 바울이 되도록 부드러운 말을 사용하려고 함을 알 수 있다. 바울이 사랑의 권면을 하고 있으므로 부드러운 어조를 취하는 것이 적당하다. 사랑이야말로 근심하는 자에게 가장 좋은 치료약이다. 위로와, 용서도 넓은 의미의 사랑이나, 완전한 사랑은 보다 적극적인 사랑의 행동으로 구체화 될 수 있다. 이 사랑은 그리스도의 아가페의 사랑으로서 무슨 세상적 유익을 바라거나 특혜를 베푸는 식의 사랑이 아니라, 그리스도의 구속의 사랑을 은혜로 받은 사람이나 공동체답게 나타내는 순수한 사랑이다.

바울은 고린도 교회가 그리스도의 교회답게 되게 하기 위하여서는 용서와 사랑을 나타내는 것이 반드시 필요하다고 본다(참조, 마 18:21-22). 그리스도의 교회에서 정죄와 징계가 계속되면 교회는 스스로 복음적인 교회의 성격을 훼손시킬 수 있기 때문이다. 11절에서 바울이 말하는 마귀의 궤계는 그리스도의 교회가 미움과 질시로 분열하게 만들거나, 징벌과 정죄로 율법주의적 회당과 구별할 수 없게 만드는 것이다. 바울은 그리스도의 화해의 사신이다(5:19-21). 바울은 세상이나 인간적인 힘이 아니라 그리스도의 약함의 능력으로 사역하는 진정한 그리스도의 사도이다(12:9, 10; 13:4, 7-10). 그는 되도록 교회를 치리하는 그의 사도권을 사용하지 않고, 권면으로 문제를 해결하기를 원한다. 이 결과 그는 반대자들에게 열등하고 약한 사도로 멸시받았으나, 그는 고린도 교인들의 유익이 최우선이고 그의 명예는 상관치 않는다고 말한다(13:7, 9). 그의 궁극적 사도로서의 사명은 교인들의 믿음을 자라게 하여 그리스도의 교회를 세우는 것이기 때문이다(10:8; 12:19; 13:5, 10). 그러므로 이제는 "근심케 하는 자"를 용서하여 사랑하는 공동체의 성격을 지켜나갈 것을 지시하는 것이다. 바울은 그 "근심케하는 자"가 회개하였다는 소식을 미리 듣고서 여기서 징계해제를 권하고 있다고 본다.

9. "너희가 범사에 순종하는지 그 증거를 알고자 하여 내가 이것을 너희에게 썼노라"(**εἰς τοῦτο γὰρ καὶ ἔγραψα, ἵνα γνῶ τὴν δοκιμὴν ὑμῶν, εἰ εἰς πάντα ὑπήκοοί ἐστε**). 9절에서는 바울이 "눈물의 편지"에서 그를 반대하는 자를 치리할 것을 명했었는데, 그때는 바울이 고린도 교인들이 자신에게 대한 충성을 의심할 때였으므로 그 반대자 치리를 명하여 그들의 충성을 확증하려고 하였다. 이제 그들의 충성을 확인하였으니(1:24), 더 이상 그 반대자를 벌 받게 할 필요가 없다. 다시 말해서 그 반대자의 책벌은 반대자 개인에 대한 훈계의 목적이 있었을 뿐만 아니라, 고린도 교인 전체의 충성을 확고히 하는 이중적 목적을 갖고 있었다. 이제 책벌의 두 가지 목적이 다 이루어졌으니 더 지체 할 필요 없이 치리를 해제시켜서 그를 교인으로 회복시켜야 한다. 이렇게 하여서 교회의 더 큰 목적을 이룰 수가 있다. 즉 기쁨을 주는 공동체가 되는 것과 또 하나의 그리스도의 몸이 되는 것이다. 이런 의미가 다음 절에 계속된다.

10. "너희가 무슨 일이든지 뉘게 용서하면 나도 그리하고, 내가 만일 용서한 일이 있으면 용서한 그것은 너희를 위하여 그리스도 앞에서 한 것이니"(ᾧ δέ τι χαρίζεσθε, καγώ καὶ γὰρ ἐγὼ ὃ κεχάρισμαι, εἴ τι κεχάρισμαι, δι᾽ ὑμᾶς ἐν προσώπῳ Χριστοῦ). 10절에서 바울은 교회란 그리스도를 중심으로 서로 용서하는 공동체라는 생각을 보여준다. "그리스도 앞에서"(ἐν προσώπῳ Χριστοῦ)라는 말은 문자적으로 "그리스도의 얼굴 앞에서"라는 말이다. 이 말을 마지막에 두어서 강조하고 있다. 너희가 누구를 용서하는 것, 내가 용서하는 것, 이 모두가 그리스도 앞에서 하는 것이다. 그리스도 앞이란 말은 그리스도인의 용서의 출발지, 혹은 근거를 가리킨다. 우리도 죄인이었음을 상기시키는 말이다. 죄인이었던 우리가 그리스도로 말미암아 죄의 용서함을 받았음을 상기시키는 말이다. 그러므로 우리가 서로 용서함이 무슨 우리 자신의 은혜를 베푸는 행위로 인식해서는 안 된다는 뜻이 있다. 순전히 그리스도께로 부터 거저 받은 용서하심의 은혜를 거저 남에게 주는 것이요, 그리스도의 이름으로 주는 것이다. 그 반대자를 용서하는 것은 우리, 혹은, 교회라는 공동체의 이름으로 용서하는 것이 아니라, 우리를 은혜로 구속하신 그리스도의 이름으로 용서하여야 한다. 이렇게 용서하는 공동체가 진정한 그리스도의 몸이 된다. 이런 공동체는 이 세상 나라에는 없으나, 하나님의 나라를 사모하는 이들의 공동체인 교회에서 발견될 수 있다(마 6:12, 14, 15).

휴즈는 "그리스도 앞에서"란 말이 우리 모두가 마지막 때에 그리스도의 심판대 앞에 서서 선악 간에 심판을 받아야 할 것을 가리킨다고 한다(5:10).[65] 그러나 이 말의 문맥은 이런 종말론적 의미보다는 그리스도의 몸 된 교회라는 바울의 교회론적인 의미를 가리킨다.

11. "이는 우리로 사단에게 속지 않게 하려 함이라. 우리가 그의(그) 궤계를 알지 못하는 바가 아니로라"(ἵνα μὴ πλεονεκτηθῶμεν ὑπὸ τοῦ σατανᾶ· οὐ γὰρ αὐτοῦ τὰ νοήματα ἀγνοοῦμεν). 여기서 바울이 말하는 "사단의 궤계"(αὐτοῦ τὰ νοήματα)는 무엇인가? 사단의 궤계란 말은 원래 복수로 나타난다. 즉 "그의 궤계들"이다. 복수는 사단의 궤계가 적어도 몇 단계로 진행되었음을 나타낸다. 첫 단계는 그 문제 있는 사람을 통해서 고린도 교회를 어지럽게 하는 것이다. 두 번째 단계는 고린도 교회가 그의 잘못을 묵인하고 "사랑하게 하는 것이다." 마지막은 그를 책벌한 경우 교회가 그를 계속 미워하게 하면서 교회의 진정한 사랑을 잃게 하는 것이다. 바울은 사단의 두 단계의 궤계를 차례로 물리쳤고, 이제 세 번째 단계의 궤계를 물리치도록 권하고 있다. 바울은 "고통의 방문"(2:1)을 통해서 교회를 어지럽게 하는 반대자의 도전을 받은 후에 "눈물의 편지"를 써서 그를 책벌할 것을 지시하였다(2:9). 아마 바울은 책벌 없는 사랑은 거짓 사랑이라고 고린도 교인들을 설득했을 것이다. 그러나 정죄를 일삼는 교회도 그리스도의 교회가 아니다. 사단은 하나님의 의를 세우기 위해 범죄자를 치리하는 그리스도의 교회를 교묘히 이용하여 사랑 없이 정죄하는 집단으로 변질케 하려고 할 수 있다. 바울은 고린도 교회를 수호하는 사도로서 이를 알고 이제는 "저에

65) Hughes, 71.

게 사랑을 나타내라" 고 권면하는 것이다. 정죄하고 미워하는 교회가 아니라 사랑하는 교회가 진정한 그리스도의 교회요 온전한 사도적 교회이다. 바울 자신도 그의 사도적 권세를 되도록 쓰지 않고 교인들을 권면하여 그들이 회개하여 스스로 믿음에 서게 한다(1:24; 13:5, 7-10). 그러나 바울의 반대자들은 강압적이고 권위주의적으로 고린도 교인들을 대했다. 문제는 고린도 교인들이 그런 권세를 오히려 진정한 사도적 권세로 보고 그들을 진정한 사도들로 인정하였다는 것이다(11:20). 나아가 고린도교인들은 바울도 그런 사도적 권세를 한번 나타내도록 바라고 있다(13:3). 바울은 이들의 믿음이 잘못되어서 이런 잘못된 판단을 하게 되는 것으로 보고 그들의 믿음을 확증할 것을 요구한다(13:5).

한편 이렇게 사단의 궤계를 아는 바울은 진정한 그리스도의 사도라는 암시가 있다. 또한 그는 그의 반대자들이 거짓 사도들이며 사단의 일꾼이라고 그들의 정체를 밝힐 수 있었다(11:13-15).

주해(2:5-11):

2장 5-11절에서 바울은 징계 받은 "근심케 한 자" 의 징계를 해제하여 그리스도의 교회의 사랑의 특성을 유지하도록 한 것이다. 이런 바울의 지시 이면에는 3차 방문을 앞두고 화해의 분위기를 조성하는 것이 필요하다는 실천 목회적 이유도 있을 수 있으나, 더 근본적인 이유는 목회 신학적인 것이라고 본다. 즉 바울은 고린도후서에서 일관되게 그리스도의 약함의 신학을 유지하고 있다. 바울은 약한 가운데서 그리스도의 능력이 나타남을 믿고 그의 목회의 모든 분야에 적용하는 것이다(4:5, 7-15; 6:4-10; 8:9; 11:7,

30; 12:9, 10; 13:4-10). 징계를 해제함으로써 그리스도의 사랑을 나타내는 것이 복음 진리와 부합하며, 그리스도의 몸 된 교회를 사랑의 진리로 하나가 되어 건전하게 성장하기를 바라기 때문이다. 정죄와 비난은 그리스도의 교회의 특성이 될 수 없다. 그렇다고 바울이 사도권이나 교회의 징계권을 전혀 무시하는 것은 아니다. 바울은 실제로 "근심케 하는 자" 의 징계를 지시하였고, 13장 1-2절에서도 "문제가 된 이들" 에 대한 징계를 계획하고 있다. 그러나 바울은 되도록 그런 권세를 쓰지 않고 그리스도의 약함의 진리를 끈질기게 지키려고 애쓴다(13:3-7). 바울은 고린도 교인들이 스스로 회개하고 믿음을 가지게 될 것을 종용한다(1:24; 13:4-5). 그리고 자신의 사도권을 되도록 쓰지 않게 되기를 바란다(13:10).

오늘날 교회에서도 책벌의 문제가 있으나, 현시대를 지배하는 개인주의와 자유주의적 특성상, 또 개신교회의 개인주의적 신앙 양심을 강조하는 성격 때문에 책벌이 예전처럼 제대로 이루어지지도 않고 이루어 진다해도 책벌의 효과나 권위가 의심된다. 그러나 책벌은 필요한 것이다. 아울러 책벌을 해야 하는 교회와 교인들이 스스로의 신령한 권위를 회복하는 것도 시급하다.

1. 징계할 때와 사랑할 때(2:5-10)

개혁자들은 징계를 그리스도의 교회에서 없어서는 안 될 고유한 증표라고 했다.[66] 교회의 치리권이 요즈음 유명무실함을 본다. 치리 받아야 할 교인들을 치리하지 못하는 경우는 대개 다음과 같다. 1) 치리 받아야 할 사람이 교회의 기둥 같은 존재로서, 그를 치

---

66) Hughes,72, 재인용.

리하는 경우 교회의 존립 자체가 위협받는 경우이다. 개신교의 개교회주의적 체제로 말미암아 한 개인에게 의존적인 약한 교회들이 많으므로 이런 경우가 적지 않다. 문제된 사람이 교회를 소유하거나, 분리하거나, 세워서 자신을 보호하는 경우가 허다하다. 2) 치리를 받은 사람을 다른 교파나 교회에서 받아주는 경우이다. 이런 경우는 자기의 교회를 확장하기 위해서 당사자의 잘못을 감싸면서 용납하는 경우다. 어떤 경우 치리의 성격이 주로 개인적 인간관계에 의한 것이라고 보고 그의 잘못을 대수롭지 않게 생각한다. 그러나 이런 경우라 해도 일단 교회에서 치리 받은 사람을 용납하는 행위는 악한 것이다. 치리의 해제는 항상 치리한 교회에서 행하는 것이지, 제3자의 입장에서 베풀 수 없다. 3) 치리 받은 사람이 세상 법정에 호소할 경우가 있다. 교회는 세상 법으로도 하자가 없게 운영되어야 한다. 교회의 문제가 일단 세상 법정에서 취급되는 경우 그리스도의 교회의 권위와 거룩한 성격은 상실된다(고전 6:1-11). 또 세상 법정에서의 판결의 결과를 교회가 그대로 수용할 수는 없다. 세상법과 교회법의 판단 기준이 다르기 때문이다. 4) 개인주의적, 반 권위주의적, 자유주의적인 현대사회의 성격에 영향 받은 대다수 교인들이 성경이나 교회법에 의해서 분명히 문제가 되는 사람의 책벌을 반대하는 경우이다. 이런 경우에는 책벌하기에 앞서 책벌의 긍정적 의미를 알리는 것이 필요하다. a) 책벌이 단순히 권위주의 시대의 산물이 아니라, 성경적인 원칙이며, 교회가 지향하는 목적, 즉 교회의 일치와 순결을 위해서 필요함을 주장해야 한다. b) 책벌은 책벌 받는 사람을 미워하는 마음으로 책벌하는 것이 아니고, 책벌을 통해서 그가 회개하고 바로 서기를 바라며 하나님의 자비와 사랑의 정신으로 행하는 것임을 알려야 한다(고전 5:5; 고후 13:1-2). 한 교인의, 혹은 일부 교인들의 책벌을 통해서 그 당사자는 물론 전체 교인들이 바로 서는 계기가 됨을 알린다(7:11, 12). c)그리스도인의 진정한 용서는 잘못에 대한 분명한 회개를 통해서 실현될 수 있음을 알린다.

이외에도 개신교의 다양한 성경적, 신학적 해석의 자유로움으로 치리의 타당성과 의의가 문제될 수도 있다. 그러나 진정한 그리스도인은 그가 속한 기독교회의 치리권을 존중하고 자신의 실수를 겸손히 인정할 수 있어야 한다. 이런 자세 없이는 진정한 그리스도인도, 그리스도의 교회도, 존립할 수 없다.

치리할 때 지켜야 할 중요한 사항들은 다음과 같다. 1) 본문에서 바울이 보여 주는 것처럼, 치리를 행사할 때와 또 치리를 해제할 때가 언제 인가를 잘 판단하는 것이다. 문제 된 사람이 치리만으로 그의 죄를 뉘우칠 수 있다고 판단될 때 치리할 것이고, 그 사람이 진정으로 그 잘못을 뉘우칠 때 그를 다시 용서하고 받아들이는 넓은 마음을 가져야 한다. 2) 치리 받은 사람을 위한 권면과 기도를 계속해야 한다. 그의 죄는 미워하되 그 인간을 미워하지 않도록 조심해야 한다. 그 사람도 하나님께서 원하시면 깨끗케 되고, 재창조 될 수 있는, 하나님의 형상임을 인정해야 한다(약 3:9). 3) 교인들은 치리 받은 사람을 여전히 사랑하고 있음을 그에게 알려야 한다. 치리 조치나 일정한 치리 기간이 끝난 후에 다시 그를 사랑으로 받아들일 수 있음을 보여 주어야 한다.

2. 순종의 대상(2:9)

목회자와 교인간의 진정한 사랑과, 존경 없는 교회 생활이나 목회는 피차 어렵다. 목사는 교인들을 사랑해야 하고 교인들은 목사에게 순종해야한다. 이런 관계를 비웃는 현대교인들이 증가하고 있음은 슬픈 일이다. 그러나 교회는 이런 순종의 관계로 그리스도의 사역을 효과적으로 수행할 수 있는 것이다. 목회자의 설교, 권면, 그리고 지도가 그에 대한 교인들의 사랑과 존경 없이는 그 열매를 거둘 수 없다. 또 목회자의 희생적 사랑과 헌신 없이 교인들은 교회 생활의 기쁨을 맛볼 수 없다. 물론 목회자나, 교인들의 진정한 순종과 헌신의 대상은 사람이 아니라 하나님이요, 진리이다(4:2; 11:10; 13:9). 사람은 거짓되므로 실패할 수 있기 때문이다. 2장 9절에서 바울은 고린도 교인들이 자신에게 순종함을 확인하였다. 그러나 그 순종은 바울 자신에게 대한 순종이라고만 볼 수는 없다. 궁극적으로 하나님께 대한 순종이다. 바울이 하나님께 부르심을 받은 그리스도의 사도이며 종이기 때문이다(1:1; 롬 1:1).

오늘날과 같이 개인주의와 자유주의가 분별없이 남용되는 시대에서도 그리스도인들은 진리에 순종하는 것이 요구된다. 무엇이 진리인지 모호한 경우에도 힘써서 진리를 구하고 찾아야 한다. 그러면 성령께서 그 진리를 성경말씀이나, 기도나, 설교나 상담이나, 자신의 양심이나, 예상하지 않은 사람이나 환경을 통해서 가르쳐 주신다. 그때 우리는 기계적이고, 인위적이고, 강요된 순종이 아닌, 그리스도의 사랑 안에서 진정한 순종을 할 수 있다.

"이 목회자는 신뢰할 수 있는 인물인가?" 란 질문도 중요하나, "나는 목회자에게 순종할 수 있는 믿음을 가졌는가?" 란 질문도 중요하다. 사실 진정한 그리스도인이라면 목회자뿐만 아니라 신자 상호간에도 진심으로 순종할 수 있어야 한다(엡 5:21). 물론 목회자들도 순종을 율법적 자세로 강요하지 말고 사랑과 믿음과 순종의 본을 먼저 보여야 할 것이다(고전 11:1; 빌 3:17; 살후 3:7). 그리스도께서 이 모든 순종의 본을 우리에게 보여 주셨기 때문이다(막 14:36, 빌 2:8).

3. 사단의 궤계(2:11)

사단은 어떤 환경에서든지 어떤 문제를 통해서든지 우리를 유혹하여 하나님과 멀어지도록 하기 위해서 애쓴다. 개인적으로, 교회적으로, 사회적으로, 사단은 이런 미혹하는 활동을 열심히 추진하는 것이다. 바울은 특히 교회를 통한 사단의 궤계를 경계하고 있다. 사단의 궤계는 주로 교회의 순결과 일치를 파괴하는 것이다. 교회의 순결이냐? 교회의 일치냐? 거룩한 교회냐? 하나의 교회냐? 라는 어려운 문제로 교회를 어지럽히고 분열시킨다. 순결을 주장할 때 교회가 분열되어 교회의 일치가 문제되고, 교회의 일치를 주장할 때 교회의 순결이 문제가 되어 교회의 기강이 해이해지기 쉽다. 본문에서 바울은 지혜롭게 이 두 가지 질문을 다 만족시키는 목회를 하였다. 교회의 순결을 위해 문제된 사람을 치리하도록 하였다. 그러나 그가 근심 중에 회개하였을 때(2:7; 7:9) 그를 사랑으로 용서하도록 함으로써 교회의 일치를 유지케 하였다. 순결과 일치의 어디에다 강조점을 두느냐에 따라서 교회나 교파의 성격이 정해지기도 한다. 그러나 이 두 가지 특징의 균형을 우리 기독교회가 계속 지켜가야 한다. 사단은 교회가 이 균형을 깨뜨리도록 힘쓸 것이다. 바울은 에베소서 4장 3-6절에서 "하나 된 것을 힘써 지키라" 고 하였다. 또 데살로니가전서 5장 14절에 "규모 없는 자들을 권계하며 마음이 약한 자들을 안위하고 힘이 없는 자들을 붙들어 주며 모든 사람을 대하여 오래 참으라" 라고 하면서 교회의 일치를 가르쳤다. 그러나 데살로니가후서 3장 6절에서는 분명히 데살로니가전서 5장 14절에 언급한 이들에게서 떠나라고 명령한

다: "규모 없이 행하고 우리에게 받은 유전 대로 행하지 아니하는 모든 형제에게서 떠나라." 그러나 교회의 일치를 포기할 수 있는 경우는 "유전 대로 행하지 않는 경우"에 한정되며, 먼저 관용과 "오래 참는 것"이 선행되어야 함을 기억해야 한다.

e. 바울은 편지의 결과를 기다리는 동안 근심 가운데 있었다 (2:12-13).

본문:

> 12. 내가 그리스도의 복음을 위하여 드로아에 이르매 주 안에서 내게(복음 전도의) 문이 열렸으되 13. 내가 내 형제 디도를 만나지 못함으로 내 심령이 편치 못하여 저희를 작별하고 마게도냐로 갔노라.

본문비평:

1. 12절의 **εἰς τὸ εὐαγγέλιον**(복음을 위하여)이 F G 라틴역에서 **διά τὸ εὐαγγέλιον**(복음 때문에), "propter evangelium"이라고 각기 쓰였다. D E는 "복음으로 말미암아" (**διά τοῦ εὐαγγέλιου**)라고 쓴다.

2. 12절의 **θύρας μοι ἀνεῳγμένης**(문이 내게 열렸었다)를 F G 라틴역에서는 분사가 주격으로 바뀌고, **ἦν**과 함께, **θύρα μοι ἦν ἀνεῳγμένη,** ostium mihi apertum esset이라고 각기 쓰였다. 번역은 같게 된다. 뜻의 차이는 없다.

3. 13절의 **τῷ μή**는 ℵ A B C G K 에서, **το μή** 는 L P에서, **τοῦ**

μή 는 a C² 에서, ἐν τῷ μὴ는 D E17에서 쓰였다. 플러머는 τo μή와 τοῦ μή는 적당치 않은 말이라고 일축해 버린다.[67]

내용개요:

이 부분은 짧은 부분이지만 바울의 고린도 교회 사역에 대한 역사적 자료를 제공해준다. 이 부분은 7장 5절과 연결이 잘된다. 바울은 "눈물의 편지"를 쓰고 난 뒤에 디도를 통해 보내고, 디도가 가져올 고린도 교회의 편지에 대한 반응이나 조처를 드로아에서 기다렸다. 그러나 거기서 디도를 만나지 못하자 마게도냐로 갔고, 거기서 얼마 후 드디어 디도를 만나서 고린도 교회가 다시 바울을 따르게 되었음을 듣고 기뻐하며 위로의 하나님을 찬양하며 고린도후서를 썼던 것이다(7:6). 서론 부분에서 논했던 바와 같이 불트만 같은 이들은 1장 1절-2장 13절과 7장 5-16절을 하나의 독립된 편지("D 편지")로 본다.[68] 실제로 불트만은 그의 주석에서 2장 13절 다음에 7장 5-16절을 주석하고, 그 후에 2장 14절-7장 4절을 "C 편지"로 분류하여 주석하고 있다.[69] 이런 주장에 대해서 현재의 본문의 통일성을 지지하는 몇 가지 반대 의견을 제시할 수 있다. 1) 지금의 순서대로도 내용상 연결이 된다. 더 많은 학자들이 지금의 순서대로 훌륭히 연결된다고 본다. 2) 지금의 순서대로 썼을 가능성을 무시하고 편집 비평적 가설만을 고집하고 있다. 3) 더구나 이런 편집 비평을 뒷받침하는 사본적 증거도 없다. 모든 사본이

67) Plummer, 67.

68) Bultmann, 19.

69) Bultmann, 52, 61; 참조, Bornkamm, "The History...," 258-64; P. Vielhaur, 153; H. Koester, *Introduction to the NT,* II (Philadelphia: Fortress, 1982), 53-54.

지금의 순서대로 쓰여 있다. 2장 14절-7장 4절이 독립된 편지라면, 2장 14절에서는 시작하는 문구가 있어야 하고, 7장 4절에서는 마치는 문구가, 있어야 하는데 이런 문구가 전혀 없다.[70] 한편, 바레트도 2장 13절과 7장 5절이 원래 연속된 편지라는 주장을 반대하면서, 2장 12-13절에서는 단수 일인칭("나")이 쓰였고, 7장 5-6절에서는 복수 일인칭("우리")이 쓰였음을 지적했다.[71] 그러나 이런 인칭의 변화는 같은 서신 안에도 자주 있는 예이다(롬 6:2, 8, 11; 7:14, 15-25; 고전 9:1, 11; 갈 5:1, 2, 7). 4) 12절에서는 "드로아"에서 복음의 문이 열렸다는 사실을 말하고 있고, 13절에서는 마게도냐로 갔다는 말을 하는 사실은 14절에 있는 "각 처"(ἐν παντὶ τόπῳ)라는 말과 잘 연결된다. 5) 문맥 이탈은 바울의 흔한 필체이다. 플러머는 고린도전서 15장 57절에서도 바울이 넘치는 감사로 인해서 여기 14절과 꼭 같이 Τῷ δὲ θεῷ χάρις(하나님께 감사하노니)라는 말을 갑자기 하고 있음을 지적하였다.[72] 6) 14절은 그 앞까지의 하나님의 도우심에 대한 역사적인 설명을 요약하는 말도 되고, 15절 이후부터 나오는 바울이 하나님이 인정하시는 사도라는 신학적인 설명을 시작하는 말도 된다. 그러므로 13절과 14절은 연결이 잘된다. 7) 12, 13절에서 근심을 말하고 14절 이하에서 기쁨을 말하는 것은 고린도후서 전체의 특징에 잘 맞는다. 바울은 1장에서부터 그의 사역의 특징을 "근심과 위로"가 서로 교차되는 것으로 설명해 왔다. 그러나 이런 교차는 단순히 "삶의 슬픔과 기

70) Jerome Murphy-O'Connor, "Paul and Macedonia," 99-103; E. Thrall, "A Second Thanksgiving Period," 109-110)

71) Barrett, 206; 참조, Furnish, 172.

72) Plummer, 67.

뿜" 의 연속과는 다르다. 그의 목회에 나타난 교차적 현상은 하나의 목적을 갖고 있다. 그것은 "회중에게 기쁨을 주는 목회" 를 하는 것이다. 그러므로 "근심하는 상태" 에서 고린도 교인들을 만나고 싶지 않아서 방문 계획을 취소 했고, 또 방문을 대신하여 보낸 "눈물의 편지" 의 결과도 근심 대신에 기쁨을 가져오지 않았느냐고 한다(7장). 지금도 바울은 "눈물의 편지" 에서 지시한 치리를 해제함으로써 치리 받은 사람뿐만 아니라 고린도 교인 전체에게 기쁨을 주는 목회자란 것을 증거하고 있지 않은가? 그리고 이런 사역이야 말로 "십자가의 죽음과 부활" 을 증거하는 그리스도의 사역이 아닌가라는 생각을 일으키게 한다. 그래서 그는 계속해서 자신의 사역 가운데서 일어난 "근심된 부분" 과 "기쁜 부분" 을 교차시키고,[73] 또한 예수 그리스도의 죽음과 부활을 번갈아 가면서 논한다. 이런 대조는 실상 고린도후서 전체에 스며 있다(고후 1:8-10; 13:4).

이상과 같은 이유들로 2장 13절과 14절을 나누는 것은 옳지 않으며, 원래 지금과 같은 순서 대로 있었다고 본다.

주석:

12. "내가 그리스도의 복음을 위하여 드로아에 이르매 주 안에서 내게 (복음전도의) 문이 열렸으되" (Ἐλθὼν δὲ εἰς τὴν Τρῳάδα εἰς τὸ εὐαγγέλιον τοῦ Χριστοῦ καὶ θύρας μοι ἀνεῳγμένης ἐν κυρίῳ,)의 원명은 알렉산드리아 드로아

73) Georgi, 51, n. 190. 여기서 Georgi는 12, 13절이 아시아에서의 고난에 대해서 계속 언급하고 있는 것이라고 했다. 이에 대해 Furnish는 1:8과 12, 13절의 문장 스타일과 기능이 다르므로, 오히려 12, 13절이 일인칭 단수를 쓴다는 점에서 1:12, 15와 관련 된다고 한다(Furnish, 170, 172).

(Ἀλεξανδρεια ἡ Τρῳάς)이다. 현재의 이름은 이스탄불이다(옛날 콘스탄티노플). 이 도시는 소아시아에서 마게도냐로 항해하는 여행자들이 배를 타는 항구이다. 바울이 드로아에 간 기록이 사도행전에 있으나(16:8, 11; 20:6; 참조, 딤후 4:13) 본문의 여행 기록은 없다. 드로아에서 "복음의 문이 열렸다"는 것은 거기서 바울이 복음을 전할 수 있는 기회뿐만 아니라 근거지가 생겼음을 말한다. 13절에 "저희를 작별하였다"는 말을 보아서 매우 성공적인 사역의 발판을 마련하였음을 짐작할 수 있다.

13. "내가 내 형제 디도를 만나지 못함으로 내 심령이 편치 못하여 저희를 작별하고 마게도냐로 갔노라"(οὐκ ἔσχηκα ἄνεσιν τῷ πνεύματί μου τῷ μὴ εὑρεῖν με Τίτον τὸν ἀδελφόν μου, ἀλλὰ ἀποταξάμενος αὐτοῖς ἐξῆλθον εἰς Μακεδονίαν). 바울은 드로아에서 디도를 기다리며 고린도 교회의 소식을 듣기 원했으나, 그를 만나지 못하자 드로아에서의 복음의 기지 건설의 좋은 기회조차 포기하면서 마게도냐로 떠나야 했다. 바울은 그만큼 고린도 교회를 염려하고 사랑하였음을 보여 준다(11:28). 플러머는 "작별하였다"(ἀποταξαμενος)란 말이 매우 주저하며 떠났음을 가리키는 말이라고 하였다.[74] 그는 배로 갔을 수도 있고 육로로 갔을 수도 있다. 고린도후서 1장 8절에 바울이 말하는 아시아에서 당한 고난이 사도행전 19장의 에베소에서에서 당한 고난으로 보고, 사도행전 20장 1절에 마게도냐로 갔다는 기록을 본문의 마게도냐로 간 것과 같은 기록으로 본다.[75] 55년 마지막 달쯤 되

74) Plummer, 66.

었을 때이다.[76] 마게도냐는 지금의 그리스반도로서, 빌립보, 데살로니가, 등 바울이 세운 교회가 북쪽에 있고, 남쪽 끝에 아덴이 있고, 아덴의 서쪽으로 94km지점에 고린도가 있다.

"심령" (πνεύμα)이란 말은 바울 자신을 가리킨다(롬 1:9; 고후 7:13; 고전 16:18).[77] 7장 5절에서는 "육체" (σάρξ)란 말이 바울 자신을 가리키기도 한다. 바울이 이런 말을 번갈아 쓴 것은 그의 심신이 모두 괴로운 상태에 있었음을 나타내고 있다.

지금까지 바울은 그의 사역이 곧 하나님의 사역임을 역사적인 사례들을 열거하면서 증거하였다. 즉 그의 모든 사역을 통해서 하나님께서 근심 가운데서도 기쁨으로 인도해주신다는 것이다. 이 사실이 1장 8절에 에베소에서 당한 고난 가운데서 구원하신 역사적 사실과, 또 "눈물의 편지"의 결과가 기쁨으로 바뀌었다는 사실, 그리고 디도를 어렵게나마 만나게 하신 사실(7:6)로서도 증명이 된다는 것이다. 고린도 교인들은 이런 사도를 신뢰할 만하지 않는가 이런 하나님의 도우심의 역사적 증거는 7장에서 다시 언급되고 끝을 맺는다. 그러나 그 사이에 2장 14절-7장 4절에서 바울은 하나님의 도우시는 그의 사역을 "근심과 기쁨", "역경과 순경", "굴욕과 영광", "죽음과 생명" 등의 대조적 표현으로써 그의 사역의 신학적인 의미를 서술하고 있다.

B. 바울의 사도직의 진실성의 증거들(2:14-7:4)

75) 참조, Furnish, 172.

76) Martin, 42; Robinson, *Redating*, 50, 55.

77) Bultmann, 51.

2장 14절에서는 7장 5절의 드로아에서 디도를 만나지 못했다가 드디어 만났다는 말로 이어져야하는데 대신에 바울은 사도직에 대한 긴 연설을 시작하고 있다. 그래서 위에서 지적한 바와 같이 어떤 학자들은 2장 14절-7장 4절을 독립된 문서로 본다. 고린도후서의 통일성을 지지하는 학자들은 2장 14절에서부터 "큰 주제 이탈"이 시작된다고 보는 것이다.[78] 그러나 디도를 만나서 기뻐한 것을 주제라고 할 수 없고 바울이 고린도후서를 쓰게 된 직접적 동기라고 해야 옳을 것이다. 오히려 사도직 변명이야 말로 바울이 스스로 밝히는 고린도후서의 주제이다(12:19). 그렇다면 주제 이탈이 아니라 주제 시작이라고 보아야 한다. 바울은 이 중심 부분에서 그의 사도직의 진실성을 신학적이고 성서적 근거를 가지고 집중적으로 설명하면서 그를 신뢰하고 화해할 것을 고린도 교인들에게 계속 호소한다. 이 부분에서 자천(自薦)한다는 말이 자주 나오는데, 이것은 그를 대적하는 고린도 교회의 거짓사도들이 그들이 갖고 다니며 자랑하는 아마도 예루살렘 사도들로부터 받은 천거서(3:1)를 겨냥하여 하는 말이라고 볼 수 있다. 그가 자신의 사역의 진실성을 주장하며, 자천을 하고, 혹은 변명을 하는 것이, 그를 대적하는 자들로 말미암은 것이며 자신이 바라는 바가 아니라고 여러 번 말한다(3:1, 13; 4:2; 5:12; 11:1, 16, 18, 30: 12:1, 5, 6, 11). 믿었던 고린도 교인들마저 바울을 멀리하는 실정에서 바울은 스스로를 진정한 사도라고 증명할 수밖에 없었다. 그러나 그리스도의 교회를 대적자들의 공격으로부터 방어하고, 하나님의 진리를 수호하는 것이 사도적 사명이므로 스스로 자신의 사역의 진실

78) Harris, 240.

성을 증거 할 수 밖에 없었다(12:6). 이 부분에서 바울은 자신이 진실한 그리스도의 사도라는 증거를 자신이 하나님의 영에 의해 사도로 부르심을 받고, 인도받으며 사역하고 있다는 사실과, 그리스도의 약함을 따라서 고린도 교인들을 위해 희생하는 사역에서 찾는다(3:3-4:15; 6:4-10). 그리스도의 약함의 유형을 따라서 하나님의 능력을 나타내는 사역이 진정한 그리스도의 사도의 사역이라고 보고 이를 진정한 사도의 판단 기준으로 제시한다. 반대로 그의 반대자들은 이런 그리스도의 십자가의 증거 대신에 이차적이며 외적인 요소들을 가지고 사욕적으로 사역한다는 의미가 암시되어 있다(5:12).

1. 바울은 순수한 복음을 전한다(2:14-17).

> 14. 항상 우리를 그리스도 안에서 이기게 하시고 우리로 말미암아 각처에서 그리스도를 아는 냄새를 나타내시는 하나님께 감사하노라. 15. 우리는 구원 얻는 자들에게나 망하는 자들에게나 하나님 앞에서 그리스도의 향기니 16. 이 사람에게는 사망에서 사망으로(사망으로 좇아 사망에) 이르는 냄새요, 저 사람에게는 생명에서 생명으로 (생명으로 좇아 생명에) 이르는 냄새라. 누가 이런 일을 할 수 있겠는가 (누가 이것을 감당하리요) 17. 우리는 수다한 사람과 같이 하나님의 말씀을 혼잡하게 하지 아니하고 곧 순전함으로, 하나님께 받은 것 같이, 하나님 앞에서와 그리스도 안에서 말하노라.

본문비평:

1. 16절의 ὀσμὴ ἐκ θανάτου("사망으로 좇아 사망에 이르는 냄새")의 ἐκ가 없는 사본이 있다(D E F G K L, 라틴역, 아람어역). 그러면 사망으로 이르는 사망의 냄새라는 뜻이 된다. NIV와 마틴은 ἐκ 없는 대로 번역한다.[79] 그러나 바레트는 *lectio difficilior*

potior, 즉 어려운 구절이 더 원래의 것이라는 일반적 사본연구 원칙에 의하여 그냥 ἐκ를 가지고 "사망에서 나와서 사망에 이르는 냄새"로 해석한다.[80] 죽은 예수만을 믿는 이는 죽을 것이다. 그러나 다시 산 예수를 믿는 이는 "예수의 생명에서부터 얻은 생명"을 얻어 살게 될 것이다.

2. 17절의 οἱ πολλοί(수다한 사람들)대신 οἱ πολλοί(다른 사람들이 하는 식으로)로 기록된 사본들이 있다(p[46] D G syrP, 말시온).[81]

내용요약:

2장 14절부터 7장 16절까지 바울은 반대자들을 염두에 두고서 그리스도의 사도로서 자신의 진실성을 설명한다. 이런 내용을 한마디로 바울의 자신에 대한 추천서, 즉 자천서(自薦書)라고 말할 수도 있다. 3장 1절에서부터 반대자들이 자천서(아마도, 예루살렘 큰 사도들의)를 가지고 자랑하는 문제를 거론하면서부터 바울은 자신의 사도직을 변명하기 시작한다. 그러나 실상 2장 14절부터 바울의 자천하는 말이 시작되고 있다. 본문(2:14-17)에 나타나는 일련의 대조구문들이 반대자들과 바울의 사역을 대조하는 것으로 보인다. 특히 17절의 "우리"와 "수다한 사람들"의 대조, 그들의 "말씀을 혼잡케 함"에 대해서 바울은 "순전함으로 그리스도와 하나님 앞에서 받은 것같이 말하는 것"은 반대자들에 대해 바울이

79) Martin, 44.

80) Barrett, 101.

81) 후자의 번역을 받아들이는 학자들과 반대하는 학자들의 견해를 Martin, 44에서 보라.

자신의 사도직을 변명하고 있음을 분명히 보여 준다. 14절에서 바울은 하나님께서 그의 사역에 직접 개입하심을 요약하면서 이렇게 하나님께서 "우리"를 각처에서 이기게 하셨다고 한다. 이 말은 실제로 자신의 사역의 주역이 하나님이심을 밝히는 말이다. 자신의 복음은 진실한 복음이다(4:2; 11:10; 13:8). 자신의 복음 사역의 주역은 하나님이시며 자신은 종으로서 순종하기 때문에 그의 사역은 어떤 역경 가운데서도 승리할 수밖에 없다. 이런 사상이 고린도후서에 있는 그의 전체 사도직 변명에서 드러난다. 그런 의미에서 본문은 사도직 변명의 서론에 해당된다.

주석:

14. "항상 우리를 그리스도 안에서 이기게 하시고 우리로 말미암아 각처에서 그리스도를 아는 냄새를 나타내시는 하나님께 감사하노라"(Τῷ δὲ θεῷ χάρις τῷ πάντοτε θριαμβεύοντι ἡμᾶς ἐν τῷ Χριστῷ καὶ τὴν ὀσμὴν τῆς γνώσεως αὐτοῦ φανεροῦντι δι᾽ ἡμῶν ἐν παντὶ τόπῳ). 희랍어 본문에는 "하나님께 감사하노라"라는 말이 이 절의 맨 앞에 온다. 13절에서 바울은 디도를 만나지 못하여 매우 심령이 상해 있었다. 그러나 14절에서는 갑자기 하나님께 대한 감사의 말이 나온다. 바울은 그의 근심 걱정을 길게 늘어 놓는 것을 원치 않았다. 그의 사역 가운데 함께 하시며 위로하시고 기쁨을 주시는 하나님께 대한 찬양을 무척이나 빨리 드리고 싶었다.[82] 그 하나님이 바울 일행을 승리하게 하시며 "그리스도에 대한 지식의 냄새를 나게 하시기" 때문이다.

---

82) Allo, 44.

다른 말로 하나님이 바울과 그 일행으로 하여금 복음을 전파하게 하시기 때문이다. 본절의 "냄새"와 15절의 "그리스도의 향기"라는 표현은 당시 희랍시대의 박카스신의 축제에서 쓰이는 말로서 제의적 용어라고 한다.[83] 또는 바울이 여기서 군인들의 개선행렬을 연상하고 있다고 한다.[84] 여기서 바울은 자신을 개선장군으로서 나타내고 있다.[85] 그러나 이런 표현이 유대교적 배경을 갖고 있다는 주장도 강하다.[86] 시락서 24장 12-15절, 39장 13절에서 지혜가 향기를 뿌리는 것으로 노래한다. 에디오피아 에녹서 24장에서는 택함 받은 자에게 생명을 주는 향기 나는 나무를 언급하고 있다. 바룩서 67장 6절에서는 "의의 향기"가 언급되고 있다. 불트만은 영지주의 서적에서 비슷한 글들을 찾았다.[87] 그러나 무엇보다 구약의 희생 제사에서 나온 말일 수 있다(창 8:21; 출 29:18; 레 1:9; 민 15:3; 겔 6:13; 단 4:34). 바울은 냄새 또는 향기(ovsmh,)라는 말을 에베소서 5장 2절, 빌립보서 4장 18절에서도 은유적 의미로 쓰고 있다. 15절에서 "우리는… 하나님 앞에서 그리스도의 향기"라는 말은 희생 양 그리스도의 향기라는 의미로서 구약의 희생 제사를 그대로 나타내고 있으므로 구약 희생 제사와 관련되어 있다

83) Hughes, 78, n. 10.

84) Plummer, 68; Hughes, 78, n. 10; Martin, 47. 바울이 다른 곳에서 종종 개선 행렬을 연상시키는 표현을 쓴다. 자신을 전쟁 포로로 표현하기도 한다(롬14:7; 고전4:9; 골4:10; 몬23).

85) Barrett, 98.

86) T. W. Manson, "2 Cor 2:14-17: Suggestions Toward an Exegesis," in *Studia Paulina* (de Zwaan FS), ed. J. Sevenster and W. C. van Unnik (Haarlem: Erven F. Bohn, 1953), 155-62; Georgi, 225; Martin, 48; 특히 Furnish, 174-75를 보라.

87) *Refutatio* V 19, 3; VII 22,14f.; *Mandaean Liturgies* II, XXX, 1ff.; Bultmann, 64-66).

고 볼 수 있다. 그러나 14절에 있는 전쟁 승리에 대한 말은 개선식 때 군인들 행렬 앞에 뿌리던 향을 연상케 한다. 또 15, 16절에 "구원 얻는 자"와 "망하는 자"란 말은 개선 행렬에서 "승리한 군인들"과 "전쟁 포로"들을 염두에 두고 하는 말일 수 있고, 또 이들에게 같은 향내가 정반대로 느껴졌을 것이라는 뜻이 있다.[88]

희랍-로마적 배경이 있든지, 유대교적 배경이 있든지, 14절은 12, 13절의 근심과는 대조적인 바울의 승리와 기쁨을 나타내고 있다. 근심도 하나님께서 주시는 것일 수 있으나(7:9), 여기서는 그런 신학적 문제를 가지고 토론하지 않고 지금까지 말해온 것, 즉 하나님께서 바울의 사역과 함께 하셨다는 역사적인 증거를 요약하고 있다. 이와 같이 하나님은 지금까지 바울 일행을 언제나 승리하게 이끌어 주셨다. 그러므로 바울 일행이 하나님이 인정하시는 사도들임을 증명할 수 있지 않는가 또한 14절은 "그리스도를 아는 냄새"라는 "신학적 표현"을 담고 있으므로 15절부터 시작되는 긴 신학적 자천서, 혹은 변명을 시작하는 구절이기도 하다.

그러므로 2:14절 이하에서 말하는 바울의 승리는 보다 구체적이고 현실적인 의미로서 앞서 말한 4절의 "눈물의 편지"가 문제가 된 사람의 치리등 엄격한 지시와 내용이 있었음에도 불구하고, 또 이런 편지의 내용에 대해서 그를 반대하는 이들의 비난에도 불구하고(10:9, 10), 고린도 교인들이 회개하고 바울에게로 다시 돌아온 사실을 가리키는 것이다(7:8-12).

88) Plummer, 68; Barrett, 97-98; Allo, 43-44; Kümmel, 198; Martin, 47; 이런 관련성을 반대하는 의견이 있다: Collange, 29.

바울이 주장하는 그의 사역의 성공은 결코 그 자신이나, 다른 인간적 공로에 기인된 것이 아니라, 오로지 하나님에게서 기인되었다. 그러므로 그는 그의 성공을 하나님께 돌린다. 그렇게 함으로 그의 사도직의 신적 기원과 인정을 증거하는 것이다. 이런 승리는 바울의 사역에 있어서 지속적으로 나타나는 많은 고난에 비하면 일시적인 하나님의 격려와 확증일 뿐임을 바울은 알고 있다(4:7 이하; 6:4 이하; 11:22-33). 그러나 이런 일시적 승리가 궁극적이고 영원한 승리를 향한 확신을 위해 필요한 것이다. 이런 승리와 영광의 조건은 "그리스도 안"에 거하는 것이다. 즉 그리스도를 믿음으로 그리스도의 권능과 권세의 영역에 속한 존재가 되어야 하는 것이다(1:20, 21; 2:17; 10:7, 17, 12:2, 19; 13:2). 그리스도의 능력과 권세 밖에서의 모든 일은 주님의 인정을 받을 수 없고, 승리와 영광을 얻을 수 없다(10:18; 11:3; 12:20, 21; 13:5).

15. "우리는 구원 얻는 자들에게나 망하는 자들에게나 하나님 앞에서 그리스도의 향기니"(ὅτι Χριστοῦ εὐωδία ἐσμὲν τῷ θεῷ ἐν τοῖς σῳζομένοις καὶ ἐν τοῖς ἀπολλυμένοις). 바울의 일행의 정체는 분명하다. 그들은 "하나님 앞에서 그리스도의 향기"이다. 위에서 지적한 바와 같이 이 말의 배경을 헬라-로마적인 것만으로 주장하는 것은 옳지 않다.[89] 유대교의 희생제사의 배경이 분명히 있다.[90] 하나님 앞에서의 드린바 된 희생 제물인 그리

89) Bultmann, 64-66.

90) Plummer(71)와 Furnish (177)는 희생 제사와의 연관을 반대한다. 70인역의 ὀσμὴν εὐωδίας가 아닌 그냥 εὐωδίας가 나왔기 때문이라고 한다. 그러나 ὀσμή가 14절에 한 번, 16절에 두 번 나온다(엡5:2와 빌4:18 참조).

스도의 향기가 사도 바울과 그 일행이라는 말이다. 바울은 자신이 그리스도의 죽음과 부활에 일치된 자아 의식을 갖고 있다 (빌 3:10). 바울의 헌신적 삶은 그리스도의 삶의 연장이요, 그런 삶은 하나님께 향기가 되는 것이다. 그리고 그 향기는 하나님께 기쁨이 된다. 또 향기는 제물을 드린 사람에게 하나님의 은혜를 받게 하는 역할도 한다. 즉 바울은 복음을 받는 이들에게 하나님의 구원을 받게 하는 역할을 한다. 그러나 복음을 받지 않는 이에게는 하나님의 진노를 받게 하는 역할을 하게 된다(16절). 그러나 여기서, 하나님께 드리는 희생 제사와 관련시켜 생각할 때, 누가 "망하는 자" 를 나타내는가를 설명하기 어렵다. 이에 대해 맨슨(T. W. Manson)은 랍비 문헌에서 율법을 약처럼 생각해서 율법을 지키는 이스라엘 백성에게는 구원이 되고, 이방인들에게는 죽음의 독이 된다고 자주 언급됨을 지적하였다(*Yoma* 72b).[91] 그렇다면 이제 율법을 대신하는 복음을 모든 사람들에게 전파하는 바울 일행이 바로 "하나님 앞에서 그리스도의 향기" 이다. 이 향기를 받아들이는 이들은 구원받게 되고, 거절하는 이들은 망하게 된다. 여기에 바울의 반대자들에 대한 경고가 포함되어 있다. 위에서 언급했듯이 맨슨은 율법을 지키는 자와 안 지키는 자에게 각기 다른 결과가 주어진다는 랍비들의 글을 인용하였다.[92]

16. "이 사람에게는 사망에서 사망으로(사망으로 좇아 사망에) 이르는 냄새요, 저 사람에게는 생명에서 생명으로 (생명으로 좇아

---

91) Manson, 158.

92) Deut. Rabba 1:6: "율법의 말씀은 이스라엘에게는 생명의 약이 되고 이방인에게는 죽음의 독이 된다." ; *Sabbat* 88b; *Taanit* 7 a; *Yoma* 72b.

생명에) 이르는 냄새니, 누가 이런 일을 할 수 있겠는가 (누가 이것을 감당하리요?)" (οἷς μὲν ὀσμὴ ἐκ θανάτου εἰς θάνατον, οἷς δὲ ὀσμὴ ἐκ ζωῆς εἰς ζωήν. καὶ πρὸς ταῦτα τίς ἱκανός;). 16절에서 바울은 "하나님 앞에 그리스도의 향기"인 자신이 그의 복음을 받아들이는 자에게는 생명의 사신이 되고, 거절하는 자에게는 죽음의 사신이 됨을 밝힌다. 바레트는 16절 안에 더 깊은 기독론적 의미가 있다고 한다. 즉 누구든지 예수가 죽은 유대인이라고 믿으면서 그의 부활을 증거하는 복음을 거절하는 자는 죽는 자가 되고, 누구든지 그의 부활을 믿는 자는 산 자가 된다는 것이다.[93]

"사망으로 좇아 사망에 이르는 냄새"에 대해서 퍼니쉬는 셈족어 영향을 받은 독특한 표현으로서 "궁극적 죽음에 이르는 냄새"를 뜻하고, "생명으로 좇아 생명에 이르는 냄새"도 "궁극적 생명에 이르는 냄새"를 뜻한다고 했다.[94]

16절 마지막에 "누가 이것을 감당하리요 " 라는 말에서 "이것" (ταῦτα)은 복수로 되어 있다. 즉 "이것들"이다. "이것들"이란 복음 사역을 총괄하여 일컫는 말이다.[95] 더 자세히 바울이 언급한 그리스도의 구원의 사도(향기)로서의 사역을 가리킨다. 여기서 "감당하리요"(ἱκανός)란 말은 "충분하다" 또는 "자격이 있다"라는 말이므로 "누가 이런 일들을 할 수 있겠는가 "란 뜻이 된다. 예

93) Kümmel은 히브리어 □□(삼)이 약을 가리키며 향을 가리키지 않는다고 반대한다(198). Barrett는 □□이 후기 성서 히브리어에서는 약으로만 쓰였으나 구약 히브리어에서는 기름에 섞는 재료(출25:6), 또는 향(출30:7)으로 쓰였음을 지적한다(Barrett, 101, 102; Martin, 48).

94) Furnish, 177; Hughes, 81, n. 18; 위의 본문 비평 부분을 보라.

95) Héring, 19.

상하는 대답은 "우리" 이다(17절). 그러나 이 질문 안에는 고린도 교회 거짓사도들의 자랑에 대한 경계가 포함되어 있다.[96] 그들이 자신들의 영적 우월감을 가지고 자랑하나 그들은 "그리스도의 희생제사의 향기"가 되지 못한다.

17. "우리는 수다한 사람과 같이 하나님의 말씀을 혼잡하게 하지 아니하고 곧 순전함으로, 하나님께 받은 것 같이, 하나님 앞에서와 그리스도 안에서 말하노라"(**οὐ γάρ ἐσμεν ὡς οἱ πολλοὶ καπηλεύοντες τὸν λόγον τοῦ θεοῦ, ἀλλ᾽ ὡς ἐξ εἰλικρινείας, ἀλλ᾽ ὡς ἐκ θεοῦ κατέναντι θεοῦ ἐν Χριστῷ λαλοῦμεν**). 17절에서 바울은 16절 마지막에서 물은 질문, 즉 "누가 이것을 감당하리요 "에 대해서 곧바로 "우리다"라고 대답하지 않고, 먼저 "우리"가 진실한 복음 사역자임을 밝힌다. "우리는 수다한 사람과 같이 하나님의 말씀을 혼잡하게 하지 아니하고 순전함으로 하나님께 받은 것같이 하나님 앞에서와 그리스도 안에서 말하노라."

"수다한 사람"(**οἱ πολλοί**)은 고린도 교회의 거짓사도들을 가리킨다. 그들은 "말씀을 혼잡케 한다"(**καπηλεύοντες**). 이 동사는 몇 가지 뜻이 있다. 1) 포도주에 물을(부정한 이익을 얻기 위해서) 탄다(사 1:22).[97] 2) 조잡한 상품을 팔아 이익을 챙긴다.[98] 3) 지식을 판다.[99] 한 마디로, 자신의 유익을 위해서 말씀을 전파하는 거

96) Georgi, 224; Barrett, 102; Martin 49.

97) Barrett, 103; Plummer, 73.

98) Windisch, *TDNT* 3:606-609.

99) Plato, *Protagoras*, 313).

짓사도들의 행위를 가리키는 말이다. 그는 "순전함에서" (ἐξ εἰλικρινείας), "하나님께 받은 것 같이" (ἐκ θεοῦ), "하나님 앞에서" (κατέναντι θεοῦ), "그리스도 안에서 말한다" (ἐν Χριστῷ λαλοῦμεν). 순전함이란 말은 진실함이란 뜻도 된다(고전 5:8). 그 진실함은 인간적 도덕적 진실함 이상이다. 왜냐하면 진실함이란 말이 하나님과 그리스도라는 말과 함께 나오기 때문이다. 바울의 말은 거짓선지자들과 전혀 다른 근원과 본질을 갖고 있다. 거짓선지자들의 정체는 "사단의 일꾼들" 이다(11:15). 그러나 바울은 신적 근원을 갖고 있다. 즉 그 자신이 그리스도와 신비한 연합을 이룬 사람으로서 그의 비밀을 말하는 것이다(고전 4:1; 7:40; 고후 12:4; 빌 1:21). 여기서 "그리스도 안" (ἐν Χριστῷ)은 5장 17, 19절, 12장 2절에서와 유사하게 "그리스도의 영적 능력이나 권위에 속한 것" 을 나타내는 말로 바울의 사도적 신분을 보다 명확히 한정시키는 반면 그의 대적자들의 신분과는 의도적으로 차별화시키는 말이다. 앞에서 말한 "하나님 앞에서" 라는 말로는 바울의 사역의 진정성을 충분히 나타내기에 너무 막연한 의미가 될 수 있다. 어쩌면 다른 허다한 많은 사람들도 같은 말로 자신들의 사역의 진정성을 설명할 수 있기 때문이다. 그래서 바울은 그의 사역을 보다 구체적으로 그리스도 중심 사역으로 명시해야 할 필요성을 느낀 것이다. 복음은 하나님께서 특별히 그리스도를 통해서 나타낸 구원의 역사를 말한다. 바울은 다름 아닌 그리스도의 사도로서 그리스도의 능력과 권위로 하나님의 구원 소식을 전하는 사람이다. 그러나 그의 대적자들은 "그리스도 안" 에서 말한다고 볼 수 없다. 그들은 자신들의 사욕을 따르는 거짓 사도들이며 "그리스도를 육체를 따라서 아는" 그리스도와 대적되는 "사단의 일꾼들" 이기 때문이다(5:16; 11:13, 15). 다시 말하면 "그리스도 안"(ἐν Χριστῷ) 이란 어귀는 바울의 사도적 진정성을 나타내는 "상표"와 같은 것이다. 즉 바울은 죽으시고 부활하신 그리스도의 영적 능력과 권세를 가진 사도이다.

한편 "순전함"은 윤리적인 의미뿐만 아니라 신학적인 의미도 있다고 본다. 3장에서 바울이 공격하는 거짓 사도들의 모세의 율법주의적 시각으로 복음을 이해함으로 "말씀을 혼잡케 하는 것"으로 볼 수 있다(11:3, 4). 이에 반해서 바울과 그 일행은 말씀을 혼잡하게 하지 아니한다(4:2). 그는 하나님에게서 받은 복음을 사람 앞에서 하듯이 사람의 구미에 맞추어 변경하지 않고 "하나님 앞에서" 그대로 전할 뿐이다(갈 1:12). "그리스도 안에서 말한다"(ἐν Χριστῷ λαλοῦμεν)는 죽으시고 부활하신 그리스도의 영적 능력과 권세에 의존하여서 말한다는 뜻이다.[100] 바울의 사도권은 그리스도의 왕권에 의해 주어진 것이다. 그러므로 바울은 자의적으로 말하는 것이 아니라 예수 그리스도의 종으로서 주되신 예수 그리스도의 명령과 지시를 따라서 말한다(4:5; 10:5-6, 8; 13:10). 그러므로 그의 가르침은 신뢰할 만하다. 반면에 그의 반대자들은 자의적으로 사욕적으로 말한다는 암시가 있다(10:12b; 18).

이렇게 고린도 정황을 염두에 두고 생각하면, 2:17절의 "하나님의 말씀을 순전함으로 전하는 것"은 바울이 보낸 "눈물의 편지"의 내용이 혹독하고 준엄한 내용들이었으나 고린도 교인들의 잘못을 고치기 위해서는 어쩔 수 없이 솔직하게 할 말들을 다 썼다

100) Calvin은 Erasmus를 따라서 "그리스도를 따라서"(according to Christ)라고 번역한다 (37).

는 것을 가리킨다(7:8-12). 반대자들은 바울이 이런 엄한 편지로 그들을 위협하려한다고 비난하지만(10:9, 10), 그는 사도로서 마땅히 할 말을 한 것 뿐이라는 것이다. 오히려 반대자들이 말씀을 순전히 전하지 않고 그릇되게 전하는 것이 문제라고 반박하는 것이다. 바울의 엄한 편지로 얻은 좋은 성과, 즉 바울의 편지를 받고 회개하고 그의 지시를 따라서 문제 된 이를 치리한 것이 바울의 사역이 그리스도의 진정한 사도로서의 정당한 사역이며 그를 반대하는 이들의 사역이 잘못된 것임을 반증한다고 말하는 것이다(14-16). 한마디로 그들의 신학과 신앙이 모두 잘못된 것이라는 암시가 있다(11:4).

주해(2:14-17):

14절에서부터 바울은 그의 사도직을 적극적으로 변명하기 시작한다. 사도로서의 자신의 진실성 은 무엇보다 그가 전하는 복음의 정통성과 순수성에 있다. 그는 복음을 하나님께로부터 받은 대로 순수하게 전한다. 그가 전하는 복음은 구원의 복음이지만, 그 복음에 대한 반응은 다르다. 즉 복음을 순종하는 이들에게는 복음이 생명이 되지만, 반대자들에게는 죽음이 된다. 여기서 바울은 그를 반대하고 비난하는 고린도 교회의 거짓사도들을 가리키면서 그들의 반대에도 불구하고 그의 사역은 반드시 승리할 것임을 믿는다.

목회자나 크리스챤 사역자들 가운데 진실성 없이 자신들의 유익에 따라 사는 이들이 적지 않다. 이런 특별한 사람들이 따로 있기도 하지만, 일반적으로, 대부분의 사역자들은 때로 진실성 없이 사역하는 자신을 발견하고 자신을 원망할 때가 있다. 무엇이 복음 사역자들로 하여금 진실치 못한 사역을 하게 하는가? 사역을 금전 문제, 이성문제, 명예문제 등 자신의 개인적 사욕과 관련시킬 때 진실치 못한 사역자가 되는 것이다. 이런 욕심으로부터 벗어나지 않으면 자신과 교회의 복음사역에 큰 손실을 가져 오게 되는 것이다. 대개 이런 사욕에 빠지게 될 때 사역자는 성경 말씀을 아전인수식 해석을 하거나 어떤 성경 구절을 문맥이나 역사적 정황을 고려치 않고 잘못 해석하여 자신의 행동을 정당화시킨다. "말씀을 혼잡케 하는 실수"를 범하는 것이다. 예수님께서 사단에게 받은 시험은, 다름 아닌, 사욕을 떠난 올바른 성경 해석에 대한 시험이었던 것이다(마 4:1-11; 눅 4:2-13). 그러므로 말씀을 사욕 없이 순전하게 하나님 앞에서와 그리스도 안에서 해석하는 것은 사역자들의 진실성과 관련된 매우 중요한 일이다.

올바른 성서 해석을 위해서는 성경 해석 방법에 대한 전문적 지식도 필요하겠으나, 1) 우선 좋은 주석책을 목회자의 도움으로 선정 받고 몇 권 이상 대조하여 읽는 것이 필요하다. 성경 본문이 객관적으로 무슨 의미가 있는가를 살핀 후에, 그 말씀이 오늘 우리에게 어떤 의미가 있는가를 살필 수 있기 때문이다. 2) 이렇게 해서 얻은 해석이 아무리 자신에게 호감을 준다 하더라도 지나치게 그 해석에 의존하기 보다는 더 많은 유사한 성경의 가르침을 찾아 분명한 해석이 되도록 정화시키는 과정도 필요하다. 3) 이 정화의 과정에 다른 저서와 전문가들의 의견을 참조하는 것도 중요하다. 4) 이런 해석의 과정에서 우리는 항상 겸손함을 유지해야 한다. 자신의 해석이 하나님의 말씀의 유일한 해석이라고 주장하는 것은 가능하지만, 또한 그만큼 그 결과에 대해서 책임을 져야하는 것이다. 우리는 성경에서 "분명히 제시된 하나님의 말씀"(예를 들면, 예수님을 믿고 구원 얻음)을 확실히 믿어야 하되, "내가 해석한 하나님의 말씀"이 분명히 하나님의 말씀인지는 기도하면서 성령의 조명을 기다리는 자세가 필요하다.[101] 이해할 수 없는 부분은 억지로 해석하지 말고 더 분명한 근거나 설명방법이 나올 때까지 계속 그 말씀의 뜻을 상고하는 자세를 가진다(행 17:11; 벧후 3:16). 또한 기록된 이상의 추정은 피한다(고전 4:6).

2. 바울의 자천서(自薦書)(3:1-7:4)

2장 14절에서 이미 바울의 자천은 시작되었다. 그러나 3장 1절에서 대적자들이 가지고 자랑하는 추천서에 대해 거론하면서 바울의 자천이 본격적으로 시작된다. 바울은 반대자들이 예루살렘 사도들로부터 받은 것으로 보이는 추천서를 가지고 자신들의 사도직을 자랑하면서 바울을 추천서도 없는 신뢰할 수 없는 사도라고 비난하는 정황에서 그가 전하는 복음의 계시와 그의 사도직이 하나님으로부터 온 것이며, 그의 사역이 그리스도의 죽으심과 부활의 유형을 따라서 고린도 교인들의 유익을 위해 수행되었으므로 하나님과 사람 앞에 부끄러움이 없다고 한다. 바울은 반대자들의 배후에는 그들에게 추천장을 써서 보낸 예루살렘 사도들이 있다는 것을 알고 있었을 것이다. 그들은 바울의 이신득의 복음에

---

101) J. Robertson McQuilkin, *Understanding and Applying the Bible* (Chicago: Moody Press, 1983), 255(『성경의 해석과 적용』 송용조역, 서울:서울성경학교출판부, 1992, 254.).

대해 불신하면서 그들의 율법주의적 복음을 다른 이방 선교지역에 전하려고 이들에게 추천장을 써서 고린도 지역으로 파송한 것이라고 볼 수 있다.[102] 고린도전서에서 말하듯이 고린도 교회에 이미 유대주의적 복음을 따르는 것으로 보이는 게바파가 있었다는 사실은 이런 반대파들이 이들과 합세하여 바울에게 대항하는 세력을 형성할 수 있었을 것으로 짐작할 수 있다. 바울은 이들의 고린도에서의 사역을 좌시할 경우에 그의 전체 복음 사역이 크게 위태로워 질 수 있다고 보고 매우 심각하게 이들의 문제를 다루고 있는 것이다(5:2; 11:2, 4, 13-15). 바울은 이들의 공격으로부터 자신의 사도직의 진실성을 증명하기 위해서 신학적, 도덕적, 목회적 증거들을 열거하고 있다. 이런 증거들은 역으로 그를 반대하는 이들의 문제점들을 반영하고 있다. 반대자들은 외적이고 육적인 것들에 관심을 가지고 가치를 두지만, 바울은 내적이고 영적인 데 집중하고 가치를 두고 있음을 강조한다. 3장에서 나타나는 유대주의 전통에 대한 언급들이 이렇게 바울을 반대하는 고린도 유대주의자들에 대한 경계라는 것을 알아야 한다.

a. 고린도 교인들 자신의 변화된 생활이 우리의 자천서이다 (3:1-3)

본문:

3:1. 우리가 다시 자천하기를 시작하겠느냐 우리가 어찌 어떤 사람처럼

102) Martin, lvii. Martin은 행전 15장의 예루살렘 사도들의 회의 이후에 이방인에 대한 유대교적 전통 준수문제를 놓고 이들과 이신득의를 주장하는 바울과의 관계가 소원해지기 시작하였다고 본다.

> 천거서를 너희에게 부치거나 혹 너희에게 맡거나 할 필요가 있느냐 2. 너희가 우리의 편지라. 우리 마음에 썼고, 뭇 사람이 알고 읽는 바라. 3 .너희는 우리로 말미암아 나타난 편지니(너희들이 우리의 사역으로 말미암은 그리스도의 편지임을 너희 스스로 증거하고 있다.) 이는 먹으로 쓴 것이 아니요 오직 살아 계신 하나님의 영으로 한 것이며 또 돌비에 쓴 것이 아니요 오직 육의 심비에 한 것이라.

본문 비평:

1. 1절에 개역성경에 번역되지 않은 "혹은" **ἢ μη**,가 ℵ B C D E F G 라틴역 등에 나타나고, **εἰ μὴ**가 A K L P 아람어 역에 나타난다. 후자의 경우는 "우리가 천거서가 필요한 경우가 아닌 한" 이라고 번역된다.[103] B D 17은 **συνιστάν**, F G 는 **συνιστάναι**라고 되어 있다. A D 는 **ὥσπερ τινες**라고 되어 있다. D E F K L P d e 시리아역은 문장 끝에, 즉 **ἐξ ὑμῶν**뒤에 **συστατικῶν**(천거서)이라고 쓰고, F G 는 더 분명히 **συστατικῶν επιστολῶν**(천거편지)이라고 쓴다.

2. 2절에 **καρδίαις ἡμῶν**(우리들의 마음) 이 p^{46} A B C D 등에 나타난다. 그러나 이 말이 문맥에 맞지 않는 것 같이 보이므로, **καρδίαις ὑμῶν**(너희들의 마음)으로 33, 88, 436, 1881 등에, 문맥에 맞추어 나타난다.

3. 3절에 **καρδίαις**가 F K 벌게이트, 시리아역, 콥틱역bo, sa에 속격인 **καρδίας**로 되어 있으나, 여격을 "어려운 읽기가 원래의

103) Plummer, 79.

104) Martin, 44.

기록"이라는 원칙에 의해서 받아들인다.[104)]

내용 개요:

자신을 자랑하는 일은 어색한 일이다. 이를 아는 바울은 2장 14-17절까지의 "그리스도의 향기"로서 자신과 일행을 자천하고서는, 3장 1절에서 "우리가 다시(계속) 자천하기를 시작하겠느냐?" 고 반문한다. 그러나 거짓 사도들이 아마 유명한 예루살렘 사도들로부터 추천서를 받아서 고린도 교회에 들어와서 고린도 교인들을 미혹하는 상황에서 바울은 고린도 교회를 진정한 그리스도의 교회로 지키기 위해서 자신이 그리스도의 진정한 사도라고 자천하지 않을 수 없었다.

먼저 바울은 반대자들이 자랑하는 자천서 같은 서류가 중요한 것이 아니고 실제적인 증거가 더 중요하다고 한다. 즉 바울이 사역하여 오늘에 이른 고린도 교인들이야 말로 바울의 사도직이 합당하다는 진정한 추천서라고 한다. 그러니 우리가 무슨 추천서가 따로 필요한가 내게 복음을 받아 구원받은 너희들이 나를 추천해야 옳지 않은가 "내가 너희에게 칭찬을 받아야 마땅하도다" (12:11).

3장 전체에서 바울은 반대자들이 예루살렘 사도들에게서 받았다고 보이는 추천서를 가지고 자랑하면서 자신들의 사도적 권위를 자랑하는 반면에 바울은 추천서가 없으므로 신뢰할 수 없는 사도라고 비하시키는 정황에서 그의 사역은 하나님으로부터 위임받아 하나님의 영에 의해 수행되는 사역이므로 반대자들이 가진 종이에 쓴 추천서는 필요 없다고 한다. 오히려 종이에 먹으로 쓴 추천장에 의지하는 반대자들의 자세와 가르침이 유대교적 형식주의적이며 외모 지향적이라고 비판한다(5:12; 10:7). 반대자들은 사람들이 쓴 종이 추천장 같은 외적인 증거로 자신들의 권위를 내세우지만 진정한 권위는 하나님의 영으로부터 오는 것이다. 그들의 외모 지향적인 사역은 일시적인 모세의 돌에 새긴 율법처럼 굳어있어 영적 자유함이 없으며 그리스도의 영광을 가리고 있다(5:12; 10:7). 그러나 바울의 내적인 영적 복음 사역은 자유함이 있으며 그리스도의 영광을 영원히 들어나게 한다. 바울은 이런 주장을 의문과 영, 낡은 언약과 새 언약, 낡은 언약의 일꾼으로서의 모세의 일시적 권위와, 새 언약의 일꾼으로서의 자신의 영원한 사도적 권위를 비교하는 대조법을 통해 나타낸다. 즉 사람들이 쓴 추천서에 의존하는 반대자들의 자세를 모세가 쓴 낡은 율법에 의존하는 유대교적 발상이라고 보고, 자신은 온전히 하나님의 영에 의해서 임명받은 그리스도로 말미암은 새 언약을 전하는 진정한 사도임을 천명한다. 바울은 후에 반대자들을 "거짓 사도들"과 "사단의 일꾼들"로 신랄하게 공격하지만(11:13, 15) 여기서는 반대자들이 그리스도의 사도들이라는 주장을 어느 정도 인정하면서도(참조, 11:23), 추천서나 말솜씨, 유대출신 같은 "외모"나 육체적 조건을 가지고 자랑하는 그들의 자세를 책망하는 것이다(5:12; 10:7; 11:22). 그러므로 본문에서 바울이 지적하는 율법주의적 가르침이 곧 반대자들의 유대주의적 교훈을 가리킨다고 말하기 어렵다.

3장에서는 돌비, 의문(儀文), 모세, 모세의 수건, 이스라엘 자손들, 일시적 영광, 정죄의 직분, 수건을 덮기 같은 구원의 낡은 시대를 나타내는 유대교 율법주의적 잔재들과 구원의 새 시대를 가리키는 심비(心碑), 하나님의 영, 새 언약, 새 언약의 일꾼, 영의 직분, 그리스도, 영원한 영광, 수건을 벗기 등의 대조가 나온다. 그러나 이런 유대교적 언급에도 불구하고 반대자들이 분명히 율법주의자들이라는 증거는 여기선 물론 고린도후서 전체에서도 나타나지 않는다. 다른 서신에서 흔히 말하는 율법이나 할례는 아예 언급되지 않고 있다(갈 2:3, 7). 반대자들은 복음을 전하는 예루살렘에서 온 선교사들이다(11:22, 23). 그들은 역사적 예수를 보았고 그의 사역의 증인임을 자랑하였을 것이다(5:16). 그들은 아마 예루살렘 사도들의 추천장을 가지고 순회하며 복음을 전하는 이들이었을 것이다(3:1). 문제는 그들이 바울의 사역지인 고린도 교회를 침범한 것이다(10:13-16). 바울은 이들이 복음의 역사적 기원과 관련된 것을 아는 지식을 자랑하고(5:16), 또 영적 능력과(12:1) 정식으로 보수를 받는 것(11:7) 등을 자랑하는 자세를 복음에 거슬리는 유대교적 율법주의에 견주어 비판하기 시작하는 것이다. 그들은 아마 실제로 유대주의자들로서 유대교적 복음의 우위를 전했을 것으로 보인다. 그러나 본문에서는 그들이 유대주의적 복음을 전한다고 직접 비난하는 증거는 없다. 다만 바울은 이들이 자신들의 유대적 배경을 자랑하는 것을 알고 이들이 자랑하는 유대주의적 전통과 율법의 한계를 말하면서 이들의 사역을 암시적으로 비판하는 것이다. 동시에 자신의 복음의 우위를 분명히 밝히고 있는 것이다(11:18-22). 11장에서 바울은 그들의 정체를 기독교적 복음 전도자로 가장하면서 잘못된 복음을 전하는 거짓선지자들이라고 폭로한다(11:2-4, 13-15). 또 그들이 유대적인 기원을 자랑하는 것을 비판한다(11:18-22). 그러나 거기서도 그들의 잘못된 복음의 내용을 "다른 예수, 다른 영, 다른 복음"이라고 규정하는 것 이외에 특별히 유대교적 율법주의적 내용을 지목하는 내용은 없다. 심지어 그들이 자신들을 "그리스도의 사도"라고 말하는 것을 그대로 되풀이하여 말하기도 한다(11:23). 아마 그들은 바울의 이신득의 사상을 직접 반대는 하지 않으면서도, 또 행위로 구원 얻음을 강조하지도 않으면서도, 스스로 복음의 정통 "원조"로 자처하면서 예수의 지상 사역에 대한 많은 정보와 이야기, 예수로부터 받았다는 영적 능력을 자랑하며, 한편으로는 사도들과의 개인적 연계를 자랑하였을 가능성이 높다(5:12; 10:7; 11:5, 18; 12:1, 9, 11, 12). 이에 대해서 바울은 자신의 복음은 그런 피상적이고 과거의 역사적인 전통과 유물에 근거한 것이 아니라(참조, 5:16) 하나님의 영으로 인도받아 하나님의 직접적 계시로 말미암은 것이며 현재와 장래의 영광으로 나타나는 참된 복음이라고 말한다(3:3-4:6). 이어서 피상적인 외모를 따라서 자랑하는 것이 아니라 그리스도의 약함을 따라서 사역하는 것이 진정한 그리스도의 사도된 증표라고 반박한다(4:7-15; 5:12; 6:4-10; 12:9, 10). 바울은 3장 전체에서 일련의 낡은 유대교적 전통과 복음의 새로운 능력을 대조함으로써 이런 반대자들의 "육체적 자랑"에 맞서 자신의 복음의 영적 우위를 나타내려는 것이다.

한편 바울의 율법과 복음의 기능이나 효과의 대조 자체에서 그의 신학사상이 나타나기 때문에, 그의 반대자 비난을 통해서 나타난 그의 신학 사상에 보다 주목할 필요가 있다. 우리는 고린도후서 전체를 이런 기대를 갖고 연구해야 한다.

주석:

3:1. "우리가 다시 자천하기를 시작하겠느냐 우리가 어찌 어떤 사람처럼 천거서를 너희에게 부치거나 혹 너희에게 맏거나 할 필

요가 있느냐 "(Ἀρχόμεθα πάλιν ἑαυτοὺς συνιστάνειν; ἢ μὴ χρῄζομεν ὥς τινες συστατικῶν ἐπιστολῶν πρὸς ὑμᾶς ἢ ἐξ ὑμῶν;). 이 첫 절의 "다시"라는 말이 고린도후서의 복합적 서신설과 관련하여 논란되었다. 플러머와 같이 1-9장이 10-13장 보다 나중에 써졌다고 주장하는 이들은 이 첫 문장의 "다시"(πάλιν)란 말이 10-13장에서 바울이 자신을 자천(自薦)한 것을 가리켜서 여기에서 "다시" 자천할 필요가 있겠느냐라고 반문하고 있다고 한다.[105] 그러나 이런 가설의 불필요성에 대해서 이미 서론에서 지적하였다. 또 고린도후서 2장 4절이 고린도전서를 가리킨다고 주장하는 이들은 "다시"라는 말이 고린도전서에서 바울이 자신을 자천한 것을 가리킨다고 한다(고전 4:16; 11:1; 9:2-4).[106] 그러나 본문에서 바울은 과거의 어떤 편지를 직접 언급하지 않는다. 그러므로 지금의 문맥에서 이 말이 가리키는 "자천하는 사실"을 찾아야 한다. 즉 지금의 문맥에서 바울이 어떤 자천한 사실을 염두에 두고 "다시" 자천할 필요가 없다는 뜻인지를 알아야 한다. 그러나 문맥에서 분명히 한 가지 사실을 반복하고 있다고 말하기 어렵다. 적어도 세 가지 사실이 "다시" 자천할 필요가 없다는 말과 복합적으로 관련되어 있다.

첫째로, "다시"란 말은 본문 바로 뒤에 오는 2절 이하의 사실을 가리킨다고 본다. 2절 이하에서 바울은 고린도 교인들 자신이 바울의 참된 천거서라고 한다. 모든 사람들이 인정하는(2절) 먹으로 쓴 것이 아닌 하나님의 영으로 쓴(3절) 이런 좋은 천거서가 이미

105) Plummer, 77.

106) Bruce, 189; Hughes, 85.

있는데, 이제 "다시" 내가 나를 위한 자천서를 쓸 필요가 있는가?

둘째로, "다시"란 말은 바울이 앞장에서 시작한 자신을 자천하는 말을 계속하는 것에 대해서 양해를 구하는 말이다. 바울은 앞에서 자신이 진실하고(1:12), 하나님께 기름 부음을 받고(1:21), "그리스도의 향기"로서 늘 승리한다는 자천을 하였다(2:14-17). 그리고 본문 자체도 자천하는 말이다. 실로 고린도후서 전체(8, 9장 제외)가 바울의 자천서라고 할 수 있다. 특히 5장 12절에서 "우리가 다시 너희에게 자천하는 것이 아니요, 오직 우리를 인하여 자랑할 기회를 너희에게 주어 마음으로 하지 않고 외모로 자랑하는 자들을 대하게하려는 것이라"라고 변명조로 말하고 있다. 또 10-13장에서 자신의 사도직을 변명하면서 독자들에게 양해를 구하는 말을 자주하고 있다(10:8; 11:1, 16; 12:1, 6). 그러므로 "다시"라는 말은 이 첫 문장에서 바울이 자신을 자천하는 것이 어색하고 쑥스러운 일이므로 독자들의 양해를 구한다는 뜻을 나타낸다.

셋째로, "다시"는 "어떤 사람" (ὥς τινες), 즉 거짓사도들이 단순히 추천서를 받는 것 뿐 아니라 자신들을 자천 혹은 자찬(自贊)하는 행위를 따라서 바울이 자천하는 것을 가리킨다. 10장 13절에 의하면 이들이 자신들을 자천하고 있었다(ἑαυτοὺς συνιστανόντων). 바울은 이들이 자천하는 것과 자신이 자천하는 것이 그 진정성에 있어서 다르다고 한다. 그들의 자랑은 분량 밖의 자랑을 하므로 정당치 않으나, 자신의 자랑은 하나님이 나눠주신 분량의 한계를 지키면서 자랑하기 때문에 정당하다고 한다. 또 12장 6절에서도 유사하게 자신의 자랑이 진실임을 밝힌다. 본문에서 바울은 "그런 거짓사도들이 자천한다고 나도 따라서 자천해야겠느냐?"라고 반문하는 듯하다. 바울은 5장 12절에서도 본문과 거의 같은 말로 "다시 자천하는 것" 을 거짓 사도들과 관련하여 말하고 있다. 5장 12절에서 거짓사도들을 10장 13절에서와 같이 "외모로 자랑하는 이들" 이라고 한 것으로 보아서 "다시" 라는 말은 거짓사도들이 자천하는 행위를 바울이 반복하는 것을 말한다고 볼 수 있다. 바울은 1절의 질문을 고린도 교인들에게 던지면서 그들로부터 적절한 응답을 바라고 있다. 바울은 12장 11절에, "내가 너희에게 칭찬을 받아야 마땅하도다" 라고 하면서, 자신이 원하는 고린도 교인들의 자세를 분명히 말하고 있다. 그러나 본문에서는 질문형식으로 "너희들에게 추천받는 것이 마땅하다" 는 암시를 준다. 거짓사도들도 너희에게 추천받는다. 우리도 너희에게 추천받아야 마땅하다. 그러나 우리는 너희를 구원받도록 인도한 사도들로서 사실 그런 종이에 쓴 추천서를 받을 필요가 없다(3절). 왜냐하면 마음으로 믿어 구원에 이르고 하나님의 자녀가 된 너희들 자신들이야말로 우리의 추천서이기 때문이다(참조, 롬 10:10). "우리가 다시 추천하기를 시작하겠느냐?"

이렇게 본문의 복합적 문맥에서 보아 "다시" 라는 말은 이상의 세 가지 사실들을 모두 가리키고 있다고 본다. 바울은 구원받은 고린도 교인들이 자신의 훌륭한 추천서인데 따로 자천하는 일이 필요 없다고 생각하는 듯하다. 또한 그가 거듭해서 자신을 자천하는 일이 어색한 일임을 인정하고 있다. 후반부에서 바울은 거짓사도들처럼 자기를 자천하는 일이 어리석은 일임을 거듭 말하고 있다(11:16-18; 12:1, 6; 11).

"자천한다" (συνίστημι)라는 말은 신약에 16번, 바울 서신에 13번, 고린도후서에만 8번 나온다. 이것으로 바울과 고린도 교회 거짓사도들 사이에서 자천하는 일이 논쟁의 중심 문제이었음을 알 수 있다.[107] 그러나 자천하는 일이 초대교회에서 매우 흔한 관습이었음을 사도행전 9장 2절, 22장 5절, 18장 27절과 로마서 16장 1절 등에서 알 수 있다(참조, 고후 4:2; 10:12). 이런 자천서가 당시 희랍 문명 사회에서 유행하고 있었다.[108] 또 이 말은 "자랑하다"(καυχάομαι)는 말로 대치되기도 하는 말이다. 반대자들은 "외모"를 자랑하고(5:12; 10:7), 반면에 바울의 "외모"를 멸시 하였다(10:10). 그들은 육체를 따라 자랑하였으므로 바울도 억지로 육체적 자랑을 하였다(11:16-18; 12:1, 11). 그러나 바울이 진정으로 자랑한 것은 그의 약한 것들이었다(11:30; 12:9, 10). 바울은 모든 육체적 자랑을 경계하면서 하나님 앞에서 겸비할 것을 가르친다. 그러나 반대자들의 자랑으로 고린도 교인들이 현혹되므로 자신도 마찬가지로 자랑할 수밖에 없다고 한다. 바울은 고린도 교인들이 반대자들의 비난에 맞서서 바울을 변호하고 자랑해주기를 원했다. 그러나 그들이 침묵하거나 중립적인 자세를 취하였기 때문에 어리석게도 자신이 자신을 칭찬하거나 자랑해야 했다(12:11).

"어떤 사람들"(τινες)이란 예루살렘에서 온 이들이든,[109] 영적 권능을 자랑하는 카리스마적 성령파이든[110] 이들은 바울을 대적하면서 그들의 사역에 관한 어떤 추천서를 가지고 자랑하는 이들이었다.

고린도 교인들은 추천서를 가진 이들을 따라야 한다는 이들과, 바울을 따라야 한다는 이들로 갈라진 상태였다. 디도가 바울의

107) Georgi, *die Gegner*, 241ff.

108) C. W. Keyes, "The Greek Letter of Introduction," *American Journal of Philosophy* 56 (1935) 28-44.

109) Käsemann, *Die Legitimat*, 25.

110) Georgi, *Die Gegner*, 245.

"눈물의 편지" (2:4)를 가지고 가서 고린도후서를 쓸 때에는 대다수가 바울 편으로 돌아 왔으나 아직도 소수의 반대하는 세력이 있었다고 생각된다. 그러므로 바울은 10장에서 이들에 대한 공격을 다시 하고 있다고 본다.

2. "너희가 우리의 편지라. 우리 마음에 썼고 뭇사람이 알고 읽는 바라" (ἡ ἐπιστολὴ ἡμῶν ὑμεῖς ἐστε, ἐγγεγραμμένη ἐν ταῖς καρδίαις ἡμῶν, γινωσκομένη καὶ ἀναγινωσκομένη ὑπὸ πάντων ἀνθρώπων,). 고린도 교인들은 바울의 사역의 결실이다. 고린도 교인들은 믿음에 섰다(1:24). 추천서가 없는 바울은 고린도 교인들이야 말로 가장 좋은 자신의 추천서라고 한다. 더구나 고린도전서 9장 2절에서 밝히듯이 바울은 고린도 교회의 사도로서의 자격을 주님으로부터 확인받았다. 추천서는 종이에 쓴 것이 아니고 바울이나 디모데의 마음에 써서 갖고 다닌다. 또 다른 사람들도 바울이 고린도 교회를 세웠고, 고린도 교인들이 바울의 복음 전도로 구원 얻게 되었음을 안다. 이 사실은 보다 객관적인 증거다. 그러므로 거짓사도들이 그들 자신의 천거서를 자랑하여도 자신은 고린도 교인들을 자신의 천거서로 자랑한다(1:14; 1:24; 7:14). 고린도 교인들이야 말로 가장 확실히 바울의 사도직의 진정성을 증거하는 증인들이다. 그들은 대부분 바울 자신의 복음 사역의 열매들이기 때문이다(고전 4:15). 물론 바울이 고린도 교회를 떠난 후 4년이 지났고(51-55, 행 18:18), 그 동안 교회가 많이 성장하였다면, 바울을 모르는 이들이 많았고, 그 사이에 들어온 거짓사도들을 따르는 이들이 적잖게 있었을 것이다. 이런 새로운 교인들의 증가도 거짓사도들의 사역과 함께 고린도 교인들의 분열에 중

요한 원인이 되었을 것이다(고전 1:11, 26; 3:6; 고후 10:13 이하). 그러나 아직 고린도 교회의 중심적 대다수는 바울을 따르는 이들이며, 바울은 사도로서의 그의 권위를 갖고 있음을 알 수 있다(13:2, 10).

"마음"(καρδια)은 원래 "심장"이란 말이다. 심장은 인간성의 중심이며, 성령이 일하는 곳이며, 종교적 성향의 근원이다(참조, 막 6:52).[111] 마음은 인간의 진실성을 나타내는 곳이며 인간 본성의 중심적 기관이다(5:12). 구약에도 마음이 인간의 진실한 본성을 나타내는 곳으로 간주되었다(창 6:5; 8:21). 헬라인들도 마찬가지로 생각했다. 마음과 마음이 연결되는 교제가 가장 진실한 교제이기 때문이다. 하나님도 사람도 마음으로부터 교제하여야 진실한 교제가 되는 것이다(신 5:29; 6:5; 10:12, 16). 고린도 교인들이 바울의 가장 진실한 곳에 자리 잡고 있다(6:11). 또한 바울은 그들이 마음으로 그를 영접하기를 바란다(7:2). 사도 바울의 마음에 쓴 고린도 교인은 곧 바울의 자천서이며, 바울 사도의 진정성을 가장 잘 들어내는 편지다. 다시 말하면 바울은 그의 사도직의 진정성을 증명하는 자천서를 요구하는 반대자들에게 지금까지 복음으로 양육한 고린도 교회 교인들이 바로 자신의 사도직의 정당성을 가장 잘 들어내는 것이므로 종이에 쓴 자천서는 따로 필요 없다고 단언한다(13:3). 반대자들이 편지 같은 증빙서류에 근거하는 외모지향적인 자세에 대하여 바울은 보다 영적이고 내면적인 가치기준을 제시한다.

바울이 고린도 교인들이 자신의 천거서라고 말하는 이면에는 그들이 바울을 스스로 변호해야 한다는 의미도 있다고 보아야 한다. 그들이 바울의 복음을 받아서 그리스도인들이 되었으니만큼,

111) J. Behm, *TDNT* 3:608-614.

이단적 반대자들이 들어와서 다른 복음을 전할 때에 이들과 맞서서 바울과 그의 복음을 지켰어야 했다. 그러나 그들은 거의 침묵하거나 반대자들을 따랐던 것으로 보인다(12:11). 바울은 이점을 안타까워하면서 고린도 교회를 복음적 교회로 지키기 위해서는 억지로 자천할 수밖에 없었다.

3. "너희는 우리로 말미암아 나타난 그리스도의 편지니 (너희들이 우리의 사역으로 말미암은 그리스도의 편지임을 너희 스스로 증거하고 있다) 이는 먹으로 쓴 것이 아니요 오직 살아 계신 하나님의 영으로 한 것이며 또 돌비에 쓴 것이 아니요 오직 육의 심비(마음의 비석)에 한 것이라" (**φανερούμενοι ὅτι ἐστὲ ἐπιστολὴ Χριστοῦ διακονηθεῖσα ὑφ᾽ ἡμῶν, ἐγγεγραμμένη οὐ μέλανι ἀλλὰ πνεύματι θεοῦ ζῶντος, οὐκ ἐν πλαξὶν λιθίναις ἀλλ᾽ ἐν πλαξὶν καρδίαις σαρκίναις**). 2절에서 "너희가 우리의 편지라"는 말이 너무 인본주의적으로 들릴 수 있으므로 여기서 바울은 그 편지의 송신인은 바로 그리스도이고 자신은 배달부라고 한다. "그리스도의 편지"는 소유격이라기보다 희랍어 소유격의 특색인 기원을 나타낸다고 본다.[112] 그래서 이 말은 그리스도에게서 온 편지, 즉 그리스도가 보낸 편지라는 뜻이다. 그러나 여기서도 바울의 깊은 관심은 편지의 대필자로서의 역할의 중요함을 고린도 교인들이 납득하는 것이다. 왜냐하면 바울은 그리스도의 편지의 대필자이기 때문이다(1:1). 또 다음절(3절)에서 **ὑφ ἡμῶν**(우리로 말미암아)이란 말이 바울의 이런 역할을 분명히

112) Martin, 51.

나타내고 있다. 즉 바울의 사역 없이 고린도 교인들은 "그리스도의 편지"가 될 수 없었다.

개역성경의 "너희는 우리로 말미암아 나타난 그리스도의 편지니"라는 번역은 문자적 번역이 아니다. "너희는 우리의 사역의 결과인 그리스도의 편지임을 너희가 나타내고 있으니"(참조, NIV)가 정확한 번역이다. "그리스도의 편지"라는 말은 고린도 교인들이 그리스도인들이 된 것을 말한다. "나타내고 있다"(φανερούμενοι)라는 말은 고린도 교인들이 그리스도인답게 변화된 삶으로 "그리스도인 됨"(=그리스도의 편지)을 증거한다는 뜻이다. 고린도 교인들을 "그리스도의 편지"로 명명하는 것은 고린도 교인들을 칭찬하는 의미가 들어 있음을 주지해야 한다. 즉 바울이 고린도 교인들을 자신의 자천서라고 하면서 자신의 사도직을 정당화함과 동시에 고린도 교인들을 추겨 세워서 긍지를 갖게 하여, 바울 자신을 지지하게 만드는 복합적인 효과를 기대할 수 있는 것이다. 그러나 우리가 언제나 기억해야 할 것은, 바울은 그의 사도권 확립이 곧 그리스도의 왕권 확립으로 생각하고 있다는 것이다(4:5; 10:5-6, 8; 13:10). 고린도 교인들을 그에게로 돌리는 일은 곧 그들을 하나님 또는 그리스도로 돌리게 하는 일이다(5:18-20; 11:2). 그는 언제나 자기의 유익을 돌아보지 않고 고린도 교인들의 유익을 위해 사역하므로 그리스도의 진정한 사도라고 분명히 말한다(4:7-15; 5:11-15; 6:3-10; 7:2-3; 11:2,7-8, 10, 22-33; 12:14-18).

"이는 먹으로 쓴 것이 아니요 오직 살아 계신 하나님의 영으로 한 것이며 또 돌비에 쓴 것이 아니요 오직 육의 심비에 한 것이라." 3절의 나머지 말은 "그리스도의 편지"의 높은 가치를 거짓사도들의 추천서의 낮은 가치에 비교하였다. 여기서 "그리스도의 편지"는 고린도 교인들을 칭찬하는 의미를 가지면서도 동시에 고린도 교인들에게 대한 바울의 사역과 복음의 진정성이 탁월함을 의미하고 있다.[113] 바울의 사역이 거짓 사도들의 사역에 비해 우월한 까닭은 그 사역이 살아계신 하나님의 영에 의한 것이며 인간의 심령을 변화시키기 때문이다. 거짓사도들의 사역은 영구적이지 못하고 일시적인 가치밖에 없다. 먹이나 돌비란 말은 모세의 율법이나 십계명을 연상시켜서(출 24:12; 31:18; 32:15; 34:1; 신 9:10),[114] 바울의 대적자들이 유대인 출신이라는 추정을 하게 한다(11:22).[115] 그러나 그들이 할례나 율법을 주장하였다는 증거가 없으므로 예루살렘 사도들의 추천을 받아 온 복음 선교사들임이 거의 분명하다.[116] 바울은 그의 사역의 우월성과 그의 대적자들의 사역의 열등함을 말하고 있다. 또 "하나님의 영"이란 말과 "육의 심비"라는 말은 예레미야 31장 31, 33절과 에스겔 11장 19절과 36장 25절을 가리킨다. "돌비"란 말은 모세의 율법을 연상시키는 말이다. 바울은 본문에 이어 3장 7-18절에서 모세의 영광과 주의 영광의 대조를 분명히 하고 있다. 반대자들의 종이 추천서에 근거한 외모 자랑의 정신을 낡고 화석화되고 구시대적인 유대종교의 낮

113) Calvin은 이 구절이 바울의 편지, 즉 고린도후서의 권위를 높이는 말로 해석 하고 있으나 문맥에 비추어 보아 이해하기 힘든 해석이다(Calvin, 73-74).

114) Collange은 여기서 율법과의 관련성이 없으며, 성령이 아닌 "영"에 대한 언급만이 있다고 한다. Collange, 51; R. P. Martin, "Writing and Materials," "Papyrus," in *Dictionary of the Bible and Religion*, ed. W. Gentz (Nashville: Abingdon Press, 1986).

115) Käsemann, *Die Legitimität*, 25; Martin, 73; Thrall, 296-7; W. J. Dumbrell, "The Newness of the New Covenant: The Logic of the Argument in 2 Corinthians 3," *RTR* vol. 61(2002), 62.

116) Thrall, 640, 942.

은 가치로 보면서, 대조적으로 바울 자신의 사역은 하나님의 영으로 인도함을 받고 그리스도의 영광을 영원히 나타내는 진정한 사역이라고 밝힌다. 아래에서 계속되는 일련의 대조어귀들-돌비와 심비, 의문과 영, 정죄의 직분과 영의 직분, 일시적 영광과 영원한 영광, 구약과 암시된 신약, 모세와 주 등-은 이런 바울과 반대자들의 사역의 차이들을 통하여 바울의 사역의 탁월성과 바울의 사도직의 진정성을 밝히는 것이다.

b. 우리의 자천은 하나님께로부터 인증 받았다(3:4-4:2)

이 부분에서 바울은 일련의 새 언약과 낡은 언약의 대조를 통해서 반대자들이 사람(예루살렘 사도들)이 쓴 추천서의 자랑에 대하여 자신의 자천은 인위적인 것이 아니라 하나님이 인증하신 것이라고 한다. 바울은 반대자들의 인위적인 추천서에 근거한 사도적 권위는 하나님의 영에 의해 인증된 사도적 권위에 미치지 못함을 지적한다. 사람이 쓴 추천서에 의존하여 사도적 권위를 자랑하는 반대자들의 "육체적 자랑"을 구원 역사에 있어서 낡아버린 율법과 모세 같은 유대교의 구시대적 유물에 비교하여 평가절하하고 있다. 이와 대조적으로 자신의 사역의 신적 기원과 그리스도 중심성, 그리고 활력 있는 영적인 특성을 강조한다.

i. 우리의 추천자는 하나님 (3:4-5)

본문:

4. 우리가 그리스도로 말미암아 <u>하나님 앞에서</u>(하나님을 향하여) 이 같

은 확신이 있으니 5. 우리가 무슨 일이든지 우리에게서 난 것같이 생각하여 스스로 만족할 것이 아니니 우리의 만족은 오직 하나님께로서 났느니라.

본문 비평:

5절의 ἀφ᾽ ἑαυτῶν이 ἱκανοί ἐσμεν 앞에 있기도 하고(ℵ B C, 콥틱역, 아람역), 뒤에 오기도 하며 (K L 시리아역h), λογίσασθαί 앞에 두기도 하고(A D E F G P, 라틴역), 혹은 아예 생략도 되었다(17, 시리아역p). ἱκανοί ἐσμεν 앞에 오는 것이 원래의 것으로 생각한다.[117]

λογίσασθαί(ℵ A B K L P)가 λογίζεσθαί (C D E F G) 보다 원래의 것으로 본다. [118] B F G 는 ἐξ ἑαυτῶν 대신에 ἐξ αὐτῶν을 가졌으나 의미상 차이는 없더라도, 전자가 더 분명히 "스스로에게서"라는 의미를 가지고 있으므로 옳은 것으로 간주한다.

내용개요:

4절과 5절은 지금까지 바울이 말한 자천의 진실함을 결론적으로 말하면서 동시에 6절에서 계속해서 말하는 새로운 자천의 서론적 진술이 된다. 즉 이중적인 역할을 하는 연결구이다. 이 짧은 구절 안에 바울이 말하려는 진의가 잘 나타나고 있다. 즉 반대자들의 천거서에 비해서, 바울의 모든 자천은 진실된 것이다(참조, 12:6). 왜냐하면 그 자천을 진실 되게 하나님 앞에서 하였고, 하나님이 인정하시는 것이기 때문이다. 바울은 그의 반대자들이 천거

117) Plummer, 85.

118) Plummer, 85.

서가 인증하는 그들의 사도권을 자랑하면서 바울은 그러한 천거서가 없는 신뢰할 수 없는 사도라는 공격에 대해서 역공하고 있다. 반대자들이 자랑하는 추천서는 결국 사람이 쓴 것이며, 그 가치는 하나님의 영에 의하여 사도직을 받은 바울의 사도권보다 열등하다(5). 그들의 추천서를 쓴 사람들의 권위를 일시적인 모세의 얼굴의 영광에 비교하고, 그들의 가르침을 율법의 낡은 언약의 가르침에 비교하기도 하면서, 자신의 권위는 하나님의 영으로 말미암은 것이며, 자신의 직책은 새 언약의 사도직임을 역설하는 것이다. 이런 암유적인 의도 가운데, 바울은 3장 4-18절까지 복음의 우월함을 유대교의 율법의 열등함에 비추어 말한다. 3장 3절에서 이미 이런 비교를 시작한 바울은 3장 6절에서 3장 18절까지 이 비교를 더욱 발전시킨다. 그리고 7장 끝까지 그는 자신의 사도직의 진실성을 증거한다. 진실성의 근거는 그의 사도직의 근거가 어디까지나 하나님 자신임을 강조하고 있다(3:5, 6: 4:6; 5:5, 18-19: 6:1). 또한 그의 자천함도 하나님 앞에서 하는 진실한 것임을 거듭 밝힌다(3:4; 4:2; 5:11, 12; 7:12; 12:6). 이렇게 3장 4-5절은 바울의 사도직의 진실성을 확신하면서 복음과 유대교의 율법을 대조하는 3장 5-18절 부분의 서론이 되고 있다.

주석:

4. "우리가 그리스도로 말미암아 하나님 앞에서(하나님을 향하여) 이 같은 확신이 있으니" (**Πεποίθησιν δὲ τοιαύτην ἔχομεν διὰ τοῦ Χριστοῦ πρὸς τὸν θεόν**). "그리스도로 말미암아" (**διὰ τοῦ Χριστοῦ**)라는 말은 바울의 그리스도 중심적 사고 방식을 나

타내고 있다. 바울은 자신에게 내재하는 인본적인 힘이 아니라 그리스도께서 주시는 능력으로 말미암아 이런 확신(자천함에 대한)을 갖게 되었다는 뜻이다. 고린도후서에서 바울은 그의 모든 사고와 행동원칙이 그리스도 중심으로 형성되어서 작용한다(3:14, 16, 18; 4:10, 11; 5:9, 11, 14, 15, 17, 20; 6:4-10, 15; 8:9; 10:5, 8, 18; 11:2, 3, 10, 23; 12:2, 9, 10, 19; 13:3, 4, 10). "그리스도 안"이라는 말과 함께 바울의 존재와 행동은 그리스도의 능력과 권세와 특성을 가지고 나타난다. 4장 7절 이하에서 바울은 자신을 질그릇처럼 연약하다고 한다. 그러나 그 질그릇 안에 있는 보배가 능력이 있으므로(능력의 매우 큰 것이 하나님께 있고) 그는 낙심하지 않고 사역을 계속할 힘을 갖게 되었다. 이렇게 약한 가운데서도 강하게 되는 힘이 죽음을 이기시고 부활하신 예수의 능력의 특징이다(4:10, 11: 12:9; 13:4). 엄밀하게 말해서, 그는 스스로 자천하는 것이 아니라 약한 자를 강하게 하시는 "그리스도로 말미암아" 자천하는 것이라는 뜻이다. 이렇게 볼 때 그는 실로 그리스도의 진정한 사도라고 할 수 있다.

"하나님 앞에서"(πρὸς τὸν θεόν)를 2장 17절에서는 같은 의미의 다른 말로 표현했다(κατέναντι θεοῦ). 2장 17절에서는 사도 바울의 사역이 하나님 앞(coram Deo)에서 이루어지므로 진실한 것이라고 한다. 본문에서는 사도 바울의 자천이 전지전능하신 하나님 앞에서 말하는 것이므로 진실한 것임을 말한다. 이 어귀와 유사하게 12장 19절에는 "그리스도 안에서 하나님 앞에서"(κατέναντι θεοῦ ἐν Χριστῷ)라는 어귀가 나온다. 모든 바울의 사도직의 진정성을 천명하는 맹세문 양식 어귀로 나타난다(1:23;

2:17; 11:11; 11:31; 12:6; 참조, 롬 9:1). 이처럼 바울은 사도로서의 진정성을 내적으로 확신할 뿐만 아니라 공개적으로 밝힌다. 반면에 이런 맹세문이 한 서신 안에 거듭하여 나타나는 것은 고린도 교인들의 사도 바울에 대한 불신의 벽이 그만큼 높다는 것을 가리킨다.

"(우리가...) 이같은 확신이 있으니" (Πεποίθησιν δὲ τοιαύτην ἔχομεν)에서 "이같은 확신"이란 바로 앞에서 말한 바울의 말, 즉 고린도 교인들이 바울의 편지이므로 따로 천거서가 필요하지 않다는 말이다(3:1-3).[119] 그러나 2장 17절의 "말씀을 혼잡하게 하지 않고 순전함으로 하나님께 받은 것 같이 하나님 앞에서와 그리스도 안에서 말하노라" 와 같이 바울의 사도적 교훈의 진실성에 대한 확신을 가리킨다고 볼 수도 있다.[120] 한 마디로 자신의 자천의 전체내용에 대한 바울의 확신이다. 바울은 그의 서신 가운데서 언제나 자신이 그리스도의 사도로서 부끄럼이 없다고 강변한다(11:5, 23; 12:11). 그러면서도 자신의 과거 교회를 핍박한 사실을 회상하면서 그가 사도가 된 것은 하나님의 은혜로 말미암은 것임을 시인한다(고전 15:10; 갈 1:13-16; 딤전 1:12-16). 그러나 바울은 그의 사도직과 복음의 진정성을 그의 과거의 실수로부터 명확히 구분한다. 그는 그의 사도직을 하나님께로부터 받았음과 그의 복음의 진리의 절대성에 대해서는 항상 당당하다(4:2; 5:20; 11:10; 갈 1:7-9).

---

119) Plummer, 84; Hughes, 93; Barrett, 152.

120) Martin, 52.

5. "우리가 무슨 일이든지 우리에게서 난 것같이 생각하여 스스로 만족할 것이 아니니 우리의 만족은 오직 하나님께로서 났느니라" (οὐχ ὅτι ἀφ' ἑαυτῶν ἱκανοί ἐσμεν λογίσασθαί τι ὡς ἐξ ἑαυτῶν, ἀλλ' ἡ ἱκανότης ἡμῶν ἐκ τοῦ θεοῦ,). 여기서 "무슨 일" (τι)은 구체적으로 지금까지 말한 자찬하는 내용을 가리킨다. 자찬의 내용이 바울 스스로 생각하고 창작하여 스스로 만족하는 것이 아니란 뜻이다. 본문에서 "만족한" 이란 형용사(ἱκανοι,)와 "만족" 이란 명사(ἡ ἱκανότης)가 함께 나온다. 2장 16절에 이 형용사가 나왔다: "누가 이것을 감당하리요 (ἱκανός) " 이 말의 원 뜻은 "감당할 능력" 이란 뜻이다. 여기서 바울은 자찬하는 말 가운데 언급한 능력(예를 들면, 그리스도의 향기의 이중적 능력, 2:16)이 자신에게 내재하는 것으로 생각지 않는다. 그의 능력(ἱκανότης)은 하나님에게서 온다(12:9).

여기서 우리는 바울의 적대자들이 아마 자신들의 영적 능력을 과시하고 자랑하고 있었음을 생각할 수 있다(고후 10:2, 7, 11; 11:15; 12:6).[121] 이에 대해서 바울은 그의 자찬 (확신)은 자신이 아닌 그리스도를 통해서, 하나님에게서 온 것이라고 말하고 있다. 자신의 자찬이 하나님께로부터 온 사실은 사도직의 진정성을 밝히는 가장 궁극적인 근거인 것이다. 만일 바울의 자랑이 바울 자신에게서 온 것이라면 반대자들처럼 자신들의 능력을 자랑하는 것일 뿐이기 때문이다.

ii. 새 언약의 일꾼 (3:6)

121) C. H. Dodd, *BT* 28, 1977; Georgi, 223; Martin, 53.

6. "저가 또 우리로 새 언약의 일꾼 되기에 만족케 하셨으니(일꾼의 자격이 있게 하셨으니) 의문으로 하지 아니하고 오직 영으로 함이니 의문은 죽이는 것이요 영은 살리는 것이라"(ὃς καὶ ἱκάνωσεν ἡμᾶς διακόνους καινῆς διαθήκης, οὐ γράμματος ἀλλὰ πνεύματος· τὸ γὰρ γράμμα ἀποκτέννει, τὸ δὲ πνεῦμα ζῳοποιεῖ). "새 언약의 일꾼"(διακόνους καινῆς)이란 말 자체가 바울의 직책을 분명히 성격지어 주는 자찬의 말이라고 할 수 있다. 새 언약이란 복음을 가리킨다. 여기서 오해된 율법에 대조되는 의미로 쓰인 것이 분명하다. 본문 이하에서 영과 의문(儀文), 그리고 "영의 직분"과 "정죄의 직분"의 대조와 모세에 대한 언급을 보아서 알 수 있다. 또한 이 말은 고린도 교회의 대적자들의 유대교적 성향을 반대하는 말이라고 볼 수 있다.[122] 그 반대자들은 구약의 통상적 개념인 "언약"(베리트, ברית)이란 말을 자주 사용하였음을 알고 바울이 "새 언약의 일꾼"이라고 자신을 달리 나타내려고 했을 수도 있다.[123] 마틴은 바울은 여기서 "새 언약"의 의미를 더 분명히 나타내려고 한다고 했다. 즉 바울은 여기서 복음이란 단순히 갱신된 유대교의 교훈이 아니라 하나님의 종말론적 구원의 새 질서 (the eschatological new redemptive order)임을 나타내려 하고 있다는 것이다.[124] 다른 말로 하나님의 절대적이고 궁극적인 구원의 약속이다. 바울이 "새 것"과 "옛 것"을 대조하는 것은 매우 흔한 일이다(고전 5:7; 롬 7:6;

122) Georgi, 31-49; J. N. Collins, *JBL* 93 (1974) 88-106; Martin, 54.

123) Martin, 54.

124) Martin, 54; E. Käsemann, "The Spirit and the Letter," in *The Perspectives on Paul*, ETr. M. Kohl (Philadelphia: Fortress Press, 1971), 150.

갈 4:24; 골 3:9, 10; 엡 4:22, 24). 여기서 예레미야 31장 33절의 새 언약이란 말이 이 말의 배경이라면, 바울은 자신의 복음이 구약의 예언의 성취라는 생각도 갖고 있었을 것이다. 물론 더 넓은 배경은 노아와 맺은 언약(창 9:9), 아브라함과 다른 족장들과의 언약(창 12:2-3; 9:9; 22:16-18; 26:24; 28:13-15), 다윗과 맺은 언약(삼하 7:9-16)이다. 그리고 새 언약이란 말은 신약 여러 곳에 나타난다(마 26:28; 눅 22:20; 고전 11:25; 히 8:8; 9:15; 12:24). 그리고 쿰란 문서에도 있다(CD: 6:19; 8:21; 19:34; 20:12; cf. QpHab 11:3).

바울은 새 언약의 일꾼이다. 그리스도의 복음의 사역자로서 임명받았다. 이런 뜻이 "일꾼의 자격이 있게 하셨으니"라는 말 가운데 들어 있다. 여기서 "자격이 있게 하셨다"는 말은 2장 16절과 3장 5절에 나온 ἱκάνωσεν이란 동사가 쓰였는데, 과거형이므로 그리스도가 바울을 다메섹 도상에서 부른 사건을 상기시키는 말이라고 볼 수 있다(행 9:3-6).

본문의 마지막은 "의문"과 "영"의 대조로 되어있다. 바울은 그의 복음을 영으로, 유대교의 곡해된 율법을 "의문"으로 대조하고 있다고 본다. 바울은 율법을 인위적인 것으로 정죄한 적은 결코 없다. 율법은 영적인 것이며 거룩한 것이다(롬 7:14). 그러나 유대교는 율법을 곡해했다. 율법으로 구원 얻는다는 생각은 잘못된 율법의 이해이다(롬 3:20). 오히려 율법은 믿음으로 구원 얻음을 가르치고 있다(롬 5:3; 창 15:6; 합 2:4). 율법은 우리의 죄를 깨우쳐 준다(롬 3:20; 7:7). 무엇보다 하나님의 구원사 가운데서 율법의 행위로 구원받는 시대는 지나갔다(롬 7:6). 구원의 새 시대에서는 예수를 믿음으로 구원 얻게 되는 것이다(롬 3:21, 22; 8:3). (본문은 로마서 7장 6절과 매우 유사하게 영과 의문이 대조되어 있다). 바울은 구원받은 자가 율법을 지키는 것을 반대하지는 않았으나, 세부적인 율법의 조항을 유대인처럼 이방인들이 지킬 필요는 없다고 생각한다(롬 1:26-32; 고전 9:1-2; 10:7-11; 갈 2:14).

그러나 바레트가 지적하듯이 본문에서 바울이 지적하려는 바는 로마서의 율법의 역기능이 아니다.[125] 오히려 더 넓은 의미로 생각해서 율법의 인본주의적 사고를 지적하고 있다고 본다(로마서에서는 이런 율법의 인간 중심적 의미가 암시적으로 나타나고 있다고 본다). 이런 율법의 인본주의적 사고는 바로 바울의 하나님 중심적 복음과 대조되는 것이다. 또 바울은 이런 인본주의적 "의문"이 바로 그의 대적자들의 교훈임을 암시하고 있다. 이미 3장 3절에서 "의문"과 관련한 말들이 있는데, 먹으로 돌에 쓰는 글로 지칭되었다. 거기서 "의문"은 대적자들의 율법주의적 사상을 암시하나, 직접적으로는 그들의 자천서를 경멸하는 뜻을 나타낸다. 반대로 여기서 "의문"은 그들의 자천서를 염두에 두고, 그들의 사상을 비난하는 뜻을 나타낸다고 본다.

반면에 바울의 복음은 "영"으로 표현되었다. "영"이란 "육"에 대조되는 뜻으로서 하나님의 뜻과 능력을 나타낸다. 바울은 위에서 "하나님 앞에서"(coram Deo) 자신을 자천한다고 했다(2:17; 3:4). 그리고 그의 자천의 내용의 근원은 하나님 자신이며 결코 자신이 아니라고 했다(3:5). 그 자신은 하나님의 뜻으로 부르심을 받은 사도이다(1:1). 본문에서도 "하나님께서 그를 새 언약의 일꾼으로 자격이 있게 하셨다"고 한다. 그러므로 여기서 "의문"은 넓은

125) Barrett, 157; Hughes, 97.

의미로는 모든 인본주의적인 사상과 행위를 가리키며, "영"은 신본주의적 사상과 행위를 가리킨다. 좁은 의미로 "의문"은 자천서를 가지고 자랑하면서 유대교의 율법 주의적 사상을 아직도 버리지 못한 바울의 대적자들을 가리키며, "영"은 바울의 복음을 가리킨다. 하나님의 "영"으로 말미암은 바울의 복음에 응답하지 않고, "의문", 즉 인본주의적 가치에 의존하는 인간들은 결국 죽게 된다. 그러나 "영"에 의존하는 이들은 산다. 앞의 2장 14절 이하에서 바울과 그 일행이 그리스도의 향기로서 믿는 자에게는 생명에 이르게 하고 믿지 않는 자에게는 죽음에 이르게 한다는 말과 유사한 말이다. 새 언약의 일꾼은 "영"의 일꾼이다. 하나님께 속한 일꾼이다. 하나님의 복음을 전하는 일꾼이다.

주해(3:1-6):

바울은 반대자들이 (예루살렘 사도들의) 추천장을 가지고 그들의 사도적 권위를 세우는 데 대해서 "의문은 죽이는 것이요 영은 살리는 것이니라"(6)고 말하면서, 추천장에 의존하는 반대자들의 사도직을 낡은 언약에 빗대어 평가절하 하는 반면에, 자신의 사도직은 하나님의 영으로 말미암은 것임으로 더 순수하고 권위가 있다고 말한다. 즉 바울은 새언약의 일군이다. 6절의 말이 당장 반대자들을 겨냥하는 말이지만, 이 말 자체가 함축하는 신학적 가르침이 있다. 원래 이 말은 율법주의에 대한 복음의 우월성을 나타내는 말이다. 이 말의 더 보편적인 가르침은 인본주의에 대한 신본주의의 우월함을 나타내는데 있다. 그러므로 이 말은 율법주의를 포함한 모든 인본주의적 사상을 경계하는 말이다. 바레트는 "율법주의건, 반 율법주의적이건, 신비주의적이건 간에 인간이 만들어 낸 종교 일반을 가리킨다" 고 지적했다.[126)]

그러나 교회에서나 신앙생활에서 이 말씀을 남용하여 기도나 영적인 노력 외에 교회의 행정적 일이나, 교회의 헌법을 준수하는 일이나, 기타 어떤 사업에 대한 계획이나 연구를 모두 "의문" 이라고 정죄해 버리는 것도 옳지 않다. 주님의 사업을 지나친 행정주의나 고정적 계획에만 의존하여 처리하는 것이 잘못된 것처럼, 모든 일을 전적으로 "영적인 노력" 에 의존하는 것도 잘못된 것이다. 영적인 노력도 동기에 따라서 인본주의적인 것이 될 수 있다. 외형적 모습으로 "의문" 과 "영" 을 구별할 수 없다. 우리의 내적 성격, 의도, 동기, 의미에 따라서 모든 사업의 본성이 구별된다. 바울의 대적자들은 외모를 가지고 자랑하고 사람을 평가하므로 그들의 사역은 "의문" 에 속한 것이라는 비난을 받는 것이 마땅하다(5:12; 10:7). 반면에 바울은 언제나 그의 사역의 주인이 하나님이심을 분명히 밝히고 있다(5:12, 16; 10:2, 7, 10; 11:13; 18). 진정한 그리스도의 일꾼의 증표는 그의 가르침과 사역에서 사욕을 버리고 그리스도의 십자가의 희생과 봉사의 정신을 밝히는 것이다. 그럼으로써 그는 그리스도로 말미암은 하나님의 영광을 나타낸다. 그렇지 않으면 하나님의 영광을 막는 거짓 교사들이 된다.

iii. 영원한 영광의 직분(3:7-11)

본문:

126) Barrett, 155.

7. 돌에 써서 새긴 죽게 하는 의문의 직분도 영광이 있어, 이스라엘 자손들이 모세의 얼굴의 일시적 영광으로(얼굴의 없어질 영광을) 인하여 그 얼굴을 주목하지 못하였거든 8. 하물며 영의 직분이 더욱 영광이 있지 아니하겠느냐 9. 정죄의 직분도 영광이 있은즉 의의 직분은 영광이 더욱 넘치리라 10. 영광되었던 것이 더 큰 영광으로(을) 인하여 이에 영광될 것이 없으나, 11. 일시적 직분도 영광의 순간이 있었다면(없어질 것도 영광으로 말미암았은즉), 길이 있을 것은 더욱 영광 가운데 있느니라.

본문 비평:

1. 7절에 복수형 γράμμασιν(의문)이 ℵ A C D² D³ E K L P, d e f g 벌게이트역, 콥틱역, 시리아역p, 고딕역에 나오고, 단수형 γράμματι가 B D* F G 에 나온다. f, 벌게이트에는 γράμμασιν 앞에 있는 ἐν이 빠졌다. ℵ D E K L, d e f 벌게이트, 아람역은 λίθοις 앞에 ἐν이 있다. 이 모든 기록의 차이에도 불구하고 의미의 차이는 없다.

2. 9절의 주격의 ἡ διακονία가 B D² E K L P, f g 벌게이트, 콥틱역, 고딕역에 나온다. 여격의 τῇ διακονίᾳ 가 p⁴⁶ a A C D* F G 17, d e 시리아역에 나온다. 마틴은 전자가 원래의 것이라 하고,[127] 바레트는 후자가 원래의 것이라고 한다.[128] 후자의 경우는 한글개역성경의 번역과 같이 되고("정죄의 직분에도 영광이 있은즉"), 전자의 경우는 "죄의 직분이 영광을 가졌다면" 으로 번역될 것이다. 어느 쪽이든지 같은 의미가 된다.

127) Martin, 58.

128) Barrett, 109.

내용 개요:

앞 절에서 말하는 "의문"과 "영"의 대조가 "정죄의 직분"과 "의의 직분"으로 바뀌어 나온다. 본문에서 비교급 "더욱"(μᾶλλον)이 세 번 나온다(7, 9, 11절). 이 비교급은 "정죄의 직분"의 일시적 영광과 "의의 직분"의 영원한 영광을 비교하는 데 쓰인다. 또 죽음(7)과 영(8), 정죄(9)와 의(9), 그리고 "없어질 것"(11)과 "길이 있을 것"(11) 등 두 직분과 관련된 특징들을 대조 시킨다.

이런 대조적 내용은 대적자들이 추천장을 가지고 그들의 사도직의 권위를 자랑하는 데 대하여 바울의 사역이 그들의 사역에 비하여 탁월함을 밝히기 위한 암유적인 설명이다. 반대자들이 유대인들인 것은 거의 분명하나(11:22), 그들의 교훈이 실제로 유대교의 율법이나 관행과 관련되어 있는지는 알 수 없다. 그들이 그리스도의 사도들이라 해도(11:23), 그들이 사람(아마 예루살렘 사도들)의 추천장을 가지고 자랑하고, 추천장이 없는 바울을 비난함으로, 바울은 그들의 가르침이나 사역을 구원 역사에서 구시대적인 유대교의 상징인 율법과 모세에 비교하여 그들의 교훈과 사역을 반박하고 하나님의 영과 그리스도 중심적인 자신의 복음과 사역의 가치의 탁월함을 강조하는 것이다. 그들의 가르침을 낡은 언약인 율법에, 그들을 추천한 사람들의 권위를 모세의 일시적 권위에 비교하여 평가절하 하는 것이다. 비록 3장 전체가 반대자들의 비난을 반격하기 위한 암유적 내용이지만, 낡은 언약과 새 언약을 대조하는 암유 자체에 바울의 신학적 사상도 들어 있으므로 그 내용에서 그의 신학적 사상을 검토할 필요가 있다.

한편 본문에서 바울은 출애굽기 34장 29-35절에서 모세가 수건으로 그 얼굴의 영광을 가린 사실에 근거하여 율법의 일시성과 복음의 영원성을 논한다. 바울이 이렇게 구약을 해석하는 방식이 유대교의 탈굼식 성경 해석이라고 하는 이들이 있다.[129)] 바울이 유대교 출신으로서 탈굼식 해석의 영향 아래 있다고 볼 수 있다. 바울은 그의 다른 서신에서 자주 구약을 탈굼식으로 해석한다. 예를 들면, 로마서 10장 6-8절에서 신명기 30장 12-14절을 해석하고 있고, 갈라디아서 4장 28-31절에서는 창세기 21장 9-12절을 해석하고 있다. 본문은 출애굽기 34장에서 모세가 두 번째 십계명 돌판을 들고 왔을 때, 그의 얼굴에 나타난 광채 때문에 수건을 두르고서 사람들을 면대한 일을 반영하고 있고, 바울은 이 기록에 근거

129) Martin McNamara, *The New Testament and the Palestinian Targum to the Pentateuch* (Rome: Pontifical Biblical Institute, 1966), 168-88; Idem., *Targum and Testament. Aramaic Paraphrases of the Hebrew Bible: A Light on the New Testament* (Grand Rapids: Wm. B. Eerdmans, 1972), 111; W. C. van Unnik, "Die Decke des Moses, Untersuchungen zu einer vorpaulinischen Uberlieferung in II Cor. 3.7-18," *ZNW* 49 (1958), 1-31; M. Theolbald, *Die überstroemende Gnade. Studien zu einem paulinischen Motivefeld* (Wurzburg: Echter, 1982), 177-90; A. T. Hanson, "The Midrash in II Corinthians 3: A Reconsideration," *JSNT* 9 (1980), 2-28; D. Patte, "Early Jewish Hermeneutics in Palestine," *SBL* series 22 (Missoula: Scholars Press, 1975), 109-115; J. A. Fitzmeyer, "Glory Reflected on the Face of Christ (2 Cor. 3:7-4:6) and a Palestinian Jewish Motif," *NTS* 42 (1981), 630-44; Schmithals, 287-88. 그러나 바울이 본문에서 탈굼식 해석을 하였다기보다 자신의 자유로운 해석을 하였다고 보는 이들도 있다: W. D. Davies, *Paul and Rabbinic Judaism: Some Rabbinic Elements in Pauline Theology* (London: SPCK, 1948), 107, n. 2. 여기서 Davies는 W. L. Knox도 본문에서 바울이 유대교의 *학가다*식 해석을 하고 있다고 보기 어렵다고 한다고 한다. 한편, Stockhausen은 "pesher"(유대교식 율법해석)라고한다: C. K. Stockhausen, "2 Corinthians 3 and the Principles of Pauline Exegesis," in C. A. Evans and J. A. Sanders eds., *Paul and the Scriptures of Israel*, JSNTSS 83 (Sheffield: JSOT, 1993), 123-53. 여러 유대교식 해석에 관한 Martin의 다른 논의를 보라(59-60).

하여 하나님의 영의 주도아래 전파된 자신의 복음의 우월성을 설명하고 있다.[130)]

어떤 학자들은 본문을 3장 18절까지 연장하거나,[131)] 혹은 4장 6절까지 연장시킨다.[132)] 내용이 서로 연결되므로 그렇게 할 수 있다. 실제로 이 영광의 직분의 주제는 본문부터 4장 18절을 거쳐 5장 5절까지 계속된다. 바울의 복음의 영원한 영광과 대적자들의 일시적 영광의 대조를 염두에 두고 있다. 5장에서 바울의 장래의 소망은 그리스도의 강림 시에 모든 그리스도인과 함께 그의 몸이 그리스도의 영광의 몸의 형체와 같이 변화하는 것임을 말하고 있다(빌 3:21). 그의 복음은 이런 영원한 영광을 약속한다. 그러나 그의 대적자들은 모세의 영광과 같이 일시적 영광을 가르칠 뿐이다(3:11).

주석:

7. "돌에 써서 새긴 죽게 하는 의문의 직분도 영광이 있어, 이스라엘 자손들이 모세의 얼굴의 일시적 영광으로(얼굴의 없어질 영광을) 인하여 그 얼굴을 주목하지 못하였거든" (**Εἰ δὲ ἡ διακονία τοῦ θανάτου ἐν γράμμασιν ἐντετυπωμένη λίθοις ἐγενήθη**

130) E. E. Ellis, "How The New Testament Uses the Old" in *New Testament Interpretation*, ed. I. H. Marshall (Exter: Paternoster Press, 1977), 199-219. 여기서 엘리스는 바울이 구약의 예언이 그의 사역에서 성취되었다고 보거나, 성령의 새 시대에서 구약을 새롭게 해석해야 한다고 보면서, 종말론적 해석 또는 카리스마적 해석(성령의 역사에 입각한 해석)을 하였다고 한다.

131) Tasker, 61; Bruce, 191; Martin, 56.

132) McNamara, 168; Furnish, 201.

ἐν δόξῃ, ὥστε μὴ δύνασθαι ἀτενίσαι τοὺς υἱοὺς Ἰσραὴλ εἰς τὸ πρόσωπον Μωϋσέως διὰ τὴν δόξαν τοῦ προσώπου αὐτοῦ τὴν καταργουμένην). 본문은 출애굽기 34장에 모세가 두 번째로 받은 십계명 돌판을 자지고 시내산에서 내려 왔을 때 백성들이 모세의 얼굴에서 나는 광채 때문에 그를 직시할 수 없어서 그 얼굴을 수건으로 가리게 하였던 일을 상기 시킨다(출 34:29-35). 바울은 여기서 모세의 얼굴의 광채가 일시적이었음을 강조한다.[133] 동시에 바울은 모세 당시에는 그 일시적 영광이 대단한 위력을 갖고 있었음을 지적한다. 모세의 얼굴의 영광의 일시성은 율법의 일시성을 암시하고(롬 7:6), 영원한 영광의 도래를 가리키는 것이다. 이런 율법에 대한 복음의 우월성을 말하면서 바울은 동시에 고린도 교회 거짓 사도들의 사역에 대한 자신의 사역의 우월성을 말하고 있음을 파악해야 한다. 거짓 사도들은 유대 출신들로 역사적 복음과의 연관성을 자랑하는 이들로 생각된다. 고린도후서 11장 22절에서 그들은 자신들이 히브리인이요, 이스라엘인임을 자랑하였던 것이 분명하다. 그들이 유대교의 교훈이나 전통을 주장한다는 증거는 없으나 역사적 예수와의 연계나 사도들과의 친분을 자랑하면서 바울의 사도직과 사역을 무시한 듯하다. 이들이 예루살렘 기독교인들의 유대교적 복음을 수호하고 자랑함으로써 바울의 복음과 마찰을 일으켰으리라는 추측은 가능하다.[134] 본

133) 모세의 얼굴의 광채가 모세가 죽을 때까지 있었다는 유대교의 어떤 자료들과는 대조적이다. *Targum Ongelos on Deut.* 34:7: "모세가 120세에 죽을 때 그의 얼굴의 광채가 변하지 않았다." (H. Strack and P. Billerbeck, *Kommentar zum Neuen Testament*, 3:516에서 인용)

134) E. Käsemann, *Die Legitimität*, 25,; cf. Georgi, *Die Gegner*, 245.

문에서 바울은 이런 거짓 사도들의 교훈과 사역의 허위성과 기만성을 모세의 율법의 제약성에 비추어 공격하고 있다. 외모와 육체를 따라 자랑하는 그들의 교훈과 사역은 율법과 같이 형식적이며 진정한 가치가 없다는 것이다(10:7, 10; 11:15-22).

그러나 "돌에 써서 새긴 죽게 하는 의문의 직분"이란 말로 바울이 율법이나 모세를 경멸하였다고 생각해서는 안 된다. 사도 바울은 율법 자체보다는 율법을 지킬 수 없는 인간의 연약함을 문제삼았다. 율법은 구원의 새 시대가 도래하기 이전에 구시대의 구원의 방편이었다(롬 3:21; 7:1, 6; 갈 3:23-25). 그러나 율법을 지킬 수 없는 인간의 연약함으로 말미암아(롬 2:23; 3:12; 5:6; 8:3) 결과적으로 율법은 인간을 정죄하고 사망에 이르는 도구가 되었다: "생명에 이르게 할 그 계명이 내게 대하여 도리어 사망에 이르게 하는 것이 되었도다"(롬7:10). 모세는 계명을 줄 때 이스라엘 백성이 그 계명을 가지고 생명에 이르기를 바랐다(신 30:15-16). 그러나 이스라엘 백성이 이를 지키지 못하므로 모세는 결국 사람을 정죄하는 직분을 가졌다고 말할 수 있는 것이다. 이러한 의미에서 율법은 인간을 죽게 하는 것이며, 율법을 준 모세의 직분은 죽음의 의문의 직분(ἡ διακονία τοῦ θανάτου ἐν γράμμασιν)이다. 그리고 "믿음에 앞서서 진정한 율법의 성취란 없다. 그러므로 율법의 사역은 죽음의 사역 혹은 저주의 사역이 되는 것이다."[135]

그러나 본문에서 바울이 강조하는 바는 이런 정죄의 직분조차 영광을 가졌다는 사실이다. 그러므로 다음절(8 절)에서 자신의 "영"의 사역의 영광의 강도를 더욱 강조하고 있다.

---

135) Bultmann, *The Theology of the New Testament,* vol. I, 262f.; 참조, Hughes, 100.

"영광" (δόξα)은 고린도후서 1-8장 사이에 19번 나오는데, 그 중에 3, 4장에만 15번 나온다. 한 마디로 영광은 신적 존재의 존귀함의 극치를 나타내는 말이다. 본문에서 이 말은 중요한 중심 말이 되고 있다.[136] 여기서 이 말을 "광채" 혹은 "광휘"라고 번역할 수도 있다. 이런 번역이 출애굽기 34장 29절의 모세의 얼굴이 빛났다는 말(카란, קרן, δεδοξάσμηνον, LXX)과 맞는다.[137] "영광" (카보드, כבוד, δόξα)이란 말이 빛과 관련되어 있음이 출애굽기 24장 16-17절, 이사야 60장 1절 이하, 에녹1서 14장 15절, 솔로몬의 지혜서 7장 25절, 바룩서 5장 9절, 마태복음 6장 29절, 요한계시록 21장 24, 26절에 나타난다.[138] 시편 19편 1절에서 하나님의 영광은 피조세계와 구별된 높은 하늘나라의 특징으로 묘사되고 있다.[139] 그러나 구약에서 대체로 이 말은 하나님의 장엄한 명예, 위엄, 권능을 나타낸다.[140] 신약에서도 명예라는 뜻으로 쓰인 곳이 있다(눅 14:10; 고전 11:15; 고후 6:8; 살전 2:6, 20; 엡 3:13; 빌 3:19 등). 여기서는 빛이란 뜻으로 쓰였다(7-11, 18). 이 빛은 구약에 있는 여호와의 위엄 있는 신적 영광에 비추어 이해 되어야 한다(출 19:16;

---

136) Martin, 62.

137) "빛난다" 란 히브리어 동사 카란, קָרַן 은 "뿔이 돋는다" 는 동사 케렌, קֶרֶן 과 구별되어야한다. 중세시대 학자들은 출 34:29 이하에 나오는 이 동사를 잘못 해석하여 모세가 뿔을 가진 것으로 번역했다("뿔이 난," "cornuta," 라틴 벌게이트). 당시 미켈란젤로가 조각한 모세의 머리에 있는 두 개의 뿔이 이런 잘못된 해석을 반영하고 있다(Bruce, 191).

138) G. H. Boobyer, *"Thanksgiving" and the "Glory of God" in Paul,* 11;참조, Kittel, *TDNT,* II, 237.

139) von Rad, *TDNT,* II, 240.

140) von Rad, 238.

24:15; 33:18; 40:34; 시 24:8; 97:1; 겔 1:1; 43:1 등). 그 빛은 이 세상의 어떤 빛에 비교될 수 없는 초자연적인 빛으로서 피조물 인간은 감당할 수 없어서 압도당한다(막 9:3; 행 9:3).

8. "하물며 영의 직분이 더욱 영광이 있지 아니하겠느냐 "(πῶς οὐχὶ μᾶλλον ἡ διακονία τοῦ πνεύματος ἔσται ἐν δόξῃ;). "영의 직분" 은 7절의 "돌에 써서 새긴 죽음의 직분"(ἡ διακονία τοῦ θανάτου)에 대칭되는 말이다. 거짓 사도들의 직분은 "죽음의 직분," "정죄의 직분,"(9) "없어질 직분" 이며(11), 지나간 시대의 언약의 직분이다. 바울의 직분은 "영의 직분," "의의 직분" 이며(9), 영원한 직분이며(18), 새로운 직분이다(6). 돌에 새긴 모세의 직분이 일시적 영광을 가졌다면, 마음에 새기는 복음의 직분(3:3)은 영원한 영광을 가질 것이다(18). "영"(πνεῦμα)이나 "성령" 으로 번역하는 이들이 많으나 뜻의 차이는 없다.

"돌에 새기는 의문의 죽음의 직분" 이나 "영의 직분" 이나 모두 하나님께로부터 온 것은 사실이다(5). 즉 같은 신적 기원을 갖고 있다. 그러나 그 가치의 차이는 크다. 후자가 더 큰 영광을 가질 것이다. 여기에 논리적인 뜻과 종말론적인 뜻이 다 있다.[141] "있지 아니하겠느냐"(ἔσται)라는 말은 미래형으로 종말론적 의미를 나타내고 있다. 그러나 바울에게 있어서 구원의 새 시대는 이미 도래 하였으므로(롬 3:21), 그의 "영의 직분" 의 영광은 이미 빛나고 있다(과거와 현재).

한편 8-11절 사이에 "더 영광이 있다" 는 말은 더 가치가 있다는

141) Bultmann, 82; Barrett, 159.

말이다. 바울은 자신의 사도직의 탁월한 가치를 나타내기 위해서 영광이란 말을 쓰고 있다.

9절은 10, 11절과 함께 γάρ라는 이유절을 이끄는 접속사로 시작되어 8절의 이유를 제시하고 있다. "영의 직분"이 "의문의 직분"보다 더욱 가치가 있다고 증거하고 있다. "영의 직분"과 "의문의 직분"의 특징들을 서로 대조함으로써 증거하고 있다.

9. "정죄의 직분도 영광이 있은즉 의의 직분은 영광이 더욱 넘치리라"(**εἰ γὰρ τῇ διακονίᾳ τῆς κατακρίσεως δόξα, πολλῷ μᾶλλον περισσεύει ἡ διακονία τῆς δικαιοσύνης δόξῃ**). 9절은 먼저 두 직분의 구원 역할의 가치를 비교하여 바울의 직분을 "의의 직분"이라하고, 모세의 직분을 "정죄의 직분"이라고 규정한다. 하나님께서 모세에게 주신 옛 언약의 직분은 이스라엘 백성에게 율법을 주어 지키도록 하여 살게 하는 직분이었으나 이스라엘 백성들이 그 법을 지킬 수 없어 정죄 받았으므로 결국 이 직분은 구원이 아닌 정죄의 직분이 되었다(롬 2:17-22; 7:10). 율법이 인간을 의에 이르지 못하게 하므로, 하나님께서는 그리스도로 말미암아 죄인을 의롭게 하셨다(롬 8:3). 이런 새 언약의 복음을 전하는 "의의 직분"의 영광이 옛 언약의 직분보다 더 빛나는 것은 논리적으로나 구원의 완성을 목적으로 하는 종말론적 관점에서 보나 당연하다. **περισσεύει**("넘치리라")라는 동사는 "새로운 질서"와 "옛 질서"를 대조하면서 전자가 후자보다 월등히 낫다는 의

142) Collange, 79.

미로 자주 쓰인다.[142] 여기서는 미래형으로 되어 있어서 종말론적 소망을 강하게 나타내고 있다. 그러나 위에서 지적한 것처럼 이런 종말론적 기대는 이미 이루어지고 있다. 바울의 "의의 직분"의 영광은 이미 더 큰 영광을 나타내고 있다. 바울은 그의 직분의 우월성을 지금 그를 반대하는 고린도 교회 대적자들에 대하여 종말론적일 뿐만 아니라 현재적으로도 나타내는 것이다(18). 바울은 그의 "의의 직분"을 지금 수행하고 있는 것이다(2:14-17; 4:2, 5, 6). 그러나 "모세는 민족을 의롭게 할 수 없었고(출 32:32-33), 단지 주께서 그의 영을 그들 모두에게 주시도록 기도할 수 있을 뿐이었다."[143] 바울의 "의의 직분"이 "정죄의 직분"보다 그 구원 역할의 성격상 더 가치가 있음은 분명하다. 이렇게 바울은 자신과 모세 그리고 그의 적들과의 계속적인 대조를 통해서 하나님의 새 언약의 일꾼임을 증거한다.

10. "영광되었던 것이 더 큰 영광으로(을) 인하여 이에 영광될 것이 없음이요"(**καὶ γὰρ οὐ δεδόξασται τὸ δεδοξασμένον ἐν τούτῳ τῷ μέρει εἵνεκεν τῆς ὑπερβαλλούσης δόξης**). 칼빈은 이 말이 9절을 다시 확인하는 말이라고 하였다.[144] 그러나 이 말은 모세의 옛 계약의 영광이 새 계약의 영광보다 못하다는 것으로 그치지 않고 아예 모세의 옛 계약의 영광을 "영광될 것이 없다"(**οὐ δεδόξασται**)라고 단정적으로 부정하고 있음이 특징이다. 희랍어 본문에서 "영광될 것이 없다"는 말이 **γάρ** 바로 다음,

---

143) Barrett, 160.

144) Calvin, 87.

맨 처음에 나오는 것은 이런 부정적 의미를 강조하려는 의도이다.

"율법의 영광"이 이를 능가하는(ὑπερβαλλούσης) "복음의 영광"의 도래로 말미암아 빛을 잃었다. 이제 복음의 구원의 능력의 탁월한 효능이 율법의 효능을 무력하게 하였다. 이것은 바울이 모세의 직책보다 월등한 직책을 가졌다는 담대한 말이다. 그러나 이 말은 바울 자신을 위한 자천이기 이전에 하나님의 구원의 경륜의 최종적 조치를 수행하고 있다는 복음 사도로서의 바울의 사도적 의식을 반영한다. "인류는 바야흐로 역사의 최종적 단계로 돌입하고 있다."[145]

"이에"(ἐν τούτῳ τῷ μέρει)는 "이 부분에서"라고 직역할 수 있으나, 보통 "이런 점에서" 또는 "이에 비해서"라는 뜻이다(고후 9:3). 이 부사구를 "영광되었던 것"(τὸ δεδοξασμένον)에 붙이면, "영광되었던 것에 비해서",[146] 또는 "한정적으로 영광되었던 것"이라고 번역된다.[147] 그러나 보통 개역한글성경처럼 "영광될 것이 없음이요"(οὐ δεδόξασται)에 붙여서 "이에 영광될 것이 없음이요"라고 번역한다. "더 큰 영광이 왔으므로, 이에 영광되었던 것이(더 이상) 영광될 것이 없다"는 뜻이 된다.

11. "일시적 직분도 영광의 순간이 있었다면(없어질 것도 영광으로 말미암았은즉), 길이 있을 것은 더욱 영광 가운데 있느니라" (εἰ γὰρ τὸ καταργούμενον διὰ δόξης, πολλῷ μᾶλλον τὸ μένον ἐν δόξῃ). 11절은 옛 계약과 새 계약의 시간적 가치를 비교

145) Plummer, 91.

146) Plummer, 91.

147) Héring, 25.

한다. 전자는 일시적이다. "없어질 것"(καταργούμενον)이란 말로 그 한시성을 지적하고 있고, "길이 있을 것"(τὸ μένον)이란 말은 영원성을 가리킨다. 그러므로 "영의 직분"이 "의문의 직분"보다 영속적인 가치가 있다.

모세의 율법의 영광은 일시적인 과거의 영광이었다(참조, 요 5:46; 9:28; 6:32). 이제 복음의 영광이 지극하므로(ὑπερβαλλούσης=뛰어난) 과거의 영광이 더 이상 빛을 발할 수 없다고 한다. 옛 계약의 시대가 지났고, 구원의 경륜 가운데 새로운 시대가 도래하였다는 믿음이 이런 이유의 근거이다(롬 3:21).

이렇게 9, 10, 11절은 각기 8절의 바울의 영의 직분이 7절의 "의문의 직분"보다, 구원을 위한 역할에 있어서, "의의 직분"으로서 더 적절하고(9), 그 전하는 바 복음의 효능에 있어서도 탁월하며(10), 또 그 복음의 영속성 때문에 더 가치가 있다(11)고 한다.

주해(3:7-11):

본문에서 바울은 반대자들이 자랑하는 유대교 전통이나 역사적 예수와의 연계성에 대해서 자신의 복음은 하나님의 영의 인도를 받아 영광에 이르는 영원한 가치를 가진 것이라고 말한다. 바울의 복음은 유대교의 구원의 도리에 비해 비교할 수 없을 정도로 그 가치가 우월한 것이다. 율법은 정죄하는 것이지만 복음은 생명을 주는 것이기 때문이다. 또 율법의 구원능력은 이제 지난 것이지만 복음의 구원 능력은 영원하다. 따라서 이 복음을 전하는 복음의 사역자 역시 옛 언약의 사역자에 비해 그 가치가 월등히 높은 것이다. 바울은 그의 반대자들이 거짓 사도들로서 거짓 된 복음을 전하고 있음을 알고서(11:4; 11:13-15), 그들과 그들의 교훈을 유대교 율법주의에 비교하여 비하시키고 있다.

바울은 언제나 자신의 복음의 우위성과 절대성을 주장한다. 고린도후서 6, 7장에서 바울은 고린도 교회와의 화해를 간곡히 부탁하면서도 6장 14절-7장 1절에서 세상과 철저히 분리된 생활을 강조한다. 물론 6장 14절-7장 1절의 진정성에 대한 논란이 있으나 거기서도 바울은 자신의 복음의 절대성에 대해서 매우 단호히 주장하고 있다. 유대교와 복음과의 타협을 찾을 수가 없다. 율법의 영광은 복음의 영광으로 말미암아 더 이상 "영광될 것이 없다"(10). 바울은 복음을 부끄러워하지 않는다. 그는 복음의 능력을 매우 확신하고 있다(롬 1:16). 또한 본문에서도 그는 이런 복음을 전파하는 그의 직분을 "의의 직분," "영의 직분"으로 인식하고 매우 담대한 사명감을 가지고 복음을 변증한다(12). 반면에 그는 그가 믿었던바 유대교의 율법의 구원 능력을 단호히 거부하고 있다. 그것은 그 자신의 숙고나 판단에 의한 것이 아니고 하나님의 새로운 구원 경륜 때문이다: "이제는 율법 외에 하나님의 한 의가 나타났으니 율법과 선지자들에게 증거를 받은 것이라. 곧 예수그리스도를 믿음으로 말미암아 모든 믿는 자에게 미치는 하나님의 의니 차별이 없느니라"(롬 3:21-22). 바울이 전하는 복음의 절대성은 바울의 개인적 결단이나 믿음에서 나온 것이 아니다. 복음의 절대성은 바울이 받은 하나님의 계시로 말미암은 것이다(고후 4:6; 갈 1:12). 그의 복음이 자신의 주관적 계시만이 아니라 객관적 계시라는 증거는 이 복음이 "율법과 선지자들"에게 증거를 받았기 때문이다(롬 1:2). "율법과 선지자"란 어귀는 구약 성경을 총칭하는 말이다. 복음은 구약의 계시에 근거하고 있는 것이다.

바울은 그의 복음의 가치가 절대적임을 확실히 믿고 있다. 그는 복음의 구원의 능력을 확신하면서 율법의 행위로 말미암은 구원을 부인한다. 바울의 기존 신앙과의 단절과 복음의 능력에 대한 확신은 다원화된 세상에서 우리 복음 전도자들이 취해야 할 태도가 무엇인지를 분명히 말해 준다(행 17:16,30). 어떤 이들은 바울의 희랍적 영향을 예로 들어 다원화 문화에서 복음의 새로운 현대 문화에의 적응의 필요성을 주장할 것이다. 그러나 바울의 희랍적 영향은 그의 유대교적 영향과 함께 고려되어야 한다. 또 복음의 희랍적 영향이란 것도 대부분 유대교적 사상과 관련될 수 있는 것들이다. 그런데 바울은 본문에서 이런 유대교의 율법조차 그의 복음의 확실성에 비추어 가치가 없음을 지적하는 것이다. 그리스도의 복음은 순전히 하나님에 의해서 시작되고 하나님이 지정한 사역자들에 의해 수행되는 독특한 구원의 권능을 가지고 있다.

iv. 바울의 복음 사역의 진정성(3:12-4:6)

3장 12절-4장 6절에서도 바울은 자찬을 계속한다. 이 부분은 바울의 복음의 특성인 그리스도의 약함의 능력을 4장 7절에서부터 논하기 전에 바울의 복음의 신적 기원과 영원한 효능을 강조하면서 그 복음을 전하는 바울의 사도직의 정당성을 증거한다. 바울은 자신의 복음 사역의 진정성을 대적자들의 복음의 시간적 효과적 한계성에 비추어 논한다. 바울의 복음은 그 능력이 영원하지만, 반대자들의 복음은 모세의 율법의 영광같이 일시적이다. 무엇보다 바울의 복음은 그리스도에게서 직접 받은 계시에 의한 것이나 (4:6), 반대자들의 복음은 과거의 역사적 기억과 유물에 근거하여

기력이 쇠하고 있다. 반대자들의 복음은 영원한 소망이 없으나 바울의 복음은 영원한 소망이 있다. 더구나 바울은 복음 전도자로서 참된 복음을 전하고 양심적으로 진실하게 사역하고 있다(4:2; 2:17). 반대자들은 거짓 복음을 전하면서 사욕적으로 일하는 거짓 사도들이다(4:2, 4; 11:13). 그러므로 이들이 비판하는 바울의 복음에는 아무런 문제가 없다. 오히려 이들과 이들의 거짓된 복음이 문제다.

a) 바울의 대적자들의 복음은 한정적이나 바울의 복음은 영적 자유로움을 가진다(3:12-18).

본문:

12. 우리가 이 같은 소망이 있으므로 담대히 말하노니, 13. 우리는 모세가 이스라엘 자손들로 장차 없어질 것의 결국을 주목치 못하게 하려고 수건을 그 얼굴에 쓴 것 같이 아니하노라 14. 그러나 저희 마음이 완고하여 오늘까지라도 구약을 읽을 때에 그 수건이 오히려 벗어지지 아니하고 있으니 그 수건은 그리스도 안에서 없어질 것이라. 15. 오늘까지 모세의 글을 읽을 때에 수건이 오히려 그 마음을 덮었도다. 16. 그러나 언제든지 그 마음이 주께로 돌아가면 그 수건이 벗어지리라. 17. 주는 영이시니 주의 영이 계신 곳에는 자유함이 있느니라. 18. 우리가 다 수건을 벗은 얼굴로 거울을 보는 것 같이 주의 영광을 보매 저와 같은 형상으로 화하여 영광으로 영광에 이르니 곧 주의 영으로 말미암음이니라.

본문 비평:

1. 13절의 "그 얼굴"은 원래 "그의 얼굴"(προ,σωπον αῦτού)이다. πρόσωπον αὐτοῦ("그의 얼굴")가 A B C G L P 17에 쓰였으나, πρόσωπον ἑαυτοῦ("그 자신의 얼굴")가 ℵ D E K에 나온

다. 또 A는 τέλος("끝") 대신에 πρόσωπον("얼굴")을 쓴다. 이 경우 "없어질 것의 얼굴을 주목치 못하게 하려고"라는 뜻이 되어 3장 7절과는 비슷하나 없어지는 영광을 논하는 전체 문맥과 어긋나므로 원래의 것이 아니라고 본다.

2. 15절에서, ἡνίκα ἂν(… 때에)이 ℵ A B C 에 나오고, D F E G K L P는 ἂν을 생략한다. 바로 뒤에 나오는 ἀναγινώσκηται(읽혀지다)가 같은 어미, ἂν으로 시작되어서 일어나는 중음탈락(重音脫落, haplography)현상이다. ἀναγινώσκηται(가정법 현재 수동태)가 ℵ A B C D E P에 나오고, ἀναγινώσκεται(현재 직설법 수동태)가 F G K L에 나온다. ἂν뒤에 가정법이 나오는 것이 옳다.

3. 16절에서 ἡνίκα δὲ ἐάν이 ℵ A 17에 나오고 ἡνίκα δὲ ἂν이 ℵ², B D E F G K L P에 나온다. 대개 ἂν은 후대의 변경으로 보고 전자를 원래의 것으로 본다.[148)]

내용 개요:

3장 1절 이후 바울은 그의 반대자들이 추천서를 가지고 자랑하면서 자신을 그런 추천서가 없는 일종의 떠돌이 전도인이라고 비난하는 것을 알고서 그들이 사람의 추천서에 의존하는 사역 자세를 오히려 어리석은 것으로 비난하고 있다. 바울은 그들이 그리스도인들이라 해도(11:23) 사람이 쓴 추천서에 의지하는 그들의 가르침과 사역 자세를 그리스도로 말미암은 구원의 새 시대의 활력

148) Plummer, 102.

과 뛰어난 효능과 영구적인 구원 방법에 비해 낡고 굳고 일시적인 모세의 율법과 사역과 동일시하여 은연중에 비난한다. 한편으로, 바울은 그의 사역의 신적 기원과 그리스도 중심성에 근거한 하나님의 영의 구원사역의 탁월성과 특성(생명력[6], 영원한 영광[8, 11], 자유[17], 소망[18])을 밝힌다. 이 부분은 내용과 사고에 있어서 로마서 8장 전반부의 구원론적 내용과 매우 흡사하다. 가장 중요한 내용은 하나님의 영의 새롭고 놀라운 구원 활동 개시다. 반대자들은 복음을 유대주의적 사상과 관습에 따라서 해석하고 제한시킴으로서 복음의 생명력을 잃게 하였다(11:4). 바울은 3장 6-11절에서 영의 직분과 의문의 직분, 의의 직분과 정죄의 직분의 대조를 통해서 바울의 복음 사역이 그의 적들의 사역에 비해서 우수함을 암시적으로 논한다. 바울은 그의 적들의 사역을 직접 공박하지 않고 모세의 사역의 한계(정죄의 역할, 일시성)에 비추어 말하는 것이다. 본문에서도 모세의 사역의 문제점(일시성)을 말하나, 또한 유대인들의 복음에 대한 완고함을 공박한다. 이 유대인의 완고한 자세는 바울의 적들이 자신들의 복음에 대한 취하는 자세를 가리킨다. 그러나 본문에서 바울의 중심 관심은 자신의 복음의 변명, 혹은 자천에 있다. 즉 바울의 복음의 진실성이다. 바울의 복음은 유대교의 잘못된 성경의 해석을 답습하지 않고 바른 해석을 하여 성경의 바른 구원의 진리, 즉 그리스도에게로 사람들을 이끈다. 더구나 바울의 복음은 부활하신 주님으로부터 받은 계시에 근거한 것이다(4:6; 행 9:5-6).

18절에서 바울의 일행이 주의 영광을 보면서 "주의 형상"으로 화하여 결국 주의 영광에 이른다고 할 때 바울의 자천은 그 극치에 이른다. 바울의 복음은 영광의 주께서 주신 것이며, 바울 자신은 곧 주의 형상이다. 다른 말로 그의 사역은 "하나님의 영의 사역"이므로 그 가치는 탁월한 것이다. 바울이 이렇게 자신의 복음을 변명하는 것은 자신의 지배적 사욕에서 나온 것이 아니라 사도로 부르심을 받은 확신과 고린도 교인들을 구원하여야 한다는 사도적 사랑과 책임감 때문이다(2:4; 4:7-15; 6:4-10; 11:2; 11; 12:15; 19; 13:7, 9, 10; 참조, 고전 16:24).

이런 대조를 통해서 바울이 강조하는 바는 유대교에 대한 복음의 진리의 구원의 능력의 우수성과 영구성이다. 또한 이 모든 복음 사역이 인간이나 자연적 근원이 아닌 하나님에게서 발원되었고, 하나님의 영에 의해서 진행되는 종말론적인 최종적인 구원의 시나리오라는 것을 강조하고 있다. 이런 사역의 중심에 바울과 그의 일행이 서서 일하고 있다. 그러나 바울의 반대파는 복음 사역을 한다고 하면서도 아직도 세상적이고 인위적인 추천장이나 인간적 배경을 가지고 자랑하므로 어리석고 거짓되다. 고린도 교인들이 이런 사실을 알고 거짓사도들을 떠나서 바울에게로 돌아오기를 원하는 것이다.

주석:

12. "우리가 이 같은 소망이 있으므로 담대히 말하노니" (Ἔχοντες οὖν τοιαύτην ἐλπίδα πολλῇ παρρησίᾳ χρώμεθα). "이 같은 소망"(τοιαύτην ἐλπίδα)은 직접적으로는 11절의 "복음 사역이 길이 영광 중에 있을 것"이라는 것을 가리킨다. "길이 있을 것"(τὸ μένον)이 미래적 의미를 갖고 있으므로, 소망이란 말이 적절하다. 그러나 실제적으로 "소망"은 7-11절에서 말하는 "영의 직분"이 "의문의 직분"에 비해 월등한 영광을 가질

것이라는 모든 기대를 말한다. 이런 소망에 근거하여 바울은 13절 이하의 자신의 말이 진실함을 담대함을 가지고(῎Εχοντες … ἐλπίδα) 말할 수 있다. 여기서 이 "소망"은 결코 역사적으로 증명되지 않아서 바울의 비판자들이 볼 때 어처구니 없는 환상적 소망에 지나지 않는 것이다. 바울도 이를 알았을 것이다. 바울은 이런 소망이 단순히 환상적이 아니라 실제적 소망임을 구태여 설명하지 않는다. 어쩌면 바울의 마음 속에 히브리서 11장 1절의 "믿음은 바라는 것들(ἐλπιζομένων)의 실상이요, 보지 못하는 것들의 증거니…"란 말씀을 갖고 있는지도 모른다. 거기서 히브리서 기자는 11장 2절 이하에서 믿음의 선진들의 믿음이 역사 가운데 실제로 이루어진 증거들을 열거한다. 그러나 이런 지난 과거의 소망이나 믿음의 증거들이 현재의 믿음이나 소망을 더욱 확신케는 할지언정 완전한 증거라고 할 수는 없다. 엄밀히 말해서 믿음이나 소망은 미래적인 개념이므로 다른 증거가 필요치 않고 그 자체가 증거이다. 그러므로 바울은 "보이는 소망", 즉 성취된 소망은 더 이상 소망이 아니라고 했다(롬 8:24). 그러므로 바울은 여기서 그의 사역의 장래의 영광에 대한 소망을 아무런 증거 없이 말하고 있다(고후 1:22; 5:5에서 바울은 우리 중에 계신 성령의 현존을 하나님이 주신 장래 소망의 보증이라고 한다. 본문 17, 18에도 성령의 현존을 암시하고 있다. 그러나 여기서 성령은 바울의 소망에 대한 보증이 아니고 바울의 사역의 진실성을 증명하는 것으로 언급되었다).

"담대히"는 희랍어 성경에서는 부사가 아니고 "담대함"(παρρησίᾳ)이라는 명사이다. 수단을 나타내는 여격으로 쓰였으므로 부사로 번역하였다. 이 말 다음에 오는 "말하노니"

(χρώμεθα)를 수식한다. 이 담대함은 위의 소망에 근거한 것이며, 바울의 적들이 그의 연약함을 가지고 경멸하는 데 대한 바울의 답이다(4:7-12, 17; 5:12, 13; 6:4-10; 10:1, 10; 11:6; 12:5-10; 13:4). "나는 외모가 연약 할지언정 속은 강하다"는 메시지가 담겨져 있다. 3장 4절에서도 바울은 "확신"(πεποίθησιν)이라는 말을 쓰면서 자신의 새 언약의 사역을 강력히 변호하고 있다. 또한 이 말은 4장 1절의 "낙심하지 아니하고"(οὐκ ἐγκακοῦμεν)라는 말과도 관련된다. 그러므로 이 말은 그의 적들의 공격을 포함한 현재 그의 사역의 여러 가지 고난 중에서, 장래의 소망을 가졌으므로 낙심치 않고 담대하게 말한다는 뜻이다.

마틴은 본문의 문맥에서 좀 더 깊은 신학적 "담대함"(παρρησίᾳ)을 찾는다. "그(바울)는 '담대함' (παρρησίᾳ) 이란 말로 모세가 하나님의 구원사의 최종적 말씀이라는 사실에 도전하여… 구원의 새로운 최종적 시대가 왔음을 확신하고 있다."[149] 앞에서와 같이 13-18절에서 바울은 담대히 모세의 구원 사역의 효능이 지나 갔으며, 이제 자신의 복음의 구원의 효능이 나타나는 시대가 되었음을 말하는 것이다. 14절에 있는 옛 언약(구약)이란 말을 6절의 새 언약이란 말과 대조하여 생각해야 한다. 바울은 모세의 옛 언약의 한시성과 바울 자신의 새 언약의 영원한 가치를 확신을 갖고 대조한다.

한편 반우니크(van Unnick)는 이 말이 18절의 "수건을 벗은 얼굴"이라는 말과 관련되어 있다고 한다.[150] 즉, 이 말은 원래 "말의

149) Martin, 67.

150) W. C. van Unnik, "With Unveiled Face: An Exegesis of 2 Corinthians iii. 12-18," *NovT* 6 (1963), 153-69.

담대함" 을 뜻한다. 또 아람어, 갈래 아핀(גלה אפן)이라는 말은 "얼굴을 벗는다" 는 뜻이고, 갈래 래쉬 (גלה ראש)라는 말은 "머리에 쓴 것을 벗는다" 뜻으로 자유를 나타내는 뜻인데, 이 두 아람어를 합쳐서 본문의 "담대함" (παρρησίᾳ)이라는 말의 뜻을 이해 해야 한다고 한다. 바울은 수건에 싸인 모세의 옛 계약의 중보자로서의 사명에 비추어 수건을 벗은 분명한 새 계약의 중보자로서의 자신의 사명을 담대히 말하고 있다는 것이다. 바울이 이렇게 깊은 의미를 의도한 것인지 아니면 반우니크의 강요된 해석인지를 판단하기 어려우나 이 말 가운데, 바울의 연약함에도 불구하고 바울의 적을 향하여 장래의 영광을 바라보면서 담대함을 가진다는 실존적인 의미와 또 13-18절에 나오는 모세의 율법의 구원의 효능의 절대성에 대해 도전을 하는 담대함이라는 신학적 의미가 모두 들어 있다. 그러나 이 담대함의 근거는 역시 하나님이시다. 1장 14절에서 바울은 이미 그의 사역 가운데 하나님이 함께 하셔서 늘 승리하게 하여 주신다고 하였다. 실존적인 담대함이나 신학적인 담대함이 결국은 결합된 하나의 통전적인 담대함인 것이다.

"말하노니" (χρώμεθα)라는 말은 원래 "사용하다" 는 뜻이나 문맥상 "말하다" 로 번역해도 된다.

13. "우리는 모세가 이스라엘 자손들로 장차 없어질 것의 결국을 주목치 못하게 하려고 수건을 그 얼굴에 쓴 것 같이 아니하노라" (καὶ οὐ καθάπερ Μωϋσῆς ἐτίθει κάλυμμα ἐπὶ τὸ πρόσωπον αὐτοῦ πρὸς τὸ μὴ ἀτενίσαι τοὺς υἱοὺς Ἰσραὴλ εἰς τὸ τέλος τοῦ καταργουμένου). 13절에서 바울은 "수건을 벗은 자" 로서 "수건을 쓴 모세" 가 하지 못한 구원의 사역을 완성

하였다는 자찬을 시작하고 있다. 바울이 모세처럼 수건을 쓰지 않는다는 것은 상징적 의미가 있다. 그는 주님의 구원의 진리를 숨김없이 전하는 전달자라는 뜻이다. 그러나 모세는 하나님의 구원 경륜의 시대(율법시대)에서 그의 옛 언약의 중보자라는 제약을 가지고 있었으므로 그리스도를 통한 새 언약의 전달자가 되지 못했다. 모세의 율법은 결국 "없어질 것"이었다. 바울은 본문에서 그의 사역의 우월성을 다루고 있으므로 모세의 수건의 원래의 기능을 제쳐 놓고 그 역기능에 집중하고 있다. 즉 모세의 수건은 원래 모세의 얼굴의 강력한 광채로부터 이스라엘 백성을 보호하기 위한 선한 역할을 하였다. 그러나 동시에 그 수건은 모세의 얼굴에 나타난 하나님의 영광을 계속해서 보지 못하게 한 부정적 역할도 하였다고 보는 것이다(출 34:34 이하). 모세의 얼굴의 일시적이나마 있던 영광도 계속해서 보지 못하게 한 그 수건의 역기능은 하나님의 영광이신 그리스도의 오심으로 정지되었다(14절). 그러나 이스라엘 백성이 율법의 완성이시며 하나님의 영광인 그리스도를 거절하였으므로 그들은 여전히 수건의 역기능의 영향 아래 있는 것이다(15절).

13절에서 바울은 모세 자신이 그의 수건의 역기능을 인식하고 있는 것으로 말한다: "우리는 모세가 이스라엘 자손들로 장차 없어질 것의 결국을 주목치 못하게 하려고 그 얼굴에 수건을 쓴 것 같이 아니하노라." "주목치 못하게 하려고"(πρὸς τὸ μή)라는 목적절이 모세의 의도를 분명케 한다. 모세는 장차 올 완전한 영광을 미리 내다보면서 그의 일시적 영광조차 이스라엘 백성에게 다 보여 주지 않았다. 이것은 히브리서 기자의 생각과 흡사하다: "저는 모세보다 더욱 영광을 받을 만한 것이 마치 집 지은 자가 그 집보다 더욱 존귀함과 같으니라" (히 3:3, 5, 6).

모세가 이런 수건의 의미를 몰랐다면, 그것은 전지 전능하신 하나님의 의도였다고 보아야 한다.[151] 하나님께서 모세로 하여금 수건을 써서 없어질 영광을 가리고 장차 올 그리스도의 영원한 영광을 나타내신 것이다. 그러나 본문에서 바울이 모세 자신이 실제로 장차 올 완전한 영광을 알았으므로 그의 불완전한 영광을 끝까지 보여 주지 않았다는 것으로 말한다.[152] 다른 말로 말하면 모세는 옛 언약이 지나가고 새 언약이 온다는 것을 알고 있었다. 신명기 18장 18절에 하나님께서 "나와 같은 선지자"를 일으켜 세우실 것이라고 모세가 예언한 것을 초대 교회는 예수님의 오심에 대한 예언으로 이해했다(행 7:37). 그리고 예수님이 모세보다 더 위대한 인물임을 증거했다(히 3:3, 5, 6; 마 17:3; 19:8; 눅 24:27; 요 1:17, 45).

한편 바울의 반대자들을 생각할 때, 13절에서 언급되는 모세는 결국 반대자들이나 반대자들을 추천한 예루살렘 사도들을 암시적으로 가리킨다고 볼 수 있다. 바울은 그들이 그리스도인들이지만 하나님의 영에 의존하지 않고 예루살렘 사도들의 종이 추천서 또는 인증서에 의지하여 사도권의 진정성을 자랑하는 자세를 비난하고 있다. 바울은 물론 그런 인증서가 없다. 그러나 그는 그런 인증서가 필요하지 않다고 생각한다. 그의 사도직과 사역은 다메섹에서 하나님께 직접 받은 것이기 때문이다(고후 4:6; 갈 1:12; 행 9:3이하). 그의 반대자들이 먹으로 쓴 추천서에 의존하여서 바울은 그런 추천서가 없음으로 믿을 만한 사역자가 못된다고 비난하

151) 참조, Barrett, 163.

152) Tasker, 64.

는 것에 대해서 반대자들의 교훈과 그들의 존재 가치를 마치 구원 대신 정죄하는 율법, 그리고 일시적 영광을 가졌던 모세에 비교하여 바울은 평가절하하는 것이다. 반대로 바울은 그의 사역은 하나님의 영으로 말미암아 수행되고 있으며, 그리스도의 영광을 영원히 들어낸다고 역설한다.

"장차 없어질 것의 결국"(τὸ τέλος τοῦ καταργουμένου)에 대해 여러 가지 해석이 있다. 1) "없어질 것"(τοῦ καταργουμένου)은 중성 또는 남성이므로 여성인 영광(δόξα)은 아닐 것이다. 수건(κάλυμμα)이나, 율법(νόμος)을 가리키거나,[153] "율법의 종교적인 틀"을 가리킨다.[154] 이렇게 보아서 이 구절은 유대교의 율법의 최후를 가리키는 말이다. 모세는 율법의 최후를 보여주지 않고 은폐했다는 뜻이다.[155] 그 까닭은 율법의 최후를 보이면 백성들이 실망하게 되기 때문이다. 2) "결국"(τέλος)은 "최종적 목적"이란 뜻이다(롬 10:4; 빌 3:19). 이스라엘 백성들(모세 시대나 바울 시대)은 모세의 빛의 사라짐의 "최종적 또는 궁극적 의미"(=복음)를 이해하지 못했다. [156]그들은 대신 없어질 영광을 "주목하였다"(ἀτενίζω). 3) εἰς τὸ τέλος를 "끝까지 계속해서"라는 뜻으로 보고 "모세는 백성들이 없어질 영광을 끝까지 보지 못하도록"으로 해석할 수 있다.[157] 즉 사라질 영광마저도 원하는 대로 끝까지 다 보게 해주지 않았다. 첫 번째 해석은 가장 보편

153) Martin, 68.

154) Barrett, 163.

155) Plummer, 97; 참조, 이상근, 285.

156) Héring, 24; Martin, 68.

157) Hughes, 109.

적인 해석이나, 모세가 속임수를 썼다는 수긍하기 어려운 의미로 되는 것이 문제다.[158] 두 번째 해석이 옳다면 왜 모세가 이스라엘 백성에게 장차 올 영광(그리스도)을 못 보게 하였는가라는 질문을 하게 한다. 그들의 강퍅한 마음의 죄에 대한 형벌로 그들이 구원을 얻지 못하게 하였다는 주장도 있으나,[159] 지나친 추론적 해석이다(참조, 막 9:4). 세 번째 해석은 모세가 장차 올 완전한 영광을 알고 있었기 때문에 자신의 얼굴의 불완전한 영광을 이스라엘 백성들에게 보여주지 않았다는 것이다. 이 뜻이 문맥에 맞는다.

요약하면, 1) 모세는 이스라엘 백성을 하나님의 영광으로부터 보호하기 위해서 그의 얼굴에 수건을 썼다. 2) 그러나 바울은 지금 모세의 옛 언약의 사역의 한계를 증명하기 위해서, 모세의 수건이 하나님의 영광을 가리는 역기능이 있었음을 중시한다. 즉 모세의 율법을 믿는 유대인들이 복음을 반대하는 것을 가리킨다. 3) 즉 모세는 이스라엘 백성에게 일시적 영광을 보여주었으나 그마저도 자주 수건으로 가리곤 했다. 4) 그러나 바울은 하나님의 말씀을 가로막는 아무런 장애 없이 완전한 영광을 드러낸다. 5) 그러므로 바울의 새 언약의 사역이 모세의 옛 언약의 사역에 비해 우월하다.

14. "그러나 저희 마음이 완고하여 오늘까지라도 구약을 읽을 때에 그 수건이 오히려 벗어지지 아니하고 있으니 그 수건은 그리스도 안에서 없어질 것이라" (ἀλλὰ ἐπωρώθη τὰ νοήματα αὐτῶν. ἄχρι γὰρ τῆς σήμερον ἡμέρας τὸ αὐτὸ κάλυμμα

158) Hughes, 109; Plummer, 97.

159) 박윤선, 318.

ἐπὶ τῇ ἀναγνώσει τῆς παλαιᾶς διαθήκης μένει, μὴ ἀνακαλυπτόμενον ὅτι ἐν Χριστῷ καταργεῖται). 14절에서 바울은 모세의 얼굴을 덮은 수건(베일)이 아니라 이스라엘 백성의 마음을 덮은 수건에 대해서 설명한다. 모세의 옛 계약의 한계성을 논한 후에 그 모세의 옛 계약을 여전히 추종하는 이스라엘 백성들의 우둔함을 책망하고 있다.

"저희 마음이 완고하여"(ἐπωρώθη τὰ νοήματα)라는 말은 유대인들이 구약에서 예언된 복음이 전해졌는데도 깨닫지 못하고 복음을 거절함을 말한다. 모세 시대 유대인들도 하나님의 말씀을 청종치 않았는데 바울 당시 유대인도 그러하다는 뜻이다.

"오늘까지라도 구약을 읽을 때에 그 수건이 오히려 벗어지지 아니하고 있으니." "오늘까지라도"(ἄχρι τῆς σήμερον)라는 말은 모세 시대부터 바울 당시까지 유대인들이 하나님의 말씀을 듣지 않은 계속된 반역의 역사를 가리킨다(행 7:39, 51-53; 롬 10:3, 21). 그들은 "구약"(παλαιᾶς διαθήκης, 문자적으로, "옛 계약")을 읽을 때에 마음에 수건을 덮고 읽기 때문이다. 앞 절에서 바울은 모세의 수건이 하나님의 영광을 가리는 역기능을 지적하였으나 여기서는 그 수건을 백성의 마음을 덮는 수건으로 의미를 바꾸어 사용하고 있다. 바울은 "바로 같은 수건"(τὸ αὐτὸ κάλυμμα)라고 함으로써 과거 모세의 수건이나 바울 당시 불신 유대인들의 수건이 결국 같은 기능, 즉 하나님의 영광 혹은 구원의 진리를 보지 못하게 하는 일을 하고 있음을 가리킨다. 구원의 진리에 대한 맹목은 그리스도 안에서 고침을 받을 수 있다(눅 24:27, 32, 45-46; 요 9:39-41 참조). 바울은 여기서 복음의 문이 이스라엘 백성에게 열려있음을 알리면서 완악함을 버리고 그리스도를 믿고 영접하라고 한다. "그 수건은 그리스도 안에서 없어질 것이라"는 말에는 "그 수건에 덮인 완악한 마음"은 그리스도의 은혜와 능력을 믿음으로 고침을 받게 된다는 뜻이다. 불신앙의 너울인 율법주의적 구원 방식인 행위로 구원 얻는다는 모세의 옛 언약을 고수하고 집착하는 생각을 버리고, 새로운 언약, 즉 그리스도를 믿음으로 구원 얻는다는 복음을 받아들이라는 말이다.

이런 가르침은 외적으로는 바울이 율법주의적 유대교를 비난하는 말이지만, 내적으로는 바울을 비난하는 반대자들이 예루살렘 사도들의 추천서를 갖고 고린도 교회에 와서 육적인 것들을 자랑하므로 바울이 이를 반박하는 것이라고 보아야 한다. 그들이 율법주의자라는 증거는 없으나 그들의 사역이 바울의 복음을 반대하는 예루살렘 신자들이나 사도들의 정서를 반영하고 있다고 보기 때문이다(행 15:1, 2).[160]

15. "오늘까지 모세의 글을 읽을 때에 수건이 오히려 그 마음을 덮었도다"(ἀλλ᾽ ἕως σήμερον ἡνίκα ἂν ἀναγινώσκηται Μωϋσῆς, κάλυμμα ἐπὶ τὴν καρδίαν αὐτῶν κεῖται). 15절은 14절의 내용 가운데 있던 말씀을 반복한다. 그러나 반복의 의도는 아마 고린도 교회의 대적자들의 잘못된 자세를 공격하기 위한 것일 것이다.[161] 그들은 외모를 중시하고, 바울의 복음을 반대하고, 유대주의적 복음을 고수하려는 예루살렘 사도들의 세력을 자신들의 배경으로 자랑하고 있다(3:1; 5:12; 11:22; 12:11). 그들은 왜곡된

160) Martin, lv-lvii.

161) Martin, 69.

복음을 가르치는 거짓 사도들이다(11:4). "그러나 오늘까지"(ἀλλ' ἕως σήμερον)라는 바울 당시를 가리키는 말과 한글 개역에는 번역되지 않은 "그들의 마음"(καρδίαν αὐτῶν)이라는 말은 모두 그 당시 고린도에서 바울을 괴롭히는 대적자들을 지칭하는 말이라고 본다. 바울의 대적자들은 패역한 이스라엘 백성의 오늘날의 후손이다. 그들은 과거부터 하나님의 말씀을 대적하고 선지자들을 핍박한 무리에 속한다(마 5:12; 행 7:52). 이런 의미에서 바울은 그들을 하나님의 구원사에 역행하는 배반사(背反史)의 주역들로 정죄하고 있다. 그러나 바울은 겉으로 일반 유대인들의 복음에 대한 배척을 말하고 있다. 바울은 당시 유대인들의 완고함이나 어리석음에 비추어서 그리스도의 일꾼들이라고 자처하는 반대자들의 비 복음적인 자세를 질타하고 있다고 본다(11:23; 참조, 롬 9:1).

16. "그러나 언제든지 그 마음이 주께로 돌아가면 그 수건이 벗어지리라"(ἡνίκα δὲ ἐὰν ἐπιστρέψῃ πρὸς κύριον, περιαιρεῖται τὸ κάλυμμα). 16절도 14절의 마지막 부분의 반복이다. 반드시 반복할 수 밖에 없는 이유는 15절에서 바울이 그의 반대자들을 정죄하였는데, 정죄 하는 것은 "정죄의 직분"을 가진 이들의 임무이며, "의의 직분"을 가진 바울의 사역이 아니라는 것을 밝혀야 하기 때문이다(9절). 그러므로 바울은 그들에게 구원의 기회를 주고 있다: "그러나 언제든지 주께로 돌아가면 그 수건이 벗어지리라." 수건은 율법주의적 구원을 가리킨다. 죄의 멍에는 율법주의적 구원관을 버리고 그리스도의 십자가 앞에서 하나님의 은혜를 믿을 때만 벗을 수 있다. 유대교 율법주의로 말미암은 구원의 도리에 대한 맹목은 주께로 가야 고침을 받을 수 있는 것이

다(롬 8:1-2; 9:1). "돌아간다"(ἐπιστρέψῃ)는 회개의 의미가 있다(갈 4:9; 살전 1:9).[162] 삼인칭 단수이지만 마음에 베일을 쓴 유대 백성 전체를 가리킨다(롬 11:14, 25-26).[163] 또한 출애굽기 34장 34절에 모세 자신이 하나님 앞에서 수건을 벗은 사실을 시사하고 있다. 바울은 모세가 하나님 앞에 설 때에 수건을 벗었다는 것은 추론적으로 생각하여 그 동안은 모세가 율법을 떠난 것이라고 본다.[164] 그렇다면 유대인들도 이제 그들의 마음을 덮은 수건을 벗어야한다. 하나님께 돌아가는 행위와 진리에 대한 맹목을 버리는 행위(베일을 벗고 율법을 읽는 것)는 결국 같은 동작이지만, 돌아가는 것, 즉 회개의 동작이 개념 설명 상 모든 동작의 시발적 동작이므로 먼저 언급되었다.

"주께로"(κύριον)란 말이 하나님인가 또는 예수 그리스도인가에 대한 논쟁이 있다(17, 18절의 "주"도 같은 논쟁을 갖고 있다). 16절이 14절의 후반부를 반복하는 것으로 보아서 그리스도를 가리킨다고 볼 수 있다. 그러나 퍼니쉬는 고린도후서에서 바울이 3장에서 그의 모든 사역을 하나님과 관련시켜 설명하고 있음을 중시하면서 본문의 "주"는 하나님을 가리킨다고 한다.[165] 그러나 주를 "예수"로 보는 이들은 이미 하나님을 믿는 유대인들에게 하나님께로 돌아가라고 말하는 것은 별 의미가 없으므로, 하나님의 율법의 성취이신 그리스도에게 돌아가라고 말했다고 보는 것이 더

---

162) Martin, 70.

163) Windisch, 124; Bachmann, 170-71; Barrett, 166; Bultmann, 89; 참조, Furnish, 210, 234.

164) Tasker, 66.

165) Furnish, 234-35; 그러나 Martin, 71을 보라.

타당하다고 한다.[166] 그러나 구약에서 이미 믿는 유대인들에게도 회개하고 여호와께 돌아오라(שׁוּב)고 했으므로 이런 반박은 설득력이 없다(신 30:2, 10; 렘 3:12; 암 4:6; 슥 1:3; 말 3:7). 그렇다면 그 아들을 보내신 하나님께 돌아오라는 의미로 보아야 한다. 여기서 바울이 "주"라고 쓴 것은 70인역 출애굽기에 "주 앞에서"(ἔναντι κυρίου)란 말이 자주 나오기 때문이다. 바울이 구약의 하나님께 대한 표현을 그리스도에 대한 것으로 바꾸어 쓸 때가 많은 것은 사실이지만, 그렇다고 이 문맥에서 주를 그리스도로 한정시킨다고 보기는 어렵다.[167] 오히려 이 부분에서는 하나님께 돌아오는 것을 말하고, 그 다음 4장에 들어가서 예수 그리스도를 통한 구원 진리를 선포하는 것이라고 본다(4:2). 그러나 어쩌면 바울은 의도적으로 하나님과 그리스도를 동시에 나타내는 "주님"이란 말을 써서 하나님의 사역과 그리스도의 사역을 함께 동심원적(同心圓的)으로 말하고 있는지도 모른다.

한마디로 16절은 유대인들이 영의 눈을 떠서 믿음으로 구약을 읽으면 예수가 하나님께서 약속하신 그리스도임을 깨닫게 된다는 것이다(롬 1:2). 타스커는 16절을 "그리스도가 구약 성경의 성취"라고 보아야 구약 성경이 제대로 이해될 수 있음을 가장 강하게 강조하는 신약 성경 구절 가운데 하나라고 한다.[168]

한편으로 16절에서 바울은 거짓 사도들의 가르침을 믿고 따라온 고린도 교인들에게 바울의 복음진리로 다시 돌아 올 것을 암시적으로 권면하고 있다고 본다(11:20; 13:5).

---

166) Tasker, 66; Hughes, 112; Barrett, 166; Plummer, 102.

167) Plummer, 102.

168) Tasker, 66.

17. "주는 영이시니 주의 영이 계신 곳에는 자유함이 있느니라" (**ὁ δὲ κύριος τὸ πνεῦμά ἐστιν· οὗ δὲ τὸ πνεῦμα κυρίου, ἐλευθερία**). 이 구절을 새로운 주제를 시작하는 구절로 보아서는 안 된다. 16절에서 주께로 돌아가면 수건이 벗어진다는 말의 이유를 말한 것뿐이다. 그러나 본문의 내용이 새로운 표현을 담고 있음은 사실이다. 즉 "주"(하나님)를 "영"(**πνεῦμα**)이라고 부르는 것과 "자유"(**ἐλευθερία**)라는 개념의 도입이다. 바울은 3장 3절 이후 하나님의 영의 활동에 대해서 말하기 시작했다. 16절에서 하나님에게로 돌아가면 수건이 벗어진다고 했는데, 17절에서는 하나님이 어떤 분이시기에 수건이 벗겨지느냐라는 질문에 대해서 답하고 있다. 즉 "하나님은 영이시며, 자유함을 주시는 분이시다." 여기서 영이란 의문에 반대되는 것이며, 자유함이란 의문의 형식적이고 율법적인 구속에 반대되는 의미라고 본다. 본문에서는 주님이 돌에 새긴 정죄와 사망과 일시적 영광의 의문에서 벗어나 의와 영원한 영광에 이르게 하는 자유를 말한다(3:6-11, 18; 롬 6:18; 8:1, 2). 여기서의 자유는 유대교의 율법주의적 구원 이해에서 은혜로 말미암은 복음적 구원이해를 말한다. 그러나 궁극적으로 그리스도로 말미암은 죄로부터의 자유를 가리킨다. 하나님은 그리스도 안에서 우리를 죄에서 해방시키셨다. 또한 칼빈은 "자유"의 의미에 대해서 "'자유'라는 말을 나는 죄와 육신의 노예살이에서의 자유로만 보는 것이 아니라" 로마서 8장 15절에 의해서 그리스도인은 두려워하는 영을 받지 않고 양자의 영을 받았으므로 그리

---

169) Calvin, 86-87.

스도께서 주시는 믿음도 이 말 속에 포함시킨다고 했다.[169)]

하나님의 "영"은 문맥에서 의문이나 율법에 매이지 않는 그리스도 안에서의 하나님의 새로운 구원의 능력을 가리킨다. 원문에 ἅγιος(聖)란 말이 없이 πνεῦμα(영)란 말만 있다. 그러나 "영"을 성령으로 이해하는 이들은 본문에서 그냥 "영"(πνεῦμα)이라고 한 것은 성령의 인격적 설명이 아니라 성령의 역동적 행위를 강조하려고 하기 때문이라고 한다.[170)] 그러나 3장 3절, 6절에서 "영"의 역동적이고 내적이고 영적인 사역을 설명할 때 하나님의 영으로 말했고 특별히 성령의 역사란 언급은 없다. 물론 하나님의 성령도 본문에서의 하나님의 영과 같이 자유함을 주시는 것도 사실이다. 성령이 율법과(갈 5:18) 공포와(롬 8:15) 죄와(롬 7:6) 부패(롬 8:21, 23)에서 자유케 하신다.[171)] 다만 본문에서 바울은 보다 유대교적인 용어를 가지고 유대인들을 대상으로 말하는 형식을 취하기 때문에 성령이라는 신약적인 용어보다는 유대인들이 수긍할 수 있는 "하나님의 영"이란 말을 쓰는 것으로 본다. 유대인이라는 문맥상의 또는 의미상의 청중을 고려하여 선택한 언어라고 볼 수 있다. 그러므로 내적으로는 성령을 가리키지만 외적으로는 단순히 "하나님의 영"으로 지칭한다고 할 수 있다.

바울은 새 언약의 일꾼으로서 주님의 사역, 하나님의 영의 사역을 돕고 있다. 그래서 이미 8절에서 그의 사역을 영의 사역이라고 했다.

여기에서도 3장 1-3절의 자천서 문제가 계속 암시되고 있다. 바

---

170) Barrett, 167; N. Turner, *Grammatical Insights into the NT* (Edinburgh: T. & T. Clark, 1965), 126f.; Martin, 71.

171) Furnish, 236-37; Tasker, 66.

울의 자천서는 잉크로 종이에 쓴 것이 아니라 하나님의 영으로 고린도 교인들의 마음에 쓴 것이다. 마음을 변화시키고 구원의 영광에 이르게 하는 영적 사역이다. 반면에 그의 대적자들이 잉크로 쓴 사도들의 자천서를 가지고 인간적 배경과 유대적 배경을 자랑하는 자세는 하나님의 영이 이끄는 복음의 성격에 배치된다고 보는 것이다. 그들은 복음이 아닌 율법의 낡은 언약을 중심으로 가르치는 사망과 정죄의 사역자들과 다름이 없다. 더구나 그들은 고린도 교인들을 무례하게 대하면서 그들을 종으로 부리고 있다. 그런데도 고린도 교인들은 이들을 용납하면서 따라가는 것을 바울은 안타까워한다(11:20). 속히 진심으로 그들을 사랑하는 그리스도의 진정한 사도인 그에게 돌아 와서 진정한 그리스도인으로서의 자유함을 누리라는 암시가 있다(1:24; 4:7-15; 6:4-10; 12:15; 13:7). 이런 복음의 자유함으로의 초청에 핵심적 반대자들이 포함되어 있다고 보기 어렵다. 바울은 그들을 거짓사도, 사단의 일꾼으로 정죄하기 때문이다(11:13-15).

18. "우리가 다 수건을 벗은 얼굴로 거울을 보는 것 같이 주의 영광을 보매 저와 같은 형상으로 화하여 영광으로 영광에 이르니 곧 주의 영으로 말미암음이니라" (ἡμεῖς δὲ πάντες ἀνακεκαλυμμένῳ προσώπῳ τὴν δόξαν κυρίου κατοπτριζόμενοι τὴν αὐτὴν εἰκόνα μεταμορφούμεθα ἀπὸ δόξης εἰς δόξαν καθάπερ ἀπὸ κυρίου πνεύματος). 18절은 넓게는 13절부터 시작된 모세의 수건을 쓴 사역과 바울의 수건을 벗기는 사역, 즉 율법을 옛 언약으로 읽게 하는 직분과 새 언약으로 읽게 하는 직분의 대조적 설명의 결론이며, 좁게는 17절의 주

의 영으로 말미암는 바울의 사역에 대한 결론이다. 여기서 바울은 복음 진리의 영구적 성격을 보여 준다. 즉 복음은 외적이고 일시적인 세상에 보이는 것을 가지고 사람들을 인도하는 것이 아니라 죄인이 그리스도 안에서 하나님의 영광을 보게 되고, 새로운 피조물로 형성되어, 현실 세상의 모든 어려움을 극복하면서 영원한 하나님의 영광을 사모하며 살아가게 하는 것이다(4:16-5:10; 참조, 5:12). 이 모든 과정이 결국 의문(율법의 행위)에 의한 것이 아니라 주의 영으로(은혜로) 말미암은 것임을 말한다. 바울은 하나님의 새롭고 영원한 구원의 언약을 전하는 새 언약의 일꾼이다. 낡은 구원의 언약은 한정적이고 일시적이지만 이 새로운 언약의 효능은 영원하다(18). 그런데도 복음 사역자라고 자처하는 바울의 반대자들은 사람이 쓴 종이 추천장을 가지고 자랑하며 바울은 추천장이 없는 열등한 사도로 비난하니, 그들이야 말로 구시대적 발상에 젖은 유대주의자들과 다를 바가 없다는 것이다.

"우리가 다 수건을 벗은 얼굴로 거울을 보는 것 같이 주의 얼굴(영광)을 보매" 에서 "우리" 는 바울과 그의 일행으로 그리스도의 복음의 일꾼들이다. 그러나 그리스도의 복음을 믿는 모든 사람들을 포함한다(4:4). 수건을 쓴 모세와는 대조적으로 바울의 일행은 수건을 벗었다. 즉 바울은 분명히 하나님의 구원진리를 나타낸다. 그리고 주의 영광을 거울로 본다. "거울로 본다" (κατοπτριζόμενοι)는 하나님의 영광을 거울로 본다는 뜻도 되고(흠정역), 비춘다는 뜻도 된다(RSV, NIV). 그러나 3장 7절에서 이스라엘 백성들의 모세의 얼굴에 나타난 "영광을 인하여 그 얼굴을 주목치 못하게 하려고" 라는 말과 또 13절에 나오는 "장차 없어질 것(모세의 얼굴의 영광)의 결국을 주목치 못하게 하려고" 라는 말에 의해서 "본다"는 뜻이 더 적절하다. 유대인들은 수건으로 주의 영광을 보지 못하나, 바울은 수건을 벗고 주의 영광을 본다. "주의 영광"은 하나님의 영광이며, 그의 형상이신 그리스도에게서 나타나는 것이다(4:4).[172] 바울과 모든 그리스도인들은 그리스도에게서 비춰는 하나님의 영광을 보고 그리스도와 같은 형상으로 변화되고 "영광으로 영광"에 이르는 것이다(롬 8:17, 29, 30; 갈 4:19). 이런 변화는 하나님의 영의 역사로 말미암는 것이다. 이것은 그리스도 안에서 죄인이 하나님의 새로운 피조물로, 새로운 존재로, 창조되는 놀라운 과정이다(5:17). 하나님의 영광을 떠난 죄인은 모든 참담한 어려움 가운데 고난 받는다. 주의 영광을 보는 것이 모든 멸망 받을 죄인의 궁극적 소망이다(롬 3:23). 하나님의 영광을 보고 그 영광에 비춰임을 받으면 죄인은 하나님의 자녀로 변화된다(롬 8:14). 그리고 현실 세상의 온갖 어려움을 이기고 궁극적이고 영원한 하나님의 영광이 나타날 것을 소망하며 살아가게 되는 것이다(롬 8:18-25). 죄인은 하나님의 형상이시며, 그들에게 하나님의 영광을 비춰시는 그리스도를 믿음으로 이런 변화와 소망을 이룰 수 있다.

한편, "주의 영광을 본다"는 말과 주의 "형상"이란 말은 바울의 다메섹 도상에서의 그리스도 현현의 체험을 암시하고 있다고 볼 수도 있다(행 9:3-9; 22:5-11; 26:12-19). 바울 자신은 새로운 하나님의 구원 계시를 다메섹의 영광의 주를 통해서 직접 받았다(갈 1:12). 그리고 그 계시의 구약적 근거를 알았다(롬 1:2). 더구나 다메섹에서 하늘의 빛으로 바울 자신이 눈이 한 동안 멀어졌던 경험

---

172) Barnett, 205; Martin, 71-72..

은 지금의 유대인들이 모세의 수건에 가리워져 성경의 복음에 대한 증거를 보지 못하는 사실과 유사하여 그 암시성을 더해 주고 있다.

"저와 같은 형상으로 화하여"라는 말은 새로운 개념을 도입한다. 여기서 "저"는 누구를 가리키는가 먼저 그리스도를 가리킨다고 볼 수 있다. 그리스도가 하나님의 형상(εἰκόν)이란 말은 고린도후서 4장 4-6절, 골로새서 1장 15절, 히브리서 1장 1-4절 등에 나온다. 요한일서 3장 2절에서도 장래에 "그가 나타내심이 되면 우리가 그와 같을 줄을 아는 것은"이라고 했다. 또 같은 동사가 마가복음 9장 2절, 마태복음 17장 2절, 로마서 12장 2절에 나온다. 이런 구절에 의하면 "형상으로 화한다"는 말은 하나님의 형상이신 그리스도와 관련된 것으로 보아야 한다. 즉 그리스도인들이 그리스도의 형상을 닮아가는 것을 말한다. 특히 로마서 8장 29절과 고린도후서 4장 4절에 그리스도를 하나님의 형상이라고 한 것을 중시해야 한다. 그러나 퍼니쉬가 지적한 것처럼 4장에서 본격적으로 그리스도를 하나님의 형상으로 밝히기 전에 현재의 문맥에서는 구약의 하나님의 사역이 주제이므로 여기서는 적어도 겉으로는 "하나님의 형상"을 가리킨다고 보는 것이 타당하다.[173] 3장에서 바울이 성령이라는 말 대신 "하나님의 영"이라고 말하는 것과 일치한다(참조, 롬 8:4-17).[174] 4장에서 복음을 드러내놓고 말하기 전

173) Furnish, 234-35.

174) 로마서 8장에서 바울은 "영"과 "성령"을 병행적으로 쓰고 있다. 그러나 8:4-15에서는 인간 구원과 관련하여 집중적으로 "하나님의 영"의 활동이 언급된다. "하나님의"구원 사역의 주체가 하나님이심을 강조하려는 것이며, 성령은 주로 구원받은 후에 신자의 인도와 양육을 담당하는 것으로 나타난다(8:16; 26, 27; 갈5:22).

에 유대인의 경험과 사고틀 안에서 복음의 의미를 설명하는 것이다. 그러므로 여기서 "저와 같은 형상"이라는 말은 유대인들이 아는 보편적인 "하나님의 형상"이란 말이며, 다만 암시적으로 "그리스도의 형상"을 가리킨다고 보아야 할 것이다. 어쩌면 바울이 여기서 "주"라는 개념을 쓰는 것도 의도적으로 쓴다고 볼 수 있다. 주라는 말이 결국 유대인에게는 하나님을, 그리스도인들에게는 그리스도를 주로 나타내는 이중적 의미로 쓰일 수 있기 때문이다. 그리스도는 하나님의 형상이며, 그리스도 안에서 우리 모두가 그리스도의 형상 또는 하나님의 형상으로 변화되는 것이다(4:4; 고전 11:7; 롬 8:29; 골 3:10; 참조, 약 3:9).

"화한다"(μεταμορφούμεθα)는 말에 대하여 칼빈은 아담이 범죄로 말미암아 일그러진 신자의 형상이 하나님의 형상으로 점차 회복된다는 뜻이라고 했다.[175] 이와 비슷하게 박윤선은 신자의 영혼이 성화되는 것으로 말한다.[176] 이상근은 성도의 미래의 변화(부활된 몸)를 가리킨다고 한다.[177] 믿는 자의 형상의 변화는 미래적이지만 또 그리스도를 믿는 순간부터 일어나므로 과거적이고 또 현재적이다. 과거의 중생의 경험과 현재의 믿음과 장래의 영광을 통해서 그의 하나님의 새로운 형상 또는 그리스도의 형상은 태아처럼 서서히 성장한다(8:9-11). 새로운 형상으로서 신자는 하나님의 영광을 현재에서 미래로 누리게 된다(롬 8:17, 18). 그러므로 "영광에서 영광"으로 이른다고 하였다. 믿는 자들의 과거, 현재 그리고 미래의 영광을 함께 표현하는 것이다(4:16-5:10; 롬 8:18-25).

175) Calvin, 88.

176) 박윤선, 320.

177) 이상근, 278.

"주의 영으로 말미암음이니라"(καθάπερ ἀπὸ κυρίου πνεύματος)를 "영이신 주로 말미암음이니라"라고 번역하기도 한다.[178] 그러나 3절에서 "살아 계신 하나님의 영"이란 말이 있으므로, "주의 영"이 더 적절하다. 물론 이런 번역의 차이로 말미암는 다른 의미는 없다. "주의 영"이든지 "영이신 주"이든지 "주"와 "영"의 가까운 관계와 역할을 나타내기 때문이다. 인간 존재의 진정한 변화는 의문의 사역에 의한 것이 아니라 하나님의 영의 사역으로만 가능하다. "하나님의 영" 또는 "여호와의 신"은 기존의 침체된 질서나 어둡고 혼돈된 상황에서 새로운 신적 활력으로 새로운 희망의 세계를 창조하는 힘을 가리킨다(창 1:2; 삿 6:3; 11:29; 13:25; 14:6, 19; 15:14; 삼상 10:6; 16:13; 롬 8:11). 성령이라고 하지 않고 "하나님의 영"이라고 쓴 것은 현재 문맥에서 의미상의 청중이 유대인이기 때문에 그들이 받아들일 수 있는 칭호를 쓴 것이다. 동시에 구원의 주체가 다름 아닌 하나님 자신이라는 뜻도 있다. "하나님의 영"은 구원의 새 시대에서 과거의 의문의 시대에서 일시적으로 허락된 율법의 행위로 구원받는 것과는 전혀 다른 방법, 즉 하나님의 영광을 보고 주님의 형상으로 변화되는 은혜의 방법으로 역사한다. 이런 하나님의 영의 역사는 과거 시대와 같이 일시적이고 단편적인 것이 아니라 영구적이고 최종적인 것이다(3:18). 바울은 바로 이런 사역을 맡아서 일하는 진정한 사도이다.

주 해(3:12–18):

178) NIV, RSV, 이상근, 278; Barrett, 125; Martin, 57, 72.

바울은 분문에서 유대교의 율법주의적 성경 해석에 의한 구원 도리를 능가하는 하나님의 영으로 말미암은 계시에 의한 복음의 구원도리의 탁월함을 논하고 있다. "하나님의 영"이나 "자유"(17), 그리고 "영광"에 대한 언급은 이 부분이 로마서 8장 전반부와 매우 흡사한 내용과 구원론적 사고구조를 가지고 있음을 보여준다. 하나님의 영으로 말미암은 그리스도의 구원 역사는 율법의 속박으로부터 죄인을 구원하여 영광에 이르게 한다는 것이다. 인간 구원에 있어서 하나님의 영의 새로운 역사가 그리스도를 통해서 인간 구원을 위한 획기적이고 영구적인 대책을 세우고 이를 놀랍게 추진하고 있다는 것이다. 바울은 바로 이런 엄청난 하나님의 구원 역사에 부르심을 받은 새 언약의 일꾼이다.

그러나 내적으로는 고린도 교회의 유대 기독교인 지도자들이 바울의 사도직이나 바울의 복음을 반대하면서 유대교적 율법주의적인 복음을 주장하는 것을 경계하면서 바울의 복음의 진정성을 설명하고 있다고 볼 수 있다. 무엇보다 바울의 복음사역은 하나님의 영에 의해서 새로운 구원의 시대를 전개해나가는 사역이다. 그리스도를 육체대로 알지 아니하고 하나님의 영에 의해서 하나님의 아들로 믿고 구원받게 하는 생명의 사역이다(3:6; 5:17). 그 기원이 하나님의 영인 것이다. 유대교 율법주의는 아직도 그 영광이 다한 구시대의 구원방식에 집착하고 있다. 바울은 이런 유대교 율법주의에 비추어서 육체적 자랑에 근거한 그의 반대자들의 복음과 그들의 사역의 어리석음을 지적하는 것이다. 바울의 반대자들은 아마도 예루살렘 사도들의 추천장을 가지고 와서 자신들이 정통 기독교 복음을 가르친다고 자랑하면서 바울의 복음은 이단적이라고 반대하도록 가르친 것으로 본다(3:1). 그들은 역사적 예수를 직접 보고 그의 복음의 목격자들로 자처하거나 예수의 제자들과의 긴밀한 관계를 내세워 자신들의 복음을 자랑하고 자신들의 권위를 세웠을 것이다(11:22). 바울은 어쩌면 이들 배후에 있는 예루살렘 사도들의 부정적 영향을 더 심각하게 의식하고 말하고 있을 것이다.[179] 그러므로 바울은 두 번씩이나 자신이 큰 사도들보다 조금도 부족하지 않다고 말하는 것이다(11:5; 12:11; 참조, 고전 15:10). 바울은 이들의 외적인 자랑에 대해서 "우리는 예수를 더 이상 육체대로(예수에 대한 피상적인 역사적 이야기를 따라서) 알지 아니한다"(5:16)로 말하고, 나아가 이들을 거짓 복음을 가르치는 가장된 거짓 사도들로, 사단의 일꾼들로 정죄하였다(11:4, 13-15). 바울은 이들이 유대교적 배경을 가지고 자랑하면서 유대교적 복음을 가리키는 것을 알고서 그의 복음은 직접 주님으로부터 받은 순수한 정통 복음임을 말하면서 이들을 경계하는 것이다(4:3, 4). 바울은 로마서나 갈라디아서에서 하나님이 약속하신 구원의 새 시대가 도래하였으며, 이제는 더 이상 율법의 행위로 말미암지 않고 그리스도를 믿음으로 말미암아 구원받는 것이라고 가르친다. 이런 바울의 구원론이 3장의 논쟁의 중심에 숨어 있다(롬 3:21; 갈 2:16). 바울을 반대하는 기독교 유대주의자들의 문제는 하나님의 복음(믿음으로 구원 얻음)에 비추어 구약성경을 이해하지 않고, 오히려 유대교 율법주의(행위로 말미암는 구원)에 비추어 복음을 이해하는 것이었다(11:4). 바울은 이를 단호히 거절하면서 믿음으로 구원 얻는 진리야말로 확고한 것이며 하나님께로부터 온 것(계시적이고, 영적인 것)이라고 한다.

179) Martin, lv-lvii.

바울은 이 구원의 중심 진리가 다메섹에서 만난 예수에게서 직접 받은 것이라고 한다(갈 1:12). 주석에서 지적한 것같이 18절의 "주의 영광을 본다"는 말과 주의 "형상"은 그의 복음이 바로 주께로 받은 계시임으로 절대적이라는 암시가 있다. 4장 6절에서도 다메섹 도상에서의 계시 경험을 다시 말하는 것으로 보인다. 바울은 주의 계시를 그대로 받아 순전하게 전하는 진정한 사도라는 암시가 있다(2:17). 바울은 여기서 그리스도의 복음의 핵심을 보여준다. 죄인은 오직 그리스도에게서 하나님의 영광을 보고, 그리스도의 형상으로, 새로운 피조물로 그 존재가 바뀌게 되는 것이다. 모든 죄인들은 죄로 말미암아 하나님의 영광에 이르지 못하고 죄의 어둡고 참담한 세력 가운데 고통당하고 있었으나 그리스도를 믿고 구원을 받아서 하나님의 자녀가 되어 하나님의 영광에 이르게 된 것이다(롬 3:23). 이 놀라운 인간 존재의 변화와 새로운 창조는 사람의 노력이나, 형식적 의문(儀文)이 아닌 하나님의 영으로 말미암는 것이다(갈 2:16).

고린도 교회 이단자들의 문제가 율법주의적 성경해석 또는 복음 이해라면, 중세 교회나 오늘의 천주교회도 행위로 말미암는 구원을 가르침으로 같은 잘못을 하고 있다. 개혁자들은 이를 반대하고 믿음으로 말미암는 구원의 진리를 굳게 세웠다. 따라서 그들은 참된 복음의 사역자들이었다.

오늘도 주관주의적이고 임의적인 성경해석에 따라 하나님의 구원 진리를 그릇 되게 가르치고 사람들을 멸망으로 이끄는 이들이 있다. 신구약 성경은 처음부터 끝까지 예수를 믿음으로 구원 얻는 유일하고 분명한 진리를 가르치고 있다(히 11장). 이 외의 어떤 다른 진리를 중심 진리로 삼아 가르치는 것은 모두 "모세의 수건"에 해당되는 인위적인 거짓 복음이며 거짓 교사의 증거이다. 16절에서 바울은 이 중심 진리의 절대성을 가지고 그의 복음을 반대하는 유대적 기독교인들의 잘못된 믿음을 분명히 정죄하고 회개하고 돌아오기를 권면한다. 복음에 대한 확신은 불신자들을 정죄할 뿐만이 아니라 회개의 권유를 하게 한다.

성경의 해석 문제는 교회 갈등의 근본적 원인이 되어 왔다. 바른 성경해석 원리는 무엇인가 예수 믿어 구원 얻는 원리이다. 그러므로 이 원리에 의해서 종교개혁자들처럼 잘못된 중세 기독교회의 성경 해석의 전통을 버려야하고 또 개별적(교파든, 개인이든) 주관적 해석을 버려야 한다. 성경의 다양한 해석이 가능하다 하더라도, 성경의 중심 진리, 즉 "예수 믿어 구원 얻는 진리"를 인정해야 하고 다른 모든 진리의 부분들이 이 중심 진리와 연관되어 설명되어야 한다. 이것이 바울의 복음의 특징이요 전체 신약 성경이 지향하는 경향이다. 복음서도 예수 믿음으로 구원 얻는 진리가 초대교회의 중심 진리로 확정된 뒤에 복음적 시각에서 예수님의 말씀과 행적을 기록한 것이다. 그러므로 모든 복음서 기사는 이신득의 진리를 가리키고 있다. 복음서에 자주 나오는 "네 믿음이 너를 구하였느니라"는 말씀과 많은 믿음과 관련된 기사는 단순한 종교적 믿음이 아닌 이신득의라는 초대교회의 구원론을 반영하고 있다. 이것이 비평적으로나 역사적으로나 인정된다. 이신득의 원칙에 의해 성경을 해석하는 것이 복음의 문을 좁히는 것으로만 볼 것이 아니라 넓히는 것으로도 이해되어야 된다. 즉 예수 믿어 구원 얻는 중심 진리를 믿는 한 다른 성경 해석 문제가 있다 해도 그리스도인이나 교회로 인정해야 한다. 물론 성경의 다른 해석 문제에 있어서 일치한다 해도 중심 진리를 벗어난다면 그리스도인이나 교회로 인정할 수 없다. 그러나 바울이 이신득의 진리로 복음을 쉽고 명료하게 요약하여 이방인들이 믿기 쉽게 만든 사실을 더 중시해야 한다.

어떤 성경해석이 바른 성경해석이냐라는 문제는 흔히 어떤 교역자가 바른 교역자냐라는 문제와 직결된다. 바른 교역자는 성경을 바르게 해석하고 바르게 가르치고 바르게 산다. 잘못된 교역자는 그 반대이다. 일반 교인들은 이런 문제로 고민하고 교회가 어지럽게 될 때가 많다. 이럴 때 교회는 성경을 바르게 해석하는 교역자와 그렇게 사는 이들을 따라야 한다. 고린도 교회의 문제도 누가 바른 교역자이며, 누구의 가르침이 성경적이냐라는 문제였다. 그러나 이 문제는 간단한 문제가 아니다. 교역자마다 성경 해석이 다를 수 있고 그 강조함이 다르기 때문이다. 그러나 아무리 다양한 성경 해석이 가능하다 해도 모든 해석 가운데 복음의 중심적 특징인 십자가의 증거의 유무를 찾는 것이 중요하다. 십자가의 고난과 겸손함과 사랑과 화해와 진리수호, 그리고 용서의 정신 같은 특징들이 모든 바른 성경해석과 모든 바른 그리스도인의 삶의 특징이다. 이런 것이 있느냐 없느냐가 관건이다. 교역자가 자기의 사역의 진실함을 변명하되 십자가의 고난과 사랑과 겸손함 그리고 화해의 정신과 진리수호의 정신을 모두 갖고 있는가를 살필 것이다.

본문에서 바울은 이런 자세로 자신의 성경해석과 가르침이 바르고 자신의 삶도 바른 것임을 강변하고 있다. 그는 자신이 예수의 복음을 그대로 가르치고 자신이 복음적으로 살기 때문에 바른 사도라고 변명한다. 복음적이냐 아니냐를 판단기준으로 삼고 있다. 복음적인 증거는 고린도후서 전체에 열거되어있는데, 3장의 고린도 교인들의 심령의 변화와 바울의 복음의 신적 기원, 4장의 예수의 생명력을 증거하는 사역과 사도의 하나님 앞에서의 양심적 사역과 화해의 정신, 6장의 사도로서의 오해와 고난 받음이 예수의 오해와 고난 받으심에 해당되는 사도로서의 오해와 고난 받음, 그리고 다시 화해의 직책을 수행하면서도 동시에 참과 거짓을 구별하는 진리수호의 직책수행, 7장의 사역의 고난 중에서도 하나님께서 위로하심, 8장 9장의 헌금에 대한 사도적 권면과 축복, 10장에서 13장의 사도적 질책과 혈통이나 영적 능력 같은 사도로서의 외적 능력의 과시보다는 그의 사역에 나타난 그리스도의 고난의 동참함을 자랑스럽게 여기는 점을 바울은 참된 사도의 증거로 삼고 있다.

b) 바울의 사도직이 문제가 아니라 대적자들의 불신이 문제이다(4:1-6).

본 문:

> 1. 이러하므로 우리가 이 직분을 (하나님의) 긍휼하심으로 받아 수행하면서 (우리가 이 직분을 받아 긍휼하심을 입은 대로) 낙심하지 아니하고, 2. 이에 숨은 부끄러운 일들을 버리고 궤휼 가운데 행하지 아니하며 하나님의 말씀을 혼잡케 아니하고 오직 진리를 나타냄으로 하나님 앞에서 각 사람의 양심에 대하여 스스로 천거하노라. 3. 만일 우리 복음이 가리웠으면, 망하는 자들에게 가리운 것이라. 4. 그 중에 이 세상 신이 믿지 아니하는 자들의 마음을 혼미케 하여 그리스도의 영광의 복음의 광채가 비취지 못하게 함이니 그리스도는 하나님의 형상이니라. 5. 우리가 우리를 전파하는 것이 아니라 오직 그리스도 예수의 주 되신 것과 또 예수로 인하여(예수를 위하여) 우리가 너희의 종 된 것을 전파함이라. 6. 어두운 데서 빛이 비취리라하시던 그 하나님께서 예수 그리스도의 얼굴에 있는 하나님의 영광에 관한 지식의 빛 (영광을 아는 빛)을 우리 마음에 비취셨느니라.

본문 비평:

1. 1절의 ἐγκακοῦμεν(낙심하다)는 C ψ 0243 TR 같은 열등한 사본에서는 ἐκκακοῦμεν(피곤해지다)로 나타나는 데 이것은 두 동사가 글자뿐만이 아니라 의미가 비슷한 데서 발생한 차이라고 본다.[180]

2. 6절의 Χριστοῦ(그리스도)의 짧은 형태(A B 33 1739 cop arm Marcion Tert. 와 후기 교부들)와 긴 Χριστου ᾿Ιησοῦ(그리스도 예수) 형태(p46 ℵ과 uncials, 그리고 D F G에서 나타남. D F G에서는 "예수 그리스도"로 순서가 바뀌어 나타난다) 가 나타난다. 이 경우 대개 짧은 형태를 원형으로 본다.[181]

내용 개요:

이 부분을 2장 14절에서 시작하는 바울의 복음과 사도직의 진정성을 논하는 긴 대목의 결론 부분이라고 볼 수 있다.[182] 이 부분에서 2장 14-17절에서 바울이 거짓 교사들을 공격하는 말들과 같거나 관련된 용어들이 나온다.[183] 3장에서 바울은 그의 복음이 유대 주의적 반대자들의 율법주의적 해석과 달리 예수 믿고 구원 얻는 진리를 하나님께 받아서 분명히 전하므로 그의 사도직이 진실

180) Martin, 75; Margaret E. Thrall, *The Second Epistle to the Corinthians*, ICC, vol. 1 (Edinburgh: T&T Clark, 1994) 299.

181) B. M. Metzger, *A Textual Commentary on the Greek New Testament* (New York: United Bible Societies, 1975), 579.

182) Thrall, 299.

183) Martin, 75.

하다고 말하였고 4장에서 바울은 계속해서 그의 복음은 신적 기원을 가졌으나 그의 복음을 받지 못하는 자들은 마귀가 장님이 되게 했기 때문이라고 결론 맺는다. 그의 복음의 진정성에 대한 증거는 세 가지로 요약되었다. 첫째로, 1절과 5절에서 바울은 다메섹 도상에서 그리스도에 의해 직접 사도로 부르심을 받은 그리스도의 종이라는 사실, 즉 그의 사도직의 신적 진정성과, 둘째로, 2절에서 바울의 사도직의 도덕적 진정성, 그리고 셋째로, 2절하반절 이하 6절까지에서 바울의 복음의 신적 기원을 설명한다. 특히 6절에서 "그 하나님께서 예수 그리스도의 얼굴에 있는 하나님의 영광을 아는 빛을 우리 마음에 비춰셨느니라"는 말이 가리키는 대로, 바울의 복음은 다메섹 도상에서의 회심경험에서 받은 계시라는 것이다. 끝으로 6절에서 창세기 1장과 이사야 9장의 구약 인용을 들어서 자신의 회심이 개인적 주관적인 체험만이 아닌 객관적 성경적 근거가 있음을 제시한다. 이렇게 진정한 그의 "새 언약의 복음"을 반대하는 이들의 "복음"은 낡은 율법주의적 해석으로 말미암아 혼잡케 된 것이며, 결국 마귀적인 것이라고 한다.

이런 내용 때문에 어떤 주석가들은 4장 1절부터 8절까지의 바울의 사도직 천명을 고린 후서의 중심주제의 요약이라고 한다.[184]

주석:

1. "이러하므로 우리가 이 직분을 (하나님의) 긍휼하심으로 받

---

184) L. T. Johnson, *The Writings of the New Testament* (Philadelphia: Fortress, 1986) 292-293; David F. Ford, *Meaning and Truth in 2 Corinthians* (London: SPCK, 1987) 28-33; Wes Avram, "2 Corinthians 4:1-18," *Interpretation* 55 (2001), 70.

아 수행하면서(우리가 이 직분을 받아 긍휼하심을 입은 대로)낙심 하지 아니하고…" (Διὰ τοῦτο, ἔχοντες τὴν διακονίαν ταύτην καθὼς ἠλεήθημεν, οὐκ ἐγκακοῦμεν). 1절은 바울의 사도직의 신적 진정성이다. "이러하므로" (Διὰ τοῦτο)는 연결구로써 바로 앞선 3장의 내용뿐만 아니라 2:14 이후 바울이 강변하는 자신의 복음과 사도직의 진정성을 가리키면서, 동시에 다음에 할 말을 가리킨다. 즉 "내가 지금까지 말한 '이런 이유 때문에' 다음과 같은 말을 할 수 있다."는 뜻이다.

바울의 복음과 사도직에 대한 진정성의 첫째 이유는 그는 사도직을 하나님의 긍휼하심으로 받았기 때문이다. "긍휼하심으로 받아" (ἠλεήθημεν)라는 말에는 하나님의 은혜의 뜻이 담겨져 있다(고전 7:25; 마 5:7). 바울은 그의 사도직의 확신을 하나님의 은혜와 관련시켰다. 그러나 이 확신은 흔히 자신의 연약함과 관련하여 언급하였다. "그러나 나의 나 된 것은 하나님의 은혜로 된 것이니…" (고전 15:10; 비교, 고후 3:4-6; 딤전 1:13-16). 그는 반대자들이 지적하는 바울의 사도직의 문제와 그의 연약함을 인정하면서도, 하나님께서 그에게 사도직을 주셨다는 확신을 늘 견지했다.

이런 바울의 사도직("이 직분")은 이미 3장에서 설명된 것이다. 그것은 하나님이 주신 영적인 직분이다(3:4-6). 반면에 거짓 교사들의 직분은 의문(儀文)의 직분이다(3:6). 영적 직분은 살리는 것이며, 의문의 직분은 죽이는 것이며(3:6), 영적 직분은 자유로운 복음을 전파하며(3:14-17), 즉 영원한, 무한한 능력의 복음을 전하나, 의문의 직분은 일시적이며 제한된 율법을 전한다(3:14). 바울은 이 직책을 스스로 맡은 것이 아니라 하나님께로부터 은혜로 받은 것이라고 믿는다(3:4, 12). "긍휼하심으로 받아" (ἠλεήθημεν)

는 단순과거형으로 바울의 다메섹 회심체험 사건을 가리킨다고 보는 학자들이 많다.[185)] 그러므로 바울은 사도직을 은혜로 받았음으로 그의 모든 연약함(일부는 그의 반대자들이 지적하는바)과 사역의 어려움으로 말미암아 "낙심하지 않는다." 1절에서 "낙심한다"(ἐγκακοῦμεν)는 뜻이 "약해지다," "태만하다," 등 몇 가지로 해석될 수 있지만, 본문에서 이 말이 은혜로 받은 사도의 직분과 직접 관련되어 있다. 그러므로 불트만이 이 말을 3장 말미의 복음과 관련시켜서 "복음을 부끄러워하지 않는다"(롬 1:16)는 의미로 보는 것은 무리다.[186)] 바울은 4장에서 그의 사도직 수행에서 당하는 고난 중에서 사도직의 가치(4:1)와 그리스도인의 최종 승리와(4:8) 영적 존재 가치(4:16)를 믿음으로 낙심하지 않는다는 것을 거듭 강조한다.

2. "이에 숨은 부끄러운 일들을 버리고 궤휼 가운데 행하지 아니하며 하나님의 말씀을 혼잡케 아니하고 오직 진리를 나타냄으로 하나님 앞에서 각 사람의 양심에 대하여 스스로 천거하노라"(ἀλλὰ ἀπειπάμεθα τὰ κρυπτὰ τῆς αἰσχύνης, μὴ περιπατοῦντες ἐν πανουργίᾳ μηδὲ δολοῦντες τὸν λόγον τοῦ θεοῦ ἀλλὰ τῇ φανερώσει τῆς ἀληθείας συνιστάνοντες ἑαυτοὺς πρὸς πᾶσαν συνείδησιν ἀνθρώπων ἐνώπιον τοῦ θεοῦ). 2절 상반절은 바울의 사도직의 양심적 도덕적 진정성을 설명한다. "숨은 부끄러움의 일들을 버리

185) Martin, 76.

186) Bultmann, 99.

고"(ἀπειπάμεθα τὰ κρυπτὰ τῆς αἰσχύνης)는 혹 바울의 대적자들이 바울을 비난하여 "숨은 부끄러운 일들"을 행한다는 비난에 대한 변명일 수 있다. 그러나 "숨은 부끄러운 일들"은 바울의 반대자들인 거짓교사들이 행하는 일들이기도 하다. 빌립보서 3장 19절에서도 바울의 대적자들에게 대해서 같은 "부끄러움"(αἰσχύνης)이란 말이 언급되었다. 문법적 번역으로는 "부끄러운 숨은 일들"이라야 옳다. 어떤 영어번역들은 문법적으로 번역한다("all shameful secrecy"-The New Jerusalem Bible). 이 경우 숨은 일들이 중심어이고 부끄러운 일은 수식어가 된다. 그러나 바꾸어 써도 그 의미가 다를 바 없다. 무엇인가 숨은 일은 대개 거짓과 부끄러운 일이기 때문이다. 개역한글 성경과 NIV는 헬라어가 기록된 순서대로 번역해서 "숨은 부끄러운 일들"("secret and shameful ways")로 번역했다. 계속해서 바울은 부끄러운 일들은 열거하고 있다.

바울은 그는 "궤휼 가운데 행하지 아니하였다"고 한다. "궤휼"(πανουργίας)은 12장 16절에서는 반대자들이 바울의 행위를 비난하는 말로 나타난다. 본문에서 바울은 이런 비난에 대해서 자신은 결코 궤휼 가운데 행하지 않음을 천명하면서 도리어 그의 반대자들의 행위로 암시한다. 실제로, 바울은 같은 말로 그의 반대자들은 비판했다. 11장 3절에서 뱀의 "간계"라는 말은 같은 단어로 써 반대자들의 행위를 지칭하는 말로 쓰인다.

2절 하반절은 바울의 복음의 성격과 복음사역의 진정성을 모두 가리킨다. "하나님의 말씀을 혼잡케 아니하고"라는 말은 2장 17절에서도 언급된 바 있는 바울의 대적자들의 비난에 대한 바울의 응답으로 볼 수 있다. 바울이 이방인들에게 할례 같은 율법을 지키도록 요구하지 않았음으로 해서 이런 비난을 받았을 수도 있다.[187] 그러나 보다 넓게 보아서 3장에서 모세의 율법을 죽은 의문(儀文)으로 간주하는 식의 바울의 구약 성경 해석이 문제되었을 것이다.[188] 그러나 바울은 하나님의 진리를 분명히 들어냄으로써 자신이 어떠한 사람임을 나타내었다(φανερώσει τῆς ἀληθείας συνιστάνοντες ἑαυτούς). 하나님의 진리란 바울이 전하는 복음과 바울의 사역에서 나타나는 하나님의 의를 말한다(참조, 11:11; 13:8). 반대자들의 비판과 상관없이 2:17에서와 같이 단순히 자신의 복음 사역의 순전함을 천명하고 있다고 볼 수 있다. 5장 14절과 15절에서도 그리스도의 희생적 죽으심의 모본을 따르는 순수한 바울의 사역을 밝히고 있다. 그의 복음이나 그의 인격은 모두 순전하다는 것이다.

여기서 바울이 자신을 자천(自薦)한다는 말이 3장 1절과 5장 12절에서 바울이 자천을 하지 않는다는 말과 상반되는 듯이 보인다. 그러나 여기서 바울은 아마 자신은 진정한 자천을 한다고 생각하는 듯하다(11:31; 12:6). 반면에 반대자들의 사욕적인 자천을 한다(10:12; 15; 11:18). 물질이나, 인기, 명예, 능력 같은 것들을 자랑하면서 복음 사역을 그릇 치는 것이다. 이런 복음 전파자의 숨은 불순한 동기들도 "숨은 부끄러운 일들" 에 해당되는지 모른다. 바울은 반대자들처럼 복음전파를 통해서 자신의 영광이나 인기를 얻기 위한 자천은 하지 않는다. 바울은 자신의 유익과는 상관없이 복음진리를 분명히 나타내는 데만 전념한다는 사실을 사람들의 양심에 의해서나, 하나님에 의해서나 검증 받아도 한 점 부끄럼 없게 말할 수 있다. 여기서 양심이란 주어진 기준에 따라서 행위

187) Barnett, 128.

188) R. H. Strachan, 91, Martin 77.

189) Thrall, 301; 1:12 주석 참조.

를 평가하는 인간의 내적 판단 기구를 가리킨다.[189] 그런데 바울이 말하는 이 양심은 어떤 양심이며 그 판단 기준이 무엇인가? 우선 문자적으로 보아 여기서 양심이란 말은 그리스도인의 양심이란 말 대신 "각 사람의 양심"(πᾶσαν συνείδησιν ἀνθρώπων)이라고 일반화된 양심으로 보인다. 이 양심은 기독교적 양심이나, 바울이 고린도후서에서 가르친 교훈에 입각한 양심이라기보다는 일반적인 인간양심을 가리킨다고 볼 수 있다. 이런 관점에서 트롤은 바울은 본문에서 일반적 인간의 양심이 복음의 진정성과 진정한 복음 전달자를 판단할 수 있는 능력을 가지고 있다고 생각 한다고 본다.[190] 그러나 바울이 인간 양심에 대한 무한한 신뢰를 했다고 볼 수 없다. 로마서 2장 15절에서 바울은 인간의 일반적 양심의 도덕적 기능을 인정하는 듯이 보이나, 복음을 인정하는 기능이 있다고 인정하는 것은 아니다. 그리고 바울은 여러 곳에서 기능이 마비되거나 약화된 양심을 논하고 있다(고전 8:7, 딤전 4:2, 딤 1:3). 그러므로 본문의 "각 사람의 양심"을 5장 11절의 "너희의 양심"과 동일시하는 것이 타당하다. 본문과 5장 11절은 의미와 문맥이 거의 같다. 거기서도 본문과 마찬가지로 바울이 그의 사도직이 하나님과 너희의 양심에 알려지기를 바라고 있고 그러므로 12절에서는 바울이 반대자들에 대하여 자신을 자천할 필요가 없음을 논하고 있다. 또 이미 1장 12절에서도 바울은 그의 사역의 진실성을 그의 양심이 증거한다고 하였다. 이렇게 보아서 본문의 "각 사람의 양심"은 자연인의 양심이 아니라 그리스도인의 양심, 특히 바울의 전도로 변화된 고린도 교인들의 양심을 가리킨다고 보는

190) Thrall, 302.

것이 옳다(고후 3:1-3). 그리스도인의 양심에 의한 판단만이 하나님에 의한 판단과 일치되는 옳은 판단이 된다(참조, 11:11). 더구나 "하나님 앞에서"라는 부사구가 "각 사람의 양심"을 제한시키고 있다. 휴매니즘적인 양심은 하나님 앞에서 다시 검증받아야 하는 것이다. 아무리 인간의 선한 양심이라도 죄인 인간의 양심은 하나님의 의로우심 앞에서 온전할 수 없다.

3. "만일 우리 복음이 가리웠으면 망하는 자들에게 가리운 것이라"(εἰ δὲ καὶ ἔστιν κεκαλυμμένον τὸ εὐαγγέλιον ἡμῶν, ἐν τοῖς ἀπολλυμένοις ἐστὶν κεκαλυμμένον,). 트롤은 3절은 고린도 교인들이 바울의 복음이 베일에 가린 듯이 불분명하다고 비판한 말을 바울이 그대로 받아서 반격하는 것으로 본다.[191] 그러나 이런 견해는 단순한 추론일 뿐이다. 바울은 그의 복음을 반대하는 이들에게 그들이 바울의 복음을 거절하는 것은 그들이 3장에서 논한 모세의 수건을 스스로 썼거나(즉 율법적 시각으로 복음을 이해하려고 하거나), 아니면, 그들에게(외부적 세력에 의해서) 복음이 가리워진 것이라고 하였다. 4절에서 더 분명하게 말하여, "이 세상의 신"이 그들로 하여금 바울의 복음을 믿지 못하게 하였기 때문이라고 논한다. "망하는 자들"(ἀπολλυμένοις) 은 주로 바울의 대적자들을 지칭하는 데 쓰였다.[192] 그러나 이들과 동일인들인 4절의 "믿지 아니하는 자들"(ἀπίστοι)은 고린도전서 14장 32절에서와 같이 교회 밖의 불신자들을 가리키는 것으로 쓰였다.

191) Thrall, 304.

192) 고후 2:15; 고전 1:18; 빌 1:28; 3:19; 비교, 살후 2:10.

그렇다면 "망하는 자들"은 3장의 바울의 대적자들인 유대인 불신자들 보다는 일반 불신자들(이방인 포함)을 가리킨다고 볼 수 있다. 사실 고린도전서 1장 18절이나 데살로니가후서 2장 10절에서 "망하는 자들"은 바울의 대적자들이 아니라 교회 밖의 일반적 불신자들로 볼 수 있다. 바울은 3장에서 유대인들의 불신을 율법적인 장벽 때문이라고 하였는데 4장에 들어와서 유대인 불신자들의 불신의 장애가 율법이라면, 일반적인 이 세상의 불신자들의 불신의 장애는 무엇인가라는 질문을 스스로 인식하고 그에 대한 답변을 스스로 한 것으로 볼 수 있다. 즉 이 세상의 신이 그들을 믿지 못하게 하였다. 이런 견해가 근거 없는 추론보다 문맥적 일치와 논리적 균형의 장점이 있다.

4. "그 중에 이 세상 신이 믿지 아니하는 자들의 마음을 혼미케 하여 그리스도의 영광의 복음의 광채가 비취지 못하게 함이니 그리스도는 하나님의 형상이니라"(ἐν οἷς ὁ θεὸς τοῦ αἰῶνος τούτου ἐτύφλωσεν τὰ νοήματα τῶν ἀπίστων εἰς τὸ μὴ αὐγάσαι τὸν φωτισμὸν τοῦ εὐαγγελίου τῆς δόξης τοῦ Χριστοῦ, ὅς ἐστιν εἰκὼν τοῦ θεοῦ). 4절에서 바울은 불신의 원인을 "이 세상 신"(ὁ θεὸς τοῦ αἰῶνος)의 방해에서 찾는다. "이 세상 신"은 마귀이다(12:13-14). 하나님의 경륜 가운데서 사단이 현 세상을 지배하고 있다. 사단은 이 악한 세상을 계속 지배하기 위해서 하나님의 나라가 오지 못하도록 방해한다. 그러므로 불신자들의 마음을 혼미케 하여 하나님의 형상이신 그리스도의 영광의 복음의 광채가 비취지 못하게 한다. "혼미케 하여"(ἐτύφλωσεν)는 원어의 뜻대로 "눈이 멀게 하여"라고 번역하는

경우 "마음이 눈을 멀게 하여"라는 뜻이 되어 어색하므로 그대로 둔다.

그리스도의 영광의 복음의 광채는 3장의 모세의 얼굴의 일시적 광채와 대조되는 표현이다. "그리스도는 하나님의 형상(εἰκὼν τοῦ θεοῦ)이니라." 이 말은 초대교회에서 그리스도는 예배와 찬양의 대상으로 부를 때 쓰였다(빌2:6; 골1:15-20; 고전15:45, 49).[193] 그리스도를 믿는 자들은 이 세상에서도 하나님의 형상이신 그리스도를 섬기며 그리고 장차 오는 세상, 하나님의 나라를 사모한다.

한편 "이 세상의 신"이란 말이 여기서만 나오고, 이 말이 유일신을 믿는 우리들에게 이상하게 보이고, 또 신으로 번역된 ὁ θεός 이란 말이 "하나님"과 같은 말이므로 하나님으로 번역하고 "이 세상"을 "신"에게서 떼어내어 대신 "불신자들"(τῶν ἀπίστων)과 연결하여 "하나님께서 이 세상의 불신자들의 마음을 혼미케 했다"고 번역하기도 하였다. 이 번역이 데살로니가후서 2장 11절과 유사하기도 하다("하나님이 유혹을 저희 가운데 역사하게 하사 거짓 것을 믿게 하심은…"). 그러나 본문에서 앞에 있는 말을 훨씬

193) εἰκών("형상")개념에 대한 영지주의 관련설이나 1세기 유대교 지혜 관련설을 보라. M. E. Thrall, 310. 바울이 영지주의적 천상의 사람에 대조하여 예수를 하나님의 형상으로 보았다는 데 대해서 Barrett는 바울이 영지주의적 지식을 가졌다 해도 바울의 자료는 구약성경이다라고 했다(Barrett, 133). Thrall은 바울이 유대교 지혜 사상에서 지혜가 하나님의 지식을 나타내듯이 예수가 하나님의 본성을 나타낸다고 보았다고 제안한다(Thrall, 310). 그러나 고린도후서에서는 지혜란 말이 언급되지 않았다. 고린도전서 1장에서 언급된 지혜는 예수의 인격과 아무런 관련이 없다. 단순히 하나님의 구원의 지혜에 대조되는 통상적인 헬라적 지식의 의미로 쓰였을 뿐이다. "하나님의 형상"이신 그리스도는 바울이 다메섹에서 만난 그리스도를 나타낸다고 볼 수 있다. "그리스도의 영광의 복음의 광채"란 말도 바울의 회심 경험을 반영한다. 6절도 이를 지지한다

194) Thrall, 307.

뒤에 오는 말과 연결시키는 것은 무리한 번역으로 보인다.[194] 더구나 빌립보서 3장 19절에서 "저희의 신은 배요"라는 말에서 바울이 그의 반대자들이 탐욕을 신으로 섬긴다는 데서 "신"(ὁ θεός)을 쓰고 있으므로 본문에서 "이 세상의 신"이란 번역이 옳은 것으로 보인다. 사단의 영향력 아래 있는 이들은 복음의 광채를 볼 수 없다.

바울은 여기서 그의 복음을 거절하는 이들은 결국 마귀의 세력 아래 있다고 함으로써 그의 반대자들을 가장 거세게 공격하고 있다. 반대로 바울과 그를 따르는 이들은 하나님 편에 있다는 것을 5절과 6절에서 밝힌다.

본문은 불신의 근본 원인은 마귀의 공작 때문이라고 한다. 그러나 데살로니가후서 2장 11절과 같이 이런 마귀의 공작도 결국 하나님의 허락에 의한 것이라면, 불신의 더 근본적 원인은 하나님의 예정이라는 예정론적 문제를 다룰 수밖에 없다. 물론 본문에서 바울의 의도는 예정론적 의미를 내세우는 데 있지 않고, 단순히 그의 대적자들의 불신이 마귀의 공작에 의한 것이므로 그들의 주장이 옳지 않다는 것을 분명히 하려는 데 있다. 그러나 불신자들이 "하나님께서 (마귀를 통해서) 멸망하기로 작정된자들"이라면, 불신의 원인이나 책임이 결국 하나님이라는 논리적 귀결을 떨치기 어렵다. 인간 불신의 배후에 구원과 멸망, 택자와 불택자의 하나님의 예정이 있다는 예정론은 하나님의 주권에 철저한 예정론적 귀결이다. 물론 예정론은 성경의 말씀에 근거하고 있다(행전 13:48; 롬 9:10 이하; 엡 1:4, 5, 9, 11; 참조, 말 1:2-3). 그러나 같은 성경은 이런 하나님의 예정에도 불구하고 하나님은 불신 인간에게 죄의 책임을 묻는다고 한다. 인간은 하나님의 형상으로 지어졌다. 즉 인간은 자유로운 선택 의지를 가진 독립적인 존재로 지어졌다. 하나님의 주권과 인간의 독립적 자유 선택 결정이 성경에 다 함께 있다. 성경은 이 두 "모순된 역설"을 그대로 나타내고 있다. 인간에게는 "모순"과 "혼돈"으로 보이는 진리를 그대로 나타난다. "모순이나 혼돈"은 인간의 눈이나 이성에 비칠 때는 기이한 현상이나, 하나님의 깊으신 경륜 가운데서는 조화와 질서로 나타난다. 하나님의 경륜의 논리에서는 인간의 합리적 논리가 안 맞을 수 있다. 이런 논리는 하나님의 지혜에 관련된 것이며, 우리 인간이 감히 들어가서는 안 되는 하나님의 거룩한 지성소에 감추어진 하나님의 거룩한 지혜에 속하는 것이다. 우리 인간은 하나님의 지식을 다 알 수 없다. 하나님의 지혜는 인간의 논리나 지혜로 측량할 수 없이 기묘한 것이다. 하나님의 경륜을 인간이 당장 이해할 수 없다고 무시하는 것은 불신적인 것이며, 이해할 수 없더라도 하나님의 경륜을 수용하는 것이 믿는 이들의 마땅한 자세이다. 불신자들은 본문을 읽으면서 예정을 논리적 모순이나 혼돈으로 여겨 불신에 더욱 빠질 것이다. 그러나 믿는 이들은 하나님의 예정하심을 은혜와 지혜로 여겨 감사하며 믿음을 더 굳게 할 뿐이다(롬 11:33).

한편 예정론을 떠나 인간사회의 재판방식이나 개인적 경험에 의해 비추어 보더라도 결국 하나님 자신이 불신의 원인이므로 인간은 책임이 없다는 주장은 옳지 않다. 범법자의 범죄를 유전이나 사회적 환경 탓으로 돌리면서 범법자의 무죄를 주장할 수는 없다. 범법자 자신의 범죄 행위는 전체 범죄 현상의 중요한 요소로 간주되는 것이다. 무엇보다 범죄한 인간 자신의 양심이 자신이 죄인임을 인정한다. 대개 범죄자 개인의 양심이 범죄의 책임을 인정한다. 그러므로 양심의 고통으로 회개함과 용서를 구하는 대신 하나님께 죄의 책임을 돌리는 것은 옳지 않다. 인간의 양심이 그의 죄를 창조주에게로 돌리는 것은 옳지 않다고 증거 한다. 피조물 인간이 행동의 주체자로서 범죄의 책임을 져야하는 것이다. "죄의 소원은 네게 있으나 너는 죄를 다스릴찌니라"(창 4:7). 더구나 창조주 하나님은 그가 지은 인간의 구원을 위해 자기의 아들을 희생시키면서 까지 창조주로서의 책임을 다했다. 인간이 이런 하나님의 사랑의 책임 있는 조치를 저버리고 하나님을 계속 배역하고 불신하는 것은 벌 받아 마땅하다.

5. "우리가 우리를 전파하는 것이 아니라 오직 그리스도 예수의 주 되신 것과 또 예수로 인하여(예수를 위하여) 우리가 너희의 종된 것을 전파함이라"(**Οὐ γὰρ ἑαυτοὺς κηρύσσομεν ἀλλὰ Ἰησοῦν Χριστὸν κύριον, ἑαυτοὺς δὲ δούλους ὑμῶν διὰ Ἰησοῦν**). 본문은 두 가지 사실을 말한다. 바울은 그리스도의 종이며, 또한 고린도 교인들의 종이라는 것이다. 첫째로 바울은 그리스도의 종으로서 그리스도의 왕권을 이룩하기 위해 힘쓴다(10:5-6, 8; 13:10). 둘째는 고린도 교인들의 종으로서 그들의 유익을 위해 힘쓴다는 것이다(12:14-16; 119; 13:7, 9). 이 두 가지 사실은 결국 바울의 사역의 순수한 동기를 말한다. 바울은 그의 대적자들과 달리 결코 자신의 유익을 위해서가 아니라 그리스도와 고린도 교인들의 종으로서 그들의 유익을 위해서 그의 사도직을 수행하므로 그의 사도직은 순수하다고 한다. 이런 변명은 11장 7절에서도 언급되었다. 2절에서 바울은 이미 그가 궤휼로 행하지 않는다고 하면서 그의 사도직의 도덕성을 천명하였다. 이것은 12장 16절에 나오는 같은 말 "궤계"와 관련 된다. 거기서 바울은 고린도 교회 반대자들이 바울이 궤계를 써서 물질을 착취한다고 비난하는데 대

해서 그들을 책망하고 있다. 본문에서는 이런 비난을 의식하고서 자신은 철저히 종으로서 행하며, 아무런 탐심이 없다고 한다.

물질에 대해서 뿐만 아니라, 복음에 대해서도 바울은 사도로서 그리스도의 복음을 순전하게 전했다. 바울은 그의 모든 서신 초두에서 바울은 그의 그리스도의 사도된 것이나 종된 것을 밝히고 있다(롬1:1; 빌1:1; 갈1:10). 그의 서신은 그의 글이 아닌 순전한 예수님의 복음임을 나타내는 것이다. 그러나 본문에서 그는 "예수로 인하여 우리가 너희의 종된 것을 전파함이라" 라고 말한다. 플러머는 바울이 여기서만 이렇게 교인들의 종으로 자신을 나타낸다고 한다.[195] 그러나 실제로 그는 어디서나 교인들에게 종으로서 희생 봉사하는 자세를 보여 준다. 바울은 고린도 교인들에게 종이 된 것은 "예수 때문" (διὰ Ἰησοῦν)이라고 한다. 즉 예수를 섬기기 위한 방편으로 사람들의 종이 되었다. 이것은 예수님이 하나님께 순종하는 "고난 받는 종" 이 되어서 사람들을 위해 종노릇한 것과 같다. 예수님이 하나님과 사람들에게 종이된 것처럼, 바울도 예수와 고린도 교인들에게 종이다. 바울이 고린도 교인들의 종이 된 것은 바울의 어떤 사욕 때문이 아니라 예수를 주로 섬기기 위함이다. 주 예수를 섬기기 위해서 고린도 교인들의 종이 된 것이다. 그러므로 그는 사도로서 그들을 가르치고 질책하기도 했다. 바울이 고린도 교인들의 종이 된 것도 사욕 때문이 아니라 주 예수를 위한 것이므로 그는 사욕 없는 순전한 종의 마음으로 그들을 위해 봉사한다. 바울의 이런 종으로서의 지도자 사상(the Servant Leadership)은 마지막 장에서도 나타난다. 바울은 회개하지 않는

195) Plummer 119. 다른 곳에서는 언제나 그리스도의 종으로 자신을 나타낸다(롬 1:1; 갈 1:10; 빌 1:1).

고린도 교인들을 그의 사도권으로 징계하기를 원치 않고, 그들이 그의 방문 전에 회개하여 스스로 바로 되기를 원한다(13:5-9). 바울의 "그리스도의 약함의 능력"의 신학이 그의 사역에 적용된다. 반대로 그의 반대자들은 권위주의적 횡포로 고린도 교인들을 그들의 종으로 삼아 좌지우지했다(11:20). 문제는 고린도 교인들이 이런 악한 권위주의 힘을 진정한 하나님이나 그리스도의 능력과 혼돈하여 그것에 미혹되고 예속되는 것이다. 진정한 그리스도의 능력의 증거는 강제가 아니고 스스로 하나님의 은혜를 깨닫고 자발적으로 결단하고 일하게 하는 것이다(1:24; 8:3, 12; 9:5, 13:5). 진정한 그리스도의 지도자의 증거는 외적인 권세의 사용을 억제하면서 자신의 유익을 구하지 않고 전체 교인들의 유익을 구하면서 희생과 용서와 인내하는 자세를 가지는 것이다(12:12; 19, 3:7-10).

6. "어두운 데서 빛이 비취리라하시던 그 하나님께서 예수 그리스도의 얼굴에 있는 하나님의 영광에 관한 지식의 빛(영광을 아는 빛)을 우리 마음에 비취셨느니라"(ὅτι ὁ θεὸς ὁ εἰπών· ἐκ σκότους φῶς λάμψει, ὃς ἔλαμψεν ἐν ταῖς καρδίαις ἡμῶν πρὸς φωτισμὸν τῆς γνώσεως τῆς δόξης τοῦ θεοῦ ἐν προσώπῳ [Ἰησοῦ] Χριστοῦ). 6절에서 바울은 그의 사도직의 기원은 바로 하나님 자신이라고 하면서 자신의 사도직의 정당성을 방어한다. 자신에게 비친 그리스도의 영광의 광채로 자신이 사도가 된 것이지 자신의 환상이나 인위적 결정이 아니라는 것이다. "그 하나님께서 예수 그리스도의 얼굴에 있는 하나님의 영광을 아는 빛을 우리 마음에 비취셨느니라." 많은 학자들이 이 말을 4절과 함께 바울의 다메섹의 그리스도 현현(Christophany) 경험을 실

제로 나타내는 말로 인정한다.[196] "비취셨다"(ἔλαμψεν)이 단순 과거 동사로 과거에 실제로 일어난 사건을 의미한다고 본다. 다메섹 도상에서 바울은 하늘에서 오는 강한 빛을 보고 눈까지 멀었다 (행 9:3, 22:6; 26:13). 관련 사도행전 기사에서도 빛, 영광, 비취다라는 말들이 있다. 바울의 복음은 하나님의 실재적 계시이며, 바울 자신의 주관적 사견이나, 환상이 아니다. 바울은 그의 회심경험을 한낱 주관적 환상으로 돌려버릴 수 있음을 알고 그의 체험을 구약 성경과 관련하여 설명하는지도 모른다. "어두운 데서 빛이 비치리라"라는 말은 창세기 1장 3-4절의 빛의 창조를 가리킨다고 한다.[197] 또 이사야 9장 1절의 내용과도 흡사하다.[198] 이 두 구절이

---

196) A. Kloepper, *Kommentar über das zweite Sendschreiben des Apostels Paulus an die Gemeinde zu Korinth* (Berlin: de Gruyter, 1874), 231; P. Bachmann, *Der zweite Brief des Paulus an die Korinther*, Kommentar zum Neuen Testament VIII (Leipzig: Verlagsbuchhandlung Werner Scholl, 1918), 191; W. Bousset, "Der zweite Brief and die Korinther," in *Die Schriften des Neuen Testaments*, II. Ed. J. Weiss (Gtingen: Vandenhoeck & Ruprechet, 1907), 180; P. W. Schmiedel, *Die Briefe an die Thessaloniker und and die Korinther*, HKNT 2.1, (Freiburg: J. C. B. Mohr, 1892), 232; J. E. Belser, *Der zweite Brief des Apostels Paulus an die Korinther* (Freiburg: J. C. B. Mohr, 1910), 138; Plummer, 121; Strachan 92; Tasker, 71-2; Hughes, 133; Barrett 135; Bruce, 196; Martin 80, Jones, 60-7, Wolff, 87; Seyoon Kim, *The Origin of the Paul's Gospel* (Grand Rapids: Wm. B. Eerdmans, 1982), 137-268.

197) J. E. Osiander, *Commentar über den zweiten Brief Pauli and die Korinthier* (Stuttgart: Calwer, 1958) 152; H. A. W. Meyer, *Critical and Exegetical Handbook to the Epistles to the Corinthians II*, ETr. W. P. Dickson (Edinburgh: T. & T. Clark, 1879), 232; Strachan, 92; Hans Windisch, *Der zweite Korintherbrief*, MeyerK 6 (Göttingen: Vandenhoeck & Ruprecht, 1924) 139, Plummer, 120; Barrett, 134-5, 이외 다수.

198) D. W. Oostendorp, *Another Jesus: A Gospel of Jewish-Christian Superiority in II Corinthians* (Kampen: Kok, 1967); P. R. Jones, *The Apostle Paul: A Second Moses according to II Corinthians 2:14-4:7*, Xerox University Microfilms (Ann Arbor, 1973), 102-7.

다 함께 관련된다고 본다. "하나님" 께서 이 말씀을 하셨다는 것은 아마 4절의 "이 세상의 신" 이 불신자들로 하여금 그리스도의 영광의 복음의 광채를 보지 못하는 시각장애인으로 만드는 것과 대조하여 언급되었을 것이다. 믿는 자들에게 복음의 광채를 비추시는 이는 빛을 지으신 창조주 하나님이시며, 불신자들의 마음을 혼미케 하는 것은 어둠의 주관자인 이 세상의 신이 하는 일이다(행 26:18; 벧전 2:9). 창조주 하나님이 믿는 자의 구원을 주도하시고 그를 새로운 피조물로 만드신다(고후5:17).

한 가지 문제는 왜 바울이 자신의 개인의 체험을 말하면서 "우리(의) 마음(들)" (ἐν ταῖς καρδίαις ἡμῶν)이라고 복수를 썼는가이다. "우리" 는 바울을 따르는 고린도 교인들을 포함한 바울의 제자들을 나타내는 대표적 집단적 대명사이다. 그러므로 누가도 바울의 회심 체험을 사도행전에서 3번씩이나 쓰고 있다. "어떤 고린도 교회 청중은 바울의 회심 체험이 바울과 유사한 심리적 변화와 무의식적 영혼의 광채와 활동을 일으키고, 하나님의 형상을 내적으로 보게 되었을 것이다." [199] 이렇게 바울의 회심 간증이 그의 청중에게 그리스도의 내적 영광을 보게 하였을 것이다. 실제로, 3장에서 바울은 고린도 교인들이 그리스도의 영광을 보는 것을 모세의 영광을 보는 것과 대조하였다.

바울은 아마도 이런 자신의 회심 체험을 고린도 교인들에게 이미 간증했을 것이다. 그리고 바로 이런 "간증" 때문에 자찬한다는 비평을 반대자들로부터 받기도 하였을 것이다(3:1; 5:12; 참조, 고전4:16; 11:1). 그러나 그의 복음과 사역의 진정성을 증명하기 위해

---

199) Thrall, 320.

서, 그 오해의 소지를 막는 말을 미리 한 후(5절), 그의 회심 경험을 다시 언급할 수밖에 없었다고 본다. 바울은 그리스도의 영광의 광채를 분명히 보았으며, 그를 따르는 이들에게도 유사한 회심 경험이 있었거나, 아니면 그의 회심 간증을 통해서 내적 감동을 받았을 것이다. 이 결과 바울의 복음의 진정성은 바울 개인의 간증이나 그의 자찬으로 끝나지 않고 그와 동조하는 많은 증인들("우리")의 집단적 증거가되어 반대자들의 비판을 막는 효과를 갖게 된다. 이렇게 추론하면, 바울 회심 경험을 단수로 하지 않고 "우리의 마음들"이란 복수로 말한 것이 적절한 것이다.

"그리스도의 얼굴에 있는 하나님의 영광에 관한 지식"은 그리스도 중심의 계시를 가리킨다. 그리스도를 통한 구원의 복음의 진리는 하나님께서 바울에게 가르쳐 주셨다. 이외의 모든 것은 피상적인 것이며 일시적인 것이다. 그리스도 구원의 진리만이 유일무이한 성경의 진리이다. 이 진리는 하나님의 내적 조명에 의해서 깨닫게 된다. 바울이 다메섹 도상에서 받은 빛은 물론 외적인 빛이었으나 또한 내적인 빛이었다. 모든 그리스도인들이 바울과 같은 외적인 빛에 의하여 복음을 믿게 되는 것은 아니다. 그러나 바울의 눈에 비친 그 밝은 하나님의 영광의 빛은 믿는 자들의 마음을 내적인 믿음의 빛으로 빛나게 한다.

한편 "하나님의 영광의 아는 빛을 우리에게 비추셨다"(6절)는 바울의 말은 곧 다음과 같은 질문을 유발시킨다. 어떻게 바울에게 있는 그 복음의 빛이 모세의 영광의 빛과 달리 영원하다고 할 수 있는가?(3:7). 그 증거는 무엇인가? 오히려 바울에게는 그의 대적자들에게서 보이는 영광이 보이지 않지 않는가?(10:1, 7, 10; 11:14, 22, 23이하). 바울은 스스로 이점을 인식하고 4장 16절 이하에서 그의 사역의 직책의 영광은 영원하나, 오히려 외적으로 나타나지 않는 내적이고(4:16), 미래(주님의 강림 시)에 나타나는 영광이라고 말한다(5:4; 빌 3:21). 그것은 십자가의 영광이 고난과 죽음으로 가려진 것과 같다(6:4-10).

주해(4:1-6):

바울은 4장에 들어 와서 고린도 교회 반대자들에 의해서 제기된 자신의 복음과 사도직의 진정성에 대해서 매우 단호하게 방어하고 있다. 첫째로, 자신의 복음과 사도직은 하나님께로부터 직접 받은 것이며, 둘째로, 구약 성경에 기초하고 있으며(창 1장, 사 9장), 셋째로, 복음사역의 수행에 있어서도 조금도 부끄러움이 없다고 단언한다. 반대로 그를 반대하는 이들의 "복음"이야 말로 새로운 그리스도의 계시와 관련이 없는, 성경을 왜곡하는 율법주의적 복음이며, 그들의 복음 사역도 이기적이며 도덕성이 없으며, 결국 사단에게서 나온 것이라고 비판한다. 이런 바울의 복음과 사도직의 진정성의 판단기준은 오늘날 교회 지도자들에게 그대로 적용되어 판단할 수 있다.

첫째로, 오늘날 교회 지도자들이 전하는 복음이 성경적이며, 복음적인가? 복음의 중심 메시지를 전하고 있는가? 아니면 변질된 복음인가? 많은 비 복음주의적인 현대 신학자들이 현대의 합리주의나, 회의주의적 철학에 영향 받아 성경을 연구함으로 복음의 중심 내용을 가르치거나 믿고 있지 않고 있다. 복음서의 대개의 내용이 후대 교회 전승에서 자연발생적으로 진화된 것이며, 원래 예수가 실재로 한 말은 몇 개의 도덕적 윤리적 진술로 압축시켜 놓았다. 그들의 관심은 윤리적 가르침뿐이다. 이런 연구를 반대하는 복음주의적 학자들 조차 적지 않은 이들이 비복음주의적 학자들의 연구를 일일이 반대하는 일에 급급한 나머지 복음의 중심 내용인 구원에 관련된 부분을 거의 무시하고 말았다. 다시 말하면, 호교론적인 입장에서 반대자들의 의견과 싸우다가 그들이 정작 집중해야할 복음의 핵심적 내용을 충분히 밝히는 일을 등한히 여기게 되었다. 바울은 본문 2절에서 자신은 "말씀을 혼잡케 아니하고 오직 진리를 나타낸다" 고 하였다. 또 그는 "그리스도의 얼굴에 있는 하나님의 영광" 에 집중 한다고 했다.

한편 목회자들 가운데 물질주의나 세속적 낙관주의에 영향을 받아 비복음적인 설교로 사람들에게 호감을 얻고 외적 물량적 교회 확장에 힘쓰는 이들이 있다. 또 많은 목회자들의 설교는 도덕적인 것이며, 교회나 세상에서 더불어 살기에 좋은 사람이 되어야 한다는 데서 그치고 있으며, 성경이 가르치는 인간 영혼 구원의 중심 메시지를 전하지 못하고 있다.

일반 그리스도인들도 이들의 물질주의적 도덕주의적 가르침을 받아서 그리스도를 윤리적 교사로 삼아 질서 있고 안정된 개인적 사회적 삶을 이루려고 하거나, 평소에는 별 상관이 없다가 위급할 때 찾아가 호소하면 들어 주는 초자연적 존재로 믿는다. 물론 하나님은 우리로 하여금 윤리적 삶도 살게 하시고 사회도 개선하게 하시고, 위기에 처할 때 구원해 주신다. 그러나 그리스도와 나와의 진정한 내적 관계없이 이런 외적인 것들만을 추구하면 우리의 믿음은 성경적 구원 진리를 잃게 된다. 본문 6절에 바울은 불신자들의 마음은 이 세상의 신에 의해 혼미케 되었으나 하나님께서 우리의 마음을 그의 영광에 관한 지식으로 비추셨다고 했다. 이 세상의 신은 본질이 아닌 외적인 것을 믿도록 미혹한다. 그러나 하나님은 우리로 하여금 그리스도의 얼굴에 있는 하나님의 영광에 집중케 한다. 같은 맥락에 서 바울은 그리스도인은 그리스도 안에서 새로운 피조물이므로 더 이상 "육체대로" 그리스도를 이해하지 않는다고 하였다(고후 5:16-17). 그리스도를 진정 내적으로 사랑해야 한다. "육체를 따라 그리스도를 믿어서는 안 된다"는 말은 오늘 우리에게 있어서 진정한 믿음이란 머리로, 책으로, 지식적으로 예수에 대한 것을 알고 논하는 것이 아니며, 또 위기 때 가슴이 답답하여 찾게 되는 일반적 종교적 감정에서 그리스도를 믿는 것도 아니라는 것이다. 또 습관적으로 교회에 가거나 습관적으로 기도하는 것도 진정한 믿음이 아니다. 그런 것은 심리적 행동에 지나지 않는다. 오래 하던 일을 안 하면 불안하게 되는 심리적 반응일뿐이다. 이런 모든 외적 추구들이 결국 "육체를 따라 그리스도를 믿는 것"이다. 일시적, 피상적, 습관적, 믿음이다. 이런 믿음은 정도에서 빗나간 믿음이므로 진정한 믿음이라고 할 수 없다. 진정한 그리스도 신앙은 "그리스도 안"에서 그리스도와의 영적인 교제를 하는 것이다. 그리스도를 나의 영혼의 구주로 믿어야한다. 나의 죄를 구속하시기 위하여 죽으신 주님으로 믿고 사랑해야 한다. 그리스도를 나의 영원한 친구와 주님으로 모시어, 자나 깨나 병드나 건강하나 가난하나 부하나 사나 죽으나 나의 인생의 모든 육체적 영적 문제를 그와 의논하며, 그의 능력과 지혜를 찬양하고, 감사하고 기뻐하는 교제를 계속하는 것이다(요 15:14). (마치 결혼할 때 서약하는 것과 같다. 어떤 환경에서도 서로 사랑하겠다고 약속하는 것이다.) 우리는 먼저 그리스도 안에 있어야한다. "너희가 내 안에 거하고 내 말이 너희 안에 거하면 무엇이든지 원하는 대로 구하라 그리하면 이루리라"(요 16:7). 그리스도 안에 있는 사람은 그를 이용하여 자기가 원하는 것을 이루는 사람이 아니라 그리스도에게 순복하고 그를 섬기며 그가 원하는 것을 이루기 위해 힘쓰는 사람이다. 이런 사람은 "사나 죽으나 우리가 주의 것이로다."(롬 14:8b)라고 말할 수 있다.

그러므로 바울처럼 우리는 우리의 신앙의 초점이 "그리스도의 얼굴에 있는 하나님의 영광"에 있는지, 아닌지를 늘 점검해야 한다.

둘째로, 바울의 복음은 자신의 경험에 근거한 주관적이고 사사로운 것이 아니라 구약 성경에 근거한 복음이었다. 바울의 대표적 서신인 로마서에서조차 1장 초두에서부터 복음의 구약적 근거를 제시하고 있다. 성경 연구가들은 자주 자신들이 아는 학문방법으로만 복음을 설명하거나, 성경의 지엽적인 문제나 주변적인 배경연구에 몰두하면서 성경 자체가 말하는 중심 메시지는 등한시한다. 설교자들은 자신들의 주관적 체험을 자신들의 하나님의 종 된 증표로 자랑삼아 내세우면서 정작 성경 말씀 자체를 등한시하는 경우가 있다. 그러나 신학자든 설교자든 이런 "이 세상신의 미혹"에서 벗어나서 성경이 가르치는 복음의 중심 메시지에 집중해야 한다.

셋째로, 복음 사역자들의 도덕성 문제이다. 복음 사역자들은 그들이 전하는 복음의 성격에 걸맞게 도덕적 완전성을 유지해야 한다. 그렇지 않고는 거룩한 복음을 전파하는 사역자로서의 자격을 상실하게 된다. 세속적 말이나 사고나, 행동을 삼가고 거룩한 사역자로서의 품위를 지켜야한다. 무엇보다 깨끗한 양심을 가져야 한다(딤전 3:9). 복음전도자들이 도덕적인 부끄러움을 가지고서 많은 이들 앞에서 거룩한 복음을 전할 수 없다. 그리스도의 영광을 바라보며 세상적 탐욕이나 세상의 모든 가치의 영광을 초월해야 한다. 이런 생활을 위해서는 사역자들은 자주 세상과 동 떨어져서 기도와 예배 생활에 전무하도록 힘쓰는 것이 좋다.

v. 바울의 사역의 그리스도적 특성 - 외적 영광이 없는 고난의 사역(4:7-15).

본문:

> 7. 우리가 이 보배를 질그릇에 가졌으니 이는 능력의 심히 큰 것이 하나님에게서 오고(하나님께 있고) 우리에게서 오지(우리에게 있지) 아니함을 알게 하려 함이라. 8. 우리가 사방으로 우겨쌈을 당하여도 짓눌리지(싸이지) 아니하며 어려움(답답한 일)을 당하여도 낙심하지 아니하며, 9. 핍박을 받아도 버린 바 되지 아니하며 거꾸러뜨림을 당하여도 망하지 아니하고, 10. 우리가 항상 예수의 죽음을(예수 죽인 것을) 몸에 짊어짐은 예수의 생명이 또한 (도) 우리의 몸에 나타나게 하려 함이라. 11. 우리가 살아있는 사람들로서(우리 산자가) 항상 예수를 위하여 죽음에 넘기움은 예수의 생명이 또한 우리 죽을 육체에 나타나게 하려 함이니라. 12. 그런즉 사망은 우리 안에서 역사하고, 생명은 너희 안에서 하느니라. 13. (기록한 바) "내가 믿는 고로 말하였다"라고 기록한 것과 같은 뜻으로(한 것 같이) 우리도 믿는 고로 또한 말하노라. 14 .(즉) 주 예수를 다시 살리신 이가 예수와 함께 우리도 다시 살리사 너희와 함께 그 앞에 서게 하실 줄을 아노니, 15. (이) 모든 것을 너희를 위하여 하는 것은 은혜가 보다 더 많은 사람의 감사함으로 말미암아 (더하여) 넘쳐서 하나님께 영광을 돌리게 하려 함이라.

본문 비평:

1. 11절에서 ἀεί("항상")이 대개의 사본에서 쓰였으나 p^{46} F G syr Iren Tert Ambrosiaster에는 εἰ("만일")이 나타난다. 두 글자가 유사해서 나타난 차이라고 본다. 후자로 하면, "만일 우리가 살아

있는 사람들로서 … "라고 번역될 수 있고 뜻의 차이는 별로 나타나지 않는다.

2. 13절의 κατὰ τὸ γεγραμμένον("기록한 바") 은 본문에 유일하게 나타난 구약 인용 양식이다.[200)]

3. 14절의 τὸν κύριον ᾿Ιησοῦν("주 예수")는 대개의 사본에서 나타난다. 그러나 더 짧은 ᾿Ιησοῦν(예수)가 p[46] B 33 그리고 라틴 사본들에서 나타난다. κύριον (주)은 경건심에서 후대에 덧 부쳐진 것으로 본다.[201)]

내용 개요:

계속해서 바울은 자신의 사도직의 정당성에 대해서 증언한다. 앞에서는 바울의 복음과 복음 사역의 신적 기원과 도덕적 진정성이 중심 주제라면, 본문에서는 바울의 사도직 수행에 있어서의 그리스도의 십자가적 고난의 증거가 중심 주제이다. 바울은 그리스도의 사도임을 주장하면서 자신과 그리스도와의 밀접한 관계를 설명한다. 바울은 자신이 빌립보서 1장 21절에서 같이 그리스도와 "존재론적 일치"(존재의 일치는 아님)를 말하면서 자신이 그리스도의 특성을 드러내는 진정한 그리스도의 사도라고 자찬한다

200) Bultmann은 A. Deissmann, *Bible Studies*(250)을 언급하면서 법적 양식이라고 하나(123), 이미 랍비 문헌에 많이 나타나는 양식이다. 참조, J. Bonsirven, *Exégèse rabbinique et exégèse paulinienne* (Paris: Beauchesne et ses fils, 1939), 32; G. Schrenk, *TDNT* I:749.

201) Metzger, *Textual Commentary*, ad loc.

(4:7-15; 6:4-10; 12:9, 10, 13:4, 9). 그 특성은 사람들을 위한 고난과 희생의 사역이다. 앞에서는 그리스도의 영광의 복음을 전하는 사도 바울의 영광스러움을 논했으나 본문에서는 오히려 그리스도의 고난에 동참하는 비영광적인 사도 바울의 모습이다. 영광의 복음의 사역자라면 왜 고난을 받느냐 복음 자체는 영광이나, 그 복음을 전파하는 이는 그리스도가 고난을 받으신 것처럼 마땅히 그의 고난에 참여해야한다. 이것이 그리스도의 사역을 통해 나타난 하나님의 뜻이다. 바울의 사역에 나타나는 고난과 희생의 증거들이 그의 사도직의 그리스도적 진정성을 보여주고 있지 않은가? (6:4-10; 11:23-33, 12:5-10, 16; 참조, 고전15:10; 갈4:19; 6:17; 빌3:10; 골1:24). 바로 얼마 전 2차 방문 시(즉, 55년 여름)에도 고린도 교인들 앞에서 반대자들로부터 어떤 모욕을 당하지 않았는가?(2:1, 서론 "저작 동기," 부분 참조).바울의 적들에게는 이런 고난의 흔적들이 없지 않은가? 자신의 유익을 제쳐두고 고린도 교인들을 위해 희생하는 바울이야 말로 진정한 그리스도의 모범적 사도가 아닌가? 이런 가르침은 고린도후서에서 바울의 사도직을 변명하는 중심 진리이며, 바울이 주님으로부터 받은 계시인, "내 능력은 약한 데서 강하게 된다" (12:9)는 진리를 가리키고 있다.

주석:

7 "우리가 이 보배를 질그릇에 가졌으니 이는 능력의 심히 큰 것이 하나님에게서 오고(하나님께 있고) 우리에게서 오지(우리에게 있지) 아니함을 알게 하려 함이라" ("Εχομεν δὲ τὸν θησαυρὸν τοῦτον ἐν ὀστρακίνοις σκεύεσιν, ἵνα ἡ ὑπερβολὴ τῆς δυνάμεως ᾖ τοῦ θεοῦ καὶ μὴ ἐξ ἡμῶν). 7절

에서는 6절에서 바울이 목격한 영광의 그리스도와는 대조적으로 바울의 현실적 사역의 고통을 열거한다. 영광의 복음을 전하는 전파자로서 바울은 고난을 받는 자임을 토로하고 있다. "이 보배"(τὸν θησαυρὸν τοῦτον)는 복음, 또는 하나님의 영광에 대한 지식을 가리킨다. 4절의 "그리스도의 영광의 복음의 광채"나 6절의 "그리스도의 얼굴에 있는 하나님의 영광을 아는 빛"과 관련되어 "이" 보배라고 말했을 것이다. 어떤 이들은 1절의 "직분"을 가리킨다고 한다.[202] 본문에서 바울은 자신의 사역이나 복음을 변명하고 있음으로 어느 쪽으로 보더라도 의미의 차이는 없으나, "질 그릇"이 바울 자신의 존재나 바울의 사역을 가리킨다고 보면, "이 보배"는 사역 보다는 그리스도의 복음을 가리킨다고 본다. "질 그릇"(ἐν ὀστρακίνοις σκεύεσιν)은 고난 받는 바울 자신 또는 바울의 사역을 가리킨다. 본문과 같은 문맥에 있는 4:16절의 바울의 "겉 사람"에 해당되는 말이다. 고린도 후서에서 바울은 자신을 변명하면서 자신에 대한 적극적인 표현과 부정적인 표현을 모두 사용하고 있다(1:12; 2:15; 3:6, 9; 4:1-6, 16; 5:18; 6:4; 7:2; 10:4, 8, 10; 11:2, 10, 22-12:10 등). 이런 표현들은 바울 자신의 자기이해를 나타내는 것일 수도 있고, 반대자들의 바울에 대한 비난을 나타내는 것일 수도 있다. 영광의 복음의 광채와는 대조적으로 복음 전도자 바울의 존재는 외적으로 너무나 보잘 것 없이 초라해서 질그릇에 비유되었다. 그러나 질그릇이라도 보배를 담고 있으면 귀한 것이듯이 약한 모습의 바울이야 말로 진정한 그리스도의 사도라는 역설적 의미가 있다. 그의 고난의 사역으로 말미암아 고린도 인들이 구원을 받았

202) Bultmann, 114; M. Rissi, *Studien zum zweiten Korintherbrief*, ATANT 56 (Zurich: Zwingli Verlag, 1969), 45.

다. 더구나 반대자들의 공격으로 바울의 외적 존재는 해체되고 더욱 초라하게 보인다. 한편 반대자들은 겉으로는 화려하나 실제로는 거짓 선지자들임을 암시하고 있다(5:12; 10:7, 10; 11:13-15).

바울의 "질그릇과 보배"의 비유적 표현과 유사한 표현들이 당시 희랍사회에 있었다. 희랍시대에 어떤 가치 있는 것과 질그릇이 자주 비교된 증거가 있다. 에픽테터스(Epictetus)는 어떤 사람과의 논쟁에서 그의 그릇은 황금이나, 그의 말은 질그릇이라고 비꼬았다.[203] 푸르타크(Plutarch)는 기원전 167년에 행해진 전쟁승리 행진에서 많은 은화를 질그릇에 담아 운반했다고 기록하고 있다.[204] 또 어떤 로마 황제의 딸이 지혜로우나 매우 못생긴 유대인 랍비(Jehoshuah ben Hananiah)를 가리켜, "천한 그릇에 들어있는 영화로운 지혜"라고 했다(*Ta`an.*, 7a).[205] 또 랍비 전승에, "포도주가 질그릇에 담겨져야 하듯이 율법은 겸손한 사람이 지킬 수 있다"는 말이 있다(*Sifre Deut.* 48).[206] 이 말이 본문의 바울의 말과 가장 흡사하다. 어떤 이들은 질그릇이 희랍시대에 인간 육체에 비유되었으므로 본문에서 바울도 그의 연약한 육체를 가리킨다고 보았다고 한다.[207] 맨슨(T. W. Manson)도 고린도나 팔레스틴에서 발견되는 작은 질그릇 등잔을 전도자들을 연약한 육체에, 그리고 등잔불을 복음의 광채에 비교하였다.[208] 그러나 본문에서 바울의 고통

---

203) Plummer, 127.

204) Aemilius, 32; Hughes 136.

205) C. Maurer, σκεῦος, *TDNT* VII, 360.

206) Barrett 138 재인용.

207) Plummer 126-7; Meyer 235; Windisch 142.

208) T. W. Manson, "2 Cor 2:14-17: Suggestions towards an Exegesis" in *Studia Paulina*, ed. by J. Sevenster and W. C. van Unnik, 156.

은 육체적 고통뿐만 아니라(10절), 정신적 고통도 있으므로(8절), 질그릇을 육체적이라고 한정짓기 어렵다. 바울의 사역에서 겪는 모든 존재론적 고통을 가리킨다.

한편 보배와 질그릇 비유가 구약에서 왔다고도 볼 수 있다. 예레미야애가 4장 2절에서 시온의 아들들이 한때는 값진 황금이었으나 이제는 질항아리로 전락되었다고 한다.[209] 그리고 예레미야 19장 11절에 예루살렘과 거민을 질그릇처럼 깨뜨린다는 말이 있고 이사야 30장 14절에도 유사한 말이 나온다. 또 예레미야 22장 28절에도 비슷한 말이 나온다. 질그릇은 질이 낮고, 깨지기 쉬우므로 일시적이란 뜻이 있다.

이런 전래적인 질그릇의 의미를 바울의 사역에 적용하여 부족하고 보잘 것 없는 사역을 가리켰을 것이다. 그러나 바울이 은밀히 강조하고 있는 것은 겉으로는 보잘 것 없는 그의 사역이 귀한 가치가 있는 복음을 전하고 있다는 사실이다. 나아가 그의 연약함과 부족함이 오히려 보배로운 복음 전파를 위해 필요하다는 점이다. 외적으로 약한 바울의 사도직으로 말미암아 하나님의 능력이 나타나게 된다는 점이다. 하나님의 능력이 그의 약함을 극복하고 나타난다는 것이다. "능력의 심히 큰 것이 하나님에게서 (오고) 우리에게서 (오지) 아니함을 알게 하려 함이라." "오고"라는 말이 "하나님"(τοῦ θεοῦ)과 "우리에게서"(ἐξ ἡμῶν)가 각기 기원(起源)을 나타내는 속격(genetive of origin)이거나 기원을 나타내는 부사구와 함께 의미를 더욱 분명히 해주기 때문이다.

이런 적극적 의미를 뒷받침하는 질그릇의 적극적 의미도 있다.

---

209) Plummer 127; Furnish 253.

스픽(C. Spicq)은 고대 사회에서 매우 비싼 고급 질그릇 제품들이 많았음을 지적했다.[210] 하기야 우리나라 고려청자나 이조백자 가운데 상류사회가 쓰던 고급제품들이 있다. 꼴란쥐(J. F Collange)도 성경에서 질그릇이 명예와 존귀, 하나님의 특별한 선택의 의미로 쓰인 경우를 들었다(사 10:15; 54:16 이하; 렘 18:1-11).[211] 바울은 하나님이 택하신 이스라엘의 고난 받는 종들의 반열에 서있는 명예로운 자신의 위치를 암시하고 있다는 것이다.

바울이 이런 질그릇의 부정적이면서도 적극적인 의미가 있음에 착안하여 그의 연약함과 사도적 권위를 동시에 암시하고 있다고 볼 수 있다. 그러나 역시 부정적 의미가 더 지배적이고 표면에 나타나 있다. "능력이 하나님에게서 오고 자신에게서 오는 것이 아니라"는 말과 이어 나오는 연약함에 대한 표현들 때문이다.

연약한 인간을 통해서 신의 능력이 나타난다는 말도 희랍 시대에 쓰인 것이다.[212] 바울은 동시대 독자들에게 자신 보다 하나님의 능력에 그 강조점을 두기 위해서 이런 동시대에서 쓰인 말을 이용했을 수도 있다. 그러나 무엇보다 위에서 본 유대전통과 구약에서의 약한 질그릇(그리고 선택받은 귀한 그릇)의 비유적 의미, 무엇보다 그리스도의 십자가에서의 죽음과 부활에서 약함과 강함의 대조점을 찾은 것이 분명하다. 다음 절에 나오는 그리스도의 죽음과 생명

---

210) C. Spicq, "L'image sportive de 2 Corinthiens 4, 7-9." *Ephemerides theologicae lovanienses,* 14 (1937), 210.

211) J. F. Collange, 146.

212) Plato, Ion 534 C-D, Windisch 인용 143, Bultmann 인용 115; Epictetus, *Diss.* II 1.39; Senca, *Ep.* 71:26; J. T. Fitzgerald, *Cracks in an Earthen Vessel: An Examination of the Catalogüs of Hardships in the Corinthain Correspondence*, SBLDS 99 (Atlanta: Scholars Press, 1988) 166-7, 171.

에 동참하는 바울의 사역에서 이런 대조점이 분명히 나타난다. 실제로 고린도후서 전체에서 바울은 그의 사역의 진정성을 그리스도의 죽음과 부활에 비추어 증거하고 있다. "우리가 저의 안에서 약하나 너희를 향하여 하나님의 능력으로 저와 함께 살리라"(13:4).

8. "우리가 사방으로 우겨쌈을 당하여도 <u>짓눌리지</u> (싸이지) 아니하며 <u>어려움</u>(답답한 일)을 당하여도 낙심하지 아니하며… "(**ἐν παντὶ θλιβόμενοι ἀλλ᾽ οὐ στενοχωρούμενοι, ἀπορούμενοι ἀλλ᾽ οὐκ ἐξαπορούμενοι,**). 8절부터 바울은 질그릇같이 연약한 자신과 자신의 어려운 처지를 말하면서 동시에 그를 도우시는 하나님의 능력과 구원을 증거한다. 그의 사역에서 십자가 같은 죽음과 같은 존재해체의 괴로운 경험들이 많지만, 부활과 같은 새로운 존재형성의 기쁜 경험들이 하나님의 특별한 구원 역사로 말미암아 나타난다는 사실을 열거함으로써 자신의 사도직의 진정성을 증거한다. "우리가 사방으로 우겨쌈을 당하여도 <u>짓눌리지</u> 아니하며" 바울 자신이 그의 사역의 능력의 근거가 아니라, 그는 그 능력을 하나님에게서 받았다(10:8; 12:9; 13:10). 그의 외모는 전혀 품위가 없었다(10:7, 10). 그러나 바울은 그런 외모에 의해 그의 사역이 좌우되지 않고, 오히려 하나님의 도우심에 의해 승리하고 있음을 알고 있었다.

ἐν παντι(앤 판티)를 뒤에 오는 "에워 쌈" (**θλιβόμενοι**)이란 말의 의미에 맞추어 "사방으로" 라고 번역해도 가능하나 문자적으로 "매사에" 또는 "모든 일 마다" 에 라고 번역하여서 이어 나오는 바울의 고난과 하나님의 구원 능력의 대조들을 가리킨다고 볼 수 있다[213].

213) Thrall, 327.

θλιβόμενοι(스리보메노이)를 "우리가 에워쌈을 당하여도"라고 번역할 수 있으나 원래 "압박을 당하다", 또는 "괴로움을 당하다"의 뜻이다. 고통 중에 하나님께 충성하는 시편 기자가 같은 표현을 자주 썼다(3:2. LXX; 12:5; 22:5; 34:19). 환난(θλῖψις)이라는 명사와 고통(στενοχωρία)이라는 명사는 원래 헬라 사회에서나 구약에서 자주 함께 쓰였다.[214] 바울은 6장 4절과 12장 10절에서도 이 두말을 함께 쓰고 있다. "짓눌리다"(στενοχωρέω)는 원래 "피할 곳이 없다, 제한되다"의 뜻인데 "눌려 부서지다"의 뜻도 있다. 여기서는 수동태 분사로 나타나 외부 힘에 의해 압력을 받는 것을 말한다. 같은 말이 6장 12절에서 쓰인다: "너희가 우리 안에서 좁아진 것이 아니라." 바울의 이런 말들은 최근에 자신이 고린도 교회에서 당한 경험을 암시한다고 본다.[215] 고린도 교회에서 사도로서 수모를 겪었으나(2:1), 하나님께서 고린도 교회에서 그의 사도적 권위를 다시 회복시키셨고(7:6) 고린도 교회에 대한 그의 사랑을 회복시켜 주셨다(6:11-13).

"어려움을 당해도 낙심하지 아니하며"(ἀπορούμενοι ἀλλ̓ οὐκ ἐξαπορούμενοι). 두 동사가 반대어 이지만 결국 같은 말로 되어 있다. 개역한글성경에 ἀπορούμενοι(아포루메노이)를 "답답한 일"로 번역했으나 "어려움을 당해도"라고 해야 옳다. 바울은 어려움을 당해도 하나님의 도우심으로 낙심치 않았다. ἐξαπορούμενοι ("낙심한다")는 말은 희귀한 동사로 70인역 시편 87편 16절에 나오고 고린도후서 1장 8절에 나올 뿐이다. 동의어로

214) Epictetus, Diss. I. 25, 26; 욥 18:11; 신 28:53이하; 사 8:22; 30:6; 에 1:1, LXX.

215) Martin, 86.

(οὐκ) ἐγκακοῦμεν(엥카쿠멘, "우리는 낙심하지 [않는다]")이 4장 1절과 16절에 나온다. 고후1:8에는 "소망이 끊어지고"라고 번역되었으나 같은 의미다. 수동태이나 우리나라 말에서 "낙심한다"는 능동태형이나 "낙심된다"는 수동태형이나 뜻의 차이가 없으므로 능동태로 썼다. 바울이 어려움들을 당해서 심지어 잠시 "낙심이 되는 경우"(1:8; 2:13)에도 궁극적으로 또는 전적으로 낙심하지 않는 것은 하나님의 능력이 바울과 함께 하는 증거이다. 고린도후서 1장 8절에서 바울은 "소망이 끊어져서" 철저히 낙심한 것같이 보이나, 그 것은 잠시 인간적인 차원의 낙심이었을 것이다. 바울은 어려움 중에 낙심하기도 했으나, 하나님을 의지함(1:9)과 그리스도의 부활의 능력이 나타남(4:7-15; 6:4-10)과 "약한 중에 강하게 하시는 하나님의 역사하심"(12:9)으로 그 낙심이 오래 가지는 않았다(1:9).

9. "핍박을 받아도 버린 바 되지 아니하며 거꾸러뜨림을 당하여도 망하지 아니하고…." (διωκόμενοι ἀλλ' οὐκ ἐγκαταλειπόμενοι, καταβαλλόμενοι ἀλλ' οὐκ ἀπολλύμενοι,) 9절에서, "핍박을 받아도 버린바 되지 아니하며"의 "핍박을 받아도"(διωκόμενοι)는 동사 διώκειν(디오케인, "핍박하다")의 수동태 분사로 나타난다. 이 말은 자주 성도들의 핍박과 관련되어 사용된다(막 4:17; 롬 8:35; 살후 1:4; 고후 12:10). 이 말이 앞에서 말한 "에워쌈"이나 "어려움 당하다"란 말들 보다 더 심각한 고난을 가리킨다고 할 수 있다. 이렇게 함으로 바울은 그의 고난의 심각성을 점증적으로 알리고 있다. 그렇지 않다면 이런 고난의 열거의 의미가 별로 없다. 여기서도 바울은 이런 핍박의 힘이 하나님의 힘을 능가하지 못함을 증거한다.

"버린바 되지 아니하며" (ἐγκαταλείπειν)은 무엇에 의해 버림받은 것을 뜻하는데(딤후 4:10, 16) 하나님에 의해 버림받은 것을 뜻하는 데도 쓰였다(막 15:34; 마 27:46; 행전 2:27). 핍박 중에도 하나님이 바울과 함께 하셨다.

8절과 9절의 고난들은 결국 하나님께서 극복하게 해주셨다. 7절에서 언급했듯이 질그릇처럼 약해서 깨지기 쉬운 사도 바울은 자신의 능력이 아닌 하나님의 능력으로 말미암아 그의 복음 사역을 감당해왔다. 바울은 여기서 하나님의 능력의 위대함과 그 능력이 자신의 사역에 함께 하였음을 증거하기 위해 자신의 연약함과 자신이 당한 고난을 한껏 강조하고 있다.

10. "우리가 항상 예수의 죽음을(예수 죽인 것을) 몸에 짊어짐은 예수의 생명이 또한 (도) 우리의 몸에 나타나게 하려 함이라" (πάντοτε τὴν νέκρωσιν τοῦ Ἰησοῦ ἐν τῷ σώματι περιφέροντες, ἵνα καὶ ἡ ζωὴ τοῦ Ἰησοῦ ἐν τῷ σώματι ἡμῶν φανερωθῇ). 10절은 8절과 9절에서 말한 바울의 고난을 그리스도적으로 해석하는 것이다. 바울은 그리스도의 사도로서 사역하므로, 그의 모든 고난은 그리스도의 고난의 의미, 즉 남을 구원하는 의미가 있는 것이다.

"항상" (πάντοτε)은 바울의 고난의 사역을 수행하는 동안을 말한다. 위에서 말한 역경들을 당하는 동안 바울은 예수의 죽으심을 몸에 짊어지고 다녔다. "예수의 죽으심을 몸에 짊어짐" (τὴν νέκρωσιν τοῦ Ἰησοῦ ἐν τῷ σώματι περιφέροντες)은 첫째로, 바울은 예수님처럼 고통당했다는 뜻으로 볼 수 있다. 바울은 여기서 예수님께서 제자들에게, "아무든지 나를 따라 오려거든 자기를 부인하고 자기 십자가를 지고 나를 좇을 것이니라"(막 8:34)의 말씀을 생각했을 것이다.[216] 물론 여기서의 고통은 외부에서 억지로 주어진 것이며 바울 스스로 자청하여 고난을 받는 것은 아니지만 여전히 그리스도의 제자로서 피할 수 없는 고난을 받는다고 생각했다고 본다. 둘째로, 바울의 고난이 예수님의 죽음과 관련된다고 볼 수 있다. 그리스도의 고난은 그의 죽음의 준비 과정, 또는 반대로 그의 죽음은 그의 고난의 절정이다. 바울의 고난은 그리스도의 고난의 참여이며, 나아가 그 고난의 절정인 죽음의 준비과정에 해당되는 것이다. 바울의 신학에 의하면, 믿는 자는 그리스도와 이미 하나가 되었다(롬 6:3-6). 그러므로 믿는 자가 고난 받는 것은 그리스도가 죽으신 죽음의 고통을 의미한다. 믿는 자는 고난을 받으며, 고난의 의미를 그리스도의 죽음과 부활에 비추어 생각한다. 그리스도인은 그의 고난을 통해서 그의 겉 사람은 죽고(16절) 속사람이 부활의 생명을 가지고 나타나는 것이다. 물론 여기서는 속사람의 부활은 언급되지 않고 다만 고난을 통해 남에게 예수의 부활의 생명을 나타내는 것이 주제다. 고난을 통해서 바울은 자기의 연약함을 생각하고 또한 과거에 자신을 의지한 자기의 옛 사람을 생각하며, 이제 구원의 새 시대에서 자신의 약함과 자기중심적 옛 사람이 그리스도의 죽음과 함께 죽은 것을 믿는다. 여기서 이런 로마서 6장의 새사람과 옛사람의 대조적 의미가 분명하지는 않더라도 16절의 겉 사람 속사람의 대조와 5장 초두의 부활의 새로운 소망에 대한 언급을 고려할 때, 이런 의미가 적어도 "예수 죽으심을 짊어진다"는 말의 배경에 있는 줄 안다.

---

216) Bruce, 197.

이런 고난과 죽음의 의미와 함께, 보다 현재의 본문의 주제에 충실하게 생각해서, 10절에서 바울은 예수의 사도로서 과거의 예수의 죽으심을 그의 사역 가운데 받는 고통을 통하여 현실화하는 사도적 책임을 말하고 있다고 본다.[217] 바울은 십자가에서 죽은 그리스도를 전하는 사도답게 그리스도의 죽으심을 자신이 현재 받는 고난을 통해 현실적으로 나타내고 증거하므로서 세상 사람들이 그리스도께서 죽으신 대속적 죽음의 의미를 고난을 받으며 증거하는 바울을 통해서 실감케하고 감동받게 하고 나아가 회개하고 그리스도를 믿게 해야 하는 책임이 있다. 물론 바울이 그 자신이 죽으신 그리스도의 실제 현현(顯現)으로 까지 생각한다는 증거는 없다(참조, 갈 6:17). 또한 그의 고난을 그리스도의 고난과 동일시한다는 증거도 없다.[218] 그러나 그의 고난이 그리스도의 고난을 나타낸다는 의미는 있다. 바울은 독자들이 그의 고난의 삶의 모습들 가운데 그리스도의 죽음에 비길 만한 것들이 있음을 보기

---

217) Thrall, 334; Barnett, 236, 주, 46; A. T. Hanson, *The Paradox of the Cross in the Thought of St Paul*, JSNTSS 17 (Sheffield: JSOT, 1987), 49; J. Kremer, *2. Korintherbrief* (Stuttgart: Verlag Katholisches Bibelwerk, 1990), 47.

218) S. J. Hafemann, *Sufferring and Ministry, in the Spirit: Paul's Defense of Hid Ministry in 2 Corinthians 2:41-3:3* (Grand Rapids: Eerdmans, 1990), 66; J. W. McCant, *2 Corinthians* (Sheffield: Sheffield Academic Press, 1999), 46; S. Wan, *Power and Weakness: The Second Letter of Paul to the Corinthians* (Harrisburg, Pa.: Trinity Press International, 2000), 80; C. B. Cousar, *Theology of the Cross* (Minnneapolis: Augusburg Fortress, 1990), 152. 이들은 바울의 고난을 예수의 고난과 일치하는 것으로 본다. 이에 대한 다른 표현들을 보라. T. B. Savage, *Power through Weakness: Paul's Understanding of the Christian Ministry in 2 Corinthians* (New York: Cambridge University Press, 1996), 173(예수의 고난의 "참여"); J. F. Collange, 151(예수의 고난에의 "동화"); Barnett, 236(예수의 고난의 "확장").

를 원하고 있다. 바울 사도는 그의 고난의 사역을 통해서 그리스도의 죽음을 그렸다. 그의 고난의 사역은 그리스도의 죽음의 복제이다. 그리스도의 죽음이 그의 사역 가운데 다시 재현되고 있다. 바울은 자주 자신이 그리스도를 대신하여 그의 사역을 대행하고 있다고 생각한다. 그러므로 5장 20절에서 바울은 그리스도를 대신하여 사신이 되어 고린도 교인들에게 하나님과의 화해를 권면한다. 또 믿는 자는 그리스도의 죽으심을 본받아 그리스도와 함께 죽고 또 그리스도의 부활을 본받아 함께 산다고 한다(롬 6:5; 빌 3:10-11). 또 그 스스로 그리스도를 본받는 자가되었고 남들도 그렇게 되기를 권한다(고전 11:1; 살전 1:6;). 물론 여기서의 바울의 고난은 자발적으로 선택한 고난이 아니라 외부에서 온 고난이다. 그러나 외부에서 오는 고난을 그리스도의 제자로서 달게 받을 때 자발적인 고난으로 그 성격이 변하는 것이다.

복음은 그리스도의 죽음뿐만 아니라 그의 부활을 선포한다. 그러므로 사도 바울의 "그리스도의 죽음 만들기" 작업은 "그리스도의 부활 만들기 작업"과 병행되어야 한다. 그렇지 못하면 바울의 사도직의 진정성을 증명할 수 없다. 그러므로 καί(또한, 역시)로 시작되는 10절 하반절에서 바울 자신이 예수의 죽음과 함께 예수의 생명도 나타내야한다는 것을 강조한다. 여기서 바울은 예수의 생명을 나타내는 것이 자기가 예수의 죽으심을 짊어지는 목적임을 밝힌다. "예수의 생명이 또한 우리 죽을 육체에 나타나게 하려 함이니라"(ἡ ζωὴ τοῦ Ἰησοῦ ἐν τῷ σώματι ἡμῶν φανερωθῇ). 이 예수의 생명은 14절에서 말하는 미래의 부활이 아니라, 그 미래의 부활의 능력이 현실적으로 그의 사역 가운데 나타나는 것을 말한다. 곧 8절 9절에서 지적한 바울의 고난의 사역 가운데서 체험한 승리가 현실적 부활 생명에 해당하는 것이다. 엄밀히 말하면 부활 생명은 예수를 일으키신 하나님의 능력이다. 같은 하나님의 능력이 바울과 함께 하고 있는 것이다. 이런 의미에서 바울의 연약함과 고난은 부활 생명이 나타나기 위한 전제 조건이 된다.

앞서 지적한 대로 로마서 6장과 또 빌립보서 1장, 3장의 믿는 자와 그리스도와의 존재론적 일치(존재적 일치는 아님) 신학에 의하여 바울은 10절에서 그의 고난의 경험과 승리를 그리스도의 죽음과 부활과 밀접히 연결시키고 있다(6:4-10; 11:23-28; 12:9, 10; 13:5). 그는 그의 사역 가운데서 그리스도를 대신 나타내고 있다. 특히 "나타내게 하려 함이라"(φανερωθῇ)는 말이 11절과 5장10, 11절에 계속 나타나 이런 의미를 뒷받침한다. 그리고 바울 사도의 사도직의 정당성을 주장하는 전체 문맥도 이를 지지한다.

11. "우리가 살아있는 사람들로서(우리 산자가) 항상 예수를 위하여 죽음에 넘기움은 예수의 생명이 또한 우리 죽을 육체에 나타나게 하려 함이니라"(ἀεὶ γὰρ ἡμεῖς οἱ ζῶντες εἰς θάνατον παραδιδόμεθα διὰ Ἰησοῦν, ἵνα καὶ ἡ ζωὴ τοῦ Ἰησοῦ φανερωθῇ ἐν τῇ θνητῇ σαρκὶ ἡμῶν). 11절은 대체로 10절의 반복이다. 10절에서 논한 바와 같이 그의 사역은 그리스도의 고난을 나타내고 또한 부활을 나타낸다. "우리가 살아있는 사람들로서 항상 예수를 위하여 죽음에 넘기움은 예수의 생명이 또한 우리 죽을 육체에 나타나게 하려 함이니라." "살아있는 사람들로서"(οἱ ζῶντες)는 엄연히 살아있는 사람들로서 생명 대신 늘 죽음에 직면해야하는 고통을 강조하기 위해 쓴 말이다. "죽음에 넘기움"

(εἰς θάνατον παραδιδόμεθα)에서 παραδίδωμι("넘기다")는 복음서의 예수님의 수난 기사에서 쓰인 말이다.[219] 바울은 다른 데서도 이 말을 쓰고 있다(롬 4:25; 8:32; 고전 11:23; 갈 2:20). 특히 고린도전서 11장 23절에서는 예수의 최후 만찬의 전승을 직접 언급하면서 쓰고 있다. 어쩌면 여기서 바울이 복음서 전승에 속한 이 말을 의식적으로 쓰면서 자신의 고난을 그리스도의 수난과 연결시키고 있다고 생각할 수 있다.[220] "넘기움"(παραδιδόμεθα)은 수동태이므로 주어는 하나님이라고 본다. 하나님이 바울을 고난에 넘기시는 것이다. 그렇다고 이런 고난이 비자발적이라고 무시할 필요는 없다. 앞서 지적한 바와 같이 제자들이 당하는 모든 고난을 제자들은 그리스도의 고난에 참여하는 것으로 기쁘게 받아들였다(행 5:41). "예수를 위하여"(διὰ Ἰησοῦν)는 "예수 때문에"라고 번역할 수 있다. 바울은 자신의 잘못 때문에 고난을 당하는 것이 아니라 사도로서 그리스도의 고난에 참여해야 하기 때문이다. 그의 고난은 사도적 고난이다. 그 고난의 목적(또는 결과)은(는) "예수의 생명"(ζωὴ τοῦ Ἰησοῦ)이 "우리 죽을 육체"(ἐν τῇ θνητῇ σαρκὶ ἡμῶν)에 나타나게 하려 함이다. 10절에서는 단순히 "우리의 몸"(σαρκὶ ἡμῶν)이라고 말 한 것을 여기서는 보다 강하게 "우리 죽을 육체"로 표현하고 있다. 죽을 육체는 질그릇 같은 약한 존재를 의미하며 동시에 8절과 9절에서 말하는 바울의 고난 받는 사역 전체를 의미한다. 고난의 사역의 결과 그리스도의 생명이 나타난다.

---

219) 막 9:31; 10:33; 14:18, 21; 마 17:22; 19:18; 26:21; 눅 18:32.

220) Thrall, 336.

12. "그런즉 사망은 우리 안에서 역사하고, 생명은 너희 안에서 하느니라." 12절에서 바울은 그의 희생적인 사역이 고린도 교회 교인들을 위한 것임을 밝힌다(ὥστε ὁ θάνατος ἐν ἡμῖν ἐνεργεῖται, ἡ δὲ ζωὴ ἐν ὑμῖν.). "그런즉 죽음은 우리 안에서 역사하고, 생명은 너희 안에서 하느니라." 이 말은 아이러니하지만, 기독교 복음의 핵심적 내용이다. 바울은 그리스도처럼 중보자로서 고린도 교인들을 구원하기 위해 대신 죽을 고난을 받는다. 바울의 사역은 그리스도의 중보 사역의 재현이다. 바울의 고난의 사역을 통해서 그리스도의 부활의 생명이 고린도 교인들에게 역사하게 되는 것이다. 겉으로 보기에 바울의 사역은 열매 없는 죽음의 사역 같이 보이지만 실제로는 자기를 희생하여 남을 구원하는 그리스도의 생명의 사역이다(12:15; 13:7, 9). 바울의 사역에 대한 대적자들의 비난을 그리스도의 죽음과 부활이라는 하나님의 신비한 구원역사에 비추어서 그 진정성을 설명하고 있다. 여기서 우리는 이런 바울의 희생적 사역의 동기를 분명히 짚고 넘어가야 한다. 그것은 죄인을 구원하신 그리스도의 사랑을 따라서 바울이 고린도 교인들을 사랑 때문이다(5:14). 비록 사랑이란 말이 본문에 나타나지 않았으나 고난의 사역의 숨겨진 동기가 사랑인 것이 분명하다(2:4; 11:11; 12:15).

13 "(기록한 바) '내가 믿는 고로 말하였다' 라고 기록한 것과 같은 뜻으로(한 것같이) 우리도 믿는 고로 또한 말하노라." 14 (즉) 주 예수를 다시 살리신 이가 예수와 함께 우리도 다시 살리사 너희와 함께 그 앞에 서게 하실 줄을 아노니(Ἔχοντες δὲ τὸ αὐτὸ

πνεῦμα τῆς πίστεως κατὰ τὸ γεγραμμένον· ἐπίστευσα, διὸ ἐλάλησα, καὶ ἡμεῖς πιστεύομεν, διὸ καὶ λαλοῦμεν, 14 εἰδότες ὅτι ὁ ἐγείρας τὸν κύριον Ἰησοῦν καὶ ἡμᾶς σὺν Ἰησοῦ ἐγερεῖ καὶ παραστήσει σὺν ὑμῖν). 13절과 14절은 의미상 연결되어 있다. 바울의 믿는 바는 하나님께서 지금은 오해와 고난을 받는 바울을 살리사 그의 정당성을 입증해 주실 것이라는 것이다. 13절에서 바울은 이런 믿음이 결코 자신의 주관적인 믿음일 뿐만 아니라 의로 말미암아 고난 받는 모든 이들의 공통된 믿음임을 보여주기 위해서 구약 시편 기자의 말을 특별히 인용하고 있다: "내가 믿는 고로 말하였다"(시 115:1, LXX; 116:1, MT). 13절의 "기록한 바와 같은 뜻으로"라고 번역한 말에 있는 τὸ αὐτὸ πνεῦμα(같은 뜻)는 "같은 영"이라고 번역할 수 있다. 그러나 "같은 영"이라는 번역은 문맥상 맞지 않는다. 시편 기자가 믿음을 가지고 말했듯이 그와 "같은 뜻으로" 바울도 하나님의 장래 구원에 대한 믿음을 가지고 말한다는 뜻이다. "우리도"(καὶ ἡμεῖς)라는 말이 바울과 시편 기자와의 유비적 관계를 나타낸다. "바울은 시편 기자의 위험과 구원의 보고를 그의 그리스도의 죽음과 부활 선포를 위한 예시적 진술로 보고 있는지 모른다. 더구나 이 선포가 바울 자신의 고난과 구원의 체험에서 생생하게 나타났기 때문이다."[221) 하나님의 의로움의 선언은 미래적인 것만은 아니다. 8절 9절에서 이미 바울은 그의 고난 중의 승리의 체험들을 언급했다. 그러나 그런 부분적 승리와 함께 최후의 승리를 바울은 소망하는 것이다. 현재의 고난으로 죽어도 결국 부활할 때 하나님으로부터

221) Thrall, 341.

그의 수고를 인정받게 될 것이다(빌 3:10-14). 이것을 고린도 교인들도 보게 될 것이다: "너희와 함께 그 앞에 서게 하실 줄을 아노니." 그러므로 여기서 부활은 현재적이고 미래적 의미가 있다. 하나님의 현존을 체험하는 현재적 의미와 재림 시에 있을 미래적 부활이다. 현재 바울은 그의 고난 중에서 하나님의 도우심으로 승리한다는 의미와 장래의 영원한 부활과 하나님에게 받을 상 또는 인정이다. 장래 부활의 어귀에 현재적 회복의 의미가 숨어 있다. 그리고 미래적, 현재적 부활의 소망은 과거의 부활의 역사적 사건에 기초해있다. 즉 "주 예수를 살리신 이가 예수와 함께 우리도 다시 살린다", "일으키신다"는 말에 이어 "서게 하신다"는 말이 나온다. 부활이 현재적이고 미래적이라면, "서는 것도" 현재적이고 미래적이어야 한다. 미래에 그를 인정하실 하나님께서 현재의 고난 중에서도 그와 함께 하사 그의 사도직의 정당성을 증거해 주실 것이다. 따라서 그는 주의 강림시에 그의 교회 사역을 자랑할 수 있을 것이다(1:14; 빌 2:16; 살전 2:19-20).

14절에 하나님께서 "예수와 함께 우리도 다시 살리사"(ἡμᾶς σὺν Ἰησοῦ γερει)라는 말씀을 문자적으로 번역하면 예수는 이미 부활하였는데 다시 부활한다는 뜻이 되므로 원래의 의미가 훼손된다. 이 구절의 바로 앞의 "주 예수를 다시 살리신 이가"라는 말에서 바울은 분명히 과거에 일어난 예수의 부활을 말하고 있으므로 그가 "예수가 다시 부활하리라"는 미래적 부활을 말한다고 볼 수 없다. 다만 바울은 그가 현재의 고난 중에서 체험하는 예수의 부활 생명을 미래의 부활 시에 완전하게 얻게 된다는 의미이거나, 또는 미래의 부활 시에 이미 부활하신 예수를 만나게 된다는 종말론적인 뜻이다(고전 15:23).[222] 한편, 바울이 다른 데서도 언급하듯이 여기서도 자신이 주의 강림 시에 여전히 살아 있을 소망을 갖고 있다고 본다면(고전 15:52; 살전 4:17), 이 경우에는, 하나님이 바울을 "예수와 함께" 살리신다는 말은 죽은 자의 부활이 아니라 고린도전서 15장 52절에서 바울이 믿는 대로 주의 강림 시에 살아있는 사람들의 몸의 변화를 의미한다고 본다.[223] 그러나 "너희와 함께 그 앞에 서게 하실 줄을 아노니"라는 말이 5장 10절과 같은 종말론적 의미를 전체 구절에 주고 있기 때문에, 13장 5절에서와 같이 바울의 목회적 승리를 가리키는 말로 볼 수 없다.

한편 10절과 11절 그리고 14절에서 "예수"란 이름이 자주 언급되는 것은 바울과 예수와의 친밀한 유대 관계를 나타내기 위한 것인지도 모른다. 예수의 고난의 지상 생애에 비추어 사도 바울의 고난을 설명하고 또 그의 육체적 부활을 기억하면서 바울의 사역에서의 실제적 승리를 암시한다고 볼 수 있다.[224]

15. "(이) 모든 것을 너희를 위하여 하는 것은 은혜가 보다 더 많은 사람들의 감사함으로 말미암아 (더하여) 넘쳐서 하나님께 영광을 돌리게 하려 함이라"(τὰ γὰρ πάντα δι᾽ ὑμᾶς, ἵνα ἡ χάρις πλεονάσασα διὰ τῶν πλειόνων τὴν εὐχαριστίαν περισσεύσῃ εἰς τὴν δόξαν τοῦ θεοῦ). 이 부분 결론적 진술로서 바울은 그의 사역 또는 장래의 영광이 보다 많은 고린도 교인

222) Michael Byrnes, *Conformation to the Death of Christ and the Hope of Resurrection: An Exegetico-Theological Study of 2 Corinthians4, 7-15 and Philippians 3, 7-11* (Roma: Editrice Pontificia Universita Gregoriana, 2003), 121.

223) Thrall, 342.

224) Martin, 89.

들이 은혜를 받고 감사하여 하나님께 영광을 돌리려함에 있다고 한다. 그는 진정한 그리스도의 사도로서 결코 자신의 유익을 위해 사역하지 않는다. 그는 교인들의 유익을 위하고 더 궁극적으로는 하나님의 영광을 위해 사역한다.

이 구절 해석을 놓고 몇 가지 문제로 논쟁이 있다.

첫째, "모든 것"(τὰ πάντα) 이 주격이나 목적격으로 될 수 있고, 이 부분 동사가 없으므로 몇 가지 다른 번역이 가능하다. 그러나 어떤 경우도 전체 의미에 영향을 주지는 않는다. 주격으로 볼 경우 현재형 εἰμί 동사가 생략되었다고 보고, "이 모든 일들이 너희들을 위한 것이다."라고 번역하거나(NIV), 미래형 εἰμί 동사가 숨어 있다고 보고, "이 모든 일 들이 너희를 위하여 일어날 것이다"라고 번역할 수 있다.[225] 전자의 경우 이 모든 일들은 바울의 고난과 영광의 사역을 말하는 것이 되고, 후자의 경우 바로 앞에서 논하는 장래의 부활과 관련된 일련의 사건들을 가리킨다.

둘째, περισσεύσῃ("넘치다")를 자동사로 볼 수도 있고 타동사로 볼 수도 있으므로 생기는 번역의 차이다. 자동사도 볼 경우 "은혜가 넘쳐서 보다 더 많은 사람들의 감사로 말미암아 하나님께 영광을 돌리게 하려 함이라."라는 번역이 된다(개역한글판, 2001 표준 새번역 개정판, NIV). 타동사로 볼 경우 주어 "은혜"(ἡ χάρις)가 "감사"(εὐχαριστία)를 목적어로 취하여, "은혜가… 감사를 넘치게 한다"라고 된다(RSV). 문법상 이 두 번역이 가능하다.[226] 어

225) Martin, 90.

226) 참조, Thrall, 345-346.

느 경우든지 근본적인 의미의 차이는 없다고 본다.

"더 많은 사람들" (διὰ τῶν πλειόνων)이 고린도 교회의 분쟁과 관련하여 다수의 교인들을 가리키는지 또는 단순히 "더 많은 사람들"을 가리키는지 논쟁이 있다.[227] 모두 가능성이 있으나 여기서 바울은 자신의 사도로서의 희생을 주제로 삼아 논하고 있으므로, "분쟁과 관련된 다수"라기 보다는 일반적인 의미의 많은 사람들이라는 것이 타당해 보인다.

주 해(4:7–15):

4장 7-15절의 주제는 바울의 고난과 승리를 그리스도의 고난과 부활에 비교하면서 바울은 고난을 통해서 질그릇 같이 연약한 존재임을 깨달았으나 동시에 역설적으로 복음의 능력도 체험하였음을 말한다. 이런 역설적 경험은 그리스도의 죽음과 부활에서 나타나는 것과 같이 약함을 통해 역사하시는 하나님의 역사의 특성이다. 바울은 이런 하나님의 역사하심의 특성이 그의 고난의 사역 가운데 나타났음을 자랑하며, 또한 그의 외적 인간 존재(여기서 "질그릇" 또는 4:16의 "겉 사람")의 해체의 고통 가운데서 그리스도의 존재 유형(죽음과 부활)이 확인된 것을 기뻐한다. 한편 이 모든 고난이 바울의 그리스도의 사도직의 정당성을 나타내는 것이기도 하다. 바울은 3장에서 거짓 사도들의 복음의 일시적 영광을 말하면서 자신의 복음의 영원한 가치를 말하고, 4장에 들어와서 그의 복음의 내용과 사도직 수행의 진정성을 말한다. 그의 복음의

227) Moule, 108, Furnish, 260, Martin, 90-91, Thrall, 345.

내용의 진정성은 그가 받은 다메섹의 체험과 계시의 신적 기원에서 기원한다. 4장 7-15절에서 바울은 그의 사역의 진정성은 예수 그리스도의 사역과의 유비로 증명한다. 바울의 고난은 그리스도의 고난과 죽음에 해당하고, 고난 중에서의 구원의 경험은 예수의 부활에 해당한다. 그리고 그는 언젠가 주의 강림 시에 그의 사역의 진정성을 고린도 교인들 앞에서 인정받을 줄을 믿는다(5:10).

목회자나 교회 지도자들도 그들의 임무를 수행하면서 바울처럼 오해와 비난을 받고 자신들을 변명해야 할 때가 많다. 그럴 때, 바울처럼 그들이 진정으로 그들의 교회와 공동체를 위해 희생적으로 부끄럼 없이 일했다면 얼마나 떳떳할까?(잠 28:1). 그들이 받는 오해나 비난은 큰 문제가 아니다. 언젠가 그것들의 진실이 밝혀질 것이다. 이 땅에서 아니면, 오는 세상에서 밝혀질 것이다(고후 5:10). 평소에 양심대로 바르게 살아야 혹 오해를 받고 어려울 때에도, 바울처럼, 양심에 부끄러움이 없이 자신을 변명하며, 하나님의 능력과 해결을 기대할 수 있다. 그러나 그 반대로 그들의 일을 자신들의 유익이나 목적을 이루기 위한 수단으로 위장하여 수행했다면 얼마나 부끄러운 일인가?(롬 16:18; 빌 3:19). 하기야 대부분 지도자들은 자신의 유익과 공동체의 유익을 분리하지 않고 하나로 보고 자신을 위한 것이 곧 공동체의 유익이라고 믿고 그렇게 변명할 때가 많다. 사실 그 구별은 어려운 것이다. 더구나 오래도록 한 기관의 수장이 되어 일하다보면 그 기관의 거의 모든 일이 지도자 중심으로 되어있어서 그 구별은 더욱 어렵다. 그런 경우는 지도자 자신의 양심에 맡길 수밖에 없다(딤전 1:19). 그가 그리스도의 희생적 죽음의 정신을 가지고 더 많은 사람들의 유익과 하나님의 영광을 위해서 일했는가?(16절). 아니면 일신의 자족과 사욕에 집착해서 그 기관의 보다 나은 발전을 위한 하나님의 능력의 기회를 막아왔는가? 지도자들은 그리스도의 희생적 정신의 척도인 십자가로, 자주 스스로 그리고 객관적이며 공개적이고 합리적인 방법으로, 그의 임무수행을 평가받아야 한다. 또 그 집단의 반대자들의 소리에도 귀를 기우려야한다. 과연 그들의 비난이 고린도교회의 경우처럼 잘못된 오해인가? 아니면 자신의 잘못을 지적해주는 하나님의 음성인가를 분별해야할 것이다. 우리 모두 온전하지 못하다. 온전치 못한 우리 자신은 덮어두고 다른 사람이나 외적 요인을 탓하면서, 위기를 일시적으로 모면하려는 유혹을 물리쳐야한다. 심지어 본문 같은 바울의 의로운 고난과 오해를 변명하는 구절들을 자신들의 이익이나 정당화를 위해 억지로 적용하는 것은 더 큰 잘못이다. 악인이 의인의 옷으로 위장하는 악한 일이다(고후 11:15). 잘못이 있을 때는 즉시 사람들 앞에서 시인하고, 하나님께 회개하고 그의 도움을 청해야한다(삼하 12:13; 대상 21:8; 시 51편).

한편, 현대 민주주의적 사고방식과 구조가 갖는 하나의 폐해적 특징은 지도자 문제로 말미암은 교회의 잦은 혼란이다. 구성원은 그들이 일단 선택한 지도자의 지도를 따르고 순종하며 사랑하는 자세를 가져야한다(갈 4:15). 지도자들의 작은 흠이나 대수롭지 않은 문제는 되도록 덮어두고, 감싸주며 따라야 한다(살전 5:12-13). 심각한 문제가 있다면 그 시정을 요구하거나 퇴임을 정당한 방법을 통해서 요구할 수 있다. 그러나 작은 문제나 하찮은 일로 지도자를 괴롭히며 분열을 획책하는 것은 그릇된 행동이며 마귀의 궤계일 수 있다(고후 2:5-11). 그리스도의 교회는 용서받은 죄인들의 집단이다. 지도자들이 구성원들의 모범이 되어야 마땅하나, 근본적으로는 그들도 죄인들이다. 수제자 베드로는 얼마나 심각한 실수를 많이 했는가 그런데도 주께서는 그를 부르시고 그를 쓰심으로 귀한 지도자가 되었다(요 21:15-22). 그 후 베드로가 초대 교회의 지도자가 되었어도 그가 온전하지는 못했던 것 같다. 바울이 그를 외식주의자로 책망한 적이 있다(갈 2:11-13). 그러나 바울 자신도 온전하지는 못했다. 그가 과거 교회를 핍박한 일은 문제 삼지 않더라도, 스스로 "내가 원하는 바 선은 하지 아니하고 도리어 원치 아니하는바 악은 행하는 도다"라고 한탄했다(롬 7:19). 그리고 자신이 많은 계시를 받았으나 오히려 그로 말미암아 스스로 교만해질 수 있는 연약한 인간 존재임을 인정하고 있다(12:7). 교회는 하나님의 사랑 안에서 교역자를 중심으로 하나가 되도록 힘써야 한다. 정죄와 비난만을 힘쓰는 교회는 이미 그리스도의 교회가 아니라, 교회의 이름만 가진 바리새적 집단이 되 버린다. 물론 그리스도의 교회는 거룩해야 한다. 그 지도자들부터 흠 없이 순전하고 온전한 거룩함에 이르기 위해 힘써야 한다. 문제가 있는 이들을 권면하고 징계해야 마땅하다(고후 2:6; 딤전 1:20). 그러나 그리스도의 교회는 자비와 사랑이 있어야 한다. 지도자들을 반대하는 자들도 미워하지 말고 감싸주며 그들이 돌아오도록 기도해야한다(고전 5:5; 고후 2:7). 한편, 교회 분쟁을 세상 법에 호소하는 것은 바람직하지 않다. 세상 사람들을 교회 문제의 판단자로 불러들임은 결국 하나님의 교회의 권위를 떨어뜨리고 조롱거리로 만드는 것이다. 그렇게 함으로 마귀의 올무에 빠지게 되고 복음전파에 장애가 되게 하는 것이다. 분쟁은 어디까지나 교회 내에서 해결하도록 해야 한다(고전 6:1-7).

교회 문제가 어렵다고 교회를 쉽게 사직하고 떠나 버리는 것도 바람직하지 않다. 목회자의 교회에 대한 사랑이나 책임을 쉽게 포기해 버리는 이기적이고 무책임한 행동으로 지탄받을 수 있기 때문이다. 목회자는 교회 문제를 기도와 지혜와 인내로 최선을 다해 해결하기 위해 힘써야 한다(갈 4:19). 그런 후에 하나님의 지시를 따라야 할 것이다.

그러나 목회자들이 아무리 선하게 사역하더라도 반대자들은 있고 마귀의 시험은 항상 있다. 바로 그것이 하나님을 믿는 의로운 이들에게 준 하나님의 시련이기 때문이다. 시련 가운데 의로운 이들은 하나님께 더 가까이 하며 그를 의지하면서, 하나님의 구원과 도우심을 경험한다. 시험 가운데 그들이 가야할 의로운 길이 무엇인지를 배우며 성숙하게 된다. 시련 가운데 있는 의로운 이들은 이 세상의 것에 관심을 갖지 않고 하늘나라의 것에 관심을 갖게 되고, 이 불완전한 세상을 넘어 오는 완전한 영광의 세상에 대한 소망을 가지고서 사욕과 편견을 버리고 보다 고상하고 넓은 시야를 얻게 된다(잠 4:18; 렘 20:12; 골 3:1-4). 모든 그리스도의 제자들의 길에는 이런 고난과 시험이 그치지 않을 것이다(막 8:34; 10:30). 그런 길이 좁은 길이며 주님의 십자가의 길이었다(마7:13-14). 그러므로 우리는 주의 일을 하다가 고난을 만나면 그리스도의 고난에 참여하는 것으로 오히려 기뻐해야 한다(행전 5:41; 잠 14:32). 바울처럼 하나님의 위로와 구원과 장래의 영광을 바라보며 현재의 고난을 인내해야 한다. 고난의 사역을 원망하지 말고 인간 존재의 해체의 고통을 달게 받으면서 하나님이 주시는 내적 성숙의 열매("속 사람" 의 성장)로 기뻐하며 하나님의 능력이 나타날 것과 장래의 영광을 사모해야 한다(4:16-5:10; 롬 5:3-4). 바울은 이런 고난의 유익에 대해서 계속 말한다.

vi. 바울은 현재의 고난 중에서도 영원한 영광의 소망을 가짐 (4:16-5:10).

본문:

16. 그러므로 우리가 낙심하지 아니하노니 우리의 겉 사람은 후패하나 우리의 속사람은 날로 새롭도다. 17. 우리의 잠시 받는 환난의 경한 것이 지극히 크고 영원한 영광의 중한 것을 우리에게 이루게 함이니 18. 우리가 관심을 두는 것(돌아 보는 것)은 보이는 것이 아니요 보이지 않는 것이니 보이는 것은 잠간이요 보이지 않는 것은 영원함이니라. 5:1. 만일 땅에 있는 우리의 장막 집이 무너지면 하나님께서 지으신 집 곧 손으로 지은 것이 아니요 하늘에 있는 영원한 집을 우리가 갖는(집이 우리에게 있는) 줄 아나니 2. 그러므로 (과연) 우리가 여기 있어 탄식하며 하늘로부터 오는 우리 처소로 덧입기를 간절히 사모하노니 3. 이렇게 입음으로써(은) 벗은 자들로 발견되지 않게 될 것이기 때문이라(않으려 함이라). 4. 우리가 이 장막 아래서 짐을 지고서(이 장막에 있는 우리가 짐진 것 같이) 탄식하는 것은 벗고자 함이 아니요 오직 덧입고자 함이니 죽을 것이 생명에게 삼킨 바 되게 하려 함이라. 5. 곧 이것을 우리에게 이루게 하시고 보증으로 성령을 우리에게 주신 이는 하나님이시니라. 6. 이러므로 우리가 항상 확실히 아는 바는 (담대하여 . . . 아노니)몸에 거할 때에는 주와 따로 거한다는 것이니(거하는 줄을 아노니) 7. 이는 우리가 믿음으로 행하고 보는 것으로 하지 아니함 이로라. 8. 우리가 확실히 (담대하여) 원하는 바는 차라리 몸을 떠나 주와 함께 거하는 그것이라. 9. 그런즉 우리는 (몸에)거하든지 떠나든지 주를 기쁘시게 하는 자 되기를 힘쓰노라. 10. 이는 우리가 다 반드시 그리스도의 심판대 앞에 드러나 각각 선악 간에 그 몸으로 행한 것을 따라 받으려 함이라.

본문 비평:

1. 16절의 ἐγκακοῦμεν(낙심하다)(p[46] ℵ B D* F G 6. 81. 326. 2464)이 같은 의미의 ἐκκακῶμεν(C D[2] ψ 0243, *m*)보다 신빙성이 있다. 후자는 비슷한 글자에서 온 필사 오류로 본다.

2. 16절의 ἔσω ἡμῶν이 일반적 기록이나 ἔσωθεν(K L y 629, 1241) 또는 ἔσωθεν ἡμῶν(D² 2495)그냥 ἔσω(P 323. 945 등)만이 나온다. 롬 7:22에 같은 말이 나오기 때문에 다른 기록은 오류로 본다.

3. 17절의 ἐλαφρόν 앞에 어떤 사본(D* F G)에는 πρόσκαιρον καί 이 추가되었다. 이것은 필사자들이 18절의 "일시적인 것"과 "영원한 것"의 대조를 보고 이 말을 넣어 뒤에 있는 αἰώνιον과 대조 어귀를 만들려고 추가 기록한 것으로 본다.

4. 5:3에서 대부분의 사본은 εἴ γε 로 읽으나 어떤 사본들(p^{46} ℵ B D F G) 은 εἴπερ로 읽는다. 후자는 보다 강한 의구심을 나타내어 5:1의 의미와 상반되므로 전자가 원래의 것으로 본다.[228)]

5. 5:3에서 ἐνκδυσάμενοι(옷을 입은)가 대부분의 사본에 나온다. 그러나 그 반대어인 ἐκδυσάμενοι(옷을 벗은)가 D* 같은 후기 소문자 사본에 나온다. 전자로 하면 앞 절에 있는 같은 말과 겹쳐 반복적이 되기 때문에 후기 필사자들이 바꾸었다고 본다.[229)] 또 전자는 이 구절의 사도의 말을 진부하게 만든다고 한다.[230)] 불트

---

228) M. E. Thrall, "'Putting on' or 'stripping off' in 2 Corinthians 5:3," *New Testament Textual Criticism, Its Significance for Exegesis*, ed. E. J. Epp and G. D. Fee (Oxford: Clarendon Press/New York: Oxford University Press), 223-29.

229) Plummer, 148.

230) Metzger, *Textual Commentary on the Greek New Testament*, 579-580.

만은 후자(옷을 벗은)가 뒤에 오는 "벗은" (γυμνοί)이란 말과 더불어 의미를 분명히 해준다고 보면서 이를 지지한다.[231] 대부분의 학자들은 전자를 따른다.[232] 전자가 오래된 기록이나, 어느 쪽이든 결국 같은 뜻이다.

6. 5절의 κατεργασάμενος를 어떤 서방사본(D. F. G 라틴어)들은 현재형 κατεργάζομαι로 읽는다.

7. p46과 라틴 번역은 10절의 διά를 ἴδια로 읽는다.

내용 개요:

4장 16-18절을 바울의 현재의 고난을 주로 다루는 4장 7-15절까지와 바울의 미래의 천국의 영광을 주로 다루는 5장 1-10절의 연결 부위로 볼 수도 있으나,[233] 결국 5장 1-10절과 같은 주제로 즉 "외적 인간 존재가 해체되는 고통을 통해 얻게 되는 영적 성장과 장래의 온전한 존재 형성에 대한 그리스도인의 자아 인식" 이라는 한 가지 주제로 보고 함께 다루기로 한다.[234] 이 주제를 더 쉽게 말하면, 그리스도인은 고난 가운데 자신이 해체되는 고통을 겪지만 동시에 역설적으로 자신의 진정한 영적 존재는 성장하고 장래의 영광의 날을 소망하게 된다는 것이다(참조, 롬 5:3, 4; 8:18). 이 부분의 내용이 지금까지의 바울의 고난과 영광의 사역에 대한 내용

231) Bultmann, 137, 138.

232) Martin, 97, Thrall, 373, 주, 1278; Barrett 149, 주, 2.

233) Thrall, 347; 참조, Martin, 91-93.

234) Furnish, 288.

과는 다른 종말론적이며 신학적인 문제를 취급하므로, 불트만은 이 부분을 바울 서신에 흔히 있는 주제를 벗어나가서 다른 문제를 다루는 것으로 본다(6:14-7:1; 10:13-18).[235] 그러나 주제를 벗어난 것은 아니다. 계속 4장 4절 이후의 영광의 복음과 그의 고난과 영광의 주제를 보다 확장하여 미래의 소망과 함께 다루고 있을 뿐이다. 더 멀리 보아 3장에서 그의 대적자들의 일시적 영광에 비해 그의 복음의 영원한 영광의 주제아래 있는 것이다(3:7). 5장 초두의 장래의 소망도 결국 바울의 복음의 영원성과 그의 사역의 진정성에 대한 것이다. 그의 복음은 지금은 보이지 않는, 그러나 장래에 나타날 영원한 영광을 전하는 바울의 복음의 우수성을 나타낸다. 이런 복음의 특징은 그의 사역에도 나타난다고 한다. 바울의 인간존재는 고난의 사역 가운데 수고와 반대자들의 비난으로 말미암은 상처로 해체되는 고통을 받으며(10:10; 11:22-33; 12:16), 외적으로는 깨어지기 쉬운 질그릇같이 보잘 것 없으나 내적으로는 새로운 피조물로서 날마다 새롭게 되고 영원한 영광을 향하여 나아가고 결국 주의 강림 시에 온전한 영광의 몸으로 변화된다는 소망을 보여 준다(4:16-5:7). 그리고 마지막으로 바울의 복음과 그의 사역의 진정성이 최후의 심판에서 인정받게 될 것이다(5:10). 단순하게 말하면, 바울은 그의 어려운 고난의 사역 가운데서 실망하고 낙심하지 않고 하나님의 영원한 약속과 그를 믿는 믿음과 소망으로 극복함을 나타내는 말이다. 그러므로 바울은 "우리가 믿음으로 행하고 보는 것으로 하지 않음이로다"(5:7)라고 한다. 이런 믿음의 자세는 하박국서의 주제, "의인은 그 믿음으로 말미암아 살리라"의

---

235) Bultmann, 132, Martin, li, 114, 328.

피상적 의미와 상통한다. 이런 피상적 의미는 바울이 로마서 1장 17절에서 하박국 2장 4절의 말씀을 이신득의의 구원론적 의미로 해석한 것과는 다른 액면적인 의미이다. 바울은 그의 고난의 사역을 하면서 그의 연약한 인간 존재("겉사람")로 말미암아 낙심하지 않는다(4:16). 현재에도 내적으로 그리스도 안에서 새로운 피조물인 "속사람"이 성장하고 있고 장래에 온전하고 영광스런 존재로 나타날 것을 믿기 때문이다(4:16-5:10).

좁게 보아서 이 부분은 4장에서 시작된 바울의 사역의 고난에 대한 결론 부분에 해당한다. 바울은 2장 14-17절과 4장 7절 이하에서 그의 고난 가운데서도 간간히 승리케 하시는 하나님의 역사를 증거하고 있으나 궁극적 승리는 역시 마지막 날에 온다. 이 낡은 세상에서 육체를 가지고 사는 한 고난을 벗어날 수 없다고 본다. 고난으로 점철되는 육체적 삶의 끝은 죽음이다. 그러나 죽음은 끝이 아니다. 믿는 자의 죽음은 새로운 존재 양식으로서 생명의 주이신 그리스도와 함께 있게 되는 것이다(5:8). 그러나 믿는 자의 궁극적인 존재 양식은 부활이다. 주님의 강림과 함께 오는 새 세상에서 온전한 존재로서 영원한 생명을 누리게 된다(5:1; 고전 15:52-54). 바울은 고난 중에서 결국 새로운 세상의 도래를 소망하면서 위로 받는다(5:1-10). 이런 믿음과 소망 가운데 그의 현재의 존재해체의 아픔을 참는 것이다(11:23-12:10). 그리고 이런 믿음과 소망은 허구가 아니라 실체로서 실제로 위로의 능력을 나타내는 것은 인간의 희망사항에 기초한 것이 아니라 신실하신 하나님의 약속에 기초하고 있기 때문이다(참조, 롬 5:2-3; 8:18; 고전 15:58; 히 11:1).

바울은 4장 4절과 6절에서 말한 그에게 비친 하나님의 영광과 영광의 복음의 빛이 일시적인 것이 아니라 영원한 것임을 밝혀야

할 필요가 있었다. 또한 그의 사역도 대적자들처럼 일시적 현상 세계의 영광을 추구하지 않고 장차 오는 영원한 세계의 영광을 추구하고 있으므로 현재의 사역의 고난이나 영광의 결핍을 대수롭지 않게 여긴다고 말한다. 고난을 받다가 죽는다 해도, 죽음 이후에 오히려 더 큰 영광이 있으므로 절망하지 않는다. 그러나 바울이 원하는 것은 죽음이 오기 전에 그리스도의 강림을 맞아 산 채로 부활의 몸으로 변화는 것이다(5:2; 고전 15:51-52). 그러나 실제로 바울이 더 원하는 것이 있다. 그것은 살든지 죽든지, 주의 강림이 오기 전에 그에게 맡겨진 복음 전달 사명을 진실되게 마치는 것이다(5:9). 왜냐하면, 종말은 결국 올 것이며, 믿는 자는 결국 신령한 몸으로 변화될 것이다. 이 땅에서 "몸"을 가지고 주를 기쁘시게 하도록 일하는 것이 종의 본분이다. 그래야 주님께 칭찬 듣는 종으로 심판받게 될 것이다(5:10). 이렇게 영원한 소망과 함께 현실을 책임 있게 살도록 권면하는 바울의 복음사역이야 말로 대적자들의 일시적 영광의 "복음" 사역에 비해 볼 때 우월하고 진정한 복음사역이 아닌가?

주석:

16. "그러므로 우리가 낙심하지 아니하노니 우리의 겉 사람은 후패하나 우리의 속 사람은 날로 새롭도다" (Διὸ οὐκ ἐγκακοῦμεν, ἀλλ᾽ εἰ καὶ ὁ ἔξω ἡμῶν ἄνθρωπος διαφθείρεται, ἀλλ᾽ ὁ ἔσω ἡμῶν ἀνακαινοῦται ἡμέρᾳ καὶ ἡμέρᾳ). "그러므로 우리가 낙심하지 아니하노니"에서 "그러므로"(διό)는 앞 구절에서 말한 바울이 장래 부활과 주의 강림 시에 그의 고난은 그치고 영광이 있다고 믿음으로라는 뜻이다. "낙심하

지 아니하노니"(οὐκ ἐγκακοῦμεν)는 4장 1절에서 말한 것을 다시 상기시켜준다(롬 5:3). 4장 8절에는 이와 유사한 말로 같은 의미를 나타낸다. 낙심하지 않는 이유는 장래 하나님 나라의 최종적 위로(5:1 이하)와 함께 현재에 이미 진행 중인 우리의 영적 존재의 성장이다. "우리의 겉 사람은 후패하나 우리의 속 사람은 날로 새롭도다." 미래의 영광이 이미 날마다 우리에게 나타나고 있다. 바울의 여러 고난의 사역 가운데서 경험하는 승리와 위로가 바로 그것이다(1:4; 2:17; 7:6). 뿐만 아니라 그리스도에게 속한 사람으로서 비록 우리의 현재의 육체적 존재는 부패하나, 그리스도 안에 있는 참된 자아는 더욱 강건하게 되는 것이다. 이런 영적 자아의 성장은, 믿음으로 말미암아 현재 이 땅에서 약화되는, 고달픈 인간존재에 대해 미련을 두지 않게 한다. "우리의 속 사람"(ἔσω ἡμών)으로 번역 된 말은 문자적으로 "우리의 속"이지만, 앞의 "겉 사람"(ἔξω ἄνθρωπος)과 병행되게 번역한 것이다. 앞서 4:7절 주석에서 "보배를 담은 질그릇"을 논할 때 지적한 바와 같이 바울은 반대자들의 비난에 직면하여 자신의 이해를 적극적인 표현과 함께 부정적 표현을 가지고 교차적으로 또는 역설적으로 사용하고 있다. 여기서 "겉 사람"은 4:7절의 "질그릇"에 해당되는 부정적 표현으로서 반대자들의 멸시로 상처받은 바울 자신을 가리키며, "속 사람"은 4:7절의 "보배"에 해당되는 적극적인 표현으로서 하나님이 인정하시는 복음의 일꾼으로서의 바울 자신을 나타낸다.

"겉 사람"(ἔξω ἄνθρωπος)과 "속(사람)"(ἔσω ἡμῶν)과 거의 유사한 말들이 희랍시대에 사용되었다.[236] 희랍시대에는 사람을 육체나 영혼의 이중적 존재로 보았으므로, "내적인 사람"은 흔히 사람의 영혼이나 신적 요소를 가리켰다.[237] 영지주의 헤르메스 문서에서 인간 구성을 이중적으로 보아서 육체를 가졌으므로 죽을 수밖에 없으나, 한편 "본질적 인간"(ἄνθρωπος ὁ οὐσιώδης)은 영원하다고 했다.[238] 히브리 사상에도 이와 유사한 경우가 있다(마 10:28). 욥은 "나의 이 가죽, 이것이 썩은 후에 내가 육체 밖에서 하나님을 보리라"(욥 19:26)이라고 했고, 필로는 영혼을 "사람 안에 있는 사람"(ὁ ἄνθρωπος ἐν ἀνθρώπῳ)이라고 했다(*Congr.* 97). 바울도 히브리적 그리고(또는) 헬라적 전통을 따라서 육체와 영혼의 대조적 개념을 가지고, 그리스도인을 두 개의 다른 존재들로 본다(롬 7:22; 고전 5:5; 7:34; 고후 7:1). 바울은 로마서 6장 6절에서 그리스도인의 "옛 사람"은 그리스도와 함께 죽었다고 한다(롬 6:6). 그러나 곧 이어서 "옛 사람"의 습관은 아직 남아있음을 인정했다(롬 6:7-7장;엡 4:8, 14, 22-24). "옛 사람"은 죄의 성향을 가진 인간 존재를 가리킨다. "새 사람"은 예수 믿고 거룩하게 사는 사람이다(엡 4:24). 그러므로 "옛 사람"과 "새 사람"은 인간 구원이나, 죄성 또는 거룩한 생활과 관련되어 사용되었다.

본문에서 바울은 "겉 사람"과 "속 사람"을 윤리적 의미 없이 생물학적, 존재론적, 종말론적, 구원론적인 의미로 쓴다. "겉 사람"은 종말이 올 때까지 이 땅에서 태어나서 고난당하며 살다가 죽고 종말에 심판 받게 되는 인간 존재를 가리킨다고 본다. "겉 사람은

---

236) Plato, *Republic*, IX 589A; Epictetus, *Diss.* II 7.3, 8.14; Philo, *Quod Det. Pot.* 22f. J. Jeremias, ἄνθρωπος, TDNT I, 366 보라. 한편 바울이 그의 대적자들의 이원론적 인간관을 이용하여 그의 사상을 설명하는 것을 보는 이들도 있다(Martin, 91; Thrall, 349; F. T. Fallon, *2 Corinthians*, New Testament Message 11 (Wilmington, Del.: M. Glazier/Dublin: Veritas, 1980), 47.

237) Thrall, 348.

238) *Corp. Herm.* I 15; J. Jermias, *TDNT* I, 366.

후패하나"라는 말에서 "부패한다"는 말은 육체의 성격을 가리킨다고 보며, 바울이 논하는 육체의 부활은 후패한 "겉 사람"의 부활이라고 본다(고전 15:42-44): "썩을 것으로 심고 썩지 아니할 것으로 다시 살며…" 한편, "속사람"은 구원받은 영원한 존재를 가리킨다. 그러나 "속사람"을 "구원받은 영혼"과 같은 말이라고 단정할 수 없다. 영혼이란 육체와 구별되는 인간 존재의 독립된 일부이며 특히 죽음 이후에 오는 인간의 존재 양식이다. 이런 영혼의 독립된 존재와 활동에 대한 관심은 오히려 이교적이며 헬라적이다. 바울이 여기서 말하는 "속사람"은 그리스도인에게서 역사하는 새로운 존재를 의미하므로 이런 사람의 육체와 분리되고 대조되는 이교적인 영혼과는 구별되야 한다. "속사람"은 그리스도를 믿음으로 말미암아 구원받고 이 세상에서 그리스도인으로써 살아가는 전인(全人)을 가리킨다. 이" 속사람"은 고린도후서 5장 17절에 있는 "그리스도 안에 있는 새로운 피조물"이요, 에베소서 4장 25절의 "새 사람"과 같은 말이다(엡 4:24). "하나님의 법"에 따라 사는 존재이며(롬 7:22), 우리의 몸을 "의의 병기"로 쓰는 존재이다(롬 6:13). 그러나 본문에는 이런 윤리적 의미 대신 존재론적 의미로 쓰였다. 나아가 이런 의미는 대적자들과의 논쟁적 문맥에서 이해되어야 할 것이다. 즉 "겉 사람"이란 원래 인간 육체를 가리키는 말이지만, 본문에서는 더 넓게 보아 이 땅에서 고생하는 인간의 삶 전체를 가리키는 말이다. 바울은 외적 영광이 없이 고난 받는 연약한 자신의 모습을 나타내기 위해서 "겉 사람"이란 말을 썼고, 그리스도 안에서 새로운 피조물이 된 모든 그리스도인들을 포함하여 바울 사도 자신의 숨겨진 내적 존재 가치와 장래의 영광을 (특히, 그의 대적자들에게) 나타내기 위해서, "새 사람"이란 말 대신 "속사람" 이란 말을 쓰고 있다. 바울의 대적자들의 말처럼 바울은 아무런 외적 영광도 없이 그의 사역을 수행하면서 고난만 당하는 것처럼 보인다. 그러나 사실은 그의 속사람은 날로 새롭게 되고 장래의 영광을 바라보는 것이다. 이런 논쟁적 의미는 아래의 18절에서 "보이는 것"과 "보이지 않는 것"의 대조에서 더 뚜렷이 나타난다. 바울은 보이지 않는 하나님이 주시는 장래의 영광에 관심을 갖는다. 그러나 8절 이하에서 말한 것처럼 그 미래의 영광은 이미 그의 사역 가운데 일부 나타나서 역사하였다. 그의 대적자들은 눈이 어두워 이것을 보지 못할 뿐이다(4:3, 18).

"겉사람"과 "속사람"은 지금 동시적으로 함께 한 인간 개인에게서 존재하고 있으나 종말에 일시적 불완전한 "겉 사람"(육체)은 영원하고 온전한 "속사람"의 특질로 덧입게 될 것이다. 5장 초두에서 "하늘로 오는 우리 처소로 덧입기를 간절히 사모한다"고 하거나 "죽을 것이 생명에게 삼킨바 되게 하려 함이라."라고 하는 말들은 "겉사람"의 "속사람"화(化)의 소망, 즉 육체의 변화 또는 부활의 소망을 가리킨다.

16절에서 바울은 고난 중에서도 소망을 가진다고 말하면서, 자신의 진술 가운데 있는 현재의 고난과 장래의 영광이라는 모순은 근본적으로 자기에게 존재하는 "두 사람"의 모순적 특징에게서 연유된 것으로 설명한다. 바울에게는 외적 영광의 증거 대신 초라함 밖에 없다는 대적자들의 비난에 맞서서 그의 외적 초라한 존재는 장래의 영광의 발현의 과정 중에 있기 때문이라고 반론하는 것이다.[239] 더구나 영적 안목으로 볼 때 그리스도 안에서 새로운 피

239) Thrall, 351.

조물로서의 "속 사람"의 영적 존재는 날마다 성장하고 있는 것이다(4:16; 5:17).

이렇게 바울은 고린도 교회 반대자들의 비난으로 사도로서의 존재 해체의 위기 가운데서 자신의 속사람의 가치를 찾아서 자신의 존재 가치를 방어한다. 이 후에도 이런 바울 자신의 존재가치(또는 사도적 방어)에 대한 변명은 계속된다. 5장 17절에서는 그리스도의 새로운 피조물로 자신을 이해하고 나아가 5:18절 이하에서는 자신을 고린도 교회의 회복을 위한 그리스도의 화해의 사신으로서 자신의 가치를 밝히고 변명하는 것이다. 해체의 위기를 맞은 바울의 존재가 그리스도 안에서 다시 살아나서 인간관계 회복(바울과 고린도 교회 그리고 그리스도와 고린도 교회)을 위한 화해의 사신으로 나타나는 것이다(6:4-10; 12:9, 10; 13:4).

17. "우리의 잠시 받는 환난의 경한 것이 지극히 크고 영원한 영광의 중한 것을 우리에게 이루게 함이니…"(τὸ γὰρ παραυτίκα ἐλαφρὸν τῆς θλίψεως ἡμῶν καθ᾽ ὑπερβολὴν εἰς ὑπερβολὴν αἰώνιον βάρος δόξης κατεργάζεται ἡμῖν). 여기서 바울은 환난의 일시적이고 가벼운 성격과 영광의 영원하고 무거운 성격을 대조하면서 현재의 고난에 대한 인내와 위로의 근거를 제시하고 있다. 현재의 고난이 장래의 영광을 이루게 한다. 그리고 장래의 큰 영광에 비해 현재의 고난은 일시적이고 약하다. 의인이 현재 받는 고난에서 장래 축복을 믿고 위로 받는 것은 유대교에서도 인정된 것이다.[240] 로마서 8장 18절에서는 성도와 그

240) 마카비 4서 9:8; 17:12; 바룩 2서 15:7-8; 48:49-50; 51:14; Furnish 290, Plummer 138.

리스도가 연합되어 있으므로 성도가 현재의 고난을 받은 후 장차 영광을 받을 것을 말한다. 그러나 영광이 전적으로 장래의 것만은 아니다. 현재적 의미도 있다. 이미 3장 18절에서 현재적 영광을 언급했다. 여기서도 "이루게 한다"(κατεργάζεται)는 말은 현재형이다. 장래의 영광이 현재에 나타나는 것이다. 앞서 바울의 고난의 경험 가운데 체험한 승리나 16절의 "속사람"의 활동 같은 것은 장래의 영광이 이미 지금 진행되고 있음을 보여 준다. 믿는 자에게는 속사람의 영적 성장이 진행되고 있다. 로마서 5장 3-4절에서도 "우리가 환난 중에도 즐거워하나니 이는 환난은 인내를, 인내는 연단을, 연단은 소망을 이루는 줄 앎이로라"면서 고난의 현재적 미래적 유익을 함께 말하고 있다.

영광이란 무엇인가? 3장 18절에서 말하듯이 그리스도와 같이 변하는 것을 말한다. 그리스도의 부활한 몸처럼 우리의 몸이 영화롭게 변화되는 것을 말한다(고전 15:43; 빌 3:21). 그 하나님의 지극한 영광으로 말미암아 우리는 완전하고 지고한 복락을 누리게 된다.

한편 여기의 영광의 주제는 앞서 3장에서 논한 모세의 일시적 영광과 바울의 복음의 영원한 영광의 대조를 염두에 두고 이해해야 한다. 바울은 그의 대적자들의 교훈에 대한 그의 복음의 우월성은 그의 복음의 영광의 영원성임을 말했다(3:7). 대적자들의 복음의 특성은 모세의 일시적 영광처럼 일시적인 것이다. 여기서도 이런 바울의 대적자들과의 논쟁점을 헤아려 살펴야 할 것이다.

18. "우리가 관심을 두는 것(돌아보는 것)은 보이는 것이 아니요 보이지 않는 것이니 보이는 것은 잠간이요 보이지 않는 것은 영원함이니라"(μὴ σκοπούντων ἡμῶν τὰ βλεπόμενα ἀλλὰ τὰ

μὴ βλεπόμενα· τὰ γὰρ βλεπόμενα πρόσκαιρα, τὰ δὲ μὴ βλεπόμενα αἰώνια.). 16절과 17절에서 바울은 장래의 영광의 객관적 사실을 주로 말했으나 18절에서 바울은 이 사실에 대한 그의 주관적인 반응을 말한다. 바울이 "관심을 두는 것"(σκοπούντων)이란 말은 원래, "눈을 한 곳에 집중한다"는 뜻이다. 바울의 중심적 관심은 아직 보이지 않는 장차 오는 세상이다. "보이는 것"과 "보이지 않는 것"의 대조는 어쩌면 플라톤적 이원론적 세계관을 반영하는 말인지도 모른다. 즉 현상세계의 일시성은 이데아의 세계의 영원성에 비해 그 가치가 낮다.[241] 그러나 이런 이 세상의 일시적 가치와 하늘나라의 영원한 가치의 대조는 유대교에도 있다(마 6:19). 여기서도 바울은 헬라 사상보다 유대교적 종말론 사상에 입각하여 장차 나타나는 하나님의 나라에 대해 관심을 두고 있다고 볼 수도 있고, 헬라 사상에 젖은 고린도 교회 교인들을 고려하여 그들의 이원론적 세계관을 이용하여 자신의 사도직을 설명하고 있다고 볼 수도 있다. 그는 "겉사람"의 고난을 "속사람"의 영광의 소망에 비추어 대수롭지 않게 여긴다. 현재의 고난 가운데 장차 주실 하나님의 보상을 바라보면서 인내한다. 이런 보이지 않는 장래 보상은 믿음의 눈으로만 볼 수 있다. 현상 세계의 보이는 것만 찾는 불신의 눈(대적자들의)으로는 이런 장래의 영광을 볼 수가 없다. 눈에 보이는 모세의 외적이고 일시적인 영광만을 찾는 대적자들의 눈에는 이런 내적 영원한 영광이 보이지 않을 것이다(3:7-18). 마찬가지로 육체의 증거를 찾는 이들도 영원한 내적 영광을 볼 수 없다. 그리스도 안에 새로운 피조물들만이

241) Plato, *Phaedo*, 79A, Windisch, 156.

이런 영원한 영광을 볼 수 있다(5:17).

"보이는 것은 잠간이요"라는 말은 앞서 지적한 대적자들의 복음과 복음 사역의 일시성을 상기시키는 말이다(3:7, 11). 대적자들은 외적이고 일시적 영광을 자랑하는 이들이다(5:12; 10:7 이하, 11:13이하). 반면에 바울이 관심을 두는 것은 보이지 않는 것이며, 영원한 것이다. 그의 복음과 사역은 내적 미래적 영원한 성격을 가리킨다. 그러므로 5장 1절 이하의 장래 소망에 대한 말은 바울이 현재의 고난의 사역 가운데 위로 받는 말도 되지만, 그보다 그의 대적자들의 외적이고 일시적인 복음과 사역에 맞서서 그의 복음과 사역의 내면적이고 영원한 진정성을 나타내는 말이기도 하다. 그러나 외적인 영광을 찾는 것은 바울의 대적자들 만은 아닐 것이다. 이것은 모든 믿음이 없는 자연인의 경향이다(아래 5:11의 주석을 보라). 그러므로 사단은 "광명의 천사"로 가장하여 사람들을 미혹한다(고후 11:14).

5:1 "만일 땅에 있는 우리의 장막 집이 무너지면 하나님께서 지으신 집 곧 손으로 지은 것이 아니요 하늘에 있는 영원한 집을 우리가 갖는(집이 우리에게 있는) 줄 아나니…" (**Οἴδαμεν γὰρ ὅτι ἐὰν ἡ ἐπίγειος ἡμῶν οἰκία τοῦ σκήνους καταλυθῇ, οἰκοδομὴν ἐκ θεοῦ ἔχομεν, οἰκίαν ἀχειροποίητον αἰώνιον ἐν τοῖς οὐρανοῖς**). 바울은 5장 1절에서 보다 일반적인 종말론적 소망을 논하기 시작한다. 지금까지 자신의 고난의 위로의 근거로서 장래의 소망을 말하다가, 보다 근본적인 그리스도인의 소망을 논한다. 그러나 실제로 바울은 3장에서 시작된 그의 복음의 우월성의 주제를 떠나지 않고 있다. 즉 그의 대적자들의 가르침은 모

세의 얼굴의 일시적 영광처럼 일시적인 것이나, 그의 복음은 영원한 영광의 복음이란 것을 계속해서 말하고 있음을 명심해야 한다.[242] 바울은 4장 7절의 질그릇 비유에서부터 계속해서 일시성과 영원성, "겉사람"과 "속사람", 보이는 것과 보이지 않는 것, 약한 것과 강한 것의 대조를 하면서 그의 복음의 영원한 가치를 설명해 왔다. 마찬가지로 본문에서 바울은 "우리의 장막 집"과 "하늘에 있는 영원한 집"을 대조하면서 그의 복음은 어디까지나 영원한 소망을 가르치고 있음을 나타낸다.

바울은 이미 고린도전서 15장 40-44절에서도 "하늘에 속한 형체(몸)"와 "땅에 속한 형체(몸)", "썩을 것으로 심고"와 "썩지 아니할 것으로 다시 살며", 육의 몸"과 "신령한 몸"을 대조하였다. 1절에서도 "이 땅의 장막집"은 일시적이고 낡게 되나, "하늘에 있는 집"은 영원하다. "땅에 있는 우리의 장막집"(ἡ ἐπίγειὀ ἡμῶν οἰκία τοῦ σκήνους)이 본문 전체에서 거듭해서 육체와 관련되어 설명되고 있으므로 사람의 육체를 가리킨다는 데는 논쟁의 여지가 없으나(벧후 1:13이하), 왜 몸을 "집"으로 표현했는가에 대한 문제를 몇 가지로 요약할 수 있다.[243]

1. 헬라 사상을 따라서 육체를 영혼의 일시적 거주지로 보았다고 한다(지혜서 9:15; 약 2:26).[244] 그러나 바울 서신에서 이와 같은 순수한 헬라 사상이 발견되지 않는다.[245]

2. "집"은 일시적이고 연약한 인간 존재를 가리키는 유대교 사상

---

242) 참조, Martin 114.

243) Thrall, 360-361.

244) Thrall, 360, 주, 1173; Bultmann, 133; Barrett, 151.

245) Furnish 293; K. Hanhart, *The Intermediate State in the New Testament* (Groningen: Druk. V. R. B. Kleine, 1966), 165.

을 따랐다고 한다(사 38:12; 욥 4:19; 벧후 1:13 이하). 그러나 이 경우 "집"은 인간의 전체적 존재를 가리키는 것이지 육체와 영혼을 따로 구분하는 것은 아니다. 본문은 두 "몸"의 집을 대조하고 있다.[246]

3. 믿는 자의 이 땅의 순례자로서의 삶을 광야 장막 성전이나 역대상 9장 23절, 또는 요한복음 2장 19절이나 고린도전서 6장 19절의 성전에 비교한 것이라고 한다. 본문에서 바울이 사도로서의 고난의 삶을 말하고 있으므로 이 견해가 어느 정도 타당성이 있으나, 5장1절 이하의 내용은 순례와 같은 시간의 과정보다는 죽음 같은 어떤 특정한 순간을 논하고 있다고 본다.[247]

4. 바울이 고린도에서 아굴라와 브리스길라와 함께 장막 만드는 일을 했으므로 그의 직업 경험으로부터 얻은 장막의 일시적 성격을 인간 존재의 일시적 성격에 비추어 비유적으로 표현한 것이라고 볼 수 있다(행 18:1-3). 어쩌면 바울은 이런 비유적 어귀를 사용함으로써 고린도 교회 교인들이 자신의 고난을 진정한 사도로서의 표로 받아들이고, 동시에 고린도 반대자들의 바울의 착취에 대한 비난(고후 12:14-18)을 반박하는 부수적 효과를 기대했는지도 모른다.

이상의 견해들이 모두 몸을 "집"으로 나타냈다고 할 수 있다. 바울이 이런 보편적인 표현을 본문에서 쓰고 있다고 볼 수 있다.

한편, "하늘에 있는 영원한 집"(οἰκοδομὴν… αἰώνιον ἐν τοῖς οὐρανοῖς)의 의미는 그 말의 암시성과 그 암시성의 해석과 2절 이후에 나오는 내용과의 관련 문제 때문에 학자들의 의견이 다양

246) M. Rissi, *Studien zum zweiten Korintherbrief*, ATANT 56 (Zurich: Zwingli Verlag, 1969), 74.

247) Hanhart, 165; Rissi, 76-7; Collange, 183-7.

하다. 이들을 요약하면 다음과 같다.[248)]

1. 성도의 부활한 몸이다. 1절에서 앞에 있는 "땅에 있는 우리의 장막집"이 인간의 육체를 가리킨다면, 뒤에 있는 "하늘에 있는 하나님의 영원한 집" 역시 인간의 몸을 가리켜야 논리적으로 옳다고 한다. 또한, 고린도전서 15장의 부활에 관한 내용에서 본문의 두 "집"에 해당하는 "땅에 속한 자"와 "하늘에 속한 자"의 대조를 가리키며(48절), "손으로 지은 것이 아니요"는 "육의 몸"과 대조된 "신령한 몸"을 가리키는 듯이 보인다(44절; 참조 53).[249)] 이런 유사한 대조적인 단서 외에 실제로 "하늘의 집"이 "신령한 몸"을 가리키는 용례가 없으므로 단정적이 아니다. 또한 이 해석은 본문의 "무너지는 때"를 개인의 죽음이 아닌 주의 재림으로 보는 것을 전제로 하는데, 그 "때"가 개인의 죽음을 가리키는지 주님의 재림인지가 분명치 않다.

2. 요한복음 14장 2절의 "내 아버지의 집에 거할 곳이 많도다"란 말에 의거하여 하늘의 처소를 보아야 한다.[250)] 바울은 단순히 몸의 죽음 후에 가게 되는 천국을 지칭한다는 것이다. 이 경우, 첫째, 앞에서 지적했듯이, 앞의 "집"은 몸을 가리키고, 뒤의 "집"은 그대로 "집"을 가리키게 되어 논리적 일치가 사라진다고 반대할 수 있다. 둘째, 요한복음의 "거할 곳"을 바울 서신 해석을 위해 사

---

248) Thrall 363-367.

249) Bruce, 202, Allo, 138-9, Windisch, 159, Hughes, 165, Thrall, 363, 367.

250) Tasker, 78; Martin, 104; C. Hodge, *An Exposition of the Second Epistle to the Corinthians* (New York: A. C. Armstrong & Sons, 1891, reprint, Edinburgh: Banner of Truth, 1959), 485-8; J. C. K. von Hofmann, *Der zwei Brief Pauli an die Korinther*, Die heilige Schrift des Neuen Testaments II 3 (Nördlingen: C. H. Beck, 1866), 126.

용하는 것은 안전하지 못하다는 반대도 있다.[251] 셋째, 2절 이하에서 "하늘에서 오는 처소를 덧 입는다"는 말도 어쩌면 집보다는 몸을 뜻하는 것 같다. 첫째와 둘째의 반대에 대하여, 죽음 후에 천국에 가는 것은 요한복음뿐만 아니라 성경의 보편적인 믿음이라고 반박할 수 있다(욥 16:19; 히 11:16; 빌 2:10; 고전 15:49). 셋째 반대에 대하여, 2절의 하늘로부터 오는 처소로 덧입는다는 말은 바울이 살아 있는 동안 하늘의 새 예루살렘이 내려와 몸이 변화되는 것을 나타낸다고 볼 수 있다. 이것도 초대교회의 보편적인 믿음이라고 할 수 있다(갈 4:26; 계 21:2).[252]

3. "일시적인 하늘의 몸"으로서 임종 시에 받는 몸을 가리키며, 부활 시에 부활하는 육체와 결합되게 된다. 다른 말로, 임종 시에 얻는 부활의 완전한 몸 이전의 일시적인 상태를 가리킨다. 이 해석은 본문의 난제, 즉 본문이 가리키는 시간이 개인의 죽음을 가리키는지 아니면, 주의 재림 때를 가리키는지에 대한 논쟁을 접어두고 두 가지 때를 함께 포괄적으로 가리킨다고 하여 전체 해석의 어려움을 덜어 주는 장점이 있다.[253] 그러나 이런 일시적인 의미는 "영원한 집"이란 말이 있으므로 인위적인 해석이라는 비난을

---

251) Thrall, 364.

252) Martin은 1절의 "하늘의 집"(οἰκοδομὴν··· ἐν τοῖς οὐρανοῖς)은 영원한 집으로 보고, 2절의 "하늘의 처소"(τὸ οἰκητήριον ··· τὸ ἐξ οὐρανοῦ)는 부활의 몸으로 본다(103-4). 그는 바울의 종말관 가운데 이 두 가지 생각이 다 있으며 여기서도 그대로 나타난다고 보는 것이다(고전 15:51이하; 갈4:26). 결국 바울이 유사한 암시적 표현으로 말미암아 혼돈을 일으켰으나 실제는 다른 것을 가리킨다고 본다.

253) F. G. Lang, *2 Korinthers 5, 1-10 in der neuren Forschung*, BGBE 10 (Tübingen: Mohr, 1973), 11-13; D. E. H. Whitely, *The Theology of St. Paul* (Philadelphia: Fortress, 1966), 260.

면하기 어렵다.

4. 세례 시에 받는 "영적인 옷"을 가리키며, 4장 16절의 "속사람"의 다른 표현이다. "물질적 겉옷"인 육체 안에 입고서 죽음 이후에도 입고 있다가 부활 시에 벗고 "신령한 몸"으로 된다.[254] 이 해석은 4장 16절의 "속사람"과 연계하여 해석하는 장점이 있다. 그러나 본문의 "하늘 집"에 대한 소망은 4장 16절의 "속사람"과 구별되는 듯이 보인다. "속사람"은 이 땅에서 믿는 자에게 이미 주어진 것이며, "하늘 집"을 갖기 이전 신분이다. 그러나 "하늘 집"은 미래적이며 "땅의 집"이 무너질 때에 대비하여 준비된 것이다. "속사람"은 "겉 사람"과 함께 있고 믿는 자가 이 땅에서 소유하는 것이나, "하늘 집"은 "땅의 집"이 무너질 때(죽음이든, 부활이든) 오는 것이다. 바울은 2절에서 "하늘 집"을 아직 갖지 못하고 얻기를 소망하고 있다. 이에 대해서 "우리가 갖는다"가 현재의 소유를 의미한다고 반대할 수도 있으나, 이것은 현재의 소유가 아니라, 앞의 조건문의 귀결절로 볼 수 있다. "땅의 집"이 무너지면, 그 결과 오는 것이다. 그러므로 여전히 미래적인 뜻이 된다.

5. 그리스도의 몸 된 교회를 가리킨다. 바울 서신에서 집이란 교회를 가리킨다(고전 3:9; 엡 2:21, 4:12, 16). 이 주장도 "우리가 갖는다"는 말은 현재의 소유를 가리키며 미래적이 아니라는 사실을 중시한다.[255] 믿는 자는 이미 그리스도의 몸이 되었다는 것이다.

---

254) Collange, 180; R. Reitzenstein, *The Hellenistic Mystery-Religions*, ETr. J. E. Steely (Pittsburgh: Pickwick Press, 1978), 354이하.

255) J. A. T. Robinson, *The Body, A Study in Pauline Theology*, SBT 5 (London: SCM Press, 1952), 76-7.

또 "무너진다"는 말을 개인의 죽음으로 본다. 그리스도인은 세례로 그리스도의 몸에 들어왔으며 죽음도 이미 그리스도의 몸에 들어온 이상 또 하나의 그리스도의 지체가 되는 과정이지 분리가 될 수는 없다.[256] 그러나 이런 "하늘 집"에 대한 교회론적 해석은 바울 서신에서 그리스도의 몸이 교회의 세상에서의 현존과 관련되어 있고 개인의 내세의 소망과 관련되어 설명한 경우가 없다는 사실을 간과하고 있다.[257] 또한 2절에서 바울이 이미 가진 것(그리스도의 몸의 지체가 된 것)을 모르고 "탄식하며" 얻기를 소망하고 있다는 어색한 해석을 하게 된다.[258]

6. 하늘의 성전을 가리킨다.[259] 고린도전서 3장 9절에서 바울은 교회를 "하나님의 집"이라고 한다. 계속해서 고린도전서 3장 16-17절에서 교회를 하나님의 전이라고 하며 고린도후서 6장 16절에도 같은 말이 나온다(참조, 고전 6:19). 예수님도 요한복음 2장 19절에서 자신의 몸을 전이라고 했다. 이 외에도 신약에서 하나님의 성전을 암시한 곳이 있다(행 7:44; 히8-9; 계11:19). 또 본문의 "손으로 지은 것이 아닌 집"(οἰκίαν ἀχειροποίητον)은 사도행전 17장 24절의 "손으로 지은 전"(χειροποίητον ναός)과 대조를 이루고 같은 말로 되어있다. 이 견해는 결국 5번의 경우와 같이 하늘의 성전이 곧 부활하신 그리스도의 몸, 즉 교회라는 같은 결론에 이른다. 신자는 교회 생활을 통해서 하나님께 나아간다. 그것은 바로 성전의 역할이다. 그러므로 죽음도 믿는 자가 하나님의 현존하

256) R. F. Hettlinger, "2 Corinthians 5:1-10," *SJT* 10[1957], 188-9.

257) Bruce, 202.

258) Hughes, 166.

259) Hanhart, 167-72; Ellis, 217-18.

심 앞으로 나아가는 것을 막을 수 없다(고후 5:1). 다만 5번의 경우와 달리 교회의 미래적 의미, 즉 죽음 후에도 하나님과의 계속적인 교제를 말함으로 보다 본문의 의미에 충실하다고 본다. 이 견해에 대한 반대는, 본문이 믿는 자의 현재와 미래에 대한 보다 분명한 선을 긋고 있다는 것이다. 6절은 신자가 이 세상에서 하나님의 현존하심에서 떠나있음을 강조하고 있다. 이것은 "하늘에서 오는 집", 즉 "하늘의 온전한 교회"가 오기 전의 불안한 상태를 설명하는 것이라고 생각할 수 있다. 또 다른 반대는, 앞에서 지적한 바와 같이 상반절에서 "땅의 집"이 개인의 "몸"을 말한다면 하반절의 "하늘의 집"도 응당 개인의 다른 "몸"을 가리키는 것으로 보는 것이 자연스럽다는 것이다. 그러나 이것은 바울이 성전을 교회로도 보고(고전 3:16-17), 또 개인 그리스도인으로도 보기 때문에 문제가 없다(고전 6:19).[260] 오히려 1절과 2절의 해석에 도움을 준다. 즉 1절의 "하늘나라의 집"은 "하늘의 성전"을 가리키고, 2절의 "하늘나라의 처소"는 "성도의 온전하고 신령한 몸"을 가리킨다고 해석할 수 있다. 그렇게 함으로써 2절의 "하늘나라 처소"도 역시 "하나님의 전"이라고 해석할 때 일어나는 어색함을 없애주고, 성도가 "신령한 몸"을 덧입는 것으로 이해할 수 있다.

7. 부활하신 그리스도의 몸이다.[261] 이 주장을 고린도전서 15장 47-48절의 "두 아담"의 기독론과 관련시켜 생각하면 더 타당성이 있다. 그리스도의 영광의 몸은 창조의 처음 열매로서 모든 그리스

---

260) 참조, Martin 105.

261) A. Feuillet, "La demeure céleste et la destinée des chretiens: Exégèse de 2 Cor 5,1-10 et contribution à l'étude des fondements de l'eschatologie paulinienne", *RSR* 44(1956) 367, 369-78; 참조, Collange, 190-1.

도인의 영광의 몸을 포함한다. 그리스도인은 임종 시에 이 영광의 몸을 소유하게 된다. 즉 부활의 주님과 함께 거하게 된다. 결국 1번과 유사한 견해가 된다. 그러나 그리스도의 부활하신 몸을 집으로 말한 예가 없다.

8. 종말의 영광에 대한 묘사이다.[262] 퍼니쉬는 고린도후서 4장 18절-5장 1절을 빌립보서 3장 12-21절과 비교하면서 유사점을 찾는다. 빌립보 본문의 시민권은 미래의 종말을 나타내는 묘사라고 한다. 이 두 본문 모두 신자는 이미 하늘나라에 속한 자로서 살아야한다는 주제를 갖고 있다. 더구나 빌립보서 3장 21절에서 바울은 "우리의 낮은 몸을 자기 영광의 몸의 형체와 같이 변케 하시리라."고 말한다. 결국 이 해석은 1번과 7번의 해석과 같다. 그리스도인의 장래의 부활뿐만 아니라 현재의 변화된 존재를 함께 인정함으로써 16절의 "속사람"과 관련되어 전체적으로 보아 균형 있는 원만한 해석이 된다.

9. 하나님의 구원 영역에 들어 있는 전인(全人="den ganzen Menschen im goéttlichen Heil")또는 현존하는 천국의 차원을 가리킨다.[263] 본문에 있는 일시성과 영원성, 구원과 멸망의 대조에 비추어 볼 때, 중심 주제는 신자가 이 세상의 삶을 마칠 때, 어떤 영원한 것을 소유하게 된다는 것이다. 영원한 것은 현재적이고 미래적인 의미를 다 포함할 수 있다. 이 해석에 의하면 천국이란 지역적인 것이 아닌 질적인 개념으로 이해함으로써 결국 실존주의적 개념으로 전이된다. 그러나 "땅의 집"이 신자의 몸이라면, "하늘

---

262) Furnish 294-5.

263) N. Baumert, *Täglich Sterben und Auferstehen: Der Literalsinn von 2 Kor 4,12-5,10*, SANT 34 (München: Kösel-Verlag, 1973), 144-46.

264) 참조, Martin, 105.

의 집"도 구체적인 몸을 가리킨다고 보는 것이 자연스럽다.[264] 존재론적 개념은 실재론적인 히브리 사상과는 멀다. 더구나 고린도전서 15장에서 바울은 존재론적 부활이 아닌 육체의 부활과 전 우주적 변화를 논하고 있다. 이런 육체적 부활과 우주론적 변화는 단순한 개념적인 존재론적 의미의 하늘 집과는 맞지 않는다.

"하늘의 집" 해석이 이렇게 복잡한 근본적 이유는 이 말의 암시성 때문이다. 위의 아홉 가지 해석 가운데 개인의 몸으로 보는 해석이 공동체로 보는 해석보다 더 많다. 우리는 위의 2번의 천국, 5번의 교회, 그리고 6번의 성전의 개념들이 합해진 공동체적 의미로 보는 것이 가장 좋다고 본다. 이 세 가지 개념은 의미가 서로 상통하며, 결국 같은 하나님이 통치하시는 포괄적인 공동체 개념에 들어 있기 때문이다. 그러나 2절의 "하늘의 처소"를 "신령한 몸"으로 해석하면 2절 전체의 의미가 분명하나, "성전"(또는 교회, 천국)으로 해석할 때 2절의 의미가 매우 어색한 해석이 된다. "성전"(또는 교회, 천국)을 덧입기를 사모한다는 어색한 해석이 되는 것이다. 그러나 바울 서신에서 성전을 교회 공동체(고전 3:16-17), 또는 성도 개인(고전 6:19)으로 달리 나타내므로 1절에서는 그대로 "하늘의 집"으로, 2절의 "하늘로부터 오는 처소"는 "성도의 신령한 몸"으로 해석하면 된다. 이런 해석이 1절의 "하늘의 집"과 2절의 "하늘로부터 오는 처소"를 모두 "부활한 몸"으로 해석할 때 생기는 어려운 문제를 해소할 수 있다.

첫째, 1절의 "하늘 집"을 "부활의 몸" 또는 "신령한 몸"으로 해석하면 1절이 가리키는 시제는 성도의 임종이 아닌 부활을 가리키게 되는데, 1절에서 바울은 부활보다는 임종을 가리킨다고 보는 것이 옳다고 본다. 임종이 먼저 오고 부활이 그 다음에 오는 것이 대체로 종말론적 순서이다. 만일 1절이 부활을 가리킨다면 2절에서도 다시 부활을 반복하는 것이 되어 어색하다.[265] 1절을 임종시의 부활의 몸으로, 2절을 재림시의 부활의 몸으로 본다면 임종시에 얻은 이미 얻은 부활의 몸을 재림 시에 다시 얻기 위해서 2절의 바울처럼 그렇게도 갈망하는 것으로 되어 이상하다. 재림 시의 부활의 몸을 임종 시에 이미 얻은 몸이므로(부분적이며, 불완전하다 해도), 주의 재림을 그렇게 갈망할 이유가 없을 것이다. 그러나 바울은 2절에서 분명히 주의 강림을 애타게 갈망하고 있다. 이것은 고린도전서 15장 29-30절에서 바울이 고난 중에서 부활을 기다리는 자세와 일치하는 것이다. 만일 죽음과 함께 오는 부활의 몸을 믿었다면 부활보다는 더 가까운 죽음을 기다렸을 것이다. 그러나 그는 죽음이 아니라 부활을 기다렸다.

둘째, 6절과 8절에서 바울이 성도가 몸에 거할 때는 주와 따로 거한다거나, 몸을 떠나 주와 함께 거하기를 원한다는 말을 하는데, 이런 말은 1절의 "하늘의 집"이 성도가 사후에 주님과 함께 거하는 하늘의 거주지를 가리킨다는 증거가 된다.

---

265) Thrall은 1절의 "하늘의 집"을 부활의 몸으로 보고 있다(363, 367). 2절의 "하늘 처소"를 부활의 몸으로 해석하는 경우 바울이 반복적으로 부활의 몸을 말하고 있는 이유를 설명하기 어려운 점을 Thrall도 시인하고 나름대로 해결 방안을 제시한다(372). 그는 2절 초두의 이유절을 이끄는 καὶ γάρ 를 "과연"으로 해석하여 1절의 내용을 다시 확인하는, 결국 1절과 병행되는 것으로 보아서 임종시에 부활 전에 부활의 몸을 받는 것으로 본다. 1절과 함께 2절도 모두 18절의 "보이지 않는 것에 집중하는" 이유를 나타내는 이유절들로 간주할 수 있다는 것이다. 그러나 이런 견해는 억지이다. 1절은 18절의 이유절이며, 2절은 1절의 이유절로 보는 것이 자연스럽다. 무엇보다, 1절과 2절에서 같은 부활의 몸을 되풀이하여 말해야할 필요가 어디 있는가 우리가 논하듯이 1절은 임종을 2절은 주의 강림을 가리킨다는 전제에서 해석하는 것이 가장 무난하다.

셋째, 1절의 "하늘의 집"을 성도의 부활한 몸이나 그리스도의 부활한 몸으로 해석하는 것은 바울의 종말관을 너무 개인적으로 축소하여 보는 문제가 있다. 1절에서 바울은 종말을 보다 넓게 공동체의 변화로 보고 있으며, 2절에서는 보다 축소하여 개인적인 변화로 보고 있다고 생각한다. 바울은 고린도전서 15장에서 부활에 대한 설명에서도 그리스도께서 "모든 정사와 모든 권세와 능력을 멸하시고 나라를 아버지 하나님께 바치고, 만물을 복종시킨다"고 우주적 종말관을 나타내고 있다(고전 15:24-28). 다른 신약의 증거에서도 부활은 개인적 사건이나, 우주적인 종말의 대변혁과 함께 일어나는 사건이다(막 13:24이하; 눅 21:25; 벧후 3:4, 7-13; 히 6:2, 7; 계 20장, 21장). 이와 같이 바울이 하나님의 전으로 교회 공동체의 의미를 나타내기도 하고 개인 성도로 설명하기도 한다는 사실을 본문 해석에 참조할 수 있다.[266] 이런 문제들 때문에 1절의 "하늘의 집"을 문자적으로 하늘의 집으로 보고 2절의 "하늘의 처소"는 "부활의 몸"으로 보는 것이 좋다. 아래 2절 주석에서 이 문제를 더 논하게 될 것이다.

이런 "하늘의 집"에 대한 해석은 "가진다"(ἔχομεν)의 의미와 관련된다. 이것은 현재 동사로서 "하늘의 영원한 집을 우리가 가진다"는 뜻이 되는데, 이 동사의 현재시제에 대한 해석이 다양하다.

1. 신자들이 천국을 "가진다"(현재형)는 말은 신령한 몸이 이미

266) 1절의 "하늘의 집"을 공동체로 볼 때 앞에 있는 "땅에 있는 우리의 장막 집"과 4절의 "장막"도 공동체 의미로 보아서, 이 멸망 받을 일시적인 이 세상을 나타낸다고 볼 수 있으나, 이런 용례가 없다. 더구나 6절, 8절에서의 "몸에 거한다" 또는 "몸을 떠난다"는 표현으로 보아 1절의 "장막"은 거의 분명히 개인의 몸을 의미한다. 참조, Martin 105; Thrall, 367.

하나의 실재라는 사실을 가리킨다고 본다.[267] 이런 뜻은 "우리가 아노니"라는 어떤 진리를 재확인하는 말이 있으므로 확인된다. 그러나 1절의 미래의 의미를 주장하는 견해는 "소유한다"는 말은 앞의 조건절에 있는 "무너지면"(καταλυθῇ)이란 말에 있는 현재 시제의 결과로 오는 시제로 보아야 옳다고 주장한다. 또 신령한 몸이 "이미 있는 천국의 실재"라는 것은 생소한 개념이라고 한다.[268]

2. 천국을 가진다는 현재형은 바울의 장래 소망에 대한 확신, 즉 종말에 신령한 몸을 가지게 된다는 미래의 사실을 강조하는 현재형이다.[269] 그러나 이렇게 "가진다"가 미래의 의미를 가졌다면 "몸이 무너지는", 즉 죽는 순간에 즉시 얻게 된다는 의미는 없이면 장래의 약속으로 되어 버려서 본문에서 강조하는 현재적 위로의 의미를 찾기 힘들게 된다는 비판을 받는다. 바울은 본문에서 신자가 죽으면 종말에는 신령한 몸을 가지게 될 것이라는 단순한 종말론적 의미보다는 지금 현재 죽음에 직면하여 다급한 상황에서 곧 얻게 되는 신령한 몸을 가리킨다는 것이다.[270] 그러나 이런 장래의 영광에 대한 주제가 3장 이후 계속되고 있으며, 장래에 대한 소망은 현재의 고난을 경감시켜주는 효과가 있다. 17절이 이런 의미를 잘 보여 준다: "우리의 잠시 받는 환난의 경한 것이 지극히 크고 영원한 영광의 중한 것을 우리에게 이루게 함이니." 고린도전서 15장 30절에서도 바울은 현재의 고난을 장래의 부활과 관련하여 위로하고 있다.

---

267) H. B. Swete, *The Life of the World to Come* (London: Macmillan, 1917), 29.

268) A. Schlatter, *Paulus, der Bote Jesu* (Stuttgart: Clawer Verlag, 1969), 544.

269) Hughes, 163; Allo, 121; Héring, 47.

270) Harris, 78.

3. 임종 즉시 신령한 몸을 받는다는 것을 말한다.[271] 이 견해에 반대하는 견해는 역시 위의 2번의 미래적 시제로 보는 견해다. 본문에서 긴박하게 즉시 받는다는 증거가 없다는 것이다.

4. "가진다"는 말은 특별한 시제가 없이 1절의 진술을 보편적 사실로 나타내고 있다. 앞의 조건절과 뒤의 귀결절의 논리적 관계를 나타내기 위해 현재형을 썼다.[272] 그러나 이 경우 가정법의 의미가 강해져서, "우리 그리스도인은 죽어야, 신령한 몸을 가지게 된다는 것을 우리는 안다" 뜻이 되어 어색하다.[273]

2번의 현재의 위로의 효과를 가지는 미래적 의미가 가장 타당하다고 본다. 바울은 현재 우리가 고난을 받으며, 심지어 죽는다 해도 하늘나라의 집에 대한 소망으로 말미암아 낙심하지 않는다는 것이다. 16절에도 나타나듯이 바울의 종말론적 사고에는 현재적 의미와 미래적 의미가 늘 함께 있다고 보아야 한다. 미래의 사실을 현재형으로 나타낸 것은 확실한 불변의 진리이기 때문이다.

2. "그러므로 (과연)우리가 여기 있어 탄식하며 하늘로부터 오는 우리 처소로 덧입기를 간절히 사모하노니…"(**καὶ γὰρ ἐν τούτῳ στενάζομεν τὸ οἰκητήριον ἡμῶν τὸ ἐξ οὐρανοῦ ἐπενδύσασθαι ἐπιποθοῦντες,**). 여기서 한글개역판의 "과연"(**καὶ γάρ**)은 앞의 말과 연결하여 "앞의 사실로 말미암아"란 이유절을 이끌고 있으므로, "그러므로"라고 해석하는 것이 옳다.[274]

---

271) Schmiedel, 239; Windisch, 160; Thrall, 369.

272) Bachmann, 219; Furnish, 265; Baumert, 159-160.

273) Thrall, 370.

274) 참조, Thrall, 주 1270, 1272, 372-3.

"탄식하며"(στενάζομεν)의 뜻은 같은 말이 나오는 로마서 8장 22, 23절에서는 "피조물의 고통"과 직접 연결되어 있고, 본문에서는 4절의 "짐진 것"과 연결되어 있어, "하나님의 집"에 들어가기 전 이 땅에서 받는 신자의 고난을 나타낸다. "여기"는 1절의 장막을 가리킨다. "하늘의 집"이 마련된 사실을 알므로 성도는 고난 중에 탄식하며 하늘의 집을 그리는 것이다. "하늘에서 오는 우리의 처소"(τὸ οἰκητήριον ἡμῶν τὸ ἐξ οὐρανοῦ)는 1절의 "하늘의 집"과는 다르게 "신령한 몸"으로 본다. 바울이 꼭 같은 말을 사용하는 대신에 유사한 말로 바꾸어 쓰고 있으므로 다른 뜻으로 보는 것이 옳다. "덧입는다"(ἐπενδύσασθαι)란 말이나 3절의 "벗은 자들"(γυμνοί)이란 말들이 "하늘에서 오는 처소"를 임종시에 가게되는 "하늘의 집"보다(1절)는 부활 시에 얻는 "신령한 몸"으로 해석하게 한다. 특히 "벗은 자들"이 죽은 자들을 가리키는 것이 분명한데, 1절의 "하늘의 집"을 부활의 몸으로 해석하는 경우, 죽은 이들이 임종했을 때 부활의 육체를 이미 가졌을 것이므로, 죽은 이들을 가리켜 "벗은 자들"이라고 말하는 것은 적절하지 않은 것이다.[275] 우리는 위에서 논한 바와 같이 바울이 성전을 교회(고전 3:16-17), 또는 성도의 몸(고전 6:19)으로 나타내므로 여기서도 이런 중복적 의미가 가능하다고 본다. 바울은 주님의 강림이나

275) 1절의 "하늘의 집"을 임종 시에 얻는 "부활한 몸"으로 보는 경우 3절에서 이를 "벗은 몸"과 동일시 해야하는데, "부활한 몸"을 "벗은 몸"으로 간주해야하는 어려움을 피하기 위해서, Thrall은 3절에서 바울은 "벗은 몸"으로 고린도 교인들의 헬라적 육과 영의 분리 사상에 대해서 경고하는 것이며, 바울은 분리가 아닌 영과 육의 만남(2절)을 원한다고 가르치고 있다고 한다. 이에 대한 반대 의견은 바울이 "벗은 몸"이란 말을 헬라식으로 "육체를 벗은 영혼"으로 쓴 적이 없다는 것과 오히려 6절과 8절에서는 영과 육의 분리를 인정하는 듯한 말을 하고 있다는 것이다(Thrall, 377-8).

부활 시에 얻을 "신령한 몸"을 이 땅에서의 고난의 궁극적 해결방안으로 보고 그 것을 갈망하고 있는 것이다. 물론 여기서 바울은 신령한 몸을 "건물"이라는 말과 "옷"이라는 이중적인 암시적 표현을 가지고 나타낸다. "하늘의 처소"를 겉옷을 입듯이 껴입기를 원한다. "덧입는다"(ἐπενδύσασθαι)는 말 자체가 복합어로써 이런 뜻을 잘 나타내고 있다. 이 동사는 신약에서 2절과 4절에서 두 번만 나오고, 명사형("겉옷")은 요한복음 21장 7절에도 나온다. 이 동사가 원래의 의미대로 덧입는다는 뜻으로 쓰였다면, 그리고 "하늘의 처소"가 "신령한 몸"을 가리킨다면, 바울은 여기서 그가 재림 시까지 살아남아서 고린도전서 15장 52절에서 그가 가르치는 살아 있는 성도들의 몸의 변화를 친히 경험하기를 원하는 것이다. "육의 몸"(σῶμα ψυχικόν)이 "신령한 몸"(σῶμα πνευματικο,ν)으로 변화되는 경험을 원하고 있는 것이다.[276)]

3. "이렇게 입음으로써(은) 벗은 자들로 발견되지 않게 될 것이기 때문이라(않으려 함이라)"(εἴ γε καὶ ἐκδυσάμενοι οὐ γυμνοὶ εὑρεθησόμεθα). "입는다"는 것은 2절의 "신령한 옷"을 입는 것을 말한다. 헬라 시대에 "벗은 자들"(γυμνοί)은 육체를 벗어난 영혼, 즉 죽은 자의 영혼을 가리킬 수 있다. 푸라톤은 (죽은 자의)" 영혼이 지하세계의 신에게 몸을 벗고 간다"고 할 때 같은 말을 쓴다.[277)] 또 "몸을 벗은 영혼"이 심판을 받는다고도 한다.[278)]

---

276) 대부분의 학자들이 같은 해석을 한다. Rückert, 144-5; Osiander, 182-3; Meyer, 256; Bachmann, 223; Lietzmann, 119; Plummer, 145-6; Allo, 121; Héring, 48; Hughes, 168; Prümm, *Diakonia Pneumatos* I, 276; Barrett, 152-3; Martin, 105; Thrall, 373.

277) *Cratyl.* 403B, Thrall, 374, 재인용.

278) *Gorg.* 523E-524D, Thrall, 374, 재인용.

필로도 모세의 죽음과 관련한 글에서 "영혼이 발가벗기 운다"는 말을 했다.[279] 영지주의에서도 "육체를 잃은 영혼을 발가벗은 영혼"이라고 했다.[280] 유대교에서는 "벗은 영혼"이란 말은 없으나, 육체와 영혼의 분리되는 것을 도리어 기쁘게 생각하는 경우가 있다.[281] 이와 관련하여 "옷을 입는다"는 말은 유대교 묵시 문헌에서 성도들이 입을 영원한 영광스런 옷과 관련될 수 있다. 에스라4서 2장 45절에 마지막 날 성도들이 썩을 옷을 벗고 썩지 않을 옷을 입는다는 말이 나온다. 어떤 영지주의 책에서도 임종 시에 영혼이 새 옷을 입는다고 했다.[282]

한편 칠십인 역(LXX)에서 "벗은 자"란 말이 "도덕적 부끄러움"을 의미할 때가 있다(사 32:11; 겔 16:39; 23:29; 호 2:5; 참조, 창 3:10). 필로도 타락한 아담의 마음이 의로움이 없이 벗은 상태였다고 했다.

이런 "벗은 자"의 언어적 배경에 의해서 주석가들은 "벗은 자"를 벗은 영혼(즉 죽은 사람) 아니면 도덕적 부끄러움을 나타낸다고 보아왔다. "벗은 영혼"의 뜻으로 쓰였다면, 바울은 3절에서 **εἴ γε**와 함께 "덧입는 소망"의 가능성에 대해서 약간의 의구심을 갖고 있다고 본다. 즉 자신이 살아 있는 동안 재림을 맞아 변화될 수도 있으나 "벗은 상태"(죽은 상태)로 재림을 맞게 될 수 있음을 알

---

279) *Virt.* Thrall, 374, 재인용.

280) M. L. Peel, "Gnostic Eschatology and the New Testament", *NovT* 12 (1970), 154.

281) *Jub.* 23:31; 참조, 욥 19:25; Barrett 153.

282) Peel, 159-62; P. Vielhaur, "Oikodome. Das Bild vom Bau in der christlichen Literatur vom Neuen Testament bis Clemens Alexandrinus," in Oikodome Aufsaetze zum Neuen Testament, 1, ed. G. Klein, TB 65 (Munich: Kaiser, 1979), 39.

고 있었다. 그러므로 2절에서 부활의 몸을 더욱 갈망한다는 것이다.[283] "벗은 자"(죽은 자)로서 주의 강림을 맞기를 원하지 않고 살아서 새 사람을 덧입고서 주의 강림을 맞기를 원한다.[284]

도덕적 부끄러운 의미로 쓰였다면, 주의 강림 시에 그리스도의 의로움으로 입지 못한 불신자들을 가리킨다는 것이다.[285] 믿던 자들도 믿음을 떠나 벗은 상태에 이를 수 있다고 본다.[286] 바울이 여기서 이 말을 도덕적 의미로 썼을 가능성은 10절에서 그리스도인들이 선 악 간에 심판을 받게 되리라는 말에 근거한 것이다. 그러나 10절까지의 본문에서는 그리스도인의 도덕보다는 현재의 신자들의 고난과 재림 시에 있을 그들의 존재의 변화가 주된 관심이다. 더구나 4절의 "벗고자함이 아니요 오직 덧입고자 함이니" 에서 "벗는다"(ἐκδυσάμενοι)란 본문의 "벗은 자"(γυμνοί)와 유사한 뜻을 가진 말이 존재 상태를 가리키는 말로 쓰인 사실로 보아서 "벗은 자" 도 도덕적 의미보다는 존재적 의미로 쓰였다고 본다. 한마디로 바울은 죽음을 원치 않는다. 영혼이 육체와 분리되는 것은 결국 온전한 인간 상태를 벗어나는 불안한 상태인 것이다. 죽으면 비록 주님과 함께 영혼이 있을 것이나, 부활 때까지 온전한 상태는 아니기 때문이다.

4. "우리가 이 장막 아래서 짐을 지고서(이 장막에 있는 우리가

---

283) Thrall, 376.

284) Thrall, 381.

285) Calvin 67; E. E. Ellis, "II Corinthians v. 1-10 in Pauline Eschatology", *NTS* 6 (1960), 221.

286) Collange, 217-18; Furnish 298.

짐진 것 같이) 탄식하는 것은 벗고자 함이 아니요 오직 덧입고자 함이니 죽을 것이 생명에게 삼킨 바 되게 하려 함이라"(**καὶ γὰρ οἱ ὄντες ἐν τῷ σκήνει στενάζομεν βαρούμενοι, ἐφ᾽ ᾧ οὐ θέλομεν ἐκδύσασθαι ἀλλ᾽ ἐπενδύσασθαι, ἵνα καταποθῇ τὸ θνητὸν ὑπὸ τῆς ζωῆς.**). 4절의 상반절은 2절의 상반절의 반복이다. 즉 이 땅에서의 신자들의 고난이다. 이런 고난은 1장 8절과 4장 8-12절의 사도의 고난을 가리킨다. 4절 하반절은 2절 하반절의 반복이다. 그러므로 전체 의미는 2절과 같이 주의 강림 시 살아서 주를 만나기를 간절히 소망하며 고난의 삶을 극복해 가는 것이다. 바울은 죽음과 강림의 중간 시기(Zwischenzeit/Zwischenzustand)를 피하고 싶어 한다.[287] 그는 주께서 강림하실 때 썩을 육체의 몸 위에 새 몸을 덧입기 원한다(2절).

여기서 바울이 왜 "벗고자함이 아니요"라고 하면서 3절의 "벗는 자"에 이어서 "벗음"(**ἐκδύσασθαι**)에 대하여 계속 혐오하고 있는가라는 문제에 대해 몇 개의 견해가 있다.

(1) "벗는다"(**ἐκδύσασθαι**)란 말은 임종 시에 영혼이 육을 떠나 나누어지는 것을 가리킨다. 바울이 고린도 교회의 헬라적 육과 영의 분리 사상을 경계하면서 그렇게 되는 것을 원치 않는다고 보는 학자들도 있다.[288] 바울은 잠시 나마 영과 육이 나누어지는 것을 싫어했다는 것이다. 그러나 8절에서는 이를 인정하고 있고, 또 유대인이나 헬라인이 모두 이런 분리를 두려워했던 것은 아니다.[289]

287) Martin, 105.

288) Bultmann, *Theology* 1:201, 202; Daives, *Paul*, 191-200; Schmithals, *Gnosticism*, 204, Martin, 106에서 인용.

289) *Jub*. 23:31, Thrall 374-75.

또 바울은 죽음 자체를 싫어했지, 죽음 이후의 육과 영이 나뉘는 것을 문제 삼고 있지 않다. "벗고자 함"은 단순과거로 일회적 동작을 가리키므로 죽음 이후의 계속되는 동작이 아니라 죽음 자체를 의미한다고 보아야 한다.[290]

(2) 죽음을 가리킨다.[291] 더 정확하게 죽음 이후 강림이 있기까지의 죽은 사람의 상태를 가리켜 "벗은 몸"이라고 한다.[292] "벗은 몸"은 창세기 3장 7절에서 아담이 타락 이전과 이후에 벗은 상태를 상기시킨다.[293] 랍비들의 주석에 의하면 타락 이전 아담은 벗었으나 실제로 영광의 옷을 입고 있었다.[294] 타락 후에는 영광의 옷을 벗고 벗은 몸이 되었고 결국 죽게 되었다. 바울에 의하면 둘째 아담이신 그리스도 안에서 죄인들은 그 영광의 옷을 입게 되었다(고전 15:47-49). 즉 주의 강림 시에 입을 부활의 몸이다. 바울은 당시 유대인들처럼 죽음을 "벗음"으로 생각했고, 죽음을 수치로 생각했다. 왜냐하면, 죽은 사람은 사람의 온전하고 적절한 모습이 아니기 때문이다.[295] 유대인들에게 사람이 죽는다는 것은 사람이 불완전하게 되었다는 뜻이다. 죽음 이후의 중간 시기는 몸이 없는 시기이며(고전 15:35-38), 그 시기가 일시적이기는 하지만(고전 15:42-44), 일정한 기간이다(고전 15:37). 바울은 흔히 죽음을 자는

---

290) Thrall, 381.

291) Allo, 146.

292) Martin, 107.

293) Thrall, 주 1330, 380.

294) C. M. Pate, *Adam Christology as the Exegetical & Theological Substructure of 2 Corinthians 4:7-5:21* (Lanham and New York: University Press of America, 1991), 115-16.

295) Barrett, 153; Knox 137; *m. Ber.* 3:5.

것으로 말했다(고전 7:39; 11:30; 살전 4:13). 아마 이것은 유대인들이 믿는 대로 죽은 자는 땅 속의 어둡고 음침한 처소인 스올로 내려가 있게 된다는 것을 가정하는 말일 수도 있다. 그러나 이보다 성도의 죽음을 주의 강림을 기다리는 상태로 보아 자는 것으로 말했을 수 있다. 바울은 비록 죽음 이후의 중간시기에 대해 자세히 설명하지는 않으나(실제로 받은 계시도 없고, 아직 경험하지 못했으므로, 또는 주의 강림과 신령한 몸으로 변화되는 것이 궁극적 관심이므로), 이 불완전한 중간 상태의 시기에 처하기를 원치 않았다. 어쩌면, 쿨만이 말하듯이, 이 중간 시기는 이 땅의 삶보다는 낫지만(5:8; 빌 1:23), 여전히 "이미 그러나 아직"("already, but not yet")의 긴장이 지속되는 시기일 것이다. 그래서 요한계시록 6장 9-10절에서 죽임을 당한 영혼들이 최후의 심판의 도래를 하나님께 탄원하고 있다고 한다(참조, 히 11:39). 아직 구원사의 정점인 주의 강림을 기다리는 시기인 것이다. 고린도 교회의 거짓 교사들은 장래의 부활의 몸을 이미 소유한 것으로 믿고 있으나(고전 15:12) 바울은 이를 여전히 기다려야 한다고 가르친다.[296)]

더구나, 4절 하반절의 "죽을 것이 생명에게 삼킨바 되게 하려 함이라"는 말은 상반절의 "벗고자함이 아니요 오직 덧입고자함이니"라는 말에서 "덧입는 것"을 더 설명하여 주의 강림 시에 얻을 "부활의 몸"을 가리킨다면, 상반절의 "벗고자 함"은 부활 이전의 "죽음"을 가리킨다고 보는 것이 논리적이다.[297)]

바울은 이 벗은 중간 시기는 주의 강림 시에 있을 완전한 부활

296) Martin, 108.

297) Thrall, 381-82.

의 몸의 상태보다는 못한 상태로 이해하고 산채로 변화되기를(덧입기) 갈망하고 있는 것이다. 그래서 죽음은 여전히 최후의 적이다(고전 15:26). 또 바울은 죽음을 피한 것을 감사한다(고후 1:10; 빌 2:27). 그러나 바울이 죽음을 싫어한 것은 주의 강림으로 변화되는 것을 더 원했기 때문이며, 죽음을 특별히 두려워했다고 볼 수 없다. 바울은 그리스도인들이 죽을 때에도 그리스도와 함께 있는다고 말하고 있다(롬 8:30) . 그는 차라리 죽어 주와 함께 있기를 원할 때도 있고(고후 5:8; 빌 1:23), 그의 목숨을 사역을 위해 기꺼히 바치기를 원하기도 했다(빌 1:23, 2:17; 살전 2:8). 바울은 이 "벗은 시기" 또는 죽음과 부활 사이의 "중간 시기"를 싫어했으나 공포의 시기로 보는 것이 아니다. 그것은 여전히 주와 함께 있는 시기다. 그의 목적은 주의 강림이지만, 그 이전에 죽는 것도 그리스도와 함께 있게 됨으로 그리스도인에게는 유익일 뿐이다(빌 1:21).

(3) 바울은 불신자들에게 임할 부활한 몸이 없는 육신의 소멸을 두려워했다. 그러나 "벗고자 함"(ἐκδύσασθαι)이 "덧 입고자함이니"(ἐπενδύσασθαι)라는 말과 대조되어 있으므로 재림전의 죽음을 가리킨다고 본다.[298)]

1번은 지나치게 헬라적 의미로서 바울의 사상에 나타나지 않으며, 3번도 바울에게 생소하게 보인다. 2번의 답이 그 설명과 함께 가장 적절하다. 바울은 죽음을 최후의 적으로 규정하였다(고전 15:26). 현재의 그의 사역에서 점증하는 고난이 가리키는 것은 죽음임을 알고 있었다(1:8-9; 4:8-12). 이런 죽음이 오기 전에 주의 강림하심을 보고 신령한 몸으로 덧입는 것이 가장 바람직한 구원의

298) A. Oepke, du,w, *TDNT* II, 319.

길이라고 생각하고 있다. 이런 뜻이 4절 하반절의 목적절에 잘 나타나 있다. "죽을 것이 생명에게 삼킨바 되게 하려 함이라." 같은 표현이 고린도전서 15장 54절에도 나온다. 주의 강림 이전까지 아직 이 땅의 장막 집의 인간은 영원한 생명을 완전히 소유하지 못했다.

5. "곧 이것을 우리에게 이루게 하시고 보증으로 성령을 우리에게 주신 이는 하나님이시니라"(**ὁ δὲ κατεργασάμενος ἡμᾶς εἰς αὐτὸ τοῦτο θεός, ὁ δοὺς ἡμῖν τὸν ἀρραβῶνα τοῦ πνεύματος**). 여기서 "이것"(**αὐτὸ τοῦτο**)에 대한 해석이 여러 가지이다.[299] 강조형으로 "바로 이것"이란 말이 되므로 바로 앞의 4절의 약속을 가리킨다고 본다. 태초에 사람을 죽을 수밖에 없는 존재로 만드신 하나님께서 종말에 그리스도 안에서 영생을 주신다는 약속이다. 더 상세히 말해서 이미 죽은 자도, 아직 살아 있는 자도 주의 강림 시에 영생의 축복을 받게 된다(고전 15:52). 그리스도의 영광에 참여하게 된다(4:16-18). 4절의 약속은 결국 앞서 말한 장래의 나타날 모든 하나님의 구원의 약속과도 관련된다. 이런 구원의 축복은 너무나 놀라운 것이어서 믿기 어려운 것이다. 더구나 지금 무거운 짐 지고 죽음에 이르는 고난 중에 사는 (바울을 포함한) 그리스도인들에게 이런 약속은 너무나 좋고 허황되게 보여 믿기 어렵고 실제적인 가치가 없는 것으로 보일 수 있다. 더

299) C. F. D. Moule, "St Paul and Dualism: the Pauline Conception of Resurrection." *NTS* 12 (1965-66), 118-20. Moule은 "이것"이 하나님께서 우리를 인생의 고난과 죽음 그리고 중간시대를 지나 주의 강림 때에 우리의 육신의 옷을 벗고 신령한 옷으로 바꿔 입게 하신 사실을 가리킨다고 본다. 이런 해석은 "덧입는다" 말의 의미를 약화시키거나 무시하는 데서 온다. 그러나 "덧입는다"는 말이 2절과 4절에서 계속 쓰인 점을 중시하는 것이 마땅하다.

구나 우리를 구원한 그리스도는 고난당하는 우리와 떨어져 계시다(5:6). 그러나 현재 모든 그리스도인의 속사람(16절) 가운데 역사하며, 또 바울 사도의 고난의 사역을 승리로 이끄는 성령의 능력을 볼 때 이런 꿈같은 약속의 성취를 믿을 수 있다. 성령은 하나님의 약속의 장래 성취에 대한 보증이다. 성령의 보증(ἀρραβῶνα)의 역할은 1장 22절에서도 언급되었다. 거기서는 성령의 현재적인 내적 임재를 말한다: "보증으로 성령을 우리 마음에 주셨느니라." 그러나 같은 성령이 장래의 영생의 약속을 확신시켜 주는 것이다. 여기서 중요한 것은 성령이 보증하는 구원의 약속이 보이지 않는 것이지만(4:18), 그렇다고 순전히 영적인, 신학적인, 신앙적인, 종교적인 것만이 아니라 물질적인 것을 포함한 과학적 사실이란 점이다. 여기서 바울은 구체적 "몸의 부활"을 믿고 있음을 주시해야한다. "죽을 것이 생명에게 삼킨바 되는 사건"이다(롬 8:10). 바울에게서 신학이나 과학의 구별이란 없다. 그것은 이 불신적 세대가 만들어낸 구별일 뿐이다. 창세기의 창조나 계시록의 종말은 신학적 사건임과 동시에 자연 과학적 사건인 것이다. 성경은 시공간 가운데서 실제로 일어난 일들과 일어날 일들을 기록하고 있다. 태초에 하나님께서 흑암과 혼돈 중에서 세상을 창조하셨고 그리스도를 통해 구원의 재창조를 시작하셨고(마 4:17; 요 1:9-14) 세상 종말에 여러 가지 어려운 환난 가운데서도 새 하늘과 새 땅의 창조와 구원 역사를 성취하실 것이다. 특히 이 땅의 몸을 가짐으로 말미암아 고난 받는 그리스도인들에게 영광의 부활의 몸을 주실 것이다. 성령이 고난 받는 모든 그리스도인들과 지금 함께 역사하고 승리로 인도하고 계시다. 그렇다면 하나님이 약속하신 엄청난 장래의 구원의 대역사도 이 성령의 역사에

근거하여 믿을 수 있다.[300)]

6. "이러므로 우리가 항상 확실히 아는 바는 (담대하여 … 아노니)몸에 거할 때에는 주와 따로 거한다는 것이니(거하는 줄을 아노니)…" (Θαρροῦντες οὖν πάντοτε καὶ εἰδότες ὅτι ἐνδημοῦντες ἐν τῷ σώματι ἐκδημοῦμεν ἀπὸ τοῦ κυρίου·). 5절의 성령이 몸의 죽음을 폐하고 영생을 주리라는 하나님의 약속의 보증이 되신다는 사실에 근거하여 바울은 6절에서 장래의 소망을 새롭게 갖는다.[301)] 또한 5절 이전까지의 내용에서 그리스도의 역할이 전혀 언급되지 않고 죽음이나 중간시기를 말하는 것처럼 보인 것을 알고 이제 믿는 자와 생명의 주이신 그리스도와의 교제와 관계에 입각하여 그리스도인의 소망을 설명하고 있다.

원문에서 "확실히"(Θαρροῦντες)란 말은 문자적으로 "용기를 갖는다"로 번역해야 한다. 그래서 "우리가 항상 즐겁게 확신하며 아는 것은"이라고 번역해야 한다. 그러나 한글 개역의 번역도("확

300) 바울은 7절에서 "우리가 믿음으로 행하고 보는 것으로 하지 아니한다"고 했다. 이 말을 바울이 하나님의 약속을 과학적 사실로 믿는 것이 아니라 신앙적, 신학적 사실로 믿는 것임을 증거하는 것이라고 우리의 견해를 반대할 수 있다. 그러나 이 말은 하나님의 약속의 내용에 대한 것이 아니라, 약속을 신뢰하는 자세를 말하는 것이다. 하나님의 약속은 분명히 과학적이며 역사적이며 실재적인 것이다. 바울은 비록 현재의 "보이는" 극심한 고난의 사역과 그의 초라한 처지로 말미암아 엄청난 장래의 영광에 대한 약속을 믿기가 어려워도 성령의 보증으로 말미암아 실재로 나타날 것을 믿는다는 것이다. 물론 여기서 바울은 앞서 말한 현재에도 나타나는 성령의 도우심과 승리를 언급하지는 않고 있다. 다만 겉으로 나타난 바울의 고난과 어려운 형편을 보고서 장래의 영광을 믿는 그를 어리석게 여길 그의 반대자들을 염두에 두고 7절을 말하고 있다고 본다.

301) Tasker, 82.

실히")가능한 번역이다(NIV). 이 말은 4장 1절과 16절의 "낙심하지 아니한다"(οὐκ ἐγκακοῦμεν)와 같은 뜻으로 쓰였다. 독자들에게 "확신하며 아는 것은"이란 말로 죽을 수밖에 없는 절박한 현재의 상황에서도 장래의 소망이 있다는 말하고 있다. 하기야 플라톤 같은 희랍의 철학자도 죽음은 영혼이 육체의 고난과 제한에서 해방되는 것으로 즐거워해야 한다고 했다.[302] 스토익 철학자들도 그랬다.[303] 에픽테터스(Epictetus)도 같은 견해를 가졌다(*Diss.* II 1:14). 필로도 그랬다(*Leg. Alleg.* II 57, 59). 바울도 이런 희랍 사상을 알고 있었는지도 모른다(행전 17:18). 그러나 바울의 확신은 어쩔 수 없는 자연적 현상을 초연히 담담히 받아들이며, 세상에 대한 미련을 버리고, 욕심의 마음을 비우는, 수도자(修道者)적인 훈련의 결과로 얻는 확신과는 다르다. 바울의 확신은 죄인을 사랑하여 아들을 희생시키신 하나님을 신뢰하는 믿음에 근거하고 있다(롬 5:11). 그 확신의 가치가 높은 것은 창조주 하나님과의 사랑의 관계에 근거하고 있기 때문이다. 하나님을 믿는 믿음이 없이, 그분의 사랑을 모르고 이 세상의 욕심에서 해방되었다는 것은 허무주의적 포기에서 오는 허탈한 감정을 스스로 미화시키는 인간의 자위적 감정이나 자발적 믿음인 것이다. 이 땅에서 그리스도인이 사는 것은 생명의 주 그리스도를 만날 때까지만 잠시 헤어져 사는 것이므로 낙심하지 않고 용기를 가질 수 있다.

"몸"은 1절의 "우리의 장막 집", 즉 우리의 육체이다. 그리스도인은 이 땅에서 그리스도와 따로 떨어져 살면서 질그릇 같이 일시

302) *Phaedo* 63DE; *Rep.* IX 577B.

303) Plummer 150; Allo 130.

적이며 약하고 언젠가는 썩을 몸을 가지고 온갖 고난을 당하게 된다. 몸을 떠나 그리스도를 만나기 전까지 우리는 "몸에 거하는 동안" 제일 아담으로부터 물려 받은 몸의 제한성으로 인한 모든 고난을 감수해야한다. 그 고난은 죽음까지 포함하는 것이다. 죽은 후 "벗은 자"로서 재림이 오기 전 까지 기다려야 하는 지루함도 포함하는 고난인 것이다. 이 모든 고난을 현실로 받아들이고 살아야 한다. 그러나 몸을 가지고 주와 헤어져 사는 기간이 일시적인 짧은 기간 일뿐이란 것을 알면 오히려 용기를 갖는 것이 당연하다.

물론, 그리스도인은 이 땅에서 몸에 거하는 동안에도 영적으로 그리스도 안에 거한다(고전 6:15; 롬 8:1). 이 광야 같이 낯선 땅에서 주님을 향해가는 순례길에 주께서 우리와 동행하신다.[304] 그러나 영적으로 그리스도 안에 거하는 것은 주의 강림 시에 신령한 몸으로 승천한 그리스도와 함께 누리게 되는 완전한 교제에 미치지 못하는 미흡한 교제 상태이다. 우리가 이 땅에서 그리스도와 헤어져 사는 동안이나, 죽음 후에 육체를 잃은 불완전한 모습으로 존재하는 동안이나, 우리 모두 그리스도 안에 있는 것이다. 그러나 그것은 완전한 의미의 그리스도는 온갖 시험과 도전으로 위기를 맞는다(롬 8:35-39). 또, 죽음으로 몸을 떠난다 해도 이 세상에서의 교제보다는 나으나 여전히 온전한 교제가 아니라, 준비적인 교제이며 부분적인 교제이다. 우리가 죽으면 이 땅에서의 그리스도와의 교제보다는 더 나은 친밀한 교제를 할 수 있겠으나(8절) 죽은 우리 자신의 존재는 아직 신령한 몸을 갖지 못한 불완전한 몸("벗은 몸")을

---

304) W. L. Knox, *St. Paul and the Church of Gentiles* (Cambridge: University Press, 1939) 140, 141. "집을 떠나 있는" (ἐκδημῆσαι)이란 말은 고향을 떠나 다른 나라에 가서 사는 뜻이 있다. BAGD, 238; 벧전2:11; 히11:13-16; *Epistle to Diognetus* 5.

가지고 있으므로 주님과의 온전한 교제를 누릴 수 없다(3, 4절). 오직 영광의 그리스도를 직접 우리의 신령한 부활한 몸으로 만나야 완전한 교제와 그의 영광을 누리게 된다(빌 3:21). 그러나 이런 온전한 교제를 누리게 될 때까지 우리는 그와 헤어져 살아야 한다. 이것은 슬픈 일이나, 일정한 짧은 기간만 지나면 그를 만날 수 있다고 믿으면 힘을 얻게 된다(7절). 이런 믿음을 가지면, 땅의 생애의 일시성은 영원한 생을 소망하는 이들에게는 슬픔이 아닌 기쁨의 근거가 되는 것이다. 바울은 4장 17절에서도 우리의 환난의 일시성을 언급했다(롬 8:18). 우리가 이 몸에 거할 때까지만 이 땅에서 당하는 고난을 참으면 된다. 고난이 극심하면 조급하게 되어 차라리 몸을 벗고 (죽어서) "벗은 몸" 으로라도 주와 함께 있고 싶을 때가 있다(8절; 빌 1:21), 그러나 그보다 더 바람직한 것은 재림으로 오시는 주를 만나 산채로 신령한 몸으로 변화되어 주와 함께 영원히 거하는 것이다(4절; 고전 15:51; 살전 4:17). 그러므로 바울은 신령한 몸을 갖게 될 때까지, 몸으로 사는 동안만 주와 헤어져서 주를 보지 못하고 사는 것임을 알고 낙심하지 말 것을 권면한다.

7. "이는 우리가 믿음으로 행하고 보는 것으로 하지 아니함이로라" (**διὰ πίστεως γὰρ περιπατοῦμεν, οὐ διὰ εἴδους·**). 5절에서 장래의 소망은 성령의 보증으로 가능한 것이라고 했는데, 여기서는 "믿음" 이 또 하나의 장래 소망의 근거로 제시되고 있다. 또 4장 18절에서도 보이는 것이 아니라 보이지 않는 것에 집중한다고 했는데, 여기서도 같은 의미가 있다. 즉 6절의 몸에 사는 동안 주와 헤어져 산다는 사실의 근거를 믿음에 두고 있다. 우리가 주와 헤어져 살면서 장래에 주를 만나게 되는 것을 어떻게 알 수 있는가?

그 약속의 구체적 증거는 무엇인가? 그리스도인은 당장 눈에 보이는 증거 보다 더 확실한 증거로 하나님의 신실하심과 그의 약속을 믿는다. 더구나 5절에서 말한 현재 우리 중에 역사하시는 성령의 보증도 있으므로 우리의 소망은 믿을 만한 근거가 있는 것이다.

"행한다"(περιπατοῦμεν)는 원래 말은 걷는다는 뜻인데, 보통 행함을 나타내는 말이다. 그러나 본문에서 앞 절의 순례적 의미가 고려된다면 "걷는다"란 원래의 뜻이 보다 적절할 수도 있다. 보이지 않는 그리스도를 반드시 만나게 되리라는 믿음을 가지고(고전 13:12) 고난의 순례의 길을 걸어 간다(벧전 1:8, 9).

여기서 "보이는 것"(εἴδους)이 수동적인 의미로 쓰였는지 또는 능동적 의미로 쓰였는지가 문제다. 킷텔은 수동적 의미로 "보이지 않는 것들"로 해석한다.[305] 보이지 않는 것들이 실재하는 것으로 믿는다는 뜻으로 본다. 그러나 큄멜은 능동적 의미로 우리가 그리스도를 볼 수 없으나 그를 믿는다는 의미로 해석한다.[306] 앞 절이 주(κυρίου)라는 말로 끝나므로 큄멜의 해석도 가능하나, 이 말과 "믿음은 바라는 것들의 실상이요 보지 못하는 것들의 증거니"(히 11:1)를 비교해 보면 킷텔의 제안이 옳다. 히브리서의 "보지 못하는 것들"(πραγμάτων … οὐ βλεπομένων)도 수동태로 되어있다(문자적으로, "보이지 않는 것들"). 더구나 바울은 지금까지 보지 못하는 것들에 대한 소망을 말해왔다(4:18, 롬 8:24, 25). 몸으로 사는 동안 그리스도를 보지 못하나 그를 만나리라고 믿는 것도 그

305) Kittel, *TDNT* 2:374, 375; Hughes, 176, n. 2; Plummer, 151이하.

306) Kümmel, *The Theology of the New Testament according to Its Major Witnesses*, ETr. John E. Steely (Nashville: Abingdon Press, 1973) 121, 203; RSV, NEB, JB; Lietzmann, 121; Héring, 49; Bruce, 205; Rossi, 95; Martin, 96; Thrall, 387-8.

중 한 가지다. 7절에서는 우리의 믿음의 원칙이나 유형을 말하면서 그에 입각한 그리스도에 대한 신앙을 말하는 것이다. 그렇다면 수동적 의미로 해석해서 믿음에 대한 일반 원칙을 가리킨다고 보는 킷텔의 해석이 옳다고 본다.[307]

한편 어떤 학자들은 "믿음으로 행하고 보는 것으로 하지 아니한다"는 말의 배후에 바울이 고린도 교회 영지주의자들의 "보이는 것에 대한 신뢰", 즉 그들의 영적 환상과 외적 영광에 대한 자랑을 경계하면서, 참된 그리스도인의 신앙은 아직 이루어지지 않은 것에 대한 소망을 두는 것이라는 뜻이 숨어 있다고 한다.[308] 물론 이런 주장은 10장과 12장에서 바울의 대적자들의 외양이나 영적 체험을 자랑하는데 대한 경계와도 관련된다고 논할 수 있다.[309] 한편, 아래 5장 12, 16절에서 대적자들이 역사적 예수에 대한 지식이나 경험을 자랑하는 것을 바울이 경계한다고 보는 것과 관련지어 생각할 수도 있다. 예루살렘에서 온 유대인 반대자들이 그들의 예수에 대한 외적 역사적 증거에 근거한 믿음을 가르치는 것을 바울이 경계하면서 진정한 믿음이란 성령의 도우심으로 예수가 그리스도임을 믿고(5:5), 그가 장차 영광중에 재림하여 우리에게 온전한 구원을 주심을 소망하는 것임을 가르치는 것이라고

---

307) 참조, Martin 111.

308) Bultmann 141; H. Jonas, *Gnosis und die spaetantiker Geist* (Göttingen: Vandenhoeck & Ruprecht, 1954) II.1.48; A. T. Lincoln, *Paradise Now and Not Yet: Studies in the Role of the Heavenly Dimension in Paul's Thought with Special Reference to his Eschatology*. SNTSMS 43 (Cambridge: University Press, 1981), 68, 213, n. 60; J. Jervell, *Imago Dei, Gen. 1:26f. im Spätjudentum, in der Gnosis und in den paulinischen Briefen*. FRLANT 76 (Göttingen: Vandenhoeck & Ruprecht, 1960), 270.

309) Martin, 111.

볼 수 있다.[310] 그러나 본문은 논쟁이나 경계보다는 장래의 소망을 집중적으로 논하고 있으므로, 단순히 그리스도인의 믿음의 원칙을 말하고 있다고 본다. 그리스도인의 믿음의 근거는 어떤 현실적인 구체적 증거가 아니라 하나님의 신실하심과 그의 약속이다. 그리스도인은 궁극적으로 이 세상 이후의 영적 세계의 약속과 심판을 믿는다. 그러므로 보이는 현실 세상에서의 실망과 낙심을 극복하고 보이지 않는 장래의 소망을 갖는다. 물론 이 세상에서도 믿음의 증거는 나타난다. 바울도 그의 사역 가운데서 하나님이 주시는 위로와 승리를 믿음의 증거로 이미 말했다(1:4; 2:14-17). 그러나 그것들은 부분적이고 일시적인 것들이요 고난은 계속되고 실망과 낙심도 따른다. 바울의 사역도 전체적으로 볼 때 고난의 사역이다(11:23-33). 그리고 바울 자신도 낙심할 때가 있음을 솔직히 받아들인다(1:8-9; 2:1-4; 13; 7:5). 그러나 바울은 고난이 점철된 현실 사역("보이는 것") 가운데서도 영적인 성장과 장래에 나타날 하나님의 영광과 위로("보이지 않는 것")를 믿기 때문에 계속해서

310) Barrett, 158.

311) 이와 유사하게 히브리서 기자도 히브리서 11장에서 고난받는 그의 독자들의 믿음을 독려 하면서, 보이지 않는 장래의 소망인 천국 믿음의 근거를 과거 조상들의 믿음의 역사에서 찾는다. 과거 조상들의 믿음이 모두 이루어 진 것을 볼 때 우리와 그들의 장래 천국에 대한 믿음도 결국 이루어 질 것이라고 말한다(히 11:1-39). 이렇게 역사적으로 증명된 하나님의 신실하심과 그의 약속에 대한 믿음을 따라 형성된 그리스도인의 장래에 대한 믿음(바라는 것, 보이지 않는 것에 대한 믿음)은 망상이 아니라 실상이요 실체(υπόστασις)라고 말한다(히 11:1). 진정한 믿음이란 불행한 현실에 집착하지 않고 하나님의 장래 약속을 믿는 것이다. 히브리서 기자가 보이지 않는 장래에 대핸 믿음을 "실상"과 "증거"라고 주장하는 데서 본문에서 바울이 제시하는 믿음이란 보이지 않는 것을 믿는 것이라는 "그리스도인의 믿음의 정의, 또는 원칙"에 대해 추가적인 해석을 하여 더욱 강화시켰다고 본다.

낙심하지 않는 것이다(4:16; 5:1; 참조, 롬 5:3-4; 히 11:1).[311] 진정한 믿음이란 연약한 자신이나 암담한 현실에 집착하지 않는 것이다(1:9; 4:16). 우리의 약한 존재나 어려운 현실로 말미암아 낙심하지 않고 장래에 나타날 우리의 신실하시고 의로우신 하나님의 위로와 영광을 믿는 것이다(참조, 롬 8:18; 딤후 4:8; 약 1:12). 믿는 자는 현실의 축복에 대해서 하나님께 감사할 것이지만 어려움에 대해서도 하나님의 장래 약속을 믿음으로 즐거워할 수 있는 것이다(참조, 롬 5:3-4; 히 11:25). 약한 자신을 의지 않고 능력의 하나님을 의지하고(1:9), 자신의 외모("겉사람", 육체)의 건강이나 쇠약을 보지 않고, 내면("속사람")적 성장을 중히 여기며(4:16-18), 어려운 현실로 말미암아 낙담하지 않고 장차 나타날 영광과 위로를 보는 것이다(5:1-10).

이런 넓은 문맥적 해석과 함께 가까운 문맥에 의한 해석은 단순히 믿는 자가 이 세상에 사는 동안 생명의 주와 헤어져 있어서 그를 볼 수 없으나(6절) 신실하신 하나님의 약속에 의해서 그를 반드시 만나게 되리라는 소망을 가지고 현재의 고난을 이기며 살자는 것이다.

8. "우리가 확실히 (담대하여) 원하는 바는 차라리 몸을 떠나 주와 함께 거하는 그것이라" (**θαρροῦμεν δὲ καὶ εὐδοκοῦμεν μᾶλλον ἐκδημῆσαι ἐκ τοῦ σώματος καὶ ἐνδημῆσαι πρὸς τὸν κύριον**). 8절은 6절의 계속이다. 6절과 같은 "확실히"란 말로 시작된다. 여기서는 동사도 쓰였으나 어떤 사본은 6절의 분사형을 따르기도 한다.[312] 의미는 마찬가지로 "우리는 기쁘게 확신을 가

312) 0243, 6, 33, 81, 630, 1739, 1881, 2464 pc Tert. Throll, 389, n. 1400에서 재인용.

진다"는 뜻이다. 몸에 거하거나(사나) 몸을 떠나거나(죽으나) 그리스도인은 기쁨을 갖는다. 몸에 거할 때는 하나님의 장래의 약속을 믿기 때문에, 그리고 몸을 떠나 있을 때에는 주님과 함께 있기 때문이다.[313] 6절에서는 현재 분사형이 쓰여서 우리가 주와 함께 헤어져 있는 현실을 말하고 있고, 8절에서는 "(몸을) 떠나 거하는 것"(ἐκδημῆσαι)와 "(주와) 함께 거하는 것"(ἐνδημῆσαι)이 각기 단순과거 부정사형으로 쓰여서 일회적 동작을 가리킨다. 신자가 사는 동안 주님과 헤어져 있으나, 죽으면, 당장 주님을 만나 교제하게 될 것이다. "차라리"(μᾶλλον)는 6절보다 8절의 내용, 즉 주님과 헤어져 사는 것보다, 죽어서 주님과 함께 사는 것이 더 좋다(εὐδοκοῦμεν)는 것을 강조한다. 바울은 육신을 입고 고난 받으며 사는 것보다는 죽는 "벗은 몸"의 상태를 원하고 있다. 물론 5장 2-4절에서는 "벗은 몸"의 상태를 원치 않고 살아서 "신령한 몸"으로 변화하는 것을 원했다. 그러나 이 세상의 고난을 피하고 주님과 가까이 거하기 위해서는 차선책으로 "차라리" 죽는 것도 좋겠다는 뜻이다. "차라리"란 말은 최선의 선택이 아니라 차선의 선택임을 나타냄으로 여전히 바울은 죽는 것을 최상으로 원하는 것은 아닌 것이다. 살아서 부활하는 것이 가장 좋은 구원의 길이나(3, 4절), 죽어서 주님과 가깝게 되는 것도 괜찮다. 다시 말하면, 바울은 죽음에 대해서 두 가지 생각을 갖고 있다. 하나는 죽음이 온전하지 못한 사람의 상태로서 가능하면 피하고 싶다는 것이며, 다른 하나는, 결국 누구나(산 자나 죽은 자나) 주님 강림 시에 부활하게 되는 것이니 만큼, 죽어서 주님과 한층 더 깊은 교제에 들어가고

---

313) Lincoln, 69.

싶다는 것이다(빌 1:20-26). 그러나 여기서 어쩌면 바울은 12장 2, 3절에서 말하는 14년 전 그리스도 안에서 3층천에 간 경험을 회상하는 지도 모른다. 그때 경험은 "그가 몸 안에 있었는지 몸 밖에 있었는지 모르는" 매우 황홀하고 그대로 머무르고 싶은 경험으로 말하고 있다.

바울이 죽어서 주님과 가까이 하는 것이 낫겠다고 말한다고 해서 바울이 실제로 지금 죽고 싶어 한다고 볼 수는 없다. 바울은 그의 사역의 완수를 무엇보다 가장 중하게 여겼다(4:1; 딤전 2:1-8; 고전 9:23 이하; 딤후 4:7). 특히 빌립보서 1장 21-26절에서 그는 죽어 주님과 함께 있기를 원하면서도 빌립보 교인들을 보살피기 위해 살기를 원하고 있다. 또 1장 10절에서 바울은 하나님께서 그를 아시아에서 죽을 지경에서 구해주신 것을 감사하고 앞으로도 구해주실 것을 바라고 있다. 바울이 그의 육체적 생명의 가치를 무시했다고 볼 수 없다. 위 4절에서도 "이 장막에 있는 우리가 짐 진 것 같이 탄식하는 것은 벗고자 함이 아니요 오직 덧입고자 함이니 죽을 것이 생명에게 삼킨바 되게 하려 함이라"라고 말하고 있다. 그럼에도 불구하고 8절에서 죽음의 선택을 비치는 것은 그의 사역이 얼마나 괴롭고 힘들었던가를 보여준다.[314)]

314) Harris는 바울이 고린도 교회에서의 고난 때문에 임박한 종말론에서 보다 현실적인 종말론, 즉 주님의 통치와 심판이 고난의 사역 현장에서 나타나는 것으로 바꾸었다고 한다. M. J. Harris, "2 Cor 5:1-10: A Watershed in Paul's Eschatology " *TynB* 22(1971) 56을 보라. 사실 4:7이하와 그리고 16절, 그리고 5:9, 10절에서 이런 고난 가운데 승리하는 현실적 종말론의 내용이 있다. 그러나 4:18 이후부터 5:8까지는 미래적 종말론이 지배적이다. 그러므로 종말론의 변화라고 하기 보다는 오히려 현재의 종말론과 미래적 종말론이 함께 나오고 있다고 본다. Martin은 "데살로니가전서부터 고전 15장에서 고후 5:1-10까지 종말론의 변화가 거의 없는 것으로 보인다"는 Vos의

어떤 주석가들은 "몸을 떠나 주님과 함께 거하는 것"을 죽음이라고 보지 않고 죄악의 지배를 받는 옛 생활에서 주님의 인도하심을 받는 새 생활로 들어간다는 것으로 해석한다.[315] 10절에 선 악간에 받는 심판에 대한 설명이 이런 해석을 뒷받침 할 수도 있다. 그러나 위에서 언급한 단순과거형의 부정사는 이런 계속적인 동작이 아닌 일시적 동작을 나타낸다. 또 1절에서도 죽음에 대해 말했고 앞의 6절은 주님과 헤어져 살아 있는 것을 말했다. 그러므로 8절은 우리가 해석하는 대로 우리가 죽어 주님과 함께 있게 되는 동작을 나타낸다고 본다.

9. "그런즉 우리는 (몸에)거하든지 떠나든지 주를 기쁘시게 하는 자 되기를 힘쓰노라"(διὸ καὶ φιλοτιμούμεθα, εἴτε ἐνδημοῦντες εἴτε ἐκδημοῦντες, εὐάρεστοι αὐτῷ εἶναι). 9절과 10절은 4장 7절 이후 고난 중에 바라는 장래의 영광에 대한 소망의 결론이다. 여기서 바울은 지금까지 말해온 장래에 대한 소망을 일단 접어두고 당면한 현실문제로 돌아온다. 바울은 주의 강림을 간절히 기다리고 부활의 몸을 얻기를 제일 바라지만, 또는 이생의 고통을 떠나 죽어서 주님과 함께 있는 것을 원하지만, 이 모든 자

견해를 받아들이면서도, 본문에서 바울은 고린도 교회에서의 고난으로 말미암아 바울이 주의 강림 전 죽을 수 있다는 사실을 보다 현실적으로 받아들이고 있다고 본다(Martin, 113). G. Vos, *The Pauline Eschatology* (Grand Rapids: Eerdmans, 1979), 172-205를 보라. 고린도후서뿐만 아니라 거의 같은 사역 시기에 쓰인 빌 1:20-26과 2:17, 그리고 롬 15:31도 유사하게 바울의 두려움과 외로움과 함께 죽음을 현실로 받아들이고 있다고 본다(Martin, 113; Héring, 39; Barrett, 159; Lincoln, 69-71).

315) Collange, 235-7; Furnish, 203; Baumert, 222; 223-5; Thrall, 389-90, 주, 1403-1405 재인용.

신의 소원이 주님이 원하시지 않는 것이라면 아무래도 좋다. 그는 그리스도의 신실한 종으로서 무엇보다 주님을 기쁘시게 해야 한다. 바울의 우선적 관심은 자신의 행복이 아니라 사나 죽으나 주님이 원하는 뜻을 행하는 것이다(롬 14:8; 고후 5:15). 믿는 자를 위해 준비된 영원한 안식과 평안을 간절히 얻기를 바라지만, 사는 동안 오늘 주님이 내게 원하시는 일을 행하는 것이 시급하다. 장래의 약속은 하나님이 이루실 것이다. 나는 그 약속이 이루어 질 때까지 내게 주신 사명을 잘 감당해야할 책임이 있다(롬 12:1 이하; 14:18; 빌 4:18; 골 3:20; 엡 5:10; 히 13:21).

어떤 학자들은 이 구절을 문법적으로 해석하여, 살아 있을 때는 물론 죽은 후에도 주님을 기쁘시게 해야 한다는 뜻으로 본다.[316] 플러머의 말대로 본문을 주님과 함께 거하는 것 자체가 주님을 기쁘시게 하는 것으로 해석할 수 있다.[317] 그러나 "잠자는 자들" 또는 "벗은 자" 들도 주님을 기쁘시게 해야 한다는 것은 바울에게 생소한 교훈이다. 본문은 문자적 의미보다는 지금까지 바울이 말한 우리의 장래 상태에 대한 주제를 말하다가 오늘 우리 각자가 맡은 사명을 완수해야할 책임으로 화제를 바꾸기 위한 화법으로 보아야한다. 마치 주인이 오기 전까지 주인을 위해 열심히 일해야 한다는 달란트 비유의 교훈과 같다(마 25:14-30). 우리는 살아 있는 동안만 일 할 수 있다. 사후에는 쉬며 잠을 자게 될 것이다. 이런 뜻에서 바울은 죽은 후에도 일해야 한다는 뜻이 아니라, 반대로, 죽기 전에 주님이 허락하신 제한된 시간 내에서 주님을 위해 일하

316) Héring, 39; Meyer, 269-70; Hughes, 178-79; Alford, 660-1.

317) Plummer, 155.

라는 뜻이 있다.[318] 우리가 죽는 문제나 또는 죽은 후의 문제는 우리가 주관할 수 있는 문제가 아니라 주님의 문제이다. 우리의 문제는 죽음이 오기 전에 주께서 우리에게 부탁하신 우리의 사명을 다 완수하는 일이다. 나아가 우리의 장래 문제는 오늘 우리가 어떻게 사느냐에 따라서 결정된다.

10. "이는 우리가 다 반드시 그리스도의 심판대 앞에 드러나 각각 선악 간에 그 몸으로 행한 것을 따라 받으려 함이라"(τοὺς γὰρ πάντας ἡμᾶς φανερωθῆναι δεῖ ἔμπροσθεν τοῦ βήματος τοῦ Χριστοῦ, ἵνα κομίσηται ἕκαστος τὰ διὰ τοῦ σώματος πρὸς ἃ ἔπραξεν, εἴτε ἀγαθὸν εἴτε φαῦλον). 바울은 9절에 이어 장래 문제에서 현실문제로 관심을 돌리고 있다. 장래의 심판에 대한 언급은 결국 오늘 우리의 바르고 선한 삶을 권면하기 위한 것이다. 나의 장래문제는 오늘 내가 "몸"에 거하는 동안 "몸"으로 행한 것을 따라 즉 이 세상에서 내가 어떻게 사느냐에 따라서 결정된다. 그러므로 막연히 "몸"을 떠나기를 바라는 것이 아니라, (또는 주님의 강림 시에 "몸"이 변화되기만을 기다리는 것이 아니라) "몸"에 거하는 동안 "몸"으로 행하는 것이 중요하다. 살아 있는 동안 주님이 원하시는 선한 일에 힘써서 주님을 기쁘시게 해야 한다(엡 6:8; 골 3:25). 그리스도께서 강림하실 때 그리스도인들의 행위를 심판하실 것이기 때문이다. 이것을 바울의 믿음으로 구원 얻는 가르침과 대립되는 것으로 생각할 필요가 없다. 사람은 믿음으로 구원 얻으나, 그의 행위에 의해 심판을 받게 된다는 뜻이다.[319] 하나

318) Windisch, 169; Hughes, 179; Martin, 113; Thrall, 393.
319) Bultmann, 146.

님께서 세상을 심판하시나(롬 3:6) 그의 아들 그리스도께서도 심판하신다(롬 2:16, 14:10; 마 25:31; 요 5:22; 행전 17:31). 즉 하나님께서 그리스도를 통해 심판하신다.[320] 바울은 최후의 보편적인 세상 심판도 말하나(롬2:7-10) 이 구절에서는 그리스도인들이 개인적으로 받을 심판을 가르치고 있다(롬 14:10, 12; 고전 3:10-15; 4:5; 11:32; 요 5:27; 행전 10:42). 세상이 받는 영원한 정죄의 심판과 구별되는 일종의 징계의 심판이다(고전 11:32). 이 개인적 심판이 재림 시에 있을 것인지 임종 시에 있을 것인지는 말하지 않는다.[321] 물론 재림 시에 심판이 있다(고전 4:5). 임종 시의 심판에 대하여서는 알 수 없으나 아무런 분별함이나 교정의 과정 없이 거룩하신 주님과 교제하게 된다고 보기 어렵다. 이 심판의 엄정함을 결코 무시해서는 안 된다.[322] 장래의 구원의 믿음과 영광의 소망을 가진 그리스도인들이라고 해서 이런 징계의 심판을 모면할 수는 없다.[323] "각각"(ἕκαστος) 일일이 심판을 받게 된다. 우리 행위의 "선과 악"을 구분할 것이다. 그 심판은 벌 뿐만 아니라 보상을 포함한다.[324] 그들이 행한 행위의 가치에 따라 상을 받게 될 것이다(고전 3:14, 15). 그러므로 믿는 자는 "항상 복종하여 두렵고 떨림으로 구원을 이루어야 한다"(빌 2:12).

여기서 바울이 특별히 고린도 교회의 대적자들도 그들의 행위

---

320) Barrett, 160.

321) Martin, 116; Thrall, 395-6.

322) Tasker, 82.

323) Tasker, 83; Denney, 185; Hughes, 180이하.

324) Hughes, 181; Barrett, 88, 89.

에 따라 심판받게 될 것이라는 암시를 한다고 볼 수 있다.[325] 4:1이후의 내용이 결국 3장의 모세의 의문(儀文)의 직책의 일시적 영광과 바울의 영의 직분이 갖는 그리스도의 복음의 영광의 크고 영원함(3:7-11,18; 4:4-7)의 대조를 통한 바울의 복음의 우월성(3:9, 11)과 그의 사역의 진정성의 주제에서 떠나지 않고 있다. 5장 10절 이후 바울은 다시 4장 1-2절의 그의 복음의 진정성 문제를 거론하고 있다. 트롤은 11절 이하에서 바울 자신이 행한 것에 대한 변명이 나오므로 10절에서 바울은 대적자들에 대한 경계를 하는 것이 아니라 오히려 바울 자신의 떳떳한 행위에 대한 하나님의 인정을 받는 심판을 말하고 있다고 한다.[326] 그러나 결국 바울의 복음의 변명은 대적자들에 대한 경계나 공격과 함께 진행될 수밖에 없는 것이다. 이것은 고린도후서의 전체에서 나타나는 특징이다.

주해(4:16-5:10):

4장 16절-5장 10절에서 바울은 로마서 5장 3-4절과 8장 17, 18절에서와 유사하게 현재의 복음 사역에서 받는 고난을 적극적으로 이해한다. 바울은 우리 부족한 사역자들이 흔히 하듯이 소극적인 자세에서 사역의 실패나 고난을 자신의 미흡함으로 돌리고 좌절하지 않는다. 바울은 미흡하고 불완전한 자신의 존재를 인정하지만(4:7, 16, 참조, 11:6 고전 15:9; 딤전 1:13), 또한 불안한 현실로 인해서 고통 받으면서 일시적으로 낙심도 하지만(1:8, 9; 고전 2:3),

325) Martin, 115; Plummer, 156.

326) Thrall, 394.

좌절하지는 않는다(4:16). 바울은 믿는 자의 외적 육체적 존재("겉사람")는 후패하지만, 영적 존재 즉 "속사람"의 성장을 확신하고(4:16-18), 또 장래에 나타날 하나님 나라에서 온전한 영광의 존재로 변화되는 소망이 있으므로(5:1-10) 낙심을 극복할 수 있었다(4:1, 8, 16). 물론 바울은 그의 고난이 그리스도의 고난에의 동참이라는 중요한 의미와 가치를 지닌다는 것을 고린도후서 전체에서 누차 강조하고 있다(4:7-15; 5:14; 6:4-10; 11:22-33). 그의 고난은 그리스도의 고난의 유형에 일치함으로써 그의 사역이 반대자들의 사역과 차별됨을 보여주는 가장 명확한 증거라고 믿는다(11:22-12:10). 바울은 고난 중에서 자아인식을 더욱 분명히 하게 되었다. 즉 고난 중에서 자신의 영적 존재의 성장과 온전하고 영광스런 존재로 변화되는 소망을 확신하고 위로받고 있다. 십자가의 그리스도의 의로운 사도로서 이 세상의 모든 고난 후에 하늘나라에서 위로와 평안을 얻게 되며, 그의 복음과 그의 사역의 진정성이 결국 증명될 수 있음을 믿는다(5:10; 13:4).

11장 15절 이하에서 바울은 반대자들의 육체적 자랑에 맞서서 그의 고난의 경험들을 자신의 육체적 자랑으로 말하지만(11:16-18) 동시에 그 성격상 그의 약한 것들로서도 자랑한다(12:9-10). 그의 고난은 4장 16절에서 언급한 바울의 외적 인간 존재("겉사람")가 해체되는 고통이라고 할 수 있다. 그런 인간 해체의 고통을 통해서 바울의 내적 인간 존재("속사람")는 성장하고 영광의 날을 기다린다(4:16-5:10). 더구나 하나님은 고난 가운데서도 현실적 승리를 주시면서 장래의 영원한 승리를 확신케 하신다(2:14-17). 즉 1장과 2장에서의 하나님의 위로와 승리, 4장 7-15절에서 말하는 연약한 질그릇 같은 존재를 통해 나타나는 복음의 능력, 그리고 6

장 4-10절에서 말하는 고난을 통한 승리의 경험이다. 끝으로 13장 4절에서 말하는 그의 사역의 궁극적인 승리이다.

그러나 바울은 자신의 약한 것들을 자신의 공로로서 자랑하기 위해서가 아니라 하나님의 섭리와 역사의 특성을 찾기 위해 말한다(4:8-10; 6:4-10; 고전4:10-13; 롬8:35-9). 아무리 "약함의 자랑" 이라 할찌라도 그것이 인간 경험에 근거한 격언 같은 진리라면 반대자들이 주장하는 인간적인 육체적 자랑의 다른 유형에 불과하기 때문이다. 그러나 바울은 하나님의 능력이 약한데서 온전하게 된다는 말씀을 특별한 계시로 받았다(12:9). 뿐만 아니라 그의 사역은 장래의 심판을 대비하여 사람을 기쁘게 하지 아니하고 주님을 기쁘게 하기 위하여 힘쓰는 사역이다(5:9; 참조, 갈 1:10). 자신을 희생하고 남을 위한 사역이다(4:7-15; 12:14-15). 그런 사역은 그리스도의 사역의 유형을 따르는 사역이다(5:14; 6:4-10). 이런 사역이 진정한 그리스도의 사도의 사역이다(4:12).

한편 외모를 자랑하는 바울의 반대자들은 영적 성장을 기대할 수 없고 하늘나라의 소망과 인정을 받을 수 없다(5:10, 12; 참조, 10:7). 그러므로 그들은 진정한 사도들이 될 수 없다(11:13-14).

본문에서 말하는 진정한 복음 사역자의 두 가지 증거는 첫째로, 외적인 육체적 자랑을 하지 않고 즉 현재의 초라한 외적 모습에 감추어져 있는 영적 자아("속사람")의 성장과 장래의 영광된 존재로 변화한다는 소망에 관심을 집중한다(4:16-18; 참조, 5:12; 10:7, 16-18). 둘째로, 현실의 고난이나 번영에 집착하지 않고 하나님의 영원한 시간 속에서 장래의 승리와 인정을 소망한다(5:1-10). 어떤 신학이나 교회는 이 점을 결여하고 있다. 근본주의 신학을 지지하는 어떤 사람들도 실제로 영적 자아의 성장이나 영원한 소망 대신에 외양과 현실적 번영에 집착하는 경우가 종종 있으나, 자유주의 신학은 현 시대 정신인, 인본주의와 상대주의적 가치를 절대시하여 성경을 해석하고, 영혼이나 천국 같은 초월적 신앙 가치들을 과거 시대의 고물로 취급하여 버렸다. 그들은 구체적 행동을 통한 사회정의 확립이나, 개인의 실존주의적 자유로운 가치판단을 존중한다. 그들은 이런 새로운 진리 추구나 행동을 예수님이나 바울의 새로운 복음 진리 운동과 동일시하며, 전통적 성경 해석자들을 예수님과 바울을 반대한 유대교 지도자들과 동일시한다. 그들은 성경의 보이지 않는 영원성이나 초월성을 유대교 묵시문학 운동이나 헬라의 플라톤주의 등에 영향 받은 시대적 유물로 보아 무시하고 보이는 현상세계의 가치에만 집중한다. 그들은 역사적 회의주의에 근거하여 성경을 연구하므로 하나님의 구원의 능력을 믿는 믿음이 없다. 하늘나라의 하나님의 영원한 영광을 보지 못하고 기껏해야 이 땅의 윤리적 종교를 추구할 뿐이다. 자유주의자들은 모든 초월적이며, 내세적인 성경의 내용을 고대인들의 신앙적, 문학적 표현으로 돌리고 실제적 역사적인 것이 아니라고 한다. 그리고 그들은 인본주의에 근거한 개인 윤리나 사회 윤리적 문제에 집중한다. 윤리적 도덕적 현실적 문제가 종교의 중요한 요소이며, 본문에서도 바울이 이 문제를 마지막 부분 5장 9-10절에서 그리스도인의 현실적 책임으로 다루고 있다. 그러나 그 책임이 주의 심판, 즉 초월적 종말론과 직접 관련되어 있다. 바울은 현실 문제를 다루고 있으나 현실의 외면에 집착하지 않고 내면에 집중하고 현재의 성과보다 장래의 성과에 관심을 둔다. 그러므로 바울은 순수한 인간적 사회적 윤리를 다루는 것이 아니라, 하나님께 대한 인간의 책임문제를 다루는 것이다. 하나님 없는 윤리나 도덕은 인간을 근본적으로 선하다고 믿고 인간 집단의 상호간에 맺어진 사회계약이어서 구속력이 약하므로 결국 그 질서 유지 기능을 잃고 개인이나 사회를 혼란으로 빠지게 한다. 인간이 선하다고 믿는 것은 인본주의에서 나온 것이며 기독교 사상은 아니다. 이런 인본주의 사상은 인간이 죄인이란 명백한 사실을 애써 감추며, 모든 전통적 세부적 도덕을 상대화시키며, 인간존중과 인간자유라는 목적에 집중한다. 그러나 매일 우리 주변에 일어나는 많은 일들은 인간의 선보다는 죄의 결과로 일어나는 소식들이며, 인간의 내면에서 일어나는 생각들은 선한 생각보다는 악한 생각들이 대부분이다(롬 7:18-19). 아무도 보르는 죄와 역사의 시간 속에 덮여진 사회악은 얼마나 많으며, 이것을 누가, 어떻게, 언제 정죄할 것인가? 죄인 인간이나 세상이 선을 선으로 판단할 능력이나 자격이 있는가? 마찬가지로 선에 대한 보상을 누가 할 것인가? 이런 질문들과는 상관없이 성경은 모든 인간은 하나님 앞에서 죄인이며, 하나님은 회개하지 않는 죄인을 그의 공의에 따라 벌하고 회개하지 않는 죄악 세상을 멸망시키고 예수 믿고 회개하고 용서받은 사람들을 중심으로 새로운 세상을 창조하신다는 가르침을 갖고 있다(창 7:13; 렘 19:15; 겔 22:31; 롬 1:5-7; 벧후 3:6-13; 계 21:1). 본문의 마지막에도 같은 말씀이 있다(5:10) 이런 구원과 심판의 메시지는 "보이는 것"만을 추구하는 인간들은 성령의 도움 없이는 믿을 수 없는 초월적이며, 영적인 것이다. 초월적이며 영적인 것은 믿음으로만 소유할 수 있다(4:18; 히 11:6).

진정한 그리스도인은 "보이지 않는 것"에 집중하고 "보이지 않는 것"을 믿는다. 그러므로 바울은 본문에서 "우리는 믿음으로 행하고 보는 것으로 하지 아니함이로다"고 말한다(4:18; 5:7; 참조,

요 20:29). 하나님의 영원성과 초월성은 소금과 같다. 영원성이 없는 복음은 시대정신과 함께 변질되거나 사라질 것이다. 성경의 무오, 동정녀 탄생, 예수님의 신성, 육체적 부활, 예수님의 재림 등의 복음의 초월성과 영원성을 믿는 신앙을 지켜야 한다. 복음은 시대정신을 초월하는 하나님의 구원의 능력이다. 복음의 초월성을 불신하는 세력은 어느 시대에나 있었다. 부활하신 예수님을 직접 뵙고도 의심하는 이들이 있었고(마 28:17), 부활을 믿지 않는 이들이 있었고(고전 15:12), 재림을 믿지 않는 이들도 있었고(벧후 3:4), 베드로나 요한 같은 말씀의 목격자의 증언을 거부하고(행 4:18), 바울 같은 능력의 종의 복음을 듣지 않고 조롱하고 반대하던 이들은 수없이 많았다(행 16:21-22; 17:5, 32; 18:6; 19:9; 22:22; 24:25; 26:24). 바울은 초월적인 복음의 내용을 그대로 전하므로 조롱과 핍박을 받았다. 복음의 초월적 내용이 많은 고대인들에게도 걸림돌이 되었다. 그러나 바울은 복음의 초월적 내용을 조금도 양보하지 않고 그대로 전했다(고전 11:23; 15:1-12; 갈 1:7 이하). 바울은 고린도후서 3장 이후 지금까지 그의 반대자들의 현실적 영광에 맞서서 그의 복음과 사역의 내면성과 영원성을 그 진정성의 판단 기준으로 제시하고 있다. 과학적인 시대에 보이지 않는 초월적이고 영원한 하나님의 구원 역사를 전하는 것은 지혜 없는 일같이 보이고 부끄러운 일이다. 현대 보다 비과학적인 헬라 시대에 살던 이들도 복음을 비웃었다(행 17:32). 그러나 바울이 말한 것처럼 이 세상의 지혜는 없어질 일시적 지혜이며(고전 2:6), 그의 복음은 하나님께로부터 온 신령한 지혜이며(고전 2:7 이하), 구원을 주시는 하나님의 능력이다(롬 1:16). 하나님은 그의 지혜로우신 섭리 가운데서 교만하고 스스로 지혜롭다고 생각하는 이들에게는 구원의 은혜를 베풀지 않으시고 그의 복음을 겸손히 믿는 이들에게 구원을 베푸신다.

그러므로 복음을 거절하고 불신하고 의심하는 이들에게 그들의 구미에 맞추어 예수 구원의 말씀이 빠진 변질된 복음을 전하는 것은 중요한 성분을 빠트려서 약효가 없어진 약을 환자에게 처방하는 것과 같다. 복음은 예수가 길이요 진리요 생명임을 담대히 증거한다(요 14:6). 그를 믿고 구원 얻는 진리만이 사람을 구할 수 있다는 것이 성경저자들의 한결같은 증언이다. 진정한 그리스도인들은 예수를 믿어 죄 회개하고 용서함 받아 구원받는 복음진리를 굳게 믿고 담대히 증거 해야 한다. 이외에 어떠한 변질된 복음을 경계해야한다.

한편 전통적 신앙이나 신학을 표방하는 그리스도인이나 교회들 가운데 실제로 변질된 복음을 전하고 배우는 경우도 있다. 이단과 다를 바 없이 외적이고 일시적 영광을 추구하는 그리스도인들과 교회들이 있다. 그들은 전통적 신앙 신조를 지키며 하나님의 초월적이고 영원하신 약속들을 믿는 다고 자랑하나 실제로는 세속적 인본주의와 물질주의, 교권주의, 그리고 눈에 보이는 현상주의와 자기만족에 빠져 있다(롬 16:18; 빌 3:19). 마음과 생활과는 분리된 정통주의적 교리를 암송 하는 것만으로는 하나님의 심판을 면할 수 없다.

고난 중에서 오래 동안 낙심하지 않고 믿음에 합당하게 사는 것이 중요하다. 바울이 본문에서, "우리가 믿음으로 행하고 보는 것으로 하지 않음이로다"(5:7)라고 한 말을 중시해야 한다. 첫째로, 우리의 세상에서의 약한 존재로 말미암아 낙심하지 말고, 고난 중에서도 영적 성장을 위해 힘써야 한다(4:16-18). 둘째로 우리의 사역의 실망스런 성과로 말미암아 좌절해서도 안 된다. 우리의 사역에 대한 영원한 하나님 나라에서의 위로와 인정을 소망하면서 우리의 사역을 계속해야 한다(5:1-10). 비록 현실이 암담하여도 하나님께서 그의 영원하신 약속과 시간 가운데서 믿는 자로 하여금 그의 영광을 보게 하실 것을 믿고 소망을 가지고 살아야 한다. 셋째로, 첫째와 관련이 되지만, 우리는 우리의 육체적 외양의 자랑을 그치고(5:12; 참조, 10:7) 주안에서 새로운 피조물로서 의식을 가지고 그에 걸 맞는 새로운 가치를 추구해야 한다(5:16-17). 즉 그리스도의 진실한 일군으로서 진실하게 일해야 한다(2:17; 5:15; 7:2; 12:18).

끝으로, 복음 전도자가 복음 진리를 전하는 일과 함께 중요한 것은 5장 9절에서 바울이 말하듯이 사나 죽으나 주를 기쁘시게 하는 자가되도록 힘쓰는 것이다(롬 14:8; 고후 5:15). 이 말에서 두 가지 교훈을 얻을 수 있다. 첫째로, 하나님을 믿는 사람이라면 하나님 중심으로 생각하고 하나님 중심으로 살아야 할 것이다. 자유주의자나 인본주의자는 이런 말에 귀를 막지 말고 겸손히 듣고 인본주의적 사고와 삶을 회개해야 할 것이다. 또 많은 외식주의자들은 그들이 쓴 가면을 벗고 마음으로부터 회개하고 하나님의 말씀에 합당하게 살기 위해 힘써야 할 것이다. 또 당장 눈에 보이는 외적 은사나 증거나 문제 해결을 찾기에 급급한 이들은 하나님의 보이지 않는 지혜와 영원하신 약속을 믿고 그를 잠잠히 바라야 할 것이다. 둘째로, 바울은 세상을 떠나 주와 함께 있기를 원하면서도 주님을 만나기 전에 주님이 맡기신 사명을 이 땅에서 완수하는 일이 더 시급하다고 생각한다. 그는 장래에 나타날 주의 영광의 날을 기다리면서, 종말론적 신학을 언급한 후에, 그가 가르치는 종말론에 합당한 경건하고 두려운 자세를 취한다. 종말을 기다리는 사역자로서 자신의 사역도 주님의 최후 심판에서 평가받을 것임을 알고 있다(5:10). 성경 연구가들도 하나님의 말씀을 연구의 대상과 논쟁거리로 삼는데서 나아가 각자에게 주신 하나님의 명령으로 삼가 받들어 그대로 살기를 힘써야 한다. 우리 그리스도인들은 우리가 가지고 있는 모든 거룩한 신앙 신조에도 불구하고 그에 합당한 삶을 살지 못한다면 엄중한 주님의 심판을 받는다는 것을 명심하자. 초월적이고 영원한 진리를 믿는다고 자랑하면서, 그 믿음에 합당하고 경건하게 의로운 삶을 살지 못한다면 우리는 복음이 약속하는 아무 것도 받을 수 없다. 우리가 믿는 복음의 진정성을 증거하기는커녕, 위선적인 복음의 훼방꾼이 될 뿐이다. 최후의 영광과 심판을 믿으면서도, 이에 대비하여 두렵고 떨림으로 우리의 구원을 이루지 못한다면 이야말로 하나님의 진노를 쌓는 일이다(빌 2:12).

vii. "우리"의 사역의 동기의 진정성(5:11-15)

본문:

> 11. 우리가 주의 두려우심을 알므로 사람(들)을 권하노니 우리가 하나님
> 앞에 알리워졌고 또 너희의 양심에도 알리워졌기를 바라노라. 12. 우리
> 가 다시 너희에게 (우리를) 자천하는 것이 아니요 오직 우리를 위하여
> 자랑할 기회를 너희에게 주어 마음으로 하지 않고 외모로 자랑하는 자들
> 을 대하게 하려 하는 것이라. 13. 우리가 만일 미쳤어도 하나님을 위한
> 것이요, 만일 정신이 온전하여도 너희를 위한 것이니, 14. 그리스도의 사
> 랑이 우리를 강권하시는 도다. 이는 우리가 확신하는 바(우리가 생각컨
> 대) 한 사람이 모든 사람을 대신하여 죽었은즉 모든 사람이 죽은 것이라.
> 15. 저가 모든 사람을 대신하여죽으심은 산 자들로 하여금 다시는 저희

자신을 위하여 살지 않고 오직 저희를 대신하여 죽었다가 다시 사신 자를 위하여 살게 하려 함이라.

본문 비평:

1. 11절에서 p46 P ψ 629 2464 pc vgms은 πείθωμεν(가정법)을 본문의 πείθομεν("권하노니")대신하여 쓰고 있다. 트롤은 이를 필사자의 오류로 본다.[327]

2. 12절에서 p46 B ℵ은 본문의 ὑπέρ ἡμῶν("우리로 인하여") 대신에 ὑπέρ ὑμῶν("너희로 인하여")를 쓰고 있다. 바레트는 후자의 진정성 가능성을 어느 정도 인정하며,[328] 꼴란쥐(Collange)은 후자를 지지하고 있다.[329] 이 경우 바울이 고린도 교인들을 양육하였으므로 그들의 양심에 호소하여(ὑπέρ ὑμῶν["너희로 인하여"]) 그의 사역의 진정성을 판단하도록 한다는 뜻으로 본다.

3. 12절의 μὴ는 ℵ B에 나타나고, οὐκ는 D C G에 나타난다. 특별한 변화의 이유를 알 수 없다.

4. 12절의 μὴ ἐν καρδίᾳ는 p46 ℵ B에서, οὐ καρδίᾳ는 C D2에서, οὐκ ἐν καρδίᾳ는 D* F G에서 나타난다. 본문의 μὴ ἐν καρδίᾳ가 원래의 것으로 본다. μὴ는 앞의 분사 καυχωμενους("자랑하

327) Thrall, 401, 주 1457.

328) Barrett, 162, 주, 1.

329) Collange, 248.

는")가 ἐν καρδίᾳ 앞에서 생략되어 있다고 보고 생략된 분사를 부정하는 데 쓰였다. 즉 "마음으로 자랑하지 아니하고"의 뜻이다.

5. 14절의 ὅτι εἰ가 ὅτι εἰ εἷς로 조건절로 되는 곳이 있으나(א² C* 048, 0243, 81, 104, 365, 629c, 1175, 1739 *pm* f vg sa boms), 이것을 후대의 삽입으로 본다.[330]

내용 개요:

마틴은 5장 11-15절이 5장 1-10절의 결론 부분이며, 5장 16절 이하와의 연결부분이라고 본다.[331] 그러나 5장 11-15절에서 바울은 4장 16절-5장 10절의 종말론적 소망(4:16-5:10)에서부터 현실적인 문제, 즉 앞에서 말한 그의 사역의 진정성 문제로 다시 돌아온다(4:1). 사실 9, 10절에서 바울은 자신의 사역의 평가 문제를 종말론적 심판(평가)과 연결하여 언급하였다. 5장 11-15절에서는 4장 1-18절의 내용을 다시 상기시키면서 바울의 사역의 진정성 문제를 다시 시작하고 있다. 여기서 바울의 사역의 고난과 승리의 양면성을 다시 언급한다. 5장 11-13절에는 하나님으로부터 받은 바울의 사도직이 언급되나, 그 후에는 종으로서의 모습이 나온다. 이런 서술은 하나님의 아들이면서 하나님의 종이신 그리스도의 역설적인 유형을 따르는 데서 나온다. 기독론과 관련된 바울의 사역에 대한 역설적인 특성 때문에 바레트는 5장 11-21절을 바울 서신 가

330) Thrall 407, 주, 1511.

331) Martin, 118.

운데 가장 포괄적이며, 어렵고, 중요한 구절이라고 했다.[332)]

여기서 새로운 점은 첫째, 바울이 자찬(自讚)을 원치 않으나 자신의 사역의 진정성을 알리기 위해서는 어쩔 수 없이 해야 하는 난처한 입장에서(고후 11:16; 12:1, 5, 6, 11), 자신이 자신을 위한 자찬을 하는 것보다는 고린도 교인들이 스스로 바울의 대적자들의 비난에 맞서서 바울의 사역의 진정성을 알아서 대변할 수 있도록 하기 위해 자찬할 수밖에 없다는 것이다(11). 둘째, 바울의 사역이 진실한 까닭은 심판주이신 주님의 두려움을 가지고 일한다는 것이다(11; 참조, 빌 2:12). 셋째, 바울의 사역의 진실성은 그 사역 동기가 외형적인 것이 아니라 내적인 그리스도의 희생적 사랑이기 때문이다(14; 참조, 2:4; 11:11; 12:14, 15; 13:7, 9). 그의 사역은 하나님을 위한 사역이며 동시에 고린도 교인들을 위한 헌신적인 것이었다(13, 15). 바울의 사역을 통해서 그리스도의 사랑과 하나님의 화해의 구원 역사가 고린도 교인들에게 나타났다(16절 이하).

주석:

11. "우리가 주의 두려우심을 알므로 사람(들)을 권하노니 우리가 하나님 앞에 알리워졌고 또 너희의 양심에도 알리워졌기를 바라노라" (Εἰδότες οὖν τὸν φόβον τοῦ κυρίου ἀνθρώπους πείθομεν, θεῷ δὲ πεφανερώμεθα· ἐλπίζω δὲ καὶ ἐν ταῖς συνειδήσεσιν ὑμῶν πεφανερῶσθαι). 바울은 10절에서 모두 주의 심판을 받게 되는 것을 말하였으므로, 심판 주이신 주에 대한

332) Barrett, 163.

두려움(τὸν φόβον)이 그로 하여금 그의 사역을 삼가 조심하며 수행하게 한다.[333] 전지전능하신 하나님을 두려워하는 것이 지혜문학의 근본사상일 뿐만 아니라 하나님을 믿는 신앙의 본질이다.[334] 이런 두려움은 인간으로서 갖는 일반적인 두려움과 구별되는 피조물 인간이 창조주 앞에서 갖는 거룩한 두려움이다. 그것은 죄인 인간이 구원의 하나님 앞에서 가질 수밖에 없는 공통적이고 필수적인 경험이다(출 19:16; 눅 5:8). 이 거룩한 두려움은 사람으로 하여금 자신을 주님의 종으로 인식하게 하여, 삼가 조심하여 거룩한 삶을 살게 하고, 겸손하게, 그리고 충실하게 주인이 맡긴 자신의 소임을 다하면서 주인의 최종적 평가(심판)에 대비한다(마 25:14-30). 여기서 바울은 그리스도에게 구약의 하나님의 경외사상을 그대로 전이시킨다. 바울은 그리스도의 사도, 또는 종으로서 그리스도의 심판을 두려워하면서 그는 그의 사역을 수행한다. 주의 두려움은 바울이 복음을 전하는 모든 사람들에게도 알려 져야 한다. 그들 모두가 예수 믿고 회개하지 않으면 주의 심판을 받아 멸망하게 되기 때문이다. 바울은 그들이 하나님을 경외하여 멸망 받을 죄의 길에서 벗어나 구원의 바른 길로 가도록 사람들을 권면한다(πείθομεν).[335] 아래에 나오는 5장 14, 15절에서도 바울의 사역은 그리스도의 구원 사역을 수행하는 것이라고 한다. 그러나 이 문맥

333) Martin은 바울의 두려움이 하나님의 앞에 서있는 두려움(롬 2:1-11)과 구별되는 하나님의 깊은 지혜로 이끄는 두려움이라고 한다(욥 28:28; 전 12:13; 잠 9:10; 시락서 1:18).(Martin 120). 그러나 5:10의 주의 심판에 대한 언급이 있었으므로 전자의 의미가 있다고 본다(Hughes 186).

334) O. Glombitza, "Mit Furcht und Zittern. Zum Verstaendnis von Phil. 2:12," *NovT* 3(1959) 105, 106.

335) Bruce, 163.

에서 보아 권면의 내용은 그의 사도직의 진정성에 대한 것을 포함하는 것이라고 보아야 한다.[336] 그리고 11절의 "사람들"(ἀνθρώπους)은 일반적인 청중을 가리키는 것이라기보다는, 외모로 사람들을 평가하는 성향을 가진 사람들을 가리킨다.[337] 아래 12절에서 외모를 자랑하는 바울의 대적자들에 대해서 바울은 마음으로 자랑한다고 했는데, 사무엘상 16장 7절의 "사람은 외모를 취하나 나는 중심을 보느니라"는 말씀이 그 배경에 있다고 본다. 여기서 "사람"도 역시 이 말씀을 상기시킨다. 사람들은 대개 "보이지 않는 것"보다 "보이는 것"을 에 집중하고 일시적인 외적 영광을 잘 따른다(4:18). 이런 사람들을 설득하는 일은 쉬운 일이 아니다. 그래서 바울은 그의 사역이 이미 하나님에게 인정받은 것처럼,[338] 고린도 교인들에게도 인정되기를 원한다. 그는 바로 앞에서 그가 주를 기쁘시게 하는 것이 그의 사역의 목표라고 했고(5:9) 하나님께 그의 사역의 진정성을 이미 인정받았다(1:23; 2:14; 고전 9:1, 2; 고후 10:8). 그러나 바울은 사역의 대상인 고린도 교인들에게 인정받는 일에 어려움을 겪고 있다. 바울의 진정성을 그들에게

336) Plummer, 168; Hughes, 186; Collange, 245; Denney, 187; Martin, 121. Bultmann은 "설득한다"(πείθομεν)는 말이 바울의 대적자들이 바울의 사역을 비웃으며 사용한 말이라고 한다. 그렇지 않다면 παρακαλεῖν을 썼을 것이라고 한다. R. Bultmann, *Exegetische Probleme des zweiten Korintherbriefes* (Darmstadt: Wissenschaftliche Buchgesellschaft, 1963) 13. Martin도 이에 동의하면서 바울은 반대자들의 비난("바울이 사람들을 꾄다")에도 불구하고 오히려 여전히 같은 말(πείθειν)을 써서 그들과 맞선다고 한다(121). 참조, Burton, *Galatians*, ICC (New York: Scribner's Sons, 1970), 30.

337) Thrall, 402.

338) 하나님 앞에 "알리워졌고"의 πεφαερώμεθα는 완료형으로서 바울이 하나님 앞에서 그의 사도로서 그의 사역을 완전히 인정받았다는 의미이다(Martin, 122).

알리는 데 방해되는 요소들이 많이 있기 때문이다(4:2-4; 6:3; 10:7, 10; 11:3). 즉 고린도 교인들은 외모 지향적인 사람들로서 "보이는 것"과 일시적 영광을 따르므로 "보이지 않는 것"과 영원한 영광을 추구하는 바울의 사역을 이해하기 어렵고, 또 이런 고린도 교인들의 성향을 이용하여 바울의 사역을 비난하는 거짓사도들의 방해이다(4:17-18; 5:7; 11:13-15). 바울은 다음에 나오는 절(12) 에서 이런 사람들을 직접 경계한다. 바울은 고린도 교인들이 거짓 사도들의 온갖 방해를 물리치고 바른 양심에 의해서 바울의 사역의 진정성을 알게 되기를 원한다(4:2). 이렇게 되기를 희망한다. "나는 바란다"(ἐλπίζω)는 말은 4장 1절과 8절에서 "낙심하지 않는다"는 말을 다시 상기시킨다(οὐκ ἐγκακοῦμεν, οὐκ ἐξαπορούμενοι). 그러나 바울은 그가 하나님께 이미 인정받았다고 말함으로써 고린도 교인들에게 자신의 결백함과 정당함을 분명히 알리고 있다. 이제 남은 것은 고린도 교인들의 결단이다. 그러므로 11절은 바울의 사도직의 진정성에 대한 고린도 교인들의 분명한 결단을 촉구하는 말이 된다.

12. "우리가 다시 너희에게 (우리를) 자천하는 것이 아니요 오직 우리를 위하여 자랑할 기회를 너희에게 주어 마음으로 하지 않고 외모로 자랑하는 자들을 대하게 하려 하는 것이라"(οὐ πάλιν ἑαυτοὺς συνιστάνομεν ὑμῖν ἀλλὰ ἀφορμὴν διδόντες ὑμῖν καυχήματος ὑπὲρ ἡμῶν, ἵνα ἔχητε πρὸς τοὺς ἐν προσώπῳ καυχωμένους καὶ μὴ ἐν καρδίᾳ). 바울은 3장 1절에서도 자신이 자천(自薦)할 필요가 없다고 했다. 고린도 교인들의 변화된 생활이 곧 바울의 자천서요, 동시에 그리스도의 추천서라고 했다(3:2,

3; 참조, 12:11). 여기서도 자신을 자천하는 것을 원치 않는다. 왜냐하면 자천이란 자신을 자랑하는 것이므로 하나님 앞에 불손한 것이 되고, 사람에게 어리석게 보이기 때문이다(10:17, 18; 11:16, 17; 고전 1:29, 31; 롬 1:30, 3:37; 엡 2:9). 그럼에도, 바울은 자신의 진실을 고린도 교인들에게 알려서 그들을 돌아오게 하기 위해서는 자천할 수밖에 없는 어려운 처지에 있었다. 반대자들이 "외모로 자랑하여" 고린도 교인들을 미혹하기 때문이다. 그 결과 우리는 고린도후서에서 바울의 자천을 하지 않는다고 하면서도 결국 자천이나 자랑을 하는 역설적인 경우들을 보는 것이다(10:8 이하; 11:16 이하; 12:1 이하).

바울은 여기서 자신에 대해 자천하지만 사실 그가 진정으로 원하는 것은 고린도 교인들이 바울의 자천하는 말을 듣고 잘 이해해서 조금도 바울을 의심하지 않을 뿐만 아니라, 바울의 진실함을 확실하게 인정하고서, 그의 대변인들이 되어서, 바울의 대적자들의 비난으로부터 바울을 막아주는 것이다(12:11). 이 목적을 위해서 바울은 계속해서 자신의 자천하는 말을 할 수밖에 없으니, 부디 고린도 교회 교인들이 이점을 이해하고 자신에 대한 자찬의 말을 참고 들어 달라고 독자들의 이해를 바라는 것이다.

그러나, 바울이 14절에서 막상 자신을 자천할 때, 자신에게서 시작하지 않고, 복음 진리에서 시작하고 있다. 즉 자신의 사역이 그리스도의 사랑과 희생에서 기원되고 있음을 나타낸다. 그의 사역은 그리스도의 복음 정신에 충실하다는 것이다. 만일 하나님의 능력이 그의 사역에 나타났다면, 바울 자신 때문이 아니라, 복음 때문이다. 바울이 진정으로 자랑하는 것은 그리스도와 그의 복음이다(갈 6:14; 빌 3:3; 롬 1:16). 그는 그리스도와 복음 정신을 따라서 그의 약한 것들을 자랑한다(11:30; 12:5, 9, 10).

본문에서 ("가진다")의 목적이 언급되지 않았으므로 생략된 목적에 대해 여러 견해가 있다. "그 어떤 무엇"(τι), "그 어떤 무엇을 말하는 것"(λέγειν τι), "자랑할 것"(καύχημα), 또는 "기회"(ἀφορνήν)라고 보기도 한다.[339] 그러나 그 내용은 새로운 것이라기보다 바울이 지금까지 고린도 교인들에게 말해온 바를 다시 상기시키는 것이라고 본다.[340] 그것은, 14절과 15절에서 보듯이, 바울의 사역을 통하여 하나님의 구원의 능력이 나타났다는 것이다. 이점을 고린도 교인들이 다시 알고 바울의 적에 대해서 바울의 사역을 천거하라는 것이다(12:11).

"마음으로 하지 않고 외모로 자랑하는 자들을 대하게 하려는 것이라." 바울이 자랑하게된 것은 순전히 바울의 적들이 "외모"를 가지고 자랑하기 때문이다(참조, 4:17, 18; 5:7; 10:7, 10).[341] 바울의 적들은 그들의 자천서를 가지고 바울의 약점들을 지적하면서 바울의 사도직을 공격하면서 고린도 교회를 어지럽게 한다. 그들이 지적하는 바울의 약점들은 다음과 같다. (1) 바울은 예수에 대한 직접적인 지식이 부족하다(5:16);[342] (2) 모교회인 예루살렘 교회와의 관계가 원만하지 않다(참조, 갈2:11-16);[343] (3) 그의 외양이

339) Bultmann, 150, Plummer, 170, Martin, 125, 재인용.

340) Hughes, 188, 189; Martin 125.

341) "자랑한다"(καυχᾶσθαι)는 동사는 신약에 59번 나오는 데 바울서신에만 55번이 나오고, 고린도후서에 29번이 나온다. 특히 10-13장에 많이 나온다(Martin 125).

342) Strachan, 106.

343) J. D. G. Dunn, "The Incident at Antioch," *JSNT* 18(1983), 3-57; P. Stuhlmacher, "Das paulinische Evangelium," in *Das Evangelium und die Evangelien*, WUNT 28 (Tübingen: Mohr, 1983), 175-78, 서론, lvi, lvii.

볼품이 없다(10:10); (4) 언변이 부족하다(10:10; 11:6); (5) 그의 자랑의 근거는 너무 부정적인 것들이다(11:21-31).[344] 한 마디로, 반대자들이 지적하는 바울의 약점들은 외모(πρόσωπόν=εἶδος, 5:7; 10:7)에 속하는 것들이다.[345] "외모를 따라 자랑하는 것"은 곧 "육체를 따라 자랑하는 것"이다(10:2, 13; 11:18; 갈 6:13) 바울의 적들은 이런 외적 부족한 것으로 바울을 평가하고 반면에 자신들의 외적인 것들을 자랑한다. 이에 대해서 바울은 사람의 중심을 나타내는 마음(καρδίᾳ)에 있는 것으로 주안에서 자랑한다(10:18; 12:6). 바울은 그리스도의 진실한 사역자로서 피상적인 가치의 외적 육체적 능력이 아니라 오히려 약함 중에서 나타나는 보다 깊은 가치의 영적 그리스도의 능력을 자랑한다(12:9, 10).[346] 외적인 것을 자랑하는 사람들은 허영주의적 가치관에 빠지게 되나, 바울은 주의 두려움 가운데 양심적으로 순수한 사역을 하고 있다. 여기서 "마음"은 앞의 11절의 "양심"과도 상관된다. 바울은 남 앞에 나서거나 대접받기를 좋아하지 않았고, 그를 종으로 부르심에 합당하기를 힘썼다(살전 2:4-8; 행전 20:24; 26:19). 이런 진실하고 희생적인 바울의 사역은 십자가 중심 신학에서 나온 것이다. 그래서 바울은 자신에 대해서는 아무것도 자랑할 수가 없고, 오직 십자가뿐이라고 했다(갈 6:14). 바로 십자가 사상이 바울의 사역의 기초이다(11:30; 12:5, 9, 10). 고린도 교인들이 이 사실을 기억하면서, 바울

344) Hodge, 131.

345) 외모 문제를 다룰 때 할례 문제가 포함되어 있는지 알 수 없다. 5:16에도 "아무 사람도 육체를 따라 알지 아니하노라"란 말이 있으나 할례와 관련된 증거는 없다(참조 10:2-3; 롬 2:25-29; 빌 3:3-5).

346) Denney, 189-90.

을 자랑하며, 그의 적들과 맞선다면, 바울이 스스로를 자찬해야하는 괴로움을 덜어 줄 것이다(12:11).

한편 트롤은 "외모"로 번역된 "얼굴"(πρόσωπόν)을 문자적으로 해석해서 세 가지 가능한 해석을 제안한다.[347] 1) 고린도 교회의 거짓 교사들의 종교적 황홀경에 들어가 변하는 얼굴 모습을 그리는 것일 수 있다고 제안한다. 13절의 "우리가 만일 미쳤어도 주를 위한 것이요"라는 말이 이를 더 지지한다고 본다. 이와 비슷하게 "얼굴"이 영적 황홀경을 나타낸 것으로 보는 이들도 있다.[348] 2) "얼굴"(πρόσωπόν)은 3장의 모세의 얼굴을 상기시킨다고 한다. 기기서 바울의 대적자들이 바울을 모세의 영광의 얼굴과 대조하여 비난하였는데, 여기서도 같은 이들을 염두에 두고 있다고 한다. 바울은 그들은 잠시 있던 모세의 영광을 자랑하던 이들이나, 고린도 교인들은 마음에 새로운 약속을 받은 이들이라고 했다(3:3). 바울은 여기서 고린도 교인들에게 이런 이들을 다시 경계하고 있다는 것이다. 3) 사무엘상 16장 7절에서 사무엘이 엘리압의 외모와 키를 보고 왕의 자격이 있다고 혼자 생각했을 때 하나님께서, "나의 보는 것은 사람과 같지 아니하니 사람은 외모(πρόσωπόν, LXX)를 보거니와 나 여호와는 중심(καρδίαν, LXX)을 보느니라"고 말씀하셨다. 사람을 외모로 보는 것은 인간의 유한성이며 인간의 사욕 때문이다. 그러므로 예수님은 적대적인 유대인들에게 "외모로(κατα ὀψιν) 판단하지 말고 공의의 판단으로

347) Thrall, 404-405.

348) D. Georgi, *The Opponents of Paul in Second Corinthians*, ETr. H. Attridge and others (Philadelphia: Fortress 1986), 282; Collange, 249; 참조, Furnish, 324. (Thrall, 404, 주, 1489 재인용).

판단하라"고 경계하셨다(요7:24). 이런 경계의 말씀들이 바울의 외모에 대한 경계의 배경일 수 있다. 이 모든 가능성 가운데 3번이 가장 좋다고 본다. 11절에서 "사람들"에게 권면한다는 말이 외모로 사람을 평가하기 쉬운 고린도 교인들에게 바울의 중심을 보도록 권면한다고 할 수 있다. 본문에서 "마음"(καρδία)이 대조적으로 나오는 것도 사무엘상 16장 7절과의 관련 가능성을 더해준다.

13. "우리가 만일 미쳤어도 하나님을 위한 것이요, 만일 정신이 온전하여도 너희를 위한 것이니…"(εἴτε γὰρ ἐξέστημεν, θεῷ· εἴτε σωφρονοῦμεν, ὑμῖν). 바울은 그의 복음 사역의 동기가 진실함을 말한다. 사람들이 "바울이 미쳤다"는 등 무슨 비난을 하든지간에 그는 그 자신의 유익을 위해 하지 않고 언제나 하나님과 고린도 교인들을 위해 하였을 뿐이다. 트롤은 "미쳤다"(ἐξέστημεν)는 말의 의미를 여러 가지로 본다. 첫째, 바울이 자찬하는 말을 듣고 그의 대적자들이 비웃을 것을 예상하고 하는 말이다. 이런 가능성은 추정일 뿐이다(참조, 12:16). 둘째, 이 말은 영적 황홀경에 들어 있는 상태를 가리킨다.[349] 트롤은 이 의미를 받아들이면서도 13절이 바울의 영적 황홀경에 취한 상태를 가리키는 말이라는 가능성을 의심한다.[350] 왜냐하면 고린도 교회에서 바로 그런 신령한 것이 바울에게 부족한 점으로 인식되어 그의 사도적 권위를 의심하게 되었기 때문이라고 한다. 그들은 바울이 영적 체험을 하였다

349) Thrall과 같이 바울 자신의 입신 체험을 가리킨다고 보는 이들은, Martin 127; J. D. G. Dunn, *Jesus and the Spirit* (London: SCM/Philadelphia: Westminster, 1975), 215, 216; Barrett, 166(고후 12:7과 관련하여서). 그리고 Denney는 바울이 방언한 것을 가리킨다고 본다(192; 고전 14:18).

350) Thrall, 406-407.

는 것을 사도의 표로 받아들이면서 환영할 지언정 비판할 까닭이 없다는 것이다. 그러나 바울이 12장 1절 이하에서 삼층천(三層天)에 올라간 경험을 말하면서 자신도 영적체험이 있음을 말하고 있으나 그의 영적 체험의 결핍에 대한 고린도 교인들의 굳은 인식을 만회하기에는 미흡하였을 것이라고 본다. 셋째, 유대인들이 바울의 회심 경험을 듣거나 예수의 복음을 전하는 사도로 변신 한 것을 두고 미쳤다고 말했을 수도 있다. 실제로 아그립바 왕이 바울을 미쳤다고 했다(행전 26:24). 이 경우에는 μανία(마니아)란 말을 쓰는데 본문의 명사형 ἐκάστασις(에카스타시스)란 말과 교체되이 쓰인 경우가 많으므로 동의어로 본다.[351] 넷째, 다른 학자들은 바울이 대적자들을 비난하는 말을 듣고(11:1, 16-32), 그들이 그를 미친 것으로 비난했다고 본다.[352] 마틴은 "미쳤다"는 말이 위의 두 번째의 황홀경의 체험과 관련된 표현이라고 본다. 본문에서 바울은 그의 사역 가운데 신비적 경험을 포함한 "예외적 행동"과 "일반적 행동"을 대별하여 말하고 있다고 한다.[353] 즉 바울의 신비한 체험은 그와 하나님과의 친밀한 경험이며 그의 대적자들이 하듯이 떠들며 자랑할 것은 못된다. 반면에, 그의 합리적 언행은 물론 고린도 교인들의 유익을 위한 것이다. 그런 것은 바울 사도가 진실한 사도라는 증거가 될 것이다. 예로, 1장에서 바울은 고린도 교회 방문 약속을 취소했었는데 그것은 바울의 유익을 위한 것이 아니라 고린도 교인들의 유익을 위한 합리적인 취소였다(1:15-17, 23, 2:1-2). 그 외에 바울이 사도로서 고린도 교인들을 가르치

351) Philo, *Phaedrus* 244; Thrall, 406, 주, 1500.

352) Hughes, 191, 192; Strachan, 106.

353) Martin, 127.

고 권면 해온 목회 사역의 대부분이 "정신이 온전한"(σωφρονοῦμεν)중에 고린도 교인들의 유익을 위해 한 것들이라 할 수 있다. 마찬가지로, 바울의 언행 중 이해하기 어려운 것들로서 반대자들의 비난거리가 된 것들은 무엇이든지 결국은 자기의 유익을 위한 것이 아니었고 하나님을 위한 것이었다.[354] 바울이 고린도 교인들에게 "미친 짓" 으로 비난받은 것이 무엇인지는 분명히 알기 어려우나 위에서 지적한 바와 같이 "바울의 개인적 영적 체험" 이라고 볼 수 있다. 바울의 회심 경험은 유대교인들에게는 비난거리는 되나 영적 은사와 증거를 찾는 고린도 교인들에게는 비난거리가 될 수 없다(13:2; 고전 12장, 14장). 따라서 그의 삼층천 경험도 비난거리가 될 수 없다. 다만 바울은 신비스런 경험을 사람들에게 자랑하는 이들에게 자신의 경우에는 그런 체험을 하나님과의 친밀하고 비밀한 교제로 간직하며, 자랑하지는 않는다는 것이다(참조, 롬 15:18). 바울은 이런 신비한 경험은 원래 내면적인 "보이지 않는 것" 에 속하나 그에 대한 자랑으로 자신의 영적 권위를 사람들 앞에서 과시하려는 것은 오히려 "보이는 것" 에 속하며, 오만한 것이며 외적 영광을 추구하는 잘못으로 보는 듯하다(12:7). 그러므로 바울은 12장에서 삼층천 경험을 말할 때 "무익하나마 부득불 자랑한다" 고 시작한다. 그의 대적자들이 영적 경험을 자랑한다고 해서 자신도 따라서 자랑함으로써 그들의 잘못을 따라 하는 어리석은 짓이기 때문이다. 그러나 바울은 영적 체험이 없다는 비난에 대해서 진실을 밝히고, 나아가 그의 사도권을 방어하기 위해서는 그의 경험을 말할 수밖에 없었다.

354) Plummer, 173.

"미친 것"에 대한 두 번째 해석 즉 "바울의 영적 체험"이 가장 본문 문맥에 맞는다. 그러나 14절에서 말하는 그리스도의 십자가의 사랑의 강권하심에 의한 바울의 열정적 사역 자세를 가리키는 것으로 해석이 가능하다.

13절은 결국 11절과 12절의 요약이다. 바울은 무슨 일을 하든지 하나님 앞에서와 고린도 교인들 앞에서 진실히 행할 뿐이란 말이다. 아무것도 자신의 유익을 위해 자랑한 것이 없다. 그의 사역은 하나님과 고린도 교인들을 위한 것이었다. 그러므로 하나님과 사람 앞에서 부끄러울 것이 없다. 이런 말 자체가 자찬하는 말이라고 할 수 있으므로, 바울은 11절에서 이미 고린도 교인들이 자신의 진심을 알아주기를 원하였다(참조, 12:11).

14. "그리스도의 사랑이 우리를 강권하시는 도다. 이는 우리가 확신하는 바(우리가 생각컨대) 한 사람이 모든 사람을 대신하여 죽었은즉 모든 사람이 죽은 것이라"(ἡ γὰρ ἀγάπη τοῦ Χριστοῦ συνέχει ἡμᾶς, κρίναντας τοῦτο, ὅτι εἷς ὑπὲρ πάντων ἀπέθανεν, ἄρα οἱ πάντες ἀπέθανον). 14절부터 바울은 자찬의 말을 그치고 화해의 사역의 주제를 시작한다. 화해의 사역의 근원은 우리를 위한 예수의 구원의 죽음이다. 바울은 언젠가 예수의 죽음의 구속적 의미를 파악하고 인식하는 능력을 가졌다(16절). 그리고 그리스도의 죽음을 대속적 죽음으로 바르게 인식하는 데서부터 자신과 이웃을 보는 시각이 달라졌다(16, 17). 그리고 그는 그의 사역의 본질을 깨달았다. 예수의 죽으심이 죄인 인간들을 향한 하나님의 화해의 사역이듯이 자신의 고린도 교회를 향한 사역도 역시 화해의 사역임을 알았다(19-20). 실로 고린도후서 전체에

서 바울은 이 하나님의 화해의 구원 사역의 정신을 따라 고린도 교회와 화해의 사역을 시도하고 있다. 그렇다면, 바울의 화해의 사역의 근거와 출발은 14절과 15절의 예수의 대속적 죽으심과 사랑이다.

문법상 "그리스도의 사랑"(ἡ ἀγάπη τοῦ Χριστοῦ)의 속격을 주격을 나타내는 속격(또는 기원을 나타내는 주격)으로 보아서, "우리를 향한 그리스도의 사랑"으로 해석 할 수도 있고, 목적을 나타내는 속격으로 보아서, "그리스도를 향한 우리의 사랑"이라고 할 수도 있다. 문맥에서 바울의 사역의 기초가 그리스도의 사랑이라는 것을 강조한다고 보고 전자의 해석을 따른다. 전자인 경우에 좁게는, 바울과 그 동역자에 대한 그리스도의 사랑이나,[355] 넓게는, 더 근본적으로는, 모든 죄인들을 위해 죽으신 그리스도의 사랑이다. 그리스도의 사랑은 곧 하나님의 사랑이다. 그의 아들을 죄인 구원을 위해 주신 놀라운 사랑이다(롬 5:8; 요 3:16). 바울의 그리스도 사랑의 원인도 그리스도의 사랑이 있었기 때문이다.[356] 바울은 여기서 고린도 교회를 향한 그의 사랑이 그의 마음에 넘치는 이유를 그리스도의 사랑 때문이라고 설명하고 있다.[357] 바울의 고린도 교회 사랑도 그리스도의 사랑 때문이다. 자기의 사리사욕에 근거한 사랑이 아니라, 그리스도의 순수한 사랑에서 배운 사심 없는 희생적인 사랑이다. 그러나 매우 강렬한 사랑이다(1:23; 2:4;

---

355) Bultmann, *Theology* 1:304-5; Denney, 193; Godet, 179; Hodge, 133; Plummer, 173; Robertson, *A Grammar of the Greek New Testament in the light of Historical Research* (Nashville: Broadman Press, 1934), 499.

356) Spicq, 132.

357) A. Schlatter, *Paulus, der Bote Jesu*, 558, 559, Martin 128, 재인용.

4:7-15; 6:4-10; 7:3; 11:11; 12:14, 15; 13:7). 고린도 교인들을 영혼을 향한 변함없는 깊은 사랑이다(1:24; 12:15; 13:7, 9).

"강권하시는 도다"(συνέκει). 원래의 뜻은 "손안에 꼭 잡다"("장(掌)" 중에 잡다)는 뜻이다. 그러나 빌립보서 1장 23절에만 다시 한 번 나타나는 희귀한 말이다. 거기서는 두 가지 다른 생각 가운데 갇혀있다는 뜻으로 쓰였다. 대부분의 학자들이 "강제로 시키다" 또는 "장악하다"는 뜻에 동의한다.[358)]

아가페 사랑의 원형은 그리스도에게서 찾을 수 있다. 그의 사랑으로 말미암아 바울은 자신의 자랑을 감히 하지 않고 희생적인 사역을 감당할 수 있었다(11, 12). 그리스도의 사랑이 바울로 하여금 그를 위해 모든 것을 분토같이 여기고, 그리스도를 얻고, 그리스도를 알고, 그리스도 안에서 발견되기 원하게 했다(빌 1:21; 3:7-11). 그리스도가 하신 일이 바울의 삶의 근거이다.[359)]

"이는 우리가 확신 하는 바"는 문자적으로 "이는 우리가 확정하는 바"(κρίναντας τοῦτο)이다. 여기서 τοῦτο("...바")는 14, 15절에서 바울이 말하는 그리스도의 구원사역을 가리키고 "이는 우리가 확정한"(κρίναντας)은 이유를 나타내는 분사로서 그리스도 구원 사역에 대한 바울의 결정이나 판단을 가리킨다. 단순과거형 분사는 바울이 일정한 때 또는 기간에 결정하였음을 나타낸다.[360)]

---

358) Barrett, 168, Hodge, 133; Lietzmann, 124; Martin 128; Thrall, 408-9; NIV; RSV. 한편 이 말은 그리스도의 사랑이 바울을 자랑하지 못하도록 "억제한다"는 뜻으로 해석하는 이들도 있으나 여기서의 바울의 의도를 나타내는 것 같지 않다(Bultmann, 152; Plummer, 173, Strachan, 107). Furnish는 보다 약한 의미로, "유지한다"는 뜻으로 본다, V. P. Furnish, *Theology and Ethics of Paul* (New York: Abingdon), 167.

359) Martin, 128.

360) Martin, 129.

즉 바울은 그의 회심 이후 선교사역을 시작하기까지의 어느 일정한 기간 동안 그리스도 사건의 의미에 대해서 최종적인 결단을 내렸을 것이다(갈 1:17; 18).[361] 바울은 그리스도의 죽음의 구속적 의미를 잘 파악하고 인식하였다. 그리스도의 고난과 죽으심에서 나타난 사랑이 바울이 그리스도 안에 거하기를 결정하게 된 결정적 동기이다.[362]

"한 사람이 모든 사람을 대신하여 죽었은즉…." 여기서 바울은 그의 화해의 교리의 기초를 놓기 시작한다. ἀπέθανεν(그가 죽었다)은 단순과거로 그리스도께서 죽으신 역사적 사건을 가리킨다. 그리스도께서 "모든 사람"을 위해 죽으신 사실과 그 결과에 대한 바울의 판단(κρίναντας)이 그의 사역의 성격을 결정하고 있다. 그러므로 바울의 사역은 진실한 것이다.

ὑπέρ(후페르, "대신하여")가 15절에도 같은 어귀에 다시 나온다. 즉 그리스도가 "모든 사람을 대신하여" 죽었다. 이 전치사의

361) Hughes, 193, 주 22; Martin 129; Plummer, 174; Thrall, 409. Thrall은 여기서 κρίναντας("우리가 확정한")라는 과거 분사가 가리키는 것은 초대교회의 전형적 신앙고백적 양식, 즉 "그리스도께서 우리를 위해 죽으셨다"을 바울이 재구성하였다고 본다(Barrett, 168; Furnish 310). 고전 15:3에서 바울은 "내가 받은 것을 먼저 너희에게 전하였노니 성경대로 그리스도께서 우리 죄를 위하여 죽으시고 장사 지낸 바 되었다가 성경대로 사흘 만에 다시 살아 나사…"라고 할 때 초대교회의 신앙전통에 대한 언급을 하고 있다. 그러나 거기서 바울은 "받았다"(παρέδωκα)는 말을 쓰고 있으므로 여기의 경우와 다르다. κρίναντας가 "과거에 정한 어떤 결정"을 가리킨다는 것은 분명하다. 바울이 그의 회심 이후 교회의 전통적 신앙고백을 진리로 믿고 확정한 것으로 본다. 분사의 주어인 ἡμᾶς("우리")가 바울 자신을 가리키므로 κρίναντας는 이런 개인적 결단을 나타낸다(Thrall, 409). 이것은 바울은 단순히 신앙전통을 전수하는 데 그치지 않고, 그 전통에 대해 스스로 동의하고 자신의 진리로 확정하는 과정을 거쳤음을 가리킨다.

362) Hughes, 193.

의미에 대한 논쟁이 있다. 원래 "대신하여"라는 전치사는 ἀντί(안티)이다(ἀντί, 창 22:13, LXX; 참조, ἀπό, 사 53:8, LXX). ὑπέρ가 신약에서는 마가복음 10장 45절(병행, 마 20:28)에서 단 한번 대속적 의미로 쓰였다. 일반적으로 ὑπέρ가 "대신하여"란 뜻보다 "위하여"라는 뜻을 나타내기 때문에 이 전치사가 여기서 단순히 모든 사람의 유익을 "위하여"라는 뜻인가, 아니면 "대신하여"라는 뜻인가란 논쟁이 있다.[363] 15절에도 두 번 나타나는데, 앞의 것은 14절의 것과 같이 "대신하여"라고 번역이 가능하나 두 번째 것은 분명히 "위하여"라는 뜻이다("다시 사신 자를 위하여 살게 하려 함이라").

그러나 여기서 ὑπέρ가 대속적 의미로 쓰인 증거는 충분하다. 첫째, 문맥이 후자의 뜻을 나타낸다. 즉 이 말 다음에 오는 말, "모든 사람이 죽은 것이라"는 말은 결국 한 사람이 모든 사람을 대신하여 죽었다는 뜻을 선호하게 한다. 막연한 의미를 가진 "위하여"란 뜻으로 번역하여, "한 사람이 모든 사람을 '위하여' 죽었으므로 모든 사람이 죽었다"는 번역은 앞 구절과 뒷 구절의 논리적 연결을 빈약하게 만든다. 둘째, ὑπέρ가 대속적 죽음을 나타내는 의미로 쓰인 곳이 있는데, 특히 바로 5장 21절에 있다. 5장 20절에서도 "대신한다"는 의미로 쓰였다(몬 13; 엡 6:20; 딤전 2:6). 특히 딤

363) "위하여": Meyer, 129; 130; Filson, 334; Thrall, 409; "대신하여": Hughes, 193; Plummer, 174; Strachan, 107; Tasker, 86; Bultmann, 152, 153; Martin, 129 재인용. Barrett는 ὑπέρ의 대속적 의미에 대해 회의적이다(168, 169). J. D. G. Dunn도 "대속한다"는 의미보다 "대표한다"는 의미를 선호한다. Dunn, "Paul's Understanding of the Death of Jesus," in *Reconciliation and Hope*, ed. Robert Banks (Grand Rapids: Eerdmans, 1974), 140, 141.

전 2:6에서 바울이 대속론을 논할 때 ἀντί를 전접어로 쓴 말과 ὑπέρ가 함께 나온다(ἀντιλύτρον ὑπέρ πάντον=[그가] 모든 사람을 위하여 속전[으로 주셨으니]). 이것은 ὑπέρ가 대속적 의미를 가지고 있다는 분명한 증거이다. 이 외에 로마서 8장 32절, 고린도전서 15장 3절, 갈라디아서 1장 4절, 2장 20절, 3장 13절에서는 그리스도께서 죄인을 "위하여" 죽었다고 번역이 되었으나 대속적 의미가 있다. ὑπέρ는 이 당시에 쓰인 많은 파피루스 서신에서 대필한 것을 나타내는 말로, 아무개가 "그(편지 보낸 사람)를 대신하여 썼다" (ἔγραψα [또는, ἔγραψεν] ὑπέρ αὐτους)라고 나온다. 또 ὑπέρ는 유리피데스(Euripides)에서, 아드메투스(Admetus)가 알세스티스(Alcestis)을 대신해서 죽겠다는 말 가운데 독립적 전치사와 전접어(ὑπερθνήσκειν)로 나온다(Alcestis, 682, 690, 700, 701).[364] 결론적으로 바울이 ὑπέρ의 일반적인 복합적 의미를 따라서 "위하여"라는 뜻을 쓰기도 하고 또 "대신하여"라는 뜻으로 쓰기도 하나, 여기서는 뒤에 오는 "모든 사람이 죽었다"라는 말의 논리적 명확성을 위해서, "모든 사람을 대신하여 죽었다"라는 번역이 필수적이다.[365]

마틴은 이 말(ὑπέρ)의 문자적 의미를 대속적이라고 규정한 뒤에 본문과 관련하여 대속의 의미를 나타내기 위해 쓰는 영어의 *substitution*(대리, 대용, 대체)이란 말이 그리스도의 구속 사역을 설명하는 데 적절한 개념인가 아니면 *representation*(대표)란 말이 적당한가에 대한 논쟁이 있음을 지적하고 이에 대해서 제안한

---

364) Plummer; 174, Hughes, 194, 주 24; Martin 130, 재인용; Henry G. Liddel and Robert Scott, *A Greek-English Lexicon* (Oxford: Clarendon, 1996), 1857.

365) Plummer, 174.

다.[366] 그는 대체로 이 두 가지 의미가 결국 모두 구속의 의미를 가르친다고 본다. 그는 본문의 배경으로 로마서 6장의 그리스도와 믿는 자의 연합이 세례에서 이루어졌다는 교훈을 지적하면서 본문에서 같은 그리스도의 대속적 죽음의 의미가 나타나 있다고 한다. 더구나 본문에서 **κρίναντας**("이는 우리가 확정한"), ὅτι(…[라는 사실])와 같은 말들은 바울이 로마서 6장의 세례에 관한 가르침에서 "그리스도께서 그의 이름으로 세례 받는 이들을 위해 죽으셨다"고 말한 것을 가리키는 증거라고 한다.[367] 세례 받는 이들은 그의 죽으심과 합하여 세례를 받는다(6:3, 4, 5). "한 사람이 모든 사람을 대신하여 죽었은즉"이란 말은 죄인들이 당해야 할 죽음을 그리스도께서 대신 담당 하셨고, 세례를 통해서 그 대속적 죽음의 유익을 받는다는 뜻이다. 그러나 마틴은 대속자의 의미가 죽음으로 받는 혜택을 설명하기에는 적절치 못하다고 본다. 마틴은 보다 엄밀하게 생각하여 그리스도의 죽음은 죄인들을 위한 대속적 죽음이되(substitution), 그 죽음으로 인한 축복은 우리를 위한 그리스도의 대표적 역할(representation)의 결과라고 한다. 마틴은 그리스도가 직접 우리의 죄를 그의 것으로 담당하셨고, 또한 사람과 하나님의 중계 역할을 하였으므로 대표자(representative)라는 말은 그 의미가 약하며(Dunn에 반대하여), 대속자(substitute)란 말은 죄를 속한 역할은 설명하나 구원의 축복의 의미를 설명하지 못으로, 그리스도의 전체 구속 사역을 설명하기 위해서는, 중보자의 의미를 가진 법정대리인(proxy)이란 말이 낫다고 한다.[368] 이런

366) 마틴, 130-1.

367) Martin, 130.

368) Martin, 131.

논쟁에도 불구하고, 본문에서는 대속적이란 의미가 가장 중요한 의미라고 본다. 더구나 이사야 53장의 "하나님의 고난 받는 종"(עֶבֶד יְהוָה, 에베드 야웨)의 대속적 죽음이 초대교회 구원론의 기초임을 상기할 필요가 있다.[369]

한편 트롤은 로마서 6장의 세례와 본문을 관련시키는 것을 주저한다. 그에 의하면 "모든 사람"은 여기서는 문자적으로 모든 세상 사람을 가리키는데, 로마서 6장은 믿는 사람의 세례 시의 죽음을 가리키므로 관련이 없다고 본다.[370] 그러나 여기서 "모든 사람"(πάντες)이 반드시 모든 세상 사람들을 가리킨다고 볼 수 없다. 15절에서 모든 자(πάντων)는 산 자들(οἱ ζῶντες)과 같은 사람들로 나타난다. 산자들은 그리스도를 믿고 그와 함께 일단 죽었다가 산 사람들이다. 그러므로 여기서 "모든 사람"은 복음 선포의 대상을 유대인뿐만 아니라 이방인도 포함하는 선교적 의미를 갖는다. 복음 전도자는 누가 구원받을 자인지를 모르기 때문에 그리스도는 모든 사람을 위해 죽으셨다고 복음을 전해야 한다. 그러나 신학적으로 그리스도는 그를 믿지 않는 사람들이 아니라 믿는 모든 사람들을 위해 죽으셨다. 트롤이 주장하는 세례 관련에 대한 또 다른 반대 이유는 본문에서 쓰인 "죽는다"는 동사가 예수와 모든 사람에게 같은 과거시제(ἀπέθανεν, ἀπέθανον)로 나타난다는 것이다. 세례를 가리킨다면 "모든 사람이 죽는다"고 현재형으로

369) O. Cullmann, *Christology of the New Testament*, ETr. Shirley C. Guthrie and Charles A. M. Hall (Philadelphia: Westminster, 1959), 51-82; H. R. Weber, *The Cross: Tradition and Interpretation*, ETr. E. Jessett (Grand Rapids: Eerdmans/London: SPCK, 1978), 50-63.

370) Thrall, 409.

371) Thrall, 410.

썼어야 했다는 것이다.[371] 그러나 여기서의 과거형은, 불변의 사실을 나타내는 과거형, 또는 연계적 과거형으로 보아야 한다. 그리스도의 죽음과 모든 (믿는)사람의 죽음이 서로 관련된다는 사실을 나타내기 위해서 같은 과거형을 쓰고 있다. 본문과 관련되는 로마서 6장 4절에서도 "우리가 그와 함께 장사되었다"(συνετάφημεν)는 과거형을 쓰고 있다. 그리스도와 그리스도인과 연합을 의미하기 위해 같은 과거형을 쓴 것이다. 우리는 지금 믿으나, 그리스도가 죽을 그 때 우리도 법적으로는 죽었다.[372]

"모든 사람이 죽은 것이라"는 말은 위에서 본 것처럼 이사야 53장의 하나님의 고난 받는 종의 대속적 죽음과 로마서 6장의 그리스도와의 연합 사상에 의한 대속적 죽음을 가리킨다(사 53:5, 10, 11). 그리스도를 믿는 이들은 그와 연합하여 이미 죽었다. 그리스도는 그를 믿는 이들을 위해서 죽으셨다.[373] 그리스도의 죽음과 연합하여 죽은 사람들은 물론 세상 모든 사람들이 아니라 그리스도를 믿는 자들이다. 그의 죽으심은 죄인들에 대한 지극한 사랑의 증거이다. 그리스도의 대속적 죽음으로 그리스도인들의 죄의 옛 사람은 법적으로 죽었다(롬 8:1). 그러나 옛 사람의 습관 또는 행위는 아직 살아 있으므로 계속 이를 죽이고 그리스도의 새 사람으로서 살아가야 한다(롬 6:8-22).

다시 바울의 사도직 진정성 문제로 돌아와 생각하면, 여기서 바울은 그리스도의 희생적인 사랑의 죽음이 자신의 사역의 근본적 동기임을 설명한다. 그리스도께서 하나님의 뜻에 순종하여 그의

---

372) Liezmann, 124; Bruce, 207.

373) Martin, 131.

생명을 희생하여 구원의 사역을 완수하였듯이 바울 사도는 그리스도의 복음을 전하는 사도로서 사심이 없이 고린도 교인들의 유익을 위해 사역해왔다. 그리스도의 죽음의 희생적 정신에 따라서 그는 결코 자랑하지 않는다. 그는 이 사실을 하나님께 인정받기를 원하고 또한 고린도 교인들이 양심을 가지고 인정하기를 바란다 (참조, 11절).

15. "저가 모든 사람을 대신하여 죽으심은 산 자들로 하여금 다시는 저희 자신을 위하여 살지 않고 오직 저희를 대신하여 죽었다가 다시 사신 자를 위하여 살게 하려 함이라"(καὶ ὑπὲρ πάντων ἀπέθανεν, ἵνα οἱ ζῶντες μηκέτι ἑαυτοῖς ζῶσιν ἀλλὰ τῷ ὑπὲρ αὐτῶν ἀποθανόντι καὶ ἐγερθέντι). 여기서 바울은 그리스도의 죽으심으로 구원받은 이들의 마땅한 삶의 원칙을 말한다. 그들은 그들을 살리신 그리스도를 위해 살아야 한다. 그것은 나를 위해 죽으신 그리스도를 사랑하는 마음에서 나오는 그리스도에 대한 헌신적인 삶이다.[374] 트롤은 14절의 모든 사람을 모든 인류라고 해석한 후에 여기서도 그리스도의 구원의 새 시대에 속한 모든 사람들이 그리스도처럼 남을 위해 살아야 한다고 본다.[375] 그러나 이런 보편주의적이며, 도덕주의적 해석은 바울이 의도한 것이 아니다. 14절이나 15절의 "모든 사람" 가운데 그리스도를 믿지 않는 사람들을 포함하는 것은 잘못이다. 그리스도를 믿지 않는 사람들은, 그리스도와 연합이 안 된 이들로서, 그리스도와 함께 죽을 수

374) Martin, 411-12.

375) Martin, 408, 411.

가 없다. 나아가, 신학적 논리에서 이들은 그리스도와 함께 죽지 않은 이들이라 그리스도와 함께 살 수가 없는 것이다. 그러므로 믿지 않는 이들에게 그리스도를 주로 모시고 살라고 말하는 것은 더욱 의미가 없다. 그러므로 본문은 그리스도를 믿어 그와 함께 영적으로 죽고, 그와 함께 영적으로 산 자들이 자기중심적 삶을 버리고 그리스도를 주로 모시고 그의 말씀을 따라서 살아야 함을 가르치는 것이다.[376] 그러므로 그리스도 중심으로 사는 것은 도덕적인 삶 이상이다.[377] 그 것은 9절에서 말한 것과 같이 그리스도를 사랑하며 그를 기쁘시게 하는 헌신적인 삶이다. 어떤 인간의 어떤 외적인 도덕적 기준이 아니라 우리가 믿는 믿음의 주를 기쁘시게 하는 것이 최종적 심판의 기준이다(10절).

"저희를 대신하여 죽었다가 다시 사신 자를 위하여 살게 하려 함이라." ὑπέρ("대신하여")가 대속적인 의미를 나타낸다는 것을 이미 위에서 논하였다. 여기서 기억할 것은 "죽었다가"(ἀποθανόντι)란 동사와 "다시 사신 것"(ἐγερθέντι)이 모두 과거 동사로서 그리스도의 죽음의 역사적 사실을 나타내고 있다는 것이다. 그리스도의 죽음과 부활을 사람의 존재를 변화시키고 그리스도를 따라 살게 하는 실존주의적 의미의 역사적 근거를 가리키는 것이다. 바울은 15절에서 그 역사적 사실에 대한 실존주의적 의미를 설명하면서도 그 사실을 과거에 실제로 일어난 역사적 사건으로 주의 깊게 나타내고 있는 것이다. 또한 "죽었다"(ἀποθανόντι)는 동사는 능동태로서 그리스도가 스스로 죽은 것

---

376) Windisch, 183; Bultmann, 154; Furnish, 311, Martin, 132.

377) 참조, Martin, 132.

을 나타내며, "다시 사심"(εγερθε,ντι)은 실제로는 수동태로서 "일으키심을 받으심"("was raised," NIV)이란 뜻으로 하나님의 개입에 의한 것임을 주의 깊게 신학적으로 나타낸다. 다시 말하면 복음 진리는 사람이 만든 인위적 사변적 종교적 진리가 아니라 하나님이 주도하는 구원 역사에서 계시된 하나님의 진리임을 나타내는 것이다. 기독교 복음은 신적 계시에 의한 것이다. 신학은 그 계시에 대한 인간의 학문적 설명 방법이다.

주해(5:11-15):

바울은 그의 사역의 기초를 그리스도의 구속 사건에 두고 있음을 밝힌다(참조, 롬 3:25; 갈 2:20). 그는 그리스도의 구속 신학의 터 이외에 세운 어떤 사역도 결국은 심판을 받을 것이라고 한다(고전 3:10-15). 그의 사역은 그리스도를 통해 나타난 하나님의 구원의 역사를 전하여 사람들을 구원받게 하는 일이다. 바울은 그리스도의 사도로서 이 사명을 가지고 고린도 교인들의 구원을 위해 수고해왔다. 그러나 거짓 사도들은 그리스도의 구속의 터 이외의 것을 가지고 사람들을 호도하는 사역을 하고 있다(5:12; 11:4). 바울은 고린도 교인들이 자신의 바른 복음의 사역을 받기를 간청한다. 자신이 자찬하는 것이 어색하지만(11절), 영적 위기에 처한 고린도 교인들을 구원하기 위해서는 어쩔 수 없다(11:3). 바울은 10장에서 13장까지 거짓 사도들의 자랑에 맞서서 어쩔 수 없이 자신의 사역을 자랑을 하다가, 결론 부분에서는 자신은 차라리 자신의 약한 것을 자랑한다고 하면서 그리스도를 위해, 복음전파와 영혼 구원을 위해 목숨까지 내놓고 수고한 것과 자신에게 있는 여러 가지 약점들을 자랑한다(11:15-12:9). 바울은 자신의 사도직이 그리스도의 구속의 본질과 유형을 따라서 수행되었음을 증거하고 있다. 보이는 것이 아닌, 안 보이는 것, 일시적인 것이 아닌, 영원한 것, 영광이 아닌 고난, 강한 것이 아닌 약한 것, 이런 것들이 그리스도의 사역의 특징들이며, 자신도 그렇게 사역하고 있다고 한다. 이런 대조적 설명은 단순히 하나님의 계시나 역사하심이 모두 역설적이라는 것을 의미하기보다는 하나님의 지혜와 능력이 인간의 지혜와 예상을 넘어서서 나타남으로 사람들로 하여금 그에게 영광을 돌리게 하는 것이 하나님의 뜻이라는 의미가 있다.

복음 사역자는 물론 모든 그리스도인은 예수 그리스도의 구속 사건을 중심 메시지로 전해야하며, 또한 그 메시지의 본질과 유형을 따라서 살아 가야한다. 모든 그리스도인은 그리스도와 함께 죽고 그리스도와 함께 살았다. 우리 몸에 거하는 동안에 이 구원 진리를 생활화해야 한다(4:7-15; 5:18-21; 6:11-13; 7:3; 9절; 롬 6:8-22). 우리의 옛 사람의 행위를 죽이고 새 사람으로 살아야한다. 그리스도께서 우리를 위해 죽으신 것처럼, 내 유익을 앞세우지 말고 남의 유익을 앞세워야 한다. 화해와 같은 모든 선한 일을 행하여 그리스도의 구속의 은혜를 증거하며, 구속의 역사를 구현하고, 하나님의 사랑과 능력을 증거해야 하는 책임이 있다. 이런 삶은 도덕적인 행위를 포함하나, 근본적으로는 주를 기쁘시게 하는 데 목적을 둔다. 나를 구속하신 그리스도의 은혜를 말과 삶으로 증거해야 한다. 자기를 죽이고 남을 살리신 주님처럼 사는 것은 주님을 사랑하는 마음에서 나온 것이므로, 사람의 칭찬이나 영광을 바라지 않는다. 이런 삶은 악이 지배하는 이 세상에서는 십자가의 삶이요 고난의 삶이다. 하나님의 능력과 승리가 가끔 나타나기도 하나

(2:14-17; 4:7-9), 전체적으로 고난의 삶이다(4:10-12; 11:23-28). 그러나 이렇게 주를 기쁘시게 하며 일생을 마친 이들에게 영원한 하나님의 축복이 있다(고후 4:16-5:10; 딤후 4:6-8).

한편, 바울이 복음을 배도하고 반대하는 자들에게 경고 하지만, 우리가 생각하기보다는 구체적인 형벌이나 심판에 대한 언급은 되도록 자제하는 것도 그리스도의 사랑과 구원을 복음의 중심 주제로 삼기 위함이다(롬 16:18; 빌 3:19; 고후 11:13-15; 살후 3:14-15; 딤후 2:16-19; 3:6-9; 4:10, 14-16; 딛 1:10-16, 3:10-11; 참조, 히 6:4-6; 벧후 3:7, 16). 복음의 사도로서 사랑과 구원의 하나님의 능력을 전하고 그에 합당하게 살아야 할 것에 집중하는 것이다. 자칫 형벌과 재난에 대해 계속 강조하는 경우에 전도자 스스로 자칫 증오와 악한 생각에 지배받게 되어, 결국 복음의 중심인 그리스도의 구속의 본질과 유형인, 사랑, 용서, 인내를 간직하지 못하고 잃어버리게 되는 오류를 경계한다(고후 2:5-11; 살후 3:14-15; 딤후 2:24-26). 심한 말이나 분노 대신 오히려 참고 부드러운 말로 권면하는 것이 죄에 대해서 오래 참으시는 아버지 하나님의 자비하심을 가르치는 사역자의 적절한 모습이다(롬 2:4; 벧전 3:20; 벧후 3:9; 딤후 2:24). 그러므로 바울은 분을 내더라도 분노의 종이 되지 말라고 한다(엡 4:26). 분을 절제하고 인내와 사랑의 목회자 본연의 자세(즉 고난 받으신 주님의 자세)를 유지해야 함을 가르친다. 죽으시고 다시 사신 주님의 능력은 약한 데서 온전케 하는 능력임을 믿어야 한다고 한다(고후 12:9). "그러므로 내가 택하신 자를 위하여 모든 것을 참음은 저희로도 그리스도 예수 안에 있는 구원을 영원한 영광과 함께 얻게 하려 함이로라. 미쁘다 이 말이여, '우리가 주와 함께 죽었으면 또한 주와 함께 살 것이요. 참으면 또한 함께 왕 노릇할 것이요. 우리가 주를 부인하면 주도 우리를 부인하실 것이라' "(딤후 2:10-12). 이렇게 주님의 구속 사건의 본질인 사랑과 용서와 희생과 인내를 힘써 나타내는 사역이 진정한 그리스도의 사역이다.

viii. 우리는 하나님의 화해의 사신(5:16-6:2).

본문:

> 16. 그러므로 우리가 이제부터는 아무 사람도 육체대로 알지 아니하노라. 비록 우리가 그리스도도 육체대로 알았으나 이제부터는 이같이 알지 아니하노라. 17. 그런즉 누구든지 그리스도 안에 있으면 새로운 피조물이라. 이전 것은 지나갔으니 보라 새 것이 되었도다. 18. 모든 것이 하나님께로 났나니 저가 그리스도로 말미암아 우리를 자기와 화목하게 하시고 또 우리에게 화목하게 하는 직책을 주셨으니 19. 이는 하나님께서 그리스도 안에 계시사 세상을 자기와 화목하게 하시며 저희의 죄를 저희에게 돌리지 아니하시고 화목하게 하는 말씀을 우리에게 부탁하셨느니라. 20. 이러므로 우리가 그리스도를 대신하여 사신(使臣)이 되어 하나님이 우리로 너희를 권면하시는 것 같이 그리스도를 대신하여 간구하노니 너희는 하나님과 화목하라. 21. 하나님이 죄를 알지도 못하신 자로 우리를 대신하여 죄를 삼으신 것은 우리로 하여금 저의 안에서 하나님의 의가 되게 하려 하심이니라. 6:1. 우리가 하나님과 함께 일하는 자로서 너희를 권하노니 하나님의 은혜를 헛되이 받지 말라. 2. 가라사대 내가 은혜 베풀 때에 너를 듣고 구원의 날에 너를 도왔다.

본문 비평:

1. 16절의 **εἰ καὶ**(비록)가 p^{46} B A* D* 에 나타나고 **εἰ δὲ καὶ**(그러나 비록) 가 소문자 사본에 나타난다. 뜻의 변화는 없다. 그러나 **καὶ εἰ**(만일…라도)(G, vg) 와 **εἰ δε**(그러나 만일)(K)는 강조를 나타낸다.

2. 17절에 마지막에 τὰ πὰντα(모든 것)이 소문자 사본에 나타나고, p46 B C D* vg 등에는 나타나지 않는다. τὰ πὰντα가 18절에 초두에도 나오므로 필사자들이 혼돈하여 덧붙여서 기록하였을 가능성이 있다(중복기록, dittography). 원래 있었다면, τὰ πὰντα(모든 것)가 γέγονεν(되었다)의 주어가 되어, "모든 것이 새롭게 되었다"라고 해석된다. 그러나 마틴은 이를 부사구로 보아 "모든 면에서 새롭게 되었다"라고 해석할 수 있다고 한다.[378)]

3. 19절의 τὸν λόγον(말씀)이 가장 신빙성이 있다. p46은 εὐαγγέλιον(복음)을 써서 "화해의 복음"이라고 하고, D F G는 말씀과 복음을 다 합하여 "화해의 말씀의 복음"이라고 한다.

4. 6:1의 παρακαλοῦμεν(권하노니)가 p46 D F G에서는 현재분사형 παρακαλοῦντες로 나타난다. 의미 변화는 없다.

내용 개요:

위에서 본 바와 같이 바울은 14절과 15절에서 자신의 희생적 사역을 그리스도의 죽음의 의미와 연결시켰다. 16절 이하에서 바울은 그리스도 사건의 주제를 더욱 확대시켜서 그리스도의 죽음이 가져온 놀랍게 변화된 우주적 개인적 결과들을 지적하면서 그리스도인은 이런 변화를 인식하고 새로운 존재로 자신과 남을 인식하며 살아가야 한다고 한다(롬 3:21). 그리스도로 말미암은 구원의 새시대의 변화들이란 새로운 창세기의 시작(17), 죄인과 하나님과

378) Martin, 135.

의 화해(18-20), 하나님의 의의 역사(21)이다.[379] 그리스도의 죽으심으로 말미암아 죽을 수밖에 없던 우리들이 새로 지으심을 받은 존재가 되었고(존재론적 변화), 하나님과 소외되었던 우리들이 하나님과 화목하게 되었고, 하나님의 심판을 받게 되었던 우리들이 심판을 면하고 은혜로 말미암는 하나님의 의로우심을 입게 되었다.[380] 이런 놀라운 복음이 바로 바울의 사역을 통해서 전파되고 있다(6:1-2). 고린도 교인들은 그리스도로 말미암아 새롭게 시작된 구원의 시대에서 변화된 인간 존재에 대한 새로운 인식과 인간에 대한 새로운 가치판단으로 자신과 이웃을 평가해야 한다. 특히 고린도 교인들은 이런 새로운 가치판단기준에 의하여 바울의 사역을 이해하고 이에 대해 열린 자세를 가져야 마땅하다(6:11-13). 바울은 그리스도의 죽으심으로 말미암은 그리스도의 사랑과 구원의 능력이 그의 사역의 중심이다(14, 15). 바울은 더 이상 "그리스도를 육체를 따라" 낡은 가치판단기준으로 이해하지 않고, 그리스도 안에서 새로운 피조물로서 자신을 인식하고 사람들을 인식한다. 고린도 교회는 이런 새로운 인간인식의 진리에 철저히 서있는 그의 복음의 진정성을 인식하고 바울과 화목해야 한다는 뜻이다. 바울이 이런 하나님의 구원 역사에 대한 인식론을 말할 때, 본문에서 잘 드러나지는 않지만, 약함 가운데서 강해지는 기독론적 진리에 대한 인식의 필요성도 아울러 암시하고 있다고 본다. 바울이 이미 반대자들의 외모의 자랑을 언급하였고(5:12), 그리스도의

379) 문학적 구성으로 보아서, 18-21사이에서 바울은 초대교회의 전통적 가르침을 가지고서 자신을 몇 개의 설명을 부치고 있다고 한다(Martin, 136).

380) Martin, 150.

희생적 죽으심을 언급하는데서, 바울이 고린도후서 전체에서 주장하는 외모나, 육체의 능력이 아닌 약함 가운데서 강해지는 진리를 암시하고 있다고 보아야 할 것이다(12:9).

더 나아가서 바울은 보다 구체적으로 자신의 정체성을 "화해의 사신"으로 밝히고 있다. 이런 특정한 칭호의 사용은 고린도 후서의 주제를 화해로 보는 근거가 된다. 4:7절의 "보배를 담은 질그릇" 같은 말에 비해서 보다 궁극적인 자아 인식의 의미를 가진 표현이다. 질그릇 같이 천히 여김을 받는 바울의 고난의 목적은 그리스도의 고난의 목적과 같이 결국 죄인과 하나님과의 화해, 즉 구원에 있는 것이다.

한편 바울의 반대자들은 이런 바울의 그리스도로 말미암은 새로운 구원의 시대가 요구하는 인간 존재 인식 대신에 낡은 인간 인식방법으로 그리스도를 인식하고 또 자신들을 인식하여 자랑하고(5:12; 11:18), 바울을 비난한다. 아마 이들은 팔레스틴 유대인 기독교인들로서 지상의 예수에 대한 지식과 경험을 자랑하였을 것으로 본다(3:13-15; 10:12-16; 11:22). 또 이에 영향 받은 많은 고린도 교인들도 거짓 사도들의 구시대적 인간인식 방법에 따라서 살고 있다(10:7; 11:, 2, 20). 바울은 고린도 교인들이 반대자들의 낡은 세계관, 인간론, 가치관을 버리고 바울이 가르치는 하나님의 계시에 근거한 세계관, 인간론 가치판단 기준에 따라서 살아야 한다고 가르친다(4:6). 그것은 하나님의 영을 따라서 그리스도를 통해 주신 새 언약을 믿고 그리스도의 영광을 바라보면서 겉 사람이 아닌 속사람의 성장을 기뻐하며 사는 삶을 가리킨다(3:3, 18; 4: 6, 16). 무엇보다 그리스도의 약함의 능력을 믿는 삶이다(12:9, 10; 13:4). 바울 자신이 바로 이렇게 사는 사람이고 이런 삶을 가르치는 사도이다. 그러므로 그는 진정한 그리스도의 사도이다. 그러므로 고린도 교인들은 거짓 사도들을 따르지 말고 바울과 화목해야 한다(5:18-21).

주석:

16. "그러므로 우리가 이제부터는 아무 사람도 육체대로 알지 아니하노라. 비록 우리가 그리스도도 육체대로 알았으나 이제부터는 이같이 알지 아니하노라"(Ὥστε ἡμεῖς ἀπὸ τοῦ νῦν οὐδένα οἴδαμεν κατὰ σάρκα· εἰ καὶ ἐγνώκαμεν κατὰ σάρκα Χριστόν, ἀλλὰ νῦν οὐκέτι γινώσκομεν). 16절은 앞의 15절과 잘 연결된다. 그리스도의 죽으심의 구속적 의미는 믿음으로 알게 되는 것이지 세속적인 "육체를 따르는"(κατὰ σάρκα) 인식방법으로 알 수 없다(16절 하반절). 예수님의 죽으심과 부활을 따라서 구원받는다는 믿음으로 사람들과 세상을 새롭게 인식하는 것이다. 예수를 믿기 이전에는 예수를 구세주로 알지도 못하였고(참조, 마16:14), 또 인간은 용서받을 수 없는 죄인으로만 여겼고, 세상은 하나님의 진노의 대상으로 여겼으나, 믿음을 가진 뒤로는 인간도 세상도 하나님의 은혜와 사랑의 대상으로 보게 되었다(17절).

중복적으로 나타나는 "이제부터는"(ἀπὸ τοῦ νῦν)은 로마서 3장 21절의 "이제는"(Νυνὶ)라는 말과 같이 구원의 새 시대의 시작을 가리키는 말이다(참조, 6:1, 2; 행 18:30; 롬 7:6; 8:1). "이제"란 말은 바울 서신에서 그리스도의 사건이 믿는 자들의 존재에 영향을 미치는 말로 자주 쓰인다.[381] 여기서 이 말은 그리스도의 복음이 전파되는 구원의 새 시대, 그리스도와 함께 죽고 다시 살아서, 그리스도 안에 거하는 사람들의 현존을 가리킨다. 그것은 역사적 그리스도 사건 자체 일 수도 있으나, 그리스도인이 그리스도의 죽음과 부활의 구원의 의미를 알게 된 시점을 가리킨다(6:4).[382] 또 16절 이하에서 바울이 그리스도에 대한 자신의 평가의 변화에 대해 말하고 있으므로 구체적으로 바울의 회심을 가리킬 수도 있다.[383] 세속적 외모만을 보는, "보이는 것" 에만 의존하는 인간의 자연적 인식 능력으로는 하나님의 구원의 새 시대를 인식할 수 없고, 그리스도의 죽음의 의미를 알 수 없고 오히려 오해만을 하게 된다(4:18, 5:12). 즉 그리스도는 결국 십자가에서 죄인으로 죽은 실패한 메시아라고 생각하게 된다. 그것이 바울이 회심 전에 그리스도를 "육체를 따라" (κατὰ σάρκα) 생각한 것이다. 바울은 회심 이전에 자연적 사고방식과, 인간적 경험적 판단으로 그리스도를 알았다. 그러나 바울은 회심 후 약하게 십자가에서 죽으신 그리스도 사건에서 하나님의 보이지 않는 구원의 능력을 보는 인식 능력(믿음)을 하나님의 은혜로 소유하게 되었다(14, 고전 2:12).[384] 즉 사도들이 선포한 복음(케리그마)을 따라서 예수를 새롭게 인식하게 되었다(행 2:14-36). 그 전에는 그리스도의 죽음을 그를 죽인 자

---

381) J. B. Souček, "Wir erkennen Christus nich mehr nach dem Fleisch", *EvT* 19 (1959), 305, 주 13, 참조, 롬 3:21, 26, 5:9, 11, 8:1, 13:11; 고후 6:2; Furnish, 312: Furnish는 사 48:6의 "내가 이제 새 일을 시작하리니" 라는 구절을 고후 5:17과 관련시킨다(Thrall, 414, 주 1563 재인용).

382) Wendland, 202; Kümmel, 205; Bultmann, 156.

383) Bachmann, 255; Belser, 181; Windisch, 184; Hughes, 197, 200; Bruce, 208. (Thrall, 415, 주 1565에서 재인용.)

384) Hughes, 197-199; Denney, 205.

들과 같이 세속적으로 이해했으나 그 이후부터 하나님의 구원의 지혜요 능력임을 알게 되었다(고전 2:8-16; 롬 1:16). 그리스도의 죽음에 대해서 이런 믿음을 가지게 되는 것(바울의 인식의 변화)은 하나님의 은혜다(6:1-2; 고전 2:12). 그리스도께서 약함으로 죽으셨으나 하나님의 능력으로 다시 사신 것을 믿게 되었다(12:9). 이런 의미에서 "육체를 따라 아는 것"은 17절의 "이전 것"과 관련되고, "육체를 따라 알지 않고 영을 따라 아는 것"은 "새 것"과 관련된다. 바울은 하나님께서 그리스도를 통해서 인간과 만물을 새롭게 하시는 구원 역사의 관점에서 그리스도와 사람을 이해하는 것을 말한다(롬 3:21: "이제는…"). 한편 반대자들은 그리스도의 사도라고 하면서도 여전히 육체를 따라 자랑함으로써 하나님의 구원 역사적 관점, 즉 그리스도의 죽음과 부활의 사건, 약한 가운데서 강해지는 그리스도의 능력을 따라서 사람(바울)을 인식하지 못하고, 외모와, 육체를 따라서 피상적으로 이해한다는 강한 암시가 있다(4:7-15; 5:12; 10:7, 10; 11:18, 23; 12:9; 13:4, 5). 그리스도를 "육체를 따라서" 생각하지 않고, 약함 가운데서 오히려 강해지는 기독론적 기준을 따라 사고하면, 바울은 반대자들이 지적하는 그의 모든 약점들 때문에 오히려 하나님의 진정한 사도라는 것이다. 여기서도 바울이 반대자들의 자신의 약점들에 대한 비난을 기독론적 역설을 근거로 반격하는 "되받아치기식" 논쟁 형식을 취하고 있다고 볼 수 있다.

또한 이렇게 그리스도 안에서 그리스도에 대한 새로운 인식 능력을 가진 이후 바울은 이제 사람도 "육체를 따라"(κατὰ σάρκα) 보지 않게 되었다(16절 상반절). 바울의 사람에 대한 평가 기준은 그가 실로 그리스도 안에 거하는 가? 그리스도를 믿는 믿음을 가지고 그와 함께 죽고 살았는가? 구원을 받았는가 이다(13:4, 5). 이것이 그리스도의 죽음 이후에 가장 본질적인 의미 있는 사람 평가 기준이다. 이외에 다른 평가 기준은 모두 외적인 것, 보이는 것에 의한 평가이므로 신뢰 할 수 없다. 사람의 인종, 지역, 풍습, 사회적 지위, 부, 직위 등 세상의 판단 기준과 인간의 경험 기준으로 사람을 평가하는 것은 피상적인 것이며 진실성이 없다(11:22; 롬 2:11; 엡 6:9; 골 3:25; 갈 3:28; 약 2:1-9).[385] 더구나 그리스도의 사도직에 대한 평가도 사도의 외모나 언변이나, 혈통이나, 영적 체험 등 보이는 것이 되어서는 안 되고, 그리스도의 죽음의 구속적 진리의 성격에 부합하는지가 관건이다(4:2; 10:7, 10; 11:6, 18; 12:12). 그러므로 바울은 10장 이후 이런 외적인 세속적 평가 기준에 의해 그의 사도직을 평가받는 것을 거절하고 십자가의 약함에 의한 평가를 받기를 원한다(10:7). 그러나 그의 대적자들은 "육체를 따라" 외모로 사람을 평가한다(5:12; 10:10; 11:18). 이들은 바울도 "육체를 따라" 평가했고 바울은 이를 비 복음적인 평가 기준으로 보아 거절했다(10:2, 3, 11:18).

이상과 같이 16절을 14절과 15절의 예수 그리스도의 죽으심과 사심과 그것이 사람에게 미치는 효과의 맥락에서 "육체대로"의 의미를 해석해야 한다(13:4, 5). 그리스도의 죽음과 부활이후 우리는 구원의 새 시대에 속해 있다. 그러므로 우리는 이 구원 사건에 비추어서 사람을 다시 인식해야 한다. 그렇게 사람을 인식하지 못하는 것은 무엇이든지(자연론적, 과학적, 합리론적, 경험론적, 사회론적, 심리학적 인식론, 등) "육체대로" 인식하는 것이며 하나님

385) Hughes, 197; Denney, 204.

이 그리스도를 통한 구원의 역사를 보지 못하는 데서 기인하는 것이다. 요약하면, 우리가 그리스도를 믿으면 우리의 세계관과 인간관도 따라서 변하게 된다는 것이다. 그러나 16절에 대해서 학자들이 지적하는 다양한 주석적 문제와 그에 따른 해석을 살피지 않을 수 없다.

이 절에서 두 번 반복되어 나오는 "육체대로"(κατὰ σάρκα)라는 구를 어떤 말과 관련시키느냐는 문법적인 문제가 있다. 즉 이 구를 "아무 사람"(οὐδένα)과 그리스도에 부쳐서 해석하면, 그리스도와 사람을 수식하는 형용사구가 되어 "우리는 육체에 의한 그리스도(육체의 그리스도, 육체적 그리스도)와 육체에 의한 사람(육체적 사람)을 더 이상 알지 아니한다"는 뜻이 된다. 즉 외적 특징이나, 타고난 특성, 사회적 지위 등에 의해 한정되는 그리스도와 사람의 특성, 즉 인식 대상의 특성, 을 강조하는 뜻이 된다.[386] 그러나 이 구를 한글개역처럼 "안다"(οἴδαμεν)는 동사와 관련시켜 부사구로 해석하면 우리가 사람이나 그리스도를 인간적인 평가기준이나, 세속적 기준에 따라서 "우리가 평가하는 것," 즉 인식 방식의 특성을 강조하는 의미가 된다.[387] 한편, "육체"가 인식 대상의 특성을 가리킨다고 보고 "육체의 그리스도"라고 번역할 때 그 표현이 다소 생소하다. 그러므로 한글개역이나 다수의 학자들의 의견을 따라서 "육체를 따르는" 회심전의 자연적 인식 방식

386) Bultmann, 156; Plummer, 176; Thrall, 412, 413.

387) 많은 학자들이 이 구가 여기서 "안다"(οἴδαμεν)는 동사와 상관된다고 본다(Martin, 151; Bachmann, 256; Allo, 167; Collange, 259; Barrett, 170; Furnish 212; Thrall, 412). 그것은 이 구가 명사를 수식하는 경우에는 해당 명사를 직접 따르는데(롬 4:1, 9:3; 고전 1:26, 10:18), 여기서는 그렇지 않다는 사실에 근거하는 듯하다(Thrall, 412, 주, 1548).

을 가리키는 것으로 본다. 사실 어느 쪽이든 전체 의미는 마찬가지다.

아래에서 더 논의하겠지만, 여기서 "육체대로 아는 그리스도"의 의미를 몇 가지로 나누어 생각할 수 있다. 첫째는 예수의 죽음과 부활의 구원의 의미를 모르고 사람이나 예수를 인식하는 것을 말한다. 즉 바울은 자신이 회심 이전에 예수를 "육체대로" 이해하여 가짜 메시아로 생각했던 것을 회상하고 뉘우치는 것을 나타낸다. 둘째는 일반 유대인들이 전통적으로 생각해 오던 민족적, 정치적 메시아라고 볼 수 있다. 셋째는 그의 반대자들이 전하는 "다른 예수"를 가리킨다고 볼 수 있다(11:4). 이런 그리스도의 이해는, 예수의 죽으심과 부활에 대한 믿음 없이, "외모를 따라서," "육체대로," 피상적으로, 자연론적으로, 보이는 것으로만 그리스도를 이해하는 것이다. 즉 역사적 예수를 강조하면서 겉으로 나타나는 이적과 기사를 행하는 예수 신앙을 가리키는 것이다(12:1). 이상의 어떤 것이든지 예수를 바로 이해하는 것이 아니다. 이런 이해방식은 한마디로 자연적 경험적 인식방식이다. 바른 예수 이해는 이런 자연적 경험적 인식론을 버리고 성령의 도움을 받아 예수를 그리스도로 믿는 신앙적 이해로만 가능하다(마 16:15, 16; 롬 8:13, 14).

한편, 바울이 반대자들의 비난을 받는 전황을 고려할 때(5:12), "육체대로 사람을 알지 아니한다"는 말은 반대자들이 이런 피상적인 예수 이해(기독론)에 따라서 자신들과 바울을 평가하는 것을 거절한다는 뜻을 담고 있다(5:12; 10:7, 9, 10; 11:18, 22; 12:16). 바울은 "그리스도의 약함"을 따라서 사역하기 때문에 이런 외적 판단 기준으로 자신을 평가 할 수 없다고 한다(10:12; 12:9). 아래에서 이를 더 논하게 될 것이다.

한편, "우리"(ἡμεῖς)는 바울 자신을 가리키는 말이다. 12절 이후 바울이 반대자들을 경계하며 자신의 사도직을 변명하는 것이 분명함으로 "우리"를 바울로 보는 것이 적합하다. 11-14절에서 같은 일인칭 복수가 분명히 바울을 가리키고 있다. 14-15절에서 "모든 사람"은 삼인칭 복수 동사를 쓰고 있으므로 "우리"를 가리킬 수 없다.[388] 여기서 "우리"는 그리스도의 죽음의 구원의 능력을 이해하고 그리스도 안에 있는 바울을 가리키며, 그리스도의 죽음의 능력을 모르고서 사람이나 그리스도를 외모나 육체를 따라서 인식하는 바울의 내적자들과 대조를 이룬다. "우리"도 그리스도를 믿기 전에는 그리스도를 육체를 따라 알았으나 이제는 더 이상 그렇게 알지 않는다는 것이다.

또 εἰ καί(비록)가 이끄는 조건절이 사실을 가리키는가 아니면 단순한 가정인지에 대한 논쟁이 있다. 불트만은 가정이라고 본다.[389] 그러나 휴즈와 마틴은 사실일 가능성이 더 높다고 본다.[390] εἰ καί가 주로 과거의 사건을 인식하는 데 쓰이기 때문이다. 또 가정일 경우 본문의 완료형(ἐγνώκαμεν)대신 "(설령)알았다고 해도"(ἔγωμεν)라고 과거형을 썼을 것이기 때문이다.[391] 가설적인 해석이 부당한 것은 16절이 분명히 바울 자신의 그리스도에 대한 지식을 가리키고 있기 때문이다.[392] 문맥에서 "우리"는 포괄적이

388) 참조, Bultmann, 155; Collange, 257-8; Furnish, 312.

389) Bultmann, 157; Lietzmann, 125; Furnish, 313; Thrall, 415-420.

390) Martin, 151; Hughes, 197-200.

391) Lietzmann, 125.

392) Hughes, 199.

아닌 바로 바울 자신을 가리키는 것이 분명하다. 전술한 바와 같이 11-14절에서 "우리"는 바울을 가리키는 것이 분명하며, **εἰ καί**는 단순한 조건문으로서 사실을 가리킨다. 즉 바울이 예수 믿기 전 생각한 예수에 대한 잘못된 견해를 가리킨다. 그러므로 바울이 예수에 대한 역사적 사실들을 알고 있었다는 의미로 본다.[393] 바울이 실제로 역사적 예수를 만났다는 사실을 말하는 것이라고 보는 이들도 있다.[394] 바울은 예루살렘에서 가말리엘의 제자였으며(행 22:3), 예수가 재판 받고 십자가를 지는 것을 보았을 수도 있었다. 어쩌면 예수께 질문한 부자 청년이었을 수도 있다(막 10:17).[395] 그러나 이를 뒷받침할 만한 근거가 없다. 본문에서 바울이 이런 역사적 예수를 의미했다면 그리스도라는 신학적인 칭호 대신 예수라는 말을 썼을 것이다.[396] 앞에서 보았듯이, 고린도후서 4장 10-14절에서 바울이 자신의 고난을, 예수의 수난과 비교해서 말할 때 그리스도라는 말 대신 예수라는 말을 쓰고 있음을 유의할 필요가 있다. 바울은 회심 전 예수는 자신의 죄로 인해 죽은 것으로 알고 있었다. 이것은 그 당시 유대교의 예수에 대한 이해였다.[397] 그러나 회심 후에 그리스도를 구주로 믿고 전파하게 되었다(행 9:4 이하; 고전 2:12). 본문이 바울이 실제로 예수를 본 사

---

393) Windisch, 187.

394) Hughes, 198; C. A. Anderson Scott, *Christianity according to St Paul* (Cambridge: Cambrdige University Press, 1961), 11-12; J. Weiss, *Paul and Jesus* (London/New York: Harper & Brothers, 1909), 41ff.; J. W. Fraser, "Paul's Knowledge of Jesus: 2 Corinthians 5.16 once more" *NTS* 17 (1971), 293, 주, 1, 2.

395) Hughes, 198.

396) Bachmann, 259.

397) Plummer, 177; Bachmann, 259.

실을 말하는 것이 아니라 해도, 그의 회심 전 예수에 대한 이해를 가리킨다고 본다.

그러나 "비록 우리가 그리스도도 육체대로 알았으나 이제부터는 이같이 알지 아니하노라"라는 말이 문법적으로는 바울 개인의 경험을 가리킨다 해도, 반대자들과 싸우는 전체 문맥, 특히 12절의 "외모를 자랑하는 이들"에 대한 바울의 경계를 고려하지 않을 수가 없다. 이 문장을 가설로 볼 때 바울뿐만이 아니라 일반적으로 유대인들이 알고 있는 역사적 예수에 대한 잘못된 지식을 버린다는 말로 본다.[398] 이 경우 "우리"(ἡμεῖς)를 포괄적인 의미로 보아서 바울과 바울의 대적자들을 포함한 모든 불신 유대인들의 그리스도에 대한 이해를 가리키는 것이 된다. 즉 가설적으로 "설령, 우리가 지금까지 어떤 이들이 자랑하는 대로 '육체대로 예수를 아는 지식'을 가졌다고 하더라도 우리는 이제 그런 지식을 버린다"라고 바울이 말하는 것으로 본다.[399] 가설로 보는 해석들은 한 마디로 "육체를 따라" 예수를 아는 것은 주로 반대자들의 예수에 대한 잘못된 인식들이다. 이것은 바울이 "십자가의 약함을 따라" 예수를 아는 것과 대조되며(13:4, 5), 결국 바울이 경계하는 "다른 예수"이다(11:4). 이 문장을 가설로 볼 때 가능한 몇 가지 잘못된 유대인들의 "역사적 예수의 이해"에 대한 제안들이 있다.[400]

첫째로, "육체대로 예수를 안다"는 것은 역사적 예수를 직접 모신 제자들이나, 초대 교회가 공유한 지상의 예수에 대한 역사적인

398) Hughes, 199.

399) Plummer, 177.

400) Thrall, 417-420.

지식을 가리킬 수 있다고 한다.[401] 고린도 교회의 바울의 반대자들은 자신들이 가진 예수에 대한 목격자들의 일차적인 지식과 자료를 가지고서 사람들에게 자랑하고 그들을 미혹하였다.[402] 그들은 고린도 교회의 "그리스도 파당"에 속한 사람들과 함께 역사적 예수의 생애에 대한 전승을 많이 아는 것을 자랑하면서 바울 같이 직접 예수에 대한 전승이 없는 이들을 열등한 교사로 보고 자신들을 우수한 교사들로 자처하는 이들일 수 있다(고전 1:12 이하; 고후 11:4, 22).[403] 이들이 바로 예루살렘 교회에서 자천서를 받아와서 그들과 역사적 예수와의 외적 연결을 자랑하므로 바울이 이들을 5장 12절에서 "외모를 자랑하는 자들"이라고 지칭했을 수도 있다(고후 2:1). 바울 자신은 이제 영으로 말미암아 예수에 대한 분명한 지식을 얻었으므로(고전 2:12-16, 고후 4:6) 이런 반대자들의 예수에 대한 지식을 거절한다는 것이다.[404]

둘째로, "육체대로 예수를 안다"는 것은 반대자들이 예수를 기적을 행하고 영광을 받는 권능의 메시아로 이해하는 것을 가리킨다. 반대자들은 복음 전통을 따라서 병고치고 귀신 쫓아내는 초월적 영적 능력을 행하면서 그들이야 말로 예수를 바로 알고 좇는 사도들이라고 자처했을 것이다. 바울은 그의 반대자들이 그리스도의 지상 사역의 영광(기적 같은)을 강조하는 것을 반대하고 오히려 그의 수난과 죽음을 강조하는 것이 마땅함을 주장한다. 이렇게 해서 바울은 기적과 이사로 외적 영광을 자랑하는 그의 대적자

---

401) Thrall, 417.

402) Plummer, 178; Denney, 200-201; Windisch, 187-188.

403) Denney, 200.

404) Bousset, 188-9.

들을 경계한다(16절 상반절; 12:12).[405] 그러나 이 두 번째 해석의 가능성은 현재 문맥에서 말하는 그리스도와는 거리가 멀다고 하기도 한다.[406] 바울도 장래의 영광의 소망을 말하거나 현재의 변화된 상태를 말하고 있다고 볼 수도 있다(4:18; 5:17). 그러나 고린도후서 전체 문맥에서 볼 때 바울이 자신의 표적과 기사와 이적을 말하면서 사도직을 변명하는 것이나(12:12), 영적 체험이나 계시의 경험을 말하면서 이를 결국 "육체적 자랑"으로 여기는 것을 보면(12:1, 5, 16, 17, 12:1, 11, 12), 반대자들의 이런 영적 능력의 과시를 "그리스도를 육체대로"아는 것과 같은 것으로 볼 수도 있다.[407] 이에 대해서 바울은 약함으로 십자가에서 죽으신 그리스도의 능력을 자랑한다. 그는 심지어 그의 사도권 행사마저 "육체를 따라서" 사용하는 것으로 알고 되도록 행사하지 않기를 원하는 것이다(13:3, 7, 9, 10).

셋째로, 둘째의 경우와 유사한 해석이지만, 반대되는 의미로써, 본문에서 바울이 이제 그리스도를 더 이상 고난 받는 그리스도로 보지 말라고 말하는 것으로 본다.[408] 지상에서는 고난 받는 그리스도였으나 이제 그리스도는 영광중에 계시기 때문이라는 것이다. 그러므로 암시적 의미로서, 바울은 고린도 교인들에게 자신의 외양을 보고 평가하지 말라고 한다. 오히려 초라한 자신의 외양

---

405) Georgi, 252-3, 276, 299, 주, 167.

406) Furnish, 313.

407) 반대자들을 영지주자들이라고 보는 Windisch, Bultmann, Schmithals, Schlatter, Bousset 등의 견해를 따르거나(Harris, 79), 또는, 해리스(M. J. Harris)가 말하는 대로 고린도전서의 영지주의적 영향이나 잔재세력이 반대자들과 함께 규합하여 바울을 반대한다고 보면 이런 해석이 가능하다(Harris, 87).

408) Bultmann, 156-57.

가운데 그리스도의 영광이 나타난다는 뜻을 나타내고 있다(2:14-16; 4:7-12). 그러나 이런 해석은 고난을 강조하는 고린도후서의 지배적인 사도직 이해와 배치된다. 영광은 언제나 고난 뒤에 감추어져 있다. 영광 보다는 바울이 현재 당하는 고통이 지배적인 문제이다(11:23-12:10). 또한 고난은 바울의 진정한 사도직의 증표로 제시되고 있다(11:23-12:10, 15; 13:9).

넷째로, "육체대로 예수를 안다"는 것은 유대교 기독교인들이 신봉한 유대교 중심적 예수 사상을 가리키는 것이다. 바울 자신도 실제로 회심 후에 이런 유대교 중심적 메시아사상에 입각한 민족주의적 기독론에 심취하였었는데 얼마 후에 그런 관심을 버리게 되었다는 것이다. 소위 바울의 제2의 회심론이다.[409] 그러나 바울 서신이나 사도행전에서 이를 뒷받침하는 어떤 증거도 없다.[410] 오히려 바울은 그의 회심 후에 같은 복음을 전파한 것으로 나타난다. 그는 다른 복음은 있어서 안 되고 자신이 다른 복음을 전할 수도 없다고 잘라 말한다(11:4; 갈 1:6이하).

이렇게 16절의 "예수를 육체를 따라 알았다"는 말을 가설적으로 해석하는 것은 바울과 고린도 교회 반대파의 입장을 고려하면서 보다 복합적인 의미를 제시하고 있다. "그리스도를 육체를 따라서 알았다"는 말을 단순히 바울이 예수를 믿기 전에 알았던 "유대교의 범죄자 예수"로만 한정시키는 것은 고린도후서 전체에서 볼 때뿐만이 아니라 문맥에서도 맞지 않는다는 것이다. 사도직 변명이라는 고린도후서의 전체 주제와 반대자들과의 논쟁적인 문맥

---

409) Hughes, 199.

410) Hughes, 199; Allo, 167.

과 함께 종말론적인 문맥을 고려해야 한다는 것이다. 즉 5장 12절에서 바울은 마음으로 하지 않고 외모로 자랑하는 반대자들을 지칭하였고, 또 17절은 그리스도로 말미암은 전혀 새로운 변화된 세계와 존재를 말하고 있다. 그러므로 "그리스도를 육체대로 알았다"는 말은 과거의 바울의 개인적 예수에 대한 이해뿐만이 아니라, 반대자들의 예수에 대한 이해와 이에 반대되는 예수의 진정한 구속론적 의미를 복합적으로 고려한 말이라고 보는 것이 옳다는 것이다. 이런 해석들의 저변에는 반대자들이 역사적 예수에 대한 지식을 자랑하는 데 대항하여 바울이 "나(바울)는 역사적 예수에 대해 전혀 몰라도 상관이 없다. 왜냐하면 나는 이제 예수에 대해 더 분명히 알고 있기 때문이다(고전 2:12; 고후 4:6)"라는 의미가 있다고 본다. 즉 유대교의 고소로 죽은 과거의 죄인 예수는 바울에게 아무런 의미도 없고 상관도 없다는 것이다. 그가 이제 아는 예수는 죄인들을 대신하여 죽고 다시 사신 그리스도이시다. 새로운 구원의 시대를 시작하여 죄인을 구원하시고 하나님과 화목케 하시고 구원하여, 새로운 삶을 시작하게 하신 그리스도라는 것이다. 다시 말하면 본문에서 바울은 과거의 역사적 예수에 대한 지식을 자랑하는 반대자들에 대해서 은혜로 말미암아 구원 얻게 되는 자신의 복음을 변명하고 있다는 것이다.

이렇게 본문의 "육체대로 예수를 알지 아니한다"는 말을 가설적으로 보는 현대 실존주의적 신학자들 가운데 전통적 초월적인 예수 신앙을 무시하면서 오늘날 내가 나의 현실에서 믿는 예수 신앙을 주장하는 이들이 많다. 이런 해석은 바울이 본문에서 말하는 의미를 왜곡시킨 해석이라고 본다. 우리는 신앙적이고 신학적 예수는 역사적 예수와 함께 중요한 것이며 분리될 수 없는 것으로 보아야 한다. 실제로 없었던 예수나 그의 이야기라도 신앙적 신학적 의미만 있으면 된다는 것은 바울의 사상이 아니고 복음적 전통도 아니다. 바울은 본문에서 유대 배경을 가지고 역사적 예수와의 접촉 경험을 가지고 자랑하며, 마치 이런 지상 예수에 대한 지식 자체가 구원의 증거나, 사도직의 증표가 되는 것으로 가르치는 것을 반대하는 것이다. 바울은 예수를 믿고 그리스도 안에서 새롭게 변화되는 것이 믿음의 증거이며, 이런 복음을 전하는 것이 진정한 사도의 증표로 본다(4:7-15; 6:4-10; 13:4, 5). 본문에서 바울이 말하는 예수에 대한 역사적 이해에 대한 경계는 복음서에서 예수 자신이 경계한 말과도 유사하다. 예수는 가버나움 집에서 그의 가족들이 그를 찾아 왔을 때, 그는 가족의 개념을 "육체를 따라서" 생각지 않고, "누구든지 하늘에 계신 내 아버지의 뜻대로 하는 자가 내 형제요 자매요 모친이니라" 고 하였다(마 12:50; 막 3:35). 그리스도인이 그리스도를 따른다는 것은 베드로나 도마의 경우처럼 예수의 외양이나, 그에 대한 외적인 지식에서가 아니라 그를 사랑하고 믿는 것이다(벧전 1:8; 요 20:29; 참조, 벧후 1:16). 당시 일반 유대인들은 예수를 세례 요한이나 선지자로 생각했고(마 16:14), 바리새인들은 그리스도를 외모나 "육체를 따라" 그릇되게 평가하였고 그를 하나님의 아들로 믿지 못했다(막 6:3; 요 7:24, 8:15, 57; 10:33). 유사하게 바울의 반대자들은 예수에 대한 역사적 이야기들을 아는 것과, 지상의 예수와의 실제적 접촉 경험을 자랑하면서 그런 경험이 없는 바울을 열등한 사도로 경멸하였다고 본다(10:7; 11:4, 18, 23; 참조, 벧후 1:16). 바울은 이런 예수 인식에 대해서 반대하면서 진정한 신앙적 예수는 죄인을 사랑하여 십자가에서 약함으로 죽으신 예수를 믿는 것이라고 말하는 것이다. 그리고 자신의 약함의 사역과 이에 반하는 반대자들의 자랑과 오만함의 사역을 암시하면서 고린도 교인들의 바른 판단을 촉구한다는 것이다(13:3, 4, 5).

특별히 불트만은 이 절을 그의 지론인 역사적 예수를 거절하고 실존주의적인 그리스도 이해를 주장하기 위해 해석한다.[411] 그는 "육체대로 예수를 아는 것"은 예수가 이 세상에 있을 때의 역사적 예수에 대한 지식을 가리킨다고 한다.[412] 그는 이런 사실적 역사적 예수에 대한 지식은 무의미하다면서 반대하고, 그의 자유주의적 실존주의적 예수 이해(즉 "진정한 존재"로서의 예수)를 위한 근거로서 본문을 이용하고 있다. 불트만은 바울이 마치 세상에서 사시고 죽으신 과거의 예수에 대해 거의 무관심한 것으로 볼 뿐만 아니라. 실제로 바울이 믿는 죄인들을 위해 죽고 사신 구주 예수

411) 그러나 Bultmann은 그의 주석책(*The Second Letter to the Corinthians*)에서 5:16과 17절을 주석할 때는 특별히 역사주의적 해석을 배재하고 실존주의적 해석을 주장하는 말이 없다. 그는 16절의 "육체를 따라 사람이나 예수을 아는 것"를 세상이나 인간의 경험적 이해를 따라서 예수를 이해하는 것(즉, 반대자들이 예수의 지상 사역을 따라서 예수를 이해하는 것)이라고 보고, 17절의 "그리스도 안에서의 새로운 피조물"을 예수를 주로 믿는 신앙과 함께 종말론적 교회론적 시각으로 해석하고 있을 뿐이다(156-158). 존재론적 해석은 그의 다른 저서에서 강조되었다(다음 주를 보라).

412) R. Bultmann, *Glauben und Verstehen,* I (Tübingen: Mohr, 1933), 10, 207; "The Primitive Christian Kerygma and the Historical Jesus" in *The Historical Jesus and the Kerygmatic Christ: Essays on the New Quest of the Historical Jesus,* ed. & ETr. C. E. Braaten and R. A. Harrisville (New York: Abingdon Press, 1964), 18; *Theology of the New Testament,* I, ETr. Kendrick Grobel (New York: Scribner, 1951), I. 239; G. Bornkamm, *Jesus of Nazareth,* ETr. Irene and Fraser with Kames M. Robinson (Minneapolis: Fortress Press, 1995), 58; J. M. Robinson, *A New Quest of the Historical Jesus* (Philadelphia: Fortress Press, 1983), 26, 31.

가 아니라 불트만 자신이나, 그를 따르는 실존주의적 제자들(the Bultmanneans)이 스스로 믿는 각자의 실존적 작은 "예수들" 이다. 그 예수는 각자가 처한 상황에 따라서 나름대로 주관적으로 의미를 부여하여 해석된 예수이며(주로 윤리적 예수) 성경이 가르치는 구주 예수와 거리가 멀다. 복음서의 예수는 그 당시 비과학적 시대의 사람들이 믿던 묵시론적 예수이며 믿는 자의 각 시대나 정황에 따라서 예수를 재해석하여 믿어야 한다는 것이다. 특히 과학적 시대에서 복음서의 초자연적 기록을 비신화화(非神話化)하여 우리에게 필요한 해석만을 찾아 내야한다고 한다. 그렇게 하는 것이 바른 성경 해석의 전통을 따르는 해석법이라는 것이다. 그러나 이런 예수는 바울이 질책하는 고린도 교회 거짓 사도들의 "다른 예수" 를 연상시킨다(11:4). 바울은 그가 전한 복음 외에 다른 복음은 없다고 단언하였다(갈 1:7). 불트만의 역사적 예수에 대한 부정과 각자가 재해석하여 믿는 예수는 결국 기독교 신앙의 혼돈과 상대화를 초래하였고 그를 따르던 유럽이나 다른 지역의 교회들은 전통적 신앙을 포기한 것은 물론 교회 자체가 약화되게 되었다.

본문에 반대파의 역사적 예수의 지식의 자랑에 대한 경계의 의미가 있다고 해서, 실제로 바울이 지상의 역사적 예수에 대한 지식이나 이야기나 말씀 같은 전승을 무시했다는 것은 아니다(고전 9:14; 11:23). 다만 지상의 예수와의 접촉이나 지식의 소유 자체가 진정한 자랑이 될 수 없고 그를 진실히 믿고 변화되어 새 사람이 되어 온전함에 이르기를 힘쓰는 것이 진정한 그리스도인의 모습임을 가르치고 있다(13:5, 10).

휴즈도 "예수를 더 이상 육체를 따라 알지 않는다" 말을 가지고 복음서의 역사적 예수에 대한 신앙을 반대하며 주관적이고 실존주의적 신앙의 근거로 삼는 이들에 대하여 비판하고 있다.

현대 신학자들 가운데 변증적, 실존주의적 진영에 속한 이들은 이 구절을 가지고 객관적 역사적 진실을 무시하려는 목적에 자주 사용해왔다. 그들은 그리스도가 역사적으로 행한 모든 행동과 사실들을 기독교의 본질적인 것이 아닌 주변적인 것으로 보고 있다. 가치판단 기준을 주관적이며 실존주의적인 경험에 두고, 현실적인 것에만 관심을 둔다. 그들은 "육체를 따라 아는 그리스도"는 그리스도를 과거의 객관적 인물로 아는 것이며, 이런 그리스도는 현대인에게 알려질 수도 없고, 맞지도 않는다고 한다. 그러나 이런 의미는 바울이 그의 모든 서신과, 적어도, 본문(18절에서 21절)에서 말하는 의도와는 먼 것이다. 바울에게 있어서 기독교 진리란 그리스도의 인격과 사역에서 나타난 모든 사실들을 포함하는 것이며 이 사실들은 논쟁 이전에 객관적인 것들로 전제되고(a priori) 있는 것들이다. 이 진리는 예수 그리스도 안에서 저작자인 하나님에 의해서 객관적인 실재로서 형성되고 계시되어 인간을 대면하고 있다. 이 진리에 대한 (개인의) 주관적인(실존주의적인) 경험은, 성령의 은혜를 통하여, 언제나 반드시 하나님의 구원 역사의 객관성에 대한 전이해(前理解)가 있어야 오는 것이다.[413]

413) Hughes, 199-200.

본문은 바로 앞 절(14, 15)에서 말하는 그리스도의 역사적 죽음의 사실에 근거하고 있다. 역사적 죽음이 없는 그리스도는 유령에 지나지 않고 그런 그리스도에 대한 신뢰는 결국 인간의 주관적 이해에 대한 신뢰일 뿐이며, 개인이 만든 "우상"에 지나지 않는다. 바울이 본문에서 "보이는 것에 대한" 경계를 한 것이 역사적 예수에 대한 지식을 무시한 것이라고 볼 수 없다.[414] 다만 역사적 예수에 대한 지식을 자랑하고 신앙의 중심으로 삼는 것을 경계하는 것이다. 바울이 역사적 예수에 대해서 거의 언급하지 않는 것은 사실이다. 그러나 그는 복음 전승에 대해서 언급하고 있는 것도 사실이다. 바울은 고린도전서 11장 23절에서 성찬에 대한 가르침을 "주께 받은 것"이라고 하면서 복음서에서 읽는 최후의 만찬의 기록과 거의 같은 글을 쓰고 있다. 그리고 고린도전서 15장의 부활에 대한 가르침에서도 "내가 받은 것을 내가 너희에게 전하였노니"(고전 15:3)라고 하여 바울은 많은 부분에서 복음전승을 그대로 따르는 것을 보여준다. 이외에 주의 말씀에 대한 언급이 희박하나 바울은 사도행전 20장 35절에서 "주 예수의 말씀에 '주는 것이 받는 것보다 복이 있다' 하심을 기억하여야 할 찌니라"라고 말한다. 그 스스로 주 예수의 말씀을 실제로 많이 알고 있었으리라고 보나, 그의 서신에서 실제로 직접 언급하지는 않는다. 이런 의문에 대해서 몇 가지로 생각해 볼 수 있다. 첫째로, 바울 당시 복음서가 공식적인 정경(正經)이 되지 않은 상태에서 예수에 대한 말씀이나 예수가 하신 말씀들 가운데 일치되지 않거나 중복되거나 그 신빙성이 불분명한 말씀들이 많이 떠돌아다니기 때문에 바울

414) Denney, 202-203.

은 예수의 말씀 인용에 보다 신중해야 했다고 생각했을 것이다. 실제로 우리가 갖고 있는 현재의 사복음서 외에 더 많은 복음서들이 있었고, 그 내용이 서로 다르고 신빙성이 없는 기사들도 많이 있었다. 바울은 사도행전 20장 35절의 경우와 같이 실제로 복음을 전하는 자리에서는 예수의 말씀을 언급하였을 것이다. 그러나 아무리 예수의 말씀이라 해도 아직 공식적으로 정경화(正經化)되지 않은 말을 자기의 기억에 의존한 채 공식적인 서신에서 인용하는 것은 말씀을 정확하게 옮기지 못할 위험이 있으므로 의도적으로 피했을 것이다. 당시 랍비들은 회당 예배에서 성경을 읽을 때에 성경을 암기하지 못하게 했다. 정확성을 위해서 반드시 보고 읽도록 했다. 바울이 그의 서신에서 구약을 자주 인용하면서도 예수의 말씀을 인용하지 않는 것은 아마 이런 정확성과 신빙성 문제 때문일 것이다. 둘째로, 앞의 경우와는 반대로, 예수의 말씀이 현재의 복음서에 있는 내용과 거의 같은 수준으로 초대 교회에 잘 알려져 있었으므로, 바울은 반복하여 언급하기를 피했을 것이다. 더구나 예수의 말씀이나 예수에 대한 말씀은 말씀의 목격자가 된 제자들이 이미 다 전하고 다녔는데, 말씀의 목격자도 아닌 바울이 이를 언급하는 것은 신빙성도 없고 권위도 없다고 보았을 것이다. 그러나 이런 추정의 가능성은 희박하다고 본다. 셋째로, 바울 자신이 다메섹 도상에서 계시된 예수에 의해서 구원받았으니 만큼, 다른 사람들에게도 이 예수를 믿고 구원 얻음을 전함으로 충분하다고 보았다(고후 4:6). 그 자신 예수에 대하여 잘 알지도 못했고 그의 말씀도 알지 모르는 상태에서 단지 부활하신 예수를 만나서 구원받았다. 그러므로 예수의 죽음이나 부활 같은 구원을 위해 중요한 예수의 역사적 사건과 그 의미에 집중하는 것이 가장 필요하고 또 충분하다고 보았다. 바울은 예수의 죽으심과 부활의 사건이 충분히 분명히 복음의 능력을 나타내므로 그 외의 "사소한" 예수에 대한 언급은 이 사건 가운데 다 포함되고 의미되는 것으로 보았다. 그는 독자들이 복음서에 있는 예수에 대한 이야기를 이미 아는 것으로 전제하고 그리스도의 의미에 대해서 집중적으로 논하는 것이다. 그는 회심이후에 예수의 생애에 대한 이야기를 많이 듣고 알았을 것이다. 그러나 그의 관심은 단순히 그 이야기를 반복하는 것보다는 과거의 예수가 그의 회심 체험에서와 같이 각자에게 현실적으로 어떤 의미가 있느냐에 초점을 맞추고 있는 것이다. 특히 이방인 선교를 위해서는 다른 것들 보다는 예수의 죽음과 부활의 의미에 대해서 집중적으로 설명하여 이해하도록 하는 것이 선교적으로 가장 효과적이라고 보았다(고전 2:2). 그의 모든 서신의 중심적 메시지는 결국 예수의 죽음과 부활과 그것이 우리 믿는 이들에게 미치는 구원의 능력에 대한 설명이다.[415] 실제로 베드로서나 요한서신이나 야고보서에도 역사적 예수에 관한 내용이 거의 없다(참조, 벧후 1:16). 더구나 지상의 예수에 대한 지식을 자랑하는 것은 진정한 신앙인의 자세가 아니다.[416] 그것은 예수를 "육체대

415) 바울의 역사적 예수에 대한 관심이 그의 서신에 나타나지 별로 않는 것에 대하여, 라드는 "바울이 예수의 죽음, 부활, 그리고 승귀의 종말론적인 의미를 선포할 때 예수의 생애와 행적과, 말씀과 그 이상을 포함하고 있다. 그의 예수에 대한 상대적인 침묵은 예수에 대한 역사적 신학적 무관심을 나타내는 것이 아니라, 구원 역사가 전개되는 실제 상황을 나타내는 것이다. 예수가 역사 가운데 의미한 모든 것이 승귀한 예수 가운데 포함되어 있고, 확대되어 있는 것이다." G. E. Ladd, *A Theology of the New Testament* (Grand Rapids: Wm. B. Eerdmans Publising Company, 1974), 413; 강창희, 『복음서의 지명과 복음서의 역사성』(서울: 솔로몬, 2001), 16-17.

416) Denney, 203.

로 아는 것"에 속한다. 문제는 14절 15절에서와 같이 그리스도의 역사적 생애 특히 죽음과 부활에 비추어서 오늘 나의 존재와 삶과 관련 시켜서 그 의미를 알고 사는 것이다. 바울의 고린도후서의 중심 신학이 바로 그것이다(4:7-15; 5:14, 15; 6:4-10; 13:4). 반대자들의 문제는 역사적 예수에 대한 지식을 가지고 자랑하였으나, 바울은 그 지식을 근거로 오늘 내가 그리스도 안에서 새사람으로 사는 것을 중시했다.

이렇게 16절 하반절의 "예수를 육체대로 알지 아니한다"는 말은 지상의 예수의 역사적 행적을 아는 것으로만 예수를 믿는 것이 아니라 예수를 그리스도로 믿고 그 안에 거하면서 인간 존재에 대한 변화된 인식을 가지고 변화된 삶을 사는 것이 진정한 그리스도인이 되는 것임을 말한다. 예수에 대한 역사적 사실만을 아는 것을 지나치게 강조하여 신앙적이고 신학적인 의미를 무시하는 역사적 실증주의에 빠져서도 안 된다는 것이다.[417] 반면에, 예수에 대한 역사적 탐구 자체를 비난하여 주관주의적 실존주의적 예수 이해만을 주장하는 것도 경계해야한다(참조, 요일 4:2). 예수에 대한 역사적 사실들도 알아야 하고, 또 성경에서 해석하는 대로 그 역사적 사실들(즉 예수님의 죽음이나 부활, 승천)의 신학적 의미를 이해해야 한다. 우리 신약이 전체적으로 예수님의 역사적 사실들을 주로 다룬 복음서와, 그 신학적 의미를 주로 다룬 서신들로 구성되어 있는 것 자체가 이런 균형된 자세를 시사한다.

이상과 같이 "육체대로 예수를 아는 것"은 보다 복합적인 의미

417) 19세기의 "역사적 예수 연구"는 초월적인 예수의 특성을 제쳐두고, 실증주의적 예수 연구에 만 집중한 나머지 결국은 예수를 단순히 윤리적 교사로만 보게 되었다.

로서 바울의 회심전의 예수에 대한 이해는 물론, 반대자들의 지상의 예수와의 친분에 의한 예수 이해, 그리고 예수가 베푼 기적이나 영적 능력을 행하는 것을 자랑하는 것, 또는 영광의 예수를 강조하는 것을 의미한다고 보아야 할 것이다. "육체대로 예수를 알지 아니한다"는 말 자체는 바울이 회심 이전의 예수에 대한 이해를 버렸다는 말이지만, 문맥에서 바울의 반대자들의 역사적 지상 예수에 대한 지식을 자랑하는 데 대한 경계도 들어 있다고 본다. 즉 바울은 12절에서 반대자들의 외모를 자랑하는 것을 경계하고, 14절에서 예수의 죽으심과 부활의 의미를 언급하고, 17절에서 그리스도의 도래로 말미암은 새로운 구원의 시대에서의 변화된 존재와 인식을 말한다. 대적자들이 "역사적 예수에 대한 사소한 이야기들"에 심취하는 것은 "예수를 육체대로"아는 것에 불과하다. 진정한 그리스도인은 예수의 죽으심과 부활과 그 의미에 집중하고 그로 말미암은 구원의 새로운 시대에 합당한 시각과 가치판단 기준을 가져야 한다. 이렇게 바울은 16절과 17절에서 그리스도의 죽음과 부활의 의미와 그 종말론적 구원론적 의미에 비추어 새로운 세계관과 인간관을 가지게 된 것을 말한다. 특히 여기서 바울은 반대자들과 대립하는 정황에서 사람(바울 자신)을 외모나 세상의 조건에 의해서 평가하는 것은 어리석으며, 그리스도의 사건의 의미, 즉 십자가의 약함과 부활의 능력에 비추어 사람을 이해해야 한다는 뜻을 암시적으로 나타내고 있다. 앞서서 바울은 자신을 "그리스도의 향기"로(2:14-17), "보배를 담은 질그릇"으로(4:7-15), 또 뒤에서는, "그리스도의 고난의 종"으로(11:23-12:10) 그의 외적 약함을 강조하면서, 고린도 교인들을 진심으로 사랑하고 그들을 위해 희생하는 진정한 그리스도의 사도임을 강변하고 있다(12:14,

15; 13:7, 9). 여기서도 그리스도의 약함을 따라서 사역하는 바울 자신에 대한 변명과 그리스도의 영광을 따라 외모를 자랑하는 반대자들에 대한 비난이 숨어 있는 것이다.

17. "그런즉 누구든지 그리스도 안에 있으면 새로운 피조물이라. 이전 것은 지나갔으니 보라 새 것이 되었도다"(ὥστε εἴ τις ἐν Χριστῷ, καινὴ κτίσις· τὰ ἀρχαῖα παρῆλθεν, ἰδοὺ γέγονεν καινά·). 이 구절은 16절의 구원의 새 시대가 도래한 지금 "그리스도와 사람을 육체대로 알지 아니한다"는 내용을 계속하여 설명한다. 본문의 "이전 것"은 16절의 "육체대로 아는 것"과 병행을 이루고 있다. 16절과 같이 결과절을 이끄는 ὥστε로 시작되고 있고, 16절에서 "이제부터는"(ἀπὸ τοῦ νῦν)라는 새로운 시점과 연계된다. 14절과 15절의 그리스도 사건에 대한 이해의 결과로(예수를 믿음으로), 우리는 그리스도 안에 있게 되었다. 16절의 "이제부터"란 예수 그리스도의 죽음과 부활로 시작된 하나님의 새로운 구원의 시대부터라는 뜻이다(롬 3:21; 참조, 행 17:30). 본문의 "그리스도 안에 있으면"은 예수를 믿어 예수의 능력과 권세를 가지게 되면 이란 뜻이고, "새로운 피조물"이란 이렇게 예수를 믿어 예수의 능력을 가진 변화된 인간존재를 가리킨다. 예수를 믿으면 우선 신분의 변화가 일어난다. 즉 제1아담 그리스도를 믿고 그의 후손이 되면 죄의 형벌의 공포 대신에 제2아담 그리스도의 생명과 영광을 얻는 하나님의 자녀로서의 변화된 존재로서의 신분과 축복을 받게 되는 것이다(롬 6:15-19; 8:1). 이 문맥에서는 특히 그리스도인의 신분의 변화로 말미암은 그리스도인의 가치평가 기준의 변화와 이에 따른 사람의 평가기준의 변화를 말하는 것이다. 바울

은 5장 12절에서 반대자들이 외모로 사람을 평가한다는 것을 지적했다. 반대자들은 바울을 외적인 조건들을 가지고 평가하여 열등한 사도로 보았다(10:7, 10; 11:6). 외모나 육체를 따라 평가하는 것은 세상적 평가 기준이며, 그 반대자들이 아직 "죽으시고 부활하신 그리스도 안"에 있지 않다는 증거이다. "그리스도 안"에 있으면 새로운 시각으로, 그리스도의 평가기준으로 세상을 보게 되고 사람을 보게 된다. 즉 그리스도의 인간관과 세계관을 가지게 되는 것이다.

"그리스도 안"(ἐν Χριστῷ)의 의미는 여러 가지로 제안되었다(1:20, 21; 2:14, 17; 10:7, 17, 12:2, 19; 13:2). 첫째, 믿음으로 그리스도에게 속하는 것, 그리스도의 죽음과 부활에 참여하는 것, 이 세상에서 구원의 새 시대로 옮기는 것이다.[418] 이 경우에 ἐν Χριστῷ와 함께 "믿는다"(πιστεύω)라는 동사가 쓰인 경우가 에베소서 1장 13절뿐이고 "믿음"(πίστις)이란 명사가 쓰인 경우는 갈라디아서 3장 26절, 골로새서 1장 4절에 있을 뿐이라는 반대가 있으나, 우리가 앞서 지적한 대로 14절과 15절에서의 예수의 대속적 죽음의 주제가 16절을 거쳐 17절까지 논리적으로 잘 연결된다. 둘째, 그리스도의 영적 능력의 영역이다.[419] 이 견해는 "그리스도 안"(ἐν Χριστῷ)에 거한다는 말이 로마서 8장 1, 9절에서 "성령 안"(ἐν πνεύματι)에 거한다는 뜻과 같고, 성령의 본질이 신적 능력이므로, 결국 이 말이 그리스도의 영적 능력의 영역을 가리킨다고 이해한다. 그러나 문제는 "그리스도 안"이란 말이 "성령 안"이라 말보다 훨씬 더 많이 나오므로 이 말 자체의 의미를 찾는 것이

418) Barrett, 173.

419) J. A. Ziesler, *Pauline Christianity* (Oxford: Oxford University Press, 1983), 63.

필요하다는 지적이다. 셋째, 믿는 자들이 그리스도와 영적으로 일치를 나타낸다. “우리 대신 죄의 형벌을 받아서 우리로 하나님의 심판을 받지 않게 하신 그 분 안에서 안정되게 있는 것, 하나님이 홀로 기뻐하시는 자(그리스도)에게 영접 받고, 부활이요 생명이신 그에게 장래를 보장 받고, 하나님의 유일한 상속자이신 그의 아들에게 있는 영광을 얻게 되고, 영원한 말씀이신 그에게서 신의 성품을 받고, 진리이신 그에게서 진리를 배우고 자유 하는 것을 말한다.”[420] 이 견해는 1과 2를 종합한 개념이므로 문제될 것이 없다.[421] 넷째, 세례로 그리스도의 몸(교회)의 지체가 된 것을 말한다.[422] 갈라디아서 3장 27-28절에서 믿는 자가 그리스도와 합하여 세례를 받고 그리스도 안에서 하나가 된다고 한다. 고린도전서 12장 12-13, 17절에도 유사한 의미가 있다. 이 구절과 관계되는 14절과 15절의 배경이 세례에서의 그리스도와의 죽음이라고 보면(롬 6:4), 이런 의미도 가능하다. 다섯째, 그리스도 중심적 영적 질서를 절대적으로 따르는 것, 또는 그리스도의 주권이나 통치에 온전히 복종함을 가리킨다(고후 2:17; 엡 6:1). 이것은 “그리스도의 영적 능력의 영역”이라는 위의 두 번째 견해와 유사하나 그리스도의 권위와 함께 그리스도 중심적 질서를 가리킨다. 이것도 두 번째와 함께 적절한 의미라고 본다. 본문에서는 이런 그리스도로 말미암아 나타난 새롭고 온전한 영적 질서 체계(하나님의 나라)가 사람에게 미치는 놀라운 능력과 혜택을 가리킨다. 믿는 자가 그리스도

---

420) Hughes, 202.

421) Meyer, 287; Windisch, 189; Hughes, 201.

422) Bultmann, 158; Plummer, 179.

를 믿음으로 그와 함께 죽고 다시 살아 그리스도와 영적으로 하나가 되어 새로운 존재(피조물)로 변화되는 것을 말한다. 결국 요한복음 3장의 중생한 사람과 같은 존재 형태이다. "그리스도 안"(ἐν Χριστῷ)에 거하는 자("새로운 피조물")는 그리스도를 "육체대로" 알기를 거부하고 그와 함께 죽고 산 자이며," 또한 사람을 "육체대로" 알기를 거부하고, 사람을 외적 세상적 조건으로 평가하지 않고, 하나님의 자녀로서 귀하게 여기거나, 또는 하나님의 사랑과 구원의 대상으로 여긴다. 바울 자신도 그의 사역을 죄인을 위해 죽으신 그리스도의 사랑으로 말미암아 수행하고 있다(14). 그러나 17절에서는 이런 개념을 하나님의 종말론적 구원 역사의 관점에서 이해해야 할 것이다. 사람이 그리스도 안에 있으면, 그를 믿으면, 하나님이 시작하시는 새로운 구원 역사의 시각에서 세상과 사람들을 인식하고 평가하게 된다는 것이다. 아래에서 이를 더 설명할 것이다.

한편 바울이 그의 대적자들과 대치된 상황을 고려할 때 "그리스도 안"이란 말은 바울의 대적자들과 차별화된 바울의 사도적 진정성을 나타내는 증표와 같은 것이다(2:17; 5:19; 12:2). 바울은 "그리스도 안"에 있다. 그는 진정한 그리스도의 사도로서 그리스도의 약함의 능력을 믿고 나타낸다. 그래서 그의 사역을 통해서 그리스도의 생명의 역사가 일어나는 것이다(4:7-15; 6:4-10; 12:9; 13:4). 또한 바울의 복음을 믿는 자는 그리스도의 능력으로 말미암아 새로운 존재가 되었고, 그의 능력으로 살아가지만 그렇지 않은 자들은 이런 존재의 변화와 이에 따르는 인식의 변화를 경험하지 못한다는 뜻이다. 바울은 4장 7절에서 "보화를 담은 질그릇," 4장 16절에서 "겉사람은 후패하나 속사람은 날로 새롭다"라고 반대자들의 비난에 맞서서 자신의 존재 가치를 방어해왔다. 여기서는 그리스도 안에서(그리스도의 능력으로) 자신이 새로운 피조물로 거듭나는 것을 암시한다(6:4-10; 12:9, 10; 13:4). 나아가 그 새로운 피조물은 그리스도의 화해의 사신으로 나타난다. 그리스도 안에서 자신의 존재 가치를 회복한 바울은, 고린도 교회와의 관계 회복을 위한 존재, 고린도 교회 신앙 회복을 위한 사도로 자신의 정체성을 확립한다(5:18-21). 바울의 대적자들은 그리스도를 "육체대로"(겉으로, 세속적 평가 기준을 따라서) 알기 때문에, 진정한 그리스도를 알지 못하는 거짓 사도들이며 사단의 일군들이므로 그들은 바울도 자기들의 세속적인 판단기준으로 낮게 평가하면서 무시한다(5:12; 10:7, 10; 11:18). 그러므로 이들을 따라서는 안 된다는 암시가 있다(11:2-4; 13, 15).

"새로운 피조물"(καινή κτίσις)은 하나님께서 마지막 때에 제2 아담 그리스도 안에서 죽을 죄인을 의인으로 창조하신 피조물 즉 구원받은 사람이다(롬 6:15-19). 이런 피조 세계의 새로운 변화에 대한 사상은 무엇보다 구약성경의 이사야 65장 17절과 66장 22절의 하나님의 새 하늘과 새 땅의 창조의 약속을 상기시킨다. 또 이사야 43장 18-19절에서도 새로운 질서 확립의 약속이 바벨론 포로 귀환 예언과 함께 나타난다. 유대교의 배경은 더 다양하다. 쿰란 문서에 종말론과 함께 우주적 인간적 변화에 대한 언급이 많다(1QS 4:25; 1QH 3:19-22, 11:10-14, 13:11). 또 쥬빌리서(*Jubilee*) 4장 26절과 에녹1서(*1Enoch*) 72장 1절에 "새 창조"란 언급이 나오고, 바룩2서(*2Baruch*) 32장 6절, 44장 12절, 57장 2절에 종말론적 피조물의 갱신에 대한 언급이 있다. 랍비 유대교에서는 주로 신년이나 속죄일과 관련하여 죄의 용서와 하나님의 새로 지음 받는 인간에 대한 설명이 있다.[423] 또 유대교로 개종한 이방인들을 새로 태어난 아기에 비교하기도 했으나, 종말론적 의미는 없다.[424] 이렇게 바울 당시 유대교에서도 종말론적 의미의 우주적 인간적 갱신의 예는 있으나, 결국 이사야서의 약속에 근거하고 있다고 본다. 바울은 갈 6:15에서 새 창조를 언급하고 있는데, 멜(Mell)에 의하면, 바울은 유대교의 종말론적 창조의 개념을 도입하여 그리스도 중심적 개념으로 발전시켰다고 한다.[425] 이에 대해 트롤은 갈라디아서 6장 15절을 5장 6절과 고린도전서 7장 19절에 관련 시켜서 볼 때 바울이 어떤 자료에 의지한다기 보다는 자신이 직접 쓴 글이라고 보았다.[426] 그 외에 신약에서는 마태복음 19장 28절, 에베소서 2장 10, 15절, 4장 24절, 베드로후서 3장 13절, 요한계시록 21장 1-5절에 새 창조에 대한 언급이 있다. 이들은 바울의 고린도후서 5장 15절과 갈라디아서 6장 15절의 언급보다 후대에 쓰인 것임으로 그 의미의 기원을 찾는 데 별 도움이 안 된다.[427] 그러나 모두 일치하여 종말론적인 우주적 인간적 창조를 그리스도 사건과 관련하여 언급하고 있다.

피조물(κτίσις)이란 말은 명사형인데, 동사형(κτίζειν)과 같이

---

423) P. Stuhlmacher, "Erwägungen zum ontologische Charakter der kainh. kti,sij bei Paulus", *EvT* 27(1967), 15.

424) U. Mell, *Neuen Schoepfung: Eine traditions-geschichtliche und exegetische Studie zu einem soteriologischen Grundsatz paulinischer Theologie*, BZNW 56 (Berlin and New York: De Gruyter, 1989), 182-185.(Thrall 422, 주 1623, 재인용.); *Joseph and Aseneth* 8:10-11, Stuhlmacher, "kainh, kti,sij", 18에서 인용, Thrall, 422, 주 1624에서 재인용).

425) U. Mell, 298-317.

426) Thrall, 423.

427) Thrall, 424.

수동태(피조물)나 능동태(창조)의 두 가지 의미를 다 갖고 있다. 창조 주체인 하나님을 중심으로 생각하면 능동적 의미가 되고, 창조 대상인 인간이나 만물을 중심에 두면 수동태가 된다.[428] 한글 성경에서는 피조물로 번역되었으나 영어 번역 성경들은 모두 "창조"(creation)라고 능동적으로 번역하고 있다. 그러나 창조나 피조물이나 문제될 것이 없는 것은 능동적 의미의 창조란 말 자체가 결국 하나님에 의한 창조로서 수동적 의미를 포함하기 때문이다. 그러므로 학자들의 관심은, 인간의 창조인가, 아니면 세계적 우주적 창조인가라는 논쟁에 집중되어 있다.[429]

대부분의 학자들은 καινὴ κτίσις(새로운 피조물)를 새 인간 창조를 가리킨다고 본다.[430] 인간이 그리스도 안에서 새로운 존재로 변화되는 것을 의미한다고 본다.[431] 그러나 다른 학자들은 새 인간 창조가 아니라 새 세계 창조가 중심 주제라고 본다. 하나님의 종말론적 새로운 세계 창조가 먼저 이며, 사람은 이런 세계 창조의 영향을 받아서 새로운 존재가 된다고 본다. 그래서 마틴은 17절 상반절을, "누구든지 그리스도 안에 들어오면, 거기에는 새로운 창조가 일어난다"라고 해석한다.[432] 바울은 17절에서 새로운 창조의 행위를 말하며, 개인의 변화를 말하는 것이 아니라고 주장

---

428) 동사형 능동적 의미: 막 13:19; 엡 3:90; 수동적 의미: 고전 11:9; 엡 4:24; 골 1:16; 명사형 능동적 의미: 막 3:19; 히 9:11; 벧후 3:4; 수동적 의미: 롬 1:25; 갈 6:15; 골 1:15.

429) J. Reumann, *Righteousness in the New Testament* [Philadelphia: Fortress Press, 1982] 51, 주 65.

430) Barrett, 173, Thrall, 424, Meyer, 287, Windisch, 189, Hughes, 201.

431) Thrall, 424.

432) Martin, 135.

한다.[433] 구원의 새 시대의 도래가 인간의 존재의 변화에 우선하는 것이라고 한다.[434] 인간의 존재변화는 새 세계 창조의 결과라는 것이다.

그러나 상반절의 "누구든지 그리스도 안에 있으면"(τις ἐν Χριστῷ)에서 τις는 분명히 인간을 가리킨다. 세계 창조는 후반절에 나타난다. "이전 것은 지나갔으니 보라 새 것이 되었도다." 또 18절에서도 나타난다. 그러므로 16절에서 인간 존재의 변화가 새 세계 창조에 앞선 우선적 요구 사항임이 분명하다. 물론 마지막 때에는 인간의 회개나 변화와 상관없이 최후의 심판이 있을 것이다(5:10; 롬 14:10; 살후 2:12; 딤후 4:1). 그러나 인간의 죄가 인간의 저주와 함께 세상의 저주를 초래한 것을 상기한다면(창 3장), 인간의 죄의 회개가 세상의 회복 이전에 자주 요구되는 사항임을 알아야 한다. 인간의 죄 사함이 없는 우주 회복은 성경적이 아니다. 그래서 바울도 "피조물의 고대하는 바는 하나님의 아들들의 나타나는 것"이라고 했다(롬 8:19). 또 예수님도, "회개하라 천국이 가까웠느니라"(마 4:17)고 하셨다. 인간의 죄의 사유함이 이 세상의 변화에 앞서서 요구된다. 무엇보다 이 세상은 인간의 죄로 말미암아 저주받았기 때문이다(창 3:18). 종말은 인간의 회개나 구원과 깊이 관련되어 있다. 하나님은 그의 인자하심으로 인간의 죄에 대한 진노를 참으시고 심판을 주저하신다(롬 2:4; 벧후 3:9).

17절 상반절은 구원의 새 시대에 일어나는 인간존재의 놀라운 변화가 주제이다. 멸망 받아야 할 죄인 인간이 예수를 믿고 죄 사

433) Martin, 152; U. Mell, 298-317.

434) Martin, 152; R. C. Tannehill, *Dying and Rising, with Christ: A Study in Pauline Theology*, BZNW 32 (Berlin: Töpelmann, 1967), 68, 69.

함을 받아 "그리스도 안에 새로운 피조물"로서 다시 태어나는 것이다. 그것은 로마서 8장 1절 이하의 그리스도 안에서 죄에서 해방된 인간이며, 갈라디아서 6장 14-15절에서 그리스도와 함께 십자가에 못 박히고 율법에서 해방된 "새로 지으심을 받은 자"이며, 에베소서 2장 10절에서 하나님이 만드신 자요, 예수 안에서 선한 일을 위하여 지으심을 받은 자이며, 에베소서 4장 21절 이하에서 예수 안에서 배우고, 썩어져 가는 구습을 좇는 옛 사람을 벗어버리고 오직 심령으로 새롭게 되어 하나님을 따라 의와 진리와 거룩함으로 지으심을 받은 새 사람을 입는 자이다(딛 3:5; 요 3:5).

17절은 이런 새 피조물이 새 시대의 변화된 특성을 인식하고 그에 따라 살 수 있는 능력을 갖고 있음을 암시하고 있다. 이미 16절에서 이런 새로운 능력을 언급했다. 거기서는 사람에 대한 새로운 인식능력, 즉 인간관의 변화에 대해서 말했다. 그렇다면 17절은 이 세계 또는 이 시대에 대한 인식능력, 즉 세계관을 말하는 것이다. 사람이 그런 인식능력을 그리스도 안에서 얻을 수 있다고 하는 것이다. 새로운 세계 창조가 시작되었으나, 그 창조의 핵심적 사건인 그리스도의 죽으심의 구원의 의미를 깨닫지 못하면, 이런 새로운 하나님의 세계 창조의 경륜을 볼 수 없다. 그리스도를 아는 지식으로 세상을 보지 못하면 세상은 변하지 않은 그대로의 세상처럼 보인다. 그러나 그리스도를 아는 지식으로 보면 하나님께서 이 세상을 새롭게 바꾸시는 것을 볼 수 있다. 주의할 것은 이런 세계관에 대한 변화를 개인의 주관적 인식의 변화로만 이해해서는 안 된다. 그리스도의 구속 사건은 역사적 객관적 사건이며, 그 후부터 이 세상은 새로운 구원의 시대가 시작된 것이다. 세상의 창조주께서 그의 아들을 통하여 구원의 새 역사를 시작하셨다. 이련 구속 사건을 이해하는 것은 단순히 개인의 주관적인 해석이 아니라, 사실을 사실대로 보는 객관적이고 과학적인 관찰이 우선이다. 예수를 믿음으로 세상이 실제로 변화한다는 사실을 보게 되는 것이다. 이런 새로운 변화를 보지 못하는 이들은 멸망 받을 세상의 사상이나 죄인 인간들의 사상에 빠져있는 것이다(요 9:41). 바울 자신이 이런 새로운 구원의 세계의 도래를 알지 못했다가 그리스도를 만나고서야 알게 되었다. 그가 다메섹 도상에서 하늘의 강한 빛으로 보지 못하다가 다시 보게 된 경험이 16절과 17절에 암시된 새로운 인식능력의 배경일 수도 있다(행 9:9, 18; 고후 4:6).

이런 인식의 변화에 대한 해석이 14, 15절의 그리스도의 죽음과 부활에 대한 언급과 일치되고, 또 16절의 "더 이상 그리스도를 육체대로 알지 아니한다"는 말과 일치된다. 바울이 그리스도를 믿기 전에는 그리스도를 "겉으로"만 알았다. 그리스도를 전통적인 유대교적 관점에서 강력한 민족적 메시아로 이해했다. 그러나 예수를 만나서 그의 메시아관이 바뀌었다. 진정한 그리스도는 외적인 능력을 과시하는 메시아가 아니라, 십자가의 약함으로 죽으시고 하나님의 능력으로 부활하신 그리스도로 인식하게 되었다. 그 후에 바울은 예수 믿는 사람의 새로운 시각에서 세상과 사람도 새롭게 인식하게 되었다. 그리스도를 "육체대로" 알지 않고 하나님의 계시를 따라 아는 사람은, 사람도, 세계도 새롭게 보게 되는 것이다. 그리스도의 구원 역사를 믿는 순간부터 "육체대로" 만물을 보던 낡은 인식방법을 버리고 하나님의 구원역사의 시각에서 새롭게 사람과 만물을 보게 된다. 이런 견해는 문법적으로도 지지를 받는다. 위에서 지적한 바와 같이 16절과 17절 모두 ὥστε라는 결과절로 시작되는데 이것은 16절과 17절이, 앞의 두절, 14, 15절에서 말한 그리스도의 죽으심과 부활의 결과에 대한 내용임을 의미한다. 그리스도의 죽음과 부활의 결과로 사람을 제대로 알게 되고 세상을 제대로 알게 되었다는 것이다. 그리스도 사건의 바른 인식에서부터 모든 인식이 바르게 된다. 그러므로 17절 상반절은 "누구든지 그리스도 안에 있으면"이라는 εἰ(만일)로 시작되는 조건문과, "새로운 피조물이라"라는 귀결절로 되어있다. 사람이 그리스도 안에 있어야 새로운 피조물로서의 안목을 가지고 하나님이 창조하시는 새로운 세상을 볼 수 있게 된다. 그리스도 밖에 있으면 하나님의 대변혁의 새 세계를 보지 못하고 구태의연한 낡은 세상으로 잘못 보고 살게 되는 것이다. 그리스도 안에 있다는 것은 그리스도의 죽음과 부활을 믿어 그와 영적으로 일치된 것을 가리킨다. 이런 사람은 하나님의 새로운 창조의 세계관을 갖게 된다. 뿐만 아니라, 17절에서 사람을 가리키는 인칭대명사 τις가 "그리스도 안"(ἐν Χριστῷ) 바로 앞에 있으므로 그리스도 안에 있는 인간 존재를 의미한다고 봐야 한다. 사람이 그리스도 안에 들어와야 새 피조물(창조) 이(가) 된다. 그래야 하나님의 새로운 세계 창조의 대변혁의 사건을 볼 수 있다. 만일 사람의 창조가 아닌 세계 창조를 나타내려고 했다면, 인칭대명사 τις대신에 18절에 있는 τὰ πάντα(만물 혹은 모든 것)란 말을 썼을 것이다(고전 15:27, 28; 골 1:17, 20).

"세계 창조"란 개념은 오히려 17절 하반절에 나타나 있다고 할 수 있다: "이전 것은 지나갔으니 보라 새 것이 되었도다"(참조, 고전 15:27; 골 1:16, 20).[435] τὰ ἀρχαῖα(이전 것)와 καίνα(새 것)는

435) Thrall은 "새로운 피조물"에 대한 인간 창조설과 세계 창조설을 융합하여, 17절 상반절에서는 누구나 그리스도 안에 있으면 그는 새로 지음 받은 존재라는 뜻이고, 하반절에서는 상반절의 근거로서 더 넓은 배경을 언급한다고 한다(427).

중성 복수형으로써 사람이 아니라 우주 만물을 가리킨다고 볼 수 있다. 그러나 이 말 조차 상반절의 새로운 피조물의 변화된 "모습"을 강조하는 것이라고 볼 수 있다.[436] 그리스도의 대속적 죽음으로 죄에서 해방이 되고, 하나님의 진노의 두려움을 벗어나고, 의롭게 된 인간의 변화된 상태를 가리킨다고 볼 수 있다. "이전 것"은 16절의 "육체"와 병행되는 개념으로서, 고린도전서 2장 14절의 "육에 속한 사람," 로마서 6장 6절의 "옛 사람," 로마서 6장 11절의 "죽은 자," 로마서 6장 16절의 "죄의 종"을 가리킨다. "새 것"은 고린도전서 2장 15절의 "신령한 자," 로마서 6장 11절의 "산 자," 로마서 6장 18절의 "의의 종"을 각기 가리킨다. 18절 이하에서는 이런 하나님과 죄인의 새로 변화된 관계를 화해라고 말하고 있다. 휴즈는 17절 하반절의 변화는 믿는 자의 썩을 육신이 영원히 썩지 않는 몸으로 변화되는 것을 포함한다고 하면서 현재적 변화와 함께 미래적 그리스도인의 변화라고 말한다.[437] 미래적 변화는 5장 초두에서 이미 말한 것이다(참조, 고전 15:44-46). 휴즈의 말대로, "그리스도로 말미암는 구원은 하나님의 창조의 영원한 목적의 성취로서, 그 영향이 매우 크므로 '새 창조'라고 부르는 것이 마땅하다."[438] 그러나 τὰ ἀρχαῖα(이전 것)와 καίνα(새 것)가 갖는 보다 포괄적 의미를 고려하여 볼 때, 또 창조론에서 인간이

---

436) Hughes, 202; Plummer, 215.

437) Hughes, 204. 그러나 Hughes는 다른 곳에서 17절 상반절의 의미가 개인적인 변화와 함께 우주적인 변화도 포함한다고 본다: "그리스도의 구원 사역은 믿는 자의 경험에서만 그 영향을 나타내는 것이 아니라 하나님의 창조의 전체 질서를 통하여 나타난다. 만물의 완성은 단순히 새로운 인간만이 아니라 새 하늘과 새 땅, 새로운 우주를 말한다"(205).

438) Hughes, 202.

하나님의 창조의 극치(the crown of God's creation)[439]임을 생각할 때, 17절 하반절은 그리스도을 통한 인간존재의 변화를 중심으로 한 하나님의 새로운 세상의 창조를 가리킨다고 보는 것이 합당하다. 피조된 세상이 저주를 받은 것은 인간의 타락이 그 원인이기 때문에, 세상의 회복은 인간 회복으로부터 시작되는 것이 마땅하다(창 3:18; 롬 8:19-22). 이런 인간과 세상의 총체적 재창조는 다음 18절에 나타나는 "모든 것" (τὰ πάντα)이란 말에서 확인된다.

이렇게 17절은 하나님의 인간존재와 세계에 대한 종말론적 총체적 재창조를 가리킨다. 이미 14절 15절에서 말한 그리스도의 죽음은 이런 하나님의 재창조의 시작으로 보아야 한다. 그것은 주관적인 일이 아니라 실제로 하나님께서 역사 가운데 행하신 일이다. 다만 사람들이 그 사실을 보지 못하는 것이 문제다. 그러나 그리스도 안에 들어오면 이 놀라운 하나님의 대변혁의 사역을 알게 된다. 17절 상반절은 제2아담, 원인간(原人間, *Ur-mensch*),[440] 그리스도로 말미암는 인간의 놀라운 존재적 변화와 그 자신이나 세계에 대한 인식능력의 변화를 말하고, 하반절은 인간 존재의 변화에 대한 재확인과, 우주적 변화까지 포함하는 총체적 변화를 말한다. 다시 말하지만, 바울은 14절과 15절에서 그리스도의 죽음을 통한 하나님의 인간 구원 역사로 변화된 인간존재를 설명하고 16절에서는 그의 변화된 인간관, 그리고 17절 상반절에서는 다시 그리스도 안에서 변화된 인간존재와 그의 인식의 변화를, 그리고 17절 하반절에서는, 놀랍게 변화된 인간존재의 확인과 변화된 세계를 말한다. 그리고 이것은 바울의 목회적 관심인 고린도 교인들과의

439) Hughes, 209.
440) Thrall, 427.

화해의 준비작업도 된다. 그리스도인은 새로 변화된 존재로서 변화된 인간관과 세계관으로 모든 문제를 새롭게 인식하고 하나님의 자녀로써 의롭게 살아가도록 힘써야 한다.[441]

17절에서의 그리스도 안에서의 새로운 존재의 변화를 통해서 바울이 강조하려는 것은 그리스도인의 실제적인 변화된 자세와 삶이다. 5장 초두의 그리스도인의 미래적인 대망이 10절의 최후 심판을 기점으로 다시 그리스도인의 현실적 책임문제로 돌아왔다. 새로운 피조물인 그리스도인이 새로운 세상에서 어떻게 살아야 할 것인가 사실 바울은 여기서 말하는 그리스도 안에서 새로 태어난 존재와 새로 지어진 세계가 아직 온전한 세계가 아님을 알고 있다. 새로운 존재와 새로운 세계가 이미 시작됐으나 아직 온전함을 이룬 것은 아니다. 인간과 세상은 온전함을 이루는 종말을 향해 가고 있는 것이다. 그러므로 바울은 바로 앞에서 종말의 영광을 대망하였고(4:17-5:10), 또 현재의 고통을 시인하고 있다(4:16; 참조, 롬 5:3; 8:18). 또 이 세상에서 그리스도인은 온갖 죄의 유혹을 이기며 살아야 할 책임이 있다. 이런 세상의 세력과 자신의 약함에도 불구하고 우리는 그리스도 안에서 새로운 피조물로, 새롭게 지음 받았다는 것과 하나님께서 세상을 새롭게 하신다는 인식을 가지고 새롭게 변화된 삶을 살도록 힘써야 한다는 것이다(롬 6:11).

여기서 바울은 고린도 교회의 화해 문제를 염두에 두고 있다(5:18-21; 6:11-13; 7:2). 그러나 지금은 먼저 고린도 교인들에게 화해의 당위성을 위한 신학적 준비 작업을 계속하고 있는 것이다. 고린도 교인들이 낡은 옛 인식을 버리고 그리스도 안에서 새로운

441) Plummer, 181.

인식력을 가짐으로써 바울과 함께 새로운 인간관계를 시작하자는 것이다.[442] 18절에는 이런 화해를 위한 의도가 보다 분명하게 나타난다. 바울은 반대자들에 비해서 약한 모습의 사도이다. 반대자들은 유대인 선교사들로서 예루살렘 사도들의 추천장을 가지고 자랑하며(3:1), 예수님에 대한 역사적 지식을 자랑한다. 물론 바울도 같은 유대인이며 그리스도의 사도이다(11:5, 22, 23; 12:12). 바울도 그들과 같이 표적과 기적과 이사를 나타낸다(12:12). 영적인 체험도 있다(12:1-4, 7). 또 지식도 있다(11:6). 그러나 바울은 온갖 고난을 받으며(11:23-33), "몸의 가시"도 있다(12:7). 언변도 부족하고 외모도 부족하다(10:10). 그러나 바울은 이런 강점과 약점에 대한 평가 자체가 결국 모두 "육체를 따라" 이해하는 낡은 구시대적 사고방식 때문이라고 본다(11:18). 심지어 영적인 능력이나 계시와 체험, 그리고 사도권까지지도 사람의 오만함을 나타낸다면 "육체를 따르는 것"에 속하게 되는 것이다(12:1; 7; 13:3, 7, 9). 거짓 선지자들이 이런 것들을 자기 과시를 위해 나타내는 것은 "육체적 자랑"이 되는 것이다(12:1, 5, 6; 마 7:15, 21-23; 막 13:22). 십자가에서 약함으로 죽으셨으나 하나님의 능력으로 부활하신 그리스도를 믿을 때 이런 모든 외적 가치 판단 기준이 별 의미가 없음을 깨닫게 된 것이다. 십자가의 능력은 오히려 약한데서 강해지는 능력이기 때문이다. 세상이 자랑하는 외모나 힘은 그리스도의 십자가 앞에서 그 가치를 잃게 되는 것이다. 그런대도 반대자들이

---

442) Jae Young Noh(노재영)은 새로운 피조물을 존재론적 의미로 보지않고 새롭게 변화된 인간관계라고 강조한다. 그러나 존재론적 변화 없이 관계의 변화가 나타날 수 없다. Jae Young Noh, *An Exegesis of 2 Corinthians 5:16-21, and Its Contribution to Pauline Theology*, A Ph.D. Dissertation, (Ann Arbor, UMI, 1997), 82.

그런 낡은 세상의 가치로 바울을 평가하고 있고, 고린도 교인들이 이를 따르고 있으니, 바울은 안타까울 뿐이다(13:3, 5, 6). 그러나 16절 주석에서 밝혔듯이 이런 넓은 의미의 "그리스도를 육체대로 아는 것"은 고린도후서 전체의 의미이고 지금의 문맥에서는 단순히 바울이 예수를 믿기 전에 유대인으로서 알았던 지상의 예수를 가리킨다고 볼 수도 있다. 예수의 진정한 신분을 모르고 핍박하였으나 그를 만난 뒤에 그의 신분이 구세주이심을 믿고 자신이 변화된 것을 가리킨다는 것이다.

이상과 같이 16절, 17절은 빌3:3-5과 갈6:13-15의 내용과 유사하다. 그리스도인들은 구원의 새시대에서 구시대적 육체적 자랑이나 구시대적 인간 존재 인식은 무가치 하게 여기며, 대신 그리스도로 말미암은 구원의 은혜의 새로운 시각에서 인간존재나, 세계에 대한 새로운 가치관을 형성하게 되는 것이다.

18. "모든 것이 하나님께로 났나니 저가 그리스도로 말미암아 우리를 자기와 화목하게 하시고 또 우리에게 화목하게 하는 직책을 주셨으니…" (τὰ δὲ πάντα ἐκ τοῦ θεοῦ τοῦ καταλλάξαντος ἡμᾶς ἑαυτῷ διὰ Χριστοῦ καὶ δόντος ἡμῖν τὴν διακονίαν τῆς καταλλαγῆς,). 18절에서 이 부분의 또 하나의 중요한 주제가 나타난다. 그리스도를 통한 새 창조에 이어 화해의 주제가 등장한다. 사실 고린도 교회에 대한 바울의 주된 관심이 화해이고 보면, 이 부분이 고린도후서의 핵심적인 부분이다. 바울의 다른 기독론적 구절과 달리 여기서부터 21절까지 그리스도의 활동이 아니라 하나님의 활동에 그 초점을 맞추는 것이 특징이다. 창조주 하나님의 창조적 활동이 그리스도의 죽으심, 부활,

재림의 배후의 근본적인 동인이다.[443]

18절 이하에서 바울은 자신의 존재인식을 "그리스도의 화해의 사신" 이라고 밝힌다. 이것은 17절에서의 "그리스도의 새로운 피조물" 이란 존재인식 보다 구체적인 것이다. 사실 바울은 여러가지로 자아인식을 표현해 왔다. 즉 "그리스도의 향기" (2:15), "새언약의 일군" (3:6), "그리스도의 종" (4:5), "보배를 담은 질그릇" (4:7), 그리고 여기서 "그리스도의 화해의 사신" 이라고 한다.

"모든 것" (τὰ πάντα)은 필로(Philo of Alexandria)나 마르쿠스 아우렐리우스(Markus Aulelius) 같은 헬라-로마시대 사상가들에게서 만물이나 사연을 나타내는 종교적 철학적 의미로 쓰이기도 했다.[444] 바울도 어떤 곳에서는 이 말을 이런 의미로 쓰기도 하기도 하나[445] 다른 데서는 전혀 그런 뜻으로 쓰지 않는다.[446] 이 말에 영지주의적 개념이 있다는 주장도 있으나 확실하게 증명이 되지 않는다.[447] 어떤 이들은 18절의 이 말을 아예 "우주" 로 해석한다.[448] 한편 어떤 이들은 "모든 것" 이 14절 이후 에 언급되는 그리스도의 죽음과 부활 같은 일련의 하나님의 구원 역사를 가리키는 대명사로 쓰였다고 한다.[449] 이제 바울은 지금까지 말한 하나님이 하신

---

443) Hendrikus Boers, "2 Corinthians 5:14-6:2: A Fragment of Pauline Christology," *CBQ* 64 (2002), 539, 546.

444) Philo, *Rev. Div. Her.*, 36; Marcus Aurelius, IV 23, Barrett, 175 재인용, Thrall, 429, 주, 1659 재인용.

445) 롬 11:36; 고전 8:6, 15:28; 빌 3:21; 골 1:16-17.

446) 고전 12:6, 19; 고후 4:15, 12:19; 골 3:8.

447) Héring, 53.

448) Héring, 53; Reicke, *TDNT* 5:885-95.

449) Thrall, 429; 참조, Martin, 152.

모든 일들을 하나님의 화해의 역사의 관점에서 논한다는 것이다. 사실 바울은 화해라는 주제에 이르기 위해서 그리스도의 죽음에 대해 미리 말했고, 그리스도를 믿는 신앙에 입각한 인간관과 세계관을 설명하였다. 뿐만 아니라 화해의 주제가 전체 고린도후서의 주제라고 할 수 있다.

그러나 **τὰ πάντα**(모든 것)는 보다 포괄적으로 해석되어야 한다. 바울이 화해의 준비과정으로써 본문에서 지금까지 말한 인간 존재의 변화와 그 인식의 변화를 가리키지만 동시에 새 세계 창조의 의미도 있다. 인간과 우주를 포함한 총체적 창조이다. **τὰ πάντα**(모든 것)는 중성복수형으로써 같은 중성복수형인 17절의 **τὰ ἀρχαῖα**(이전 것)와 **καίνα**(새 것)란 말을 가리킨다.[450] 바울이 14-16절까지 말한 것은 곧 이전 것과 새 것의 교체를 가리키기 때문이다. 전에 보지 않던 식으로 그리스도를 보고, 사람들을 보고 사물을 보기 때문이다. 그러나 "모든 것"은 인간 존재와 그의 인식의 변화뿐만 아니라, 창조 세계의 변화도 가리킨다고 본다. 실제로 **κτίσις**(창조, "피조물")란 말이 17절에 언급되었다. 이 말은 창세기의 아담의 창조에 빗대어서 제 2 아담 그리스도의 유형을 따른 인간의 재창조를 가리키는 것이다(고전 16:45). 인간 창조는 세계 창조와 구별되지만, 창조 세계의 몰락의 원인이 인간의 타락이라고 볼 때, 인간 회복과 세계 회복은 불가분리적인 관계이다. 인간의 회복으로 저주받은 전체 창조 질서 회복도 이루어 질 것이다.[451]

이렇게 바울이 지금까지 말한 것은 인간적인 면과 우주적인 면

---

450) Hughes, 204.

451) Hughes, 207.

을 다 포함하는 총체적인 변화이다. 창조주 하나님은 태초에 세상을 그리스도를 통해 창조하셨고(골 1:16; 요 1:2), 말세에도 그를 통해 재창조하신다(고전 15:28; 골 1:20). 창조의 핵심은 창조세계를 다스리도록 창조된 인간의 창조이다. 그러나 인간의 타락으로 창조 세계도 타락되었다. 이제 인간의 죄를 속하고 그를 새롭게 창조하는 것이 새 창조의 핵심적인 일이다. 이 모든 일이 제2아담 그리스도로 말미암아 이루어졌다(고전 16:45; 롬 6:15-19). 바울은 하나님의 새 창조 역사에서 나타난 화해에 대한 영적 안목을 가지고 고린도 교인들과의 갈등을 풀고 화해의 사역을 수행하고 있다. 그러므로 "모든 것이 하나님께로서 났다"는 말은 바울이 이제 강조하려는 새로운 주제인 화해도 창조주 하나님께로부터 시작되었다는 말이다. 그리스도인의 화해는 인간 중심적인 인본주의적 화해가 아니라 하나님 중심적 화해이다. 화해의 근원, 화해의 주인은 인간과 세상을 지으신 하나님이시다. 그가 화해를 먼저 시작하셨다(19절). 그가 아직 원수 된 인간에게 그의 아들을 죽게 하시어 죄의 담을 허셨다(롬 5:6, 10). 그러므로 바울의 고린도 교회와의 화해도 그가 먼저 화해의 이니시어티브를 가진다. "고린도인들이여 너희를 향하여 우리의 입이 열리고 우리의 마음이 넓었으니 너희가 우리 안에서 좁아진 것이 아니라 오직 너희 심정에서 좁아진 것이라"(6:11, 12). 또 그 화해는 아무런 기준도 없이 하나가 되는 화해가 아니라 하나님의 거룩하심의 기준에 인간이 다가가는 화해이다. "너희는 믿지 않는 자와 멍에를 같이하지 말라…너희는 저희 중에 나와서 따로 있고 부정한 것을 만지지 말라. 내가 너희를 영접하여 너희에게 아버지가 되고 너희는 내게 자녀가 되리라"(6:14-18).

마틴은 18절의 내용이 초대교회의 전래되는 신조를 가지고 바울이 약간의 설명을 달았을 것이라고 한다. 그렇게 하여 독자들과 자신과의 어떤 공통된 지식을 바탕으로 해서 화해의 가능성을 넓히려고 했다고 한다.[452] 그는 18절부터 21절 사이에서 바울의 용어와 그렇지 않은 용어를 구별하고, 또 초대교회 신앙고백적인 대칭적 문장 구조와 운률을 지적하면서 바울이 사용한 찬양이나 교독문의 흔적을 찾는다.[453] 피차에 아는 지식, 더구나 하나님의 화해에 대한 내용은 바울과 고린도 교회의 목회적 화해를 위해서 도움이 되었을 것이다.

"화해한다"(καταλλάσσειν) 또는 "화해"(καταλλαγή)말은 헬라사회에서도 쓰였으나 특별히 종교적인 의미로 쓰인 것 같지는 않다.[454] 그러나 마카비2서에 많이 나타나고 있다. 주로 백성들의 기도와 순교를 통한 하나님과의 화해가 그 주제이다.[455] 트롤은 여기서 바울이 의식적으로 마카비 2서의 화해에 대조하여서 하나님과의 화해로 발전시키고 있다고 제안한다. 그러나 고린도 교회 같은 이방교회에서 이런 유대 민족주의자들의 화해의 기도를 가지고 화해하려했다는 것은 지나친 발상이라고 본다. 바울은 그리

---

452) Martin, 152.

453) Martin, 138-40; Martin은 이런 예를, 롬 3:24-26, 빌 2:6-11, 골 1:15-20, 고전 15:11에서도 찾는다(Martin, 139, 그리고, *The Spirit and Congregation: Studies in 1 Corinthians 12-15* [Grand Rapids: Eerdmans/Exeter: Paternoster Press, 1984], ch.6). 그러나 Thrall은 Martin, Käsemann, Stuhlmacher, Furnish, Collange 등의 이 같은 견해에 대해 반대한다(Thrall, 445-449). 바울이 사용한 자료라는 것들을 바울이 추가하여 쓴 글들이라는 것들과 비교해 본 후에 결국 모두 바울 자신이 쓴 글이라고 볼 수 있다고 한다.

454) I. H. Marshall, 'Meaning of "Reconciliation"', in *Unity and Diversity in New Testament Theology*, ed. R. A. Guelich, (Grand Rapids: Eerdmans, 1978) 119-120.

455) 마카비 2서 1:5, 7:33, 8:29, Thrall, 430, 재인용.

스도의 죽음에서 충분한 화해의 근거를 보았으므로 이런 외적 자료나 근거의 도움이 필요했으리라고 보지 않는다.

18절에서 "화목하게 하시고"(καταλλάξαντος)는 과거능동태 분사로서 하나님께서 그리스도를 통해 행하신 화해의 역사를 지칭한다. 화해 사역은 하나님이 시작하신 것이다. 인간이 여전히 하나님께 적대적이었을 때 하나님께서 먼저 화해 조처를 취하셨다(롬 5:8, 9). 이와 관련하여 트롤은 20절에 나오는 "하나님과 화목하라(καταλλάγητε)"는 명령형은 하나님이 자신의 화해 제안에 대하여 인간의 적절한 반응을 요구하신다는 것이라고 한다.[456] 그러나 화해가 상호간의 소외 관계의 해소라면, 인간의 반응만이 아니라, 하나님의 변화도 필요한 것이 아닌가?[457] 하나님도 인간의 죄에 대해 진노를 품지 않으셨던가 하나님은 인간의 반역에 대해서 진노하실 수 있는 권세와 능력이 있다. 그는 인간을 지으신 분이며, 이 세상의 절대적인 지배자이시다. 그러므로 인간에게 진노하실 수 있다. 인간의 죄에 대해서 아무런 진노 없는 사랑의 하나님만을 논할 때 하나님은 무능하고 무관심한 하나님이 될 것이다.[458] 사실, 진노도 하나님의 사랑의 표현이다. 하나님이 인간의 죄를 보고도 무시한다면, 그것은 사랑이 아니라 무관심인 것이다.[459] 하나님은 그리스도를 죄인들을 위해 대속하게 하심으로, 진노 대신 자비와 사랑으로 화해의 조치를 취하신 것이다. 물론 엄밀히 말하면 하나님은 십자가에서 진노와 사랑을 다 나타내셨

456) Thrall, 431.

457) Thrall, 431; Plummer, 182; Hughes, 205.

458) Hughes, 205.

459) Thrall, 431.

다. 그리고 이런 화해의 조처에도 불구하고 그를 멀리하는 자들에게 최후의 심판을 준비하신다. 그러나 사랑하는 그의 아들 그리스도를 화목제물로 삼으신 것은 그의 긍휼하심 가운데 죄인들을 구원하시기로 결단하신 것이다(5:12; 롬 3:25). 그러므로 이런 하나님의 화해의 소식을 전하는 것이 모든 세대의 죄인 인간들에게 "가장 유일하게 필요한 것" 이다.[460)]

하나님은 이 화해의 소식을 전하는 직책을 바울에게 맡기셨다. "우리에게" (ἡμῖν)는 일반 그리스도인들이 아니라 바울을 가리킨다. 그리스도의 원수로서 행하다가 회개한 바울이 누구보다도, "그리스도 안" 에 있는 것이 무엇을 의미하는 것인지를 잘 알고, "옛 것은 지나가고 새것이 왔다" 는 말을 가장 깊이 알고, 하나님과 화해하는 것이 무슨 뜻인 지를 누구보다 잘 알고 있을 것이다. 그러므로 하나님께서는 그에게 이 화해의 직책을 맡기셨다. 이런 "화해의 사신" 으로서의 바울의 자아 이해는 4:7의 "보배를 담은 질그릇" 으로서의 자아 인식보다 더 적극적이고 궁극적인 바울의 정체성을 나타낸다. "보배를 담은 질그릇" 의 자아 인식은 화해를 위해 필요한 과정과 수단으로써 고난 받는 바울 자신을 가리킨다. "화해의 사신" 은 바울의 궁극적인 사명을 가리킨다. 이런 자아 인식은 고린도 후서의 전체 주제를 화해로 보는 중요한 근거가 된다. 바울은 복음의 근본 정신인 화해를 실제 목회에도 적용하는 것이다.

19. "이는 하나님께서 그리스도 안에 계시사 세상을 자기와 화

---

460) Hughes, 206: "*the one thing needful*".

목하게 하시며 저희의 죄를 저희에게 돌리지 아니하시고 화목하게 하는 말씀을 우리에게 부탁하셨느니라"(ὡς ὅτι θεὸς ἦν ἐν Χριστῷ κόσμον καταλλάσσων ἑαυτῷ, μὴ λογιζόμενος αὐτοῖς τὰ παραπτώματα αὐτῶν καὶ θέμενος ἐν ἡμῖν τὸν λόγον τῆς καταλλαγῆς). 이 절은 "이는"으로 번역되는 ὡς ὅτι로 시작되는데 ὡς(…같은)가 동사 없이 쓰였으므로 ὅτι(…라는 것)를 따라오는 문장 전체에 주는 의미가 무엇인지 분명하지 않다. 한글 성경은 본문을 이유절로 해석하고 있는데("이는…"), 19절이 앞 절(18절)과 같은 내용, 즉 화해의 직책을 반복하여 말하고 있으므로 이유절로 보는 것은 어색하다. 트롤도 19절은 18절의 반복으로서 ὡς ὅτι는 "이와 같이" 또는 "마찬가지로"라고 번역해야 한다고 한다.[461] 어떤 이들은 다른 사람의 말이나 다른 자료를 인용할 때 쓰는 방법으로 본다.[462] 이 견해가 옳다면 바울은 여기서 바울에게 전해진 "하나님께서 그리스도 안에서 행하신 화해사역"에 대해서 재확인한다는 뜻이 된다. 어떤 경우든지 전체 문장의 의미에 주는 영향은 미미하다.[463]

이 뿐만 아니라 19절의 단어들을 어떻게 서로 연결시키느냐에 따라 19절 전체의 해석이 달라질 수 있으므로 몇 가지 가능한 해석들이 제시되었다.[464] 첫째로, 한글 개역과 같이, "하나님께서 그리스도 안에 계시사(과거), 세상을 자기와 화목하게 하시며…"로

---

461) Thrall, 432.

462) Hughes, 206, 주, 45; Martin, 153; 참조, Thrall, 432, 주 1680.

463) T. Muraoka, "The Use of WS in the Greek Bible," *NovT* 7 (1964) 51-72, 특히 65, (Martin, 153 인용).

464) Plummer, 183.

번역한다.[465] 헬라어 본문에서 "그리스도 안" 이란 어귀가 "화목하게 하시며"(καταλλάσσων)라는 현재분사에 긴밀하게 연결된다고 보고 해석한다. 즉 하나님이 그리스도 안에 계셨다는 뜻보다, 그리스도를 통해서 화목하셨다는 뜻을 강조한다. (엄밀하게, 여기서 ἦν이 미완료로서 현재분사와 함께 미완료의 뜻 즉 과거 진행의 의미로 나타난다: "화목하시고 계셨다.") 둘째로, "그리스도 안에 있는 세상을 자기와 화목하게 하셨으며…" 이 해석은 본문에서 "그리스도 안" 앞에 세상의 관사가 있다고 가정하고 있으나 실제로는 없으므로 부당한 해석이다([τὸν] ἐν Χριστῷ κόσμον). 더구나 "그리스도 안에 있는 세상" 이란 말은 생소한 말이다. 또한, "그리스도 안에 있는 세상" 이 화해할 필요가 있는가 셋째로, "하나님께서 계셨다. 그 분이 그리스도 안에서 세상을 그와 화목하게 하셨다. 이 해석의 경우에는 하나님의 관사가 따로 없기 때문에 관사를 부쳐서 ὁ θεός라고 해야 하는 데 본문과는 다르다. 넷째로, "그리스도 안에 있는 하나님께서 세상을 자기와 화목하게 하셨다."[466] 이 경우에 "그리스도 안에 있는 하나님" 이란 말이 이상하다.[467] 믿는 자가 그리스도 안에 있는 것은 익숙하나 하나님이 그리스도 안에 있다는 것은 어색하다. 이 해석은 그리스도를 하나님의 계시의 장소로 삼는 계시적 의미, 또는 성육신적 의미를 강조함으로써 구원론적 의미("화목하게 하셨다")를 약화시킨다.[468] 그

---

465) Luther, Calvin, Beza, Bengel 등. Hughes, 206 재인용; Plummer, 183, Martin, 154 등 대다수의 학자들.

466) Allo, Bachmann, Collange, Martin, 153, 재인용.

467) Denney는 "그리스도 안에 하나님이 계셨다" 란 말은 바울은 물론 신약 어디에서도 찾을 수 없다고 했다(Denney, 214).

468) Martin, 154.

러나 해리스가 제안하듯이 하나님께서 그리스도 안에 계시기로 선택하심으로써 세상을 자기와 화목하게 하셨다는 뜻으로 보면 가능한 해석이다.[469)]

많은 학자들이 지지하는 첫 번째 해석이 무난하다고 본다. 두 번째를 제쳐 놓고, 하나님의 성육신을 나타내는 네 번째 해석과 그리스도로 말미암은 해석을 강조하는 첫 번째 해석을 함께 생각할 수 있다. 의미가 이렇게 다양한 경우는 어쩌면 저자가 그 모든 의미를 다 나타내려는 의도가 있다고 볼 수도 있다. 둘째를 제외한 모든 해석들이 결국은 같은 의미를 가리킨다. 즉 하나님의 화해의 역사가 그리스도의 사역으로 한정된 것을 의미한다. 하나님께서 성육신하신 그리스도를 통해서 화해의 사역을 행하셨다는 뜻이다. 그리스도의 사역이 곧 하나님의 사역이다. 하나님이 그리스도를 통해서 사역을 시작하셨고 그를 통해서 마치신다. 하나님의 사역이 그리스도의 구원 사역으로 한정된 사실은 그리스도가 복음의 진정성의 증표 또는 사도직의 진정성의 증표가 된다는 것이다. 그리스도로 말미암지 않는 복음이나 사도직은 하나님에게서 나온 것이 아니다. 아래에서 바울은 그의 복음을 화해의 의미로 설명하고, 그의 사도직을 화해의 사신의 직책으로, 말하면서 그의 사역이 곧 그리스도로 말미암은 사역이며, 동시에 하나님께서 인정하는 진정한 사역임을 밝힌다. 이렇게 말하면서 바울은 고린도 교인들이 자신을 반대자들과 구별하여 진정한 복음의 사도로서 인정하고 영접하라는 요청을 하려는 것이다(7:2).

469) M. J. Harris, "Prepositions and Theology in the Greek New Testament," *The New International Dictionary of New Testament Theology*, ed. C. Brown, vol. 3 (Grand Rapids: Zondervan Publishing House, 1978), 1193. Martin, 154, 재인용.

"하나님께서 그리스도 안에 계시사" 에서 "계셨다" 는 동사는 ἦν 으로써 미완료로 나온다. 마틴은 이 동사는 뒤에 따라 오는 현재분사 καταλλάσσων("화목하다")와 함께 동작의 진행을 가리킨다고 보면서, 하나님 편에서의 화해 사역은 완수되었으나, 사람들이 아직 하나님의 화해의 조치에 완전히 가담하지 않았다는 불확정적 뜻이 있다고 한다.[470] 이 경우 미완료는 하나님의 인간과의 화해 사역이 계속된다는 뜻을 나타낸다. 그러나 휴즈는 이 미완료를 과거에 일어난 십자가 사건을 가리키는 것으로 본다.[471] 트롤도 이와 유사하게 여기서 미완료는 리듬 형식 때문에 사용되었으나 실제로는 과거를 나타낸다고 본다.[472] 그리스도인의 화해는 하나님의 역사적 화해 사건에 근거하고 있음을 강조하고 있다고 한다. 그러나 마틴의 견해대로 그리스도로 말미암아 완성된 화해가 사람들의 화해의 응답을 바라면서 지속되고 있다고 보는 것이 좋을 것 같다. 이것은 미완료의 특성을 고려하는 것뿐만 아니라, 화해의 실재가 그렇다. 우선 고린도 교회의 화해 문제도 아직 끝난 것이 아니라 진행 중이다.

"세상을 자기와 화목하게 하시며…" 이 구절은 화해의 사역의 확장을 말한다. 18절에서 우리에서 세상으로 확대 되었다. 세상(κόσμος)이란 말을 하나님이 누구든지 아무나와 화해한다는 무차별적인 보편구원설로 보아서는 안 된다.[473] 이 말은 하나님의 화해의 성격이 광범위함을 가리킨다. 모든 인종적 사회적 장벽들

470) Bruce, 209; Martin, 154, Plummer, 183.

471) Hughes, 208.

472) Thrall, 434.

473) Thrall, 434.

을 넘어 하나님이 보내신 그리스도를 믿는 모든 사람에게 그 화해의 능력이 미친다. 나아가 종말론적 대변혁을 고려 할 때 하나님의 창조는 하나님이 지으신 우주만물의 새로운 질서까지도 포함한다(고전 15:24-28; 골 1:20). 위에서 논의 한 바와 같이 하나님의 모든 창조의 총체적인 화해다. 그러나 인간이 하나님의 창조의 극치임을 고려 할 때 인간과의 화해를 만물과의 화해와 동등하게 볼 수 없고 화해의 중심적 목적으로 보아야 할 것이다. 인간과의 화해의 결과로 만물과의 화해도 이루어 질 것이다. 만물의 회복은 인간의 타락의 결과로 저주를 받게 된 것을 다시 환원시키는 것이므로, 인간의 화해가 우선적으로 요구되는 것이다.

"저희의 죄를 저희에게 돌리지 아니하시고"는 그리스도의 대속의 결과로 죄인들이 죄 사함을 받은 것을 말한다(롬 4:3이하; 참조, 시 32:2). 하나님께서 죄인들을 진노하심을 그치시기로 하신 것이다. 우리가 하나님과 화해하기 전에 먼저 하나님께서 화해의 조치를 취하셨다는 것이 은혜의 복음의 특성이다. 더 이상 그리스도 안에서 정죄는 없다(롬 8:1). 하나님께서 죄인들이 응답하실 수 있도록 하나님 편에서 해야 할 화해의 장애를 다 거두셨다. 죄인들은 이런 하나님의 화해의 제안에 대해서 하나님과 화해하기 위해 힘쓰는 것이 마땅하다. 한편 하나님과 일단 화해한 그리스도인들도, 고린도 교인들의 경우와 같이, 실제적 신앙생활에서 화해의 삶에 실패할 경우도 있으나 이를 계속해야 한다. 그리스도와의 화해를 삶 속에 구현해야할 책임이 있다.

"화목하게 하는 말씀"은 다름 아닌 복음이다. 바울은 하나님이 그리스도로 말미암아 단행하신 화해의 소식을 전하는 직책을 수임 받았다. 바울은 "말씀"(λόγος)를 복음과 같이 사용한다(엡

1:13; 골 1:5; 고전 1:18). 요한복음 서론에서 그리스도를 "말씀"으로 표현한 것은 심각하게 말씀과 신화를 구별하고 있기 때문이다. 헬라 사상에서 "말씀"(λόγος)이란 사실과 사실로 믿을 수 있는 것임을 나타내며, 반면에 "신화"(μύθος)는 지어낸 것이나 믿을 수 없는 것을 의미한다.[474] 소크라테스는 어떤 이야기를 지어낸 신화("미토스," μύθος)가 아닌, 사실적 "로고스"(λόγος)라고 말한 적이 있다(Plato, *Timaeus*, 26E). 바울은 복음의 확실성을 믿고 신화와 구별하였다(갈 1:12; 딤전 1:4; 4:7). 복음은 사실이며 의미이지만 신화는 의미는 있으나 사실이 아니다. 하나님이 바울에게 복음 사역자로 삼으신 이유는 분명하다. 바울 스스로 복음 진리에 의해서 변화되었기 때문이고, 하나님과 화목하였기 때문이다. 하나님이 보내신 복음 전파자들 중에 하나님 하신 일이 무엇인지, 무엇을 하나님의 복음으로 전해야 하는 지에 대해서 바울보다 더 깊이 이해하는 사람은 없다.[475]

20. "이러므로 우리가 그리스도를 대신하여 사신(使臣)이 되어 하나님이 우리로 너희를 권면하시는 것 같이 그리스도를 대신하여 간구하노니 너희는 하나님과 화목하라"(Ὑπὲρ Χριστοῦ οὖν πρεσβεύομεν ὡς τοῦ θεοῦ παρακαλοῦντος δι᾽ ἡμῶν· δεόμεθα ὑπὲρ Χριστοῦ, καταλλάγητε τῷ θεῷ). 19절에서 바울은 하나님께로부터 화해의 말씀을 전하는 직책을 위임 받았고, 여기서는 "그리스도의 사신"의 자격으로 일하는 것을 밝힌다. "그리스도를 대신하여"(ὑπὲρ Χριστοῦ)라는 말이 두 번 반복해서 나온

474) Hughes, 207.

475) Denney, 215.

다. 여기서 ὑπὲρ가 "그리스도를 위하여"라는 뜻으로 쓰였는지,[476) 아니면, 그리스도를 대신한다는 뜻으로 쓰였는지 분명하지 않다.[477)] 14절과 15절에서 이 전치사의 의미를 대속적 의미의 해석 문제와 관련하여 이미 위에서 논의한 바 있다. 여기서는 어떤 뜻이든지 전체 문장의 의미에 중요한 변화를 주지 않는다. "위하여"라는 뜻이든 "대신하여"라는 뜻이든지 바울이 말하는 것은 그리스도의 사신으로서 그리스도의 말씀을 전하는 것이다.[478)] "사신"(πρεσβευτής)이란 말은 로마 황제의 지방장관을 가리키는 말이다. 이 말이 동사(πρεσβύεω)나 명사(πρεσβευτής)로 당시 비문에서 많이 발견된다.[479)] 원래 사신은 그를 보낸 왕을 위해서 말할 뿐만 아니라 그를 대신하여 말하기도 한다.[480)] 바울은 하나님께서 그를 통해서 독자들에게 말씀하신다는 확신을 갖고 말하고 있다. 바울이 말하는 것은 하나님이 말씀하시는 것이다.

"하나님이 우리로 너희를 권면하는 것 같이 그리스도를 대신하여 간구하노니…." 플러머는 이 구절을 이끄는 ὡς(…와 같이)를 비교절로 보지 않고 동시적인 병행절로 본다.[481)] "하나님이 우리로 너희를 권면하는 것을 알고서…"라고 번역한다. ὡς가 이끄는 말이 사실인 경우에는 "알고서"라고 번역하고(벧후 1:3), 사실이 아니거나, 옳지 않은 경우에는 "마치…같이"라고 번역해야 한다고 한다(고전 4:18; 벧전 4:12; 행전 27:30). 여기서는 "하나님이 너

---

476) Plummer, 186.

477) Thrall, 437.

478) Hughes, 209.

479) Deissmann, 379; Plummer, 184-5; Thrall, 436, 주, 1722, 재인용.

480) Hughes, 209-10, Bultmann, 165.

481) Plummer, 184.

희를 권면하는 것"이 진정한 사실이므로 "알고서"라고 번역하는 것이 옳다고 한다.[482] 그러나 본문에서는 바울이 하나님의 사신으로서 하나님의 역할을 대신하고 있으므로, ὡς를 "마치…같이"로 해석하는 것이 전체 의미를 더 분명히 해준다. 바울은 그가 하나님과 그리스도를 모두 대변한다고 본다. 구원역사는 그리스도의 일이요(14, 15), 또한 하나님의 일이다(18, 19). 성부와 성자 하나님은 실제로 한 분 하나님이시기 때문이다. 그들은 함께 세상을 창조하셨고, 이제 종말에 다시 함께 구원 역사를 시작하고 계신다.

"권면하다"(παρακαλέω)는 동사는 뒤에 따라 나오는 "간구하노니"(δεόμαι)와 거의 같은 의미를 갖고 있다. 모두 "권하다", "호소하다", "간청하다"는 뜻이 있으나, δεόμαι가 더 간절히 애원하는 뜻이 있다.[483] 여기서는 하나님이 "권면하고"(παρακαλοῦτος), 바울이 "간구하노니"(δεόμαι)라고 하나, 6장 1절에서는 바울이 직접 "권한다"(παρακαλοῦμεν)는 말을 쓰고 있다. 죄인 인간에게 거룩하신 하나님께서 화해하기를 간곡히 애원하신다는 것은 어색하게 들리지만, 실제로 그의 아들 그리스도를 희생시키신 것은 간곡한 애원의 자세에 부합된다. 그리스도가 스스로 죄인의 모습으로 죽으신 것도 이런 의미와 일치된다. 14절에서 말하는 그리스도의 사랑이 이런 표현과 일치된다. 이제 그리스도의 화해의 사신이 된 바울은 옛날 오만한 바리새인 사울과는 다른 변화된 모습으로 겸손하게 고린도 교인들을 달래고 있다.

"너희는 하나님과 화목하라." 하나님은 그리스도를 통해서 그의 편에 있는 이미 화해의 장애(죄에 대한 진노)를 없애고, 사람들

482) Plummer, 184.

483) BAGD, 175, 617.

이 화해하기를 원하신다. "화목하라"(καταλλάγητε)는 말이 명령형이지만, "간구하노니"(δεόμεθα)라는 말의 겸손한 어감에서 하는 말이므로 오만한 명령은 아니다. 그럼에도 이 명령형은 중요한 문제에 대한 결단을 촉구하는 의미가 있다. 하나님과의 화해는 인간의 운명을 완전히 바꾸는 매우 심각한 일이다. 영생이냐 영벌이냐의 선택의 문제이므로, 하나님께 위임받은 사도의 권위로 화해하도록 명령하는 것은 적절한 것이다. 명령형이 단순과거로 나온 것도 이런 결단을 촉구하는 의미를 보여준다.[484)]

한편 "화목하라"는 말이 일반적 복음전파의 성격을 가진 것이지, 바울과 고린도 교인들과의 화해를 말하는 것은 아니라고 보는 견해가 있다.[485)] 휴즈는 바울은 고린도 교회를 염두에 둔 것이 아니라 모든 세상 사람들을 향한 복음전도의 직책을 말하고 있다고 한다. 고린도 교회를 위한 간구는 6장에서 시작된다고 한다.[486)] 트롤은 속죄일에 모세의 계약에 따라 죄의 속함을 받음을 믿는 당시 유대인들에게 그리스도를 통한 속죄를 강조하고 있다고 본다. 앞의 3장에서 모세의 "사라지는 영광"에 대한 말을 했으나, 이제 갑자기 유대교 문제를 논한다고 보기 어렵다. 바울이 여기서 고린도 교회를 염두에 두고 화해를 말하고 있음은 6장 이하나 전체 내용을 통해 자명하다. 다만 여기서는 바울의 사도직책의 본질적인 성격을 보다 분명히 할 필요가 있으므로 화해의 직책에 대해서 보다 일반적으로 말하고 있는 것이다. 19절에서 바울은 하나님의 화해 사역의 대상을 세상 전체라고 했다. 바울은 그의 사신으로써 마땅

484) Thrall, 438.

485) Hughes, 211; Thrall, 438.

486) Hughes, 211.

히 세상 전체를 화해의 대상으로 알고 화해의 복음을 전해야 한다. 그러나 구체적인 사역지를 도외시하는 세상 전체를 위한 사역이란 있을 수 없다. 고린도후서에서 바울은 당장 고린도 교회의 문제를 당면하고 있으므로, 고린도 교회와의 화해를 염두에 두고 있다고 봐야 한다. 곧이어 나오는 6장 1절에서 언급하는 고린도 교회의 화해 문제를 여기서는 잊고 있다고 볼 수 없다.

21. "하나님이 죄를 알지도 못하신 자로 우리를 대신하여 죄를 삼으신 것은 우리로 하여금 저의 안에서 하나님의 의가 되게 하려 하심이니라"(τὸν μὴ γνόντα ἁμαρτίαν ὑπὲρ ἡμῶν ἁμαρτίαν ἐποίησεν, ἵνα ἡμεῖς γενώμεθα δικαιοσύνη θεοῦ ἐν αὐτῷ). 여기서 19절로 돌아가 "저희의 죄를 저희에게 돌리지 아니하시고"를 더 부연 설명한다. 한마디로 죄인 인간의 의롭게 됨에 대한 설명이다. 20절은 화해에 대한 설명이므로, 여기서는 화해의 원인이 되는 의롭게 됨의 과정을 설명하는 것이다. 바울이 그리스도의 죽음과 하나님과의 화목을 말하는 것은 고린도 교회의 문제만을 위해 발견한 새로운 개념이 아니다. 로마서에서도 에베소에서도 화해의 개념은 바울 신학의 지배적인 개념이다(롬 3:25; 4:25; 5:1, 10; 엡 2:14-16).

이 문장의 주어는 하나님이다. 하나님이 화해의 사역을 시작하시고 주도하고 계신다. 5장 18절에서 "모든 것이 하나님께로서 났나니"라는 말은 하나님이 친히 모든 화해의 과정을 주장하고 계신다는 뜻이다. 그의 아들 그리스도는 그의 뜻에 복종하여(일치되어) 의의 과정에 참여하고 있다(빌 2:8; 막 14:36). 구원은 하나님께로부터 나오는 것이다. 인간은 인간을 스스로 구할 수 없다. 그는 자신을 구할 수 없는 죄인이기 때문이다. 창조주 되시고 구속자 되시는 하나님만이 인간을 구원하실 수 있다. 이것이 성경의 구원론의 전제이다.[487)]

"죄를 알지도 못하신 자"는 물론 그리스도를 가리킨다. 그리스도는 원래 죄가 없으신 하나님이시거니와(요 10:30; 14:10 이하; 17:11, 21이하), 지상 사역에서도 죄를 짓지 않으셨다(요 8:46; 벧전 2:22; 히 4:15 , 7:26; 요일 3:5; 눅 23:4, 14, 22, 41, 47, 48). 죄가 없는 자만이 남의 죄를 대신 질 수 있다. 모든 사람이 범죄하였으므로, 속죄는 사람이 된 하나님이신 그리스도만이 할 수 있다(롬 3:10, 23). 사람이 되신 그리스도만이 속죄의 일을 담당하는 중보자가 될 수 있다(요 1:14; 롬 8:3; 빌 2:7).[488)] 그리스도는 우리의 중보자로서 우리의 죄에 대한 하나님의 진노를 받으시고 죽으셨다. 그 결과 그리스도 안에서 우리의 죄는 속함을 받고 또한 그 의를 얻게 되었고, 하나님과 화해하게 되었다(롬 4:25; 5:1, 10).

본문에서, "죄를 삼으신 것"(문자적으로, "죄를 만드신 것", **ἁμαρτίαν ἐποίησεν**)이란 말의 정확한 의미에 대해서 논란이 있다. 이 말은 로마서 8:3의 "(하나님이) 죄를 인하여 자기 아들을 죄 있는 육신의 모양으로 보내어 육신에 죄를 정(정죄)하사"라는 말과 같다. 그러나 학자들은 이 "죄"란 말이 "속죄제물"의 뜻이냐, "죄인"이냐를 놓고 논쟁한다. "속죄제물"이란 뜻으로 보는 근거는 레위기 4장과 5장 여러 곳에서 속죄제물과 죄라는 말이 같은 히브리어 **חַטָּאת**(하타트)로 번갈아 나타나고 있고 또 70인역도 이

487) Denney, 218.

488) Hughes, 212.

를 ἁμαρτία(죄)로 번역하고 있기 때문이다.[489] 또 로마서 8장 3절의 헬라어 원문에 있는 περὶ ἁμαρτίας("죄에 대하여")라는 말이 (한글개역본에는 번역되지 않음) 70인 역에서 이사야 53장 10절의 고난 받는 종이 자신을 "속건제물"(περὶ ἁμαρτίας, 70인역)로 드렸다라고 번역하는 것과 일치하므로 여기서의 "죄"도 70인역의 이 번역("속건제물")의 영향을 직접 받았다고 말할 수 있다. 이사야 53장 10절의 אָשָׁם(아삼)은 레위기서의 חַטָּאת(하타트)와 같이 "죄"와 "속건제물"을 모두 가리키는 이중적 의미가 있다.[490] 이외에 로마서 3장 25절("화목 제물")와 고린도전서 5장 7절("우리의 유월절 양")에서도 제물과 관련하여 그리스도의 죽음을 설명한다. 더구나 본문에 "죄를 알지 못하신 자"란 말은 "흠 없는 희생제물"의 뜻을 나타내고, 의롭게 됨에 대한 말("하나님의 의가 되게 하려 하심이니라")이 나오고 있는 것은 이사야 53장 9-11절에서 고난 받는 하나님의 종이 죄가 없고, 많은 사람을 의롭게 했다는 말과 일치한다.[491]

다른 학자들은 본문의 "죄"는 "죄인"을 나타낸다고 본다.[492] 바울이 본문에서 그리스도의 죽음을 희생적 의미로 말하고 있고, 또한 이사야 53장 9-11절을 생각하고 있다고 보면, "속죄제물"보다

489) John R. Kohlenberger III and James A. Swanson, *The Hebrew English Concordance to the Old Testament with the New International Version* (Grand Rapids: Zondervan Publishing House, 1998), 525-26.

490) Kohlenberger, 856-6; Bruce, 210..

491) H. Ewald, *Die Sendschrieben des Apostels Paulus* (Göttingen: 1857), 277; Bruce, 210; Martin, 157.

492) De Wette, 10; Goudge, 60; Allo, 172; Meyer, 295, Rückert, 185, Thrall, 441, 주 1762, 1763 재인용.

는 "죄인" 이란 의미가 더 적합하다고 본다.[493] 그리스도는 죄인을 대신하여 죽었으므로 여기의 "죄"는 곧 "죄인"을 말한다는 것이다. 갈라디아서 3장 13절에도 그리스도가 저주를 받은 자로 우리를 대신하여 죽으셨다고 한다. 그리스도는 결국 죄인과 자신을 일치시킨 것이다. 그러므로 "죄를 삼으신 것" 이란 말의 "죄"란 그리스도를 가리킨다. 그러므로 본문은 그리스도가 죄인으로 죽으셨다는 뜻이다.

그러나 21절의 "죄"를 그냥 죄로 해석해야 한다는 학자들도 많다.[494] 데니는 "죄"를 "속죄제물"로 해석하는 것을 반대한다.[495] 우선 두 말 자체가 다른 말들이고, 뒤에 나오는 "의"(δικαιοσύνη)란 말과 병행되어 있으므로 "속죄제"라는 말은 적절치 않다고 본다. 데니는 그리스도가 죄가 되었다는 말은 그리스도가 우리가 받을 죄의 형벌을 대신 받아 죽은 것을 말한다고 한다.

> "하나님이 죄를 모르는 자를 죄로 삼으셨다"는 말은 그리스도 안에서 십자가 위에서 정반대 적인 세상의 죄와 하나님의 의(성육신 하신 그리스도)가 서로 만나서 하나가 되었다는 것을 의미한다. 하나님이 죄를 '죄 없으신 자' 위에 놓고, 그 죄의 대가를 받게 하시고, 정죄하여 죽게 하셨다. 그가 죽을 때 그는 죄를 물리쳤다. 이제 죄는 더 이상 세상과 하나님 사이를 막지 않고 있다. 반

493) Thrall, 442.

494) Osiander, 229; Goudge, 60; Hughes, 213, 215; Collange, 278; Plummer, 187-88; Denney, 218-20.

495) Denney, 220.

> 대로, 하나님은 이 엄청난 거래를 통해 화평을 이룩하셨다. 그는 화해의 장을 여셨다. 이제 화해의 사역자들을 이 엄청난 소식을 가지고 어디든지 갈 수 있다.[496]

(데니는 이런 바울의 속죄론이 바울의 전체 사상 체계의 핵심이며, 기독교 계시에 있어서 항상 붙고 있는 횃불이며, 모든 사람들이 쳐다보는 불기둥이라고 했다).[497]

휴즈도 "죄"를 "죄인"이라고 해석하는 것을 반대한다. 그는 바울이 그리스도를 "죄인"이라고 하는 경우 죄인이 다른 죄인 인간을 구원하는 것이 되어 구원의 원칙에서 벗어남으로 주의 깊게 "죄"라고 표현하고 있다고 한다.[498] "말하자면 아버지 하나님이 죄 없으시고 성육신 하신 그의 아들을 우리를 위하여 그의 진노와 심판의 대상으로 삼으셨다. 그 결과 그리스도 안에서 십자가 위에서 세상의 죄는 심판받고 씻음을 받았다" 라는 뜻이라고 한다.[499] 그리고 "죄"(ἁμαρτίαν)라는 말이 앞의 "죄"(ἁμαρτίαν)라는 말과 뒤의 "의"(δικαιοσύνη)라는 말에 맞는다고 하였다.[500] 그리스도가 (우리의) "죄" 자체가 되어 우리 대신 형벌을 받았고, 우리가 그 안에서 하나님의 의를 받게 하심이다. 이렇게 휴즈는 "그리스도를 죄로 삼으신 것"의 "죄"를 단순히 "죄"로 해석할 수 있는 가능성을 보여 준다. 그러나 바울이 과연 휴즈가 말하는 대로 예수를 "죄

---

496) Denney, 220.

497) Denney, 218.

498) Hughes, 213.

499) Hughes, 213.

500) Hughes, 215.

인" 이라고 하는 것이 부적절 하다고 판단해서 그저 "죄" 로만 말하는 것인지는 여전히 확실하지 않다. 아래에서 논하는 바와 같이 "죄" 라는 표현이 그리스도의 속죄 사역에 대한 종합적이고 일반적인 의미를 위해 적절한 표현이라고 볼 수도 있기 때문이다.

플러머는 "죄로 삼으심" 이란 말은 하나님이 죄인을 하나님의 의로 만들기 위해서 그리스도를 죄로 만들었다는 설명하기 어려운 신비스런 사실을 그대로 가르치는 것이라고 한다. 플러머는 이 말은 믿는 자와 그리스도의 연합을 가리킨다고 한다. 이 말을 "그리스도가 우리 안에, 우리가 그리스도 안에" 라는 연합 관계로 이해되어야 한다고 한다.[501] 그리스도가 인간과 일치되는 원칙에 따라서 그리스도는 인간의 "죄" 와 하나가 되고, 사람은 하나님의 "의" 와 하나가 된다. 플러머는 이런 신비스런 진리를 설명하는 것은 불가능하다고 한다.[502] 인간의 사고나 언어로 파악되기 어려운 바울이 받은 하나님의 계시라고 한다. 그러나 이런 연합관계는 플러머가 말하듯이 그렇게 어렵고 신비스러운 것은 아니다. 그리스도와의 관계의 일치 개념은 레위기에서 희생제물의 머리에 제물을 드리는 사람이 안수하는 제의의식에 이미 나타나 있다. 안수라는 상징적 행위는 희생제물을 바치는 자의 죄가 그 제물에 전가된다는 대속에 대한 하나님의 약속에 근거한 것이다(레 1:4). 제물과 제물을 드리는 사람의 정체적 일치는 상징은 곧 실체라는 제의적인 상징주의적 원칙에 근거한다. 속죄제 의식같이 하나님이 정하고 약속하신 상징적 행위 또는 실체의 형상은 실체와 같다. 속죄제로 죄를 씻기를 단순히 원하고 바라는 것이 아니라, 속죄제는

501) Plummer, 187.

502) Plummer, 187.

실제로 죄를 씻는 방법이다. 그리스도의 죽음도 마찬가지다. 하나님께서 정하신 대속적인 구원의 방법이다. 죄인은 그리스도와 같이 일치되어 죽고 사는 것이다. "그리스도와의 연합에 의한 구원"은 하나님이 제정하신 인간 구원의 유일한 방법이다(갈 1:7, 8, 9). 이것은 죄인과 같이 낮아지시고 그를 위해 아들을 죽도록 하신 하나님의 지극한 사랑의 구원방법이며, 이에 대한 믿는 자의 적극적이고 심각한 믿음으로 성취된다.

트롤은 이런 전통적인 견해들을 수정하여 "그리스도로… 죄를 삼았다"는 말은 "그리스도가 죄의 결과 하나님으로부터 소원하게 되어 하나님의 진노의 대상이 되는 하나님과의 관계에 들어 왔다"는 뜻이라고 한다.[503] 그는 본문의 "죄"를 "속죄제", 또는 "죄인"로 보는 것은 "죄"의 배경을 말할 뿐이고, "죄"란 말 자체의 뜻은 아니라고 본다. 그는 죄의 개념을 파괴된 인격적 관계로 보면서 "그리스도가 이런 죄의 관계에 들어왔다"고 해석한다. 트롤이 주장하는 대로 바울이 여기서 죄를 하나님과의 소원한 관계로 생각했을 수 있다. 로마서 1장 18절 이하에서 바울이 죄를 정의 할 때 하나님을 떠나 마음대로 사는 것을 가리킨다. 특히 1장 28절과 29절에서 바울은 죄를 하나님께서 인간을 "상실한 마음"대로 버려두어 "모든 불의"(πάσῃ ἀδικίᾳ)를 행하게 되는 것으로 정의한다. 하나님이 죄 짓는 인간을 "버려두었다"(παρέδωκεν)는 말이 24, 26, 28에 계속 나온다. 특히 "불의"(ἀδικία)란 말은 물론 "의"(δικαιοσύνη)에 반대되는 말이며, 본문에서도 "의"(δικαιοσύνη)란 말이 "죄"(ἁμαρτίαν)란 말에 대조적인 말로 따라 나온다. 이런

---

503) Thrall, 442.

바울의 죄에 대한 정의는 트롤이 죄를 하나님과 인간의 소원한 관계로 정의하는 것과 다르지 않다고 본다(참조, 창 3:8; 4:14). 더구나 이 문맥에서 바울은 고린도 교회와의 소원한 관계를 회복하는 화해의 주제를 가지고 논하고 있다.

그럼에도 불구하고 바울이 여기서 그의 일반적인 그리스도의 속죄를 나타내는 개념들을 무시하고 "죄"를 단순히 "하나님으로부터 소원한 관계"로만 생각한다고 보기 어렵다. 바울이 "죄"와 관련하여 사용하는 다른 표현이나 구약의 배경들을 무시하고 이 말을 쓰고 있다고 할 수 없다. 위에서 지적한 바와 같이 레위기 4장이나 이사야 53장의 죄와 속죄제의 용어 사용과, 레위기의 안수를 통한 제물과 제물을 드리는 자의 일체, 또는 죄의 전가는 그리스도와 죄인과의 일체 사상의 배경이다. 그러므로 바울이 여기서 그리스도를 "죄"로 만들었다고 한 것은 뒤에 나오는 "의"와 대조를 위해서 "속죄제", "유월절 양", 또는 "죄인을 위해 죽으셨다"(롬 5:8; 참조, 갈 3:13)같은 바울의 다른 표현들을 종합하고 개념화해서 "죄"로 말한 것으로 보인다. 바울이 로마서 1장 29절에서 여러 죄를 구체적으로 제시하기 전에 보다 추상적이고 개념적인 말로 "모든 불의(πάσῃ ἀδικίᾳ), 추악, 탐욕, 악의" 라고 표현한 것이나 갈라디아서 5장 19절에서 여러 죄를 말하기 전에 "육체의 일"이란 말로 요약한 것을 볼 때 여기서도 "죄"란 말로 다른 죄와 관련된 의미들을 취합하여 개념화한 것이 가능하다.

하나님이 그리스도를 죄가 되게 하셨으나 그리스도 또한 자발적으로 하나님의 구원의 뜻에 따라 "죄"가 되셨다(빌 2:7; 요 10:17). 이것은 "우리를 대신하여(ὑπὲρ ἡμῶν) 하신 것이다." 14절의 "그리스도의 사랑"이 죄인을 구하기 위해 "죄"가 되신 것이다.

여기에 그리스도와 죄인의 일치의 뜻이 있다. 그리스도가 죄인을 위해 대신 죽었으므로 죄인들이 죽은 것으로 간주되었다(참조, 19절).[504] 즉 대속적 죽음이다. 뒤에 따라 나오는 "그리스도 안에서 하나님의 의가 되게 하려 하심이라"는 말이 그리스도와 죄인의 일치를 더 분명히 나타낸다. 그리스도께서 우리의 죄를 가져가고 그의 의를 우리에게 주신 것이다 (롬 6:4). 죄인들의 죄를 대신 지시고 죽으심으로 그 결과 그의 의를 우리에게 주셨다. 일치와 교환이 그리스도의 중보적 사역으로 일어났다.[505] 뿐만 아니라 "하나님의 의를 얻게 되었다." 이것은 사람의 마음에서나 행위의 의로움을 말하는 것이 아니라, 사람이 그리스도 안에서(ἐν αὐτῷ) 그리스도와 일체가 되어 하나님의 의를 받게 되었다는 뜻이다(롬 8:1).

그리스도의 죽음으로 죄에 대한 하나님의 진노가 풀어져서 속죄를 받게 된다는 전통적 속죄론에 대하여 유치한 이방 종교적 속죄론으로 보고 반대하는 이들이 있다. 데니는 이들의 불신적 비판을 열거하며 답한다.[506] 첫째로, 그들은 죄가 그리스도에게 전가되는 것은 불가능하고, 그렇게 된다 해도 그것은 죄 없으신 그리스도를 죄인으로 만들어 죽이는 엄청난 비도덕적인 것이므로 하나님이 이런 구원 방법을 인정하셨다고 볼 수 없다고 한다. 그러나 창세기 22장에서 하나님은 아브라함에게 그가 사랑하는 아들 이삭을 제물로 바치라는 "비도덕적"인 명령을 하면서 아브라함의 믿음을 시험하셨다. 욥의 시험도 그렇다. 그렇다면 하나님은 인간 구원을 위해서 "비도덕적"으로 보이는 극단적인 조치를 취하셨다

504) Martin, 154.

505) Plummer, 187; Thrall, 442.

506) Denney, 220-222.

고 보아야 할 것이다. 그만큼 인간의 죄와 그 결과는 참담한 것이므로 어려운 결정을 할 수밖에 없었던 것이다. 즉 하나님은 죄 없으신 그의 아들을 희생 제물로 받아야하는 힘들고 어려운 방법을 통해서라도 화해의 사역을 시작하셔야 했다. 죄의 값은 비싼 사망이며, 사망에서의 구원도 비싸고 엄격한 것이 있다. 죄 없으신 하나님의 아들의 죽음은 죄인들에게 엄청나게 두려운 사건이다. 그 죽음은 하나님 앞에서 모든 교만한 마음을 두렵게 만들고 모든 입을 막아버린다(막 16:8). 기독교의 구원이란 하나님의 심판을 피하는 것으로 얻게 되는 것이 아니라, 그의 심판을 거침으로써 얻게 되는 것임을 알아야 한다. 이것이 예수 그리스도 안에 있는 구원 방법이다. 둘째로, 반대자들은 하나님의 사랑을 중시하면서 하나님의 진노하심을 풀어드린다는(to appease) 생각을 반대한다. 반대자들은, "우리는 성난 하나님을 달랠 필요가 없다. 이것은 이방 종교에서 들어 온 개념이다. 그리스도인은 이를 마땅히 부끄러워해야 한다. 그것은 사랑이시며, 은혜로우신 주 예수의 하나님과 아버지에 대한 모멸적인 언사이다"라고 말한다.[507] 이것이 사실이라면 이런 진리를 가르치는 사도들은 주님의 본성을 잘못 알고, 가장 중요한 구원 진리를 왜곡시킨 생각이 좁고 편협한 사람들이 된다. 이에 대해서 데니는 "물론 우리는 성난 하나님을 달래야 할 필요가 없다. 우리가 이런 일을 할 수 없다는 것을 가르치는 것이 바로 복음이 말하는 바이다. 그러나 이 사실은 하나님의 진노하심을 푸는 것(to propitiate)이 아예 필요치 않다는 말은 아니다(다만 우리에게 하나님의 진노를 풀 수 있는 방법이 없다는 말이다). 죄

507) Denney, 221.

악이 매우 실제적인 사안인 것처럼, 죄에 대한 하나님의 저주도 실제적이어야 한다. 그러므로 하나님의 진노를 풀어드리는 것(a proptiation)이 필요하다."고 한다.[508] 반대자들은 "하나님은 사랑이시다. 그러므로 진노를 푸심이 필요치 않다"고 말한다. 그러나 사도들은 가르치기를, '하나님이 사랑이시므로 진노하심을 푸신 것이다' 라고 한다. 이런 사도들의 가르침이야말로 죄를 지어 아파하는 우리 양심에 호소하는 호소력이 있고, 하나님의 사랑에 실재와, 내용과, 실체를 더하여 준다. 반대자들의 주장은 바울과 요한이 가르치는 하나님의 사랑의 핵심이 되는 요소(하나님의 진노를 푸는 것)를 잘라 버리는 것이다. "우리가 아직 죄인 되었을 때에 그리스도께서 우리를 위하여 죽으심으로 하나님께서 우리에게 대한 자기의 사랑을 확증 하셨느니라"(롬 5:8); "이 예수를 하나님이 그의 피로 인하여 믿음으로 말미암는 화목 제물(ἱλαστήριον)로 세우셨으니 이는 하나님께서 길이 참으시는 중에 전에 지은 죄를 간과하심으로 자기의 의로우심을 나타내려 하심이니…"(롬 3:25); "사랑은 여기 있으니 우리가 하나님을 사랑한 것이 아니요 오직 하나님이 우리를 사랑하사 우리 죄를 위하여 화목제(ἱλασμόν)로 그 아들을 보내셨음이니라"(요일 4:10). 그러므로 사도들의 사랑의 가르침에서 하나님의 진노의 푸심을 빼버리고 하나님은 사랑이라고만 가르치는 것은 잘못이다. "십자가의 저주를 빼버리는 것은 복음의 힘줄을 빼버리는 것과 같다. 복음이 하나님의 화해가 자비하심만 있고, 심판이 없다고 가르치면 복음은 사람들의 마음을 붙잡는 그 고유한 힘을 잃게 된다. 복음의 가치와, 복

508) Denney, 221.

음의 하나님의 고유한 성품과의 일치와, 복음의 인간의 필요에 대한 충족과, 복음의 하나님의 사랑의 계시로서의 진정한 차원은 궁극적으로 하나님의 자비하심은 심판을 통해서 우리에게 온다는 진리에 근거하고 있다."[509)]

여기서 이렇게 우리의 죄가 사함 받고 우리가 하나님의 의를 얻게 되는 것은 하나님의 은혜임이 암시되어 있다. 그리스도와 죄인의 일체로 말미암아 그리스도 안에서의 인간 존재의 변화는 하나님의 은혜로 말미암는 것이다. "의롭게 되었다"라고 하지 않고 대신에 "하나님의 의가 되게 하려 하심이니라"란 표현은 실제로 의로운 사람이 되었다는 뜻이 아니라 법적으로 의롭다는 뜻을 나타낸다고 본다. 단순히 "의롭게 되었다"고 하면 그리스도 안에서 인간의 인격이나 생활이 실제로 흠 없이 의롭게 되었다고 오해 될 수 있기 때문이다. 물론 사도 바울이 여기서도 15절에서와 같이 믿는 자가 의로운 생활을 살아야 함을 당연하게 알고 있겠으나 "하나님의 의가 되게 하려 하심이니라"말 자체의 뜻은 하나님의 은혜로 말미암는 의를 말한다고 본다. δικαιοσύνη θεοῦ(하나님의 의)의 속격은 기원을 나타내는 속격으로 보아서 "하나님으로부터 오는 의"로 해석해야 한다. 죄인들이 하나님의 은혜로 방면되었다.[510)] 그 뿐만 아니라 방면된 죄인들이 하나님의 자녀로 의롭다함까지 얻게 된 것이다. 정죄하여 심판을 해야 할 재판장과 화해를 하게 된 것이다. 부정적인 관계가 적극적인 관계로 바뀌게 되었다. 그러나 이것은 단순히 주관적인 해석이 아니라, 하나님의 새로운 세계 창조 개시를 알리는 중요한 역사적 사건인 십자가의

509) Denney, 222.
510) Barrett, 180.

사건으로 증명된 것이다.[511] 다만 하나님의 사역이니 만큼 영적인 안목이 없이는 알 수가 없다(5:16, 17).

6:1. "우리가 하나님과 함께 일하는 자로서 너희를 권하노니 하나님의 은혜를 헛되이 받지 말라"(**Συνεργοῦντες δὲ καὶ παρακαλοῦμεν μὴ εἰς κενὸν τὴν χάριν τοῦ θεοῦ δέξασθαι ὑμᾶς·**). 바울이 이미 20절부터 그리스도의 사신으로 그리스도를 대신하여 하나님과 화목하라고 권면하였으므로 이 절은 같은 화해의 권면을 계속하는 것으로 본다.[512]

"우리가 하나님과 함께 일하는 자로 너희를 권하노니"에서 "하나님"이란 말이 헬라어 성경에는 없으나 한글과 영어 성경에 보충되어 나온다. 5장 18, 19, 20절에서 바울이 하나님의 화해의 직책을 맡은 것으로 언급되므로 "하나님"이란 말을 보충하여 의미를 더 분명하게 할 수 있다. 고린도전서 3장 9에서도 "우리는 하나님의 동역자들이요"라고 한다. 대부분의 주석가들도 이를 인정한다.[513] 그러나 "하나님"이란 말 대신 다른 제안들도 있다. (1) 독자들[514]; (2) 복음전도의 동역자들(고후 12:17; 살전, 3:2)[515]; (3) 그리

---

511) ἐποίησεν(삼으셨다)는 말은 과거형이다. 5:14절과 15절의 ἀπέθανεν과 같이 역사 가운데 일어난 예수의 죽으심의 신학적 의미를 말하고 있다.

512) Bruce, 211; Barrett, 182; Martin, 159; Thrall, 449; Plummer, 189; Denney, 224 등이 6:1 이후를 새로운 내용으로 분류한다. 그러나 Hughes는 예외이다(216).

513) J. A. Bengel, *Gnomon of the New Testament III: Romans, I and II Corinthians*, ET (Edingburgh: T. & T. Clark, 1863), 792; Plummer, 189; Barrett, 183; Bruce, 211; Denney, 225; Thrall, 451; Héring, 55; Martin, 165; Hughes, 216; Tasker, 91, 등.

514) Chrysostom, *PG* 61 col. 481 (*NANF* XII, 336); Bachmann, 275; Allo, 173; Thrall, 451, 주, 1821 재인용.

515) J. A. Bengel, 792.

스도(고후 5:20: "우리가 그리스도를 대신하여")[516]; (4) 다른 교사들("우리가 권하노니"[παρακαλοῦμεν]라는 주동사가 바울 자신을 가리키는 1인칭 복수형으로 나타나고, 함께 일하는 자들[συνεργοῦντες]이라는 말은 다른 교사들을 가리킬 수 있다)[517]; (5)우리의 권면들(이 경우 "우리의 권면에 합당하게 일하는 자들로서 너희를 권하노니"라고 번역해야 한다).[518] 1번(독자들)은 여기서 독자들은 바울의 권면의 대상이므로 동역자란 말은 문맥상 맞지 않는다.[519] 2번(복음의 동역자들)과 4번(다른 교사들)으로 하는 경우 문장의 의미가 맞지 않는다. 이 경우 바울이 동역자들과 함께 일하며 권한다는 뜻이 되는데 "우리가 권하노니"(παρακαλοῦμεν)라는 주동사가 1인칭 복수형으로 바울만을 가리키는 의미가 되어 어색하다. 바울이 자신을 나타내기를 원했다면 일인칭 단수를 써서 자신과 동역자들을 구분해서 썼어야 했다. 만일 이 복수형이 모든 동역자들을 가리킨다고 한다면 "우리 동역자들이 우리들 자신들과 함께 일하는 자로서"라는 매우 이상한 번역이 된다.[520] 3번(그리스도)은 다른 예가 없으며, 5번(우리의 권면들)이라면, 더 분명한 말로 나타냈어야 했을 것이다. 앞 절들과의 연계로 보아 1번의 "하나님"이란 말이 가장 적절하다. 바울은 하나님과 함께 일하는 동역자이다. 그는 하나님의 화해의 동역자로서 하나님의 화해의 심정으로 고린도 교인들을 권면한다: "하나

516) Plummer, 189.
517) Plummer, 189.
518) Plummer, 190.
519) Martin, 165.
520) Martin, 165.

님의 은혜를 헛되이 받지 말라." 그리스도의 속죄의 죽으심으로 하나님의 죄에 대한 진노는 사라지고 하나님 편에서 화해의 길은 열렸다. 하나님과 죄인 사이에 막힌 죄의 담은 무너졌다. 이 화해의 조치는 하나님의 아들의 죽음이라는 엄청난 희생으로써 이루어진 매우 귀한 것이다. 이런 하나님의 화해의 조치는 하나님이 그를 믿는 모든 인간에게 베푸시는 넘치는 선물이요 은혜다. 이제 인간이 그의 놀라운 은혜에 대해서 적절한 반응을 보이는 것이 마땅하다. 사실 고린도 교인들은 이미 회개하고 예수를 믿어 의롭게 되었고(고전 6:11), 하나님의 화해의 축복을 받았고(고후 5:18), 하나님의 많은 영적 은사를 받은 이들이다(고전 12장, 14장). 이제 고린도 교인들의 해야 할 것은 하나님과의 지속적인 화해이다. 하나님의 화해를 계속 받아들여 좋은 성과를 이루어야 할 것이다. **δέξασθαι**("받는다")는 단순과거부정사로써 고린도 교인들이 과거에 이미 받은 은혜를 헛되이 하지 말라는 뜻이다.[521] **εἰς κενόν**("헛되이")라 말은 "유익이 없는" 이란 뜻이다(살전 3:5; 갈 2:2; 빌 2:16).[522] 이미 받은 하나님의 화해의 복음의 씨앗을 열매 없이 지키지만 말고, 계속 성장 시켜야 한다는 뜻이다. 하나님의 화해의 복음을 받아서 실생활에 접목시켜 열매를 맺으라는 말이다. 트롤은 이런 권면 뒤에는 일말의 염려가 있다고 한다. 바울은 고린도 교인들이 그리스도 안에서 새로운 피조물이 된 것을 잊고서 온전한 도덕적 삶을 살지 못하게 될까 염려한다는 것이다(12:20-21).[523] 이런 염려는 바울의 리더십과 사도직의 진정성 문

521) Hughes, 218; 참조, Plummer, 190, Furnish, 341.

522) Plummer, 190

523) Thrall, 451.

제와 연계되어 있다. 고린도전서에서 보듯이 고린도 교인들은 여러 도덕적 문제에서 바울의 지시를 일일이 받아야 했다. 그들이 바울의 가르침을 받지 않고 그리스도 안에서 새로운 삶은 지속하지 않는나면 그들에게 베푸신 하나님의 놀라운 은혜를 헛되게 만드는 것이기 때문이다.

2. "가라사대, '내가 은혜 베풀 때에 너를 듣고 구원의 날에 너를 도왔다' 하셨으니 보라 지금은 은혜 받을 만한 때요 보라 지금은 구원의 날이로다"(**λέγει γάρ· καιρῷ δεκτῷ ἐπήκουσά σου καὶ ἐν ἡμέρᾳ σωτηρίας ἐβοήθησά σοι. ἰδοὺ νῦν καιρὸς εὐπρόσδεκτος, ἰδοὺ νῦν ἡμέρα σωτηρίας**). 1절에서의 바울의 화해의 권면을 이사야 49장 8절의 부분적 인용으로 강화시키고 있다. **λέγει γάρ**(가라사대)로 시작 되는 이런 구약 인용법이 쿰란식, 또는 랍비식이라고도 보면, 바울이 당시 유대교의 구약 인용법에 익숙했다고 말 할 수 있다.[524] 즉 성경을 영감 받은 책으로 인용하여 실생활에 적용하기도하고, 설교나 강론에서 사용하기도 한다. 바울은 이사야 49장 8절을 인용하여 자신의 문제에 적용하

524) **λέγει γάρ**("가라사대")로 시작되는 인용이 바울 서신에 잦다(롬 4:3, 6; 9:15, 17, 25; 10:6, 8, 11, 16, 20, 21; 11:2, 4, 9; 12:19; 14:11; 15:10, 12; 갈 4:30). 흔히 주어가 없으며 암시적인 주어는 하나님이다. E. E. Ellis, *Paul's Use of the Old Testament* (Edinburgh: Oliver and Boyd, 1957) 24 n. 5, Thrall 452, 주, 1832, 재인용. 구약 인용이 현실과 적용되어 해석되는 것은 쿰란식이라고 한다(Bruce, 211, Thrall, 452, 주 1833, 재인용). 그러나 여기에 랍비식 인용방법과 유사한 점도 있다. 어떤 주제를 성경 인용으로 강화시키는 것이다. 여기서는 1절의 내용을 2절에서 사 49:8의 인용으로 강화시킨다고 본다. 바울은 결국 그 당시 쿰란식, 랍비식 성경 인용에 익숙해져 있다는 증거다(D. Cohn-Sherbok, "Paul and Rabbinic Exegesis", *SJT* 35 (1982), 120; E. E. Ellis, *Paul's Use of the Old Testament*, 143; Thrall, 452, 주 1833 재인용).

고 있다. 바울은 인용문에서 이사야가 메시아를 가리켜 한 말임을 알고 있었을 것이다. 그러나 바울은 자기 상황에 따라 해석하여 적용하고 있다. 이사야 본문에서 하나님이 메시아를 이방의 빛으로 선택하여 그 의 말씀을 땅 끝까지 전하게 했으나 메시아는 낙심하게 되었다. 이사야 49장 8절은 낙심한 메시아를 위로하는 말이다. 사람은 그를 실망시키나 하나님은 그의 말씀으로 위로하신다. 플러머가 지적하듯이 바울의 상황도 이와 유사하다고 볼 수 있다.[525] 그러나 트롤이 지적하듯이 이 문맥에서 문법적으로 바울은 고린도인들을 향하여 "은혜를 받을 때"라고 말하고 있고 자신을 위하는 말이 아니다. 이사야와 유사한 정황이 있으나, 바울이 그 유사성을 알고 의도적으로 인용했다는 증거는 없다.

바울은 무엇보다 지금이 하나님의 구원의 "은혜를 받을 수 있는 때"(**καιρὸς εὐπρόδεκτος**)라고 한다. 왜냐하면 지금이 하나님이 그의 구원의 은혜를 "베푸는 때"(**καιρὸς δεκτός**)이기 때문이다. **δεκτός**(데크토스)는 "받을 만한"이란 뜻인데 하나님 편에서 보아 "베푼다"는 뜻으로 해석하였다(구약인용). **εὐπρόδεκτος**(유프로데크토스)는 같은 뜻이지만 강조형이다. 사람 편에서 보아 "받을 만한 때"라고 해석하였다. 어째서 지금이 하나님이 은혜를 베푸는 때라고 하는가

첫째, 지금(**νῦν**)은 현재 바울이 복음을 전하는 역사적인 시간을 가르친다. 앞의 21절에서 말한 대로, 하나님이 그리스도를 우리를 위해 "죄"가 되게 하고 하나님의 의가 되게 하는 놀라운 은혜의

---

525) Plummer, 190-1; G. K. Beale, "The Old Testament Background of Reconciliation in 2 Corinthians 5-7 and its Bearing on the Literary Problem of 2 Corinthians 6:14-7:1", *NTS* 35 (1989-90), 561-62; Thrall, 453, 주 1837, 재인용.

조치를 취하여 하나님과 화해의 길이 열린 것을 바울을 통해서 사람들에게 지금 전하기 때문이다. 그러므로 바울이 이 은혜의 소식을 전하는 지금 이 시간에 은혜의 소식을 듣는 자들은 마음을 열어 하나님의 은혜를 받을 때이다. 그러므로 2절에서 반복되어 나오는 "지금"(νῦν)은 모두 무슨 최근에 일어나 특정한 사건의 발생을 가리키는 것이 아니라, 바울이 그리스도가 우리를 위해 죽으심으로 하나님과 화해의 길이 열린 것을 전하는 현재를 가리킨다(참조, 5:16; 롬 3:21; 행 17:30). 이 현재는 하나님의 구속사에서의 정점이다.

둘째, 지금(νῦν)은 그리스도 안에 이미 있는 개인(고린도 교인들)의 현재 상태를 가리킨다. 위에서 지적한 바와 같은 대부분의 고린도 교회 교인들은 이 때 이미 복음을 받고 성령의 은사도 받은 이들이다. 그러나 바울은 이들이 이미 받은 은혜에 합당하게 살지 못하는 것을 보고 고린도전서에서 이를 고치도록 하였다. 고린도후서에서도 거의 같은 뜻으로 말하고 있다(6:14-7:1; 12:19-13:2). 1절에서 이미 받은 은혜를 헛되이 하지 말라는 경고를 하였다. 그 받은 은혜를 계속 유지하고 성장시키라는 말을 하였다. 사실 이런 복음은 이미 전한 과거의 소식이다. 그러나 고린도전서에서 보듯이 고린도 교인들은 나태해져서 구태의연한 옛 사람의 삶으로 돌아가 살거나, 생명이 없는 굳어진 종교적 습관으로 살거나, 눈으로 보이는 영적 증거를 자랑하였다. 이제 이들은 우리를 위해 죽으신 그리스도를 본받아 살아야 하고(15), 그리스도 안에서 변화된 인생관과 세계관을 가진 새로운 피조물로서 복음에 합당하게 살기를 부단히 결단해야 한다. 누구나 그리스도 안에 있는 한 언제나 부단히 그리스도의 죽음과 부활의 진리에 비추어서 자신의 존재를 이해하고, 자신의 삶에 대해 결단해야 한다.

주 해(5:16-6:2):

5:18-21에서 밝히는 "그리스도의 화해의 사신"이라는 바울의 정체성 인식은 고린도 후서 전체 구조에서 볼 때 중심에 위치하고 있으며 전체 내용에 있어서도 종합적, 결론적, 중심적인 주제이다. "그리스도의 화해의 사신"이라는 바울의 자아 인식은 6장을 지나 7장까지 계속되는 주제로서(더 크게 보아서 고린도 후서 전체의 주제) 1장부터 시작한 여러 가지 사도직 변명들의 요약적이며 결론적 진술이라고 본다. 바울은 바로 앞서 5장 17절에서 자신을 포함한 모든 그리스도인들의 공통적 정체성을 "그리스도 안의 피조물"이라고 하면서 5장 18절에서는 자신의 정체성, 또는 존재가치를 보다 구체적으로 "화해의 사신"이라고 밝힌다. 4장 7절에서 "질그릇"이나 4장 16절에서 "후패한 겉사람"등 같은 바울의 자아 인식의 표현에 나타난 바와 같이 반대자들의 비난으로 존재해체의 위기를 맞은 바울은 그리스도 안에서 그리스도의 능력으로 새로운 피조물로 거듭 태어나는 것이다(6:4-10; 12:9, 10; 13:4). 그리고 나아가 고린도 교회의 신앙회복(관계 회복)을 위한 그리스도의 화해의 사신으로서 자신의 정체성을 밝히는 것이다. 자신을 반대하는 고린도 교회의 반대자들과 당장 다가오는 3차 방문을 생각하면서 사도로서의 자신의 역할을 "화해의 사신"으로서 자신의 사도직을 인식하고 변명하는 것이다. 물론 그의 화해의 사역은 궁극적으로 그리스도의 구원의 사역에 근거하고 있다(5:15). 그러나 고린도 교회의 반대하는 이들을 진정시키고 화해의 분위기로 이

끌어 가는 것이 바울이 당면한 목회 과제이다. "화해의 사신"으로서의 자아인식은 1장의 하나님의 양심적 일군, 2장의 순전한 말씀의 일군, 3장의 "새 언약의 일군", 그리고 4장의 "그리스도의 계시를 받은 진정한 일군"과 "보배를 담은 질그릇"같은 바울의 자아인식의 표현들과 연결되는 것이다. 이런 자아 인식의 표현들은 그를 반대하는 이들의 여러 가지 비난에 대한 바울의 사도적 변명들이기도 한다(12:19). 바울의 변명들은 반대자들이 바울과 그의 사역에 대해 여러 가지로 비난해왔던 것을 암시해 준다(2:4, 16, 17; 3:14; 4:3, 4; 5:12; 7:2; 10:2, 9, 10, 12; 11:13-15; 12:16-13:2). 이런 바울의 자신의 정체성 또는 자아인식은 적극적이거나 부정적, 또는 역설적 표현들을 사용하면서, 발전적으로 나타나고 있다. 우선 1장에서 반대자들은 바울이 방문 약속을 자의로 취소하고 지키지 않은 것을 비난 해온 것으로 나타난다. 이에 대해서 바울은 자신이 방문을 취소한 이유는 바울 자신의 어떤 이기적 이유에서가 아니라, 고린도 교인들이 2장에서 지적된 어떤 문제된 사람의 치리를 아직 결행 하지 않는 등 방문을 위한 준비를 채 하지 않았기 때문에 원만한 방문을 위해 방문을 일단 중지하고 나중으로 미룬 것이라고 했다(1:23; 2:1-3). 바울은 하나님의 양심적 일군으로 자처한다(1:12, 21). 계속해서 2장에서도 바울이 편지로 고린도 인들을 위협한다고 비난하는 이들에 대하여 자신의 사역의 중심은 사랑이라고 말하면서 "그리스도의 향기"로서 비난을 받으나 결국 승리한다고 말한다. 결국 바울의 강경한 편지("눈물의 편지")로 고린도 교인들이 회개하여 바울에게로 돌아 온 것이다(참조, 7:8-12). 3장과 4장에서는 자신의 복음 사역의 정체성에 대한 유대 배경을 가진 반대자들의 비난에 대해서 율법의 일시적 영광이 아닌 영원한 그리스도의 복음의 일군이며, "새 언약의 일군" 이라고 한다.

4장 7절부터 16절까지 반대자들이 자신의 사역이 초라하며, 외적 성과가 부족하다는 지적에 대해서, 바울은 자신을 보배를 담고 있는 질그릇에 비유하여 그의 초라한 고난의 사역이 바로 그리스도의 진정한 복음 사역의 증거임을 설명하고 있다. 바울이 복음 사역으로 겪는 온갖 고난을 그리스도의 고난에 비교하면서 결국 생명과 승리를 향한 고난으로 그 가치를 확인하고 있다.

4:7절의 "보배를 담은 질그릇" 의 역설적 표현은 4:16절의 "겉 사람" 과 "속 사람" 의 교차적, 역설적 표현과 이어진다. 4:16에서 5장까지 바울은 그의 고난의 사역의 영원한 가치를 반대자들의 외적 성과 중심의 일시적 세상적 영광의 사역과 암시적으로 대조하여 부각시킨다(5:12; 참조, 10:7). 그의 어려운 고난의 사역으로 말미암아 그의 "겉 사람" (육적 인간)과 "속 사람" (영적 인간)의 존재 해체의 아픈 경험을 하면서도 육적 가치는 일시적이고 영적 가치와 영적 세계의 가치가 영원하기 때문에 위로의 근거가 있다고 한다. 바울은 계속하여 5:1에서 5:10까지 영원한 장래 소망과 그리스도의 의로운 심판의 기대하며 현실의 고난의 사역의 의미를 재확인한다. 이런 현실의 고난은 잠간이고 장래의 소망은 영원하기 때문에 현실의 고난을 참을 가치가 있다는 것이다. 5:11부터 이런 고난의 사역을 인내하면서 다시 하나님의 진실한 일군으로서 그리스도의 사랑과 화해의 사역을 계속해야 하는 당위성을 재확인한다. 반대자들의 가치 판단 기준은 진실성이 없는 즉 외적 성과와 외적 영광("외모")이다(12). 예수를 "육체를 따라서" 생각하면 즉 "외모" 로만 보면 그의 존재와 사역의 가치를 바르게 평가할 수 없고, 그에 대한 바른 믿음을 가질 수 없으나, 진실한 신앙의 눈으

로 보면 예수를 그리스도로 믿고 인식하게 되듯이 그리스도를 믿는 신앙인은 내적 판단 기준을 가지고 사람을 평가해야 한다는 것이다. 바울 자신도 외적으로는 질그릇같이 연약하나 분명히 그리스도의 진정한 사도이다. 예수께서 외적으로는 약하셨으나 진정한 그리스도로서 화해의 사역을 하셨듯이 바울도 외적으로는 약하나(반대파들이 지적하듯이) 그리스도의 진정한 사도이다. 그의 약함이 오히려 그리스도의 진정한 사도라는 증거가 되는 것이다(11:21-30; 12:9, 10). 5:17에서 바울은 자신을 포함한 모든 그리스도인들이 그리스도 안에서 새로운 피조물이라고 한다. 그가 비록 반대자들에 의해서 사도로서의 존재 해체의 수모를 겪었으나(4:7-16) 그리스도 안에서 그리스도의 능력으로 다시 살아나게 되었다는 암시가 있다(6:4-10; 12:9, 10; 13:5). 더 나아가 이 새로운 피조물은 이제 그리스도의 화해의 사신으로서 그 존재 가치를 인정받아서 고린도 교회 신앙공동체의 신앙회복과 관계회복(그리스도와 바울과 고린도 교회와의 관계 회복)을 위해 일한다는 것이다.

이렇게 보면, 5:18-21절에서 말하는 "그리스도의 화해의 사신"이라는 바울의 자신의 존재인식은 1장에서 시작된 반대자들의 바울의 사도로서의 정체성에 대한 비난에 대한 적극적인 결론적 변명이라는 것이 분명하다. 즉 바울은 자신은 반대자들의 비난에 대해서 자신을 변명하고 그들과 맞서서 싸우는 싸움꾼이 아니라 오히려 그리스도의 진정한 사도로서 그리스도의 화해의 사역을 고린도 교회에서 이루려는 화해의 일군이라고 적극적으로 자신의 정체성을 반증하여 요약하는 것이다. 4:7의 "보배를 담은 질그릇" 같은 고난 받는 사도로서의 정체성도 "화해의 사신"이라는 궁극적 정체성을 나타내기 위해 필요한 과정적인 성격이 강하다. 이런 화해의 사역의 증거와 성과에 대한 진술이 6장을 지나서 고린도후서의 임시적인 결론에 해당하는 7장까지 계속된다.

우리는 바울이 고린도 교회에 화해의 복음을 전하면서, 화해를 이루지 못하고, 오히려 그로 말미암아 분쟁을 초래하고 분쟁에 말려들어 고난당하는 것을 본다. 이런 아이러니는 화해의 복음의 성격이 세속적인 의미의 평등한 화해가 아니라 하나님 중심적인 일방적이고 수직적인 화해이기 때문이다. 그러므로 예수님은 "내가 세상에 화평을 주러 온 줄로 생각지 말라. 화평이 아니요 검을 주러 왔노라(마 10:34)" 고 말씀하셨다. 우리는 바울이 전하는 화해의 의미를 우리가 생각하는 쌍방의 일대일(一對一)식의 민주적 화해의 개념으로만 이해해서는 안 된다. 하나님은 그리스도를 통해서 화해의 이니시어티브를 가지고 죄인들을 위하여 일방적인 화해의 은혜를 베푸셨다. 바울도 자신을 하나님의 화해의 사신으로서(5:19, 20), 고린도 교인들의 영적 아버지로서 고린도 교인들을 설득한다(6:13; 12:14). 하나님은 죄인들을 위해 그의 아들 그리스도를 보내시고 죽게 하심으로 자신을 사람들의 수준에 낮추셨듯이, 바울도 고린도 교인들을 부모가 자녀를 달래듯이 자세를 낮추어서 화해의 어조를 유지하지만(6:13), 고린도 교인들과의 근본적인 관계에 있어서 하나님의 주권과 그의 사도적 권위가 늘 전제되어 있음을 알아야 한다. 이런 바울의 근본적인 신학적인 사고를 인식하지 못하면 고린도후서의 어떤 말들을 오해할 수가 있다. 결과적으로 다른 교리와 마찬가지로 화해의 교리에 있어서도 하나님의 의와 하나님의 사랑, 하나님의 주권과 낮추심의 역설적인 진술들이 있고, 이에 따른 바울의 말과 자세에 있어서도 유사한 역설적인 유형이 있다. 이런 역설적인 진술들을 논리적 혼돈으로 볼 것이 아니라,

복음진리의 온전함과 풍성함을 나타내는 것으로 이해하여야 한다.

바울은 4장 16절 이후에서 자신의 사도직의 진정성의 증거를 외적인 것이 아닌 내적인 데서, 일시적 영광이 아닌 영원한 영광을 추구하는 데 있다고 하면서 영원한 장래의 소망에 관심을 갖고 설명하다가 5장 11절 이후부터 다시 현실적인 문제를 취급하기 시작한다. 즉 고린도 교회와의 화해의 문제다. 바울은 이 문제 해결의 근거를 그리스도의 죽으심과 부활에 두고 14절 이후 그리스도의 죽으심과 부활에서 출발하여 변화된 그리스도인에 대해서 설명한다. 그리스도 안에서 새롭게 변화된 인간존재가 16절에서 21절까지의 주제이다. 그리스도인은 옛 사람은 죽고 새 사람이 되었고 또 새 사람으로 살아야한다. 하나님의 아들 그리스도의 죽음으로 새로 창조된 사람답게 살아야 한다. 그리스도의 죽음과 부활의 의미를 그리스도인의 새로운 존재와 또 그 존재의 현존과 관련시켜 설명하고 있다. 특히 5장 21절에서 바울은 하나님께서 그리스도를 죄로 삼아 인간의 죄를 속죄하심으로 죄인과 화해의 길을 먼저 여신 것을 말한 후에 고린도 교인들도 이런 하나님의 화해의 은혜에 보답하라고 한다. 즉 하나님과 변화된 존재의 증거를 화해의 삶으로 나타내라는 것이다. 여기에는 화해의 복음의 전도자 바울에게로 돌아오라는 암시적 의미도 있다. 바울은 하나님이 임명하신 화해의 사신이기 때문이다(5:19, 20). 하나님과의 개인적 차원의 화해에서 화해의 복음 전도의 직책을 맡은 바울과의 화해로 발전적 적용을 하는 것이다.

그러므로 바울의 화해의 사역은 일반적인 인간관계의 쌍방 화해와는 다른 하나님 중심적 화해이다. 하나님의 화해, 하나님에 의한 화해, 하나님을 위한 화해이다. 다른 말로, 하나님께 속한 화해, 하나님이 시작한 화해, 하나님의 거룩하신 뜻을 이루기 위한 화해이다. 그러므로 바울은 화해의 주제를 시작하면서 "모든 것이 하나님께로부터 났다"(5:18)고 선언하였다. 바울은 하나님께로부터 화해의 사역을 직접 위임받았다(5:19-20). 그러므로 이 화해는 거절해도 상관없는 인간 상호 간의 화해가 아니라, 인간의 생사가 달린 문제이며, 인간의 심각한 결단을 요구하는 화해이다. 이 화해는 하나님이 시작하신 화해이며(5:21; 롬 5:6, 10), 하나님이 요구하시고 명령하시는 화해이므로(5:14, 15), 이 화해에의 초대를 거절하는 것은 하나님의 영원한 진노를 자초하게 되는 것이다(마 22:1-7). 그러므로 바울은 "하나님의 은혜를 헛되이 받지 말라"고 경고한다(6:1).

이렇게 바울이 제시하는 복음의 신적 화해에는 강요된 성격이 있다. 이런 강요된 성격의 화해의 복음을 전하는 바울은 그리스도를 통한 화해를 하나님의 구원의 새 시대의 유일한 화해의 방법으로 내세움으로써 결국 이 세상에 더 심각한 분쟁을 초래하는 것이다. 사도행전에서 보듯이 그가 복음을 전하는 곳마다 분쟁이 일어났다. 그리스도 안에 있는 자와 그리스도 밖에 있는 자의 새로운 갈등이 일어났다. 이런 갈등은 피할 수 없는 것이다. 빛의 세계와 어둠의 세계의 대립이다(요 1:5). 그러나 여기서 바울의 관심은 그리스도 교회의 대내적 갈등에 대한 것이다. 그리스도인들이 그리스도의 화평의 모델을 따라서 개인적으로 화평한 인간관계를 유지하도록 권한다. "할 수 있거든 너희는 모든 사람과 더불어 평화하라"(롬 12:18, 참조, 14:9; 갈 5:22). 그리스도의 몸 된 교회가 하나가 되도록 힘써 지키기를 원한다(고전 3:3-9, 7:15; 엡 2:13-22; 4:1-16). 더 나아가 종말론적인 우주적인 화평을 기대한다(골 1:20; 참조, 고전 15:28). 바울은 그리스도 중심적 평화론자였다. 그러므로 그리스도 중심이 아닌 평화는 반대하였다(10:5). 바울은 결코 분쟁은 무조건 피해야 한다는 평화주의자는 아니다. 다만 "육신을 따라 행하는 분쟁"을 반대하였다(10:3, 4; 고전 3:3). 이 세상의 악과 하나님의 의와의 대결은 피할 수 없는 것이다(딤전 6:12). 이것은 예수님의 입장과도 일치한다. 예수님은 개인적인 화해와 교회의 화해를 가르치셨으나, 반 복음적인 세력과의 분쟁을 예상하셨다(마 5:9, 44; 10:34; 눅 12:51). 낡은 포도주와 새 포도주, 낡은 부대와 새 부대로 표현되는 그리스도로 말미암는 구원의 새 시대와 모세의 율법으로 말미암는 옛 시대의 긴장으로 예수님도 일생 분쟁에 시달렸다. 또 화해의 복음을 전하는 바울도 그가 세운 교회의 각종 분쟁에 시달려야 했다. 대개의 바울 서신에 나타나는 싸움들은 외적인 핍박보다는 교회 자체 내에서의 싸움들이었다. 유대교와의 갈등과 같은 신학적, 신앙적인 문제로 인한 분쟁도 있었고(고전 6:1; 7:1; 8:1; 9:3; 15:12; 고후 3:1; 갈 1:6 등), 바울의 개인적인 문제로 인한 분쟁도 있었다(행 15:39; 고전 3:3 이하; 고후 10:10; 12:16; 갈 2:11; 빌 1:17, 4:19; 살전 2:2; 딤후 2:17, 3:11, 4:14, 등). 특히 고린도 교회는 이 모든 문제들이 서로 엉켜서 심각한 분쟁으로 시달린 교회이다. 그래서 바울은 "하나님은 어지러움의 하나님이 아니요 오직 화평의 하나님이시니라"(고전 14:33)고 가르쳤다. 바울 이후 1세기 말(A.D. 97) 클레멘트(Clement of Rome)가 고린도 교회에 보낸 첫 번째 편지에 보면 그 때까지도 교린도 교회의 분쟁은 그치지 않았음을 보여 준다.[526] 바울은 교회의 화평

526) Clement of Rome, *ANF*, vol. 1, 5-21, 특히 18; 이에 대한 F. F. Bruce의 견해 참고하라 (256).

을 되도록 유지하기를 원했으나, 분쟁의 원인이 신앙적이거나 신학적인 문제였을 때에는 분쟁을 인정하였다. 심지어 데살로니가 교회에게는, "규모 없이 행하고 우리에게 받은 유전대로 행하지 아니하는 모든 형제에게서 떠나라" 고 명령했다(살후 3:6; 롬 16:17).

바울은 분쟁을 원치 않았으나 어쩔 수 없는 경우 분쟁조정에 직접 개입했다. 고린도 교회가 그 경우이다. 그는 분쟁 조정도 하고 분쟁의 해결 노력도 한다. 그에 대한 비난에 대해서 이해시킬 것은 이해시키고(고후 1:16-23), 주장할 것은 주장하였다(고후 10장-13장). 그러나 바울은 결코 인간적인 화평을 위한 분쟁 해결을 한 것은 아니다. 그의 입장은 언제나 그리스도 믿는 신앙에서 이탈 여부가 관건이었다(11:2-4). 그리스도 안에서 타협하는 것이지 그리스도 밖의 어떤 타협도 있을 수 없었다. 그리스도의 구속적 진리에 위반되는 모든 것들은 정죄하고 타협하지 않았다(10:6; 12:20-13:2). 그의 관심은 오히려 더 많은 사람들을 그리스도의 십자가의 원칙을 좇도록 하는데 있었으므로 반 십자가적 문제로 인한 분쟁에 대해서는 더욱 적극적이었다(고후 10:8, 13:2; 갈 3:1; 빌 3:18). 바울의 분쟁의 결정은 단순히 예수를 믿느냐 안 믿느냐가 아니라 상대방이 진정으로 그리스도의 모델을 따라서 사느냐 안 사느냐에 달려 있다. 고린도 교회의 바울의 대적자들은 분명히 예수 믿는 이들이었다. 그들은 사도들의 추천서를 가지고 다니는 사람들이었다(3:1). 그러나 그들은 유대교 전통을 자랑하고(3:14-15), "외모를 자랑하고" (5:12), "육체를 따라 자랑하였다" (11:18). 바울에게 그들의 자랑은 겉으로는 복음과 관계된 영적인 자랑인 걸처럼 보이나 실제로는 속죄주이신 그리스도 안에서의 자랑이 아니라 그리스도 밖에서의 인간적인 자랑에 불과했다. 그러므로 바울은 "자랑하는 자는 주안에서 자랑하라"고 했다(고전 1:31; 고후 10:17; 참조, 시 34:2). 그리고 자신은 "십자가 외에는 결코 자랑할 것이 없다"고 했다(갈 6:14; 참조, 고전 1:18; 고후 12:5). 그리스도의 속죄의 모델을 따르는 신앙인가 아닌가가 분쟁의 관건이었다. 그리스도의 속죄의 신앙을 따르는 신앙이나 태도가 아니면 모두 분쟁의 대상이 될 수 있었다(롬 16:17, 18; 빌 3:18, 19).

바울은 언제나 자신은 십자가의 진리에 든든히 서서 행하고 있다고 확신하였다(11:10; 13:8). 그는 자신을 희생하는 그리스도 중심적 사역에 대해서 조금도 거리낌이 없었다(고후 4:1-2). 그러므로 그는 분쟁의 탓을 자기에게 돌리지 않는다. 혹 이런 점을 가지고 그가 자기도취적 독선적 지도자라고 볼 수도 있으나,[527] 우리는 그가 하나님의 택함 받은 종으로서 그의 영적 권위와 높은 도덕성을 믿는다(1:12; 4:2; 행 9:1-22; 롬 15:18; 고전 7:40; 갈 6:17). 바울은 스스로 완전한 그리스도의 인격에 도달하였다고 믿었다(빌 1:20-21; 딤후 4:6-8). 그러나 우리가 그의 내면적 인격을 닮지는 않고 그의 외적 권위주의적 스타일만을 배우는 것은 옳지 않다. 또 바울이 권위주의적 자세만을 가졌다고 보아서는 안 된다, 그리스도의 겸비함과 온유함을 함양한 사람이다(고후 10:1; 12:9, 10). 또 그렇게 살며 하나가 되도록 가르쳤다(롬 12, 14, 15; 빌 2:1-11). 바울의 모든 인격과 삶의 중심은 그리스도의 죽으심이다(고후 5: 14-21; 빌 1:20-21). 그러므로 그리스도 안에 거하는 것이 무엇보다 중요하다. 바울이 말하는 화해는 언제나 그리스도 중심적인 화해이다. 세속적, 타협적인 화해가 아니다. 바울의 싸움은 단적으로 말

527) Thrall, 961-62.

해서 그리스도 중심적이 아닌 것을 그리스도 중심적으로 돌리기 위해서 싸운 것이다(10:5). 그리스도 안에서만 진정하고 영원한 화해가 있음으로 어떤 세속적인 모양의 화해도 인정치 않았다.

교회 내의 분쟁이 어떤 개인이나 소수의 잘못으로 인한 경우 문제된 이들을 질책함으로 분쟁이 종결 될 수 있다(마 18:15-17; 고전 5:5; 고후 2:6). 그러나 세상에서 흔히 있는 인간적인 감정이나 편견으로 싸움하는 경우가 더 많다. 분쟁 당사자들이 피차 진정으로 한분 그리스도 안에 있는 형제들임을 자각한다면 싸울 필요 없는 싸움들이 대부분이다. 많은 교회들은 이런 싸움으로 부끄럽고 추악한 분쟁 집단으로 전락하고 말았다. 분쟁으로 교회가 갈라지는 것이 하나님의 교회 확장을 위한 섭리라고 볼 수도 있으나, 그런 선한 결과가 있다고 분쟁을 긍정적으로 볼 수는 없다. 하나님은 우리의 악을 가지시고도 선으로 바꾸시는 능력이 있으신 분이지만, 여전히 우리의 악에 대한 책임도 물으실 것이다. 그리고 하나님께서 우리의 실수에도 불구하고 선을 이루실 수 있다면 우리의 선으로는 더 큰 선을 행하실 것이다. 교회의 분쟁이 교회를 구성하는 인간들의 악이나 연약함으로 일어난 경우 회개하여 다시 하나가 되는 경우가 드물다. 분쟁이 타결되지 않는 경우 격화되기 전에 교회를 나누는 것이 차선의 방법이다. 그러나 교회가 나누어짐으로 외적인 분쟁은 종식이 되더라도 분쟁 당사자들 간의 내적인 개인적인 감정은 오래 지속될 수 있을 것이다. 그러므로 늘 개인 상호간의 화해의 정신을 함양하는 것이 필요하다. 서로 불화한 것을 회개하고 화해의 노력을 계속해야 한다. 화해가 그리스도인 된 중요한 증거이다. 교회의 분쟁을 남의 일처럼 비웃거나 걱정하기 전에 우리 자신들을 돌아보자. 나는 진정으로 그리스도 안에서 화평케 하는 자로 살고 있는가? 내 모든 인간관계에서 그리스도의 화평을 추구하였는가? "화평케 하는 자는 복이 있나니 저희가 하나님의 아들이라 일컬음을 받을 것임이요"(마 5:9). "그는 우리의 화평이 신지라 둘로 하나를 만드사 중간에 막힌 담을 허시고 원수된 것 곧 의문에 속한 계명의 율법을 자기 육체로 폐하셨으니 이는 둘로 자기의 안에서 한 새 사람을 지어 화평하게 하시고 또 십자가로 이 둘을 한 몸으로 하나님과 화목하게 하려 하심이라…"(엡 2:14-16).

본문에서 바울은 고린도 교회와의 화해의 준비 작업으로, 그리스도인들이 그리스도의 속죄의 진리를 깨달아 삶에 적용하여 살 것을 가르치고 있다. 인간의 죄를 사하시고 구원하기 위해 그의 아들을 희생시킨 거룩하신 하나님의 사랑을 생각하고 실천하는 것이 그리스도 안에서 새로운 구원의 시대를 여신 하나님의 화해의 방법을 심각하게 받아드리고 각자의 삶에 적용할 것을 권면한다. "하나님의 은혜를 헛되이 받지 말라"(고후 6:1). 12:20-21에서도 바울은 그의 3차 방문 이전에 진정한 화해를 위해서 고린도 교인들의 분열의 죄와 성적인 죄를 제거할 것을 요구한다.

법정 싸움이나 다른 인간적인 방법은 진정한 화해가 될 수 없다. 법이나 사회적 억제력에 의해 어느 쪽이 굴복하게 되고 어느 한 쪽이 승리하게 되는 경우 외적 싸움이 종식이 된다 해도, 진정한 화해가 아니므로 갈등은 지속될 것이다. 한편 도덕주의나, 휴머니즘이나, 공리주의적, 합리주의적, 또는 자연주의적 원칙에 의한 분쟁 해결도 가능하나 이런 인간의 감정이나 이성에 의한 화해는 여전히 순수하지 못한 인간의 궤계나 욕심이나 오만함이나 다른 인간적 제약성이 게재된 경우가 많다. 흔히 도덕적인 인간에게 숨어 있는 문제는 자기 기만적 외식과 자기의 도덕의식과 기준에 의거하여 다른 이들을 경멸하는 오만한 태도이다. 이것은 인간의 내면에 있는 근본적인 죄의 문제를 해결하지 않고 외적으로 고상한 도덕적 계율과 행위로 치장하기 때문이다. 옛날 유대교 바리새인들뿐만 아니라, 우리나라의 과거의 양반층이나 유교적 도덕주의적 교훈을 따르는 이들에게서, 현대의 합리주의적 메너리즘, 그리고 변화되지 않은 오래 믿는 그리스도인들에게서 자주 발견되는 문제라고 할 수 있다(마 23장; 롬 2장). 휴머니즘이 현대의 지배적인 가치로서 등장하였다. 하나님에 대한 신앙 없는 인간중심적 휴머니즘은 인간의 근본적인 죄의 문제를 심각하게 다루지 않고 상대화시켜 버리고 인간의 양심이나 인권 같은 권리만을 강조하기 때문에 죄로 말미암은 인간문제의 근본적 해결책이 될 수 없다. 합리주의 역시 인간의 이성적 판단을 가치기준으로 삼아서, 인간을 논리적으로나 기계적으로만 이해하고 다루는 문제가 있다. 자연주의적(또는, 과학주의적) 사고는 자연 자체에 존재하는 일정한 원칙에 따라서 가치기준을 세운다. 자연에서 발견되는 원칙과 질서(창조 질서)도 있으나 혼돈과 모호함도 있다. 자연주의는 근본적으로 사람의 가치를 동물이나 다른 자연의 가치와 구별하지 않는다. 이런 자연주의적 가치 판단 기준으로는 사람이 일반 자연과 구별되는 하나님의 형상으로서 가치를 세우고, 궁극적 삶의 의미를 세울 수 없다. 모든 자연물의 동등한 권리를 인정하는 나머지 인간 중심의 궁극적 가치나 질서를 세우는 것도 원칙적으로 불가능 하다(이런 자연주의 사상은 힌두교, 불교, 범신론은 물론 많은 자연주의적 환경론자들의 지배적인 사고이다). 성경은 자연 세계도 하나님의 저주 아래 있어서 회복이 필요함을 가르친다(창 3:18; 롬 8:20-22). 인간이나 자연이나 모두 피조물들이기 때문에 창조주 하나님의 구원 조치가 없이는 스스로를 구원할 수 없다.

바울은 모든 사람들이 다 죄인이라고 선언한다(롬 3:10). 그것은 사람의 모든 사고방식까지도 죄성을 가진 것임을 뜻한다. 사람은 원래 하나님을 무시하고 반역하는 죄의 성향이 있다(창 3:5, 4:9, 6:5, 8:21, 11:4; 욥 31:5-40; 롬 1:19-23). 바울은 하나님의 아들 그리스도 안에서 하나님이 모든 죄인들에게 베푸시는 은혜를 받아 구원받고, 그리스도 안에서 인간들이 서로 사랑하고 용서하는 정신을 함양하는 것이 가장 효과적이고 근본적인 인간사회 갈등의 해소책 이라고 한다(롬 12:5-21; 고후 5:15-21). 이것은 모든 인간 사회나 교회 내에 있는 기존의 구체적인 다양한 분쟁 해결 방법을 모두 무시하자는 것이 아니다. 그런 방법을 그리스도의 속죄의 정신에서 수정하고 개선하여 보다 수준 높은 화해로 승화시키고 발전시켜야 한다는 것이다. 인간의 내면적인 변화가 없는 집단이나 사회적 개선은 허구적인 미봉책에 불구하다. 그러나 오늘의 자유주의적이고 개인주의적인 사회조직의 특성상 이런 전반적인 사회개혁은 당장 어려워 보인다. 그러나 위에서 지적한 현대의 각종 사상 자체가 가지고 있는 약점들 때문에 현대 사회도 절대적 하나님의 구원의 필요성을 인정하기도 한다고 본다. 사실 이 세상의 전체적인 개혁은 주님이 오시기 전까지 이루어 질 수 없다. 주님의 재림 때까지 오히려 이 세상은 더 악해 지고 큰 혼돈에 빠지게 될 것이다(살후 2:1-12; 딤후 3:1-5). 그러나 우리 그리스도인들이 있는 곳 어디에서나 작은 밀알들로서의 사명을 감당해야 한다(4:14-17; 요 12:24-25; 마 25:14-30). 우리의 희생적인 사역의 외적인 성과가 있더라도 자랑하지 말고 하나님께 영광을 돌릴 것이다. 우리의 희생적인 사역이 때로는 아무런 성과가 없을 수도 있을 것이다. 그 때에도 낙심할 필요가 없다. 지나친 낙심은 자신에게 집착되어 있는 증거이다. 바울은 하나님께 의지하므로 그의 현재 보잘것없는 사역의 성과에 대해서 낙심하지 않는다고 하였다(고후 4:1, 8, 16). 그것은 장래에 나타날 위로와 영광을 믿기 때문이다(5:1). 또한 그가 철저히 그리스도의 죽고 사는 모델을 따라서 살기 때문이다(고후 4:7-9; 6:3-10; 13:4). 그는 그리스도의 "약함의 능력"을 늘 믿는다(12:9, 10; 13:4). 그러므로 13장에서 고린도 교회의 문제 있는 이들을 징벌할 계획을 밝히면서도, 그들이 먼저 회개하여 그의 사도권을 쓰지 않게 되기를 바란다(13:7, 10). 그 자신이 사도권을 쓰지도 못하는 약하고 무능한 사도라는 소리를 들어도 그는 개의치 않고 오직 고린도 인들의 유익만을 위해서 일해도 기쁠 것이라고 한다(4:5; 13:3, 7, 9).

우리의 사역의 성과는 최후에 하나님께서 공정히 심판해 주실 것이다(고후 5:10). 그러므로 앞서 복음을 받은 우리들은 죄인을 구하여 주신 하나님의 크신 은혜를 우리 이웃에게 전하는 하나님의 화해의 사신들임을 자각하자(고후 5:19-20). 또한 오늘 지금 내가 어떻게 하나님의 은혜와 화해의 말씀을 구현시킬 수 있는지를 살피고 결단해야 할 것이다: "보라 지금은 은혜 받을 만한 때요 보라 지금은 구원의 날이로다" (고후 6:2).

ix. 우리는 고난 받았으나 승리했다(6:3-10).

본 문:

> 6:3. 우리가 이 직책이 훼방을 받지 않게 하려고 무엇에든지 아무에게도 거리끼지 않게 하고 4. 오직 모든 일에 하나님의 일군으로 자천하며 많이

> 견디는 것과 환난과 궁핍과 곤난과 5. 매 맞음과 갇힘과 요란한 것과 수고로움과 자지 못함과 먹지 못함과 6. 깨끗함과 지식과 오래 참음과 자비함과 성령의 감화와 거짓이 없는 사랑과 7. 진리의 말씀과 하나님의 능력 안에 있어 의의 병기로 좌우하고 8. 영광과 욕됨으로 말미암으며 악한 이름과 아름다운 이름으로 말미암으며 속이는 자 같으나 참되고 9. 무명한 자 같으나 유명한 자요 죽는 자 같으나 보라 우리가 살고 징계를 받는 자 같으나 죽임을 당하지 아니하고 10. 근심하는 자 같으나 항상 기뻐하고 가난한 자 같으나 많은 사람을 부요하게 하고 아무 것도 없는 자 같으나 모든 것을 가진 자로다.

본문 비평:

1. 3절에서 서방 사본들(D F G it vg syr)은 ἡ διακονία(직책) 앞에 ἡμῶν(우리들의)이 추가되어 "우리들의 직책"이라고 한다(RSV, NIV). 그러나 바레트는 ἡ διακονία(직책)가 반드시 바울의 사역이 아니라 일반적인 사역을 나타낸다고 본다.[528]

2. 4절에서 "하나님의 일군들"은 주격으로서 "우리는 모든 일에 하나님의 일군들로서 우리 자신들을 자천하며"로 해석해야 한다. "우리를 하나님의 일군들로서 자천한다"는 뜻이 아니다. 후자의 경우에는 하나님의 일군으로 자천하는 일이 모든 일의 중심적 관심이란 뜻이 되어 어색하다. 전자의 경우는 하나님의 일군이라는 의식을 가지고 모든 일을 하고 있다는 뜻이다.

3. 4절에서 우리 본문의 συνιστάντες는 말은 p[46] ℵ* C D* F G에서 나타나고 συνίστημι(자천하다, 고후 4:2, 6:4)의 분사이다. 같

528) Barrett, 182, 주, 1.

은 뜻의 다른 말 **συνιστάντες**는 B P 104 1175 2495에 나오는 데 **συνιστάνω**(자천하다, 고후 3:1, 5:12)의 분사이고, **συνιστῶντες**는 a² D² y TR에 나타나며, **συνιστάω**(자천하다)의 분사다. 이 말들은 모두 동의어이다. 그러나 마지막 **συνιστῶντες**는 바울이 쓴 적이 없음으로 후대의 오류로 본다.[529)]

4. 6절에서 **πνεύματι ἁγίῳ**(성령) 앞에 원문에는 관사가 없으나 대부분 학자들은 관사가 빠진 것으로 보고 성령으로 번역한다. 바레트는 이를 문자적으로 "하나님의 영" 으로 번역한다.[530)]

5. 9절에서 **παιδευόμενοι**(징계를 받는 자들)대신 일반적으로 잘 쓰이는 **πειραζόμενοι**(시험을 받는 자들)가 서방 사본에 나타난다(D* F G it Ambst). 그러나 어려운 말을 원래의 것으로 보는 원칙(*lectio difficilior*)에 따라 전자를 따른다.

내용 개요:

이 부분에서 바울은 여전히 사도로서의 변명, 또는 자아인식을 논한다고 볼 수 있다. 바울은 그리스도의 사도로서 철저히 그리스도의 죽고 사는 모델에 따라서 그의 사도직이 수행되고 있음을 증거한다. 바울의 사역의 명암에 대한 표현은 4장 8-9절에서도 잠시 언급되었으나 여기 만큼 조직적으로 충분히 언급되지는 못했다. 학자들은 바울이 본문에서 매우 조직적인 구조로 서술하였다고

529) Henry George Liddell and Robert Scott, *A Greek-English Dictionary*, 1718, Thrall, 318, 주 888, 456, 주, 1858 보라.

530) Barrett, 186-7.

하면서 희랍어 구문 특징에 따라서 3-4a절은 서론이며, 그 이후는 네 개의 단위로 나타나는 데, 4b-5절(열 개의 ἐν으로 시작되는 절들로서 바울의 어려운 고통을 나타낸다.), 6-7a절(여덟 개의 ἐν절을 가지고서 바울의 사역의 장점들을 나타낸다), 7b-8a절(세 개의 διά절을 가지고 바울의 사역의 도구와 환경을 언급한다), 8b-10절(일곱 개의 ὡς로 시작하는 대조적 구문들이 바울의 역설적 존재에 대해 설명한다).[531] 어떤 학자들은 이 부분이 매우 조직적인 글이므로 원래 초대교회에서 쓰던 모범적인 주의 종에 대한 요약적 발췌문을 바울이 여기서와 11장 23절과 27절에서 사용했을 것이라고 본다.[532] 그러나 트롤은 바울 사신이 쓴 것으로 본다.[533] 이런 배경이 되는 문서에 대한 추정은 흥미는 있으나, 어디까지나 추론에 그칠 뿐이다. 그러나 여기 나오는 고난과 덕목은 바울 자신에게 한정된 것이라고 볼 수 없다. 그리스도의 사도나 신실한 종들이라면 누구나 거의 공통적으로 겪게 되는 것들이다.[534]

바울의 역경 중에서의 승리는 예수 그리스도의 구속 사역의 모델의 특성이다(4:7-15; 11:23-33; 12:7-10).[535] 바울은 이런 공통적 특성을 서술하여 고린도 교인들에게 자신의 사역의 순수성과 진

531) Hughes, 222이하, 226, 주, 67; Martin, 160-164; Thrall, 454; Collange, 281-301.

532) Collange은 여기서 바울은 이미 기술된 하나님의 종에 대한 요약적 문서(breviary)를 가지고 있었다고 한다(290). Martin도 그 가능성을 인정한다(172).

533) Thrall, 457.

534) Hughes, 223.

535) 본문의 역경을 나타내는 말들에 대하여 스토익 관련설을 주장하기도하고, 또는 유대교의 고난받는 의인 사상을 나타낸다는 주장도 있다. R. Hoeistad, "Eine hellenistische Parallele zu 2 Kor 6, 3ff." coniectanea neotestamentica IX (1944), 22-27; "A. Fridrichsen, "Paulus und die stoa," *ConNT* IV (1944) 27; K. T. Kleinknecht, *Der leidende Gerechtfertigte*, WUNT 13, (Tübingen: J. C. B. Mohr, 1984), 264, 265, 268.

정성을 증명하는 것이다. 즉 11절에서 바울이 고린도 교인들과의 화해를 직접 언급하기 전에 왜 고린도 교인들이 바울과 화해해야 하느냐에 대한 답을 미리 말하는 것이다.

주 석:

3. "우리가 이 직책이 훼방을 받지 않게 하려고 무엇에든지 아무에게도 거리끼지 않게 하고…" (**Μηδεμίαν ἐν μηδενὶ διδόντες προσκοπήν, ἵνα μὴ μωμηθῇ ἡ διακονία,**). "직책" (**ἡ διακονία**)이란 말은 앞서 5장 18절에서 언급되었다. 플러머는 3절과 1절이 모두 직책을 말하면서 잘 연결되므로 2절을 삽입구로 보지만,[536] 2절은 1절의 의미를 재확인하고 있을 뿐이다[537]. 바울은 하나님과 동역하는 자로서 고린도 교인들이 복음을 받고 복음대로 살기 원하여 그 방해되는 것들을 미리 제거하려고 한다. **Μηδεμίαν ἐν μηδενὶ διδόντες προσκοπήν, ἵνα μὴ μωμηθῇ ἡ διακονία,** ("우리가 이 직책이 훼방을 받지 않게 하려고 무엇에든지 아무에게도 거리끼지 않게 하고…")에서 부정형이 겹쳐 나오는 것은 바울이 비판적인 견해에 대한 반대를 강조하고 있음을 나타낸다. "아무에게도 거리끼지 않게 하고" 에서 **προσκόπη**(거치는 것, 장애)는 바울의 복음 전도에 대한 장애물을 가리킨다. 바울은 자신의 사역이 전혀 하나님의 은혜를 받는 데 장애가 되지 않았음을 확신하고 있다. 휴즈는 바울은 평소에 그리스도를 위한 그의 사역에 있어서 조그마한 "거치는 것" (**προσκόπη**, stumbling)도 주의 깊게 피하였

536) Plummer, 191.

537) Windisch, 202; Thrall, 455, 주, 1850.

음을 지적한다.[538] 여기서 "거리끼는 것"은 대적자들의 비난으로 인한 고린도 교인들의 바울에 대한 오해를 가리킨다. 바울은 그의 화해의 사역을 수행함에 있어서 모든 비난의 여지를 미리 봉쇄하려는 것이다.

바울은 "거리끼는 것"으로 말미암아 자신의 개인적 명예훼손이 문제가 아니라 복음 사역이 훼방 받는 것(μωμηθῇ)이 문제 였다. 원래 μωμηθῇ(비난받다)라는 말은 조롱과 비웃음의 헬라신의 이름인 μῶμος에서 왔다.[539] 바울은 그의 사역이 조롱거리가 되는 것이 두려웠다. 그러므로 바울은 고린도 교인들에게 자신의 비난에 대해 분명히 해명함으로써 하나님께로 사람들을 인도하는 그의 사역이 훼방 받지 않기를 원했다. 만일 해명이 실패할 경우 그 모든 조롱은 복음 사역이 아닌 바울 자신에게로 돌아가게 되기를 바라는 것이다.[540] 바울은 복음 전도자로서 회중에게 모범이 되어야 하는 자신의 책임을 잘 알고 있다. 고린도 교인들은 바울의 정직성을 의심했을 것이다. 바울의 변덕스러운 여행 계획취소(1:17), 그의 고통을 참지 못하는 성품(4:7-12), 또는 자천을 하지 않는 다고 하다가 자천하는 것(3:1, 4:1), 금전 문제(7:2; 11:7; 12:14-18) 등일 수 있다. 그는 이제 고린도 교인들이 문제 삼는 것들을 다 털어놓고 설명해야 한다고 생각했다. 그래야 고린도 교인들이 하나님의 은혜를 받을 수가 있다. 그러나 그는 꺼리길 것이 전혀 없었다.

538) Hughes는 여기서 "훼방"(προσκόπη)이란 말이 희귀한 말이지만 바울이 자주 쓰고 있음을 지적한다(롬 9:32, 33, 14:13, 20; 고전 8:9; 벧전 2:8). ἐγκοπή("장애", 고전 9:12)도 역시 희귀한 말이다(Hughes 221, 주 63).

539) Hughes, 221.

540) Martin, 171, Plummer, 192.

자신은 아무 것도 "거리끼는 것" 을 고린도 교인들 앞에 놓은 것이 없기 때문이었다. 그는 "육체를 따르는 자찬" 도 즐겨하지 않았다. 그는 욕심도 없었다(12:14-18). 그는 하나님의 변화시키는 능력을 가로막는 어떤 이기적인 동기나 그 어떤 무엇도 없었다(1:12; 4:2). 다시 말하지만, 바울의 관심은 자신의 개인의 명예회복을 위한 변명이 아니었다(12:19).[541] 사실 5장 11절 이후 바울의 그의 사역의 순수성과 진정성에 대해서 말해왔다. 그의 사역의 동기는 죄인을 위해 죽으신 그리스도의 사랑으로 말미암은 것이었다. 구원의 새 시대를 선포하는 하나님의 말씀을 그대로 전해왔다. 그는 전혀 자신의 유익을 위해 사역하지 않았고(5:15), 다만 복음의 진보를 위한 것이었다. 그러나 이제 보다 구체적으로 다시 자신에 대한 고린도 교인들의 의구심을 언급하면서 깨끗이 씻어 내야 한다. 문제는 이런 사도직의 순수성을 자신이 스스로 변명하고 자찬함으로써(아무리 진실이라 해도) 자찬한다는 오해를 받아야 하는 어려움이다. 그러나 그렇게 안 하면 고린도 교인들의 오해가 지속되거나, 적들에게 계속 미혹 받아서 결과적으로 고린도 교인들이 하나님의 은혜를 받지 못하고 복음 사역이 훼방 받게 됨으로 자찬을 하는 수밖에 없었다(5:12; 6:2; 11:16-18; 12:1).

복음은 오만한 불신자들에게는 거치는 것이 되게 마련이다(고전 1:23; 갈 5:11). 그러나 화해의 복음 전도자가 적절치 못한 행위나 그의 전하는 말씀과 상치되는 행위로 불신자 앞에 "거치는 돌" 을 놓는 것은 용서받을 수 없다(마 23:13). 그리스도 안에서 변화시키는 하나님의 능력을 전하는 목사가 그와는 상반된 행위를 했

541) Barrett, 184; Martin, 171, 재인용.

을 때 불신자들로 하나님을 조롱하게 만든다.[542] 바울은 고린도 교회에 대해서 양심에 거리끼는 일없이 거룩하고 진실하고 정직하게 일했다(4:2; 12:11). 그래도 이렇듯이 많은 오해가 생겼다면, 바울 보다 못한 우리는 얼마나 더 주의해야 할 것인가 칼빈은, "사단은 궤계를 써서 교역자들의 실수를 찾아서 복음을 불명예롭게 하려 한다. 사람들이 복음사역 자체를 경멸하도록 만들면 모든 복음의 진보가 파괴되기 때문이다. 그러므로 그리스도를 잘 섬기려고 결심한 이들은 그의 복음 사역의 명예를 보전하기 위해 온갖 조심을 다하여 처신해야 한다" 고 경계한다.[543]

4. "오직 모든 일에 하나님의 일군으로 자천하며 많이 견디는 것과 환난과 궁핍과 곤난과…" (**ἀλλ᾽ ἐν παντὶ συνίσταντες ἑαυτοὺς ὡς θεοῦ διάκονοι, ἐν ὑπομονῇ πολλῇ, ἐν θλίψεσιν, ἐν ἀνάγκαις, ἐν στενοχωρίαις**). "모든 일에" (**ἐν παντὶ**)은 4절 이하에서 6절까지 언급되는 일련의 바울의 고난과 특징들을 가리킨다. 그 모든 고난과 특징 앞에 여기서와 같이 모두 **ἐν**이 붙어있다. 이 모든 일에 있어서(**ἐν**) 바울은 "하나님의 일군으로 자천한다 (자신들을 나타낸다, 증거한다, 평가한다)" 는 뜻이다. "하나님의 일군" (**θεοῦ διάκονοι**)으로 자천하는 내용은 4장 2절이나 11장과 12장에 나타나는 자찬의 성격과 크게 다름없이 그리스도적 모델을 닮은 바울의 인격과 행위에 대한 것이다. 주의할 것은 **διάκονοι**가 주격으로서 "우리가 우리 자신들을 하나님의 일군들

---

542) Filson, 346.

543) Hughes, 221 재인용.

로 자천하는 것(나타내는 것)"이 아니라, "우리가 하나님의 일군으로서 모든 일에 자신들을 자천한다(나타낸다)"는 것이다. 우리를 자천하는 것이 강조되는 것이 아니라, 모든 일을 하나님의 일군답게 수행하는 것이 강조된다. 이 말은 역으로 생각하면 바울은 자신을 사도로 자천할 필요가 없는 것이다. 그는 스스로 사도인 것을 분명히 알고 있었기 때문이다. 다만 사도로서 수행한 일들을 말할 필요가 있다는 것이다. 바울은 사도로서 진실성을 가지고 (5:11-13), 환난과 핍박 중에도(6:4-10; 11:23-33) 복음을 고린도 교인들에게 전했다.

고린도전서 4장 3-5절에서 그는 사람의 판단에 대해서는 관심을 갖지 않는다고 했다. 또 고린도후서 3장 1절에서는 자신은 자천이 필요 없다고 했다. 그러나 고린도후서 4장 2절과 5장 12절에서 바울은 사람들의 자신에 대한 평가에도 관심을 갖고 있다. 본문에서 다시 사람들의 평가에 주의를 하는 것으로 나타난다. 바울의 의도는 자신은 사람들의 평가에 그렇게 관심을 두지 않으나(언제나 주님의 종으로서 양심대로 살기 때문에), 대적자들의 자신에 대한 악의적인 평가로 인해서 혹 고린도 교인들이 오해하지 않도록 하기 위해서 대적자들의 잘못된 평가에 대해서 관심을 갖는 것이라고 본다. 마틴은 고린도 교인들을 향한 바울의 사랑하는 마음과 어려운 고린도 교회 상황이 자찬을 하지 않겠다는 처음 생각을 이겼다고 한다.[544] 그는 그의 대적자들과 같이 육체를 따라 자랑하는 것을 원하지 않으나, 역시 고린도 교인들의 오해를 불식시키고 자신과의 교제를 계속할 수 있게 하기 위해서 육체적 자랑을

544) Martin, 172.

억지로 한다(11:16-18; 12:11).[545] 사실 10장 이하에서 바울은 "육체적인 자찬"도 하고 있으나 그의 대적자들이 "육체적 자찬"과 함께 바울의 "육체적 결핍"을 지적함에 따라 어쩔 수 없는 대응 조치라고 해명한다. 그런 자찬의 내용도 진실만을 말한다고 했다(4:2; 12:6). 여기서도 그의 자찬의 목적은 자신의 자랑을 통한 유익이 아니라 어디까지나 복음 사역에 훼방 받지 않고 복음을 받은 고린도 교인들이 자신을 오해하여 복음자체를 불신하는 일이 없도록 하기 위한 것이다.

"많이 견디는 것"(ὑπομονῇ πολλῇ)은 "시험 중에 참으면서 구원을 기다리는 자세"이다.[546] 바울은 계속되는 여러 가지 환난에서 인내함으로 견디었다. 고린도후서 12장 12절에서는 인내를 사도의 자격 가운데 첫 번째 요소로 언급하였다. 명사형은 주로 고린도후서와 로마서에 나온다(고후 1:6과 12:12; 롬 5:3, 4, 15:4, 5). 동사형(ὑπομένειν)으로도 다른 바울 서신에서 골고루 나온다(롬 2:4, 7, 3:25, 8:35, 9:22; 고전 4:12, 9:12, 13:7; 살전 3:1, 5; 딤후 2:10, 12, 24). 이 덕목이 자주 사랑 다음으로 언급되어 그 중요성을 들어낸다(살전 1:3; 딤전 6:11; 딤후 3:10; 딛 2:2; 참조, 갈 5:22). 예수님은 종말론적 구원과 관련하여 인내의 중요성을 강조하셨다(마 10:22; 24:13; 막 13:13; 눅 8:15; 21:19). 70인 역에도 희망을 갖고 견디는 뜻으로 나오고 시락서에도 덕목 가운데 자주 나온다(2:14, 16:13, 17:24, 41:2). 마카비4서에는 신약의 경우처럼 종말론적인 인내에 대한 언급들이 있다(17:12, 17, 23). 바울은 이런 인내의 자

545) Barrett, 185; Furnish, 354.

546) C. Spicq, "ΥΠΟΜΟΝΗ, patientia," *RsPhTh* (1930), 83-106, 특히 103이하(Martin, 173, 재인용).

세로 아래 기록된 환난과 핍박을 견디었음으로 이 덕목을 제일 먼저 썼다. 환난은 그리스도인들에게 인내를 얻게 한다(롬 5:3; 약 1:3). 그러나 그리스도인이 환난 중에 얻는 인내를 그리스도의 인내와 직접 연결하는 경우가 없는 것이 이상하나 암시적인 것은 있다(참조, 고전 4:12; 살후 3:5; 행전 5:41; 히 12:2-3). 바울은 4절 하반절에서부터 말하는 그가 당한 여러 가지의 고난 중에서 인내하면서 복음 전도자의 책임을 다했다고 함으로서 사도로서의 진정성을 증거 한다.

"많이 견디는 것"에 이어 나오는 4절 하반절에서 5절에 걸쳐 언급되는 고난의 조목들은 3개로 되어있고 각기 3개의 항목으로 되어 있다. 첫째 항목은 일반적인 고난의 개념으로서 "환난과 궁핍과 곤란"이고, 둘째 항목은 구체적으로, "매 맞음과, 갇힘과, 요란한 것(난동, ἀκαταστασία)"이며, 셋째 항목은 생존의 고통들로서, "수고로움과 자지 못함과, 먹지 못함"이다. 더 자세한 바울의 고통에 대한 기록은 11장 23이하에 있고 또 사도행전에 있다. 트롤은 이 부분이 Dio Chrysostom의 고상한 인격자에 대한 묘사와 비슷하다고 한다.[547)] 그러나 그는 에녹서2서 66장 6절과의 관련설에 대해서는 회의적이다.[548)] 그러나 5절에 나오는 6개의 단어 가

547) Thrall, 457; R. Hoiestad, 22-27.

548) Thrall, 457을 보라. Windisch(206), Bultmann(171), Kleinknecht(264-5)은 에녹2서에서 에녹이 자기 아들을 훈계하는 대목에 나오는 덕목들에 바울이 의존하고 있다고 보나, Thrall은 Fitzgerald의 주장을 따라서 더 초기의 것으로 보이는 에녹2서의 다른 판(B)에는 본문의 고난에 대한 기록이 없다는 사실을 중시하면서, 에녹2서 A판은 후대의 것으로 바울의 말이 첨가된 것으로 본다. 그러므로 에녹2서와 고린도후서는 관련이 없다는 것이다. J. T. Fitzgerald, *Cracks in an Earthen Vessel: An Examination of the Catalogues of Hardships in the Corinthian Correspondence*, SBLDS 99(Atlanta, Ga.: Scholars Press, 1988), 16-17.

운데 5개가 11장 23절과 27절에 나오고, 그 중에 4개의 말은 바울 서신에서 이 두 본문에만 나온다. 위에서 지적했듯이 본문의 배경으로 "주의 종의 지침서"를 제안하는 것은 추론적일 뿐이다.[549] 본문의 고난과 덕목들은 사도행전이나 바울 서신에 나오는 바울의 실제적 고난과 덕목과 일치되므로 바울이 자기 경험에 비추어 썼다고 보는 것이 자연스럽다. 만일 독자들도 아는 어떤 추론적인 문서가 있었다면, 바울의 열거한 고난들이 그런 주의 종의 지침에 합당하므로 바울의 사도직의 순수성을 인정받는데 더욱 설득력이 있었을 것이다.[550]

첫째 항목의 첫 조목은 "환난"(ἐν θλίψεσιν)이다. 바울은 그리스도의 종이 겪어야할 일반적인 고난의 개념을 먼저 말한 후에 보다 구체적인 고난을 말한다. 바울은 전도 여행 중 도처에서 많은 환난을 겪었다(행 13:5, 14:19, 17:5, 18:12, 19:29). 빌립보에서는 바울은 옥에 갇히기도 하고 매도 맞았다(행 16:22-23). 고린도에서도 유대인들에게 잡혀서 아가야 총독 갈리오에게 갔으나 갈리오는 유대교 문제를 간섭하지 않겠다고 함으로 더 큰 화는 면했다(행 18:12-17). "환난"(θλῖψις)이란 다른 서신에서는 그렇게 많지 않고(히 10:33, 11:37; 약 1:27), 주로 바울 서신에 집중되어 있고, 그 중에서도 고린도후서에서 가장 많이 나온다(1:4, 6, 8, 2:4, 4:8, 17, 7:4, 5, 8:2, 13). 로마서와 데살로니가 전서에 각기 4번씩 나오는데 두 번째로 많은 것이다(롬 2:9, 5:3, 8:35, 12:12; 살전 1:6, 3:3, 4, 7; 살후 1:4, 6, 7). 고린도전서와 에베소서, 디모데 전서에는 각기 한 번씩만 나온다(고전 7:26; 엡 3:13; 딤전 5:10). 요한복음에서 환난

549) Thrall, 457.

550) 6:4-10의 문장구조에 더 자세한 토의는 Martin, 160-164와 Hughes, 226, 주 67을 보라.

은 제자들의 세상에서의 존재 형태 그 자체이다(요 16:33). 그러나 신실한 그리스도의 사람에게는 환난 중에 오히려 하나님의 능력이 나타나므로 그를 그리스도의 사랑에서 끊을 수 없다고 했다(롬 8:35). 그의 사역은 고통으로 점철되어 있으나, 그는 하나님의 진실한 사역자로 인정받는다는 것이다.[551]

둘째 조목은 "궁핍"(ἐν ἀνάγκαις)이다. "궁핍"(ἀνάγκη)은 스트레스를 받는 것을 의미한다.[552] 그러나 결핍의 개념이 들어 있다.[553] 복음을 전하면서 경험하는 궁핍의 고난은 진정한 사도의 표시이다(빌 4:12). 그러나 그의 가장 큰 궁핍함은 복음을 다 전하지 못하는 데서오는 궁핍이다.[554] "복음을 전하지 아니하면 내게 화가 있을 것임이로라"(고전 9:16).

셋째 조목은 "곤란"(ἐν στενοχωρίαις)이다. στενοχωρία(스테노코리아)는 원래 벗어나기 힘든 좁은 틈이라는 뜻이며 괴로움이란 의미가 된다(고후 4:8, 12:10; 롬 8:35).[555] 4장 8절에서는 "우겨쌈을 당하여도 '싸이지 아니한다'(οὐ στενοχωρούμενοι)"고 했다. 사역 중에 곤란한 일을 만나도 그 일이 그의 사역을 막지는 못했다. 진퇴양난의 상황에서 결국 하나님께서는 언제나 피할 길을 마련해 주셨다(고전 10:13).

이상의 3가지 조목들은 그 의미의 차이에도 불구하고 거의 동의어에 가깝다.[556] 그리스도인은 이런 환난 가운데 처할 때 그 어

---

551) Martin, 173.

552) Martin, 173.

553) Tasker, 93.

554) Hughes, 224.

555) Filson, 347, Martin, 173, 재인용.

556) Thrall, 458; Martin, 173; Furnish, 343; Plummer, 194.

려움이 그리스도를 위해 당하는 것이거나 다른 믿는 형제들을 위해 겪는 것이라면, 그리스도의 능력이 나타나는 기회로 알고 환난 중에 참으며 기뻐할 수 있었다(6:4-10; 12:10; 13:5). 이것이 바울이 그의 환난의 경험을 통해서 배운 귀중한 하나님의 교훈이다.

5. "매 맞음과 갇힘과 요란한 것과 수고로움과 자지 못함과 먹지 못함과…" (ἐν πληγαῖς, ἐν φυλακαῖς, ἐν ἀκαταστασίαις, ἐν κόποις, ἐν ἀγρυπνίαις, ἐν νηστείαις,). 두 번째 항목은 보다 구체적인 고통이며 주로 외부에서 부가된 것들이다. 첫째 고난은 "매 맞음" (ἐν πληγαῖς)이다. 이사야 53장 4절(LXX)의 고난 받는 종의 "맞음" (נָגוּעַ מֻכֵּה)과 같다. 단수와 복수의 차이 뿐이다. 11장 23, 24절에서 바울은 거짓 사도들의 편안한 사도 생활에 비해서 그는 비참하게 맞으면서 사도 생활을 했음을 밝힌다(11:13). 그는 "유대인들에게 사십에 하나 감한 매를 다섯 번 맞았으며" (11:24), 로마인들에게 세 번 몽둥이(태장)로 맞았다(11:25; 참고, 행 16:23). 이런 매 맞은 기록은 바울의 사역의 마지막 기록이 아니라 아직 진행 중임을 기억해야 한다. 이 글을 쓴 뒤에도 사도행전에서 보듯이 그는 아직도 숱한 고난을 겪었어야 했다. 여기서 바울은 이사야서의 고난 받는 종의 고난과, 그리스도의 고난에 비추어 그의 희생적인 고난을 암시한다고 본다.

둘째 고난은 투옥(ἐν φυλακαῖς)이다. 11장 23절에서 바울은 여러 번 옥에 갇혔었다고 한다. 사도행전에는 단 한번 빌립보에서의 투옥만 기록하고 있으나(로마 감옥 생활은 고린도후서 이후이다), 실상 더 많은 감옥 생활(φυλακή)이 있었음을 밝힌다.

셋째 고난은 난동(ἐν ἀκαταστασίαις)이다. 사도행전에서는 군중들에 의한 여러 소요사건들을 기록하고 있다. 비시디아 안디옥(행 13:50), 이고니온(14:5), 루스드라(14:19), 빌립보(16:22), 데살로니가(17:5), 고린도(18:12), 에베소서(19:23-41), 예루살렘(21:27-36)에서 유대인들을 비롯한 군중들의 난동(ἀκαταστασία)으로 위협을 받았다. 한 개인의 위협에 비해, 군중에 의한 위협은 무책임하고, 예측할 수 없는 위험에 노출된다. 그러므로 더 두려운 것이다.

"수고로움과 자지 못함과 먹지 못함과…"는 앞의 외부적인 고난에 비해서 주로 바울 스스로 선택한 고난들이다.[557]

"수고로움"(ἐν κόποις)은 원래 "피로"를 의미하나 사도직을 수행하는 일의 어려움과 일의 결과 피곤함을 다 포함한 괴로움이다.[558] 여기서 바울이 직접 일을 하여 생활하므로 겪는 수고를 포함하는지는 의문이다(행 18:2; 살전 2:9; 살후 3:8; 고전 9:12, 15; 고후 9:7, 9, 10). 여기서 순수한 사도직의 수행만을 언급한다고 보고 바울의 천막 만드는 일을 포함시켜서는 안 된다고 볼 수도 있으나,[559] 그런 일도 넓은 의미에서의 사역이라고 볼 때 "수고로움"(κόπος)에 포함시킬 수도 있다.[560] 그렇게 함으로 교인들에게 경제적 부담을 주지 않겠다는 것이 바울의 사역의 특징이기 때문이다(고후 11:9).

"자지 못함"(ἐν ἀγρυπνίαις)은 단순한 불면증이 아닌 의도적으로나 외적 요인으로 자지 못함(ἀγρυπνία)을 뜻한다. 또 이 말은 "깨어 있음"으로도 번역된다.[561] 바울은 사역에 집중하기 위해서

---

557) Martin, 174.

558) Martin, 174.

559) Hughes, 225.

560) Barrett, 186; Thrall, 458.

561) Hughes, 225; Martin, 174.

일부러 잠을 자지 않았을 것이다. 신변이 위험하여 잠을 잘 수 없었던 때도 있었겠으나, 깨어 기도하면서 자지 못한 적도 있었을 것이다(11:27; 엡 6:18; 히 13:17).

"먹지 못함" (ἐν νηστείαις)은 원래 종교적 금식을 가리키는 말이다[562]. 단순히 음식이 없어서 "굶는다"는 말은 11장 27절에 나오는 λιμός(리모스)이다.[563] 트롤은 "먹지 못함" (νηστεία)이 여기서는 종교적 금식이 아니라 바울이 복음 사역에 깊이 몰두하다가 먹지 못한 경우라고 한다.[564] 그러나 마틴은 종교적 금식을 가리킨다고 본다(마 6:16, 17).[565] 휴즈의 견해는 보다 포괄적이다. "먹지 못함"은 종교적인 금식을 가리키며, 또한 사역에 집중하여 먹지 못한 경우도 가리킨다. 그러나 바울의 선교정책상 남에게 짐이 되기 싫어서 그냥 굶은 것도 포함한다고 했다.[566] 아무도 먹을 음식이 없어서 굶은 경우는 생각지 않으나, 바울의 선교 여행 중 이런 경우가 있었을 것이다. 예를 들어 감옥에 갇혔을 때나, 군중들에게 잡히거나, 배가 파선하였을 경우, 얼마든지 억지로 굶어야 했을 때가 있었을 것이다. 바울이 "먹지 못함" (νηστεία)을 11장 27절의 "굶주림" (λιμός)과 엄격히 구별하여 종교적 금식을 말한다는 증거가 없다. 그러나 여기서 바울은 그의 사역 중에 일어난 모든 먹지 못한 것을 실제로 하나의 종교적 금식으로 취급했을 수도 있다.

562) Liddell & Scott, *A Greek-English Lexicon*, 1175.

563) Thrall, 458.

564) Thrall, 459.

565) Martin, 175; Barrett, 186.

566) Hughes, 226.

6. "깨끗함과 지식과 오래 참음과 자비함과 성령의 감화와 거짓이 없는 사랑과…"(ἐν ἁγνότητι, ἐν γνώσει, ἐν μακροθυμίᾳ, ἐν χρηστότητι, ἐν πνεύματι ἁγίῳ, ἐν ἀγάπῃ ἀνυποκρίτῳ). 6절부터는 이런 어려운 환난들 가운데서 바울이 복음 전도자로서 어떤 내적 반응을 보이며 살았는가에 대한 설명이다.[567] 그 반응은 모두 적극적인 덕목들로 나온다. "깨끗함"(ἐν ἁγνότητι)은 "순결함과 흠이 없음"을 말한다.[568] 특히 도덕적인 깨끗함을 말한다.[569] 어쩌면 7장 2절과 12장 16절에 있는 바울에 대한 비난을 염두에 두고 하는 말일 수도 있다. 또 이것은 성적 순결함을 가리킬 수도 있다(12:20, 21).[570] 그러나 여기서는 무엇보다 바울의 양심이나 의도에 있어서 순결함(ἁγνότης)을 말한다(3:13, 4:2).[571]

"지식"(ἐν γνώσει)은 무엇보다 예수 그리스도 안에 있는 구원의 지식을 가리킨다(5:16, 18-20).[572] 빈디쉬는 고린도전서 12장 8절에 있는 "성령을 따라 얻는 지식"을 가리킨다고 하나 "오래 참음과 자비함"같은 이웃에게 유익을 끼치는 덕목과 함께 있는 이 "지식"(γνῶσις)이란 말이 지식주의적 오만함을 나타낼 수 있는 특정한 개인에게만 계시된 비밀의 지식을 가리킨다고 볼 수 없다[573]. 고린도 전 후서에서 중심 주제와 문제는 하나님의 구원을 아

---

567) Tasker, 93.

568) Martin, 175; Barrett, 186; Filson, 348.

569) Tasker, 93, 94.

570) G. Friedrich, *Amt und Lebensführung: Eine Auslegung von 2 Kor. 6:1-10* (Neukirchen-Vluyn: Neukirchener Verlag, 1963) 42.

571) Martin, 175.

572) Hughes, 187; Tasker, 94; Filson 348; Martin, 175 재인용.

573) Hughes, 227; Martin, 175.

는 지식이며, 이 지식이 헬라주의적 비밀의 지식과 대조되어있는 것이다(2:14, 4:6, 11:6; 고전 8:7; 골 2:3).[574] 특히 고린도후서 4장 6절에서 바울은 자신에게 그리스도와 하나님에 대한 지식이 특별히 계시되었다고 한다. 그러나 그 지식은 이미 다른 이에게도 알려진 소식이며 비밀은 아니다(고전 14:6; 고후 2:14). 고전 4:1에서 "사람이 마땅히 우리를 그리스도의 일군이요 하나님의 비밀을 맡은 자로 여길 지어다"라는 말에서 "하나님의 비밀"(μυστηρίων θεοῦ)은 남이 모르는 바울에게 한정된 계시라는 뜻이라기보다(즉 밀의종교적[密儀宗敎的] 계시가 아니라) 이전에는 감취었다가 이제는 계시된 하나님의 놀라운 구원진리라는 뜻으로 보아야한다.[575] 하나님이 바울에게 이 구원의 지식을 명확하게 계시하였다는 사실을 강조하고 있다(갈 1:8, 9, 12). 그러므로 바울의 사도적 권위를 인정하는 것이 마땅하다는 뜻이다. 본문에서도 바울에게 특별히 계시된 복음 진리에 대한 명확한 지식을 말한다고 본다. 하나님의 계시를 가진 바울은 믿을 만한 사도라는 독자들의 반응을 기대하는 것이다.

그러나 여기서 "지식"(γνῶσις)은 속죄하신 그리스도를 아는 지식과, 이 지식의 목회적 적용까지 포함한다고 본다. 이 말이 "오래 참음과 자비함" 같은 덕목과 함께 쓰인 것은 이 말의 계시적 의미

574) C. K. Barrett, *Essays on Paul* (Philadelphia: Westminster, 1982) 6-14; E. E. Ellis, *Wisdom and Prophecy and Hermeneutic in Early Christianity: New Testament Essays* (Grand Rapids: Wm. B. Eerdmans, 1978); J. Dupon, *Gnosis: la connaissance religieuse dans les épîres de Saint Paul* (Louvain: E. Nauwlaerts/Paris: Gabalda, 1949), 379-416. Martin, 175, 재인용.

575) F. W. Grosheide, *Commentary on the First Epistle to the Corinthians,* NICNT, (Grand Rapids: Wm. B. Eerdmans Publishing Company, 1955), 99.

와 함께 목회 사역적인 의미를 반영한다고 보는 것이다. 그러므로 사도나 하나님의 종이 갖고 있는 하나님의 뜻이나 기독교의 진리를 아는 이해력이나 통찰력, 또는 목회 상황에의 적용능력을 가리킨다(벧전 3:7).[576] 바울의 대적자들은 그리스도를 아는 지식을 오용하고 있으나(10:4, 5, 11:13-15), 바울은 이 지식을 하나님의 뜻에 따라 바르게 사용하고 있다. 복음을 바로 이해하고 바르게 전할 뿐만 아니라 복음에 합당하게 살고 있다. 그러나 어떤 고린도 교회 사람들이 이를 모르고 그의 본질적이 아닌 하찮은 약점들을 가지고 그를 비난한다(10:10; 11:6).

"오래 참음"(ἐν μακροθυμίᾳ)은 주로 인간관계에서 받은 상처나 어려움들에 대한 분노나 복수심을 참는 것을 의미한다.[577] 급한 성미에 반대되는 개념이다. 위의 "인내"(많이 견디는 것, ὑπομονή)는 역경을 불평이나 낙심하지 않고 용기 있게 이기는 힘을 말한다.[578] 휴즈는 "오래 참음"(μακροθυμία)은 교인들이 저지

576) Barrett, 186. Barrett는 Kennedy의 견해를 언급한다. J. N. D. Kelly, *The Epistle of Peter and Jude*, (New York: Harper & Row, Publishers, 1969), ad loc.; C. K. Barrett, *The First Epistle to the Corinthians* (New York: Harper & Row, Publishers, 1968) 37; Martin, 175; Thrall은 여기서 "지식"(γνῶσις)이 벧전 3:7의 경우와 같이 상황을 파악하고 적용하는 통찰이라는 의미를 반대한다. 바울 서신에서 그런 의미로 "지식"(γνῶσις)이 쓰인 경우가 없기 때문이라고 한다. 여기서의 지식은 바울이 전파하는 그리스도와 하나님께 대한 지식을 가리킨다고 한다(459). 그러나 Martin이 지적하는 대로 "지식"(γνῶσις)이란 말과 함께 나오는 "오래 참음과 자비함" 같은 인간관계와 관련된 덕목들은 "지식"(γνῶσις)이란 말이 복잡한 인간관계에 대처하는 기독교적 지식도 포함한다고 볼 수 있다(175). 그 지식은 물론 하나님과 그리스도를 아는 지식에 기초한 지식이다.

577) 약 1:19; 롬 12:19, Martin, 176; Plummer, 196.

578) Plummer, 196.

른 잘못에 대한 바울의 자세를 가리키고, "많이 견디는 것"(ὑπομονή)은 교회 밖의 적들의 악행에 대한 바울의 반응을 나타낸다고 한다.[579] 에베소서 4장 2절에서 바울은 에베소 교인들에게 "모든 겸손과 온유로 하고 '오래 참음'으로 사랑가운데 서로 용납하라"고 권면한다(골 3:12, 13). 마틴은 이런 견해에 수긍하면서도 두 말의 의미의 차이가 별로 없으므로 서로 바꿔 쓸 수 있다고 한다.[580]

"자비함"(ἐν χρηστότητι)은 친절 또는 온유라는 말로 번역된다.[581] 하나님에 대한 사랑의 결과로 다른 사람에 대한 사랑이 나타나는 것을 말한다. 이 말은 여기서와 같이 흔히 "오래 참음"(μακροθυμία)과 함께 쓰인다(갈 5:22; 고전 13:4; 엡 2:7; 딛 3:4). 고린도전서 13장 4절에서 바울은 "사랑은 오래 참고 온유하며(χρηστεύεται)"라고 하는데 여기서는 6절 끝에서 모든 덕목을 마무리하는 의미로 사랑을 언급한다. 진정한 하나님의 사역자는 다른 여러 특성과 함께 자비함(χρηστότης)과 오래 참음으로 그 진정성을 나타낸다(골 3:12, 13). 바울은 자기들의 유익을 찾는 거짓 사도들과 달리 고린도 교인들을 사랑하고 그들의 유익을 위해 일한다.

"성령 안에서"(ἐν πνεύματι ἁγίῳ)라는 말의 번역과 이 구절에서의 역할에 대한 논쟁이 많다. 6장 4절 이후 모든 고통과 덕목 앞에 ἐν이 붙어 있어서 4절에 있는 "모든 일에 하나님의 일군으로 자천한다"는 말과 직결되어 있는데, 우리는 덕목들에 대해서만 주석 해왔으나, 여기서는 "성령"을 따로 놓고 설명하는 것보다 "성령 안에서"라고 설명하는 것이 바울의 사역의 원동력으로서의

579) Hughes, 227.

580) Martin, 176.

581) Martin, 176; Hughes, 227.

성령의 원래의 의미를 더 잘 나타낼 수 있을 줄 안다. 그래서 "성령 안에서 우리는 하나님의 일군으로 자천한다"는 뜻이 된다. 그러나 이 말이 성령인지 인간의 "거룩한 영"인지에 대한 논쟁이 있다. 또 왜 이 말이 여러 덕목들을 열거하는 중간에 나와 있는지에 대해 논의가 있다.

플러머는 성령을 모든 덕의 처음이나 결말에 두지 않고 종속적인 위치에 둔 것은 있을 수 없다고 하면서 여기서 **πνεῦμα ἅγιον**을 성령이 아닌 "거룩한 영"으로 보았다.[582] 바울은 거룩한 영으로 거짓 사역과 진정한 사역을 구별한다는 것이다. 그리고 바울은 하나님의 영인지 사람의 영인지 분간이 안되게 말할 때가 있다고 한다(살후 2:13; 롬 1:4). 특히 에베소서에서 자주 나오는 **ἐν πνεύματι**를 어떤 의미로 사용하였는지 분명하지 않다고 한다(엡 2:22, 3:5, 5:18, 6:18). 그리고 여기서와 같이 관사 없는 **πνεῦμα ἅγιον**가 관사를 가진 경우 보다 더 많음을 지적하였다.[583] 플러머는 웨스트카트(Westcott)의 말을 인용하여, 여기 **πνεῦμα ἅγιον**의 대강의 뜻은 "사람이 하나님과의 친교의 극치에 이르러서 사람의 능력이 최고조에 달해있을 때의 상태로서, 사람이 성령 안에, 성령이 사람 안에 있는 상태를 나타낸다"고 하였다.[584] (여기서 웨스트카트는 플러머와 달리 성령으로 번역하고 있다).

휴즈는 이런 번역에 반대하면서 "성령"으로 번역하는 것이 자연스럽다고 한다.[585] 만일 플러머가 제안하듯, 바울이 여기서 "거

582) Plummer, 196.

583) Plummer, 197.

584) Plummer, 197.

585) Hughes, 228.

룩한 영" 이란 뜻으로 쓰려고 했다면, ἐν πνεύματι ἁγίῳ라고 쓰지 않고 로마서 1장 4절에서의 κατά πνεῦμα ἁγιοσύνης("성결의 영을 따라")의 형태를 따라서 ἐν πνεύματι ἁγιοσύνης("성결의 영 안에서")라고 썼을 것이라고 한다.[586] 그리고 여기서 ἐν πνεύματι ἁγίῳ("성결의 영안에서")이 다른 덕목들 사이에 나오는 것은 이 말 뒤에 오는 말들이 앞의 말들과 달리 두 단어들로 구성된 말들이 나오기 때문이라고 보았다.[587] 이렇게 보면 ἐν πνεύματι ἁγίῳ도 두 단어로 되어 있으며, 이 말 다음에 나오는 두 단어로 된 어군들의 선두에 위치한다. 휴즈는 칼빈을 인용하면서 성령의 열매들과 성령이 함께 나오는 것은 자연스럽다고 한다.[588] 또 그는 스웨트(Swete)의 말을 인용하여, 바울의 글체가 논리적이라기보다는 자유스런 비공식적 편지 글에 가깝다고 하고, 여기서는 바울의 관심은 성령의 인격이 아니라 성령의 은사이며, "성령은 여기서 모든 사역자들의 인격의 중심적 특징이 되어야 하며, 거짓 사도들과 구별되는 하나님의 진실한 사역자에게 공통적인 거룩한 영과 거의 동일하다"라고 한다.[589] 이렇게 스웨트의 견해를 따르면서 위에서 반대한 플러머의 "거룩한 영" 의 번역이 원칙적으로는 틀리지만, 결과적으로는 옳다고 양보한다. 그러나 마틴은 이 말을 "성령" 으로 번역해야 함을 주장하면서 바울이 다른 곳에서 분명히 성령을 말할 때 여기와 같이 관사 없이 쓰인 곳이 많다는 사실을 지적하였다.[590] 계속하여 마틴은 플러머와 같이 사

586) Hughes, 주, 69.

587) Hughes, 226, 주, 67.

588) Hughes, 228.

589) Hughes, 228; H. B. Swete, *The Holy Spirit* (London: Macmillan, 1910), 196-97.

590) 롬 5:5, 9:1, 14:17, 15:13, 16; 고전 6:19, 12:3; 고후 13:13; 살전 1:5, 6, 4:8. Martin, 176-77.

람의 "거룩한 영"으로 보는 바레트의 견해를 반대한다. 바레트는 바울이 πνεῦμα(푸뉴마)를 "인간의 영"으로 말한다는 바울 서신의 예들을 제시하였는데, 마틴은 그 모든 경우 모두 ἅγιος("거룩한")가 없는 것들로서 이 경우와 상관없는 말들임을 바르게 지적하였다.[591] 바울은 인간의 영을 나타낼 때는 πνεῦμα("영")만 쓰고, 성령을 나타낼 때는 반드시 ἅγιος("거룩한")와 함께 써서 구별한다는 것이다.[592]

그러므로 바울이 여기서 성령을 가리키는 것이 확실하다. 그러나 여기서와 같이 관사 없이 쓰인 경우는 성령의 능력을 강조하고, 관사가 있는 경우는 성령의 인격을 나타낸다.[593] "인간의 영"이란 번역은 전혀 틀린 번역이다. 대개의 성경 번역과 학자들이 이를 따른다. 바울은 성령이 그가 나열하는 덕목들을 은사로 주는 것을 나타내고 있으며, 그 덕목들 자체가 성령이 바울의 사역 안에서 역사한다는 증거이다.[594] 그의 직책은 성령이 주신 직책이다(고후 3:8). 더구나 7절의 "하나님의 능력"이란 말도 여기서 성령으로 번역하는 것이 옳다는 것을 지지해준다. 성령의 능력으로 말미암아 혼자서는 질그릇처럼 약한 바울이 하나님의 사역을 성공적으로 수행해 왔다. 성령의 능력이 함께 한다는 사실이 바울의 사도된 증거이다.

"거짓이 없는 사랑"(ἐν ἀγαπῃ ἀνυποκρίτῳ)은 가장 특징적인

---

591) Martin, 177.

592) Thrall은 이를 재확인한다(460).

593) D. P. Francis, "The Holy Spirit. A Statistical Inquiry," *Exp Tim* 96 (1985), 136이하. Martin, 177, 재인용.

594) Bruce, 212; Thrall, 460.

기독교인의 덕목으로서 지금까지 말한 진정한 사도(또는 그리스도인)의 인격의 덕목들을 극적인 고조로 종결 짓는다. 이것이 성령의 첫 열매이므로(갈 5:22) 앞의 ἐν πνεύματι ἁγίῳ을 "성령"으로 해석하는 것이 더욱 옳다는 것이 재확인된다. 아가페 사랑은 하나님의 본성이다(고후 13:11; 요일 4:8, 16). 하나님이 먼저 우리를 사랑하셨고(고후 5:14; 요 3:16), 그리고 우리를 통해 나타나는 사랑이다(요일 4:11). 고린도 교인들이 배우고 따라야할 "더 좋은 길"이다(고전 12:31; 13장 이하). "거짓이 없는"이란 말은 이런 하나님의 사랑에 배치되는 거짓 사랑이 있음을 암시한다. 모든 인간의 사랑이 다 순수한 것은 아니나. 모두에게 유익을 주는 것은 아니다. 바울이 여기서 거짓 사도들의 가장과 위선을 염두에 두면서 자신의 사랑의 순수함을 말한다고 본다. 그러나 바울은 진정한 사랑으로 그의 사역을 수행한다(롬 12:9; 참조, 벧전 1:22). 그의 사랑은 그의 복음 사역을 강권하시는 그리스도의 사랑을 모델로 삼고 있기 때문이다(5:14). 그러므로 그의 사역은 신빙성이 있다.

7. "진리의 말씀과 하나님의 능력 안에 있어 의의 병기로 좌우하고…" (ἐν λόγῳ ἀληθείας, ἐν δυνάμει θεοῦ· διὰ τῶν ὅπλων τῆς δικαιοσύνης τῶν δεξιῶν καὶ ἀριστερῶν). 7절부터 바울은 그의 내적 자질에서 그의 설교 사역으로 주제를 바꾼다. 이제 바울은 자신이 진리의 말씀을 전했음을 자찬한다.

"진리의 말씀"(ἐν λόγῳ ἀληθείας)은 ἀληθείας(진리의)가 속격으로 되어 있어서 이 속격을 어떤 종류의 속격으로 보느냐에 따라서 해석이 달라질 수 있다. 이 속격을 형용사적 의미로 볼 때, "진실한 말씀"이라고 번역된다.[595] 이 같은 경우가 여러 곳에 나타난다(1:12, 13, 2:17, 4:2, 10:11). 그러나 속격을 서술적 의미로 보아서 "진리인 말씀"으로 번역도 가능하다(골 1:5; 엡 1:13).[596] 속격을 목적으로 보고 말씀(λόγος)을 동적인 의미로 보면, "진리의 선포"라는 뜻이 된다. 4장 2절에서 바울 사도가 "진리를 나타낸다"고 하였는데, 그런 의미에서 "복음 진리의 선포"라는 뜻이 가장 적합할 것 같다.[597] 말씀을 선포하는 것은 하나님의 은사이다(고전 12:8). 바울은 하나님께로부터 이 은사를 받아서 말씀을 전하고 있다(고전 15:10, 11). 휴즈는 "복음 진리 말씀"이라고 하면서도 바울의 일반적인 말의 진실함을 나타낼 수도 있다고 한다.[598] 1장에서 바울이 그의 방문 약속의 번복에 대한 이해를 구하는 것에 비춰 보아서 가능한 제안이다. 바레트는 "진리"란 말은 바울의 대적자들의 메시지를 경계하는 의미도 들어 있다고 한다.[599]

"하나님의 능력"(ἐν δυνάμει θεοῦ)은 앞서 3장 초두에서 말한 바와 같이 바울의 사역의 주체가 바울이 아니라 하나님에 의한 것임을 말한다.[600] 오히려 바울은 질그릇같이 연약한 존재이며, 대적자들이 비난하는 것 같이 외적 영광은 없다(4:7, 16). 하나님의 능력은 그의 사역 전반에서 나타났다(4:7-10). 주로 약한 데서 하나님의 능력은 나타났다(12:9; 13:4). 바울의 메시지의 진실성은 그의 설교에서 나타난 하나님의 능력으로 증명되었다(고전 1:18,

595) RSV, Plummer, 197; Héring, 47.

596) Windisch, 206.

597) Hughes, 229, 230; Tasker, 94; Bultmann, 173.

598) Hughes, 230.

599) Barrett, 187.

600) C. H. Powell, *The Biblical Concept of Power* (London: Epworth Press, 1963).

2:4-5, 고후 4:7; 살전 1:5).[601] 하나님의 능력은 그의 대적자들이 생각하는 것처럼 외적인 것으로만 나타나는 것이 아니라 내적인 면이 있다. 즉 새로운 피조물로 변화되는 것이다. 그러므로 12장 12절에서 사도의 표를 말할 때 모든 참음(ἐν πάσῃ ὑπομονῇ)이 표적과 기사 보다 먼저 언급되었다. 위의 사도로서의 덕목 가운데 제일 먼저 언급된 것도 "인내"(ὑπομονή)이다. 어쩌면 인내가 십자가를 참으신 그리스도의 고난에 동참하는 가장 확실한 제자도의 표로 보았기 때문일 것이다(히 12:2; 딤후 2:12; 막 8:34). 인내는 약한 자에게 주시는 하나님의 능력이다.

"의의 병기로 좌우하고…"(διὰ τῶν ὅπλων τῆς δικαιοσύνης τῶν δεξιῶν καὶ ἀριστερῶν). 여기서부터 8절 상반절까지 διὰ로 시작되는 절이 3개가 계속 나온다. 이 전치사의 의미가 조금씩 다르게 쓰였는데, 여기서는 뒤에 나오는 "병기"(ὅπλων)라는 말과 앞에 나온 "진리의 말씀"과 "하나님의 능력" 때문에 도구적인 의미(…로 말미암아)를 나타낸다.[602] 8절의 두 개의 절은 어떤 상황을 통해서 일어나는 부대상황적(附帶狀況的)의미이다. 여기서 διὰ를 쓰는 것은 앞에 나온 열여덟 개의 ἐν과 구별하여 문장 스타일을 바꾸는 것 외에 별다른 의미를 주기 위한 것이 아니라고 본다.

"의의 병기"는 희랍어 속격이 갖는 다양한 의미 때문에 여러 가지 번역이 가능하다.[603] (1) 내용을 나타내는 속격으로 보아서 "의로 만들어진 병기"라고 할 수 있다. 이 경우에 의는 인간의 의로운

601) Hughes, 230.

602) Windisch, 206.

603) Thrall, 461.

행위를 의미한다. (2) 속격은 형용사의 역할로서 관련 명사의 질을 나타낸다. 이 경우에는 "의로운 병기"라고 번역되어 (1)의 경우와 같이 여전히 인간의 의로운 도덕적 행위를 나타낸다. 그러나 이 경우 인간의 의는 은혜의 구원의 시대에 대적자들의 "율법적 의의 복음"에 맞서는 하나님의 은혜로 말미암는 의의 복음을 전하는 바울의 사역을 나타낼 수도 있고, 도덕적으로 불의한 대적자들과 맞서는 사도 바울의 의로움을 나타낼 수도 있다(3:9).[604] (3) 속격을 주격의 의미(또는 기원[起源]의 의미)로 보면 "의가 준비한 병기"로 되어 사람의 의로운 행위가 아닌 하나님의 의가 준비한 병기라는 뜻이 된다.[605] 이 경우 앞에 있는 성령의 역할을 고려하면, 바울에게 내주하는 성령이 주시는 "'의의 병기"라는 뜻이 된다.[606] 이 문맥에서 바울은 자신의 덕목을 열거하고 있으므로 인간의 의로운 행위를 가리킨다고 보는 것이 타당하다.[607] 로마서 6장 13절에서 "너희 지체를 의의 병기로 하나님께 드리라"라고 할 때에도 역시 인간의 의로운 행위를 나타낸다.

"좌우하고"는 우는 공격무기를, 좌는 방패 같은 방어용 무기를 잡는 것을 가리킨다.[608] 한마디로 완전무장을 갖추어 전쟁에 임하는 군인의 자세로서 사도적 임무 수행에 있어서 바울은 오로지 의로운 일만 하였음을 가리킨다. 이것을 바울이 그를 모함하는 대적

604) Martin, 178; Bultmann, 174; Barrett, 189.

605) Plummer, 198.

606) Bruce, 212; Tasker, 94; J. Reumann, *Righteousness in the New Testament*, 52, 53, Martin, 179, 재인용.

607) Thrall, 462, Barrett, 189.

608) Plummer, 198; Windisch, 207; Bultmann; 174; Thrall, 462, 주, 1917, 재인용.

자들에 대해 자신을 항전하는 모습으로 묘사된 비유적 표현이라고 생각하는 것은 너무 지엽적이다. 바울은 평소에도 세상의 악과 맞서 싸워야 하는 그리스도인의 신앙생활과 복음 전파 사명을 이런 군인의 전투자세로 설명한다(10:3, 4; 롬 6:13; 13:12; 엡 6:11 이하; 빌 2:25; 딤전 6:12; 딤후 2:3, 4; 몬 1:2). 트롤은 바울은 유대교의 고난 받는 의인 사상에 입각해서 이렇게 말한다고 한다.[609] 또 쿰란에서도 의와 불의의 싸움을 개인의 영적 싸움과, 또 종말론적 싸움의 차원에서 논하며, 이 때 의의 편에 나타나는 선과 불의의 편에 나타나는 악을 대조한다.[610] 그러나 바울의 말과 일치하는 예는 없다.[611] 뿐만 아니라 냉소주의학파 크레테스(The Cynic Crates)도 철학자의 겉옷과 가방을 가리켜 "신들의 무기들"이라고 한다.[612] 물론 이것과 바울의 표현은 관련이 없다.

8. "영광과 욕됨으로 말미암으며 악한 이름과 아름다운 이름으로 말미암으며 속이는 자 같으나 참되고…"(διὰ δόξης καὶ ἀτιμίας, διὰ δυσφημίας καὶ εὐφημίας· ὡς πλάνοι καὶ ἀληθεῖς). 8절에는 두 개의 διά("…통하여", "말미암아")로 시작되는 절들이 나온다. 앞에서(7절 하반절) 이미 διά가 나왔으나 여기서와 같이 대조적인 말이 없다. 바로 앞에서는 "진리의 말씀과 하나님의 능력, 그리고 의의 병기"같은 바울의 말씀 전파 사역의

609) Thrall, 462.

610) 1QS 1:4-5, Thrall, 462; Barrett, 188; *Testaments of the Twelve Patriarchs*, 6:10; Murphy-O'Connor, *Paul and Qumran*, 57, Martin, 178 재인용.

611) Kleinknecht, *Der leidende Gerechtertigte*, 265, 주, 73을 보라. Martin, 178, 재인용.

612) Windisch, 207; Furnish, 346; A J. Malherbe, *The Cynic Epistles*, SBLSBS 12, (Missoula: Scholars Press, 1977), 66-7; 참조, *Ep.* 23, 72-3. Thrall, 462, 주 191, 재인용.

특징을 말했고, 여기서는 대조적인 단어들을 통해서 바울의 말씀 사역에 대한 적극적인 반응과 부정적인 반응을 보여주고 있다. 역설적인 표현들을 사용하여 고린도 교인들이 바울 자신에 대한 온갖 오해를 버리고 진실한 그의 모습을 보기를 원한다.

"영광과 욕됨으로 말미암으며"(διὰ δόξης καὶ ἀτιμίας). 헬라어 δόξα("영광")은 원래 호평이나 찬사를 의미한다(참조, 요 5:44, 12:43).[613] 어떤 이들의 눈에는 바울은 매우 존경해야 할 사람으로 비쳤고(갈 4:14), 어떤 이들에게는 무시당했다(10:10; 11:23-33; 고전 4:10; 빌 1:15-18; 살후 2:2).

"악한 이름과 아름다운 이름으로 말미암으며"(διὰδυσφημίας καὶ εὐφημίας). 이 절은 앞 절과 다른 뜻이 없이 앞 절의 반복이다. 바울은 교회 안과 밖에서 비난을 받았다(고전 4:13; 롬 3:8). 바울은 아무리 악한 소문도 그에게 해가 될 수 없으며, 반대로 아무리 좋은 소문도 그의 사도로서의 한결 같은 자세를 흐트러뜨리지 못한다고 증거 한다.[614] 어느 정도 훈련받은 복음 사역자라면 자신에 대한 비난에 대해서 적어도 참거나 때로는 반성의 기회로 삼기도 하나, 자신에 대한 칭찬에 대해서는 대개 쉽게 미혹 받아서, 자만심에 취하도록 기회를 노리는 자신의 옛 사람에 대한 경계심을 늦춘다(12:7).[615] 사람들의 비난이나 칭찬에 아랑곳하지 않고 하나님의 평가와 인정만이 그의 관심이라는 의미가 있다. 그런 자세가 바로 그리스도의 자세였다(막 10:17-18; 벧전 2:23).

"속이는 자 같으나 참되고"(ὡς πλάνοι καὶ ἀληθεῖς). 여기서

613) Hughes 231, 주, 74.

614) Hughes, 232.

615) Martin, 180.

부터 10절까지 일곱 개의 ὡς("…같이")가 나온다. 원래 "…같이"라는 뜻의 전치사이나 여기 문맥에서는 오히려 대조적 의미로 쓰인다.[616] 바울의 외적 모습과 참된 실재를 대조적으로 묘사하면서 참된 실재를 역설직으로 강조하고 있다.[617] 그런데 그의 외적 모습이 사실을 그대로 나타내는 경우도 있고, 그렇지 않은 경우도 있다. 여기서는 바울은 실제로 속이지 않았으나 속이는 자로 오해받았다고 한다. 그의 고린도 방문 계획 취소 때문일 수도 있고(1:15-22), 그의 재정 관리 문제 일 수도 있다(7:2; 12:16-18). 그의 사도로서의 자격이나 그의 메시지에 대한 비난일 수도 있다(10:7, 10).[618] 어쩌면 기독교를 증오하는 유대인들로부터 받는 비난일 수도 있다.[619] 바울은 이런 비난에 대해서 여러 번 변명한다(롬 9:1-2; 고후 11:31; 갈 1:20). 심지어 바울이 죽은 후에도 이런 오명이 따라 다녔다.[620]그러나 누가 뭐라고 해도 바울은 양심적으로나 하나님 앞에서나 떳떳했다(4:2, 5:11). 그는 하나님의 부르심에 합당하게 행했고, 고린도 교인들에게 대해서 진실했다. 11장에서와 달리 바울은 여기서 비교적 조용하게 이런 비난을 받아들이면서 자신의 진실함을 밝힌다. 그는 결국 진실이 드러나리라는 확신을

616) Martin, 180; 참조, Plummer, 199.

617) Thrall, 463.

618) Hughes, 233; Barrett, 189.

619) Thrall, 464.

620) 2세기 위서(僞書)인 클레멘트의 글(Pseudo-Clementine Literature)에서 바울이 마술사 시몬(Simon Magus)에 비교된다. 2 세기 작품, Hughes, 233, 재인용; H. J. Schopes, *Theologie und Geschichte des Judenchristentums* (Tübingen: J. C. B. Mohr, 1964), 128, 431; D. A. Hagner, "Paul in Modern Jewish Thought," in *Pauline Studies: Essays Presented to F. F. Bruce (Exeter:* Paternoster Press, 1980), 143-65.

갖고 있다. 한편 그리스도도 속이는 자로 소문이 났었다(마 27:63). 그러나 실제로 속이는 자는 적그리스도이다(요2서 7; 고후 11:3-5).

9. "무명한 자 같으나 유명한 자요 죽는 자 같으나 보라 우리가 살고 징계를 받는 자 같으나 죽임을 당하지 아니하고"(ὡς ἀγνοούμενοι καὶ ἐπιγινωσκόμενοι, ὡς ἀποθνῄσκοντες καὶ ἰδοὺ ζῶμεν, ὡς παιδευόμενοι καὶ μὴ θανατούμενοι,). "무명한 자 같으나 유명한 자요"(ὡς ἀγνοούμενοι καὶ ἐπιγινωσκόμενοι)에서 두 개의 분사가 모두 수동태이므로 바울에 대한 평가가 외부에서 온 것임을 나타낸다. 여기서는 바울이 "무명한 자"라는 것이 어느 정도 사실임을 의미한다. 바울은 현재 고린도 교인들에게 그의 사도직의 진정성을 스스로 변호해야 할 정도로 무명하다고 느꼈을 것이다. 휴즈는 바울이 옛날 유명한 길리기아 다소의 사울에서 무명의 사도 바울로 바뀐 것을 의미한다고 한다.[621] 옛날에는 유명했으나 지금은 무명해졌다는 말이다. 바울은 비록 세상에서는 알려지지 않았으나 하나님께 알려지고 인정받게 되기를 원했다(고전 13:12). 또는 바울은 세상에는 알려지지 않았으나 교회에서는 알려졌음을 나타내는 것일 수도 있다.[622] 그러나 한편 바울은 교회 내에서도 사도로서의 자격이 부족하다는 평을 받았다(5:12; 12:12). 초대교회에서 적어도 초창기에는 그는 다른 기둥 사도들에 비해서 잘 알려지지 않은 사도였다.[623] "무명하다"는 것이

621) Hughes, 234.

622) Windisch, 208; Plummer, 199; Thrall, 465.

623) Filson, 350; Plummer, 199; Tasker, 95.

세상에서 그렇다는 것인지, 교회 안에서도 그렇다는 것인지, 아니면 모두에서 다 그렇다는 것인지 분명치 않다. 그러나 분명한 것은 바울 자신은 이런 외적인 명성의 유무에는 관심이 없었다. 다만 하나님께 자신이 알려 지기를 원했다(고전 13:12).[624]

"죽는 자 같으나 보라 우리가 살고"(ὡς ἀποθνῄσκοντες καὶ ἰδοὺ ζῶμεν). 이 말은 시편 118편 17절(117:17, LXX), ("내가 죽지 않고 살아서," οὐκ ἀποθανοῦμαι, ἀλλὰ ζήσομαι)과 유사하다. 아래에서 보듯이 다음 말도 같은 시편의 말과 유사하다. 그러나 이 말은 그리스도의 죽음과 부활을 암시하는 가장 핵심적인 바울의 사역의 특징이다(5:15). 바울이 여기서 말하는 모든 역설적인 사역의 신학적이고 목회적인 의미는 그리스도의 죽음과 부활의 역설에 의존한다.[625] 그리스도의 죽음과 부활의 역설 때문에 바울의 역설적인 사역은 그 신빙성과 설득력을 갖는다. 그러나 "죽는 자 같으나"는 신학적인 의미뿐만이 아니라 바울의 실제적인 모습이다. 그는 실제로 여러 번 죽음에 직면했다. 바울의 사역은 항상 죽음에 노출된 위험을 무릅쓴 사역이었다(행 14:19; 고전 4:9; 15:30; 고후 1:8, 9; 11:23-26). 그럼에도 그는 죽지 않고 지금까지

624) Héring은 이런 바울의 입장을 이사야서의 고난받는 종에 비교한다(사 52:2, 3). 고난의 종처럼 하나님에게도 버림받은 비참한 처지라는 것이다(57). 바울이 안디옥 교회에서 선교사 파송을 받을 때 이사야 42:6과 49:6을 인용하고 있다(행전 13:47). 그러나 Martin과 Thrall은 이에 동의하지 않는다. Thrall은 실제로 병행구가 하나도 없다는 것을 지적한다(Thrall, 464, 주 1937; Martin 181). 그러나 위에서 본 바와 같이 5절의 "매맞음"(ἐν πληγαῖς)과 이사야 53:4의 "맞음"(ἐν πληγῇ)과, 아래에서 9절의 "징계를 받는 자"(παιδευόμενοι)는 이사야 53:5의 "징계"(παιδεία)와 병행하는 말들이 있다..

625) Bultmann, 189.

살아서 일하고 있다. 그리스도를 살리신 하나님의 능력이 그와 함께 하기 때문이다(13:4). 바로 이것이 그의 사도직의 진정성을 확실히 보여 주지 않는가

때로 바울은 죽는 것과 사는 것을 신학적인 의미로 말할 때가 있다. 그리스도인이 그리스도와 함께 죽과 사는 것은 신학적인 의미이다(5:14; 롬 6:1-4; 갈 2:20). 실제적으로나, 신학적 의미로 보거나, 바울은 늘 죽고 산다. 그러므로 외적으로는 볼모양이 없으나, 실제적으로나, 신학적으로나, 바울은 그리스도의 죽고 사는 모델을 닮은 모범적인 그리스도의 사도이다.[626] 그리스도의 죽고 사는 효능은 그리스도 안에 있는 사람에게만 나타나는 것이다(5:17). 그리스도 안에 있는 사람도 옛 시대의 잔존 세력인 죽음에 의해 여전히 위협받으나 그리스도의 생명력으로 다시 사는 것이다(4:7-10). 현재의 사역에서는 죽고 사는 것이 계속되나, 영원한 영광이 기다리고 있다(4:17; 롬 8:18). 그리고 최후의 심판 때에 이 땅에서의 사역에 대한 최종적 평가를 받게 될 것이다(5:10; 고전 3:13-15). 그러나 본문에서 바울은 현재의 자신의 사역에서 그리스도적 죽음과 다시 사는 유형이 나타남으로 최후 심판 이전에 하나님의 인정을 받았다고 본다(1:23; 3:5; 4:2, 6, 7-10, 5:11; 6:1, 참조, 11:13). 일종의 예비적 재판에서 승소했다고 본다(13:6).

"징계를 받는 자 같으나 죽임을 당하지 아니하고" (**ὡς παιδευόμενοι καὶ μὴ θανατούμενοι**). 이 말도 앞의 말과 같이 시편 118편 18절(117:18, LXX)과 유사하다: "주께서 나를 시험하셨으나 죽지는 않게 하시고" (**παιδεύων ἐπαίδευσέν με ὁ κύριος**

626) Plummer, 200; Barrett, 189-90; Bultmann, 175; Furnish, 358.

καὶ τῷ θανάτῳ οὐ παρέδωκέν με). 앞 절과 마찬가지로 그리스도의 죽고 사는 유형이 암시되어 있다. 그러나 징계란 말은 신학적 사고보다는 실제적 사역을 반영하는 말이다. "징계"라는 말은 실제로 죄에 대한 징계라기보다 여러 가지 모양의 고난과 어려움을 가리키는 말이라고 본다. 시편 118편은 시편기자가 고난을 하나님의 징계로 보고 있다. 또 유대교에서 하나님의 징계는 사랑의 매로 생각한다.[627] 또 바울 자신도 고린도전서 11장 32절에서 징계는 그리스도인들의 유익을 위한 것이라고 한다.[628] 문제는 바울 스스로가 이런 고난들을 징계로 보는지 아니면 그의 대적자들의 생각인지 불확실하다. 대부분의 주석가들은 두 가지 가능성을 다 받아들인다. 바울 자신, 또는 그의 적들이 그의 고난을 그에 대한 징계로 생각하고 있다고 한다. 고난을 통해서 바울은 그리스도의 현존을 깨닫고 하나님과 더 가깝게 된다고 보았다고 한다.[629] 또는 과거 기독교를 핍박하던 교만한 바리새인으로서 징계를 받는다고 생각했다고 한다.[630] 그래서 그는 자신을 죄인의 괴수라고 생각하는가 (딤전 1:15). 아니면 그의 대적자들이 그의 고난을 그의 과거와 현재의 죄에 대한 징계라고 하는가.[631] 여기의 말이 시편 118편의 내용과 유사하다 해도 바울 자신이 징계를 받는다고 생각했다고 볼 수 없다. 바울이 시편 기자의 글을 인용하였다 해서 반드시 그와 자신을 동일시하고 있다고 볼 수는 없다. 다만 시

---

627) 잠 3:11; 욥 5:17; 시 94:12; 119:67, 75; 예 31:18; 히 12:5-13; 계 3:19, 등. Hughes, 235 재인용; Martin, 182.

628) Windisch, 208; Barrett, 190.

629) Plummer, 200; Martin, 183; Filson, 350; Thrall, 466.

630) Plummer, 200; Hughes, 235.

631) Plummer, 200, Hughes, 235; Martin, 183; Thrall, 466.

편 기자의 받는 고난과 그가 받는 고난의 유사성 때문에 귀에 익은 시편 구절과 유사하게 말하고 있을 뿐이다. 그의 대적자들이나 다른 이들이 보기에 극심한 여러 고난을 겪는 바울이 하나님께 징계를 당한다고 잘못 생각할 수 있다는 것이다. 퍼니쉬는 여기의 ώς를 "마치 … 같이"(as though)로 보고 있다.[632] 즉 실제와 다르다는 뜻이다. 또 ώς(마치… 같이)와 καί(그리고)는 대조적 의미를 가지고 있으므로, "마치 징계를 받는 자 같으나 죽임을 당하지는 않고"라고 번역해야 한다.[633] 위의 학자들은 이런 대조적인 의미를 인정하면서도 시편 118편(117편, LXX)과의 유사성에 집착하여 바울이 받는 징계로 보고 있다.[634] 그러나 몇 가지 이유로 바울은 앞에서 지적하였듯이 본문에서 ώς로 시작하는 모든 말들은 외적인 현상을 나타내는 것뿐이며, καί 다음에 오는 두 번째 말이 진실을 나타낸다. 물론 본문에서 경우에 따라 외적인 현상이 사실을 나타내는 경우도 있다. 바로 앞의 "죽는 자 같으나 보라 우리가 살고"도 실제로 바울의 사역에서 죽음에 직면하는 사실을 가리킨다고 했다. 그러나 그 앞의 "속이는 같으나 참되고"란 말은 바울이 실제로 속였다는 사실을 가리킬 수 없고, 다만 속이는 자처럼 오해받은 사실을 가리킬 뿐이다. 여기서도 바울이 받는 여러 고난으로 볼 때 극심한 징계를 당하는 것 같이 보인다. 그러나 죽지는 않는 걸로 보아서 그 징계가 바울의 죄에 대한 것이 아니라 의인의 고통 같은, 그리스도의 고난과 같은 희생적인 것이라는 의미가 있

632) Furnish, 358; Thrall, 466 재인용.

633) Martin, 180; C. F. D. Moule, *An Idiom Book of New Testament Greek* (Cambridge: University Press, 1979), 178.

634) Hughes, 235; Martin, 182-83; Thrall, 466.

다. 이런 해석이 다른 해석과 일치된다. 한편으로 그런 징계로 보이는 고난 중에 그는 영적으로 더욱 강해 졌다(12:9). 전체 어휘는 시편 118편과 같으나 의미는 오히려 이사야 53장 4-5절에서의 고난받는 종의 대속적인 고난의 묘사와 흡사하다. 실제로 이사야 53장 5절에서 그가 "징계를 받음으로 우리가 평화를 얻었도다"에서 παιδεία("징계")라는 명사가 쓰였다. 이 말의 분사형(παιδευόμενοι, "징계를 받음")이 본문에 나타난다. 더구나 앞에서 본 대로 6장 5절에서의 "매맞음"(ἐν πληγαῖς)이 이사야 53장 4절의 "맞음"(ἐν πληγῇ)과 상관된다고 볼 때 관련성을 무시할 수 없다. 더구나 바울이 그가 받는 고난을 그의 죄에 대한 징계로 생각했다면 그리스도 안에서 새로운 피조물로서 새로운 구원의 시대를 선포하고 죄에서의 해방을 선언하는 그의 복음에 역행하는 것이 된다(5:17; 롬 8:1). 그러므로 여기서 바울은 외적으로 볼 때(그의 대적자이든, 고린도 교인들이든지) 바울이 징계를 받는 것처럼 보이나, 실제로는 그렇지 않다는 뜻이다.

10. "근심하는 자 같으나 항상 기뻐하고 가난한 자 같으나 많은 사람을 부요하게 하고 아무 것도 없는 자 같으나 모든 것을 가진 자로다"(ὡς λυπούμενοι ἀεὶ δὲ χαίροντες, ὡς πτωχοὶ πολλοὺς δὲ πλουτίζοντες, ὡς μηδὲν ἔχοντες καὶ πάντα κατέχοντες). "근심하는 자 같으나 항상 기뻐하고"(ὡς λυπούμενοι ἀεὶ δὲ χαίροντες)에서 바울은 실제로 온갖 어려운 일들로 근심할 수밖에 없을 때가 있었음을 말한다. 불신 유대인들의 구원에 대한 염려도 있었고, 교회에 대한 염려도 늘 있다고 했다(고후 2:1, 4; 11:28).[635] "염려"(λύπη)라는 말이 바울 서신에서

23번 나오는 데 그 중에 18번이 고린도후서에 나온다. 이것을 보면 바울의 염려 중에서 고린도 교회에 대한 염려가 제일 큰 비중을 차지한다고 말할 수 있다. 빌립보서에 "기뻐하라" (χαράχαίρειν)는 말이 16번 나오는 것과 대조적이다.[636] 그러나 고린도후서에서도 이와 거의 같은 횟수로 바울은 기뻐한다는 말을 자주 한다(2:3; 7:4; 7, 9, 13; 13:9; 롬 12:12, 15; 14:17; 15:13, 32; 16:19; 고전 16:17; 갈 5:22; 빌 1:4; 2:17; 3:1; 4:10; 살전 2:19 이하; 3:9; 5:16; 몬 7). 슬픔과 기쁨은 바울에게 항상 함께 있는 감정들이었다.[637] 그러나 그 균형이 같은 것은 아니었다. 바울은 항상 주안에서 기뻐하는 자세를 유지했다.[638] 여기 본문에 "항상" (ἀεί)이란 말이 있다. 같은 부사가 기뻐하라는 말과 함께 빌립보서 4장 4절과 데살로니가전서 5장 16절에도 나온다. 기쁨의 이유는 그리스도 안에서 그가 갖는 믿음과 소망 때문이다. 주 안에 있는 하나의 슬픔은 결국 또 하나의 기쁨의 기회가 되기 때문이다(빌 2:17). 그것은 "하나님의 능력은 약한 데서 온전하여 짐" 과도 관련된다(고후 12:9). 좀 더 원론적으로 보아서 이것이 그리스도를 통해 나타나는 하나님의 능력의 역설적인 모습이기도 하다. 하나님께서는 그가 부르신 자들에게는 모든 일들이 합력하여 선을 이루시도록 하시는 전능하신 분이시다(롬8:28). 바울은 하나님의 부르심을 받은 종이며, 그가 하는 일은 하나님의 일이므로 바울은 기뻐한다. 슬픈 일을 만나도 결국은 기뻐하게 된다. 예수께서도 제자들에게 같은 교훈

635) Hughes, 236; Barrett, 190; Martin, 183, Thrall, 466.

636) Martin, 183.

637) Barrett, 190.

638) Tasker, 96.

을 가르치셨다(요 16:33). 바울은 결국 그리스도의 교훈을 따라 살고 있는 것이다.

"가난한 자 같으나 많은 사람을 부요하게 하고"(ὡς πτωχοὶ πολλοὺς δὲ πλουτίζοντες). 실제로 바울은 물질적으로 가난한 사람이었다(11:9, 27; 고전 4:11-12). 그는 스스로 자비량 사역을 하였으나 간혹 교회의 물질적 도움을 받았다(9:9; 빌 4:15). 이 말을 영적으로 해석해서 다른 이들에 비해서 영적 은사가 빈약하다는 뜻으로는 볼 수 없다(12:1, 7). 혹 그런 반대자들의 비난에 대하여 반박한다고 볼 수도 있다. 그러나 여기서 사도 바울은 그의 실제 고난들을 열거하고 있으므로 물질적인 어려움으로 보는 것이 좋다.[639] 그러나 부요하게 한다는 말은 물질적인 의미보다는 영적으로 풍요하게 한다고 보아야 할 것이다. 그가 각지에서 거둔 헌금으로 예루살렘 성도들을 돕지만 그것으로 그들을 부요하게 했다고 보기는 어렵다. 그러므로 여기서 "부요하게 한다"는 말은 주로 예수 믿고 구원 얻는 믿음의 축복을 포함한 영적 축복을 말한다고 본다(엡 2:7; 3:8).[640] 그것이 복음의 핵심이기 때문이다. 바울은 그리스도를 아는 지식의 뛰어난 가치로 말미암아 그가 이 세상의 다른 것은 모두 분토처럼 버리고 영원한 천국의 상을 받기 위해 달렸다(빌 3:7, 8, 14). 바울의 보배는 그리스도의 영광의 복음이다(4:7). 그러나 물질적 육체적 축복을 전혀 제외할 수는 없다. "하나님이 능히 모든 은혜를 넘치게 하시나니 이는 너희로 모든 일에 항상 모든 것이 넉넉하여 모든 착한 일을 넘치게 하게 하려 하심

639) Thrall, 467.

640) Martin, 184; Collange, 299; J. D. G. Dunn, *Christology in the Making* (Philadelphia: Westminster, 1980), 122.

이라"(고후 9:8). 또 그의 재정 독립형 사역으로 실제로 고린도 교인들이 재정적으로 부담을 덜었을 것이다(11:7-10; 12:13, 14). 그러므로 여기의 부요함이 주로 영적인 부요함을 말하되 넓은 의미의 부요함을 의미한다고 본다(행 3:6; 빌 4:19). 이 말이 가리키는 것은 바울의 사역은 자기의 유익을 얻는 사역이 아니라 남을 유익하게 하는 사역이라는 것이다(고후 12:14). 이것이 바로 예수 그리스도의 모델이다. "예수 그리스도의 은혜를 너희가 알거니와 부요하신 자로서 너희를 위하여 가난하게 되심은 그의 가난함을 인하여 너희로 부요케 하려 하심이니라"(고후 8:8; 참조, 마 8:20). 여기서도 역시 역설적인 의미가 있다. 그러나 이런 역설적 진리는 바로 바울이 그리스도의 진정한 사도라는 증거가 된다. 그리고 바울의 희생적 사역 모델이 모든 그리스도인의 삶의 모델임을 암시하고 있다(5:14, 15; 13:4, 5). 나아가서 그리스도의 약함을 본받아서 스스로 약함 가운데 사역하여 그리스도의 능력이 나타나는 "진리"를 따르는 것이다(11:10; 12:9, 10; 13:8). 재정적으로도 가난하고 남에게 의지 하지 않음으로써 하나님이 주시는 풍성하신 은혜에 의존하는 "그리스도의 약함의 능력"을 그의 모든 사역에 일관되게 적용하는 것이다(9:15; 빌 4:11-13).

여기서 가난 자체를 미덕으로 삼아 청빈의 행복을 누리려 하는 어떤 희랍 철학자들과는 사뭇 다르다. 바울의 관심은 어떤 형편에 처해있더라도 모든 것을 풍족하게 하시는 하나님의 은혜이다(고후 12:9; 빌 4:11-12). 이와 같은 생각이 다음 말에서도 나타난다.

"아무 것도 없는 자 같으나 모든 것을 가진 자로다"(ὡς μηδὲν ε;χοντες καὶ πάντα κατέχοντες)."아무 것도 없는 자"란 앞의 "가난한 자 같으나"의 강화된 반복이다. 역시 물질적 결핍을 나타낸다.[641] 그러나 보다 넓게 바울이 갖지 않은 다른 것들도 나타낼 수 있다. 바울은 그의 대적자들처럼 자천서를 받을 만큼 예루살렘 사도들의 지지를 받는 것도 아니다.[642] 또 그들의 대적자들이 자랑하는 사람들에게 인기를 얻을 만한 영적 은사도 없다.[643] 그가 가진 것은 그리스도뿐이다.

"모든 것을 가진 자로다"는 영적인 성격을 담고 있다.[644] 그러나 모든 것이란 영적인 것만을 의미하는 것이 아니라 영적인 것을 포함한 모든 것의 소유를 의미한다. 로마서 8장 32절의 "모든 것"(τὰ πάντα)은 문맥에 의해서 그리스도로 말미암는 구원의 축복(영적 축복)을 말하고 있다. 그러나 고린도전서 3장 20-21절에서 바울은 고린도 교인들이 모든 사도들이나 세계나 생명이나 사망이나 지금 것이나 장래 것이나 다 너희 것이라고 하여 보다 포괄적인 소유를 의미한다.

당시 희랍 철학자들 가운데 스토익 철학자들이나 냉소주의 철학자들은 흔히 빈궁을 행복으로 자랑했다.[645] 냉소주의 철학자 크라테스(Crates)는 "우리는 아무것도 없으나 모든 것을 가졌다"고 했다.[646] 디오게네스(Diogenes)는, "지혜로운 자는 만물을 다 가지고 있다. 왜냐하면 그는 만물을 가진 신들의 친구이며, 친구들이란 재산을 함께 공유하기 때문이다"라고 했다.[647] 필로는 바로

641) Martin, 184.

642) Martin, 184.

643) Collange, 300.

644) Martin, 184.

645) Martin, 184.

646) Windisch, 209; Malherbe, *Cynic Epistles, Ep.* 7, 58-9, Thrall, 467, 주 1965, 재인용.

647) Diogenes Laertius VI 72; D. L. Mealand, "'As Having Nothing and yet Possessing

이 논쟁을 인용하면서 하나님께서 모든 세상을 모세의 손에 두셨다고 했다.[648] 아폴로니우스(Apollonius of Tyana)는 "나는 인도의 브라만들이 아무 것도 없으면서도 모든 사람들의 소유를 가지고 있음을 보았다" 고 했다.[649] 트롤은 의사소통의 편리를 위하여 바울이 독자들이 잘 아는 희랍의 철학자들의 생각을 기독교화 하여 말하고 있다고 본다.[650] 미랜드(Mealand)는 인용이라기보다는 널리 알려진 개념들을 바울이 사용하는 것이라고 한다.[651] 그러나 여기서 크라인크네흐트(Kleinknecht)는 유대교 전통의 "경건한 자의 고통" 의 흔적을 본다.[652] 어떤 경우든 간에 바울의 이 마지막 반제도 앞의 5개의 반제와 같이 역설적인 성격을 갖고 있다. 바울은 외적으로 아무것도 없는 불쌍한 사람처럼 보이나, 그는 사람들을 사랑하고, 언제나 기뻐하고, 장래의 영광을 바라보며 현재의 모든 난관을 극복해가는 그리스도의 놀라운 능력을 지닌 사도이다. 그리스도 안에 있는 사람은 모든 것을 잃었으나, 또한 모든 것을 가진 사람이다. 바울의 삶은 역시 그리스도의 "죽어도 사는 역설적인 유형" 에 기초하고 있다고 본다. 여기서도 바울의 사역이

Everything', 2 Cor 6:10c", *ZNW* 67 (1976), 278 인용; Malherbe, *Cynic Epistles, Epp.* 26, 27, 77, Thrall, 467-78, 주 1966 재인용.

648) Philo, *Vit. Moses* I 156-7, Mealand, 278 인용, Thrall, 468, 주 1967 재인용.

649) Philostratus, *Vit. Apollonius*(*Life of Apollonius*) III 15, Wettstein, 193 인용; Windisch, 209; Furnish, 348, Thrall, 468, 주 1968 재인용.

650) Thrall, 468.

651) Lietzmann은 Epictetus(*Diss.* 2:14, 24)를 인용하여 여기서 바울이 대조적으로 말하는 것과 유사하다고 한다: "병드는 것과 행복한 것, 죽는 것과 행복한 것, 포로로 잡히는 것과 행복한 것, 불명예와 행복한 것." Martin, 185, 재인용;D. L. Mealand, 277-79.

652) K. T. Kleinknecht, *Der leindende Gerechtfertigte*, WUNT 2nd series, 13 (Tübingen: Mohr, 1984), 267, 268.

그리스도의 역설적 유형에 잘 들어맞기 때문에 그의 사역은 신뢰할만한 것이라는 의미가 있다.

휴즈는 그의 10절 주석 마지막에 다음과 같이 3절부터 10절의 바울의 글을 바울 서신 가운데 최고봉 가운데 하나라고 격찬하고 있다:

> 이 감동적인 아름다운 찬송 같은 글은 사도의 지식과 체험의 깊은 가슴에서 흐르는 것이다. 이 글의 시적인 강렬함, 짜임 있는 균형, 진솔한 자연스러움은 시대를 초월하여 찬사와 감사의 반향을 일으켰다. 에라스무스(Erasmus-15세기 신학자)는 이 글의 효력은 지대하여 어떤 글도 이보다 애독될 수 없고, 열렬하게 할 수 없다고 했다. 이 글은 이 놀라운 인간적인 서신(고린도후서)에서 뿐만이 아니라 모든 바울 서신 중에서 최고봉의 하나임이 확실하다. 이 글은 그 어떤 인위성도 없이 바울의 새로 거듭난 성품이 갖는 열의와 헌신과 진지함을 보여준다. 그러므로 이 글은 이 글을 심각하게 읽으려는 모든 사람들에게 하나님 앞에서 십자가에서 죽으시고 다시 사시고 승천하신 주님과 자신과의 관계를 재점검하고, 그의 삶과 재능을 오로지 그리스도를 위한 임무수행을 위해서 배가된 진지함으로 다시 새롭게 헌신 하도록 도전한다.[653]

653) Hughes, 238.

바울은 자신의 고난의 사역과 그의 인격에서 그의 십자가의 메시지가 그대로 배어있음을 나타내고 있다. 바울은 언행일치의 본을 보여주고 있다. 이것이 그의 자찬의 중심적이고 지배적인 성격이다. 이 같은 언행일치의 사도 바울을 고린도 교인들이 마땅히 믿어야 하지 않겠는가 그와 다시 화해하는 것이 당연하지 않은가?

주해(6:3-10):

바울은 6장 3절에서 10절까지 고린도 교인들과의 화해를 위해서 자신의 사역이 얼마나 그리스도의 사역과 닮았는가를 보여 준다. 그는 구원의 소식을 전하는 그의 복음 사역이 대단히 소중한 것인가를 잘 알고 있다. 그 사역이 자칫 외적, 내적 훼방을 받아 복음을 듣는 이들에게 장애가 되지 않도록 매사에 주의해야 함을 잘 알고 있었다(6:3). "아무에게도 거리끼지 않게 하려고" 그는 모든 고난을 감수했다(6:4). 그 것이 하나님의 일군으로서 마땅히 해야 할 임무였다. 4절의 "모든 일에 하나님의 일군으로 자천했다"는 말은 매사에 하나님의 일군으로 자신들을 나타냈다는 뜻이다. 과연 여기서 바울은 그의 사역 가운데 그리스도의 죽고 사는 유형을 따라서 고난당하나 승리하는 것을 보여주고 있다. 바울의 사역을 익히 아는 사람이라면 바울의 이런 증거를 의심 없이 받아들였을 것이다. 그러나 이런 글을 읽고도 그를 의심하는 이들도 있었을 것이다. 바울은 그의 진실된 사도직 수행에 대해 최선을 다해 증거하고 있으나 그 결과는 알 수 없다. 오히려 고린도후서 마지막 장들을 보면 바울의 자천에 대한 고린도 교회의 반응에 대한 바울의 예상이 그렇게 낙관적인 것은 아님을 보여준다. 그럼에도 불구하고 고린도후서를 통해서 바울은 시종일관 자천하는 일을 쉬지 않고 하고 있다. 이것이 화해의 직책을 맡은 하나님의 일군의 임무이기 때문이다. 하나님의 화해의 사신은 예상되는 결과에 상관없이 화해를 위해 최후까지 일해야 하는 것이다. 이것이 화해의 종 그리스도가 하신 일이다. 죽기까지 하나님의 화해의 뜻에 복종하신 것이다. 바울도 그렇게 끝까지 최선을 다해 화해의 일을 하고 있다.

이런 바울의 화해를 위한 자천의 글에서 우리는 바울 사도처럼 그리스도의 화해의 종으로써 남과의 화해를 위해서 최선을 다해야 한다는 것을 배운다. "할 수 있거든 너희는 모든 사람과 더불어 평화하라"(롬 12:18). 어느 인간관계나 어떤 인간 사회에서 가장 일반적인 문제는 화해의 문제이다. 어떤 장애로 인해서 인간관계나 인간 사회가 어려워졌든지 간에 화해는 모든 목회의 공통된 목표이다. 불화는 모든 불행의 씨가 된다. 문제는 누가 먼저 화해를 어떻게 시작하느냐가 문제다. 첫째로, 바울은 본문에서 인내를 첫 번째 화해의 단계로 제시하고 있다(6:4). 인내하는 사람이 화해를 시작하고 이룰 수 있는 사람이다. 도덕인 인내와 그리스도인의 인내는 구별돼야 한다. 도덕적인 세계에서의 인내란, 상당한 시간이 지나서 상대방이 스스로 깨닫고 제대로 돌아오게 되거나, 또는 주위 환경이 자연적인 순리에 따라서 바뀌어서 화해의 방향으로 진정될 수 있거나, 또는 단순히 인내가 미덕이라는 관념에서 그 가치를 인정받는 것이다. 그러나 그리스도인의 인내란 거룩하신 하나님 앞에서 자신의 감정과 논리를 겸손히 접어두고 하나님의 개입과 처리를 겸손히 기다리는 자세이다. 그러므로 상대방이나 환경의 변화도 모두 하나님의 개입과 도우심으로 본다. 또는 보다 적극적으로 그리스도 안에 있는 하나님의 은혜와 사랑의 교제로 말미암아 상대방을 용납하고 사랑하는 마음을 갖는 것이다. 그리스도께서도 하나님께 의지하여 십자가를 참으셨다(막 14:36; 히 12:2). 하나님께서는 십자가를 통해서 그의 진노하심을 참으시고 죄인들을 용서하셨다. 인간들의 죄에 대한 진노하심을 참으셨다. 하나님께서는 십자가를 통해서 그의 진노하심을 참으시고 죄인들을 용서하셨다(5:21). 인간들의 죄에 대한 진노하심을 참으셨다. 현대문화는 무엇이든지 개방하는 자세를 선호한다. 인내하는 미덕보다는 인간의 감정을 감추지 말고 발산하도록 권한다. 그 결과 현대 사회는 무절제한 개인의 자유와 무책임한 인권의 요구로 걷잡을 수 없는 혼돈과 불안으로 치닫게 될 것이다. 잘못된 철학은 사람을 오도하되 원래 그 잘못된 결과에 대해 어떤 책임도 지지 않는다. 결국 그 잘못된 철학을 선택한 사람이나 사회가 그 결과로 말미암는 고통을 받게 되는 것이다.

둘째로 바울은 구체적으로 화해의 장애가 되는 오해를 제거하고 있다. 우리도 보다 적극적으로 화해를 위해 우리에게 있는 화해의 장애의 요소를 먼저 제거해야 한다. 본문의 사도 바울은 완벽하게 그리스도의 종으로서 산 것을 자찬했다. 우리 같은 갑남을녀(甲男乙女)들은 바울같이 완전한 그리스도적 삶을 살기는 어렵다 해도 적어도 그리스도 안에 있는 우리에게 실제적인 화해의 장애를 파악하고 그 장애를 제거할 수 있는 능력이 있다. 화해는 나와 상대방의 문제이기 이전에 나와 하나님과의 문제이다. 나와 그리스도와의 문제이다. 내가 진정으로 그리스도 안에 있어 그의 죽으심과 사심의 원리에 따라 행하느냐가 문제다. 그리스도인은 언제나 먼저 화해를 시작해야 한다. 우리가 죄인 되어 하나님과 불화 했을 때 그리스도께서 먼저 우리를 위해 죽으셨기 때문이다(롬 8:8, 10). 화해의 이니시어티브는 그리스도인이 가져야 한다. 그것이 인간관계의 평화유지가 주는 유익을 위할 뿐만 아니라 그리스도를 통한 하나님의 화해의 복음을 증거하는 중요한 방법이기 때문이다.

오늘날 그리스도인들에게, 특히 목회자들에게 구체적인 화해의 장애 요소는 무엇인가? 바울의 자찬하는 내용에 비추어 볼 때, 인내도 부족하고, 그리스도를 위한 헌신도 부족하고, 깨끗함도 부족하고, 의로움도 부족하고, 영적 부요함도 약하다. 많은 그리스도인들이 안일주의적, 세속주의적 가치관에 많이 물들어 있다. 많은 그리스도인들이 자신들도 모르게 세상의 물량주의적 가치관에 빠져있다. 세속적 인본주의, 과학적 합리주의, 그리고 무절제한 낙관주의에 의해서 그리스도 중심적 거룩한 가치는 무의식 중에 조롱거리가 되고 있다. 이런 세속적인 가치들이 그리스도인의 마음과 그리스도의 교회 안에 자리 잡고 있는 한 그 개인과 교회는 하나님의 화해의 직책을 감당할 수 없고 대신 불화와 혼돈 속에 갇히게 된다. 뿐만 아니라 세상을 향한 화해의 복음의 증거의 책임도 감당할 수 없게 된다.

그리스도 안에 있는 우리는 십자가를 참으신 그리스도처럼 세상의 조롱거리가 된 그리스도의 거룩하신 십자가의 가치와 인격을 힘써 지켜 나가야 한다. 참된 힘과 참된 진리와 참된 영광과 참된 기쁨과 참된 부요함은 모두 그리스도 안에 있는 것이다. 이 좋은 것들을 갖기 위해서는 내게 있는 세상의 잘못된 모든 가치관을 찾아내어버려야 한다. "그러나 무엇이든지 내게 유익하던 것을 내가 그리스도를 위하여 다 해로 여길 뿐더러 또한 모든 것을 해로 여김은 내 주 그리스도 예수를 아는 지식이 가장 고상함을 인함이라…" (빌

3:7-8). 교회를 핍박하던 바울이 회개하여 새사람이 되었으나 그가 이 세상을 떠나 다른 세상으로 가서 살았기 때문에 그렇게 완전한 그리스도인으로 살게 된 것이 아니다. 오히려 그는 우리가 사는 세상보다 더 악조건 가운데서도 그리스도 안에서 그리스도를 따라 살기를 힘쓰며 살다가 승리했다(딤후 4:7). 그렇다면 우리는 아무런 핑계도 할 수 없다. 우리도 이세 상에서 그리스도 안에서 그리스도를 따라 살 수 있다. 그렇게 함으로 진정한 하나님의 화해의 복음의 사신이 되어 하나님의 화해의 사역을 수행할 수 있다.

한편 바울의 화해의 신학을 남용하여 세속주의적 가치나 타종교와의 화해로 발전시켜 생각하는 것은 바울의 뜻과는 거리가 멀다. 그러므로 6장 14절부터 바울은 무분별한 화해를 막기 위해서 화해의 선을 긋고 있다. 바울이 말하는 화해는 그리스도 안에서의 새로운 피조물의 화해이며 그리스도를 믿는 신앙의 테두리 안에서의 화해이지 그리스도를 대적하는 불신 세력과는 오히려 단절할 것을 엄명하고 있다. "그리스도와 벨리알이 어찌 조화되며 믿는 자와 믿지 않는 자와 어찌 상관 하며 하나님의 성전과 우상이 어찌 일치가 되리요?" (6:15-16a). 이런 무절제한 화해는 그리스도의 교회를 오염시키고 파괴하는 적 그리스도적 행위일 뿐이다. 오늘날 어떤 신학이나 교회는 무분별한 화해의 신학으로 말미암아 "그리스도의 십자가의 원수" 로 행하고 있다(빌 3:18).

x. 우리와 화해하자 (6:11-7:4).

본 문:

11. 고린도인들이여 너희를 향하여 우리의 입이 열리고 우리의 마음이

넓혀졌으니(넓었으니) 12. 너희가 우리 안에서 좁아진 것이 아니라 오직 너희 심정에서 좁아진 것이니라. 13. 내가 자녀에게 말하듯 하노니 보답하는 양으로 너희도 마음을 넓히라. 14. 너희는 믿지 않는 자와 멍에를 같이 하지 말라. 의와 불법이 어찌 함께하며 빛과 어두움이 어찌 사귀며 15. 그리스도와 벨리알이 어찌 조화되며 믿는 자와 믿지 않는 자가 어찌 상관하며 16. 하나님의 성전과 우상이 어찌 일치가 되리요. 우리는 살아 계신 하나님의 성전이라. 이와 같이 하나님께서 가라사대, "내가 저희 가운데 거하며 (그들 가운데)두루 행하여 나는 저희 하나님이 되고 저희는 나의 백성이 되리라"하셨느니라. 17. 그러므로 주께서 말씀하시기를 너희는 저희 중에서 나와서 따로 있고 부정한 것을 만지지 말라. 내가 너희를 영접하여 18. 너희에게 아버지가 되고 너희는 내게 자녀가 되리라. 전능하신 주의 말씀이니라 하셨느니라. 7:1. 그런즉 사랑하는 자들아 이 약속을 가진 우리가 하나님을 두려워하는 가운데서 거룩함을 온전히 이루어 육과 영의 온갖 더러운 것에서 자신을 깨끗케 하자. 2. 마음으로 우리를 영접하라. 우리가 아무에게도 불의를 하지 않고 아무에게도 해롭게 하지 않고 아무에게도 속여 빼앗은 일이 없노라. 3. 내가 정죄하려고 이 말을 하는 것이 아니라. 이전에 말하였거니와 너희로 우리 마음에 있어 함께 죽고 함께 살고자 함이라. 4. "내가 너희를 무척 신뢰하며 (향하여 하는 말이 담대한 것도 많고), 너희를 위하여 자랑하는 것도 많으니, 내가 우리의 모든 환난 가운데서 위로가 가득하고 기쁨이 넘치는 도다.

본문 비평:

1. 11절에서 ἡμῶν(우리들의) 대신 ὑμῶν(너희들의)이 p[46] ℵ B에 나온다. 그러나 이것은 문맥에 전혀 맞지 않으므로 배제한다.[654] 이것이 더 오랜 기록이나, 브루스의 말대로, 고대의 것이라고 해서 모두 진실을 나타내는 것은 아니다.[655]

---

654) Metzger, *The Text of the New Testament*, 191, 192.

655) Bruce, 213.

2. 15절의 벨리알(βελίαρ)의 희랍어 철자가 사본에 따라 다르다: βελίαν(D K y), βελίαβ(F G), βελίαλ(pc lat; vg).[656] 다만 βελίαλ의 경우는 βελίαρ의 ρ이 λ로 변한 것이다. 우리나라 사람들이 영어의 R (r)발음이 없어서 L(l)발음으로 바꾸어 말하는 것과 같은 이화현상(異化現像, dissimilation)이 희랍인들에게 생긴 것이다.[657] 휴즈는 중국 사람들이 R발음을 L발음으로 한다고 예를 든다.[658] 그리고 희랍인 Alcibiades가 희랍어 ρ을 λ로 혼돈한다고 Aristophanes가 말했다는 것을 인용한다. 그러나 반대로 L(λ)을 R(ρ)로 혼돈해서 원래 βελίαλ의 끝 자음 λ을 ρ로 혼돈하여 βελίαρ로 잘못 썼다고 볼 수도 있다. 실제로 βελίαλ이 히브리어 בליעל을 바르게 옮겨 적은 것으로 보인다. 그러나 학자들은 모두 βελίαρ가 원래의 글로 본다. 이 경우 처음부터 히브리어 בליעל의 마지막 자음 ל을 헬라어 ρ로 잘못 적었다고 본다.[659]

3. 16절에서 대다수의 소문자 사본(MSS)이 ἡμεῖς(우리)대신 ὑμεῖς(너희)로 쓴다(p[46] [ℵ] D* C D2 F G itg vg). 그러나 알렉산드리아 사본과 서방사본은 Nestle-Aland 판의 ἡμεῖς(우리)를 지지한다(ℵ* B D* 33 81* it[d] cop[sa, bo]). 메쯔거(Metzger)는 고린도전서 3장 16절, "하나님의 성령이 너희 안에 거하시는 것을 너희가 알지 못하느냐 "에서부터 ἡμεῖς(우리)대신 ὑμεῖς(너희)로 고쳐 썼다고 본

656) 철자의 변화에 대한 설명은 Hughes, 248-48, 주 12, 그리고 Martin, 190을 보라.

657) Bruce, 214; Martin, 190.

658) Hughes, 250, 주 12.

659) 이에 대한 더 자세한 논의는 Hughes, 250, 주 12를 보라.

다.[660] 마틴도 이에 동의하면서 같은 혼돈의 문제가 7장 12절, 8장 8, 19절, 고린도전서 7장 15절에도 있다고 한다. 반면에 ὑμεῖς(너희)가 ἡμεῖς(우리)로 바뀔 이유는 없다고 한다.[661]

4. 7:1에서 단지 p[46]만이 φόβῳ(두려움)대신 ἀγάπῃ(아가페, 사랑)를 쓴다. 커(R. E. Ker)는 ἐν ἀγάπῃ θεοῦ(하나님의 사랑)가 ἐν φόβῳ θεοῦ(하나님의 두려움)보다 신약에서 더 친숙한 표현이라고 한다.[662] 그는 후자를 70인역의 영향이라고 본다(유다서 21). 그러나 대부분 학자들은 p[46]의 φόβῳ(두려움)가 오류라고 본다.[663]

5. 7:3의 πρὸς κατάκρισιν οὐ λέγω는 ℵ B C P를 따른 것이며, οὐ πρὸς κατάκρισιν λέγω가 D E F G K L에서 나온다. 그러나 이것은 후대의 변경으로 보인다.[664]

6. 7:3에서 B는 ἐστε를 생략한다.[665]

7. 7:3에서 συζῆν(B[3] K L P)은 같은 뜻의 συνζῆν(ℵ B* C D E F G)보다 신빙성이 약하다.[666]

---

660) Metzger, *Textual Commentary*, 580; Barrett, 193, 주, 1.

661) Martin, 190.

662) R. E. Ker, "Fear or Love A Textual Note," *The Expository Times* 71-72 (1959-61), 195.

663) Barrett, 193, 주, 2; Martin, 190; Thrall, 480, 주, 2059.

664) Plummer, 215.

665) Plummer, 215.

666) Plummer, 215.

내용 개요:

이 부분은 바울이 적극적인 화해를 위해 부모가 잘못된 자식을 타이르듯이 고린도 교인들을 설득하는 말로 시작하고 같은 말로 맺는다(참조, 12:14). 그러나 중심 본문인 6장 14절부터 7장 1절까지에서 바울은 고린도 교인들에게 있는 온갖 부정한 것과 세속적인 것을 버리고 거룩하게 되어야 그리스도 안에서 참된 화해와 친교를 가질 수 있다고 보다 단호하게 말한다. 화해를 말하던 바울의 어조가 바뀌어 세상과의 단절을 말하므로, 어떤 학자들은 이 본문에 다른 외적 요소가 게재되어 있거나 심지어 다른 자료가 삽입되었을 가능성도 추정하고 있으나, 바울은 본문에서 화해의 문맥 안에서 그리스도 중심의 진정한 화해를 위해 이에 방해되는 세상과의 단절을 제안하고 있을 뿐이다. 바울은 화해를 위해 자신의 사도직의 진정성에 대해서 숨김없이 다 말했다. 본문에서 바울은 이제 내가 화해에 장애가 되는 오해들을 풀기 위해 모든 것을 다 밝혔으니 이제는 고린도 교인들 편에서 화해에 장애가 되는 요소들을 제거해야 할 차례라고 한다. 유사하게 바울은 12:20, 21에서도 3차 방문을 앞두고 진정한 교제에 방해가 되는 죄를 버릴 것을 권면하고 있다. 그리스도인의 화해는 그리스도 중심, 하나님 중심의 화해이어야 하며, 이에 방해되는 우상과 같은 기존의 세속적인 요소들을 제거하고 하나님과 같이 거룩한 품성을 회복해야 진정한 화해가 이루어진다. "내가 거룩하니 너희도 몸을 구별하여 거룩하게 하라"(레 11:44). 그리스도 안에 있는 새로운 피조물로서 하나님의 화해의 역사에 참여하기 위해서는 하나님과 그리스도인 사이에 남아 있는 반 하나님적 요소를 제거해야 한다. 그리스도인의 화해는 무분별한 혼합적 화해가 아니라 하나님 중심적, 그리스도 중심적 거룩한 화해이기 때문이다.

6장 14절부터 7장 1절의 문맥의 위치와 내용에 대해서 많은 논란이 있어 왔다. 본문에 대한 논쟁점들에 대해서 서론에서 이미 논의하였으므로 여기서는 논쟁점들을 요약하여 설명하기로 한다.

첫째, 우선 이 글의 문맥의 위치에 대하여 살펴보자. 학자들은 6장 13절과 6장 14절이 연결이 잘 안된다고 본다. 6장 13절은 화해를 설득하는 말이나, 6장 14절은 갑자기 화해와는 상반되는 과격한 분리의 말처럼 보이기 때문이다. 마찬가지로 7장 1절은 분리를 말하나, 7장 2절은 화해를 다시 말하고 있으므로 서로 연결이 안되는 듯이 보인다. 더구나 6장 13절은 7장 2절과 내용이 잘 연결된다. 그래서 6장 14절부터 7장 1절까지를 바울이 이전에 보낸 "엄격한 서신"(고전 5:9)의 일부가 여기에 삽입되었다고 보는 견해도 많다.[667)]

둘째, 이 부분에 바울 서신에서 나타나지 않는 희귀한 용어들(*hapax legomena*)이 9개나 있고,[668)] 이원론적(二元論的) 사상과, 율법주의적인 배타주의 사상이 있으므로 많은 학자들이 쿰란의 분리주의적 영향을 논하기도 한다.[669)]

---

667) J. Moffatt, *First Epistle to the Corinthians* (London: Hodder & Stoughton, 1938), xxiv; Strachan, 3; Denney, 238; T. W. Manson, "The Corinthian Correspondence," *Studies in the Gospels and Epistles*, ed. M. Black (Manchester: Manchester University Press, 1962), 222; J. C. Hurd, Jr., 135-139; E. Stange, "Diktierpausen in den Paulusbriefen," *ZNW* 18 (1917-18) 115f.; G D. Fee, "I Corinthians vi.14-vii.1 and Food Offered to Idols," *NTS* 23 (1976-77) 140-61; Martin, li-lii, 191.

668) ἑτεροζυγοῦντες, μετοχή, συμφώνησις, βελίαρ, συγκατάνθεσις, ἐμπεριπατέω, εἰσδέχομαι, παντοκράτωρ, μολυσμός.

마틴은 바울은 많은 지식을 가지 사람으로서 충분히 쿰란 등 다른 사상에 대해서도 알고 있었으리라고 보면서 바울의 글이 아니라는 견해를 반대한다.[670] 또한 마틴은 아무런 사본 상의 증거가 없음을 지적하며 삽입설을 반대한다.[671] 모든 고린도후서 사본은 이 부분을 갖고 있기 때문이다.[672] 마틴은 주로 랜스버거(Rensberger)와 그닐카(Gnilka)의 견해를 따라서 이 부분은 바울이 엣센파(쿰란)에 속했다가 기독교인이 된 어떤 사람이 이미 썼던 글을 사용하여 썼다는 가능성을 제기 한다.[673] 원래의 글은 유대인 기독교인들에게 우상과 간음죄를 짓는 이방인과의 접촉을 피하라는 내용이었는데, 바울이 여기서 사용하였다고 본다. 이글이 독립적인 구조를 가지고 짜임새 있게 쓰였기 때문이다. 그러나 이 글이 고린도전서 5장의 음행에 대한 경고하는 바울의 편지(고전 5:9)와 관련되었는지는 알 수 없다고 한다.[674] 그러나 이런 제안은 추정일 뿐이다. 마틴은 이 독특한 내용이 이곳에 위치하고 있는

669) 쿰란 관련설을 처음 주장한 이는 K. G. Kuhn, "Die Schriftrollen vom Toten Meer", *EvT* 11(1951), 72-5, Thrall, 32, 주, 209 재인용. 쿰란 관련설에 대하여 Martin, 191-93; Hughes, 242, Thrall, 29-36을 보라.

670) Martin, 192; Hughes, 242; 참조, W. G. Kümmel, *Introduction to New Testament*, 288.

671) 많은 학자들이 이 부분이 바울이 직접 쓴 것이라고 한다: Filson, 352; Tasker, 30; Bruce, 214; Barrett, 194; Plummer, 208; Héring, 49; Hughes, 243, 44; Martin, 서론, lii; Thrall, 35.

672) Plummer, 205.

673) D. Rensberger, "2 Corinthians 6:14-7:1–A Fresh Examination," *StBibT* 8 (1978) 41; J. Gnilka, "2 Cor 6:14-7:1 in Light of of the Qumran Texts and the Testaments of the Twelve Patriarchs." *Paul and Qumran*, ed. J. Murphy-O'Connor, *Paul and Qumran*, 59: 성전 주제와 관련하여 1QS 5:1-6을 언급한다; Martin, 193.

674) Martin, 194.

타당한 이유를 전체 문맥의 흐름에 비추어서 이해한다. 즉 바울이 5장 이후 화해의 주제를 논하면서 그의 사역을 변명한 후에 고린도 교인들 쪽에서 화해에 방해가 되는 문제들을 지적하기 시작하고 있다는 것이다. 그것은 불신자들과의 접촉으로 인한 불신적이고 세속적인 요소들이다. 이것들을 제거해야 진정한 화해를 이룰 수 있다는 것이다.[675] 이렇게 생각하면 이 부분은 전체 화해의 문맥에 매우 잘 맞는다.

트롤도 본문에 바울이 다른 곳에서 쓰지 않는 말과 독특한 권면이 있지만, 바울이 고린도 전후서와 로마서 같은 다른 서신에서 잘 쓰는 말과 어휘가 많이 있음을 지적한다.[676] 또한 쿰란 문서에 나온다고 지적된 용어들은 다른 바울 서신에서도 나오는 것이며,[677] 불의와 의의 대조는 유대교 문서인 *Testament of Dan*(단의 증언) 6장 10절에도 나오고, 빛과 어두움, 주와 벨리알의 대조가 *Testament of Levi*(레위의 증언) 19장 1절에도 나온다고 한다(34).[678]

이상의 학자들의 견해를 검토해 본 결과 6장 14절-7장 1절은 문맥적으로나, 신학적으로나, 사본의 일치된 증거나, 바울의 글이 아니라고 할 만한 확실한 근거가 없다. 본문의 진정성을 반대하는 견해의 공통된 문제점은 거의 모든 주장들이 분명한 증거가 없는

675) Martin, 194.

676) Thrall, 34-35.

677) Bruce, 214; Barrett, 197, 199.

678) Murphy O'Connor, "Philo and 2 Cor 6:14-7:1", *The Diakonia of the Spirit (2Co 4:7-7:4)*, ed. L. de Lorenzi, Monographic Series of "Benedictina": Biblical-Ecumenical Section 10, (Rome: Abbaye de S. Paul, 1989)137-9; Bruce, 215: 벨리알(Belial/Beliar)이 *Jubilee* 1:20; *T. Levi* 19:1; *Ascension of Isaiah* 1:8이하, 2:4에 나옴을 지적한다.

추정에 근거하고 있다는 것이다.

첫째로, 문맥에 대한 문제는 바울이 온전한 화해에 장애되는 요소를 제거하도록 강조하는 것이라고 보면, 달라진 어조가 전체 화해의 주제와 관련된다고 이해할 수 있다. 14절 상반절 이후에 5개의 반제(反題)들로 이루어져 있다(14절 중반절, 14절 하반절, 15절 상반절, 15절 하반절, 16절 상반절). 이 5개의 반제들은 14절 상반절의 말을 강화하는 역할을 한다("너희는 믿지 않는 자와 멍에를 같이 하지 말라"). 거룩하게 되기 위해서 악에서의 분리를 강조한다. 이 모든 내용은 불신자들과 더불어 사는 고린도 교인들에 대한 경고이다. 고린도전서에서 볼 수 있는 고린도 교회 안에 있는 세속적 문제를 여기서 다시 엄중히 다루면서 이런 것들이 아직 진정한 화해의 장애로 남아 있음을 지적하는 것이다. 또한 바울은 여기서 화해의 의미를 보다 분명하게 할 필요가 있었을 것이다. 바울이 말하는 화해는 세속적인 무분별한 화해나, 하나님을 나의 목적이나 탐욕에 이용하는 우상숭배식 화해가 아니라, 하나님의 백성으로서 하나님의 거룩하신 성품을 본받음으로써 하나님께로 나아가는 상향식 화해인 것임을 분명히 가르칠 필요가 있었다(참조, 벧후 1:4). 이렇게 보면, 오히려 문맥적으로는 사도 바울이 자신의 사도직 수행의 선명성을 밝힌 후에 고린도 교인들 편에서도 화해의 장애가 되는 불신적이고 세속적인 요소를 제거하라는 권면으로 보아서 문맥에 잘 맞는다. 바울은 6장 1절에서 하나님의 은혜를 헛되이 받지 말라고 하면서 하나님의 은혜에 합당한 삶을 살 것을 권면하였다. 또 3장에서 바울은 고린도 교인들을 그의 자천서라고 하면서 새 언약의 백성으로서 살지 못하면 새 언약의 말씀과 사역이 그 타당성을 잃게 될 것이며, 따라서 유대인들의 의심과 비판이 강화될 것임을 말하였다.[679] 에베소서 2장에서도 본문과 같이 먼저 화해를 말한 후에 성전에 비추어 그리스도 교회와 성도들의 존재 의미와 존재 양식을 말한다. 물론 여기서와 같이 세상과 분리가 아닌, 교회의 통일성이 주제로 되어 있으나, 화해와 성전의 주제가 연결되어 나오는 것은 여기와 유사하다.

한편, 위에서 쓴 것 같이 바울은 여기서 자신이 원하는 화해가 어떤 것인지를 분명히 말해둘 필요를 느꼈을 것이다. 부분별한 화해가 아니라 하나님의 거룩하심을 본받아 하나가 되는 화해를 지향해야 함을 말하는 것이다.

둘째로, 바울의 사상과 다르다고 지적된 이원론적인 대조나 배타주의적 진술이 반드시 바울 사상에 어긋난다고 볼 수 없다.[680] 오히려 바울 서신에 분리주의적인 대조를 암시하는 곳은 많다. 불신자와의 결혼문제(고전 7:12-15), 우상의 제물 먹는 문제(고전 10:27이하), 불신자들 앞에서 형제를 고소하는 문제(고전 6:5이하), 의와 불의의 대조(롬 6:13), 죄의 종과 의의 종(롬 6:18), 의와 불법(롬 6:19), 선과 악의 대조(롬 7:18 이하), 육과 영의 대조(롬 8:4이하), 빛과 어두움의 대조(롬 13:12; 살전 5:5) 등이다.[681]

셋째로, 본문에 나타난 바울이 쓰지 않는 어휘도 결국 유대교적 배경을 갖고 있으므로, 바울이 절대로 쓸 수 없다고 할 수는 없다.[682] 본문의 크기에 비해 많은 9개의 희귀어도 큰 문제는 아니다. 본문뿐만 아니라 고린도후서에만 50개의 희귀용어(*hapax*

679) Thrall, 472.

680) Hughes, 242; Martin, 193.

681) Barrett, 197; Plummer, 207; Thrall, 474.

682) Hughes, 242; Martin, 192.

legomena)가 있다.[683] 바울은 무분별한 화해에 대해 제동을 걸려는 의도가 보다 강력하고 독특한 언어를 사용하게 만든 것이다.

넷째로, 트롤이 지적한 대로 본문에 바울이 다른 곳에서도 사용하는 어휘들이 나온다.[684] 그 중에서 6장 14절의 ἄπιστος("믿지 않는 자")란 말이 고린도전후서에 12번 나오는 데, 그 외 신약 전체에서는 9번만 나온다. 7장 1절의 ἐπιτελέω(온전히 이루다)는 고린도후서 8장 6, 11절에 두 번 나오고, 로마서 15장 28절, 갈라디아서 3장 3절, 빌립보서 1장 6절에 나오는데, 그 외 신약에서는 3번 나온다(히 8:5, 9:6; 벧전 5:9). ἁγιωσύνη("거룩함")는 바울에게서만 발견되는 용어이다(롬 1:4; 살전 3:13).

그러므로 6장 14절-7장 1절은 다른 바울의 글과 문학적, 신학적 독특성이 있음에도 불구하고 상응하는 동질성이 있으므로 바울의 글이라고 보아야 한다. 뿐만 아니라 이런 본문의 독특한 요소는 본문에서 바울이 의도적으로 사용하였을 충분한 이유가 있다고 볼 수 있다. 본문의 이질적 요소는 고린도 교회와의 지속적인 화해관계 유지를 위해 이 시점에서 반드시 집고 넘어가야 할 문제라고 보았을 것이다.[685] 바울은 문제가 되는 것들을 그냥 지나쳐 버리고 마는 임시 처방식 피상적인 화해는 지속적인 진정한 화해가 될 수 없다고 보았을 것이다. 바울은 여기서 진정한 화해를 위해서는 부정적으로는 피차의 장애적 요소를 제거하고 적극적으로는 일치된 요소를 찾아야 한다고 생각한다. 바울은 우선 피차 마음속

683) Hughes, 242.

684) Thrall, 35.

685) David A. deSilva, "Recasting the Moment of Decision: 2 Corinthians 6:14-7:1 in Its Literary Context," *AUS* 31 (1993), 3-16.

에 있는 장애의 요소를 찾아서 제거하는 작업이 필요하다고 보았다. 바울은 6장 3-10절에서 자신에게 있는 화해의 장애의 문제, 즉 사도직의 진정성에 대한 의구심을 일으킬 수 있는 문제들을 털어놓고 말했나. 이제는 고린도 교인들도 그들 편에 있는 장애를 제거해야할 차례가 되었다. 바울은 남아 있는 화해의 장애 요소를 눈감아 버리는 일시적이고 피상적인 거짓 화해를 원치 않는다. 그러므로 보다 분명하게 세속적인 삶을 떠나서 거룩한 그리스도인으로서의 삶을 위한 결단을 촉구하고 있다. 그러나 바울은 화해의 어조를 계속 유지하고 있다. 그러므로 이 부분의 처음과 끝인 6장 13절과 7장 1절은 바울의 간절한 화해의 말로 되어 있다. 바울은 주의 깊게 고린도 교인들을 달래면서 그들의 잘못을 구체적으로 지적하기를 피한다. 오히려 일반적인 "세상에서 사는 그리스도인의 거룩한 삶의 지침서" 같은 내용을 가지고 고린도 교인들을 우회적으로 설득하고 있다. 만일 이런 글이 초대교회에 이미 알려진 어떤 그리스도인의 지침서였다면 오히려 고린도 교인들을 설득하는데 좋은 자료가 되었을 것이다.[686] 때로 상대방에게 직접 하기 어려운 말은 남의 말을 빌려서하는 것이 화해나 좋은 관계를 유지하기 위해 보다 설득력이 있기 때문이다. 우리 그리스도인들 모두 이렇게 거룩하게 사는 것이 당연하니 너희 고린도 교인들도 이렇게 살아야 하지 않겠는가라고 설득할 수 있다(7:1). 그러나 트롤이 지적하는 대로 본문 전체가 바울의 글이며 원래 이곳에 있는 것이라고 보는 데 무리가 없다.[687]

---

686) Martin, 193: 유대교 종파인 쿰란인으로 있다가 기독교인이 된 작가의 글; Thrall, 36, 479: 초대 교회 세례준비를 위한 학습지.

687) Thrall, 35.

그러므로 본문에서 바울은 고린도 교인들에게 세속적이고 반기독교적인 화해의 장애를 제거하고, 무분별한 화해를 경계하여 하나님과의 진정한 높은 차원의 화해를 이루도록 권면하고 있다. 바울이 원하는 화해는 다원주의적 혼합적인 분별없는 화해가 아니라 거룩한 하나님의 백성으로서 그리스도 안에서 새로운 피조물로서 그에 합당한 거룩한 삶을 사는 것을 전제로 한 화해이다. 그러므로 이런 바울의 의도는 6장 14절-7장 1절 이전과 이후의 화해의 문맥과 주제에 일치된다고 본다.

주 석:

11. "고린도인들이여 너희를 향하여 우리의 입이 열리고 우리의 마음이 넓혀졌으니(넓었으니)" (**Τὸ στόμα ἡμῶν ἀνέῳγεν πρὸς ὑμᾶς, Κορίνθιοι, ἡ καρδία ἡμῶν πεπλάτυνται**). "너희를 향하여 우리의 입이 열리고" (**τὸ στόμα ἡμῶν ἀνέῳγεν πρὸς ὑμᾶς, Κορίνθιοι**). 원문에는 "고린도인들이여" (**Κορίνθιοι**)라는 말이 마지막에 있으나, 개역한글판을 따라 먼저 주석한다. 이런 직접적인 호칭은 드물게 나온다(갈 3:1; 빌 4:5). 호칭은 고린도 교회에 대한 바울의 특별한 애정을 나타낸다.[688] "너희를 향하여 우리의 입이 열리고…"란 말이 이런 바울의 애정을 확인해준다. "표현의 자유는 열린 마음의 증거이다."[689] 친한 사람에게만 우리는 마음에 있는 말을 다 할 수 있다. 바울은 고린도 교인들이 그를 괴

688) Plummer, 203; Hughes, 239.

689) Hughes, 239.

롭혔지만 여전히 친구로 생각하고 있다.[690] 여기서 바울의 고린도 교인들에 대한 사랑의 진정성을 볼 수 있다. 바울은 6장 3-10절에서 자신의 편에 있는 대화에 방해되는 장애 요소라고 할 수 있는 마음속에 품고 있던 "울분"을 솔직하게 다 내 놓았다. 사도로서 겪어야 했으나 다 말할 수도 없는 입장으로서 지금까지 갖고 있던 심정을 다 털어놓았다. 그는 더 이상 마음속에 감춘 것이 없었다. 그러므로 그는 이제 자유롭게 진지하게 대화할 수 있게 되었다.

"우리의 마음이 넓혀졌으니"(ἡ καρδία ἡμῶν πεπλάτυνται). 바울은 앞에서 마음속에 있던 "울분 섞인 불만"과 하고 싶었던 자찬의 말을 다하고서 이제는 속이 시원해진 상태가 되었다. 그리고 고린도 교인들을 진정으로 사랑하는 마음을 다시 확인하였다. **πεπλάτυνται**(넓혀졌으니)는 여기서 수동태로 번역하였으나 중간태로도 번역할 수 있다. 그 경우에는 "넓었으니"(개역한글)라고 바울의 보다 적극적인 자세는 나타낼 수 있으나, 어감이 어색하므로 수동태로 번역하였다. 수동태로 되어도 적극성이 그렇게 감소되지는 않는다. 바울의 마음속에 고린도 교인들에 대한 생각이 자리 잡고 있다(3:2; 7:3; 빌 1:7).[691] 특히 바울이 편지를 쓸 때면 그의 고린도 교인들에 대한 애정이 더 넘친다. 적어도 이 점만은 고린도 교인들도 인정할 것이다(고후 10:10). 이 점은 고린도 교인들이 바울에 대하여 스스로 자랑할 수 있는 바이다(5:12). 6장 11절은 시편 119편 32절 하반절(118:32, LXX)과 유사하나 문자적인 것뿐이며 의미는 다르다.[692]

---

690) Martin, 185.

691) Martin, 186.

692) Thrall, 469. Thrall은 "네 마음을 넓히라"는 말이 있는 신 11:6(LXX)과 시 118:32(LXX)

12. "너희가 우리 안에서 좁아진 것이 아니라 오직 너희 심정에서 좁아진 것이니라" (οὐ στενοχωρεῖσθε ἐν ἡμῖν, στενοχωρεῖσθε δὲ ἐν τοῖς σπλάγχνοις ὑμῶν). "너희가 우리 안에서 좁아진 것이 아니라" (οὐ στενοχωρεῖσθε ἐν ἡμῖν). στενοχωρέω(스테노코레오, "좁게 만들다," "압축하다")는 4장 8절에서 좁은 틈새에 끼워서 "눌려서 으깨어진"의 의미로 쓰였다. 여기서 이 말은 고린도 교인들이 바울을 멀리하였다고 해서 그들을 바울의 마음의 중요하지 않은 한 귀퉁이에 따로 제쳐놓은 것이 아니라는 뜻이다.[693] 바울은 고린도 교인들을 향하여 열린 사랑의 마음을 갖고 있다.

"오직 너희 심정에서 좁아진 것이니라" (στενοχωρεῖσθε δὲ ἐν τοῖς σπλάγχνοις ὑμῶν). σπλάγχνα(스프랑나, "심정"), 히브리어 רחמים(라하밈)은 문자적으로는 "창자"란 뜻이나 실제로는 "정"이란 뜻이다. 희랍인들은 사람의 몸의 중요한 장기(심장, 간, 허파)는 인간의 마음의 근원이라고 보았다.[694] 한편 σπλάγχνα(스프랑나, "심정")은 καρδία(마음, 심장)와 마찬가지 의미이므로[695] 개역한글판에 "심정(心情)"이라고 번역한 것은 이

를 본문과 대조 한 후 의미와 정황이 서로 다르다고 한다. 그 대신 사 60:5(히브리 원본)가 이스라엘 백성들의 회복을 말하고 있고, 본문에서도 바울이 고린도 교회와 바울과의 회복을 말하고 있으므로 적절한 배경이 될 수 있다고 한다. 그러나 문제는, Thrall 자신이 인정하듯이, 언어적인 연관성이 없다(470).

693) W. Bauer, *A Greek-English Lexicon of the New Testament and Other Early Christain Literature,* ed. W. F. Arndt, F. W. Gingrich, and F. W. Danker (Chicago: University of Chicago, 1979), 766.

694) Filson, 352.

말의 종합적인 의미를 잘 나타내주는 번역이다. "그러나 너희는 우리에게 너희의 정을 주지 않는다"란 뜻이다. 비록 바울에 대한 중상과 모략으로(12:20) 고린도 교인들은 바울을 잘 대해 주지도 않고 마음에도 없었으나 바울의 마음은 그들에 대한 사랑으로 차 있다. 바울이 고린도 교인들을 꾸짖는 것이 아니라, 그들을 부모가 아이를 달래듯이 설득하는 어조로 말하고 있다.

13. "내가 자녀에게 말하듯 하노니 보답하는 양으로 너희도 마음을 넓히라"(τὴν δὲ αὐτὴν ἀντιμισθίαν, ὡς τέκνοις λέγω, πλατύνθητε καὶ ὑμεῖς). "내가 자녀에게 말하듯 하노니"(ὡς τέκνοις λέγω)가 원문에서는 "보답하는 양으로"(τὴν δὲ αὐτὴν ἀντιμισθίαν)의 뒤에 나오나 번역 상 바꾸어서 앞에 쓴 개역한글 성경을 따라 먼저 주석한다. 바울은 다른 곳에서도 그의 독자들을 그의 자녀로 본다(12:14; 고전 3:1; 4:14, 17; 갈 4:19; 딤전 1:2, 18; 딤후 1:2; 2:1; 딛 1:4; 몬 10; 참조, 요일 2:1, 28; 3:7, 18; 4:4; 5:21). 바울은 그의 교인들의 영적 아버지이며, 그들은 영적 자녀들이었다. 아버지가 자녀에게 사랑을 요구하는 것은 당연하다.[696] 그러나 그는 그들의 애정을 사도적 권위로써 강요하여 얻을 수 없는 것임을 잘 알고 있다.[697]

"보답하는 양으로…"(τὴν δὲ αὐτὴν ἀντιμισθίαν). 바울은 영적 아버지로서 그의 자녀 된 고린도 교인들에게 그의 사랑에 상응

695) Hughes, 240, 주 2; Bultmann, 177; Collange, 301, 주 1; H. Koester, *TDNT* 7:548-59, Martin, 186 재인용.

696) Plummer, 204.

697) Barrett, 192; 1:24; 참조, 13:7-10.

하는 사랑을 요구한다(8:8, 24; 11:11; 12:14, 15). 바울은 고린도 교인들이 바울을 떠난 것을 질책할 수도 있었으나, 아직 믿음이 약한 그들에게 상처를 주지 않기 위해서 사랑의 자세로 그들을 설득하고 있다.[698] 부모가 성난 아이를 달래면서 "그러지 말고 이리 와서 나와 같이 놀자. 자 내가 이렇게 너를 좋아 하는 데 이리 와라" 라고 말하는 모습이다.[699] τὴν δὲ αὐτη.ν ἀντιμισθίαν(보답하는 양)의 격이 대격(목적격)인데 "가져라" 라는 타동사가 생략되었다고 본다.[700] 이 말은 이 절의 주제인 "열린 마음" 을 가리키며 "너희도 그와 같은 것, 즉 열린 마음을 (가져라)" 는 뜻이다.[701] 그러나 개역한글성경이나 다른 번역(RSV/NIV)과 같이 대격 명사 앞에 "양으로" (as a return of/ as a fair exchange/ in return/ in the same manner/ in the same way/ by way of)와 같은 전치사가 생략되어 있다고 볼 수도 있다. 이 경우 "너희도 ("나의 열린 마음")에 보답하는 양으로 마음을 열어라" 라고 번역하게 된다.

"너희도 마음을 넓히라" (πλατύνθητε και. ὑμεῖς). 이것이 이 부분의 바울의 호소의 결론이다. 고린도 교인들이 바울과 같이 마음을 열고 바울을 받아들이지 않는 한 화해가 될 수 없다. 아이들은 부모의 애정 어린 말을 잘 듣는다. 그 말에 순종하게 되는 것은 그 말의 내용은 싫더라도 그 말에 담겨 있는 부모의 자식에 대한 사랑과 기대를 저버림으로 부모를 실망시켜서 부모와 소원하게 되는 것을 원치 않기 때문이다. 자식은 자식대로 부모와의 원만한

698) Martin, 186.

699) Tasker, 97; Bruce, 213.

700) Hughes, 240, 주 3; Plummer, 204.

701) Hughes, 240, 주 3.

관계를 원한다. 바울도 고린도 교인들이 바울과의 관계를 완전히 깨뜨리는 것을 원하지 않고 있음을 알기 때문에 그들에 대한 사랑과 정을 가지고 접근한다(7:12). 여기서 중요한 점은 바울이 고린도 교인들을 자녀로 본다는 의미가 그들을 낮추어 본다는 의미보다는 그들에게 영적인 아버지로서 순수한 정과 사랑을 가지고 있다는 의미이다. (고전 3장에서는 바울이 고린도 교인들을 아직 영적으로 성숙하지 못한 젖 먹는 아이들로 보고 있다). 실제로 바울은 고린도 교회를 세웠고 고린도 교인들에게 복음을 전한 영적인 아버지이다(고후 3:3). 권위주의를 싫어하고 개인주의화되어 가는 오늘의 시대에서 바울이 제시하는 부모와 자녀의 관계를 오늘날의 교인들과 교역자의 관계에 그대로 적용시키기는 어렵다 해도, 부모와 자식 사이의 순수한 정과 사랑은 진정한 인간관계의 모델이 된다. 바울은 이처럼 순수한 희생적인 부모의 사랑에 근거하고 있음으로 진정한 그리스도의 사도이다.

14. "너희는 믿지 않는 자와 멍에를 같이 하지 말라. 의와 불법이 어찌 함께하며 빛과 어두움이 어찌 사귀며…" (Μὴ γίνεσθε ἑτεροζυγοῦντες ἀπίστοις· τίς γὰρ μετοχὴ δικαιοσύνῃ καὶ ἀνομίᾳ, ἢ τίς κοινωνία φωτὶ πρὸς σκότος;). 지금까지의 부드러운 화해의 어조와는 대조적으로 6장 14절부터 7장 1절까지의 어조는 매우 단호하고 배타적인 어조이다. 그래서 위에서 지적한 이런 특성을 가진 이 부분에 대한 여러 가지 제안들이 있음을 지적했다. 학자들의 이 부분에 대한 의심은 이 부분의 내용이 전후와 연결이 잘 안 된다는 데 있다. 또 바울이 잘 쓰지 않는 어휘도 있고, 바울의 사상과 다르다는 배타주의적 사상도 나온다. 어떤

성경학자들은 성경에 새로운 말들이 나오거나 문맥이 부드럽게 흐르지 않으면, 외부에서 온 것으로 간주하거나 후대 편집자의 삽입으로 간주해버린다. 그러나 글을 쓰는 저자들이 학자들이 찾는 통일된 논리와, 통일된 문장 구조나 사상을 따라 쓰지 않을 수도 있다. 더구나 바울의 글의 특징은 자주 주제를 벗어나는 것임은 잘 알려진 것이다.[702] 고린도후서에서의 주제 이탈은 더욱 심하다. 예로, 고후 2:12, 13에서 바울이 드로아에서 디도를 만나지 못해서 실망했다는 말을 한 후에 바울은 전혀 다른 말로 이어 가다가 7:5, 6에 와서야 마게도냐에서 디도를 만나게 된 것을 말한다.

그러나 6장 14절-7장 1절은 다른 학자들이 보는 대로 주제 이탈의 예도 아니고, 화해의 부드러운 어조가 달라진 것도 아니고, 바울이 모르는 외래 문서의 삽입도 아니다. 5장 18절 이후의 화해의 주제를 더욱 강화시키기 위해서 화해에 방해가 되는 장애를 제거하라고 훈계하는 내용이다. 바울은 6장 13절까지 화해를 위해 고린도 교회를 위해 충성되게 수고한 자신의 사역의 진정성을 다 말한 후에(6:3-10), 화해를 위해 그들을 부드럽게 달래는 말을 시작한다(6:11-13). 그러면서 바울은 아직도 고린도 교인들에게 화해의 장애가 되는 문제들이 남아 있다는 것을 생각하고(어쩌면 고린도전서에 언급한 있는 많은 세속적인 문제들을 상기하면서) 그것들을 제거하기를 권면하는 것이다(6:14-7:1). 실제로 6장 14절-7장 1절의 내용은 고린도 교인들과 직접적으로 관련된 구체적인 문제를 논하는 것은 아니다. 그리스도인이라면 누구나 세상과 분리된 분별된 삶을 살아야 한다는 일반적인 훈계인 것이다. 이런 훈계가

702) Martin, 187.

초대교회에 이미 알려져 있었거나, 아니면 바울이 어디서 찾아 사용한 것일 수도 있다.[703] 그래서 이질적 용어가 많고 배타주의적 사상이 있는 지도 모른다.[704] 그러나 이런 외래 문서설은 이질적으로 보이는 특성에 대한 추정일 뿐이다. 여전히 바울의 용어가 나타나 있고 배타적인 내용도 화해를 위해 적극적인 의미로 볼 수 있다. 바울은 보다 지속적인 화해를 위해 세속적 요소를 제거하도록 요구하고 있다고 볼 수 있다. 이런 요구는 6장 1절에서 고린도 교인들이 하나님의 은혜를 헛되이 하지 말고 은혜에 합당하게 살라는 말씀이나 3장에서 바울의 자천서로써, 또는 새 언약의 백성으로서 의롭게 살라는 말씀과 일치한다. 더구나 12장 21절에서도 바울은 고린도 교인들의 세속적인 죄를 회개하도록 촉구한다.

바울은 계속 화해의 어조를 유지하면서 고린도 교인들이 세속적인 것들을 버리고 거룩하게 살아야 할 것을 권면한다. "사랑하는 자들아"로 시작되는 7장 1절 이후에서의 우호적인 어조는 6장 14절-7장 1절이 화해의 전체 문맥에서 벗어나는 것이 아니라 여전히 화해의 어조 가운데 있음을 나타낸다. 바울은 화해에 방해되는 세속적인 비기독교적인 요소들을 제거함으로써 진정한 화해가 성

703) J. A. Fitzmeyer, "Qumrân and the Interpolated Paragraph in 2 Cor 6:14-7:1," *Essays on the Semitic Background of the New Testament* (London: Chapman, 1971), 205-17, 59-89. Fitzmeyer는 1QFlor에서 구약이 많이 인용된 것은 어떤 구약인용문집이 따로 있음을 가리킨다고 보며, 여기서도 구약인용이 많이 나오므로 바울이 testimonia와 같은 이미 있는 구약 인용 문서를 사용하고 있다고 본다(215-216). Martin은 쿰란에 속했다가 기독교인이 된 사람이 쓴 글을 바울이 사용했을 가능성을 제안한다(195). Thrall은 초대교회 세례준비를 위한 교훈집에서 왔을 것이라는 제안을 한다(31). 두 사람 모두 바울이 이런 자료들을 사용하여 직접 썼다고 본다.

704) Hughes, 242, Martin, 193; Betz, "2Cor 6:14-7:1."

사되기를 바라고 있다. 만일 이것이 바울의 의도라면 6장 14절-7장 1절은 오히려 이 문맥에 맞는 적절한 내용인 것이다. 바울은 이와 유사하게 로마서 12장에서도 믿는 자가 세상을 본받지 말고 마음을 새롭게 함으로 변화를 받아 하나님의 온전하신 뜻이 무엇인지 분별하라고 한다(롬12:2). 또 로마서와 같이 믿음으로 구원 얻는 도리를 강조하는 갈라디아에서도 "너희는 성령을 좇아 행하라. 그리하면 육체의 욕심을 이루지 아니하리라" (갈 5:16)고 세속적인 삶과 구별된 성도의 거룩한 행위를 강조한다.

"너희는 믿지 않는 자와 멍에를 같이 하지 말라" (μὴ γίνεσθε ἑτεροζυγοῦντες ἀπίστοις). ἑτεροζυγούντες("멍에를 같이하지 말라")는 말은 이 부분에 나오는 첫 번째 희귀어로써 다른 신약에서는 나타나지 않는다. 그러나 ζυγός(멍에)라는 명사는 여러 곳에서 쓰인다(마11:29, 30; 21:5; 행 15:10; 갈 5:1; 딤전 6:1). 빌립보서 4장 3절에는 σύζυγος가 "멍에를 같이 한 자"란 뜻으로 이 나온다.

그러므로 바울에게 "멍에를 멘다"는 개념은 익숙한 개념이라고 할 수 있다. ἑτεροζυγοῦντες("멍에를 같이하지 말라")는 흔히 레위기 19장 19절에서 이종교합(異種交合)을 금하는 것과 신명기 22:10에서 황소와 나귀를 함께 경작에 쓰지 말라는 말과 관련시킨다. 두 다른 동물의 혼합은 창조질서에 어긋나므로 금지 된 것이다. 바울은 이런 율법에 근거하여 신자와 불신자가 함께 관계하는 것을 금했다는 것이다.[705] 불신자와의 관계를 더 자세히 말하면, 성적인 관계나 혼인,[706] 상업거래,[707] 이방신전에서의 식사(고전

705) Martin, 196; Thrall, 472, 473.

706) Denney, 249; Plummer, 206.

707) J. D. M. Derrett, "2 Cor 6,14ff. a Midrash on Dt 22,10", *Bib* 59 (1978), 231-50.

10:27, 28),[708] 불신자와의 식사,[709] 불신자에게 재판받는 것(고전 6:1-8),[710] 또는 이런 모든 관계를 포함한 불신자와의 일반적인 접촉을 가리킨다고 한다.[711] 이 경우 당장 바울이 고린도전서에 취하는 세상 사람과의 관계에 대한 보다 개방적인 자세와 다르다고 지적할 수 있다(고전 5:10; 9:20-23). 그러나 역시 정도 문제라고 말할 수 있다. 바울이 세상 사람과 아무렇게나 지나도 좋다는 것은 아닐 것이다. 어쩌면 고린도전서에서 바울이 보인 개방적인 자세를 고린도 교인들이 남용하였으므로 이에 대한 경고를 하게 되었을 수도 있다.[712] 한마디로 바울은 믿음을 버리고서 불신자와 교제하는 것을 경고하고 있다.[713] 무엇을 하든지 거룩한 하나님의 백성들임을 망각하는 것을 경고하고있다.[714] 이런 의미에서 "멍에"는 복음 사역이나 그리스도의 몸(교회)의 조화나 일치를 나타내며, 바울은 이에 방해하는 모든 관계를 청산 할 것을 명하는 것이다.[715]

"의와 불법이 어찌 함께하며?"(τίς γὰρ μετοχὴ δικαιοσύνῃ καὶ ἀνομίᾳ). 이 말과 함께 다섯 개의 반제로 된 질문이 계속된다. 그 질문들 가운데 이미 부정적인 답들이 암시되고 있다. 이 질

708) G. D. Fee, "II Corinthians vi.14-vii.1 and Food Offered to Idols", *NTS* 23 (1977), 157-60).

709) Barrett, 196.

710) Martin, 197.

711) Martin, 197; Thrall, 473.

712) Tasker, 98.

713) Hughes, 246.

714) Barrett, 196; Strach, 4; Martin, 197.

715) Hughes, 194.

문에서도 의와 불법이 함께 할 수 없다는 답이 암시되는 것이다. 이 문장이 γάρ(이는…)로 시작된 이유절이므로 이 뒤에 나오는 모든 질문과 예상된 답은 "너희는 믿지 않는 자와 멍에를 같이 하지 말라"는 명령에 대한 이유(근거)들임을 보여 준다. 한글 개역이나 영어 번역판에서 번역 상의 어려움으로 이유절로 번역되지 않았다. 무리해서 번역하면, "이는 의와 불법이 어찌 함께 하겠는가 이며"라고 할 수 있다.

μετοχή("함께 함," "동반자 관계," partnership)는 또 다른 희귀어이다. δικαιοσύνῃ("의")는 장소를 나타내는 여격으로 보아서, 문자적으로, "의와 불법에 있어서 어떤 관계가 있는가 "라고 번역할 수 있다. 바울은 그의 서신에서 "의"(δικαιοσύνη)를 도처에서 사용하고 있다. 이 사실은 이 부분이 바울의 것이라는 또 하나의 증거가 된다.[716] 하나님의 선물의 의미로서의 의, 즉 이신득의(以信得義)와 인간의 행위로서의 의, 즉 이행득의(以行得義)가 함께 언급된다. 물론 바울은 일반적으로 전자를 더욱 강조하는 것은 사실이다. 여기서는 인간의 행위를 가리키며, 하나님의 은혜로 말미암은 의를 가리키지 않는다(롬 6:13-19; 14:17; 고후 6:7; 11:15; 빌 1:11; 참조, 1QH 14).[717]

"의"(δικαιοσύνη)와 "불법"(ἀνομία)은 롬 6:19에서 대조되어 있다. 그리스도께서 의롭게 하신 자들은 불법에 따라 살면 않된다

716) Barrett, 197; Martin, 198. Martin은 이 부분이 비 바울적이라는 Betz의 견해를 반대한다(H. D. Betz, "2 Cor. 6:14-7:1: An Anti-Pauline Fragment " *JBL* 92 [1973] 91, 주 12). 그러나 여기서 바울이 11:15절의 자칭 "의의 일군"이라는 거짓 사도들을 반대하여 자신의 의의 복음을 방어하는 것일 수 있다는 가능성을 열어 둔다.

717) Collange, 306.

(딛 2:14; 고전 1:30). 바울은 의로운 삶에 있어서 믿는 자가 믿지 않는 자와 명확하게 분리되어야 할 것을 요구하고 있다. 스트라찬(Strachan)은 바울은 추상적인 신학적 의미의 분리가 아닌 이방 도시의 삶에 있어서 실제적인 인간관계의 분리를 말하고 있다고 했다.[718] 바울은 하나님의 은혜와 사랑을 받는 사람들로서 여기에 제시된 일종의 청교도적 경건주의는 하나님의 은혜에 대한 자연스럽고 필요한 반응으로 본다(6:1, 2).[719] 스트라찬은 혹 여기서 바울의 원래 바리새적 분리주의가 다시 나타난 것이 아닌가 생각한다.[720] 그러나 이런 분리주의적 자세는 바울의 선교를 위한 연합적인 자세들과 더불어 균형있게 이해되어야한다.

"빛과 어두움이 어찌 사귀며?"(ἢ τίς κοινωνία φωτὶ πρὸς σκότος;) 빛과 어두움은 양립할 수 없는 도덕성으로 바울 서신과 그 외의 신약에서 자주 대조된다(롬 13:12; 살전 5:5; 엡 5:11-14; 요 1:4-9; 12:36; 눅 16:8; 벧전 2:9). 또 빛은 고린도후서 4장 6절에서 "예수 그리스도의 얼굴에 있는 하나님의 영광을 아는 빛"으로 복음의 빛(4:4)과 동일시되었다. 이 복음의 빛은 구원의 능력, 또는 생명을 나타낸다. 믿음을 가진 이들은 빛을 소유하고 있으며, 믿음이 없는 자들은 상대적으로 구원의 가망이 없는 어두움에 처한 것으로 나타난다. 어두움은 구원에 반대되는 사망이나 멸망을 나타낸다. 여기서 바울이 그리스도 자신을 빛으로 말하지는 않으나 암시하고 있으며(고후 4:4-6), 사단도 어둠의 세력으로 암시된 곳은 있다. 고후 11:14에서 암흑은 불신자들의 운명이며, 고린도 교

718) Strachan, 5.

719) Denney, 237-47.

720) Strachan, 4.

인들은 광명의 천사로 가장한 사단을 따르는 위험에 노출되어 있다. 그러나 다음 15절의 "그리스도와 벨리알"의 대조구가 여기의 "빛과 어두움"의 대조와 병행한다면, 그리스도는 빛(구원)의 주요 벨리알은 어두움(사망)의 주가 된다고 볼 수 있다. 요한복음에서 분명하게 그리스도를 빛으로 나타낸다(요 1:4 이하; 3:19; 8:12; 9:5). 쿰란의 "전쟁문서"(the War Scroll)에서 빛의 아들들이 어두움이다의 아들들과 싸운다는 기사가 여러 곳에 있다(1QM 1:1, 3, 9, 11, 13; 13:5-6, 9, 15-16; 1QS 1:9-11; 1QH 12:6; 4QFlor 1:9). 어두움의 아들이란 말이 신약에는 나오지 않는다. 데살로니가전서 5장 5절에 매우 비슷한 말이 나오지만 다르다("우리가 어두움에 속하지 아니하나니"). 이런 차이가 쿰란과의 관련을 부인하기 위해 사용되기도 하고,[721] 인정하는 데 쓰이기도 한다.[722] 바울은 당시 잘 알려진 빛과 어두움의 대조를 통해서, 또는 빛과 어두움이라는 매우 대조적인 비유적 개념으로,[723] 고린도 교인들이 그리스도인들로서 멸망 받은 세상 사람과 명확히 분별된 구원받은 사람들로서 도덕적이고 영적인 생활을 살아야 할 것을 강조한다.

15. "그리스도와 벨리알이 어찌 조화되며 믿는 자와 믿지 않는 자가 어찌 상관하며?"(τίς δὲ συμφώνησις Χριστοῦ πρὸς Βελιάρ, ἢ τίς μερὶς πιστῷ μετὰ ἀπίστου;). "그리스도와 벨리알이 어찌 조화되며"(τίς δὲ συμφώνησις Χριστοῦ πρὸς Βελιάρ)에서 앞 절의 빛과 어두움의 대조에 맞추어 보면 그리스

721) Barrett, 197.

722) Martin, 199.

723) Hughes, 247.

도는 빛(구원)의 주요 벨리알은 마귀로서 어두움(사망)의 주이다. 빛과 어두움이 함께 할 수 없듯이 그리스도와 벨리알도 함께 할 수 없다. "조화"(συμφώνησις)도 희귀어로서 "동의", "일치"라는 말이다.[724] 트롤은 바울은 고린도후서에서와 다른 데서 사단(σατάν)이라는 말을 쓰는데 왜 여기서 "벨리알"(בליעל)이란 희귀한 말을 쓰는가에 대해 알기 어렵다고 한다(고후 2:11, 11:14, 15; 12:7).[725] 트롤은 본문이 바울의 글임을 믿으나, "벨리알"이 본문에 나오는 유일한 희귀어로서 본문이 바울의 글임을 의심케 하는 단 한 가지 근거라고 한다.[726] 우선 이 말이 구약과 70인역에 이름으로는 나오지 않으나, "가치 없는", "악한", 또는 "불법"이란 뜻으로 쓰인다(신 13:13; 15:9; 삼하 22:5; 시 18:4; 나훔 1:11, 15).[727] 이 말은 후기 유대교 문서, 특히 쿰란 문서에 많이 나온다.[728] 한편

724) Barrett, 198.

725) Martin, 200; Thrall, 474.

726) Thrall, 474.

727) 마귀는 ὁ διάβολος(디아볼로스, 영어 the Devil, 데블의 어원)이며, "반역자" 또는 "고소자"란 뜻이 있다. 전자는 하나님의 역사 방해하는 데서 온 이름이고, 후자는 죄를 지은 인간을 비난, 또는 고소한다는 뜻이라고 본다. 성경에 흔히 쓰이는 고유한 이름은 히브리어로 שָׂטָן, 헬라어로, σατάν(사탄), 또는 σατανᾶς(사타나스)이다. Foerster, "σατανᾶς" *TDNT* v. vii, 151-163; H. G. Liddell & R. Scott, *A Greek-English Lexicon*, 1585.

728) 후기 유대교 문서 중, *쥬빌리서* 1:20; *레위의 증언* 19:1; *단의 증언* 4:7; 5:1; *납달리의 증언* 2:6; 3:1; *이사야의 승천* 1:8-9; 2:4; *시빌린의 신탁*(*Sibylline Oracles*); 1QM 13:1-4; 특히 레위의 증언 8:12에는 벨리알이 메시아에 대항하는 것으로 나온다. 사해 문서의 벨리알에 대한 언급은 어쩌면 12 족장의 증언에게 영향을 받았는지도 모른다(J. T. Milik, *Ten Years of Discovery in the Wilderness of Judea,* SBT 26 [London: SCM, 1959] 34, 35). 쿰란문서에 나오는 벨리알에 대해 서는, H. W. Huppenbaur, "Belial in den Qumrantexten", *TZ* 15(1959) 81-89; Gnilka, ibid., 55-6를 보라. 쿰란을 포함한 후

랍비문헌 가운데 "(율법의) 멍에를 벗은 자(בלי עול, 벨리 올)"라는 말이 있는데(*Sifre on Deut* 117 on 15:7-9; 산헤드린 111b), 그 말이 하나님의 율법을 버렸다는 뜻으로 발전하고, 결국은 하나님을 대적하는 세력(בליעל, 벨리알)을 나타내는 말로 발전되었다는 견해도 있다.[729] 이런 견해는 14절에 불신자와 멍에를 같이 하지 말라는 말이 나오고 15절에는 벨리알이 나오므로 "율법의 멍에를 벗은 자"가 곧 하나님을 대항하는 악한 세력, 즉 "벨리알"이란 말로 발전되어 여기에서 암시적으로 쓰였다고 볼 수 있다고 한다.[730] 즉 14절의 불신자(바울의 대적자들)는(은) "율법의 멍에를 버린 자"("벨리 올")를 가리키고, 그는 15절의 사단("벨리알")의 추종자라는 뜻으로 연결된다. 이런 뜻은 바울이 11:14에서 대적자들을 사단의 추종자로 정죄하는 사실에 비추어 더 분명하게 된다. 물론 벨리알이 이런 랍비문헌의 말("율법의 멍에를 벗은 자", "벨리 올")로부터 발전했다는 것을 고린도 교인들이 알았을 가능성은 희박하다. 그러나 그들이 그 말의 어원을 알든 모르든 고린도 교인들이 이 말을 알고 있었다고 볼 수는 있다. 쿰란과 후대 유대교 문헌에 자주 쓰인 것으로 보아서, 이전에 바울을 통해서나, 고린도 교회에 있는 유대인들을 통해서 이 말을 알고 있었을 수도 있다(고린도에 유대인 회당도 있었다[행 18:4]). 그러므로 바울이 그들이 잘 아는 말로 알고 썼을 가능성이 높다. 바울이 의도적으로

---

den Qumrantexten", *TZ* 15(1959) 81-89; Gnilka, 55-6를 보라. 쿰란을 포함한 후기 유대교 문헌에 나오는 "벨리알"에 대해서, Martin, 199-200; Hughes, 248-50, 주 12를 보라.

729) Barrett, 197.

730) Martin, 198.

잘 모르는 말을 써서 고린도 교인들의 경각심을 불러일으키려고 했을 가능성은 낮다.[731]

"벨리알"은 마귀로서 거짓말쟁이이며 처음부터 살인자이다(요 8:44). 그의 한결같은 목적은 하나님의 목적(특히 구원역사)을 훼방하는 일이다. 그래서 그의 원래 이름인 사단(사탄, שָׂטָן)의 뜻은 "반역자"란 뜻이다. 그가 예수님을 시험했고(마 4:1-11), 그 후 유다에게 들어가 예수를 죽이도록 했다(눅 22:3; 요 13:27). 그러나 주께서 사망 권세를 이기시고 부활하심으로 생명의 주가 되셨다. 히브리서 2장 14절에 의하면 마귀는 "사망의 권세를 잡은 자"이며, 예수는 이 마귀를 이기셨다(참조, 요일 3:7이하; 고전 15:54-56). 이 마귀는 예수님의 구원 사역으로 그 근본적인 힘과 위치를 잃었다(눅 10:18; 참조, 롬 8:1). 그러나 종말에 무저갱에 이어서 지옥에 갇힐 때까지 하나님을 대적하고 믿는 자를 미혹하는 일을 계속한다. 그러므로 여전히 경계의 대상이다(고후 2:11; 11:14, 15; 12:7; 엡 4:17; 6:11; 딤전 3:6, 7; 딤후 2:26; 약 3:15; 4:7; 벧전 5:18; 요일 3:8, 10, 계 2:10; 12:9; 20:2, 3, 7-10).

여기서 "벨리알"과 관련된 세력은 누구인가 11장 14절에서 바울이 그의 대적자들을 사단의 추종자들로 보고 있으므로 여기서도 고린도 교인들이 그의 대적자들을 따르지 말 것을 암시한다고 보기도 한다.[732] 그러나 만일 바울이 그의 대적자들을 본문에 나오는 모든 불의의 편에 속한 자들로 보았다면 보다 분명하게 말했어야 했다. 바울의 대적자들을 제외할 수는 없으나, 보다 넓은 의

731) Martin, 200; Thrall, 474-75.

732) Martin, 200.

미의 그리스도인의 거룩한 생활을 위협하는 세상의 악한 세력을 지칭한다고 보는 것이 안전하다. "그리스도와 벨리알이 어찌 조화되며"라는 말은 따라 나오는 "믿는 자는 믿지 않는 자가 어찌 상관하며"와 직결된다.

"믿는 자와 믿지 않는 자가 어찌 상관하며 "(ἢ τίς μερὶς πιστῷ μετὰ ἀπίστου;). 이 말은 이 부분의 초두에 나온 14절의 "너희는 (믿는 자로서) 믿지 않는 자와 멍에를 같이 하지 말라"는 말을 다시 확인하고 있다. "상관"으로 번역된 μερίς는 "몫" 또는 "분깃"이란 뜻으로 골로새서 1장 12절에도 나온다. "믿는"(πιστός)이란 말이 여기서 예수를 "믿는 자"를 가리키는 전문용어로 쓰인다(딤전 4:10, 12; 5:16). 마찬가지로 "믿지 않는 자"(ἄπιστος)도 형용사에서 명사로 바뀌어 "예수를 믿지 않는 자"란 의미의 전문용어로 쓰이게 되었다(고전 7:12-15; 10:27; 14:22-24; 고후 4:4).

불신자의 삶은 자신에 집착하는 삶이다. (우상을 믿는 것도 결국은 자기의 욕심에 대한 집중이다.) 그러나 그리스도를 믿는 자는 그리스도 중심으로 산다. 불신자는 이 세상의 생존에 집중한다. 믿는 자는 오는 하나님의 나라를 대망한다. 불신자는 인간과 세상의 영화를 찾으나, 믿는 자는 하나님의 영광을 위해 산다(4:18). 그러나 이런 대조적인 차이에서 그리스도인의 삶을 바리새적 분리주의나 수도원적인 세상으로부터 분리된 삶으로 이해되서는 안 된다. 칼빈은 그리스도인들의 분리된 삶이란 사람으로서 살아가는 일상생활에서의 분리를 말하는 것이 아니라 "불신자에게 독특한 것들로부터의 분리"를 가리킨다고 했다.[733]바울도 이미

733) Hughes, 251 재인용.

유사한 말을 하였다(고전 5:10, 11).

16. "하나님의 성전과 우상이 어찌 일치가 되리요. 우리는 살아 계신 하나님의 성전이라. 이와 같이 하나님께서 가라사대, '내가 저희 가운데 거하며 (그들 가운데) 두루 행하여 나는 저희 하나님이 되고 저희는 나의 백성이 되리라' 하셨느니라" (**τίς δὲ συγκατάθεσις ναῷ θεοῦ μετὰ εἰδώλων; ἡμεῖς γὰρ ναὸς θεοῦ ἐσμεν ζῶντος, καθὼς εἶπεν ὁ θεὸς ὅτι ἐνοικήσω ἐν αὐτοῖς καὶ ἐμπεριπατήσω καὶ ἔσομαι αὐτῶν θεὸς καὶ αὐτοὶ ἔσονταί μου λαός**). "하나님의 성전과 우상이 어찌 일치가 되리요 "(**τίς δὲ συγκατάθεσις ναῷ θεοῦ μετὰ εἰδώλων;**)에서 성전과 우상을 대조하는 말이 14절 이후 5개의 반제적인(대조적인) 질문들을 마감하는 질문이다. 이 말은 너희 몸은 "너희 가운데 계신 성령의 전" 이라는 말을 상기시킨다(고전 6:19). **συγκατάθεσις**(일치)란 말도 희귀어로 성경에는 다시없는 말이다.[734] 개역한글성경에 성전으로 번역된 **ναός**는 실제로는 지성소이다(고전 3:16-17; 6:19). 성전은 **τὸ ἱερόν**이다. 바울에 의하면, 성전은 그리스도인이나 그리스도인들이 모인 교회이다. 그러므로 여기서 실제로 예루살렘 성전과 우상의 전을 대조한다고 볼 수 없다. 그리스도인이 우상 숭배하는 죄에 대해서 말하는 것이다(고전 6:10, 11; 6:9; 8장; 10:7, 14, 19; 12:2; 갈 5:20; 골 3:5; 살전 1:9). 한편 바울은 우상 숭배의 죄를 음란함과 연결시켜 말한다. 실제로 당시 우상 숭배 시에

---

734) Philo, *De Post. Caini* 175; Epictetus; Dionys. Hal. 8, 79; Polybius 2, 58, 11:21, 26, 16, Martin, 201 재인용.

음란한 행위를 동반하였기 때문이다(솔로몬의 시편, 14:12).[735] 말하자면 거짓과 탐욕의 우상 숭배 행위가 도덕적인 무질서로 이어졌다. 그러므로 그리스도인들은 우상 숭배자들과 깊은 교제를 할 수 없다(고전 5:10, 11; 6:9, 10; 10:7, 14). 실제 우상이 예루살렘 성전을 더럽히듯이 우상 숭배 행위는 영적 성전인 믿는 자들과 그들의 교회를 더럽힌다. 고린도 교회에서 우상숭배문제와 더불어 음란한 문제는 실제로 바울이 고린도전서에서 언급할 만큼 심각한 문제였다(5장). 고린도에는 당시 다른 도시와 마찬가지로 여러 신전들이 있었을 것이다. 필자가 1994년 5월 초에 가서 본 바로는 옛 고린도 시의 한가운데 아폴로 신전이 서 있었고, 도시의 남쪽 도시와 지중해를 내려다보는 서울 남산 같은 산봉우리에는 고린도 시의 주신(主神) 아프로디테의 신전이 있었다. 서론에서 말했듯이 아프로디테 신전에는 음란한 예배를 위해 천 여명의 창녀들이 있었다고 한다.[736] (2006년 현재 관광객들을 모으기 위해 그리스 정부는, 그리스 정교회의 반대에도 불구하고, 많은 돈을 드려서 유스티니아누스 황제[483-565]때 파괴한 우상과 신전을 애써서 복원하고 있다. 필자가 아테네에 간 1994년에도 그리스 정부가 그리스 정교회의 반대를 무시하고 관광 수입을 위해서 아테네의 파르테논 신전을 복구하고 있었다.)

쿰란 문서에서 성전관련 교훈들이 많이 나온다. 그러나 여기서 보는 성전과 우상과의 대조는 없다.[737] 그러므로 이점에서도 본문

735) Martin, 201.

736) H. Conzelmann, "Korinthian und die Madichen der Aphrodite. Zur Religionsgeschichte der Stadt Korinth," *NAG* 8 (1967), 247-61; Murphy-O'Connor, *St. Paul's Corinth*, 126, 127.

과 사해문서와의 관련설은 지지를 받지 못한다.[738] 성전과 우상의 대조는 역시 성경의 성전의 거룩한 관리에 대한 가르침에 기초한 것으로 본다(레 21:3, 23; 대하 7:2, 16, 19, 20 36:14; 시 79:1; 겔 5:11; 고전 3:17; 6:19 이하).[739] 이스라엘의 멸망은 우상 숭배로 성전을 더럽혔기 때문이다(대하 36:14). "누구든지 하나님의 성전을 더럽히면 하나님이 그 사람을 멸하시리라. 하나님의 성전은 거룩하니 너희도 그러하리라"(고전 3:17).

"우리는 살아 계신 하나님의 성전이라"(ἡμεῖς γαρ ναὸς θεοῦ ἐσμεν ζῶντος). 이 구절의 γάρ(이는…)는 앞 절에서 말한 우상 숭배가 왜 불가한가에 대한 이유를 나타내는 추론적인 접속사이다. 한글 개역 번역에는 이유가 분명히 나타나 있지는 않고 암시되어 있다(참조, NIV). 이 말이 이 본문 가운데 가장 핵심적인 진술이다. 다른 말들은 이 진술에 대한 보조적 설명들이다. 이 진술은 성전의 암시적이고 복합적인 개념에 비추어 그리스도인들의 책임과 사명을 나타내고 있다.

첫째, 성전은 하나님이 이 땅에 임재하는 거룩한 곳이다. 더러운 세상과 구별되어 하나님이 자기의 거룩한 이름을 두신 거룩한 곳이다(레 6:16; 10:17; 대하 7:16, 23:6; 30:8; 고전 3:16, 17; 6:19, 등). 성전 건물은 물론 그 안에 있는 기구들이나 제사장들을 포함한 레위인들이나 제물들은 모두 거룩하게 구별되었다(출 22:31;

737) 1QS 2:11, 17; 4:5; 1QH 4:19; CD 20:9; 참조, 르우벤의 증언, 4:6; J. A. Fitzmeyer, "Qumrân and the Interpolated Paragraph in 2 Cor 6:14-7:1", *Essays on the Semitic Background of the New Testament* (London: Chapman, 1971), 213; Martin, 202.

738) Barrett, 199; Thrall, 477.

739) Martin, 202.

29:34; 40:9; 레 10:17; 스 8:28, 등). 그러므로 그리스도인들이 하나님의 성전이라는 것은 하나님의 거룩한 백성으로 세상에서 구별된 존재라는 뜻이다. 둘째로, 성전은 사람이 지은 것이다. 구약에는 성전을 짓는 것과 성전 기구를 만드는 일을 되도록 자세히 설명하고 있다(출 36-39; 왕상 6-7). 그것은 역사적으로 성전이 어떻게 지어졌는가를 보여주는 자료도 되지만, 성전은 모름지기 사람이 하나님의 지시하심을 따라서 온갖 정성을 다하여 지어야 한다는 교훈도 있다. 여기서 바울은 고린도 교인들이 도덕적으로 영적으로 책임 있는 그리스도인으로 살아가야 함을 가르치고 있다(고전 6:19). 어쩌면, 세상에서의 분리는 쉽다. 그러나 거룩함을 온전히 이루는 일은 우리 평생의 과업이다. 셋째로, 성전은 중보적 기능이 있다(참조, 요 2:21). 성전은 하나님이 죄인들을 만나서 그들의 죄를 용서하시고, 그들의 기도를 들으시는 만남의 장소이다(왕하 8:38; 대하 6:24이하; 마 21:13). 고린도 교인들은 성전으로써 이 세상 사람들에게 그리스도를 통한 하나님의 은혜를 전하고 하나님 앞으로 인도하는 복음 사역자로서의 책임을 가지고 있다.

그러나 여기서 바울이 강조하는 성전의 개념은 첫 번째와 두 번째이다. 그리스도인은 하나님이 임재하시는 거룩한 존재로서 세상에서 분리되고 또 그의 거룩한 존재임을 거룩한 삶으로 증명해야 한다. 하나님이 거주하실 가장 적합한 곳은 성전에 해당되는 인간의 마음이다.[740] "살아 계신 하나님" (θεοῦ ··· ζῶντος)은 새로운 피조물이 된 고린도 교인들에게 계속하여 새로운 삶을 요구하시는 하나님이시란 의미가 있다고 본다(5:17). 온 세상의 주인이신

740) Plummer, 209.

하나님이 이제 "손으로 지은 성전"이 아닌 그를 믿는 이들의 "마음 성전"에 거하신다(행 7:48; 17:24). 돌과 나무로 된 성전도 우상과 함께 있을 수 없다면, 살아 있는 돌들로 지어진 성전은 더욱 거룩해야 한다(벧전 2:5).[741] 성전 된 믿는 자들의 임무는 새로운 삶으로 그들이 하나님의 성전 됨을 증거 해야 한다. 생명을 주시고 다시 태어나게 하시는 하나님의 개념이 성전 개념과 함께 나타나고 있다.[742] 요 2:21에는 예수님의 몸을 성전으로 나타낸다. 유사하게 에베소서 2:20-22에서는 교회가 하나님의 거룩한 전으로 묘사되고, 예수는 모퉁이 돌, 사도들은 성전 터, 성도들이 서로 연결하여 성전을 지어가는 것과, 또 개인적으로도 "하나님의 거하실 처소가 되기 위하여 예수 안에서 함께 지어져 가는 것"을 말한다.

"우리"(ἡμεῖς)는 일인칭 복수로서 하나님의 성전의 집단적 의미와 개인적 의미를 다 나타낸다.[743] 바울은 성전을 집단적으로 영적 교회로 나타내기도 하고(고전 3:16, 17), 개인의 마음으로도 설명한다(고전 6:19 이하; 엡 2:21; 벧전 2:5). 에베소서 2장 20-21절에도 교회를 예수와 사도와 연결되는 집단적 의미의 성전으로 말함과 동시에 개인적으로 "하나님 안에서 성령이 거하시는 처소"로 설명하고 있다. 특히 에베소서 2장이 본문과 같이 화해의 주제를 가지고 있으면서 성전에 비추어 교회와 그리스도인의 존재 의미와 양식을 설명하는 사실은 본문도 바울의 쓴 글임을 지지해준다. 칼빈은 "하나님께서는 각 사람에게 거하심으로 그들 중에 거

741) Hughes, 252.

742) Hughes, 252, 253.

743) Hughes, 252; Martin, 202.

하신다" 고 하였다.[744] 거룩한 교회는 거룩한 개인으로 구성된다.

바울은 교회를 그리스도인들의 집단으로서 구약 언약의 합법적 전수자들이며, 그러므로 당연히 성전이라고 보았다(고후 3:7, 8, 18).[745] 성전은 하나님이 거하시는 땅위의 장소이며, 유대인들의 신앙의 중심이다. 이제 구원의 새 시대에 성전의 의미는 새롭게 해석되었다. 고린도전서가 쓰인 시기(A.D. 55년-56년)가 성전 파괴(A.D. 70년 3-4월) 15년 이전이지만, 이미 바울은 성전을 지역적 의미를 떠나서 그리스도의 교회와 그리스도인 자신들로 존재론적으로 영적으로 해석하고 있었다(고전 3:16, 17; 6:19 이하). (이런 바울의 영적 의미의 성전은 스데반의 설교[행 7:48이하]를 듣고서 생각하기 시작했다면 지나치게 추정적인 주장이 될 것이다.) 그러므로 여기서도 하나님의 거룩한 성전에 비추어 고린도 교인들이 그리스도인으로서 세상과 분리되고 구별되는 거룩한 삶을 살아야 함을 말하고 있다. 그리스도인의 공동체 조직과 개인의 매일의 삶을 유대인 신앙의 중심인 성전에 비추어서 생각하는 것은 바울의 독특한 생각이며, 세상에서의 교회와 그리스도인의 존재의 의의와 성격과 양식을 함께 설명하는 적절한 비유적 표현이다. 비록 성전이 땅에 있으나 하나님이 거하시는 처소이듯이, 그리스도의 교회나 그리스도인은 하나님이 거하시는 곳으로서 비록 세상에 위치하고 있으나 흠 없이 거룩해야 한다. 하나님의 거룩하신 성전이 이 추한 세상에 존재한다는 역설적인 의미는 그리스도의 교회와 그리스도인이 거룩한 하나님의 백성으로서 이 더러운 세상에

744) Martin, 202 재인용.

745) Barrett, 199

서 거룩하게 살아야하는 역설적인 의미와 유사하므로, 바울이 성전 비유를 사용하고 있다.

한편, 논쟁적인 고린도후서의 상황을 고려할 때, "우리"(ἡμεῖς)는 하나님께서 복음의 사역자로 삼으신 바울을 가까이 따르는 고린도 교인들을 포함하는 "우리"라고 보아야 한다.[746] 5장 20절에서 바울은 하나님께서 자신을 하나님의 화해의 사신으로 삼아 보내셨다고 했다. 그를 따르는 이들은 하나님과 화해하면서 모두 다 같이 하나님의 영적 성전이 된다. 그러나 그를 따르지 않는 이들은 결국 우상 숭배자들과 같다. 바울과 함께 그리스도 안에 거하는 이들이 참된 신앙 공동체이며 영적 하나님의 전이다. 고린도후서 자체가 바울의 반대자들을 염두에 두고 있으므로 이런 논쟁적 요소를 거의 배제할 수는 없다. 바울은 원칙적인 그리스도의 교회의 거룩함을 말하면서 고린도 교인들이 그("우리")와 대적자들 사이에 선택할 것을 간접적으로 암시하고 있다고 봐야 할 것이다.

"이와 같이 하나님께서 가라사대"(καθὼς εἶπεν ὁ θεὸς). 바울은 권위 있는 하나님의 말씀인 구약 인용을 통해서 고린도 교인들에게 거룩한 생활의 당위성을 강조한다. 그런데 바울의 이런 인용 양식은 다른 인용 양식과 다르다. 그는 구약 인용 시, 흔히 ("이르시되")라고만 한다(롬 9:15, 25; 고후 4:6; 6:2; 갈 3:16). 그닐카(Gnilka)는 이 독특한 인용 양식은 쿰란 문서에서 발견된다고 한다(CD 6:12-13; 8:9; 참조, 19:22).[747] 물론 이런 표현의 유사성만 가지고 쿰란과의 연계성을 증명할 수는 없다.[748] 바울은 구약인용

746) Martin, 203.

747) Gnilka, "2 Cor 6:14-7:1," 58.

748) Barrett, 200; 참조, Martin, 203.

(70인역 사용)을 문자적으로는 하지 않되 중심 의미는 살리면서, 고린도 교인들이 세속적인 생활로부터 분리된 거룩한 생활을 해야 하는 근거로 삼는다. 이렇게 현재의 해석자의 처지에 따라 구약을 적절히 의역하여 해석하고 적용하는 것을 유대교식 또는 쿰란식 성경 해석, 즉 페쉐르(פֵּשֶׁר)라고 한다. 바울은 여기서 레위기 26장 11, 12절을 메시아적으로 해석한다고 한다.[749] 위의 6장 2절의 구약인용에서와 같이 메시아로 말미암는 구원의 새 시대가 시작되었다는 의미를 강조하고 있다.

"내가 저희 가운데 거하며 (그들 가운데)두루 행하여" (**ὅτι ἐνοικήσω ἐν αὐτοῖς καὶ ἐμπεριπατήσω**). 이 구절은 초대교회에서 메시아 도래와 사역을 증명하기 위해 구약 성경에서 발췌하여 만든 "구약성경 인용집" (*testimonium*)에서 왔다고 본다.[750] 6장 16절 하반절은 레위기 26장 11, 12절과 에스겔 37장 27절로 결합되어 있다. 바울은 여기서 **ἐνοικήσω**(내가 거하리라)란 말을 에스겔 37장 27절의 **ἡ κατασκήνωσις**(거처)를 의역하여 쓴다고 본다. 70인역은 히브리 성경 레위기 26장 11절의 "거주지" (מִשְׁכָּנִי, 미스카니, "내 장막")를 언약(**διαδήκη**, 디아데케)으로 번역하여 "내가 너희 중에 언약을 두겠다" 라고 한다. "두루 행하여" (**ἐμπεριπατήσω**)는 예수님의 지상 사역의 성취를 가리키는 구절이다(행 10:48). 예수의 땅위의 사역이 문자적으로 성취된 사실에 비추어 볼 때 70인역의 의역보다는 히브리 성경의 문자적 번역 ("내가 내 장막을 너희 중에 세우리니")이 바울에게 더 호감을 주

749) Georgi, *Die Gegner*, 265-82; Ellis, "A Note," 130.

750) Martin, 204.

었을 것이다. 이 말을 포함한 다른 말들은 레위기 26장 12절과 거의 같다.

"'나는 저희 하나님이 되고 저희는 나의 백성이 되리라' 하셨느니라"(καὶ ἔσομαι αὐτῶν θεὸς καὶ αὐτοὶ ἔσονταί μου λαός). 이것은 하나님의 백성에게 주시는 세 개의 약속 중 첫 번째 약속이다. 7장 1절에서 이런 약속들을 가리켜 직접 "이 약속(들)(ταύτας…τὰς ἐπαγγελίας)"이라고 언급하고 있다. 이 부분은 레위기 26장 12절(LXX)의 "너희"(ὑμῶν)가 "저희"(αὐτῶν)로 바뀐 것 외에는 문자적으로 인용되었다. 앞서 하나님이 모세에게 약속하신 언약의 말씀과 문자적으로 약간 다르다(출 6:7). 이 옛 언약의 성취는 구약 시대에 예언자들을 통해서 약속되었다(겔 11:20; 36:28; 참조, 계 21:3; 겔 37:26, 27; 렘 31:31-34). 하나님은 그를 믿는 백성들 가운데 좌정하시기를 작정하셨다. 옛 언약의 양식은 에스겔 37장 26절과 레위기 26장 11절에 있는 언약에 대한 암시와 관련 있어 보인다(참조, 렘 32:38). 내용이나 어휘에 있어서 큰 변경은 없다. 바울은 새 언약이 이 땅에서 오셔서 사역하신 그리스도에게서 성취되었고 또 그의 일군으로서 그가 세운 새로운 그리스도 공동체에서, 또 각 개인의 마음 가운데, 이 언약이 계속 성취되고 있다고 생각한다(마 1:23; 요 1:14; 엡 3:17; 고전 6:19이하). 그리고 이 언약은 최종적인 성취를 기다리고 있다(계 21:3). 하나님은 그리스도를 통해서 구원의 새 시대를 시작하셨다(6:1, 2). 하나님께서 그의 백성 가운데 거하시겠다는 약속이 성취된 것이다. 그리고 그의 거주하심은 새로운 영적 의미와 깊이를 더하게 되었다. 즉 아무도 이 언약을 파기할 수 없다. 이 언약에 참여한 사람은 새로운 피조물이 된다(5:17). 그러나 이런 특권은 거룩한 백성으로 살아야할 책임과 함께 부과된 것임을 알아야 한다(레 11:44; 19:2; 마 5:48). "너희는 거룩하라 나 여호와 너희 하나님이 거룩함이니라."(레 19:2). 하나님의 백성으로서 거룩함을 이루는 것이 본문전체의 주제이다. 거룩함은 고린도 교인들이 하나님과, 그리고 그의 사도 바울과 화해적 관계의 공통적이고 필수적인 성격이다.

17. "그러므로 주께서 말씀하시기를 너희는 저희 중에서 나와서 따로 있고 부정한 것을 만지지 말라. 내가 너희를 영접하여" (**διὸ ἐξέλθατε ἐκ μέσου αὐτῶν καὶ ἀφορίσθητε, λέγει κύριος, καὶ ἀκαθάρτου μὴ ἅπτεσθε· κἀγὼ εἰσδέξομαι ὑμᾶς**). 17절은 14절에서 16절까지의 실제적 의미의 결론이라고 할 수 있다.[751]

"너희는 저희 중에서 나와서"(**ἐξέλθατε ἐκ μέσου αὐτῶν**). 바울은 계속해서 구약 성경을 인용하여 거룩한 생활의 필요성을 강조하고 있다. "나와서"(**ἐξέλθατε**)는 단순과거 명령형으로 "즉시 단번에 나오라"는 뜻이다. 바울은 세상의 죄의 더러움에 의한 오염의 위험이 매우 높다고 보았다. 세상에서 나오지 않으면 거룩하신 하나님이 그들과 함께 거하실 수 없다. 거룩한 생활을 위해서는 일단 더러운 곳에서 분리되어야한다. 그 분리는 세상과의 결별 같은 물리적인 분리를 말하는 것이 아니라, 영적인 분리를 말한다. 물론 수도사 같은 특별한 은혜를 받은 이들은 이 말을 문자적으로 지켜서 세상에서 분리된 삶을 살 수는 있다. 그러나 바울이 고린도 교인들에게 이렇게 실제로 분리된 생활을 의미하는 것은

---

751) Plummer, 209.

아니라고 본다(고전 5:10).[752)]

"따로 있고"(ἀφορίσθητε). 이 말도 단순과거 명령형으로서 앞의 "나오라"는 명령을 뒷받침하는 말이다. 세상에서 나올 뿐만 아니라 분명히 구별되는 생활을 지속하라는 말이다.

"부정한 것을 만지지 말라"(ἀκαθάρτου μη. ἅπτεσθε). 이 말도 마찬가지로 단순과거 명령형이다. 이 두 말 모두 17절 상반절의 "너희는 저희 중에서 나오라"는 말을 강화시키는 말들이다. "주께서 말씀하시기를"(λέγει κύριος)이라는 말은 주의 말씀을 인용함으로써(사 52:11; 겔 20:34), 바울의 말이 성경과 일치되는 것을 보여줌으로써 고린도 교인들을 설득하는 효과가 있다. 성전에서 봉사하는 제사장들은 자신을 거룩하게 지키기 위해서 부정한 것을 만질 수 없듯이(레 21:11), 성전 된 그리스도인들도 마찬가지로 죄를 멀리해야 한다는 뜻이다.

"내가 너희를 영접하여"(κἀγὼ εἰσδέξομαι ὑμᾶς). 세상의 더러움에서 분리되고 부정한 것을 피하는 결과는 주님과 함께 살고 교제하는 것이다. 이 약속은 6장 14절-7장 1절에 있는 세 가지 약속 중에 두 번째 약속이다. 이 약속은 구약의 약속에 근거한 것이다(겔 11:17; 20:34, 41; 참조, 습 3:20). 고린도 교인들의 세상의 더러움을 버리고 분리되어 살고, 바울의 복음을 받으면, 하나님과 화해하게 된다.

17절은 두 개의 구약 성경 인용이 결합되어 있다. 이사야 52장 11절: "너희는 떠날찌어다. 떠날찌어다. 거기서 나오고 부정한 것

---

752) 이런 분리주의적 특성 때문에 이 부분이 고전 5:9의 "잃어버린 편지"(the Lost Letter)에서 온 것이라고 보는 견해도 있다. J. C. Hurd Jr., 135-39; Jewett, 389-444; Schmithals, 265; Suhl, 208.

을 만지지 말찌어다. 그 가운데서 나올 찌어다(참조, 렘: 51:45: "나의 백성아 너희는 그 중에서 나와…"). 에스겔 20장 34절: "…너희를 열국 중에서 나오게 하며 너희의 흩어진 열방 중에서 모아내고." 지금까지 바울은 부정적으로 믿지 않는 자와 함께 멍에를 메지 말고, 그리스도와 벨리알이 조화가 될 수 없으며, 하나님의 성전과 우상이 일치 될 수 없다고 하였다. 그러나 17절에서는 적극적인 표현을 써서 이방인들에게서 나오고 부정한 것을 피하라고 한다. 인용된 구약 성경은 하나님의 백성이 그들의 죄 때문에 포로로 잡혀 있는 악하고 우상을 섬기는 나라에서 나올 것을 말한다. 특히 이사야 52장 11절은 주의 전의 그릇들을 관할하는 제사장들에게 말한 것이다.[753] 이 말씀이 그리스도인들에게 적절한 말씀인 까닭은 다음과 같다.[754] 첫째로, 그리스도인은 하나님의 백성으로서, 그리스도의 피로 죄의 속박과 더러움에서 속량되었다. 둘째로, 그들도 왕 같은 제사장이다(벧전 2:9; 계 1:6). 셋째로, 그들이 다루는 주의 전의 그릇들은 다름 아닌 그들의 몸들이다(행 9:15; 롬 9:21이하; 고후 4:7; 살전 4:4; 딤후 2:20 이하). 바울은 고린도 교인들이 고린도와 같은 음란한 우상숭배의 도시에 살면서 바

---

753) Betz는 인용된 이사야 52:11이 제사장들의 제사 의식적 정결을 말한 것과 같이 본문도 제사 의식적 정결을 말하는 것이라고 한다("2 Cor 6:14-7:1," 95, 96). 이에 대해서 Martin은 고후 6:1, 2에서 바울이 하나님의 은혜를 헛되이 받지 말라고 말함으로서 제사 의식적 정결함이 아니라 도덕적 정결함을 가르치고 있다고 한다(Martin, 205; Bruce, 215). 그들은 은혜로 말미암아 법적으로는 거룩한 백성이 되었으나, 실제적으로는 아직 거룩함을 이루지는 못했다(고전 5:7, 8; 참조, 마 5:48). 직설법("의롭게 되었다")과 명령법("의롭게 되라")의 긴장에 대해서, P. Tachau, *"Einst" und "Jezt" im Neuen Testament,* FRLANT 105 (Göttingen: Vandenhoeck & Ruprecht, 1972), 116-29를 보라.

754) Hughes, 256.

벨론에 포로가 되었던 유대인들처럼 부주의와 타협으로 흘러버릴 위험에 처해 있다고 보았다. 비슷한 상황에 처해있던 에베소 교회에도 비슷한 경고를 하였다: "그러므로 저희와 함께 참예하는 자 되지 말라. 너희가 전에는 어두움이었더니 이제는 주안에서 빛이라. 빛의 자녀들처럼 행하라"(엡 5:7-8). 칼빈은 이런 분리주의적 교훈의 균형적 이해를 위해서 다음과 같이 말한다. 우리가 세상의 더러움에서 건짐을 받았으므로 세상에 등을 돌리라는 말이 아니라, 다만 세상의 더러움을 피하라는 것이다.[755] 우리는 세상의 빛으로 세상 사람들에게 빛을 비춰야 한다(마 5:14 이하). 세상에서 몸으로의 분리가 아니라, 도덕적 영적으로의 분리이다. 세상에 살면서 세상의 더러움을 피해야 한다. 이것은 성전이 이 세상에 있으면서도 거룩해야하는 것과 마찬가지이다. 바울은 이런 성전의 역설적인 존재 의의와 양식이 교회와 성도의 세상에서의 역설적인 존재 의의와 존재 양식과 일치하므로 여기서 그리스도인을 살아 계신 하나님의 성전이라고 말하는 것이다.

18. "너희에게 아버지가 되고 너희는 내게 자녀가 되리라. 전능하신 주의 말씀이니라 하셨느니라"(**καὶ ἔσομαι ὑμῖν εἰς πατέρα καὶ ὑμεῖς ἔσεσθέ μοι εἰς υἱοὺς καὶ θυγατέρας, λέγει κύριος παντοκράτωρ**). 이것이 세 개의 약속 중에 마지막 약속이다. 이 말씀은 삼하 7:14에 나단 선지자가 다윗에게 한 예언과 흡사하다. "나는 그 아비가 되고 그는 내 아들이 되리니…" 바울이 3인칭 단수대명사("그")를 2인칭 복수 대명사("너희")로 바꾸었다고 볼 수

---

755) Hughes, 256 재인용.

있다. 이렇게 하여 고린도 교인들에게 관련된 의미로 전달될 수 있기 때문이다. 그런데 바울은 "내 아들" 뒤에 "딸들"(θυγατέρας)이란 말을 보충하고 있다. "딸들"이란 말이 추가되었다고 해서 바울이 여성을 남성과 동등하게 보는 증거로 활용하는 것은 본문의 의도와는 상관없는 지나친 확대 해석이다.[756] 바울은 다른 데서 창조질서에 의한 교회와 사회나 가정에서의 남녀유별의 견지를 확고히 하고 있으므로, 여기서는 아들과 함께 딸들이란 말이 추가된 것은 남녀 상호관계에 있어서 동등을 말하는 것이 아니라, 하나님 앞에서 하나님의 구원의 대상으로서 여자는 남자와 동등하다는 뜻으로 보아야 한다(골 3:18; 고전 11:11-16; 14:33-36; 엡 5:22-33; 딤전 2:11-15). 오히려 이사야 43장 6절("내가… 내 아들들을 원방에서 이끌며 내 딸들을 땅 끝에서 오게 하라")의 이스라엘 회복의 날에 대한 대망에 기초하여 그리스도 안의 새로운 피조물 된 남녀가 모두 하나님의 공동체, 즉 하나님의 성전이 된다는 종말론적인 뜻으로 보아야 할 것이다(사 49:22; 60:4). 또 이사야 52장 11절의 "아들"(υἱόν, 단수)이 여기서는 "아들들"(υἱούς, 복수)로 표기된 것도 이사야 43장 6절의 "아들들"을 반영하여 이제 구원의 새 시대에 모든 그리스도인들이 하나님의 자녀가 되는 약속의 축복을 받게 되었다는 의미로 볼 수 있다. 바울은 다른 데서도 그리스도인들을 하나님의 아들로 표기하고 있다(롬 8:14-17; 9:25-26; 갈 3:26; 4:6-7). 로마서 9장 25-26절에서 하나님의 백성은 하나님의 아들이라고 한다. 롬 1:3의 다윗의 아들 그리스도의 도래의 약속은 갈라디아서 4장 4-5절에서 모든 그리스도인들에게

---

756) Plummer, 210; Barrett, 201; Martin, 207.

적용되어서 그리스도의 도래로 그리스도인들이 하나님의 아들이 되는 특권을 가지게 되었다고 한다.[757]

여기의 시제는 모두 미래로 되어있으나("되고"[되리라, ἔσομαι], "되리라"[ἔσεσθέ]), 이 미래의 약속들이 여기에 제시된 명령에 사람이 순종하는 여부에 따라서 성취될 것이다. 그리고 지금은 아직 아무런 약속의 효과가 나타나지 않았다고 보아서는 안 된다. 믿는 자는 이미 하나님의 자녀가 되었다(갈 3:26-27). 그러므로 여기의 미래 시제는 그리스도를 믿음으로 말미암아 이미 성취된 것이다. 그들은 이미 하나님의 성전이다(16). 그럼에도 불구하고 그들은 하나님의 자녀, 성전으로서 합당하게 살아야 하나님의 약속의 성취와 축복을 계속해서 누릴 수가 있다(17). 또한 미래적 의미는 남아 있다. "이미" 그러나 "아직 아니"(already, but not yet)의 긴장이 여기에 있다. "믿는 자는 하나님의 자녀가 된 사실과 일치되어야 한다(believers must become what they already are.)."[758]

"전능하신 주의 말씀이니라 하셨느니라"(λέγει κύριος παντοκράτωρ). 이 말은 16절에도 나온 "주께서 말씀하시기를"(λέγει κύριος)이라는 말과 함께 바울의 말의 신적 근거를 밝혀서 바울의 말의 권위를 높이는 효과가 있다. "전능하신"(παντοκράτωρ)이란 말은 다른 바울 서신 가운데 나타나는 예가 없다. 계시록에서 9번 나타난다. 구약에서는 "전능하신 하나님"

---

757) 쿰란문서(4QFlor 1:2)에서 다윗 계보의 메시아와 관련하여 사 52:11을 인용한다. J. A. Fitzmeyer, "Qumrân and the Interpolated Paragraph in 2 Cor 6:14-7:1," *Essays on the Semitic Background of the New Testament*, 120.

758) Thrall, 479.

보다는 "전능하신 이"로 많이 나타난다(창 17:1; 출 6:3; 민 24:4, 욥 5:17; 사 9:6; 겔 1:24, 8:5; 10:5). 70 인역은 "만군의 여호와"를 "전능하신 하나님"으로 자주 번역한다(삼하 7:8; 렘 51:7). 그러나 "전능하신 주의 말씀이니라"는 말은 성경전체에서 여기에만 있다. 이런 양식이 독자들에게 바울의 말의 권위를 의식하게 하는 효과도 있고, 또 그들이 하나님의 말을 순종해야 한다는 의식도 갖게 한다. 그들이 우상을 섬기던 방식으로 하나님을 자신의 욕구를 충족시키는 대상으로 의식하지 않고, 오히려 하나님의 뜻에 따라서 움직이는 신앙을 가지도록 하게 한다. 우상과의 화해는 우상이 원하는 욕심을 충족시킴으로 가능하나, 하나님과의 화해는 그의 거룩하심을 본받으므로 가능하다. 선과 의와 거룩하신 하나님의 고상한 본성을 닮음으로 그와의 교제가 가능해진다. 바울은 단순히 고린도 교인들과 같이 되어 그들이 원하는 대로 허락하거나 따름으로써 화해하려는 것이 아니다. 그가 아이를 달래는 부모처럼 자신을 낮추어서 고린도 교회를 대하는 것은 결국 하나님의 온전하심으로 그들을 이끌어 올리려는 데 있다. 바울의 하향식 접근 방식은 결국 하나님과의 상향적인 관계 수립을 위한 것이다.

바울은 여기에 나오는 일련의 구약 인용들을 "전능하신 하나님의 말씀이니라"라는 말로 맺는다. 바울은 하나님의 종으로서 고린도 교인들에게 하나님의 말씀을 전하고 있음을 나타낸다. 여기의 권면은 자기의 유익을 위한 것도 아니고 자신의 생각에서 나온 말이 아니다. 오로지 하나님의 명령을 순수히 전할 뿐이다. 그런 면에서 거짓 사도들과 구별된다(2:17; 4:2; 11:13-15; 12:12-13; 참조, 롬 16:18; 빌 3:19). 마틴은 여기서 바울이 마치 구약의 예언자처럼 예언자의 두루마기("망또")를 입고 예언하는 듯이 보인다고 한다(207; 참조, 고전 14:37). 그가 전하는 하나님의 뜻은 그의 자녀가 그들의 아버지의 거룩하심을 알고 그와 같이 거룩하게 되는 것이다.

7:1. "그런즉 사랑하는 자들아 이 약속을 가진 우리가 하나님을 두려워하는 가운데서 거룩함을 온전히 이루어 육과 영의 온갖 더러운 것에서 자신을 깨끗케 하자"(ταύτας οὖν ἔχοντες τὰς ἐπαγγελίας, ἀγαπητοί, καθαρίσωμεν ἑαυτοὺς ἀπὸ παντὸς μολυσμοῦ σαρκὸς καὶ πνεύματος, ἐπιτελοῦντες ἁγιωσύνην ἐν φόβῳ θεοῦ). "그런즉 사랑하는 자들아 이 약속을 가진 우리가"(ταύτας οὖν ἔχοντες τὰς ἐπαγγελίας, ἀγαπητοί). 이 약속들은 앞에서 언급한 세 가지 약속들이다(16, 17, 18). 하나님께서는 우리가 그의 명령을 잘 이행하면 그의 약속을 잘 지키실 것이다. 그러나 하나님께서 그의 백성들과 함께 계신다는 약속을 실행하시기 위해서는 먼저 그 백성들이 정결케 되어야 한다.[759] 그러므로 바울은 하나님의 약속에 근거하여 고린도 교인들에게 거룩하게 되기를 권면하고 있다.

바울이 자기 유익을 위해서 화해를 요청하는 것이 아니라 고린도 교회를 위한 것이라는 증거가 "사랑하는 자들아"(ἀγαπητοί)라는 호칭이다. 이런 말이 바울의 서신에서 자주 나올 것으로 예상되지만, 바울은 이 말을 매우 아껴 쓰는 편이다(고후 12:19; 고전 10:14; 15:58; 빌, 2:12, 4:1; 롬 12:19). 고린도 교인들은 바울을 잘

---

759) Plummer, 211.

대해 주지 않았으나(고전 2:3; 고후 2:1), 바울은 고린도 교인들을 여전히 사랑하고 그들을 향하여 마음을 열고 있다(6:11). 이 말은 또한 이 부분이 바울이 쓴 것이라는 또 하나의 증거이다. 바울 외에 그 누구도 고린도 교인들을 이렇게 부를 수 있는 사람은 없다. 그들을 자기의 자천서라고 부르는 바울만이 그렇게 부를 수 있다(고후 3:2). 제 삼자인 편집자가 이런 말을 삽입할 수 없다.[760] 이런 다정한 말은 다시 화해의 주제로 전체 문맥을 다시 돌리는 부수적인 효과도 있다.

"하나님을 두려워하는 가운데서 거룩함을 온전히 이루어"(ἐπιτελοῦντες ἁγιωσύνην ἐν φόβῳ θεοῦ). 이 말도 헬라 성경에는 맨 뒤쪽에 나오는 말이나 한글 개역에는 번역상 앞으로 나와 있다.

"하나님을 두려워하는 가운데서"(ἐν φόβῳ θεοῦ). 거룩한 삶은 하나님을 두려워함에서 시작된다. 5:11에서도 주님의 최후 심판을 받아야 할 것을 말한 후 "주의 두려우심"으로 너희를 권한다고 했다. 이미 구원받은 사람도 주님의 심판을 받을 것이다. 그리고 심판 이전이라도 "살아 계신 하나님"(θεοῦ … ζῶντος)은 그의 자녀들이 하나님을 두려워함으로 거룩하게 삶으로써 하나님의 영광을 세상에 증거할 것을 끊임없이 요구하신다(2:14; 롬 3:18; 참조, 엡 5:21). "하나님을 두려워함"이 유대지혜전통의 중심 사상이다(욥 1:1; 2:3; 시 2:11; 5:7; 잠 1:7, 29, 8:13; 전 12:13; 시락서 1:11-30). 사람이나 다른 피조물(세상이나 무슨 "운명" 같은 것)을 두려워해서가 아니라 하나님을 두려워함이 지혜의 근본이다. 하나님의 지

760) Hughes, 257.

혜의 깊이와 신묘막측 하신 경륜을 유한된 지혜를 가진 인간은 마땅히 경외해야 한다. 여기서도 이런 유대 지혜의 전통이 나타난다고 보아야 한다. 지혜 있는 자는 지혜의 근원이신 하나님의 말씀을 듣고 행함으로 생명의 길로 간다. 그러나 어리석은 자는 그 반대이다. 고린도 교인들은 하나님의 자녀로서 하나님을 두려워하면서 더러운 것을 버리고, 거룩함을 온전히 이루어서 하나님의 약속의 축복을 받아야 한다. "가운데서"(ἐν)라는 전치사가 거룩함을 온전하게 이루는 영역을 가리키는지, 아니면, 수단을 가리키는지 분명하지 않다. 즉 하나님을 두려워하는 정신적 자세에서 거룩함을 이루라는 것인지, 하나님을 두려워함을 통해서 거룩함을 이루라는 말인지 알 수 없으나, 어느 쪽이든지 거룩함을 이루라는 전체 의미는 분명하다.[761]

"온전히 이루어"(ἐπιτελοῦντες)는 원래 "거룩함을 이루다"(ἐπιτελεῖν)라는 뜻이다.[762] 이 말은 본문에서 바울의 관심이 무엇인가를 다시 분명히 나타낸 준다. 바울은 고린도 교인들이 거룩한 삶을 살기를 원하고 있다. 이 말은 어쩌면 완전주의적 삶을 반대하는 빌립보서 3장 12-15절과 불일치되는 것처럼 보인다. 빌립보서에서 바울은 모든 것을 다 이루었다고 자처하는 빌립보 이단을 가리켜서 "그리스도의 십자가의 원수"라고 했다(빌 3:18). 바울은 거기서나 여기서나 거룩함을 다 이루었다고 자처하지 말고 계속해서 정진할 것을 권면하고 있다. 다만 여기서는 고린도 교회의 세속주의적 영향이 강하므로 보다 완전주의적인 말로 그들을 권

761) Plummer, 212; Martin, 211.

762) Hughes, 258, 주, 22.

면한다고 봐야 한다.[763] 이 세상에서 믿는 자는 거룩함의 목적을 향해 계속 전진할 뿐이다(참조, 8:6, 11; 빌 1:6; 살전 3:3; 롬 1:4).[764] 거룩함을 이루었다고 자만하는 것은 하나님을 무시하는 도덕주의나 율법주의적 자세이다. 아무도 하나님 앞에 완전하다고 자랑할 수는 없다(롬 3:27). 이것 역시 하나님의 은혜를 헛되게 하는 것이다(6:1, 2). 한편 바울은 고린도 교인들이 이미 하나님의 성전이라고 했으나(16절), 계속해서 성전답게 살 것을 권면해왔다(17). 여기서도 고린도 교인들이 예수를 믿음으로 법적으로는 이미 거룩하나, 명실공(名實共)히 하나님의 성전이 되기 위해 힘쓰라고 권한다. 여기에도 역설적인 또 하나의 현재와 미래의 긴장이 있다. 바울의 구원론과 성화론의 교훈에서는 "이미" 그러나 "아직 아닌"(already, but not yet)의 긴장이 항상 있다. 어느 한 부분만을 보면 불일치로 보이나 전체적으로는 조화를 이룬다. 사실 이런 역설적인 조화는 기독론을 비롯한 기독교의 모든 교리나 가르침의 특징이며 그 특징이 그들이 온전한 진리임을 증거해 준다. 이단들은 이런 역설적인 진리의 "건전한 긴장"을 "불일치로 인한 긴장" 또는 "혼돈"으로 보고 어느 한 쪽만을 가르쳐서 진리를 "분명하게" 만든다고 하나, 결국 온전한 진리가 갖는 건전한 긴장을 깨어 버리고 단순하고 치우친 거짓 진리에 빠지게 되는 것이다. 그리스도인들은 부정적인 면으로 육과 영의 더러움을 깨끗하게 씻고(죄의 회개), 적극적으로는 그들의 거룩함을 이루어야 하는 이중적 의무를 갖고 있다.[765] 더구나 고린도 교인들은 거짓 사도들의 말을 듣

763) Plummer, 212.

764) Bruce, 216.

지 말고 하나님이 택하신 예수 그리스도의 사도 바울(고전1:1; 고후 1:1)의 말을 잘 듣고 따라서 하나님의 거룩한 자녀로 살아야 한다.

"육과 영의 온갖 더러운 것에서 자신을 깨끗케 하자"(καθαρίσωμεν ἑαυτοὺς ἀπὸ παντὸς μολυσμοῦ σαρκὸς καὶ πνεύματος). 바울은 복수 일인칭("우리")을 써서 너나 할 것 없이 모두 하나님 앞에서 하나님을 두려워하는 자세를 가지자는 뜻으로, 바울 자신을 포함시켜서, "우리 자신을 깨끗케 하자"(καθαρίσωμεν ἑαυτού.)라고 명령법이 아닌 사역적 가정법으로 말한다. 여기서 다시 바울의 고린도 교인들을 향한 애정과 열린 자세를 보여 준다.[766] 어린 아이를 달래는 부모의 자세가 6장 13절 이후 계속되는 것이다. 하나님과 같이 거룩하게 되는데 방해 되는 것은 무엇이든지 제거해야 하는 것이다. 이것이 6장 14-18절에서 바울의 주된 관심이다. 하나님의 자녀가 되기 위해서는 깨끗하게 되는 것이 선결조건이다. 물론 고린도 교인들은 하나님의 은혜로 거룩하게 되었다. 본문에서도 그들을 하나님의 성전이라고 선언했다(16). 그러나 바울은 고린도 교인들이 이런 하나님의 부르심의 은혜를 헛되이 할까 염려하면서 계속하여 하나님의 은혜에 보답하여 깨끗하기를 권면하는 것이다(6:1, 2). 이런 면에서 도덕주의자나 완전주의자 같이 거룩함 이루는 자체가 목적이 아니라, 구원받은 증거로 거룩함을 이루라는 뜻이다.

깨끗하게 해야 할 대상은 모든 더러움(παντὸς μολυσμοῦ)이

765) Tasker, 100.

766) Hughes, 257; Thrall, 480.

다. 이것이 본문의 마지막 희귀어이다. 고린도전서 8장 7절에 동족어가 나오지만 이 같은 말은 여기에만 있다. 그러나 "더러움"이란 개념은 흔히 우상숭배와 관련되어 나온다(에스라1서 8:80; 마카비 2서 5:27; 렘 23:15, LXX). 16절에서 우상숭배를 경계하는 말이 나왔으므로 이 말이 다른 데서와 같이 우상숭배와 관련된다고 본다. 고린도 같은 고대 도시에서는 우상숭배가 삶의 중심이 되고 우상숭배와 관련되지 않은 것이 거의 없을 정도였다. 그래서 고린도전서에서는 시장에서 파는 고기는 거의 모두 우상의 제물이지만, 바울은 묻지 말고 먹으라고 할 수 밖에 없었다(고전 10:25). 또 위에서 지적한 바와 같이 음란한 행위도 우상숭배와 관련되었다. 고린도 교인들이 우상숭배의 영향을 여러모로 받고 있었을 것이다. 바울은 이를 알고 "온갖 더러움"에서 깨끗하게 될 것을 권면하고 있다.

"육과 영의"(σαρκὸς καὶ πνεύματος). 더러움을 수식하는 말이 육과 영으로 대조되어 나온다. "육적인 더러움과 영적인 더러움에서 깨끗하게 되자"는 것이다. 바울 서신에서 "육"(σάρξ)은 본래 더러움을 나타내는 것이고 "영"(πνεῦμα)은 깨끗함을 나타내는 것인데(롬 8:12이하; 갈 5:16이하) 여기에서 영의 더러움을 말하고 육을 씻어 깨끗게 한다고 말함으로 이 부분은 바울의 글이 아니라는 주장이 있다.[767] 어거스틴도 "육과 영"을 함께 더럽다고 한 것을 이상하게 보면서 독자들이 "영과 육"을 나누어 생각해서 육은 "더러움"(πολυσμοῦ)이란 말과 관련시키되, 영은 뒤에 나오는 "거룩함"(ἁγιωσύνην)과 관련시킬 수 있지 않을까 생각한

767) Collange, 313.

다.[768] 즉 육의 더러움은 씻고, 영은 온전하게 한다는 의미로 보았다.[769] 그러나 이런 해석은 무리한 해석이다.[770] 쿰란 공동체는 이런 영과 육의 청결에 관심이 집중되어 있었다(1QH 13:13, 14; 15:21, 22; 17:25). 거룩한 성전(聖戰)에 임하는 빛의 아들들은 영과 육이 온전해야 한다(1QM 7:5). 그러므로 피츠마이어(J. A. Fitzmeyer)는 고린도후서 7장 1절이 쿰란 사상과 매우 유사하다고 한다.[771] 영지주의자들은 육은 그 자체가 더러운 것이므로 씻을 수 없다고 했다.[772] 그러나 당시 사람들은 사람 전체를 가리켜서 "육과 영"으로 표현하곤 했다.[773] 바울은 여기서 "영과 육"을 특별히 신화적인 의미가 아닌 당시 대중의 통상적인 의미로 썼을 것이다.[774] 실제로 바울은 다른 곳에서 "영과 육"을 사람의 두 가지 면을 가리키는 말로 쓰고 있다. 고린도후서 7장 5절에서 바울은 "우리 육체(σάρξ)가 편지 못했다" 고한다. 그리고 2장 13절에서 "내 심령"(πνεύματι μου)이 편치 못했다" 고한다. 골로새서 2장 5절에서도 바울은 "내가 육신(σαρκί)으로는 떠나 있으나, 심령(πνεύματι)으로는 너희와 함께 있어"라고 말한다. 고린도전서 5

---

768) *De Doc. Chris.* iii.2, Plummer, 212, 재인용.

769) Hughes, 260.

770) Plummer, 212에서 Plummer는 어거스틴의 제안을 무리한 해석이라고 반대하면서 "영과 육"을 보통 사람을 나타내는 말로 보아야 한다고 한다. 계속해서, "바울이 육과 영의 더러움"과 같은 표현을 절대로 쓸 수 없다고 말하는 것은 무비판적인 교조주의(uncritical dogmatism)이다."라고 한다.

771) J. A. Fitzmeyer, "Qumrân and the Interpolated Paragraph in 2 Cor 6:14-7:1," in *Essays on the Semitic Background of the New Testament* (London: Chapman, 1971), 215.

772) Plummer, 211.

773) Plummer, 211.

774) Hughes, 259; Barrett, 209; Plummer, 211.

장 3절에 "내가 몸(σώματι)으로는 떠나 있으나 영(πνεύματι)으로는 함께 있어서"라고 말한다. (이 경우 σάρξ 대신 σῶμα를 쓰나 바울이 이 두 말을 서로 엇바꿔 쓰는 경우가 많음으로 같은 예로 볼 수 있다). 이외에도 유사한 예가 갈라디아서 2장 20절과 고린도전서 7장 34절에 있다.

바울은 "육과 영"으로 대분되는 이분법적 인간론에 근거하여 그리스도인들이 모든 면에서 정결해야 함을 가르치고 있다.[775)]

2. "마음으로 우리를 영접하라. 우리가 아무에게도 불의를 하지 않고 아무에게도 해롭게 하지 않고 아무에게도 속여 빼앗은 일이 없노라" (Χωρήσατε ἡμᾶς· οὐδένα ἠδικήσαμεν, οὐδένα ἐφθείραμεν, οὐδένα ἐπλεονεκτήσαμεν). "마음으로 우리를 영접하라" (Χωρήσατε ἡμᾶς). 이 말은 문자적으로, "너희 마음에 우리가 들어 갈 방을 만들라"라는 뜻이다. 바울은 6장 11-13절의 말을 다시 반복하고 있다. "고린도인들이여… 너희가 우리 안에서 좁아진 것이 아니라, 오직 너희 심정에서 좁아진 것이라… 마음을 넓히라." 바울이 고린도 교인들을 향하여 애정과 관심을 가지고 있듯이 고린도 교인들도 바울을 깊은 애정을 가지고 받아들이라는 말이다.[776)] "마음으로 영접하라" (χωρήσατε)는 "마음으로 영접하다" (χωρεῖν)에서 온 단순과거 명령법이다.

"우리가 아무에게도 불의를 하지 않고" (οὐδένα ἠδικήσαμεν).

---

775) 11:4에서는 "다른 영" (ἢ πνεῦμα ἕτερον)이란 말이 나오는데, 반대자들의 잘못된 가르침을 가리킨다.

776) Barrett, 203; Bultmann, 179; Strachan, 124.

다시 바울은 자신과 고린도 교인들 사이에 있는 오해와 불신의 장애가 있음을 기억하고 이를 부인하면서 자신은 실제로 순수하다고 한다(4:2; 5:12, 13; 6:3; 참조, 행 20:26, 27). 이 말과 뒤에 나오는 두 말들이 모두 단순과거로 되어 있어서 과거에 실제로 일어난 일을 바울이 언급하고 있다고 본다.[777] 바울은 과거에 고린도 교인들로부터 그가 이런 일을 했다는 비난을 실제로 들었다(고전 2:3; 고후 2:1). 바울은 이런 비난에 대해서 단호히 거부한다. 각 비난의 말 앞에 "아무도"(οὐδένα)라는 말이 붙어 있어서 단호한 부정을 나타낸다.[778]

"불의를 행하다"(ἠδικήσαμεν, ἀδικεῖν)는 말은 다른 사람을 불의하게 취급했다는 뜻이다(7:12; 갈 4:12; 몬 18; 골 3:25).[779] 바울은 아무에게도 불의를 행하지 않았다. 사실 그 자신이야 말로 억울하게 고린도 교회 반대자들에게 불의를 당한 사람이다. 즉 그가 교묘한 방법으로 고린도 교회를 착취한다는 비난 같은 것이다(12:16).

"아무에게도 해롭게 하지 않고"(οὐδένα ἐφθείραμεν). φθείρειν(프데이레인)은 "망치다"는 말로, 재정적으로나, 도덕적으로 망하게 했다는 뜻이 있다. 12장 16-18절에서 바울은 재정적으로 묘하게 갈취한다는 비난을 받았다고 한다. 겉으로는 재정지원을 받지 않는다고 하면서 뒤로는 예루살렘 성도들을 위한 헌금을 착복하는 것으로 비난받았다고 본다. 그 외에 인간관계에서 어

777) Hughes, 260, 주 26.

778) Martin, 217.

779) Filson, 356.

떤 오해가 있었던 것을 생각할 수 있다. 혹 고린도전서 8장 11절에서 우상의 제물을 먹는 것에 대한 바울의 보다 자유로운 태도에 대해서 보다 엄격한 유대인 기독교인들이 비난했을 수도 있다.[780] 또는 바울의 할례에 대한 관용적인 견해일 수도 있으나, 고린도후서에서는 할례 문제가 거론되지는 않았다(참조, 고전 7:18, 19;갈 1:19; 5:6; 6:15; 빌 3:3; 골 2:11). 바울의 반 율법주의적 복음이 모세의 율법 전통이나 도덕적 기준을 붕괴시켜버렸다는 비난일 수 있다.[781] 이런 비난에 대해 바울은 언제나 자신의 결백함을 떳떳하게 주장할 수 있었다.

"아무에게도 속여 빼앗은 일이 없노라"(οὐδένα ἐπλεονεκτήσαμεν). πλεονεκτεῖν(프레오네크테인)은 "사기로 돈을 빼앗다"는 뜻도 있으나, "재정적으로나, 다른 면으로, 사람을 이용하여 자기 유익을 취하다"는 더 보편적인 뜻이 있다.[782] 바울을 미워하는 반대자들은 바울이 걷는 예루살렘 성도들을 위한 헌금도 바울이 착복한다는 의심을 한 것 같다(12:16-18). 또 하나님의 부름 받은 그리스도의 사도라는 권위로 명하는 어떤 명령이나 시정 요구도 모두 상처를 주는 것으로 비난할 수 있다. 예를 들면 고린도전서 5장 5절의 근친상간한 자에 대해 사단에게 내어주도록 명령한 조치에 대해서 반대자들이 비록 그를 형벌하는 것 자체는 반대하지 않았을 찌라도 교회를 떠난 바울이 계속 교회에 독재적 권력을 행사하는 것이라고 반발했을 수도 있다.[783] 고린도후서 2장 5-7절에서 그에 대한 징계조치를 칭찬하면서도 다시 그 징

780) Filson, 857; Plummer, 213; Martin, 217.

781) Thrall, 482.

782) Martin, 218.

계를 풀어주라고 하는 것은 반대자들의 비난을 인식하면서 스스로 내린 조치인지도 모른다. 어쩌면 이런 비난을 디도를 통해서 들었을 것이다(7:6-16).[784] 그리고 그 비난에 대해서 바울은 변명할 필요가 있었다.

이런 세 가지 비난이 구체적으로 무엇을 말하는지 분명히 알 수 없으나, 편지를 받는 고린도 교인들은 그 문제들이 무엇을 가리키는지를 잘 알고 있었을 것이다. 바울은 그를 오해하게 만들고 고린도 교회와 소원하게 만든 이 문제들에 대해서 단호하게 부인하면서, 자신의 정직성과 진심을 고린도 교인들에게 전하고 있다. 사실 착취를 당한 쪽은 오히려 바울 쪽이다. 그가 고린도 교회를 위해 받은 일반적인 고난은 고사하더라도(6:4-10), 그는 고린도 교회에 재정적인 폐를 끼치지 않기 위해 매사에 조심하였다(11:9; 12:13). 그럼에도 그는 돈을 사취한다는 누명까지 썼다(고후 12:16). 그는 이런 비난을 받으면서 6장 10절에서 "가난한 자 같으나 모든 사람들을 부요케 하고"라고 말한다. 그는 오히려 재정 독립형 사역을 함으로써 고린도 교인들에게 폐를 끼치지 않고 결과적으로 재정적 도움을 준 셈이 되었다고 생각한다(11:7-10; 12:14, 15; 참조, 행 18:2; 20:33-35).

어떤 이들은 바울이 이런 비난을 실제로 들은 것이 아니라 그를 반대하는 이들의 비위 사실을 가지고 자신은 그런 문제가 없다고 말하고 있다고 한다.[785] 그러나 우리가 고린도전서나 후서에서 보는 고린도 교인들의 바울에 대한 오해나 비난을 생각할 때 여기에

783) Martin, 218.

784) Hughes, 260.

785) Hughes, 261, 재인용; Plummer, 211.

서의 바울의 말들이 바울에 대한 비난과 무관하다고 보기 어렵다. 더구나 다음에 나오는 3절 상반절의 말은 바울에 대한 비난이 실제로 고린도 교인들이 한 것이라는 거의 확실한 증거이다.

3. "내가 정죄하려고 이 말을 하는 것이 아니라. 이전에 말하였거니와 너희로 우리 마음에 있어 함께 죽고 함께 살고자 함이라" (πρὸς κατάκρισιν οὐ λέγω· προείρηκα γὰρ ὅτι ἐν ταῖς καρδίαις ἡμῶν ἐστε εἰς τὸ συναποθανεῖν καὶ συζῆν). 바울은 앞서 고린도 교인들이 자신을 비난한 말들(7:2)로 인해서 혹 그들의 마음이 상하지 않도록 다독거린다. 바울은 고린도 교인들을 정죄하기를 원치 않는다(πρὸς κατάκρισιν οὐ λέγω). 여기서 "정죄"(κατάκρισις)라는 명사는 판사가 죄인을 정죄하는 법정적인 용어다.[786] 바울의 마음속에 이들에게 보다 단호하게 잘못을 꾸짖어야겠다는 생각이 있을지는 몰라도(10:1), 디도를 통해서 전해들은 고린도 교회의 보다 낙관적인 형편에 비추어서(7:7-16), 지금은 화해의 기회라는 생각이 지배적이다. 그가 세운 고린도 교회와 다시 돈독한 관계를 이루는 것이 급선무이다. 그러므로 그는 씁쓸한 마음을 감추고 사랑으로 그들을 대한다. 물론 이것은 결코 가식적으로 고린도 교인들을 대하는 것은 아니다. 그는 진심으로 그들과 "함께 죽고 살고자 하는" 진실한 심정을 가지고 있다. 그의 사랑의 진정성은 고린도전서 13장에서 제시되었고, 그가 말하는 "함께 죽고 산다"는 말의 진정성은 그의 목숨을 건 사도직 수행에서 증명된다(1:6; 6:3 이하; 11:23 이하). 바울은 사랑을 말로만 가르치는

---

786) Martin, 218.

사도가 아니라 행동으로 그 사랑을 증명하는 진정한 사도이다. 그러나 바울은 이미 다 아는 비난에 대해서 자신의 입장을 분명히 밝혀야 진정한 화해가 이루어 질 수 있으므로 자신으로서는 되뇌고 싶지도 않고, 고린도 교인들에게는 듣기 거북한 비난의 말들을 다시 반복하는 수밖에 없다. 바울은 이런 그의 입장을 고린도 교인들이 이해주기를 바라면서 이런 화해적인 말을 덧 붙이 는 것이다.

"이전에 말하였거니와 너희로 우리 마음에 있어 함께 죽고 함께 살고자 함이라"(προείρηκα γὰρ ὅτι ἐν ταῖς καρδίαις ἡμῶν ἐστε εἰς τὸ συναποθανεῖν καὶ συζῆν). "이전에 말하였거니와"는 바울이 앞서 6장 11절과 12절에서 고린도 교인들에 대한 사랑하는 마음이 활짝 열려있다고 말한 것을 가리킨다(2:4; 11:11; 12:15).[787] 이제 바울은 이런 사랑의 관계를 유지하기 위하여 그의 입장이 매우 단호하며 진실하다는 것을 말한다. 고린도 교인과의 결속을 위해서 바울은 자신의 목숨도 아끼지 않고 바칠 각오가 되어있다(4:12). 여기서 그리스도의 죽고 사심이라는 주제와 직접 연결은 되지 않았으나, 목회자 바울의 고린도 교인들을 향한 심정은 예수께서 말한 양을 위해 목숨을 버리는 선한 목자의 사랑과 같은 것이다(요 10:11, 15; 막 10:45).[788] 한편 충성된 인간 상호 상호관

787) "이전에(조금 전에) 말하였거니와"는, Tasker가 지적하였듯이, 6:14-7:1이 삽입된 것이 아니라 바울이 직접 썼다는 증거가 된다. 바울이 6:11-13에서 화해를 말하다가, 보다 단호하게 세속적인 것을 버리라고 말했음(6:14-7:1)을 잘 알고 있다는 증거가 된다(Tasker, 102).

788) R. C. Tannehill, *Dying and Rising with Christ: A Study in Pauline Theology*, BZNW 32 (Berlin: Töpelmann, 1967) 93-4; 대부분의 학자들은 그리스도의 죽음과 부활과는 상관 없는 단순한 목회적 애정을 나타내는 것이라고 한다. Thrall, 483; Martin, 219; 214; Plummer, 214.

계를 나타내는 데, "함께 죽고 함께 산다"는 말이 공식적인 말로 잘 나타난다. 사무엘하 15장 21절에서 잇대가 다윗 왕에게 "…진실로 내 주 왕께서 어느 곳에 계시든지 무론 사생(死生)하고 종도 그곳에 있겠나이다"라고 말한다. 비기독교 세계에서도 이런 말은 자주 쓰인다. 호레이스(Horace)가 리디아(Lydia)에게, "내가 기꺼이 당신과 함께 살고 죽겠습니다."라고 말한다.[789] 유리피데스(Euripides)가 쓴 오레스테스(Orestes)에서도 엘렉트라(Electra)가 오레스테스(Orestes)에게, "당신과 함께 죽고 살기를 결단하겠습니다"라고 말한다.[790] 그 외에 호머의 일리아드 18:32이하, 푸르다크 영웅전, 안토니우스 편, 71에서 안토니우스의 클레오파트라에 대한 사랑의 고백, 등의 고전적 예를 들 수 있다.[791] 그러나 바울의 말은 이런 세속적인 인간관계의 충절에서 라기 보다 그의 평소 그리스도 중심적 사고에서 자연스럽게 나온 것이다. 5장 14, 15절에서 바울은 그의 사역은 그리스도의 사랑에 힘입은 것이며 그의 죽으심과 사심을 따라서 살아야 함을 이미 말했다(빌 1:20). 그리고 그는 그의 사역에서 사도로서 죽을 고난을 많이 받은 것은 모두 그리스도의 생명이 고린도 교인들에게 나타내게 하기 위함이었다고 했다(4:8-15). 그의 사도로서의 모든 삶은 철저하게 그리스도의 죽고 사심과 직결되어 있다(고후 1:4-7; 13:4; 딤후 2:11; 행 9:16).

789) Odes 3.9.24, Martin, 219 재인용.

790) Euripides, Orestes 307 이하, Bultmann, 179, 인용, Martin, 219, 재인용.

791) "함께 죽고 사는" 예를 더 찾아 볼 수 있다. F. Olivier, Συναποθνὴσκω. D'un article de lexique à Saint Paul, II Corinthiens, vii, 3," *RsThPh* 17(1929) 103-33; G. Stählin, "Um mitzusterben und mitzuleben. Bermerkungen zur 2 Kor. 7.3," *Neues Testament und christliche Existenz*, FS Herbert Braun, ed. H.-D. Betz and L. Schottroff (Tübingen: J. C. B. Mohr, 1973), 503-21.

베드로, 도마, 그리고 다른 제자들도 그리스도와 함께 죽을 각오를 하였다(막 14:31; 요 11:16; 마 20:22, 23; 눅 22:33). 그리고 그들의 주님에 대한 사랑과 헌신은 그들의 헌신적 목양(牧羊)과 연결되었다(요 21:15-19; 마 10:38).

"너희로 우리의 마음에 있어"(ἐν ταῖς καρδίαι ἡμῶν ἐστε). 이 말은 6장 12절을 다시 확인하는 말이다. "너희가 우리 안에서 좁아진 것이 아니라…" 바울이 고린도 교인들에 대한 사랑의 마음은 변함이 없다. 여기서 "나의 마음"이라고 하지 않고 "우리의 마음"이라고 하여 팀 사역의 관심을 보여 주는 것도 특이하다. 상반절(3절)에서는 "내가… 말하는 것이 아니라"(οὐ λέγω)에서는 일인칭 단수로 바울 자신을 가리키나, 여기서는 일인칭 복수로 디도를 포함한 바울을 돕는 고린도 교회 사역자들을 다 가리키고 있다(7:12). 바울은 고린도 교회와의 좋은 관계를 유지하는 것을 강조할 때는 "우리"를 쓴다. "우리"가 곤경에 처했을 때도 결국 승리함으로 고린도 교회에 확신을 주고 기쁨을 줌으로써 결과적으로 "우리"와의 관계를 더 돈독하게 만들었다(4:7-10; 7:5).[792] 지금도 고린도 교인들은 "우리"의 마음에 있어 여러 오해에도 불구하고 돈독한 관계를 갖고 있다는 것이다.[793] 이렇게 바울은 "마음"과 "마음"이 연결된 관계를 지향한다는 데서 "외모로 자랑하는 이들"(즉 바울의 반대자들)과 분명히 대조를 이루고 있다(5:12).

---

792) Martin, 220.

793) M. Carrez, "Le 'nous' en 2 Corinthians," *NTS* 26(1979-80) 474-86. Carrez는 바울이 "나"와 "우리"를 단순히 문학적인 표현이상으로, 신학적인 의미로 주의 깊게 쓰고 있다고 한다. 즉 바울은 그리스도/ 바울/ 사도들/ 사역자들/ 교회(공동체)의 연결구도를 가지고 대명사를 골라서 쓰는데, "우리"는 "나"와 "너희" 사이의 풍성하고도 복잡한 그리스도를 포함한 긴장관계를 나타내는 대명사라고 한다(Martin, 220 재인용).

4. "내가 너희를 무척 신뢰하며 (향하여 하는 말이 담대한 것도 많고), 너희를 위하여 자랑하는 것도 많으니, 내가 우리의 모든 환난 가운데서 위로가 가득하고 기쁨이 넘치는 도다" (πολλή μοι παρρησία πρὸς ὑμᾶς, πολλή μοι καύχησις ὑπὲρ ὑμῶν· πεπλήρωμαι τῇ παρακλήσει, ὑπερπερισσεύομαι τῇ χαρᾷ ἐπὶ πάσῃ τῇ θλίψει ἡμῶν). "내가 너희를 무척 신뢰하며" (πολλή μοι παρρησι,α πρὸς ὑμᾶς). 이 절이 6장 11절부터 시작된 바울의 화해의 제의의 마지막 부분이다. 이 절은 또한 2장 12, 13절에서 드로아에서 고린도에서 오는 디도를 기다리다가 만나지 못해서 답답한 심정으로 떠났던 이야기로 다시 돌아가는 대목이다. 2장 14절에서 시작된 그의 사역에 대한 변명이라는 지금까지의 주제를 맺고, 1장에서 2장 13절까지의 디도를 만나서 고린도 교회가 다시 바울을 따르게 되었다는 기쁜 소식을 듣고 위로를 받았다는 주제로 다시 돌아가는 연결고리 역할을 한다.

헬라어 원문을 보면 이 구절에 π(파이)로 시작하는 말들이 8개나 있음을 본다(πολλή, παρρησία, πρός, πολλή, πεπλήρωμαι, παρακλήσει, ὑπερπερισσεύομαι, πάσῃ). 이것은 바울이 특별히 이 글자를 좋아해서 문장을 그렇게 만들었다고 본다(8:22; 9:5, 8; 13:2).[794] 특히 "많다"는 뜻의 πολλή가 2번 나온다. 그리고 "신뢰" (παρρησία)라는 이 절의 핵심적인 단어도 π로 시작한다. 이 핵심 단어("파래시아")의 원래의 뜻은 "말을 담대하게 함"이다.[795] 우리 한글 개역 성경의 번역과 다른 번역들이 이 번역을 지

794) Plummer, 215.

795) Filson, 356; Tasker, 102.

지한다.[796] 불트만은 이 번역을 반대한다.[797] 6장 11절에서 바울이 입을 벌리고, 마음을 넓혀서 말한다고 하였으므로(속에 있는 하고 싶은 말을 다 털어놓고 솔직히 말하겠다), 여기서도 그와 같은 뜻으로 "직언을 하다"는 의미로 볼 수 있다고 한다. 그러나 전체 신약에서는 주로 "담대함" 또는 "확신"이라는 뜻으로 쓰였다(엡 3:12; 딤전 3:13; 히 3:6; 6:16; 10:19, 35; 요일 2:28; 3:21; 4:17; 5:14).[798] 고린도후서 3장 12절에서도 "담대함"("담대히")으로 번역하여 "확신"을 나타낸다. 여기와 같은 문맥인 고린도후서 7장 16절에서도 바울이 고린도 교인들을 "신뢰한다"는 의미로 θαρρῶ라는 동사를 쓰고 있다. 그러므로 여기서도 바울이 고린도 교인들을 "신뢰한다"는 뜻으로 παρρησία를 쓰고 있다고 볼 수 있다. 디도를 통해 고린도 교회의 소식을 들은 바울은 고린도 교인들을 믿게 되었다. 그러나 휴즈는 이 두 가지의 번역이 서로 큰 차이는 없다고 한다. 신뢰를 하므로, 직언을 할 수 있기 때문이라고 한다.[799] 그러나 "말을 담대하게 하는 것"이나 "솔직함"은 말하는 사람의 자세로서 그에게 국한 된 개념이지만, "확신"은 상대방에 대한 반응을 나타내는 개념이므로 차이가 있다.

"너희를 위하여 자랑하는 것도 많으니"(πολλή μοι καύχησις

---

796) KJV; Barrett, 193, Denney, 248; 3:12; 참조, NEB("frankness"); W. C. van Unnik, "The Christian's Freedom of Speech," *BJRL* 44 (1961-62) 466-88는 NEB의 번역 "frankness"의 의미를 지지한다 (Martin, 221 재인용.). Barrett, 193, 204; Furnish, 193, 384; Thrall도 이를 지지한다(485).

797) Bultmann, 180.

798) Plummer, 215; Héring, 53; Tasker, 102; Bruce, 217; Strachan, 125; Filson, 356, RSV; NIV.

799) Hughes, 262.

ὑπὲρ ὑμῶν). 고린도 교회에 대한 확신은 더 나아가서 바울이 고린도 교회를 자랑하게(καύχησις) 되는 이유가 된다. 7장 14절에 의하면 바울은 디도를 보내기 전에 고린도 교회를 믿고 자랑하였다. 그러므로 지금 고린도 교회를 믿고 자랑하는 것은 아무런 근거 없이 잘된다는 막연한 낙관주의적 자세에서 나온 것이 아니라 진리가 승리한다는 그의 평소의 소신에 근거한 것이다(9:2; 13:8). 디도의 소식으로 이제 더욱 고린도 교인들의 충성심을 믿게 되었다.

"내가 우리의 모든 환난 가운데서 위로가 가득하고 기쁨이 넘치는 도다"(πεπλήρωμαι τῇ παρακλήσει, ὑπερπερισσεύομαι τῇ χαρᾷ ἐπὶ πάσῃ τῇ θλίψει ἡμῶν). 바울은 이 구절을 두 겹 "크라이막스"로 맺는다.[800] 바울은 위로받는 심정이면서도 기쁨이 넘치는 상태이다(ὑπερπερισσεύομαι τῇ χαρᾷ). 바울에게 있어서 확신과 기쁨은 위로의 수단이다. 위로(παρακλήσει)는 고린도후서 초두(1:3-7)에 반복적으로 나왔던 말이다. 디도가 가져온 고린도 교회의 회복의 소식은 그의 복음 사역에서 겪은 온갖 고초를 말끔히 씻겨주었다. 힘든 복음 사역의 보람을 느낀 것이다. 그러나 이 위로의 참된 근원은 그리스도이었다. "그리스도의 고난이 우리에게 넘친 것 같이 그리스도의 위로도 우리에게 넘치는 도다"(1:5). 그러므로 바울은 자신을 자랑하는 것을 절제하면서 하나님의 은혜를 선포하는 도구로서의 그의 역할을 견지하였다(5:20; 참조, 5:10, 11; 6:1). 여기서 바울의 기쁨은 큰 환난과 근심 중에 얻은 기쁨이므로 더 큰 기쁨이다. 물론 이런 기쁨은 오래 가지는 못했다. 10-13장의 극심한 내용은 아직 바울의 마음속에는 고린도 교

800) Plummer, 215.

회에 대한 염려가 남아 있으며, 앞으로 사태가 어떻게 변하게 될지 알 수 없는 일말의 두려움이 있었을 것이다(12:28). 그리고 바울은 그의 사역의 일시적이고 외적인 성공적 사역에 의하여 고무된 것만이 아니라, 그가 모든 사역일을 수고하면서 양심적으로 수행하였으므로(2:17; 4:2), 하나님께서 그의 사역을 인정하시고, 그에게 위로의 선물을 주시는 것이므로 이로 말미암아 기뻐하는 것이다(1:3-7).

"우리의 모든 환난 가운데서"(ἐπὶ πάσῃ τῇ θλίψει ἡμῶν)는 1장 4절에서도 발견된다. 바울이 여기서 다시 초두의 진술로 돌아감을 나타내는 하나의 증거가 된다. 이것은 1장 8절에서 언급한 아시아에서 겪은 환난, 2장 4절에서 "눈물의 편지"를 쓸 때에 겪은 환난(소아시아에서의 환난), 바로 뒤 7장 5절에서의 마게도냐에서 겪은 환난, 등 바울이 사역 중에 겪은 환난들(6:4)을 가리킨다.

어떤 학자들은 2장 14절-7장 2-4절(6:14-7:1제외하고)은 바울의 독립된 편지로 보고("변명의 편지"), 디도가 이 편지를 가지고 고린도에 가서 거짓 사도들을 대면하고 반박한 후에 돌아왔다고 한다. 사태가 아직 유동적인 가운데 바울은 고린도 교회를 다시 방문하고 돌아왔다("임시 방문"). 그리고 10-13장의 "눈물의 편지"를 썼고, 그 결과 사태가 호전되었다는 소식을 디도를 통해 듣고 고무되어 다시 1장 1절-2장 13절과 7장 5-16절을 써서 보냈다는 것이다. 이런 설명은 고린도후서에 몇 가지 다른 어조가 나타나 있으므로 이에 기초하여 바울의 여행 일정과 서신발송에 대해 추정하는 것일 뿐이며, 아무런 사본 상의 증거가 없다. 우리가 가진 고린도후서 사본은 모두 같은 위치에 같은 순서로 되어 있다. 더구나 그 누군가 어떤 권위로 아무런 설명도 없이 사도 바울의 글을 한 편지 인양 편집하고 단일화시켜 모든 교회에 빠짐없이 보급했겠는가라는 어려운 질문에 대한 답이 없다. 그리고 누가 그 어떤 권위로 이런 바울의 중요한 여러 편지들을 한 조각도 남김없이 모두 없애 버렸겠는가에 대한 답도 없다.

주 해:(6:11–7:4):

본문에서 바울은 하나님과의 화해를 가르치면서도 세상과의 결별을 역설적으로 가르치고 있다. 6장 11절-7장 4절에서 바울은 고린도 교인들에게 화해의 주제를 가지고 다정한 자세로 시작하였다가 단호한 말(6:14-7:1)로 그의 마음에 있는 말을 다하고 다시 다정하고 온유한 어조로 마친다(7:2-4). 진정한 화해는 겉치레 말이나 감정의 표현으로 이루어지는 것이 아니라 진실한 마음의 자세를 요구한다. 사람이 거룩하신 하나님과 교제하기 위해서는 세상의 더러운 것을 버리지 않으면 안 된다. 바울은 비록 화해의 어조를 지켜 가지만, 반드시 해야 할 말은 하는 사도로서의 임무를 수행하고 있다. 이것은 하나님의 말씀을 전하는 모든 사람들의 역설적인 임무이다. 하나님의 은혜와 사랑의 메시지를 전하면서도 거룩하신 하나님의 요구와 심판의 메시지도 함께 전해야 한다. 사랑의 하나님과 거룩하신 하나님을 다 같이 전해야 한다. 이것을 전하는 일이 결코 쉬운 일이 아니다. 역설이란 논리적 모순으로 듣는 자에게 혼돈을 주기 때문이다. 그러나 온전한 진리는 흔히 역설적인 성격을 갖는다. 오히려 역설적이 아닌 단순한 진리는 반쪽 진리이며 그것은 위험한 진리이다.(서양 속담 가운데, "적은 지식은 위험한 것이다." ["A little knowledge is a dangerous thing"]; "반쪽 진리는 흔히 큰 거짓말이다" ["Half the truth is often a great lie."

Poor Richard's Almanac, 1758]).

역설적인 진리를 전할 때 설교자가 당면하는 또 하나의 고충은 그런 역설적인 진리를 자신의 인격이나 삶에서 충분히 소화하여 성숙하지 못한 상태에서 그 진리를 지식으로만 이해하고 전할 때 생기는 지식과 확신 사이의 괴리 문제이다. 아직 완전히 자신의 경험을 통해서 확신하는 진리가 되지 못할 때, 말씀을 전하는 자신부터 확신이 없으므로, 청중에게 아무런 감동을 줄 수 없다. 이런 설교를 통해서도 성령이 역사 할 수 있을까 바울의 경우 그는 이런 역설적인 진리를 그의 인격과 삶에서 잘 터득하였다고 한다. "내게 사는 것이 그리스도니 죽는 것도 유익함이라" (빌 1:21). "어떠한 형편에서도 자족하기를 배웠노니 내가 비천에 처할 줄도 알고 풍부에 처할 줄도 알아 모든 일에 배부르며 배고픔과 풍부와 궁핍에도 일체의 비결을 배웠노라" (빌 4: 11-12). 바울은 각종 역설적인 환경에서 자족하는 원숙성을 갑자기 배운 것이 아니라 그가 만나는 온갖 역설적인 경험을 통해, 특히 그리스도의 죽으심과 사심의 진리를 자신의 삶에 적용하는 연습을 통해서 배웠던 것이다(ἔμαθον, 빌 4:11; 고후 4:7-18; 5:15, 16; 갈 4:19; 6:17). 바울은 4장 7-18절과 6장 8-10절에서 말하는 역설적인 사역의 경험들을 통해서 습득한 것이다(참조, 11:23-28). 이런 원숙한 경지에 이른 바울은 본문에서도 이 어려운 역설적인 말씀의 전달자 역할을 훌륭하게 수행하여 모든 그리스도의 복음 사역자들에게 모범적 지침을 제시하고 있다.

첫째, 바울은 처음부터 끝까지 고린도 교인들을 향한 화해의 어조를 흩뜨리지 않고 지키고 있다. 6장 14절부터 7장 1절의 그리스도인의 단호한 세상과의 결별을 가르침이 끝날 때 7장 2절부터 4절까지 6장 11-13절의 화해의 어조를 다시 계속하고 있다. 자신이 하나님의 "정죄의 사신"이 아니라(7:3) "화해의 사신"(5:18)임을 견지하고 있다(13:10).

둘째, 바울은 고린도 교인들에게 "세상과의 결별" 촉구하면서 자신의 사도로서의 권위를 내세워 말하지 않고 자신을 낮추어 말한다(참조, 고전 9:18; 행 10:25-27). 부모가 자식을 달래듯이 부드러운 자세와 깊은 정을 가지고(6:13, 참조, 12:14), 세상과의 결별과 거룩한 생활을 촉구하는 것이다. 그리스도의 성육신과 연약함으로 십자가에 달리신 것이 바울의 기본적인 행동 지침이다(고후 13:4; 빌 2:5-8). 7장 1절에서도 고린도 교인들에게 명령하지 않고 자신을 포함하여 모두 다 함께, "'육과 영'의 온갖 더러운 것에서 자신을 깨끗케 하자"고 말한다.

셋째, (위의 둘째 사항과 관련하여)바울은 자신의 사도적 권위 대신 하나님의 권위를 내세운다. 다른 데서와 같이 본문에서도 바울은 구약에서 여러 하나님의 말씀을 직접 인용하고 있다. 특히, "하나님이 가라사대"(16), "그러므로 주께서 말씀하시기를"(17)이라는 인용 양식을 먼저 써서 구약을 인용한 후에, "전능하신 주의 말씀이니라"라는 말로 맺으면서(18) 본문의 명령과 약속들이 자신의 말이 아니라 하나님의 말씀임을 강조하여 그 신뢰성과 권위를 높인다(겔 37:26; 레 26:12; 사 52:11; 삼하 7:14, 등). 그러나 이렇게 자신을 감추고 하나님을 나타냄으로써 결국은 바울 자신의 신령한 권위도 나타나는 것이다. 사도의 권위는 하나님의 말씀을 그대로 전하는 데서 하나님의 은혜로 나타나는 것임을 바울은 알고 있다. 인간의 지혜나 "육체"에 의지하지 않고 하나님의 지혜에 의지함으로써 복음 전달자의 권위가 나타남을 알고 있다(고전 2:1 이하). "내 말과 내 전도함이 지혜의 권하는 말로 하지 아니하고 다만 성령의 나타남과 능력으로하여 너희 믿음이 사람의 지혜에 있지 아니하고 다만 하나님의 능력에 있게 하려 하였도다."(고전 2:4, 5). "이 복음은 하나님이 선지자들로 말미암아 그의 아들에 관하여 성경에 미리 약속하신 것이라"(롬 1:2).

넷째, 바울은 6장 14절-7장 1절에서 "하나님의 거룩하심과 온전함을 이루는 것이 모든 그리스도인의 삶의 공통적 목표"라고 말하면서, 고린도 교인들의 동참을 촉구하고 있다. 사실 세상과의 결별은 당시 어느 교회보다 고린도 교회에게 해당되는 문제라고 본다. 당시 도시 중 고린도가 가장 타락한 도시였기 때문이다(서론 참조). 그러나 바울은 믿음이 약한 고린도 교인들을 몰아 세워서 다른 교인들과 비교하여 "너희들이 가장 문제"라는 식으로 말하지는 않는다. 그것은 바울이 그들이 문제가 있다는 것을 솔직히 말하면 고린도 교인들의 감정이 상할 것을 걱정하였기 때문에 감추고 있는 것이라기보다, 바울이 하나님의 은혜와 능력을 믿음으로 그들도 하나님의 능력 안에서 새롭게 변화될 수 있는 "가능성이 있는 사람들"로 보기 때문이다. 그러므로 7장 4절에서 바울은 이들에 대해 신뢰하고 자랑하는 것이 많다고 한다(7:14). 하나님의 도우심으로 고린도 교인들이 과거에 이룩한 좋은 점들과 장래의 가능성을 보고 기뻐하는 것이다.

다섯째, 바울은 마음과 마음이 연결이 된 진정한 인간관계를 지향하고 있다(7:3). 이런 자세는 외모지상주의적인 바울의 반대자들의 자세와 뚜렷한 대조를 이룬다(5:12). 외적인 것과 육체적인 자랑과 눈에 보이는 것을 추구하는 것은 거짓사도들과 궤휼의 역군들의 증거이다(11:13-15).

이상에서 본 바울의 복음전도자로서의 여러 자세들은 서로 관련된다. 이것들은 바울이 어떤 위기를 극복하는 재치나 기술을 가졌다는 것이 아니라, 바울의 하나님 중심 신앙과 신학을 나타내는 증거들이다. 바울은 그가 세운 교회들이 그의 말을 듣지 않을 때, 사도로서의 권위를 내세우려는 충동을 가끔 받았는지도 모른다(고전 9장). 실제로 그의 사도직의 진정성이나 복음의 진정성에 대한 논란이 있을 때, 자신의 복음과 사도직이 하나님에게서 직접 온 것임을 분명히 밝힌다(고전 7:40; 고후 4:6; 12:12; 갈 1:12). 또 그의 모든 편지 초두에서 자신이 하나님의 택하심을 받은 그리스도의 사도임을 언제나 나타낸다. 그러나 바울이 진정으로 원하는 것은 그의 사도직이 그의 삶 속에서 스스로 입증되기를 원했다. 그의 그리스도 죽음과 부활의 유형을 따르는 역설적인 삶을 통해서 저절로 나타나기를 원했다(2:14, 17; 4:2, 10-12; 12:10; 갈 4:19; 6:17). 본문에서도 그의 사도로서의 권위를 되도록 감추고, 자기를 낮추어서 그들을 권하고 격려하고 있다. 이것은 화해라는 당면한 문제를 의식하기 때문만이 아니라 바울의 사도직이나 신학에 대한 기본적인 인식 때문이라고 생각한다. 그의 인격과 정신이 그리스도의 십자가 신학에 의해 조성되어 있기 때문이다. 그러므로 1-9장의 화해의 어조와 상반되는 10-13장에서 고린도 교인들을 질책할 때에도 바울은 육체적 자랑을 억지로 하면서 동시에 자신의 육체적 조건의 약함을 시인하면서 십자가의 능력에 의지한다(13:4). 십자가의 능력이란 나를 의지하지 않고 내게 능력 주시는 자를 의지하는 데서 나타나는 것이다. 바울은 죽으시고 다시 사신 그리스도를 믿는 믿음 안에서 모든 역설적인 혼돈과 무질서가 조화와 풍요함으로 전이되는 놀라운 역사가 일어나는 것을 알고 있다. "영광과 욕됨으로 말미암으며 악한 이름과 아름다운 이름으로 말미암으며, 속이는 자 같으나 참되고, 무명한 자 같으나, 보라 우리가 살고, 징계를 받는 자 같으나 죽임을 당하지 아니하고, 근심하는 자 같으나 많은 사람을 부요하게 하고, 아무 것도 없는 자 같으나 모든 것을 가진 자로다"(6:8-10). 바울의 글이 능력과 권위가 있는 한 가지 이유는 그의 그리스도 중심 신앙과 신학을 말로써 뿐만이 아니라 그의 실제 사역을 통해서 입증하기 때문이다.

그러므로 진실한 목회자는 그리스도의 죽으심과 사심, 하나님의 사랑과 거룩하심, 하나님의 구원과 심판의 역설적인 진리를 주저하지 말고 분명히 가르쳐야한다. 그리고 무엇보다 이런 역설적인 진리를 지신의 인격과 삶에 잘 적용하여 증거하야 한다. 설교자는 이런 역설을 알고 논하는데 그쳐서도 안 되고, 이런 역설적인 진리로 말미암아 혼돈되어서도 안 되며, 오히려 그리스도 안에서 성숙된 사람이 되기를 기도해야 한다. 그렇지 못 할 때 위선적인 거짓 교사가 되고 울리는 꽹과리가 될 것이다. 실로 이런 "역설적 진리의 구현"조차 역설적이다. 그것은 성령의 은사이면서도, 설교자의 노력과 연습의 결과이기 때문이다(빌 4:11-12; 딤전 4:7). 하나님께서는 이렇게 준비된 사람을 그의 합당한 도구로 쓰신다.

3. 하나님께서 우리의 사역을 도우신다(7:5-16).

본문:

> 7:5 우리가 마게도냐에 이르렀을 때에도 우리 육체가 편치 못하고 사방으로 환난을 당하여 밖으로는 다툼이요 안으로는 두려움이라. 6. 그러나 비천한 자들을 위로하시는 하나님이 디도의 옴으로 우리를 위로하셨으니 7. 저의 온 것 뿐 아니요 오직 저가 너희에게 받은 그 위로로 위로하고 너희의 사모함과 애통함과 나를 위하여 열심 있는 것을 우리에게 고함으

로 나로 더욱 기쁘게 하였느니라. 8. 그러므로 내가 편지로 너희를 근심하게 한 것을 후회하였으나 지금은 후회하지 아니함은 그 편지가 너희로 잠시만 근심하게 한 줄을 앎이라. 9. 내가 지금 기뻐함은 너희로 근심하게 한 까닭이 아니요 도리어 너희가 근심함으로 회개함에 이른 까닭이라. 너희가 하나님의 뜻대로 근심하게 된 것은 우리에게서 아무 해도 받지 않게 하려 함이라. 10. 하나님의 뜻대로 하는 근심은 후회할 것이 없는 구원에 이르게 하는 회개를 이루는 것이요. 세상 근심은 사망을 이루는 것이니라. 11. 보라 하나님의 뜻대로 하게 한 이 근심이 너희로 얼마나 간절하게 하며 얼마나 변명하게 하며 얼마나 분하게 하며 얼마나 두렵게 하며 얼마나 사모하게 하며 얼마나 열심있게 하며 얼마나 벌하게 하였는가 너희가 저 일에 대하여 일절 너희 자신의 깨끗함을 나타내었느니라. 12. 그런즉 내가 너희에게 쓴 것은 그 불의 행한 자를 위한 것도 아니요 그 불의 당한 자를 위한 것도 아니요 오직 우리를 향한 너희의 간절함이 하나님 앞에서 너희에게 나타나게 하려 함이로라. 13. 이로 인하여 우리가 위로를 받았고 우리의 받은 위로 위에 디도의 기쁨으로 우리가 더욱 많이 기뻐함은 그의 마음이 너희 무리를 인하여 안심함을 얻었음이니라. 14. 내가 그에게 너희를 위하여 자랑한 것이 있더라도 부끄럽지 아니하니 우리가 너희에게 이른 말이 다 참된 것같이 디도 앞에서 우리의 자랑한 것도 참되게 되었도다. 15. 저가 너희 모든 사람이 두려워하고 떪으로 자기를 영접하여 순종한 것을 생각하고 너희를 향하여 그의 심정이 더욱 깊었으니 16. 내가 너희를 모든 일에 신뢰할 수 있음을(내가 너희를 인하여 범사에 담대한 고로) 기뻐하노라.

본문 비평:

1. 5절의 ἔσχηκεν(완료형, "가졌다")은 ℵ C D ψ 0243에 나타나고, ἔσχεν(단순과거형, "가졌다")은 p[46] B F G K 같은 소문자 사본에 나타난다. 후자가 시제를 바르게 고치느라고 후대에 쓴 것이거나,[801] 아니면 가운데 η를 필사자가 빠뜨렸을 수 있다.[802]

801) Martin, 213.

802) Thrall, 487, 주 4.

2. 5절에서 p^{46}은 단수형 φόβος("두려움")을 쓴다.

3. 8절은 두 가지 본문 문제가 있다. 첫째는, βλέπων(분사형, "본다")이 p^{46} vg에, βλέπω(현재형)가 P^{46} B D* it sa Ambrosiaster에, 또는 βλέπω γὰρ가 ℵ C D^1 F G ψ 0243 vgmss syrbo 에 나타난다. 학자들마다 이에 대한 이견이 있다. 휴즈는 βλέπων(분사형)을 지지한다.[803] 끝의 ν이 기록과정에서 생략되거나 상실되었을 가능성을 본다. 그러나 필사자가 어색한 문장을 다듬기 위해서 βλέπω에 ν을 추가하였을 가능성이 있다.[804] 바레트는 βλέπω(현재형)를 지지한다.[805] 그러나 그는 βλέπων(분사형)으로 할 경우 가장 의미가 분명해진다고 한다. 이것은 결국 분사형이 후대의 수정이라는 가능성을 보여주는 것이다. 바울이 자주 문법적으로 맞지 않는 말을 쓰기 때문이며, 다른 것들은 후대에 이를 고치려는 시도들로 보기 때문이다.[806] 그러나 대부분 βλεπω γὰρ를 지지한다(Nestle-Aland).

둘째는, 위의 문제와 관련하여 문장을 적절히 나누는 문제인데(punctuation), εἰ καὶ μετεμελόμην("비록 내가 후회했지만")절을 그 앞의 문장에 연관시켜 읽을 것인가 아니면, 뒤에 오는 문장에 관련시켜 읽을 것인가의 문제이다. 앞의 문장과 관련시키는 경우에는 "비록 내가 편지로 너희를 근심하게 하였으나, 지금은 후회하지 않는다. 비록 과거엔 후회했지만…" 으로 번역된다. 이 경우

803) Hughes, 269.

804) Thrall, 491.

805) Barrett, 210.

806) Metzger, *A Textual Commentary on the Greek New Testament*, 581.

에 **οὐ μεταμέλομαι**("후회하지 않는다")는 문장이 주문장이 된다. 그리고 이 문장은 귀결절도 되어 앞뒤로 조건절을 두 개 갖는다. 그리고 **βλέπω [γὰρ] ὅτι ἡ ἐπιστολὴ ἐκείνη εἰ καὶ πρὸς ὥραν ἐλύπησεν ὑμᾶς**("그 편지가 너희로 잠시만 근심하게 한 줄을 앎이라")라는 절이 **γάρ**를 가지는 경우에는 근심하게 만든 이유를 설명하는 이유절로 볼 수도 있고, 주문장 **οὐ μεταμέλομαι**("후회하지 않는다")가 이유절로 볼 수도 있다. 어떤 사본에는 없는 **γάρ**를 제하고 번역하면, 이 절은 단순히 근심하게 만든 것에 대한 보충적 설명이 된다. 그러나 이 경우 문제는 9절("내가 지금 기뻐한다")이 8절과 문법적으로 연결이 안 되는 것이다. 트롤은 이런 어려움에도 불구하고 이 경우가 다음 경우보다 8절의 논리적 통일성을 세워줌으로 낫다고 본다.[807] 바울은 편지로 고린도 교인들을 근심케 한 것을 과거에는 후회하였으나 이제는 더 이상 후회하지 않는다는 뜻이다. 한글개역도 이런 문장 구성을 따라서 번역하고 있다.

한편, **εἰ καὶ μετεμελόμην**("비록 내가 후회했지만")을 뒤에 오는 9절과 연결시켜서, "그러므로 내가 편지로 너희를 근심하게 한 것을 후회하였으나, … 내가 지금은 기뻐함은…" 으로 번역하기도 한다.[808] 문법적으로 **εἰ καὶ μετεμελόμην**("비록 내가 후회했지만")절이 9절의 조건절이 되고, 9절이 귀결절이 되는 것이다. 이 경우에 가운데 있는 **βλέπω [γὰρ] ὅτι ἡ ἐπιστολὴ ἐκει,νη εἰ καὶ πρὸς ὥραν ἐλύπησεν ὑμᾶς**("그 편지가 너희로 잠시만 근심하게

807) Thrall, 491.

808) NIV; Hodge, 181; Tasker, 105; Hughes, 269, 2n 6.

한 줄을 앎이라")라는 절을 삽입구로 보게 된다. 이 경우 문법적으로 직설법 동사 βλέπω를 분사형 βλέπων으로 고쳐야 한다.[809] 그러나 삽입구가 8절과 9절 사이에 거추장스럽게 있다고 보는 것이 문제다.[810] (B 사본은 εἰ καὶ μετεμελόμην["비록 내가 후회했지만"]의 εἰ와 καὶ사이에 δὲ를 넣어서[εἰ δὲ καὶ μετεμελόμην, "그러나 내가 후회하였으나…"] 그 뒤의 βλέπω절을 새로이 시작되는 문장으로 생각하고 있다).[811]

한편 흠정역은 εἰ καὶ μετεμελόμην("비록 내가 후회했지만")의 절을 9절이 아니라 βλέπω("내가 앎이라")로 시작되는 절과 직접 연결시켜서 "너희를 잠시나마 근심하게 한 것을 후회했다"고 번역한다. 지와 타스커는 그렇게 보면 9절이 연결이 안 되고 전체 의미가 분명치 않다고 한다. 지에 의하면, 흠정역 번역은 결국 "내가 너희를 근심케 하였다. 이것을 지금은 후회하지 않는다. 이것을 전에는 후회했다. 왜냐하면 내가 잠시나마 너희를 근심케 하였기 때문이다"라고 "근심케 하였다"는 말이 쓸데없이 반복되는 번역이 되고, 편지 보낸 것을 후회하는 것이 아니라, 근심케 한 것을 후회한다는 뜻이 되어 어색하다고 한다.[812] 실제로 바울은 근심케 한 것을 후회하는 것이 아니라, 편지 보낸 것을 후회하고 있다는 것이다. 지와 타스커는 εἰ καὶ μετεμελόμην("비록 내가 후회했지만")절을 9절과 연결시키고 βλέπω("내가 앎이라")로 시작되는 절을 삽입절로 보고, "비록 내가 너희를 편지로 근심하게 하였으나

---

809) Barrett, 210.

810) Thrall, 491.

811) Martin, 213; Thrall, 491.

812) Hodge, 181, Tasker, 104, 105; Martin, 213, 229.

편지 보낸 것을 후회하지 않는다. 비록 (과거에는) 후회했지만, (내 편지가 잠시만 너를 근심하게 하였음을 알게 되었기 때문에…) 이제는 기뻐한다(9절 상반절)"로 번역한다.

이렇게, 조건절, **εἰ καὶ μετεμελόμην**("비록 내가 후회했지만") 을 앞쪽으로 아니면, 뒤쪽으로 부쳐서 읽느냐에 따라서 번역이 달라지지만, 문장 분석과 상관없이 "근심케 한 것" 또는 "편지를 부친 것" 중 어느 쪽을 주제로 보느냐에 따라서도 해석이 달라질 수 있다. 그러나 엄격하게 보아서 편지를 보낸 것이 곧 근심케 한 것이므로 "편지를 보낸 것"이 주제이든지, "근심케 한 것"이 주제이든지 전체의 뜻을 크게 변하게 하지는 않는다.[813] 본문에 **λύπειν**(근심하다)이란 말이 8-11절 사이에 8번(10절의 명사형 **λύπη** x2 포함) 나오므로 근심케 한 일이 주제라고 보고 한글개역을 따른다.[814] 바울은 편지로 근심케 한 것을 후회하였으나 이제는 더 이상 후회하지 않는다.

4. 10절의 ἐργάζεται(이룬다)가 א* B C D P 81 1175,

---

813) 참조, Hodge, 181; Tasker, 205.

814) Thrall, 491; P. Barnett, *The Second Epistle to the Corinthians* (Grand Rapids: Wm. B. Eerdmans Publishing Company, 1997) 371, 372, 주 2: Barnett은 여기서 Thrall을 따라서 "나는 후회하지 않는다"를 앞쪽으로 부쳐서 번역하나, 371에서는 뒤쪽으로 부쳐서 번역하고 있어서 그 자신 혼돈하고 있음을 보여 준다(372, 주 4를 보라) (Thrall, 486; Martin 212). 뒤쪽으로 부쳐서 번역하면 Barnett의 번역은 Thrall의 번역과는 다르고 오히려 Martin의 번역과 거의 같다(Thrall, 486; Martin 212와 비교 해보라). 한편 어떤 이들은 "나는 후회하였다"를 뒤로 부쳐서, "내가 편지로 잠시 너희를 근심하게 한 것을 알고서 후회하였다"라고 해석하고 있다(Hodge, 181; Tasker, 104, 105; Martin, 228-229).

κατεργάζεται("이뤘다")로 ℵ² F G ψ 0243. 다음 절에 나오는 κατεργάζεται("이뤘다")에 동화된 것이라고 본다.[815)]

5. 11절에 소문자 사본(ℵ² D ψ vg)에 λυπηθῆναι(부정사, "근심하는 것") 뒤에 ὑμᾶς("우리")가 나오나 p⁴⁶ ℵ* B C F G 0243 33 81 630 1739 1881 Ambrosiaster에는 없다.

6. 11절에 ὑμῖν("너희들")앞에 ἐν("…안")이 있는 경우(ℵ² C F G P 104 326 629 2464 2495 Ambrsiaster)와 없는 경우([p⁴⁶] ℵ* B D K L y 0243 33 81 630 Clement)가 있다.

7. 11절에 ἐν이 τῷ πράγματι("일, 사건") 앞에 나오는 경우가 있다(D¹). 그러나 원래는 없는 것으로 본다(ℵ B C D* F G, f g).[816)]

8. 12절에 ἄρα("그러면", "그러므로")는 여기서 ὥστε("그 결과")의 뜻으로 결과절을 이끈다.

9. 12절에서 ἡμῶν τὴν ὑπὲρ ἡμῶν("우리를 위한 우리의")은 G d vgms에서, ὑμῶν τὴν ὑπὲρ ὑμῶν("너희를 위한 너희의")는 ℵ D* F 0243 629에 나타난다. 전자가 문맥에 맞다(Nestle-Aland). 후자는 7장 4절의 ὑμῶν에 맞추려고 한 것으로 보인다.[817)]

---

815) Plummer, 222.

816) Plummer, 224.

817) Martin, 214; Bultmann, 62.

10. 13절의 διὰ τοῦτο παρακεκλήμεθα("이로 인하여")를 12절에 포함시키는 학자들이 있다.[818)]

11. 13절에서 δέ가 빠진 경우가 있다(p[46] 81 104 365 629 630 1175).

12. 14절의 πάντα("모든 것들")(ℵ B C D F G K L P, Latt. Goth) 대신에 πάντοτε("언제나")(C F G 81 syh co)가 쓰이는 경우와 πάντων("모든 것들의")(326)으로 읽는 경우도 있다.

13. 14절에서 B F에는 ἡμῶν("우리들의") 대신에 ὑμῶν("너희들의")이 나온다.

14. ἡ ἐπὶ Τίτου("디도 앞에서", p[46] ℵ[2] C 0243) 대신에 ἡ πρὸς Τίτου("디도에게", D F G P ψ 365 614 1175)이 나온다. 의미상의 차이는 없다.

내용 개요:

바울은 고린도 교인들에 대한 그의 신뢰를 밝힌 후(4), 오랜 강해(2:14-7:4) 끝에 드디어 디도가 가져온 소식에 대해서 다시 말한다. 2장 13절에서 바울은 드로아에서 디도가 가져올 그의 "엄격한 편지"에 대한 고린도 교회의 반응에 대한 소식을 애타게 기다리면서도 디도를 만나지 못해 괴로웠던 것을 회상하고 있었다. 얼마

---

818) RSV, Héring, 56, 주.

후 디도가 가져온 소식은 고린도 교회가 다시 바울에게로 돌아섰고 다시 바울과 화목하게 되었다는 것이었다. 그래서 바울은 감사와 기쁨으로 고린도 교인들을 격려하고 있다. 바울은 디도의 소식을 들은 당장에는 기쁨으로 가득 찼다. 그가 보낸 디도가 고린도 교인들에게 많은 사랑을 받고 온 것도 큰 기쁨이었다(7:13). 7장 8절에 언급된 바울이 보낸 "엄격한 편지"는 2장 4절에 언급된 편지와 같은 것으로 본다. 이 편지의 내용은 구체적이고 매우 엄격한 내용의 편지라고 할 수 있다(2:5 이하). 그러므로 바울은 일종의 극약 처방 같은 이 편지에 대해서 고린도 교인들이 행여 완전히 부정적인 반응을 보이지 않을까 근심하면서 디도를 통해 오는 소식을 애타게 기다렸던 것이다. 그러나 바울의 근심은 디도가 가져온 기쁜 소식으로 이내 사라졌다. 고린도 교인들이 그들의 잘못을 회개하고 다시 바울에게 돌아온 것이었다. 하나님께서 그 편지를 통해서 역사하셨던 것이었다. 그러므로 바울은 너무 기뻤다(16). 바울은 고린도 교인들이 디도에게 보여준 환대에 대해서 기뻐하는 것으로 끝맺는다(13-15). 바울이 기뻐한 중요한 원인은 비록 고린도 교인들의 반응이 어떻게 나올지 몰라 초조했으나 그가 원래 편지 쓰기 전부터 갖고 있던 고린도 교인들에 대한 신뢰가 다시 확인되었기 때문이다(14). 본문은 4절에 나오는 세 가지 핵심적인 단어들(즉, παρακλήσει, 위로; χαρά, 기쁨; θλίψει, 환난)이 본문에 있는 다른 동족어들과 함께 병행적으로 짜여져 있는 것이 흥미롭다.

παρακλήσεὶ; παρακαλῶν; παρεκάλεσεν(6); παρακλήσει ἧ παρεκλήθη(7); παρακεκλήμεθα(13)("위로", "위로하다").

χαρᾷ χαρῆναι(7); **χαίρω**(9); **ἐχάρημεν, χαρᾷ**(13)("기쁨", "기뻐하다").

θλίψει; θλιβόμενοι(5)("환난", "환난당하다").

이 중에서 **παρακλήσει**("위로")라는 말이 첫 절(4절)과 마지막 절(16절)에 나와서 환형문장구조(環形文章構造)을 이루고 있다. 이 외에도 4절에서 **καύχησις**("자랑")이란 말이 14절에서 다시 나온다. 이런 언어들이 조직적 연결되어 있는 것은 7장 2-4절과 7장 5-16절이 원래 하나의 글임을 보여 줌으로써, 2장 14절-7장 4절의 독립문서설을 반대하는 중요한 근거가 된다.[819)]

바울과 고린도 교회와의 관계회복이 일시적이거나 불안한 요소들이 아직 남아 있다고 보아야 한다. 10장 이후의 엄격한 내용을 볼 때, 아직도 반대하는 세력이 남아 있거나, 상태가 다시 악화될 수 있는 가능성이 있다. 만일 우리가 견지하는 대로 10-13장이 1-9장 이후에 계속 쓰인 것이라면, 왜 바울의 어조가 그토록 달라질 수 있는가? 바울이 7장 4절에서 고린도 교인들을 신뢰한다는 것은 오직 그를 따르는 사람들에 대한 것인가 10-13장은 아직 그를 반대하는 소수에 대한 질책인가 아니면 디도가 바울을 만난 뒤에 다시 고린도 교회 상황이 악화되었는가? 서론에서 이 문제를 다루었음으로 여기서는 다만 이런 문제가 있음을 상기할 뿐이다.

주 석

7:5. "우리가 마게도냐에 이르렀을 때에도 우리 육체가 편치 못

819) H. Lietzmann, *An die Korinther 1/2*, 131.

하고 사방으로 환난을 당하여 밖으로는 다툼이요 안으로는 두려움이라"(Καὶ γὰρ ἐλθόντων ἡμῶν εἰς Μακεδονίαν οὐδεμίαν ἔσχηκεν ἄνεσιν ἡ σὰρξ ἡμῶν ἀλλ' ἐν παντὶ θλιβόμενοι· ἔξωθεν μάχαι, ἔσωθεν φόβοι). 이 절은 καὶ γάρ(그리고…이라)로 시작되어 논리적으로는 4절에 대한 이유를 제시하고 있고, 실제로 "사방으로 환난을 당하여"(ἐν παντὶ θλιβόμενοι)는 4절의 "우리의 모든 환난"(ἐπὶ πάσῃ τῇ θλίψει ἡμῶν)과 같다. 그러나 크게는 2장 13절로 다시 돌아가서 드로아에서 디도를 만나지 못해서 애태우며 고린도 교회 소식을 기다리던 일을 회상하고 있다. 드로아에서 걱정하면서 떠났으나 마게도냐에 이르러서도 쉴 수 없었다. 육체적으로나 영적으로 괴로운 날들이었음을 계속하고 있다. 그러나 이런 어둡고 괴로운 설명은 그의 기쁨을 설명하기 위한 준비적인 것이다. 실패와 절망 뒤에 오는 더 큰 위로와 기쁨과 승리를 강조하는 대조적 표현 방법이다.

바울은 실제로 마게도냐 지방의 어느 도시에 있었는가 바은 빌립보라고 본다.[820] 마게도냐의 항구도시 네압볼리(Neapolis)에서 4, 5킬로 정도 떨어진 곳이며, 드로아 다음에 지나는 곳으로서는 이 곳 외에 없기 때문이며, 또 6년 전에 바울이 세운 교회가 여기 있기 때문이다(빌 4:14-16). 사도행전 16장 8-12절에서 바울이 2차 전도 여행 시에 드로아를 떠나 마게도냐로 갈 때, 네압볼리에서 곧장 빌립보로 갔다고 했다. 그리고 그곳을 "마게도냐 지경의 첫 성" 이라고 했다(행 16:12). 그러나 바이 지적하듯이 실제로 고린도후서에서 이에 대한 언급이 전혀 없는 것은 이상하다. 타스커는

---

820) Barnett, 368-69.

좀 더 막연하게 네압볼리에서 다른 여러 도시들을 잇는 큰길가(Via Ignatia) 어디선가에서 디도를 만나려 했었다고 본다.[821]

"육체가 편치 못했다"(οὐδεμίαν ἔσχηκεν ἄνεσιν ἡ σὰρξ ἡμῶν)는 말은 2장 13절과 7장 5절의 구체적인 바울의 환난을 생각하면, 여기서 "순수한 육체적 고통"을 가리킨다고 본다. 7장 1절에서와 같이 여기서의 "육체"(σάρξ)는 패역한 인간 자아를 나타내는 신학적인 의미가 아니고, 일반적 의미로, 바울의 연약한 육체를 가리키는 의미로 쓰였다.[822] 나아가 "육체"는 몸은 물론 정신까지도 포함하여 바울의 전인(全人)을 나타내는 것이다.[823] "현재의 문맥에서 바울은 πνεῦμα(프뉴마, "정신")와 σάρξ(사르크스, "육체")를 동의어로 쓰고 있다."[824] 이 절에서 "밖으로는 다툼이요"(ἔξωθεν μάχαι)는 육체적인 피곤함을 가리킬 수 있으나, "안으로는 두려움이라"(ἔσωθεν φόβοι)는 정신적인 고통을 가리킨다. 또 7장 5절이 연결되는 2장 13절에서도 이 말과 유사한 형태로, "내 심령이 편치 못하여"(οὐκ ἔσχηκα ἄνεσιν τῷ πνεύματί μου)라는 말이 나온다. 마게도냐에서 바울은 육체적으로나(7:5), 정신적으로나(2:13) 몹시 고통스러운 상태에 있었다. 그 고통은 드로아에서부터의 항해에 기인한 피로보다는 주로 이방인이나 유대인과의 접촉에서 오는 고통이라고 본다.[825] 어쩌면 그의 "육체의 가시"도 그의 육체의 불편함의 한 원인이었을 것이다(12:7).[826]

---

821) Tasker, 20.

822) Martin, 223.

823) Thrall, 487; Furnish, 384.

824) Martin 223; 참조, Hughes, 265; Bultmann, 56.

825) Thrall, 488.

826) Bruce, 217.

"편하다"(ἄνεσιν)는 개념은 긴장을 풀고 쉰다는 뜻이다(참조, 2:13; 8:13).[827] "바울은 고린도 교인들의 눈에 사도로서 가치를 인정받게 되기 전까지는 고통으로부터 벗어나 쉴 수 없었다."[828] 바울은 매우 민감한 사람으로서 일상생활의 스트레스와 압력으로 시달리는 나약한 인간으로 자신을 나타내고 있다.[829] 이런 고통이 계속적인 현상이라는 사실은 문자적으로 "(아무 것도) 갖지 못했다"는 말의 ἔσχηκεν이 ἔχειν(가지다)의 완료형으로 계속을 나타내기 때문이다. 이것은 고린도 교회의 기쁜 소식에도 불구하고 바울은 여전히 (아마 고린도 교회 문제로) 스트레스를 받고 있는 상태에 있음을 보여 준다고 볼 수 있다.[830] 고린도 교회의 문제가 아직도 바울의 마음 가운데 있음을 나타낸다(11:28).

"밖으로는 다툼이요 안으로는 두려움이라"(ἔξωθεν μάχαι, ἔσωθεν φόβοι). 이 말은 앞에 있는 "사방으로 환난을 당하여"라는 말을 더 절실하게 설명하는 말이다. μάχαι(마카이, "다툼")는 "싸움," "분쟁"을 가리키는 말로서 마게도냐에 있는 바울의 반대자들을 가리키며(고전 15:30-32, 16:9),[831] 그들은 기독교인이거나 비기독교인들 일 수 있으며(행 16:23; 17:5; 빌 1:30; 살전 2:2),[832] 또는 역경을 가리킬 수 있다.[833] "안으로는 두려움"은 "고린도 교

---

827) Bruce, 217.

828) Martin, 223.

829) Tasker, 102, 103.

830) Denney, 252.

831) Bruce, 217; Plummer, 217, 218.

832) Barrett, 207; Tasker, 103; Filson, 357.

833) Bultmann, 56.

인들로 말미암는 두려움"을 가리킨다고 본다.[834] 고린도전서 2장 3절에서 바울은 이전의 고통스런 고린도 교회 방문을 회상하면서, "내가 너희 가운데 거할 때에 약하며 두려워하며(καὶ ἐν φόβῳ) 심히 떨었노라"고 말한다. 바울은 디도를 통해서 고린도 교회에 편지를 보내고 그 반응이 어떻게 일어날 것인가에 대해서 불안했다. 더구나 디도의 도착이 지연되면서 그 초조함은 더해졌을 것이다. 바울의 "엄격한 편지" 또는 "눈물의 편지"(2:4)는 죽어가는 다급한 환자에게 마지막 수단으로 쓰는 의사의 극약 처방과 같은 것이었다. 바울은 그 극약의 효과가 환자에게 어떻게 나타나는가를 초조하게 기다리는 의사와 같았다. 더구나 그 환자가 의사의 사랑하는 아들이라면 그 불안과 초조함은 더할 것이다. 바울에게 고린도 교회는 지극히 사랑하는 믿음의 자녀였다(2:4; 6:13; 7:1; 12:14, 15).

6. "그러나 비천한 자들을 위로하시는 하나님이 디도의 옴으로 우리를 위로하셨으니"(ἀλλ' ὁ παρακαλῶν τοὺς ταπεινοὺς παρεκάλεσεν ἡμᾶς ὁ θεὸς ἐν τῇ παρουσίᾳ Τίτου). "비천한 자들"(τοὺς ταπεινοὺς)은 여기 문맥을 따라서 "낙심한 자들"이라고 번역할 수도 있다.[835] 디도의 옴으로 위로 받기 전의 바울의 기분을 나타내기 때문이다. 이 말은 원래 "비천한 자들", "세상에서 버림받은 이들"을 가리킨다. "여호와가 그 백성을 위로하였은즉 그 고난당한 자를 긍휼히 여길 것임이니라"(καὶ τοὺς ταπεινοὺς

834) Bultmann, 56.

835) RSV; NIV; Plummer, 218; Strachan, 124; Barrett, 205; Furnish, 384; Tasker, 103; Martin, 225.

τοῦ λαοῦ αὐτοῦ παρεκάλεσεν, 사 49:13, LXX)는 말씀과 비슷하다. 또 "(여호와 우리 하나님) … 가난한 자를 진토에서 일으키시고"(καὶ τὰ ταπεινὰ ἐφορῶν, 시 113:7, LXX), "낮은 자를 높이 드시고"(τὸν ποιοῦντα ταπεινοὺς[עני, 아니, "낮은 자"] εἰς ὕψος, 욥 5:11, LXX)와 유사하다. 이사야서 49장 13절과의 연계는 앞서 6장 2절에서 이사야서 49장 8절이 나오기 때문에 더 깊어 보인다. 또한 하나님의 위로와 "고난당한 자"가 함께 나오는 것도 우연한 일치는 아닌 것으로 보인다. 이외에도 이사야서에는 하나님이 그의 백성을 위로하신다는 약속이 많다(사 40:1; 51:3, 12, 19; 52:9; 61:2; 66:13). "이스라엘의 위로"(눅 2:25)는 오랫동안 고대하던 메시야 시대를 가리킨다. 바은 "고린도후서에서 위로의 말이 많이 사용되는 것은 메시아 시대가 도래했음을 나타내며, 그리고 6장 2절에서 이점이 더 명확히 나타난다고 본다.[836] 나아가서, "비천한 자들을 위로하시는 하나님" 이란 구절은 디도를 통해 기쁜 소식을 주신 것만을 의미하는 것이 아니라, 새로운 언약을 받은 그의 백성을 향한 하나님의 구원 행위를 가리킨다고 한다.[837]

"디도의 옴으로"(ἐν τῇ παρουσίᾳ Τίτου). 여기서 전치사 ἐν은 수단의 여격이다. "디도가 옴으로써" 사태가 반전이 되었다. 디도는 하나님이 보내 주신 바울의 기분을 전환시키는 수단이었다. 디도는 고린도 교회 사역을 전담하는 사역자였다. 그는 충성스러운 사람이었고(2:13), 바울의 동역자였으며(8:23), 바울과 한마음이 된 사람이었다(8:16). 그는 단순히 편지 배달부만은 아닌 듯하

836) Barnett, 370.
837) Barnett, 370.

다.[838] 바울의 편지를 가지고 고린도 교인들의 마음을 돌리는 역할도 하였을 것이다.[839] "옴"(παρουσία, "파루시아")은 흔히 쓰는 일반적인 말인데, 신약신학에서 주님의 강림을 나타내는 전문적인 용어로 쓰이고 있다. 물론 여기서는 단순히 디도의 도착을 가리킨다. 바울의 기쁨은 엄격히 말해서 디도를 만났기 때문이 아니라 디도가 가져온 기쁜 소식 때문이었다.[840] 그가 디도를 통해 받은 소식은 실제로 하나님께로부터 받은 위로이다. 하나님의 이름을 언급한 것은 하나님이 자신의 사역의 주체라는 바울의 깊은 믿음을 나타낸다.

"우리"(ἡμᾶς)라고 한 것은 고린도 교회 사역을 바울의 개인적 일이 아니라 보다 공식적인 사도적 사역으로 보기 때문이다.[841] 실제로 그 기쁨은 디도를 포함한 바울의 사역을 돕는 모든 고린도 교회 사역자들의 기쁨이었다(8:18). 디도의 도래는 고린도 교회의 사태로 침울했던 바울에게 새로운 희망과 용기를 준 계기가 된 것은 분명하다. 그러나 디도의 소식은 고린도 교회의 헌금의 지연문제, 그리고 아직 바울을 반대하는 소수의 사람들에 대한 보고도 포함되어 있었을 것이다. 이런 문제가 바울로 하여금 10장 이후에 엄격한 글로써 보다 단호하게 고린도 교회문제를 처리하려는 계획을 집필 처음부터 하였을 것이다. 그러나 디도의 소식은 바울의 초조함과 불안을 씻어 내기에 충분했다. 고린도 교인들이 자신이

---

838) 디도가 바울의 "엄격한 편지"를 가지고 갔는지 가기 전에 미리 보냈는지에 대한 논란이 있다(Héring, 54, 주, 8). Martin은 후자를 지지한다(226).

839) Barnett, 370.

840) Bultmann, 57.

841) Martin, 225.

기대했던 것 이상으로 자신의 편지에 대해 적극적인 반응을 보였기 때문이다.

7. "저의 온 것 뿐 아니요 오직 저가 너희에게 받은 그 위로로 위로하고 너희의 사모함과 애통함과 나를 위하여 열심 있는 것을 우리에게 고함으로 나로 더욱 기쁘게 하였느니라"(οὐ μόνον δὲ ἐν τῇ παρουσίᾳ αὐτοῦ ἀλλὰ καὶ ἐν τῇ παρακλήσει ᾗ παρεκλήθη ἐφ᾽ ὑμῖν, ἀναγγέλλων ἡμῖν τὴν ὑμῶν ἐπιπόθησιν, τὸν ὑμῶν ὀδυρμόν, τὸν ὑμῶν ζῆλον ὑπὲρ ἐμοῦ ὥστε με μᾶλλον χαρῆναι). "저의 온 것(으로)"(ἐν τῇ παρουσίᾳ αὐτοῦ)은 다음에 나오는 "저가 너희에게 받은 그 위로"(καὶ ἐν τῇ παρακλήσει ᾗ παρεκλήθη ἐφ᾽ ὑμίν)와 함께 바울이 받은 위로의 수단을 나타낸다. 지금까지 본문의 주제인 "위로"(1:3-7; 7:6, 13)와 디도의 "돌아옴"에 대해서 여기서 더 자세히 풀어 설명하고 있다. 고린도 교인들이 바울의 사신인 디도를 잘 대해 주어서 디도가 위로를 받고(παρεκλήθη) 돌아와서 바울에게 보고할 때에 바울도 위로를 받게 된 것이다. 디도 자신도 바울과 같이 고린도 교회에 대해 근심하면서 고린도에 갔었을 것이다. 그리고 디도는 바울을 반대하는 고린도 교인들에게 바울이 쓴 엄격한 내용의 편지를 전하는 일도 쉬운 일이 아님을 잘 알고 있었을 것이다. 바울은 멀리 떨어져서 관망하며 초조한 입장이나, 디도는 문제의 고린도 교회에 직접 가서 그들과 대면해야 하는 어려운 입장이었다. 그러나 고린도 교인들의 바울에 대한 편지의 반응이 의외로 좋게 나오고 그들이 디도를 잘 대해줄 때에 그런 근심이 사라지고 기쁨으로 차게 되었다. 그러나 7절의 초점은 바울이 디도의 위로로 말미암

아 받은 위로에 있다. 바울의 동역자인 디도가 받은 위로는 곧 그의 위로이기 때문이다. 이제 바울이 방문해도 그들의 따뜻한 영접을 받게 될 것이다.

"너희에게 받은 그 위로로(도)" (καὶ ἐν τῇ παρακλήσει ᾗ παρεκλήθη ἐφ᾽ ὑμίν). 바울이 위로를 받은 근본적 이유는 그의 동역자 디도가 고린도 교인들에게 받은 위로였다. 디도가 고린도 교인들의 변화로 말미암아 위로를 받고 돌아온 것은 고린도 교인들이 디도의 사역을 따라 바울로 돌아왔다는 가장 확실한 증거이기 때문이다. "너희에게" (ἐφ᾽ ὑμῖν)의 정확한 해석을 놓고 "너희에 대해서" (over you)란 해석과[842] "너희 안에" (in you) 라는 해석이 있다.[843] 전자는 고린도 교인들의 변화된 사실 전체로 말미암아 위로 받았다는 뜻이 되고, 후자는 고린도 교인들의 내면적 변화를 강조하는 뜻이 된다. 7장 하반절의 고린도 교인들의 내적 특징들은 이를 지지한다.

"너희의 사모함과" (τὴν ὑμῶν ἐπιπόθησιν). 7절 하반절에서 바울은 디도를 통해 들은 고린도 교인들의 내적 변화의 특징들을 다시 적고 있다. 첫째로, 고린도 교인들은 바울을 그리워하고 있었다(7:11; 겔 23:11). 동사형(ἐπιποθεῖν)은 자주 나오나(롬 1:11; 살전 3:6; 빌 2:26; LXX 여러 곳) 명사형은 드물다(7:11; 겔 23:11). 이 말은 주로 사람을 그리워하는 뜻으로 쓰인다. 그리움의 대상은 뒤에 나오는 "나를 위하여" (ὑπερ ἐμοῦ)라는 말에 있듯이 바울이다. 바울이 여행 계획을 취소한 일도 있으므로(2:11), 고린도 교인들이

842) Plummer, 219; Bultmann, 57.

843) Tasker, 103; Martin, 226.

그를 더 보고 싶어 하였을 것이다. 바울 대신 디도가 갔으므로 디도 편에 바울을 그리는 그들의 그리움을 전했다. 이제 화해의 문은 열렸고 바울 자신도 따뜻한 영접을 받게 될 것이다.

여기에서 ὑμῶν(너희)이 3번 연거푸 관사와 명사 사이에 나오는 것이 흥미롭다(τὴν ὑμῶν ἐπιπόθησιν, τὸν ὑμῶν ὀδυρμόν, τὸν ὑμῶν ζῆλον ὑπὲρ ἐμοῦ).[844] 데니는 이것은 고린도 교인들의 마음의 변화를 가리키는 것이라고 한다.[845] 변덕스런 고린도 교인들이 바울을 사모하는 마음으로 바뀌었다. 바울이 고린도 교인들을 향해 갖고 있던 일방적인 행동이 이제는 고린도 교인들이 갖고 있는 행동들로 바뀐 것을 대조적으로 나타내는 것이라고도 할 수 있다.[846] 고린도 교인들의 사모함이 원래의 수준으로 되돌아갔음을 말한다.[847]

"(너희의) 애통함" (τὸν ὑμῶν ὀδυρμόν)이 어떤 것에 대한 슬퍼함인지 언급하지 않았으나 바울을 괴롭힌 것에 대한 애통함일 것이다.[848] 바울이 그들을 방문할 수 없다는 통보를 받고 애통했을 수도 있다.[849] 바울은 방문을 원했으나, 고린도 교인들 편에서 화해적 방문을 위한 여건이 성숙하지 않아서 방문을 취소하고 대신 디도를 보냈던 것이다(1:23-2:3). 여기서의 "애통함"은 10절의 회개(μετάνοια)와 관련된다.

---

844) 이런 예가 1:6(ὑπὲρ τῆς ὑμῶν παρακλήσεως, "너희의 위로와 …을 위함이요", 2번)과 12:19(ὑπε.ρ τῆς ὑμῶν οἰκοδομῆς, "너희의 덕을 세우기 위함")에도 나온다.

845) Tasker, 103; Denney. 252, 253.

846) Denney, 252, 253; Hughes, 267, 주, 5.

847) Filson, 358.

848) Tasker, 103; Hughes, 267; Bruce, 218.

849) Barrett, 208.

"나를 위하여 열심 있는 것"(τὸν ὑμῶν ζῆλον ὑπὲρ ἐμοῦ)은 "사모함", "애통함"의 클라이맥스에 해당되는 자세이다.[850] 이 "열심"은 고린도 교인들이 바울의 지시를 따라서 실제로 잘못을 고치고 바로잡는 조치에서 나타난 것이다.[851] 또 바울이 그를 비난하는 대적자들에 맞서서 변호하는 충성에서 나타났다(5:12).[852]

"우리에게 고함으로"(ἀναγγέλλων ἡμῖν). 원문에서는 위의 3개의 절 앞에 나오지만 한글개역에 따라 뒤에서 다룬다. "알린다", "보고한다"는 뜻이다. 주동사로 나와야 하지만 분사형으로 나온 것은 바울이 기쁨으로 고조된 상태에서 보다 적극적인 메시지를 나타내기 위함이라고 한다.[853]

"나로 더욱 기쁘게 하였느니라"(ὥστε με μᾶλλον χαρῆναι). 이상의 고린도 교인들의 확실한 변화의 증거들로 말미암아 바울이 더욱 기뻐하게 되었다. 디도를 만나서 고린도 교회의 변화의 소식을 들을 것도 기쁜데, 이런게 확실한 변화의 구체적 증거들을 들으니 더욱 기쁜 것이다. 혹 증폭된 기쁨의 원인을 위로를 받은 데서 찾기도 하고, 편지를 보낸 뒤에 바울이 불안과 초조함에 있던 것에 비해서 그 기쁨이 더 크다는 뜻으로 해석하기도 한다.[854]

여기서 바울의 목회에 대한 바넷의 통찰력 있는 견해를 읽는 것이 본문의 이해에 도움이 된다.

---

850) Bultmann, 58.

851) Bruce, 228.

852) Barrett, 208.

853) Martin, 226.

854) Bultmann, 58; Windisch, 228; Martin, 227; Thrall, 489.

> 이상의 구절들은 (1) 바울의 사역 접근 자세, 그리고 (2) 그의 감정을 보여 준다. (1)에 관해서, 우리는 바울에게 어떤 객관성이 있음을 알게 된다. 고린도후서의 대부분이 그렇듯이, 비록 고린도 교회가 여전히 중요한 문제들로 어려운 가운데 있었으나 바울은 이 특별한 일(고린도 교회의 변화)을 따로 분리해 내어서 기쁨의 기회로 삼고 있다. 이런 객관성은 바울의 신학적 관점에서 나온 것으로서, 바울은 아직도 죄에 젖어 있는 고린도 교회를 종말론적 완전함의 시각에서 보면서도, 한편으로는 현재의 어떤 은혜의 증거를 찾으면 감사하는 자세를 갖는다. 그러나 역설적으로 동시에 (2)에 관해서 생각하면, 바울은 고린도 교회와 매우 친밀한 관계를 원하는 인간적인 소망을 갖고 있음을 본다(6:11-13; 7:2를 보라). 인간관계에 관한 한, 목회는 결코 단순히 "객관적"인 것이 될 수 없다. 목사들도 감정이 있으며, 목회사역은 인간관계의 정황에서 수행되게 마련이다.[855]

바넷의 지적과 같이 바울은 고린도 교인들에게 종말론적 긴박감 가운데서 그들이 그리스도 안에서 새로운 피조물(5:17)이라고 하기도 하고, 하나님의 성전(6:16)이라고도 하며 그들이 태만한 옛사람의 생활을 벗어나서 거룩하게 살기를 독려한다(5:17). 고린도전서 7장 29절에 바울은 "때가 단축하여 진고로 이후로 아내 있는 자들은 없는 자같이 하며"라고 긴박한 종말에 대한 교훈을 간직하

855) Barnett, 371.

고 있다. 그리고 고린도후서 5장 10절에서 "우리가 다 반드시 그리스도의 심판대 앞에 드러나 각각 선악 간에 그 몸으로 행한 것을 따라 받으려 함이라" 고 종말론적 긴박감에서 고린도 교인들의 변화의 필요성을 촉구하고 있다.

그러나 바이 바울의 이런 객관성(신학적 견해)을 주관성(감정)과 분리하는 것이 문제다. 본문에서 바울은 사도로서 또 개인으로서 고린도 교인들이 죄를 회개하고(7:10) 거룩한 삶을 결심하였기 때문에 기뻤다. 이를 객관성과 주관성으로 나누어 생각하는 것은 어려운 일이다. 바울의 근본적인 관심은 개인적 감정이라기보다 고린도 교인들을 그리스도의 흠 없는 신부로 단장시키려는 사도적 사명감이다(11:2). 바울의 개인적인 감정은 이런 사명감에 의해서 오히려 억제될 수 있다. 앞서 6장 4절에서 말하는 "인내"(ὑπομονή)와, 특히 12장 12절에서 말하는 사도된 증거로서의 "모든 인내" (πάσῃ ὑπομονῇ)는 바울의 고난뿐만 아니라 이런 사사로운 감정의 억제도 포함한다고 본다. 그러나 실제로 개인적 감정과 공적인 사도로서의 일의 성취에 대한 보람의 느낌을 구분하는 것은 어려운 것이며 또 그럴 필요도 없는 것이다.

그러나 바넷의 진술은 목회자의 자세에 대해서 필요하고 중요한 점을 상기시켜 준다. 목회자는 종말론적 긴장감을 가지고 교인들을 경계할 필요도 있으나, 반대로 "종말론적 여유" 를 가지고 "즉 지금은 저래도 언젠가는 나아지겠지" 라고 인내하며 기다리는 자세도 필요하다(참조, 마 13:29-30). 종말의 주이신 하나님 자신이 이런 인내를 가지고 지금까지 죄인들의 회개를 기다리시기 때문이다(롬 2:4; 벧후 3:9, 15). 종말론적이며 완전주의적 목표를 향해 꾸준히 전진하는 가운데, 작은 실패와 좌절에 대해서 관용하며, 반대로 작은 성취와 진보를 업신여기지 말고 격려하고 그로 인해 기뻐하는 기회로 삼는 여유가 필요하다. 본문에서 바울이 기뻐하는 것도 고린도 교회의 문제가 완전히 해결되었기 때문이 아니라, 비록 작은 성취와 진보이며, 불완전하고 일시적인 것일지언정, 지금 고린도 교회가 바울에게 돌아온 것은 바울의 화해사역의 진보이며, 또 그의 사역에 대한 하나님의 개입과 인정의 증거이므로 바울이 기뻐하는 것이다(1:4; 2:14; 5:19; 6:1). 그 것은 장래의 또 다른 성취를 예견케 하며, 더 나아가서 종말론적 영원한 성취와 보상의 예비적인 증거로 알고 기뻐하는 것이다. 이렇게 신학 사상과 신앙 감정은 연관되어 나타나는 것이다.

8. "그러므로 내가 편지로 너희를 근심하게 한 것을 후회하였으나 지금은 후회하지 아니함은 그 편지가 너희로 잠시만 근심하게 한 줄을 앎이라"(Ὅτι εἰ καὶ ἐλύπησα ὑμᾶς ἐν τῇ ἐπιστολῇ, οὐ μεταμέλομαι· εἰ καὶ μετεμελόμην, βλέπω [γὰρ] ὅτι ἡ ἐπιστολὴ ἐκείνη εἰ καὶ πρὸς ὥραν ἐλύπησεν ὑμᾶς,)

위의 본문 비평에서 이 절의 문장을 두 가지로 나누는 방법이 있다고 했다. 첫째는 "후회하였으나"(εἰ καὶ μετεμελόμην)를 희랍어 본문에서의 앞 문장인 "지금은 후회하지 아니한다"(οὐ μεταμέλομαι)를 한 번 더 설명하는 것으로 보고, 뒤에 오는 βλέπω(나는 [본다]안다)로 시작되는 문장("그 편지가 너희로… 아노니")을 이유절로 해석하는 것이다. 본문비평에서 이에 대한 논쟁을 이미 언급하였다. 우리의 입장은 첫 번째 견해로서, "그러므로 내가 편지로 너희를 근심하게 한 것을 비록 (과거에는)후회하였으나 지금은 후회하지 않는다. 왜냐하면 그 편지가 너희로 잠시만 근심하게 한 줄을 알기 때문이다. 내가 지금 기뻐한다"라고 번역한다. 결국 개역한글성경이나 흠정역과 같은 의미이다.

둘째는 "후회했으나"를 9절의 "지금 내가 기뻐한다"에 연결하여 "후회했으나… 이제는 기뻐한다"로 해석하여 8절과 9절을 대조적인 문장 구조로 보고, βλέπω(나는 [본다]안다)로 시작되는 문장("그 편지가 너희로 잠시만 근심케 한 줄을 앎이라")을 삽입구로 보는 방법이다(NIV). 이 방법대로 번역하면, "그러므로 내가 편지로 너희를 근심하게 한 것을 지금은 후회하지 않는다. 비록 (과거에는) 후회하였다. (왜냐하면, 그 편지가 너희로 잠시 근심하게 한 줄을 알기 때문이다.) (그러나) 내가 지금 기뻐한다."

이렇게 우리말로 번역하면 첫 번째와 두 번째 번역이 별 차이가 없어 보이나, 헬라어나 영어로 볼 때, 두 번째 번역은 대체로 "편지로 근심케 한 것을 (과거에) 후회하였으나(8절), 지금은 기뻐한다(9절 상반절)"로 되어 과거의 후회함과 현재의 기뻐함의 대조가 뚜렷해지는 반면에, 첫 번째 번역으로는 이 대조가 약해지고, "지금 후회하지 않는다"(οὐ μεταμέλομαι)는 것과 "후회하지 않는 이유"(βλέπω [γὰρ] ὅτι…)가 강조된다. 과거에 "후회했다"(εἰ καὶ μετεμελόμην)는 것은 앞에 있는 "지금 후회하지 않는다"(οὐ μεταμέλομαι)는 주문장의 보조적인 의미로 약화된다. 첫 번째 번역은 9절의 "지금은 기뻐한다"(νῦν χαίρω)는 말을 8절과 문법적으로 연결시키지 못한 채, 따로 시작하는 문장으로 보는 것이 문제다. 두 번째 번역은 βλέπω로 시작되는 문장("그 편지가 너희로 잠시만 근심케 한 줄을 앎이라")을 삽입구로 보아서 문장의 계속성과 통일성을 깨뜨리는 것이 어색하다. 첫 번째 해석을 따르는 경우 γάρ(왜냐하면)가 원래 사본에 있던 것으로 보아도 βλέπω [γὰρ]절을 "지금 후회하지 않는 이유"(οὐ μεταμέλομαι)를 나타내는 이유절로 그대로 이어서 해석할 수 있다. 또 9절 상반절의 "지금 내가 기뻐한다"도 "지금 후회하지 않는다"는 말에 대해서는 추가적인 의미로, "(과거에는) 후회하였다"는 말에 대해서는 대조적인 의미로 연결이 된다. "편지를 보내어 마음을 괴롭게 한 것을 후회하기도 했으나, 잠시만 괴롭힌 것을 알기에, 지금은 더 이상 후회하지 않고 기뻐한다." 이제 바울은 "엄격한 편지" 또는 "눈물의 편지"로 고린도 교인들을 근심하게 한 것을 더 이상 후회하지 않는다. 그 편지가 그들을 잠시만 슬프게 하였을 뿐이다. 하나님의 도우심으로 고린도 교인들이 회개하고 돌아온 것이다. 하나님의 도우심으로 바울의 근심이 기쁨으로 바뀌었다.

여기서 우리는 목회자 바울의 심정을 이해할 수 있다. 편지를 쓸 때 그는 고린도 교인들의 잘못을 책망해야하는 당위성을 알면서도 그들이 상처받지 않는 적절한 책망의 선을 정하기 위해 고민하였음을 보여준다. 편지를 보낸 후에도 자신이 쓴 책망의 내용을 생각하면서 고린도 교인들의 부정적 반응을 예상해 보면서 괴로워했다. 이런 바울의 자세는 그가 사도가 된 후에도 과거의 독선적인 바리새적이고 율법주의적인 자세를 여전히 가지고 있지 않는가라는 의구심을 버리게 한다. 빌립보서에서도 그는 로마 감옥에서 사느냐 죽느냐의 문제로 고민하는 모습을 본다(빌 20-23). "만일 육신으로 사는 것이 내 일의 열매일진대 무엇을 가릴는지 나는 알지 못하노라"(빌 1:22). 고민 끝에 그에게는 차라리 이생을 떠나 주와 함께 있는 것이 더 좋은 것이지만 빌립보 교인들을 위해서는 아직 자신이 살아서 그들을 돕는 것이 더 좋다고 생각한다. 이렇게 바울은 독선적 자세로 자신의 생각만을 고집하는 성격의 소유자는 아니었다. 그는 복음 진리에 대해서는 조금도 양보하지 않는 확고한 자세를 지켰다. 그가 받은 계시는 변개될 수 없는 진리임을 확고하게 믿었다(갈 1:7-12). 그러나 목회적 딜레마에서는 모든 목회자들과 마찬가지로 고민하였다. 사람들을 복음 진리에 따라 살게 해야 하는 당위성과 복음 진리를 따라 살지 못하는 인간의 연약함과 취약한 현실을 이해하고 그들을 설득하여 적절히 조정하여 나아가야 하는 어려운 "목회적 조절 문제"로 인해서 모든 목회자들처럼 고통 받았다. 바울도 당장 그의 눈앞에 나타난 모든 목회적 문제에 대해 즉각적이고 확고한 답을 찾지는 못했던 것이다. 어떻게 편지를 써야할지 어느 정도로 어떤 말로 꾸짖어야 할지 언제 편지를 보내야 할지 내가 이제는 죽는 것이 차라리 낫지 않는가? 이런 목회적 고통은 모든 목회자들이 져야하는 십자가이다. 주님의 겟세마네의 고통도 이런 목회적 고통과 유사한 것이었다. 그렇다면 이런 목회적 고통은 목회자들의 증표이며 특권이기도 하다.

9. "내가 지금 기뻐함은 너희로 근심하게 한 까닭이 아니요 도리어 너희가 근심함으로 회개함에 이른 까닭이라. 너희가 하나님의 뜻대로 근심하게 된 것은 우리에게서 아무 해도 받지 않게 하려 함이라"(νῦν χαίρω, οὐχ ὅτι ἐλυπήθητε ἀλλ᾽ ὅτι ἐλυπήθητε εἰς μετάνοιαν· ἐλυπήθητε γὰρ κατὰ θεόν, ἵνα ἐν μηδενὶ ζημιωθῆτε ἐξ ἡμῶν). "내가 지금 기뻐함은"(νῦν χαίρω)은 8절에서 바울이 편지를 보낸 것을 후회하지 않는다고 소극적으로 말했으나, 9절에서는 적극적으로 오히려 기뻐한다고 한다. 그 이유는 그들을 잠시 근심케 한 편지가 그들을 회개하도록 했기 때문이다.

바울은 앞의 4절과 7절에서도 이미 기뻐한다고 했는데 그것은 고린도 교인들의 바울에 대한 적극적 반응과 그 소식에 대한 바울의 전체적인 기쁨이었다. 여기서는 그 기쁨의 근거를 보다 자세히 논한다.

"너희로 근심하게 한 까닭이 아니요"(οὐχ ὅτι ἐλυπήθητε)는 바울의 기쁨의 이유에 대한 가능한 오해를 먼저 불식시키는 말이다.[856] 바울은 고린도 교회 반대자들은 바울의 모든 말을 왜곡시키는 데 주력하기 때문에 이를 미리 해소해야 한다고 보았다.[857] 바울이 본문에서 거듭 기뻐하는 것이 결국 남을 근심하게 해놓고 기뻐한다는 것으로 이상하게 들릴 수도 있기 때문에 그 오해의 소지를 씻어 내는 말을 하는 것이다. 바울이 기뻐하는 것은 단순히 고린도 교인들이 편지를 받고 근심하게 된 것으로 기뻐하는 것이 아니다. 또는 바울이 그들과의 싸움에서 결국 그들을 굴복시키고 이겼으므로 통쾌해서 기뻐한다는 것이 아니다. 바울은 8절에서와 말한 바와 같이 편지로 그들을 괴롭게 하는 것 자체를 좋아하지 않는다.[858] 바울은 그의 교인들이 기뻐하는 것을 좋아한다(1:24; 살전 2:19; 20). 그는 고린도 교인들의 "기쁨을 돕는 자"가 되려고 한다(1:24). 그는 남의 슬픔의 대가로 기뻐하는 그런 잔인한 사람이 아니다. 그는 오히려 "즐거워하는 자들로 함께 즐거워하고 우는 자들로 함께 울라"(롬 12:15)고 가르치는 동정적인 사람이다.

"도리어 너희가 근심함으로 회개함에 이른 까닭이라"(ἀλλ᾽ ὅτι ἐλυπήθητε εἰς μετάνοιαν). 바울이 기뻐하는 이유는 그의 편지

856) Hughes, 269.

857) Hughes, 269; Barnett, 374.

858) Plummer, 221; Barnett, 374.

의 효과가 우려했던 바와 달리 적극적으로 나타났기 때문이다. 고린도 교인들이 회개하게 된 것이다. 바울은 고린도 교인들이 편지를 받고 바울이 전한 복음 진리를 떠나거나 바울을 오해하고 질시할 것을 두려워했을 것이다. 그런데 그 편지가 고린도 교인들로 하여금 그들의 잘못에 대해서 슬퍼하고 회개하기에 이른 것이다. 그러므로 바울은 기뻐하게 되었다. 나아가 바울이 기뻐하는 것은 단순히 고린도 교인들이 자신의 편이 되었다는 것으로 기뻐하는 것이 아니라, 고린도 교인들이 자신에게 돌아 왔다는 것은, 복음 진리로 돌아온 것이 되기 때문이다. 바울의 복음은 언제나 하나님의 진리이며, 바울의 편에 서는 것은 하나님 편에 서는 것이라는 확신이 항상 전제되어있다(4:6; 5:20).

바울이 "회개"(μετάνοια)란 말을 의외로 적게 쓰고 있다(고후 7:10; 롬 2:4; 딤후 2:25).[859] 동사형(μετανοιεῖν)은 단 한 번 고린도후서 12장 21절에만 나온다. 물론 바울은 죄의 용서에 대한 말씀은 화해의 주제와 더불어 자주 있다.[860] 어쩌면 "회개"란 말이 바울이 강조하는 하나님의 은혜와 구원 역사보다는 인간편의 반응을 나타내기 때문인지도 모른다.[861] 회개는 원래 히브리어 תשובה(테수바, "되돌아감")에서 온 것이다. 예언자들은 타락한 이스라엘 백성들이 하나님께 돌아올 것을 말했다(사 10:21; 44:22; 렘 3:12; 단 14:1; 호 7:10; 욜 2:12 등). 여기서 바울은 고린도 교인들이 하나님께 자신들이 잘못한 것을 깨닫고 회개한 것을 의미한다. 동

859) Windisch, 233-4.

860) Plummer, 221.

861) F. T. Fallon, *2 Corinthians*, New Testament Message 11 (Wilmington, Del.: M. Glazier/Dublin: Veritas, 1980), 64.

시에 고린도 교인들은 하나님의 사신이며 종인 사도 바울에 대해 잘못한 것도 깨달았을 것이다. 하나님의 사자를 업신여기는 것은 하나님을 업신여기는 것과 같이 매우 심각한 일이다. 바울은 고린도 교인들이 하나님께 대하여 회개하기를 원했을 것이다. 그러나 동시에 바울에 대한 그들의 잘못도 회개하기를 원했을 것이다.[862] 왜냐하면 바울은 하나님께 부르심을 받은 사도이므로(5:20), 그를 거절하는 것은 곧 하나님을 거절하는 것과 마찬가지기 때문이다.[863] 바울이 원하던 대로 고린도 교인들은 바울의 책망을 받아들이고 회개하기에 이르렀다. 하나님께서 "엄격한 편지"를 통해서 화해의 역사를 이루신 것이다.

"너희가 하나님의 뜻대로 근심하게 된 것은"(**ἐλυπήθητε γὰρ κατὰ θεόν**). 이 말은 고린도 교인들의 근심은 단순히 인간의 가치나 감정으로 인한 피상적인 근심이 아니라, 하나님이 원하시는 자세를 확립하기 위하여 자신의 잘못을 부끄러워하고 두려워하며 심각하게 뉘우치는 근심이다. 유대교 위경인 열두 족장의 증언 중 "갓의 증언" 5장 7절에서 회개에 대하여 다음과 같이 말하고 있다. "하나님의 진리를 따라 하는 회개는 불순종함을 파괴시키고, 어두움을 사라지게 하며, 소망을 밝히며, 영혼의 지식을 갖춰주며, 심사숙고하게 하여 구원으로 인도한다."[864]

"우리에게서 아무 해(害)도 받지 않게 하려 함이라"(**ἵνα ἐν μηδενὶ ζημιωθῆτε ἐξ ἡμῶν**). "하나님의 뜻대로 하는 근심"은 어

---

862) Filson, 358, 359.

863) Bultmann, 149.

864) J. H. Charlesworth, ed., *The Old Testament Pseudepigrapha*, vol. 1, H. C. Kee의 번역, Martin, 230-231, 재인용.

떤 해도 없다. 여기서 "우리로 말미암아 받는 해"란 어떤 것인가 휴즈와 마틴은 고린도전서 3장 10-15절에 언급하는 최후 심판 때에 사도들의 공력이 각각 들어날 터인데, 바울은 영적인 아버지로서 고린도 교인들을 바르게 인도하기 위하여 최선을 다해야 할 책임을 느꼈다고 한다.[865]. 그러므로 "우리로 말미암는 해"란 말은 고린도 교인들이 그의 편지에 대해 적절한 반응을 보이지 않았을 경우에 사도의 권위로서 더 혹독한 조치를 내렸을 것이라는 것이다.[866] 그 혹독한 조치는, 10절에서 말하는, 고린도 교인들이 "세상의 근심"으로 빠져서 바울을 질시하고 복음에서 떠나 결국 사망에 이르게 된다는 사도적 경고나 징계를 가리킨다(13:2).[867] 징계를 가리키는 말이 아니라면, 단순히 바울의 편지로 말미암은 더 악화된 관계를 가리킨다고 볼 수도 있다.

여기서 하나님과 그의 사도인 바울의 긴밀한 관계가 설정되어 있어서 하나님께 대한 회개는 곧 바울에 대한 회개와 연계되어 있다.[868] 앞서 하나님과의 화해가 바울과의 화해와 직결되어 있는 것과 마찬가지다(5:18, 20; 6:11-13). 그럼에도 바울은 그의 사도적 권한을 되도록 제한하면서 쓰려고 한다. 오히려 고린도 교인들의 종으로 자처한다(4:5). 이것은 그리스도의 유형을 따라서 종노릇하는 것을 말한다. 또 1장 24절에서 그들의 "믿음을 주관하려고 하지 않고 기쁨을 돕고자 한다"고 한다. 그는 겸비하며, 그리스도

---

865) Chrysostom, *PG* 61 col. 503 (*ANF* XII 350); Hughes, 269, 270; Martin, 231; Plummer, 221; 6:13; 5:9, 11.

866) Filson, 359; Thrall, 492.

867) Martin, 231-232; Thrall, 492.

868) Barnett, 374.

의 온유와 관용으로 권한다고 한다(10:1). 바울의 사도로서의 자세는 항상 역설적이다.

목회자들의 권위는 사도들의 권위와 같을 수는 없다(4:2, 6; 12:12).[869] 사도 시대 이후 사도들의 "절대적 권위"가 이어지지는 않았으나, 보다 "약화된 권위"가 복음을 전하고 가르치는 목사와 교사들에게 전해졌다고 본다. 그들의 성경해석이 온전하지 않고, 오류가 있을 수 있음을 인정해야 한다(벧후 3:15, 16). 또 종교개혁 이후 누구나 성경을 읽고 해석할 수 있게 되었다. 그러므로 누구든지 말씀에 대해서 바울 사도와 같은 절대적인 권위를 주장할 수 없게 되었다. 그러나 목사들은 성경 해석을 바로 하도록 훈련받은 사람들로서 실제로 사도적 권위를 가지고 있다고 보아야 한다. 다시 말하면 사도적 권위는 성경의 말씀을 사도들이 가르쳐 준대로 잘 보존하고 각 말씀의 뜻을 보다 분명히 가르치는 사람에게 주어진다. 예로 바울 사도의 말씀을 가장 바르게 이해하는 사람이 바울 사도의 권위를 이어 받는 사람이다. 나아가 그를 본받아 말씀대로 사는 사람이 더욱 그의 권위를 실제로 나타내는 사람이다.

10. "하나님의 뜻대로 하는 근심은 후회할 것이 없는 구원에 이르게 하는 회개를 이루는 것이요. 세상 근심은 사망을 이루는 것이니라"(ἡ γὰρ κατὰ θεὸν λύπη μετάνοιαν εἰς σωτηρίαν ἀμεταμέλητον ἐργάζεται· ἡ δὲ τοῦ κόσμου λύπη θάνατον κατεργάζεται). 바울은 계속해서 "하나님의 뜻대로 하는 근심"(ἡ γαρ κατὰ θεὸν λύπη)을 주제로 삼고 있다. 이것은 "하나님이

869) Barnett, 375.

지시하시는 근심" 이라고 할 수도 있다.[870] 바울의 편지를 받고 고린도 교인들은 회개함으로써 "하나님의 뜻에 맞는 자세"를 취했다.[871] 그리고 회개의 결과 구원에 이르게 되었다.

"후회할 것이 없는 구원에 이르게 하는 회개를 이루는 것이요" (μετάνοιαν εἰς σωτηρι,αν ἀμεταμε,λητον ἐργα,ζεται). "후회할 것이 없는" (ἀμεταμέλητον)이란 말이 "회개" (μετάνοιαν)를 수식하는지,[872] 아니면 "구원" (σωτηρίαν)을 수식하는지,[873] 아니면 이 두 말 모두에게 관련되는지,[874] 또는 회개와 구원을 합친 종합적인 생각과 관련되는지에 대한 논쟁이 있다.[875] 바이 지적하듯이 본문에서는 "하나님의 뜻대로 하는 근심"과 "세상 근심", 그리고 "후회할 것이 없는 구원"과 "사망"이 병행 대조를 이루고 있으므로, "사망" 앞에 "후회할 수 있는"이란 말이 생략되었다고 보아서 "후회할 수 있는 사망"이라고 읽을 수 있다.[876] 그렇다면 "후회할 것이 없는"이란 말은" 회개"가 아니라 "구원"을 수식한다고 보는 것이 옳다. "구원을 후회한다"는 개념이 성립될 수 없다고 반대할 수 있으나,[877] 바울은 여기서 "후회하게 될 사망"이라는 말에 "구원"을 의도적으로 대조시켜 부정적으로 표현하는 방법

870) Tasker, 106.

871) Hodge, 182.

872) Calvin, 99; Hodge, 183; Lietzmann, 132; Bachmann, 302-3; Windisch, 232; Allo, 196; Bultmann, 60; Furnish, 388; Thrall, 492, 주 42.

873) NIV; Strachan, 128; Bruce, 218; Plummer, 221; Tasker, 105, 106; Héring, 55.

874) Hughes, 271, 주, 11.

875) Barrett, 211.

876) Barnett, 376.

877) Plummer, 221; Martin, 232.

(litotes="긍정적 의미를 부정적으로 낮추어 표현하는 방법", 또는 oxymoron=반어법)을 쓰고 있다고 본다.[878] 이렇게 부정적인 표현을 써서 도리어 독자들의 적극적이고 긍정적인 반응을 기대하는 것이다. 즉 "'후회 없는 구원' 이라니 구원은 그 이상이지" 같은 반응이다. 바울은 구원이 좋은 것이라는 것을 독자들이 다 알고 있으므로 이렇게 소극적으로 구원을 표현해도 독자들은 "후회할 사망"에 대해 대조적으로 표현된 "구원"의 의미를 부정적으로 이해하지 않고 적극적으로 이해할 수 있다고 가정하고 있다.

"이루는 것이요"(ἐργάζεται, 에르가제타이)라는 말이 같은 의미의 "세상 근심을 하다"(**κατεργάζεται**, 카테르가제타이)와 같이 나타난다. 전자는 "하나님의 뜻대로 하는 근심"의 동사고, 후자는 "세상 근심"의 동사이다. 같은 의미라는 증거는 바로 다음 절(11)에서 여기서는 "세상 근심을 이룬다"는 뜻으로 쓰인 **κατεργάζεται**가 "하나님의 뜻대로 하는 근심이 이루는 것"을 나타내기 때문이다(11절을 한글개역에서는 "… 하며"로 약하게 번역하고 있다). 사람이 어떤 "근심"을 하느냐에 따라서 살기도 하고 죽기도 한다. 근심은 정신적인 것이나 결국 사람을 그에 따라 움직이게 하는 큰 힘을 가지고 있어서 실제적이고 구체적인 일을 이룬다는데서 유심론적(唯心論的) 사상과 유사하다. 사람이 지금 어떤 근심을 하느냐에 따라서 그 사람의 장래가 결정되는 것이다. 물론 이런 표현은 순수한 유심론적인 표현은 아니다. 바울의 말에는 하나님의 역사하심이 전제되어 있다. 마음의 상태는 하나님의 역사의 도구이거나 반응일 뿐이다(1:22; 8:16; 참조 3:2, 14; 4:4). 긍

878) Furnish, 388; Thrall, 492, 주 42; Barnett, 376, 주 17.

극적인 능력은 인간의 마음가짐이 아니라 하나님에게서 나온다 (1:21-22; 3:2-3; 13:5). "내게 능력 주시는 자 안에서 내가 모든 것을 할 수 있느니라" (빌 4:13). 그러나 사람은 그 마음을 하나님의 뜻에 합당하게 다스려야할 책임이 있다(3:2, 14, 15, 롬 12:2; 빌 2:5; 4:7; 골 3:23; 살전 2:4). 감사하게도 고린도 교인들은 하나님의 뜻대로 하는 근심을 하여서 회개하고 구원에 이르게 되었다. 바울은 7장 8절에서 고린도 교인들을 편지로 근심케 만든 것을 후회하였으나, 고린도 교인들의 회개하고 바울에게로 돌아 왔음으로 더 이상 후회하지 않고 오히려 기뻐하게 되었다. 복음은 사람을 생명으로 이끈다(2:16). 그러므로 하나님의 뜻대로 하는 근심은 구원으로 인도하기 때문에 좋은 결과와 유익을 이루는 것이다.

칼빈은 이 절을 철저히 구원론적으로 이해한다. "하나님의 뜻대로 하는 근심"은 죄에 대한 근심이며, 그 근심은 회개로 이어지며, 회개는 구원으로 이어진다. 칼빈은 회개로 구원을 얻을 수 없으나, 회개도 구원과 같이 하나님의 은혜로 가능하다고 한다.[879] 회개는 구원의 원인이 아니라(만일 그렇게 된다면 믿음이 아니라 행위로 구원받게 된다는 의미가 된다), 구원과 거의 동시에 주시는 하나님의 선물이다. 회개 없이 죄 사함을 받지 못하며, 죄 사함 받는 근거는 하나님의 자비하심이다.[880]

"세상 근심은 사망을 이루는 것이니라" (ἡ δὲ τοῦ κόσμου λύπη θάνατον κατεργάζεται). "세상" (κόσμος)은 하나님 없이 하나님과 적대적인 영역을 말한다.[881] "세상 근심"은 여러 가지

879) Calvin, 99-100.

880) Calvin, 100.

881) Bultmann, 60; Thrall, 493 재인용.

죄로 말미암는 것으로 "하나님의 뜻대로 하는 근심"과 같이 고통이 수반되나, 그 결과는 반대로 사망이다. 세상 근심은 하나님을 떠난 죄인이 빠지는 불안한 상태를 가리킨다. 죄인은 죄의 결과인 근심을 벗어나려고 하지만 그의 죄에 대한 후회만 할 뿐 진정한 회개를 잘 할 수 없다. 진정한 회개는 그리스도 안에서 죄를 용서하시고(5:14, 15, 20), 새로운 존재로 만들어 주시는(5:17) 하나님 앞에서만 가능하다. 그리고 회개는 인간의 지(知), 정(精), 의(意)가 합쳐서 일어나는 전인적(全人的) 현상이며 과정이다.[882] 정서적인 변화뿐만 아니라 인간 존재의 영적 변화이다.[883] "죄를 인식하는 것만으로는 회개라고 할 수 없다. 그것은 저항일 뿐이다. 죄에 대해서 근심하는 것도 회개라고 할 수 없다. 슬픈 마음만 가지고 회개할 수 없다. 그 것은 슬픈 감정이나 실망일 뿐이다. 죄를 안 짓는 것만으로는 회개가 아니다. 그것은 절제일 뿐이다."[884] 회개는 죄인이 생각과 감정과 의지로써 죄와 세상을 멀리하고 하나님을 가까이 하고 하나님의 은혜와 의와 선하심의 영역 안에 거주함으로 일어난다. 반면에 회개 없는 세상적인 근심은 결국 "죽음에 이르는 병"이다(키엘케골). 이삭의 아들 에서는 눈물을 흘리며 장자의 축복 받기를 원했으나 "회개할 기회를 얻지 못하였다"(창 27:38; 히 12:17). 다윗은 그의 죄를 회개하고 하나님의 인정을 받았다(시 51:1-19). 베드로는 주를 배반하였으나 회개하여 용서를 받았고(눅 22:31-34: ἐπιστρεψας), 유다는 "후회하였을 뿐이다"(마 27:3=21:30, 32: μεταμεληθείς).

882) Strachan, 128.

883) Denney, 257.

884) Strachan, 128.

여기서 "세상 근심"은 고린도 교인들이 바울의 편지를 받고 회개하지 않았을 경우에 그들이 가질 수 있는 바울에 대한 적대적인 감정을 가리킬 수도 있다. 바울의 "엄격한 편지" 내용이 고린도 교인들을 불쾌하게 만들어 바울을 미워하며 비난했을 경우에 나타날 모든 부정적인 것들을 "세상 근심"이라고 할 수 있다.[885] 이런 근심은 결국 고린도 교인들을 바울에게서 멀게 만들고 바울의 생명의 복음을 거절하게 함으로써 결국 사망으로 빠지게 할 것이다.

그러나 바울이 보기에 (적어도 디도가 전한 현재의 소식에 의하여 판단할 때) 적어도 현재의 고린도 교인들은 외적인 후회가 아니라 진정한 회개를 하였다. 그들은 주님께 돌아왔고, 바울에게 돌아왔다. 거짓 선지자들을 떠났다(2:16, 17). 그들은 바울의 편지를 받고 잘못된 과거를 버리고 새로운 삶을 결심하였다. 그들은 사망으로 이르는 죄의 길을 떠나서 생명으로 인도하는 길로 들어섰다(2:16). "사망은 구원과 대조될 때 바르게 정의될 수 있다. 하나님에게 맡기지 않는 슬픔은 영혼을 지치게 만들고, 영혼의 조직을 마르게 하며, 영혼의 희망을 사라지게 하고, 모든 것을 소멸시키고, 죽게 만든다."[886]

여기서 다시 우리는 복음과 그 복음 사역자인 바울과의 밀접한 관계를 본다. 바울은 하나님의 아들의 도래하심과 대속적 죽으심으로 하나님이 약속하신 구원의 새 시대가 시작되었음을 선포하였다(1:18-20; 6:1-2). 바울을 거절하는 것은 구원의 새 시대의 은혜

885) Thrall, 493; 참조, Barnett, 377.

886) Denney, 256.

를 받지 못하게 되는 것이다(6:1-2). 하나님의 동역자이며, 그리스도의 화해의 사신인 바울에게 돌아오는 것은 곧 하나님께로 돌아오는 것이다(5:20; 6:1). 그러므로 고린도 교인들이 편지를 받고 근심하며 자신들의 잘못을 회개하는 것은 바울의 복음을 받고 구원받은 자들로서 매우 적절한 자세이다.

11. "보라 하나님의 뜻대로 하게 한 이 근심이 너희로 얼마나 간절하게 하며 얼마나 변명하게 하며 얼마나 분하게 하며 얼마나 두렵게 하며 얼마나 사모하게 하며 얼마나 열심있게 하며 얼마나 벌하게 하였는가 너희가 저 일에 대하여 일절 너희 자신의 깨끗함을 나타내었느니라" (ἰδοὺ γὰρ αὐτὸ τοῦτο τὸ κατὰ θεὸν λυπηθῆναι πόσην κατειργάσατο ὑμῖν σπουδήν, ἀλλὰ ἀπολογίαν, ἀλλὰ ἀγανάκτησιν, ἀλλὰ φόβον, ἀλλὰ ἐπιπόθησιν, ἀλλὰ ζῆλον, ἀλλὰ ἐκδίκησιν. ἐν παντὶ συνεστήσατε ἑαυτοὺς ἁγνοὺς εἶναι τῷ πράγματι). 이 절은 여러 가지로 강조적이다. "보라"(ἰδού)라는 독자들의 주의를 끄는 말을 쓰고 있으며, 고린도 인들의 회개로 말미암아 변화된 일곱 가지의 자세를 차례로 쓰고 있고,[887] "바로 이 것(근심)"(αὐτὸ τοῦτο)이란 말도 그렇고, "얼마나"라는 말 때문에 번역이 안 된 ἀλλά(그러나)가 거듭 나와 강조적이다.[888] "너희로 얼마나 간절하게 하며"(πόσην κατειργάσατο ὑμῖν σπουδήν)도 강조형이다. 실제로 πόσην(얼마나)라는 말이 뒤에 따라 나오는 모든 고린

887) Calvin, 101.

888) Meyer, 333; Bachmann, 303; Lietzmann, 132; A. T. Robinson, *Grammar*, 1185.

도 교인들의 회개로 말미암아 변화된 자세와 그 의미를 강조하는 역할을 하고 있다.[889] 바울은 고린도 교인들의 일곱 개의 태도를 나열하면서 그의 기쁨의 범위나 근거를 넓힌다고 볼 수도 있고, 바울의 마음과 고린도 교인들의 마음 가운데 있는 모든 의심의 요소를 제거하고 있다고 볼 수도 있다.[890] 바울은 그의 기쁨 가운데서 근심을 극복한 고린도 교인들을 격려하고 칭찬한다(7:14). 무엇보다 일곱 가지 자세는 고린도 교인들의 회개의 열매이며, 근심의 적극적인 결과이다. 그들의 근심이 세상근심이 아니라 하나님의 뜻대로 한 근심이라는 증거이다.

"보라 하나님의 뜻대로 하게 한 이 근심이 너희로 얼마나 간절하게 하며"(ἰδοὺ γὰρ αὐτὸ τοῦτο τὸ κατὰ θεὸν λυπηθῆναι πόσην κατειργάσατο ὑμῖν σπουδήν). "하나님의 뜻대로 한 이 근심"이란 말이 세 번째 나오고 있다(9, 10, 11). 고린도 교인들은 바울의 편지의 지시를 따라 신속하게 그러나 진지하게 대처하였다.[891] "간절함"(σπουδήν)은 "진지함", "열의"란 뜻이 있으며 12절에도 나온다. 12절에서 같은 "간절함"(σπουδήν)이 문제가 된 사람의 처리를 나타내는 의미로 쓰이고 있고, 바울의 편지에서 문제된 사람에 대한 조치를 지시했다고 말하고 있으므로, 이 말은 고린도 교인들이 문제가 된 사람을 바울의 지시에 따라 신속히 처리했다는 뜻으로 보는 이들이 많다.[892] 그러나 이 말이 그 문제를 포함한 다른 지시사항들에 대한 고린도 교인들의 열의를 나타낸

889) Plummer, 222.
890) Windisch, 234.
891) Windisch, 234; Bultmann, 61.
892) Windisch, 234; Bultmann, 61; Thrall, 493; Barnett, 379.

다고 볼 수도 있다.[893] 고린도 교인들은 바울의 편지의 지시에 대해서 열의를 가지고 신속하게 따름으로 바울과의 관계를 다시 회복하였고, 화해의 길을 열었다.[894]

"얼마나 변명하게 하며"(ἀλλὰ ἀπολογίαν)는 고린도 교인들의 변명이다. 이 말은 역으로 바울이 고린도 교인들에 대해서 오해한 부분들이 있었음을 추측하게 만든다.[895] 그러나 바울이 오해했다는 말을 어디에서도 하고 있지 않으므로 추측에 불과하다. 변명은 어떤 오해에 대한 해명이라기보다, 과거의 잘못을 솔직히 인정하고 앞으로는 같은 잘못을 범하지 않겠다는 변명이라고 볼 수 있다.[896] 또는 고린도 교인들이 거짓 교사들을 실제로는 따르지는 않았다는 변명일 수도 있다. 아니면 그들이 문제가 된 사람의 행위를 따르지 않았다는 변명일 수도 있다.[897] 어느 경우든지 진지한 변명은 회개의 한 형태이다.

"얼마나 분하게 하며"(ἀλλὰ ἀγανάκτησιν)는 그들의 잘못에 대한 분노이거나,[898] 거짓 선지자들,[899]또는 "문제가 된 사람"에게 대한 분노일 수 있다.[900] 칼빈은 이 모든 가능성을 다 인정한다(101). "분노"도 회개의 열매라고 볼 때 외적인 것에 대한 분노보다 자신들의 잘못에 대한 반성이라고 보는 것이 타당하다. 거짓

893) Martin, 234.

894) Hughes, 274; Bultmann, 61; Barnett, 378; Martin, 234.

895) Windisch, 235; Thrall, 494.

896) Strachan, 128.

897) Plummer, 222.

898) Windisch, 235; Denney, 256; Plummer, 223; Tasker, 106; Strachan, 129; Hughes, 274.

899) Filson, 360; Fallon, 65.

900) Barrett, 211; Héring, 55; Bultmann, 61; Bachmann, 303; Furnish, 395.

선지자들이나, 문제가 된 이에 대한 것이나 결국은 이런 이들을 용납한 것은 고린도 교인들 자신들이므로 그들의 잘못에 대해서 분개하는 것이 타당하다.

"얼마나 두렵게 하며"(ἀλλὰ φόβον)는 고린도 교인들이 바울을 사도로서 경외하는 자세를 가리킨다.[901] 바울은 언제나 자신이 하나님의 사도임을 강조하고 확신시키고 있다(1:23; 5:20; 13:1-3; 고전 4:1). 바울은 고린도전서 4장 21절에서, "내가 매를 가지고 너희에게 나아가랴 "라고 사도적 권위로 말하고 있다. 또 7장 15절에서는 고린도 교인들이 바울의 동역자 디도를 두렵고 떪으로 영접하고 순종하였다고 한다. 그러나 일반적인 하나님에 대한 경외심을 가리킨다고 볼 수도 있다(5:11). 죄인들은 심판주 하나님 앞에서 그들의 죄에 대해서 심판을 받는다는 두려움을 갖는다.[902]

"얼마나 사모하게 하며"(ἀλλὰ ἐπιπόθησιν)는 바울에 대한 고린도 교인들의 사모함이다(7:7). 그들은 자신들의 잘못을 청산하고 바울과의 관계 개선을 원한다. 고린도 교인들이 바울을 매우 근심케 하여 고린도 교인들과 소원한 관계가 되어서 지난번 여행 계획마저 취소한 바 있다(2:1). 그러므로 바울에게 미안하고 이제 다시 만나서 모든 오해를 풀고 주 안에서 친밀하게 교제하기를 원한다.

"얼마나 열심 있게 하며"(ἀλλὰ ζῆλον). "열심"은 좋은 의미도 있고(출20:5; 왕상19:10; 롬 10:2; 고후 9:2; 11:2; 갈 4:18), "시기, 질투" 같은 나쁜 의미도 있다(롬 13:13; 고전 13:4; 고후 12:20; 약

901) Barrett, 211; Filson, 360; Denney, 257; Hughes, 274; Fallon, 65.

902) Calvin, 101.

3:14, 16).[903] 물론 여기서는 회개의 열매로서 전자의 의미다. 위의 7절에서도 바울은 디도를 통해서 고린도 교인들의 바울에 대한 "열심"이 회복되었다는 말을 듣고 기뻐하였다. 이제 고린도 교인들은 바울을 사도로서 존경하고 그의 가르침을 따르게 되었다.[904] 반면에 그들은 바울의 대적자들을 반대하며, 바울이 지적한 잘못된 모든 것을 고치는 데에도 열심을 가지게 되었다.[905] 사람에게 뿐만 아니라 하나님께 대한 열심도 포함한다.[906] NIV 영어 성경은 "관심"(concern)이라고 번역하였는데, 이 말은 바울이 말하는 깊은 정서를 충분히 반영하고 있지 못한다.[907]

"얼마나 벌하게 하였는가 "(ἀλλὰ ἐκδίκησιν;) 위의 고린도 교인들의 분노와 바울에 대한 사모와 열심이 그의 지시대로 문제가 된 사람을 벌하게 하였고,[908] 이 조치는 고린도 교인들이 이 문제

903) 물론 인간의 질투와 의 하나님의 질투(קנא, 카나, 출20:5)는 구별 되어야 한다. 하나님은 그의 택한 백성과의 언약 관계에서 절대적 사랑이 있으므로 그 관계를 깨뜨릴 때에 "질투"하시는 것은 당연하다. 인간관계에 있어서도 부부간의 언약 관계같은 절대적 사랑이 요구되는 관계에 있어서 질투는 용인되어야 마땅하다. 한편, 질투(קנא)란 히브리어는 열심이란 말과 같다(왕상19:10).

904) Hughes, 275.

905) Denney, 257; Meyer, 333.

906) Plummer, 223.

907) Martin, 235.

908) 본문에서 "불의 행한 자"가 누구인가에 대해서 고린도전서 5장 5절의 근친상간한 사람이라고 보는 이도 있으나(Calvin, 101; Hughes, 59-65, 275), 바울을 반대한 이들의 수장으로 보는 이들이 더 많다(Plummer, 25; Bruce, 184-185, 218; Barrett, 213; Furnish, 166-68, 396; Martin, 38, 237-238; Barnett, 380-81, 주 45). 고전 5:5-13의 근친상간한 사람에 대한 바울의 조치는 매우 엄격한 것이었으나, 고후 2:5-9에서는 매우 완화된 자세로 그 어떤 사람을 용서하라고 한다. 근친상간 같은 심각한 죄에 대해서 바울이 용서하라고 했다고 보기 어렵다(Barrett, 212). 그러므로 같은 사람으로 동일

에 관한한 깨끗하다는 것을 반증해주는 증거였다. "너희가 저 일에 대하여 일절 너희 자신의 깨끗함을 나타내었느니라"(ἐν παντὶ συνεστήσατε ἑαυτοὺς ἁγνοὺς εἶναι τῷ πράγματι). "저 일"(τῷ πράγματι)은 고린도전서 5장의 근친상간 사건이거나, 바울을 반대하여 소란케 한 일일 것이다(2:5-9). 바울은 말하기조차 부끄러운 일이므로 구체적 언급을 피하고 그저 "그 일"이라고만 말하고 있다.[909] 고린도 교인들이 그들의 "일절 깨끗함"을 증거하였다는 것은 그 문제된 사람을 징계함으로써 그들도 그 사람과 관련되어 있다는 "혐의"를 벗었다는 뜻이다(2:5, 6). 고린도 교인들의 잘못은 그 범죄자를 신속하게 징계하지 않음으로서 그들이 이 사람의 범죄에 대해 심각하게 생각하지 않고 있다는 의구심을 갖게 한 것이다. 만일 이 문제가 된 사람이 도덕적인 범죄자가 아니라 바울의 복음과 지도에 반대하여 교회를 어지럽게 한 사람이라면, 고린도 교인들이 이제 바울의 복음과 지도를 따르기로 작정하고 그 반대자를 제거하였다는 뜻이 된다. 그러나 바울은 고린도 교인

시하는 이들이 적어지는 추세다. 한편, 고후 2:5이하에서와 7:12에서 바울은 같은 특정한 개인을 지목하여 말하고 있는 것으로 본다. 2장과 7장이 연결되기 때문에 같은 사람에 대해서 바울이 말하는 것으로 본다. 바울을 반대하는 무리의 수장으로 본다. 그러나 바울은 일단 고린도 교회 분쟁문제가 해결된 이상 분쟁을 주도하여 말썽을 일으킨 이 사람에 대해서 유화적인 자세를 취하여 다시 문제를 삼지 않고 넘어 가기를 원한다고 볼 수 있다(12절). 터툴리안은 고후 2:5의 인물을 고전 5:5의 근친상간한 사람과 동일시하는 것을 반대하고 있다. 심각한 죄에 대한 바울의 조치가 너무 약하다고 보기 때문이다(*De pudicitia* 13-15, A.D. 218, 부루스, 185 재인용). 한편 바울이 1-9장을 쓴 후 고린도교회의 사태가 다시 악화되었다는 소식을 듣고 10-13장을 썼다고 보는 학자들은 10-13장의 대적자들은 2:5-9, 5:12; 7:11, 12의 대적자들과 다른 디도가 온 이후에 도착한 이들로 본다(Barnett, 380-81, 주 45).

909) Plummer, 223; Martin, 236.

들이 단순히 자신의 편이 되어서 그를 벌하였다는 것보다는 잘못된 것을 고치고 복음 진리를 확립하였다는 사실을 중시하였을 것이다.[910] 어쨌든지 고린도 교회 문제는 이제 일단락되었다. 고린도 교인들은 전체적으로 더 이상 혐의가 없는 사람들로 바울 사도에 의해서 인정받게 된 것이다. 마치 노회에 상정된 고린도 교회 소송사건을 맡은 재판장 사도 바울이 사건 조사 후에 무죄로 확정한 것과 같은 것이다. 실제로 불트만은 11절과 12절에서 몇 개의 당시 법정에서 쓰는 용어를 쓰고 있음을 지적하였다.(11절의 "벌"[ἐκδίκησις], 12절의 "불의"[ἀδικήσας], "깨끗하다"="결백"="무혐의"[ἁγνός], "일"="소송사건"[πρᾶγμα], "나타내다"="증명하다"[συνιστάναι]; 참조, 2:6의 "벌"="형벌"[ἐπιτιμία]).[911]

고린도 교인들이 이일로 자신들을 "깨끗하게"(ἁγνός) 하였다는 것은 구원론적인 의미가 있다. "깨끗하게 된 것"이 회개의 뚜렷한 증거이기 때문이다. 구원을 받기 위해서 죄인은 회개하고 죄사함을 받아야 하는데, 고린도 교인들 모두(ἐν παντί)가 회개하여 죄 사하심을 받아 구원을 받게 되었다는 의미가 있다고 본다.[912] 더구나 "깨끗하다"는 말이 7개의 회개의 열매를 언급한 후 "모두"라는 최종평가를 의미하는 말과 함께 마지막에 언급되었으므로 이런 암시적 의도가 있다고 볼 수 있다. 물론 표면적으로는 "모두"는 고린도 교인들의 "문제가 된 사람과의 혐의"를 가리키며, "깨끗하다"는 그 혐의를 벗었다는 의미다. 그러나 이 말들이 회개의 열매들이 열거된 후에 최종적으로 언급되었음을 고려할 때, 그

910) Martin, 236.

911) Bultmann 61, Martin, 236 재인용.

912) Calvin, 100.

리고 10절의 "구원에 이르는 회개"라는 말에 비추어 보아서 구원과 관련된 암시적 의미가 있다고 본다.

12. "그런즉 내가 너희에게 쓴 것은 그 불의 행한 자를 위한 것도 아니요 그 불의 당한 자를 위한 것도 아니요 오직 우리를 위한 너희의 간절함이 하나님 앞에서 너희에게 나타나게 하려 함이로라"(ἄρα εἰ καὶ ἔγραψα ὑμῖν, οὐχ ἕνεκεν τοῦ ἀδικήσαντος οὐδὲ ἕνεκεν τοῦ ἀδικηθέντος ἀλλ' ἕνεκεν τοῦ φανερωθῆναι τὴν σπουδὴν ὑμῶν τὴν ὑπὲρ ἡμῶν πρὸς ὑμᾶς ἐνώπιον τοῦ θεοῦ). 12절은 앞서 바울이 2:4에서 언급한 "엄격한 편지"를 쓴 진정한 목적을 다시 밝힌다. 그 편지의 목적은 문제가 된 사람을 처리하기 위한 것도 아니고 그 사람으로 말미암아 피해를 본 사람("불의 당한 자," ἀδικηθέντος=바울 자신)[913]을 보호하기 위한 것도 아니며, 바울에 대한 고린도 교회의 진정한 열의("간절함," σπουδὴν)가 하나님 앞에서 드러나게 하기 위함이었다. 유사하게

913) 피해자가 3인칭("불의 당한 자," ἀδικηθέντος)으로 나타났음으로 바울이 아니라는 견해도 있으나(Windisch, 238; 참조, Allo, 199), 2:5과 10을 비교하여 검토해보면, 결국 바울을 가리키는 말이라고 보는 것이 타당해 보인다(Thrall, 496, 그러나 69를 보라). Bruce도 "불의를 당한 자"("피해자")란 말이 바울을 가리킨다고 본다. 만일 본문이 문제의 사람을 고전 5장의 근친상간한 사람으로 보면, 피해를 입은 자는 결국 그의 아버지가 될 것이라고 한다. 그러나 바울이 이런 사람을 다시 용서하라고 믿기 어려우므로(2:5-8), 여기서 "불의 행한 자"는 바울을 대적한 사람, "불의 당한 자"는 바울로 본다(Bruce, 218-219; Furnish, 164-66; Martin, 238; Barnett, 380-81, 주 45). 2:5에서도 바울 자신이 피해자라고 한다. 아마 바울이 두 번째 방문 할 때에 공중 앞에서 그를 모욕한 사람으로 보인다(2:1). 그리고 바울이 1-9장을 쓴 후에 고린도 교회의 사정이 악화되어서 10-13장을 계속 썼다는 이들은 여기의 대적자를 디도가 온 후에 나타난 10-13장의 대적자들과 구별한다(Barnett, 380-381, 주 45).

2:4에서는 그 편지의 목적이 고린도 교인들을 향한 바울의 "넘치는 사랑"을 나타내기 위함이라고 하였다. 여기서는 바울의 사랑에 대한 고린도 교회의 간절함의 반응을 보기 위한 것이었다고 말한다. 결국 같은 목적을 발신자의 입장과 수신자의 입장에서 말할 때 다른 표현으로 나타낸 것이다. ἄρα("그런즉")는 결과를 나타내는 접속사[914] 그 편지가 고린도 교인들에게 미친 영향들이(11절), 바울의 편지의 숨은 진정한 목적을 상기 시켜준다는 것이다.[915] 고린도 교인들이 그 편지로 말미암아 그들의 바울에 대한 진정한 열의("간절함," σπουδὴν)를 다시 갖게 된 것이 우연이 아니다(11절). 바울이 편지를 쓸 때 품은 목적이 고린도 교인들에게 전달되었고, 그로 인해서 고린도 교인들이 바울에게 다시 열의를 갖게 되었던 것이다. 그러나 이 말은 바울에게 찬사를 돌리려는 것이 아니라 바울에게 그들의 열의가 나타나서 화해를 이루게 하시는 하나님의 은혜로운 섭리를 가리키는 말이다. 물론 여기서 바울이 문제가 된 사람의 처리가 편지의 목적이 전혀 아니라는 것이 아니라, 보다 궁극적인 목적은 고린도 교인들의 진정한 열의를 통한 화해라는 것이다. 이것은 히브리 어법에서 어떤 부정을 절대적으로 부정하는 것이 아니라 약한 부정으로써 다른 사실을 강조하는 부정이다.[916] 이렇게 보면 바울은 문제가 된 바울을 공격한 사람을 잊은 것은 아니다. 그러나 바울은 그 보다 더 궁극적인 관심

914) Plummer, 224.

915) 참조, Thrall, 495.

916) Plummer는 이런 히브리식 부정의 예를 호 6:6에서 찾는다. "나는 인애를 원하고 제사를 원치 아니하며 번제 보다는 하나님 아는 것을 원하노라." 그렇다고 하나님이 실제로 제사를 폐기하라는 뜻이 아니라 내적 자세 즉 인애가 더 중요함을 가리키는 것이다(참조, 막 9:37; 눅 10:20; 14:12; 23:28).

을 갖고 그 편지를 썼다. 고린도 교인들이 그들의 진정한 사랑과 열의를 나타내어서 자신과 화해하기 위해 썼다. 화해의 사신으로서의 바울의 역할은 고린도후서를 쓸 때에만 수행된 일시적인 것이 아니라, "엄격한 편지"를 쓸 때도 마찬가지로 인식한 역할이었다.

εἰ(비록…이지만)는 여기서 조건을 나타내는 것이 아니라, 양보를 나타내면서, "엄격한 편지"의 강한 책망과 요구에 대한 미안함이나 또는 이에 대한 반대자들의 비난을 염두에 두고 시작하는 말이라고 본다.[917] "그런즉 비록 내가 너희에게 썼지만…"

ἀλλά("그러나")뒤에 나오는 ἕνεκεν(헤네켄)이란 전치사를 일반적으로 "위하여"라는 목적을 나타내는 전치사로 보지만, 이유를 나타내는 전치사로 보아서, "우리를 위한 너희의 간절함이 하나님 앞에서 나타남으로 말미암아 우리가 위로 받았다"라고 번역하는 이들이 있다.[918] 그러나 ἕνεκεν은 목적의 의미로 쓰이는 것이 통례이며, 여기서도 같은 의미로 번역하는 것이 타당하다고 본다. 이 전치사가 세 번 계속 나오면서 바울이 쓴 편지의 진정한 목적을 말한다.

여기서 "그 불의 행한 자"(ἕνεκεν τοῦ ἀδικήσαντος)가 고린도후서 2장 7절의 사람과 다른 사람이라고 위에서 논하였다.[919] 여기서의 문제는 이 사람이 고린도 교인인가 아니면 외부인인가에 대한 논쟁이 있다. 바레트는 외부인으로서 고린도 교회에 들어와서 바울을 반대하는 파당을 일으킨 사람일 것이라고 한다.[920] 그

917) Barnett, 378.

918) Héring, 56.

919) Bruce, 218-219; Martin, 237-238.

920) Barrett, 213; Martin, 238; 참조, Thrall, 67, 177, 496.

러나 바울의 편지로 말미암아 그를 따르던 고린도 교인들이 그를 떠났다는 것이다. 고린도 교인들이 속히 그를 떠난 것을 보아서 고린도 교인들과 깊은 관계가 없는 외부 인사란 것이 이해도 되지만, 동시에 어떻게 고린도 교인들이 외부 인사를 그렇게 속히 따르게 되었을까라는 의문이 있다. 이에 대해 고린도 교인들이 바울이 생각한 것처럼 바울을 떠난 것이 아닌데, 바울이 잘못 알고 있었다고 생각할 수도 있으나,[921] 이렇게 되면, 고린도후서 전체가 디도의 잘못된 정황판단에 의한 그릇된 보고로 말미암아 쓴 편지가 될 뿐이다. 그리고 하나님 앞에서 진실을 말한다는 바울의 복음의 진실성마저 흔들리게 될 수 있다(2:17; 4:2). 이렇게 상황을 잘 알지도 못하고 편지를 쓰는 이의 복음을 어떻게 신뢰하고 받을 수 있는가?

그러나 10-13장에서 바울의 공격적인 내용은 반대자가 외부인사라는 것을 지지하는 근거가 될 수 있다(11:4, 20). 이 경우 본문의 문제가 된 사람은 11장 4, 20절의 인물과 같은 자로 볼 수 있다. 디도가 "엄격한 편지"를 가지고 고린도 교회에 다녀온 후 바울이 1-9장을 쓰는 얼마 동안 이 사람은 조용했으나 그 후 다시 고린도 교회를 괴롭힌다는 소식을 듣고 10-13장을 더 쓰게 되었다는 추론이 나온다.[922]우리도 본문의 반대자가 10-13장의 반대자들 중의 하나라고 보지는 않는다. 1-9장을 쓴 후에 들어 온 사람이라고 보지 않고, 원래 있던 사람이라고 본다.

한편, 트롤은 이 사람이 고린도 교회 내부인으로서 예루살렘 성도들을 위한 헌금을 훔쳐 교회 문제를 일으켜서 바울이 경계하는

921) Martin, 238; Thrall, 497.

922) Martin, 238.

인물로 본다.[923] 그러나 이런 추측이 2장의 문제를 일으킨 사람과 본문의 사람을 동일인으로 볼 수 있게 하고, 2장의 징계를 풀어주라는 조치를 이해하게도 만드나, 피해자가 바울이 아니라 다른 사람이라는 설명이 석연치 않다(트롤은, 바울이 재정을 유용한 특정인을 지목하고 치리를 명령하였으나 고린도 교인들이 듣지 않고 있다가 디도가 가져 간 "엄격한 편지"를 통해 재차 명령한 후에야 겨우 치리를 하였고, 고린도후서를 쓰면서 다시 이를 용서하도록 했으며, 이 경우 피해자 "불의 당한 자,"[ἀδικηθέντος]는 바울이 아니라, 돈을 맡고 있었던 사람이라고 한다).[924]

"하나님 앞에서"(ἐνώπιον τοῦ θεοῦ, *Coram Deo*)란 말은 이중적인 의미가 있다. 첫째는 고린도 교인들이 하나님 앞에서 사도 바울에 대한 바른 자세("간절함")를 취하는 책임이 있음을 말하는 것이며, 둘째는 바울이 하나님의 사도로서 그렇게 그들을 하게 해야 할 책임이 있다는 말이다.[925] 트롤은 여기서 바울이 고린도 교인들의 변(辯)은 듣지 않고 자기중심적으로만 말하는 것으로 들릴 수 있다고 생각한다.[926] 이런 생각을 발전시키면, 고린도후서 자체의 목적이 반대자를 공격하고 자신의 편으로 고린도 교인들을 돌아서게 하는 이기적인 것이었는데도, 바울이 고린도 교인들의 유익을 위하는 것으로만 말하는 듯하다. 그러나 여기서 바울은 이기적이고 권위주적인 의도를 부인하고 다만 "하나님 앞에서"의

---

923) Thrall, 68.

924) 그러나, 서론에서의 이런 주장과 달리(68), Thrall은 7:12절 주석에서는 "관련된 글로 미루어 보아서" 바울이 피해자라는 가능성을 받아들이고 있다(496).

925) Plummer, 226; Martin, 239.

926) Thrall, 496.

진실한 "간절함"을 나타내려고 했다고 말하고 있다.[927] "하나님 앞에서"(ἐνώπιον τοῦ θεοῦ)는 문장의 끝에서 강조를 나타내고 있다.[928] 바울은 고린도후서에서 자신의 결백을 나타내기 위해서 이 말을 자주 쓴다(2:17; 4:2; 5:10, 11; 12:19; 참조, 8:21). "하나님 앞에서" 행하는 일을 어떤 인간적인 평가로 정죄할 수 없다. 즉 권위주의나, 독선적 행위, 그리고 이기주의 등 인간평등주의에 반대되는 사상이나 행위도 "하나님 앞에서" 수행된 것이라면 그 진의를 선한 것으로 보아야 한다. "하나님 앞에서" 모든 인간의 가치는 새롭게 창조되고 해석되고 이해되어야 한다. 그러므로 바울은 어떤 독자들이 자신의 어떤 행위에 대해서 이기적이고 독선적이라고 비난할 수 있음을 감지하고서 그런 오해에 대한 경계를 자주 하고 있다(5:10, 11). "내가 내 영혼을 두고 하나님을 불러 증거하시게 하노니 다시 고린도에 가지 아니한 것은 너희를 아끼려 함이라"(1:23). "우리가 무슨 일이든지 우리에게서 난 것 같이 생각하여 스스로 만족할 것이 아니니 우리의 만족은 오직 하나님께로서 났느니라"(3:5). "주 예수 아버지 영원히 찬송할 하나님이 나의 거짓말 아니하는 줄을 아시느니라"(11:31). 인간 앞에서 행하는 인간의 행위나 인간에게 인정받는 가치는 온전할 수 없다. 그러나 "하나님 앞에서"의 행위나 가치는 영원한 가치를 갖는다. 바울은 그가 하나님의 사도라는 확고한 신념을 가지고 가르치고 행한다(4:6; 5:20). 그의 말은 곧 하나님의 말씀이다(고전 7:40; 고후 5:20). 다만 그 사실을 어떻게 고린도 교인들에게 확신시키느냐가 문제

927) Barnett, 381.

928) Barnett, 381.

다. 고린도 교회 대적자와 그를 따르는 이들의 문제가 바로 바울의 이런 사도적 권위와 그의 정직성을 의심하고 그의 말을 믿지 않는 데 있었던 것이다(12:12, 16). 고린도 교회와 화해를 위하여 무엇보다 바울이 하나님의 사도로서 하나님의 영을 가지고 말하고 있음과 그러므로 그의 정직성을 그들이 인정하는 것이 필요하다고 보았다(고전 7:40). 그러므로, 여기서 "하나님 앞에서"란 말도 결코 바울의 사사로운 권위나 입장을 세우려는 것이 아니라, 하나님의 사도로서의 신성한 책임감에서 나온 말이다. 그는 그의 사도로서의 증거를 스스로 자천하는 일이 싫어서 고린도 교인들이 스스로 해주길 바랐으나 결국 자기가 자신을 증거하는 괴로움을 참을 수밖에 없었던 것이다(5:12; 12:11;참조, 10:8; 11:1, 16-18; 12:1, 6, 등). 여기서 바울은 고린도 교인들이 언제나 "하나님 앞에서" 그가 보내신 자신을 진실히 따르게 해야 할 책임이 있음을 천명하고 있는 것이다. 그것은 오로지 하나님의 영광을 위한 것이다. 그래서 그는 그가 사도로서의 진실성을 항변하는 것과 함께 그가 받은 수많은 고난의 사역을 제시하고 있다(4:7-18; 11:23-33). 바울이 복음으로 인해 고난 받은 사실은 그가 자신의 유익을 위해 사역하지 않는다는 가장 확실한 증거이다. 또 그것은 그가 죄인을 위해 고난 받으시고 죽으신 주 예수의 참된 사도라는 증거이기도 하다. 그의 독선적이고 일방적으로 들리는 항변은 그의 겸비한 고난의 종으로서의 사역과 균형을 이루고 있다.

13. "이로 인하여 우리가 위로를 받았고 우리의 받은 위로 위에 디도의 기쁨으로 우리가 더욱 많이 기뻐함은 그의 마음이 너희 무리를 인하여 안심함을 얻었음이니라" (διὰ τοῦτο

παρακεκλήμεθα. Ἐπὶ δὲ τῇ παρακλήσει ἡμῶν περισσοτέρως μᾶλλον ἐχάρημεν ἐπὶ τῇ χαρᾷ Τίτου, ὅτι ἀναπέπαυται τὸ πνεῦμα αὐτοῦ ἀπὸ πάντων ὑμῶν). "이로 인하여 기뻐함"(διὰ τοῦτο παρακεκλήμεθα)은 좁게는 12절에서 한 말 즉, 바울의 편지가 고린도 교인들의 간절함을 드러내게 하기 위한 목적을 달성하였음으로 바울은 기뻐하였다는 뜻이다.[929] 그러나 넓게는 바울의 편지에 대한 고린도 교인들의 모든 적극적인 반응(회개)으로 인하여 기뻐한다는 뜻도 된다.[930] 위의 7장 6절 이하에서 디도의 옴으로 받은 "위로"와 고린도 교인들의 적극적 변화를 이미 언급하였고, 또 이 "위로"는 1장 3-7절의 초두에서의 "위로의 주제"를 다시 상기시키기 때문이다.[931]

"우리의 받은 위로 위에 디도의 기쁨으로 우리가 더욱 많이 기뻐함은"(Ἐπὶ δὲ τῇ παρακλήσει ἡμῶν περισσοτέρως μᾶλλον ἐχάρημεν ἐπὶ τῇ χαρᾷ Τίτου). 전치사 ἐπί는 "…에"라는 위치를 가리키는 전치사이나, 여기서는 "그에 더하여"라는 부수적인 뜻이 있다.[932] 그러나 뒤에 나오는 "디도의 기쁨"(ἐπὶ τῇ χαρᾷ Τίτου)이라는 말에 있는 같은 전치사는 "…으로"라는 인용의 의미를 가지는 전치사이다. 디도의 기쁨은 고린도 교인들의 회개에 대한 것이었고, 그의 기쁨이 바울에게 전달되어 그를 또한 기쁘게 하였다.[933] 바울은 디도의 기쁨으로 그가 기뻐하게 되었음을 강조

929) Tasker, 107.

930) Thrall, 497.

931) Martin, 239.

932) Tasker, 107; Plummer, 226; Bultmann, 63.

933) Martin, 240.

하기 위하여 비교급 περισσοτέρως(더욱)와 μᾶλλον(많이)라는 말을 함께 써서 "더욱 많이 기뻐함"이라고 한다.[934] 이렇게 바울이 디도의 기쁨으로 기뻐하는 것은 바울이 디도를 고린도로 보낼 때에 고린도 교인들이 보일 반응에 대해 불안하고 회의적이었음을 보여 준다. 그러나 바울은 디도를 격려하면서 잘 될 것이라고 적극적인 자세로 갈 것을 권하였을 것이다. 14절을 보면 바울이 디도에게 고린도 교인들에 대해서 자랑한 것이 그대로 사실로 드러나서 기쁘다고 말하는 것은 바울이 고린도에 가기를 두려워하고 염려하는 디도를 격려하면서 보낼 때에 한 말을 가리키는 것이다. 의외로 고린도 교인들이 적극적인 반응을 보임으로써 디도 자신이 하나님의 역사하심을 의식하여 크게 감동을 받고 바울에게 이런 감동을 전하였을 것으로 보인다(7:7). 그러므로 바울의 기쁨은 더욱 컸다. 그가 디도에게 고린도 교회가 그래도 가능성이 있다고 격려한 말이 빈 말이 아니었음이 나타났기 때문이다. 물론 바울의 10-13장에서의 돌변한 자세는 여기와 크게 대조되므로 여러 가지 추측을 낳게 한다. 그 중에서 디도가 고린도 교회의 상황을 잘못 판단하였다는 의심 할 수 있고,[935] 고린도 교회의 돌변적인 사태가 그 원인이라고 볼 수도 있다. 그러나 우리가 누차 주장하듯이 10-13장은 돌변한 고린도 교회 사태에 대한 글이 아니라 잔존하는 반대 세력에 대한 경고라고 본다. 그래서 플러머는 고린도 교회의 상태를 가리켜서, "평화가 아닌 휴전"이라고 말하였다.[936] 사실 하나님 나라가 오기 전까지 이 세상에는 궁극적인 평

---

934) Plummer, 226; Hughes, 278, 주 21.

935) Thrall, 497.

936) Plummer, 226.

화란 없다. 인간역사는 투쟁의 역사이다. 모든 평화라는 것은 결국 휴전일 뿐이다. 그러나 휴전이라도 장래에 나타날 궁극적인 평화의 예비적인 성취로 보고 감사할 수 있어야 한다. 바울과 디도의 기쁨은 종말론적인 예비적 기쁨으로 보아 헛된 일시직 기쁨이라고 일축할 필요가 없다. 하나님의 영원한 위로의 약속을 믿는 자들의 기쁨은 일시적인 것이라 해도 영원한 소망의 기쁨의 선상에서 가치가 있는 것이다. 그러므로 그 기쁨은 하나님의 약속이 없는 허망한 일시적인 세속적인 기쁨과는 분명히 구별되어야 한다. 바울과 디도는 그들의 고린도 교인들을 위한 수고가 헛되지 않고 하나님의 도우심으로 개선된 것을 기뻐하였다. 그것이 일시적인 현상이라 해도 주 안에서의 완전한 승리를 얻을 때까지 고달픈 사역자들에게 하나님께서 잠시 동안 주시는 위로의 효과가 있음을 알고 있다. 그러므로 바울은 "항상 기뻐하고 범사에 감사하라고 가르쳤다."(빌 4:4; 살전 5:18 등). 우리 모든 그리스도인의 이 세상의 기쁨은 종말론적인 궁극적인 기쁨에 비추어 재해석될 때 같은 세상의 기쁨과 구별되어 영원한 하나님 나라의 기쁨으로 이어지는 작은 기쁨이 되는 것이다. 세상에서의 잔치는 주님과 함께할 영원한 잔치의 예표로(막 6:21; 눅 13:29; 14:24), 출생의 기쁨은 중생의 기쁨으로(요 3:5), 재산의 증식의 기쁨은 하늘나라 소유의 증식의 기쁨으로(막 10:30; 마 5:20), 우정의 기쁨은 하늘나라의 교제의 기쁨으로 승화시켜 해석되는 것이다(행 2:42; 빌 2:1; 몬 6). 스토익 철학(stoicism)같이 하나님의 종국적인 구원의 종말론이 없는 사상이나 종교는 기뻐할 이유가 없고 기껏해야 고통에 대해 무감각한 사람이 되기를 가르치고 훈련할 뿐이다. 기쁨을 가르치는 세상 종교는 하나님의 약속에 기초한 기쁨이 아니라, 자기도취적인 믿음에 기초한 기쁨일 뿐이거나, 헛된 환상에 기초한 최면적인 기쁨이다. 기독교의 기쁨은 구체적 역사적 사실에서 계시된 하나님의 약속에 근거한 기쁨이다. 무엇보다, 예수의 부활은 사람의 소원이 아니라 역사적 사실이며, 부활하신 예수는 장래 우리의 부활에 대한 약속을 확신케 하는 기쁨을 준다(고전 15:20). 또한 성도의 기쁨은 우리 가운데 역사하시는 성령이 주시는 것이다(갈 5:22). 성령이 우리 중에 내주하심은 우리의 심리적 감정이 아니라 객관적인 사실로서 장래의 영원한 소망의 보증이 된다(5:5; 롬 8:23). 그러므로 그리스도인의 기쁨은 비록 순간 적인 것이라 해도 하나님의 영원한 기쁨의 약속을 반영하는 것이므로 그 가치가 있다.

"그의 마음이 너희 무리를 인하여 안심함을 얻었음이니라"(ὅτι ἀναπέπαυται τὸ πνεῦμα αὐτοῦ ἀπὸ πάντων ὑμῶν). 여기서 πνεῦμα(프뉴마, "영")는 신학적인 의미가 아니고 일반적인 사람의 "마음"을 나타낸다(고전 16:18; 참조, 몬 7, 20).[937] ἀπό("…에게")보다는 ὑπό(…에 의하여)가 적절하게 보이지만, 여기서 ἀπό("…에게")는 "…로 인하여"라는 이유를 나타낸다.[938] "너희 무리"로 번역된 πάντων ὑμῶν은 문자적으로 "너희 모두"이다. 10-13장의 상황을 고려할 때 고린도 교인들이 모두 완전히 바울을 따른다고 보기는 어려우므로, 이 말은 대체적인 의미를 가지고 있다고 보아야 할 것이다. 15절에도 같은 말이 나온다. 이런 고린도 교회의 일치된 모습을 나타내는 말은 바울의 고린도 교회에 대한 자랑(14)의 근거가 되고 어쩌면 8장과 9장의 헌금을 독려하기 위

937) Barrett, 214; Martin, 241; Thrall, 497.

938) Martin, 241.

한 사전 준비적인 말이라고 볼 수도 있다(8:6, 16).[939] 바울은 소수의 반대자가 있다는 사실을 알면서도 "너희 모두"라는 말로 그 소수들도 결국 하나가 되리라는 소망을 가지고 말했다고도 볼 수 있다.

14. "내가 그에게 너희를 위하여 자랑한 것이 있더라도 부끄럽지 아니하니 우리가 너희에게 이른 말이 다 참된 것같이 디도 앞에서 우리의 자랑한 것도 참되게 되었도다"(ὅτι εἴ τι αὐτῷ ὑπὲρ ὑμῶν κεκαύχημαι, οὐ κατῃσχύνθην, ἀλλ᾽ ὡς πάντα ἐν ἀληθείᾳ ἐλαλήσαμεν ὑμῖν, οὕτως καὶ ἡ καύχησις ἡμῶν ἡ ἐπὶ Τίτου ἀλήθεια ἐγενήθη). "내가 그에게 너희를 위하여 자랑한 것이 있더라도 부끄럽지 아니하니"(ὅτι εἴ τι αὐτῷ ὑπὲρ ὑμῶν κεκαύχημαι, οὐ κατῃσχύνθην). 위에서 말한 바와 같이 바울이 고린도로 디도를 보낼 때 그를 격려하면서 고린도 교회가 편지를 받아 읽으면, 잘 될 수 있으라 라고 한 말이 그대로 이루어졌으므로 바울은 기뻤던 것이다. "자랑한다"(κεκαύχημαι)는 개념이 고린도후서에서 30번 가량 나오며, 이것은 나머지 바울 서신 전체에서 나오는 수보다 더 많다. 바울은 모든 일이 잘 될 것이라는 말을 하는 담대한 자랑을 하였는데, 그 담대한 자랑이 사실로 나타났으니, 부끄럽지 않게 되었다(οὐ κατῃσχύνθην). 여기서 바울은 그의 신뢰성을 의심하는 그의 대적자들에 대하여 그의 말이 모두 진실이라는 것을 다시 나타내고 있다(1:13f. 15-23).[940] 즉 "우리가 너

939) Thrall, 497.

940) Hughes, 279; Martin, 242.

희에게 이른 말이 다 참된 것같이"(ἀλλ᾽ ὡς πάντα ἐν ἀληθείᾳ ἐλαλήσαμεν ὑμῖν)라는 말은 바울이 1장 13-17절에서 그의 여행 계획 취소에 대해서 변명하는 것과 관련된 듯하다.[941] 거기서 바울은 고린도 방문계획 취소가 고린도 교인들의 유익을 위한 것이며 자신의 유익을 위한 것이 아니므로 자신의 계획 취소는 진실하다고 한다. 고린도후서 전체에서 바울의 가장 큰 관심은 그의 복음의 진실성과 사도직을 증명하는 일이다(4:2). 디도가 고린도 교회에 있는 동안에는 고린도 교회 형편이 좋았던 것이 분명하다.[942] 이때에는 바울은 현명하게도 돈에 관한 문제를 논하지는 않았다. 돈 문제는 좋지 않은 고린도 교회 상황에 부정적인 영향을 미칠 수 있기 때문이다. 그러나 지금은 사태가 진정되고 화해의 분위기가 조성되었으므로 헌금에 관한 부탁(8, 9장)을 할 수 있게 되었다. 트롤은 14절의 격려도 헌금에 대한 요구를 하기 전에 고린도 교인들을 부추기는 구실도 한다고 본다.[943]

바울이 디도를 보낼 때 고린도 교인들을 신뢰한 근거는 무엇인가 바울은 고린도 교인들이 이미 하나님의 은혜를 받은 사람들로서 진리의 말씀을 들을 수 있으며(6:1), 하나님의 영이 그들에게

---

941) Thrall, 499; Barnett, 384.

942) Windisch, 240; Barrett, 215; Furnish, 397; Thrall, 498. Thrall은 디도가 방문하였을 때에도 어느 정도 바울에 대한 저항 세력이 있었을 것이라고 본다(498). 14절의 εἰ(만일)은 바울이 고린도 교회에 대한 정황이 유동적임을 알고 있다는 증거라고 한다. "([εἰ "만일"]내가 그에게 너희를 위하여 자랑한 것이 있더라도…" 그러므로 바울이 2:9에서 고린도 교인들의 복종을 시험하기 위해서 편지를 보냈다고 한다. 그러면서도 바울은 자신의 편지의 적극적 효과를 기대하였다고 본다. 한마디로 바울은 반신반의(半信半疑)하면서 그 편지를 보냈고, 그러므로 그는 더욱 고린도 교회의 소식을 애타게 기다렸을 것이다.

943) Thrall, 497.

있으며(1:18-22; 3:2-3, 18), 그리고 그리스도가 그들에게 있었음을 알고 있었다(13:5). 결국 바울은 고린도 교인들을 신뢰한 것이 아니라 고린도 교인들을 주장하시는 하나님을 신뢰하였다.[944]

15. "저가 너희 모든 사람이 두려워하고 떪으로 자기를 영접하여 순종한 것을 생각하고 너희를 향하여 그의 심정이 더욱 깊었으니"(**καὶ τὰ σπλάγχνα αὐτοῦ περισσοτέρως εἰς ὑμᾶς ἐστιν ἀναμιμνῃσκομένου τὴν πάντων ὑμῶν ὑπακοήν, ὡς μετὰ φόβου καὶ τρόμου ἐδέξασθε αὐτόν**). 15절은 디도의 방문과 관련하여 고린도 교인들의 반응에 대한 디도 자신의 소감을 쓰고 있다. 주절은 "너희를 향하여 그의 심정이 더욱 깊었으니"이다. 이 절이 원문에는 앞에 나오나 한글개역에는 번역상 뒤에 나온다.

"저가 너희 모든 사람이 두려워하고 떪으로 자기를 영접하여"(**ὡς μετὰ φόβου καὶ τρόμου ἐδέξασθε αὐτόν**). 이 절이 희랍어 성경에는 맨 뒤에 나오나 한글개역성경을 따라 먼저 주석한다. 여기서 **ὡς**는 이유절을 이끄는 접속사로 해석될 수 있다.[945] "너희 모든 사람이 … 자기를 영접하였으므로", "두려워하고 떪"(**μετὰ φόβου καὶ τρόμου**)으로는 바울이 잘 쓰는 어귀이다(고전 2:3; 빌 2:12; 엡 6:5). 신약에서 바울 서신 외에 다른 데서는 이 말이 나타나지 않는다(출 15:16; 신 2:25; 사 19:16). 이 어귀는 종말론적 구원이나 심판과 관련하여 맡은 일을 매우 주의 깊게 수행하는 자세를 가리킨다.[946] 이 말은 어쩌면 고린도 교인들이 바울을 괴롭힌 죄

944) Barnett, 385.

945) Martin, 244.

946) Hodge, 190; Barnett, 385.

책감에서 디도를 조심스럽게 만나는 자세를 가리키는 지도 모른다.[947] 또는 고린도 교인들이 바울의 편지를 받고 근심하는 태도를 가리킬 수도 있다(7:11).[948] 무엇보다 이 말은 사도적 권위를 존중하고 그에 대해 순종하는 자세를 가리킨다. 바울은 필요하면 언제나 담대하게 자신의 사도적 소명과 권위를 분명히 밝힌다(2:9; 5:20-6:2; 6:11-13; 10:8; 13:1-2, 10). 그러나 때로는, 특히 설득이 필요할 때에는, 의도적으로 사도적 권위를 내 세우지 않기도 한다(1:24; 8:9). 디도를 정중히 모신 것은 바울의 사도적 권위를 인정한 것과 같다. 그는 바울의 사신이기 때문이다. 그리고 아마 디도가 가져간 바울의 편지에서 바울은 8장 23-24절에서도 말하는 것처럼 디도를 정중히 모실 것을 명령하였을 것이다. 고린도 교인들이 바울의 말대로 그를 정중히 대한 것을 디도가 고마워하고 있음을 말하면서 바울은 그렇게 한 고린도 교인들을 칭찬하고 있다. 한편 "두렵고 떪"은 앞서 말한 하나님의 뜻대로 한 고린도 교인들의 근심과 회개의 열매와 관련된다(9-11).

"순종한 것을 생각하고"(ἀναμιμνῃσκομένου τὴν πάντων ὑμῶν ὑπακοήν). 고린도 교인들이 바울의 사신 디도에게 순종한 것은 곧 그를 보낸 바울에 대한 순종이다. 바울에 대한 고린도 교회의 순종은 가장 확실한 화해의 증거이다. 바울은 복음에 대한 인간의 반응을 순종으로 자주 나타낸다. 바울은 디도가 가져간 편지에서 고린도 교회 사태에 대해서 구체적인 조치들을 지시하였을 것이며, 고린도 교인들은 이런 조치들을 모두 따른 것으로 보

947) Filson, 303.

948) Bruce, 219.

949) Plummer, 228.

인다.[949] 특히 2장 9절과 7장 11, 12절에서 말하듯이 고린도 교인들은 "불의 행한 자"에 대한 바울의 조치를 잘 따랐다. 디도는 그런 조치들이 들어 있는 "눈물의 편지"를 직접 전하였고 그들의 순종을 확인하였을 것이다. 그러므로 디도는 그들의 순종을 생각하고 깊은 정을 가지고 있다고 한다. 이렇게 바울이 디도의 깊은 감정을 언급하므로써 이제 다시 고린도후서를 가지고 고린도로 가야하는 디도에 대한 고린도 교인들의 충성이 더욱 확고하게 지속되기를 바라는 것이다. 그에 대한 충성은 곧 하나님의 사신인 자신에 대한 충성이요, 그것은 결국 하나님께 대한 것이기 때문이다. 고린도 교회는 바울 사도에게 순종하지 않음으로 어려움에 처하게 되었었는데, 이제 다시 그에게 순종함으로 질서와 안정을 찾게 되었다(참조, 고전 1:11-12; 2:16; 3:4, 21-23; 4:1; 14:34).

어떤 면에서 고린도 교회의 문제는 순종의 문제가 아니라 순종의 대상을 정하지 못한 것이 문제라고 할 수 있다. 바울이냐, 게바냐, 아볼로냐, 그리스도냐라는 문제였다(1:12). 비록 바울이 고린도 교인들에게 바울이나 아볼로나 모두 하나님의 동역자라고 했으나(고전 3:9), 실제로 어느 사도를 선택하여 순종할 것인가는 고린도 교인들에게 맡겨진 어려운 문제였다. 누구에게 대한 순종이냐의 문제는 상대적으로 다른 이에 대한 비판이나 배반을 동반할 수도 있다. 실제로 다른 이가 나타나서 바울을 반대하는 운동을 일으켰다(2:5-9; 7:11, 12). 바울은 이들을 공격하는 "엄격한 편지"를 써서 고린도 교인들이 그 문제된 사람을 정죄하고 바울을 따라야 할 것을 명확하게 전하였다. 그 "엄격한 편지"의 효과와 함께 디도의 사역이 매우 유효하여 그들은 이제 바울 사도에게 순종하기를 결정하였다.

현대 교회에서는 순종이라는 미덕 자체가 멸종위기 동물처럼 사라지고 있다. 그러나 순종은 그리스도인과 그리스도 교회의 중요한 특성 중의 하나이다(빌 2:1-11). 많은 현대 교회에서 세속주의의 영향으로 교회의 전통적인 순종보다는 저항이 미덕으로 간주되기도 한다. 교회 지도자에 대한 반대와 비난으로 많은 교회가 어지럽다. 그러나 주안에서 신앙의 지도자의 지도를 따르는 것이 기독교인의 기본적 자세이다. 모든 어린 아이들에게 순종의 미덕을 가르치듯이 믿는 사람들은 순종을 힘써 가르치고 배워야 한다. 어느 시대나 어느 조직 사회도 위계질서(位階秩序)가 그 조직의 설립목적을 수행하기 위해 필요하다. 현대 민주 사회에서도 군대는 물론 회사 같은 조직 사회에서도 윗사람에게 대한 "순종적" 자세가 요구되고 있다. 또한 카톨릭이나 정교회 같은 전통적 그리스도의 교회에서도 아직 순종이 미덕으로 존중되고 있고 교회 성장에 도움이 되고 있음을 간과해서는 안 된다. 그러나 유독 개신교에서는 다른 조직체에 비해서 순종적인 자세가 자주 무시당하는 것은 잘못된 것이다. 실제로 개혁교회(Reformed Church)전통은 성경의 진리를 떠나 행위구원을 가르치는 구교를 반대하고 믿음으로 구원 얻는 성경적 진리를 복구하는 개혁 교회 신앙전통을 계승하고 있다. 그러나 이런 개혁 교회 전통을 가지고 지도자에게 반항하는 자세를 합리화해서는 안 된다. 개혁 신앙 진리에 순종하듯이 지도자들이 분명히 잘못을 범하지 않은 한 지도자들에게 순종하는 자세를 견지해야 한다(살전 5:12-13). 개신교회는 교인들에게 그 지도자들에게 순종하는 미덕을 가르쳐서 그리스도의 교회의 분열을 막고, 하나가 되기를 보다 힘써야 한다(엡 5:21; 살전 5:12, 13).

16. 내가 너희를 모든 일에 신뢰 할 수 있음을(내가 너희를 인하여 범사에 담대한 고로) 기뻐하노라(χαίρω ὅτι ἐν παντὶ θαρρῶ ἐν ὑμῖν). 이 절은 이 부분과 7장 3절 이전 부분을 연결하는 4절에서 언급하는 디도를 만난 기쁨을 다시 반복하고 있다. ὅτι는 이유절(RSV, 한글개역), 또는 기쁨을 설명하는 서술절로 볼 수 있다(KJV, 참조, NIV). 바울의 기쁨은 본문에서 누차 동사(7, 9, 13)와 명사(4, 13)로 표현되었다. 각 절의 기쁨은 각기 특징이 있다. 4절의 기쁨은 개론적이고 일반적인 것이고, 5-7절은 디도를 만남과 그의 보고에 대한 기쁨, 8-12절의 기쁨은 고린도 교인들의 회개에 대한 기쁨, 13-15절의 기쁨은 동역자 디도의 기쁨을 함께 나누는 기쁨이다. 16절은 4절과 같이 이모든 기쁨을 대표하고 종합하는 기쁨이다.[950] 이제 다시 디도를 보내어서 이 편지를 읽게 하고(8:16-24), 또 헌금도 준비케 함으로써(8:6) 사역을 계속 수행할 수 있게 된 것이 기쁜 것이다.

θαρρῶ는 "나는 확신한다" 또는 "나는 용기를 갖는다", "나는 담대하다"라고 번역할 수 있다.[951] 그러나 여기서는 ἐν("…안에")라는 전치사가 있으므로 "신뢰한다"로 해석해야 한다.[952] 10장 1절에는 이 말이 εἰς("…으로", "향하여")와 함께 쓰여서 "나는 너희를 신뢰한다"(θαρρῶ εἰς ὑμῖν)로 해석해야 한다. 플러머는 이 말을 10장 1절과 관련시켜서 "너희에게서 담대함을 갖는다"라고

950) 바클레는 본문의 기쁨을 세 개로 나눈다: (1) 화해의 기쁨; (2) 변화된 사람에게 있는 믿음과 확신을 발견하는 기쁨; (3) 사랑받고, 인정받고, 잘 대접받은 사람을 보는 기쁨. W. Barclary, *The Letters to the Corinthians* (Edinburgh: St. Andrews Press/Philadelphia: Westminster Press, 1975), 246.

951) Calvin, 102; Denney, 249; Plummer, 228; 개역한글판.

952) Thrall, 501.

해석해야 할 것을 주장한다.[953] 바울을 따르는 이와 반대하는 이들에게 "담대함"이 각기 다른 의미로 나타난다는 것이다. 그러나 이 말이 5장 6, 8절에서는 신뢰한다는 의미로 쓰였다(개역한글판= "담대함"). 그러나 여기서는 위에서 트롤이 지적한 다른 전치사가 사용된 것을 고려하고, 또 고린도 교인들을 신뢰한다고 해석하는 것이 우리말 어감상으로도 좋으므로 "신뢰한다"로 번역한다.[954]

이렇게 16절은 지금까지 바울이 변화된 고린도 교인들을 칭찬하고 그들을 신뢰함을 확인하면서 8장, 9장의 헌금에 대한 요청을 하기 위해 준비하는 연결절의 역할을 하고 있다.[955]

주 해(7:5-16):

7장 5-16절은 화해의 결과인 기쁨이다. 그런데 그 기쁨은 화해를 위해 온갖 고난을 거친 결과로 얻은 기쁨이다. 이것은 바울의 "고난 중의 기쁨"의 구체적인 예이다. 크리소스톰은 바울의 기쁨은 그가 당한 고난을 능가하는 기쁨이라고 했다.[956] 숫자와 시간으로 논하면 아마 바울의 고난이 나 슬픔이 기쁨보다 더 많았을 것이다(12:28; 참조, 6:10). 뿐만 아니라 때로는 농도에 있어서도 바울의 슬픔이나 고난이 그의 기쁨보다 더 할 수도 있었을 것이다(2:4="많은 눈물"). 그런데도 바울의 기쁨을 그의 고난에 비교하여

---

953) Plummer, 228; Bultmann, 64.

954) Hodge, 190; Barrett, 215; Bruce, 219; Tasker, 108; Martin, 245; Thrall, 501; Barnett, 386.

955) Hughes, 282; Martin, 245, Thrall, 501.

956) *Homiletics in 2 Cor*, 14.1, 2.

분명히 더 크다고 할 수 있을까 나아가 바울이 자주 그의 독자들을 격려하는 것처럼 그 자신이 고난 중에서도 실제로 기뻐할 수 있었을까 (6:10; 롬 12:1; 빌 2:17; 골 1:24; 12:10). 그렇다면 그 기쁨의 비밀은 무엇인가

첫째, 바울은 고난 중에서 그리스도의 고난에 동참한다고 믿고 기뻐할 수 있었다. "우리가 그와 함께 영광을 받기 위하여 고난도 함께 받아야 될 것이니라"(롬 8:17절 하반절; 참조, 빌 1:29; 3:10; 골 1:24; 행 5:41). 믿음의 주이시며 장래의 승리와 영광을 이루어 주실 그리스도와 함께 현재의 고난을 당하는 것은 주를 믿는 자의 자랑이요 기쁨이다. 둘째, 바울은 현재의 고난 중에서 최후의 종말론적 승리 이전에도 주시는 일종의 예비적 승리를 믿고 기뻐하였다(2:14). "핍박을 당하여도 버린바 되지 아니하며, 꺼꾸러뜨림을 당하여도 망하지 아니하며"(4:9). "죽는 자 같으나 보라 우리가 살고…"(6:9); "그러므로 내가 그리스도를 위하여 약한 것들과 능욕과 궁핍과 핍박과 곤란을 기뻐하노니 이는 내가 약할 그 때에 곧 강함이니라"(12:9). 셋째, 아무런 가시적인 현재의 승리가 없을 때에도 속사람의 성장과 최종적인 하나님의 승리의 약속을 믿고 바라며 기뻐했다. "우리의 잠시 받는 환난의 경한 것이 지극히 크고 영원한 영광의 중한 것을 우리에게 이루게 함이니"(4:17; 참조, 롬 8:18).

우리 많은 그리스도인들이 바울보다 못한 고난을 당하면서도 바울의 기쁨을 누리지 못한다면, 그것은 우리가 이상의 바울과 같은 믿음과 소망을 갖고 살지 못하기 때문이다. 하나님을 믿지 않는 세상 사람들도 흔히 낙관적이고 적극적인 사고방식이 사람의 신념과 정신을 든든하게 하여 보다 즐겁고 성공적인 삶을 살게 할

수 있다고 한다. 그러나 모든 인본주의적 자랑은 하나님 앞에서 무력해 질 수 밖에 없다. 하나님을 믿는 우리는 바울처럼 온갖 고난 중에서도 선한 믿음과 소망을 가지는 것이 중요하다. 하나님께서 나를 사랑하시고 나를 구원하시고 나를 인도해 주신다는 믿음을 늘 새롭게 하는 것이 어떤 고난 중에서도 기쁨을 누리는 조건이다. 또한 믿음을 지키며 죄를 짓지 않도록 해야 한다. 죄를 지으면 하나님의 구원과 축복의 믿음이 약해지고 대신 하나님의 진노와 형벌의 두려움으로 불안하게 된다. 그러나 죄를 지었을 때에도 속히 회개하고 하나님께 돌아와서 그의 자비하심에 호소하여 용서함을 구하고 용서함을 확신하는 것이 필요하다. 죄 사함의 확신은 다시 같은 죄를 반복하여 짓지 않으므로 얻을 수 있다. 죄 사함의 확신이 없으면 기쁨을 누릴 수가 없다. 결국은 죄 사함의 확신도 믿음이 있어야 한다. 믿음이 굳건한 사람은 죄를 짓기 어려우며, 죄를 지어도 용서받는 믿음의 힘으로 다시 정상적인 믿음의 상태로 회복될 수 있다. 그러므로 믿음이 좋은 사람은 건강한 사람과 같다. 평소에 건강관리를 잘하는 사람은 병이 잘 걸리지 않으며, 병이 걸려도 곧 회복되는 것과 같다. 반대로 평소에 건강관리를 잘 못하는 사람은 병에 잘 걸리고 한 번 병에 걸리면 잘 낫지 않는 것과 같다. 죽고 다시 사신 그리스도를 굳게 믿는 사람은 어떤 시험에서도 이기며, 혹 실패해도 다시 일어서는 힘을 갖게 된다. 그리스도를 믿는 믿음이 없이 다른 무엇을 믿는 사람은 결국은 실패하고 좌절하게 된다. 그 믿음의 대상이 결국 창조주 하나님이 아닌 썩을 피조물(인간, 자연)이거나 피조물과 관련된 원칙이나 사상이기 때문이다. 죽으시고 다시 사신 하나님의 아들 그리스도에게서만 세상을 이기는 궁극적 힘이 있다. "누가 우리를 그리스도의 사랑에서 끊으리요 환난이나, 곤고나 핍박이나 기근이나 적신이나 위험이나 칼이랴 그러나 이 모든 일에 우리를 사랑하시는 이로 말미암아 우리가 넉넉히 이기느니라. 내가 확신하노니 사망이나 생명이나 천사들이나 권세자들이나 현재 일이나 장래 일이나 능력이나 높음이나 깊음이나 다른 아무 피조물이라도 우리를 우리 주 예수 안에 있는 하나님의 사랑에서 끊을 수 없으리라" (롬 8:35-39, 중략). 이런 요지부동의 믿음에 수반되는 것이 안전과 승리의 기쁨이며 그 기쁨은 하나님 신앙에 근거한 것이므로 참되고 영원한 기쁨이다.

바울은 이런 믿음과 기쁨을 자랑하고 있다. 우리 믿는 이들도 그런 믿음과 기쁨을 가지고 있다. 그러나 많은 그리스도인들이 바울과 달리 현대 세속주의적 가치관의 세력을 두려워하여 이런 기쁨을 주는 복음을 세상 사람들에게 감히 증거하지 못하고 자신의 개인이나 가정의 소장물로 감추고 있다. "내가 복음을 부끄러워하지 아니하노니 이 복음은 모든 믿는 자에게 구원을 주시는 하나님의 능력이 됨이라. 첫째는 유대인이요, 또한 헬라인에게로다" (롬 1:16). 복음을 담대히 증거 할 수 있는 능력을 주시도록 기도하자.

Ⅳ. 헌금 요청(8-9장)

바울은 7장까지 사도직에 대한 자신의 변명을 마치고, 8장에서 9장까지 헌금이라는 새로운 주제를 시작하고 있다. 특히 7장에서 고린도 교인들이 바울의 "엄격한 편지"를 읽고서 회개하고 바울과 새로운 관계를 가지고 출발하게 된 것에 대하여 디도와 바울이 받은 위로와 기쁨이 강조된 것은 적어도 부분적으로는 어려운 헌금 요청을 위한 바울의 "사전 작업"으로도 볼 수 있다.[1] 이 헌금은 바울의 사사로운 용도를 위한 것이 아니고, 예루살렘 성도들을 위한 것이며, 이방교회가 예루살렘 교회에 진 복음의 빚을 갚는 상징적 수단인 것이다. 물론 이런 헌금 전달을 통해서 바울이 얻는 부수적인 개인적인 유익도 있다고 본다. 첫째, 헌금은 바울의 성공적인 이방 선교의 구체적 표로써 예루살렘 사도들과 성도들에게 인식되고 따라서 바울의 이방사역이 인정을 받게 될 것이다. 둘째, 헌금은 이방인들에게 "믿음으로만 구원얻는다"는 복음을 전하면서 율법을 가르치지 않는 바울의 "느슨한 복음"에 대한 유대교 기독교인들의 불만을 어느 정도 달랠 수 있을 것이다(행 21:20이하). 셋째, 바울의 교회를 핍박했던 과거의 잘못에 대한 사죄의 목적도 있다고 본다(고전 15:9). 그러므로 바울은 예루살렘 성도들이 그의 헌금을 잘 받아 줄지에 대해서 일말의 의심을 하고 있다(롬 15:31).

디도가 보고한 고린도 교회의 변화는 적극적이었으나, 헌금 문제는 유동적이었던 것 같다. 벌써 일 년 전부터 헌금을 시작하였

1) Barnett, 387.

으나 성과가 좋지 않았던 것 같다(8:6, 10; 9:2; 참조, 고전16:1-4). 하기야 고린도 교인들이 변화되었다고 해서 바울이 요청한 헌금을 쉽게 모으게 되는 것은 아니다. 시간이 필요한 것이다. 더구나 바울에게 돌아온 지 얼마 안 되는 고린도 교인들에게 이내 헌금을 부탁하는 것은 매우 어려운 일이다. 바울은 본문에서 자신의 헌금 요청이 급작스러운 것이 아니며 일 년 전부터 시작한 것임을 거듭 말하고 있다(8:10; 9:2). 그리고 그는 직접 헌금을 거두지 않고 디도와 "두 형제들"을 보내어 그의 방문 전에 미리 헌금을 거두어서 그의 사역이 "돈을 걷는 사역"으로 상대방을 약취하는 인상을 주지 않으려고 주의하고 있다(12:16). 바울에게 돌아 온지 얼마 되지 않은 고린도 교인들에게 헌금 요청을 하기에는 다소 부적절한 시기임을 알고서 매우 조심스럽게 헌금 요청을 하고 있다(8:8, 10-12). 고린도 교회의 헌금 문제를 떠나서 바울은 사도로서 돈 문제에 대해서는 초연하고 말씀 전하고 기도에 전무해야 한다는 예루살렘 교회 전통을 알고 있었을 것이다(행 6:4). 그러므로 그는 더욱 더 헌금 요청에 대해서 조심스럽게 접근하고 있다.

이렇게 헌금 문제를 다루는 것이 어려운 일이지만, 바울은 예루살렘 가난한 성도들을 위한 구제 헌금의 신학적 당위성을 찾는다. 헌금은 "평균케 하시는 하나님의 세상 경륜"을 실행하는 마땅한 의로운 행위이며(고후 8:13-15), 우리를 위해 가난하게 되신 그리스도를 믿는 이들이 그의 은혜를 실제적으로 보답하는 중요한 방법이라고 보았다(8:9). 또 이 헌금의 인간적, 도덕적 당위성은 헌금 약속 때문이다. 그는 그 헌금 사역을 담당하기로 예루살렘 사도들과 약속까지 한 바 있다(갈 2:10). 이제 바울은 그의 선교일생의 막바지에 이르러 헌금을 가지고 예루살렘으로 가는 계획을 가지고 있었다. 다시 말하면 바울은 그의 전체 선교 사역 계획을 차질 없이 수행하기를 원했다. 그러나 아가야 지방의 중심 교회인 고린도 교회의 헌금이 일 년이 넘도록 지연되는 것이 안타까웠다(8:10; 9:2). 바울이 헌금에 대해서 2장이나 쓴 것은 바울의 헌금에 대한 관심이 매우 큰 것을 보여 준다. 이 헌금을 수령하는 것이 당장 다가오는 그의 고린도 교회 방문 목적과 직접 관련되어 있기 때문이다(8:16-24; 9:5). 그러나 헌금 사역은 고린도 교회에 국한되지 않는 바울의 범교회적 중요한 사역이었음을 이해하는 것이 중요하다. 바울의 헌금 사역은 그의 예루살렘 사도들에 대한 신뢰 유지(갈 2:10)와 이방교회와 예루살렘 교회의 유대 관계 확립(9:11-14), 하나님의 은혜의 공유(8:13-15) 등 목회적 선교적 신학적 의미가 있다. 또 앞에서 말한 대로, 헌금으로 바울과 예루살렘 사도들과 성도들과의 관계가 원만해지고 싸여 있던 문제들도 해소되기를 바라는 소망도 있다. 그러므로 바울이 두려워하는 것은(9:4) 고린도 교회의 헌금이 지연되는 것이 고린도 교회의 체면 손상을 넘어서, 헌금에 참여한 다른 교회들의 실망(9:4), 바울의 사도로서의 리더쉽과 신뢰성 손상(8:8; 참조, 11:11), 그리고 그의 전체 선교 여행 계획과 그가 헌금과 관련된 목회적 신학적 선교적 계획에도 막중한 손실을 가져올 수 있기 때문이다. 이렇게 바울은 사도로서 돈에 관련된 일에 초연해야 함을 알면서도 헌금을 요청할 수밖에 없는 긴박하고 난처한 입장에 있었다. 그러므로 8장 9장에서 바울은 헌금 요청을 하면서 절대로 강요하지 않고 믿음이 약한 고린도 교인들을 달래고 있다(8:8, 12; 9:7, 8). 그러나 바울은 이러한 조용한 접근도 그를 반대하는 이들의 비난을 완전히 피하기가 어려울 것이라고 짐작하고 있었을 것이다(7:2; 12:13-18).

학자들은 8장과 9장의 통일성 문제를 논의해왔다. 8장과 9장이 같은 헌금에 대한 주제를 다루면서 문장과 내용의 연결이 되지 않는 것처럼 보이는 증거들이 있기 때문이다. 첫째, 9장에서 바울은 8장의 헌금주제를 전혀 의식하지 않고 새롭게 시작하는 것처럼 보이기 때문이다. 8장에서 헌금에 대해 계속하여 말한 후에 9장을 "성도를 섬기는 일에 대하여 내가 너희에게 쓸 필요가 없나니…" (9:1)라고 시작하여 중복되는 주제를 반복하고 있다. 바울은 8장 1절에서 마게도냐 교회가 헌금을 많이 했다는 사례를 말한 후에 고린도 교인들에게 이미 시작한 헌금을 마치도록 권면하고, 9장 2절에서는 바울이 마게도냐 교인들에게 고린도 교인들이 헌금을 이미 시작했다는 말로 자랑하여 그들로 많은 헌금을 하게 하였음을 말하면서, 그 자랑에 걸맞는 헌금하기를 부탁한다. 그래서 불트만은 고린도 교인들의 헌금을 자랑한 일을 언급한 9장이 8장보다 먼저 쓴 것이라고 한다.[2] 둘째, 8장은 고린도 교인들에게 헌금을 독려하고, 9장은 더 넓게 남부 그리스, 즉 아가야 지방에 있는 교인들에게 헌금을 독려하는 것처럼 보인다. 그러므로 8장 9장은 따로 쓰인 것이라고 한다.[3] 셋째, 8장은 7장의 위로와 기쁨에 이어 고린도 교인들을 신뢰하는 어조에서 헌금을 독려하는데, 9장은 8장, 18절과 22절에서 추천하는 형제들의 사역에 첨부하여 쓰는 것으로 보인다.[4] 이 경우 8장과 9장은 내용은 다르나 같은 편지로 본다. 넷째, 빈디쉬는 8장과 9장의 통일성을 반대하면서 8장 18절 이하에서 디도와 다른 두 형제들과 9장 3-5절의 "형제들" 은 다른 이

2) Bultmann, 255.

3) Windisch, 268.

4) Martin, 249-50.

유를 가지고 보냈다고 한다. 8장 18절 이하의 디도와 두 형제들을 헌금을 위해 보내는 이유는 재정에 관한 바울의 신뢰성 문제를 위한 것이며, 9장 3-5절에서 "형제들"을 보내는 이유는 바울이 고린도 교회를 방문하기 전에 이들이 미리 가서 헌금을 걷는 일을 마치도록 하려는 다른 이유를 갖고 있다고 본다.[5] 그러나 이런 다른 이유들이 8장, 9장의 통일성을 저해한다고 보기 어렵다. 바울이 이런 이유들을 다른 경우를 가리키는 것이 아니라 같은 경우에 대해서 한 편지에서 연속해서 말하고 있다고 볼 수 있다. 오히려 이런 증거들은 8장과 9장의 독립 대신에 연결을 지지하는 증거로 볼 수도 있다. 바울은 9장에서 마게도냐 사람들에게 고린도 교인들이 헌금을 이미 시작하였음을 말하여 좋은 성과가 있었으니 먼저 시작한 너희 고린도 교인들이 그 일을 꼭 마치도록 하라고 8장에서 말한 것을 반복 강조하면서 특히 바울의 임박한 방문 전에 헌금을 마칠 것을 부탁하고 있고, 헌금과 관련하여 하나님께서 주실 축복을 다짐하고 있다고 보면 통일성이 유지된다.

그러나 8장 24절과 9장 1절의 연결이 어색한 것, 같은 주제를 지나치게 반복적으로 언급하는 것 등은 사실이다.[6] 위의 다른 지적들과 같이 이를 다른 독립된 서신의 내용을 편집하여 합쳤기 때문으로 보느냐,[7] 아니면 한 편지의 내용을 시간이 경과한 후 다른 경우에 썼기 때문이라고 보느냐,[8] 또는 단순히 반복적으로 썼느냐

5) Windisch, 268.

6) Héring, 65.

7) J. S. Semler, *Paraphrasis II. Epistolae ad Corinthos* (Halle: Carl Hermann Hemmerde, 1776); B. Rigaux, *The Letters of St. Paul*, tr. S. Yonick (Chicago: Franciscan Herald Press, 1968, 110; Windisch, 268.

8) Martin, 249-250; Thrall, 38-43, 77, 503-4.

에 대한 선택이 있다.[9] 우리는 바울이 대필을 하면서 8장까지 마친 후에 얼마간 쉬었다가 다시 쓰면서 8장의 내용과 주제를 다시 읽어 본 후에 자신이 8장에서 말한 것들을 9장 초두에 다시 언급하면서 자신의 방문 전에 헌금을 마칠 것과, 하나님의 축복의 약속을 하고 있다고 본다. 데니가 지적했듯이 9장 1절의 "(성도를)섬기는 일에 대하여"(περὶ…τῆς διακονίας)라는 어귀는 바울이 미묘한 사항을 다룰 때 쓰는 것이며, τῆς διακονίας(섬기는 일)의 관사와 "쓸 필요가 없나니"라는 말은 이미 언급한 헌금에 관한 논의를 다른 시각에서 다루기 위해 쓰는 "부드러운 연결어귀"(a smooth transition)라고 본다(참조, 빌 3:1).[10] 또한 8장과 9장이 하나의 편지인 증거는 그 내용의 연결성이다. 8장에서는 헌금의 당위성을 적어도 두 가지 신학적 원칙에서 논한다. 첫째는 우리를 위하여 가난하게 되신 그리스도의 은혜에 대한 감사이다(8:9). 둘째는 그의 백성들에게 공평하게 주시는 하나님의 사역의 원칙이다(8:13-15). 9장에서는 헌금하는 이에게 주시는 하나님의 축복을 여러 하나님의 말씀에 근거하여 설명한다. 바울은 마치 중개인처럼 헌금하는 자가 받을 축복과 헌금을 받으시는 하나님의 축복의 약속의 책임을 확약시키는 것이다. 바울은 헌금하는 고린도 교인들과 헌금을 받는 예루살렘 성도들 그리고 "평균케 하시기"를 원하시는 하나님 사이에 서서 서로 유익이 되는 헌금에 대해 말한다. 고린도 교인들은 헌금으로 더 많은 축복을 받게 될 것이고(9:6-11), 하나님은 예루살렘 성도들을 통해서 감사함과 영광을 받게

9) Barnett, 388.

10) Denney, 279-280.

된다(9:11, 13). (여기에서 바울은 그의 반대자들이 비판하는 대로 그가 헌금이라는 명목으로 고린도 교인들의 재물을 탐하는 사람이 아니라 오히려 하나님의 축복의 매개자라는 암시가 있다[참조, 11:2; 12:13-18]).

한편, 8장과 9장의 헌금이 갈라디아서 2장 10절에서 약속한 예루살렘 성도들을 위한 것인가 아니면 새로운 헌금인가에 대한 논쟁이 있다. 트롤은 비록 역사적으로는 가난한 예루살렘 성도들과 관련된 것이라 해도 8장과 9장의 헌금 계획은 갈라디아서 2장 11절에서 베드로와의 논쟁이후에 거의 무산되었다가 다시 시작하는 예루살렘 성도들을 위한 새로운 헌금계획이라고 생각한다.[11] 그러나 대체로 학자들은 예루살렘 성도들과 관련된 헌금기사들에 근거하여 예루살렘 성도들을 위한 애초의 헌금계획을 계속 추진하는 것을 가리키는 것이라고 본다(행 20:16; 22; 24:17; 고전 16:1-4; 고후 8, 9장; 갈 2:10; 롬 15:26-29). 예루살렘 성도들은 "거룩하고" "가난한" 성도들이라고 보는 근거는 사도행전 2장 44-45절의 예루살렘 공동체의 생활 모습과 마태복음 5장 3절의 "심령이 가난한 자"에 대한 말씀과도 관련된다.[12] 그러나 학자들은 이 헌금에 자선이나 구제 목적이외에 신학적 목회적 의미가 있다고 본다. (1) 헌금은 바울이 예루살렘 기둥 사도들과 약속한 것이었다(갈 2:10;

11) Thrall, 504-507.

12) Karl Holl, "Der Kirchenbegriff des Paulus in seinem Verhaeltnis zu dem der Urgemeinde," *Gesammelte Aufsaetze zur Kirchengeschichte* (Tübingen: J. C. B. Mohr, 1928), 2:44-67; D. Georgi, *Die Geschichte der Kollekte*, 10, 11, 17; G. Bornkamm, *Paul*, 40, 41; B. Holmberg, *Paul and Power*, 77; W. D. Davies, *The Gospel and the Land*, 199; L. E. Keck, "The Poor among the Saints in the New Testament," *ZNW* 56 (1965), 100-29; R. N. Flew, *Jesus and His Church* (London: Epworth, 1938), 156, 157.

롬15:25-27). 그러나 갈라디아서 2장 11절 이하에서 바울이 베드로와 논쟁한 이후에 헌금의 약속 이행에 차질이 있었던 것으로 가정한다.[13] (2) 헌금은 이방 교인들이 예루살렘 교회에 대한 사랑과 동정을 나누는 표시이다(8:13-15; 롬 15:25-27). (3) 이방교회가 예루살렘 어머니 교회에 대한 영적 빚을 갚는 한 가지 수단이었다(고후 9:13-14; 롬 11:30-31). (4) 이방인들이 선물을 가지고 예루살렘에 순례 온다는 종말론적 예언의 성취로 보았다(사 2:2-5; 60:5-22; 미 4:1-5; 행 15:15-18; 롬 11:30-31). 이것은 이방인과 유대인이 모두 예수를 믿음으로 말미암아 구원 얻는 바울의 종말론적 구원사상과 일치된다(갈 3:23-4:7; 엡 2:11-22).[14] (5) 헌금을 통해서 예루살렘 교회와 이방교회가 서로에 대한 불신을 극복하고 같은 하나님의 백성임을 확인하게 하는 수단이었다(9:13, 14). 예루살렘 교회는 선택된 백성으로서, 또 예수 전승의 계승자로서 이방 교회에 대한 오만함을 가지고 있었고, 이방교회는 당시 반유대적 풍조와 예루살렘 교회의 율법주의적 태도에 대한 비판적인 자세를 가지고 있었다고 본다. (6) 바울은 자신의 사도직과 이방 선교에 대한 예루살렘 교회의 남아 있는 의구심을 인식하고, 특히 예루살렘

---

13) Lüdemann, *Paul, Apostle to the Gentiles: Studies in Chronology*, 87, 88; Martin, 251.

14) Munck, *Paul and the Salvation of Mankind*, 288-92, 295-97. 헌금의 종말론적 의미에 동의하는 학자들은 Furnish, 412; Martin, 251; F. T. Fallon, *2 Corinthians*, New Testament Message 11 (Wilmington, Del.: M. Glazier/Dublin: Veritas, 1980), 68-9; Thrall은 바울이 롬 15:24, 28에서 스페인 선교를 언급하고 있으므로 헌금을 종말론적 의미와 연계하는 것은 타당하지 않다고 한다. 아직 이방 선교가 끝나지 않았으므로 이방인들이 예루살렘으로 선물을 가져오는 종말론적 환상과 연계될 수 없다고 한다(513). 그러나 바울의 임박한 종말에 대한 가르침에 비추어 보아서(고전 7:29; 16:22) 이런 추정은 여전히 가능하다.

신자들의 유대교적 율법주의적 잔재와 자신의 이신득의의 갈등을 극복하고,[15] 사도직의 표시를 예루살렘 교회에 나타내고 화해하기를 원했다.[16] (7) 헌금은 그리스도의 약함을 따라 자신도 하나님 앞에서 스스로 약해지는 것이며 하나님 외에 다른 것은 의지하지 않고 하나님만 의지하겠다는 구체적인 신앙고백 행위이다(8:5, 9).

이러한 헌금의 신학적 목회적 또는 심리적 의미를 논할 수 있지만 바울의 헌금은 우선 성경의 구제에 대한 많은 가르침과 유대교의 구제와 자선의 전통적 가르침에 입각한 것이라고 볼 수 있다.[17] 이에 따라 바울은 직접 구제를 가르치기도 하고(롬 12:8; 고전 13:3; 엡 4:28; 딤전 5:10), 헌금을 가난한 이들을 위한 구제의 의미를 나타내는 "은혜"(χάρις)로 설명하고 있다(고후 8:1, 4, 6, 7, 13-14). 그러나 대다수의 학자들은 감추어진 신학적 목회적 의미를 찾는 데만 관심을 가지고 헌금이 주로 예루살렘 성도들을 위한 구제의 행위라는 것을 거의 망각한다.[18] 바울은 헌금을 성도를 섬기는 봉사의 직무, 즉 구제의 의미로 생각한다(8:4; 13-15; 9:9; 12). 한편 유대교의 구제의 가르침은 하나님의 긍휼하심에 기초하고 있다. 하나님이 가난한 자를 긍휼히 여기심을 알고, 그의 백성으로서 가난한 자와 궁핍한 자를 긍휼히 여기며 구제하는 것이다(신

15) Martin, lvii.

16) J. Hainz, *Koinonia*, "Kirche" als Gemeinschaft bei Paulus BU 16 (Regensburg: Verlag Friedrich Pustet, 1982), 139. Martin, 254, 재인용.

17) Barrett, 27; Thrall, 511; 참조, Martin, 257, 특히, 296. 출 23:6, 11; 레 19:10; 23:22; 25:35; 신 15:7; 24:14; 삼상 2:8; 에 9:22; 욥 29:12; 30:25; 31:16; 시 35:10; 112:9; 113:7; 잠 17:5; 19:17; 22:9; 28:27; 31:20; 사 58:7; 61:1; 렘 22:16; 겔 16:49; 18:12; 22:29; 암 4:1; 5:11; 8:4; 슥 7:10.

18) Martin, 296.

15: 9, 11; 시 69:33; 72:4; 82:4; 109:16; 잠 28:27; 살전 4:12; 딛 3:13; 요일 3:17 등).

어떤 학자들은 바울이 헌금에 대한 그의 신학적 목회적 목적을 이루지 못하였다고 본다. 바울이 헌금을 가지고 마지막으로 예루살렘을 방문하였을 때 유대 당국에 의해 체포되었고(행 21:27 이하), 예루살렘 교회가 이에 대해 적절히 바울을 변호하고 돕지 못한 것은 바울의 이방선교나 사도직에 대한 불만과 의구심을 떨쳐버리지 못했기 때문이라는 것이다.[19] 그러나 이것은 근거 없는 추정에 지나지 않는다. 당시 예루살렘 교회가 유대 당국에 맞서서 바울을 법적으로 보호할만한 세력이 되지 못한 것이 바울 체포의 주된 이유이며 의도적인 방조는 아니라고 본다. 바울의 체포는 이방의 세력이나 풍조를 증오하는 열심당 같은 유대인들의 충동에 의한 것으로 보는 것이 타당하다(행 21:28-30).

한편 "예루살렘의 가난한 성도들"이란 말이 물질적으로 가난함을 지칭한다고 보는 견해가 지배적이나, 영적인 가난함(마 5:3)이나 경건한 이들을 지칭한다는 주장도 있다.[20] 어머니 교회의 이런 경건한 이들을 돕는 것은 당연한 것이다. 이런 생각의 배후에는 당시 해외에 거주하는 유대인들(디아스포라 유대인들)의 회당이

---

19) Martin, 258.

20) Karl Holl, "Der Kirchenbegriff des Paulus in seinem Verhaeltnis zu dem der Urgemeinde," *Gesammelte Aufsaetze zur Kirchengeschichte* (Tübingen: J. C. B. Mohr, 1928) 2:44-67; D. Georgi, *Die Geschichte der Kollekte des Paulus für Jerusalem*, TF 38 (Mamburg-Bergstedt: H. Reich. Evangelischer Verlag, 1965), 23. 여기서 Georgi는 구약과 유대교에서의 "가난함"의 의미가 경건함을 나타낸다고 한다. 솔로몬의 시편 10; 15; 18:1-5; 1QpHab 12:3, 6, 10; 14:7; 1QM 11:9, 13; 13:14; 1QH 5:13, 14, 16, 22; Thrall, 507; Martin, 257.

예루살렘에 성전세금을 보내야 하는 법적 의무나 관습과도 관련되었다는 견해도 있다(마 17:24-27).[21] 그러나 이런 견해는 지나친 추정이라는 비난을 받았다.[22] 바울이 밝히는 대로 예루살렘의 가난한 성도들에게 이방교회인 고린도 교회가 물질적 도움을 주는 것을 구원받은 만민들이 모두 함께 하나님께 감사와 영광을 돌리는 표로 보고 헌금을 독려하는 것이 8장과 9장의 중심 주제이다.

A. 마게도냐 교인들의 모범적 헌금 사례 (8:1-6)

본문:

1. 형제들아 하나님께서 마게도냐 교회들에게 주신 은혜를 우리가 너희에게 알게 하노니 2. 환난의 많은 시련 가운데서 저희 넘치는 기쁨과 극한 가난이 저희로 풍성한 연보를 넘치도록 하게 하였느니라. 3. 내가 증거하노니 저희가 힘대로 할 뿐 아니라 힘에 지나도록 자원하여 4. 이 은혜와 성도 섬기는 일에 참여함에 대하여 우리에게 간절히 구하니 5. 우리의 바라던 것 뿐 아니라 저희가 먼저 자신을 주께 드리고 또 하나님의 뜻을 좇아 우리에게 주었도다. 6. 이러므로 우리가 디도를 권하여 너희 가운데서 시작하였은즉 이 은혜를 그대로 성취케 하라 하였노라.

본문 비평:

1. 2절의 **κατὰ βάθους**(극한)가 p^{46} D^{*} pc에는 **βάθος**로 나타난다.

2. 4절 끝에 **δέξασθαι ἡμᾶς**(우리가 받은)라는 말이 대문자 사본(MS) 가장자리에 추서되어, "다른 많은 사본에도 이같이 쓰여

---

21) Holl, 62.

22) Martin, 257.

있음" 이라는 필사자들의 설명이 붙어있다.[23]

3. 5절의 τῷ κυρίῳ(주께)대신 p^{46}은 θεῷ(하나님께)라는 말을 쓴다. 그러나 이것은 부정확한 기록이다. 뒤의 "하나님의 뜻" 에 동화된 기록이라고 본다. 여기서 "주" 는 바울의 사도권을 주신 예수 그리스도를 나타내야 한다(1:1; 고전 9:1, 2; 갈 1:1, 16). 더구나 뒤에 나와 있는 "하나님의 뜻" 이란 어구를 1장 1절의 "하나님의 뜻으로 말미암아 그리스도 예수의 사도된 바울" 이란 말에 비추어 볼 때, "주" 는 그리스도를 나타내는 것이 마땅하다. 마게도냐 사람들은 바울 사도의 "주" 즉 그리스도에게 자신을 드렸다.

내용 개요:

바울은 8장 6절에서 고린도 교인들에게 헌금 요청을 하기 전에, 마게도냐 교인들의 풍성한 헌금의 예를 들어서 헌금 촉구를 위한 예비적 진술을 하고 있다. 마게도냐 교인들이 많은 시련 가운데서, 그리고 극한 가난 중에서도 많은 헌금을 하였다면, 고린도 교인들도 같은 열의를 가지고 헌금을 하여야 할 것이라는 것이다. 위에서 지적하였듯이, 바울은 헌금을 구제와 경제적 도움으로 생각하지만, 동시에 신학적 목회적 의미도 숨어 있다고 본다. 바울은 헌금을 하나님의 이스라엘을 통한 이방인 구원 역사와 관련시켜 생각한다. 그래서 본문에, "은혜" (8:1, 4, 6), "참여함" =교제(8:4; 참조, 9:13), "섬기는 일" (8:4; 참조, 9:1, 13), "자신을 주께 드리고"

23) B. M. Metzger, *The Text of the New Testament*, 2nd ed. (New York: Oxford University Press, 1968), 194.

(8:5) 등 하나님과 인간관계를 나타내는 신학적이고 목회적인 말들이 나온다. 그러므로 알로(Allo)는 헌금을 가리켜 바울의 사역에 있어서 하나의 위대한 과업이라고 했고(204), 게오르기(Georgi)는 "바울신학의 예시적 모델"이라고 중요하게 평하였다.[24)]

주석:

8:1. "형제들아 하나님께서 마게도냐 교회들에게 주신 은혜를 우리가 너희에게 알게 하노니"(**Γνωρίζομεν δὲ ὑμῖν, ἀδελφοί, τὴν χάριν τοῦ θεοῦ τὴν δεδομένην ἐν ταῖς ἐκκλησίαις τῆς Μακεδονίας**). "하나님의 은혜"가 바울의 헌금을 위한 호소의 중심적 언어이다. 이 은혜는 9절의 "예수 그리스도의 은혜"를 가리킨다. "부요하신 자로서 너희를 위하여 가난하게 되심은 그의 가난함을 인하여 너희로 부요케 하려 하심이니라." 이런 고상한 은혜로 말미암아 마게도냐 사람들도 자신을 주께 드리고, 또 바울 사도 일행에게도 맡기면서 헌금을 했다(5절). 이런 행동은 그리스도께서 죄인을 위해 자신을 드리신 은혜의 능력으로 말미암은 것이다(갈 4:1).[25)] "은혜"라는 말에는 헌금의 신학적 근거는 그리스도의 구속의 은혜에 대한 보답이란 암시가 있다.

마게도냐는 북쪽 희랍지방이며(고린도는 희랍 남쪽 아가야 지방), 바울일행이 빌립보 옥에서 나와서 암비볼리와 아볼로니아와 데살로니가에 이르렀다는 사도행전 17장 1절의 기록에서 보듯이

---

24) Georgi, *Die Geschichte der Kollekte*, 79.

25) J. D. G. Dunn, *Jesus and the Spirit* (London: SCM Press/Philadelphia: Westminster, 1975) 202-4.

바울이 모두 거쳐서 전도한 곳이다. 바울이 빌립보서 4장 15절에서 말하듯이 이 지방에서의 바울의 사역은 매우 중요했다.

2. "환난의 많은 시련 가운데서 저희 넘치는 기쁨과 극한 가난이 저희로 풍성한 연보를 넘치도록 하게 하였느니라" (ὅτι ἐν πολλῇ δοκιμῇ θλίψεως ἡ περισσεία τῆς χαρᾶς αὐτῶν καὶ ἡ κατὰ βάθους πτωχεία αὐτῶν ἐπερίσσευσεν εἰς τὸ πλοῦτος τῆς ἁπλότητος αὐτῶν). 문법적으로 ὅτι(…라는 것, 사실)는 1절의 "알게 하노니" (Γνωρίζομεν)의 목적절(2절 전체)을 이끌고 있다. "…라는 사실" 을 "알게 하노니" 가 된다. 즉 마게도냐 사람들은 극심한 가난으로 인한 환난의 시련을 겪었다는 사실을 알린다. 그들이 겪은 환난은 주로 가난함과 관련된 것이라고 본다.[26] "넘치는 기쁨" 은 "환난의 많은 시련" 과 대조 되며, "풍성한 연보" 는 극한 가난과 대조 된다. "넘치는 기쁨" 은 하나님의 은혜로 말미암아 구원받은 기쁨이다(빌 4:4; 살전 1:6). 그 기쁨으로 말미암아 환난의 시련을 이기고 풍성한 연보를 하게 하였다. 또 역설적으로 가난함이 헌금을 넘치도록 하게 하였다. 이것은 그들의 가난한 형편에 비추어 상당히 많은 액수의 헌금을 하였다는 뜻이다. 문자적으로 "(그들의) 풍성한 연보" (τὸ πλοῦτος τῆς ἁπλότητος αὐτῶν)는 "그들의 관대함의 풍성함" 이란 말이나 실제적 헌금의 풍성함을 가리키는 말이다.[27] 물론 풍성한 헌금은 그리스도의 넘치는 은

26) Martin, 253.

27) "풍성함" (ἁπλότης)이란 말이 "순전함, 성실함" 이란 뜻도 되고(1:12; 11:3), "진정한 관심" 의 뜻도 되나(BAGD, 86), 물질적으로 넉넉하게 베푸는 뜻으로 번역되는 곳이 많다(9:11, 13; 롬 12:8; Barrett, 220).

혜와 희생으로 말미암아 "관대해지고 희생하는 마음"의 표시이다.[28]

3. "내가 증거하노니 저희가 힘대로 할 뿐 아니라 힘에 지나도록 자원하여"(ὅτι κατὰ δύναμιν, μαρτυρῶ, καὶ παρὰ δύναμιν, αὐθαίρετοι). 앞의 2절의 말이 의례적인 찬사의 말이 아니라 사실임을 밝힌다. 문법적으로 "내가 증거하노니"가 주동사이며, ὅτι가 이끄는 문장을 목적절로 하고 있다. 즉 "…을 내가 증거한다"는 뜻이다. 증거의 내용은 마게도냐 사람들이 그들의 경제적 능력을 능가하는 헌금을 스스로 했다는 것이다. "힘대로"(κατὰ δύναμιν)와 "힘에 지나도록"(παρὰ δύναμιν)이 같은 말을 점증적으로 강화시키고 있다. "힘대로"는 문자적으로 "힘의 한계"에 이르기까지이므로 한글개역보다 그 의미가 실제로는 더 강하다. 마지막 말, "자원하여"(αὐθαίρετοι)는 8장 17절에도 나오는 말로서, 외압이나 강제성이 없는 자발적인 헌금이라는 뜻이다. 헤링은 바울이 실제로 헌금을 거두라고 요청하였을 것임으로 "자원하였다"는 말은 적절치 않다고 한다.[29] 그러나 바울이 실제로 요청하였다 하더라도 그 요청을 기꺼이 받아들여서 헌금에 적극적으로 참여한 것을 가리키는 말이라고 본다. 4절에서 이런 의미가 나타나고 있다.

4. "이 은혜와 성도 섬기는 일에 참여함에 대하여 우리에게 간

28) Martin, 253.

29) Héring, 59.

절히 구하니"(μετὰ πολλῆς παρακλήσεως δεόμενοι ἡμῶν τὴν χάριν καὶ τὴν κοινωνίαν τῆς διακονίας τῆς εἰς τοὺς ἁγίους).

마게도냐 사람들은 바울에게 헌금하기를 스스로 "간청하였다"(δεόμενοι).[30] "은혜", "섬기는 일(봉사)", "참여함"은 모두 헌금과 관계된 말들이다. "은혜"(χάριν)는 하나님의 은혜를 본받아 행하는 인간의 은혜로운 행위를 가리킨다(8:1). 헌금은 하나님이 베푸신 은혜(선물)에 따라 인간이 보이는 반응(선물)이므로 역시 은혜라고 말 할 수 있는 것이다. "섬기는 일"(διακονίας)은 가난한 예루살렘 성도들을 돕는 것을 가리킨다(롬 15:25, 26; 고전 16:1, 2; 고후 9:12). "참여함"(코이노니아, κοινωνία)은 여기서 사람들과의 친교만이 아니라, 친교를 가능하게 하고 원활하게 하는 어떤 구체적인 사업에 참여함을 가리킨다.[31] 물론 여기서 그 목적이란 헌금을 가리킨다. 이와 같이 바울은 헌금을 "은혜"라는 말로 표현하면서, 구속론적 의미와 관련시켜서, 헌금이 남에게 베푸는 선물이지만, 그 근본적 의미는 주님의 구속의 은혜에 대한 보답이란 뜻을 암시하고 있다. 한편 여기서 바울은 고린도 교회 반대자들이 자신이 헌금을 유용한다는 의구심을 갖고 있다는 것을 알고서(7:2; 12:16-18), 의도적으로 "은혜와 성도 섬기는 일"이란 말로 헌금의 성격과 목적을 분명히 명시하고 있다고 볼 수도 있다.

---

30) 여기서 δεόμενοι("간청하다")는 분사형이나 직설법으로 주동사의 역할을 하고 있다. 보라. C. F. D. Moule, "Peculiarities in the Language of II Corinthians," in *Essays in New Testament Interpretation* (Cambridge: University Presss, 1982), 1581-61.

31) Martin, 254; A. R. George, *Communion with God in the New Testament* (London: Epworth Press, 1953); J. M. McDermott, "The Biblical Doctrine of KOINONIA," *BZ* 19(1975) 64-77.

5. "우리의 바라던 것 뿐 아니라 저희가 먼저 자신을 주께 드리고 또 하나님의 뜻을 좇아 우리에게 주었도다"(καὶ οὐ καθὼς ἠλπίσαμεν ἀλλὰ ἑαυτοὺς ἔδωκαν πρῶτον τῷ κυρίῳ καὶ ἡμῖν διὰ θελήματος θεοῦ). 마게도냐 그리스도인들은 헌금만을 드렸을 뿐만이 아니라 자신들을 주님과 바울에게 드렸다. 이런 헌신의 자세는 온전한 헌금의 전제조건이다. 그들을 주님에게 드렸다는 것은 하나님의 구속의 은혜에 감사하여 하나님에게 그들의 존재를 완전히 의탁하고 그의 뜻에 완전히 순종하는 것을 가리킨다. 어쩌면 여기에 성전에서 희생제물을 드리는 사람이 자신의 제물에 안수함으로 결국 자신을 드리는 의미가 암시되어 있는지도 모른다(레 1:4). 바울은 아래 9장 12절에서 헌금을 "봉사의 직무"라고 말하는데, "봉사"(λειτουργία)라는 말은 헬라사회에서는 공직(公職)을 가리키고, 70인역에서 흔히 제사장이나 레위인들의 제사임무와 관련되어 사용된다. 그리고 같은 말이 빌립보서 2장 17, 30절에서 빌립보 교인들이 바울에게 주는 돈을 가리키는 말로 쓰였는데 제례적인 의미를 나타내고 있다. "만일 너희의 믿음의 제물과 봉사(λειτουργίᾳ)위에 내가 나를 관제로 드릴지라도…나는 …기뻐하리라." 또 로마서 15장 16절에서 바울은 그의 복음 사역을 가리켜 그 자신이 이방인의 제사장으로서 이방인을 제물로 하나님께 드리는 사역이라고 설명하고 있다.

이런 구약의 희생제사 배경에 비추어 보는 헌금의 봉사적 의미 이외에, 마게도냐 교인들이 "먼저 자신을 주께 드렸다"는 말은 보다 복음적인 헌금의 의미를 제시하고 있다. 헌금이란 우리를 구원하시기 위해 아들을 아끼지 않으신 하나님의 사랑과 은혜에 감사의 응답도 되지만, 죄인들을 위해 희생하신 그리스도의 모본을 따라서 구원받은 죄인들이 스스로를 가난하게 만들고 약하게 만드는 행위이다(8:9). 약한 가운데서 강하게 하시는 하나님 앞에 재물에 대한 믿음을 포기하고 우리 자신을 온전히 능력의 하나님께 우리 자신을 의탁하는 것이다(12:9). 이런 의미에서 헌금은 다름 아닌 주님께 우리를 헌신하는 것이다. 주님께만 충성하고 그분에게만 온전한 축복과 권능이 있음을 확신하며 그분 앞에서 우리 자신의 소유와 재물의 힘을 불신하고 포기하고 우리 스스로를 약하게 만들어 온전히 주님께 의탁하는 상징적이며 실제적인 신앙행위인 것이다. 우리를 위해 가난하게 되신 주님 앞에서 우리 스스로 가난하게 되는 것이다(8:9). 그렇게 할 때 주님은 우리를 부요케 하시는 것이다. 우리를 주안에서 영육 간에 진정한 의미에서 부요케 하시는 것이다(9:8: "하나님이 능히 모든 은혜를 너희에게 넘치게 하시나니…"). 이렇게 헌금에도 바울의 약함의 신학이 자리 잡고 있는 것이다. 이 헌금을 "우리"(바울)에게 주었다는 것은 바울이 그리스도의 진정한 사도로서 그리스도의 약함의 능력을 가르치고 몸소 경험하는 분으로서 그를 신뢰하고, 또한 약한 예루살렘 성도들을 돕기 위해서 그가 주도하는 헌금 사역을 후원한다는 뜻이다. 다른 말로, 마게도냐 교인들은 바울을 하나님의 일꾼으로 신뢰하고 있다는 것이다. 바울은 고린도 교인들이 이런 마게도냐 교인들의 믿음을 따라서 하나님을 믿고 자신을 신뢰하기를 원하는 것이다. 여기서 마게도냐 교인들이 헌금을 "우리"에게 주었다는 바울의 표현은 바울이 헌금을 직접 거두지 않고, 디도와 다른 형제 등 그의 동역자들을 통해서 거둔 사실을 그대로 나타내는 표현이라고도 볼 수 있다(8:16, 18, 22-24; 9:3, 5). 한편, 어쩌면, 현재 고린도 교회에서 바울이 헌금을 유용하고 있다는 의구심이 있음을 바울이 알고서(12:16-18), 자신에게 주었다는 표현 대신에 의도적으로 "우리"라는 복수형을 써서 헌금 관리의 투명성을 제고(提高)하는 것이라고 볼 수도 있다.

여기서 마게도냐 교인들이 자신들을 바울에게 주었다는 것과 하나님께 드렸다는 것이 함께 관련되어 언급되었다. 바울은 마게도냐 교인들의 헌금의 동기는 하나님에 대한 믿음과 함께 바울 자신에 대한 신뢰였음을 말하면서 이것을 고린도 교인들에게 하나의 모범적인 사례로 제시하여 고린도 교인들도 이와 같이 바울에 대한 신뢰 회복의 증거(헌금)를 제시하도록 촉구하는 것이다(8:8, 24). 마게도냐 교인들의 헌금의 동기는 몇 가지로 정리해볼 수 있다.

첫째, 마게도냐 교인들은 그리스도를 통해 나타난 하나님의 구속의 은혜에 감사하고, 그리스도안에서 새로운 존재로 하나님께 헌신하는 자세로 헌금을 드렸다.

둘째, 마게도냐 교인들은 바울이 하나님이 택하신 예수 그리스도의 사도임을 믿었다(1:1, 고전 9:1, 2; 갈 1:1, 16). 그는 하나님의 사신이다(5:18, 20). 바울에게는 예수 그리스도의 권세가 있다. 그의 사역의 궁극적인 목적은 각 교회에서 그리스도의 왕권을 확립하는 일이다(4:5; 10:5-6, 8; 13:10). 마게도냐 교인들은 바울을 일종의 하나님의 제사장으로 알고 있었을 것이다. 그러므로 그들은 자신을 하나님께 드리고, 또 하나님의 제사장 바울에게 주고, 그에게 순종하며 따랐다. 앞에서도 보았듯이 고린도 교인들이 바울의 가르침과 그에게 복종하는 것은 곧 그리스도의 가르침과 그에게 복종하는 것이다(4:6; 5:14, 19, 20). 바울에게 있는 그리스도의 권세는 바울이나 그리스도의 유익을 위한 권세가 아니라, 그들의 권세에 복종하는 이들의 유익을 위한 것이다(4:10-12). 마게도냐인들은 실제로 그 헌금을 거두어 바울에게 주었을 것이다. 그러나 여기서는 그들이 먼저 자신들을 바울에게 바친 것을 말하고 있다. 마게도냐 교인들의 헌금의 동기는 바울이 전한 예수 그리스도의 은혜의 복음에 대한 보답과 사도 바울의 사역 가운데 그리스도가 함께 한다는 확신이었다.

셋째, 바울에 대한 사랑의 동기도 있다(7). 고린도 교회에서 바울의 사도직의 신빙성 문제가 논의되었던 만큼, 마게도냐 교인들의 바울의 사도직에 대한 인정과 신뢰는 바울에게 소중한 것이었다. 바울은 여기서 그들의 분에 넘치는 헌금이 바로 그들의 바울에 대한 충성과 사랑의 증기임을 암시하면서 고린도 교인들에게도 같은 증거를 보이기를 바라고 있다(8:8, 24; 9:13).

6. "이러므로 우리가 디도를 권하여 너희 가운데서 시작하였은즉 이 은혜를 그대로 성취케 하라 하였노라" (εἰς τὸ παρακαλέσαι ἡμᾶς Τίτον, ἵνα καθὼς προενήρξατο οὕτως καὶ ἐπιτελέσῃ εἰς ὑμᾶς καὶ τὴν χάριν ταύτην). 마게도냐 교인들이 예루살렘 교인들을 위한 헌금에 적극적으로 참여한 사례를 들면서 바울은 디도에게 1년 전에 부탁했던 고린도에서의 헌금 사역을 이제 완수하도록 명하였다고 하면서 고린도 교인들의 협조를 당부한다(8:1; 9:2). 그러나 여기서 바울이 καί(역시)로 어떤 의미를 나타내는지 분명하지 않다. 디도에게 하는 말로 처음에 헌금을 시작한 것 "같이" 이제는 마치라는 뜻으로 쓰였거나(본문, 한글개역), 아니면 고린도 교인들에게 하는 말로서 그들이 지난번에 디도를 잘 대해주고 바울의 명령에 따른 것"같이"(처럼) 이제 헌금 계획을 완수하라는 부탁을 받고 다시 가는 디도를 잘 영접하

고 작정한 헌금을 내기를 바란다는 뜻일 수도 있다.[32] 어느 쪽이든 상관없고 전체 의미에 영향을 미치지 않는다. 위의 4절에서와 같이 여기서도 헌금을 "은혜"로 표현하고 있다. 주 안에 있는 사람들은 모든 것을 하나님의 은혜로 설명할 수 있다. 헌금을 내는 사람들이나 헌금을 거두는 바울이나 하나님의 은혜를 받은 사람들이다. 특히 바울이나 그의 동역자들에게는 헌금 사역도 그리스도를 통한 하나님의 은혜의 사역의 일부인 것이다(8:9).

주해(8:1-6):

마게도냐 교인들이 극심한 가난함 중에서 오히려 넘치는 헌금을 하였다는 것은 매우 감동적인 일이다. 아마 고린도 교인들이 이 소식을 듣고 분발하여 헌금에 참여하였을 것이다(롬15:31).[33] 오늘날 우리는 헌금은 "여유가 있을 때"나 "은혜를 받았을 때" 뿐만이 아니라 늘 감사하는 마음으로 항상 꾸준히 드려야 한다. 헌금은 액수보다 우리의 믿음의 분량을 나타내는 중요한 표시와 척도로서 하나님께 드려야한다. 믿는 자 자신을 하나님의 것으로 인정하고 맡기는 구체적 행위이다. 돈과 물질에 의존하는 존재가 아니라 하나님께 의존하는 존재임을 증거하는 신앙 행위이다(마 6:24). 그러므로 마게도냐인들이 "먼저 자신을 주께 드렸다"(5)는 것은 습관적으로 하거나 남이 하니 어쩔 수 없이 억지로 한 것이

32) Martin, 255; Thrall, 528.

33) 바울은 로마서를 고린도후서를 보내고 나서 3차 고린도 교회 방문 중 썼다. 롬 15:31은 고린도 교회가 헌금 사역에 제대로 협조하여서 바울이 고린도에 있을 때 예루살렘 성도들에게 헌금을 전달할 수 있게 되었음을 보여준다.

아니라 헌금의 참된 자세를 가지고 헌금하였다는 것을 말한다. 또한 헌금은 원래의 주인이신 하나님께 되돌려드리는 행위로서 하나님을 우리의 진정한 주님으로 인정하고 섬기는 구체적 신앙적 행위이다. 그러므로 있는 자나 없는 자나 액수에 상관하지 말고 각자의 진정한 믿음의 분량에 따라서 헌금해야 할 것이다. 그러므로 예수님도 가난한 과부의 작은 헌금을 부자의 많은 헌금보다 귀중한 것으로 여기셨다(막 12:42-44; 눅 21:2-4). 진정한 믿음이 없으면 아무리 많은 헌금을 한다 해도 그것은 참된 헌금이 되지 못한다. 주님은 "네 보물이 있는 그곳에는 네 마음도 있느니라"고 말씀하셨다(마 6:21). 사람이 돈을 귀중하게 생각하는 것만큼 그 돈을 어디다가 쓰는가에 따라서 그 사람의 궁극적인 가치나 관심의 향방을 알 수 있는 것이다. 하나님의 사업을 위해 헌금을 하는 사람은 그의 관심이 하나님의 나라라는 것이 실제로 증명된다(마 6:33). 정말로 생계조차 어려워 헌금을 전혀 할 수 없을 때도 있으나, 진정한 그리스도인은 하나님 나라 사업을 위해 할 수 있는 대로 헌금해야 한다.

어떤 이들은 구약 시대에는 십일조가 곧 세금이었음으로 반드시 내야했으나, 지금은 따로 세금을 내고 있음으로 십일조를 그대로 할 필요가 없다고 말한다. 구약 이스라엘 백성에게 부과한 십일조는 제정일치의 사회조직에서 국가적이고 종교적인 목적에 함께 쓰일 수밖에 없었을 것이다. 그러나 국가를 위한 세금도 따로 내야 했다(왕상 12:4; 대하 10:4).[34] 예수님 당시 유대인들은 로마

34) Raymond B. Dillard, *2 Chronicles* (Waco, TX.: Word Book, Publishers, 1987), 86. 대하 10:4에서 "멍에"는 중과세를 가리킨다고 한다.

에 바치는 세금도 내면서 십일조도 내었다. 예수님도 이를 인정했다(막 12:14-17; 마 22:17-21; 눅 20:22-25; 마 23:23). 이 세상 시민으로서의 세금의 의무도 해야 하나, 하나님 나라 시민으로서 하나님이 친히 정하신 세금의 의무(십일조)를 이행하는 것이 당연한 것이다. 이 세상의 세금은 내면서 하나님 나라를 위한 헌금을 이런 저런 이유로 아낀다면 하나님 나라의 시민의 자격이 없다. 그리고서 어떻게 하나님 나라의 성장을 바랄 수 있는가? 헌금을 세금으로 감면 받는 문제와 상관없이 십일조를 해야 한다. 설령 높은 세금도 내면서 십일조를 내는 것이 경제적으로 어렵게 만든다 해도 그 어려움조차 천국 시민으로서 현재 누리는 특권과 장차 누릴 영광을 생각하고 극복해야 한다. 그러나 실제로 믿는 사람들은 불신자들이 세상적 목적에 쓰는 돈을 쓰지 않고 절약할 수 있으므로 십일조 헌금을 한다고 해도 크게 경제적으로 지장받는다고 생각되지 않는다. 막스 베버(Max Weber)는 그의 "개신교 윤리와 자본주의 정신" 이란 책에서 검약한 서양 개신교인들의 생활 방식으로 말미암아 낭비가 줄어들어 오히려 자본이 축적되고 그 결과 근대 자본주의가 형성되었다고 한다.[35] 우리는 이 세상에 살면서 이 세상 나라의 시민으로서 국가가 요구하는 세금을 내야 한다. 그러나 동시에 하나님 나라의 시민으로서 "하나님이 정하신 하나님 나라의 정한 세금" (십일조)을 드려야 한다. 그래야 이 땅위에 하나님의 나라가 실제적으로 계속 확장될 것이다. 그렇게 하지 않으면 하나님 나라는 외적으로는 물론 영적으로도 위축될 것이 확실하다. 구

35) Max Weber, *The Protestant Ethic and the Spirit of Capitalism* (London: Unwin Papberbacks, 1985).

약이나 신약 시대의 사람들도 이런 "이중적 과세"의 부담을 안고 살았으나, 진실한 하나님의 백성들은 계속 십일조를 드렸다. 우리 신실한 그리스도인들은 마게도냐 교인들이 "힘에 지나도록 자원하여" 헌금에 적극 참여한 것을 본받아서 세금과 관계없이 십일조는 물론 모든 헌금에 적극 참여하여야 한다.

이 부분에서 특별히 중요한 부분은 5절에서 마게도야 교인들이 먼저 자신을 주께 드렸다는 말이다. 헌금은 하나님의 구원의 은혜에 대한 보답이다. 그러나 동시에 그리스도의 희생의 모본을 따라서 우리를 위해 죽으신 그리스도 앞에서 자신과 재물의 힘을 포기하고 하나님만 전적으로 신뢰하고 그에게 나의 존재를 의탁하는 거룩한 행위인 것이다. 여기에서도 바울의 약함의 신학이 나타나는 것이다(8:9; 12:9). 또한 그 물질을 바울에게 의탁한 것은 바울이 진정한 사도로서 하나님의 의로운 일, 즉 가난한 예루살렘 성도들을 돕는 일을 하는 것을 인정하고 함께 돕는다는 뜻이다. 바울은 이런 마게도냐 교인들의 바른 헌금 자세를 소개하면서 고린도인들도 그와 같이 바른 믿음을 갖고 자신을 지지할 것을 암시하는 것이다.

B. 바울의 헌금 호소 (8:7-15)

본문:

> 7. 오직 너희는 믿음과 말과 지식과 모든 간절함과 우리에게서 나와 너희에게 거하는 사랑 등 (우리를 사랑하는)이 모든 일에 풍성한 것같이 이 은혜에도 풍성하게 할지니라. 8. 내가 명령으로 하는 말이 아니요, 오직 다른 이들의 간절함을 가지고 너희의 사랑의 진실함을 증명코자 함이로라. 9. 우리 주 예수 그리스도의 은혜를 너희가 알거니와 부요하신 자로

> 서 너희를 위하여 가난하게 되심은 그의 가난함을 인하여 너희로 부요케 하려 하심이니라. 10. 이 일에 내가 뜻만 보이노니 이것은 너희에게 유익함이라. 너희가 일 년 전에 행하기를 먼저 시작할 뿐 아니라 원하기도 하였은즉 11. 이제는 행하기를 성취할지니 마음에 원하던 것과 같이 성취하되 있는 대로하라. 12. 할 마음만 있으면 있는대로 받으실 터이요 없는 것을 받지 아니하시리라. 13. 이는 다른 사람들은 평안하게 하고 너희는 곤고하게 하려는 것이 아니요 평균케 하려 함이니 14. 이제 너희의 유여한 것으로 저희 부족한 것을 보충함은 후에 저희 유여한 것으로 너희 부족한 것을 보충하여 평균하게 하려 함이라. 15. 기록한 것같이 많이 거둔 자도 남지 아니하였고 적게 거둔 자도 모자라지 아니하였느니라.

본문 비평:

1. 7절에서 ἐξ ἡμῶν ἐν ὑμῖν ἀγάπῃ(“우리를 사랑하는=너희에게서 나와서 우리에게 거하는 사랑”)이 ℵ C D F G ψ TR lat syr에 나타나고, ἐξ ὑμῶν ἐν ἡμῖν ἀγάπῃ(“우리에게서 나와서 너희에게 거하는 사랑”)이 p46 B copsa bo와 어떤 교부들의 기록에서 나타난다. 개역한글성경, NIV, RSV, GNB 등이 전자를 따른다. 마틴은 후자가 더 어려운 표현으로서 원래의 것이며 전자는 수정된 것이라고 본다.[36)]

2. 10절에서 προενήρξασθε(“너희가 먼저 시작하였다”)가 ℵ B C K L P에 나오고 더 부드러운 표현인 ἐνήρξασθε(“너희가 행하였다”)는 D F G에 나온다.

3. 13절의 θλῖψις(“곤고함”)를 끝으로 보고 그 다음에 오는 ἀλλ᾽ ἐξ ἰσότητος(“평균케 하려 함이니”)를 14절에 부쳐서 해석할 수

---

36) Martin, 260.

도 있다.[37] 그러나 이 경우 14절 뒤에 비슷한 말이 다시 나오므로 (ὅπως γένηται ἰσότης, "평균하게 하려 함이라"), 중복되어 어색하다.[38] 또 이 문장이 앞의 두 개의 짧은 문장과 함께 리듬을 이루고 있으므로 13절에 그대로 두는 것이 좋다: οὐ γὰρ ἵνα ἄλλοις ἄνεσις(1), ὑμῖν θλῖψις(2), ἀλλ' ἐξ ἰσότητος(3).[39]

내용 개요:

본문에서 바울은 헌금을 요청하되 매우 조심스럽게 강제로 명령하는 것을 피하고(8), 고린도 교인들이 자발적으로 참여 하기를 원한다. 그러므로 바울은 처음 헌금을 시작했을 때 그들이 자발적으로 참여했음을 상기시킨다(10). 또한 마게도냐 교인들이 분에 넘치도록 헌금하였다는 말(3)이 고린도 교인들에게 부담이 될 수 있음을 감지하면서, 지나치게 하지 말고 각자가 가지고 있는 대로 할 것을 권한다(12). 무엇보다 바울은 그의 "헌금 신학"을 제시한다. 그리스도께서 우리를 부요케 하려 하시기 위해서 약하게 되신 은혜에 감사로 보답하는 반면에, 그의 모본을 따라서 우리 자신을 하나님께 헌신하는 의미가 있는 것이다.

또한 본문에서는 헌금의 두 가지 신학적 근거를 제시하면서 헌금을 독려한다.

첫째, 이 헌금이 가난한 예루살렘 성도들을 위한 이방인들의 구제헌금이라는 점을 감안하고, 바울은 보다 일반적인 하나님의 긍

37) Plummer, 244; Allo, 220; Barrett, 226.

38) Windisch, 257; Martin, 259; Furnish, 399, 407; Betz, *2 Corinthians 8-9*, 37; Thrall, 539, 주, 229.

39) Thrall, 539, 주, 229.

휼하심의 원칙을 말하는 대신, 하나님의 평등의 원칙 또는 상호 호혜의 원칙을 제시한다(13-15). 이방인들은 이스라엘에게 영적 빚을 지었으므로 곤궁한 유대인들을 돕는 것은 당연하다(롬 15:30-31). 이스라엘은 이방인을 영적으로 구원하였고, 이방인은 이스라엘을 육적으로 구원하였다. 그러므로 이방인이 이스라엘의 빈궁함을 돕는다고 자랑할 것도 없고, 반대로 도움을 받는 예루살렘 성도들은 열등감을 가질 필요도 없다. 다만 하나님의 "평균케 하시는 경륜"을 따라서 서로 돕는 것으로 생각하면 부담감이 없다. 대신 9장 후반부에서 헌금을 받은 예루살렘 성도들이 하나님께 감사하고 영광돌린다(9:11, 12, 13)는 말을 한다. 이 말은 헌금을 드리는 고린도인들에게 감사하지 않는다는 뜻이 아니라 원수되었던 이방인들을 구원하여 그들을 통해서 경제적으로 어려운 이스라엘 백성을 구원하시는 하나님의 놀라운 섭리에 감사하고 영광을 돌린다는 뜻이다(롬 15:30-31).

둘째, 또 하나의 근본적인 그리스도인의 헌금의 근거는 인간 구원을 위해 그의 부요함을 버리고 가난하게 되신 그리스도의 모본이다(9). 구원받은 사람은 그리스도로 말미암아 영적으로 부요해 진 사람이다. 이 부요한 사람이, 그가 받은 영적 부요함, 즉 구원의 은혜를 감사하며 그를 구원하신 하나님께, 그의 복음 사역에, 즉 영적으로 가난한 사람을 부요케 하는 사역에, 물질적으로 보답하는 것은 당연하다. 특히 고린도후서에서 약함의 능력을 강조하는 바울은 헌금에 있어서도 그리스도께서 우리를 위해서 약하게 죽으심을 헌금의 근거로 삼아서 설명하고 있다. 헌금은 우리를 위해 죽으신 그리스도에게 우리를 헌신하는 것이다. 우리를 위해 약하게 되신 그리스도에게 우리 자신의 일부인 재정 능력(물질)을 드림으로써 우리 자신을 약하게 만드는 것이다. 헌금을 드린다는 것 자체가 우리 자신을 약하게 만드는 것이다. 우리의 것을 드림으로 우리는 우선 재정적으로 약해진다. 그러나 헌금을 드리면서 우리는 재물의 힘에 우리 자신을 맡기지 않고 하나님의 능력의 손에 우리를 맡기는 믿음을 증거하고 강화시키는 것이다. 그리고 약한 가운데 강하게 해주시는 주님께서 헌금으로 우리를 약하게 만드는 우리를 또한 은혜로 채워주심을 믿는 것이다(9:8; 12:9).

이런 확고한 "헌금의 신학" 이 있더라도, 여전히 헌금은 연약한 인간으로서 시험받기 쉬운 부분이므로 바울은 매우 조심스럽게 헌금을 독려하고 있다.

이런 구제 헌금이 사도직 변명과 무슨 관계가 있는가? 바울은 다수의 고린도 교인들이 다시 바울에게 돌아와 바울을 그들의 사도로 영접 하게 된 것을 알고 예루살렘 사도들과의 약속인 예루살렘 성도들을 위한 헌금 사업을 계속하기를 원했다(참조, 갈 2:10). 고린도 교인들이 이제 바울에게 돌아와서 그를 진정 그들의 사도로 따른다면, 헌금동참으로 그 증거를 보여 달라고 간청하는 것이다(8:8, 24). 물론 헌금 문제를 논할 적절한 시기는 아니라 해도 예루살렘 방문을 앞두고 있는 바울에게 약속한 구제 헌금을 가지고 가야하는 책임을 느끼고 있었던 것이다. 방금 화해한 고린도 교인들에게 돈 문제를 거론하는 것 자체가 어려운 일이므로 바울은 매우 조심스럽게 말하며, 자의적으로 할 것을 강조하는 것이다. 또한 이 헌금이 소기의 목적을 위해서 잘 쓰일 것임을 바울이 보내는 디도와 형제들의 높은 신임도에 대한 찬사의 말 가운데 암시하고 있다.

주 석:

7. "오직 너희는 믿음과 말과 지식과 모든 간절함과 우리에게서 나와 너희에게 거하는 사랑 등(우리를 사랑하는) 이 모든 일에 풍성한 것같이 이 은혜에도 풍성하게 할지니라"(Ἀλλ᾽ ὥσπερ ἐν παντὶ περισσεύετε, πίστει καὶ λόγῳ καὶ γνώσει καὶ πάσῃ σπουδῇ καὶ τῇ ἐξ ἡμῶν ἐν ὑμῖν ἀγάπῃ, ἵνα καὶ ἐν ταύτῃ τῇ χάριτι περισσεύητε). 6절에서의 "은혜"를 7절에서는 "이 은혜"라고 강조적으로 언급하면서 더 분명하게 "헌금의 당위성"을 가리킨다. 고린도 교인들은 원래 풍성한 성령의 은사를 받았다(고전 12:4 이하). 더구나 디도의 방문 이후 회개하고 변화되었다. 그렇다면 이제 풍성한 헌금으로 그 풍성한 은사에 보답해야 하고, 또 은혜로 말미암은 그들의 변화의 진정성을 증거 해야 할 것이다. 바울은 먼저 고린도 교인들의 은혜와 변화, 또는 적극적 반응들을 차례대로 쓰고 있다. "믿음"은 "기적을 일으키는 믿음"이거나(고전 13:2), 일반적인 믿음을 가리킨다고 본다.[40] "말"은 예언이나 방언 은사를 가리킬 수도 있다(고전 13:1, 2).[41] 지식은 무엇보다 그리스도를 통한 하나님의 구원 역사에 대한 지식이다(고전 1:4-5; 빌 3:8). "간절함"(σπουδῇ)은 7장 11절에도 나온 고린도 교인들의 변화된 모습이다. "사랑"의 은사는 위에서 지적한 바와 같이 사본상의 차이가 있다. 즉 "너희에게서 나와 우리에게 거하는 사랑"

40) Thrall, 529.

41) Barrett, *First Corinthians*, 37.

(ἐξ ὑμῶν ἐν ἡμῖν ἀγάπῃ)이거나 "우리에게서 나와 너희에게 거하는 사랑"(ἐξ ἡμῶν ἐν ὑμῖν ἀγάπῃ)이다. 가까운 문맥으로는 고린도 교인들의 은사를 나열하고 있으므로 "너희의 사랑"이라고 볼 수 있으나, 넓은 문맥으로는 "우리의 사랑"이 옳다. 바울은 고린도후서 전체에서 그리스도의 희생적 사랑의 유형을 따른 모범적 사랑으로 고린도 교인들을 위해 사역하였음을 증명하려고 애쓰면서, 또 그들에게 자신의 진실한 사랑에 대해 같은 진실한 사랑의 반응을 보이도록 설득하고 있기 때문이다(1:23; 4:10-12; 5:14-15; 7:3; 6:4-10; 11:11; 12:15). 바울은 7장 1절에서 고린도 교인들을 "사랑하는 자들아"(ἀγαπητοί)라고 부르고 있다. 바울의 사랑의 선도적인 성격은 무엇보다 12장 15절에서 가장 잘 나타난다: "내가 너희 영혼을 위하여 크게 기뻐함으로 재물을 허비하고 또 내 자신까지 허비하리니 너희를 더욱 사랑할수록 나는 덜 사랑을 받겠느냐?" 고린도 교인들에게 사랑의 은사가 있다면 그것은 바울에게서 나온 것이다. 그리고 그 사랑은 "그리스도의 강권하는 사랑"과 희생적인 사랑에서 나온 것이다(5:14, 15). 그러므로 "우리에게서 나와서 너희에게 거하는 사랑"이란 말이 옳다고 본다. 바울이 고린도후서 전체에서 고린도 교인들에게 이런 진실한 사랑을 가지고 있음을 증명하는 것이 중요한 목적이라고 위에서 논했다. 여기서 바울은 자신의 진실한 사랑에 대한 보답을 헌금으로 나타내기를 권면하고 있다(8, 24; 참조, 11:11).

이 모든 은사에 풍성한 것같이 헌금에 있어서도 풍성해야 할 것이다. 여기서 특기할 것은 바울이 성령의 은사나 헌금을 모두 "은혜"(선물, χάρις)라는 같은 말로 부르는 것이다. 성령의 은사가 하나님의 선물인 것처럼, 헌금은 내 것이 아니라 하나님에게서 받은 선물이다.[42] 원칙적으로 헌금은 내 것을 드리는 것이 아니라 헌금을 내게 주신 원주인은 하나님이시며, 그 하나님에게 받은 것을 되돌려 드림으로써 하나님을 우리의 진정한 주님으로 고백하고 증거하는 신앙행위이다.

"이 은혜에도 풍성하게 할지니라"는 ἵνα("…이 되도록", "…을 위해서")가 이끄는 결과절(또는 목적절)로 되어 있는데, 퍼니쉬와 마틴은 이 절을 명령적 의미를 가지는 것으로 본다.[43] 한글개역도 명령적 의미가 있다. 그러나 버브루그(Verbrugge)는 1세기 사용에서 ἵνα가 이끄는 절은 명령적 의미가 거의 없으며 단순히 바람을 나타내는 의미라고 한다.[44] 8절에서 바울이 분명히 명령이 아니라고 부인하고 있으므로 이런 주장이 인정될 수도 있다. 그러나 바울의 일관된 의도는 고린도 교인들로 하여금 헌금을 하도록 만드는 것이므로 명령적인 의미가 있다고 보는 것이 옳다. 8절에서 바울이 "명령하는 것이 아니라"고 이내 부인하지만 이것은 이제 겨우 돌아온 고린도 교인들에게 민감한 돈 이야기를 하여 시험받지 않게 하려고 주의하려는 것이다. 공평하게 말한다면, 바울은 고린도 교인들의 감정을 고려하여 직접적인 명령은 피하고 간접적인 명령을 하고 있다고 본다.

8. "내가 명령으로 하는 말이 아니요, 오직 다른 이들의 간절함

---

42) Barrett, 216, 222.

43) Furnish, 403; Martin, 262; Windisch, 257; Martin, 259; Furnish, 399, 407; Betz, *2 Corinthians 8 and 9*, 37; Thrall, 539, 주, 229.

44) V. D. Verbrugge, *Paul's Style of Church Leadership Illustrated by his Instructions to the Corinthians on the Collection: To Command or not to Command* (San Francisco: Mellen Research University Press/Lewiston, NY.: Edwin Mellen Press, 1992), 251.

을 가지고 너희의 사랑의 진실함을 증명코자 함이로라"(Οὐ κατ᾽ ἐπιταγὴν λέγω ἀλλὰ διὰ τῆς ἑτέρων σπουδῆς καὶ τὸ τῆς ὑμετέρας ἀγάπης γνήσιον δοκιμάζων). 8절에서 바울은 헌금 문제를 매우 조심하면서 언급한다. 자칫하면 바울은 헌금문제로 오해를 살 수 있음을 잘 알고 있다. 실제로 그를 반대하는 이들은 바울이 그들을 교묘하게 착취하였다고 비난했다(7:2; 12:16). 우리는 이런 비난을 어떤 이들이 생각하듯이 고린도 교인들이 8장의 헌금 요청을 하나의 독립된 편지로 받고 난 뒤에 일어난 것이라고 보지 않는다. 바울은 8장을 쓰면서 그런 비난을 이미 알고서 충분히 감지하고 있는 것으로 생각한다. 바울은 고린도 교인들을 완전히 신뢰하여 헌금을 요청하기에는 아직도 어려운 상대임을 감지하고 있기 때문에 거듭해서 조심스럽게 헌금 문제에 접근하고 있는 것이다(8:20-21). "다른 이들의 간절함"(τῆς ἑτέρων σπουδῆς)은 앞에서 말한 대로 마게도냐 교인들이 분에 넘치는 헌금으로 바울에 대한 그들의 사랑을 증명한 것을 가리킨다. 그러나 속격을 목적을 가리키는 속격으로 보아서 "다른 이들에 대한 간절함"으로 번역하여, 고린도 교인들의 예루살렘 성도들을 위한 간절함으로 해석하기도 한다.[45] 그러나 앞의 "내가 명령으로 하는 말이 아니요"라는 말에 비교하여 이 말을 생각하면, 역시 전자의 해석이 옳다. 명령이 아니라 고린도 교인들이 고린도와 같은 지역의 북쪽에 있는 마게도냐 교인들의 모범을 따르도록 설득한다는 뜻이다.[46] 바울은 이제 자기에게 돌아온 고린도 교인들에게도 그들의

45) Thrall, 532.

46) 참조, Hughes, 298-9.

바울에 대한 사랑을 헌금으로 증명하기를 원한다. 7절에서 고린도 교인들의 사랑이 바울의 희생적인 사랑에서 배운 것임을 말하였으므로, 바울의 헌금요청을 따라 헌금을 하는 것은 바울에 대한 그들의 사랑의 확실한 증명이 될 것이다(8:24). 바울은 고린도후서 전체에서 고린도 교인들을 향한 그의 진실한 사랑을 애써 증거하고 있고 이에 대해 고린도 교인들이 같은 사랑의 반응을 보이도록 권면하고 있다(1:23; 2:4; 4:10-12; 5:14-15; 7:3; 6:4-10; 11:11; 12:15). 앞에서 여러 차례 논하였듯이 바울의 고린도 교회에 대한 사랑은 바울이 고린도후서를 쓰게 된 내적 동기이다. 이 사랑이 그가 진실한 사도임을 증명하는 가장 중요한 증거이다. 이 사랑은 그리스도의 희생적 사랑에 근거한 것이다(5:14, 15). 그러므로 고린도 교인들의 헌금은 결국 주님께 대한 사랑의 증명이 된다. 바울은 주님의 사도로서 고린도 교인들의 사랑을 받으나 그 사랑은 결국 주님을 향한 사랑이다.[47]

바울이 여기서 자발적인 사랑을 헌금의 동기로 삼는 것은 헌금의 율법주의적이고 타성적인 동기를 예방하려는 뜻도 있다고 본다.[48] 그러나 그보다 바울은 이제 막 돌아온 고린도 교인들을 조

47) Barrett는 "사랑의 진실을 증명코자 함이라"는 말 가운데 고린도 교인들의 풍성한 헌금을 함으로써 그들이 실제로 바울에게 돌아 왔다는 확실한 증거를 보이라는 뜻이 있다고 한다(222). 7장에서 고린도 교인들이 회개하고 바울에게 다시 돌아옴을 기뻐한다고 말한 즉시 8장에서 헌금요청을 하고 있으므로 이런 의미가 암시되어 있다고 본다. 또 7절에서도 고린도 교인들의 바울에 대한 사랑을 말하고 있다. 그러나 바울은 자신의 유익에 개의치 않는다고 여러 번 공언하고 있다(4:10-13; 5:15; 12:15). 그러므로 바울은 그에게 돌아오는 것이 곧 주님께 돌아온 것이며, 그에 대한 사랑이 곧 주님께 대한 사랑이라고 믿는다.

48) Tasker, 114.

심히 다루며 사랑으로 설득하는 목회적 방법을 쓰고 있다고 볼 수 있다. 바울의 의도는 어떻게 해서든지 그들을 설득하여 헌금을 하도록 만드는 것이다. 바울은 온유한 자세를 취하여 자발적인 헌금을 종용하지만 반드시 헌금하도록 해야 한다는 생각을 견지하고 있다. 바울이 여기서 명령을 하지 않고 온유한 자세를 취하는 것은 헌금의 필요성에 대한 우유부단한 자세 때문이 아니라 아직도 믿음이 연약한 고린도 교인들을 설득하여 헌금하게 하는 가장 효과적인 방법이기 때문이다(고전 3:1; 고후 6:13; 12:14). 이런 자세를 이중적으로 남을 속이는 사람의 자세와 같이 보아서는 안 된다(7:2; 12:16). 위에서 말한 바와 같이 헌금 자체가 신앙적 행위이기 때문에 바울은 자기의 유익을 위함이 아니라 고린도 교인들의 신앙적 발전을 위해 헌금요청을 하고 있는 것이다(12:13 이하). 바울은 헌금과 관련하여 가능한 오해를 감지하고 있었다(7:2; 8:20-21). 실제로 바울을 비난하는 이들도 있었다(12:16). 그러므로 여기서의 바울의 온유한 화법은 주께로부터 직접적 계명을 받지 못했을 경우에 바울이 쓰던 "이 말은 권도요 명령이 아니니라"(고전 7:6; 25)는 말과는 구별 되어야 한다.[49]

9. "우리 주 예수 그리스도의 은혜를 너희가 알거니와 부요하신 자로서 너희를 위하여 가난하게 되심은 그의 가난함을 인하여 너희로 부요케 하려 하심이니라"(**γινώσκετε γὰρ τὴν χάριν τοῦ κυρίου ἡμῶν Ἰησοῦ Χριστοῦ, ὅτι δι' ὑμᾶς ἐπτώχευσεν**

49) H. -D. Betz, *2 Corinthians 8 and 9*, 59. Betz는 이런 유화적인 대화법이 당시 희랍사회에서 자선기금을 모으는 데 쓰인 것이라고 한다.

πλούσιος ὤν, ἵνα ὑμεῖς τῇ ἐκείνου πτωχείᾳ πλουτήσητε). 모든 그리스도인의 삶의 지침은 이 땅에 성육신하시고 죄인을 위해 죽으신 그리스도의 희생적 사랑에 근거하고 있다(빌 2:6). 헌금도 예외는 아니다. 그리스도를 통해 베푸신 하나님의 구원의 큰 사랑과 은혜에 보답하여 하나님께 드리는 것이다. 위에서 지적한 바와 같이 실제로 헌금은 내 것이 아니다. 내게 주신 하나님의 은혜를 은혜의 근원이신 주님에게 다시 돌려드리는 것일 뿐이다. 그래도 이런 행위는 우리의 하나님께 대한 진정한 사랑과 하나님의 구원에 대한 믿음을 증명하는 중요한 수단이 되는 것이다. 더구나 그리스도인들에게 있어서 가장 큰 하나님의 은혜는 그리스도를 통한 구원의 은혜이다. 그러므로 헌금을 하나님의 은혜에 보답한다는 일반적인 의미로만 생각할 것이 아니라 보다 분명하게 복음적으로 생각하여 아들을 아끼지 않으시고 희생 제물로 내어 주신 하나님의 구원의 은혜와 관련지어 생각하는 것이 마땅하다.

한편 이러한 구원의 감사에 대한 보답의 뜻도 있으나, 헌금의 다른 측면은 5절에서 마게도냐 교인들이 한 것과 같이 그리스도께 우리 자신을 드리는 것이다. 우리를 위해 헌신하신 모본을 따라서 우리를 헌신하는 것이다. 헌금은 우리를 위해 약하게 되신 사랑을 본받아 우리를 가난하고 약하게 만드는 행위인 것이다. 재물이 우리의 힘의 일부라는 것을 하나님 앞에서 부정하며, 하나님의 은혜의 손에 우리를 맡기는 것이다. 이렇게 바울의 약함의 신학이 헌금에도 나타나는 것이다.

"우리를 위하여 가난하게 되심"은 그리스도의 성육신의 의미(높은 하늘 보좌의 영광의 주께서 낮고 천한 인간의 몸을 입으시고 이 땅에 오심)를 우리의 구원의 절실한 상태와 또 헌금을 요청하는 정황에 비추어 선택한 표현이라고 본다.[50] 바울은 이런 그리스도의 성육신과 함께 구속론적 유형과 그 가운데 나타난 하나님의 구속의 은혜와 사랑이 고린도 교인들의 믿음을 일깨워서 풍성한 헌금을 할 수 있는 동기와 힘을 준다고 보았다. 바울은 영적인 부요와 물질적 부요는 통전적인 관계가 있다고 가정한다(갈 6:6; 고전 9:11; 롬 15:27). 복음서는 그리스도께서 실제로 가난하게 사셨음을 보여준다(마 8:20; 칼빈, 111). 바울은 여기서 그리스도의 지상 생애의 물질적 가난함이 그리스도인들에게는 영적 부요함이 되었다는 것도 생각한다고 볼 수 있다. 그러나 중심 사상은 그리스도의 성육신과 구속이 포함하는 영적이고 육체적인 총체적인 가난함을 의미한다고 보아야 한다. 특히 그의 고난과 죽으심이 "가난함" 의 중심 개념이다. 바레트는 그리스도의 "가난 함" 은 "십자가에서 완전히 벗으신 가난함" 으로서 그의 죽으심을 가리킨다고 했다.[51] 그가 죄인을 사랑하여 자신을 드려 하나님의 희생양이 되신 것이 "가난함" 의 중심적 개념이다. 그의 희생적 죽음으로 그를 믿는 자는 이 세상과 오는 세상에서 영적으로나 물질적으로나 "부요하게" 되었다. 그리스도는 그의 희생적 죽음으로 죄인에 대한 하나님의 지극하신 사랑과 은혜를 구체적인 행위로 나타내었다. 바울은 이 구체적인 사랑과 은혜에 대한 보답을 헌금이라는

---

50) Martin, 263-4; Thrall, 534; 참조, J. D. G. Dunn, *Christology in the Making: A New Testament Inquiry into the Origins of the Doctrine of Incarnation* (London: SCM Press, 1980), 121, 122. Dunn은 바울서신에서 "은혜" 란 말이 성육신과 관련하여 나타나지 않는다고 하면서 본문에서 "부요한 것" 은 그리스도와 하나님과의 영적 교제를 나타내며 "가난하게 되었다" 는 십자가에서 하나님이 버리신 것을 나타낸다고 한다. 그러나 넓은 의미에서 그리스도의 성육신 자체도 그리스도의 고난에 속한다고 볼 수 있다.

51) Barrett, 223.

구체적인 행위로 나타낼 것을 권면하는 것이다. 여기서 바울이 영적인 부요뿐만 아니라 물질적 부요를 언급하는 것은 바울이 말하는 믿는 자의 종말론적 영광은 육체적인 부활을 포함하는 구체적인 것이며(고전 15:13; 고후 5:4), 또 같은 문맥에서 바울이 풍성한 헌금과 함께 오는 하나님의 구체적인 물질적인 축복을 언급하고 있기 때문이다(9:8-12).

10. "이 일에 내가 뜻만 보이노니 이것은 너희에게 유익함이라. 너희가 일 년 전에 행하기를 먼저 시작할 뿐 아니라 원하기도 하였은즉"(**καὶ γνώμην ἐν τούτῳ δίδωμι· τοῦτο γὰρ ὑμῖν συμφέρει, οἵτινες οὐ μόνον τὸ ποιῆσαι ἀλλὰ καὶ τὸ θέλειν προενήρξασθε ἀπὸ πέρυσι**). 여전히 바울은 헌금을 강요하는 자세를 피하고 자발적으로 하도록 권하는 자세를 취한다. "이 일에 뜻만 보이노니"는 헌금에 대한 바울의 조심스런 권면을 나타내는 것이다. "이것은 너희에게 유익함이라"(**τοῦτο γὰρ ὑμῖν συμφέρει**)에서 "이것"(**τοῦτο**)이 바울의 충고를 가리키는지,[52] 아니면 헌금을 가리키는지[53] 분명하지 않다. 전자에 따르면, 강제로 하지 않고 자발적으로 하도록 하는 것이 진정한 헌금이므로 그들에게 유익이 된다는 뜻일 수도 있고, 후자에 따르면, 헌금을 하는 것 자체가 유익이 된다는 뜻일 수도 있다. 그러나 8절에서 바울이 명령이 아니라 권면하는 것임을 말하였으므로 "이것"은 "헌금을 자발적으로 하도록 권하는 것"을 가리킨다.

---

52) Lietzmann, 134; Martin, 264.

53) Windisch, 254; Barrett, 224.

주석가들은 바울이 여기서 "행하는 것"과 "원하는 것"을 비교하면서 바울이 "원하는 것"을 "행하는 것보다" 더 중하게 여기는 이유가 무엇인가를 논한다. 이런 의문은 일반적으로 보기에 헌금을 실제로 시행하는 것이 단순히 원하는 것보다 중요하게 보이기 때문이다. 아마 순수한 동기가 없는 단순한 행위는 기계적인 의미밖에 없는 것이기 때문일 수도 있다.[54] 그러나 11절에서 마음에 원하는 것을 행하라고 함으로써 동기의 순수함이 바울의 주된 관심이 아니라 오히려 행동이 주된 관심으로 보인다. 아니면 고린도 교인들이 마게도냐 교인들보다 헌금의 시행뿐만 아니라 의도에 있어서도 앞서 있었다는 뜻인가?[55] 그리하여 고린도 교인들을 격려하는 것인가? 실제로 9장 2절에서 바울은 마게도냐인들에게 헌금을 걷도록 격려할 때 고린도(아가야) 교인들은 이미 일 년 전부터 "예비하였다"고 했다. 이와 관련하여 (헌금을) "행하는 것"과 "원하는 것"이 분명히 시간상 다른 시점을 가리키는 것으로 논의할 수도 있다.[56] 바레트는 고린도 교인들이 헌금의 의도가 헌금 시행보다 실제로 먼저 있었다는 것을 가리킨다고 본다.[57] 의도가 있었으나 디도가 방문한 뒤에야 시행하게 된 것이라고 본다(8:6). 9장 2절의 "예비하였다"는 말을 "의도했다"는 뜻으로 본다. 여기서 분명한 이유를 알기 어려우나 바울이 "행하는 것" 보다 "원하는 것"을 강조하는 것은 일 년 전 고린도 교인들이 헌금을 시작할 때에 자발적으로 원해서 적극적으로 참여한 것 같이 이제도 자발

54) Betz, *2 Corinthians 8 and 9*, 64.

55) Meyer, 354; Tasker, 116.

56) Thrall, 536.

57) Barrett, 225.

적으로 하라고 자발성을 강조하기 위함이다(9:2). 일 년 동안 바울에 대한 반대 분위기로 말미암아 헌금의 수행에 차질이 생기게 되었는데, 이제 다시 바울에게 돌아왔으니 초기의 헌금에 대한 자발적인 자세를 가지고 다시 시작하라는 말이다.[58]

11. "이제는 행하기를 성취할지니 마음에 원하던 것과 같이 성취하되 있는 대로 하라" (**νυνὶ δὲ καὶ τὸ ποιῆσαι ἐπιτελέσατε, ὅπως καθάπερ ἡ προθυμία τοῦ θέλειν, οὕτως καὶ τὸ ἐπιτελέσαι ἐκ τοῦ ἔχειν**). 여기서 바울은 보다 직접적인 말로 헌금 수행을 성취하라(**τὸ ποιῆσαι ἐπιτελέσατε**)고 당부한다. 그러나 여전히 바울은 강요하는 자세를 애써 피하고 있다. 자발적인 헌금과 힘에 지나지 않는 적절한 헌금을 권하고 있다. 자발적인 헌금은 10절에서 언급한 대로 고린도 교인들이 원래 헌금을 작정했을 때 보인 자세이며, 마게도냐 교인들이 보인 자세이다(8:3). 그러나 "있는 대로 하라"는 것은 마게도냐 교인들이 "힘대로 할 뿐 아니라 힘에 지나도록" 한 것에 비하면 한 단계 낮은 열성이다. 바울은 목회자로서 고린도 교회의 미묘한 정황을 이해하고 있다. 고린도 교인들이 바울에게 돌아온지 얼마 되지도 않은 형편에서 헌금을 부탁하는 것은 자칫하면 고린도 교인들에게 바울이 기회를 타서 자신들을 이용한다고 오해할 수 있기 때문이다.[59] 그러므로 비록 마게도냐 교인들의 자발적이고 열성적인 모범을 들면서도, 그들과 같은 수준의 요구를 하지는 않고 한 단계 낮은 헌금에

---

58) Martin, 264-5; Thrall, 536.

59) Martin, 265.

대한 성의를 보이기를 바라고 있는 것이다.[60] 여기서 바울의 예민한 목회적 감각을 엿볼 수가 있다. 그럼에도 여기서 "이제는 행하기를 성취할지니"라고 헌금을 다그치는 말이 중심적인 진술이며, "있는 대로하라"는 말은 강요의 인상을 주지 않으려는 부수적인 말이다.

12. "할 마음만 있으면 있는 대로 받으실 터이요 없는 것을 받지 아니하시리라"(**εἰ γὰρ ἡ προθυμία πρόκειται, καθὸ ἐὰν ἔχῃ εὐπρόσδεκτος, οὐ καθὸ οὐκ ἔχει**). 개역한글성경은 바울이 헌금을 받으시는 하나님 편에서 하나님의 생각을 짐작하여 말하는 것으로 번역한다. 그러나 문자적으로는 "할 마음만 있으면, 있는 대로 내는 것이 받을 만한 것이며, 없는 것을 내는 것은 아니다"라고 번역된다. 개역한글성경은 "(헌금을) 받을 만한"(**εὐπρόσδεκτος**)이란 말의 대상이 하나님이라는 가정에 의한 것이며, 이 가정은 유사한 다른 성경 구절에 의해서 증명된다(5:9; 빌 4:18; 벧전 2:5; 참조, 롬 15:31). 이 헌금이 실제로 예루살렘 성도들에게 가는 것이라고 볼 때 예루살렘 성도들에게 받을 만한 것이라고 볼 수도 있다. 그러나 문맥에서 이것은 가난한 성도들을 위한 구제금이기 전에 하나님께 드리는 헌금이라는 뜻이 강하므로 역시 헌금의 대상은 하나님이라고 보아야 한다. 13절 이하에서 이런 헌금의 의미가 강조되고 있다. 중심적 진술은 헌금을 할 마음이 있어야 한다는 것이다. 남이 하라고 해서 마지못해 하는 헌금이 되어서는 안 되며 자원하는 심령으로 해야 함을 말하고 있다. 바울은 여전히 고린도 교인

---

60) Windisch, 257.

들의 자발성을 강조하면서 자신의 강요가 헌금의 동기가 되어서는 안 된다는 것을 말하고 있다. 이것은 헌금의 바른 자세를 가르치는 것이지만, 동시에 헌금과 관련하여 고린도 교인들이 오해하고 시험을 받지 않도록 계속 주의하고 있음을 보여 준다(8:20). 평소에 자비량 선교를 하면서 고린도 교회의 재정적 지원을 절대로 받지 않는다고 공언한 바울이 이제 헌금을 요청하는 것은 매우 힘들고 어려운 일이라고 생각된다(고전 9:18; 11:7-9).

13. "이는 다른 사람들은 평안하게 하고 너희는 곤고하게 하려는 것이 아니요 평균케 하려 함이니" (οὐ γὰρ ἵνα ἄλλοις ἄνεσις, ὑμῖν θλῖψις, ἀλλ᾽ ἐξ ἰσότητος). 바울은 자신의 헌금 요청이 고린도 교인들에게 부정적 생각을 불러일으킬 수 있음을 알고 예방적인 진술을 계속한다. 바울이 우리가 수고한 것을 받아 가지고 우리와는 상관없고 자신만이 아는 다른 사람들(예루살렘 교인들, 사도들)에게 주어 자신의 유익을 노리는 것이 아닌가란 가능한 의구심을 사전에 차단하고 있다. 첫째, "다른 사람들" (ἄλλοις)은 고린도 교인들과 같이 모두 그리스도 안에 있는 형제자매이다. 둘째, 하나님은 그의 백성들이 경제적으로 고르게 살기를 원하시는데 자신의 헌금 사역이 바로 그러한 하나님의 일을 수행하는 것이며, 결국 고린도 교인들도 헌금을 통하여 하나님의 사역에 동참하는 것이 된다(15). 셋째, 구원론적 시각에서 볼 때 가난한 자를 구제하는 헌금은 하나님이 원하시는 것이며, 그의 인간 구원의 뜻을 이루는 것이다. 바울은 단순히 헌금만을 거두는 사람이 아니라 하나님의 구원 사역을 돕는 일을 하고 있는 것이며, 고린도 교인들은 하나님의 구원 사역에 동참하는 것이다. 이방인과 유대

인들이 상호 유익을 나눈다는 개념은 로마서 9-11장의 하나님의 종말론적 구원 섭리와 로마서 15장 27절에도 나타난다.[61] 이방인들이 유대인들로 말미암아 구원 얻었고, 또 불신 유대인들도 이방인의 구원올 보고 구원을 얻게 된다. 14절과 15절에서 이 같은 하나님의 구원섭리에 입각한 평등주의와 호혜주의적 원칙을 분명히 보여준다.

14. "이제 너희의 유여한 것으로 저희 부족한 것을 보충함은 후에 저희 유여한 것으로 너희 부족한 것을 보충하여 평균하게 하려 함이라"(ἐν τῷ νῦν καιρῷ τὸ ὑμῶν περίσσευμα εἰς τὸ ἐκείνων ὑστέρημα, ἵνα καὶ τὸ ἐκείνων περίσσευμα γένηται εἰς τὸ ὑμῶν ὑστέρημα, ὅπως γένηται ἰσότης). 예루살렘 성도들을 위한 헌금은 "상부상조"의 방법을 통한 "평균의 원칙"에 의한 것이다. "유여하다"는 것과 "부족하다"는 것이 영적인 의미인지 물질적인 의미인지 당장은 분명치 않다. 마틴은 "너희의 유여한 것"은 경제적으로 유여한 것일 수도 있으나 이방인 고린도 교인들이 "은혜로 값없이 받은 구원"을 의미한다고 본다.[62] 멸망 받을 자들이 은혜로 구원 받은 것을 가리킨다고 한다. 크리소스톰은 땅위의 물질의 나눔으로 영적인 유여함을 누리게 된다고 한다.[63] 이런 이유들로 예수를 통한 하나님의 인간구원의 역사의 증인들인 예루살렘 성도들의 경제적 고통을 덜어주기 위해 구원받은 이방인들이 헌금하는 것이 마땅하다는 것이다. 마틴은 로마서 9-11장의 종

61) Martin, 267.

62) Martin, 267.

63) John Chrysostom, *Patrologia Graeca*(이하, *PG*), 61 col. 519; *NPNF*, vol, XII, 361.

말론적 구원의 완성의 시각에서 헌금 사역을 이해한다. 헌금은 하나님의 구원의 종말론적 성취를 돕는 것이며, 이스라엘이 회개하여 돌아오고 구원 받은 모든 이방인들이 모이는 마지막 날에 대한 소망을 확인하는 것이라고 한다(롬 9-11).[64] 그러나 트롤은 이런 마틴의 견해를 헌금에 지나치게 신학적 의미를 부가시키는 것으로 반대한다. 트롤은 당시 흉년과 예루살렘 멸망 전의 어려운 경제 상황에 비추어 경제적인 어려움으로 이해할 것을 제안한다.[65] 고린도 교회는 어려운 예루살렘 교회에 비해 그래도 경제적으로 유여했을 것이 분명하다. 그리고 바울이 예루살렘 교회의 가난함을 다른 데서 말하고 있고(롬 8:26; 갈 2:10), 또 위에서 본 바와 같이 8장 2, 9절에서 경제적 가난함을 말하고 있음으로 여기서도 단순히 경제적 빈곤과 넉넉함을 가리킨다고 볼 수 있다. 그러나 위의 마틴이 제안하는 신학적, 영적 해석도 로마서 15장 27절에 근거하여 볼 때 전혀 타당성이 없는 것은 아니다. 바울은 로마서 15장 26절에서 예루살렘의 가난한 성도들을 위한 마게도냐 교인들의 헌금을 언급한 후에 27절에서 마게도냐 인들이 이방교인들로서 예루살렘 교인들에게 신령한 빚을 진 것이므로 육신의 것(헌금)으로 그들을 섬기는 것이 마땅하다고 한다. 결국 바울은 여기서도 영적인 빚과 육적인 도움을 함께 말하면서 이방교회와 예루살렘 교회가 상호 도움을 주는 것을 말하고 있다고 본다. 이런 의미에서 고린도 교회가 예루살렘 교회에 경제적 도움을 준다고 교만해서는 안 된다는 경계까지도 포함하고 있는지 모른다. 바울이

---

64) Chrysostom, *PG*, 61 col. 519.

65) Thrall, 547.

거듭 쓰는 "평균케 한다"(ἰσότης)[66]는 말 가운데 하나님의 구원의 섭리 차원에서 상호 유익을 주고받는 관계임으로 주는 자는 지나치게 우월감을 가져서는 안 되고 받는 자도 지나치게 열등감을 가질 필요가 없다는 뜻이 있을지 모른다. 주고받는 것이 모두 하나님의 구원의 섭리 가운데서 이루어지는 것이기 때문이다.

실제로 바울은 9장 10-15절에서 헌금의 결과로 얻게 되는 물질적 축복과 함께 영적 축복을 언급하고 있다. 그러나 헌금의 공평케 하는 원칙은 이런 신학적 의미와 함께 초기 예루살렘 교회의 기독교 공동체의 모본을 따라서 서서히 형성된 초대교회의 함께 나누며 사는 공동체 생활의 특징인 것 같다(행 2:44-46). 바울의 헌금은 이런 공동체 전통을 그의 이방 선교 상황에 적용하는 것이라고 볼 수 있다. 모든 이방 교회가 각기 다른 경제적 문화적 형편으로 말미암아 예루살렘 교회와 같은 공동체 생활을 할 수는 없었을 것이다. 그러나 고린도 교회의 애찬이나 데살로니가 교회의 경우처럼 이런 예루살렘 공동체 삶을 부분적으로나마 적용하여 공동체 생활을 나름대로 시행하였던 것 같다(고전 11:17-22). 이에 대

66) ἰσότης("공평함")는 헬라 철학에서 쓰이던 중요한 개념으로 우주적이고 신비한 의미를 가지고 있다. 필로는 이 말을 "인격화된 신적인 능력" 또는 "창조된 세계의 균형과 질서의 현상"(빛과 어두움, 남녀, 봄, 가을 등)으로 보았고, 그러므로 하나님의 품성과 동등한 개념으로 보았다(*Quis Rerum Divinarum Heres(누가 하나님의 소유를 상속할 것인가?)* 141-206, Georgi, *Kollekte*, 62, 재인용). ἰσότης는 전쟁을 그치고 평화가 오게 한다. 반면에 ἀνισότης("불공평함")는 온갖 전쟁을 일으킨다(*Rev. Div. Her.* 162). 트롤은 본문에서 바울이 이 말의 헬라적 개념을 가지고 사용한다고 보기 어렵고, 단순히 일반적인 "공평함"을 나타낼 뿐이라고 본다(Thrall, 539-540). 그러나 바울의 사역이 곧 하나님의 구원 사역이라고 볼 때 결국 이 말 자체의 신적 의미는 아니지만 이 말이 가져오는 신적 의미를 유추해 낼 수는 있다. 즉 헌금과 관련하여 하나님의 구원 계획 가운데서 예루살렘 사람들과 이방인들이 서로 돕는다는 것이다.

한 부작용도 있어서 "규모 없이 행하며" 일하지 않고 놀고먹는 이들을 바울은 경계하였다(살전 5:14; 살후 3:6-12).

15. "기록한 것같이 많이 거둔 자도 남지 아니하였고 적게 거둔 자도 모자라지 아니하였느니라"(**καθὼς γέγραπται· ὁ τὸ πολὺ οὐκ ἐπλεόνασεν, καὶ ὁ τὸ ὀλίγον οὐκ ἠλαττόνησεν**). 이 말은 출애굽기 16장 18절의 인용이다. 이 구절은 70인역(초대 기독교인들이 쓰던 기원전 3세기에 번역된 헬라어 구약성경)의 단어와 어귀가 거의 같다(**οὐκ ἐπλεόνασεν ὁ τὸ πολύ καὶ ὁ τὸ ἔλαττον οὐκ ἠλαττόνησεν**, LXX). 바울이 **ἔλαττον**(적음)대신 **ὀλίγον**(적음)을 쓰고 있는 것이 다르고, 첫 구절의 순서가 바뀌었으나 의미는 같다.[67] 바울은 어순을 바꾸어 보다 "많이 거둔 자"와 "적게 거둔 자"의 대조를 높이고 있다. 중심 의미는 하나님의 공평하심으로 인한 백성들 사이의 평화와 만족이다. 고린도 교인들은 "새 이스라엘 백성"으로서 "옛 이스라엘 백성"들이 광야에서 서로 공평하게 나누어 가진 것을 따라서 자원하여 헌금해야 하는 것이다.[68] 핸슨(R. P. C. Hanson)은 광야에서 공평하게 베푸신 하나님의 기적이 새 이스라엘이 된 그리스도인들에게는 그리스도의 공평한 은혜와 사랑으로 나타난다고 보았다.[69] 트롤은 이런 해석들을 구약의 의미를 지나치게 확대시키는 것이라고 반대하면서 단순히

67) 기록의 차이에 관한 설명을 보라. C. D. Stanley, *Paul and the Language of Scripture: Citation Technique in the Pauline Epistles and Contemporary Literature*, SNTSMS 74 (Cambridge: University Press, 1992), 231-3; Thrall, 542, 주, 249.

68) Plummer, 245; Windisch, 259.

69) R. P. C. Hanson, *The Second Epistle to the Corinthians* (London: SCM Press, 1954), 71.

헌금과 관련하여 공평한 원칙을 말하고 있을 따름이라고 보았다.[70]

주 해(8:7–15):

본문에서 바울은 헌금의 모든 원리를 말하려고 하지 않으나, 몇 가지 헌금의 신학적 근거와 신앙적 유익을 말하고 있다. 첫째, 물질을 드리기 이전에 자신을 먼저 하나님께 드리는 것이 필요하다(8:5). 헌금은 자신의 희생물로 드리는 제사에 해당하는 것으로 본다. 여기서 헌금이 구제의 목적으로 드리는 것이지만 그것은 결국 하나님께 드리는 거룩한 제물과 같은 것이다. 제물을 드리는 사람은 그 제물의 머리에 안수함으로 그 제물과 하나가 된다(레 1:4). 그 제물을 드리는 것은 곧 자신을 드리는 것이다. 바울의 약함의 신학에 근거하여 볼 때, 이 말은 자신이 그리스도의 약함의 모본을 따라서 스스로 약하게 되는 것이다(헌금도 결국 자신의 일부를 드리는 것이다). 둘째, 그리스도인의 헌금은 예수 그리스도의 구속의 구체적인 사랑과 은혜에 대한 구체적인 보답이다(9). 셋째, 헌금의 자세는 자발성이다(10-12). 넷째, 하나님의 자녀들로서 그의 자식들에게 공평하게 나누어주시는 하늘 아버지의 뜻을 실천하는 것이다(13-15). 다섯째, 헌금은 하나님의 축복을 계속 받는 방법이자(9:8) 성도의 교제의 방법이다(9:12-15). 여섯째, 하나님께 감사와 영광을 드리는 방법이다(9:11-13).

그리스도인의 헌금은 근본적으로 하나님께서 그리스도를 통해

70) Thrall, 543.

베푸신 구원의 은혜에 대한 구체적 보답이다. 물질 자체가 더러운 것이 아니다. 인간의 주인의식과 소유욕이 문제다. 하나님께서 세상 만물을 지으셨다. 물질은 우리의 수고의 대가이며 축복이다. 더구나 물질을 하나님의 구원 사역을 위해 구별하여 바칠 때 하나님의 영광을 드러내는 거룩한 성물이 되는 것이다(8:23; 9:13). 헌금은 하나님 앞에서 인간의 주인 의식을 포기하고 하나님의 주되심을 인정하는 구체적 행위이다. 모든 헌금은 구체적인 목적을 위해 쓰인다. 본문의 헌금은 가난한 예루살렘 성도들을 위한 구제금이다(8:4; 9:1; 고전 16:1; 갈 2:10). 그러나 그 구제금은 결국 하나님의 구원 사역을 돕는 것이므로 거룩한 헌금이 되는 것이다. 하나님은 이스라엘 백성을 통하여 이방 구원 역사를 시작하셨다. 그러므로 그 구원의 혜택을 받은 고린도 교회가 어려운 이스라엘 백성을 물질적으로 돕는 것은 마땅하다. 이스라엘 백성이나 이방인이나 그리스도 안에서 모두 하나님의 백성이 되었으므로 하나님의 공평하심을 따라서 서로 가진 은혜를 나누는 것은 마땅한 일이다. 여기에서 헌금의 자발적 동기와 호혜적 의미를 찾을 수 있다.

바울은 본문에서 헌금 목적을 달성하기 위해 고린도 교인들을 설득하면서 신학적 근거와 서로 유익을 주고받는 것임을 상기시키는데, 특히 헌금이 자발적이어야 함을 강조한다. 고린도 교인들의 연약한 믿음이 손상될 것을 염려하여 강요하는 자세를 보이지 않는다. 고린도 교인들의 형편이나 마음을 고려하지 않고 헌금의 당위성만을 주장할 때, 헌금의 목적을 이룰 수 없을 뿐만 아니라, 고린도 교인들이 물질로 시험 받게 되고, 어렵게 돌아온 그들을 다시 잃게 된다는 것을 바울은 알고 있다. 반대로, 고린도 교인들의 형편과 어려움만을 고려하여 헌금요청을 하지 않을 수도 없다.

이런 목회적 딜레마로부터 바울은 조심하며 헤쳐 나온다. 바울은 매우 조심스럽게 헌금 요청을 하는데, 주로 자발적으로 마음에서 우러나는 대로, 있는 대로 하라고 권하는 것이다(8, 10-12). 그러나 헌금의 필요성과 당위성을 힘주어 말한다(7, 11; 참조, 갈 1:10). 헌금의 필요성을 논하면서도 강요하는 자세를 피한다. 거듭 고린도 교인들이 스스로 헌금을 하도록 호소하는 것이다. 여기에서 바울은 인내하며 교인들을 사랑하는 모습과 원칙을 고수하는 목회자의 모습을 모두 보여준다. 그는 이제 막 회개하고 돌아온 고린도 교인들을 갓난아이들을 다루듯이 매우 조심스럽게 대한다. 그러나 부모는 아이를 애지중지해서 버릇없이 키우면 안 된다. 그들을 가르쳐 성숙한 어른으로 자라게 할 책임이 있다(고전 3:1; 고후 6:14; 12:14). 이런 바울의 목회적 자세는 목회자가 신학적, 성경적 원칙을 따라 목회해야 하면서도, 실제 목회 형편을 신중히 파악하고 고려하여 다양한 목회적 목적들을 이루어 가야할 책임을 갖는 것을 보여 준다.[71] 그는 목회를 위해 필요한 헌금을 말하고 있으나 목회자로서 무엇보다 교인들을 사랑해야한다는 목회원칙을 잊지 않고 있다. 목회의 궁극적인 목적은 사람을 사랑하고 구원하는 일이다. 그 외의 목적들은 부수적인 것이며 이차적인 것이다. 이런 부수적인 작은 목적과 사람을 구원하고 제자화 하는 우선적 목적의 순서를 혼동하지 않도록 주의해야 한다. 어떤 목회적인 목표가 있더라도 사람을 잃지 않도록 최선을 다해야 한다. 목회자는 사람을 낚는 어부이지, 고기를 낚는 어부가 아니다. 사람과 고기를 구별해야 한다. (물론 사람을 귀히 여기는 자세는 사람을 얻기

71) Verbrugge, *Collection*, 367.

위해 수단 방법을 가리지 않는 인본주의적 처세론과는 구별되어야한다. 목회자는 복음의 진리의 테두리 안에서 사람을 품어야 한다. "이제 내가 사람들에게 좋게 하랴? 하나님께 좋게 하랴? 사람들에게 기쁨을 구하랴? 지금까지 사람의 기쁨을 구하는 것이었다면 그리스도의 종이 아니니라"(갈 1:10). 바울은 갈라디아서에서 갈라디아 교인들이 믿음으로 구원 얻는 진리를 떠난 것을 알고 그들을 경책하기를 주저하지 않았다. 유사하게 고린도후서에서도 복음 진리를 떠난 고린도 교인들을 향하여 바울은 고린도후서 10-13장에서 호되게 질책하고 있다.)

목회자들이 흔히 직면하는 유사한 원칙과 현실의 갈등에서도 목회자들은 어느 한쪽을 포기하거나 치우치지 말고 모두 만족시키도록 최선을 다해야 한다. 결과에 대한 지나친 낙관이나 비관적 자세는 금물이다. 그 결과를 하나님께 맡기고 원칙을 고수하면서도 현실의 문제점을 파악하여 대처하는 것이다. 어느 한 쪽으로 치우치지 않는 이런 균형의 기술에 따라 목회자의 목회 능력이 평가되고, "성공적 목회"도 가능하겠으나, 목회자의 진정한 자세는 결과에 집착하지 않고, 이러한 조화의 원리를 따라서 최선을 다하고 그 결과(성공이든 실패든)를 하나님께 맡기는 것이다. 이런 사람이 진정한 하나님의 사람이다. 바울의 헌금 요청의 결과는 알 수 없다. 위에서 지적한 바와 같이 로마서 15장 31절의 진술을 보다 적극적으로 해석해서 고린도 교회가 예루살렘 성도들을 위한 헌금을 모두 마친 증거로 볼 수도 있다. 그러나 회의적 견해도 있다.[72] 바울이 예루살렘에 갔을 때, 각 지방과 교회에서 온 사람들

72) Thrall, 516.

이 언급되었으나, 고린도에서 온 사람은 아무도 언급되지 않았다(행 20:4). 실제로 사도행전에서 누가는 헌금에 대해서 그렇게 중요하게 다루지 않고 있다. 그 이유를 잘 알 수는 없으나, 아마도 헌금에 대한 기대와 결과가 만족스럽지 못했기 때문이라고 볼 수도 있다.[73] 바울이 기대했던 헌금 목표가 찼는지도 알 수 없고, 그 헌금을 예루살렘 성도들에게 전하여 바울이 기대했던 반응을 얻었는지도 알 수 없다. 오히려 바울은 예루살렘에 가서 체포되어 죄인이 되고 가이사랴 감옥에 갇히는 몸이 되었다. 그러나 그 헌금의 결과가 어떻든지 아무도 바울을 실패한 목회자로 보는 사람은 없다. 바울 스스로는 외적으로 실패같이 보이는 그의 사역을 성공적인 것으로 믿고 있다. 그는 최선을 다하여 일했기 때문이다. 바울은 목회의 실패와 성공의 개념을 그리스도의 죽음과 부활, 또는 종말론적 개념으로 이해하기 때문에 당장 나타난 현상이나 증거로 평가받기를 거부한다(4:16-5:10; 6:8-10; 딤후 4:8, 16, 17).

C. 디도와 두 형제들의 파송 (8:16-24)

본문:

> 16. 너희를 위하여 같은 간절함을 디도의 마음에도 주시는 하나님께 감사하노니 17. 저가 권함을 받고 더욱 간절함으로 자원하여 너희에게 나아갔고 18. 또 저와 함께 한 형제를 보내었으니 이 사람은 복음으로서 모든 교회에서 칭찬을 받는 자요 19. 이뿐 아니라 저는 주님 자신의(동일한 주의) 영광과 우리의 원을 나타내기 위하여 여러 교회의 택함을 입어 우리의 맡은 은혜의 일로 우리와 동행하는 자라. 20. 이것을 조심함은 우리

---

73) Thrall, 518; J D. G. Dunn, *Unity and Diversity in the New Testament*, (London: SCM Press, 1977) 257; Georgi, *Kollekte*, 88-9.

가 맡은 이 거액의 연보로 인하여 아무도 우리를 훼방하지 못하게 하려 함이니 21. 이는 우리가 주 앞에서만 아니라 사람 앞에서도 선한 일에 조심하려 함이라. 22. 또 저희와 함께 우리의 한 형제를 보내었으니 우리가 여러 가지 일에 그 간절한 것을 여러번 시험하였거니와 이제 저가 너희를 크게 믿은 고로 더욱 간절하니라. 23. 디도로 말하면 나의 동무요 너희를 위한 나의 동역자요 우리 형제들로 말하면 여러 교회의 사자들이요 그리스도의 영광이니라. 24. 그러므로 너희는 여러 교회 앞에서 너희의 사랑과 너희에(를) 대한 우리의 자랑의 증거를 저희에게 보이라.

본문 비평:

1. 16절의 **διδόντι**(δίδωμι[주다]의 현재분사)가 ℵ B C Byz에 나타나고, **δόντι**(δίδωμι[주다]의 과거분사)가 p[46] ℵ[3] D F G L lat bo Ambrosiaster에 나오고 Nestle-Aland도 이를 따른다. 후자는 7장 11절에서 언급한 "고린도 교회의 간절함"과 관련하여 "디도의 간절함"을 말하면서 고린도 교인들에게 간절함을 주셨을 그때에 디도에게도 "같은 간절함"을 주신 것으로 생각하고 "과거분사"로 고쳤다고 본다면 전자가 원래의 것이다.[74)]

2. 19절의 **σὺν**(함께)이 p[46] ℵ D G K Byz에 나타나고, **ἐν**이 B C P lat syrp cop arm eth에 나타난다. 전자가 원래의 것이다. 후자는 비인격 목적에 **ἐν**을 사용하는 경향을 따라 바뀐 것으로 본다.[75)]

3. 19절에서 Nestle-Aland 판에서는 괄호 속에 **αὐτοῦ**(그의)를 두고 있다([αὐτοῦ]). 이 대명사가 B C D* F G L에는 없고 A D[1]

74) 참조, Barrett, 217; Plummer, 247; Martin, 271.

75) B. M. Metzger, *Textual Commentary*, 581, 582; Martin, 271.

Byz에는 나타나기 때문이다. 원래 이 대명사가 τοῦ κυρίου와 함께 있었으나, 의미가 겹친다고 보고 생략한 것으로 본다. 원래 "그의, 즉 주의 영광"(τὴν αὐτοῦ τοῦ κυρίου δόξαν)이라고 중복적으로 쓰였을 것이다.[76)]

4. ἐνδεικνύμενοι(ἐνδείκνυμι[나타내다]의 현재분사)가 B D* E F G에 나타나는데, ℵ C D^b,c K L P lat와 기타 많은 사본에는 ἐνδείξασθε(현재명령형)이 나타난다. 후자는 셈족어 현재분사의 명령의 의미를 모르는 필사자들이 수정한 것으로 본다.[77)]

내용 분해:

본문은 바울이 헌금을 위해 디모데와 함께 가는 다른 두 형제들을 추천하는 내용이다. 디도 외에 두 형제들을 추천하여 보내는 이유는 다음과 같다.

첫째, 헌금 내역의 투명성을 지키고 헌금을 예루살렘 교회에 안전하게 전달하게 하려는 의도가 있다(8:20). 헌금에 관한한 바울의 동기가 순수하며 추호의 욕심도 없다는 것을 보여 주어야 했다(20, 21; 참조, 4:2; 6:3; 7:2; 8:20; 11:10; 12:15-18). 그러므로 바울이 직접 헌금을 거두러 가지 않고 대신 디도와 다른 두 형제들을 보내어 헌금을 수거하게 한다.[78)] 그리고 바울은 헌금과 관련하여 자신뿐만 아니라 자기와 교회들이 파송하는 디도와 두 형제들을 가

---

76) Barrett, 217.

77) Moule, *Idiom Book*, 158, 179; Moulton, *Grammar* 3:343; Lietzmann, 137; Martin, 272; 참조, Windisch, 267, 268; Plummer, 252.

78) Héring, 62.

능한 의심과 오해로부터 보호해야할 필요를 느끼고 이들은 각 교회에서 추천된 깨끗하고 신뢰할 수 있는 사람들이란 것을 강조하고 있다. 디도가 바울의 측근임으로 디도 한 사람만으로는 헌금관리의 투명성을 객관적으로 증명하기 어려우므로 헌금에 참여한 교회들(마게도냐 교회와 안디옥이나 에베소 교회 같은 소아시아 교회들)이 지명한 사람들의 재정 감시가 필요하다고 보았다. 이들은 모두 검증을 거친 믿을 만한 사람들이므로 마땅히 존경하며 영접할 것을 강조한다(23-24).

둘째, 고린도 교회에 아직도 추천서를 가지고 들어온 이들이 바울을 저항하는 세력으로 남아 있으므로(3:1-3), 바울은 이런 세력에 대항하여 바울 자신뿐만이 아니라 모든 교회가 선택하고 추천하여 파송하는 신뢰할 수 있는 사람들을 직접 추천하여 보냄으로서 반대파들의 헌금 관련 비난을 억제하려는 의도도 있을 수 있다(12:16). 두 형제는 "여러 교회"에서 추천을 받은 재정 전문가들로서 헌금을 투명하게 관리할 수 있는 사람들로 보인다.

셋째, 바울이 직접가지 못하지만 헌금 수거가 더 이상 늦출 수 없는 속히 마쳐야 할 매우 중요한 사역이므로 바울이 방문하기 전에 고린도 교인들이 이 일에 적극 가담하도록 해야 하는 문제이다(9:4). 바울이 한 번에 세 사람씩이나 보내는 것도 그가 이 일을 이번에 마치기를 원하고 있다는 증거다.

주석:

16. "너희를 위하여 같은 간절함을 디도의 마음에도 주시는 하나님께 감사하노니"(Χάρις δὲ τῷ θεῷ τῷ δόντι τὴν αὐτὴν

σπουδὴν ὑπὲρ ὑμῶν ἐν τῇ καρδίᾳ Τίτου). "같은 간절함"(τὴν αὐτὴν σπουδὴν)은 누구의 간절함과 같다는 말인가? 마게도냐인들의 정성인가(8:8)? 고린도 교회의 간절함인가(7:12, 8:7)? 아니면 바울 자신의 간절함인가? 대부분의 주석가들은 바울 자신의 간절함이라고 본다.[79] "너희를 위하여"(ὑπὲρ ὑμῶν)라는 말이 마게도냐인들이나, 고린도 교인들을 제외시키고 고린도 교인들을 향한 바울의 간절함을 가리킨다고 본다.[80] 그러나 본문에서 분명하게 바울의 간절함이란 말이 없으므로 바울을 포함한 마게도냐 교인과 고린도 교인들 같은 모든 이들의 간절함을 의미할 수도 있다.[81] 디도가 간절함으로 고린도 교회에 다시 돌아가고 싶어 하는 것은 헌금 자체가 아니라 헌금을 통해서 나타날 그들의 순종과 믿음을 다시 확인하기 위해서이다(8:17). 디도는 전번 방문 시에 고린도 교인들의 융숭한 영접과 순종으로 크게 감동되었는데(7:15), 그들의 열심을 헌금을 통해서 다시 확인할 수 있게 되었음으로 다시 돌아가기를 소원하고 있다. 바울도 같은 기대를 갖고 있다(24).

"하나님께 감사하노니"(Χάρις δὲ τῷ θεῷ)는 디도의 간절함이 단순히 디도의 인간적인 감정이나 의지로 말미암은 것이 아니라 하나님이 감동케 하신 것을 보여준다. 따라서 헌금은 바울이나 디도의 계획에 의한 것이 아니라 하나님에 의해 지시된 거룩한 사업으로 모두 참가해야 한다. 사실 고린도 교회의 형편을 누구보다 잘 아는 디도는 고린도 교회의 호전된 분위기에도 불구하고 헌금

---

79) Meyer, 359; Bachmann, 321; Plummer, 247; Lietzmann, 135; Barrett, 227; Wolff, 176; Furnish, 421; Martin, 273.

80) Thrall, 544-545.

81) Furnish, 421.

을 요청하기에는 너무 이르다는 생각을 할 수도 있었다. 그가 헌금의 임무를 가지고 가면, 교회가 안정되었다는 보고를 하자마자 이내 헌금 거두라는 지시를 받아 가지고 왔다는 비난을 반대자들로부터 들을 각오를 해야 했다. 바울도 디도의 난처한 입장을 잘 알고 있었으므로 그에게 헌금에 대한 임무를 맡기기가 미안했을 것이다. 그러나 의외로 디도는 헌금에 대해서 적극적인 자세를 갖고 있었던 것이다. 바울은 앞서서 말한 모든 이들의 "간절함" 이 디도에게도 있다는 것은 헌금과 관련하여 하나님께서 디도의 마음을 감동 감화시키셨음으로 알고 하나님께 감사하는 것이다.

17. "저가 권함을 받고 더욱 간절함으로 자원하여 너희에게 나아갔고" (ὅτι τὴν μὲν παράκλησιν ἐδέξατο, σπουδαιότερος δὲ ὑπάρχων αὐθαίρετος ἐξῆλθεν πρὸς ὑμᾶς). 명령이 아닌 온화한 "권함" (παράκλησιν)이란 말을 쓴 것은 바울이 헌금에 관한한 강요하지 않고 설득한다는 일관된 자세를 보여준다. 평소에도 바울이 그의 조력자들에게 이런 낮은 자세로 사역을 한다고 본다.[82] 그러므로 그들은 바울의 인격에 이끌리어 더욱 자발적으로 충성하게 되었다고 본다.[83] 바울이 헌금 문제를 제기하자 디도는 적극적으로 호응하며 고린도 교회에 다시 가기로 했다.

"더욱 간절함" (σπουδαιότερος)이란 말은 비교급이나 문자에

---

82) Barrett, 228.

83) Betz는 παράκλησιν("권함")이란 말이 헬라시대에 법적 명령이라고 하나 Thrall은 이에 대한 증거가 부족하다고 반대한다(Betz, *2 Corinthians 8 and 9*, 71; Thrall, 546). 더구나 8장은 전체가 호소와 권면이지 명령이란 말은 바울이 의도적으로 피하는 개념이다(8).

서 비교의 대상이 없으므로 적극적인 간절함에 대한 표현이라고 본다. 단순히 권면을 받아들이는 것 이상으로 호응하는 자세이다.

"자원함으로"(αὐθαίρετος)는 바울의 권면한 사실과 모순되는 말이다. 어떻게 바울의 권면과 디도의 자원함이 동시에 일어날 수 있는가? 그것은 하나님의 은혜와 섭리 때문이다. 바울이 권면하기 전에 디도에게도 같은 생각이 있었다. 바울의 권면은 디도의 의중을 확인하는데 지나지 않았다. 바울 자신이 헌금에 대하여 직접 나서지 않아도 다 되었다는 뜻이다. 여기에 헌금에 대한 자발성과 은혜라는 점을 다시 강조함으로써 바울 자신이 헌금과 관련되어 일어날 수 있는 어떤 잡음의 소지를 아예 차단하려는 의도가 있다(4:22; 6:3; 7:2; 12:16-18). 헌금은 모두가 자발적으로 한 것이며 이것이 하나님의 도우심의 증거라는 점을 강조하면서 자신은 되도록 직접 관여하지 않으려는 자세를 견지하고 있다. 이런 자세는 바울의 이기적인 자세로 볼 수 없고 전체 교회의 평화를 위해 필요한 것이다. 일찍이 예루살렘 교회에서 사도들은 공궤에 관한 책임을 집사들에게 넘기고 말씀과 기도에 전무하였다(행 6:1-4). 어쩌면 바울도 이런 전통을 알고 존중하기 위해 이런 소극적 자세를 의도적으로 취하고 있는지도 모른다. 헌금의 필요성을 말하면서도, 헌금을 수거하는 일은 직접 관여하지 않는다는 자세를 견지하고 있다.

"너희에게로 나아갔고"(ἐξῆλθεν)는 서신에서 쓰이는 과거형이다. 즉 그의 편지를 디도가 가지고 갔을 때에는 이미 디도가 고린도에 도착하였다는 가정을 하고 과거로 쓰는 것이다. 어떤 학자들이 이 과거동사를 문자적으로 해석하여 디도가 먼저 고린도로 떠난 후에 바울이 편지를 보냈다고 해석하는 것은 불필요한 추정이다[84] 18절에도 같은 "서신용 과거"가 나온다(συνεπέμψαμεν, "보내었으니").

18. "또 저와 함께 한 형제를 보내었으니 이 사람은 복음으로서 모든 교회에서 칭찬을 받는 자요"(**συνεπέμψαμεν δὲ μετ' αὐτοῦ τὸν ἀδελφὸν οὗ ὁ ἔπαινος ἐν τῷ εὐαγγελίῳ διὰ πασῶν τῶν ἐκκλησιῶν**). 이 형제의 이름과 22절에 나오는 다른 형제의 이름이 무명으로 쓰인 것이 이상하다. 또한 "복음으로서 모든 교회에서 칭찬을 받는 자"라는 설명도 분명하지 않다. "복음으로서"(ἐν τῷ εὐαγγελίῳ)란 말이 복음 사역이라는 광범위한 의미의 말인지(빌 1:5; 4:3), 복음 전도자란 뜻인지, 아니면 마가나 누가 같은 복음서를 기록한 사람이란 뜻인지 알 수 없다. 이 마지막 제안은 복음이란 말이 복음서를 지칭하게 된 것이 역사적으로 주후 150년 이후라고 보기 때문에 제외될 수 있다.[85] 더구나 마가복음이나 누가 복음서가 고린도후서보다 먼저 쓰였다고 보기 어렵다. 희랍시대 추천서에서 무명으로 쓰는 경우는 드물다.[86] 바울은 로마서 16장 1절과 고린도전서 16장 10-15절에서 이름을 직접 언급하며 추천한다. 마틴은 빌립보서 4장 2절에서 이름이 언급되지 않은 경우가 있다고 한다.[87] 어떤 이들은 원래 이 두 형제들의

84) 과거로 해석하는 이들: Bachmann, 322; Wendland, 221; Allo, 223; 반대하는 이들: Meyer, 360; Plummer, 247; Tasker, 119; Furnish, 422; Thrall, 547.

85) R. P. Martin, "Gospel," *International Standard Bible Encyclopedia*, ed. G. W Bromiley et al. (Grand Rapids: Eerdmans, 1982) 2:529.

86) C. H. Kim, *Form and Structure of the Familiar Greek Letter of Recommendation*. SBLDS 4 (Missoula: Scholars, 1972), 40, 여기서 4개의 이름이 언급되지 않은 추천의 경우를 들고 있다. (Betz, *2 Corinthians 8 and 9*, 73, 주 275에 인용됨.)

이름이 있었으나 그들이 고린도 교회에 가서 어떤 불미스런 일에 관련되었으므로 후에 그들의 이름을 지웠다고 본다.[88] 닉클(Niclke)은 두 형제를 사도행전 15장 22절의 유다와 실라로 본다.[89] 그들은 사도회의의 이방인들을 위한 요약된 율법을 각 교회에 전하는 임무를 맡았던 이들이다. 닉클(K. F. Nickle)은 사도행전 18장 22절에서 바울이 예루살렘에 잠시 들린 것을 헌금과 관련하여 예루살렘 교회의 자문을 구하기 위한 것으로 보고, 이때 예루살렘 교회가 실라와 유다를 헌금을 위한 책임자들로 임명하였다는 것이다. 닉클은 예루살렘 교회의 관심은 바울의 헌금으로 말미암아 디아스포라 유대인들이 예루살렘으로 보내는 성전 헌금이 저해 받지 않게 하는 것이었다는 것으로 추정한다. 그러나 이들의 이름이 지워진 이유는 고린도 교회가 이들이 전한, 이방인들을 위한 사도들의 약식 율법을 거절하였기 때문이라고 닉클은 추정하지만 이는 지나치다. 더구나 예루살렘 교회를 비롯한 유대의 교회들이 이들을 지명하였다는 주장은 바울이 로마서 15장 31절에서 예루살렘 교회에서 헌금을 거절할지도 모른다는 염려에 상치된다. 더구나 일반적으로 실라는 실루아노와 동일한 인물로 보는데, 실루아노는 고린도 교회에 복음을 전하였다고 고린도후서 1장 19절에 언급되고 있다. 그렇다면 왜 여기서는 무명으로 언급되는가?

플러머는 디도가 이 두 형제를 데리고 가서 직접 소개할 수 있다고 보았고, 고린도 교인들이 잘 모르는 사람들을 따로 언급할

---

87) Martin, 275.

88) Lietzmann, 137; 참조, Windisch, 262; Héring, 62.

89) K. F. Nickle, *The Collection*, SBT 48 (London: SCM Press, 1966), 21-2, 55, 61-2.

필요를 느끼지 않았다고 한다.[90] 베츠는 이 두 사람(18, 22)이 교회에서 임명된 사람들이었으므로 바울은 자신의 사람 디도에게 보다 힘을 실어 주기 위해서 이들의 이름을 언급하지 않음으로 그들을 디도의 권위에 종속시키려고 하였다고 본다.[91] 이런 견해는 매우 가능성이 있는 추정이다. 그러나 바울이 이들을 극찬하고 있으므로, 이들을 경계하려는 의도보다는 고린도 교회가 잘 아는 디도를 헌금 사역의 책임자로 제시하고, 그들이 잘 모르는 형제들을 그의 보조자로서 헌금의 투명성을 높이고, 또 각 교회가 모두 참여함을 보여주어 고린도 교인들의 헌금에 대한 의욕을 높이기 위해서, 필요한 사람들로 언급만 할 필요를 느꼈다고 본다.

18절의 "형제"가 디도의 친형제이므로 이름이 언급되지 않았다는 견해는 23절에 "우리들의 형제들"(ἀδελφοὶ ἡμῶν)이란 말이 있어 타당성이 약화된다.[92] 더구나 본문에서 바울은 자신의 측근인 디도 외에 다른 형제들을 보냄으로서 헌금의 투명성을 높이려는 의도가 있다고 보는데 디도의 친형제를 보내는 것은 투명성에 도움을 주지 않을 수도 있다. "한 형제"가 바나바를 가리킨다는 견해도 있다.[93] 바나바는 바울의 선교 동역자이며, 복음 전파자이다(행 13:2-5). 그러나 바울과 동역자인 바나바가 바울의 조수 격

---

90) Plummer, 248.

91) Betz, *2 Corinthians 8 and 9*, 73.

92) L. J. Rückert, *Der zweite Brief Pauli an die Korinther* (Leipzig: K. F. Koehler, 1837) 259; A. Souter, "A Suggested Relationship between Titus and Luke," *The Expository Times* 18 (1906-7), 280; Plummer, 561; E. E. Ellis, "Paul and his Co-workers," *NTS* 17 (1971), 445-48; Thrall, 560-561.

93) Chrysostom, *Patrologia Graeca*, 61 col. 524; Thrall, 561, 주 387, 인용.

인 디도에게 종속될 수가 없고 이미 고린도 교회에 알려진 그를 초면 인사로서 소개할 이유가 없다(고전 9:6). 또 "한 형제"가 아리스다고일 것이라는 견해도 있다.[94] 그는 마게도냐 인이며 바울의 동역자였다(행 19:29; 참조, 20:4; 27:2). 아볼로라는 견해도 있다(행 18:24-28).[95] 누가라는 견해는 크리소스톰, 오리겐, 제롬, 다른 교부들로부터 현대에 이르기까지 오랜 역사를 가지고 있다.[96] 사도행전의 저자 누가가 "우리"라는 말 가운데 자신을 포함하여 쓰고 있다고 보면, 사도행전 20장 3-6절에서 바울과 동행하여 헌금을 가지고 예루살렘에 갔다는 것이다(골 4:14; 몬 24). 사도행전 21장 15, 17절에는 보다 분명히 누가는 바울과 동행한 것으로 보인다. 그러나 본문에서 누가가 동행했다는 기록이 없으므로 역시 추정일 뿐이다.

19. "이뿐 아니라 저는 주님 자신의(동일한 주님의) 영광과 우리의 원을 나타내기 위하여 여러 교회의 택함을 입어 우리의 맡은 은혜의 일로 우리와 동행하는 자라"(οὐ μόνον δέ, ἀλλὰ καὶ χειροτονηθεὶς ὑπὸ τῶν ἐκκλησιῶν συνέκδημος ἡμῶν σὺν τῇ χάριτι ταύτῃ τῇ διακονουμένῃ ὑφ᾽ ἡμῶν πρὸς τὴν [αὐτοῦ] τοῦ κυρίου δόξαν καὶ προθυμίαν ἡμῶν). 이 형제는 헌금을 위해서 고린도 교회에 가도록 교회들이 선택한 사람이다. 이 형제는 결국 바울을 동행하여 헌금을 가지고 예루살렘까지 갈 사람이

94) Windisch, 263.

95) Martin, 275.

96) Thrall, 561, 주 390을 보라. 현대학자들로, Bachmann, 325-6; Plummer, 248; Hughes, 313; Tasker, 120.

다(고전 16:3). 그러나 더 중요한 이들의 임무는 20절에서 바울이 말하듯이 헌금을 투명하게 관리하여 바울이나 디도가 직접 혼자서 헌금을 관리할 때 발생할 수 있는 오해의 소지를 미리 막는 일이었다. 바울은 헌금과 관련하여 자신의 "안전함" 뿐만 아니라 디도의 "안전" 도 고려하여 이 형제를 보냈다.[97] 여기서도 헌금이 하나님의 선물(χάρις)이라는 말로 쓰인다. 그러므로 이 헌금은 "주의 영광과 우리의 원을 나타내게 된다." "주의 영광과 우리의 원" 이 나란히 연결된 것은 헌금이 바울의 요청일 뿐만 아니라 또한 하나님의 뜻임을 나타낸다. 바울의 요청을 따르는 것일 뿐만이 아니라 하나님의 뜻을 따르는 것이 된다.

한글개역판의 "동일한 주의 영광" 이란 번역보다는, "바로 주님의 영광" (τὴν [αὐτοῦ] τοῦ κυρίου δόξαν)이라고 지정하는 의미로 번역해야 이해가 쉽다. 그러나 "주님 자신의 영광" 이라고 강조하는 의미로 번역하는 경우가 더 많다.[98]

"여러 교회들" 은 사도행전 20장 4절에서 언급된 바울과 함께 헌금을 가지고 예루살렘으로 동행한 사람들이 그들이 소속된 교회들에 의해 파송된 것에 비추어 이해할 수 있다. 고린도전서 16장 3절에도 바울이 유사하게 예루살렘 성도를 위한 헌금을 고린도 교인들이 인정한 사람들을 통해 전달하겠다고 말한다. 여기서는 고린도 교회의 헌금을 위해 여러 교회들이 이 두 사람을 헌금을 관리하도록 파송한 것이다. "여러 교회들" 은 어떤 교회들인가? 닉클은 위에서 말했듯이 예루살렘 교회라고 하고(21-2; 갈 1:22; 살전

97) Betz, *2 Corinthians 8 and 9*, 75.

98) NIV; Thrall, 543; Martin, 275.

2:14), 테일러(Taylor)는 안디옥 교회라고 하고,[99] 아시아 교회들이라고 하기도하고(행 20:33-34), 또는 고린도후서를 썼던 마게도냐의 교회,[100] 나아가 아시아 교회와 마게도냐 교회가 함께 보낸 이들이라고도 한다.[101] "우리의 원"(προθυμίαν ἡμῶν)이란 말의 해석이 다양하다. 마틴은 "우리의 준비"라고 하고,[102] 데니(Denney)는 "우리의 선한 마음"으로 번역하며,[103] 트롤은 "우리의 열의"라고 한다.[104] 8장 12절과 9장 2절에 비추어 한글 개역의 "우리의 원"은 무리 없는 해석이라고 본다.

20. "이것을 조심함은 우리가 맡은 이 거액의 연보로 인하여 아무도 우리를 훼방하지 못하게 하려 함이니"(**στελλόμενοι τοῦτο, μή τις ἡμᾶς μωμήσηται ἐν τῇ ἁδρότητι ταύτῃ τῇ διακονουμένῃ ὑφ' ἡμῶν**). 이 구절은 본문에서 헌금과 관련된 바울의 염려가 무엇인지를 가장 분명히 나타내고 있다. 즉 헌금으로 인한 비난의 여론이다(7:2; 12:16). "이것을 조심함은"(**στελλόμενοι τοῦτο**)에서 "이것"(**τοῦτο**)이 무엇을 가리키는지 당장 알기 어렵다. 우선 **στέλλεσθαι**는 "멀찍이 서다, 피하다"는 뜻이다(살후 3:6).[105] 이 말은 **φοβεῖσθαι**(두려워하다)와 동의어이

99) N. Taylor, *Paul, Antioch and Jerusalem: A Study in Relationships and Authority in Earliest Christianity*, JSNTSS 66 (Sheffield: Sheffield Academic Press, 1992) 202.

100) Barnett, 433.

101) Thrall, 560-1.

102) Martin, 276.

103) Denney, 277.

104) Thrall, 543.

105) *TDNT* 7:588-99; Chrysostom, *PG* 61 col. 325 (*Nicine and Post Nicean Fathers* XII, 364).

다.[106] 그러나 "정리하다" 또는 "개시하다"의 뜻도 있다. 헤링은 이 마지막 의미를 적용하여, "모든 일을 주의 깊게 처리하여 우리가 맡은… .아무도 우리를 훼방 못하게 하려 함이니"라고 번역한다.[107] NIV는 한글 개역과 같이 "피한다"는 뜻을 살려서 번역하되 "이것"(τοῦτο)을 바울 일행의 헌금 관리에 대한 "비난"(criticism)으로 해석한다. 뒤에 나오는 "훼방하지 못하게 하려 함이니"라는 말의 의미가 분명하기 때문에 이 동사의 어느 쪽의 의미로 번역해도 전체 의미는 같다. 바울은 예상되는 비난에 대비하여 헌금을 투명하게 관리할 형제를 보내는 것이다. 베츠는 당시 지중해 연안에 "종교적" 목적으로 모금하여 유용하는 이들이 있었으며 이들로부터 바울은 자신을 분명히 구별해야할 필요를 느꼈다고 본다(참조, 살전 2:3-12).[108]

"이 거액의 연보"(τῇ ἁδρότητι ταύτῃ τῇ διακονουμένῃ)에서 "큰, 풍성한"의 뜻을 나타내는 말 αδρότης(아드로테스)는 희귀어(*hapax legomenon*)이며, 고린도 교인들에게 바울 일행의 헌금 관리의 막중한 책임을 알리면서, 동시에 이미 많은 교회에서 헌금에 호응하여 큰 액수가 되었으니만큼, 그들도 적극적으로 헌금에 참여하라는 기대가 암시되어 있다.[109] 연보라고 번역된 말(διακνουμένῃ)은 4절에서도 언급된("섬기는 일") "봉사한다"는 동사의 분사형이다. 유사하게 9장 12절에서는 "봉사의 직무"(ἡ διακονία τῆς λειτουργίας)로 표현한다. 위의 2절과 아래의 9장

106) BAGD, 766.

107) Héring, 63; 참조, Furnish, 423; Martin, 276; Thrall, 543, 551.

108) Betz, *2 Corinthians 8 and 9*, 76.

109) Thrall, 550.

11, 13절에서 "연보"로 번역된 말은 "관용" 또는 "관대함"(generosity)이라 뜻의 ἁπλότης(하프로테스)이다. 8장 4절에서는 "은혜"라는 말과 "성도들을 위한 봉사의 교제"(τὴν χάριν καὶ τὴν κοινωνίαν τῆς διακονίας τῆς εἰς τοὺς ἁγίους)라는 말을 함께 쓴다. 또 9장 5절에서는 "축복"이라는 뜻의 εὐλογία(유로기아)를 쓰고 있다. 이렇게 헌금이 다양하게 번역된 것은 헌금이 단순히 모금이 아니라 다양한 신학적 목회적 의미를 함축하기 때문이다.

21. "이는 우리가 주 앞에서만 아니라 사람 앞에서도 선한 일에 조심하려 함이라"(προνοοῦμεν γὰρ καλὰ οὐ μόνον ἐνώπιον κυρίου ἀλλὰ καὶ ἐνώπιον ἀνθρώπων). 이 말은 잠언 3장 4절(LXX)에 근거하여 확장시킨 것이다(참조, 고전 10:32; 롬 12:17; 딤전 5:8; 솔로몬의 지혜서 6:8). "그리하면 네가 하나님과 사람 앞에서 은총과 귀중히 여김을 받으리라"라는 말의 강조형이다. 바울은 헌금 관리에 대해 하나님 앞에서는 일절 거리끼는 것이 없다. 그러나 아무리 거리낌이 없이 한 일이라 해도 사람들에게 오해를 일으키는 것도 하나님의 뜻이 아니므로 헌금을 따로 관리하고 감독할 형제를 보내기로 하였음을 밝힌다. 실로 바울은 여기서 뿐만 아니라 고린도후서 전체를 통해서 고린도 교인들에게 바울 자신과 그의 사역에 대해서 오해가 없도록 조심하는 자세로 일관하고 있다. 행여나 그의 실수로 오해를 일으켜 하나님의 구원 사역에 방해가 되지 않도록 주의한다(4:2; 참조, 2:17; 5:11). 여기서 바울은 복음서의 예수의 말씀을 기억하고 있는지도 모른다. "누구든지 나를 믿는 이 소자 중 하나를 실족케 하면 차라리 연자 맷돌을 그

목에 달리우고 깊은 바다에 빠뜨리는 것이 나으리라. …실족케 하는 일이 없을 수는 없으나 실족케 하는 그 사람에게는 화가 있도다" (마 18:6-7). 여기서 바울이 특별히 잠언을 인용하는 뜻이 무엇인가? 바울은 그를 지지하는 이들이나 그를 반대하는 적들로부터 이 형제를 보내는 것도 결국 바울 자신의 방어와 안전을 위한 조치라는 또 다른 오해나 비난을 받을 수 있음을 예견하고 형제 파송은 자신의 생각이 아니라 하나님의 말씀 또는 지혜에 근거한 것임을 밝혀서 고린도 교인들이 오해와 비난의 유혹에 빠지지 않도록 하려는 것이다. 여전히 바울은 목회자로서 회중의 가능한 반응을 예견하고 그에 대한 예민한 목회적 감각과 통찰력을 가지고 글을 쓰고 있음을 보여준다. 그러나 바울이 하나님의 일을 하면서 사람의 눈치만 살피는 목회자가 아님은 고린도 교인들의 마음과 감정을 이해하면서도 헌금 수행의 당위성을 계속 강조하는데서 증명된다.

22. "또 저희와 함께 우리의 한 형제를 보내었으니 우리가 여러 가지 일에 그 간절한 것을 여러 번 시험하였거니와 이제 저가 너희를 크게 믿은 고로 더욱 간절하니라" (συνεπέμψαμεν δὲ αὐτοῖς τὸν ἀδελφὸν ἡμῶν ὃν ἐδοκιμάσαμεν ἐν πολλοῖς πολλάκις σπουδαῖον ὄντα, νυνὶ δὲ πολὺ σπουδαιότερον πεποιθήσει πολλῇ τῇ εἰς ὑμᾶς). 앞서 언급된 형제의 경우와 같이 또 다른 형제의 이름도 무명이다. 18절에서 그의 이름을 밝히지 않은 이유에 대해 논하였으므로 여기서는 그에 대한 바울의 추천 내용에만 집중하기로 한다.

그 형제는 일에 대한 "간절함" (σπουδή)을 가진 사람이다.

σπουδή(스프데, "간절함")는 "열성"이라는 의미도 갖는다. 그는 매사에 열성을 가지고 일하는 사람이란 것이 여러 차례 증명되었다고 한다. 바울이 과거에 그에게 일을 맡겨 보았더니 열성을 가지고 잘했다는 것이다. 그는 바울의 사역을 위한 여러 시험에 통과한 사람이다. 더구나 그는 고린도 교인들에게 큰 신뢰(πεποιθήσει πολλῇ)를 가지고 있다. 그의 신뢰는 앞서 말한 디도가 고린도 교인들에 대해 품고 있는 깊은 신뢰(7:13-15)와 또한 바울의 신뢰와 기쁨에 의해 고무된 것이라고 본다. "내가 너희를 모든 일에 신뢰 할 수 있음을 기뻐하노라"(7:16). 보다 구체적으로 이 형제는 고린도 교인들이 바울의 헌금 요청을 받아들여 순조롭게 참여할 것이라고 크게 믿고 기대하고 있다는 것이다. 한편 바울이 이 형제의 고린도 교인들에 대한 "열성"과 "큰 신뢰"를 언급할 때 고린도 교인들이 이 형제를 믿고 또 그의 간절한 기대를 저버리지 말고 성의 있게 헌금해야 할 것을 암시하고 있다고 본다.

23. "디도로 말하면 나의 동무요 너희를 위한 나의 동역자요 우리 형제들로 말하면 여러 교회의 사자들이요 그리스도의 영광이니라"(εἴτε ὑπὲρ Τίτου, κοινωνὸς ἐμὸς καὶ εἰς ὑμᾶς συνεργός· εἴτε ἀδελφοὶ ἡμῶν, ἀπόστολοι ἐκκλησιῶν, δόξα Χριστοῦ). 여기서 바울은 파송되는 세 사람들의 신분을 보다 분명히 밝힌다. "나의 동무"(κοινωνὸς ἐμὸς)에서 속격 ἐμοῦ("나의") 대신 주격 ἐμὸς("나는" 혹은 "내가")가 쓰인 것은 분명히 잘못이다.

디도는 두 형제 보다 먼저 언급되면서 그가 그들의 위치보다 높다는 것을 암시한다. 그리고 두 가지 칭호로 그의 신분이 소개 된다. 첫째는 "나의 동무"(κοινωνὸς ἐμὸς)이다. "동무"(κοινωνός)

란 일반적으로는 신뢰와 기쁨의 친분관계를 나타내며, 신약에서는 복음 진리의 동참자란 뜻이 있다.[110] 둘째는 "(나의) 동역자" (συνεργὸς)이다. 바울과의 동역자란 의미도 있으나, 고린도 교인들과의 동역자란 의미도 있을 수 있다(1:24). 더구나 바울이 하나님과 동역자란 말도 했으므로(6:1) 하나님과의 동역자란 뜻도 된다. "동역자"는 (1) 하나님이 부르신 사람이며(고전 3:9; 살전 3:2), (2) 복음전파의 연합 사업에 임무를 맡은 자이며(고전 15:48; 16:10; 빌 2:30), (3) 선교지역 교회에서 설교를 맡은 사람이다(살전 3:2; 고전 3:9; 16:16; 참조, 4:11).[111] 이들은 바울의 단순한 조수라기보다는 같은 기업의 동업자 또는 공동 소유자로 생각된다(참조, 빌 1:7; 2:22).

"우리들의 형제들"(ἀδελφοὶ ἡμῶν)은 먼저 여러 교회의 "사자들"(ἀπόστολοι)이라고 소개되었다. 사도들이란 말과 같은 말이나 여기에 관사가 없는 것에 유의해야 한다. 그러므로 전체 교회에서 공인된 "사도들"이 아니라 일부 교회들의 "사자들"이란 말이 적절한 번역이다. 빌립보서 2장 25절에서 에바브로디도의 호칭도 여기서와 같이 관사 없는 ἀπόστολος로서 "사자" (messenger, NIV)로 번역되었다. 바레트는 1세기 유대 회당에서 일하던 전달자(샬리아, שליח)의 역할에 해당하는 것으로 생각한

110) Martin, 277; Hauck, *TDNT* 3:804.

111) W. H. Ollrog, *Paulus und seine Mitarbeiter*, WMANT 50 (Neukirchen-Vluyn: Neukirchener Verla, 1979), 67, Martin, 278, 재인용.

112) C. K. Barrett, "Shalia? and Apostle," *Donum Gentilicium. New Testament Essays in Honour of David Daube*, ed. E. Bammel, C, K, Barrett, and W. D. Davies (Oxford: Clarendon Press, 1978), 95-7; Ollrog, 79-92; Martin, 278, 재인용; 디아스포라가 예루살렘에 내는 세금에 대한 기록에 대해서, Philo, *Special laws* 1:78; *Embassy to Gaius*,

다.[112] 트롤은 이런 견해에 대해서 확실한 증거가 없다고 회의적이나,[113] 바넷은 수긍한다.[114] 트롤은 여기서의 ἀπόστολοι(아포스토로이)의 의미가 단순히 교회들이 선택한 "사자들"일 뿐이며 "그리스도의 사도들"(예루살렘 사도들과 바울 같은)과는 엄격히 분리되고, 나아가 더 넓은 의미의 사도권에 속한 "사도"도 아니라고 본다(고전 15:7; 빌 2:25). 그리고 일반 헬라어에서 이 말이 가끔 "사자"라는 말로 쓰였음을 지적한다.[115]

두 번째로 이 형제들을 가리켜 "그리스도의 영광"(δόξα Χριστοῦ)이라고 극찬하고 있다. 이 말은 "두 형제"가 그들의 사역으로 그리스도의 영광을 나타낸다는 말이다.[116] 빈디쉬(Windisch)는 이 말이 그리스도의 권위를 지니고 있다는 뜻이라고 본다.[117] 벤드란트(Wendland)는 3장에서 바울이 복음 사역자가 그리스도의 영광의 직분이라고 한 것과 관련시켜서 그들이 사도로서 그리스도의 영광을 나타낸다고 본다.[118] 그러나 이런 견해는 본문에서 이 두 형제들을 디도에게 종속된 것으로 나타내는 사실에 배치된다. 더구나 디도 자신도 사도가 아니다. 베츠는 이들이 그리스도의 사자로서 그리스도의 영광에 해당되는 영광을 나타내

216; Josephus, *Antiquities of the Jews*, 16:172), P. Barnett, 426, 주 654를 보라.

113) Thrall, 554.

114) Barnett, 426, 주, 65.

115) Thrall, 554; W. Schmithals, *The Office of Apostle in the Early Church,* ETr. John E. Steely (Nashville: Abingdon Press, 1969) 97-8; BAGD, avpo,stoloj.

116) Bachmann, 326.

117) Windisch, 267.

118) H. D. Wendland, *Die Briefe an die Korinther*, NTD 7 (Göttingen: Vandenhoeck & Ruprecht, 1972), 222; Thrall, 555 재인용.

는 것이라고 본다.[119] 그러나 바울이 이들이 개인적으로 그리스도의 영광을 나타내는 사람들로 보았는가? 아니면 그들의 사역이 그리스도의 영광을 나타내는 것으로 보았는가? 그들의 신분이 디도의 조수라는 것과 단순히 무명의 사람들임을 고려할 때, 후자의 가능성이 크다. 그들이 헌금 사역에 종사함으로써 그리스도의 영광을 드러내는 일이다. 그러나 중요한 것은 바울이 마치 그리스도의 영광이 이들에게서 직접 나타나는 것처럼 말하고 있다는 사실이다. 바울은 무명의 이 두 사람을 그리스도의 영광이 나타나는 통로로 묘사하면서 그 통로의 가치를 한껏 높이고 있다. 그들은 단순한 통로가 아니라 하나님의 선택받은 귀한 통로임을 강조하는 것이다. 이 무명의 형제들은 이런 강력한 추천으로 말미암아 그들의 사명의 존귀함을 더욱 깨달았을 것이며, 고린도 교인들은 이들의 헌금 사역에 참여하는 일이 얼마나 중요한가를 알았을 것이다.

아울러 "그리스도의 영광"이란 말은 이 두 형제의 헌금 사역뿐만 아니라 바울이 주도하는 헌금 사역의 당위성과 목적을 헌금 사역에 대해서 이의를 제기하는 이들에게 분명히 밝히는 말이다. 예루살렘 성도들을 위해 헌금하는 것은 그리스도의 영광이 나타나는 귀한 일이다. 그리스도가 죄인을 위해 희생하였듯이 이스라엘과 원수 되었던 이방 교인들이 구원을 받아 가난한 예루살렘 성도들을 위해 자신들의 물질을 희생제물로써 하나님께 드리는 것은 바로 그리스도의 구원 사역과 화해의 사역을 성취하는 일로써 그리스도의 영광을 나타내는 일이 된다(아래 9:12의 주석을 보라).

119) Betz, *2 Corinthians 8 and 9,* 81-2.

이런 의미를 가지고 고린도 교인들의 적극적인 헌금 참여를 권하고 있다.

24. "그러므로 너희는 여러 교회 앞에서 너희의 사랑과 너희에(를) 대한 우리의 자랑의 증거를 저희에게 보이라"(**τὴν οὖν ἔνδειξιν τῆς ἀγάπης ὑμῶν καὶ ἡμῶν καυχήσεως ὑπὲρ ὑμῶν εἰς αὐτοὺς ἐνδεικνύμενοι εἰς πρόσωπον τῶν ἐκκλησιῶν**). 마지막으로 형제들을 위해 당부하는 말이다. 이제 디도와 두 형제들이 헌금 사역을 위해 고린도에 가는데, 고린도인들이 앞서 디도를 잘 영접하여 바울의 그들에 대한 그의 자랑이 확인되었다고 기뻐한 것 같이(7:14), 이들을 잘 영접하고 헌금에 협조해 달라는 것이다. 더구나 이번 고린도 교회의 헌금에 대한 반응은 두 형제들이 파송한 여러 교회들에게도 알려지게 된다는 것을 상기시키면서 고린도 교인들의 헌금에 대한 적극적인 반응을 요청한다. 그러므로 핵심적인 말은 "보이라"(ἐνδεικνύμενοι)이다. 이 말이 분사형으로 되어 있으나 실제로는 셈족어 영향으로 명령형을 나타낸다.[120] ℵ C 라틴어, 콥틱어, 시리아, 그리고 비잔틴 소문자 사본에 나오는 명령형(ἐνδείξασθε)은 셈족어의 영향으로 분사가 명령의 의미를 가질 수 있음을 모르고 고친 것이라고 본다. "보이라"는 말의 목적어는 증거(ἔνδειξιν)이며 바로 "너희의 사랑"(τῆς ἀγάπης ὑμῶν)과 "너희에 대한 우리의 자랑"의 증거이다. 헌금은

---

120) Moule, *Idiom Book*, 179-80; David Daube, "Participle and Imperative in 1 Peter" in E. G. Selwyn, *The First Epistle of St. Peter* (London: Macmillan & Co. Ltd, 1946), 467-88; Furnish, 425; Martin, 272, 279; Thrall, 555-556. 그러나 Verbrugge의 반대의견을 보라, *Collection*, 254-8.

가난한 예루살렘 성도들에 대한 그들의 사랑의 표시일 뿐만 아니라, 헌금 사역을 주도하는 바울과 파송 받은 디도와 두 형제와 이들을 파송한 교회들과 나아가 하나님께 대한 사랑의 표시이기도 하다. 더구나 바울과 반목 관계에 있었던 고린도 교인들이 바울에게 대한 진실한 사랑의 회복의 증거가 되는 것이다. 이것은 8장 8절에서 "너희의 사랑의 진실을 증명하는 것이 헌금 요청의 참된 의도" 라고 한 것과 일치된다. 위에서 여러 번 지적한 것처럼 바울은 고린도 교인들에게 자신이 그들을 진실히 사랑한다는 것을 증명하기 위해서 애쓴다(2:4; 12:14, 15). 동시에 그의 사랑에 상응하는 그들의 사랑의 증거를 보여 달라고 간청한다(8:8; 11:11). 8절에 이어 9절에서 예수의 구원과 사랑을 언급하여 믿는 형제에 대한 사랑이 궁극적으로는 예수에 대한 사랑의 증거이며, 우리를 구원하신 예수 사랑이 헌금의 근본적 동기임을 보여 준다. "너희에 대한 우리의 자랑" 은 바울이 마게도냐인들에게 고린도 교인들이 헌금을 시작하였다고 자랑한 것(9:2)뿐만이 아니라, 그들에 대한 전반적인 신뢰를 가리킨다(7:14). 바울은 목회자로서 고린도 교인들을 칭찬하고 격려하여 그들 스스로 헌금에 대한 열의를 갖게 하려고 애쓴다. 그러나 바로 이러한 말들이 바울의 적들로 하여금 "(바울이) 공교한 자가 되어 궤계로 너희를 취하였다" 라고 바울을 공격하게 만들었을 것이며(12:16), 이런 공격이 바울이 10-13장의 강력한 반격의 편지를 쓰게 된 하나의 이유가 되었을 것이다.

주 해(8:18-24):

바울은 헌금에 대한 언급을 하면서 시종일관 매우 조심하는 자세를 보이고 있다(8, 10-13, 22). 그러나 헌금의 관리를 맡은 디도와 두 형제들을 소개할 때는 매우 고조된 기분으로 그들을 소개하고 있다. 디도는 "간절함"을 가지고 헌금 사역을 맡기로 하였고, 첫 번째 형제는 모든 교회에서 칭찬받는 사람이며(18), 주의 영광을 나타내는 사람이고, 두 번째 형제는 일에 열의를 가진 사람이며, 고린도 교인들을 신뢰하는 사람이라고 한다(22). 또한 디도는 바울의 동무요, 동역자이며, 형제들은 교회가 파송한 사자들이며, 그리스도의 영광이다(23).

이들에 대한 적극적인 평가는 위에서 지적한 바와 같이 이들이야말로 헌금을 공정하고 투명하게 관리할 수 있는 믿을 수 있는 사람들이므로 이들을 믿고 헌금을 해달라는 의미가 있다. 또 바울을 반대하는 이들이 바울과 디도 혼자서 마음대로 헌금을 유용할 수 있다고 선동하지 못하게 하려는 의도도 있을 수 있다. 이 두 형제가 믿을 만한 사람들이란 것은 이들이 교회라는 공동체가 검증하여 추천하였고(19, 23), 바울 자신이 개인적으로 검증한 사람들이므로(22), 이런 의구심이나 선동을 차단할 수 있다. 이런 바울의 조치는 바울이 치밀한 교회 행정가로서의 면모를 보여 준다.

또 앞서 지적한 고린도 교인들의 마음과 감정을 상하지 않게 하기 위해서 헌금을 강요하지 않고 스스로 할 수 있도록 격려하고 설득하는 자세에서 목회자적 자세를 볼 수 있다.

여기서 이 두 형제들을 적극적으로 평가하는 데서 또 하나의 바울의 목회자적 또는 인간적 면모를 찾을 수 있다. 그는 사람을 적극적으로 신뢰하는 모습이다. 바울 같이 예리한 영적 통찰력을 가진 사람이(2:11, 11:15) 사람들의 약점을 모를 리가 없다. 그는 사람의 악한 본성을 누구보다 잘 안다. "사람은 거짓되되 오직 하나님은 참되시다 할지어다"(롬 3:4). 바울은 하나님의 일을 위해 나선 디도와 두 형제들의 부정적인 면을 알고 있을 것이다. 그러나 비록 그들이 부족한 점이 있더라도, 좋은 점이 있는 이상 하나님께서 그들의 약점을 감추거나 메워 주시고, 그들의 장점들을 통해서 그의 일꾼으로 들어 쓰신다고 믿는다. 바울이 이 사람들을 적극적으로 추천하고 신뢰하는 근본적인 이유는 그들을 신뢰하기 때문이 아니라 그들과 함께 일하실 하나님의 전능하심을 믿기 때문이다. 우리가 사람에 대한 우리 자신의 평가에만 의지하는 것은 하나님의 지혜와 능력을 무시하는 인본주의적인 것이다. 실제로 사람들을 지나치게 가리는 자세는 결국 우리 주위로부터 사람들을 떠나게 하며, 하나님의 사역을 위해 다른 일꾼들과 함께 일할 기회를 놓치게 될 것이다. "사람을 잘 써야 한다"는 원칙이 "하나님의 능력을 의지해야 한다"는 원칙보다 우선할 수 없다. 바울 자신도 많은 사람들에게 배신도 당하고 고통도 당하여 "사람 잘 써야 한다"는 데 반대할 리가 없다(빌 1:17; 딤전 1:10; 딤후 2:17; 4:10, 14-16; 딛 1:10). 실제로 본문에서도 두 번째 형제는 여러 번 시험을 받아 그 열성이 증명되었다고 한다(22). 그러나 바울은 사람을 경계하는 자세보다 우선 믿고 사랑하는 자세가 더 중요함을 알았다(롬 12:18 이하). 속임을 당하지 않으려고 사람을 경계하는 것 보다 사람을 사랑하며 속는 것이 낫다(고전 6:7). 우리가 사람을 경계만 하면 결국 우리 스스로 그리스도인의 중요한 사랑의 품격을 잃게 되기 때문이다. 그는 첫 선교 여행 후에 중간에서 돌아온 마가를 불신하고 두 번째 선교 여행에 데려가지 않기로 하여, 그 일로 바나바와 다투고 헤어졌다(행 15:38, 39). 그러나 그 후 디모데후서 4장 11절에서 다시 마가에 대한 적극적인 평가를 하고 있다. 그의 생애의 마지막에 그를 돕던 사람들이 그를 버리고 배반하였으나 그들을 저주하지 않았다. "…다 나를 버렸으나 저희에게 허물을 돌리지 않기를 원하노라"(딤후 4:16). 하나님은 우리가 보기에는 가망이 없는 사람이라도 구원하시어 그의 능력의 도구로 쓰실 수 있기 때문이다(눅 22:31-32). 어떤 사람도 하나님이 원하시면 그의 영광을 들어내는 도구가 될 수 있다. 모든 사람은 주 안에서 가능한 존재이다. 하나님은 예상치 않은 일을 행하시어 그의 능력을 나타내시며 그로 말미암아 찬양 받으시기를 좋아하시는 분이시기 때문이다. 무엇보다 바울 자신도 "죄인 중의 괴수" 였으나 하나님이 은혜로 부르시어 그를 큰 구원의 그릇으로 쓰셨다.

그러므로 바울은 디도와 무명의 두 형제들의 사역을 통해서 하나님의 영광이 나타날 것을 믿고 그들을 증거 하였다. 데니는 23절에서 두 형제들을 "교회들의 사자요, 그리스도의 영광" 으로 극찬한 의미를 다음과 같이 말한다. "바울은 인간 본성의 어두운 면과 접촉하면서도 (사람 가운데 있는) 그리스도의 찬란함을 보지 못하는 소경이 되지는 않았다. 인간의 영혼 가운데 있는 그리스도의 영광으로 말미암아 그는 모든 것을 믿고, 모든 것을 바라고, 모든 것을 참았다."[121] "그리스도의 영광" 이란 말은 원수 되었던 이방인 고린도 교인들이 구원받아서 가난한 예루살렘 성도들을 물질로 돕는 것이 그리스도의 구원과 화해의 사역을 확장시키는 일임을 가리킨다(엡 2:11 이하).

바울이 무명의 두 형제를 통해서 그리스도의 영광이 나타날 것을 믿었다면, 오늘 우리 자신들이나 형제들의 사역을 통해서도 그

121) Denney, 278-279.

리스도의 영광이 나타날 것을 믿자. 현대 과학적 문명은 기계화되고 숫자화 되어 점점 각박하고 피곤한 세상을 만들고 있다. 이런 세상에서 지친 사람들은 진정한 사랑과 영적 피난처를 갈구하게 마련이다. 한동안 기계문명에 의지하여 행복을 찾던 사람들은 이제는 오히려 탈기계화 또는 탈도시화, 탈문명화의 방법, 즉 자연요법이나 명상 등의 방법으로 안식을 찾으려고 애쓴다. 기계문명화든, 탈기계문명화든, 죄인들 스스로의 방법으로는 자신들을 구원할 수 없다. 또 자연이 아무리 좋아도 피조물의 허무함에서부터 자유로울 수 없다(롬8:18-21). 하나님의 아들 그리스도 안에서만 진정한 평안과 자유함이 있다. 우리가 먼저 그리스도 안에서 평안과 자유를 경험하고 그 경험을 곤핍한 사람들에게 증거하면, 그들도 하나님의 놀라운 구원의 역사를 믿고 하나님께 돌아오게 될 것이다. 그때 그리스도의 영광이 나타나게 될 것이다. 우리도 감히 그리스도의 영광의 통로가 되는 기쁨을 얻게 될 것이다.

D. 형제들의 파송과 신임 (9:1-5)

본 문:

9:1. 성도를 섬기는 일에 대하여 내가 너희에게 쓸 필요가 없나니 2. 이는 내가 너희의 원함을 앎이라. 내가 너희를 위하여 마게도냐인들에게 아가야에서는 일 년 전부터 예비하였다 자랑하였는데 과연 너희 열심히 퍽 많은 사람들을 격동시켰느니라. 3. 그런데 이 형제들을 보낸 것은 이 일에 너희를 위한 우리의 자랑이 헛되지 않고 내 말한 것같이 준비하게 하려 함이라. 4. 혹 마게도냐인들이 나와 함께 가서 너희의 준비치 아니한 것을 보면 너희는 고사하고 우리가 이 믿던 것에 부끄러움을 당할까 두려워하노라. 5. 이러므로 내가 이 형제들로 먼저 너희에게 가서 너희의 전에 약속한 연보를 미리 준비케 하도록 권면하는 것이 필요한 줄 생각

하였노니 이렇게 준비하여야 참 연보답고 억지가 아니니라.

본문 비평:

1. 4절에 ἵνα μὴ λέγω ὑμεῖς(너희는 고사하고)에서 λέγω("내가 말한다," 가정법 일인칭 단수)가 p^{46} C* D F G copsa goth.에서 나타나고, λέγωμεν(가정법 일인칭 복수)는 ℵ B C^2 y Byz lat syr bo에서 나타난다. 플러머는 더 많은 사본에서 나타나므로 λέγωμεν을 선택한다.[122] 그러나 일반적으로 λέγωμεν은 앞에 있는 다른 가정법 일인칭 복수형인 καταισχυνθῶμεν(우리가 부끄러움을 당한다)을 필사자가 따른 것으로 본다.[123]

2. 4절 끝에 τῆς καυχήσεως("자랑의")라는 말이 $ℵ^2$ Byz^{pl} syr에 추가되어 나온다. 필사자가 의미를 더 분명히 하려하여 썼거나, 고린도후서 11장 17절의 마지막에 나오는 유사한 구절을 따라 추가한 것으로 본다.[124] 이 경우 "기탄없이 자랑함으로 부끄러움을 당할까 하노라"의 뜻이 된다.

내용 개요:

앞에서 8장과 9장의 연결이 잘 되지 않으므로 독립된 두 개의 글이라고 보는 이들이 많다는 것을 지적하였다. 마틴은 같은 편지이나, 8장은 보다 좁게 고린도 교인들을 위해 썼고, 9장은 보다 넓게 아가야의 모든 교회를 상대로 같은 헌금문제에 대해서 썼다고

122) Plummer, 255.

123) Metzger, *Textual Commentary*, 582.

124) Koester, *TDNT* 8:584, n. 117; Furnish, 427.

한다.[125] 그러나 우리는 다른 학자들과 함께 같은 고린도 교인들에게 9장을 계속 썼다고 보는 데 무리가 없다고 본다. 우선 9장 1절에서 헌금 주제를 중복적으로 말하는 것을 바울이 자인하고 있다. 8장 16-24절에서 말하는 디도와 두 형제들의 추천의 주제를 계속하면서도 9장의 내용에 새로운 요소들이 추가된 것으로 보인다. 9장에서 바울은 마게도냐 사람들에게 고린도 교인들이 헌금을 이미 시작하였음을 말하여 좋은 성과가 있었으니 먼저 시작한 너희 고린도 교인들이 그 일을 꼭 마치도록 8장에서 말한 것을 반복 강조하면서 특히 임박한 바울의 방문 전에 헌금을 마칠 것을 부탁하고 있고, 헌금과 관련하여 하나님께서 주실 축복을 다짐하고 있다고 보면 8장과 9장의 통일성이 유지된다. 더구나 학자들이 제시하는 8장과 9장의 독립된 서신들로서의 증거들은 결정적인 증거들이 아니다. 반대로 8장과 9장의 통일성을 지지하는 증거들이 적지 않다. 데니는 8장 16-24절을 모르면 9장 3-5절을 이해하기 어려웠을 것이다" 라고 말하면서 8장과 9장이 하나의 편지임을 주장했다.[126]

8장과 9장의 내용의 차이가 있다. 8장은 헌금을 내야하는 당위성을 헌금의 신학적 원칙과 함께 말한다. 즉 우리를 위하여 가난하게 되신 그리스도의 은혜에 감사와(8:9) 하나님의 평균케 하시는 경륜을 따르는 것이다(8:13-15). 9장은 헌금하는 고린도 교인들에 대한 하나님의 축복의 약속을 고린도 인들에게 확신케 한다(9:6 이하). 바울은 그의 대적자들이 비판하는 대로 헌금이라는 명

125) Martin, 281.

126) Hughes, 322, 재인용.

목으로 고린도 교인들의 재물을 탐하는 사람이 아니라(고후 12:13-18), 그들에게 헌금을 받으시는 하나님의 넘치시는 축복의 약속을 보증하는 중개인의 역할을 한다. 바울은 사심이 없는 중개인으로서 헌금하는 고린도 교인들과 헌금을 받는 예루살렘 성도들 그리고 "평균케 하시기"를 원하시는 하나님 사이에서 헌금이 피차 어떤 유익이 되는가에 대해 말한다. 즉 고린도 교인들은 헌금으로 더 많은 축복을 받게 될 것이고(6-11), 하나님은 예루살렘 성도들을 통해서 감사함과 영광을 받게 된다고 한다(9:11, 13). 바울의 이런 중개인으로서의 이메지 형성은 그가 헌금 자체를 탐한다는 반대자들의 비난을 의식하고(12:16) 헌금을 탐하는 것이 아니라 헌금의 결과 고린도 교인들에게 돌아가는 유익이 무엇인지를 객관적으로 설명하는 입장이라는 것이다. 바울은 고린도 교인들의 헌금을 받아가는 것만이 아니다. 오히려 하나님의 구제에 관한 축복의 말씀에 근거하여 하나님의 더 큰 축복을 그들에게 확약하는 것이다. 이런 시각에서 볼 때 8장과 9장은 헌금에 관한 하나의 통일된 서신이며, 바울이 8장을 쓴 후에 고린도로 돌아가는 디도가 맡은 헌금의 중요성을 다시 인식하고서 8장에 이어서 9장을 계속해서 썼다고 생각된다.[127]

주석:

9:1. "성도를 섬기는 일에 대하여 내가 너희에게 쓸 필요가 없나니" (Περὶ μὲν γὰρ τῆς διακονίας τῆς εἰς τοὺς ἁγίους

127) 9장 4절 주석에서 바울 사역에 있어서 헌금 사역의 중요성에 대한 설명을 보시오.

περισσόν μοί ἐστιν τὸ γράφειν ὑμῖν·). 8장 24절과 9장 1절의 연결이 어색한 것은 주제를 반복적으로 언급하기 때문이다.[128] 8장과 9장의 연결문제에 대한 논쟁은 대체로 세 개로 요약된다. 즉 이를 다른 독립된 서신의 내용을 편집하여 합쳤기 때문으로 보느냐,[129] 아니면 한 편지의 내용을 시간이 경과한 후 다른 경우에 썼기 때문이라고 보느냐,[130] 또는 단순히 반복적으로 썼느냐에 대한 논란이 있다.[131] 우리는 바울이 8장까지 마친 후에 8장의 내용과 주제를 다시 읽어 본 후에 자신이 8장에서 말한 것들을 9장 초두에 다시 언급하면서 자신의 방문 전에 헌금을 마칠 것과, 하나님의 축복의 약속을 하고 있다고 본다. 데니가 지적했듯이 9장 1절의 "(성도를) 섬기는 일에 대하여"(Περί··· τῆς διακονίας)라는 어귀는 바울이 다루기에 미묘한 사항을 다룰 때 쓰는 말이며(고전 7:1, 25; 8:1; 12:1; 16:1, 12), τῆς διακονίας("섬기는 일")의 관사와 "쓸 필요가 없나니"라는 말은 이미 언급한 헌금에 관한 논의를 다른 시각에서 다루기 위해 쓰는 "부드러운 연결구"(a smooth transition)라고 본다(참조, 빌 3:1).[132] Περὶ μὲν γάρ("그러므로 ··· 에 대하여")은 8장 24절까지의 주제를 다시 시작하는 연결구로서 문제가 없다.[133] 바울은 독자들이 같은 주제로 거듭 말하는 것을

128) Héring, 65.

129) J. S. Semler, *Paraphrasis II. Epistolae ad Corinthos* (Halle: Carl Hermann Hemmerde, 1776); B. Rigaux, *The Letters of St. Paul*, tr. S. Yonick (Chicago: Franciscan Herald Press, 1968), 110; Windisch, 268..

130) Martin, 249-250; Thrall, 38-43, 77, 503-4.

131) Barnett, 388.

132) Denney, 279-280.

133) Plummer, 252; S. K. Stowers, "Peri men gar and the Integrity of 2 Corinthians 8 and

지루하게 생각할 것을 알고 있으므로 이렇게 양보적인 말로 시작하는 것이다. 그리고 주제를 반복하는 것은 바울의 특징이다.[134)]

고린도 교회의 어려운 형편이 끝나자마자 헌금 요청을 해야 하는 바울의 입장은 매우 난처했다. 그러나 이 헌금 문제는 바울이 그의 사역에 있어서 매우 중요한 일로 보았다(9장 4절 주석을 보라). 어쩌면 예루살렘의 반대자들에게 그들이 영향을 미치려고 했던 고린도 교인들이 여전히 바울을 지지하고 그의 사역을 돕고 있다는 확실한 증거를 보이기를 원했는지도 모른다. 그러므로 같은 헌금에 대해서 2장씩이나 거듭 쓰면서 헌금의 지연 문제를 해결하려고 애쓰는 것이다.

"성도를 섬기는 일"은 8장 4절에서 예루살렘 성도들을 위한 헌금으로 이미 언급되었다.

2. "이는 내가 너희의 원함을 앎이라. 내가 너희를 위하여 마게도냐인들에게 아가야에서는 일 년 전부터 예비하였다 자랑하였는데 과연 너희 열심이 퍽 많은 사람들을 격동시켰느니라" (οἶδα γὰρ τὴν προθυμίαν ὑμῶν ἣν ὑπὲρ ὑμῶν καυχῶμαι

9," *NovT* 32 (1980) 340-48. 스타워는 Περὶ μὲν γάρ(그러므로 …에 대하여)가 신약에서 행 28:22에 다시 나오나 새로운 글을 시작하는 데 쓰인 것이 아니며, 신약 외 90개의 쓰인 경우도 모두 단순한 연결구로 쓰였다고 하여, 이 연결구가 8장과 9장이 하나의 글임을 증거한다고 주장한다. 이에 대해 Thrall은 8장과 9장이 독립된 글임을 주장하면서 γάρ는 편집적인 추가이며, Περὶ μὲν 은 Demosthenes의 편지 초두에 나온다고 한다. 그러나 이런 주장은 사본 상의 증거가 없다. Barnett, 429-430. 고린도전서 Περί로 새로운 주제를 시작하는 경우가 있으나("…대하여는"), 여기와 양식이 다르다(고전 7:1; 8:1; 12:1).

134) Plummer, 252.

Μακεδόσιν, ὅτι Ἀχαΐα παρεσκεύασται ἀπὸ πέρυσι, καὶ τὸ ὑμῶν ζῆλος ἠρέθισεν τοὺς πλείονας). "이는 내가 너희의 원함을 앎이라."라는 말은 9장 1절에서 바울이 말하는 "헌금에 대해서 다시 쓸 필요가 없다"는 말에 대한 이유이다. 바울은 고린도인들에게 헌금에 대한 간절함이 있다고 이미 언급했다(8:10). 그런 간절함이 있는 이들에게 헌금하라고 반복할 이유가 없다는 것이다. 바울은 같은 주제를 가지고 반복하는 것을 독자들이 싫어할 것을 염두에 두고 말한다. 이것이 8장과 9장이 하나의 글임을 증명하는 가장 확실한 증거이다.

아가야는 고린도 교회가 속해 있는 지방 이름이며, 이 지방 다른 곳에도 교회가 있었으나 고린도 교회가 가장 중심적인 교회이다. 고린도 교회가 헌금을 시작할 때 아가야 지방의 다른 교회들도 함께 시작하였을 것이다(8:10). 바울은 이 사실을 마게도냐인들에게 알려서 그들이 이에 자극받아 열심히 헌금토록 하였다(8:2-5). 그러나 고린도 교회 보다 1년 후에 시작한 마게도냐 교회의 헌금 성과가 좋은 데 반하여 1년 먼저 시작한 고린도 교회의 헌금 성과는 부진한 것이 문제다. 그동안 바울을 반대하는 이들의 소요사태를 겪으면서 헌금도 지연된 것이 분명하다. 바울은 디도 편에 고린도 교인들이 변화되었다는 소식을 들었으나 1년 전에 시작한 헌금이 아직도 끝나지 않았다는 것을 가장 시급히 해결되어야 할 중요한 문제로 보았다. 헌금은 바울이 세운 모든 교회들이 참여하고 있는 범교회적 사업이며, 더구나 고린도 교회에서 먼저 시작한 일인데 이 사역이 부진한 것은 바울에게 당황스런 일이다. 바울이 다른 교회에 헌금을 독려할 때에 고린도 교회를 비롯한 아가야 교회들의 헌금 결정의 예를 들었는데, 이제 그 헌금 결과가 부진한 것을 다른 교회들이 알면 바울은 물론 고린도 교회도 면목이 없게 될 것이기 때문이다(9:4). 바울이 헌금을 걷기 위해서 준비도 안 된 고린도 교회의 예를 들어 우리를 속이고 헌금을 거두었다는 비난을 받을 수도 있기 때문이다. 그러나 바울은 고린도 교인들이 헌금에 대한 관심이 아직 있다고 믿으며 고린도 교인들에게 헌금을 독려하고 있다. 아직도 늦지 않으니 빨리 시작하라는 것이다. 특히 이 형제들을 보내는 이 기회를 놓치지 말라는 것이다.

바울이 고린도 교회가 헌금을 시작하였다고 마게도냐 교인들에게 말한 것은 교회 사이에 건전한 경쟁심을 일으키려는 의도이다. 8장 1-5절에서는 반대로 마게도냐 교회의 헌금에 대한 열의를 들어 고린도 교인들을 격려하고 있다. 또한 이런 말은 바울이 일상적으로 그의 동역자나 교회를 되도록 좋은 말로 치켜 세워주는 목회적 자세에서 비롯되었다고도 볼 수 있다(1:14; 3:2-3; 7:14; 8:10, 18-23).

3. "그런데 이 형제들을 보낸 것은 이 일에 너희를 위한 우리의 자랑이 헛되지 않고 내 말한 것같이 준비하게 하려 함이라" (ἔπεμψα δὲ τοὺς ἀδελφούς, ἵνα μὴ τὸ καύχημα ἡμῶν τὸ ὑπὲρ ὑμῶν κενωθῇ ἐν τῷ μέρει τούτῳ, ἵνα καθὼς ἔλεγον παρεσκευασμένοι ἦτε). 바울이 그의 형제들을 보내는 목적을 말한다. 즉 이 형제들을 헌금문제("이 일"=τῷ μέρει τούτῳ)를 위한 해결팀으로 보내어 헌금의 지연으로 인하여 발생할 고린도 교회의 미안함을 줄이고(4절), 바울의 권고로 이미 헌금에 참여한 마게도냐 교회 같은 다른 교회들의 실망 가능성(4절)과, 바울 자신이 한 말의 신뢰성 손실(즉, 바울이 9장 2절에서 "아가야 교회[고린도

교회]는 일 년 전부터 예비하였다"라고 마게도냐 교회에 말하여 열심히 헌금하게 했는데, 고린도 교회는 그동안 헌금을 하지 않음으로 인해서 마게도냐 교인들에게 바울의 신뢰성이 손상 받게 된 것) 등을 예방하려고 한다.

"내가 말한 것 같이"(καθὼς ἔλεγον)는 8장 11절에서 말한 바울의 헌금의 독려를 가리킨다. 바울이 형제들을 그의 방문에 앞서 보내는 중요한 이유는 그 자신이 헌금에 직접 관여하는 인상을 주지 않기 위함이다. 아무리 헌금이 중요한 사역이라 해도 바울 사도가 구원의 말씀을 값없이 전하면서 동시에 헌금을 요청하는 것은 은혜롭지 못할 수 있기 때문이다. 더구나 이제 막 돌아온 고린도 교인들에게 헌금으로 인한 시험을 받게 할 수도 있다. 형제들이 미리 가서 헌금을 모두 수거한 연후에 자신은 말씀을 전하고 헌금의 결과에 대해 칭찬을 하면 은혜로운 방문이 될 것이라고 생각한다. 이것은 이기적인 생각이 아니라 그렇게 하는 것이 바울은 물론 전체 교회의 덕이 되기 때문이다. 바울의 개인적 유익을 교회의 유익과 분리하여 생각하는 것은 잘못이다. 바울은 교회의 사도이며 그는 양심적인 사람이다(1:12, 23; 2:17; 4:2, 12; 5:9-10; 6:6; 7:2; 12:14 이하).

8장과 9장이 독립된 서신으로 보는 이들은 "형제들"을 8장의 "형제들"과 다른 이들이라고 한다.[135] 그러나 이들을 다른 이들로 보아야 할 근거가 없다. 오히려 바울은 9장 초두에서 앞서 말한 것들을 다시 반복하고 있다. 9장 1절의 "성도들을 섬기는 일"은 8장 4절에도 나오고, 2절의 "너희의 원함"은 8장 10, 11절에, 같은 2절

135) Héring, 65; Windisch, 272, 286-88; Georgi, 58.

의 "일 년 전"은 8장 10절에, 3절의 "우리의 자랑"은 8장 24절에 이미 나온 것들이므로 이 "형제들"이란 말만을 특별히 골라서 다른 이들로 보는 것은 어색하다. "형제들"이란 말이 그들의 독립문서설에 반대되는 증거이므로 억지로 다른 "형제들"로 말해버리는 것으로 보인다.

4. "혹 마게도냐인들이 나와 함께 가서 너희의 준비치 아니한 것을 보면 너희는 고사하고 우리가 이 믿던 것에 부끄러움을 당할까 두려워하노라"(μή πως ἐὰν ἔλθωσιν σὺν ἐμοὶ Μακεδόνες καὶ εὕρωσιν ὑμᾶς ἀπαρασκευάστους καταισχυνθῶμεν ἡμεῖς, ἵνα μὴ λέγω ὑμεῖς, ἐν τῇ ὑποστάσει ταύτῃ). 형제들로 구성된 헌금팀을 보내는 목적은 헌금 지연으로 말미암아 발생하는 여러 문제들을 해결하기 위함이다. 첫째, 당장 고린도 교인들의 믿음과 열성이 그들을 방문할 마게도냐 교인들에게 의심받게 될 것이다. 마게도냐 교인들은 이미 헌금을 모두 거두어서 대표자들을 뽑아서 바울을 동행하여 예루살렘으로 곧 갈 터인데, 그 때 고린도에 들려서 그들이 고린도교회의 헌금이 지연된 것을 보면 우리보다 먼저 시작하였다더니 아직도 준비되지 않았다고 실망하게 될 것이다. 둘째, 그것은 고린도 교인들의 체면 손상뿐만 아니라 바울의 사도로서의 신뢰성에 대한 다른 교회들의 실망으로 이어지게 될 것이다. 바울이 각 교회에게 고린도 교인들이 헌금을 시작하였다고 말해서 힘써 헌금을 걷어 고린도 교회에 와서 보니 실제로 매우 미진한 상태인 것을 보면 바울의 사도로서의 신뢰성과 리더십이 손상될 것이 분명하다(갈 2:10). 바울이 헌금을 걷기 위해 거짓말했다는 의심을 받게 될 것이다. 그것은 고린도후서 전

체의 주제인 그의 사도로서의 진정성이나, 그의 사역에 대한 하나님의 도우심에 대한 의구심으로까지 확대될 수 있다. 그러므로 헌금 지연 문제는 결코 고린도 교회의 지엽적인 문제만이 아닌 것이다. 그것은 바울의 사역의 신뢰성 문제와 관련되어 있다. 셋째, 고린도 교회가 바울에게로 돌아와 그를 사랑하게 되었다는 증거도 찾기 어렵게 될 것이며, 바울의 기쁨과 칭찬도 모두 허사가 될 것이다(8:7, 24). 넷째, 헌금 지연은 그의 전체 선교 여행 계획의 차질을 불러 올 수 있는 심각한 문제이다. 그는 곧 고린도 교회를 방문하여 헌금을 받아서 예루살렘으로 향하는 계획을 하고 있다(행 20:3-4). 다섯째, 이와 관련하여 고린도 교회의 헌금이 실패할 경우, 자신을 반대하는 예루살렘 사도들과 성도들(롬 15:31)에게 고린도 교회뿐만 아니라 그의 이방 선교 사역의 성공을 증명하기 어려워지고, 자신의 이신득의 복음의 활로가 막히게 되어 그의 전체 이방교회 사역이 큰 난관에 봉착하게 될 가능성을 내다보고 있다. 마지막으로, 헌금 사역이 순조롭지 못할 경우에 헌금의 선교적 신학적인 바울의 다른 목적도 이룰 수 없다. 예루살렘 성도들과 이방인 교인들의 유대 관계 확립, 이방인들의 종말론적 구원의 증표, 이방인을 위한 사도 바울의 유대인 성도들에 대한 관심과 사랑의 표시 같은 것이다(9:13-15). 바울은 이 모든 어려운 문제들이 고린도 교인들의 헌금 지연으로 말미암아 발생할 수 있음을 "두려워하는 것이다."

여기서 바울이 형제들과 함께 방문한다는 것은, 바울이 방문 시에 만난 사람들을 그의 편지에서 기억하면서 자주 언급하는 관습을 상기시킨다. 즉 바울은 그가 세운 교회에 그의 동역자들을 보내고, 그리고 들을 통해 편지를 보내고, 또 편지에서 형제들을 문안함으로써 그가 세운 교회에 그의 사도적 현존(apostolic "parousia")이 지속되게 하는 목회 방법을 쓰고 있는 것이다(고후 10:1; 빌 1:7; 살후 2:15; 골 4:16).[136)]

"너희는 고사하고"(ἵνα μὴ λέγω ὑμεῖς)는 "너희는 말할 것도 없고 (우리가…)"라는 뜻이다. 이 구절은 바울의 입장과 고린도 교인들의 입장을 비교하면서 헌금 지연으로 말미암은 바울의 (난처한) 입장을 강조하기 위해 쓴 표현이다(대조강조법).

"이 믿던 것"(ὑποστάσει ταύτῃ)은 헌금을 가리킨다.[137)]

5. "이러므로 내가 이 형제들로 먼저 너희에게 가서 너희의 전에 약속한 연보를 미리 준비케 하도록 권면하는 것이 필요한 줄 생각하였노니 이렇게 준비하여야 참 연보답고 억지가 아니니라"

---

136) R. W. Funk, "The Apostolic Parousia: Form and Significance," in *Christian History and Interpretation*, FS John Knox, ed. W. R. Farmer et al., 249-68 (Cambridge: University Press, 1967), 249, 254.

137) "믿던 것"(ὑποστάσει)의 전통적 의미는 "신뢰하는"이란 뜻이다(KJV, RSV, NEB; Calvin, 120; Meyer, 372; Bachmann, 328; Lietzmann, 137; Plummer, 255; Allo, 231; Hughes, 325). 대부분의 현대 주석가들은 이 말을 "사업" 또는 "일"로 번역한다. H. Koester, ὑπόστασις, *TDNT* VIII, 572-589; Thrall, "project"(제안) 568이하; Martin, "eventuality"(성과) 284, "ground"(입장) 363; Barnett, "undertaking"(사업) 433; 특히 Koester의 견해를 지지하는 Thrall의 논의를 보라(568이하). 이들의 견해는 ὑπόστασις가 LXX에서 주로 "사업"이란 의미를 나타내고 있다는 것이다(렘 23:32; 겔 19:5). 그리고 이 말이 실제로 히브리서 1:3, 3:14, 11:1에서 "본체", "실상"(reality)으로 번역되는 경우를 지적한다(NIV, 개역한글성경은 히 1:3, 11:1은 reality[실체]로 번역하나 히 3:14은 confidence[확신]로 번역함.) 그리고 고후 11:17에서도 같은 의미로 번역한다. Barnett은 고후 11:17에서 "확신"으로 번역한다(530). 통일된 의견이 없고, "믿던 것"이라는 개역한글성경 번역이 사실상 "사업"이라는 의미를 포함하고 있다고 보고 전통적 번역을 그대로 따르기로 한다.

(ἀναγκαῖον οὖν ἡγησάμην παρακαλέσαι τοὺς ἀδελφούς, ἵνα προέλθωσιν εἰς ὑμᾶς καὶ προκαταρτίσωσιν τὴν προεπηγγελμένην εὐλογίαν ὑμῶν, ταύτην ἑτοίμην εἶναι οὕτως ὡς εὐλογίαν καὶ μὴ ὡς πλεονεξίαν). 앞에서 언급한 바와 같이 바울은 자신이 직접 헌금에 관여하는 것이 자신에게나 고린도 교회에 유익이 되지 않는다고 보았다. 헌금과 관련하여 일어날 수 있는 여러 가지 오해는 바울에게 뿐만 아니라 고린도 교회에 덕이 되지 않을 것이다. 그러나 여기서 형제들의 방문에 대하여 바울이 제시하는 이유는 형제들이 바울이 가기 전에 가서 헌금을 미리 준비하는 것은 자발적인 헌금을 낼 수 있도록 하기 위함이라고 한다. 바울이 온 후에야 헌금을 내는 것은 바울이 헌금을 강요하는 결과가 되어 피차 오해를 불러일으킬 수 있기 때문이다.

바울은 여기서 헌금을 "연보"(εὐλογία)라고 하는데, 원래의 뜻은 "축복"이란 뜻이다. 바울은 헌금의 근원이 하나님의 은혜와 축복임을 강조하기 위해서 이 말을 쓰고 있다. 헌금은 하나님의 은혜에 대한 감사로 드리는 것이다.[138] 이 말에 대조되어 "억지"(πλεονεξία)란 말이 쓰였는데 물질에 대한 탐욕이란 뜻이다(NIV=grudgingly given).[139] 12장 17, 18절에서 바울이 "이를 취했다"(ἐπλεονέκτησεν)는 비난을 받았다고 하면서 쓰는 말이다. 여기서 이 두 개의 말로 바울은 자발적인 헌금과 인색한 헌금을 대조하면서 전자를 가르치고 있다. 헌금은 하나님의 구원의 은혜에 대한 감사이므로 근본적으로 자발적인 성격이 있다. 이런 말로 바

---

138) Dieter Georgi, *Remembering the Poor: The History of Paul's Collection for Jerusalem* (Nashville: Abingdon Press, 1992), 67, 68. (번역자 이름 표기 않됨).

139) 롬 1:29; 참조 골 3:5; 유대의 증언 19:1; Delling, *TDNT* 6:266-74.

울은 자신이 고린도 교인들을 착취하였다는 비난을 의식하고 있다(12:14 이하). 최근까지 바울을 반대했던 고린도 교회를 생각하면 바울이 이런 비난을 실제로 들었을 수도 있다.

주 해(9:1–5):

본문에서는 바울이 헌금의 지연문제를 심각하게 생각하면서 헌금을 담당할 형제들을 보내니 약속한 헌금을 실시해서 자신의 방문할 때는 헌금 지연 문제로 피차 오해나 불편함이 없도록 하자는 것이다. 바울은 헌금 사역을 통해서 하나님의 공평의 원칙을 하나님의 백성의 삶 가운데 실현하는 것이라고 믿으며 헌금 사역에 적극적이다(8:14-15). 그러나 바울은 목회자로서 헌금의 당위성을 가르치면서도, 헌금에 직접 관여하지 않아야 한다는 원칙을 보여준다. 바울은 형제들에게 헌금 사역을 일임시키면서 헌금에 직접 관여하지 않고 주의 깊게 소극적 자세를 취하고 있는 것이다. 헌금과 관련한 이런 바울의 이중적 자세는 고린도 교회의 특수한 상황을 고려하면 당연한 것이다. 최근까지 바울을 반대하던 고린도 교회의 불안한 분위기를 고려할 때 헌금을 요청하는 것은 어려운 일임을 알고 있었다. 그가 돈을 직접 관리함으로 일어날 수 있는 어려움도 알고 있었을 것이다. 실제로 그가 고린도 교회에 헌금을 요청한 이후 고린도 교회가 어려워졌음을 고려할 때 그가 돈을 착취한다는 비난을 이미 들었다고 볼 수도 있다(고후 12:16 이하).

그럼에도 불구하고 바울이 헌금 요청에 대해서 조심하는 자세를 고린도 교회의 특수한 형편에 국한된 자세라고 볼 수만은 없다. 바울은 물질과 관련하여 자신의 개인적 명예 훼손을 피하려는 직접적인 이유 외에 보다 근본적인 이유들 때문에 헌금에 직접 관여하지 않고 있다고 본다.

첫째, 자칫하면 헌금으로 말미암아 바울의 복음사역이 훼방을 받을 수 있음을 알았기 때문이다. 복음은 돈으로 계산할 수 없는 하나님의 매우 귀한 선물이므로 값없이 주어야 한다. 돈과 관련될 때 복음의 가치는 떨어진다(참조, 행 8:18-20). 마찬가지로 복음 전도자의 가치도 떨어진다. "너희 목마른 자들아 물로 나아오라. 돈 없는 자도 오라. 너희는 와서 사 먹되 돈 없이 값없이 와서 포도주와 젖을 사라" (사 55:1; 참조, 52:3). 바울은 예루살렘 교회를 위한 헌금을 거두면서 자신은 전혀 아무런 이를 탐하지 않았음을 거듭 천명하였다(고후 12:14-18). 그의 청빈한 삶이 그의 말이 진실임을 증명한다. 실제로 바울은 청빈한 삶에 있어서도 모본을 보였다. 그는 사역을 하면서도 교인들에게 부담을 지우지 않으려고 손수 장막 만드는 일로 생활비를 마련하였다(행 18:3; 20:33-35; 고후 12:13, 14). 물론 때로는 교회의 도움도 받았으나(빌 4:18) 주로 자비량 선교사역을 하였다. 그의 말년에 로마 감옥에서 남은 재산이란 결국 겉옷 한 벌과 가죽책뿐이었다(딤후 4:13).

둘째, 바울은 복음 전승에 근거한 초대 교회에서 형성된 일종의 불문율 같은 "사도들의 윤리 강령" 을 따라 헌금 문제에 직접 관여하지 않으려고 했을 것이다. 바울은 돈과 관련된 복음 전승을 알고 있었다. "주는 것이 받는 것 보다 복이 있다" (행 20:35)는 말씀을 알고 있었고, "거저 받았으니 거저 주어라" (마 10:8)는 말씀도 알고 있었을 것이다. "너희가 하나님과 재물을 겸하여 섬기지 못하느니라" 는 말씀도 알았을 것이다(마 6:24). 바울은 어쩌면 초대 예루살렘 교회에서 사도들이 공궤를 집사들에게 맡기고 기도와 말씀

전하는 일에 전무하였던 전통도 알고 있었을 것이다(행 6:2-4).

셋째, 사도가 돈 문제를 언급하는 것이 은혜롭지 못하다는 그의 이방인 교인들의 생각을 존중했는지도 모른다. 당시 로마의 철학자 시세로(Cicero)는 "모든 공무 행정과 집행에서 추호의 탐욕의 의심이라도 없도록 해야한다"(*ut avaritiae pellatur etiam minima suspicio*)고 했다(*De officiis* 2.21.75). 헬라 문화에 젖은 고린도인들도 사도 바울 같은 공인이 돈에 직접 관여하는 것은 바람직하지 않다고 보았을 것이다. 바울이 디모데에게 돈을 멀리하라는 경계를 거듭하는 것은 부분적으로 나마 이런 헌금과 관련된 그의 경험에 근거한 것인지도 모른다(딤전 3:3; 6:10; 딤후 3:2; 참조, 히 13:5).

그러나 근본적으로 바울의 헌금 요청에 대한 조심스런 자세는 첫 번째로 지적한 헌금으로 말미암아 복음 사역이 훼방 받지 않게 하려는 데 있다고 본다.

한편, 헌금은 그리스도인들의 청빈한 삶과 관련된다. 믿는 사람이라 해도, 사치하고 낭비하는 사람은 진정한 헌금을 드릴 수 없다. 모름지기 모든 그리스도인들은, 특히 교회의 재정적 지원을 받는 교역자들은 "인자는 머리 둘 곳도 없다"고 말씀하신 주님처럼(마 8:20; 눅 9:58) 청빈하게 살기를 힘써야 하며, "두 벌 옷이나 신이나 지팡이를 가지지 말라"고 제자들을 가르치신 말씀도 기억해야 할 것이다(마 10:10). 바울이 8장 14, 15절에서 말하는 하나님의 균형의 원칙에 따라 가진 것을 없는 이들과 나누면서 최소한의 생활비로 만족해야 할 것이다. 청빈한 사람이란 흔히 아무것도 없이 하나님께 의지하여 경건하게 사는 사람들을 가리키는 말이지만, 많은 재력을 가졌으나, 청빈의 정신을 가지고, 자기 것이라고 하지 않고 청지기로서 남을 위해 적절히 쓰는 "청빈한 부자들"도 진정한 의미에서 청빈한 사람들이다. 참된 그리스도인들에게 청빈은 부끄러움이 아니고 주님의 제자 된 자랑스러운 증표이다. 부유한 교회는 그 부를 가난한 국, 내외 교회를 위한 전도 사업이나 구제 사업을 위해 써야 할 것이다. "풍성한 헌금"을 통한 청빈한 삶은 하나님의 나라를 확장시킬 것이며(8:2), "인색한 헌금"은 결국 하나님 나라보다 세상 나라를 확장하게 할 것이다(9:7).

E. 헌금의 의의—하나님께 영광 (9:6-15)

본문:

> 6. 이것이 곧 적게 심는 자는 적게 거두고 많이 심는 자는 많이 거둔다 하는 말이로다. 7. 각각 그 마음에 정한대로 할 것이요 인색함으로나 억지로 하지 말지니 하나님은 즐겨 내는 자를 사랑하시느니라. 8. 하나님이 능히 모든 은혜를 너희에게 넘치게 하시나니 이는 너희로 모든 일에 항상 모든 것이 넉넉하여 모든 착한 일을 넘치게 하게 하려 하심이라. 9. 기록한 바 "저가 흩어 가난한 자들에게 주었으니 그의 의가 영원토록 있느니라" 함과 같으니라. 10. 심는 자에게 씨와 먹을 양식을 주시는 이가 너희 심을 것을 주사 풍성하게 하시고 너희 의의 열매를 더하게 하시리니 11. 너희가 모든 일에 부요하여 너그럽게 연보를 함은 저희로 우리로 말미암아 하나님께 감사하게 하는 것이라. 12. 이 봉사의 직무가 성도들의 부족한 것만 보충할 뿐 아니라 사람들의 하나님께 드리는 많은 감사를 인하여 넘쳤느니라. 13. 이 직무로 증거를 삼아 너희의 그리스도의 복음을 진실히 믿고 복종하는 것과 저희와 모든 사람을 위한 너희의 교제의 후한 연보(모든 사람을 섬기는 너희의 후한 연보)를 인하여 하나님께 영광을 돌리고 14. 또 저희가 너희를 위하여 간구하며 하나님의 너희에게 주신 지극한 은혜를 인하여 너희를 사모하느니라. 15. 말할 수 없는 그의 은사를 인하여 하나님께 감사하노라.

본문 비평:

1. 7절의 προῄρηται("선택하다"의 과거형)가 ℵ B C F G에 나오고, 현재형 προαιρεῖται가 D ψ Byz에 나온다. 본문은 Nestle-Aland를 따라 전자를 택한다.

2. 10절에서 미래형 χορηγήσει("주실 것이다"), πληθυνεῖ("풍성하게 하실 것이다"), αὐξήσει("더하실 것이다")가 ℵ* B C D*와 소문자 사본에 나오고, 희구법 χορηγήσαι("주실 지어다"), πληθύναι("풍성하게 하실 지어다"), αὐξήσαι("더하실 지어다")가 대문자 사본에 나온다. 다만 p[46]은 미래형 χορηγήσεί πληθυνει("풍성하게 주실 것이다")와 희구법 αὐξήσαι("더하실 지어다")를 함께 쓰고 있다. 문맥이 바울의 기도라기보다는 확신적 주장을 나타내므로 미래형을 택한다.[140] 희구법은 신약에는 드물게 나오므로, 필사자의 실수나, 헬라식 어형화(語形化, atticisim)에 의한 현상이라고 본다.[141]

3. 12절의 εὐχαριστιῶν("감사들의", 복수속격)이 ℵ B C D G K Byz 등 대부분의 사본에 나온다. εὐχαριστίαν("감사를", 단수대격)은 p[46part] Cyp. Aug.에, εὐχαριστιας("감사의", 단수 속격)는 arm, Ambrosiaster에 각기 나온다. 이 단수형들은 11절의 εὐχαριστίαν τῷ θεῷ("하나님께 [드리는] 감사를", 단수대격)에 동화된 것으로 본다.

---

140) Barrett, 232.

141) Thrall, 585.

4. 14절의 ὑμῶν(너희들의)이 지배적이다. ἡμῶν(우리들의)이 ℵ* B 와 다른 사본들에 나오나 보다 쉬운 의미를 찾아서 고친 것으로 보인다.

내용 개요:

9장 6절부터 15절은 9장을 8장에서 시작된 헌금 요청 대목을 마무리 짓는 부분이다. 바울은 앞서 방문할 형제들을 추천하였고, 그들의 방문 목적(헌금), 그리고 헌금의 신학적 의미를 말했다. 마지막으로 바울은 헌금에 대한 하나님의 축복 또는 은혜로운 결과를 말하면서 성의 있는 헌금이 되도록 호소한다. 바울은 헌금을 거두기만 하는 사람이 아니다. 헌금하는 이들에게 주시는 하나님의 축복을 확신시키는 사도이다. 본문에서 바울은 구약 성경에서 구제에 대한 하나님의 축복과 관련된 여러 개의 말씀에 근거하여 고린도 교인들에게 헌금은 손해 보는 것이 아니라 오히려 유익을 얻는 것임을 확신시키려고 한다. 앞에서도 말했으나, 바울은 일종의 중개인처럼 헌금하는 고린도 교인들과 헌금을 받는 예루살렘 성도들 그리고 "평균케 하시기"를 원하시는 하나님 사이에서 피차 유익이 되는 점에 대해 말한다. 즉 고린도 교인들은 헌금으로 더 많은 축복을 받게 될 것이고(6-11), 예루살렘 교인들은 하나님께 감사함과 영광을 돌리게 된다(9:11, 13). 고린도 교인들에게 헌금이 미치는 적극적인 효과를 전망하여 헌금을 독려하는 것이다.

첫 번째 헌금의 결과는 하나님의 물질적 축복이다. 하나님은 선한 일을 계속하도록 필요한 물질을 채워 주신다(6-10). 두 번째 헌금의 결과는 이방인 고린도 교인들이 예루살렘 성도들과의 교제이다. 헌금을 받은 예루살렘 성도들이 고린도 교인들을 위해 기도

함으로써 성도의 교제가 이루어지게 되는 것이다(13, 14). 이런 교제를 통해서 지역적으로 인종적으로 나누어진 이방인 고린도 교회와 예루살렘 교회가 실제로 주님의 몸 된 교회로 일치된다는 더 큰 목회 신학적 의미도 있다.[142] 이런 교제는 그리스도의 화해의 구원 역사로 말미암아 가능해진 것이다. 바울의 사역은 한마디로 그리스도의 구원을 통한 화해의 사역이다(5:18-21; 6:1-13). 죄인이 회개하고 하나님을 만나서 하나님의 백성이 되는 놀라운 역사이며, 서로 질시하던 사람들이 미움을 버리고 다시 만나 사랑을 고백하며, 바울을 떠난 고린도 교회가 회개하고 다시 돌아오는 하나님의 놀라운 역사이다. 여기서 바울은 그가 에베소 교인들에게 말한 것과 같은 생각을 하고 있을 것이다. "이제는 전에 멀리 있던 너희가 그리스도 예수 안에서 그리스도의 피로 가까워졌느니라. 그는 우리의 화평이신지라. 둘로 하나를 만드사 중간에 막힌 담을 허시고…십자가로 이 둘을 한 몸으로 하나님과 화목하게 하려 하심이라. 원수된 것을 십자가로 소멸하시고 또 오셔서 먼 데 있는 너희에게 평안을 전하고 가까운 데 있는 자들에게 평안을 전하셨으니 이는 저로 말미암아 우리들이 한 성령 안에서 아버지께 나아감을 얻게 하려 하심이라" (엡 2:13-18). 고린도 교인들의 헌금이 이스라엘을 통하여 구원받은 만민이 실제로 하나가 되는 하나님의 오랜 약속을 이루는 첫 신호가 되는 것이다(사 2:2-5; 60:5-22; 미 4:1-5; 행 15:15-18; 롬 15:30-31). 이런 구속론적 종말론적 관점에서 헌금이 가져올 풍성한 열매를 미리 바라보는 바울은 감격해 마지않는다. "말할 수 없는 그 은사로 인하여 하나님께 감사하노라" (15).

142) Martin, 288.

이러한 하나님의 놀라운 은혜에 대한 하나님의 백성들의 많은 감사는 결국 거룩하신 하나님의 큰 영광을 들어내게 되는 것이다.

주석:

6. "이것이 곧 적게 심는 자는 적게 거두고 많이 심는 자는 많이 거둔다 하는 말이로다" (**Τοῦτο δέ, ὁ σπείρων φειδομένως φειδομένως καὶ θερίσει, καὶ ὁ σπείρων ἐπ' εὐλογίαις ἐπ' εὐλογίαις καὶ θερίσει**). 이 말은 파종과 수확의 농사를 주제로 한 잠언 형태로 되어있다. 파종의 양에 따라 수확량이 결정되는 것이 농사의 원리이다. 이 원리에 따라 구제를 장려하고, 도덕적 의를 권하는 경구들이 많다. "악을 뿌리는 자는 재앙을 거두리니" (잠 22:8). "구제를 좋아하는 자는 풍족하여 질 것이요 남을 윤택하게 하는 자는 윤택하여 지리라. 곡식을 내지 아니하는 자는 백성에게 저주를 받을 것이니 파는 자는 그 머리에 복이 임하리라" (잠 11:25-26; 참조, 레위의 증언, 13:6). 또 당시 희랍 사회에서도 유사한 말들이 있었다. "너는 수치로 씨를 뿌려서, 불행을 거두었다" (아리스토텔레스, *Rhetoric*, III 3.4); "네가 뿌린 대로 거둘 것이다" (시세로, *Orator*, II lxv[II 261]); "그들은 부정을 뿌려서, 부도덕을 거두었다" (필로, *Confusion of Tongues*, 152).[143] 본문에서의 바울의 의도는 되도록 많은 헌금을 내도록 독려하는 것이다. 확고한 인과응보의 논리로서 헌금은 많이 하면 그 대가도 많은 법이라는

---

143) 이외에도, Plato, *Phaedrus*, 260C-D; Philo, *Confusion of Tongues*, 21; *Change of Names*, 269.

단순한 설명이다. 이것은 물론 하나님의 자연 섭리 법칙에 근거한 가르침이다.

앞의 8장 14절에서 바울은 "상부상조(相扶相助)"의 유익에 대해서 말하였다. 거기서는 고린도 교인들의 경제적 도움은 예루살렘 성도들의 어떤 "보충"으로 암시되었다. 9장에서는 그 "보충"을 구체적으로 설명하고 있다. 8절에서 14절 사이에서, 후한 연보의 결과를 열거하고 있다. (1)물질적 축복을 더욱 풍성하게 받을 것이다. (2)헌금을 받은 예루살렘 성도들이 하나님께 감사할 것이다. (3) 이방인 고린도 교인들의 믿음의 진실성을 확인하게 될 것이다. 그로 인해 예루살렘 성도들이 하나님께 영광을 돌릴 것이다. (4) 그들이 고린도 교인들을 위해 기도하고 사모함으로써 이방인 성도와 유대인 성도 사이에 아름다운 성도의 교제를 하게 되고, 이방 교회와 예루살렘 교회의 유대가 강화되고, 이로써 그리스도의 한 몸 된 교회로서의 일치가 이루어질 것이다.

바울은 앞에서 "있는 대로" 하라고 했으나 여기서는 다시 후한 헌금을 독려한다(8:11, 12). 이것은 말씀을 받는 자들의 믿음의 분량이 다르기 때문이다. 믿음이 약한 자에게 많은 헌금을 요구하면 시험을 받기 쉽기 때문이다. 그러나 믿음이 없는 자도 후한 헌금이 후한 축복을 받게 된다는 원칙을 배워야 한다. 물론 여기서 바울은 단순한 번영신학을 말하는 것은 아니다. 앞에서 헌금의 전제적 원칙을 말할 때 "먼저 자신을 드리는 것"과 "바울을 사랑하고 사모하는 마음의 증거"(7), 그리고 우리를 구하시기 위해 "가난하게 되신 그리스도"의 구원하신 은혜에 대한 감사의 표시라고 말했다(8:5, 9). 이런 원칙에 입각한 후한 헌금은 탐심에 도취한 이방종교의 헌금과 다르다. 후한 헌금은 하나님의 구속의 은혜를 깊이 깨달은 사람이 할 수 있다. (물론 실제로 믿음이 깊은 사람이라도 물질이 없는 경우 후한 헌금을 할 수 없다. 그러나 그들도 "과부가 드린 동전" 같은 진정한 의미의 후한 헌금을 할 수 있다.)

7. "각각 그 마음에 정한대로 할 것이요 인색함으로나 억지로 하지 말지니 하나님은 즐겨 내는 자를 사랑하시느니라"(ἕκαστος καθὼς προῄρηται τῇ καρδίᾳ, μὴ ἐκ λύπης ἢ ἐξ ἀνάγκης· ἱλαρὸν γὰρ δότην ἀγαπᾷ ὁ θεός). 이 말은 6절의 말을 보완하는 말이다. 풍성한 축복을 받게 되는 헌금의 조건이다. 이미 5절에서도 억지로 마지못해서 내는 헌금이 아니라 미리 준비해서 드리는 참 연보가 되도록 형제들을 앞서 보낸다고 하였다. 7절에서도 이 점을 다시 강조하고 있다. 헌금은 억지로 내거나 인색하게 내서는 안 되고 "즐겨 내는 참 연보"이어야 하는 것이다. 즉 많이 냈으니 많이 얻는다는 것이 아니다. 어떤 마음의 자세로 냈느냐가 문제가 된다. 헌금의 양이 아니라, 헌금의 질이 관건이다. 인간의 중심을 보시는 하나님은 헌금의 액수보다 헌금자의 마음을 보신다. 하나님은 부자의 많은 돈보다 과부의 동전의 가치를 더 크게 보신다(눅 21:1-4; 막 12:41-44).

바울은 6절에서 많은 헌금을 하도록 말했으나, 이내 액수와는 상관없이 헌금을 드리는 사람의 자발적이고 진정한 자세가 중요함을 다시 강조한다. 그리하여 바울이 헌금을 강요한다거나 헌금 액수 자체에 관심을 가졌다는 오해의 소지를 없애는 것이다. 거듭 바울은 헌금의 당위성과 자발성을 함께 말하고 있다. 그러나 전체적으로 보아 당위성보다 자발성을 강조하고 있다. 그는 풍성한 헌금을 원하지만, 그보다 더 원하는 것은 자발적인 헌금이다. 그러나 그가 가장 원하는 것은 자발적인 풍성한 헌금이다. 그것이 고린도 교인들의 믿음의 참된 증거가 되고(9:13), 하나님의 물질적 영적 축복을 받는 길이 되기 때문이다(9:8-14).

"각각 그 마음에 정한대로 할 것이요 인색함으로나 억지로 하지 말지니." 당시 스토익 철학자들은 진리를 따르지 못하게 하거나, 진리가 아닌 것을 진리로 받아들이도록 강요하는 모든 외압으로부터 자유롭다고 했다. Epicteus의 *Diss.* I 17.21에 나오는 말 가운데 ἀναγκάζω("강요하다"), ἀναγκαστός("강요하는"), ἀνανάγκαστος("강요당하지 않는") 등 본문의 ἀνάγκης("억지")의 동족어들이 나오므로 어떤 관련이 있다는 견해도 있다.[144] 고린도전서 10장 29절에서도 바울이 "우상의 제물을 먹는 문제"에 대하여 개인의 양심의 자유에 입각하여 결정하는 예를 보여줌으로 여기서도 다른 이의 헌금액수에 구애받지 말고 각자가 스스로 양심대로 하라는 의미가 있다. 그러나 표현의 유사성에도 불구하고, 바울이 말하는 "개인적 결단의 자유"가 스토익 철학자들이 말하는 자유와 같은 것이라고 볼 수는 없다. 하나님을 모르는 모든 사람들이 그렇듯이 스토익 철학자들은 그들이 누린다고 생각한 자유로운 판단에 사실상 속박된 노예들이다. 그들의 진리란 철저한 금욕주의적 체념과 포기 그리고 혹독한 인내의 훈련을 통해서 무감각적인 상태에 이르는 것이다. 이런 진리는 기독교의 생명과 소망의 진리와는 대조되는 것이다. 바울이 말하는 자유는 이런 스토익 철학의 도덕적, 철학적인 진리에 대한 철저한 개인주의적 판단을 말하는 것이 아니다. 하나님의 복음 진리를 믿고 순종하며

144) Georgi, *Kollekte*, 69; 참조, *Diss*, I 16.40; Thrall, 575.

스스로 선한 일에 힘쓰는 자유다(13). 그러므로 바울은 "주의 영이 계신 곳에는 자유함이 있느니라"(고후 3:17)고 말한다. 주님의 종은 주 안에서 자유하는 종이다. 스토익 철학자들이 말하는 자유로움은 결국 방황, 소외, 고독, 그리고 영원한 절망에 이르게 된다.

μὴ ἐκ λύπης("인색함으로" 혹은 "억지로")라는 말이 동사 명령형으로 앞에 있는 **τῇ καρδίᾳ**("마음에")라는 말과 함께 신명기 15장 10절에 나온다. "구제할 때는 아끼는 마음을 품지 말 것이니라"(**οὐ λυπηθήσῃ τῇ καρδίᾳ**). 구제와 관련된 말이므로 관련이 있다고 볼 수 있다. 결국 **μὴ ἐκ λύπης**("인색함으로" 혹은 "억지로")은 **ἐξ ἀνάγκης**("억지로")라는 말과 같은 의미로서 헌금의 자발성을 강조하기 위해 쓰인 것이다.

"하나님은 즐겨 내는 자를 사랑하시느니라"(**ἱλαρὸν γὰρ δότην ἀγαπᾷ ὁ θεός**)는 말은 잠언 22장 8절 상반절(9절, LXX)과 유사하다. "하나님은 즐겁게 내는 사람을 축복하신다"(하나님은 즐겨 내는 자를 사랑하시느니라"(**ἄνδρα ἱλαρὸν καὶ δότην εὐλογεῖ ὁ θεός**). 이 외에도 시락서 4장 10, 14절, 13장 26절, 26장 4절, 35장 9절(LXX 35:8), 솔로몬의 시편 7편 28절 등에서도 같은 말이 나온다. 하나님께서는 즐겁게 바치는 자를 기뻐하신다는 생각은 유대교의 뿌리 깊은 신앙 사상이다.[145] 바울은 LXX의 "축복하신다"(**εὐλογεῖ**)대신 "사랑하신다"(**ἀγαπᾷ**)는 말을 쓰고 있다. 우리의 70인역과 다른 역본을 쓰거나,[146] 잘못 기억하여 쓰고 있거나,[147]

145) Plummer, 259-60; Barrett, 236; Windisch, 277; Martin, 290; Furnish 441; Betz, *2 Corinthians 8 and 9*, 107-9.

146) Hughes, 331, 주, 65.

147) Plummer, 259; Betz, *2 Corinthians 8 and 9*, 107.

아니면 하나님의 사랑이 그의 어떤 축복 보다 가장 고상한 축복이라고 보고 의도적으로 고쳐 썼다고도 한다.[148] 바레트는 여기서 "사랑한다"는 말은 "귀하게 여긴다" 또는 "인정한다"는 뜻이라고 한다.[149] 게오르기(Georgi)는 하나님의 사랑이 사람들을 즐겁게 내도록 만든다고 보았다. 즉 하나님의 사랑이 헌금의 결과가 아니라 동기로 보았다.[150] 그러나 이런 의미는 헌금의 근본적 의미는 되나, 본문에서 말하는 뜻은 아니라고 본다. 이 말을 오직 즐겁게 내는 자만을 하나님이 사랑한다고 문자적으로만 보아서는 안 될 것이다.[151] 여기서는 단순히 하나님께서는 헌금 드리는 자의 중심을 보시므로, 성의 있게 자발적으로 헌금을 해야 한다는 뜻이다. 그러나 이런 말로 바울은 자신이 헌금을 강요하는 인상을 주지 않으려고 계속 조심한다.

8. "하나님이 능히 모든 은혜를 너희에게 넘치게 하시나니 이는 너희로 모든 일에 항상 모든 것이 넉넉하여 모든 착한 일을 넘치게 하게 하려 하심이라"(**δυνατεῖ δὲ ὁ θεὸς πᾶσαν χάριν περισσεῦσαι εἰς ὑμᾶς, ἵνα ἐν παντὶ πάντοτε πᾶσαν αὐτάρκειαν ἔχοντες περισσεύητε εἰς πᾶν ἔργον ἀγαθόν**). 8절에서부터 바울은 일종의 중개인으로서 헌금하는 고린도 교인들과 헌금을 받으시는 하나님의 중간에 서서 헌금하는 고린도 교인들이 받게 되는 하나님의 축복과 또 헌금을 받으시고 축복하시는

---

148) Windisch, 277; Thrall, 576.

149) Barrett, 236.

150) Georgi, *Kollekte*, 70.

151) Thrall, 577; 참조, Barrett, 236.

하나님이 사람들로부터 받으실 감사와 영광에 대해서 말한다. 8장에서와 본 바와 같이 이런 중개인으로서의 이메지는 바울이 아무런 사심이 없이 오로지 고린도 교인들의 유익을 위해서 헌금을 독려하는 입장이라는 것을 나타내는 것이다.

8절에서 바울은 즐거운 마음으로 드린 "참 연보"로 말미암는 결과로 하나님의 모든 은혜를 받게 된다고 한다.[152] 이 은혜가 "참 연보"의 결과이다. 하나님의 은혜가 선한 일의 결과이지만 동시에 원인으로 볼 수도 있다.[153] 하나님이 성도를 섬기는 일, 즉 헌금에 참여하도록 하게 하신 것이 은혜인 것이다. 그러나 현재 문맥에서 하나님의 은혜는 헌금의 결과나 보상을 가리킨다. 본문을 따라 나오는 말들이 분명히 헌금에 대한 보상을 논하고 있다(참조, 고전 3:8, 14). 그리고 바울은 즐거움으로 구제하는 이들에 대한 하나님의 축복의 약속을 알고 있었을 것이다(잠언 11:25: "구제를 좋아하는 자는 풍족하여 질 것이요"; 참조, 11:24; 28:27).

"모든 은혜"(πᾶσαν χάριν)는 물질적, 영적인 축복을 함께 의미하는 말이다. 10절 이하에서 나오는 하나님의 축복은 물질적 축복과 함께 영적인 축복들을 아울러 말하고 있기 때문이다.[154] "모든 은혜"란 말과 함께 나오는 "모든 일"(παντί), "모든 것"(πᾶσαν), "모든 착한 일"(πᾶν ἔργον ἀγαθόν)에서 "모든"(πᾶν)은 물질적 영적 선한 일을 함께 의미한다고 본다. 또 여기서 "모든 은혜를 넘치시게 하신다"는 말은 하나님의 전능하신 능력을 가리킨다. 헌금을 드려 당장은 물질적으로 빈약해질 것이나, 결국 하

---

152) Windisch, 277.

153) Furnish, 447; Thrall, 578, 주, 101.

154) Windisch, 277-8.

나님께서 그 빈 곳을 넘치게 채워주신다. 하나님께서 헌금을 드린 자에게 "모든 착한 일을 넘치게 하게 하려 하시기" 때문이다. "모든 착한 일"은 남에게 유익이 되는 일을 말한다. 여기서는 9절에서 가리키듯이 구제를 가리킨다.

그러나 여기서 헌금을 많이 할수록 더 많은 축복을 받아 부자가 된다는 단순한 유추는 사욕을 자극하는 말로서 본문에서 가르치는 헌금의 교훈과 배치된다. 오히려 바울은 물질에 대한 탐욕을 버리고 선한 일에 힘쓰는 이들을 하나님께서 더욱 축복하신다는 것을 가르치고 있다.

"넉넉함"(αὐτάρκειαν)은 스토익 철학에서 말하는 "내적 자족함"이란 뜻도 있으나 여기서는 물질적 "충족함"을 나타낸다고 본다.[155]

우리는 바울이 이 글을 마게도냐에서 쓰고 있음을 상기해야 한다. 바울은 그곳 마게도냐 교인들이 매우 가난했으나 분에 넘치는 풍성한 헌금을 하였다고 하면서 고린도 교인들의 헌금을 독려하였다(8:2, 3). 바울은 선한 일을 위해 물질을 쓰면 하나님이 선한 일을 위해 쓰도록 더욱 주신다는 확고한 믿음을 모든 그리스도인들(부자나 가난한 자나)이 가지고서 헌금에 적극적으로 참여해야 할 것을 말하고 있다(참조, 13:3; 엡 4:28). 이런 말이 고린도 교인들에게는 물론 풍성한 헌금을 한 마게도냐 교인들에게도 격려와 소망을 주었을 것이다.

9. "기록한 바 '저가 흩어 가난한 자들에게 주었으니 그의 의가

---

155) Kittel, *TDNT* 1:466; Thrall, 579; 참조 빌 4:11-13="그리스도 안에서의 자족함."

영원토록 있느니라' 함과 같으니라"(καθὼς γέγραπται· ἐσκόρπισεν, ἔδωκεν τοῖς πένησιν, ἡ δικαιοσύνη αὐτοῦ μένει εἰς τὸν αἰῶνα). 이것은 8절의 "모든 착한 일"을 구체적으로 구제 행위와 관련시켜 말하는 것이다. 이 말은 시편 112편 9절(LXX 111:9)의 인용이다. 시편의 문맥에서 "의인"이 주어이며, 의인의 구제 행위가 주제이다. 다니엘 4장 27절, 마태복음 6장 1-4절에서 구제 행위가 "의"(צדקה: 체데카, 또는 צדק, 체데크=δικαιοσύνή, 디카이오스네)로 언급된다.[156] 본문의 의가 하나님의 의인지 사람의 의인지에 대해서 논쟁이 있으나, 시편 문맥은 물론 본문의 문맥에서도 사람의 의의 행위에 대해 말하는 것이 분명하다.[157] 바울은 9절에서 구제 행위가 의로운 행위임을 말하고, 8절과 10절에서는 하나님이 이런 의로운 사람(여기서는 참된 헌금을 드리는 사람)에게 주시는 축복을 말하면서 헌금을 독려하고 있다.

---

156) H. Strack and P. Billerbeck, *Kommentar zum Neuen Testament* 3:525; J. Reumann, *Righteousness in the New Testament* (Philadelphia: Fortrress Press, 1982), 52f., 234; J. A. Ziesler, *The Meaning of Righteousness in Paul: A Linguistic and Theological Enquiry*, SNTSMS 20 (Cambridge: University Press, 1972), 134.

157) Georgi, *Geschichte der Kollekte*, 71-74, 는 10절에서 씨를 주시는 하나님을 9절의 주어로 보고 있다. Martin은 Georgi를 따라 예루살렘 성도를 위한 이방인들의 헌금을 하나님의 종말론적 행위로 보면서 하나님의 의로 본다(291). P. Barnett도 8절과 10절의 주어가 하나님으로써 9절의 주어도 하나님으로 보고 있다고 한다(440). 그러나 많은 주석가들이 바울이 9절에서는 단순히 의인의 구제 행위를 말하고 있다고 본다 (Meyer, 378; Plummer, 261; Strachan, 143; Allo, 234-5; Lietzmann, 138; Barrett, 238; Hughes, 332-33; Windisch, 278, 279; Thrall, 580-853). 물론 이런 도덕적 의는 하나님에 대한 순종이나 하나님과의 바른 관계에 기초한 행위임으로 일반적인 도덕적 행위와는 구별되야 한다. 더구나 그리스도인의 구제는 그리스도의 구속의 진리와 연결되어 있다. A. T. Hanson, *Studies in Paul's Technique and Theology* (Grand Rapids: Eerdmans, 1974), 179-80.

물론 본문이 인용하는 시편 112편에서 의인의 의로운 행위는 하나님에 대한 순종과 바른 관계에서 비롯된 것이므로 일반적인 도덕적 의와는 성격이 다르다. 광야에서 이스라엘 백성에게 만나를 공평하게 나누어주신 하나님의 평균의 원칙을 따라서 자신의 것을 부족한 사람에게 주는 것이 하나님의 백성으로서 마땅한 의로운 행위이다(8:13-15). 특별히 그리스도인의 구제는 우리의 부요를 위해 가난하게 되신 그리스도의 은혜에 감사하는 행위이다(8:9).

"그의 의가 영원토록 있도다"란 말은 의인의 구제의 행위를 찬양하는 말이며, 동시에 그 행위의 가치가 영원하다는 말이다. 구제의 행위가 영원한 의가 되는 것은 그 행위가 사람들의 기억 속에 남아 있다는 것이라기보다, 영원하신 하나님의 기억하신 바가 된다는 의미가 있다. 천사가 고넬료에게, "네 기도와 구제가 하나님 앞에 상달하여 기억하신바 되었으니"라고 했다(행 10:4, 31). 구제뿐만 아니라 사람의 모든 행위가 사람의 기억 속에는 사라질지언정 하나님에게는 기억된다.[158] 믿는 사람이 선악 간에 그 몸으로 행한 것을 따라 그리스도의 심판을 받게 된다는 것은 선악에 대한 하나님의 영원한 기억을 전제하는 것이다(고후 5:10; 참조, 벧전 1:17; 계 20:13). 그러나 여기서 바울은 구제(헌금)를(을) 의로운 행위로 권장하는 것이지, 행위로 말미암은 구원이나 자동적 인

158) 죄에 대한 기억과 망각에 대한 말씀이 모두 있다. 인간의 죄에 대한 하나님의 기억: 시 10:11, 25:7; 79:8; 109:14; 렘 14:10; 17:1; 호 7:2; 8:13; 9:9; 암 8:7. 인간 죄에 대한 하나님의 망각: 사 38:17; 43:25; 렘 31:34; 미 7:19. 그리스도 안에서 죄 사하시는 역사가 일어난다(롬 4:7=시 32:1, 2; 8:1; 고후 5:19). 그럼에도 불구하고 믿는 자도 그의 행위에 대해서 심판 받게 된다(고전 3:13-15; 4:4-5; 고후 5:10; 빌 3:14; 골 3:6; 살전 5:23; 딤후 4:1; , 8; 참조, 마 25:41이하; 벧전 1:17; 벧후 3:11, 14; 계20:13).

물질적 보상을 말하는 것이 아니다. 오히려 "그 의가 영원히 있도다"라는 말은 종말론적 보상으로서, 희생적인 사랑의 정신에 따라서 당장의 보상보다는 영원한 보상을 바라는 진실한 구제의 자세를 가리킨다.

10. "심는 자에게 씨와 먹을 양식을 주시는 이가 너희 심을 것을 주사 풍성하게 하시고 너희 의의 열매를 더하게 하시리니"(**ὁ δὲ ἐπιχορηγῶν σπόρον τῷ σπείροντι καὶ ἄρτον εἰς βρῶσιν χορηγήσει καὶ πληθυνεῖ τὸν σπόρον ὑμῶν καὶ αὐξήσει τὰ γενήματα τῆς δικαιοσύνης ὑμῶν**).

본문은 8절에서 말한 선한 일을 하는 이에 대한 하나님의 점증되는 축복을 자연계시(농사)를 들어 말한다. 하나님은 선한 일을 하는 이에게 선한 일을 더 많이 하도록 선한 일을 위한 자원을 더 많이 주신다. 여전히 잠언 11장 24, 25절을 연상케 한다. "흩어 구제하여도 더욱 부하게 되는 일이 있나니 과도히 아껴도 가난하게 될 뿐이니라. 구제를 좋아하는 자는 풍족하여질 것이요 남을 윤택하게 하는 자는 윤택하여 지리라." 그러나 농사 표현과 관계되는 다른 구약 구절들도 있다. "파종하는 자에게 종자를 주며 먹는 자에게 양식을 줌과 같이…"(사 55:10 하반절); "의를 심고 긍휼을 거두라"(호 10:12 상반절). 바울은 이런 구약의 표현에 잠언의 구제에 대한 하나님의 축복의 응답을 담고 있다.

농사를 짓는 것은 농부이지만, 농사를 지을 수 있게 하고 그 수확을 얻게 하는 것은 하나님이시다. 유사하게 고린도전서 4장 5-9절에서 바울은 복음사역을 농사짓는 일에 비유한다. 복음을 전한 자신이나 아볼로를 농사짓는 일꾼으로 보고, 하나님은 자라게 하시는 분으로 본다. 일꾼은 아무것도 아니나, 자라게 하시는 하나님이 복음사역의 주역이라고 한다. 결국 우리의 모든 소유는 우리의 것이 아니라 하나님의 것으로서 우리는 그 소유의 일시적 관리인으로 본다. 소유자 하나님의 평균케 하시는 원칙에 따라서 부족한 이들에게 나누어주는 선한 일을 하면, 주인 되신 자비하신 하나님의 평균케 하시려는 세상 경륜과 일치하는 일을 하므로 하나님의 신임을 받아서 더 많은 소유를 맡기신다는 것이다(마 25:28, 29). 고린도 교회가 유여한 것으로 빈궁한 예루살렘 교회를 도우면 하나님께서 더욱 채워주실 것이라는 믿음을 가지고 헌금하라는 것이다(6). 이런 말의 이면에는 고린도 교인들에게 헌금을 할 때 재물이 적어진다는 부정적인 생각으로 하지 말고, 반대로 온 세상의 주인 되시는 하나님의 축복의 약속을 믿고, 결국에는 더욱 선한 일을 할 수 있도록 더 많은 재물을 주신다는 적극적인 생각을 하라는 의미가 있다. 여기서 바울은 일종의 중개인처럼 헌금하는 고린도 교인들과 헌금을 받는 예루살렘 성도들 그리고 "평균케 하시기"를 원하시는 하나님 사이에서 피차 유익이 되는 점들을 말한다. 고린도 교인들은 헌금으로 더 많은 축복을 받게 될 것이고(6-11), 하나님은 감사함과 영광을 받게 된다(9:11, 13). 물론 이런 축복의 약속들도 바울의 대적자들이나 불신자들에게는 결국 헌금을 풍성히 내게 하려는 바울의 궤휼이라는 비판을 받을 수 있다(12:13-18). 그러나 바울은 단순히 중개인으로서 아무런 사욕없이 헌금의 축복에 대해서 말하고 있다.

"너희 의의 열매"(τῆς δικαιοσύνης ὑμῶν)는 8절의 "모든 착한 일"(πᾶν ἔργον ἀγαθόν)에 해당되는 말이다. 그러나 위에서도 지적하였듯이 바울의 이신득의 사상에 비추어 볼 때 이런 의의 행위는 단순한 도덕적 행위가 아니라 이미 믿고 구원받은 자들의 선한 행위이다. "의의 열매"는 바울이 5장 21절에서 말한 그리스도의 구속으로 말미암아 의롭게 된 사람들의 내적 성숙과, 외적 행동을 가리킨다(롬 6:13; 참조, 갈 5:22-23).

11. "너희가 모든 일에 부요하여 너그럽게 연보를 함은 저희로 우리로 말미암아 하나님께 감사하게 하는 것이라" (**ἐν παντὶ πλουτιζόμενοι εἰς πᾶσαν ἁπλότητα, ἥτις κατεργάζεται δι' ἡμῶν εὐχαριστίαν τῷ θεῷ**). 바울은 계속해서 하나님과 사람들과 관련하여 헌금이 가져 오는 다른 선한 결과들에 대해서 말한다. 이 구절은 6장 10절과 8장 9절을 상기시킨다. "모든 일에 부요하여" (**ἐν παντὶ πλουτιζόμενοι**)는 물질 뿐만 아니라 영적인 부요함도 의미한다고 본다.[159] 지금까지 가난한 예루살렘 성도들을 위한 헌금의 결과로 얻게 되는 물질적인 축복에 무게를 두었으나, 11절 이하에서는 하나님께 대한 감사와 영광의 영적 축복을 언급하기 때문이다.

"저희"라는 말은 원문에 없는 말로 의미상의 대명사이다(참조, NIV). 이 축복은 고린도 교인들이 직접 받는 축복이 아니라 헌금을 받는 예루살렘 성도들이 하나님께 감사하는 것이다. 그러나 고린도 교인들의 헌금이 예루살렘 성도들의 감사를 유발시키는 것이므로 고린도 교인들의 축복도 될 수 있다. 그들의 선한 일이 또 다른 "의의 열매"를 맺게 하는 것이다. 그것은 그리스도의 믿음의

159) Windisch, 281; Martin, 292; C. Wolff, *Der zweite Brief des Paulus an die Korinther*, THKNT 8 (Berlin: Evangelische Verlagsanstalt, 1989), 187; Thrall, 585.

중인되는 예루살렘 성도들이 "우리로" 말미암아 하나님께 감사하는 것은 대단한 일이다. "우리"는 헌금을 하는 고린도 교인들과 함께 바울도 가리킨다. 바울이 고린도 교인들과 함께 헌금 사역을 주도하고 있기 때문이다. 이방인들이던 고린도 교인들이 하나님이 선택하시고 구원의 근원이 되는 예루살렘 성도들을 돕는 것은 그리스도의 구속으로 일어난 기적 같은 사건이다.[160] 이방인과 유대인이 그리스도로 말미암아 하나님의 같은 자녀들이 되었다(엡 2:11-22). 헌금으로 주 안에서 이방인과 유대인이 하나로 연결되는 것이 만민 구원에 대한 하나님의 약속의 전초적인 성취로 알고 예루살렘 성도들이 약속을 이루시는 하나님께 감사하게 되는 것이다(사 2:2-5; 60:5-22; 미 4:1-5; 행 15:15-18; 롬 11:30-31). 퍼니쉬는 헌금이 하나님의 오랜 만민 구원의 약속을 더 가까이 앞당기는 역할을 한다고 말한다.[161]

문법적으로 예루살렘 성도들을 하나님께 감사하게 하는 것은 우리들의 "너그러운 연보"(πᾶσαν ἁπλότητα, "모든 관대함")이다. 여기서 바울은 앞에서 말한 바 "있는 대로 내라"(8:11, 12)는 말과 달리 많은 헌금에 대하여 관심을 보인다. 9장 6절에서도 이미 많은 헌금에 대한 암시를 하였다. 바울은 독자들의 믿음의 분량에 따라서 말하는 것 같이 보인다. 시험받지 않고 후하게 낼 수 있는 믿음이 깊은 이들을 위해서 말하는 것이다. 물론 믿음이 약한 사람도 이런 말을 듣고 믿음을 가질 수 있을 것이다. 그러나 바울은 이들이 시험받기를 원하지 않으므로 "있는 대로 하라"고도

---

160) Martin, 292.

161) Furnish, 451.

말하는 것이다. 여기서 바울은 후한 헌금을 내라고 직접 말하지는 않는다. 관련 성경구절을 인용하거나 원칙을 말한다. 여기서는 고린도 교인들이 마치 "너그러운 연보"를 이미 한 것처럼 기대하며 말할 뿐이다. **κατεργάζεται**("하게 한다", "이루다", "성취하다")가 현재로 되어서 바울이 장래의 결과 즉 후한 헌금을 낙관하고 현재 이루어진 것처럼 말하는 것이다.

12. "이 봉사의 직무가 성도들의 부족한 것만 보충할 뿐 아니라 사람들의 하나님께 드리는 많은 감사를 인하여 넘쳤느니라"(**ὅτι ἡ διακονία τῆς λειτουργίας ταύτης οὐ μόνον ἐστὶν προσαναπληροῦσα τὰ ὑστερήματα τῶν ἁγίων, ἀλλὰ καὶ περισσεύουσα διὰ πολλῶν εὐχαριστιῶν τῷ θεῷ**). 11절의 말을 더 분명하게 말하여, 헌금의 물질적 효과와 영적 효과를 말하면서 후자를 강조하고 있다. 여기서 헌금을 "봉사의 직무"(**ἡ διακονία τῆς λειτουργίας**)라는 말로 표현하고 있다. 8장 4절에서도 유사하게 헌금을 "성도 섬기는 일"(**τῆς διακονίας τῆς εἰς τοὺς ἁγίους**)로 말했다. 그러나 거기에는 "봉사"(**λειτουργία**)란 말이 없다. 바넷은 "봉사의 직무"를 8장 13-15절에서 말한 하나님의 균등하게 하는 사역에 참여하는 의미로 해석한다.[162] 그러나 이런 해석은 이 말의 제의적 의미를 무시한 해석이다. "봉사"(**λειτουργία**)라는 말은 헬라사회에서는 공직(公職)을 가리키나, 70인역에서는 흔히 제사장이나 레위인들의 제사임무와 관련되어

162) Barnett, 444.

사용된다.[163)] 이런 의미와 관련하여 8장 5절에서 마게도냐인들이 "먼저 자신을 주께 드리고"라는 말을 위에서 제의적 의미로 우리는 해석하였다. 고린도인들의 헌금도 하나님께 자신들을 드리는 제의적 의미가 있다고 봐야한다.[164)] 특히 이 말이 빌립보서 2장 17절에서 빌립보 교인들이 바울에게 주는 선물을 가리키는 말로 쓰일 때 제의적 문맥에서 쓰였음을 주지할 만하다. "만일 너희 믿음의 제물과 봉사위에 내가 나를 관제로 드릴지라도 나는 … 기뻐하리니." 로마서 15장 16절에서 바울의 이방인을 위한 사역을 바울이 하나님의 제사장으로서 이방인을 하나님께 제물로 드리는 제의 의식으로 설명하는 것에 비추어 보아서 이 말의 제의적 의미는 거의 확실하다. 그러므로 고린도 교인들의 헌금은 하나님께 드리는 제물과 같이 거룩한 것이다. 고린도 교인들의 거룩한 제물과 같은 헌금이 예루살렘 성도들의 물질적 빈곤 문제를 해결할 뿐만이 아니라 약속대로 만민을 구원하신 하나님께 감사를 드리게 하는 큰 효과를 가지고 온다는 뜻이다.

"사람들"이란 말은 원문에 없으나, "많은 감사"(**πολλῶν εὐχαριστιῶν**)는 앞의 성도들(τῶν ἁγίων)과 성, 수, 격이 일치하므로 서로 관련 시켜서 예루살렘 성도들의 많은 감사로 보아야 한다.[165)] 더구나 13절에서 헌금의 다른 결과를 말할 때 "그들이" 하나님께 영광을 돌린다고 하였고, "그들은" 문맥에서 분명히 예루살렘 성도들을 가리킨다. 여기서는 같은 "그들이" 하나님께 감사

---

163) H. Strathmann, on leitourgi,a in *TDNT* IV, 226-231; BAGD, 591; H. G. Liddell and R. Scott, *A Greek-English Lexicon* (Oxford: Clarendon Press, 1961)1036-7.

164) Strathmann, 234; Leitzmann, 139; Windisch, 281-2; Allo, 236; Furnish, 443, 451.

165) Georgi, 74, 주 289; 참조, Martin, 293; Barnett, 443, 주, 41.

하는 것으로 본다. 이방 교인들로부터 구제헌금을 받은 예루살렘 성도들은 예루살렘에 모여드는 구원받은 이방인들에 대한 하나님의 오랜 약속의 실현의 시작으로 보고 감개무량하게 생각하며 이를 이루신 하나님께 감사할 것이다(사 2:2-5; 60:5-22; 미 4:1-5; 롬 11:30-32).

11절에서와 같이 여기 나오는 동사의 시제는 모두 현재로서(ἐστὶν προσαναπληροῦσά περισσεύουσα) 바울은 장래의 소망을 이루어진 것으로 믿고 현실로 말하고 있다. 이것은 고린도 교인들의 헌금을 독려하기 위하여 헌금의 좋은 결과들을 미리 말하기를 원하기 때문이다.

13. "이 직무로 증거를 삼아 너희의 그리스도의 복음을 진실히 믿고 복종하는 것과 저희와 모든 사람을 위한 너희의 교제의 후한 연보(모든 사람을 섬기는 너희의 후한 연보)를 인하여 하나님께 영광을 돌리고…"(διὰ τῆς δοκιμῆς τῆς διακονίας ταύτης δοξάζοντες τὸν θεὸν ἐπὶ τῇ ὑποταγῇ τῆς ὁμολογίας ὑμῶν εἰς τὸ εὐαγγέλιον τοῦ Χριστοῦ καὶ ἁπλότητι τῆς κοινωνίας εἰς αὐτοὺς καὶ εἰς πάντας). "이 직무로 증거를 삼아"(문자적으로, "이 직무의 증거에 의해서")에서 "이 직무"는 앞 절에서 말하는 "봉사의 직무" 곧 고린도 교인들의 헌금 봉사의 직무를 가리킨다. 고린도 교인들이 헌금 봉사를 성공적으로 잘 수행하면 다음에서 말하는 좋은 결과들이 따르게 된다는 뜻이다.

앞서 12절에서 말한 예루살렘 성도들이 하나님께 감사하는 것이 본문에서는 하나님께 영광을 돌리는 것으로 바뀌어 나타나고, 영광의 이유를 자세히 설명한다. 예루살렘 성도들이 하나님께 영광을 돌리게 되는 이유는 두 가지이다. 첫째로, 이방인의 순종(ὑποταγῇ)이다. 순종이란 그리스도의 복음을 믿고 따르는 것을 가리킨다. 예루살렘 성도들은 이방인 고린도 교인들이 예수 그리스도를 믿는 믿음을 가지고 있음을 알고 하나님께 영광을 돌린다. 둘째는 그들의 교제(κοινωνίας)의 후한 헌금이다("교제"란 말이 한글 개역에서는 "섬기는" 이란 말로 부드럽게 번역되었다). 헌금은 예루살렘 성도들에게 고린도 교인들이 그들과 또 다른 그리스도인들과 더불어 한 마음 한 뜻으로 복음 사역에 참여하고 있음을 확인케 하는 것이다. 이런 두 가지 이유로 그들은 그리스도를 통해 인간을 구원하시는 하나님께 영광을 돌릴 것이다.

"하나님께 영광을 돌리고"(δοξάζοντες τὸν θεὸν)의 주어가 분명하지 않으나 대부분의 주석가들이 12절에 언급된 예루살렘 성도들로 본다.[166] 한편, 브루스와 트롤은 주어를 고린도 교인들로 보고 있고(RSV, 참조, NIV="men"),[167] 마틴은 특별히 바울을 따르는 다수의 고린도 교인들이라고 본다.[168] 그는 12절의 "많은 감사들"(πολλῶν εὐχαριστιῶν)을 "많은 고린도 교인들의 감사들"로 해석한다. 13절의 주어를 고린도 교인들로 보고 있다. 그러나 이런 해석은 분명한 근거가 없다. 바울은 11절에서 시작되는 헌금에 대한 예루살렘 성도들의 적극적 반응을 계속해서 말하는 것이다.[169] 본문의 "반응"은 고린도 교인들의 "봉사의 직무"로 말미암아 나타난 것이다.[170] 더구나 마틴도 인정하고 있듯이 본문의 "저

166) Lietzmann, 139; Barrett, 240; Furnish, 440; Héring, 68; Plummer, 266; Thrall, 588.
167) Bruce, 228; Thrall, 588.
168) Martin, 294.
169) Thrall, 588.

희"(αὐτοὺς)는 분명히 예루살렘 성도들을 가리킨다.[171] 또한 따라오는 14절의 "저희"(αὐτῶν)도 마찬가지며, 특히 이 말에 있는 καί("그리고" 혹은 "또한")는 같은 주어(예루살렘 성도들)의 연속적인 동작을 가리킨다고 보는 것이 자연스럽다.

지금까지 지적해 왔듯이 고린도 교인들의 헌금은 구제금이나 그 이면에는 여러 가지 복합적인 의미가 있다. 무엇보다, 예루살렘 사도들에 의해서 이방인을 위한 바울 사도의 역할과 그의 사도적 권위를 보다 적극적으로 인정하는 계기가 될 수 있다(행 13:46; 15:7 이하; 갈 2:10). 이런 인정은 바울의 고린도 교회에서의 입지뿐만 아니라 다른 이방교회에서의 바울의 입지를 더욱 강화시킬 수 있는 반사적 효과도 있다. 특히 고린도 교회에서 바울을 반대하는 이들은 주로 예루살렘 사도들의 추천서를 가져온 이들로서 바울과 그의 복음을 정통성이 결여된 것으로 보았다(3:1; 11:5; 22, 23). 만일 고린도 교회에서의 헌금 사역이 부실하게 끝날 경우에 바울이 예루살렘 방문 시에 그곳의 사도들과 성도들에게 그의 이방인을 위한 이신득의 사역의 당위성을 잃게 될 것이 확실하다. 그러나 고린도 교회의 풍성한 헌금으로 인하여 예루살렘 교회가 바울의 이방선교사역을 인정하는 경우에 이방인 교회와 예루살렘 교회 간에 성도의 교제 이루어 질 것이다. 그리고 이로 말미암아 이방인 그리스도인들과 유대인 그리스도인들이 한 몸 된 그리스도의 교회를 이루는 것이다(롬 3:29; 30; 10:9-13; 갈 3:28; 29; 고전 10:32). 이런 교제를 통한 한 몸이 되는 사건은 고

170) Barrett, 232; Furnish, 440.

171) Martin, 294.

린도 교인들과 예루살렘 교인들에게만 국한 되는 것이 아니라 결국 "모든 교인들"(εἰς πάντας)에게로 확대될 것이다.[172] 그리고 종국적으로는 만민을 구원하시는 하나님의 영광이 나타나게 될 것이다. 성도의 친밀한 교제와 그로 인한 위로와 기쁨이야 말로 하나님 나라 백성이 누리는 특권이며 바울의 사역이 지향하는 목회이다.

이러한 헌금 사역의 목회적 신학적 동기를 생각할 때 바울이 고린도 교회의 헌금을 중시할 수밖에 없는 이유를 알 수 있다.

14. "또 저희가 너희를 위하여 간구하며 하나님의 너희에게 주신 지극한 은혜를 인하여 너희를 사모하느니라"(καὶ αὐτῶν δεήσει ὑπὲρ ὑμῶν ἐπιποθούντων ὑμᾶς διὰ τὴν ὑπερβάλλουσαν χάριν τοῦ θεοῦ ἐφ' ὑμῖν). 위에서 지적하였듯이 접속사 καί(그리고)는 13절의 예루살렘 성도들의 헌금에 대해 예상되는 적극적인 반응을 계속 말하고 있다. 앞에서는 예루살렘 성도들이 감사를 하나님께 드리고(11, 12), 또 영광을 돌릴 것이라고 했다(13). 여기서는 고린도 교인들을 위해 기도하고, 그들을 "사모하게", 또는 "그리워하게"(ἐπιποθεῖν)될 것이다. 바울은 기도를 성도간의 교제의 수단으로서 그의 서신의 초두와 말미에 자주 언급하고 있다.[173] 기도는 13절에서 말하는 고린도 교인들과 예루살렘 성도들 간에 시작된 교제를 강화시키고 지속하는 수단

172) Tasker, 129; Héring, 68, 주, 10; J. Hainz, *Koinonia*, "Kirche" als Gemeinschaft bei Paulus, 144.

173) 롬 1:9; 15:30; 엡 1:16; 빌 1:9; 골 1:3, 9; 4:12; 살전 1:2; 5:25; 살후 1:11, 3:1.

이다. "하나님의 너희에게 주신 지극한 은혜를 인하여"(διὰ τὴν ὑπερβάλλουσαν χάριν τοῦ θεοῦ ἐφ' ὑμῖν)에서 "은혜"는 지금까지의 의미(즉 헌금)와는 달리, 8장 1절에서와 같이 하나님의 일반적인 은혜를 가리킨다. 그러나 그 일반적 의미의 은혜는 8장 1절에서나 여기에서 모두 헌금과 관련된다. 즉 "헌금을 하도록 마음을 움직여 주신 하나님의 은혜"라는 뜻이다.

지금까지 바울이 말한 헌금의 사역은 무엇보다도 이방인과 이스라엘의 구원하시는 하나님의 구원 역사와 관련되어 있다. 이런 큰 하나님의 구원 사역에 고린도 교인들 같은 이방인들을 참여케 하신 은혜는 하나님이 베푸시는 지극한 은혜(τὴν ὑπερβάλλουσαν χάριν)이다. 하나님께서 그의 크신 은혜로 이방인인 고린도인들을 같은 하나님의 자녀로 삼으신 것이다. 그러므로 이제 고린도 교인들이 주 안에서 한 형제 된 것을 확인한 예루살렘 성도들은 그들을 그리워하게 된다는 것이다. 고린도 교인들의 헌금 교제(τὴν κοινωνίαν τῆς διακονίας τῆς εἰς τοὺς ἁγίους, 8:4)가 이렇게 풍성하고 지속적인 아름다운 성도의 교제의 파급효과를 가져온다는 것이다. 이런 교제가 바울의 사역이 궁극적으로 지향하는 것이다.

15. "말할 수 없는 그의 은사를 인하여 하나님께 감사하노라"(Χάρις τῷ θεῷ ἐπὶ τῇ ἀνεκδιηγήτῳ αὐτοῦ δωρεᾷ). 바울은 하나님을 찬양하는 말로 헌금 요청의 글을 맺는다. 이 말은 원문에서는 다시 "하나님께 은혜"(Χάρις τῷ θεῷ)라는 말로 시작된다. 그러나 여기서 은혜는 모두 "감사"라는 말로 번역하고 있다. 끝에 있는 "은사" 또는 "선물"(δωρεᾷ)이란 말이 있으므로 "감사"로 번

역하는 것이다. 8장 1절에서 하나님의 은혜로 시작하고 9장 마지막 절을 은혜로 맺는 것은 헌금요청의 서신에 매우 적합한 양식이다. 결국 우리의 모든 것이 주의 것이라는 엄숙한 고백이 내포되어 있나. 앞에서 말한 하나님이 베푸시는 물질적 은혜와 영적 은혜(감사, 영광, 기도, 교제)를 모두 가리킨다. 그러나 "말할 수 없는 그의 은사"는 이런 모든 은혜 외에 그의 아들 예수 그리스도를 주신 은혜를 가리킨다고 보는 것이 옳다.[174] 예수 그리스도의 선물은 죄인들이 감히 받을 수 없는 그러나 어쩔 수 없이 받을 수밖에 없는 "말로 다 표현할 수 없고", "측량할 수 없는" 은사이다(롬 11:33). 이 은사는 사람들이 줄 수 없는 하나님만이 주실 수 있는 특별한 은사(αὐτοῦ δωρεᾶ)이다.

바울의 이 마지막 찬양의 말의 의미 가운데에서도 헌금의 당위성이 암시되어 있다. 이렇게 "말할 수 없는 은사"를 받은 우리가 헌금하는 것은 마땅하다는 반응을 기대할 수 있다.

주해(9:6-15):

바울은 헌금의 원칙을 하나님의 상호평등주의 원칙에 두었다(8:13-15; 참조, 12:13). 하나님이 그의 자비하신 성품에서 그의 백성들이 평등하게 살도록 나누어주신다. 이 평등의 원칙에 따라서 고린도 교인들이 예루살렘 성도들을 돕는 것이다. 그러나 고린도 교인들도 예루살렘 성도들로 말미암아 구원을 얻은 셈이므로 결국 서로 돕는 것이 된다. 바울은 구제 헌금은 일종의 상호 이익이

174) Martin, 295; Thrall, 594.

보장된 투자와 같은 것으로 설명한다.

바울은 고린도 교회, 예루살렘 교회, 그리고 하나님 사이에서 헌금으로 말미암아 피차 얻는 유익에 대해서 제3자로서 말하고 있다. 물론 이런 축복들은 직접적으로나 간접적으로 헌금을 하는 고린도 교인들이 받게 되는 것이다. 헌금의 결과는 물질적으로 갚아주시는 하나님의 축복과 예루살렘 교인들의 중보 기도와 깊어지는 교제는 물론, 그들이 하나님께 많은 감사를 드리는 것과 하나님께 영광을 돌리는 것이다. 이런 축복의 열거는 헌금을 독려하는 방법이기도하다. 바울이 헌금을 요청하는 것만으로 끝나지 않고, 9장에서 헌금의 결과로 받게 되는 축복을 일일이 열거하면서 바울은 헌금을 거두기만 하려는 것이 아니라, 고린도 교인들이 헌금으로 말미암아 발생하는 유익한 효과를 말해주는 것이다. 그는 구약에서의 하나님의 말씀 가운데 구제하는 자에게 주시는 물질적 축복을 열거하고(9:8-10), 또한 감사(11, 12, 15), 영광(13), 교제(14), 중보기도(14) 같은 축복들을 말한다. 그리고 바울조차 이렇게 이방인 고린도인들이 구원받아 예루살렘 성도들을 돕는 것이 너무 감사하여 이런 모든 헌금의 과정과 축복의 결과로 이끄실 하나님을 찬양하면서 글을 맺는다. 그는 그의 반대자들이 비난하듯 고린도 교인들을 착취하는 악한 사람이 아니다(12:16-18). 그는 복음의 사도로서 고린도 교인들에게 여전히 좋은 소식을 전해 주고 있는 것이다. 즉 고린도 교인들이 헌금을 하는 것은 손해 보는 일이 아니라 결국 유익이 되는 일이라는 것을 가르치는 사도로서의 선한 사역을 하고 있는 것이다. 이런 의미에서 바울은 9장 끝에서 고린도 교인들에게 귀한 선물을 나누어 주고 있는 것이다. 그 자신이 "상호 평등의 원칙"을 준수하고 있는 셈이다.

교역자들이 헌금 요청을 자주하거나 직접 하는 것은 은혜롭지 못한 것이 사실이다. 영적 지도자들로서 사람들에게 은혜를 베푸는 대신 물질적 요구를 하는 것이 적절치 못한 것으로 생각되는 것은 당연하다. 그래서 바울도 특히 8장에서 본대로 강요하지 않고 "있는 대로" "원하는 대로" 하라고 고린도 교인들의 자발적 결정에 맡기면서 조심하면서 헌금을 부탁한다. 그리고 자기가 직접 나서지 않고 형제들을 파송하여 헌금 사역을 맡긴다.

그러나 어떤 경우 다른 사람 보다 목회자가 직접 헌금의 필요성을 말해야 할 때가 있다. 그럴 경우 9장에서의 바울처럼 헌금을 교인들의 돈을 축내는 것이라고만 생각지 말고, 목회자 자신이 헌금이 하나님의 축복의 통로가 됨을 확신하고 또한 교인들을 그렇게 확신시켜야 한다. 목회자의 확신은 그 말을 듣는 이들에게도 전달되어서 은혜로운 결과가 있을 것이다. 헌금 요청도 어려운 일이나 문제는 헌금으로 오는 하나님의 축복과 유익의 약속에 대해 확신을 하는 것이 더 어려운 일이다. 헌금 요청 이전에 기도로 이런 확신에 이르도록 해야 한다. 확신이 없는 요청은 오히려 하지 않는 것이 좋다. 자신과 교인들 그리고 하나님을 속이는 것이기 때문이다. 일단 확신에 이르면 헌금으로 인한 오해나 어려움에도 아랑곳하지 말고 목회자는 신앙 양심에 따라서 헌금 요청을 "복음" 외의 행정적 사안으로서가 아니라 엄연한 "복음"의 내용으로서 전할 수 있을 것이다. 9장 본문에 의하면 헌금이야말로 온갖 복을 받게 하는 복된 소식이기 때문이다. 이런 확신 있는 헌금 요청은 목회자가 믿음이 있는 교인들에게 주는 은혜로운 선물이 되는 것이다. 그러나 이럴 때에도 바울이 주의하는 바와 같이 믿음이 약한 이들을 고려해야하고, 강요하는 것이 되어서는 안 된다. 축복의 결과를 확신하며 설교하는 것은 강요하는 것과는 다르다. 전자는 하나님의 말씀을 그대로 전하는 것이며, 후자는 인위적이고 사욕적인 것이다.

또한 이런 하나님의 축복을 믿는 믿음이 세상 탐욕과 같아서는 안 되고 무엇보다 구원의 은혜에 감사하고, 또한 하나님의 깊으신 지혜와 사랑의 섭리에 순종하는 자세로 헌금할 것을 가르쳐야 한다. 탐욕적인 헌금은 "참 연보"가 될 수 없고 흠 있고 온전치 못한 제물과 같이 하나님이 받으시지 않을 것이다(출 12:5; 레 1:3; 삼상 15:22; 말 1:14; 잠 21:27). 마게도냐인들처럼 먼저 자신을 하나님께 드려서(5), 하나님의 거룩하시고 합당하신 뜻에 맡기듯이 사심 없이 기쁘게 드려야 할 것이다(5, 7). 축복도 하나님의 뜻에 온전히 맡기는 것이 "참 연보"답다. 그 축복이 물질적일 수도 있고, 영적일 수도 있고, 또 모두 일 수도 있다. 원하는 때에 올 수도 있고 원하는 때에 오지 않을 수도 있다. 하나님이 우리를 축복하시는 것은 우리의 원대로 하실 수도 있으나, 우리의 원대로만 하시지는 않으신다. 하나님은 그의 무궁한 지혜에 따라 우리를 축복하신다. "깊도다, 하나님의 지혜와 지식의 부요함이여, 그의 판단은 측량치 못할 것이며 그의 길은 찾지 못할 것이로다. 누가 주의 마음을 알았느뇨? 누가 그의 모사가 되었느뇨? 누가 주께 먼저 드려서 갚으심을 받겠느뇨?("내가 먼저 하나님께 드렸으니 이제 그가 갚아주실 것이다"라고 말할 사람이 어디 있느냐?[35]) 이는 만물이 주에게서 나오고 주로 말미암고 주에게로 돌아감이라. 영광이 그에게 세세토록 있을지어다 아멘"(롬 11:33-36). 이런 말씀(특히 35절)은 단순한 기계적이고, 주면 받는다는 식의 축복관을 버리고, 하나님의 전지 전능하심과 깊으신 뜻에 순종하는 축복관을 가져야

"참 연보"를 할 수 있음을 보여준다. 어쩌면, 바울이 12장 16절에서 "어떤 이의 말이 내가 너희에게 짐을 지우지는 아니하였을지라도 공교한 자가 되어 궤계로 너희를 취하였다하니"라는 비난을 듣게 된 것은 본문과 같은 바울의 헌금에 대한 축복의 말을 곡해하였기 때문일 수도 있다. 축복을 내세워 헌금을 하라고 한다는 비난일 수 있다. 또는 바울이 평소에 다른 사도들처럼 보수를 받지 않는 것도 사실은 헌금으로 그 보수를 대신 충당하려한다는 반대자들의 악의에 찬 비난일 수도 있다(7:2). 그러나 본문의 바울의 말씀은 하나님의 약속에 따라 확신을 가지고 말하였음으로 "궤계"일 수 없다. 그러나 하나님의 깊으신 지혜와 섭리에 대한 믿음이 없는 이들이 본문을 기계적으로 "주면 더 받는다"는 식으로 사욕적으로 곡해하고, 또 그를 반대하는 이들은 바울이 그들에게서 재물을 "궤계로 빼앗는다"고 바울을 비난할 여지가 있다.

헌금으로 인한 시험과 곡해의 가능성에도 불구하고 복음 사역자는 필요에 따라 헌금을 복음 사역의 일부로서 거두어야 할 책임이 있다. 교인들이 하나님께 헌신하는 자세로서, 선한 일에 힘써야 하는 마땅한 임무로서, 하나님의 축복을 받는 선행으로서, 헌금을 하도록 가르쳐야한다.

V. 사도직에 대한 변명 혹은 자천(自薦) (10:1-13:10)

이 마지막 부분에서 바울은 고린도 교인들이 반대자들의 선동과 비난으로 말미암아 바울이 진정한 사도인가에 대한 증거를 요구하고 있음을 알고서 자신의 사도직과 관련된 몇 가지 문제들을 적극적으로 논하면서 자신의 사도직을 변명한다(13:3). 바울은 그의 변명 가운데 반대자들을 질책하며, 고린도 교인들에게는 자신의 사도직의 진정성을 묻기 전에 스스로 자신들의 믿음이 진정한 믿음인지를 검토하라고 명한다(13:5).

서론 부분에서 논의한 바와 같이 10장부터 13장은 1장부터 9장과 대조적으로 바울이 고린도 교인들에게 매우 격앙된 어조와 신랄한 자세로 말하고 있으므로 이 부분이 1-9장과 같은 편지인가, 다른 편지인가에 관한 논쟁이 있어왔다. 서론에서 이미 논했으나 지금까지 제안된 의견들을 정리해보면, 대체로 세 가지로 분류될 수 있다. (1) 원래 독립된 편지로서 고린도후서에 편집적으로 추가된 것이다. 이 견해는 다시 (a) 바울이 이전에 디도를 통해서 보낸 "엄격한 편지"의 일부라는 견해,[1] 그리고 (b) 1-9장을 쓴 후에 보낸 편지라는 두 가지 견해로 나뉜다.[2] (2) 독립된 편지가 아니며,

---

1) J. S. Semler, 310, 주, 350; J. Weiss, *Earliest Christianity*, 356-7.

2) Thrall, 5-20, 595, 596. Thrall 특유의 종합적인 견해는 다음 학자들의 연구에 기초하고 있다. J. Zmijewski, *Der Stil der paulinischen 'Narrenrede': Analyse der Sprachgestaltung in 2 Kor 11, 1-12, 10 als Beitrag zur Methodik von Stiluntersuchungen neutestamentlicher Texte*, BBB 52 (Bonn/Koeln: Hanstein, 1978; M. M. DiCicco, *Paul's Use of Ethos, Pathos, and Logos in 2 Corinthians 10-13*, MBPS 31 (Lewiston: Mellen Biblical Press, 1995); Hans G. Sundermann, *Der schwache Apostel und die Kraft der Rede*, 29-30.

1-9장은 주로 바울을 지지하는 다수를 향해 쓴 것이고, 10-13장은 주로 바울을 반대하는 소수를 염두에 두고 대해 쓴 것이다.[3] (3) 독립된 편지가 아니나, 1-9장을 쓴 뒤에, 얼마 있다가 고린도 교회 형편이 다시 어려워지자 다시 덧 부쳐 쓴 것이다.[4] 우리는 (2)와 같이 1-13장은 하나의 편지로 처음부터 계속해서 썼다는 견해이다.[5] 첫 번째 견해, 즉 독립된 편지라는 견해는 이를 지지하는 사본 상의 증거가 없다. 모든 고린도후서의 사본은 1장부터 13장까지 하나의 서신으로 나와 있다. 그리고 초대교회에서의 바울 사도의 권위를 생각할 때, 그의 독립된 두 편지를 누군가 감히 거두절미(去頭截尾)하여 하나의 서신으로 편집할 수 있다는 것을 생각하기 어렵다.[6] 더구나 그렇게 함으로써 후대의 독자들의 이해를 돕는 것이 아니라 우리가 지금 겪는 것과 같은 혼란을 초래할 수 있음을 알면서도 편집을 강행했다고 볼 수 없다. 두 번째와 세 번째는 모두 하나의 서신을 말하면서도, 두 개의 다른 수신자들을 대상으로 보거나(두 번째), 고린도 교회의 바뀐 형편을 고려하고 있다(세 번째). 서론에서 고린도후서의 통일성을 다루는 부분에서 이 문제에 관해서 이미 논의하였으므로 더 자세히 논의할 필요가 없다고 본다. 다만 여기서는 이 부분에서 조차 바울은 화해의 주제를 잊지 않고 있다는 것이다(5:18-21; 7:2). 자신이 화해의 사도로서 고린도 교인들을 그리스도에게로 이끄는 책임을 잊지 않고서 간간히 화해의 말을 하고 있다(11:2, 11; 12:14, 15). 무엇보다 이

3) Tasker, 32-35; Hughes, xxiii-xxxv; D. Guthrie, *New Testament Introduction*, 446.

4) Martin, vlvi, 298.

5) Barnett, 17-23; 451.

6) Barnett, 452.

부분의 처음과 마지막을 화해적인 말로 시작하고 맺는다(10:1; 13:7, 9, 10).

이 마지막 부분의 여러 논쟁적 진술 가운데서 어떤 경우에는 바울 자신이 인정하듯이 이기적으로 보이는 자랑들이 있다(11:16-18; 12:1). 이런 자랑이 섞인 부분을 읽을 때 우리는 바울이 단순히 고린도 교인들을 자신에게로 가까이 이끌고 거짓 사도로 부터는 멀리하게 해야 한다는 이기적 동기에서 변명을 하고 있다고 보지 말아달라는 바울의 부탁을 기억해야 한다(12:19; 13:7). 그의 진정한 마음은 그들을 주님에게로 이끄는 것이다. 고린도 교회에서 그리스도의 주권을 확립하는 것이다(10; 8, 13:10). 자신이 주님의 진정한 사도라는 확신이 있으므로, 또 그것을 지금 증명하고 있으므로, 고린도 교인들이 자신을 믿고 돌아오는 것이 곧 주님에게로 돌아오는 것으로 말하는 것이다(4:14; 3:5; 5:20; 6:11-13; 7:2; 10:11). 바울이 제시하는 진정한 그리스도의 사도된 증거는 그가 그리스도처럼 고난을 받은 것이다(11:23-33). 단순히 고난 받은 것이 아니라 그리스도의 고난과 같은 사랑의 동기에서 고난 받았으므로 그 고난은 가치가 있는 고난이다(5:14-15). 또한 재정적으로 교회에 폐를 끼치지 않은 것도 이런 순수한 사랑을 증거하는 한 가지 예이다(7:2; 11:7-11; 12:14-15).

흔히 대부분의 학자들이 말하는 대로 바울이 고린도 교회에서 그의 대적자들과 맞서서 자신의 사도권을 방어하기 위한 변명에만 집중하고 있다고 말하는 것은 사안(事案)의 중심을 흐리게 만든다. 고린도후서 후반부에서의 바울의 관심은 화해의 큰 주제 아래서 단순히 자신의 사도권 변명을 넘어 그리스도 교회를 그리스도의 구원 진리를 따라서 세우는 것이다(10:8; 13:10). 고린도 교인들의 믿음을 세우는 것이다(12:19, 13:5, 7, 10). 이 목적을 위해 자신은 희생이 되어도 좋으며, 실제로 희생의 사역을 하고 있다. 그것은 교회를 세우신 그리스도의 희생의 유형을 따라서 필수불가결의 사도적 사역이다(2:4; 4:7-15; 5:14, 15; 6:4-10; 11:23-29; 12:15; 13:4; 참조, 빌2:17). 바울은 이 큰 사도적 사명 아래서 이 사명에 합당한 사람이 되기 위하여 늘 의롭고 부끄럼이 없이 살기 위해 부단히 힘쓰는 사람이라는 것을 믿어줄 것을 호소한다(4:2; 7:2; 10:7; 11:29; 12:12, 15; 13:7). 그리스도의 몸 된 교회의 사역과 자신의 사도권 확립이라는 이 두 가지 주제가 불가분리의 관계이지만 적어도 바울은 자신이 그리스도의 종이므로 그의 모든 것은 그리스도의 교훈과 모본에서 온 것임을 말한다.

한편, 바울은 그의 사도적 진정성을 자신의 능력이나 고린도 교회 교인들의 다수의 인기나 지원에 의존하여 방어하지는 않는다. 바울은 반대자들이 지적한 자신의 약점 가운데 말이 부족하다는 점을 인정한다(10:10; 11:6). 10장 6절에서 아직도 고린도 교인들 다수가 바울을 완전히 따르지 않고 있음을 알고 있다(6:11-13; 7:2). 나아가서 바울은 그의 사도적 진정성 문제를 단순히 하나님께 맡기지도 않는다. 1장에서 보여 주듯이 바울은 어려운 궁지에서 도우시는 하나님을 믿으며 스스로 위로받았으나 그 것으로 그치지 않는다. 그는 자신의 지도력이나, 사람들의 지지에 의존하지 않지만, 그렇다고 해서 피해의식에 젖어 어쩔 수 없이 막연하게 하나님만 의지해야 한다고 생각하지도 않는다. 바울은 그의 목회적 궁지에서 보다 구체적이고 특별한 하나님의 구원의 능력을 믿는다. 즉 그리스도의 부활의 생명력이 자기에게서 역사하심을 믿는다. 이 끈질긴 그리스도의 부활의 생명력이 그를 그의 모든 약점들에도 불구하고 고린도 교회의 어려움에서 반드시 구원한다고 믿고 바라는 것이다(13:4). 그리스도의 부활을 통해 나타난 하나님의 구원의 능력은 과거의 부활사건으로 그치는 것도 아니고, 장래의 부활로만 약속된 것도 아니다. 오늘 여기에서 고통 받는 모든 하나님의 백성에게 승리로 나타나는 것이다(2:14-16; 4:16; 5:14; 13:4). 그러므로 고린도후서에서의 바울의 중심적 관심 또는 동기는 십자가를 통한 그리스도의 고난과 죽음을 통한 구원의 능력을 복음의 근간으로 삼아서 그리스도의 왕권을 각 개인과 교회에 확립하여 그의 몸 된 교회를 굳게 세우는 것이다. 그러므로 바울은 그리스도의 고난과 죽음을 교회의 근간이 되는 사도권을 포함한 모든 그리스도 교회의 사역을 위한 유일하고 정확한 평가기준으로 삼는다. 그리스도의 고난과 죽음을 통한 구원의 객관적 평가기준에 의해서 그 자신과 그의 반대자들을 평가하고 있고 그 결과 자신은 분명히 그리스도의 사도이며, 의의 일꾼을 반대하는 자들은 사단의 불의한 일꾼들임을 밝히거나 암시한다.

준더만(A. G. Sundermann)이 제시하는 10-13장의 내용개요에 기초하여 이 부분의 전체 구조를 보면 다음과 같다.[7]

(i) 서론 10:1-11

(ii) 거짓 사도들의 자랑에 대한 바울의 자랑의 당위성 10:12-18

(iii) 어리석은 자의 변명 11:1-12:18

(a) 반론 11:1-15

---

7) H. G. Sundermann, *Der schwache Apostel und die Kraft der Rede: Eine rhetorische Analyse von 2 Kor 10-13*, 45; Thrall, 596, 재인용.

(b) 증명 11:16-12:18

(iv) 결론 12:19-13:1-10[8)]

이런 내용 개요는 1세기 헬라시대의 변명문의 문학적 유형에 따라서 고린도후서의 내용을 분석해 볼 때 고린도후서 전체의 주제인 "약함을 통해 강하게 역사하시는 하나님" 이 바울의 변명의 핵심적 사상으로서 명백히 들어나는 것을 알 수 있다.

A. 바울의 변명(10:1-11)

본문:

1. 너희를 대하여 대면하면 겸비하고 떠나 있으면 담대한 나 바울은 이제 그리스도의 온유와 관용으로 친히 너희를 권면하고 2. 또한 우리를 육체대로 행하는 자로 여기는 자들을 대하여 내가 담대히 대하려는 것 같이 너희와 함께 있을 때에 나로 하여금 이 담대한 태도로 대하지 않게 하기를 구하노라 3. 우리가 육체에 있어 행하나 육체대로 싸우지 아니하노니 4. 우리의 싸우는 병기는 육체에 속한 것이 아니요 오직 견고한 진을 파하는 하나님의 능력이라 (오직 하나님 앞에서 견고한 진을 파하는 하나님의 강력이라) 5. 모든 이론을 파하며 하나님 아는 것을 대적하여 높아진 것을 다 파하고 모든 생각을 사로잡아 그리스도에게 복종케 하니 6. 너희의 복종이 온전히 될 때에 모든 복종치 않는 것을 벌하려고 예비하는 중에 있노라 7. 너희는 외모만 보는 도다 만일 어떤 사람이 자기가 그리스도에게 속한 줄을 믿을진대 자기가 그리스도에게 속한 것같이 우리도 그러한 줄을 자기 속으로 다시 생각할 것이라 8. 주께서 주신 권세는 너희를 파하려고 하신 것이 아니요 세우려고 하신 것이니 내가 이에 대하여 지나치게 자랑하여도 부끄럽지 아니하리라 9. 이는 내가 편지들로 너희를 놀라게 하려는 것 같이 생각지 않게 함이니 10. 저희 말이 그 편

8) Sundermann, *Kraft der Rede*, 205-7, 210-11 에서 12:19-21을 전이(轉移, transfer) 또는 연결부분으로 보고, 13장을 결론으로 보나 12:19-21을 결론에 포함시켜도 무리가 없을 줄 안다.

지들은 중하고 힘이 있으나 그 몸으로 대할 때는 약하고 말이 시원치 않다 하니 11. 이런 사람은 우리가 떠나 있을 때에 편지들로 말하는 자가 어떠한 자이면 함께 있을 때에 행하는 자도 그와 같은 자인 줄 알라.

본문 비평:

1. 7절에서 D* F G vg[3mss]는 Χριστοῦ앞에 δοῦλος를 써서 "그리스도의 종" 이라고 한다. p[46]은 ὁ Χριστός라고 쓴다.

2. 8절에서 ℵ C D y는 ἐάν 뒤에 τε를 넣는다. 그러나 p[46] C B와 소문자 사본에는 τε가 없다.

내용 개요:

10장부터 바울은 강경한 어조로 자신의 사도직의 진정성을 의심하는 고린도 교인들과 그들을 선동하는 외부에서 들어온 거짓 사도들의 여러 비난에 대해서 자신을 변명한다. 바울은 그의 세 번째 방문 이전에 그에 대한 비난과 오해를 미리 해명함으로써 방문 시에 어려움이 없도록 조치하는 것이 필요하다고 보고 고린도 후서의 마지막을 자신에 대한 변명을 집중적으로 쓰고 있다 (12:20-13:2). 물론 앞에서도 많은 부분(2:14-7:4)에서 그의 사도직을 변명하였으나, 거기서는 주로자신을 따르는 고린도 교인들을 상대로 말하고 있으며, 10장부터는 자신을 비난하는 거짓 사도들이나 이에 동조하는 고린도 교인들을 염두에 두고 그들의 자신에 대한 비난을 일일이 열거하며 말하고 있다. 학자들은 10장 1-11절이 10-13장의 서론에 해당한다고 한다. 바울은 초두에서부터 그의 반대자들이 자기들의 자랑이면서, 동시에 바울의 약점들이라고 비웃는 것들을 열거하면서 "약한 자를 강하게 하시는 하나님의 사역" 이라는 그의 주제를 향해서 나아간다(12:9, 10). 그 과정에서 바울은 자신의 강점들을 열거하고 자랑하면서도 오히려 자신의 약점들을 보다 높은 영적 가치로 승화시킨다. 반대자들의 "육체적 자랑" 을 가치가 낮은 것으로 보고, 자신의 약함의 능력을 그리스도 중심적 사도직의 가장 확실한 증거로 제시하고 있다(10:8; 11:18; 12:9-11).

10장에서 13장까지의 반대자들에 대한 바울의 강경한 자세는 1-9장에서의 거짓 사도들과 그의 동조자들에 대해서 가끔 암시적으로 말하는 것과는 대조적이다(3:1, 7-9; 5:12; 7:2). 소위 "어리석은 자의 변명" (11:1-12:18)으로 사도권을 방어하면서 반대자들의 주장을 적극적으로 공격하는 것이다. 이렇게 단호한 결심을 하게 된 동기는 고린도 교회에서의 자신의 사도권 문제를 방치할 경우 고린도 교회가 속한 아가야 지방, 나아가서는 그의 사역전체에 부정적 영향을 미치게 될 것이라고 보았기 때문이다(고전 6:7; 고후 6:14-7:1). 그러나 더 중요한 동기는 반대자들이 단순히 같은 복음을 전하는 같은 믿음의 형제들이 아니라 이단적 교훈을 전하는 거짓된 사단의 추종자들이라는 확신 때문이었다. 그는 그리스도의 사도로써 잘못된 교훈과 적그리스도를 찾아 제거해야하는 사도적 사명을 이행해야 하기 때문이었다(11:1-15). 그러므로 위에서 지적한 바와 같이 다수의 학자들이 동의하는바 고린도 교회의 주제가 반대자들에 맞서서 바울의 사도권을 방어하기 위한 변명이라는 것은 너무 일방적이다. 고린도후서 특히 후반부에서의 주제는 사도권 변명과 함께 그리스도 교회를 그리스도의 구원진리를 따라서 세우려는 더 큰 주제를 포함하고 있는 것이다(10:8; 13:10).

10장에서 바울의 반대파들에 대한 단호한 입장을 취하면서 투쟁을 선언하는 것은 1장에서 그를 지지하는 대다수 교인들에게 우호적으로 은혜와 평강을 축원하던 것과는 사뭇 다르다. 바울은 그리스도의 왕권이 개인과 세상에서 수립되기 전까지는 궁극적인 평강은 없다고 본다(엡 2:14, 15; 고전 15:24, 25). 바울은 현실적으로 그를 포함한 모든 그리스도인들이 그리스도 중심적 평강을 반대하는 세력과 싸울 수밖에 없음을 잘 알고 있다. 그래서 그의 삶 전체를 선한 싸움으로 규정짓는다(딤후 4:7). 또한 그리스도인의 복음 사역과 삶을 무장한 군인으로 묘사하기도 했다(엡 6:11; 빌 2:25; 딤후 2:3, 4). 그는 궁극적 그리스도 중심의 평화를 이루기까지는 이를 방해하는 세력과 타협하거나 방관하여 얻는 비겁하고 구차한 평안을 원치 않고 기꺼이 싸우기를 원했다(참조, 롬 12:18).

주 석:

1. "너희를 대하여 대면하면 겸비하고 떠나 있으면 담대한 나 바울은 이제 그리스도의 온유와 관용으로 친히 너희를 권면하고" (**Αὐτὸς δὲ ἐγὼ Παῦλος παρακαλῶ ὑμᾶς διὰ τῆς πραΰτητος καὶ ἐπιεικείας τοῦ Χριστοῦ, ὃς κατὰ πρόσωπον μὲν ταπεινὸς ἐν ὑμῖν, ἀπὼν δὲ θαρρῶ εἰς ὑμᾶς**). 학자들은 "겸비하다"(**ταπεινὸς**)는 말이 인격적인 겸손함을 가리키는 것이 아니라, 바울이 고린도 교회의 대적자들이 그를 비난하는 말을 빌어서 "무능하고 부족한" 사람이라고 자신을 빗대어 하는 말이라고 한

다.[9] 또는 바울이 이전의 고통스런 고린도 교회 방문을 회상하는 것이라고 한다. 그 때 바울은 그를 공격하는 이들의 비난을 받으며 제대로 변명도 못하고 사태를 악화시키는 무능한 모습을 보였다(고전 2;3).[10] 마찬가지로, 현재 우월감에 사로잡혀 자신들의 "외모"를 자랑하는 고린도 교회의 반대자들을 염두에 두고 이렇게 말한다고 한다(10:11; 5:12; 11:15, 18). 10절에서 고린도 교인들에게 비친 바울의 말과 외모가 보잘 것이 없다는 말도 반대자들의 비난을 반영하는 말이다.

바울은 "겸손함"에 대조되는 "담대한"이란 말을 함께 쓰고 있다. 학자들은 이 말도 10절에 비추어 이해해야 한다고 한다. 10절에 고린도 교인들이 "그 편지들은 중하고 힘이 있으나"라고 말했다고 한다. 그러므로 여기서 "담대함"(θαρρῶ)은 바울의 편지쓰기를 빗대어서 한 말이라는 것이다. 즉 고린도 교인들이 바울에 대해 불평하여 말하기를, "설교도 부족하고 인물도 볼품이 없이 함께 있을 때는 별 볼일 없는 사람이, 떠나 있으면 편지를 보내어 이래라 저래라 말을 많이 한다"는 것이다. 이런 비난을 알고 있는 바울은 초두에 "너희들이 말하는 대로 너희들과 함께 있을 때는 꼼짝 못하고 '어리석고 부족한' 나 바울이 이제 떠나와서 또 글로 너희들을 괴롭히게 됐으니 용서하라"는 풍자적인 말을 하고 있다는 것이다. 10-13장에서 다른 유사한 풍자적이고 냉소적인 표현들이 자주 나오는 사실에 비추어 보아 이런 견해는 자못 흥미로운

---

9) Chrysostom, *NPNF*, XII, 375; Meyer, 391; Plummer, 273; Hughes, 346-347; H. -D. Betz, *Der Apostel Paulus und die sokratische Tradition*, 46, 52; Thrall, 602; Martin, 303; Barnett, 457-58.

10) Lietzmann, 140; Windisch, 293.

것이다.

한편 이런 비난과 상관없이 바울 스스로 고린도 교회와의 관계를 회고하면서 "함께 있으면 무능하고 떠나있으면 편지로 괴롭히는 나 바울은" 이라고 말했을 수도 있다. 바로 몇 달 전에도 "엄격한 편지" 를 써서 이들을 근심하게 하였는데(고후 7:8), 또 다시 이런 강경한 편지를 연이어 보내게 된 것을 유감스럽게 생각한다는 의미가 게재되어 있다고 볼 수 있다. "그리스도의 온유와 관용으로 친히 너희를 권면하고" 라는 정중한 말 가운데 냉소적인 어조가 있다고 보기 어렵다. 이 말이 헬라어 원문에는 맨 앞에 나와 있다. 바울은 그의 모든 편지의 초두에서 자신을 하나님과 그리스도의 종이라고 밝힌다. 여기서도 그에 준하는 정중함과 사도로서의 품위를 지키고 있다고 본다. 특히 바울은 "그리스도의 온유와 관용" 으로 권한다는 말을 하고 있음을 주지해야 한다(참조, 롬 9:3; 15:4; 갈 5:2). 이 말과 관련하여 "겸비하다" (ταπεινὸς)는 말은 역시 그리스도의 겸손함을 가리키는 것으로써, 그리스도의 성육신과 그의 지상 생애를 가리킨다(마 11:29; 21:5; 18:4; 막 9:33; 요 13:14-17).[11] 바울은 그리스도의 제자로서 그리스도의 겸비한 삶의 유형을 따라 사역하면서 모본을 보였다(4:7 이하; 5:21; 6:3-10; 8:9; 빌

11) Kümmel, 208; Windisch, 292; G. N. Stanton, "Matthew 11:28-30," *Expository Times* 94 (1982) 3-9; Plummer, 173; Martin, Carmen Christi, xxiii-xxv; Barrett, 246. Thrall은 Furnish를 따라서 마 11:29의 진정성을 의심한다(609). Furnish에 의하면 마 11:29은 지혜문학전통을 따라서(시 131; 시락서 45:4) 예수의 말씀으로 저절로 형성된 것이지 실제 예수의 말이 아니라고 한다(455, 460). 그러므로 Thrall은 "온유함" 을 복음전승에서 찾지 않고 8:9과 빌 2:7-8에 있는 예수의 성육신과 겸비한 삶 가운데서 찾는다(Thrall, 609). 그러나 이것 또한 복음전승에서 받은 것이 아닌가? Thrall이 Furnish의 주장을 자세히 검토하지 않고 그대로 수용하는 것이 문제다.

2:6-11; 4:5, 8, 12; 골 3:12; 딤전 3:3; 딛 3:2). 바울은 평소에 고린도 교인들과 함께 있을 때는 사랑의 교제를 중심으로 사역하면서 반대하는 이들의 비난도 참으며 그들에게 역겨운 말을 하지 않았다. 그러나 그들을 떠나서는 편지로는 그들에게 엄격하게 말하기도 하였다. 이제 그의 방문을 앞두고 그 방문이 보다 우호적인 방문이 되게 하기 위해서는, 방문 중에 평소와 같이 그들을 겸비하게 대면하기 위해서는, 아무래도 다시 편지로 어려운 말을 할 수밖에 없다는 양보적인 의미의 말이라고 보아야 할 것이다(2절). 더구나 1-9장에서는 주로 유화적인 말로 고린도 교인들에게 권면하였는데, 이제 편지를 끝내기 전에 마지막으로 강경한 어조로 할 말을 할 수밖에 없다는 말이다.

"담대한"(θαρρῶ)이란 말은 "겸비함"에 대조되는 "오만한" 자세를 가리키는 말이다. 이런 "담대한" 자세는 고린도 교인들과 함께 교제할 때의 바울의 "겸손한" 모습과는 대조적인 모습이지만, 이런 자세는 바울 자신의 변덕스런 이중적 인격으로 말미암은 것이 아니라, 어디까지나 그리스도의 온유와 관용에 근거하여 고린도 교회를 세우기 위해 필요한 자세이다(8절, 13:10). 바울은 자기의 유익에 따라서 변덕스럽게 사람들의 환심을 사기 위해서 그들과 함께 있을 때는 우유부단하고, 떠나면 마음대로 명령하는 것이 아니다. 그는 고린도 교인들과 함께 지낼 때는 교회의 일치와 사랑의 교제를 위해서 모든 것을 참으며 지냈다. 그러나 이제 그의 세 번째 방문을 앞두고 이 방문이 다시 그전과 같은 어려운 방문이 되어서는 안 되겠다고 생각하고, 속에 있던 어려운 말을 모두 함으로써, 고린도 교인들과 피상적인 화해가 아닌, 진정한 관계 개선을 이루어야겠다고 결심한 것이다(2절; 12:19-21). 그러므로 바울의 말은 단순한 인간적인 토로(吐露)가 아니라 그리스도의 사도로서 "그리스도의 온유와 관용"을 따라 권면하는 것임을 분명히 한다. 그러므로 앞으로 하는 바울의 모든 말 가운데, 비록 바울의 개인적이고 "육체적인 자랑" 같이 들리는 말이나, 듣기 싫은 언짢은 말이라 할 찌라도, 모두 "그리스도의 온유와 관용" 가운데서 결국 고린도 교인들의 덕을 위하고 그들을 주안에 든든히 세우기 위한 것임을 이해해달라는 부탁이 들어있다(8절, 12:19; 13:5-10). 그리스도의 온유(ἤπιος)와 관용(πλήκτης)은 바울이 디모데에게 가르치는 주의 종의 자세와 일치된다. "마땅히 주의 종은 다투지 아니하고 모든 사람을 대하여 온유하며(ἤπιον) 가르치기를 잘하며 참으며 거역하는 자를 온유함으로(πραΰτητι) 징계할지니 혹 하나님이 저희에게 회개함을 주사 진리를 알게 하실까 하며…" (딤후 2:24-25). 또 바울은 감독의 자질 가운데, 관용(πλήκτης)을 포함시키고 있다. 바울이 인간적인 증오의 감정에 의해 지배받지 않고 그리스도의 성품을 가지고 권면한다는 것은 하나님이 부르신 사도로서의 소임을 수행하고 있다는 증거이다.

이렇게 바울은 "나는 자신을 낮추신 그리스도를 따르는 그의 겸비한 제자이다. 그러나 동시에 그의 몸 된 교회를 수호하는 책임과 권위를 위임받은 그의 사도이다"라는 이중적 자세를 취하고 있다. 이런 이중적 자세는 이상한 것이 아니라 복음서에 나타나는 그리스도의 겸비하심과 권위를 동시에 나타내는 것이다. 그는 겸비하셨으나 성전 청소(요 2:14 이하)와 바리새인들에 대한 공격(마 23장)에서 하나님의 아들의 권위로 그들을 책망하셨다. 바울은 사도로서 이런 이중적 자세를 나타내는 것이다. 사실로 이런 이중적 자세는 이곳에서 뿐만 아니라 다른 데에서도 나타난다. 예를 들면 갈라디아서에서도 바울은 강경한 입장을 보이면서도 여전히 갈라디아 교인들에 대한 사랑의 관심을 나타낸다(갈 3:1 이하; 4:16; 5:2, 7, 10, 12; 4:19; 5:22 이하; 6:1 이하). 고린도후서 전체에서 이런 사도의 사랑과 권위가 함께 나타나는 것이다(2:4; 6:3 이하; 5:21; 7:8; 6:14-7:1; 10-13). 더구나 10-13장에서 그의 사도적 권위로 권면할 때에 그리스도의 온유와 관용이 전제되어 있음을 다시 확인하는 것이다.

한편, 아래 6절과 7절에서 바울은 이 번 방문이 예전 방문과 같이 "겸비함으로 우호적인 방문"이 아니라 고린도 교인들이나 문제가 되는 이들의 자세에 따라서는 편지를 쓸 때의 "담대한" 자세로 일관되는 방문이 될 수도 있음을 경고한다. 13:2에서도 방문 시에 문제되는 사람들의 징계를 다짐하고 있다. 그러나 이런 강경한 자세에도 불구하고 바울이 진정으로 원하는 것은 그의 방문이 역시 우호적인 방문이 되고, 바울이 평소와 같이 겸비한 자세로 그들을 만나는 것이다(12:20; 13:10). 그러므로 1절의 "함께 있을 때는 겸비하고, 떠나 있으면 담대한" 바울의 평소의 자세를 근본적으로 바꾸는 것은 아니다.

2. "또한 우리를 육체대로 행하는 자로 여기는 자들을 대하여 내가 담대히 대하려는 것 같이 너희와 함께 있을 때에 나로 하여금 이 담대한 태도로 대하지 않게 하기를 구하노라"(**δέομαι δὲ τὸ μὴ παρὼν θαρρῆσαι τῇ πεποιθήσει ᾗ λογίζομαι τολμῆσαι ἐπί τινας τοὺς λογιζομένους ἡμᾶς ὡς κατὰ σάρκα περιπατοῦντας**). 우선 여기서 바울은 그의 수신자가 일반적인 고린도 교인들임을 암시한다. "구하노라"는 말은 "너희(에게)"라

는 대상(간접목적어)을 요구하기 때문이다. 바울은 다가오는 3차 방문 시에 그들과의 원만한 교제를 갖기 위해서 그들과 바울 사이에 문제가 되는 것들을 미리 해소하기 위한 것이 그의 서신의 목적임을 말하고 있다. 한편, 바울은 여기서 또 다른 수신자로서 그를 반대하는 대적자들을 염두에 두고 있음을 밝힌다. 즉 그들은 "우리를 육체대로 행하는 자로 여기는 자들"이다. 바울을 대적하는 이들의 존재와 이들의 사욕적인 자랑과 구원의 구시대적 인식론에 대해서 이미 앞서서 언급하였다(3:1, 14-16; 4:3; 5:12, 16). 여기서 바울은 더 집중적으로 더 구체적으로 이들의 태도와 자신에 대한 비난에 대해서 성토하고 자신을 변명할 것임을 시사한다(10:10-18; 11:2-4, 7-10; 11:18-23; 12:11-18; 13:1-2). 바울은 1-9장에서 이들의 정체를 분명히 밝히지 않음으로써 이들의 존재를 의도적으로 무시하려고 하였으나 3차 방문 시까지 이들이 일반 교인들을 선동하여 바울과의 이간을 책동하는 경우 문제가 심각하게 발전되어 원만한 방문 계획이 위협받을 수 있다고 판단하여 그들을 "거짓 사도들"과 "사단의 일꾼들"로 정죄하면서 정면공격을 하게 되었다(11:3, 13-15). 바울은 이미 한 차례 방문을 취소하여 그로 인하여 고린도 교인들의 오해를 샀고 또 변명을 하였는데(1:15-23), 이제 그의 대적자들의 선동으로 다시 방문을 취소하는 사태에 이르게 되면 헌금 같은 중요한 목회적 목적은 물론(8장, 9장) 모처럼 회복된 고린도 교회와 바울과의 화해가 큰 난관에 봉착하게 될 것이라고 내다보았다. 이들의 선동을 사전에 차단하여 바울이 3차 방문 시에 이들과 직접 격돌하는 일이 없도록 해야 한다고 판단하였다(12:14; 13:1). 바울은 고린도에서 그들과 싸움으로써 "온유하고 관용하시는 그리스도의 사도로서의 품위"를 잃어 그를 반대하는 자에게는 조소를 당하고 그를 지지하는 이들에게조차 실망을 주는 일이 없도록 하기 위해서 미리 편지로 엄하게 이들의 잘못을 꾸짖어서 이들의 난동을 막아야 한다는 생각을 하고 있다(10:8; 12:19-21; 13:10). 이렇게 이 구절은 바울의 10-13장의 두 수신자(반대자와 지지자)를 가리키면서 이 글이 다가오는 바울의 삼차 방문을 위해서 준비하기 위해 썼다는 목적을 분명히 제시하는 중요한 구절이다(9:4-6; 10:6; 12:145, 20, 21; 13:1, 2, 10; 참조, 2:1, 3).

"육체대로 행하는 자"(κατὰ σάρκα περιπατοῦντας)는 대적자들의 바울에 대한 여러 가지 비난을 가리킨다고 볼 수 있다.[12] 즉 바울이 성령의 지시를 받지 않고 자기 마음대로 행하는 사람이란 뜻이거나,[13] 영지주의자들이 바울을 영적 체험이나 능력이 결핍되었다고 비난한 말이거나,[14] 사도적 지도능력 결핍이라거나,[15] 다른 사도들과 달리 자급자족으로 생활함으로써 사도직을 비하시킨다는 비난일 수도 있고(12:13),[16] 또는 보다 일반적 의미로 세속적 동기와 자세를 가진 자기중심적인 사람이란 뜻이다(1:12-24; 2:17; 4:2).[17] 마지막 경우라면, 더 구체적으로 12장 16절에서와 같이 헌금과 관련하여 돈만 챙기는 사람이라고 비난했을 수 있다. 그러나 이런 여러 비난들은 서로 관련되는 것들이며, 바

---

12) Thrall, 605-607.

13) Rückert, 292; Meyer, 393; Bruce, 229.

14) Barrett, 250; Windisch, 295.

15) Martin, 304; Thrall, 607; Barnett, 461, 주, 29.

16) Furnish, 461; G. Theissen, *The Social Setting of Pauline Christianity*, 42-8.

17) Martin, 304.

울이 10-13장에서 이런 여러 가지 비난에 맞서서 "담대하게" (θαρρῆσαι) 그 부당성을 지적하고 그의 결백을 밝힌다. 이런 비난을 하는 사람들은 외부에서 들어온 사람들이다(4절). 바울은 오히려 그의 반대자들이 "육체를 따라" 행하는 사욕적인 이들로 본다(5:12; 10:7, 10-18; 11:13-15, 18; 12:20, 21).

3. "우리가 육체에 있어 행하나 육체대로 싸우지 아니하노니" (Ἐν σαρκὶ γὰρ περιπατοῦντες οὐ κατὰ σάρκα στρατευόμεθα,). 이 말은 그의 대적자들이 바울이 "육체를 따라 산다"고 비난하는 말을 받아서(12:21-13:3), "우리는 육체를 가지고 사나, 육체를 따라 사는 것은 아니다"라고 정정하는 말일 수 있다.[18] "우리가 육체에 있어 행하나"에서 "육체"(σαρκί)는 영적이거나 도덕적이 아닌 중립적인 의미로서 "한계를 가진 우리의 연약한 몸"을 의미한다.[19] 즉 "우리가 이 세상에서 육체적 한계와 연약함을 가지고 힘들게 살아가고 있다"란 뜻이다. 그러나 "육체대로 싸우지 아니하노니"의 "육체"(σάρκα)는 도덕적이거나 영적인 의미이다. 그를 비난하는 대적자들의 말과 관련하여, 바울은 모든 연약함을 가지고 세상에 살면서도 세상적인 욕심을 채우기 위하여 이기주의적 방법으로 살지 않는다고 한다(10:2; 12:21-13:3). 반면에 그를 "육체를 따라 산다"고 비판하는 자들이야말로 외모와 육체를 자랑하며 육체를 따라 사는 거짓 사도들이다(5:12; 10:7, 10-18; 11:13-15, 18; 12:20, 21). 바울은 그리스도의 새로운 피조물

18) Barnett, 463.

19) Furnish, 457.

로서 새로운 하나님의 나라의 삶의 기준을 따라 산다(1:12; 2:17; 4:2; 5:9, 14, 15, 17; 6:4-10; 14-7:1, 2; 11:2; 12:19; 13:7). 그리스도인은 세상 속에 살고 있으나 하나님의 거룩한 성전으로서 구별된 존재로 살아야 한다는 그의 가르침과 같다(6:16). 그는 세상에서 질그릇 같은 연약한 존재로 살면서 온갖 육체적 정신적 고초를 겪는다(4:7-15; 6:4-10; 11:23-28). 그러나 연약함을 통해서 하나님의 능력이 나타난다. 이것이 그리스도의 십자가의 역설적 능력의 비밀이며, 그리스도의 참 제자들에게 나타나는 현상이다(4:7-10; 6:4-10; 11:23-12:10). 더구나 이런 역설적인 구원의 진리는 바울의 경험에서 얻은 것도 아니고, 바울의 주관적 해석도 아니라, 그가 그리스도로부터 직접 얻은 계시의 말씀이다(12:9).

"싸운다"(στρατευὀμεθα)는 말은 악한 사단의 세력과의 영적 싸움을 뜻한다. 여기에 근본적으로는 종말론적 의미가 포함되는 것이지만,[20] 본문에서는 4절 이하에서 말하는 바와 같이 바울 사도가 그의 사역에서 싸워야 하는 일반적인 영적 싸움을 가리키는 것으로 보아야한다(6:4-7; 11:23-33; 엡 6:11 이하; 딤전 6:12; 딤후 2:3; 4:7). 더 구체적으로는 당장 바울이 싸워야 하는 고린도 교회의 거짓 사도들과의 싸움이다(11:13-15, 20, 23, 24). 바울은 이 영적 싸움을 세상적이고 인위적인 방법으로 싸우지 않고, 약한 것을 강하게 하시는 하나님의 능력의 원리, 즉 그리스도의 십자가의 능력의 원리를 따라 싸운다(12:9).

4. "우리의 싸우는 병기는 육체에 속한 것이 아니요 <u>오직 견고</u>

20) Windisch, 295-6.

한 진을 파하는 하나님의 능력이라(오직 하나님 앞에서 견고한 진을 파하는 강력이라)"(τὰ γὰρ ὅπλα τῆς στρατείας ἡμῶν οὐ σαρκικὰ ἀλλὰ δυνατὰ τῷ θεῷ πρὸς καθαίρεσιν ὀχυρωμάτων,). 바울은 그의 반대자들과 자신의 싸움이 하나님의 능력이 함께하는 의로운 영적 싸움이라고 말한다(참조, 딤전 6:12; 딤후 4:7). 바울의 "병기들"(ὅπλα)은 구체적으로 알 수 없으나, 바울이 10-13장에서 말하는 모든 논리와 경험들을 가리킨다고 본다.[21] 그러나 바울이 사용하는 병기들은 세상의 싸움(전쟁이 아닌 일반적인 인간들의 투쟁과 갈등)에서 사용되는 모든 인간적인 능력이나 자랑(5절; 11:18)이 아니라 오히려 "하나님의 강력"(δυνατὰ τῷ θεῷ), 곧 "하나님의 능력"(divine power, NIV)이다(롬8:35-39). 여기서 하나님(τῷ θεῷ)의 여격을 해석하는 견해가 몇 개 있다. (1) "유익의 여격"으로서 "하나님을 위하여" 싸우는 힘있는 병기하는 뜻이다[22]; (2) 히브리어 영향을 받아 "강조의 여격"으로서 "매우 강한" 병기라는 뜻이다. 같은 하나님의 여격이 요나서 3장 3절에서는, πόλὶ μεγάλη τῷ θεῷ(LXX), 문자적으로는, "하나님께 대하여 강한"이라는 뜻이나, 의미상으로, "극히 큰 성읍"(한글 개역)으로 번역된다. 여기서는 "매우 강한" 병기라는 뜻이다[23]; (3) "주관적 판단의 여격"으로서 "하나님이 보시기에" 또는 "하나님 앞에서"(한글 개역) 강력하다는 뜻이다.[24] (4) "매개적 여

---

21) Barnett은 바울의 병기들은 "엄격한 편지"를 통해 문제가 된 이를 징계조치하고(2:5-9), 다수의 고린도 교인들을 회개하게 하는 바울의 일련의 엄격한 조치들을 가리킨다고 한다(464-65). 그러나 10-13장에서 대적자들에 대한 논쟁에 대항하는 바울의 논쟁과 그들의 비난에 대한 바울의 변명들을 포함해야 할 것이다.

22) Lietzmann, 141; Thrall, 609-610.

23) Moule, Idiom Book, 184; Barrett, 251; Thrall, 609.

격"으로서 "하나님으로 말미암는 능력"이란 뜻이다(눅 23:15). 결국 하나님과 관련된 능력을 나타내고 있으므로 의미상 큰 차이는 없다. 2번째와 4번째 해석이 가장 의미가 분명하다. 많은 학자들도 이 해석을 따르고 있다.[25] 바울의 병기들은 곧 "하나님의 능력"으로서 인간의 자랑과 논리를 복종케 만들어, 마침내 하나님의 절대적인 통치가 인간 세상에 자리 잡게 하는 것이다. 여기에 바울의 선한 싸움의 최종적 목적이 있다. 실제로 10-13장에서 바울의 대적자들이 사용하는 병기들은 모두 세상적이고 육체적인 자랑이다. 바울 자신도 그런 세상적 육체적 병기를 가지고 있으나 사용하지 않고 오히려 약한 자를 강하게 하시는 하나님의 능력, 곧 "그리스도의 약함의 능력"을 그의 주무기로 사용한다(4:7-15; 6:4-10; 12:9, 10; 12:15 13:4, 7, 10; 참조, 롬 6:13; 엡 6:12-17).

바울의 병기들의 위력은 "견고한 진을 파하는"(καθαίρεσιν ὀχυρωμάτων)데서 나타난다. 이 구절은 잠언 21장 22절에도 나온다. "지혜로운 자는 용사의 성에 올라가서 그 성의 견고하 의뢰하는 것을 파하느니라(καθεῖλεν τὸ ὀχύρωμα)." 필로는 이 구절로 소피스트 철학자들(sophists, 희랍의 궤변학파 철학자들)의 논리를 공격한다.[26] 필로도 같은 잠언을 인용하여 그의 적들을 공격하는 것은 흥미로운 것이다. 그러나 마틴은 마카비서에서도 비슷한 말들이 나옴을 지적한다(ὀχύρωμα, "진," "요새," αἰχμαλωτίζοντες, "사로잡아," [5절] 마카비 1서 5:65; 8:10).[27] 이

24) Plummer, 276; Barrett, 251.

25) Martin, 305; Plummer, 276; Barrett, 251; Windisch, 296; Hughes, 351, 주, 6.

26) De Conf. Ling. 129-31; Windisch, 297, 298; Bruce, 230; Betz, *Der Apostel Paulus und die sokratische Tradition*, 68.

런 말들이 나온다고 해서 바울이 여기서 필로나 마카비서의 내용을 상기하고 있다고 볼 필요는 없다.[28] 반대자들과의 논쟁을 전쟁에 비유하는 것은 누구나 할 수 있는 표현이다.[29] 그러나 트롤이 지적하는 대로 희랍 철학자들(소피스트)의 논쟁과 유사하기는 하나 바울이 특히 이를 의식하고 사용한다고 보기 어렵다.[30] 바울은 전쟁 용어도 쓰고 있기 때문이다.

"견고한 진"은 고린도 교회의 반대자들과 그들의 잘못된 가르침과 권세를 가리킨다(11:4, 18, 20). 바울은 이들의 세력을 고린도 교회에서 몰아내기 위해서 이 글을 쓰고 있는 것이다. 고린도 교회가 그리스도의 왕권을 가진 사도적 교회로 세우기 위해서 희생을 무릅쓰고 싸움에 나아가는 것이다(4:5; 10:5-6, 8; 12:19; 13:7, 10). 그러나 바울은 이런 영적 싸움을 세상의 싸움에 비교하여 설명하면서도 세상 싸움과 구별하여 말하는 것에 주의해야 한다. 그의 싸움은 육체대로 싸우는 싸움이 아니며, 그의 무기는 육체에 속한 무기가 아니라고 말하는 것이다. 이런 표현은 그의 싸움이 단순히 영적인 싸움일 뿐만 아니라 일반적인 영적인 싸움과도 구별되는 싸움임을 암시한다고 본다. 아래에서 보듯이 그리스도의 권세에 불복종하는 모든 세력을 복종케 하는 일종의 종말론적 싸움이며, 그 무기는 뛰어난 수사학적 논쟁술이나 세상적 논리가 아니라, 그리스도의 약함의 능력이다(12:9, 10; 13:4, 7, 9). 바울도 대적자들과 같이 수사학적 표현과 논리를 사용하지만, 바울은 궁극

---

27) Martin, 305; Plummer, 276, 277.

28) 참조, Betz, *Der Apostel Paulus und die sokratische Tradition*, 68-9; Martin, 305.

29) Furnish, 458.

30) Thrall, 617.

적으로 하나님의 능력에 의지하고 있다(13:4).

5. "모든 이론을 파하며 하나님 아는 것을 대적하여 높아진 것을 다 파하고 모든 생각을 사로잡아 그리스도에게 복종케 하니" (λογισμοὺς καθαιροῦντες καὶ πᾶν ὕψωμα ἐπαιρόμενον κατὰ τῆς γνώσεως τοῦ θεοῦ, καὶ αἰχμαλωτίζοντες πᾶν νόημα εἰς τὴν ὑπακοὴν τοῦ Χριστοῦ,). 4절에서의 "견고한 진을 파하는" 바울의 병기들의 강력한 파괴력이 계속 언급된다. 원문에서 "파한다"(καθαιροὺντες)는 말은 한번 나오고, "이론"과 "대적하여 높아진 것"을 목적으로 하고 있다. 그 다음의 분사 "사로잡아"(αἰχμαλωτίζοντες)도 결국 바울의 병기의 파괴적인 힘의 모습이다. 바울은 대적자들의 이론(λογισμοὺς)과 하나님을 대항하는 "모든 교만함"(πᾶν ὕψωμα)을 파괴할 수 있으며, 그리고 그들의 "모든 생각"(πᾶν νόημα, 2:11, 3:14, 4:4)을 "포로로 만들어"(αἰχμαλωτίζοντες) 그리스도에게 복종시킬 수 있다. 희랍어 ὕψωμα("높아진 것")는 원래 "높은 곳"이란 말이며, 다른 희랍어 πρύγωμα(푸르고마), "높은 진지" 또는 "망루"라는 군사적 용어와 같다.[31] 빈디쉬는 고대 헬라 시대의 신전이 있던 높은 언덕을 가리킨다고 본다.[32] 그러나 이 말은 내적 교만함을 의미하기도 한다(욥 24:24, LXX).[33] 바넷은 복음을 반대하는 유대교 회당의 서기관들의 율법주의적 오만함(참조, 고전 1:20)과 고린도에 처음 오기

31) Chrysostom, *NPNF*, XII, 376-7; Windisch, 298; BAGD, 858.

32) Windisch, 298.

33) Thrall, 612.

전에 들렀던 아덴에서 만난 복음을 비웃던 당시 희랍 철학자들의 지식적 오만함(행 17:17-34)을 가리킨다고 본다.[34] 그들에게 모두 복음이 거치는 돌이 되었던 것이 사실이다(고전 1:23). "모든"(πᾶν)이란 말이 거듭 나와서 바울의 병기의 위력을 강조한다. 이런 군사적 용어들과 함께 바울은 그리스도를 위해 싸우는 용맹한 장군 같은 모습도 보여주고(참조, 롬 1:18-23; 7:23; 딤후 4:7), "이론"이나 "모든 생각" 같은 말들은 철학자들의 논쟁적 상황도 연상케 한다. 그러나 여기서는 반대파들의 "다른 복음"이나 바울과 바울의 복음에 대한 공격이라고 본다(10:10, 12, 15; 11:2-4, 16-18). 어떤 경우든지, 바울은 언제나 하나님 편에 서있고 그의 대적자들은 그 반대편이라는 전제가 여기에도 깔려 있다(4:2-7; 6:7; 13:8). 대적자들은 주로 외부에서 들어온 거짓 사도들과 그들의 동조자들을 가리킨다(11:5-6, 20). 바울은 그가 가진 하나님의 강력한 병기들을 가지고 있으므로 아무리 대적자들의 세력이 강할 찌라도 그들을 이길 수 있다(참조, 2:14; 4:14; 6:7-9; 13:4).

그러나 다시 말하지만 바울의 병기는 결코 "육체적인 세상의 병기"가 아니다. 십자가의 약함을 통해 나타나는 그리스도의 능력이다(4:7-15; 6:4-10; 12:9, 10; 13:4). 하나님의 강력한 능력은 역설적으로 그리스도의 온유와 관용 특히 그의 약함 가운데 나타난다.

6. "너희의 복종이 온전히 될 때에 모든 복종치 않는 것을 벌하려고 예비하는 중에 있노라"(καὶ ἐν ἑτοίμῳ ἔχοντες ἐκδικῆσαι

34) Barnett, 466.

πᾶσαν παρακοήν, ὅταν πληρωθῇ ὑμῶν ἡ ὑπακοή). 이 구절은 2-5절의 결론적 구절이다. 2절에서 언급한 10-13장의 목적을 "고린도 교회 방문을 위한 사전 준비작업"으로 다시 분명히 말하고 있다. 바울은 고린도 교회를 방문할 때 1절에서 말한 바와 같이 우호적인 분위기에서 그리스도의 온유함과 관용 그리고 겸손함으로 그들을 대하기를 원한다. 그러기 위해서 그의 방문 전에 고린도 교회의 반대자들의 비난에 대해서 보다 적극적으로 공격하거나 해명하여 자신에 대한 오해를 없애는 것이 중요하다고 보았다. 그런 작업을 통해서 바울은 고린도 교회의 대다수의 교인들이 바울에게 완전히 돌아서게 되면, 그와 그리스도에게 복종하지 않는 그의 대적자들을 그가 고린도 교회를 방문할 때에 벌할 계획을 하고 있다(12:2-13:2). "너희"는 대다수의 고린도 교인들을 가리키고, "모든 복종치 않는 것들"(πᾶσαν παρακοήν)은 그의 대적자들을 가리킨다. 이 대적자들은 다시 외부에서 들어온 거짓사도와 내부 동조자들(2절, 11:4-5, 13; 12:20), 그리고 회개치 않은 음란한 자들(12:21; 13:2)로 나뉜다. 이중에서 바울이 이 문맥에서 가리키는 대적자들은 거짓사도들이다. 이 글에서 그가 가지고 있는 하나님의 강력한 병기들(10-13장에서의 바울의 논리적 신학적 논쟁과 변명)이 이들의 세력을 격파하고 굴복하게 할 것이다. 그러나 먼저 다수의 교인들이 대적자들의 잘못된 복음을 버리고 바울의 바른 복음으로 돌아와야 한다. 그러므로 10-13장은 바울의 대적자들에 대한 공격과 그들을 가까이 따르는 고린도 교인들에 대한 경고, 그리고 이들의 비난과 선동으로 흔들리는 교인들에게 대한 질책 등으로 구분될 수 있다. 그러므로 여기에서 "복종"(ὑπακοή)은 바울과 그의 대적자들 사이에서 머뭇거리는 다수의 교인들의 마땅한

자세를 가리키며, "모든 복종치 않는 것들"(πᾶσαν παρακοήν)은 외부에서 들어온 거짓사도의 자세를 가리킨다. "벌"(ἐκδικῆσαι)은 외부의 대적자들이 받게되는 교회에서의 추방일 것이고, 그의 동조자들이 받는 벌은 징계일 것이다(13:2). 어떤 이들은 12장 12절에 비추어 볼 때 어쩌면 사도의 특별한 기적같은 초자연적 능력으로 이들을 벌한다는 의미가 있을 수도 있다고 한다.[35] 그러나 이런 능력의 사용은 오히려 반대자들이나 그들의 추종자들이 사도의 표로 나타내기를 원하는 것이다(13:3). 바울은 편지의 마지막 부분에서도 반대자들에 대한 강력한 경고 메시지를 보내지만(12:20-13:2), 동시에 "그리스도의 약함의 능력"에 근거한 온유하고 겸비한 자세를 끝까지 견지한다(13:7, 9, 10).

한편, 이 구절은 바울이 고린도 교회에 가면 그의 반대자들을 징계한다고 말함으로써 1절의 "너희를 대면하면 겸비하고 떠나 있으면 담대한" 바울이란 말에 상치되는 듯이 보인다. 1절은 바울이 지금까지 취한 평소의 자세이다. 그러나 실제로 바울은 "함께 있을 때"에 피차 화목한 분위기에서 고린도 교인들을 만나기를 원하며 "담대함"으로 대하는 것을 원치 않는다(12:20). 그러기 위해서는 평소와 같이 편지로 "담대한" 자세를 취하여 문제가 되는 것을 해결하려고 한다(2절). 그래도 해결되지 않은 부분이 있다면 평소와 달리 방문 시에라도 어쩔 수 없이 벌할 수밖에 없다고 생각하고 있다(13:2). 그의 강경한 자세에도 불구하고 바울이 진정으로 원하는 것은 그의 방문이 역시 우호적인 방문이 되고, 바울이 평소와 같이 겸비한 자세로 그들을 만나는 것이다(11:20; 13:7, 10).

---

35) B. Holmberg, *Paul and Power*, 78-79; Thrall, 615-616.

그러므로 1절의 "함께 있을 때는 겸비하고, 떠나 있으면 담대한" 바울의 평소의 자세를 근본적으로 바꾸는 것은 아니다.

7. "너희는 외모만 보는도다. 만일 어떤 사람이 자기가 그리스도에게 속한 줄을 믿을진대 자기가 그리스도에게 속한 것같이 우리도 그러한 줄을 자기 속으로 다시 생각할 것이다"(Τὰ κατὰ πρόσωπον βλέπετε. εἴ τις πέποιθεν ἑαυτῷ Χριστοῦ εἶναι, τοῦτο λογιζέσθω πάλιν ἐφ' ἑαυτοῦ, ὅτι καθὼς αὐτὸς Χριστοῦ, οὕτως καὶ ἡμεῖς). 바울은 위에서 자신이 말한 권면이 그리스도의 온유와 관용을 따르는 것이나, 동시에 하나님의 능력을 따르는 것이라고 전제하면서 그 내용이 "담대한" 것임을 미리 예고한다. 7절부터 직접 그가 받는 비난에 대해서 변명하고 공격한다. 그러나 아직 그의 대적자들의 비난의 분명한 내용이 나타나지는 않는다. 그런 의미에서 이 구절은 11장 16절-12장 18절에 나오는 사도의 진정성에 대한 "어리석은 자의 연설"의 서론에 해당된다.

"너희는 외모만 보는 도다"(Τὰ κατὰ πρόσωπον βλέπετε)에 대해서 3가지 해석이 가능하다. (1) 직설법으로 보아서, "너희는 외모만 본다."[36] (2) 의문문으로 보고, "너희는 외모만 보느냐?"[37] (3) 명령형으로 보고, πρόσωπον(프로소폰, "외모")을 "현실"로 번역하여, (1)과 (2)와는 다른 뜻으로, "너희 앞에 있는 현실을 직시하라"("바울이 그리스도에게 속하지 않았다고 비난받는 이 현실을 보라" 또는 "바울이 하나님의 사도로서 고린도 교회를 세우고 사역하는 현실을 보라"[8절]).[38] (1)과 (2)의 번역을 주장하는 이

36) 개역한글성경, J. A. T. Robinson, *The Body*, 26.

37) KJV, J. H. Kennedy, *The Second and Third Epistle*, 184; Bultmann, 198.

들은 (3)이 명령법이라면 βλέπετε(보라)라는 말이 문장 앞에 있어야하는데, 뒤에 오며, πρόσωπον이 1장 1절에 나오는 같은 말과 관련되어 바울의 괴로웠던 과거 방문을 다시 가리키는 것이 되어서 이 문맥에서는 어색한 의미가 된다고 한다. (3)의 번역을 주장하는 이들은 βλέπετε(보라)라는 말이 강조를 위해 뒤에 왔으며, 또 바울이 이 말을 26번(또는 27번)사용하는 가운데, 9번(또는 10번)이 명령형이고 직설법은 하나도 없다는 것이다.[39] πρόσωπον은 바울 서신의 18번(또는 19번)의 사용에서 대부분(16번 또는 17번)이 "외모"의 의미로 해석해야할 필요가 없듯이 여기서도 그렇다는 것이다. 그러나 이런 주장은 βλέπετε를 명령법으로 번역해야 하고 πρόσωπον을 "현실"로 반드시 번역해야 한다는 결정적인 근거가 될 수 없다. 바울이 대적자들을 대면하여 질책하는 문맥을 고려할 때 이런 주장은 타당성이 약하다. 바레트는 고린도전서 1장 26절에서 βλέπετε가 직설법으로 사용된 경우가 있다고 보고 있고,[40] 더구나 πρόσωπον은 고린도후서 5장 12절, 갈라디아서 2장 6절에서 "외모"라는 의미로 번역되었으므로 (1)과 (2)의 번역을 지지해준다고 한다. 그러나 (1)과 (2)의 번역은 "외모를 자랑하며 진실을 보지 못하는 이들"(5:12)에 대한 경고가 되며, (3)은 (바울이 그리스도에 속한) 사실을 잘 파악하라는 뜻이 되므로(참조, 10:1), 이 모든 번역이 결국 대적자들의 거짓된 신분(1과 2), 또는 바울의 정당한 사도직(3)에 대한 독자들의 올바른 인식을 촉구

---

38) NIV, RSV, NEB; Windisch, 300; Héring, 79; Barrett, 256; Furnish, 465; Hughes, 355; Martin, 307; Thrall, 619; Kleinknecht, *Der leidende Gerechtfertigte*, 285-89.

39) 고전 1:16; 8:9; 10:18; 16:10; 갈 5:15; 빌 3:2(세 번); 골 2:8; (엡 5:15); Thrall, 619.

40) Barrett, *First Corinthians*, 56

하는 말이므로 어떤 번역이든지 전체 의미에 영향을 주지는 않는다. 우리는 한글개역과 바레트의 제안과 같이 (1)을 따라서 "너희는 외모만 보는 도다"라고 번역한다.

사람을 "외모"를 보고 판단하는 것이 인간의 약점이다(삼상 16:7). 바울은 앞서 5:12에서 이미 반대자들이 "외모로 자랑함"을 비판하였다. 여기서는 "외모로 자랑하는 자들"을 따라서 미혹받은 고린도교인들을 책망한다. 삼상16:7에서 사무엘이 다윗을 왕으로 기름 부을 때 하나님은 "나의 보는 것은 사람과 같지 아니하니 사람은 외모(πρόσωπον, LXX)를 보거니와 나 여호와는 중심을 보느니라"고 말씀하셨다. 사람을 외모로 보는 것은 이런 인간의 유한성과 함께 인간의 죄성이나 사욕을 나타낸다. 그러므로 예수님은 적대적인 유대인들에게 "외모로(κατα ὄψιν) 판단하지 말고 공의의 판단으로 판단하라"고 경계하셨다(요7:24). 이런 경계의 말씀들이 바울의 외모에 대한 경계의 배경일 수 있다. 외모를 자랑하는 바울의 반대자들은 곧 자신들을 가장하여 미혹하는 거짓사도들이며 사단의 일군들이다(11:13-15).

이런 뜻에서 "외모만을 보는 것"은 "육체를 따라 자랑하는 것"과 같이 사욕을 따르는 것으로서 그리스도의 연약함을 자랑하고 희생과 봉사로 남을 섬기며 그리스도의 진리를 따르는 것과 대조된다(4:5; 7-15; 5:14, 15; 6:4-10; 11:23-28; 12:9, 10; 13:7). 바울이 주장하는 그의 사도직의 진정성은 외적인 데 있지 않고 내적인 데 있다. 그러므로 바울은 그의 사도직을 변명할 때, 하나님의 영(3:3, 6), 하나님 앞(2:17; 3:4; 4:2; 5:11), 양심(1:12; 4:2), 사랑(2:4; 5:14) 같은 내적인 요소를 나타내는 말을 써서 반대자들의 외모와 육체를 따르는 자세와 대조 한다. 그리고 한편으로 반대자들의 사욕적 사역을 약하고 고난 받는 자신의 사역과 대조시키기도 한다(4:7-15; 6:4-10;

11:23-30; 12:9, 10). 이런 대조를 통해서 독자들이 누가 진정한 그리스도의 사도인지를 스스로 판단하도록 돕는 것이다. 물론 바울은 그가 진정한 그리스도의 사도임을 입증하고 있고 그의 변명을 이해하는 독자들 대다수가 자신을 선택할 것으로 알고 있다(12:11).

바울의 이런 모든 말은 "어떤 사람"(τις)이 자신이 그리스도에 속하였다고 주장하고 바울은 그렇지 않다는 주장에 대해 반박하는 말이다. 이 사람은 누구인가? 같은 말이 11:20에서는 보다 분명히 바울의 외부에서 들어온 대적자를 가리키므로 여기서도 같은 외부인사라고 볼 수 있다.[41] 바레트는 대적자들의 대표자를 가리키는 말이라고 한다.[42] 그러나 퍼니쉬는 바울 서신에서 εἴ τις가 특정인이 아닌 사람 일반을 가리키는 말로 쓰였다고 한다(8:9; 고전 3:12; 빌 3:4).[43] 누구든지 간에 이 사람은 자신이 그리스도에 속했다고 한다(Χριστοῦ εἶναι). 바울이 11장 13-15절에서 이 사람과 관련되는 것으로 보이는 이들을 "거짓 사도들," "궤휼의 역군들," "사단의 일꾼들"로 규정하면서도 여기서는 이 사람이 그리스도에 속한 것으로 일단 인정하고 있다.[44] 그러나 자세히 보면, 빈디쉬가 지적하듯이, πέποιθεν ἑαυτῷ(자기가 믿는)라는 말이 그리스도에게 속했다는 것이 그의 주관적인 주장일 뿐이며 바울이 인정하는 바는 아니라는 것이다(롬 2:19; 빌 3:4). 이들은 결국 "외모로 자랑하는 이들"이며(5:12), 또한 거짓 사도들이다. 거짓사도들의 특성이 가장하는 것이기 때문이다(11:13~15).

---

41) Plummer, 280.

42) Barrett, 256.

43) Furnish, 466.

44) Windisch, 300, Wolff, 200-1.

"그리스도에 속한 어떤 사람"(τις … Χριστοῦ εἶναι) 이란 말은 누구를 가리키는가?[45]

1. 단순히 그리스도인이란 뜻인가?[46] 고린도전서 3장 23절, 15장 23절, 갈라디아서 3장 29절, 5장 24절에서 Χριστοῦ(그리스도)라는 말과 함께 유사한 형태로 단순히 그리스도인이란 의미로 쓰인 예들이 있다. 그렇다면 그 대적자가 바울을 아예 그리스도인이 아니라고 한다는 말인가? 하기야 2절에서 바울을 "육체대로 행하는 자"라고 까지 정죄한 것을 보면 이런 비난도 가능하다. 그러나 여기서 바울이 그의 대적자가 그에 대한 비난의 말을 문자적으로 사용한다는 증거는 없다. 또 대적자들이 자신들의 사도직의 정당성과 권위를 높이는 상황에서 단순히 그리스도인인가 아닌가라는 논쟁은 큰 의미가 없어 보인다. 이 보다는 "그리스도 파"같은 파당의 수장을 가리키는 말 같다(고전 1:12).

2. 고린도전서 1장 12절에 나오는 "그리스도 파"와 관련되는 말인가?[47] 슈미탈스(Schmithals)는 "그리스도 파"는 영지주의자들(노스틱스, Gnostics)이라고 한다[48]. 그들은 자신들이 그리스도의 분신이라고 믿었고, 그리스도는 성령과 같은 존재로 보았다. "그리스도와 같이 되는 것"은 성령을 가진 "영적인 사람"(πνευματικός)이 되는 것이다. 그들은 사도는 이와 같은 영적인 사람이어야 한다고 했다. 슈미탈스는 고린도 교회에서 이런 "영적

45) Thrall, 620-23.

46) D. W. Oostendorp, *Another Jesus. A Gospel of Jewish Christian Superiority in II Corinthians* (Kampen: Kok, 1967), 18-19; Barnett, 471.

47) Allo, 246-7, 272-4; Hughes, 356.

48) W. Schmithals, *Gnosticism*, 199-201; 192, 113-14, 205.

인 사람들"이 바울을 반대하였다고 한다. 그러나 이런 주장은 바울 자신이 "그리스도 파"에 속했다는 의미가 되므로 받아들이기 어렵다. 뿐만 아니라, 고린도전서 1장 12절의 "그리스도 파"는 고린도 교회 내부의 조직으로 보이는데 반해서 본문의 "어떤 사람"은 외부에서 들어온 사람같이 보인다(10:16).[49]

3. 고린도전서 1장 12절의 "그리스도 파"와는 상관없이, 자신들이 그리스도와 특별한 영적 관계를 가지고 있다고 주장하는 이들인가?[50] 10-13장에서 이런 주장을 지지하는 근거가 거의 없다.

4. 이들은 역사적 예수를 직접 따라 다니면서 그의 행적을 목격했다는 유대인 그리스도인들이 아닌가?[51] 이들이 유대교 전통을 강조한 징후는 3장 6절 이하, 11장 15, 22절에 있다. 이런 주장을 하는 이들이 역사적 예수를 직접 보지 못한 바울의 사도적 권위에 도전했을 가능성이 있다.[52] 그러나 위에서 지적한 바와 같이 본문에서 이들이 "자신들을 그렇게 믿는다"(πέποιθεν ἑαυτῷ)는 사실은 그들이 실제로 역사적 예수와 상관없다는 말이라고도 볼 수 있다. 그러나 우리는 이들이 예루살렘 사도들의 자천서를 가지고 온 유대인 기독교 선교사들이라고 본다(3:1; 11:22).

5. 그리스도의 사도나 일꾼이란 말이다. "그리스도"(Χριστοῦ)란 말에서 사도(ἀπόστολοι)나 일꾼(διάκοναι)이란 말이 생략되

49) Bruce, 231; Barrett, 257.

50) Bultmann, 189; Héring, 79; Windisch, 301.

51) Albert Kloepper, *Kommentar über das zweite Sendschreiben des Apostels Paulus an die Gemeinde zu Korinth* (Berlin: G. Reimer, 1874), 433; F. C. Baur, *Paul the Apostle of Jesus Christ*, ETr. E. Zeller (London: Williams & Norgate, 1876) 276; 대니, 301; Hughes, 356.

52) Furnish 476.

었다고 볼 수 있다. 11장 13, 23절에서 대적자들은 자신들을 그리스도의 사도들(ἀπόστολοι Χριστοῦ), 또는 일꾼들(διάκονοι Χριστοῦ)이라고 했다.[53] 그러나, 이 경우, 본문에 따라서("만일 어떤 사람이 자기가 그리스도에게 속한 줄을 믿을진내 자기가 그리스도에게 속한 것같이") 바울이 이들을 "그리스도의 사도"라고 일단 인정하는 셈이 되어(아무리 자칭한다고 하여도), 11장 13-15절에서 이 사람들과 같은 사람들이라고 보이는 이들을 "거짓 사도들", "궤휼의 역군들", "사단의 일꾼들"로 부르는 것과 상반된다.[54] 뿐만 아니라, 이런 번역은 여전히 이들의 정체를 알려 주지 못한다.

6. 타이슨(G. Theissen)은 "그리스도에 속한 어떤 사람"(τις … Χριστοῦ εἶναι)이란 말은 "순회 은사집회 설교자들"(itinerant charismatic preachers)로서 자신들이 그리스도의 가족에 속한다고 하면서 고린도 교회에 그들의 의식주 문제를 맡기고서 사역하였던 이들을 가리킨다고 한다.[55] 이들의 생활 유형은 예수가 제자들의 전도 여행 파송 시에 말씀한 마가복음 9장 41절의 "그리스도에게 속한 자"(Χριστοῦ ἐστε)라고 하여 냉수 한 그릇을 주는 행위에서 근거하였다고 본다(마 10:10; 눅 10:7). 바울은 이런 이들과 달리 자비량 사역을 함으로써 이들로부터 "바울은 그리스도에 속하지 않았다"는 지탄을 받았다는 것이다(11:7-11; 12:4; 행 18:2; 20:33-35).[56] 이런 해석은 흥미로운 것이지만, 경제적 생활 유형의 차이에 따라 "그리스도에 속한 사도"로 인정받거나 받지 못하게

---

53) Barrett, 257.

54) Windisch, 302.

55) G. Theissen, *Social Setting*, 46-7.

56) Furnish, 476.

된다는 것은 너무나 단순한 평가기준이다. 10-13장에서 바울의 변명 가운데 경제적인 문제는 그 일부일 뿐이다(11:7-11; 12:13-15). 그리고 Χριστοῦ εἶναι와 Χριστοῦ ἐστε가 실제로 연관된 표현인지, 우연한 일치인지를 알 수도 없다.

이와 같이 "그리스도에 속한 어떤 사람"(τις …Χριστοῦ εἶναι)이란 말이 고린도 교회의 거짓 사도들의 정체를 밝히는 데 특별한 도움을 주지 못하고 여러 가지 가능한 정체를 추측하게 할 뿐이다. 우리는 트롤이 말하는 대로 τις(어떤 사람)가 특정인이 아닌 거짓 사도 전체를 나타내는 말이라고 본다(11:13).[57] 문맥에서 이 사람들은 바울을 육체를 따라 행한다고 비난하였고(2절), 또 12장에서 바울이 특별히 그의 영적 체험을 (그의 대적자들의 영적 체험 자랑에 맞서서) 언급하고 있으므로, 이들은 아마도 영적인 은사를 자랑하는 예루살렘으로부터 온 순회 전도사들이라고 볼 수 있다(3:1; 11:22).[58]

바울의 대적자들이 자신들을 "그리스도에 속한 자들"이라고 자랑했으나 바울은 이런 주장을 받아들일 수 없고 오히려 자신이 "그리스도에 속한 자"라고 한다. 바레트는 여기서 바울이 자신을 "그리스도인"이라고 하면서, 동시에 사도인 것을 나타내고 있다고 한다.[59] 나아가 그가 고린도 교회의 설립자임을 나타낸다. 바울은 고린도 교인들이 이런 사실들을 보기를 원했다고 한다. 그렇다면 여기서 바울의 궁극적 관심은 거짓 사도들의 정체의 규명보다는 진정한 사도가 누구인가에 대한 고린도 교인들의 바른 판단

57) Martin, 307; Thrall, 623; 참조, Barrett, 260.

58) Barnett, 470.

59) Barrett, 257.

기준이다. 이제 고린도 교인들은 외모로 판단하지 말고 사람의 중심을 보고 참 사도와 거짓 사도를 구별해야할 것이다(5:12). 바울이 지금까지 고린도 교인들을 위해 아무런 삯을 받지 않고 정직하게 열심히 사역한 것을 보아야 한다(3:2; 4:2-5; 5:11; 15, 18-21; 6:4-13; 7:2; 11:7, 11, 23-12:10, 14, 15; 참조, 행18:2; 20:33-35). 이제부터 바울이 증거하는 사도의 진정성에 대한 증거들을 주시해야 한다. 바울은 거짓 사도들이 그들의 사도직의 외적 증거를 이미 내세웠으므로, 그의 사도직의 내적 증거와 함께 외적 증거들도 마지 못해 열거하게 된다. 억지로 육체를 따라서 자랑하게 된다(11:18). 그러나 결론적으로는 이런 육체적 자랑을 제쳐두고 반대로 그의 연약함을 자랑하여 약함으로 십자가에서 죽으신 그리스도의 진정한 사도임을 입증한다(12:9, 10; 13:4). 그러나 또한 이런 약함의 논리가 자신의 논리가 아니라 하나님의 계시에 의한 것임을 밝힌다(12:9). 그러므로 바울의 병기는 결국 육체의 병기가 아니고 "모든 이론을 파하며 하나님 아는 것을 대적하여 높아진 것을 다 파하고 모든 생각을 사로잡아 그리스도에게 복종케 하는"(10:5-6) 하나님의 능력이며, 그리스도의 십자가의 능력이다.

2절 이후 바울은 이 번 방문이 예전 방문과 같이 "겸비함으로 우호적인 방문"이 아니라 고린도 교인들이나 문제가 되는 이들이 회개하지 않으면, 편지를 쓸 때의 "담대한" 자세로 일관되는 방문이 될 수도 있음을 경고한다. 실제로 바울은 11장 20절과 13장 2절에서 방문 시에 문제되는 사람들의 징계를 다짐하고 있다. 그러나 이런 강경한 자세에도 불구하고 바울이 진정으로 원하는 것은 그의 방문이 역시 우호적인 방문이 되고, 바울이 평소와 같이 겸비한 자세로 그들을 만나는 것이다(11:20). 바울의 자세는 고린도 교인들의 복종의 여부에 달려 있다. 바울은 평소와 같이 겸비하고 온유한 자세를 일관되게 유지하는 것을 원하지만, 그리스도의 사도로서 그리스도의 교회를 안전하게 세우는 것이 더 중요하다고 생각하고 있다(10:8, 13:10). 그러므로 그는 평소의 방문과 달리 이번 방문에서 강경한 자세를 취하여 문제가 되는 이들을 징계할 수 있음을 미리 경고한다.

8. "주께서 주신 권세는 너희를 파하려고 하신 것이 아니요 세우려고 하신 것이니 내가 이에 대하여 지나치게 자랑하여도 부끄럽지 아니하리라"(ἐάν [τε] γὰρ περισσότερόν τι καυχήσωμαι περὶ τῆς ἐξουσίας ἡμῶν ἧς ἔδωκεν ὁ κύριος εἰς οἰκοδομὴν καὶ οὐκ εἰς καθαίρεσιν ὑμῶν, οὐκ αἰσχυνθήσομαι). 바울은 2절 이후 그의 강경한 자세와 7절에서의 "그리스도에 속한 사도"로서의 자격과 권위를 주장한 후에 여기서는 그에 대한 보충적이고 양보적인 설명을 한다. 그가 담대하게 그의 사도적 권위로 대적자들을 벌한다고 말하는 것은 개인적이고 인간적인 감정에서가 아니라 사도로서 그리스도의 교회를 "세우기 위한 사도적 책임"에서이다(13:10). 더구나 바울은 고린도 교회를 세운 창립자이다. 바울은 여기서 이 교회를 "세우는 권한"(ἐξουσίας⋯εἰς οἰκοδομὴν)이 주님에게서 왔음을 언급한다. 여기서 주님은 하나님 보다, 그리스도를 가리킨다고 본다. 앞 절에서 바울이 "그리스도에 속한 자"라고 하였기 때문이다. 따라서 그는 "그리스도에게 속한 사도"로서 고린도 교회의 사역에 대한 합법적인 권한이 있다는 것이다. "주께서 주신 권세"는 바울이 사도로서 부르심을 받은 것과 그리스도의 교회를 세우고 사역하는 권한을 가리킨다(고전

9:1-2; 갈 1:1, 15-16). "세우는 권세"는 교회의 창립 뿐만아니라 교회의 건전한 성장을 위한 사역도 가리킨다. 그러므로 바울은 그의 방문이나, 편지로나 그의 교회를 사역할(세울) 책임과 권한이 있는 것이다. 교회의 갈등은 결국 그리스도의 사도인 바울에게 복종함으로써 해결되어야 한다(6절). 그의 "담대한" 말이나 조치는 교회를 파괴하려는 것이 아니라, 교인들이 바울에게 복종케 함으로써 문제를 해결하여 교회를 든든히 세우려는 것이다.[60] 4절에서 언급한 바울의 파괴하는 병기는 이 교회를 세우는 데 방해되는 세력(그의 대적자들의 세력)을 파괴하는 데 쓰이는 것으로써 그의 논쟁적 변명이다(2:9; 7:12).[61] 그러나 바울은 그리스도의 사도로서 그의 궁극적인 목적은 그리스도의 교회를 건전하게 세우데 있다.[62] 바울이 "담대하게" 말한다고 해서 바울을 교회를 파괴하는

---

60) Thrall, 625.

61) Chrysostom, PG col. 548(*Nicene and Post-Nicene Fathers* XII, 379-80.

62) 많은 학자들은 "파괴한다"(καθαίρειν)는 말이 바울의 대적자들의 교회 파괴행위를 비난하는 말로 본다(Meyer, 401; Bachmann, 351; Windisch, 303; Héring, 79, 주, 6; Wolff, 201; Thrall, 626). 그러나 4절에서 바울이 같은 말을 쓰고 있으므로 여기서 바울은 그의 사역의 과정에서 파괴하는 일같은 일들(즉 "엄격한 편지"나 10-13장의 "담대한 말"같은 조치들)이 있으나, 그것은 결국 교회를 세우려는 과정일 뿐이라고 해명하는 것으로 본다. 한편, Barnett은 바울의 대적자들이 바울을 비난하는 중요한 이유는 바울이 고린도 교회의 도덕적으로 문란한 이들의 징계를 잘 처리하지 못했다는 것이다(461, 주, 29; 472, 614). 이에 대해서 바울은 주님이 주신 사도로서의 권한이 "파하려는 것이 아니요, 세우려는 것"이라고 변명하고 있다고 본다(참조, 2:5이하; 12:21; 3:2, 13:10; G. W. H. Lampe, "Church Discipline and the Interpretation of the Epistles to the Corinthians," in *Christina History and Interpretation, Studies presented to John Knox*, ed. W. R. Farmer et al, [Cambrdige: University Press, 1967] 352-55; J. Munck, *Paul and the Salvation of Mankind*, 190; Bultmann, 191. 그러나 바울의 징계의 부실함이 대적자들의 비난이라는 확실한 증거가 없다. 이 같은 견해는 역시 추정적 제안일 뿐이다. "파괴한다"

사람이라고 비난하거나 오해해서는 안 된다(9절). 실제로 바울의 사역은 징계(2:4, 9; 7:12)와 화해(2:6-7; 6:18-21)의 양면성을 보여주고 있으나 이 모든 사역은 궁극적으로 건전한 그리스도의 교회를 세우기 위한 것이다(13:10). 바울은 3차 방문 시 사도권을 사용할 것이다. 그러나 어디까지나 건설적으로 사용할 것이며 파괴적으로 사용하기를 원치 않는다. 사도권을 건설적으로 사용할 것인지 파괴적인 사용할 것인지는 고린도 교인들의 회개여부에 달려있다(12:19-13:5, 10). 그의 사역의 궁극적 목적은 어디까지나 그리스도의 왕권 확립이기 때문이다. 또 이러한 바울의 사도적 권한이 주님에게서 온 것이 분명한 사실임을 거듭하여 강조하는 것("이에 대하여 지나치게 자랑하여도")이 문제가 될 것이 없다. 더구나 지금 바울의 사도적 권세를 부인하는 무리들이 있는 고린도 교회의 현실을 고려하면 부끄러움을 무릅쓰고 그의 권세를 스스로 자랑할 수밖에 없다(7절). 바울의 자신의 사도적 권세에 대한 자랑은 10장 13-18절에서 시작하는 자신의 육체적 자랑과 연계된다.

9. "이는 내가 편지들로 너희를 놀라게 하려는 것 같이 생각지 않게 함이니"(ἵνα μὴ δόξω ὡς ἂν ἐκφοβεῖν ὑμᾶς διὰ τῶν ἐπιστολῶν). 이것은 8절과 문법적으로 연결이 되지 않는다.[63] 그러나 의미상으로는 잘 연결된다. ἵνα(…하게 함이니)로 시작되는

(καθαιρεῖν)는 말이 징계의 의미로 쓰인 예는 없다. "세운다"(οἰκοδομεῖν)는 동사나, 명사(οἰκοδομή)도 교회의 설립이나 성장, 또는 개인의 영적 성장을 나타내는 목회적인 의미로 쓰였으나, 징계와 관련해서 쓰인 적은 없다(고전 3:10-14, 8:1, 14:3, 5; 엡 4:12, 16, 29; 5:7; 골 1:22, 28; 살전 5:11). P. Vielhaur, Oikodome, 77, 108.

63) Martin, 309; Thrall, 626.

절을 쓰면서 바울은 문법적으로 생각지 않고 단순히 8절에서 한 말의 이유를 밝히고 있다. 즉 그의 "파괴하는 권세"도 결국 교회를 세우기 위함이라고 말한 이유를 말한다. 그것은 지금 말하려는 "담대한" 내용의 글(10-13장)을 말할 수밖에 없는 그의 입장을 독자들이 오해하지 않고 이해하기를 원하기 때문이다. 바울은 이전에 보낸 "엄격한 편지" 같은 편지들로 고린도 교인들을 놀라게 한 것처럼 이 글로 또 다시 그들을 놀라게 하려는 것이 그의 진의가 아니라(2:4; 7:8; 10:1) 고린도 교회를 건실히 세우려는 것이 그의 진의라는 것이다. 그를 미워하는 대적자들은 바울이 함께 있을 때는 별 볼일 없이 있다가 떠나간 후에는 편지질을 하여 자꾸 우리를 괴롭힌다고 말할 수 있음을 감지하고 미리 그들의 생각을 막으려는 것이다(10:1; 10:10). 바울은 결코 인위적인 권세를 가지고 사람들을 자기 유익에 따라 마음대로 부리는 독재자가 아니라, 주님께로부터 받은 사도적 권한 또는 임무("파괴하고 세우는")를 충실히 수행하고 있을 뿐임을 독자들이 알기를 원한다(1:24). 여기서 바울은 지난번에 보낸 "엄격한 편지"(눈물의 편지)를 받은 교인들이 회개하고 바울에게 돌아오는 등, 그 성과가 좋았듯이 지금 이 편지도 좋은 반응을 얻기를 기대하는 것이다(2:4; 7:12).[64] 그래야 그의 말대로 그의 권한이나 사역이 결국 세우는 것이며 파괴하는 것이 아님을 입증될 수 있을 것이기 때문이다.

10. "저희 말이 그 편지들은 중하고 힘이 있으나 그 몸으로 대할 때는 약하고 말이 시원치 않다 하니"(ὅτι αἱ ἐπιστολαὶ μέν,

64) Barnett, 475.

φησίν, βαρεῖαι καὶ ἰσχυραί, ἡ δὲ παρουσία τοῦ σώματος ἀσθενὴς καὶ ὁ λόγος ἐξουθενημένος). 바울이 그의 사도적 권세에 의하여 교회를 세우려는 선한 의도를 가지고 이런 편지를 보내지만,[65] 편지를 받는 사람의 반응에 따라서 그의 사도적 권세나 사역의 효과가 제한될 것이다. 이미 바울의 반대자들은 바울은 고린도 교회를 떠나 있으면서 편지로만 사도적 위엄을 부리고 실제로 대면하면 무능한 사도라고 비난했다. 그의 인격이나 능력은 별것이 아니라는 선입견을 가지고 있다. 바울은 그의 대적자들이 바울을 비난하는 말을 직접 인용하고 있다. 바울은 아마 이런 비난을 디도를 통해서 들었을 것이다(7:5-7). 그들은 바울을 낮게 평가하고 있다. 그들의 말 가운데 "편지들은 중하고 힘이 있다"는 말은 액면 그대로 바울의 편지에 대한 적극적인 평가로 보기보다는, "떠나서는 제법 문장력이 좋은 편지로써 우리를 설득시키려고 하지만, 실제로 바울의 사람됨은 그렇지 못하다"는 바울에 대한 부정적인 평을 강조하기 위한 대조적 어귀로서 풍자적 의미가 있다. 만일 그들이 문자적으로 편지가 "중하고 힘이 있다"고 믿었다면 편지에 있는 사도의 가르침을 따랐어야 했다. 그러나 그들이 바울의 글도 무시하고 듣지 않은 것이 분명하다. 그들의 바울에 대한 평가는 잘못된 것이다. 그들은 "외모"와 "육체를 따라" 바울을 평

65) 바울의 "편지 사역"에 대해서 홀츠(T. Holtz)는 바울이 예루살렘 사도회의(주후 49/50) 이후에 그가 세운 교회를 사역하는 방법으로 편지를 이용했다고 본다(갈 2:11-16). 바울은 편지를 자신의 분신(alter ego)으로서 여기고("사도적 현존"- apostolic presence), 그가 떠난 교회를 다른 순회전도자들이 들어와서 교회를 교란하는 것을 막는 데 사용했다고 한다. 흔히 순회전도자들은 바울이 편지로만 목회하고 실제로는 교회와 거리를 두고 인격적인 접촉이 없다고 비난했다고 한다. T. Holtz, "Die Bedeutung des Apostelkonzils für Paulus," *NTS* 16 (1974), 110-48(147, 주, 5).

가하고 있기 때문이다(5:12, 16). 바울이 주께서 세우신 사도라는 본질적 사실을 무시한 채 피상적인 것으로 평가하고 있다(10:2). 그러므로 이것은 잘못된 평가이고, 이런 평가를 하는 이들은 위험한 인물들이며, 그들의 평가에 동조해서는 안 된다. "그 몸으로 대할 때는 약하고 말이 시원치 않다 하니,"라는 비난은 실제로 그의 육체적인 연약함과 언변의 부족함을 가리키는 것이라고 보아야 한다.[66]바울 자신이 이를 사실로 받아들이기 때문이다(11:6).[67] 그러므로 어떤 학자들이 말하듯이 이 말을 직접 바울의 영적 능력의 결핍을 가리킨다고 보는 것은 옳지 않다.[68] 그 학자들은 바울의 대적자들이 바울의 언변과 외모가 부족하다고 비난한 것은 바울의 그리스도와의 관계가 약한 증거(즉 7절에서 "바울은 그리스도에 속하지 않았다"고 하는 비난의 증거)로, 즉 바울의 영적능력의 결핍으로 보고 비난하였다고 생각한다.[69] 그러나 바울에 대하여 영적 체험이 부족하다는 비난을 했을 가능성이 있으나(7절, 12:1

---

66) Windisch, 293; 참조, 12:7; H. Clavier, "La santé de l'apôtre Paul," in *Studia Paulina in honorem Johannis de Zwaan* (Haarlem: 1953), 66-82, 특히, 77; J. Jervell, "Der schwache Charismatiker," in *Rechtfertigung*, FS E. Käsemann, ed. J. Friedrich, W. Poehlmann and P. Stuhlmacher, 185-98(Tübingen/Göttingen: Mohr/Vandenhoeck & Ruprecht, 1976), 109-14; Acts of Paul and Thekla, 3장. (데크라 라는 여인이 바울을 사모하여 그녀의 약혼자를 떠났다는 이야기). 이에 대한 연구를 보라: E. M. Howe, "Interpretations of Paul in the Acts of Paul and Thelka," *Pauline Studies*, FS., F. F. Bruce, ed. D. A. Hagner and M. J. Harris (Grand Rapids: Eerdmans/Exeter: Paternoster, 1980), 33-49.

67) 11:6; 12:7; 고전 2:1; 갈 4:13, 14, 6:17; Furnish, 478-9; Martin, 312; Lietzmann, 142; Hughes, 362; Barrett, 261; Bultmann, 192.

68) H. D. Betz, *Der Apostel Paulus und die sokratische Tradition*, 46이하; Georgi, Die Gegner, 145이하, 220-229. 바울의 영적 능력의 결핍을 말한다고 보는 다른 학자들을 Martin, 312에서 찾아 보라.

69) Schmithals, *Gnosticism*, 176-9; Martin, 312.

이하), 여기서는 문자적으로 외모와 언변의 부족을 의미한다고 보는 것이 옳다.[70] 바울 스스로 그는 성령의 능력으로 말한다고 한다. "내 말과 내 전도함이 지혜의 권하는 말로 하지 아니하고 다만 성령의 나타남과 능력으로 하여 너희 믿음이 사람의 지혜에 있지 아니하고 다만 하나님의 능력에 있게 하려 하였노라"(고전 2:4-5). 또 바로 위의 4-5절에서도 바울의 병기는 하나님의 능력이라고 말하고 있다. 바울은 뒤에서 반대자들이 지적하는 이런 약함들을 오히려 자신의 자랑이라고 하면서 진정한 그리스도의 사도의 표로 역이용한다(12:9, 10). 엄밀하게 그것은 바울 자신의 지혜나 경험이나 논리적 역공이 아니라 하나님이 주신 계시에 근거한 바울의 변명이다. 무엇보다 바울은 실제로 많은 고난을 겪었다(11:23-33). 그에게는 "몸의 가시"도 있었다(12:7). 이런 모든 약한 것들이 바울이 이론이나 말뿐이 아닌 진정한 의미에서의 그리스도의 사도임을 강력하게 증거한다고 보는 것이다.

마틴은 "말이 시원치 않다"(ἐξουθενημένος)는 말은 매우 경멸하는 말로서, 실제로는, "바울의 언변은 형편없다"는 뜻이라고 한다.[71] 이런 모욕적인 표현의 이면에는 바울의 사도직의 진정성과 권위에 대한 의심뿐만 아니라 심지어 사기꾼이라는 비난까지 숨어 있다는 것이다(7:2; 12:16).[72] 어떤 학자들은 바울의 대적자들이 바울이 속임수를 쓴다는 비난을 그의 외모가 "약하다"(ἀσθενὴς)는 말과 관련시킨다.[73] 그러나 이것은 "약함"이란 말의 의미를 지

70) Thrall, 631.

71) Martin, 312; Furnish, 465.

72) Martin, 312.

73) Windisch, 306; Furnish, 479; Hock, *The Social Context of Paul's Ministry*, 35, 60.

나치게 확대하는 것이다. 그러나 이 말과 관련됨이 없이, 반대자들이 바울이 속임수로 사람들을 다룬다는 비난을 하였다는 것은 가능하다(12:16). 직접 현장 목회는 자신이 없으므로 피하고, 원거리에서 편지로만 사람들을 마음대로 부린다는 비난을 했을 수도 있다(10:11; 참조, 1:24; 고전 5:3).

한편 헬라시대 냉소주의 철학자 에픽테투스(Epictetus)의 "외양의 단장"이라는 글에서 헬라시대 수사학을 공부하는 학생들에게 외모의 단장이 청중에게 미치는 영향이 크다는 것을 말한다.[74] 여기서 바울의 대적자들이 바울의 외모와 언변을 연계하여 경멸하는 것도 이런 경향과 연관되어 있다고 볼 수 있다. 그들이 유대에서 온 사람들이라도(11:22), 스데반이나 빌립 같이 헬라 문화에 익숙한 이들일 수 있고, 또 헬라 문화에 젖은 고린도 교인들의 헬라식 지도자 평가 기준에 의해서 바울을 폄하하는 말을 할 수 있기 때문이다.

이와 같이 바울은 그의 대적자들이 그를 "육체를 따라" 평가함으로써 "육체대로 행하는 이"가 자신이 아니라(2절) 그들임을 스스로 입증하는 것이라고 반박하는 셈이 된다. 또한 이들의 비난을 가지고 "약함 가운데서 강해짐"의 하나님의 역사가 바로 자신의 사역의 특징임을 말함으로 역전의 기회로 삼고 있다(12:9).

한편 바울의 일반적인 지도자 평가 기준은 "마음"이라고 생각한다. 반대자들이 외모나 육체를 따라 자랑하는데 반해서 바울은 자자주 "마음"이라는 말로 자신의 진정성을 표현한다(3:2; 5:12;

---

74) B. W. Winter, *Philo and Paul among the Sophists*, SNTSMS 96 (Cambridge: University Press, 1997) 116-17; Furnish, 468, 인용, Epictetus, *Diss.* III 22.86-89.

7:3; 11:3; 13:11; 참조, 삼상 16:7).

11. "이런 사람은 우리가 떠나 있을 때에 편지들로 말하는 자가 어떠한 자이면 함께 있을 때에 행하는 자도 그와 같은 자인 줄 알라"(τοῦτο λογιζέσθω ὁ τοιοῦτος, ὅτι οἷοί ἐσμεν τῷ λόγῳ δι' ἐπιστολῶν ἀπόντες, τοιοῦτοι καὶ παρόντες τῷ ἔργῳ). 바울은 그의 대적자들을 향하여 8절에서 인용한 그들의 비난을 일축한다. 1절에서의 그의 말을 상기시키면서, 그가 그들과 함께 있어 말로 가르칠 때나, 떠나서 편지로 명령할 때나, 같은 사도의 권위와 능력을 가지고 있음을 확언한다. 더구나 여기서 바울이 자신을 가리켜 "말하는 자"라는 말 대신에 "행하는 자" 라고 한 것은 6절에서 언급한바 바울이 고린도 교회를 방문하여 행할 일련의 엄한 조치들, 가령, 문제된 이들을 치리하는 것을 의미한다고 볼 수 있다(13:2).[75] 여기서 단수로 나타나는 "이 사람"(τοῦτο)은 한 개인이라기보다 그의 대적자들 전체를 하나의 대상으로 삼아 말하고 있다. 이들은 외부에서 들어온 거짓 사도들이다(12절, 11:2, 3, 13). 이들은 바울이 여러 가지 면에서 사도로서의 자신도 없고 실력도 없으니까 편지로만 고린도 교회를 이리저리 원격조정만 하려하고, 실제로 정정당당히 얼굴을 맞대고 문제를 해결하려 들지 않는다고 비난하였을 것이다. 이에 대해서 바울은 직접 현장에서 목회하든, 편지로 간접 사역을 하든, 자신은 사도로서의 사역을 하는 것임을 분명히 알아야 하고, 사도인 자신의 지시에 순종하는 것이

75) W. L. Knox, St. Paul, 101, 102; J. Munck, *Paul and the Salvation of Mankind*, 190, Martin, 313, 재인용.

마땅한 교인 된 도리임을 역설한다. 더구나 이번 3차 방문 시에는, 6절에서 말한 것처럼, 또 13장 2절에서 재차 다짐하는 것처럼, 바울이 "떠나 있을 때와 마찬가지로 함께 있을 때"에도 같은 사도로서의 권위를 가지고 사역할 터이니 두고 보라고 경고하는 것이다. 대적자들이 비난하는 대로 바울이 말과 언변이 부족하여 직접 사람들을 만나면 기가 죽고 무능하게 될 것이 아니라, 편지의 사도적 위엄을 그대로 가지고 말하고 행하여 모든 잘못된 것을 복종시키게 될 것이라고 한다.

트롤은 바울이 그의 2차 방문 시에는 그토록 의기소침하였다가 여기서는 무엇 때문에 이토록 그의 대적자들에 대하여 의기양양한 어조로 말하고 있는가라고 질문한다.[76] 그 때는 아마 바울이 병으로 고통당했고, 교회의 상황이 그를 반대하는 분위기였으나(2:1), 이제는 다수의 고린도 교인들이 바울을 지지하는 상황으로 호전되었기 때문이라고 생각한다(7:4 이하). 뿐만 아니라 이렇게 편지로 재차 엄히 경고하여 그의 반대자들의 입을 막고, 디도가 가서 방문을 위한 여건을 잘 마련할 수 있다고 믿었기 때문이다(8:16).

주해(10:1–11):

10장 1-11절은 10-13장의 서설에 해당하는 부분이다. 10-13장에서 바울은 그의 대적자들을 대면하여 그들의 거짓 정체를 직설적으로 드러내고, 자신의 사도직의 진정성을 자찬을 통해 증거한다. 서설 부분에서 바울은 이런 본문의 근본적 방향과 틀을 제시하고

76) Thrall, 634.

있다. 즉 그의 사도직의 정당성의 항변과 그의 대적자들의 사도직의 부당성이다. 그의 대적자들의 부당함의 증거는 하나님께로부터 받은 사도직을 외모와 육체를 따라 평하는 것이다. "외모"와 "육체"는 그들의 지상의 예수와의 친분과 지식(5:12, 16), 예루살렘 사도들과의 친분관계나 그들의 자천서(3:1; 11:22), 교회의 재정적 지원을 받는 공식적인 사역 방식(11:5-12), 웅변적 화술(10:10), 유대인 정통성 (11:22) 등이다. 그들은 그 모든 외모와 육체적 은사를 받았으나 바울은 그렇지 못하다고 무시하는 것이다. 그들의 외적 조건(뛰어난 화술과 풍채)이 하나님의 은사라고 하여도, 그것들을 소유함에 대한 자랑과 오만함, 그리고 이런 것을 가지지 못했다고 바울을 경멸하는 자세는, 그들 스스로가 거짓 사도들임을 입증하고 있는 것이다(11:13). 반대로 바울의 사도직의 정당성은 외모와 육체적 조건에 있지 않고, 그리스도의 죽음과 부활의 유형을 따라서, 약함 가운데서 강함을 그의 사역 가운데서 증거하기 때문이다(12:9-10). 이런 그리스도의 유형은 12장에서 분명히 언급되고 있으나, 10장에서 바울의 언변과 용모를 경멸하는 말을 인용할 때에 암시된다.

10절에서의 대적자들의 바울에 대한 직접적인 공격은 바울은 교회를 떠나서 편지로만 이래라저래라 하고 실제로 그들처럼 현장에서 목회를 하지 않는다는 것일 수 있다. 이것은 사도로서 무책임하고 비겁한 일이라는 것이다. 직접 만나서 대화로 잘잘못을 따지지 않고 원거리에서 숨어서 뒤로 편지로 사람들을 조정하려는 드는 것은 부당하다는 것이다. 자신들이 현재 고린도 교회를 직접 현장에서 사역하고 있으니 자신들이야 말로 헌신적인 사도들이라는 논리다. 또한 바울이 직접 만나서 말하지 못하는 것은 그의 언변과 외모가 부족한 탓이라고 보는 것이다. 이런 비난이 사실이라면, 더구나 바울이 헌금까지 요구하고 있으므로(8장, 9장; 11:8-9; 12:17, 18), 바울의 입장이 매우 난처했을 것이다. 이에 대해서 바울은 자신은 결코 자신의 유익을 따라("육체대로") 목회하지 않으며 자신의 사도적 권위와 부정적 또는 적극적 모든 종류의 사역("파하고 세우는")은 하나님의 능력에 의한 것이며, 결국 하나님의 교회를 세우기 위한 것임을 단언한다. 이런 자신의 말을 듣지 않고 계속 반대하는 이들은 그의 3차 방문 시에 엄한 징벌 조치를 받게 될 것임을 경고한다(참조, 13:2). 바울은 이번 방문이 고린도 교인들이나 문제가 되는 이들의 자세에 따라서는 편지를 쓸 때의 "담대한" 자세로 일관되는 방문이 될 수 있음을 경고한다. 실제로 12장 20절과 13장 2절에서 방문 시에 문제되는 사람들의 징계를 다짐하고 있다. 그러나 이런 강경한 자세에도 불구하고 바울이 진정으로 원하는 것은 그의 방문이 역시 우호적인 방문이 되고, 바울이 평소와 같이 겸비한 자세로 그들을 만나는 것이다(13:10). 그러므로 1절의 "함께 있을 때는 겸비하고, 떠나 있으면 담대한" 바울의 평소의 자세를 근본적으로 바꾸는 것은 아니다. 강경한 자세와 조치는 그의 방문이 평화롭고 우호적인 것이 되도록 고린도 교인들이 회개하고 변화되기를 바라는 마음에서 제시하는 것이다. 그러므로 바울은 1절에서 엄한 경고를 시작하면서 그의 질책이 그리스도의 온유(ἤπιος)와 관용(πλήκτης)으로 권하는 것임을 상기시키고 있다(마 11:29). 그의 이런 목회적 자세는 그가 디모데에게 가르치는 주의 종의 자세와 일치된다. "마땅히 주의 종은 다투지 아니하고 모든 사람을 대하여 온유하며(ἤπιον)

가르치기를 잘하며 참으며 거역하는 자를 온유함으로(πραΰτητι) 징계할지니 혹 하나님이 저희에게 회개함을 주사 진리를 알게 하실까 하며…"(딤후 2:24-25). 또 바울은 감독의 자질 가운데, 1절에 나오는 관용(πλήκτης)을 포함시키고 있다.

이렇게 바울이 인간적인 증오의 감정이나 사사로운 유익에 의해 매이지 않고 그리스도의 온유한 성품을 가지고 불순종하는 이들을 엄하게 권면하는 것은 그가 사도로서의 소임 즉 "그리스도의 몸 된 교회를 세우는" 책임을 잘 수행하고 있다는 증거이다. 그는 진정한 그리스도의 사도이다.

B. 바울이 자천하려는 바는 반대자들의 경우와 달리 하나님이 허락하신 한계 안에 있으므로 문제없음 (10:12-18)

본문:

> 12. 우리가 어떤 자기를 칭찬하는 자로 더불어 감히 짝하며 비교할 수 없노라 그러나 저희가 자기로서 자기를 헤아리고 자기로서 자기를 비교하니 지혜가 없도다 13. 그러나 우리는 분량 밖의 자랑을 하지 않고 오직 하나님이 우리에게 분량으로 나눠주신 그 분량의 한계를 따라 하노니 곧 너희에게까지 이른 것이라 14. 우리가 (이왕에) 너희에게 가지 않았더라면 (지금 우리의 사역이) 우리의 한계를 지나치는 것이라고 하겠으나, 그런 것이 아니라.(우리가 너희에게 미치지 못할 자로서 스스로 지나쳐 나아간 것이 아니요) 우리는 그리스도의 복음으로 (이왕에) 너희에게까지 이른 것이라. 15. 우리는 남의 수고를 가지고 분량 밖에 자랑하는 것이 아니라 오직 너희 믿음이 더할수록 우리의 한계를 따라 너희 가운데서 우리의 활동 영역이 더 크게 확장되기를 바라노라 (더욱 위대하여지기를 바라노라). 16. 이는 남의 한계 안에 예비한 것으로 자랑하지 아니하고 너희 지경을 넘어 복음을 전하려 함이라 17. 자랑하는 자는 주 안에

서 자랑할지니라 18. 옳다 인정함을 받는 자는 자기를 칭찬하는 자가 아니요 오직 주께서 칭찬하시는 자니라.

본문 비평:

12절의 끝 부분과 13절의 시작 부분의 원문이 긴 것과 짧은 것으로 된 사본들이 있어 불분명하다. D* G it^{d,g,61} Ambrosiaster 등에는 **οὐ συνιᾶσιν. ἡμεῖς δὲ**.("[저희가]…지혜가 없도다. 그러나 우리는")이 없다. 이 경우, 12절 하반절의 주어는 "저희"가 아니라 "우리"가 되어, "그러나 우리로서 우리를 헤아리고, 우리로서 우리를 비교하니, 우리가 우리의 분량 밖의 자랑을 하지 않고…"가 된다. 따라서 12절 하반절은 대적자들의 자랑을 비난하는 말 대신 바울의 자랑의 타당성을 가리키는 말이 된다. 케제만(Käsemann)은 이 짧은 사본의 구절을 지지한다.[77)] 바울은 이 세상의 인준이 필요 없는 하늘의 성령의 인준만을 필요로 하는 영적 존재라고 말한다는 것이다.[78)] 여러 학자들이 짧은 사본을 지지한다.[79)]

그러나 짧은 구절을 반대하는 이유는 다음과 같다, 첫째, 짧은 구절일 경우 **ἐν ἑαυτοῖς ἑαυτοὺς μετροῦντες**가 바울을 가리킨다고 보아 "우리로서 우리를 헤아리고"라고 해석하는 것이 문제다.[80)] 둘째, 짧은 구절일 경우 3인칭 복수인 **αὐτοί**(그들)를 바울 또는 "우리"로 보는 것도 문제다.[81)] 물론 짧은 구절을 지지하는 이

---

77) Käsemann, *Die legitimität*, 45.

78) Schlatter, Paulus, 623; Georgi, *Die Gegner*, 230.

79) Windisch, 309; Bultmann, 194, 5; Strachan, 15, 16; Héring, 73.

80) Kümmel, *Introduction to the New Testament*, 208, 209.

81) Plummer, 285.

들은 이것(αὐτοί)을 바울("우리")을 강조하는 재귀대명사로 볼 수도 있으나, 그것은 자연스럽지 못하다.[82] 셋째, 12절과 13절의 바울의 평가와 그의 대적자들의 평가의 대조적 의미가 사라지는 것도 문제다.[83] 바울은 스스로 평가하지 않고 하나님이 주신 척도에 의해서 평가하는데, 그의 대적자들은 스스로 척도하니 "지혜가 없다"는 뜻이 원래의 의미로 보이기 때문이다.[84] 짧은 구절의 경우에는 바울 자신의 자신에 대한 두 가지 평가 방법이 대조되는 것이 된다. "우리가 우리를 자기를 자랑하는 이들과 비교하지 않는다. 그러나 우리는 우리들 자신들과 비교하며, 지나치게 자랑하지 않는다." 그러나 바울을 그의 대적들과 비교하는 문맥에 비추어 볼 때 전자의 비교가 보다 적절하다.

우리는 긴 구절을 지지하여, 첫째, 필사자가 **οὐ συνιᾶσιν. ἡμεῖς δε. οὐκ**를 복사할 때, **οὐ**를 써야 할 때 실수로, 그 이후의 글은 빠뜨리고, 같은 글자인 **οὐκ**부터 쓰기 시작했다고 본다.[85] 둘째, 주요 사본들(MS)이 긴 구절을 지지한다. 셋째, **οὐ συνιᾶσιν**(지혜가 없다)이란 중요한 말이 나중에 덧 부쳐진 것이라고 보기 어렵다.[86]

한편 ℵ* 88은 **οὐ συνιᾶσιν ἡμεῖς.**라고 **οὐ συνιᾶσιν** 다음에 **ἡμεῖς**를 부쳐서 읽는다. 이렇게 되면 "그들은 그들이 무엇을 하는지 모르는 채 그들을 그들 자신과 비교한다"는 뜻이 되는데, 이런

82) Thrall, 638.

83) Martin, 315.

84) 참조, Thrall, 639.

85) Metzger, *Textual Commentary*, 514; Plummer, 285; Barrett, 264; Martin, 315; Thrall, 638.

86) Meyer, 388; Hughes, 365, 주, 22; Furnish, 470; Woff, 204, 주, 74; Thrall, 639.

말을 바울이 했을 리는 없다.[87] 메츠거(Metzger)는 필사자가 의도적으로 정정한 것이라고 본다.[88]

내용 개요:

10장 12절부터 바울이 그의 대적자들, 특히 거짓 사도들에 대한 "담대한" 주장이 시작된다. 바울은 1절에서 그의 편지의 "담대함"(τόλμα)에 대해서 이미 말했다. 거기서는 그의 편지의 내용의 거친 질책이나 노골적인 말에 대해서 미리 양해를 구하는 말이라고 했다. 바울이 고린도후서에서 사용하는 "담대함"이란 말은 이중적인 의미가 있다. 바울의 사도로서 하나님으로부터 받은 소명과 권위와 능력에 대한 "담대한" 신념과 함께(1:15, 3:4, 8, 22, 10:2), 잘못하는 고린도 교인들을 "담대하게" 질책한다(7:4).

그러나 바울의 대적자들에게는 이런 담대함이 비난거리가 될 수 있었을 것이다. 그들은 바울의 담대함이 결국 자만함과 자기선전이며, 이로 인하여 자기 자랑과 자찬을 늘어놓는다고 비난 할 수 있었을 것이다(10:17, 18). 이외에도 나중에 언급되는 바울에 대한 비난은 공교한 자로서 궤계로 헌금을 착취한다든가(12:16), 자신의 병도 못 고치면서 남을 구원한다는 병약한 사람이라는(12:7-10) 것이다.

10장 12-18절에서의 쟁점은 바울이 고린도 교회에서 사역할 권한이 있느냐는 것이며 이에 대하여 바울은 자기의 사역의 타당성을 방어하고 있다. 바레트는 10장 13절에서의 "하나님이 우리에게 나누어주신 분량의 한계"라는 말은 바울 사도가 맡은 복음 사

87) Martin, 315.

88) Metzger, *Textual Commentary*, 583.

역의 영역을 가리킨다는 견해를 갖고 있으나(10:15),[89] 이런 해석이 무리하다는 견해도 있다.[90] 10장 13절에서 바울은 지나치게 "분량 밖의 자랑"을 하지 않는다고 일반적인 의미로 말을 시작하였으나 이내 그에게 할당된 선교사역자의 한계를 가리키는 말로 전환하여 의미를 바꾸고 있다. 사도들의 복음 활동의 영역의 할당은 초대교회에서 결정된 사항이었다(롬 15:19, 20; 갈 2:7-9). 그러므로 외부(아마도, 예루살렘)에서 온 그들이 고린도에서 사역할 권한이 없다고 바울이 비난한 것이 거의 분명하다(10:16).[91] 바울은 사도들의 회의에서 결정된 대로 이방의 사도로서 그 자신이 고린도 교회를 창립한 사도라고 주장했을 것이다(14절; 고전 3:6-10). 그러므로 그는 현장에서나 원거리에서나 고린도 교회를 사역할 마땅한 권한이 있으며(10:10, 11), 이런 권한은 근본적으로 하나님께로부터 받은 것임을 항변한다(참조, 11:12). 문제는 이런 할당된 영역을 무시하고 들어 온 거짓 사도들이다. 바울은 고린도 교회를 선교의 근거로 삼아 더욱 더 그의 선교 영역을 넓혀 나갈 것이다(16, 참조, 11:11). 한편, 어떤 학자들은 바울을 대적하는 세력의 정체를 규명하기 위해서 바울이 고린도 교회를 세우고, 고린도전서를 쓰기 이전에(52년에서 55년 사이) 베드로가 고린도 교회

89) C. K. Barrett, "Christianity at Corinth" in *Essays on Paul* (London: SPCK, 1982), 18.

90) Martin, 320-21.

91) F. C. Baur, *Paul the Apostle of Jesus Christ*, tr. E. Zeller (London: Williams & Norgate, 1872) 281; Ernst Käsemann, *Die Legitimität des Apostels: eine Untersuchung zu II Korinther 10-13* (Darmstadt: Wissenschaftliche Buchgesellschaft, 1956) 34;B. Holmberg, Paul and Power, 502; C. K. Barrett, "Cephas and Corinth," in *Essayns on Paul, 35-38.;* Martin, 316.

92) Barrett, "Cephas and Corinth" 35-39; Martin, 323; Holmberg, 50; J. J. Günther, *St. Paul's Opponents and their Background: A Study of Apocalyptic Jewish Sectarian Teachings* (Leiden: Brill, 1973) 301-3.

를 방문한 사실을 중시한다. 그들은 본문에서 바울을 반대하는 유대주의적 세력의 배후에는 베드로가 있다고 본다(11:22).[92] 바울은 베드로의 높은 위치를 생각하여 그의 이름을 일부로 언급하지 않고 단순히 "이런 사람"(11절)이나 "어떤 자"(12절)로 말하고 있기 때문이라는 것이다. 그러나 이런 견해는 분명한 근거가 없으므로 역시 추정적일 수밖에 없다.[93] 바울은 여기서 자신을 반대하는 세력을 개인화 시켜서 말한다고 본다(16절).

바울은 하나님이 인정하신 평가 기준에 따라 자신을 평가한다. 그 증거는 바울 자신이 고린도 교회의 창립자라는 사실과 거짓 사도들은 나중에 그의 교회를 침범한 이들이란 사실이다. 바울은 남의 영역을 침범하여 사역하는 것이 아니다(고전 3:10; 롬 15:20). 그의 사역의 영역은 하나님이 지정하신 대로 모든 이방인의 영역이다(갈 2:7-9; 행 9:15). 남의 영역을 침범한 것은 오히려 거짓 사도들이다. 그들은 자신들의 행동을 자신이 만든 척도로 평가하므로 어리석다.

주석:

12. "우리가 어떤 자기를 칭찬하는 자로 더불어 감히 짝하며 비교할 수 없노라 그러나 저희가 자기로서 자기를 헤아리고 자기로서 자기를 비교하니 지혜가 없도다"(Οὐ γὰρ τολμῶμεν ἐγκρῖναι ἢ συγκρῖναι ἑαυτούς τισιν τῶν ἑαυτοὺς συνιστανόντων, ἀλλὰ αὐτοὶ ἐν ἑαυτοῖς ἑαυτοὺς μετροῦντες καὶ συγκρίνοντες ἑαυτοὺς ἑαυτοῖς οὐ συνιᾶσιν). 11절에서 바울

93) Barnett, 481.

은 그의 대적자들을 세게 다룰 것이라고 경고하였다. 12절에서 바울은 대적자들을 본격적으로 공격하기 시작한다. 접속사 γὰρ("이는 …함이라")는 여기서 11절과 직접 관련시켜 생각하는 것 같지 않다. 12절이 11절의 이유로 보는 것은 어색하고 의미가 분명하지 않다.[94] 여기서 이 접속사는 이유 접속사가 아니라 단순히 계속적인 설명을 위한 별 의미 없는 "설명적 접속사"로 보는 것이 좋다.[95] 바로 앞 11절에서 편지로 사역하는 바울과 실제로 현장에서 사역하는 바울이 같은 하나님의 사람이라는 사실을 알아야 한다고 말하지만, 그럼에도 불구하고, 자신들을 스스로 높이 평가하는 오만한 사람들과는 감히 비교하지 않겠다고 한다.[96] 바울은 문자적으로 자신을 대적자들과 비교할 수 없다는 것이 아니라, 대적자들의 오만한 자랑을 비난하는 것이다.[97] 사실 7절에서도 바울은 반대자들과 비교를 하였고, 나머지 10-13장에서 많은 비교를 하고 있다.

바울은 반대자들의 어리석음을 공격한다. "그러나 저희가 자기로서 자기를 헤아리고 자기로서 자기를 비교하니 지혜가 없도다." 바울의 대적자들의 문제는 스스로 만든 기준으로 자신을 평가하여 잘난 체하는 것이다. 이런 판단 기준으로 스스로를 높게 평가하여 자랑하고, 바울을 낮게 평가하여 열등한 사도로 업신여기는 것은 어리석은 것이다. 바울 자신은 하나님의 사도로서 하나님의 인정을 받는다는 사실을 굳게 믿고 있고 그것을 거듭 증명하고 있다(3:1; 10:8, 18; 11:12; 갈 1:1). 이에 반해서 그의 대적자들은 하나

94) 참조, Thrall, 640.

95) Windisch, 308; Barnett, 481.

96) Windisch, 308; Bultmann, 194; Furnish, 480; Martin, 318; Thrall, 640.

97) 참조, Barnett, 482.

님의 사도라는 증거 대신, 오히려 사단의 거짓 사도라는 증거만 있다(11:13-15). 그들의 판단 기준은 자기 자신들이 높은 평가를 받도록 스스로 고안한 주관적이고 독선적인 것이기 때문이다. 그들의 판단 기준 가운데는 언변이나 외모(10:7, 10) 이외에도,[98] 복음서의 예수님이 정하신 사도들의 경제생활 규범(11:8-9; 12:13; 마 10:42),[99] 기사나 영적 능력(12:1-12) 등이 있을 수 있다.[100] 본문에서도 대적자들은 2절에서 바울을 "육체대로 행하는 자"로 비난하며, 7절에서 외모로 사람을 평가하여, 바울은 진정한 그리스도의 사도가 아니고, 자신들만이 그리스도의 사도라고 주장하며, 10절에서도 바울을 비난하여 외모와 언변이 없다고 하였다. 이런 육체적 평가 기준을 가지고 자랑하거나 비난하는 것 자체가 거짓 사도의 표이다.[101] 바울 시대에 헬라 철학자들이 청중이나 학생들을 끌기 위하여 자신을 높이고 남들과 비교하였다. 바울의 대적자들도 이런 유행을 따랐을 수도 있다.[102] 이 대적자들의 배경이 예루살렘인 것이 거의 확실하지만(3:1-2; 11:23), 헬라문화에 영향받은 유대인 기독교인들이라고 볼 수 있다.

13. "그러나 우리는 분량 밖의 자랑을 하지 않고 오직 하나님이

---

98) P. Marshall, *Enmity in Corinth: Social Convention in Paul's Relations with the Corinthians*, WUNT 2, Reihe 23, (Tübingen: Mohr, 1987), 325.

99) Theissen, *Social Setting*, 52.

100) Furnish, 480.

101) 푸르타크(Plutarch)는 자기칭찬을 경계하였으나, 자신에 대한 비난을 위한 변명을 위해서는 필요하다고 보았다(*Moralia*. 539E-47; C. Forbes, "Comparison, Self-Praise and Irony: Paul's Boasting and the Conventions of Hellenistic Rhetoric", *NTS* 32 (1986), 8-10

102) Furnish, 342; Frobes, 7; B. W. Winter, *Philo and Paul among the Sophists*, SNTSMS 96 (Cambridge: University Press, 1997), 223.

우리에게 분량으로 나눠주신 그 분량의 한계를 따라 하노니 곧 너희에게까지 이른 것이라" (ἡμεῖς δὲ οὐκ εἰς τὰ ἄμετρα καυχησόμεθα ἀλλὰ κατὰ τὸ μέτρον τοῦ κανόνος οὗ ἐμέρισεν ἡμῖν ὁ θεὸς μέτρου, ἐφικέσθαι ἄχρι καὶ ὑμῶν). 바울은 그와 그의 대적자들의 "자랑"을 비교하면서 대적자들을 공격한다. 대적자들은 자신들이 정한 판단기준에 의해 자랑하지만, 바울은 하나님이 정해 주신 분량 밖의 자랑을 하지 않는다(13-17절). 12절에서 말하는 자랑과 자기평가 그리고 13절의 "분량 밖의 자랑"은 보다 넓은 의미를 가지고 있으나, 13절 후반에서는 구체적인 선교지역의 한계라는 뜻으로 좁혀서 말하고 있다. 13절에서 바울은 그의 자랑이 "분량 밖의 자랑"이 아니라면서 자신의 자찬 내용이 결코 지나친 것이 아니라고 말을 시작하지만 이내 구체적인 선교사역지의 한계라는 유사한 말로 전환한다. 대부분의 학자들은 "분량의 한계"(τὸ μέτρον τοῦ κανόνος)라는 말은 지역적인 의미를 가리킨다고 한다.[103] 그러나 바레트와 마이어는 그리스도에게 속한 사도적 신분을 가리킨다고 한다.[104] 퍼니쉬는 "분량"(κανόν)이란 말이 지역적 의미와 함께 사도적 권위를 가리킨다고 보면서, "법적 영역"(jurisdiction)으로 본다(465). 유사하게 저쥐(E. A. Judge)도 "분량"(κανόν)이란 말을 지역적 의미를 가진 봉사라고 한다.[105] 케제만, 게오르기, 큄멜은 "판단기준"으로 본다.[106] 실

---

103) Hughes, 366; Furnish, 471; Bultmann, 196; Martin, 319, 321; Barnett, 484, 485; Thrall, 644.

104) Barrett, 263; Meyer, 408.

105) 재인용, G. H. R. Horsely, *New Documents Illustrating Early Christianity I* (North Ryde: Macquarie University, 1981), 45.

106) Käsemann, *Die Legitimität*, 43-51; Georgi, *Die Gegner*, 229, 230; Kümmel, 209.

제로 대적자들은 그들이 그리스도의 사도의 신분임을 자랑한다(7절). 바울은 이들의 주관적인 사도직 주장과 거리를 두면서 자신의 사도직의 객관성을 입증하려고 한다고 본다. 이런 여러 가지 제안에도 불구하고, 본문에서는 선교 지역적인 의미가 뚜렷하게 나타나 있다. 더구나 "너희에게까지 이른 것이라"는 말은 바울이 고린도 교회를 세운 것을 말한다. 바울은 하나님께서 정해주신 그의 선교지역의 한계 안에서 사역함으로써 마음대로 사역지를 정하거나 침범하는 대적자들과 달리 하나님의 진정한 사도임을 입증하는 것이다(고전 9:1-3; 15-18; 15:8-11; 참조, 고전 7:17; 롬 12:3). 그는 하나님으로부터 이방사도로 부르심을 받았고, 또한 사도회의에서 이방을 위한 사도로 결정된 것이나, 그의 대적자들은 이런 규정을 알고도 이를 무시하고 바울의 선교지역, 즉 고린도 교회로 들어 왔다(갈 2:7-9).[107] 바울은 고린도 교회를 그의 선교 사역의 열매로 자랑하고 있다(3:2, 3; 10:15). 고린도 교회는 하나님이 정해주신 정당한 바울의 선교사역지이며 그가 그의 선교의 열매를 자랑하는 것은 지극히 타당한 것이다. 바울이 고린도 교인들의 영적 아버지로 자처하는 것은 당연하다(12:14; 고전 4:14-15). 문제는 대적자들이 바울의 선교지역을 침범하고 그가 수고한 선교의 열매를 거두는 것이다.[108] 이런 시각에서 트롤은 "분량의 한계"란 말을 지역적 의미와 함께 선교적 성과를 나타내는 말이라고 한다(646). 바울은 그의 선교지역에서 그가 이룬 선교적 성과를 따라서만 자신의 사역을 평가한다는 것이다. 무엇보다 바울은 지중

107) D. A. Carson, *From Triumphalism to Maturity: An Exposition of 2 Corinthians 10-13* (Grand Rapids: Baker Book House, 1984), 75.

108) Martin, 319.

해 연안을 따라서 선교해야 한다는 사명감을 갖고 있었다(16; 롬 15:23). 이 사명감은 하나님께로부터 받은 것이다(롬 15:16; 행 9:15). 여기서 바울이 그의 대적자들이 이방의 선교를 아예 할 수 없다는 것을 말하는 것인지 분명하지 않다. 분명한 것은 그들이 그가 시작한 선교지를 침범하는 것을 문제 삼는 것이다(15:20). 바넷은 바울이 사도회의의 규정을 엄밀하게 적용하였다고 보면서 그 대적자들은 유대인들로서 회당 같은 데서 유대인들을 상대로만 복음을 전할 수 있다고 한다.[109] 그러나 이 경우에 바울이 처음 고린도에서 유대인 회당에서 헬라인들뿐만 아니라 유대인들에게도 복음을 전한 사실은 바울 자신이 먼저 그의 대적자들의 선교영역를 침범한 것이 됨으로 여기서 바울이 사도회의의 규정을 엄밀하게 적용하고 있다기 보다는 바울이 시작한 선교지에 이들이 침입한 것을 문제 삼는 것으로 보아야 한다(행 18:4).

14. "우리가 (이왕에) 너희에게 가지 않았더라면 (지금 우리의 사역이) 우리의 한계를 지나치는 것이라고 하겠으나, 그런 것이 아니라.(우리가 너희에게 미치지 못할 자로서 스스로 지나쳐 나아간 것이 아니요) 우리는 그리스도의 복음으로 (이왕에) 너희에게까지 이른 것이라" (οὐ γὰρ ὡς μὴ ἐφικνούμενοι εἰς ὑμᾶς ὑπερεκτείνομεν ἑαυτούς, ἄχρι γὰρ καὶ ὑμῶν ἐφθάσαμεν ἐν τῷ εὐαγγελίῳ τοῦ Χριστοῦ). 여기서는 13절에서 바울이 그의 선교 지역의 한계를 벗어나지 않았다는 말을 보다 분명하게 설명하고 있다. 바울은 고린도 교회를 세운 사람이기 때문에 그의 고

---

109) Barnett, 488.

린도 교회의 사역은 합법적이다(고전 3:10; 4:15). 바울은 이방의 사도로서 마땅히 고린도 교회를 세울 자격이 있었다. 한글개역에 "미치지 못할 자"(ἐφικνούμενοι)라는 현재분사가 명사로 번역되었으나 실제로 동사적 용법으로서 "우리가…가지 않았다면"으로 해석 한다(RSV; NIV). 한 가지 문제는 시제가 과거분사이어야 하는데 현재분사인 것이다. "우리가 너희에게 (이왕에) 가지 않았더라면 (지금 너희를 위한 우리의 사역이) 우리의 한계를 지나치는 것이라고 하겠으나, (실제로는) 그런 것이 아니다. 우리는 너희들에게 (이미) 복음을 전하였다."[110] 현재형(ἐφικνούμενοι)(["우리가]… 가지 [않았다면]")을 써서 바울의 고린도 교회에 대한 계속적인 사역의 권한을 가리킨다고 볼 수도 있다.[111] 또는 ὑπερεκτείνομεν(한계를 지나치다)은 동사의 현재형에 동화된 것으로 보기도 한다.[112] 이런 시제의 문제가 있으나 의미는 분명하다. 바울이 고린도 교회를 세우지 않았더라면, 고린도 교회에 대해서 그의 사도적 권한을 행사하는 것이 월권적 행위가 되지만, 바울이 이왕에 고린도 교회를 세웠으므로 월권이 아니라 당연한 것이다. 실제로는 바울의 대적자들이 이런 월권적인 행위를 하고 있음을 나타내고 있다. 휴즈는 φθάνειν(프다네인)이란 말은 원래 "먼저 이르다"란 뜻임을 지적하면서, 이런 의미를 여기서 충분히 살려서 이해해야 한다고 한다(참조, 살전 4:15).[113] 바울은 대적자들이 오기 전에 먼저 그 교회를 세웠다. "우리는 그리스도의 복음

110) Martin, 315; Thrall, 648.

111) Furnish, 472.

112) Thrall, 646.

113) Hughes, 366, 주, 24.

으로 (이왕에) 너희에게까지 이른 것이라"라는 말은 대적자들이 다른 예수를 전하고 다른 복음을 전한다는 사실(11:4)과 대조되어 바울의 고린도 교회에 대한 사역권이 타당한 것임을 나타낸다.

15-16절: "우리는 남의 수고를 가지고 분량 밖에 자랑하는 것이 아니라 오직 너희 믿음이 더할수록 우리의 한계를 따라 너희 가운데서 우리의 활동 영역이 더 크게 확장되기를 바라노라 (더욱 위대하여지기를 바라노라). 이는 남의 한계 안에 예비한 것으로 자랑하지 아니하고 너희 지경을 넘어 복음을 전하려 함이라" (οὐκ εἰς τὰ ἄμετρα καυχώμενοι ἐν ἀλλοτρίοις κόποις, ἐλπίδα δὲ ἔχοντες αὐξανομένης τῆς πίστεως ὑμῶν ἐν ὑμῖν μεγαλυνθῆναι κατὰ τὸν κανόνα ἡμῶν εἰς περισσείαν εἰς τὰ ὑπερέκεινα ὑμῶν εὐαγγελίσασθαι, οὐκ ἐν ἀλλοτρίῳ κανόνι εἰς τὰ ἕτοιμα καυχήσασθαι). 13절과 14절에서의 바울의 분량을 따르는 합당한 "자랑"과 반대자들의 분량을 넘는 부당한 "자랑"이 대조되고 있다. 여기서 "분량"은 13절에서와 같이 피상적으로는 지나친 자랑을 가리키나 실제적으로는 바울에게 할당된 합법적인 선교지역을 가리킨다. 바울의 대적자들은 교권에 굶주려서 바울이 시작한 고린도 교회에 침범하여 바울이 이룩한 성과들을 자기들의 것으로 자랑하는 불한당들이다.[114] 이들과는 대조적으로 바울은 정해진 선교 사역지 (고린도지역) 안에서 그가 이루는 성과로 말미암아 그의 사역이 계속 확장되기를 바라고 있었다.

"오직 너희 믿음이 더할수록 우리의 한계를 따라 너희 가운데

114) Carson, 78.

서 우리의 활동 영역이 더 크게 확장되기를 바라노라(NIV) (더욱 위대하여지기를 바라노라)." 고린도 교인들의 믿음이 자라서 바울의 선교를 돕게 되면 그의 사역의 영역은 더욱 넓어지게 될 것이며, 그의 사노적 역량과 권위가 더욱 커지게 될 것이다. "믿음이 더할수록"은 영적 성장을 가리키는 말이지만, 구체적으로 고린도 교인들이 바울의 반대자들의 미혹을 뿌리치고 완전히 바울의 편으로 돌아오는 것을 암시한다고 볼 수 있다.[115] 그들이 바울에게 돌아와 그의 선교를 지원할 수 있을 때 그는 보다 원대한 선교지 개척의 비젼을 실현할 수 있을 것이다. 그러나 바울은 그의 대적자들처럼 남의 선교 영역을 결코 침범하지 않고, 어디까지나 "우리의 한계를 따라"(κατὰ τὸν κανόνα ἡμῶν) 선교할 것임을 다짐하고 있다(롬 15:20). 바울의 사역은 그의 선교지 안에서도 얼마든지 성장을 할 수 있음을 자신하는 것이다. 부정사 μεγαλυνθῆναι(위대하여지기)의 주어가 분명하지 않아서 학자들의 견해는 두 개로 나누어진다. "우리",[116] 또는 "우리의 사역"이다.[117] 문맥상 어느 것이나 가능하나, "우리"(바울)라는 말이 바울의 사도적 권위와 사역을 복합적으로 나타내므로 더 적합한 번역이라고 본다. 그러나 여기서 "(우리가) 더욱 위대해지기 바라노라"는 의미가 어색하므로 NIV를 따라 활동영역으로 번역하였다.

"너희 지경을 넘어 복음을 전하려 함이라." 고린도는 안디옥에서 시작된 바울의 선교 여행 중 현재까지 가장 먼 곳이다. 바울은

---

115) Windisch, 312; Thrall, 650.

116) Hughes, 367; Thrall, 635; M. Zerwick and M. Grosvenor, *A Grammatical Analysis of the Greek New Testament*, II (Rome: Biblical Institute Press, 1979), 556.

117) Martin, 322; Barnett, 490, 주, 53.

고린도를 거점으로 삼아 더욱 먼 곳까지 그의 선교지역을 확장할 계획임을 밝힌다. 어쩌면 이미 스페인 선교 계획을 하고 있는지도 모른다(롬 15:24, 28-29).[118] 이를 위해서는 아가야 지방의 중심 도시인 고린도 교인들의 지원이 필요한 것이다.

이렇게 바울은 이방지역 개척 선교를 하는 데 반하여, 그의 대적자들이 바울이 이미 개척한 고린도 교회에 침입하여서 바울이 이룬 성과를 마치 자기들의 것인 양 자랑하니 부당하다.[119]

17. "자랑하는 자는 주 안에서 자랑할지니라"(Ὁ δὲ **καυχώμενος ἐν κυρίῳ καυχάσθω**). 바울은 남의 영역에 침입하여 선교하는 것과, 남의 선교적 성과를 가지고 자랑하는 것을 부당하다고 말해왔다. 그렇다면 적절한 자랑은 할 수 있다는 것인가? 여기서 바울은 사람의 자랑하는 것이 도대체 부당하다고 말한다. "주 안에서 자랑하라"는 말은 예레미야 9장 23절(70인역)의 인용으로서 고린도전서 1장 31절에도 인용되었다. 예레미야 9장 23-24절은 사람의 궁극적인 평가는 인간이 설정한 조건으로 할 것이 아니라, 다만 여호와의 인애와, 공평과 정직에 따라야한다는 뜻이

118) Bachmann, 360; Plummer, 289; Barrett, 268; Martin, 324; Thrall, 652.

119) Barrett는 바울의 대적자들은 바울이 아니라 베드로가 처음으로 고린도 교회를 세웠다고 하면서 오히려 바울이 그들의 영역을 침범했다고 비난하였을 것이라고 한다(Barrett, "Cephas and Corinth," 35-6). 그러나 베드로가 고린도 교회를 방문하였다는 것은 추측에 불과하다(고전 1:12; 3:22; 9:5; 15:5). 또한 고린도에 유대인 회당이 있었으므로 바울의 대적자들은 고린도가 자기들 같은 유대인 기독교인들의 마땅한 선교지라고 주장했을 수도 있다는 것이다. 그러나 바울은 그들이 자신이 세운 고린도 교회에 침입한 것을 문제로 삼고 있다. 물론 고린도 교회 전체가 완전히 이방인 교회라고 할 수는 없을 것이다. 적어도 브리스길라와 아굴라는 유대인들이었다(행전 18:2). 그러나 전체적으로 이방인이 지배적이었을 가능성이 짙다.

있다. 로마서 15장 17-18절에서 바울은 "그리스도 안" 에서 자신의 사역에 대하여 자랑한다고 말한다. "주 안에서" 란 말은 "주님의 인격과 권위를 존중하는 주님을 중심으로" 란 말이다. 다시 말하면 우리의 구속자로서 우리를 위해 죽으신 주님을 기준으로 삼아서 그의 종 된 우리들의 인격과 자세를 평가받아야 한다고 신적인 평가 기준을 제안하는 것이다. 주를 섬기는 종들은 결코 세상의 판단기준이나 인간적인 사욕을 따라 사역해서는 안 된다. 세상의 판단 기준이나 자기 사욕을 따라 자랑하는 사람들은 결코 진정한 주의 종들이 될 수 없다. 그러므로 바울이 "주 안에서" 또는 "그리스도 안에서" 라는 제한적인 말을 붙인 것은 자랑을 삼가라는 부정적인 의미로 보아야한다. 죄인 인간은 주 앞에서 아무것도 자랑할 수 없기 때문이다(3:27). 갈라디아서 6장 4절에서 "각자 자기의 일을 살피라. 그리하면 자랑할 것이 자기에게만 있고 남에게는 있지 아니하리니" 라고 남에게 자랑하는 것을 경계하는 말과 같다(참조, 롬 1:30; 고전 1:29). 그리고 아래에서 바울은 반대자들의 자랑에 대하여 "육체를 따라" 자랑하는 것을 어리석다고 말한다(11:18; 12:1, 11). 바울의 진정한 자랑은 십자가뿐이다(갈 6:14; 롬 15:18-19). 우리의 모든 것은 하나님께로부터 왔으므로 자랑하는 것 자체가 어리석다(고전4:7). 주님께 감사하고 그에게 영광을 돌려야 한다. 그럼에도 바울은 반대자들의 부당한 비난에 맞서서 억지로 자랑할 수밖에 없다고 하면서 그의 복음 전도자로서 받은 고난을 자랑한다(11:22-33; 참조, 갈 6:14). 그러나 엄밀히 말해서 그의 진정한 자랑은 자신이 고난을 받은 것에 대한 것이 아니라 "고난을 통해 나타난 하나님의 능력" 에 대한 것이라고 한다(12:9). 그리스도의 고난과 죽음, 즉 약함을 통해서 하나님의 능력이 나타났듯이 바울의 약함을 통해 하나님의 능력이 나타났음을 말하면서 바울은 약한 것들을 자랑한다고 말한다(12:9, 10). 또한, 바울은 12장 1-5절에서 영적 체험을 자랑한다. 그러나 곧 이어서 영적 체험으로 말미암아 자신이 자고(自高)하게 되는 것을 막기 위해 "몸의 가시"를 주신 것을 언급하면서 자신의 약한 것들을 자랑한다고 한다(11:30; 12:7-10). 이런 약함에 대한 자랑은 자신의 연약함을 인정하면서 하나님의 능력과 은혜에 의존하는 자세이므로 진정한 의미의 "주 안에서의 자랑"으로 본다. 약함의 자랑은 자신이 영광을 받으려는 것이 아니라 자신을 비우고 약한 가운데서 역사하시는 하나님께 영광을 돌리기 때문이다. 또한 바울은 그가 사도로 다른 사도들 보다 더 많은 고난 받았으나 그것을 자신의 공로를 내세우지 않고, 주님의 은혜로 하였으며, 주님의 종으로서 마땅히 할 일을 했을 뿐이라는 겸비한 자세를 함께 가지는 것이다(11:23; 고전 15:10; 눅 17:10).[120] 이와 달리 반대자들은 "육체를 따라 자랑"하는 일에 적극적이고, 그로 말미암아 자신들이 영광을 받으므로 그리스도의 사도들이라고 할 수 없다. 그들은 "가장된 사단의 일꾼들"이다(11:13-15).

그리스도인의 인격과 삶의 궁극적 평가 기준은 그리스도의 겸비한 인격과 희생적 삶이다(4:7-15; 빌 2:1-10). 이 평가 기준이 또한 진정한 그리스도의 종의 유일하고 진정한 판단 기준이 되는 것이다. 바울의 대적자들은 바울의 선교 영역에 들어와서 바울이 이룬 업적을 가지고 자랑하고(10:13-15), 자신들의 권위와 능력을 과시하는 사욕적 관심을 가지고 있으므로 진정한 주님의 사도들이라고 볼 수 없다.

---

120) Martin, 325.

18. "옳다 인정함을 받는 자는 자기를 칭찬하는 자가 아니요 오직 주께서 칭찬하시는 자니라"(οὐ γὰρ ὁ ἑαυτὸν συνιστάνων, ἐκεῖνός ἐστιν δόκιμος, ἀλλὰ ὃν ὁ κύριος συνίστησιν). 바울의 대적자들이 주님의 종들이라면 자신들이 만든 기준에 따라서(12절) 자랑해서는 안 되고, 주님의 기준에 따라 인정받고 칭찬 받아야 진정한 칭찬이며, 진정한 주님의 종들이다. 그러나 바울의 대적자들은 자신들이 스스로 만든 기준에 따라 자찬하는 사람들이니 어리석고 거짓되다. 여기서 암시적인 의미는 바울은 그의 사역을 주님의 기준에 따라서 행해왔음으로 칭찬받을 것이며. 따라서 진정한 주님의 사도라는 것이다. 반면에 그의 대적자들은 자신들의 사욕에 따라 만든 육체적 평가 기준을 따라 자찬하므로 진정한 주님의 사도가 아니라는 것이다. 바울은 이미 2장 14절에서 7장 4절까지 그의 사도직의 진정성을 변명해왔고 자신을 자찬했다. 그 자찬의 기준은 그리스도의 약함의 능력에 의존하는 것이었다. 바울은 자신이 이런 주님의 약함의 평가 기준에 따라서 실제로 사역하였음을 계속 밝힐 것이다(11:2-3; 12:12). 그리스도의 고난과 죽음을 통해서 하나님의 능력이 나타났듯이 그리스도의 고난에 참여하여 하나님의 능력에 의지하는 사람들이 진정한 그리스도의 사도라는 것이다. 자신의 사욕이나 세상의 가치 기준을 따라 스스로 자랑하는 이들은 진정한 사도들이 될 수 없다. 그리스도를 주로 모시는 공동체에서는 그리스도가 제시한 객관적 가치판단 기준, 즉 약함을 통해 나타나는 하나님의 능력에 의존 여부가 관건이다. 바울은 자신이 이런 판단 기준에 의해 사역한 것이 실제로 증명되므로 자신이 고린도 교인들에 의해 당연히 칭찬받아야 한다고 믿는다(11:22-33; 12:11). 여기서는 복음 사역에 대한 평가나 칭찬은 주님

이 각자에게 설정해준 선교 영역에 한정되어 사역한 경우에만 가능하다는 것이다. 다시 말하면 아무리 일을 많이 해도 규칙을 따라 합법적으로 임무를 수행하지 않으면 평가나 칭찬의 대상에서 제외된다는 것이다. 바울은 설정된 자신의 선교 지역에서 일했으나, 반대자들이 그의 지역을 침입해서 자신들의 공과를 자랑하고 있으니 그들은 주님의 진정한 종들이라고 볼 수 없다(10:13-16; 11:13).

주해:(10:12–18):

바울 사도는 12절부터 그의 대적자들에 대한 공격과 방어를 함께 하고 있다. 무엇보다 바울은 그의 대적자들이 자기들이 스스로 만든 기준으로 진정한 사도직과 그 사역을 평가하여 자신들을 높이는 반면 바울을 낮추는 것이 부당함을 지적한다. 여기서 바울이 문제를 삼는 것은 사도들이 자신들이 할당받은 선교지역에서 벗어나 일하는 것이다. 바울이 맡은 고린도 교회 사역은 주후 50년에 열린 예루살렘 사도 회의의 결정에 따라 이방사역을 담당한 자신이 해온 것이므로 합법적이다(갈 2:9). 뿐만 아니라 이방사역은 하나님께서 친히 그에게 맡기신 임무이다(13절). 그러나 대적자들은 (유대인 사도들로서) 누구에게서도 승인받지 않은 채 한계를 벗어나 이방인 고린도 지역에서 사역하고 있으므로 불법을 행하고 있다(11:3, 4, 20). 바울은 처음 고린도 교회를 세웠다(14; 참조, 고전 3:6). 그는 아무런 사심 없이 고린도 교회의 사역을 해왔다(15, 16; 참조, 롬 15:20). 그러므로 그의 대적자들은 그의 사역지를 침범한 범법자들이다(고전 9:1; 고후 3:2). 그들의 행위는 인간적인 계약(사도회의)을 어긴 것일 뿐만 아니라 주님의 지시와 뜻을 어긴 것이다(17, 18절). 그들의 주 관심은 선한 하나님의 백성을 모으는 데 있는 것이 아니라, 그들의 사욕적 세력 형성에 있다.[121)]

이렇게 바울은 목회의 어려움에 봉착하여 막연히 하나님의 뜻에 맡기는 수동적인 자세를 취하지 않고 적극적으로 반대 세력을 대면한다. 그렇다고 사사로운 감정에 사로 잡혀서 그의 반대자들을 공격하지도 않는다. 그는 그리스도의 사도로서 사욕을 버리고 교회를 수호해야한다는 책임을 통감하면서(10:8) 객관적인 목회 윤리적 문제(10:13-16)와 신학적인 문제들(11:4, 13-15)을 가지고 반대자들의 부당성을 공격하고, 한편으로는 자신의 사도직의 정당성을 방어한다.

바울의 항변은 오늘날 복음사역에도 적용이 된다. 사실 교역자들이라면 언제 어디서나 복음화 사역을 위한 소명을 받았다. 그러나 그 소명을 합법적 윤리적 신학적인 근거를 가지고 적절하게 수행하지 않을 때 소모적인 분쟁에 휘말리게 되고, 복음사역에 역행하는 결과를 초래할 수 있으므로 주의해야 한다. 본문에서 우리가 배울 것은 목회적 곤경에 처해서 바울이 사욕이나 감정에서 상대방을 비방하고 헐뜯기 쉬운 입장에서 이를 잘 극복하고 있다는 것이다. 본문에서 바울의 지배적인 관심은 그의 대적자들에 대한 객관적인 윤리적 신학적인 문제를 지적하고 자신의 사도직의 진정성에 대해서도 객관적인 자료를 가지고 항변하는 것이다(11:2-12:16). 여기서 우리가 관심을 가지고 배워야 할 중요한 목회원칙은 복음 사역자들이 자신의 감정이나 사사로운 원칙을 주장해서는 안 되고 그리스도 중심적 신학적 원칙과 평가 기준을 가지고

121) Denney, 309.

사역해야 한다는 것이다. 그리스도 중심이라고 해서 희생이나 봉사의 정신만이 아니고 막연히 하나님의 뜻에 맡기는 수동적 자세도 아니다. 사태가 어렵다고 피하지만 말고 시시비비를 가려서 그리스도의 교회를 바로 세우는 일이 책임 있는 목회자의 직무임을 배워야 한다. 문제는 바울처럼 그리스도 중심적 신학에 입각하여 사욕을 떠나서 진실을 분명히 밝히는 바른 목회적 자세가 필요하고, 또한 사태를 신학적 토대 위에서 합리적으로 정확하게 판단하고 분석하는 목회자의 능력도 필요하다(11:10). 이런 자세와 능력이 없을 때 막연히 "만사를 하나님의 뜻에 맡겨 버리는" 무능한 목회자가 될 수밖에 없다. 이것은 목회자의 오래 참는 기다림의 지혜를 부인하는 것이 아니다. 다만 인내하고 기도하며 기다려야 할 때에도 목회자는 교회의 현실 문제에 대한 정확한 신학적 도덕적 분석을 하고 이에 상응하는 대책을 부지런히 강구하는 것이 마땅하다는 것이다.

본문에서 문제가 된 것은 배정된 선교지역의 한계를 벗어나 불법으로 선교하는 것이다. 바울은 모든 전도자들이 하나님으로부터 복음화의 사명을 받았으나, 각자가 맡은 사역의 지역이나 대상을 벗어나지 않도록 주의해야 한다고 경계 하면서 반대자들을 공격한다.

현대 사회는 교통의 발달로 전통적인 지리적인 지역의 개념의 의미가 퇴색되고, 보다 인간적이고 사회계층적인 "지역"의 의미가 더 중요한 것도 사실이다. 더구나 개신교는 여러 신조들과 교단들에 따라 같은 지역에서도 선교하는 현실이므로 지리적 한정의 개념이 무색하다. 그러나 같은 신조나 같은 교단의 경우에도 교역자들은 되도록이면 자기 교회로 교인들을 모으기 위해 애쓰며, 이로 인해 적지 않은 갈등을 일으킨다. 그래서 "교인쟁탈전"이라는 말도 생겼다. 그러나 진정한 사역자는 물량적인 면보다 영적으로 성숙한 교회가 되도록 힘써야 한다. 목회자의 학력이나 설교실력, 교회 건물, 교인수, 교단 규모 등, 외모에 집중하는 것은 바울이 지적한 거짓 사도들의 증표이다(5:12; 7절; 참조, 빌 1:18). 자신의 인격을 그리스도의 인격을 따라 형성하고, 다른 사역자들을 동역자들로 존중해야 하고, 교인들을 깊이 사랑하여, 지역 복음화를 위해 힘쓰는 자세가 필요하다. 내가 섬기는 교회는 내 교회가 아니라 주님의 교회임을 자각하고 무엇이 진정으로 주님의 교회를 위해 유익이 되는지를 생각해야 한다.

한편 어떤 교역자들의 성공적인 사역이 어쩔 수 없이 같은 지역의 다른 교역자들의 사역에 "피해"를 입히는 수도 있다. 교인들이 그 교회로 떠나가기도 하고, 그 교회의 번창은 다른 교회에 상대적인 박탈감을 갖게 한다. 이런 경우 성공적인 목회자는 다른 이웃 목회자들의 사역을 돕기 위해 힘써야 하며, 또 다른 목회자들은 성공적인 목회자를 질시하지 말고 축복해야 한다. 모두 주님의 교회의 사역자들이요, 모두 세계 복음화를 위해 일하고 있음을 잊지 말아야 한다. 바울은 고린도 교회와 유사하게 빌립보 교회에서도 경쟁적인 대적자들에 의해 도전을 받았다. 그 때는 여기서와는 달리 유연한 자세를 취하면서 대적자들의 사역이 결과적으로 복음의 진전에 공헌할 수 있다고 하면서 도리어 기뻐한다(빌 1:17-18).

C. 바울이 자천(自薦) 함(11:1-15)

본문:

1. 원컨대 너희는 나의 좀 어리석은 것을 용납하라 청컨대 나를 용납하라 2. 내가 하나님의 열심으로 너희를 위하여 열심 내노니 내가 너희를 정결한 처녀로 한 남편인 그리스도께 드리려고 중매함이로다 3. 뱀이 그 간계로 이와를 미혹케 한 것 같이 너희 마음이 그리스도를 향하는 진실함과 깨끗함에서 떠나 부패할까 두려워하노라 4. 만일 누가 가서 우리의 전파하지 아니한 다른 예수를 전파하거나 혹 너희의 받지 아니한 다른 영을 받게 하거나 혹 너희의 받지 아니한 다른 복음을 받게 할 때에는 너희가 잘 용납하는구나 5. 내가 지극히 큰 사도들보다 부족한 것이 조금도 없는 줄 생각하노라 6. 내가 비록 말에는 졸하나 지식에는 그렇지 아니하니 이것을 우리가 모든 사람 가운데서 모든 일로 너희에게 나타내었노라 7. 내가 너희를 높이려고 나를 낮추어 하나님의 복음을 값없이 너희에게 전함으로 죄를 지었느냐 8. 내가 너희를 섬기기 위하여 다른 여러 교회에서 요를 받은 것이 탈취한 것이라 9. 또 내가 너희중에 있을 때 (너희에게 있어) 용도가 부족하되 아무에게도 누를 끼치지 아니함은 마게도냐에서 온 형제들이 나의 부족한 것을 보충하였음이라 내가 모든 일에 너희에게 폐를 끼치지 않기 위하여 스스로 조심하였거니와 또 조심하리라 10. 그리스도의 진리가 내 속에 있으니 아가야 지방에서 나의 이 자랑이 막히지 아니하리라 11. 어떠한 연고뇨 내가 너희를 사랑하지 아니함이냐 하나님이 아시느니라 12 .내가 하는 것을 또 하리니 기회를 찾는 자들의 그 기회를 끊어 저희로 하여금 그 자랑하는 일에 대하여 우리와 같이 되게 하려함이로라 13. 저런 사람들은 거짓 사도요 궤휼의 역군이니 자기를 그리스도의 사도로 가장하는 자들이니라 14. 이것이 이상한 일이 아니라 사단도 자기를 광명의 천사로 가장하나니 15. 그러므로 사단의 일군들도 자기를 의의 일군으로 가장하는 것이 또한 큰 일이 아니라 저희의 결국은 그 행위대로 되리라.

본문 비평:

1. 1절에서 ὄφελον("원컨대")이 p^{46} ℵ B에 나오고, 이 동사에 접두모음이 붙은 ὤφελον이 D^3 F G K L ψ에 나온다. 모두 이루어지지 않은 소원을 나타낸다. 이 말은 동사라기보다는 반어적 의미를 나타내는 삽입어로 쓰인다(갈 5:12; 고전 4:8).

2. 1절에서 τι는 p^{46} ℵ B D y등의 대문자 사본의 지지를 받고 있으나 F^{1} G H it Ambrosiaster에는 아예 없다. 이들 중 F G같은 사본에는 τῆς가 나온다. 또 다른 유형은 τῇ ἀφροσύνῃ("어리석음")를 쓴다(H). 트롤은 이렇게 다른 유형들이 나오는 것은 한 필사자가 τι를 τη로 잘못 써서 τῇ ἀφροσύνῃ로 쓴 이후에 다른 이들이 이를 여러 가지로 고쳐서 쓰려고 한 결과라고 본다.[122)]

3. 1절 하반절에서 ἀνέχεσθε("참다" 혹은 "용납하다")는 직설법 현재형이나 명령형이다. 한글개역에서는 "용납하라"는 명령형을 쓰고 있다. 직설법 현재로 보는 경우는, "너희가 이미 그렇게 하고 있다(용납하고 있다)"는 뜻으로 앞의 같은 말(ἀνείχεσθε)을 반복하여 강조한다고 본다.[123)] 그러나 ἀλλὰ καί("그러나 역시")에 대한 번역이 다르다. 이를 앞의 말과 대조하여 강조하는 의미로 보기도하고,[124)] 계속 연결하여 강조하는 의미로 보기도 한다.[125)] 의미상 큰 차이는 없으나 후자의 번역이 보다 부드럽게 된다("그래, 너희가 이미 용납하고 있지.").

4. 3절에 καὶ τῆς ἁγνότητος("깨끗함과")가 원래 ἀπὸ τῆς ἁπλότητος("진실함에서") 뒤에 있었는가 아니면 후에 첨부되었는가의 논쟁이 있다. 이 말이 p^{46} ℵ* B G syr^{h} $cop^{sa,bo}$ goth eth에는

---

122) Thrall, 주, 18, 657.

123) NIV: "but you are already doing that,"; Plummer, 293; Lietzmann, 144; Bultmann, 201; Barrett, 217; Martin, 327.

124) NIV, Plummer, 293; Lietzmann, 144; Bultmann, 201.

125) Barrett, 217; Martin, 327.

있고, ℵ^{c} D^{c} H K P y lat syr^{p,h} arm에는 없기 때문이다. 한편, 암부로스, 어거스틴, 루시퍼같은 라틴 교부들에게서는 ἀπὸ τῆς ἁπλότητος("진실함에서")가 빠져 있다. 두 말의 어미가 모두 -ότητος로 되어 있어서 필사자가 혼돈하여 어느 하나를 빠뜨리는 데서 생긴 오류(*homoeoteleuton*)라고 본다.[126] 한편, D* it^{d} Epiphanius는 두 말의 순서를 반대로 쓰고 있다. Lietzmann은 2절의 ἁγνὴν("정결한")이란 형용사로부터 ἁγνότητος"("깨끗함")이 형성되었다고 본다.[127] 마틴은 이를 수긍한다.[128] 바레트는 ἁγνότητος의 위치가 다양한 것은 이 말이 후에 첨부된 증거라고 한다(*lectio brevior potior*).[129] Allo와 휴즈는 이를 원래 있었는데 빠뜨린 것으로 보는 반면(haplography, 중복글자탈락),[130] 빈디쉬는 원래 없었는데 중복된 것으로 본다(dittography, 중복오사[誤寫]).[131] καὶ τῆς ἁγνότητος("깨끗함과")가 2절의 ἁγνὴν("정결한")이란 말과 관련되므로 원래 있던 말로 보는 것이 자연스럽다.[132]

5. 4절 마지막의 καλῶς ἀνέχεσθε("잘 용납하는구나")는 반어적인 말로 p^{46} B D* 33 sa에 나온다.[133] 미완료형 ἀνείχεσθε("너희

---

126) Martin, 328.

127) Lietzmann, 145.

128) Martin, 328.

129) Barrett, 270.

130) Allo, 276; Hughes, 376.

131) Windisch, 325; B. M. Metzger의 *Textual Commentary*, 583, 584를 보라.

132) Thrall, 663.

133) Plummer, 297.

가 [의례] 용납할 것이다")은 ℵ D3 uncial lat에 나온다. 여기서 미완료형은 과거의 의미가 아니라 "용납할" 미래적 가능성을 나타낸다.[134] 그러나 바울은 고린도 교인들이 대적자들의 가르침을 따라왔음을 이미 알고서 냉소적으로 말하고 있다. 그러므로 현재형이 적절하다(NIV).

6. 15절의 οὐ θαῦμα("이상한 일이 아니다")는 ℵ B D* F G에 나오고, 같은 의미의 οὐ θαυμαστόν("이상한 일이 아니다")은 Db,c E K에 나온다. 전자는 드물게 쓰이는 말이고, 후자는 신약과 LXX에 자주 나오는 말이므로, 전자가 원래의 것으로 보인다.[135]

내용 개요:

일반적으로 11장 1절-12장 18절까지를 독립된 문단으로서 "바보의 연설"이라고 한다. 이 부분에서 바울은 자주 역설적인 진술들로 독자들을 혼돈케 한다. 그러나 주제는 분명하다. 반대자들이 하는 육체적 자랑을 바울도 할 수 있으나, 그의 진정한 자랑은 오히려 그의 약한 것들에 대한 자랑이다(12:9, 10). 그것들이 고난 받으신 그리스도를 전하는 사도의 가장 분명하고 구체적인 증거이기 때문이다. 물론 11장에서 바울이 "원컨대 너희는 나의 좀 어리석은 것을 용납하라"는 말로 시작하여 12장 13절까지 바울이 스스로 어리석은 줄 알면서도 자신에 대한 "외모와 육체적인 자랑"을 하고 있다(11:16, 17, 19, 21; 12:6, 11). 이런 자랑은 그의 진정한

134) Martin, 328.
135) Martin, 328.

자랑을 강조하기 위한 예비적이고, 보조적인 것이다. 그의 대적들의 "외모와 육체에 대한 자랑" 에 대해 나도 그런 자랑을 할 수 있다고 응수하면서 반대자들의 육체적 자랑에 대하여 자신의 육체적 자랑을 열거한다. 그러나 결국 그의 진정한 자랑은 그의 반대자들의 자랑과는 다른 것이라고 하여 대조적이고 반어적인 효과를 나타내고 있다. 그의 진정한 자랑은 그가 그리스도의 약함을 가지고 있다는 데 있다. 그의 육체의 가시와 그의 사역에서 받은 수많은 고난이 바로 그것이다. 그의 대적자들은 이런 고난의 증표가 없으므로 진정한 그리스도의 사도가 아니다. 이런 그리스도 중심적 논리를 전개하기 전에 바울은 먼저 자신에 대한 "어리석은 육체적 자랑" 을 시작한다. 바울이 진정으로 그런 자랑을 원하는 것은 아니지만 반대자들의 공격에 맞서서 어쩔 수 없이 한 것이다. 바울은 적극적으로 이런 자랑이 참말이기 때문이 진실을 밝히기 위해서 자랑하는 것이 타당하다고도 말한다(12:6). 또 고린도 교인들이 반대자들의 자랑에 미혹받지 않게 하기 위함이다.

중요한 것은 바울의 자랑이 "육체를 따르는 자랑" 이라고 하나 주로 고난 받은 자랑이므로 반대자들의 "육체적 자랑" 과는 질적으로 구별된다는 것이다. "약한 것의 자랑" 이란 나는 죽고 하나님의 능력이 나타나는 것에 대한 자랑이기 때문이다. "육체적인 인간적인 자랑이 아니라 하나님의 영광에 대한 자랑이다. 그러므로 고난의 자랑이 "육체의 자랑" 의 모양은 가졌으나 그리스도의 십자가의 능력을 믿는 믿음 안에서 주안에서의 자랑이 된다. 바울의 고난은 진정한 사도의 표가 된다. 반대로 영적 체험이라 해도 사욕에 의해 자랑하는 것은 "육체적 자랑" 에 속한다(4:2; 12:1; 7; 고전 2:2). 즉 "육체의 한계" 와 같이 피상적이며 부패할 수밖에 없는 가치로 전락되는 것이다. 바울의 고난의 자랑은 같은 육체적 자랑의 모양을 가졌으나, 그 동기와 성격이 반대자들의 육체적 자랑과 다르기 때문에 주님이 인정하는 주안에서의 신령한 자랑이 된다고 볼 수 있다(10:17-18).

한편, 바울이 "육체적 자랑"을 하는 것이 단순히 대적자들과 맞서서 싸우기 위한 것만은 아니다. "육체적 자랑"은 10장 11절에서 말하는 바울의 사도의 자격과 권위를 분명히 나타내기 위한 것도 된다(12:12; 롬 15:18). 바울은 적어도 두 번 자신이 "지극히 큰 사도들 보다 조금도 부족하지 않다"고 말한다(11:5; 12:11). 고린도후서 전체에서 바울은 그의 대적자들의 비난에 맞서서 그리스도의 사도로서의 인격과 그의 사역을 번갈아 가며 변명하고 있는 것이다. 바울은 대적자들의 비난에 직면하여 자신이 과연 진정한 사도로서의 증거를 가지고 있는가에 대해서 심각하게 자성(自省)하는 계기를 갖게 된 것이다(13:3). 이런 자성은 주로 그의 말(λόγος)과 일, 사역(ἔργον)의 효력에 대한 것이라고 할 수 있다.[136] 바울은 자성의 결과 그가 말로는 약하나, 말씀을 순수하게 가르치며(2:17), 윤리적으로 깨끗하며(1:12), 궤휼을 쓰지 않으며(4:2), 할당된 지역에서만 사역해왔으며(10:13-15; 롬 15:20), 교회에 재정적 부담을 주지 않았다는 것을 재확인한다(11:8-9; 12:16-18). 물론 기사와 표적의 능력도 있다(12:12). 그리고 무엇보다 적극적인 복음 사역을 하면서 많은 고난을 받았다(6:4; 11:23-33). 반면에 바울은 반대자들의 오만하고 부당한 행위를 열거한다. 반대자들은 예루살렘 사도들의 권위를 내세워 오만하게 바울에게 할당된 사역지에 들어

136) Windisch, 307.

와서(10:15-17), 바울이 그동안 이룩해 놓은 목회적 성과를 자기들의 것으로 삼고(10:15), 자신들의 설교 실력을 자랑하며(10:10), 거짓된 복음을 전하며(11:4), 교회의 재정을 축내는 사욕적 사역을 하면서도(11:7), 이런 사역을 자랑하며(10:17; 11:12, 18), 바울과 대등하게 되려고 함으로써(11:12) 그들의 행위의 부당함을 스스로 들어내었다. 바울은 자성을 통해서 사도로서의 모든 자격을 다 갖추었음을 확신하게 된 것이다(10:10-11; 11:5). 반대자들의 자랑에 대하여 바울은 마지못해 그러나 확실한 어조로 그의 자랑을 열거하는 것이다. 물론 사도의 진정한 표는 그리스도의 십자가의 고난과 능력임을 거듭 강조한다. 또한 바울은 제3차 방문 시에는 사도로서 "그 몸으로 대할 때에도" 강하다는 것을 나타내 보일 것임을 시사하고 있는 것이다(10:2; 13:2). 즉 사도권으로 반대자들을 치리할 것을 공언한다(13:2). 그럼으로써 그가 진정으로 그리스도의 사도임을 부분적으로 나마 증명할 수 있다고 한다(13:3). 그러나 그가 진정으로 원하는 것은 어디까지나 그리스도의 온유함과 겸비함으로 고린도 교인들을 만나는 것이다(10:1; 12:20; 13:7, 9, 10). 그런 자세가 그리스도의 사도의 진정한 표로 보기 때문이다. 3차 방문이 원만하게 하기 위해서 바울은 3차 방문 이전에 고린도 교인들이 스스로 회개하여 온전하여 지기를 바라는 것이다(12:19-21; 13:5).

11장 1절부터 바울의 중심적인 연설이 시작되는 것이라는 데에는 이의가 없으나, 끝나는 부분에 대해서는 학자들의 의견이 다르다. 즈미주스키(Zmijewski)는 12장 10절까지라고 보는데, 12장 11절에서 "내가 어리석은 자가되었으나"라는 말을 "어리석은 자의 연설"을 앞 절(12:10)에서 끝맺었다는 말로 보기 때문이다. 그러나

12장 11-13절을 연설의 결론 부분으로 볼 수도 있다는 견해가 있다.[137] 14절부터 바울은 그의 새로운 주제(세 번째 방문)를 발하기를 시작하고 있다는 것이다. 18절까지의 내용이 여전히 바울의 사도직 변명에 대한 말이므로 이를 포함시키는 견해도 있다.[138] 19절의 "이 때까지 우리가 우리를 너희에게 변명하는 줄로 생각하는구나"라는 말이 18절에서 그의 연설을 마쳤다고 보게 한다. 우리는 이 견해를 따른다.

11장 1-15절은 11장 1절-12장 18절의 "바보의 연설"의 서론 부분으로서 바울은 자신을 거짓 사도들과 비교하면서 자신을 자찬하기 시작한다. 이 부분의 내용을 분석하면 다음과 같다.[139]

1. 고린도 교인들을 그리스도에게 중매한 바울 (교회의 설립자)은 고린도 교인들이 계속 그리스도와 교제하기를 원함 (11:1-3)
2. 고린도 교인들이 거짓 사도를 용납하였음을 질책함 (11:4)
3. 바울은 자신이 큰 사도들 보다 부족함이 없다고 생각함 (11:5)
   a. 말은 못하나 지식은 깊음 (11:6)
   b. 삯을 받지 않고 사역했음 (11:7-9)

---

137) Furnish, 484; Wolff, 208.

138) H. G. Sundermann, Kraft der Rede, 45.

139) cf. Sundermann, 45: insinuatio(도입부분): 11:1-6; propositio(명제부분): 11:7; argumentatio(논쟁부분) 11:8-11; Peroratio(결론부분) 11:12-15. 그러나 이런 분류는 대체적인 것이며 절대적이라고 할 수 없다. 예를 들어 바울은 Sundermann이 서론에 포함시키는 1:6에서 바울은 자신이 "말에는 졸하나 지식에는 그렇지 아니하니…"라고 본론적인 말(propositio)을 하고 있다.

c. 그리스도의 진리가 있음 (11:10)
d. 고린도 교인들을 사랑함 (11:11)
e. 거짓 사도들은 우리와 대등하게 되려고 하지만 사단의 일꾼들임(11:12-15)

11장 1-15절의 문학적 특징들은 다음과 같다.[140] 반복법을 쓴다(9, 12), 보다 강도 높은 정서적인 용어들을 구사한다("탈취하다," συλᾶν, 8절; "막히다," ἐκκόπτειν, 10절; "사랑," ἀγαπᾶν, 11절; "끊다", φράσσειν, 12절); 명사형을 많이 쓴다; 병행구가 많이 나타난다; 유사한 말들을 중복하여 쓴다(13절); 13절, 14절, 15절은 명제(a=c), 논증(b=c), 결론(a=b)의 삼단논법으로 구성되어 있다(즉 거짓사도들은 가장한다; 사단도 가장한다; 고로 거짓사도들은 사단의 일꾼들이다); 경중(輕重)을 대비하는 랍비들의 논쟁 양식이 있다(6절), 등이다.

사도직 방어를 위한 바울의 변명이라는 큰 주제 아래서 11장 1-15절의 역할은 10장에서 지적한 반대자들의 오만한 자랑의 거짓됨을 지적한 후에, 11장 16-33절에서의 자신의 "겸손한 약함의 자랑" (고난의 사역)을 더 자세히 대조적으로 말하기 전에, 독자들에게 반대자들의 정체를 폭로함으로서, 독자들이 중립적 자세를 벗어나서 바울의 입장을 지지하여 반대자들을 축출해야할 근본적 이유를 제시하는 것이다. 또한 여기서 바울은 11장 16-33절에서의 그의 사도로서의 "선행들"을 말하기 전에 그의 "선한 신분"을 반대자들의 "악한 신분"과 대조하여 독자들에게 분명히 알

140) Zmijewski, 187; Martin, 331.

려야 할 필요가 있다고 보았다. 독자들이 반대자들의 "악한 신분"과 바울의 "선한 신분"을 일단 이해하게 되면, 비록 바울이 반대자들과 유사하게 "육체적 자랑"을 하더라도 독자들이 그 진의를 알고 이해해줄 것을 기대하고 있다. 물론 11장 1-15절에서도 바울은 사도로서의 자신의 자격을 증명하는 구체적 사례도 든다. 즉 6절에서는 자신의 뛰어난 지식, 7-12절에서는 자비량 선교로 나타난 재정적 투명성을 지적하면서 자신의 사도적 신분의 우월성을 증거한다.

서론("바울의 사도직 이해")에서 지적한 바와 같이 바울이 보기에 반대자들은 그들의 사도직을 그리스도 중심으로 이해하지 못하고 "영광과 능력의 직책"으로 이해하고 있었다(3:14; 4:4). 또한 반대자들은 "다른 예수, 다른 복음, 다른 영"을 전하는 이들이었다(11:4). 그들은 "외모"와 "육체적 조건"을 중시하는 이들이었다(5:12; 10:7). 그러므로 그들은 그리스도의 사도직을 제대로 이해할 수가 없었다(11:4). 바울은 앞서 밝힌 바와 같이 복음을 분명히 하나님의 계시로 받았고, 그 계시가 그리스도의 죽으심과 부활에서 구체적으로 나타났음을 알고 있다(3:5, 18; 4:4; 5:15). 그리스도의 사도는 그리스도의 고난을 겪고 그리스도의 인내를 함양한 사람이어야 하고 또 그것을 그의 사역에 적용하고, 그의 사역에서 그리스도의 약함의 승리를 입증할 수 있어야 한다(4:7-15; 6:4-10; 12:9-12; 13:4). 그래서 바울은 고린도 교회에서 반대자들로 말미암아 훼손된 그의 사도직을 회복하기 위해서 그의 사도직의 정당성과 반대자들의 사도직의 부당성을 이런 기독론적 판단 기준에 의해서 설명한다. 바울은 그리스도의 고난을 통한 구원 사역을 중심으로 해서 자신의 사역과 생애가 전개됨을 일일이 지적하면서 반대자들의 사역이 그렇지 못함을 지적하고 있다. 바울은 그의 사도직의 정당성 문제와 관련하여 고린도 교회의 대적자들의 사도직의 부당한 여러 가지 점들도 지적하고 있다. 무엇보다 그들의 가장 큰 문제는 복음을 그리스도의 고난을 중심으로 명확히 이해하지 못하고, "다른 예수." "다른 영," "다른 복음"을 가르쳐서 고린도 교회를 정통적 인 사도적 교회가 되지 못하게 하는 것이다 (11:2-4).

그러므로 바울은 반대자들에 대하여 고린도 교회 일반 교인들에게 보인 유화적인 자세를 취하지도 않고(5:20-22; 6:1; 7:2), 어려운 사태가 저절로 잘 되리라고 낙관하지도 않는다. 바울은 반대자들의 뒤에는 사단의 역사가 있다고 본다(11:15). 반대자들은 단순히 바울을 반대하는 자들이 아니라 하나님의 뜻에 역행하는 사단의 일꾼들이다. 그들은 특히 사도들로 가장한 거짓 사도들이므로 속기 쉽다(11:13). 그러므로 바울은 이들과의 정면 대결을 결심했다. 또한 바울은 고린도 교인들이 자신을 단순히 자신을 변명하거나 자랑하는 것으로 보지 말고 그들을 영적 전쟁에서부터 구원하는 진정한 사도로서 신뢰하고 인식하기를 바라는 것이다. 바울은 1-15절에서 16절부터 시작되는 바울의 고난의 사역에 대한 자기 자랑을 할 수밖에 없는 이유를 미리 제시하는 것이다. 즉 반대자들이 거짓 사도들이라는 것이다. 그들의 거짓된 신분에 대조되는 자신의 진정한 신분(그리스도와 고린도 교회의 중매자, 11:2)을 밝혀서 고린도 교인들이 바르게 판단하도록 도와야 한다고 생각한 것이다. 더구나 16절 이하에서 밝힐 자신의 사역은 고난의 사역이다. 고난의 사역은 자기를 위한 것이 아니라 그리스도의 복음을 위한 것이므로 진실한 자랑이며, "주안에서의 자랑"이라는 것이다(10:18). 바울은 자신의 고난 받은 자랑은 반대자들의 "강함의 자랑"과 그 성격이 전혀 다른 "약함의 자랑"임을 강조하고 있다(12:9-10). 바울은 "약함의 자랑"조차도 여전히 "육체적 자랑"이며 어리석은 자랑이라는데 동의한다(11:15-18). 그러나 역설적으로 "약함의 자랑"은 진정한 그리스도의 사도의 표라고 확신한다(12:12). 그리스도의 사역이 약함을 통한 능력의 사역이었기 때문이다. 이런 자신의 선행의 자랑을 할 수 밖에 없는 이유는 11장 1-15절에서 보듯이 반대자들이 매우 위험한 이단자들이기 때문이다. 본문에서 바울은 진실을 밝히기 위해서는 반대자들처럼 자기 자랑을 할 수 밖에 없는 입장이지만 자기와 반대자들은 아예 그 정체부터 다르다는 것을 미리 지적할 필요가 있다고 본다. 같은 자랑을 하더라도 그 사람이 누구냐에 따라서 자랑의 성격이나 의도도 다름으로 독자들이 자랑하는 사람의 정체를 분명히 알 것을 원한다. 다시 말하면 이 부분은 외견상 앞서 10장에서 시작한 "육체적 자랑"의 주제를 떠난 것 같이 보이지만 실제로는 같은 주제 안에 있다고 보아야 한다. 그런 의미에서 11장 1-15절은 11장 16-33절의 바울의 육체적 자랑"의 예비적인 진술이다.

1. 고린도 교인들을 그리스도에게 중매한 바울은 그들이 그리스와의 교제를 계속하기를 원함(11:1-3).

주석:

1. "원컨대 너희는 나의 좀 어리석은 것을 용납하라 청컨대 나를 용납하라"(Ὄφελον ἀνείχεσθέ μου μικρόν τι ἀφροσύνης·

ἀλλὰ καὶ ἀνέχεσθέ μου). 외형적으로 이 구절이 10장 17-18절과 잘 연결되지 않는다.[141] 10장 17-18절에서는 바울은 대적자들의 자랑에 맞서서 "주안에서 자랑하라"고 말했는데, 11장 1-15절에서는 자신의 신분(그리스도와 고린도 교회의 중매자)과 반대자들의 신분(사단의 일꾼)을 대조적으로 말하기 때문이다. 또 11장 16절 이하에서 10장의 자랑의 주제가 다시 나타남으로 이 부분은 삽입 문단이라고 볼 수 있다. 이 부분은 11장 16절 이하에서 바울이 비록 자신이 반대자들과 같이 어리석은 육체적 자랑을 하지만 자신과 반대자들의 정체가 다르다는 것을 독자들에게 미리 알려줄 필요가 있다고 보고 삽입적으로 쓴 것이다. 말하는 사람이 누구냐에 따라서 같은 말이라도 그 의도가 다른 것같이 바울은 그가 하는 자랑의 의도가 반대자들과 다르다는 것을 독자들이 알기를 원하는 것이다. 그러나 그리스도와 고린도 교인들의 중매자(2절)로서의 자신의 선한 정체를 밝히는 것부터 이미 육체적 자랑이라고 볼 수 있다. 그러므로 "나의 좀 어리석은 것을 용납하라"고 독자들의 양해를 구한다. 그 자신도 그가 비난하는 대적자들과 결국 마찬가지로 육체를 따라 자찬한다는 비난을 받을 수 있음을 알기 때문이다. 그는 이런 "외모나 육체적인 자랑"의 어리석음을 알고 있다. 10장 17-18절에서와 같이 진정한 자랑은 주 안에서의 자랑뿐이다. 즉 주님이 인정하는 자랑만이 참된 자랑이다. 아마 거기서 바울은 뒤에서 말할 자신의 그리스도의 고난의 참여를 염두에 두고 있었을 것이다(12:9). 바울은 무엇보다 그가 다른 사도보다

---

141) Martin, 331. 그러나 Thrall은 ἄφρων(어리석은)/ ἀφροσύνη(어리석음)라는 말들이 11:1부터 12:11사이에 자주 나오고 있는 것은 이 부분이 하나의 통일된 문단임을 지지해 준다고 한다(Thrall, 654).

더 주님의 고난에 참여하여 수고한 것이 참된 자랑의 근거이다(11:23-33; 12:11; 고전15:10). 바울은 이런 고난의 자랑을 하기 전에 먼저 고난 받는 자신이 누구인가를 밝혀야 할 필요가 있다고 보았다. 그러므로 자신의 "선한 신분"을 반대자들의 "악한 신분"과 대조적으로 설명한다. 실제로 11장 1-15절에는 반대자들의 정체 폭로가 대부분이다. 그러므로 남을 비판하면서 상대적으로 자신은 선하다고 자랑하는 "어리석음"에 대해서 독자들의 양해를 구하는 것이다. 아무리 타당한 진술이라 해도, 남을 비판하면서 자신을 자랑하는 것은 오만하다는 느낌을 주어서 청중의 거부감을 불러일으킬 수 있다고 보기 때문이다. 유사하게 곧 이어 나오는 그의 고난의 자랑을 시작하기 전에도 독자들의 양해를 구한다(11:15-18). 그는 육체적 자랑을 늘어놓아야 하는 것이 못마땅하나, 그의 대적자들의 저질적인 비난에 미혹되는 고린도 교인들을 구하기 위해서는 이런 저질적인 육체적 외모의 자랑을 할 수밖에 없음을 거듭 말한다(12:1, 5, 11). 육체적 자랑은 그가 이스라엘 출신이라는 인종적 혈통적인 자랑 뿐만 아니라(11:22), 그의 영적 체험까지도 포함한다(12:1-5). 육체적 자랑은 육체와 관련된 것뿐만이 아니라 영적인 것이라 해도 우리로 하여금 우리를 위해 죽으신 주님에게 복종하는 낮은 위치를 벗어나서 자만케 하는 모든 것들을 포함한다(12:7). 그런 일들은 어리석은 것들이다. 십자가의 죽으심이 참된 지혜이며, 그렇게 사는 것이 지혜로운 삶이기 때문이다(고전 1:18-2:6). 그래서 바울은 11장 19절에서 "너희는 지혜로운 자로서 어리석은 자들을 기쁘게 용납하는구나"라고 말한다. 어리석음은 지혜와 함께 유대 지혜문학의 전문용어이지만 바울은 삶의 지혜를 그리스도의 죽음과 부활 사건에서 나타난 하나님의 신학적인 지혜와 연결하여 사용한다.[142] 하나님의 지혜는 "육체의 지혜"를 초월한다(고후 1:12). 바울은 이것을 알면서도 "어리석은 자랑"을 할 수 밖에 없는 입장이다. 이렇게 볼 때 1-15절은 삽입적 문단이지만 "육체의 자랑"이라는 큰 주제의 한 부분일 뿐이다.

1절에서 바울은 자신의 선한 신분을 자랑을 하는 어리석음에 빠질 수밖에 없는 자신의 입장에 대한 독자들의 양해를 우선 구한다. 16절에서의 고난 받은 자신의 선행을 자랑하기에 앞서서 자신의 선한 신분과 반대자들이 가장한 거짓 사도들이라는 악한 신분을 미리 밝혀서 비록 바울이 그들과 같이 어리석은 자랑을 하더라도 자신은 그리스도의 진정한 사도로서 그 자랑의 진의에 있어서 반대자들과 분명히 다르다는 것을 독자들이 알아야 한다고 보았다. 그는 그리스도의 진정한 사도로서 거짓 사도들의 미혹으로부터 고린도 교인들을 구해내야 한다는 사도적 책임의식을 가지고 진실을 밝힌다. 한편 바울은 고린도 교인들이 그의 대적자들의 자신에 대한 비난에 대해서 그가 어떻게 답변할 것인가를 기다리고 있다는 것을 알고 있었다. 즉 바울에게도 그의 대적자들이 말하는 사도적 권위를 나타내는 그런 자랑거리들이 과연 있느냐는 것이다(13:3). 이에 대해 바울은 그런 자랑거리들이라면 내게도 있노라고 맞서서 말하기를 시작하는 것이다(11:6; 12:12; 13:4). 그렇게 함으로 교만한 대적자들을 겸손하게 만들고 또 일반 고린도 교인들에게도 자신이 일반적인 사도로서의 증표들 - 아무리 육체적인 것

142) Windisch, 318; Barrett, "Christianity at Corinth," *Essays on Paul* (Philadelphia: Westminster Press, 1982), 6-14; E. E. Ellis, "Wisdom and Knowledge in 1 Cor," in *Prophecy and Hermeneutics in Early Christianity* (Grand Rapids: Eerdmans, 1978), 45-62.

들이라 해도 - 을 가지고 있음을 보여줌으로서 그들을 자기에게로 이끌어야 했다(12:12; 13:10). 바울은 그렇게 하는 것이 자신의 유익보다 결국 고린도 교인들을 위한 것이고 결국 주님을 위한 것임을 굳게 믿고 있었다(10:5; 11:2; 11, 12:15, 19; 13:6, 7, 9). 더구나 그가 제시하는 "육체적 자랑 거리"는 반대자들의 그것들과 근본적 성격이 다르다. 즉 그리스도를 따르는 희생과 고난의 복음 사역이기 때문이다. 이렇게 그의 육체적 자랑거리는 실제로 거룩한 사도적 증표로 제시되고 있다. 그러므로 바울은 강한 것들이 아닌 약한 것들을 자랑한다고 한다고 하면서 반대자들과의 차별화를 강조하고 있다. 그리고 고린도인들의 현명한 판단을 촉구하는 것이다.

"원컨대" (Οφελον)는 위에서 말했듯이 삽입구이다. 우리말로는 "원하건대"의 준말이다. "바라는 것은" 이라고 번역할 수 있다. 미완료형으로서 아직 이루어지지 않은, 또는 이룰 수 없는 소원을 나타낸다. 이런 부정적인 의미는 어쩌면 고린도 교인들의 바울에 대한 의구심이 깊다는 것을 반영하는 것인지도 모른다.[143] 또는 반어적인 의미에서 생각하면, 고린도 교인들이 스스로 매우 지혜 있다고 생각하므로(고전 4:10) 그들이 바울의 이런 "어리석은 자랑"을 용납할 것 같지 않다는 풍자적 의미도 있을 수 있다.[144] 그러나 1절 상반절의 이런 주저하는 표현과는 달리, 하반절과 11:16-18에서 바울은 그의 자랑이 용납되기를 요구한다. 위에서 본 바와 같이 1절 하반절에서 ἀνέχεσθε("참다" 혹은 "용납하다")는 직설법 현재형이나 명령형이다. 한글개역에서는 "용납하라"는 명령형

143) Thrall, 658.

144) Thrall, 658.

을 쓰고 있다. 명령형으로 보는 경우 ἀλλά(그러나)는 명령을 강조하는 뜻의 "이제"로 번역하여, "이제 나를 용납하라"로 하든가,[145] 또는 뒤에 오는 καί(역시)의 의미에 흡입시켜 "그래, 나를 용납하라"고 번역할 수 있다.[146] 11장 6절에서 "나로 조금 자랑하게 어리석은 자로 받으라"에서 "받으라"(δέξασθε)는 분명히 명령형이다. 직설법 현재로 보는 경우도, "그러나 (내가 틀렸어) 너희가 이미 그렇게 하고 있다(용납하고 있다)"는 뜻으로 앞의 같은 용납하라는 말(ἀνέχεσθε)을 반복하여 강조하는 효과가 있다. 어쩌면 바울의 대적자들이 바울을 가리켜 "어리석다"고 말했기 때문에 고린도 교인들은 바울이 "어리석음"이란 말의 풍자적이고 암시적 의미를 잘 알고 있는지도 모른다. 바울이 자주 그의 대적자들의 말을 그대로 받아들이면서 그의 대적자들을 공격하듯이, 여기서도 그들의 어리석다는 말을 되받아서 그들의 어리석음을 들어내려는 논리를 준비한다고 할 수 있다. 한편 "용납하라"는 말이 4절에도 나오는데, 4절의 의미에 비추어 생각해 볼 때 "너희들이 잘못된 대적자들을 용납했다면, 이제 나의 어리석음도 용납하는 것이 공평하지 않느냐?"라는 의미가 여기에 있다.[147] 이런 의미에서 바울은 그의 자랑하는 어리석음을 고린도 교인들에게 용납하라고 명령할 근거가 있다.

2. "내가 하나님의 열심으로 너희를 위하여 열심 내노니 내가

145) Thrall, 659.

146) Martin, 331.

147) Thrall, 659.

너희를 정결한 처녀로 한 남편인 그리스도께 드리려고 중매함이로다"(ζηλῶ γὰρ ὑμᾶς θεοῦ ζήλῳ, ἡρμοσάμην γὰρ ὑμᾶς ἑνὶ ἀνδρὶ παρθένον ἁγνὴν παραστῆσαι τῷ Χριστῷ). 바울은 그리스도와 그의 교회를 혼인관계로 나타낸다(엡 5:22-23; 참조, 마 25:1-13; 계 19:7-9; 21:2).[148] "중매함이로다"(ἡρμοσάμην)라는 말에서 바울의 입장이 중매자로서 인가, 아니면, 신부의 아버지로서 인가의 논쟁이 있다.[149] 유대교의 풍습에는 주로 신부의 아버지가 결혼을 주선하는 것이 관습이며 딸의 정결을 책임 져야 한다(신 22:15-21).[150] 바울이 자신을 고린도 교인들의 아버지로 묘사하고 있다(12:14; 고전 4:15). 그러므로 여기서도 신부의 아버지로서의 역할을 생각하고 있다고 볼 수 있다. 그러나 결혼을 시키는 아버지의 역할도 결국은 중매자의 역할과 같다. 바울은 중매하는 사람이 바라는 바와 같이 고린도 교인들이 신랑인 그리스도만 사랑하여 그의 재림 시에 그와 온전히 하나가 되기를 원한다(살전 4:17). 문제는 다른 대적자들이 이를 훼방하여 고린도 교인들을 다른 그리스도와 다른 복음을 듣게 하여 그리스도를 사모하지 못하게 함이다. 이에 바울은 열심으로 고린도 교인들을 대적자들로부터 보호하고 그리스도로 인도하기 위해 애쓰는 것이다. 특히 그리스도

148) C. Chavasse, *The Bride of Christ* (London: Religious Book Club, 1930); J. P. Sampley, *"And the Two Shall Become One Flesh": A Study of the Traditions in Ephesians*, SNTSMS 16 (Cambridge: University Press, 1971), 34-51; R. Batey, *New Testament Nuptial Imagery* (Leiden: Brill, 1971).

149) Thrall, 660; Martin, 332. Martin은 바울이 유대관습에 따라서 그리스도와 그의 신부인 고린도 교인들의 혼인을 위한 "둘러리"(신랑의 친구)로서 중매 역할을 한다고 본다(요 3:29; 1 Macc 9:39; Str-B, 2:429; cf. 1:500-4).

150) Plummer, 294; Furnish, 499.

를 "한 남편"(ἑνὶ ἀνδρί)으로 강조한 것은 그리스도인의 그리스도를 향한 절대적 충성을 나타내는 뜻이다.[151] 열심(ζῆλος)은 바울의 복음사역의 특징이다(갈 4:17, 18). 이 말은 원래 이스라엘의 유일한 남편으로서 하나님이 그의 신부 이스라엘에 대한 절실한 사랑을 나타내는 말이다(출 20:5; 호 6:4; 겔 16; 사 50:1-2; 54:1-8; 62:5). 열심은 진정한 사랑의 표시이다. 히브리어 열심은 질투와 같은 말이다(קנא). 하나님의 질투는 인간의 질투와 달리 거룩한 것이며, 그의 백성을 사랑하는 열심과 같은 것이다. 또 하나님의 사람의 열심도 거룩한 것이다. 그러므로 엘리야는 그가 "여호와를 위하여 열심이 특심하다"고 했다(왕상 19:10). 바울도 하나님이 선택하신 종으로서 그의 열심은 거룩한 열심이다. 바울은 "열심을 품고 주를 섬기라"고 했다(롬 12:11). 바울은 회심 이전에 율법에 대한 열심이 있었으나 회심 후에 그 대상이 복음으로 바뀐 것이다(갈 1:14; 빌 3:6). 바울의 고린도 교회에 대한 열심은 고린도 교회에 대한 그의 참된 사랑의 증거이다. 그리고 그의 열심은 "하나님의 열심"(θεοῦ ζήλῳ)으로서 사심이 없는 하나님의 영광을 위한 열심이다.[152]

바울이 여기서 자신의 역할을 중매자의 역할에 비교하는 것은 그의 사도직 이해에 근거하고 있다. 여기서 중매자는 사심 없이 객관적 입장에서 혼인 당사자들의 유익을 위해 일하는 사람으로 제시된다. 마찬가지로 사도는 아무런 사심 없이 그리스도의 신부된 교회의 유익을 위해 일 하는 것이다(4:5; 12:19; 고전15:10). 그러나 반대자들은 사욕을 가지고 고린도 교인들을 미혹하여 종으

151) Tasker, 145; Bultmann, 202.

152) θεοῦ ζήλῳ에서 하나님의 속격은 기원을 나타내기 보다는 성격을 나타내는 속격이라고 본다(Windisch, 319).

로 삼고 있다(11:22).

"그리스도께 드리려고"(παραστήσαι τῷ Χριστῷ)에서 "드린다"(παραστῆσαι)는 말은 재림과 관계된다.[153] 중매의 역할은 신랑이 나타날 때 흠 없는 신부로 바치는 것이다(4:14). 이것이 바울의 교회 사역의 일관된 목표이다(고전 4:15; 고후 4:14; 6:12; 7:4). 자신의 사도직 유지나 지도력 회복이 궁극적 목표가 아니라 그리스도의 몸 된 교회에서 그리스도의 왕권 확립이 그의 지고의 목표이다(4:5; 10:5-6, 8; 13:10). 사도권 확립은 그리스도로부터 받은 이 엄숙한 사도적 사명을 달성하기 위해 필요한 수단일 뿐이다. 이 목적을 달성하기 위해서 그는 온갖 시련과 어려움을 달게 받는 것이다(고후 1:13-15; 5:10; 11:28; 갈 4:19). 자기 유익이 아닌 고린도 교회의 유익, 더 궁극적으로 그리스도를 존귀케 하려는 것을 진정한 사역의 목표로 삼는 바울이야 말로 그리스도의 진정한 사도이다(4:11; 5:15; 빌 1:20).

3. "뱀이 그 간계로 이와를 미혹케 한 것 같이 너희 마음이 그리스도를 향하는 진실함과 깨끗함에서 떠나 부패할까 두려워하노라"(φοβοῦμαι δὲ μή πως, ὡς ὁ ὄφις ἐξηπάτησεν Εὕαν ἐν τῇ πανουργίᾳ αὐτοῦ, φθαρῇ τὰ νοήματα ὑμῶν ἀπὸ τῆς ἁπλότητος [καὶ τῆς ἁγνότητος] τῆς εἰς τὸν Χριστόν). 여기서 창세기 3장에서 뱀이 하와를 미혹한 사실을 인용하는 것은 바울이

153) 그러나, H. Schlicher, *Der Brief an die Epheser* (Düsseldorf: Patmos Verlag, 1968), 252-80, 는 엡 5:27에서 "드린다"(παραστήσῃ)는 말이 종말론적 의미가 없이 윤리적인 의미로 쓰였다고 지적한다. 그러나 신약 전체에서 종말론적 가르침은 윤리적 가르침과 분리될 수 없다.

고린도 교인들이 바울의 그리스도에 대한 가르침을 떠난 것을 매우 심각한 일로 본다는 것과 함께, 사도로서 이를 반드시 막아야 하는 그의 책임감을 나타낸다. 바울은 고린도 교회의 문제가 단순히 인간집단의 갈등문제와 다르다고 보았다. 이 싸움은 하나님과 사단의 영적 전쟁이라고 본 것이다(참조, 엡 6:12). 그리고 그는 이런 싸움에서 하나님 편에 서서 싸운다고 확신하였다. 고린도 교회 갈등이 결국 심각한 영적 싸움이기 때문에 고린도 교인들이 중립적 자세를 가지고 바울과 그 반대자들이 싸우는 우연적인 싸움으로 볼 것이 아니라 분명히 바울 편에 서서 승리해야 함을 촉구하는 것이다.

"두려워하노라" (φοβοῦμαι)는 말이 그 싸움의 심각성을 더해준다. 하와가 뱀의 미혹을 받아서 남편 아담의 말을 듣지 않고 배반하여 선악과를 먹었고, 나아가서 아담에게 그 열매를 먹게 한 이중적 죄를 지은 것 같이 고린도 교인들이 바울의 반대자들의 미혹을 받아 바울을 떠나고, 이어서 제2 아담인 그리스도를 떠나 비참한 지경에 이르게 될 수 있다고 본다. 이렇게 바울은 고린도 교회 사태를 단순한 집단 분쟁으로 보는 것이 아니라 인간의 타락과 같은 심각한 영적 타락으로 보는 것이다(롬 5:12). 빈디쉬(Windisch)는 이 부분이 창세기 3장 1-7절에 대한 바울의 유대교 탈굼식 해석이라고 보았다.[154] 당시 유대교에서는 뱀을 마귀로 해석하였다(솔로몬의 지혜서2:23). 그리고 뱀이 하와를 성적으로 더럽혔다는 랍비들의 해석도 여러 곳에서 발견된다.[155] 같은 사상이 2세기 영지

---

154) Windisch, 323.

155) 에녹1서 69:6; 에녹2서 31:6; 탈무드, *Yebamot* 103b; *Aboda Zara* 22b; 미쉬나, *Sabbat 146a*.

주의 이단 사상에서 발견된다.[156] 교부들은 이런 성적 해석을 반대하였다. 본문의 "진실함과 깨끗함"(τῆς ἁπλότητος [καὶ τῆς ἁγνότητος])[157]은 윤리적 영적 순결함뿐만 아니라 교리적 순수함을 의미할 수도 있다.[158] 바울은 고린도 교인들이 바른 진리를 찾아야 할 것을 말하는 시점에서 성경의 순수한 바른 해석을 지지하는 것이 당연하다. 그러므로 바울이 창세기 3장의 뱀과 하와의 성적 해석을 따른다는 증거는 없다. 다만, 뱀을 사탄으로 해석하는 지혜서 2장 24절을 알고 있었다고 볼 수 있다. 실제로 아래 11장 13-15절에서 반대자들을 사탄의 일꾼으로 규정하고 있다. 그 반대자들은 단순히 의견을 달리하는 믿음의 형제들이 아니라 복음의 적이다. 그들이 원하는 것은 간계로 고린도 교인들의 마음(τά νοήματα ὑμῶν)을 미혹하여 그리스도를 떠나게 하는 것이다. 바울은 고린도 교인들의 마음이 단순히 바울의 그리스도를 향하게 하는 것이 아니라 그와 모든 사도들이 전하는 그리스도를 향하게 하는 것이 소원이다. 바울이 받은 복음은 그가 만든 복음이 아니라 사도들이 그리스도로부터 받은 복음이었고 그는 그것을 그대로 고린도 교인들에게 전했다(2:17; 4:2; 고전 11:23; 15:3, 11; 참조, 갈 1:12). 이런 사욕이 없는 순순한 뜻에서 그는 고린도 교인들의 마음도 언제나 "진실함과 깨끗함"으로 그리스도를 향하기를 원했다(고전 1:8). 그러나 바울은 자신의 사도로서의 권세가 그리스도에게서 온 것임을 굳게 믿기 때문에 고린도 교인들이 자신에게로

156) *Protevangelium of James 13; Apocryphon of John 23.* 이를 비판한 이레네우스의 *Refut.* 5:26와 Epiphanius, *Haer.* 40.5.3을 보라. H. Windisch, 323에서 자세한 자료를 찾으라.

157) 두 단어의 사본상의 다른 형태에 대해서 위의 본문비평부분을 보라.

158) Lietzmann, 145.

돌아오는 것이 곧 그리스도에게로 돌아오는 것이라는 확신을 가지고 있다(2:17; 5:20; 6:11-13; 7:2; 10:8; 13:10).

2. 고린도 교인들이 거짓 사도를 용납하였음을 질책함(11:4)

4. "만일 누가 가서 우리의 전파하지 아니한 다른 예수를 전파하거나 혹 너희의 받지 아니한 다른 영을 받게 하거나 혹 너희의 받지 아니한 다른 복음을 받게 할 때에는 너희가 잘 용납하는구나"(**εἰ μὲν γὰρ ὁ ἐρχόμενος ἄλλον Ἰησοῦν κηρύσσει ὃν οὐκ ἐκηρύξαμεν, ἢ πνεῦμα ἕτερον λαμβάνετε ὃ οὐκ ἐλάβετε, ἢ εὐαγγέλιον ἕτερον ὃ οὐκ ἐδέξασθε, καλῶς ἀνέχεσθε**). 케제만은 이 구절이 고린도후서의 반대자들의 이해를 위한 열쇠라고 한다.[159] 바울은 고린도 교인들이 현재의 갈등 문제를 단순히 바울과 그 반대자들의 싸움이라고 보는 중립적 자세를 버리고 반대자들을 이단자들로 정죄하면서 고린도 교인들이 자신을 지지해야 할 근본적인 이유를 제시하고 있다. 이런 바울의 강경한 자세는 바울이 고린도전서에서 게바파, 아볼로파, 그리스도파 같은 파벌에 대해서 유화적인 자세를 취하는 것과는 대조적이다(고전 3:5-6). 베드로나 아볼로와 달리 반대자들은 단순히 바울의 반대자들이 아니라 이단적 복음을 전하는 거짓사도들이요 사단의 일꾼들이기 때문이다(11:13). 바울은 앞에서 자신이 하나님의 말씀을 받은 대로 순전히 전한다고 말하면서, 반대자들은 말씀을 혼잡케 한다는

---

159) E. Käsemann, *Die Legitimität des Apostels: eine Untersuchung zu II Korinther 10-13* (Darmstadt: Wissenschaftliche Buchgesellschaft, 1956, originally in *ZNW* 41[1942] 33-71), 14, Martin, 334..

것을 암시한 바 있다(2:17; 4:2, 4). 여기서 바울은 드물게 강한 어조로 반대자들을 질책하고 있다(갈 1:8; 2:11; 5:10; 골 2:8). 바울은 반대자들로 말미암아 고린도 교회가 비사도적 교회로 전락하는 위기에 처했으며, 동시에 고린도가 속한 전체 아가야 지방에서의 바울의 사역이 위기의 국면을 맞았다고 보았다. 한 교회의 싸움이지만, 그대로 방치할 경우 그의 전체의 사역과 그의 사도적 권위에 치명적인 결과가 올 수 있다고 보았다. 바울은 이들의 배후에는 사단의 세력이 작동하고 있다고 보았다(3, 13). 그래서 반대자들에 대한 확고한 신학적 비판을 통해서 이들을 정죄할 것을 결심했다. 여기서 "만일"(ἐι)은 가정의 의미가 아니라 "지금 보듯이"라는 실제상황을 나타내는 말이다.[160] 여기의 대적자들은 10:5, 6, 12에서 바울과 자기들을 비교하면서 바울을 멸시하는 이들이다. 바울은 이들의 사도직 평가 기준이 자신의 그것과 다름을 지적하고 있다. "누가 가서"(ὁ ἐρχόμενος)는 "누가 와서"라고 번역할 수도 있다. 어떤 이가 고린도 교회에 와서 다른 예수를 전파하는 사실을 말한다. 단수로서 한 사람이 오는 것을 가리킨다. 그러므로 이 반대자들의 수장은 어느 한 개인임을 시사한다. 10장 7, 10, 11절, 11장 20-21절에도 반대자가 단수로 나와 있다. 물론 이런 단수를 일반화 단수로서 전체 반대자들을 총칭하여 이른 말이라고 볼 수도 있다.[161] 그러나 많은 구절들에서 단수로 나타난 것은 특정한

160) Strachan, 18.

161) Plummer, 296; Allo, 279, Zmijewski, 99, 100, 413, H. D. Wendland, *Die Briefe an die Korinther*, NTD 7 (Göttingen: Vandenhoeck & Ruprecht, 1964), 234; K. Prümm, *Diakonia Pnuematos I: Theologische Auslegung des zweiten Korintherbriefs* (Rome/Freiburg/Wien: Herder, 1967), 602; Thrall, 665.

인물을 지칭한다고 볼 수 있다.[162] 뿐만 아니라 복수로 나타나는 부분도 있는데 이 경우는 그 구성원들을 가리킨다고 볼 수 있다(11:12, 13, 18). 이 수장이 이끄는 일단의 무리는 외부에서 왔으며(10:14-15), 하나님이 인정하는 단체가 아니므로, 진정한 사도들이 아니고, 거짓사도들이다(11:13). 이들이 헬라 영지주의 사상의 영향을 받아 기적을 중시하는 사람들인지, 스데반, 빌립 같은 헬라 영향을 받은 유대인들로서 은사와 유대교 전통을 존중하는 순회 선교단체인지(행 6:8; 8:6), 마태복음 28장의 대위임을 중시하며 다니는 선교단체인지, 분명한 증거는 없으나 예루살렘 사도들과 나아가 역사적 예수와의 친분을 내세워 자신들의 권위를 내세우는 유대인들임이 거의 분명하다(11:22).[163]

이들이 전한 메시지는 무엇인가? 그 메시지는 3중적으로 나타난다. 즉 "다른 예수, 다른 영, 다른 복음"이다(ἄλλος Ἰησοῦς, ἢ πνεῦμα ἕτερον, ἢ εὐαγγέλιον ἕτερον). "다른 예수"의 전파의 결과로 "다른 영"과 "다른 복음"이 전파된다고 볼 수 있다.[164] "다른 예수"는 믿음 보다 율법전통을, 고난 보다 기적과 영광의 옷을 입은 예수, 행복과 기쁨만을 주는 예수를 가리킨다.[165] 이에 따라서 "다른 영"은 "능력과 영적으로 황홀한 상태"(ecstacy)를 지고의 가치로 중시하는 영이다(참조, 딤전 4:1). 바울은 1장 22절에서 그와 그의 동역자들(디모데, 실루아노)이 모두 한 성령의 보증을 받

---

162) Martin, 335, Barrett, 275.

163) 서론-"바울의 반대자들"을 보라; Martin, 335-42; Thrall, 665-70.

164) C. Wolff, *Der zweite Brief des Paulus an die Korinther*, THKNT VIII (Berlin: Evangelische Verlaganstalt, 1989), 215, 주, 142.

165) Carson, 90; W. Bieder, "Paulus und seine Gegner in Korinth" *TZ* 17(1961), 319.

았음을 말하고, 또 12장 18절에서 바울은 그의 동역자와 한 성령으로 행한다고 말하면서 그의 사도직의 정당성을 말한다. "다른 복음"은 갈라디아서 1장 6, 7절에서 나오는 다른 복음(ἕτερον εὐαγγέλιον)이란 말과 문자적으로만 같고 뉴앙스는 다르다. 갈라디아서는 율법주의적 복음을 가리키며, 여기서는 고난 없는 "능력과 영광의 복음"이란 뜻을 가리킨다. 참고로, ἕτερος(헤테로스)와 ἄλλος(알로스)가 갈라디아서 1장 6, 7절에 번갈아 "다른" 복음을 나타내고 있으므로 같은 뜻임을 알 수 있다.

논쟁의 중심은 이들이 전하는 예수가 바울이 전하는 예수와 "다른 예수"라는 것이다. 반대자들은 능력과 은사를 베푸는 예수에 집중한 것 같다. 이들이 유대에서 온 것이 분명하므로(11:22), 초기 예수의 사역의 형태와 이를 계승한 예루살렘 사도들의 사역의 형태를 그대로 답습하고 있다고 볼 수 있다(마 10:1; 행 3:6; 4:30; 5:12). 이에 대해서 바울은 자신도 영적 체험이 있으며(12:1-5), 고린도 교인들에게 표적과 기사도 행했음을 상기시키고 있다. 그러나 바울은 이런 것들을 "육체적 자랑"으로 보면서 대적자들이 자랑하니 자신도 "부득불 자랑한다"는 것이라고 하면서 이런 은사능력을 자랑하기를 꺼리면서 오히려 자신이 전파하려는 것은 그리스도의 약함이라고 아이러니한 복음의 핵심을 말한다. 4장 5절에서 바울은 자신의 복음의 핵심이 (반대파가 주장하듯이) 자신이 아니라, 그리스도의 주되심과 자신이 고린도 교인들의 종된 것임을 이미 언급했다. 그리고 12장 10절에서 그리스도의 약함을 따라서 사역하는 것을 자랑하겠다고 한다. 바울은 사도의 진정성은 그를 사도로 부르신 그리스도를 바르게 이해하고 바르게 전하고 그리스도를 따라 바르게 사는 삶에서 나타난다고 믿고 있다. 바울이 전하고 따르는 그리스도의 복음의 핵심은 그의 죽으심과 부활이다. 그는 그리스도의 희생하는 유형을 따라서 고린도 교인들의 종으로서 사역하고 있다(4:5; 5:15). 그러므로 바울은 5장 16절에서 "우리가 그리스도를 육체를 따라 알지 아니한다"고 선언했다. 이것은 이런 유대 교사들의 역사적 예수와의 "육체적" 연결을 자랑하며, 외적인 영적 권능을 행사하는 것을 염두에 둔 말로 생각할 수 있다(3:1; 5:12; 10:7, 10).[166] 그들은 아마도 말씀의 목격자들로서 예수의 복음사역에 익숙한 이들임을 자랑하는 이들이었을 것이다(마 10:1; 28:18-20). 바울은 자신이 직접 예수님을 생전에 뵙고 따르지 못했고 오히려 교회를 핍박하였으나 하나님의 은혜로 말미암아 사도로 피택 되었다고 피력한다(고전 15:9-10). 그 대신 하나님의 은혜로 더 많이 수고하였고, 그 결과 (반대자들에게 추천서를 써 준) 다른 사도들 보다 결코 부족한 사도가 아님을 밝힌다(고전 15:10; 고후 11:23; 12:11). 바울은 역사적 예수와의 접촉은 없으나 부활하신 그를 다메섹 도상에서 만났다(고전 15:8). 그러나 그는 그것을 자랑하지 않고 십자가의 그리스도를 전하고 따른다(고전 1:22-23; 고후 12:10). 그는 과거의 역사 속의 예수가 아니라, 오늘 날 죄인을 새로운 피조물, 하나님의 자녀로 만드는 능력의 예수를 믿는다(5:16). 그의 반대자들은 외적 능력과 영광의 주를 강조하나, 그는 오히려 약함으로 십자가를 지신 그리스도를 자랑한다. 그것이 하나님의 진정한 구원의 능력이 나타나는 복음의 핵심으로 믿는다(롬 1:16; 고전 1:24; 2:2; 고후 5:15-16; 12:10;

---

166) Käsemann, *Die Legitimität*, 48-9; Bultmann, 204; Furnish, 502.

13:4). 사도의 진정성은 그가 전하는 그리스도의 바른 이해에 근거한다. 그리스도의 죽으심과 부활의 능력이 진정한 기독론의 핵심이다. 반대자들은 이런 핵심이 없는 외적인 역사성과 영적 능력의 그리스도를 전하므로 사도적 진정성을 잃었다.

여기서 "다른 영"(ἣ πνεῦμα ἕτερον)은 그 의미가 분명하지 않다. 헤링은 이단적 복음서인 "히브리인의 복음서"에서 성령이 예수의 어머니로 나타나는 것을 예로 들면서 성령에 대한 이와 유사한 잘못된 이단적 가르침을 지칭한다고 한다.[167] 케제만(Käsemann)은 사도직은 성령의 은사가운데 첫째 은사인데(고전 12:28), 반대자들은 바울의 사도직을 반대함으로 분명히 "다른 영"이라고 볼 수밖에 없다는 논리다.[168] 그러나 바울의 사도직을 반대한다고 해서 "다른 영"이라고 하는 것은 이상하다. "다른 영"은 반대자들이 영적 은사를 강조하는 것과 관련하여 "능력과 영광의 영"을 가리킨다고 본다. "영"은 개인이나 단체를 인도하는 본질적이고 초월적인 신적 특성 또는 능력이나 사상을 가리키는 말이다. 즉 요한1서 4장 3절을 상기할 수 있다. 즉, "예수를 시인하지 아니하는 영마다 하나님께 속한 것이 아니니 이것이 곧 적그리스도의 영이니라." 반대자들은 예수의 고난과 죽으심을 등한히 하는 나머지 그들의 사역이나 삶 전체에서 그리스도의 겸비와 고난을 통한 구원의 특징이 나타나지 않는다는 뜻으로 생각 할 수 있다. 유사하게 마틴은 바울의 겸비와 상반되는 그들의 오만한 삶의 자

---

167) Héring, 79. 주 10: 히브리 복음서에서 성령을 어머니로 보는 것은 성부를 아버지로, 예수를 아들로 보는 이단적 삼위일체라고 한다.

168) Héring, 79.

세라고 한다.[169)]

"다른 복음"(ἢ εὐαγγέλιον ἕτερον)은 반대자들의 가르침이 바울의 "그리스도의 고난과 죽음을 통한 구원의 가르침"과는 달리 "영광과 능력"을 강조하는 것임을 가리킨다. 반대자들은 예수가 지상에서 행한 놀라운 일들을 중점적으로 가르켰으나, 복음의 구원론의 핵심인 그리스도의 죽으심의 의미를 충분히 강조하지 못했던 것으로 보인다.[170)]

이렇게 반대자들의 복음은 "희생적 사랑"에 근거하지 않은 사욕적 "능력과 영광"의 특성을 지닌 것으로 본다.

"너희가 잘 용납하는구나"(καλῶς ἀνέχεσθε). 이 말은 거짓 사도들과 그들의 가르침을 받아들이는 고린도 교인들의 느슨한 자세를 책망하는 말이다(11:19, 20). 그들의 느슨한 자세는 다른 사상에 대한 관용적인 헬라의 지혜 문화 전통을 따르는 것이라고 볼 수도 있다(고전 1:18 이하). 11장 19, 20절에서 바울은 고린도 교인들의 "용납하는 자세"를 질책하면서도, 동시에 자신의 변명을 들어 주어야 하는 근거로 삼고 있다. "용납함"이 11장 1절 이하에서부터 11장 19절까지에서 바울의 육체적 자랑하기 위한 개론적 진술의 중요한 주제이다.

고린도 교인들이 바울이 가르쳐준 복음을 잊고 새로 들어 온 교

---

169) Martin, 336.

170) J. Murphy-O'Connor, "Another Jesus(2 Cor 11:4)," *Revue Biblique* 97 (1990), 238-51; Wolff, 214-15.

사들의 복음을 듣고 따르는 것은 바울에게 크나큰 실망감과 함께 배신감을 안겨 주었음에 틀림없다. 이들이 바울과 같은 복음을 가르쳤다면 바울도 크게 상관하지 않았을 것이다(고전 3:5; 15:11). 그러나 이들은 전혀 다른 복음을 가르치고 있었다. 자신은 정성을 다해 그리스도의 신부로 단장 시키려 했건만 어느새 이렇게 자신을 배반하고 다른 사람을 따르는 것은 괴로운 일이다. 더구나 그 교사들은 잘못된 교리를 가리키면서 자신의 사도직까지 공격하니 바울은 더 이상 침묵할 수 없었던 것이다(10:1). 바울은 단순히 자신의 사도직이나 지도력을 회복해야겠다는 개인적 생각에서가 아니라 자신이 희생하더라도 고린도 교인들은 구해야겠다는 심정에서 설득하고 있는 것이다(4:5). 고린도 교인들이 바울이 처음에 전해준 예수를 버리고 거짓 사도들이 전해 준 "다른 예수"를 따르면 결국 멸망에 이르기 때문이다. 바울은 사도로서, 영적 "부모"로서 그것을 방관할 수 없었다(11:29; 12:14-15). 반대자들이 "다른 예수, 다른 영, 다른 복음"을 전하는 이들이다 보니, 그들의 사도직을 제대로 이해할 수가 없었다(11:4). 그들은 사도직을 그리스도 중심으로 이해하지 못하고 구약 전통을 오해하여 "영광과 능력의 직책"으로 이해했다(3:14; 4:4). 그들은 사도의 "외모"와 "육체적 조건"을 중시하는 이들이었다(5:12; 10:7). 바울은 복음을 분명히 하나님의 계시로 받았고, 그 계시가 그리스도의 죽으심과 부활에서 구체적으로 나타났음을 알고 있다(3:5, 18; 4:4; 5:15). 다시 말하면 사도는 그리스도의 종으로서 그리스도의 특성을 인격적으로 함양한 사람이어야 하고 또 그것을 그의 사역에 적용하는 사람이어야 한다. 그래서 바울은 고린도 교회에서 반대자들로 말미암아 훼손된 그의 사도직을 회복하기 위해서 그의 사도직의 정당성과 반대자들의 사도직의 부당성을 기독론적 판단 기준에 의해서 설명한다. 즉 그리스도의 고난을 통한 구원 사역을 중심으로 해서 자신의 사역과 생애가 전개됨을 일일이 지적하면서 반대자들의 사역이 그렇지 못함을 지적하고 있다. 바울은 그의 사도직의 정당성 문제와 관련하여 고린도 교회의 대적자들의 사도직의 부당한 여러 가지 점들도 지적하고 있다. 그러나 그들의 가장 큰 문제는 복음을 막연하게 이해하고, 그리스도 중심, 특히 그의 고난을 중심으로 명확히 이해하지 못하는 것이다. 그들의 사역은 복음의 특성인 희생적 사랑이 없는 사욕적인 사역이었다.

3. 바울은 자신이 큰 사도들 보다 부족함이 없다고 함(11:5).

5. "내가 지극히 큰 사도들보다 부족한 것이 조금도 없는 줄 생각하노라"(Λογίζομαι γὰρ μηδὲν ὑστερηκέναι τῶν ὑπερλίαν ἀποστόλων). "지극히 큰 사도들"(τῶν ὑπερλίαν ἀποστόλων)이 예루살렘 사도들을 가리키는지 아니면 거짓 사도들을 풍자적으로 가리키는지가 논쟁되어 왔다.[171] 고린도후서 10장 2-7절에서 거짓 사도들이 외모나 육체를 따라 자랑한다고 했는데, 유사하게, 갈라디아서에서 바울은 베드로를 포함한 예루살렘 사도들을 "유명하다는 이들"(갈 1:6)로 언급하면서 "하나님은 사람의 외모를 취하시지 아니하시나니"라고 말한다. 그러나 고린도 교회 거짓 사

171) 대부분이 "지극히 큰 사도들"을 예루살렘 사도들로 보지만 이를 반대하는 학자들은 다음과 같다: Héring, 79; Käsemann, *Die Legitimität*, 28; Zmijewski, 116, 117; 특히 Thrall의 두 논쟁을 비교한 것을 보라, 671-676; 정규남, 164.

도들이 역사적 예수와의 접촉이나 예루살렘 사도들의 추천서를 가지고 자랑하는 것을 보면, 본문의 "지극히 큰 사도들"은 거짓 교사들이 아니라, 예루살렘 사도들을 가리키는 것으로 보아야 한다. 더구나 바울이 11:13에서 반대자들을 "거짓 사도요 궤휼의 역군"으로, 11장 15절에서는 "사단의 일꾼"으로 부르고 있는데, 이들을 본문과 12장 11절의 "지극히 큰 사도들"과 바울이 동일시하였다고 보는 것은 무리다. 여기서 바울은 거짓 사도들이 "지극히 큰 사도들"과의 교분을 빙자하여 자신들의 위치나 권세를 높이려는 것을 경계하는 것으로 생각한다. 고린도후서 12장 11절에서 바울이 자신을 "지극히 큰 사도들"과 비교하면서 "조금도 부족하지 않다"고 말하는 것이나, 그렇게 자랑하는 자신을 어리석은 자라고 양해를 구하면서 말하는 겸비한 자세는 예루살렘의 유명한 기둥사도들(갈 1:9)을 지칭하는 것일 때 가능하다. 거짓 사도들에게 이렇게까지 겸손하게 말할 필요가 없을 것이다. 더구나 고린도전서 15장 9절에서 자신을 다른 사도들과 비교하면서 "사도 중에 지극히 작은 사도"라고 겸손하게 말하고 있으며, 또한 거기서 게바와 야고보 같은 "기둥 같이 여기는 사도들"(pillar apostles)을 언급하고 있다(고전 15:5, 7). 또 계속해서 "모든 사도보다 더 많이 수고하였음"을 언급하는 것은 11장 후반부에서 자신의 수고를 열거하는 것과 일치한다. 물론 고린도후서 11장 23절에서 바울이 분명히 거짓 사도들을 대하여 "저희가 그리스도의 일꾼이냐?"라고 말하면서 바울 자신의 고난의 사역을 그들의 사역에 비교하기도 하지만, 10장 12절에서는 "우리가 어떤 자기를 칭찬하는 자로 더불어 감히 짝하며 비교할 수 없노라"라고 거짓 사도들과의 비교자체를 거절한다. 한 마디로 바울은 거짓 사도들을 멸시하지만 그들

뒤에 있는 예루살렘 사도들의 권위에 대해서는 조심하면서 말하는 것이라고 보아야 한다.[172] 그러므로 여기서 "지극히 큰 사도들"은 거짓 사도들이 자신들을 인정하고 파송하였다고 말하는 예루살렘 사도들을 가리킨다.

바울은 자신을 자랑하는 것 자체를 어리석은 것으로 알고 있음을 상기해야 한다(11:1). 반대자들이 외모로 자랑한다고 해서 자신도 그 수준으로 떨어져서 같이 자랑하고 있으니 자신이 어리석다는 것이다. 그러나 바울은 이렇게 어리석은 자랑을 고린도 교인들을 진리로 인도하기위한 과정으로 선택하고 있다(4:2; 11:16-18, 12:11). 즉 자신의 진정한 자랑은 연약함이며 이것이 그리스도의 죽음과 부활의 역동적 힘을 입어서 강하게 나타나는 구속의 진리의 특성과 일치함을 알리려는 것이다(12:9-10). 즉 사도직의 진정성을 말로만 하지 않고 구체적으로 증명된 사례를 열거하여 증거하는 것이다(11:22-33). 그 결과 누가 진실로 그리스도의 사역자인가를 독자들이 스스로 판단할 수 있게 하는 것이다. 다시 말하지만 바울의 이런 자랑은 결코 자신을 위한 자랑이 아님을 우리는 알아야 한다. 12장 11절에서도 여기서와 같이 자신이 "지극히 큰 사도들 보다 조금도 부족하지 않다"고 말하기 전에, 자신은 "아무것도 아니라"고 비하시킨다. 바울의 관심은 사욕적 자랑이 아니라

---

172) Käsemann, *Die Legitimiät*, 44-8에서 5절의 "지극히 큰 사도"는 6절의 비교 대상과 다르다고 한다. Thrall은 5, 6절이 잘 연결되어 있기 때문에 이런 구별을 반대한다(675). 즉 5절의 "지극히 큰 사도들"은 곧 6절의 "거짓 사도들"을 가리킨다는 것이다. Carson도 거짓사도들에 대한 풍자적 표현이라고 한다(91). Martin은 13절의 "사단의 일꾼"들과 바울이 자신을 비교하는 것을 생각할 수 없기 때문에 5절의 "지극히 큰 사도들"은 거짓 사도들이 아니라 그들이 의지하는 예루살렘 사도들로 본다(342).

어디 까지나 자신이 희생하더라도 고린도 교인들을 그리스도의 진리 가운데 든든히 서게 하는 것이다(2:4; 4:12; 5:15; 7:2-3; 11:2; 12:19; 13:8-10). 문제는 고린도 교인들이 바울의 약함을 따라 섬기는 사도직을 의심하고 잘못된 거짓 사도들의 외양이나 외적 능력을 진정한 사도의 증거로 잘못 알고 받아들이는 것이다(11:4).

이렇게 "지극히 큰 사도들" 에 대한 바울의 사도직에 대한 언급이 반대자들을 비난하는 문맥에서 갑자기 돌출된 말로 보이지만, "지극히 큰 사도들의 인정과 친분" 이 반대자들이 내세우는 정당성의 근거이기 때문에 바울은 그들과 같은 위치에 있는 사도임을 천명하는 것이다. 또한 반대자들이 바울을 열등한 사도로 비하하는 현실에서 6절에서 말하는 지식의 우월성 같은 자신의 장점(육체적 자랑)을 제시하기도 한다. 여기서 바울이 자신을 "지극히 큰 사도들" 과 비교하는 것은 7절부터 시작되는 바울의 자비량 선교에 나타난 희생적이고 투명한 재정관리와 관련지어 생각할 수 도 있다(7:2; 11:10; 12:14-15). 고린도전서 9장에서 바울은 교회의 재정적 지원을 받는 다른 사도들을 언급하면서 자신도 그들과 꼭 같이 재정 지원을 받을 마땅한 권한이 있으나 스스로 받지 않는 것이라고 말하는 것을 상기하면, 여기서도 바울은 자신의 자비량 선교를 비난하는 반대자들에게 대해서 자신이 다른 사도들에 비해서 무엇인가 부족하기 때문에 교회의 재정지원을 받지 않는 것이 아니라 단순히 교회에 폐를 끼치지 않는다는 순수한 마음으로 받지 않는 것임을 밝히고 있다(12:14, 15). 이렇게 바울은 "지극히 큰 사도들의 신분" 에 대한 그의 사도로서의 신분 비교를 하면서 자신의 지식의 탁월성(6절)이나 재정의 투명성(7-12) 같은 것들을 자신의 사도로서의 자격의 구체적 증거로 제시하는 것이다.

a. 언변은 약하나 지식은 깊음(11:6)

6. "내가 비록 말에는 졸하나 지식에는 그렇지 아니하니 이것을 우리가 모든 사람 가운데서 모든 일로 너희에게 나타내었노라" (**εἰ δὲ καὶ ἰδιώτης τῷ λόγῳ, ἀλλ᾽ οὐ τῇ γνώσει, ἀλλ᾽ ἐν παντὶ φανερώσαντες ἐν πᾶσιν εἰς ὑμᾶς**). 원문에는 "이것을" 이란 말이 없으나, **φανερώσαντες**(나타내었다)는 동사의 목적이 필요한데, 앞의 문장의 **τῇ γνώσει**(지식)을 목적으로 보아서, "이것" 이란 대명사로 나타내었다(4:2).[173] 그러나 쉬라터(A. Schlatter)는 다른 여러 가지 가능한 목적어들을 제안한다.[174] 리쯔만은 "지식의 비밀" 또는 "믿음의 비밀" 로 제안한다.[175] 라이쩬쉬타인(R. Reitzenstein)은 "우리가 책망 받을 것이 없음" 이라는 문장을 제시한다.[176] 어느 것이든 빠진 목적어를 두고 바울의 생각을 추정한 것으로써 전체 의미에 지장을 주지는 않는다.

"말에는 졸하나 지식에는 그렇지 아니하니" 에 대하여 불트만은 바울이 고린도전서 2장 4절에서와 같이 반대자들의 "영지주의적 말(**λόγος**)" 을 멸시하면서 그의 복음적 지식에 대한 집중을 나타내는 것이라고 본다.[177] 케제만은 다른 반대자들에 비해서 자신이

---

173) Martin, 343.

174) A. Schlatter, Paulus, *der Bote Jesus* (Stuttgart: Calwer Verlag, 1969), 642.

175) Lietzmann, 147.

176) R. Reitzenstein, *Hellenistic Mystery-Religions*, tr. J. E. Steely(Pittsburgh: Pickwick Press, 1978), 465.

방언을 잘 못하는 것을 의미한다고 본다(참고, 고전 14:18).[178] Betz는 바울이 λόγος("말")를 외적 표현으로 보고, γνῶσις("지식")를 내용으로 보는 희랍 철학의 개념을 나타낸다고 본다.[179] 그러나 바레트는 특별한 의미가 아닌, 일반적 의미의 지식을 나타낸다고 본다.[180] 유사하게 휴즈는 바울은 그의 설교 스타일은 평범하게 말하면서, 수사학적 웅변을 오히려 의도적으로 피한다는 뜻으로 본다.[181] 바레트와 휴즈의 주석이 전체 흐름에 가장 적절한 것으로 본다. 바울은 반대자들의 "말이 시원치 않다"(10:10)는 비판에 대하여 답변하고 있다고 봐야 한다. 그러나 λόγος("말")나 γνῶσις("지식")의 헬라 철학에서의 중요한 용도를 생각할 때, 또 고린도 교회의 "지혜"에 대한 바울의 비판적 반응(고전 2장)을 고려할 때 헬라 지혜와 수사학적 배경이 본문 이해에 도움이 될 수 있다. 실제로 궤변학파(Shophists="지혜자들")들로서 웅변에 능숙한 이들이 헬라시대에 존경을 받았고, 특히 고린도에서도 이들의 사회적 영향이 있었다는 연구도 있다.[182] 그렇다면 고린도 교인들이 바울과 그의 반대자들의 수사학적 언변을 비교하면서 사도로서의 능력을 평가하는 것은 당연하게 보인다.

바울은 "말이 신통치 않다"는 반대자들의 비판을 수용하면서도 말보다 더 중요한 것은 말의 근거인 지식임을 지적한다. 말은 왜

177) Bultmann, 205, 206.

178) Käsemann, *Die Legitimität*, 9.

179) H. D. Betz, *Der Apostel Paulus und die sokratische Tradition*, 59.

180) Barrett, 280.

181) Hughes, 380-82.

182) B. W. Winter, *Philo and Paul among the Sophists*, SNTSMS 96 (Cambridge: University Press, 1997), 135. Thrall, 679-681에서 이에 대한 토의를 보라.

곡하거나, 호도될 수 있으나 지식은 그렇게 될 수 없다. 말은 "육체" 나 "외모" 에 해당되는 피상적인 것이나, 지식은 본질적인 영적인 계시에 속한다고 본다(3:3-5). 바울이 "말" (λόγος)을 무시한 것은 아니지만, "지식" (γνώσις)을 보다 본질적인 개념으로 파악하는 것으로 보인다(고후 8:7). 바울은 그리스도를 아는 지식에 관한 한 분명히 바른 지식을 가지고 있다(6:6; 11:4; 빌 3:8). 바울은 고린도전서 2장 4절에서 이미 "지혜의 말" 에 대해서 반대하였고 "성령의 능력" 에 힘입어 전도한다고 하였다. 바울은 반대자들의 언변의 자랑을 육체적 자랑이라고 폄하하면서(10:10), 자신의 영적 지식을 보다 중요한 사도직의 자격 요건으로 제시하는 것이다. 바울은 그의 복음 사역에 있어서 "매사에" " 모든 사람들에게" 육체의 자랑은 피하고 영적인 가치를 우선시 한 것을 상기 시키고 있다.

그러나 우리가 10장 이후 13장 마지막까지에서 보듯이 바울은 실제로 여러 가지 수사학적인 기법을 동원하여 그의 반대자들을 역공하고 있는 것이 사실이다. 반대자들이 육체를 따라 자랑하기 때문에 바울도 어리석게나마 육체적인 자랑을 한다고 하는데, 바울은 언변실력이 부족하다고 해도 그의 글 솜씨는 역시 대단하다는 것을 은연중에 암시하는 지도 모른다(10:10).

b. 삯을 받지 않고 일했음(11:7-10)

7. "내가 너희를 높이려고 나를 낮추어 하나님의 복음을 값없이 너희에게 전함으로 죄를 지었느냐?" ("Η ἁμαρτίαν ἐποίησα ἐμαυτὸν ταπεινῶν ἵνα ὑμεῖς ὑψωθῆτε, ὅτι δωρεὰν τὸ τοῦ

θεοῦ εὐαγγέλιον εὐηγγελισάμην ὑμῖν;). 희랍어 본문 처음에 있는 Ἢ는 의문문을 이끄는 것으로 본다.[183] 이런 아이러니한 질문은 당연하게 부정적인 답을 예상하게 한다. 바울이 값없이 복음을 전한 것은 전혀 문제가 되지 않는다. 이 반어적 질문은 아무런 문제가 될 것이 없는 사실을 가지고 문제 삼는 이들이 오히려 문제가 있다고 생각하게 하는 역공적 효과가 있다. 트롤은 7절을 8절부터 15절까지의 논쟁의 서두로 본다.[184] 논쟁의 초점은 바울의 독특한 사역 스타일로서 자신의 교회에 경제적으로 의존하지 않는 다는 것이다. 이런 자비량 사역의 동기는 무엇인가? 이 문제에 대해서 서론 부분에서 이미 논했으므로 여기서는 간략히 정리해본다.

첫째, 바울의 반대자들은 바울의 재정독립형사역이 예수님께서 제자들을 파송하실 때 지시한 재정의존형 사역에 배치되는 것이라고 비난했을 것이다(마 10:10-11; 눅 9:4; 10:7). 그러나 바울은 온전히 그리스도의 가르치심을 본받아 값없이 복음을 전해 주고(고전 9:18), 또한 그리스도의 사도로서 겸비하게 그리스도의 가난함을 본받는 생활을 하기 위한 것이다(고후 9:9). 바울은 그리스도의 제자도에 대한 가르침을 알고 있었을 것이고 이를 철저히 지키기 위해 힘썼다(마 10:8; 행 18:3; 20:33-35). 고린도후서에서 바울은 그리스도의 약함을 본받아 약함으로 사역하는 것을 그의 반대자들의 오만한 목회 사역과 대조하여 말하면서 그리스도의 진정한 사도의 증표로 제시한다(4:7-15; 6:4-10; 11:18-33; 12:9, 10, 12; 13:4). 그러므로 본문에서 "나를 낮추어"(ἐμαυτὸν ταπεινῶν)라

183) Martin, 344.

184) Thrall, 681.

는 말의 의미를 단순히 재정 문제를 떠나서 바울의 "약한 가운데서 온전하게 하는 그리스도의 능력"이라는 기본적인 목회 사상(12:9, 10)에 비추어 이해해야할 필요가 있다. 바울은 십자가의 그리스도처럼 희생적인 정신과 하나님만 온전히 의지하는 자세가 진정한 그리스도의 사도된 자세라고 보고 그의 사역의 모든 분야에서 이 원칙을 적용하는 것이다(1:9; 4:5, 7-15; 6:4-10; 5:15; 12:15; 13:4). 그것은 단순히 고난을 자초하여 자신을 단련시키는 고난주의나 금욕주의와는 다르다. 십자가를 지는 진정한 의미는 단순히 고난을 인내하는 것이 아니라, 고난을 허락하신 하나님의 뜻에 온전히 의존하고 순종하면서 동시에 하나님의 구원을 소망하는 자세이다(4:17; 롬 8:17, 18). 즉 모든 것을 주관하시는 하나님을 믿는 신뢰관계가 전제되어 있다. 바울은 고난의 사역 중에서 스토익 철학자들처럼 고난을 담담히 견디는 것이 아니라 고난으로부터 벗어나서 하나님의 구원을 바랬고, 구원받은 후에 감사했다고 솔직히 말한다(1:8-10). 재정문제와 관련하여서도 바울은 사람이나 물질에 의존하지 않고 하나님만 의존하는 제자도의 큰 원칙에 따라서 고린도 교회의 지원을 거절했던 것이다. 이런 바울의 고난을 인내하는 사역은 겸비하신 그리스도를 인격적으로 본받고 또 교회에 폐를 끼치지 않으려는 것이다. 그러므로 스토익 사상 같은 인본주의적인 오만한 금욕주의적 자족주의 사상과는 구별되어야 한다.

둘째, 바울은 교회에 재정적 부담을 주지 않는 사역이 전도의 문을 넓히는 효과도 있다고 보았다. 즉 복음 사역이 이(利)를 위해 일하는 것이 아니라 오히려 복음을 받는 자에게 유익을 주기 위한 것임을 실제로 증거하여 사람들이 그의 복음에 순종하도록 하는 것이다(11:9; 12:13-15; 고전 9:12, 19). 그러나 이런 바울의 사역은 다른 사역자들의 빈축을 살 수 있었다. 즉 바울의 독선적인 자세는 교회로부터 경제적 지원을 받는 다른 사도들의 입장을 난처하게 만드는 것이라고 보기 때문이다. 바울은 이에 대해서 고린도전서에서 경제적 지원을 받는 것이 하등 문제될 것이 없는 성경적인 것이라고 긍정적으로 말하면서도 자신은 경제적 지원을 거절하는 사역을 계속하겠다고 말했다(고전 9:3-19). 또 반대자들은 바울이 교회의 경제적 지원을 거절하는 이유는 자신이 사도로서 무엇인가 부족하다고 생각하기 때문에 스스로 받지 않는 것이라고 비난했을 수도 있다. 그래서 11장 5절에서 "내가 지극히 큰 사도들 보다 부족한 것이 조금도 없는 줄 생각하노라"라고 말한 것으로 보인다. 한편 고린도 교회의 반대자들은 바울이 다른 교회의 지원은 계속 받으면서도 자신들의 경제적 지원을 거절하는 것을 그들에 대한 무관심이나 사랑의 결핍이라면서 비난거리로 삼았다(8:1-5; 11:, 8-11; 12:13, 15;행 16:11-17:15; 빌 4:10-20). 위에서 제시한 신앙적 이유 외에도, 바울은 고린도 교회와 같이 갈등이 심한 교회로부터 경제적 지원을 받는 것은 그에 대한 물질적 오해를 불러일으켜 전체 사역이 어렵게 될 수도 수 있기 때문에 의도적으로 피했을 것이다. 바울은 고린도 교회뿐만 아니라 다른 교회에게도 재정적 부담을 주지 않도록 애썼다(12:16; 살전 2:9; 살후 3:8; 딤전 5:16). 그러나 바울이 적어도 두 가지 경우에는 교회의 경제적 지원을 받기도 했다고 본다: (1) 그가 교회를 세우고 떠난 뒤에는 그 교회의 지원을 받았다(11:8, 9). (2) 빌립보, 데살로니가, 베뢰아와 같이 상호 협력 관계가 지속되는 교회로 부터는 지원을 받았다(고

185) Martin, 345; Plummer, 205.

후 8:1-3; 행 16:11-17:15; 빌 4:10-20).[185] 그렇다면 바울의 경제적 도움은 신조와 같이 제한 된 것이 아니라 교회의 형편에 따라 신축적으로 적용되었으며, 바로 이런 일관되지 않은 자세 때문에 다른 사도들이나 고린도 교인들에게 비판받았을 것이다. 더구나 바울은 고전 9장에서 이미 자비량 선교를 선언하였으므로 이제 와서 정책을 바꾸면 그에 대한 반대자들의 비판을 감당하기 어렵다고 판단하여 계속하여 고린도교회의 재정 지원을 거절했을 것이다. 바울은 비록 일관되게 적용하지 않는다고 있더라도 경제적 독립 사역의 동기가 선한 동기임으로 문제될 것이 없는데도, 이것을 문제 삼는 이들을 책망하고 있다. 그의 모든 동기는 십자가를 지신 겸비하신 그리스도의 복음 정신과 일치되게 살려는 일관된 바울의 목회 신학에서 나온 것임을 암시하고 있다(11:21; 12:13).

셋째, 한편 바울의 경제적 자립형 사역의 동기를 보다 비판적인 시각에서 찾으면, 자립형 사역이 반대자들의 의존형 사역과 차별화되는 효과가 높다고 보았기 때문일 것이다. 반대자들과 사도권 문제로 갈등이 많은 교회에서 바울은 자신이 돈을 받지 않고 희생적으로 사역하는 진정한 그리스도의 사도임을 분명히 밝혀서 그의 사도권 위신과 명예를 지키는 반면, 반대자들의 입지를 약화시키려 했다고 볼 수도 있다. 그러나 이런 목회적 동기는 그리스도의 희생의 본을 따르는 바울의 순수한 신앙적 동기보다 우선적이라고 볼 수 없고, 순수한 신앙적 결단의 결과나 효과로 보아야 할 것이다. 바울은 그의 사역의 동기가 인간적 궤휼이나 사욕이 아니라 언제나 순수한 윤리적이고 기독론적 동기임을 독자들에게 알리는 것이 고린도후서의 중심 목적이기 때문이다(1:12; 2:17;

4:2; 4:7-15; 5:14, 15; 6:4-10; 12:14, 15, 19; 13:4, 7). 그는 일반 목회 사역에 있어서 뿐 아니라, 재정 문제에 있어서도 언제나 약하심으로 죽으신 십자가의 그리스도처럼 약하고 가난한 모습으로 사역하려고 힘쓴 것이다. 그러므로 바울은 이런 자신을 가리켜 "약한 자 같으나 많은 사람을 부요하게 하고 아무것도 없는 자 같으나 모든 것을 가진 자로다"라고 말한다(6:10b). 바울의 이런 삶의 스타일은 그리스도의 삶의 그것과 같다: "우리 주 예수 그리스도의 은혜를 너희가 알거니와 부요하신 자로서 너희를 위하여 가난하게 되심은 그의 가난함을 인하여 너희로 부요케 하려 함이로라" (8:9). 문제는 고린도 교인들이 바울의 이런 진실한 그리스도의 사도로서의 겸비한 자세를 오히려 다른 사도들에 비해서 어딘가 열등하고 모자란 데가 있거나 아니면 예루살렘 성도들을 위한 헌금을 착복하기 때문에 양심상 스스로 재정 지원을 거절하는 것으로 오해하는 것이다(12:13-18).

넷째로, 서론에서 논의한 바와 같이 바울은 예루살렘 회의 이후 예루살렘 사도들과 소원한 관계가 되었다(행 15장). 그 여파가 바울을 지원하던 예루살렘 교회와 가까운 안디옥 교회까지 미쳐서 안디옥 교회가 바울에 대한 재정 지원을 끊었다고 본다.[186] 안디옥 교회가 후원하는 바나바와 마가의 문제로 더 이상 함께 사역하지 않은 것도 재정지원을 받지 못하는 하나의 요인이 되었을 것이다(행 15:36-41). 그래서 바울은 고린도에 왔을 때 천막 만드는 자비량 선교를 할 수 밖에 없었다(행 18:3). 그리고 차제에 아예 교회 지원을 스스로 받지 않는 자비량 선교 사역을 선언하였던 것으로

186) Martin, lvii.

본다(고전 9장).

이상의 동기들은 모두 하나의 기본적 동기와 관련된다. 즉 바울은 스스로 그리스도의 약함을 본받아 사역할 때 그리스도의 내적 능력이 나타난다고 믿었다(12:9, 10). 바울은 그의 모든 사역의 분야에서 이 원칙을 적용하였다. 그러므로 재정적으로도 남에게 의존하지 않고 가난하게 지내면서 하나님의 도우심에 절대적으로 의존하는 자세를 가진 것이다. 여기서 바울 자신이 자비량으로 선교했다고 하는 것을 지나치게 강조해서는 안 된다고 본다. 바울의 관심은 자신이 벌어서 사역한다는 데 있는 것이 아니라 하나님의 은혜로 사역한다는 데 있다(9:15). 바울은 그의 자비량 사역을 그의 희생적 사랑의 구체적 증거로 제시하고 있는 것이다(5:14-15; 11:11; 12:14-15).

8. "내가 너희를 섬기기 위하여 다른 여러 교회에서 요를 받은 것이 탈취한 것이라"(ἄλλας ἐκκλησίας ἐσύλησα λαβὼν ὀψώνιον πρὸς τὴν ὑμῶν διακονίαν,). 계속해서 바울은 아이러니한 말로 고린도 교회의 반대자들의 비판을 논박한다. 반대자들은 바울이 고린도 교회의 도움은 안 받는다고 하면서도 다른 교회에서는 도움을 받는 것이 결국은 다른 교회를 약탈하여 우리를 돕는 것이라고 비판했을 것이다. 즉 바울의 재정 독립 사역이 일관되게 적용되지 않는 것은 바울의 신뢰성을 의심케 하는 증거라는 것이다. 이에 대해서 바울은 그가 다른 교회에서 경제적 도움을 받은 것을 인정하지만, 그렇다고 해서 자신의 재정 독립 선교 정책 원칙을 바꾼 것이 아니고 오히려 되도록 교회의 도움을 받지 않는다는

그의 선교 정책의 기조를 지키고 있음을 증명하는 것이라고 한다. 즉 다른 교회의 도움을 받은 결과 적어도 고린도 교회로부터의 도움을 받을 필요가 없어졌고, 결과적으로 고린도 교회에 유익을 준 것이라고 반박하고 있다. 그런대도 반대자들은 바울이 다른 교회에서 지원 받은 사실을 악의적으로 과장하여 "탈취한 것이라" 고 비난하는 것이다. "탈취한 것이라" (ἐσύλησα= "약탈하다")는 말은 매우 강한 말로서 원래 전쟁터에서 죽은 적군들을 약탈하는 데서 유래한 말이라고 한다.[187] 반대자들이 실제로 이런 말로 바울을 비판했을 것이다(12:16-18). 여기서도 바울의 선한 동기를 무시하고 역시 진실을 왜곡하는 반대자들의 말을 인용함으로써 바울이 반대자들을 공격하는 데 독자들이 함께 참여하게 하는 효과가 있다.

9. "또 내가 너희 중에 있을 때 (너희에게 있어) 용도가 부족하되 아무에게도 누를 끼치지 아니함은 마게도냐에서 온 형제들이 나의 부족한 것을 보충하였음이라 내가 모든 일에 너희에게 폐를 끼치지 않기 위하여 스스로 조심하였거니와 또 조심하리라" (καὶ παρὼν πρὸς ὑμᾶς καὶ ὑστερηθεὶς οὐ κατενάρκησα οὐθενός· τὸ γὰρ ὑστέρημά μου προσανεπλήρωσαν οἱ ἀδελφοὶ ἐλθόντες ἀπὸ Μακεδονίας, καὶ ἐν παντὶ ἀβαρῆ ἐμαυτὸν ὑμῖν ἐτήρησα καὶ τηρήσω). "내가 너희에게 있어" (καὶ παρὼν πρὸς ὑμᾶς)라는 말은 "내가 너희와 함께 일을 때" 라고 시간을 나타내는 절로 번역해야 옳다. 즉 바울이 고린도에 처음방문 했을 때이다(행 18:1-17). 2차 전도여행 시 바울이 마게도냐의 빌립보,

187) Hughes, 385; Furnish, 492.

데살로니가, 베뢰아 등을 거쳐 고린도 교회에 갔는데(행 16:12-17:15), 그 때 여행경비를 마게도냐 교회에서 도운 것으로 보이며, 고린도에 가서 생활비가 모자라서 천막을 만들며 살 때에도(행 18:3), 마게도냐 교인들이 부족한 것을 보충하였다. 결국 바울은 고린도 교인들에게 아무런 경제적 누를 끼치지 않았음(οὐ κατενάρκησα)을 거듭 강조한다. 그런데 이것을 도리어 바울이 고린도 교회에 대한 사랑이 없기 때문이라고 말하는 것은 당치않다(11:11; 12:13). 또 반대로 교묘히 재정적인 누를 끼쳤다고 주장하는 이들도 있었다(12:16). 그러나 바울은 원칙적으로 다른 교회들 에게도 재정적 부담을 주지 않도록 조심하였고, 또 교인들을 그렇게 가르쳤다(12:16; 살전 2:9; 살후 3:8; 딤전 5:16). "폐를 끼치지 않도록"(ἀβαρῆ)은 원래 "재정적인 짐"을 나타내는 말이나, 바울은 다른 의미의 부담도 가리킬 때 쓴다(고후 1:8; 2:5; 4:17; 5:4).[188] 12장 13절에서 "폐를 끼치지 않았다"는 말은 이 말이 아니고 본문에 나오는 "누를 끼치지 않았다"(οὐ κατενάρκησα)는 말과 꼭 같은 말을 다르게 번역한 것뿐이다. "마게도냐에서 온 형제들"이 실라와 디모데를 가리킬 수 있으나(행 18:5), 확실한 증거는 없다.

이렇게 바울이 독립 재정 원칙을 지키면서도 필요에 따라서 다른 교회로부터 어느 정도의 재정 지원은 받았다. 그러나 고린도 교회는 교회 설립 당시부터 재정 지원을 받지 않겠다고 선언하였으므로(고전 9:15) 그 원칙을 엄격히 지켰던 것으로 보인다. 만일 바울이 이 원칙을 무시하고 고린도 교회의 재정 지원을 조금이라

188) J. G. Strelan, "Burden-Bearing and the Law of Christ: A Re-Examination of Galatians 6:2," *JBL* 94(1975) 266-76; G. Schrenk, on βάρος, βαρέω, in TDNT I, 551-9: 파피루스에서 이런 말들이 재정적인 폐를 가르키는 말로 쓰인다고 한다(552, 559).

도 받았다면 반대파들은 더욱 심하게 바울의 신뢰성을 공격하였을 것이다. 바울은 이를 알고서 끝내 고린도 교회의 지원만은 받지 않았던 것이다.

10. "그리스도의 진리가 내 속에 있으니 아가야 지방에서 나의 이 자랑이 막히지 아니하리라"(**ἔστιν ἀλήθεια Χριστοῦ ἐν ἐμοὶ ὅτι ἡ καύχησις αὕτη οὐ φραγήσεται εἰς ἐμὲ ἐν τοῖς κλίμασιν τῆς Ἀχαΐας**). 여기서의 "그리스도의 진리"는 "그리스도의 약함에서 강해지는 진리"를 가리킨다. 이 진리를 12장 9, 10절에서 분명히 말하고 있고, 또 13장 8절에서의 "진리"도 거의 같은 맥락에서 말한 것이라고 생각한다. 그리스도의 약함의 능력의 진리는 앞부분에서 여러 번 바울의 목회 신학 또는 원칙으로 언급되었다. 4장 7-15절에서 바울 자신의 존재를 보화를 담은 질그릇을 언급하고, 그의 고난의 사역을 그리스도의 죽음과 생명의 사역에 비교하여 고린도 교인들을 위한 희생으로 설명할 때, 그리고 유사하게 6장 4-10절에서 그의 사역의 약함과 강함을 대조하면서 설명할 때, 8장 9절에서 우리를 부요케 하시기 위해 그리스도께서 가난하게 되심을 말할 때, "그리스도의 약함의 능력"을 말했다. 바울은 자신의 자비량 선교도 사람에게 의지하지 않는 "약함" 가운데 하나님이 주시는 은혜와 능력으로 수행하는 것이다. 위의 7절에서 "나를 낮추어 하나님의 복음을 값없이 전함으로"라는 말도 이런 의도를 나타낸다. 그리스도께서 "약함"으로 십자가에서 죽으시고 하나님의 능력으로 부활하신 복음 진리를 바울은 재정 분야에도 적용하는 것이다(12:14-15; 참조, 8:9). 이 진리는 단순히 이론뿐만이 아니라 바울의 사역에서 실제로 증명되는 진리로서

그의 사도직의 진정성을 알려주는 가장 분명한 증거로 제시된다(13:4). 바울의 반대자들에게 이 진리의 증거가 없으므로 그들은 거짓 사도들이다. 반대자들은 재정적 지원을 받으나 자신은 아무런 지원을 받지 않는 사실이 자신이 순전히 고린도 교인들을 위해 희생적으로 사역하는 사도라는 것을 보여 주는 중요한 증거가 된다고 믿는다(12:13-15). 그러므로 그는 오해와 어려움이 있더라도 이 선교 정책을 끝까지 포기하지 않을 것이라고 천명한다. 경제적으로 교회에 의존하지 않는 그의 사역은 실제로 그의 "약함"의 자랑이다. 비록 그의 자립적 사역에 대한 반대가 있으나(고린도 교회 반대자들에 의한) 특히 아가야 지방(고린도를 포함한 그리스 남쪽 지방)에서는 결코 이런 형태의 사역이 중단 되지 않을 것이라고 한다.[189] 여기서 그의 재정 독립 사역을 아가야 지방에만 국한 시켜 말하는 것은 바울이 북쪽 마게도냐 지방의 교회로부터는 이미 재정 지원을 받았기 때문에(11:9) 주의 깊게 아가야 지방에 한정 시켜 말하는 것으로 본다. 고린도전서 9장 15절에서도 바울은 그가 복음을 값없이 전하는 데 대하여 반대하는 이들이 있지만 그의 자립형 사역을 중단하지 않을 것이라고 말했다. 본문의 "자랑"이란 말이 고전 9:15에서도 나오는데, 모두 바울의 자립형 사

189) 여기서 바울이 경제적 독립을 주장하는 것이 고린도 교회를 비롯한 아가야 지방의 교회로부터 전혀 경제적 지원을 받지 않겠다는 말인지, 아가야 지방의 선교를 위한 재정 지원을 받지 않겠다는 것인지, 즉 다른 지방을 위한 선교 지원은 받는다는 것인지가 분명하지 않다. 전자의 경우라면 고린도 교회와의 갈등이 수긍이 되나(바울이 고린도 교회의 재정 지원을 거절하여 호의를 무시한다고 보고), 후자의 경우는 다른 지방 교회들의 도움을 받는 것처럼 아가야 지방의 교회, 특히 고린도 교회의 지원을 받는 것이므로 아예 갈등이 발생될 이유가 없을 것이다. 그러므로 전자의 경우일 가능성이 높다(Thrall, 707).

역에 대한 자랑을 가리킨다. 바울은 앞서 육체적인 "자랑"을 경계하면서 그리스도 안에서 자랑하라고 한다. 고린도전서 1장 29-31절에서도 세상 지혜의 자랑을 다른 육체적 자랑들과 함께 경계하였고, 고린도후서 10장 17-18절에서는 하나님께서 자신에게 할당해주신 지역, 즉 아가야 지방에서 전도하는 것을 주안에서 자랑하면서, 그의 지역을 침입하여 바울을 멸시하며 자신들의 사역을 자랑하는 반대자들을 공격하고 있다. 여기서 바울은 "그의 자랑"과 "반대자들의 자랑"을 대조하고 있다(11:10-12). 그의 사역에 대한 자랑은 주님이 보시고 인정하는 한도 내("그리스도 안")에서의 자랑임으로 정당한 자랑이지만, 반대자들의 자랑은 "육체를 따라 하는 자랑"임으로 그렇지 않다. 모든 것을 아시는 주님 앞에서 자랑할 수 있는 사람이 얼마나 되겠는가? 그러나 바울은 적어도 할당된 선교지역 내에서의 선교나, 자립형 선교를 하면서 깨끗하게 욕심이 없이 교회에 부담을 주지 않고 사역해 왔다. 바울은 그의 자랑은 주님이 인정하는 자랑이라고 확신한다. 물론 바울은 문맥에서 이런 "주안에서의 정직한 자랑, 주님이 인정하는 자랑" 조차도 사욕이 개제될 때 어리석은 "육체를 따르는 어리석은 자랑"이 될 수도 있음을 인정하고 있다(11:16-18; 12:1). 그러나 오해를 불식시키기 위해서는 바울은 어쩔 수 없이 어리석은 자가 되었다고 한다. 어리석은 자들에게는 어리석은 자가 되어 어리석은 말(자랑)을 할 수 밖에 없다는 논리다. 그러나 바울은 자신이 그리스도의 "약함의 능력"의 복음진리에 따라서 늘 정직하고 의롭게 사역하고 있다는 것을 말한다(1:12; 4:2). 그의 반대자들은 바울의 선교지역인 아가야 지방에 불법적으로 침투해 들어와서 사욕적인 사역을 하면서 아가야 지방의 원래 선교사인 바울의 순수한 사역을 비난하고 있는 것이다(10:13-16). 그러나 바울은 합법적인 지역에서, 청빈하게, 고린도 교인들에게 유익을 주는 사역을 하기 때문에 주안에서 자랑할 수 있다고 믿는다. 이렇게 청빈하게 사역하는 것에 대한 자랑은 바울의 또 하나의 약한 것들의 자랑일 뿐이다. 바울은 그리스도의 "약하심" 을 따라서 스스로 가난하게 되어 하나님의 은혜로 사역하는 것을 소신으로 삼고 있다. 바울은 고린도 교인들이 이런 그의 입장을 이해하고 바울이 그들의 재정 지원을 받지 않는 문제에 대한 오해를 풀기를 바라고 있다.

c. 고린도 교인들을 사랑함(11:11)

11. "어떠한 연고뇨 내가 너희를 사랑하지 아니함이냐 하나님이 아시느니라" (διὰ τί; ὅτι οὐκ ἀγαπῶ ὑμᾶς; ὁ θεὸς οἶδεν.). "어떠한 연고뇨?" 반대자들은 바울이 다른 교회의 재정적 지원은 받으면서도 유독 고린도 교회의 경제적 지원을 거절하는 이유를 그의 고린도 교회에 대한 사랑과 관심의 결핍 때문이라고 하였다. 그러나 바울은 반대자들의 비난에 개의치 않고 독립된 사역을 계속하겠다고 다짐한다. 바울이 이렇게 독자적인 사역을 계속 고집하는 이유는 무엇인가? 그 이유는 반대자들이 말하듯이 바울이 고린도 교회를 사랑하지 않기 때문이 아니다. 자신의 고린도 교회에 대한 사랑을 하나님께는 아신다고 잘라 말하고 있다. 유사하게 11장 31절에서도 바울은 "하나님이 나의 거짓말 아니하는 줄을 아시느니라" 고 단호하게 말한다. 그리고 12장 15절에서도 거듭해서 고린도 교회를 향한 그의 희생적이고 진정한 사랑을 고백한다. 이런 바울의 사랑은 "그리스도의 강권하는 사랑" 에서 비롯된 것이

다(5:14). 바울의 재정 독립 사역은 고린도교회를 향한 그의 사랑이 순수한 것임을 구체적으로 증명한다.

d. 거짓 사도들은 사단의 일꾼들임(11:12-15)

12. "내가 하는 것을 또 하리니 기회를 찾는 자들의 그 기회를 끊어 저희로 하여금 그 자랑하는 일에 대하여 우리와 같이 되게 하려함이로라"(Ὃ δὲ ποιῶ, καὶ ποιήσω, ἵνα ἐκκόψω τὴν ἀφορμὴν τῶν θελόντων ἀφορμήν, ἵνα ἐν ᾧ καυχῶνται εὑρεθῶσιν καθὼς καὶ ἡμεῖς). "기회를 찾는 자들"의 "기회"(ἀφορμήν)란 말은 반대자들이 바울의 희생적 사역을 반대하고, 자신들의 여러 가지 사욕적이며 육체적 자랑을 가지고 고린도 교회를 설득하여 자신들의 지배를 노리는 것을 가리킨다. 바울은 이에 대해서 지속적으로 그의 반대자들의 그릇된 사역을 막겠다는 의지를 보인다("내가 하는 것을 또 하리니…"). 바울은 반대자들("기회를 찾는 자들")이 그의 사역을 더 이상 왜곡하여 반대하지 못하게 하기 위해서 자신에게 할당된 아가야 지방에서 그의 자립형 사역을 계속하여 반대자들이 "자랑하는 일," 즉, 남의 선교지역을 침입하여 사욕적으로 하는 사역을 더 이상 계속할 수 없게 할 것이다. 플러머는 바울이 그들로 하여금 그들의 교회 의존형 선교 방식을 포기하게 하여 고린도 교인들에게 "우리처럼" 더 이상 경제적인 짐이 되지 않게 만들 것이라고 해석한다.[190] 문맥이 자비량 사역에 대한 논쟁이므로 이런 해석이 가능하다. 그러나 반

---

190) Plummer, 307, 308.

대자들은 바울의 자립형 사역뿐만 아니라 바울의 아가야 지방 선교권(10:13-16)과 나아가서 사도권의 정통성에 대해서 도전하고 있다. 그들은 예루살렘 교회와 사도들과의 친분관계를 자랑하면서 남의 영역을 침범하여 자신들의 사도적 정통성을 주장하며 바울과 대등하게 되려는 이들이다.[191] 그러므로 바울의 자립형 사역은 그리스도께서 값없이 은혜로 주신 구원에 근거한 바울의 전체 사역의 성격에 비추어 보아야 한다. 바울은 이런 희생적 사역을 계속하여서 이들의 육체적 자랑에 근거한 사역을 더 못하게 만들 것이라고 한다.[192]

"(그들이) 자랑하는 일에 대하여 우리와 같이 되게 하려 함이로라"에 대한 해석이 어렵다. 바울("우리")을 이문장의 실제적 의미상의 주어로 보고, 두 번째 ἵνα절을 이끈다고 보면, 바울이 "그의 반대자들을 그와 같이 되게 하려 한다"라고 사역의 의미로 번역하게 된다(개역한글판). 그러나 문자적 주어인 반대자들을 실제적으로 주어로 보면(εὑρεθῶσιν), "반대자들이 그와 같이 되려고 한다"로 능동적으로 번역된다(NIV, GNB). 대부분의 학자들이 반대자들을 주어로 보고, 그들이 바울에게 할당된 선교지역에 침투하여, 재정적으로 의존하는 사역을 바울의 할당 받은 지역에서의 자립형 사역과 대등하게 보이려는 것으로 보아 능동적으로 해석한다.[193]

191) Thrall, 693.

192) Martin, 349: Kümmel, 210, 211; Thrall, 693. Thrall은 예루살렘에서 온 반대자들이 베드로 식의 교회 재정 지원을 받는 선교원칙을 고수하면서(마10:11, 40-42; 참조, 10:8; 고전9:5), 바울의 재정 독립형 선교원칙에 맞서려고 했다고 본다(693). 그러나 이들이 실제로 베드로의 선교방식으로 바울의 선교방식에 맞대응하여 교회의 지배권을 노렸다는 것은 역시 흥미로운 추상일 뿐이다.

193) Martin, 348; Thrall, 693; Barnett, 521.

반대자들이 불법적으로 일하면서도 스스로 바울과 같이 대등하게 되려고 한다는 뜻이다. 그러나 개역한글성경과 같이 바울을 의미상의 주어로 볼 수도 있다. 이 경우 바울이 반대자들을 자랑하는 일에 대하여 "자신과 같이 되게 하도록 만든다"는 뜻이 된다. 주어를 정하는 문제에 따라서 이 마지막 구절의 해석이 달라진다. 바울을 주어로 보는 경우에는 바울 자신의 사역 형태를 반대자들이 따르게 만드는 것으로 해석 되고(개역한글성경), 반대자들을 주어로 보는 경우에는 자신들의 사역 형태를 바울이 따르게 만드는 것을 의미한다(NIV, GNB). 그러나 이 경우에도 바울이 반대자들의 그런 의도("기회")를 끊는 것(ἐκκόψω)을 목적하고 있으므로, 결국 전체 의미는 같게 된다. 우리는 개역한글성경을 따라서 바울을 주어로 삼고 번역한다.

이 구절은 전체적으로 바울이 희생적 재정 독립적 선교 사역을 계속하여서 반대자들이 바울의 선교 영역에서 고린도 교회의 재정적 지원을 받으면서 자랑하는 선교를 그만두고 떠나게 만들겠다는 의미로 본다. 그러나 이 구절이 실제로 반대자들로 하여금 바울의 희생적 선교 형태 전체를 따르게 만들겠다는 말로 보기는 어렵다. 그들에 대한 바울의 적대적 표현들이 너무 많고 반대자들이 바울의 사역을 순종하리라고 기대하기 어렵기 때문이다. 보다 좁게 생각하여 10장 마지막 부분에서 그들이 남의 영역에 침입하여서 사역하나, 바울은 하나님이 정해 주신 한계를 따라서 선교한다고 했는데, 그들도 바울처럼 남의 선교의 영역을 침범하지 않고 존중하며 합법적인 선교할 것을 의미한다고는 볼 수 있을 것이다. 그러나 역시 13절 이하에 나타나는 이들에 대한 바울의 적대적 표현들을 고려할 때 12절의 진의는 이들이 바울의 희생적 선교 방식을 따라 사역할 수 없다면 결국 아가야 지역을 떠나야 할 것이라는 뜻으로 본다.

13. "저런 사람들은 거짓 사도요 궤휼의 역군이니 자기를 그리스도의 사도로 가장하는 자들이니라"(οἱ γὰρ τοιοῦτοι ψευδαπόστολοι, ἐργάται δόλιοι, μετασχηματιζόμενοι εἰς ἀποστόλους Χριστοῦ). γάρ는 반대자들이 어떤 주장을 하던지 그들의 주장을 거절할 수밖에 없는 이유절을 이끈다. "저런 사람들"(οἱ τοιοῦτοι)은 "이런 사람들"로 번역하는 것이 보다 가까운 의미다. 그러나 이 대명사(οἱ τοιοῦτοι)가 거의 같은 뜻인 οἱ οὗτοι보다 더 부정적인 의미로 쓰이기 때문에, 우리 나라말로 "이런 자들"이라고 번역하는 것이 좋을 듯하다.[194] 바울은 지금까지 그의 반대자들의 오만하고 부당한 행위를 열거해왔다. 반대자들은 예루살렘 사도들의 권위를 내세워 바울에게 할당된 사역지에 들어와서 사도로 자처하면서 바울이 그동안 이룩해 놓은 목회적 성과를 자기들의 것으로 삼고, 자신들의 설교 실력을 자랑하며, 교회의 재정을 축내는 사욕적 사역을 하면서도, 이런 사역을 자랑하며, 바울과 대등하게 되려고 함으로써 그들의 행위의 부당함을 스스로 들어내었다. 이제 바울은 이런 사람들의 정체를 폭로한다. 그들은 거짓 사도이며, 궤휼의 역군들이다. 그들은 결코 믿는 형제들이 아니며, 단순히 세속적이거나 중립적인 사람들도 아니라 하나님과 복음의 적이다.

첫째로, "이런 자들"은 "거짓사도들"(ψευδαπόστολοι)이다. 사도란 그리스도로부터 보내심을 받는 그리스도의 대변자인데,

194) Martin, 350.

거짓 사도는 그리스도의 사도로 위장하여 다른 복음(이단적 복음)을 전하면서 바울의 사도직에 대항하는 위험한 이들이다(고전 15:15; 갈 2:4; 고후 11:4, 26; 마 7:15). 그들은 전혀 그리스도로부터 "보내심을 받은" 사도들이 아니다. 그들의 위험성은 겉으로 보기에는 사도처럼 보이나 속은 그렇지 않은 데 있다(11:12, 23). 진정한 사도의 표는 기독론적 평가 기준에 의해 결정되는데, 메시지와 일상생활에 있어서 진정한 그리스도의 표를 가지고 있느냐가 관건이다(4:7-15; 6:4-10; 12:9, 10, 12; 13:4).[195]

둘째로, 그들은 "궤휼의 역군들"(ἐργάται δόλιοι), 즉 "간교하게 속이는 일꾼들"이다(11:3; 2:17; 4:2). 이들은 그리스도의 일꾼들로 자처하지만 바울은 이들을 "궤휼의 일꾼들"로 규정하고 있다(11:23). 바울은 그들이 12장 16절에서 자신을 향해 비난할 때 사용하는 "궤휼"(δόλῳ)이란 말을 그대로 사용하고 있다.

셋째로, 그들은 그리스도의 사도들로 "가장하는 자들", 또는 "변장하는 자들"(μετασχηματιζόμενοι)이다. 이들은 5장 12절에 언급된 "외모로 자랑하는 자들"이다. 겉으로는 그리스도의 사도들처럼 보이나, 속으로는 그리스도의 적인 사단의 일꾼들이다. 고린도 교인들은 가장한 반대자들의 외모만 보고 이들을 따르지만, 진정한 그리스도의 사도인 바울은 그들의 정체를 분명히 아는 분별력을 가지고 있다는 의미가 있다(2:11; 5:12; 10:7). 반대자들의

---

195) C. K. Barrett, "ΨΕΥΔΑΠΟΕΤΟΛΟΙ(2 Cor 11.13)" in *Mélanges Bibliques en Hommage au R. P. Béda Rigaux*, ed. A. -L. Descamps and A. de Halleux, (Gembloux: Duculot, 1970) 377-96; reprinted in *Essays on Paul* (London: SPCK 1982), 87-107; 93-4: Barrett는 ("거짓사도")라는 말이 아마 바울이 지어낸 말로서, 그의 반대자들이 바울을 마 7:15의 ψευδαπόστολοι("거짓 예언자들")의 전통에 따라서 "거짓 예언자"라고 공박함에 대해서 응수한 말이라고 한다. Thrall도 이에 동의한다(694).

정체를 분명히 밝히고 또한 이들의 미혹을 받은 고린도 교인들에게 경고하는 것이다.

14. "이것이 이상한 일이 아니라 사단도 자기를 광명의 천사로 가장하나니." (**καὶ οὐ θαῦμα· αὐτὸς γὰρ ὁ σατανᾶς μετασχηματίζεται εἰς ἄγγελον φωτός.**). "이것" 이란 말은 본문에는 없으나 이해를 돕기 위해서 첨가된 번역어이다. "이상한 일이 아니라" (**καὶ οὐ θαῦμα**)는 원문에는 동사가 없는 불완전한 문장으로서, 독자들의 주의를 환기 시키는 경계의 의미가 있다.[196] "이상한 일" 은 앞 절에서 반대자들이 그리스도의 사도들로 "변장하는 것" 을 가리킨다. 만일 반대자들이 사단의 일꾼이라면 어떻게 그들에게서 사도들의 능력과 역사가 일어날 수 있는가란 예상된 질문에 대한 대답이다. "변장" 은 사단이 곧잘 쓰는 술책이다. 사단은 어둠의 권세자이나 사람들을 미혹하기 위해서 광명의 천사로 둔갑하는 것이다. 유대교 위경(僞經)인 "아담과 하와의 일생" 9장 1절에 사단이 타락 이후에 두 번째로 화와를 유혹하는 이야기에서 사단이 빛나는 천사로 둔갑하여 하와에게 말을 거는 이야기가 나온다.[197] 유사하게 같은 유대교 위경인 "모세의 묵시록" 17장 1절에서도 하와에게 사단이 천사처럼 찬송을 부르면서 천사의

---

196) Martin, 351.

197) Windisch, 342: Windisch는 바울이 *Life of Adam and Eve*에 나오는 이 이야기를 생각하고 있다고 본다. 다른 학자들도 이에 동조한다. Lietzmann, 149; Héring, 86; Bruce, 239; Barrett, 286; Bultmann, 211; Furnish, 495. Barrett와 Furnish는 *The Apocalypse of Mose*도 언급한다. 그러나 Plummer 같은 학자들은 이를 반대하고 여기서 바울이 일반적인 사단의 변장술에 대한 통념을 반영하는 것일 뿐이라고 한다: Plummer, 309; Allo, 287; Tasker, 153; Hughes, 393-4, n. 57.

모습으로 나타난다. 또한 당시 랍비 문헌에도 태초에 사단이 타락하기 전에 영광의 천사인 루시퍼였다는 전승이 있다(참조, 겔 28:13).[198] 이런 책들의 내용을 바울과 당시 유대교인들은 잘 알고 있었을 것으로 추정된다.[199] 바울은 이미 4장 6절, 6장 14절-7장 1절에서 빛과 어두움의 대조를 통해서 거룩한 생활에 대해서 가르쳤다(골 1:12; 13; 엡 5:11-14; 6:12). 3장에서도 자신을 영원한 그리스도의 영광을 나타내는 영광의 직분을 맡은 사도로 말하고 반대자들을 일시적 모세의 영광에 비교하여 그들의 가르침과 직분의 가식적인 성격을 암시적으로 말했다. 바울은 여기서 반대자들이 자랑하는 능력과 역사는 진정한 사도의 표가 아니라 광명의 천사로 가장하는 사단의 특성에 따른 것임을 역설하고 있다. 반대자들이 자랑하는 것들이 오히려 그들의 정체가 사단의 일꾼들임을 드러내는 증거가 되는 것이다(마 7:21-23; 24:11; 막 13:22). 겉으로는 화려한 그들의 궁극적 목적은 그들이 따르는 사단의 목적과 같이 사람들을 멸망으로 빠뜨리는 데 있다는 것을 암시한다. 천사들의 임무가 하나님의 말씀을 전하는 전달자임을 생각할 때, 앞서 11장 4절에서 지적한대로 반대자들은 다른 예수, 다른 영, 다른 복음을 전하는 사단의 일꾼들이다(참조, 갈 1:8). 그들은 잘못된 메시지로 사람들을 멸망으로 인도하는 것이다(11:4).

바울의 논쟁의 초점은 시종일관 반대자들의 "육체와 외모의 자랑"에 관한 것이다. 여기서는 반대자들이 사도의 표로 내세우며 자랑하는 것들이 결국은 사단의 변장술에 지나지 않는다는 것이다. 그들의 예루살렘 사도들과의 교분, 그들의 추천서(3:1), 굉장한 웅변술

198) K. L. Schmidt, "Luzifer als gefallene Engelsmacht," *TZ* 7(1951) 261-79.

199) 일반적으로 천사들이 빛과 관련되어 인식된 것은 분명하다(눅2:9; 24:4).

과 영적 능력도 진정한 사도의 표가 아니라 사람들을 미혹하기 위한 사단의 화려한 "변장"에 지나지 않는다고 말하고 있다(10:7, 10; 12:1). 중요한 것은 바울은 이런 위장을 꿰뚫어 보는 능력을 가지고 있다는 사실이다(2:11). 그러므로 이런 능력을 가진 바울이야말로 진정한 사도라는 암시가 있다. 그러나 문제는 이런 사람들에게 미혹받아 따르면서 바울을 여전히 의심하는 고린도 교인들이 있다는 것이다. 그래서 바울은 더욱 반대자들에 대한 공격의 수위를 높인다.

15. "그러므로 사단의 일군들도 자기를 의의 일군으로 가장하는 것이 또한 큰 일이 아니라 저희의 결국은 그 행위대로 되리라" (**οὐ μέγα οὖν εἰ καὶ οἱ διάκονοι αὐτοῦ μετασχηματίζονται ὡς διάκονοι δικαιοσύνης· ὧν τὸ τέλος ἔσται κατὰ τὰ ἔργα αὐτῶν.**). 이구절도 **οὐ μέγα οὖν εἰ καί**로 시작되어 앞 절(**καί οὐ θαῦμα**)과 유사하게 불완전한 문장으로 시작된다. **οὐ μέγα οὖν εἰ καί**는 문자적으로 번역하면 이해가 어려우므로 한글개역의 번역("그러므로 만일 …하여도 또한 큰일은 아니라")은 타당하다. 앞 절과 유사하게 시작하고, 그 내용도 병행적인 내용이다. 즉 앞 절에서 말한 대로 반대자들이 사단을 따라서 가장하듯이 그들은 또한 사단을 따라서 "의의 일군들"(**διάκονοι δικαιοσύνης**)로 가장한다고 계속 비판한다. 원문에 사단이란 말은 "그"(**αὐτοῦ**)라는 3인칭 대명사로 나타나고 있다.

주제는 여전히 반대자들의 "육체와 외모에 대한 자랑들"이 가식적인 것이며 진실성이 없다는 것이다. 앞에서는 그들의 가식적 가르침에 대한 공격이었다면, 여기서는 그들의 가식적이며 위선적인 행위에 대한 공격이 계속된다. 바울은 앞서 그의 사역을 "의의 사역" 이라고 규정했다(3:9; 5:19-21; 6:7). 또한 바울 자신을 "의의 일군" 이라고 하였다(참조, 3:6; 4:5; 6:7; 7:2; 10:15-16). 그러나 반대자들은 다른 예수, 다른 영, 다른 복음을 가르쳐서 고린도 교인들을 미혹하는 반면에, 행동과 삶에 있어서 불의하다. 그들은 외모와 육체적 조건들을 자랑하면서 사람들을 미혹하는 거짓사도들이다(5:12, 10:7). 그들은 역사적 예수를 직접보았다고 자랑하고(5:16), 예루살렘 사도들의 추천장을 자랑하며(3:1), 또 웅변과 풍채를 자랑한다(10:7,10). 뿐만아니라, 그들은 남의 선교영역에 침범하여 바울이 이루어 놓은 목회적 성과를 자기들의 것으로 삼아 자랑하고 있으니 불의하지 않은가?(10:12-16). 특히 11장에서 그들은 바울이 고린도 교회에 재정적 후원을 받지 않는 것을 고린도 교회를 무시하는 처사라고 비난하면서 바울과 고린도 교회를 이간질하고, 도리어 교회에 재정적으로 의존하는 자신들을 의로운 일꾼으로 자랑한다. 이런 이들을 어떻게 "의의 일군들" 이라고 할 수 있는가?(11:7-9). 이들의 사역으로 고린도 교인들의 형편이 참담하게 되었으니(12:20-21) 이들이 사단의 일꾼들이란 사실이 더욱 분명하다(11:1-6).

"의의 일군" 에 대한 해석이 다양하다. (1) 반대자들이 "의로운 일꾼들" 로 자처했다. 그들은 자신들의 의로운 사역에 대해 자랑하면서 그렇게 선전했다[200]; (2) 반대자들이 자신들도 바울과 같이 "믿음으로 구원 얻는 복음" 을 가르친다고 주장했다. "가장한다" 는 말은 바울의 복음으로 가장한다는 뜻으로 본다.[201] 그러나 3절에서 바울이 이들이 "다른 예수," "다른 영," "다른 복음" 을 전한다고 했으므로 이런 주장을 받아들이기 어렵다; (3) 반대자들은 바

---

200) Barrett, 287.

201) Meyer, 439.

울과 반대로 의의 행위로 말미암는 구원을 가르쳤다.[202] 이 견해에 대해서 일반적으로 행위 구원을 주장하는 유대인들이라면 자신들을 "가장한다"는 말이 적절치 않다고 본다. 이런 사람들은 대체로 율법 행위를 들어 내놓고 자랑하는 이들이기 때문이다. 바울이 이런 율법주의자들을 "사단의 역군"들이라고까지 부른다는 것도 받아들이기 어렵다(3:6-16); (4) 반대자들은 3장 9절에서 바울이 자신의 사도직을 "의의 직분"이라고 한 것을 알고 이에 대항하여 자신들을 "의의 일군"이라고 주장하였는데, 바울이 이를 여기서 비난하는 것이다.[203] 이런 주장은 1-9장이 10-13보다 늦게 보낸 분리된 편지라는 것을 전제해야 하는 문제가 있다. 그리고 "의의 직분"과 "의의 일군"이란 유사하나 같지는 않다. 이상의 주장들은 바울이 반대자들을 비방하기 위해서 "의의 일군들"이란 말을 지었는가(2, 3번) 아니면 반대자들이 스스로 자신들을 가리켜 한말인가(1, 4번)로 나눌 수 있다. 우리는 바울이 "매사에 있어서 육체와 외모를 자랑하는 반대자들의 오만한 자세"를 싸잡아서 그들을 "의의 일군들"로 표현했다고 본다. 이 경우에 "의"(δικαιοσύνη)란 신학적 의미가 아닌 일반적인 도덕적 의미로 보는 것이다. 반대자들은 매사에 그들이 옳다는 자세를 취하나, 바울은 이들이 스스로 기만하고 있다고 본다.

여기서 바울은 그의 반대자들을 직접 거명하지 않고 간접적으로 풍자적인 용어로 비난하는데, 직접 거명할 경우에, 오히려 바울의 사도로서의 위신이 손상될 수 있기 때문이라고 볼 수 있

202) Tasker, 154; Plummer, 310; Hughes, 395.

203) Thrall, 697-698.

다.[204]간접적으로 풍자적으로 반대자들의 잘못됨을 나타내더라도 고린도 독자들은 쉽게 누구를 가리키는가를 알 수 있었을 것이다. 독자들은 반대자들의 권위와 바울의 사도적 권위를 보다 객관적으로 비교하게 되면서 반대자들을 비난하는 바울의 견해에 스스로 동조하게 되는 효과도 있을 것이다.[205]

"저희의 결국은 그 행위대로 되리라." 바울은 그의 반대자들의 "가장된 행위"에 대한 최종적 심판을 하나님께 맡긴다. 사단의 일꾼들로서 속이는 행위는 결국 하나님께서 심판하실 것이다.[206]바울은 다른 서신에서도 하나님의 심판에 맡긴다는 언급을 한다(롬 2:16; 3:8; 고전 4:5; 빌 3:19; 참조 행 17:31). 반대자들의 자신들에 대한 모든 주장에도 불구하고 그 주장들이 거짓임을 하나님께서 들어내실 것이다. 바울은 단순히 그를 반대하는 인간 집단과 싸우는 것이 아니라 그 배후에 있는 사단의 세력과 싸우는 것이며, 그의 판단이 옳다는 것을 하나님께서 밝혀 주실 것이라고 믿는다. 현재 반대자들은 사단 편에서 싸우고, 바울은 하나님 편에서 싸우고 있다. 이것은 매우 심각한 영적 싸움이다.[207] 이 중요한 사실을 고린도 교인들 가운데 분명히 모르고 우왕좌왕하는 이들도 있다. 그러나 바울이 지금 이 사실을 명확하게 밝힐 때 이를 인정해야

---

204) C. Forbes의 말이 인용됨: P. Marshall, *Enmity in Corinth: Social Conventions in Paul's Relations with the Corinthians*, WUNT 2, Reich 23(Tübingen: Tübingen University, 1987), 90.

205) Martin, 353.

206) 시 62:13; 잠 24:12; 바룩서 11:9; *Testament of Abraham* 9:8; 행 10:35; 약 2:14-26; 3:13; 요일 3:7, 12, 18. 사람은 그 행한 대로 보응을 받는다는 유대인의 보편적인 사상이 나타나있다.

207) K. T. Kleinknecht, *Der leiden Gerechtfertigte*, WUNT 2nd ser. 13 (Tübingen: Mohr, 1984), 293, Thrall의 인용, 698, 주 300.

할 것이다. 바울은 반대자들을 정죄하면서 고린도 교인들이 누구를 따를 것인가를 분명히 결단할 것을 촉구하는 것이다(13:5).

그러나 이런 강력한 비판도 반대자들이나 그들의 동조자들에게는 여전히 바울의 개인적이며 주관적인 주장일 뿐이라고 일축할 수 있다. 바울은 이에 대해서 그의 반대자들이 결여하고 있는 가장 확실하고 진정한 사도의 준거(準據)를 제시한다. 반대자들이 내세우는 사도적 표들이 진짜가 아닌 모두 가짜라는 결정적 증거는 그들이 제시하는 자랑거리 가운데, 그리스도의 사도로서 그리스도의 고난에 참여한 예가 없다는 것이다. 그들은 복음의 중심인 그리스도의 십자가의 고난과 상반되는 "육체나 외모의 자랑" 에 심취해 있다. 그러나 바울은 그리스도의 고난을 그의 복음과 사역의 중심으로 삼고 있다(4:5, 7-15; 5:14-15; 6:4-10; 8:9; 11:29; 12:10; 13:4). 이제 고린도 교인들은 진정한 사도의 가장 확실한 표가 무엇인지 알고 누가 진정한 사도인지를 결정해야 할 때가 되었다.

주해(11:1–15):

11장 1-15절에서 바울은 어려운 궁지 가운데서 모든 일이 저절로 잘되리라는 유연한 자세 대신에 반대자들과의 정면 대결을 불사한다. 그것은 그리스도의 사도로서 그리스도의 교회를 악한 세력으로부터 보호해야하는 책임이 있기 때문이다. 또한 고린도의 반대자들을 방치할 경우에 그의 전체 사역에 미치는 파급 효과가 클 것으로 보고 이들에 대해서 단호하게 대처하기로 결심한 것이다. 바울은 자신의 사도직의 정당성을 변명하면서 동시에 반대자들의 사악한 정체를 폭로한다. 그들은 바울이 전한 예수, 영, 복음과는 "다른 예수, 다른 영, 다른 복음"을 전하는 "사단의 역군들이다"(11:4). 이들은 고린도 교회를 미혹하여 멸망으로 이끄는 이들이므로 결코 용납해서는 안 된다. 더구나 이들은 바울이 고린도 교회에 신세를 지지 않고 사역하는 것을 가지고 바울이 다른 사도들에 비해서 사도적 열등감을 가졌기 때문이고(12:11), 고린도 교회를 무시하거나 사랑하지 않는다고 하면서 바울과 고린도 교회를 이간하였다(11:3, 7-8). 이에 대해서 바울은 마치 그리스도를 위한 신부로 단장시키는 중매자의 자세를 가지고 고린도 교회를 각별히 돌보고 있으며, 자비량 선교의 취지도 고린도 교회에 재정적 폐를 끼치지 않으려는 것이지 고린도 교회에 대해 어떤 편향성을 가졌기 때문이 아닌 것으로 변명한다.

바울이 반대자들을 강도 높게 비난한 것은 그들의 사역이 바울의 이방 교회 사역을 포함한 그리스도 교회 전체에 심각한 위협이 되었고, 그들의 사역의 배후에는 그리스도의 교회를 교란시키려는 사단의 계획이 있음을 보았기 때문이다.

첫째, 그들은 고린도 교인들의 마음을 그리스도를 향한 마음으로부터 멀게 한다(11:3, 13; 갈 1:6-10; 막 8:33; 마 7:15-23; 요일 4:1-6; 계 2:20-24).

둘째, 이들은 바울이 전하는 "예수, 영, 복음"과 배치되는 "다른 예수, 다른 영, 다른 복음"을 전하여 교회를 교란 시키는 무리들이다. 이들이 전하는 예수, 영, 복음이 실제로 무엇인지 밝히지 않고 있으나, 이들이 예루살렘에서 온 이들이라는 사실과, 그들에 대한 바울의 대응을 살피면, 이들은 대체로 예수의 역사적 행적을 중시하고, 이적과 기사 중심의 사역을 행하는 유대주의적 선교사들로 보인다. 바울은 이들의 복음이 자신의 복음과 다를 뿐만 아니라 다른 사도들이 전하는 전체 기독교 복음과도 다르다고 보았을 것이다.

셋째, 이들은 예루살렘 사도들의 인정과 권위를 가진 사도들이라고 자랑하면서, 바울에게 맞섰다(11:5, 6; 3:1). 특별히 이들은 바울이 고린도 교회에서 지원을 받지 않는 것 자체가 바울이 자신들처럼 인정받은 정식 사도가 아니기 때문에 열등감 가운데서 스스로 피하는 것이라고 비난했을 것이다. 바울은 이미 고린도전서 9장에서 복음 사역자들이 교회의 지원을 받는 것이 타당함을 인정하였으나, 자신은 지원을 받지 않는 원칙을 고수해왔으며, 이것은 자신의 열등감이나, 교회의 성의를 무시하기 때문이 아니라 그리스도의 제자도를 따르는 개인적인 목회적 신념이라고 보았다. 물론 바울은 고린도 교회와 고린도 교회가 속한 아가야 지방 사역에서만 이 원칙을 고수했다. 바울이 고린도 사역을 시작했을 때(50년 말), 예루살렘 교회의 신학 노선을 따르던 안디옥 교회가 아마도 바울의 극단적인 반유대주의적 신학적 노선을 문제 삼고(행 15:1) 또, 바울과 바나바와의 분쟁(행 15:39), 이방인과 식사하다 유대인들이 오자 자리를 뜬 베드로와 바나바에 대한 바울의 공격(갈 2:12) 등을 문제 삼아서 바울에 대한 선교지원비를 끊었다고 본다.[208] 그러므로 바울은 어쩔 수 없이 천막을 만들며 살아야 했다(행 8:2). 그때 그는 어떤 교회에도 재정적으로 매이지 않는 독립 사역을 선언하였던 것 같다(고전 9장). 물론 다른 지역의 지원을 모두 거부한 것은 아니다. 실제로 그는 마게도냐 교회의 지원도 받았음을 밝힌다(11:9, 빌 4:15-19). 그러나 고린도전서 9장에서 이미 독립적 선교를 공식적으로 선언한 이상 고린도 교회에서의

208) Martin, lvii.

재정지원만은 받지 않기로 결심한 것이다. 반대자들은 계속해서 바울이 돈을 받지 않는 척하면서도 뒤로는 받는다고 비난했다(12:16). 이것은 아마 예루살렘 성도들을 위한 헌금(8-9장)을 가리키는 말로 보인다. 이에 대해서 바울은 전혀 그렇지 않다고 부인한다(12:17-18). 바울은 이들이 전혀 사도가 아니라 "사단의 역군들"이며 가장한 "거짓 사도"라고 공격한다. 바울은 고린도 교인들이 이들의 말만 듣고, 이들의 외적 조건만을 보고 믿지 말고 그들이 전하는 예수의 성격과, 그들의 복음의 성격을 분명히 알고, 그들의 영적 배후의 세력을 분명히 알아야 한다고 말하는 것이다(11:4). 바울은 아래에서 그들은 그리스도의 고난에대해서 말할 수는 있으나 스스로 고난을 받지는 않은 사람들임을 지적한다(11:15-33). 그러므로 그들은 성도들을 미혹하는 거짓된 사도들이라고 한다.

목회적 궁지에 몰려서 바울은 자신의 능력이나, 사람들의 지지에 의존하지도 않으며, 그렇다고 피해의식에 젖어 어쩔 수 없이 막연하게 하나님만 의지해야 한다고 생각하지도 않는다. 그는 목회적 궁지에서 보다 구체적인 하나님의 구원의 능력을 믿는다. 즉 예수 그리스도의 죽으심과 부활을 통해 나타난 하나님의 구원의 능력이다. 그리스도의 부활의 생명력이 곤경 가운데 처한 자신에게 역사하심을 믿는다. 이 끈질긴 그리스도의 부활의 생명력이 그를 고린도 교회의 어려움에서 반드시 구원한다고 믿고 바라는 것이다(12:10; 13:4). 부활 사건 가운데 나타난 하나님의 구원의 능력은 과거의 사건으로 그치는 것이 아니고, 장래의 구원으로만 약속된 것도 아니다. 언제 어디서나 그리스도 안에서 새로운 피조물로 살아가는 모든 하나님의 백성에게 언제나 나타나는 것으로 믿는 것이다(5:17).

11장 1-15절에서 바울은 매우 적극적으로 반대자들에 대해서 혹독한 공격을 가한다. 이런 심한 공격은 다른 서신에서 그 예를 찾을 수 없다. 반대자들의 문제가 그만 큼 심각한 이유도 있으나, 바울 자신이 그리스도의 사도로서 조금도 양심에 거리낌이 없이 최선을 다해 사역해왔다는 확신이 있기 때문이다(4:2). 그는 주님을 위해서 일체 부끄러움이 없는 사역을 해왔기 때문에 떳떳하다(1:12; 4:2). 주 예수 그리스도의 부활의 생명력이 그의 종으로서의 자신의 사역 가운데 재생된다(4:7-15; 6:4-10; 13:4).

이런 부활의 생명력에 대한 믿음은 역시 바울처럼 헌신적이며 양심적이고 정직한 목회자들만이 가질 수 가 있다. 불의한 사람들은 자신들의 불의함으로 말미암아 하나님의 도우심을 기대하거나 믿을 수가 없다. 그들은 죄책감과 열등감에 빠져서 하나님의 심판을 두려워하게 된다. 그들은 위선적인 설교를 할 수 밖에 없다. 그러나 바울처럼 온전한 목회자가 실제로 있는가? 대개 하나님의 사람들도 나름대로의 결함을 가지고 있지 않은가? 하나님은 죄인들을 징벌하시지만, 그의 긍휼하심과 자비하심으로 그들을 불러 쓰시기도 하신다. 베드로도 실수가 많았으나 주님께서 그를 쓰셨다. 우리는 하나님의 "인자하심과 용납하심과, 길이 참으심을 멸시하지 말고" 죄를 깊이 회개하면서 하나님의 정직하고, 선한 일꾼이 되기 위해서 부단히 힘써야 한다(롬 2:4). 그래야 바울처럼 "예수 그리스도의 죽으심과 부활에서 나타난 하나님의 능력" 이 우리 중에 역사하심을 믿을 수 있다.

D. 바울이 거짓 사도들의 비난에 대하여 자천(自薦)(자랑)을 계속함 (11:16-12:18)

바울은 바로 앞 절에서 고린도 교회의 거짓 사도들의 정체를

"사단의 일꾼들"로 최종 판단하였다. 그리고 나서 주저하면서 자신의 자천 또는 자랑을 시작한다. 거짓사도들의 주장을 반박하면서 주로 그의 사역이 고난의 사역임을 식접 예를 들어서 말하는 것이다. 바울은 그리스도의 사도의 가장 중요한 증거가 바로 그리스도의 약함을 따라서 겸손히 사역하는 것이라고 본다. 이것이 그에게는 진리다(11:10; 13:8). 이 진리 기준에 의하여 바울은 자신을 변명하고, 또 거짓 사도들을 비판하는 것이다. 고린도 교인들이 이 진리를 기준으로 자신의 사도직에 마땅한 판단을 내리기를 원하는 것이다. 그는 다른 사도들처럼 "표적과 기사와 능력"을 행했다. 그러나 이런 외적 기준으로는 진정한 사도직의 판단이 불가능하다고 본다. 그가 가장 중하게 여기는 궁극적인 그리스도의 사도된 표는 그리스도께서 약함으로 십자가에서 죽으셨으나 하나님의 능력으로 다시 사신 것과 같이 자신도 모든 약함 가운데서 사역하면서 그리스도의 능력을 나타내는 것이다(4:7-15; 6:4-10; 11:23-33; 12:12; 13:4. 7, 9; 고전 15:10). 그리스도의 외적인 능력이나 영광보다 먼저 그리스도의 고난에 동참할 수 있는 자라야 진정한 그리스도의 사도라고 굳게 믿는 것이다(12:1). 어쩌면 바울이 예수님의 거짓사도들에 대한 경고를 알고 있었을 것이다(마 7:22-23; 24:11; 막 13:22). 또한 예수님의 제자들에게 자기 십자가를 지고 그를 따르라고 하신 말씀도 알고 있었을 것이다(마 10:38; 막 8:34; 눅 9:23 등). 십자가의 고난과 인내는 진짜 메시아와 가짜 메시아, 그리고 진정한 사도와 거짓 사도를 시험하는 리트머스 시험지와 같은 것이다. 십자가를 참으시고 죽으신 그리스도를 따라서 고난을 참는 것은 진실한 사랑의 가장 확실한 증거이기 때문이다(5:14-15).

그리스도의 약함과 함께 그리스도의 희생적 사랑의 모본을 따라 고린도 교인들을 위해 희생하는 것도 중요한 사도의 표로 제시한다. 바울은 교인들의 재정적 지원을 받지 않고 자비량 선교를 하는 것이 그가 진정한 사도라는 구체적 증거로 제시한다(11:7-10; 12:14-18; 참조, 행 18:2; 20:33-35). 그런데도 이것을 가지고 오히려 바울이 궤휼로 재물을 취한다고 악선전하는 반대자들이야말로 거짓 사도들이다(12:16).

바울은 이런 자랑을 자신이해야 하는 것을 부끄럽고 어렵게 생각했다(11:16-17). 그러나 고린도 교인들에게 진실을 밝혀서 미혹받지 않게 하는 것도 중요하다고 보았다. 한편, 자신을 위해 나서서 변명해야할 고린도 교인들이 침묵하기 때문에 어쩔 수 없이 자기가 해야 했다며 고린도 교인들의 무관심을 탓하기도 한다(12:11).

1. 자천을 계속함에 대한 변명(11:16-21)

본문:

> 16. 내가 다시 말하노니 누구든지 나를 어리석은 자로 여기지 말라 만일 그러하더라도 나로 조금 자랑하게 어리석은 자로 받으라 17. 내가 말하는 것은 주를 따라 하는 말이 아니요 오직 어리석은 자와 같이 기탄없이 자랑하노라 18. 여러 사람이 육체를 따라 자랑하니 나도 자랑하겠노라 19. 너희는 지혜로운 자로서 어리석은 자들을 기쁘게 용납하는구나 20. 누가 너희로 종을 삼거나 잡아 먹거나 사로잡거나 자고하다 하거나 뺨을 칠지라도 너희가 용납하는도다 21. 우리가 (지금까지 늘) 약하게 살아온 것을 부끄럽게 말하노라 (우리가 약한 것 같이 내가 욕되게 말하노라). 그러나 누가 무슨 일에 담대하면 어리석은 말이나마 나도 담대하리라.

본문 비평:

1. 18절에서 κατὰ τὴν σάρκα(육체를 따라)가 ℵ² B D1 ψ TR에 나타나고 관사가 없는 짧은 κατὰ σάρκα는 p⁴⁶ ℵ* B D* G 에 나타난다. 후대에 빠진 관사를 첨부했다고 보아서 후자가 원형이라고 본다.[209] 의미는 모두 같다.[210]

2. 21절에서 ἠσθενήκαμεν(우리가 약한 것 같이)가 p⁴⁶ ℵ B 에 있고, 더 부드러운 형인 ἠσθενήσαμεν이 D E G와 소문자 사본에 나타난다.[211]

내용 개요:

11장 16-21절은 11장 1절-12장 18절까지의 이른 바 "바보의 연설" 에서 여전히 서론에 해당되는 부분이다.[212] 11장 1-15절도 서론에 해당되지만, 16-21절은 보다 직접적인 서론으로서, "바보의 연설" 의 본격적인 내용에 앞서서 자신이 받은 고난의 자랑, 즉 반대자들과 같이 "육체적인 자랑"을, 말 할 수밖에 없는 자신의 입장에 대한 바울의 변(辯)이다. 이 부분은 문학적으로 보아 주로 아이러니, 역설, 패러디, 대조법등의 논쟁형태로 되어 있다. 바울의 고난의 생애를 열거하는 대목은 논쟁의 한 부분이긴 하지만 성격상 논쟁과는 구별되는 부분이다(11:24-33).[213] 일반적으로 연설의

---

209) Windisch, 346, 주, 3.

210) 참조, Allo, 290; Prümm, *Diakonia*, 1:631.

211) 참조, Allo, 290, 292.

212) 11:1-12:18을 "바보의 연설" 이라고 부른다. 명사형 "어리석음" (ἀφροσύνη)이란 말이 11:1, 분사형 ἄφρων이 12:11에서, 형용사형 ἄφρονα가 11:16에서 나온다.

서두에서는 청중들을 칭찬한다. 여기서 바울은 아이러니하게 청중을 칭찬한다. 즉 그들을 "지혜로운 자들"이라고 치켜세운다(19a). 그러나 지혜 있다는 사람들이 어리석은 자들의 말을 잘 들으니 문제라고 냉소한다(19b).

바울은 반대자들이 "육체적 자랑"을 한다고 비난하면서도 자신도 마찬가지로 "육체적 자랑"을 하는 어리석음을 범하는 것에 대해서 독자들의 양해를 구한다.[214] 이런 바울에 대한 변호는 바울을 잘아는 고린도 교인들이 해야 마땅한 것이지만(12:11) 그들이 침묵하기 때문에 바울 스스로 자신을 변호해야 하니 양해 하라는 것이다. 이 부분은 12장에서 주장하는 바울의 중심적인 논지, 즉, 그의 고난의 사역이 그의 반대자들과 구별되는 자신의 사역의 특징으로서, 진정한 그리스도의 사도의 표인, "약한 것을 통해 나타나는 하나님의 구원 능력에 전적으로 의지하는 자세"를 보여 준다는 것을 말하기 위한 준비 과정이다(12:10). "약한 것을 자랑하는 것"도 역시 "육체를 따르는 자랑"이 되어 "어리석은 것"이라고 할 수 있지만(11:16-18) 자랑하는 사람의 의도에 따라서 육체적 자랑과는 다른 차원의 의미를 가질 수 있다. 바울의 고

---

213) 여러 학자들이 11:15-33의 부분에서 헬라식 패러디나 논쟁의 특징이 있음을 지적한다(Martin, 357-360을 보라). 그러나 디아스포라 유대교적 특징도 지적되었다(H. Thyen, *Der Stil der jüdisch-hellenistischen Homilie*, FRLANT 65 [Göttingen: Vandenhoeck & Ruprecht, 1955]; W. Bujard, *Stilanalystische Untersuchungen zum Kolosserbrief*, SUNT 11 [Göttingen: Vandehoeck & Ruprecht, 1973] 132, 221); K. T. Kleinknecht는 바울의 고난의 생애에 대한 자서전적 특징을 중시해야 한다고 주장한다(*Der leidende Gerechtfertigte*, 293).

214) J. Zmijewski, *Der Stil der paulinischen "Narrenrede,"* 17: 11:15-21을 "아이로니칼한 양보"라고 한다.

난과 약함의 자랑은 바울의 사역이 그리스도의 희생적인 사역의 유형을 따르는 것이며 자신의 유익이 아닌 남의 유익을 추구하는 희생적 사역이라는 것을 증거한다. 바울은 십자가의 희생적 정신을 따라서 사역하고 있다(4:2-15; 5:14-15, 20; 6:3-13; 11:10). 이렇게 말하면서 고린도 교인들의 신앙적 감성에 호소한다고 볼 수 있다.[215] 나아가 바울의 사역은 약한 것을 통해서 나타나는 하나님의 영광과 구원의 능력을 나타내는 사역이므로 죽음과 부활의 그리스도의 사역과 일치한다. 반대자들은 자신의 영광을 나타내는 사욕적인 사역을 함으로서 그리스도의 사역에 배치된다(고후 10:17, 18; 참조, 고전 1:29, 31). 그러므로 그들을 "가장된 사단의 일꾼들"이라고 정죄한 것이 타당하다는 암시가 있다(11:15). 본문에서 바울은 진실을 밝히기 위해서는 반대자들처럼 자기 자랑을 할 수 밖에 없는 입장이지만 자기와 반대자들은 아예 그 정체가 다르다는 것을 이미 말했으므로 양해해 달라고 부탁한다.

주석:

16. "내가 다시 말하노니 누구든지 나를 어리석은 자로 여기지 말라 만일 그러하더라도 나로 조금 자랑하게 어리석은 자로 받으라"(Πάλιν λέγω, μή τίς με δόξῃ ἄφρονα εἶναι· εἰ δὲ μή γε, κἂν ὡς ἄφρονα δέξασθέ με, ἵνα καγὼ μικρόν τι καυχήσωμαι). 이 구절은 11장 1절에서 "청컨대 나의 좀 어리석은 것을 용납하라"는 말을 반복하면서 10장 17, 18절에서의 "육체

215) M. M. DiCicco, *Paul's Use of Ethos, Pathos and Logos in 2 Corinthians 10-13*, Mellen Biblical Press Series 31 (Lewiston: Biblical Press, 1995), 78-9.

를 따라하는(κατὰ σάρκα) 자랑"과 "주를 따라하는(κατὰ κύριον) 자랑"(11:17="주 안에서[ἐν κυρίῳ]의 자랑", 10:17)의 대조적 주제를 다시 상기시킨다. 11장 1-15절을 "자랑의 주제"를 논하는 10장 18절과 11장 16절 사이의 연결을 방해하는 주제이탈(digression)로 보는 이들도 있다. 그러나 11장 1-15절은 같은 "자랑의 주제"를 더 효과적으로 설명하기 위해 필요한 진술이라고 볼 수 있다. 즉 10장에서의 "육체적 자랑"의 어리석음을 말한 후에 곧 이어서 자신의 "육체적 자랑" 즉 고난의 사역을 말하는 것보다는, 먼저 11장에서 그의 선한 정체(중매자)와 반대자들의 악한 정체를 밝힌 후에 자신의 "육체적 자랑"을 하는 것이 독자들의 오해를 줄이고 이해를 넓힐 수 있다고 보았기 때문이다. 같은 "육체적 자랑"이라도 말하는 사람이 누구냐에 따라서 그 의미가 다를 수 있기 때문이다.

바울은 역설적인 말로 시작한다. 자신을 어리석은 자로 여기지 말라고 하면서도 어리석은 말을 하겠다고 한다. 바울이 반대자들의 육체적 자랑을 어리석은 자랑이라고 말하면서도, 그 자신도 육체적 자랑"을 하는 것이 어리석다는 것을 잘 알고 있다. 그러나 반대자들의 공격에 맞서서 진실을 밝혀야 하는 사도적 책임이 있으므로, 어쩔 수 없이 반대자들과 같이 어리석게 자신에 대한 육체적 자랑을 할 수 밖에 없다는 것이다. 그러나 독자들이 결국 바울도 반대자들과 마찬가지로 어리석다고 생각하지 말아 달라는 것이다. 그가 말하려는 그의 고난의 사역에 대한 "육체적 자랑"은 반대자들의 것과 구별되어야 하기 때문이다. 그의 고난의 사역에 대한 자랑은 "주를 따라하는 타당한 주안에서의 자랑"이다(10:17, 18). 그의 고난의 사역이 겉으로는 "육체적 자랑"이라고 하겠으나, 실제로는 "주를 따라 하는 약한 것들에 대한 자랑"으로서,

이중적인 의미가 있다고 봐야 할 것이다.[216] 바울의 고난의 자랑은 반대자들의 육체적 자랑과는 질적으로 구별되는 자랑이라 하더라도 그의 고난의 자랑도 의도에 따라서는 육체적 자랑이 될 수 있음을 바울 스스로 인정하고 있다. 그러나 여기서 그의 진의는 그리스도의 사도로서 그리스도의 사역의 유형(죽음과 부활)을 따라 약한 가운데 나타나는 하나님의 능력을 증거 하기를 원한다. 자신의 "약한 것"을 자랑하여 사도의 진정성을 밝혀야할 사도적 책임이 있기 때문이다. 비록 자신에 대하여 자랑하지만, 독자들에게 진실을 밝혀야할 사도적 책임을 엄숙히 수행하는 것이다. 다시 말하면 바울은 지혜로운 자로서 어리석은 자처럼 행동해야하는 어려운 처지에 놓여 있음을 독자들이 이해하기를 바라는 것이다.

"조금 자랑하게"는 반대자들의 과장된 육체적 자랑에 비해서 그의 자랑은 약하다는 뜻도 있으나, 자신의 자랑을 늘어놓는 데 대해서 겸비하게 낮은 자세를 취하면서 청중의 양해를 구하는 수사학적 표현이라고 본다.[217] 즉 "제 반대자들이 자랑을 많이 하는데 나도 조금 하겠습니다."라는 식의 의미이다.

17. "내가 말하는 것은 주를 따라 하는 말이 아니요 오직 어리석은 자와 같이 기탄없이 자랑하노라"(ὃ λαλῶ, οὐ κατὰ κύριον λαλῶ ἀλλ᾽ ὡς ἐν ἀφροσύνῃ, ἐν ταύτῃ τῇ ὑποστάσει τῆς καυχήσεως.). 바울은 계속해서 그가 하려는 자랑에 대해서 독자들의 양해를 구한다. 그가 하려는 자랑은 우선 듣기에 "주를 따라

216) Thrall, 713.

217) Martin, 362.

하는 말이 아니요"(οὐ κατὰ κύριον λαλῶ) "육체를 따라 하는 말"이므로 어리석은 자랑 임을 인정한다. 그런 말을 하는 자신도 어리석은 자와 같다. "어리석은 자와 같이"(ὡς ἐν ἀφροσύνῃ)란 말이 가정의 뜻을 나타내고 있다. 그렇다고 해서 어떤 학자들이 제안하는 것과 같이 바울이 헬라 연극에서의 "바보의 역할"을 생각하고 있다는 것은 지나친 추론이다.[218] 트롤은 헬라 문화를 잘 아는 교부들의 해석 가운데 이런 제안을 볼 수가 없다고 지적한다.[219] 바울은 단순히 가정하는 것이다. 반대자들은 어리석은 자랑을 하지만, 자신은 단순히 그렇게 가정하고 말하는 것이며 실제 목적은 다른 데 있다는 것이다. 즉 연약함의 자랑(12:10)을 하기 위한 예비적인 발언인 것이다. 자신이 이제 하려는 말이 겉으로 듣기에 어리석은 자, 또는 반대자들의 말과 다를 게 없는 이기적인 내용임을 인정한다는 것이다. 그러나 실제로는 기독론적인 연약함의 자랑을 하기전의 예비적 진술이다(11:30).

"기탄없이 자랑하노라"라는 말은 문자적 번역인 "자랑의 이런 확신 가운데서 말하노라"([λαλῶ] ἐν ταύτῃ τῇ ὑποστάσει τῆς καυχήσεῶ)를 의역한 말인데, ὑπόστασις(후포스타시스)의 의미에 대해서 9장 4절에서 논의 한 바와 같이 논쟁이 있다. 전통적으로는 "확신"으로 번역해왔으나(NIV),[220] "일(matter)," "사업"이나 "계획", "의도", 또는 "실제", "실상"(히 1:11), 또는 "입장"으로 번

218) Windisch, 316; Betz, *Der Apostel Paulus und die sokratische Tradition*, 79-82; Wolff, 208-9.

219) Thrall, 712.

220) Meyer, 441; Plummer, 314; Barrett, 188.

역하는 예가 있다.[221] 어떤 번역이든지 전체의미에 영향을 주지는 않지만, 헤링이 제안하는 "입장"이란 의미가 가장 포괄적이면서도 문맥에 맞는다.[222] "이렇게 자랑하는 입장에서 말하노라" ("어리석은 자와 같이 말하노라")고 번역할 수 있다. 한글개역의 의역도 문맥과 우리 어감에 맞는다.

18. "여러 사람이 육체를 따라 자랑하니 나도 자랑하겠노라" (ἐπεὶ πολλοὶ καυχῶνται κατὰ σάρκα, κἀγὼ καυχήσομαι.). 바울은 10장에서 반대자들을 공격하면서 그들이 주님을 따라서 자랑하지 않고 육체를 따라서 자신들을 자랑한다고 하였다(10:12, 13, 17, 18; 11:22). 이들의 육체적 자랑의 내용이 재산, 출생신분, 조상, 성공, 외양적인 과시나 신유은사라는 제안들이 있다.[223] 이들의 자랑이 외양적이고 물질적인 것뿐만 아니라 내적이고 영적인 자랑도 포함한다는 제안이 옳다고 본다.[224] 또 이들의 사욕적인 자세도 육체적인 자랑으로 보았을 것이다. 바울은 언제나 고린도 교인들을 위해 희생하는 종으로서 섬기는 겸비한 자세로 사역하였음으로 오만한 반대자들과는 쉽게 구별된다(4:5; 10:12, 17). 자랑의 종류나 내용에 있어서 반대자들이 자랑하는 것들을 다 갖추지는 못했을 지라도, 바울도 그들에게 못지않은 것들을 갖추었음을 알릴 필요가 있다고 보았다. 이들의 자랑이 위장된 허위임을 들어내고 자신의 사역의 진실성을 증거하기 위해서는 어쩔 수 없

221) Martin, 363; Thrall, 714.

222) Héring, 82; Martin, 363.

223) Thrall, 715.

224) Zmijewski, "*Narrenrede*," 203-4.

이 육체를 따라 자랑할 수밖에 없다고 판단하였다. 무엇보다 그의 사역의 진실성은 고난 받으신 주님을 따르는 그의 희생적이고 헌신적인 복음사역에서 나타난다. 사도의 진정성은 죽으심과 부활을 중심으로 한 진정한 그리스도의 이해와 그리스도의 삶의 구현에 있다고 보았다(5:14; 6:3 이하). 육체를 따라 그리스도를 알고 따르며 사욕과 육체를 따라 자랑하는 것은 진정한 사도의 도리가 아니다. 그러나 반대파들이 자신들만이 육체적 자랑 거리가 있고 바울은 전무한 것처럼 선전하는 상황에서 바울은 자신에게도 육체적 자랑거리가 없는 것은 아니며 오히려 더 분명히 그리스도에 근접한 육체적 자랑거리가 있다고 생각하였다. 그것은 그가 누구보다도 그리스도의 고난에 많이 참여한 것이다(11:23 이하). 반대파들의 "육체적 자랑거리 목록" 에는 이 고난의 항목이 없음을 지적하려는 것이다. 이렇게 보아서 18절은 독자들에게 양해를 구하는 말도 되고, 반대자들을 냉소하는 말도 되지만, 그의 사도직에 대한 변명의 시작이다.

19. "너희는 지혜로운 자로서 어리석은 자들을 기쁘게 용납하는구나" (ἡδέως γὰρ ἀνέχεσθε τῶν ἀφρόνων φρόνιμοι ὄντες·). 이 구절은 앞의 구절에서 바울이 한 말, "여러 사람이 육체를 따라 자랑하니 나도 자랑하겠노라" 에 대한 고린도 교인들의 반응을 예측한 말로 볼 수 있다. 즉 바울은 18절의 말을 고린도 교인들이 읽으면서 아마도 잠언 26장 4-5절 같은 말을 상기하면서 '바울이 반대자들의 육체적 자랑을 어리석다고 비난하면서도, 자신도 그들을 따라 육체적 자랑을 하는 것이 또 다른 어리석음이 아닌가? 라고 반문할 수 있으리라고 생각했을 것이다. 바울은 고린도 교인들

의 이런 생각을 지혜로운 생각으로 인정한다. 그러나 그렇게 "지혜로운" 고린도 교인들이 어떻게 반대자들을 용납하는 어리석음을 범하였는가라고 바울은 그들을 냉소적으로 책망하고 있다. 이 구절을 이런 유대교의 지혜 전통에 따라서 해석할 수 있는 반면에, 헬라 지혜 전통을 따라서 해석할 수도 있다. 고린도 교인들이 스스로 지혜를 존중하는 헬라 문화 전통 가운데서 지혜로움을 자랑하면서도(고전 1:19, 3:18, 19, 4:19), 어리석게도, 육체적 자랑을 하는 어리석은 자들을 받아들이고 그들의 가르침을 따르고 있음을 책망하는 것이라고 볼 수 있다. 학자들은 고린도 교회의 지혜의 배경에 비추어 "지혜로운 자들"이란 말이 단순히 냉소적인 의미로 보지 않고 실제로 존재하는 "지혜 기독론"(wisdom christology)이나 아볼로파를 가리키는 것이라고 보기도 한다.[225)]

그러나 현재의 문맥에서 그 의미를 생각할 수도 있다. 이 구절은 앞서 11장 1절에서 "원컨대 너희는 나의 좀 어리석은 것을 용납하라"고 한 말을 연상케 한다. 거기서는 "현명하신 고린도 교인 여러분들께서 제가 하는 말이 좀 어리석게 보이더라도 양해해 주시기를 바랍니다"라는 냉소적인 의미가 암시되어 있다. 11장 4절에서는 여기서와 같이 분명하게 고린도 교인들이 반대자들의 "다른 예수, 다른 영, 다른 복음"을 용납하는 것을 책망하고 있다. 여기서는 "여러분들이 어리석은 자들의 어리석은 말까지도 들으시는 너그러우신 지혜로운 분들이라면 어리석은 저의 어리석은 말도 들어주시는 것이 당연하지 않습니까?"라는 냉소적 의미로 해석할 수

---

225) R. Richardson, "The Thunderbolt in Q and the Wise Man in Corinth," in *From Jesus to Paul*. FS. F. W. Beare(Waterloo, Ont.: Laurier University Press, 1984), 91-111. Martin 363에 재인용.

있다. 고린도 교인들이 이런 공정하고 합리적인 청원을 충분히 이해할 수 있는 지혜로운 분들이라고 냉소적으로 그들을 책망한다.

그러나 냉소적인 말로 고린도 교인들을 비판하는 것 자체가 바울의 중심 의도는 아니다. 그의 진심은 아무런 사욕 없이 중매하는 사람으로서 고린도 교인들을 위해 봉사하는 것이며, 또한 부모의 애타는 심정으로 고린도 교인들을 반대자들로부터 떠나게 하는 것이다(11:3; 12:14; 참조, 5:18; 7:2). 냉소적인 표현은 고린도 교인들을 깨우치기 위한 수사학적 기법이다. 냉소적 표현이 20절에도 계속된다.

20. "누가 너희로 종을 삼거나 잡아먹거나 사로잡거나 자고하다 하거나 뺨을 칠지라도 너희가 용납하는도다"(**ἀνέχεσθε γὰρ εἴ τις ὑμᾶς καταδουλοῖ, εἴ τις κατεσθίει, εἴ τις λαμβάνει, εἴ τις ἐπαίρεται, εἴ τις εἰς πρόσωπον ὑμᾶς δέρει.**). 19절에 이어서 바울은 계속하여 반대자들에 대한 고린도 교인들의 어리석은 자세를 질타한다. 그들의 어리석음은 반대자들의 무례하고 무리한 짓들도 참으면서 용납하는 데서 분명히 증명되었다고 냉소적인 책망을 한다. 바울은 고린도 교인들이 반대자들을 용납함을 냉소적인 말투로 책망하면서 자신이 하려는 육체적 자랑도 관용적인 자세로 들어주는 것이 마땅하다는 냉소적인 청원을 하고 있다. 한편, 어리석다고 자처하는 바울이 지혜로운 고린도 교인들의 어리석음을 지적하고 있으므로, 결국 바울이 어리석은 것이 아니라 고린도 교인들이 어리석은 것으로 나타나는 것이다. 이런 의미에서 이 구절은 18절과 함께 이중적 아이러니이다. 고린도 교인들이 지혜로운 자들로서 반대자들에게 어리석게 당하는 것이 아이러니이고, 어리석은

자(바울)에게 그들의 어리석음을 책망 받는 것이 또 다른 아이러니다. 바울은 여기서 자신이 자랑하려는 것이 어리석은 것임을 솔직히 인정한다. 그러나 특별한 입장 때문에 지혜로운 자이지만 어리석은 자로 이중적인 행세를 할 수 밖에 없다는 것이다(11:16).

"종으로 삼거나"는 반대자들의 사욕적 사역을 바울의 그리스도의 약함을 따르는 희생적 사역에 대조하는 말이다. 4장 5절에서 바울은 그가 고린도 교인들에게 그리스도의 주 되심과 고린도 교인들의 종 된 것을 전했다고 했는데, 그의 반대자들의 행대는 이와는 전혀 대조적이다. 자신들이 고린도 교인들의 주인이 되어 고린도 교인들을 종으로 삼아 무례하게 대했다. 이런 지도자들은 세상의 탐욕적이고 폭력적인 지도자들과 다를 바 없는 것이다. 그리스도 교회의 지도자는 그리스도의 종의 지도자의 본보기를 따르는 것이다(the Servant Leadership). 바울은 13장 5절 이하에서도 그리스도의 종으로서 문제가 되는 고린도 교인들을 법으로나 힘으로 다스릴 수 있는 사도권을 되도록 자제하면서 고린도 교인들이 스스로 믿음을 가지고 바르게 서기를 바란다고 말한다. 거짓 사도들의 행태는 앞서 바울이 지적한 그들의 거짓된 신분을 잘 들어내는 것이다(11:13). 문제는 이들의 행태를 고린도 교인들이 용납하였다는 것이다. 그러므로 이렇게도 너그러우신 분들이라면 자신의 어리석은 말도 참고 들어주는 것이 도리가 아니겠느냐라고 냉소적으로 말하고 있다.

"잡아먹거나" (κατεσθίει)는 반대자들의 물질적 수탈행위를 나타낸 말인데, 앞서 말한 재정적으로 교회에 의존하는 거짓 사도들의 사역과 바울의 독립적 희생적 사역을 대조적으로 암시한다고 볼 수도 있다(11:7-9; 12:14-15; 참조, 행 18:2; 20:33-35). 이 말은 다음의 "사로잡거나" (λαμβάνει)와 거의 같은 말이나, 이 말은 난폭한 의미를 가졌고 후자는 간교하게 속임수로 착취하는 의미가 있다.[226] 반대자들은 바울이 겉으로는 재정적 도움을 받지 않는 척 하면서도 "공교한 자가되어 궤계로" 고린도 교인들을 착취하였다고 비난했으나, 사실은 그 반대이다(12:16).

"자고하다고 하거나" (ἐπαίρεται)라는 말은 반대자들의 오만한 자세에 대한 표현이다(10:12). 그들은 육체적 자랑을 하는 사람들이었고(10:7, 10), 오만하게도 남의 영역에 들어 와서 남이 쌓은 수고를 가지고 자랑하며 사역하였다(10:13-16). 바울은 자신의 "분량의 한계" 를 따라 "주안에서" 자랑한다(10:13). 즉 그는 이방인의 사도로서 이방지역인 고린도에서 사역하는 것이다.

"뺨을 칠지라도" (εἰς πρόσωπον ὑμᾶς δέρει). 표면적 의미로는 앞에서 "종을 삼거나" 라는 말과 관련하여 종을 무례하게 대하는 것을 가리킨다. 그러나 실제적으로 반대자들이 고린도 교인들을 때렸다는 것을 가리키는 것인지, 암시적인 의미인지 분명하지 않다.[227] 크리소스톰은 비유적인 의미로서 이들이 권위 의식을 가지고서 고린도 교인들을 함부로 대했음을 의미한다고 보았다.[228] 바

226) Plummer, 319; Hughes, 400; Thrall, 717.

227) 실제 체벌을 했다는 이들이 있다: Windisch, 347; Tasker, 158; Bultmann, 213; Zmijewski, "*Narrenrede*," 212; Furnish, 497; Wolff, 228; Allo, 290-1(Thrall, 717, 주 443, 444, 재인용).

228) Chrysostom, NPNF, vol. XII, 392

울이 고린도전서 4장 21절에서 "내가 매를 가지고 너희에게 나아가랴"는 말을 직역으로 이해할 수 없는 것과 같다는 것이다. 트롤은 이 말이 반대자들의 오만한 행태에 내한 풍자적 패러디라고 한다.[229] 반대자들도 종교적인 지도자들인데 그런 사람들이 실제로 상대방의 빰을 때릴 수 있겠냐는 것이다. 그러나 유대교 전통에서 보면 이것도 가능하다. 종교지도자들이 상대방의 불경스런 말에 대해서 입을 치게 하기도 했다(행 23:2; 딤전 3:3; 딛 1:7). 예수님도 그런 말씀을 하셨고(마 5:39), 실제로 자신이 심문 받으면서 빰을 맞았다(**κολαφίζειν**, 마 26:67=고후 12:7).[230] 또 헬라 전통에서도 철학자들의 비열한 행위에 대해서 빰을 쳐서 경멸하는 경우가 있었다(*Life of Apollonius*, 7.23).

이런 행동들은 자체가 거짓 사도들의 오만함과 사욕을 가리킨다. 바울은 자신의 겸비함과 희생을 이미 지적했다(10:1). 그런 겸비함이 바로 그리스도의 겸비함이며, 희생이요, 약함이다(4:10; 6:3-10; 12:4). 이렇게 그리스도의 "형상"을 닮은 바울이야 말로 진정한 그리스도의 사도이다(3:18; 4:7이하).

21. "우리가 (지금까지 늘) 약하게 살아 온 것을 부끄럽게 말하노라(우리가 약한 것 같이 내가 욕되게 말하노라). 그러나 누가 무슨 일에 담대하면 어리석은 말이나마 나도 담대하리라" (**κατὰ ἀτιμίαν λέγω, ὡς ὅτι ἡμεῖς ἠσθενήκαμεν. Ἐν ᾧ δ' ἄν τις**

229) Thrall, 719.

230) 유대 전통에서 손등으로 상대방의 오른 빰을 치는 것은 매우 큰 모욕으로 여겨서 미쉬나에는 이런 행위에 대해 특별히 많은 벌금을 물도록 하게 하는 규정이 있다(*Baba Qamma*, 8.6). Martin, 365 재인용.

τολμᾷ, ἐν ἀφροσύνῃ λέγω, τολμῶ κἀγώ). 바울은 그를 반대하는 이들의 교만한 행동을 용납하는 고린도 교인들의 어리석은 지혜를 책망한 뒤에 다시 자신의 방어를 위한 변명으로 돌아온다. "우리가 (지금까지 늘) 약하게 살아 온 것을 부끄럽게 말하노라 (우리가 약한 것 같이 내가 욕되게 말하노라)" 는 말은 바울이 지금까지 약함의 사역을 해왔으나, 이제는 육체적 자랑을 하겠다는 말이다.[231] 개역한글성경의 "내가 욕되게 말하노라" (κατὰ ἀτιμίαν λέγω)는 "내가 부끄럽게 말하노라" 고 보다 쉽게 번역할 수 있다. "부끄러움이" ("욕")이 바울 자신의 부끄러움이 아니라 반대자들을 받아들인 고린도 교인들의 잘못을 가리킨다고 보는 견해도 있으나, 뒤에 "우리" 라는 말이 나오므로 바울 자신의 수치라고 보는 것이 타당하다.[232] 여기서 "부끄럽다" 는 말은 그가 육체적 자랑을 하기 때문에 부끄럽다는 뜻이 아니라 냉소적인 의미를 가지고 있다. 반대자들은 고린도 교인들에게 마음대로 횡포를 부리면서도 그들을 종으로 삼아 부리는데, 고린도 교회 설립자인 자신은 약해서 아무것도 하지 못하는 어리석은 자였으므로 부끄럽다는 것이다. 그러나 이제는 반대자들이 자신들의 능력을 자랑한다면 그도 담대하게 할 수 밖에 없다는 것이다. 다시 말하면 바울이 이제 약

231) 대부분의 학자들은 21절 상반절까지를 16절 이하에서 시작된 양보적인 문단으로 취급하고 21절 하반절을 바보의 연설의 시작으로 본다(Martin, 365; Thrall, 718). 그러나 22절에서 본격적인 자랑 또는 변명이 시작된다고 보면 21절 전체를 양보적 문단을 맺는 말로 볼 수 있다.

232) Chrysostom(NPNF, XII, 392)과 Lietzmann(149)은 고린도 교인들의 수치로 보지만, 대다수의 주석가들은 바울의 수치로 본다(Windisch, 348; Kümmel 211; Plummer 317; Allo, 290; Bachmann, 381; Furnish 497; Martin 366; Thrall 718).

함에서 벗어나서 갑자기 육체적 자랑을 할 수 밖에 없는 이유는 고린도 교인들이 육체적 자랑을 하는 거짓 사도들의 횡포를 마다하지 않고 그대로 받아들이고 그들을 따랐기 때문이라는 것이다. 그렇다면 자신도 한번 담대히 육체적 자랑을 하여 고린도 교인들을 다시 자기편으로 이끌어 오겠다는 것이다.

개역한글성경의 "우리가 약한 것 같이" (ὡς ὅτι ἡμεῖ ἠσθενήκαμεν)는 "우리가 지금까지 늘 약하게 살아 온 것처럼" 또는 "우리가 지금까지 늘 약하게 살아왔기 때문에"라는 의미로 앞의 말("내가 욕되게 말하노라")을 설명하는 것으로 볼 수 있으나, 희랍어 원문에서의 앞의 말("내가 욕되게 말하노라")의 목적절로 보아 "우리가 약해온 것을 부끄럽게 말하노라"라고 해석할 수도 있다.[233] 그러나 어떤 경우도 의미는 크게 다르지 않다. 트롤은 종합적으로 앞서 5장 19에서 ὡς ὅτι이 인용하는 말을 시작하는데 쓰인 예를 들어서, 여기서, "너희가 우리가 약하다고 말하는 것처럼(ὡς ὅτι)" 이라는 번역을 제안한다.[234] 그러나 주어가 바울이든 고린도 사람들이든지 전체 의미는 크게 달라지지 않는다. 바울이 약하다는 비난인가 아니면 바울 스스로 약하다고 보는가의 차이일 뿐이다. 전자의 경우 10장 10절에서 반대자들과 고린도 교인들이 바울을 약하다고 말한 사실이 뒷받침한다.[235] 후자의 경우 12장 10절에서 바울 자신이 그가 약하다고 말하고 있다. 바울이

---

233) Plummer 498; Kümmel 211; Hughes 401, 주 68; Barrett 176, 288; Furnish 485; Zmijewski 215.

234) Thrall, 720.

235) Bachamnn 381; Plummer 317; Hughes 401, Thrall, 721.

자신을 약하게 생각한다고 보는 것이 당장 다음에서 말하려는 바울의 고난의 사례와 관련하여 볼 때 보다 타당하다고 본다.[236] 한편, 이 말("우리가 약한 것 같이")은 우리가 위에서 언급한 바와 같이 바로 앞 절에서 언급한 반대자들이 고린도 교인들에게 행한 무례한 행위와 관련하여 해석할 수도 있다. "우리는 그런 행위를 하기에 너무 약했다"(To my shame, I must say, we were too weak for that!)라고 번역 할 수 있다(English Standard Version, 2001). 즉 우리는 너무 약해서 반대자들처럼 너희들을 막 다루지 못하여 너희들을 그들에게 빼앗겼다라고 빈정대는 의미라고 본다. 가까운 문맥에서는 이런 해석이 적절하다. 그러나 바울은 여기서 22절 이하에서 열거하려는 그의 모든 사역에서 나타난 고난의 경험을 염두에 두고 그의 사역 전체에서 그가 약했음을 의미하는 것이라고 볼 수도 있다. 즉, "우리가 지금까지 늘 약하게 살아 온 것을 부끄럽게 말하노라."

"그러나 누가 무슨 일에 담대하면 어리석은 말이나마 나도 담대하리라"(Ἐν ᾧ δ᾽ ἄν τις τολμᾷ, ἐν ἀφροσύνῃ λέγω, τολμῶ κἀγώ). 바로 앞에서 한 말("우리가 지금까지 늘 약하게 살아 바를 부끄럽게 말하노라.")과는 대조적으로, 반대자들이 담대하게 여러 가지 육체적 자랑을 하면서 자신들의 사도적 진정성을 주장한다고 하니, 나도 어리석은 줄 알지만 나의 육체적 자랑을 하겠다는 뜻이다. 아래에서 보듯이 바울의 육체적 자랑은 바울이 고난받은 사례이며 약한 면을 보여주고 있으나, 반면에 반대자들의 오

236) Zmijewski, 216-17.

만한 자랑처럼 11장 23절 이하에서 보듯이 자신이 고생한 것을 자랑하는 면이 있음을 인정하기 때문에 약하게 살아 온 것을 부끄럽다고 하는 앞의 말과는 대조적으로 강하게 말하고 있는 것이다. 그래서 이미 앞에서 바울은 자신이 하려는 말을 어리석은 자랑이라고 하면서 독자들의 양해를 부탁하였다(11:16-18). 즉 자랑인줄 알면서도 반대자들에 맞서야 하고, 또 그들에게 동조하는 고린도 교인들을 설득하기 위해서는 어쩔 수 없이 해야 하는 일종의 필요악(a necessary evil)이라는 것이다.[237] 바울은 이 연설의 끝에서 사실은 그의 사역으로 구원받은 고린도 교인들이 먼저 바울을 칭찬하고 변호했었다면 자신이 이런 어리석은 일을 하지 않았어도 됐었을 것이라고 자랑한 것을 후회스럽게 말한다(12:11). 그러나 그들이 침묵하였기 때문에 바울이 나서서 그를 공격하는 말에 능숙하고 자랑하기를 좋아하는 그의 반대자들을 향해서 자신을 칭찬할 수밖에 없다는 것이다. 이것 또한 그리스도의 왕권을 확립하고 교회를 세우도록 그리스도로부터 위임받은 바울 사도의 막중하고 어려운 책임이다(4:5; 10:5-6, 8; 13:10; 갈 4:19). 결국 이 구절에는 거짓 선지자들을 용납한 고린도 교인들에 대한 냉소적인 책망과, 이제 시작하려는 자신의 육체적 자랑의 당위성에 대한 변명이 함께 들어 있다.

주해(11:16-21):

11장 16-21절에서 바울은 구체적 사례를 들면서 반대자들의 공격에 맞서서 자신의 사도권의 정당성을 강변한다. 22절에서부터

---

237) Martin, 430.

시작되는 적극적인 자신의 사도권 방어를 하기 전에 16절에서부터 21절까지 냉소적인 어조로 고린도 교인들이 자신의 어리석은 육체적 자랑을 양해하고 들어달라고 부탁한다. 그들이 반대자들의 육체적 자랑과 무례한 자세를 받아들일 만큼 관대한 이들이므로 자신의 어리석은 자랑도 받아줄 수 있다고 믿는다고 냉소적으로 말한다. 바로 앞에서(1-15) 바울은 이미 반대자들의 정체는 "사단의 일꾼들" 임을 폭로했다. 그 보다 더 앞서서(10장) 이들이 육체적 자랑을 하는 이들임을 지적했다. 그들은 타 지역(아마도, 예루살렘)에서 바울의 선교지인 고린도 지역에 들어 온 이들로서(3:1; 10:16; 11:22) 예수의 말씀과 행적을 익히 아는 이들이었고, 그러므로 역사적 예수에 대한 그들의 지식을 자랑하였던 것으로 보인다. 그리고 아마 표적과 기사의 능력을 가진 것으로 보인다(12:12). 그러나 바울은 5장 16절에서 이미 "우리는 더 이상 육체를 따라 그리스도를 알지 아니한다" 고 선언했다. 우리가 "과거의 예수에 대한 지식" 만으로는 진실한 그리스도인이 될 수 없다. 오늘 우리가 그리스도 안에서 새로운 피조물이 되어 그리스도의 형상을 따라 살아야 진실한 그리스도인이 되는 것이다(5:17; 3:18). 이런 실존적 의미의 그리스도의 이해를 따라서 바울은 반대자들의 모든 "육체적 자랑" 을 거부하고 "주 안에서의 자랑" 을 제안했다(10:17). 이제 바울은 "주 안에서의 자랑," 즉 "그의 고난 받은 자랑," 또는 "그의 약한 것들의 자랑" 을 하려고 한다(11:30; 12:9, 10). 그리스도인의 진정한 판단 기준은 그리스도의 겸비한 인격과 행동뿐이다. 그러나 이런 그리스도 중심적 자랑 조차 또 하나의 "육체적 자랑" 이 될 수 있음을 인정한다. 이런 진실한 자랑도 그 자랑하는 사람의 자만심을 야기 시킬 수 있기 때문이다(12:7). 그래서 바울은 미리 고린도 교인들의 양해를 구하는 것이다. 사실 바울은 이런 자랑 하기를 원하지 않았다. 다만 고린도 교인들이 반대자들의 자랑에 미혹되어, 바울을 오히려 비정통적인 사도로 오해하고, 진실한 복음에서 떠나기 때문에, 원치 않는 자랑을 하여서라도 바울 자신은 억울한 누명을 벗고 고린도 교인들은 오해를 풀고 화해하기를 원하였던 것이다. 그러나 바울은 외견상 반대자들의 육체적인 자랑과 다를 바 없는 그의 자랑을 반대자들의 자랑과 구별할 것이다. 즉 반대자들은 강한 것들만을 자랑하나 자신은 강한 것들뿐만이 아니라 약한 것들과 부끄러운 것들도 자랑하기 때문이다(12:9-10). 그러나 바울은 당장은 반대자들의 육체적 자랑에 맞서서 자신의 육체적 자랑을 할 수 밖에 없다고 생각한다. 자신의 진정한 내적 사도적 증거(즉 "약한 것들의 자랑")를 제시하기 전에, 외적 사도적 증거를 고린도 교인들에게 제시하여 우선 그들이 바울을 적어도 그들이 따르는 거짓 사도들과 외견상으로는 같은 수준의 사도로 인정하기를 원한다. 그러나 실제로는 바울의 외적 증거가 복음 사역을 하면서 고난 받은 사례들이므로 그 외적 증거조차 "약한 것"이 된다. 사도로서 자신의 권능으로 고난을 피하지 못하고 고난을 당한 것이라고 비난받을 수 있다. 그러나 바울은 바로 그 "약한 것"이 진정한 그리스도의 사도의 증거라고 자랑하는 것이다(11:30). 그러나 그의 "약한 것"의 자랑은 인간적 오만함이 아니라 그리스도를 통해 주시는 하나님의 능력에 의지하는 진정한 겸비함의 표현이다(12:9,10). 즉 주안에서의 자랑이다(10:17).

2. 거짓 사도들의 자천에 대한 바울의 자천(11:22-12:10)

본 문:

22. 저희가 히브리인이냐 나도 그러하며 저희가 이스라엘인이냐 나도 그러하며 저희가 아브라함의 씨냐 나도 그러하며 23. 저희가 그리스도의 일꾼이냐 정신없는 말을 하거니와 나도 더욱 그러하도다 내가 수고를 넘치도록 하고 옥에 갇히기도 더 많이 하고 매도 수없이 맞고 여러 번 죽을뻔 하였으니 24. 유대인들에게 사십에 하나 감한 매를 다섯 번 맞았으며 25. 세 번 태장으로 맞고 한 번 돌로 맞고 세 번 파선하는데 일주야를 깊음에서 지냈으며 26. 여러 번 여행에 강의 위험과 강도의 위험과 동족의 위험과 이방인의 위험과 도시에서의 (시내[市內])의 위험과 광야의 위험과 바다의 위험과 거짓 형제 중의 위험을 당하고 27. 또 수고하며 애쓰고 여러 번 자지 못하고 주리며 목마르고 여러 번 굶고 춥고 헐벗었노라 28. 이 외의 일은 고사하고 오히려 날마다 내 속에 눌리는 일이 있으니 곧 모든 교회를 위하여 염려하는 것이라 29. 누가 약하면 내가 약하지 아니하며 누가 실족하게 되면 내가 애타하지 않더냐 30. 내가 부득불 자랑할진대 나의 약한 것을 자랑하리라 31. 주 예수의 아버지 영원히 찬송할 하나님이 나의 거짓말 아니 하는 줄을 아시느니라 32. 다메섹에서 아레다 왕의 방백이 나를 잡으려고 다메섹 성을 지킬 새 33. 내가 광주리를 타고 들창문으로 성벽을 내려가 그 손에서 벗어났노라. (고린도후서 12장) 1. 무익하나마 내가 부득불 자랑하노니 주의 환상과 계시를 말하리라 2. 내가 그리스도의 안에 있는 한 사람을 아노니 십 사년 전에 그가 셋째 하늘에 이끌려 간 자라 (그가 몸 안에 있었는지 몸 밖에 있었는지 나는 모르거니와 하나님은 아시느니라) 3. 내가 이런 사람을 아노니 (그가 몸 안에 있었는지 몸 밖에 있었는지 나는 모르거니와 하나님은 아시느니라) 4. 그가 낙원으로 이끌려가서 말할 수 없는 말을 들었으니 사람이 가히 이르지 못할 말이로라 5. 내가 이런 사람을 위하여 자랑하겠으나 나를 위하여는 약한 것들 외에 자랑치 아니하리라 6. 내가 만일 자랑하고자 하여도 어리석은 자가 되지 아니 할 것은 내가 참말을 함이라 그러나 누가 나를 보는 바와 내게 듣는 바에 지나치게 생각할까 두려워하여 그만 두노라 7. 여러 계시를 받은 것이 지극히 크므로 너무 자고하지 않게 하시려고 내 육체에 가시 곧 사단의 사자를 주셨으니 이는 나를 쳐서 너무 자고하지 않게 하려 하심이니라 8. 이것이 내게서 떠나기 위하여 내가 세 번 주께 간구하였더니 9. 내게 이르시기를 내 은혜가 네게 족하도다 이는 내 능력이 약한데서 온전하여짐이라 하신지라 이러므로 도리어 크게 기뻐함으로

> 나의 여러 약한 것들에 대하여 자랑하리니 이는 그리스도의 능력으로 내게 머물게 하려함이라 10. 그러므로 내가 그리스도를 위하여 약한 것들과 능욕과 궁핍과 핍박과 곤란을 기뻐하노니 이는 내가 약할 그 때에 곧 강함이니라.

본문 비평:

1. 28절에서 ἐπίστασίς가 p46 ℵ B D F G에서, 동의어이지만 더 강한 어조의 ἐπισύστατις가 K L M P에서 나타난다. 그리고 μοι(p46 ℵ* B)가 μου(ℵ2 D ψ TR lat Ambrosiaster)보다 더 강한 어조를 준다. μου로 되는 경우 바울이 남에게 압박을 준다는 의미가 되어 문맥상 적절치 않다.[238)]

2. 32절에서 θέλων이 με 뒤에 첨부된 곳이 많으나(ℵ D2 ψ syrh bo TR), 없는 것이 원문이라고 본다. 이 말은 아레다 왕의 방백이 바울을 잡으려고 "의도했으나" 실패했음을 강조하려고 첨부된 것으로 보인다.[239)] 마틴은 보다 부드러운 문장을 만들기 위해 첨부된 것으로 본다.[240)]

3. 12장 1절에서 ℵ2 H vg등 소문자 사본(MSS)에는 καυχᾶσθαι 앞에 εἰ가 나타난다. 또 ℵ D2 ψ bo에는 δεῖ 대신에 δέ가 나타난다. 복사자가 마지막 이오타를 빠뜨린 것이다.[241)] 또 δεῖ 대신에 δή가 나타나는 사본들도 있다(K Athanasius Chrysostom). 이것은 유사

---

238) Martin, 368.

239) Thrall, 763, 주 764.

240) Martin, 368.

241) Hughes, 428, 주 97.

한 모음으로 인한 오류로 추정된다.[242] 그러나 같은 이유로 생각하여 δή가 δεῖ보다 원래의 것이라고 할 수도 있다.[243] 메츠거(Metzger)는 δεῖ로 기록하는 Nestle-Aland를 지지한다.[244] 휴즈와 빈디쉬는 원본이 훼손됐다고 본다.[245]

συμφέρον 대신에 συμφέρει가 D*에 나타난다. 또 συμφέρον μοι가 D¹ H ψ it vg 에 나타난다. γάρ가 D ψ syr에, δέ καὶ가 B에 나타난다.

4. 4절에 ἐκτός가 ℵ D² F G H ψ 0243에 나타나는데, 2절의 영향으로 추가된 것으로 보이며, χωρίς가 p⁴⁶ B D*에만 나타나지만, 원래 있던 것으로 보인다.[246]

5. 5절에 μου가 p⁴⁶ B D* 0243에는 없지만, A D* F G y Ambrosiaster에서 ταῖς ἀσθενείαις 뒤에 나타난다. 우리의 본문에 μου가 없지만 전체 의미를 위해 있는 것으로 보고 번역한다.

6. 6절에 θέλω가 p⁴⁶에 나온다. τι가 p⁴⁶ ℵ² D* ψ 0243 vg Ambrosiaster를 따라서 Nestle-Aland 판에 괄호 안에 넣어 나온다. τι가 있는 것이 어색하므로 τι가없는 α* B D² G cop^sa,bo^의 기록이 원래의 것으로 보인다.[247]

---

242) Martin, 389.

243) Hughes, 428, 주 97.

244) Metzger, *Textual Commentary*, 584

245) Hughes, 428, 주, 97; Windisch, 367.

246) Metzger, 585.

247) Metzger, 585.

7. 7절의 시작부분("여러 계시를 받은 것이 지극히 크므로", **καὶ τῇ ὑπερβολῇν τῶν ἀποκαλύψεων**)을 앞의 6절에 붙여서 결론적 진술로 읽어야 하느냐(이 경우, "여러 계시를 받은 것이 지극히 크다"로 번역해야 함) 아니면 새로운 문단을 시작하는 문장으로 볼 것인가에 대한 논쟁이 있다.[248] 이 문장 다음에 나오는 **διό**는 p[46] D ψ it vg syr copsa에는 나오지 않으나 ℵ A B G 33 81 1739의 지지를 받고 있으며, 또한 "보다 어려운 말이 보다 신빙성이 있다"(*difficior lectio potior*)는 원칙에 따라서 원래 있던 것으로 본다.[249] 그러나 **διό**가 전 후 어느 문장에 붙어야하는가에 대한 이견이 있다. 7절 시작하는 문장에 붙어야 한다는 의견은 **διό**는 흔히 새 문장을 시작하는 말이므로 7절의 앞부분은 6절에 붙여서 결론적 진술로 보아야 한다고 본다.[250] 그러나 **διό**를 7절 전체의 이유를 말하는 절 앞에서 이유를 강조하면서 7a와 7b를 연결한다고 보아도 무리가 없다.[251] 어떤 경우에도 문장의 의미는 같다. 문장의 끝에 있고, 두 번째로 나오는 **ἵνα μὴ ὑπεραίρωμαι**은 ℵ* A D F G 33같은 소문자 사본에는 없으나 p[46] B ψ 81 1739 syr cop goth arm에는 나온다. 원래 있던 것인데, 되풀이할 필요가 없다고 보고 어떤 복사자가 삭제한 것으로 본다.

8. 9절에서 **ἡ γαρ δύναμις μου**라고 보다 후기의 ℵ[2] A[2] D[2] ψ

---

248) Martin, 389.

249) Metzger, 585, Hughes 448, 주 138.

250) Zmijewski, 354; Furnish, 528; Martin, 389.

251) Hughes, 449, 주, 138.

0243 syrbo 같은 소문자 사본과 TR(Textus Receptus)에 나오나, 초기의 사본들인 p^{46vid} ℵ* A* B D* F G it vg cop goth eth에는 μου가 없다. 앞에 있는 ἡ χαρις μου를 따라서 의미를 분명히 하기 위해서 μου가 추가된 것처럼 보인다.[252] τελειοῦται가 ℵ^2 D^2 E K L P에 나오나 τελεῖται가 보다 신빙성이 있는 사본 ℵ* A B D* F G에 나온다.

9. 10절에 p^{46} ℵ*에 καί가 ἀνάγκαις앞에 나온다. 본문의 καί στενοχωρίαις가 p^{46vid} ℵ* B 104 326 1175 1838에 의해 지지받는다. καί ἐν이 0243 630 1739 1881에, ἐν이 ℵ^2 A D G K P ψ 33 614 1241에 나온다. 이 모두 바로 앞에 있는 ἐν이 있는 구와 연결되는 문장으로 후에 다듬은 것으로 보인다.[253]

내용 개요:

바울은 어려운 고린도 교회 사태를 방관만하면서 막연히 잘 해결되리라고 생각하지 않는다. 긴 "바보의 연설"(11:22-12:10)에서 그의 사도직의 진정성을 적극적으로 방어한다. 그의 사도직의 진정성의 구체적 증거를 제시한다. 그 증거는 (그를 반대하는 거짓 사도들에 비해서) 그가 많은 고난을 겪었다는 사실이다(참조, 고전 15:10). 그의 고난은 단순한 고난이 아니라 그리스도와 그의 교회를 위한 지극한 사랑의 증거이며 따라서 진정한 사도적 증거로

252) Metzger, 585.

253) Metzger, 586.

제시하고 있다.[254] 이미 앞에서도 그의 고난을 그리스도의 고난에 빗대어 말하였고(4, 5, 6장), 아래 12장 10절에서도 그가 받은 고난을 그리스도를 위한 것으로 말하고 있다. 그러나 바울은 이런 고난 외에 다른 고난을 더 추가 한다. 그래서 계속해서 다메섹 아레다 왕에게서 도망하면서 광주리를 타고 들창문으로 빠져 나간 사실을 말한다. 또한 삼층천에 올라갔던 그의 영적 체험에도 불구하고(12:1-4) 그의 "육체의 가시" 곧 "사단의 사자"가 있음을 계속해서 지적한다(12:7-8). 즉 그의 약함을 그가 받은 많은 고난위에, 다메섹에서의 망신적인 경험과, 고질적인 그의 육체적 병을 언급함으로써 점증적으로 보충강화 한다. 무엇보다 이런 고난의 사역이 그리스도의 고난의 사역의 유형에 잘 맞는다는 것을 암시한다. 반대자들의 사역은 주로 영광과 능력을 강조하는 사역이지만 바울의 사역은 고난으로 점철된 사역이다. 이렇게 바울은 그리스도의 약함의 능력을 신학뿐만 아니라 실제 사역에 적용하여 설명함으로써 자신의 사도직의 진정성을 증명한다.

"바보의 연설"은 매우 조심스럽게 논리적으로 짜여 있다. 학자들 마다 조금씩 차이는 있으나 대개 11장 22-33절을 전반부로 보고, 12장 1-10을 후반부로 본다. 준더만(Sundermann)은 "바보의 연설"을 11장 23b-33절, 12장 1-7a절, 12장 7b-10절의 세부분으로 나누어서, 마지막 부분이 약함을 강조하는 말로 맺고 있다고 지적

254) 바울의 고난 이야기(Peristasenkataloge, 또는 Hardship-lists)는 그리스-로마 문화권에서 흔한 문학 장르에 속한다. 예로 푸르다크의 영웅전이나 호머의 오딧세이 같은 특별한 인물의 고난의 여정이 있다. M. Ebner, *Leidenslisten und Apostelbrief. Untersuchungen zu Form, Motivik und Funktion der Peristasenkataloge bei Paulus*, FB 66 (Würzburg: Echter Verlag, 1991).

했다.[255] 바울은 전반부를 시작하기 전에 11장 16-21절에서 독자들의 오해를 불식시키기 위해 바울 자신이 육체적 자랑의 어리석음을 알고 있음을 거듭 강조하고 있고, 전반부(11:22-33절)가 시작되는 22절부터 자신의 신분을 밝히면서 23-29절에서는 고난의 목록을 제시한다. "수고" 같은 일반적인 사례에서 죽음의 위험 같은 심각한 사례로 옮아가는 점층법을 써서 고난의 경험을 강화시킨다.[256] 점층적 효과를 높이기 위해서 헬라어 음절을 적절히 정리하여 사용하고 있다는 견해도 있다. 즉 22절의 Ἑβραῖοί에서 세 개의 음절이 23절에서는 διάκονοι Χριστοῦ로 여섯 개의 음절로 나타난다는 것이다.[257] 몇 개의 같은 희랍어가 반복되어 나타나고 또 다섯 번, 세 번, 한 번 등의 숫자도 점증적 효과를 높인다.[258] 명사가 둘씩 짝지어 나온다.[259] 이외에 과거 시제의 반복적 사용과 대화체가 바울의 일생을 드라마틱하게 나타낸다고 한다.[260] 이런 바울의 일생에 대한 회고가 진실임을 하나님께 맹세하는 말로 나타냄으로서 전체 진술의 진정성을 강화하고 있다(31). 11장 마지막의 다메섹에서의 도피의 이야기는 바울의 사도적 신분에 맞지 않는 부끄럽고 우스꽝스러운 에피소드로서 바울의 신분과 사역의 낮고 천한 단면을 솔직하게 보여주고 있다. 12:1-10에서는 약함과

255) H. G. Sundermann, *Kraft der Rede*, 135-6.

256) Thrall, 734.

257) Zmijewski, 254; 주 166; cf. E. A. Judge, "Paul's Boasting in Relation to Contemporary Professional Practice," *ABR* 16(1968)," 48-50.

258) K. T. Kleinknecht, *Der leidnde Gerechtfertigte*, 288에서 더 자세한 희랍어 사용을 보라.

259) Fridrichsen, 27; W. Bujard, *Stilanalystische Untersuchungen zum Kolosserbrief*, SUNT 11 (Göttingen: Vandenhoeck & Ruprecht, 1973), 187; Zmijewski, 263.

260) A. T. Robinson, *Grammar*, 896, 897; Windisch, 350.

강함을 나타내는 병행구(2, 3절), 대조귀(chiasmus, 7절 하반절)로 구성되어 있고, 역설적 논지가 지배적이다. 이러한 역설, 아이러니, 수사학적 비교 등의 모든 표현법은 결국 "바보의 연설"의 주제인 "약한 가운데 강함"의 큰 역설적 진리를 가리키도록 적절히 배정되었다고 본다. 이렇게 "바보의 연설"이 결국 논리적으로 짜임새 있고, 청중에게 도전적인 언어와 수사법으로 이루어져 있으며, 구조적으로도 "약함의 주제"를 강조하도록 구성되어 있음을 보여 준다.

"바보의 연설" 전반부(11:22-23)에서 바울은 그가 고난을 받은 사실을 예로 들면서 "육체적 자랑"을 하며 사도직을 변명한다. 후반부(12:1-10)도 그의 영적 체험의 자랑으로 시작되지만(12:1-4) 결국 "육체적 자랑"을 포기하면서 도리어 "자신의 약함"을 자랑한다. 자신의 약함을 통해서 나타나는 하나님의 능력의 역사를 강조하며 결론 짓는다. 그러면서 바울은 그가 진정으로 원하는 것은 "자신의 육체적 자랑"(즉 고난 받은 것)이 아니라 "자신의 약함을 통해 나타나는 하나님의 능력"이라는 것을 강조한다(12:9-10). 사실 12장 1-4절의 삼층천의 체험을 제외한 그의 모든 "육체적 자랑"은 결국 그의 약함을 들어낸 것들이다. 여기서 바울은 자신이 받은 고난을 자신의 약함과 동일시하는 것처럼 보인다. 헬라 철학자들도 고난의 인내를 자신들의 도덕적 가치로 생각했다.[261] 그렇

261) Epictetus, *The Discouses*. 1:11, 33; 18, 22; 11:19, 24; Seneca, *Letters*, 411.4; 82.14; Bultmann, *Der Stil der paulinischen Predigt und die kynisch-stoische Diatribe*, FRLANT 13 (Gtötingen: Vandenhoech & Ruprecht, 1910), 19, 71-80; A. Bonhöffer, *Epiktet und das Neue Testament* (Giessen: Töpelmann, 1911; 1964 reprint), 301; J. Zmijewski, *Der Stil der paulinischen "Narrenrede," Analyse der Sprachgestaltung in 2 Kor 11, 1-12, 10*

다면 그의 고난은 육체적 자랑거리임과 동시에 약한 것들의 자랑거리도 된다. 그의 고난은 4장 16절에서 언급한 바울의 외적 인간 존재("겉사람")가 해체당하는 고통이라고 할 수 있다. 그런 인간 해체의 고통을 통해서 바울의 내적 인간 존재("속사람")는 성장하고 영광의 날을 기다린다(4:16-5:10). 더구나 하나님은 고난 가운데서도 현실적 승리를 주시면서 장래의 영원한 승리를 확신케 하신다. 즉 1장과 2장에서의 하나님의 위로 승리, 4장 7-15절에서 말하는 연약한 질그릇 같은 존재를 통해 나타나는 복음의 능력, 그리고 6장 4-10절에서 말하는 고난을 통한 승리의 경험과 같은 것이다. 그러나 바울은 자신의 약한 것들을 자신의 공로로서 자랑하기 위해서가 아니라 하나님의 섭리와 역사의 특성을 찾기 위해 말한다(4:8-10; 6:4-10; 고전 4:10-13; 롬 8:35-9). 아무리 "약함의 자랑"이라 할찌라도 결국 반대자들이 주장하는 육체적 자랑의 다른 유형에 불과하다는 비판을 의식하기 때문이다. 그래서 바울은 그의 약함의 자랑을 반대자들의 자랑과 구별하고 있다. 그는 자랑을 하기 전에 독자들의 오해를 미리 감지하고서 길게 변명하였다(11:16-21). 약함의 자랑 조차 "주를 따라 말하는 것이 아니라" 면서

---

als Beitrag zur Methodik von Stiluntersuchungen neutestamentlicher Text, BBB 52 (Köln-Bonn: Hanstein, 1978), 322; A. Fridrichsen, "Zum Stil des paulinschen Peristansenkatalogs. 2 Cor 11,23ff." *SO* 7 (1928), 25-29; "Peristasenkatalog und res gestae: Nachtrag zu 2 Cor. 11, 23ff." *SO* 8 (1929), 78-82; Kümmel, 211; J. Jervell, *The Unknown Paul*, Chap. 5: "The Signs of an Apostle," ETr. R. A. Harrisville (Minneapolis: Augsburg, 1984), 436; Thrall, 755-758: 푸르타크의 알렉산더 대왕의 고난과 비난에 대한 자세 등에서 바울의 고난과 반응을 비교하고 있다. 특히 주후 14년에 오거스터스 황제가 죽었을 때 그의 묘지 기둥 앞에 그의 공적 내용을 청동판에 Res Gestae 라고 새겼는데, 그 내용과 어조와 단어가 11:22-29과 매우 흡사하다고 하는 A. Fridrichesen의 견해를 소개한다.

그의 어리석음을 자인한다(11:17). 그리고 자랑의 결론 부분에서 그가 한 모든 자랑에 대해서 억지로 한 것이라고 말하고 있다(12:11). 무엇보다 "약함의 자랑"은 자신의 주관적 주장이 아니라 하나님의 객관적인 계시의 말씀에 근거한 것이라는 것이다(12:9). 바울은 하나님께서는 자신이 "자고하는 것"을 원치 않으심을 잘 알고 있다(12:7). 그러므로 바울이 진정으로 원하는 것은 "약함의 자랑"이 아니라 그의 약함을 통해서 온전케 하시는 전능하신 하나님을 높이고 증거하는 것이다. 즉 기독론적 구원 역사에 초점을 맞추고 있다. 물론 이런 하나님의 사역이 자신의 사역을 통해 나타나므로 자신이 진정한 그리스도의 사도라는 사실을 나타내는 것도 바울의 중요한 목적이다. 그러나 그것도 하나님의 능력에 의지하여 얻게 되는 것이다(2:14; 4:7-15; 6:4-10; 13:4). 그는 십자가의 희생적 그리스도의 모본을 따라서 언제나 고린도 교인들의 유익을 위해 일하지만(4:5, 12, 15; 12:19), 이 보다 그리스도의 주권을 중시한다(5:15; 갈 1:10). 그의 약함이란 하나님과 그리스도의 사랑과 은혜와 능력이 나타나는 수단이다. 약함을 통해 그리스도의 능력을 나타남을 믿는 것이 주께 복종하는 자세이며, "주안에서의 자랑"하는 자세이다(10:5, 6, 17). 하나님과 그리스도의 주권에 순종하지 않는 "약함의 자랑"은 진정한 약함이 아니며, 또 하나의 오만한 "육체적 자랑"에 불과하기 때문이다. 그러나 그의 "약함" 통해서 나타나는 하나님의 능력을 증거하기 위해서 바울은 어쩔 수 없이 "바보의 연설," 즉 "나의 약함의 자랑"을 할 수 밖에 없는 역설적인 입장에 있었다.

"바보의 연설"의 후반부(12:1-10)에서 바울은 자신의 신비한 경험을 하지만 곧 이어서 고질적인 육체의 가시를 말함으로써 의도적으로 자랑하는 것이 아님을 거듭 밝힌다. 그러나 적어도 지금까지 자신만이 알고 있던 내적 경험을 밝히는 것은 그의 반대자들이 그가 신령한 체험이 부족하다고 비판하였기 때문에 이에 대해서 "나도 그런 경험이 있으나, 자고하지 않으려고 공개하지 않고 나만의 경험으로 알고 있었을 뿐이라" 고 말한다. 그러므로 삼층천 경험은 바울의 "육체적 자랑" 이지만 "약한 것의 자랑" 이라는 큰 주제를 위한 예비적 진술인 것이다. 이런 영적 경험은 오히려 반대자들이나 자랑하는 것이며 진실한 그리스도인은 이런 경험을 자신의 내적 경험으로 숨기며 약함 가운데 승리하신 그리스도를 따라서 오히려 자신의 약함을 자랑할 것이다(13:3-5).[262] 이미 12장 1절에서 이점을 밝혔고 12장 1-10절 전체에서도 이를 거듭 강조한다. 3층천 체험에서 자신을 "한 사람" 이라고 3인칭으로 나타내는 것은 이 경험의 초월적인 특성을 나타낸다. 동시에 이 경험이 자신에게서 난 주관적인 것이 아니라 하나님이 주신 객관적인 경험임을 나타낸다.[263] 이 경험의 객관성에 대한 강조는 2절과 3절에 "나는 모르거니와 하나님은 아시느니라" 라는 반복되는 말 가운데에서도 나타난다. 이런 강조는 반대자들이 자랑하는 유사한 초월적 경험의 진위 여부에 대해서도 고린도 교인들이 마땅히 점검해야할 것을 촉구하는 것이다. 반대자들은 가장된 거짓 사도들로서 그들의 자랑하는 초월적 경험은 다분히 주관적이고 허황되거나 거짓된 환상임을 암시하는 것이다(11:13-14). 반대로 바울은 그의 "몸의 가시" 를 언급함으로서 그의 영적 자랑을 약화시킨다. 계속해서 그의 약함이 하나님의 능력이 되는 신비함을 강조한다. 이 신비함은 곧 그

262) Käsemann, *Die Legitimität*, 64.

263) J. Dunn, *Jesus and the Spirit* (Philadelphia: Westminster Press, 1975), 214, 215.

리스도의 죽으심과 부활의 신비함을 암시하며, 따라서 순수한 하나님의 능력이다. 이렇게 바울의 약함 가운데 나타난 하나님의 능력이 그의 사도직의 진정성을 강력히 증거한다. 이렇게 보면 바울의 몸의 가시는 전혀 예상치 않은 방법으로 고통 대신 기쁨이 된 것이다. 결과적으로 바울은 가시의 고통을 받으면서도 그 고통에 의해 지배받지 않고 벗어난 것이다. 역설적으로 바울은 약하나 강한 것이다. 이 역설적인 현상은 그리스도의 죽음과 부활에서 나타난 하나님의 능력과 같다.[264] 그러므로 바울은 진정한 그리스도의 사도이다. 육체적 자랑에만 몰두하는 반대자들에게는 이런 역설적 증거가 전혀 없다. 그러므로 그들은 거짓 사도들이다(11:13-15).

주석:

a. 나도 히브리인이다 (11:22).

22. "저희가 히브리인이냐 나도 그러하며 저희가 이스라엘인이냐 나도 그러하며 저희가 아브라함의 씨냐 나도 그러하며" (Ἑβραῖοι εἰσιν; καγώ. Ἰσραηλῖταί εἰσιν; καγώ. σπέρμα Ἀβραάμ εἰσιν; καγώ). 이 구절은 반대자들이 말하는 세 가지 "육체적 자랑"을 인용한다고 본다. 이 말은 그들이 유대인들이란 사실을 입증한다. 반대파들이 자신들이 유대인임을 강조한 것은 그들이 복음의 근원지인 팔레스틴 유대인들이며, 말씀의 목격자들로서 예수를 나중에 믿게 된 바울 보다 더 정통적 복음을 전한

264) Güttgemanns, *Der leidende Apostel und sein Herr* (Göttingen: Vandenhoeck & Ruprecht, 1966), 170.

다고 자랑하기 위한 것일 수 있다.[265] 바울은 이들의 유대인 우월주의에 대한 더 자세한 이유를 덮어 두고, 단순히 유대인임을 나타내는 이 세 가지 자랑에 대해서 세 번 "나도 그러하다"(κἀγώ)라는 말로 자신도 유대인이므로 그들과 대등함을 주장한다. 그들의 이런 육체적 자랑만으로는 자신을 압도 할 수 없다는 뜻이다. 바울은 점증적 효과를 나타내기 위해서 이런 육체적 신분은 다음 절에 나오는 "그리스도의 일꾼"이라는 근본적 신분에 비해 보다 가치가 낮은 신분으로 보고 미리 언급하고 있다. 그러나 바울 자신이 이 세 가지 유대 민족과 관련된 칭호가 "그리스도의 일꾼"이 되기 위한 의미 있는 조건으로 보는 것도 분명하다. 구원은 택함받은 이스라엘 백성으로 말미암기 때문이다(창21:12; 롬9:4이하). 세 가지 신분은 광범위 한 개념에서 보다 구체적인 개념으로 기록되었고 결국 하나님의 계속된 구원역사의 시각에서 "그리스도의 일꾼"이라는 최종적 신분과 관련지어 보아야 한다. 반대파들이 자랑하는바 "히브리인"은 주로 인종을 나타내고,[266] "이스라엘인"은 택한 백성을 나타내며,[267] "아브라함의 씨"란 말은 하나님의 언약 백성, 또는 믿음의 조상의 후예라는 뜻이 있다.[268] "그리스도

265) Thrall, 730.

266) 팔레스틴 유대인만을 가리키느냐, 디아스포라 유대인도 포함하느냐로 의견이 갈라진다. 전자를 주장하는 학자는 Kümmel이고(211), 후자는 Windisch이다(350). 전자의 경우 반대자들은 바울이 디아스포라 유대인으로서 그들 보다 덜 정통적 유대인이라고 보았을 것이다. Ἑβραῖοι에 대한 다른 견해들을 Thrall 723-27에서 보라.

267) 요 1:47; 롬 9:4; 11:1; 참조, 갈 6:16. Barrett, 293.

268) 요 8:33, 37; 히 2:16; 롬 9:7; 11:1; 갈 3:16. R. Jewett, "The Agitators and the Galatian Congregation," *NTS* 17 (1970-71), 198-212; H. J. Holtzmann, *Lehrbuch der historisch-kritischen Einleitung in das Neuen Testament* (Freiburg: J. C. B. Mohr, 1886), 243; Georgi, *Die Gegner des Paulus im 2. Korinther*, 74-76.

의 일꾼"(διάκονοι Χριστοῦ)은 이런 칭호의 끝에 위치하여 오랜 구원 역사의 완성을 이루는 의미로 언급된다(참조, 롬10:4).[269] 바울이 믿는 바대로 구원의 새 시대에서 이런 민족적 "외모"나 "육체"가 더 이상 의미가 없어졌으나(롬 2:11; 3:21; 9:15이하; 고후 5:16; 10:7), 유대인이 하나님의 택한 백성으로서 하나님의 계시의 말씀을 가진 특별한 민족이란 사실은 인정한다(롬 9:4). 이들은 하나님의 율법을 가졌고 이제 그들을 통해 복음의 계시가 세상에 전해지고 있기 때문이다.[270] 그러나 반대자들은 기껏해야 유대인들이라는 구시대의 자격("육체적 외모")을 가지고 그들의 사도직을 자랑하고 있다(3:3-16; 5:12). 그들이 "그리스도의 일꾼"이라고 자처하는 것은 거짓된 주장일 뿐이다(11:13-15). 이에 대해 바울은 자신도 유대인임으로 그들과 같은 육체적 자랑을 할 수 있을 뿐만 아니라, 진정한 "그리스도의 일꾼"으로 자처할 수 있다고 한다(23). "나도 더욱 그러하도다(ὑπὲρ ἐγώ)"는 말은 바울은 이들과 대조적으로 "그리스도의 일꾼"의 자격이 충분히 있다는 말이다. 이에 대한 증거로 그의 고난의 사역을 열거하기 시작한다.

b. 나는 진정한 그리스도의 사도로서 많은 고난을 겪었다(11:23-27).

23. "저희가 그리스도의 일꾼이냐 정신없는 말을 하거니와 나

---

269) W. L. Knox, "Abraham and the Quest for God" *HTR* 28(1935) 55-59; Zmijewski, 240; Jeremias, *TDNT* I:8, 9. Thrall, 727-30에서 "아브라함의 씨"에 대한 다른 견해들을 보라.

270) D. Georgi, 76-82.

도 더욱 그러하도다. 내가 수고를 넘치도록 하고 옥에 갇히기도 더 많이 하고 매도 수없이 맞고 여러 번 죽을 뻔 하였으니" (διάκονοι Χριστοῦ εἰσιν; παραφρονῶν λαλῶ, ὑπὲρ ἐγώ· ἐν κόποις περισσοτέρως, ἐν φυλακαῖς περισσοτέρως, ἐν πληγαῖς ὑπερβαλλόντως, ἐν θανάτοις πολλάκις). 바울은 앞에서(11:13-15) 반대자들을 "사단의 일꾼들"로 정죄했기 때문이 그들이 "그리스도의 일꾼"이란 주장은 터무니 없는 주장이라고 일축할 수 있으나, 여기서는 자신의 사도직을 밝히기 위해서 편의상 그들의 주장을 그대로 반복한다고 본다.[271] 바울은 이와 유사한 "그리스도의 사도"라는 칭호를 그의 서신 초두에 늘 밝혀 왔기 때문에 "그리스도의 일꾼"이란 칭호는 이미 익숙하다. 문제는 반대자들의 같은 주장이 거짓이고 자신의 주장이 진실임을 증명하는 문제다. 바울은 "나도 더욱 그러하다"(ὑπὲρ ἐγώ)는 말로 이들의 자랑을 반박한다. 이 말의 정확한 의미에 대한 제안이 다양한다. 첫째, "나는 그리스도 일꾼 보다 더 높다"라는 뜻이다.[272] 그러

271) Barrett는 여기서 바울이 거론하는 사람은 반대파들이 아니라 반대자들을 지원하는 예루살렘 사도들이라고 본다(292-3). 그러나 다수의 학자들은 여기서 21절의 거짓 사도들을 지칭한다고 본다(Plummer, 321; Windisch, 352; Allo, 294; Bultmann, 216; Furnish, 535). Thrall은 반대자들이 원래 "그리스도의 사도들"이지만 그들의 고린도에서의 비행으로 인해서 "사단의 일꾼들"이 되었다고 바울이 생각한다면, 그가 이런 두 가지 칭호를 동시에 사용하는 것이 가능하다고 한다(732). 그러면서 베드로를 사단의 대리자로 부른 예를 든다(마 16:16-23). 사실 10:7에서 바울이 반대자들을 "그리스도에 속한 것"으로 인정하는 듯한 어귀도 있다. 그러나 거기서도 바울이 그들을 인정한다는 것이 아니라 그들의 생각을 그대로 인용하는 것뿐이라고 본다. 본문에서 바울은 그의 반대자들을 분명히 사단의 일꾼들로 정죄하였고(11:15), 예수님은 베드로를 사단의 일꾼들로 부르지는 않았고, 그의 배후에서 일하는 사단을 꾸짖었다고 본다.

272) Plummer, 321.

나 "그리스도의 종"으로 자신을 나타내는 바울이 이런 교만한 생각을 할 이유가 없다. 둘째, ὑπὲρ를 "더"(more)로 보지 않고, "도리어"(rather)로 보아서 "그리스도의 일꾼은(그들이 아니고) 도리어 나다"라고 번역한다고 보는 견해가 있다.[273] 이런 절대적 의미는 비교문이 계속되는 상황에서 어색하며, 이런 의미를 나타내려 했다면 μᾶλλον을 썼을 것이다.[274] 셋째, "나는 더욱 그리스도의 일꾼이다"이라고 번역한다. 이 번역이 반대자들과 비교하는 문맥에 가장 맞는 자연스런 해석이다. 바울은 또한 그런 말을 하는 것을 수취스럽게 여긴다. 넷째, ὑπὲρ를 최상급으로 해석하여 "내가 가장 탁월한 그리스도의 일꾼이다"라고 번역한다.[275] 이런 해석도 비교적인 문맥에 맞지 않는다. 다섯째, "나는 더 나은 그리스도의 일꾼으로서 그들과 비교할 수 없다." 이 번역은 3번의 비교적 의미의 번역과 4번의 최상급 의미의 번역을 혼합한 해석으로서 가능한 해석이다.[276] 10장 12절에서 바울은 이들과 비교하기를 거절하는 말도 했으므로 비교급과 더불어 최상급의 의미 있다고 보는 것이 가능하다. 그러나 문맥의 흐름에서 볼 때 역시 3번의 비교적인 의미가 타당하다고 본다.[277]

바울은 그리스도의 사역의 특성을 고난의 사역으로 보고 자신

---

273) Zmijewisik, 242.

274) Thrall, 733.

275) Hughes, 405-6, 주 71.

276) Hughes, 405-6, 주 71.

277) Thrall은 23절에서 ὑπὲρ를 포함한 다른 비교급 동사에 최상급의 의미가 포함되어 있다고 본다(734). 바울은 복음 사역에 있어서 반대자들에 비해 훨씬 뛰어 나게 일했다. 이런 해석이 반대자들이 "그리스도의 일꾼"이라는 주장이 타당하지 않다는 바울의 견해와 일치한다고 보는 것이다.

의 사역도 고난의 사역임을 말하여 자신의 고난의 사역이야 말로 진정한 그리스도의 사역의 유형을 따른 것이지만 반대자들에게서는 그런 증거가 빈약함을 지적하려는 것이다. 바울은 반대자들 가운데서도 그와 유사한 고난을 경험한 이들도 있을 수 있음을 예상하고 주의 깊게 비교급을 쓴다. 희랍어 원문에는 "수고를 넘치도록 하고"가 "더 많이 하고"(περισσοτέρως)로 비교급으로 나오고, 그 다음 말("옥에 갇히기도 더 많이 하고[περισσοτέρως]")도 한글개역이 번역한대로 같은 비교급이 쓰였다. 바울은 다만 그들보다 더 많은 횟수의 고난과 더 극심한 고난을 겪었음을 강조한다(참조, 고전 15:10). 그러나 단순히 비교하는 표현일 수도 있다.[278)]

여기서도 고난의 사례들이 일반적인 것들로부터 보다 구체적인 것들로, 보다 심각한 것들로 점증적으로 고조시키고 있다.

"내가 수고를 넘치도록 하고" 에서 수고(κόπος)는 원래 육체적 노동을 가리키는 말이나 바울은 그리스도인의 봉사를 가리키는 말로 주로 썼다(고전 15:58; 살전 1:3; 2:9; 3:5; 고후 6:5; 10:15; 빌 2:16). 여기서도 바울의 어려운 복음 사역을 나타낸다. 바울은 힘든 복음 사역을 하였으므로 그렇지 못한 반대자들보다 더 나은 "그리스도의 일꾼" 이라는 것이 암시된다.

감옥에 갇힌 경험은 사도행전 16장 23-30절에 나오고(참조, 고전 15:32; 고후 1:8-10; 롬 16:3-7), 클레멘트 1서 5장 6절에서는 바울이 7번 감옥에 갇혔다고 나온다.[279)] 실제로 얼마나 감옥에 갇혔는지는 알 수 없다. 어떤 이들은 감옥에 갇힌 경험이 과장되었다

278) Martin, 276.

279) R. P. Martin, *Colossians and Philemon*, NCB(1981) 26-32.

고도 본다.[280] 그러나 실제 기록에서는 확인할 수 없는 많은 투옥된 경험을 바울이 기억하면서 말하고 있다고 본다.

"매도 수없이 맞고"에서 여러 가지 형태의 매질을 나타내고 있으나 23절과 24에서 보다 구체적으로 언급된다. 24절에서 "사십에 하나 감한 매"는 유대 회당에서 맞은 것이며 25절에서 세 번 맞은 태장은 로마 관원들에게 맞은 것으로 보인다. 그 한 예가 사도행전 16장 19-24절에서 바울이 빌립보에서 귀신을 쫓아 낸 뒤에 맞고 옥에 갇힌 것이다. 이외에 14장 19절에서 루스드라에서 안디옥과 이고니온으로부터 온 유대인들에게 돌로 맞았다.

23절에서 바울은 그의 고난이 "수고"라는 일반적인 고통으로부터 투옥, 매질, 그리고 죽음에 이르는 고통까지 많고 심각한 것이었다는 일반적인 진술을 한 후에 계속해서 그 고난의 사례를 더 자세히 열거하고 있다.

"여러 번 죽을 뻔하였으니…" 바울은 계속적으로 죽음의 위협을 받았다(1:9; 10; 4:11; 고전 15:32; 롬 8:36; 행 21:31). 죽음의 위협에 직면한 경험뿐만 아니라 실제로 가사상태에 빠졌던 경험도 포함 한 것이다(행 14:19).

24. "유대인들에게 사십에 하나 감한 매를 다섯 번 맞았으며"(Ὑπὸ Ἰουδαίων πεντάκις τεσσεράκοντα παρὰ μίαν ἔλαβον,). "유대인들에 의한"이란 말을 초두에 한 것은 앞에서(22절) 바울의 반대파가 자신들이 유대인이란 것을 자랑하고 있음을 상기시키기 위한 것일 수 있다.[281] 또한 바울 자신이 유대인으로

280) Furnish, 354.

281) Windisch, 354; Furnish, 515.

서 같은 동족에게 고난 받았다는 사실을 부각시켜서 바울이 당한 고난의 부당함에 대해서 독자들의 경각심을 높이기 위한 것일 수도 있다. 더구나 5번이라는 횟수까지 언급한 것은 바울의 이런 의도를 나타낸다고 본다. 한편 유대인 반대파들은 동족들에게 이런 고난을 받지 않았음을 의미할 수도 있다. 반대파들은 "다른 복음"을 가리키는 이들로서(11:4) 아마도 모세의 법을 존중하는 부류라고 생각되기 때문이다(3장).

바울이 유대인들에게 매를 맞은 것이 어느 율법 조항에 어긋난 것인지를 알 수 없다. 유대인의 신앙 규정집 미쉬나에 있는 마코트(Makkoth) 3장 1-9절에 기록된 회당에서 태형으로 벌할 수 있는 범죄의 유형은 부정한 상태에서 성전에 들어가는 행위, 제사 의식 규정 위반, 성적 문란 행위, 문신 새기기 등 대개 바울에게는 해당되지 않는 것들이다. 사도행전 21장 28절에서 바울이 성전에 헬라인과 함께 들어와 성전을 더럽혔다는 혐의는 고린도후서 이후에 일어난 사건이므로 해당되지 않는다. 아마 할례 규정 같은 모세 율법에 대해 바울이 이방인 선교 입장에서 취한 율법에 대한 보다 신축적인 가르침에 대한 징벌이었을 것이다.[282] 회당에서 율법에 대해 잘못 가르치는 거짓 교사에게 가하는 형벌로 받았는지도 모른다(고전 9:20-21).[283]

---

282) E. P. Sanders, "Paul on the Law, His Opponents, and the Jewish People in Philppians3 and 2 Corinthians 11," in *Anti-Judaism in Early Christianity vol. I: Paul and the Gospels*, ed. Peter Richardson and David Granskou, Studies in Christianity and Judaism 2 (Waterloo/ Ontario: Wilfrid Laurier University Press, 1986), 75-90, 86-7; Wolff, 233.

283) W. A. Meeks, *First Urban Christians* (New Heaven and London: Yale University Press, 183), 26; G. Lüdemann, *Paul, Apostle to the Gentiles*, ETr. F. Stanely Jones (Philadelphia: Fortress Press, 1984), 121, 주 91에서 반대 하는 견해를 보라. 사도행전과 바울 서신에서 바울이 특별히 율법에 어긋나게 가르쳤기 때문에 벌 받았다는 증거가 없다는 것이다. 그러나 사도행전에 바울에 대한 모든 기록이 있는 것이 아니므로 이런 추정이 가능하다(Martin, 377).

한편, 이런 "유대인에 의한" 징벌에 대한 바울의 부정적인 의미와 함께, 바울은 그의 고난을 유대인의 구원을 위한 고난으로써 기꺼이 받았다는 의미도 있었을 것이다. 로마서 11장 17-24절에서 그가 유대인의 구원을 위해 희생도 감수하겠다고 한 말을 생각해 볼 때 그렇다. 그는 그의 동족의 구원한 고난을 기꺼이 받았다는 의미일 것이다. 바울이 유대인들의 고난을 받은 것은 주께서도 유대인들에 의해 고난 받았다는 사실과 병행된다. 그러나 바울이 이런 사실까지도 염두에 두고서 그의 사도직의 정당성을 암시하고 있는지는 알 수 없다.

"사십에 하나 감한 매"는 신명기 25장 2-3절에 나온다. 이 규정은 심각한 범법 행위에 대한 형벌 규정이다. "사십에 하나 감한 수"는 "사십에 가까운 수"로 번역할 수 있다(*Makkoth* 3:10: "Forty less one").[284] 재판장은 악인의 죄의 경중에 따라서 매의 횟수를 조정하여 때리게 해야 하며, 사십 횟수을 지나쳐 때리지 못하도록 금하고 있다. 실수로 지나쳐서 율법을 어기지 않게 하기 위해서 실제로 서른 아홉 번을 때리게 하였으나, 피해자에 대한 자비심도 고려한 것이라고 본다.[285]

실제로 언제 바울이 다섯 번에 걸쳐 태형을 받았는지는 알 수 없으나, 복음을 본격적으로 전하기 이전의 바울의 회개 후 "침묵의 시기"(AD 37-41)에 당한 경험들일 수도 있다.[286]

---

284) *Mishnayoth*, vol. iv: *Order Negikin*, ETr. P. Blackman (New York: Judeica Press, 1963), 325.

285) Plummer, 324; Bruce, 296.

25. "세 번 태장으로 맞고 한 번 돌로 맞고 세 번 파선하는데 일주야를 깊음에서 지냈으며…" (τρὶς ἐρραβδίσθην, ἅπαξ ἐλιθάσθην, τρὶς ἐναυάγησα, νυχθήμερον ἐν τῷ βυθῷ πεποίηκα). "세 번 태장으로 맞고"는 사도행전 16장 19-24절에서 빌립보에서 로마 관원들에게 아마도 공공질서 위반 행위로 맞고서 옥에 갇힌 사건 외에 다른 두 건이 더 있음을 가리킨다.[287] "태장"은 막대기로 때리는 로마 관원들의 형벌이다. 빌립보에서 바울은 로마 시민으로서 이런 형벌을 피할 수 있었으나, 무시당하고 맞았다(참조, 살전 2:2). 실제로 로마 시민들이 무시당하고 매를 맞았다는 기록도 있다.[288] 바울이 이를 항의하였을 때 관원들은 당황했다(행 16:37-38). 바울이 법적인 하자가 있음을 항의하였으나 내심으로는 매 맞음을 그의 유대 동족의 구원을 위한 마땅한 고난으로 생각하고 기꺼이 수용하였다고도 본다(롬 11:17-24).[289] 또한 다른 그리스도인 형제들은 고난을 당하는 데 유독 자기만 로

---

286) R. E. Osborne, "Paul's Silent Years," *JBL* 84 (1965) 59-65; E. Schürer, *The History of the Jewish People in the Age of Jesus Christ*, ed. G. Vermes and F. Millar, vol. II (Edinburgh: T. & T. Clark, 1973), 262.

287) Barrett, 297.

288) 때로는 로마 시민들도 맞는 경우가 있었다: Josephus, *The Jewish War* 2.308; Cicero, *In Verrem*, 5.62-66: 메시나(Messina)에서 어떤 사람이 "나는 로마 시민이요"라고 외쳤으나 무시당하고 매를 맞았다한다; T. Mommsen, "Die Rechtsverhaeltnisse des Apostels Paulus," *ZNW* 2 (1901), 90; A. N. Sherwin-White, *Roman Society and Roman Law in the New Testament* (Oxford: Clarendon, 1963), 48-98.

289) Thrall, 742; 참조, Bultmann, 216; Martin은 바울이 로마 시민권 소지자임을 미리 말했으나 로마 관리들이 이런 권리를 무시하고 나름대로 판단하여 매질하였다고 본다(377). 로마 시대에 이런 관행이 잦았기 때문이다. 그러나 빌립보에서 바울이 로마 시민 권자인 자신을 때린 것을 항의 했을 때는 관리들이 당황하였다(행 16:37-38). 어쩌면 법을 무시한 하급 관리들("아전들")의 실수로 볼 수 있을 것이다.

마 시민권을 가지고서 고난을 피하는 것은 그리스도의 고난에 동참하는 사도적 자세가 아니라고 보았을 것이 거의 분명하다(행 5:41). 이런 그리스도의 고난에 참여하는 것이 바로 본문에서 바울이 말하는 사도의 중요한 표이기 때문이다.

"돌로 한번 맞고"는 사도행전 14장 19절에서 유대인들에게 아마도 레위기 24장 16절의 "여호와의 이름을 훼방한 죄" 즉 "참람 죄" 또는 "신성 모독죄"로 정죄 받아 맞은 것을 가리킨다고 본다.[290]

"세 번 파선하는데 일주야를 깊음에서 지냈으며"에서 바울이 여러 번 해상 여행하는 중에 발생된 것으로 보이나 사도행전 27장의 경우는 고린도후서 이후 사건(AD 62년?)이므로 제외 된다.[291] 일주야를 깊음에서 지냈다는 표현은 바울의 뇌리 가운데 깊이 자리 잡은 괴롭고 무서운 경험이었음을 나타낸다(시 68:3; 67:23).[292] 유대인들에게 바다의 "깊음"(תְּהוֹם, 테홈)이란 말은 감정이상의 신학적 혼돈의 의미도 있으나(창 1:2), 여기서 그런 의미를 찾는 것은 지나친 추론이다. 바울은 그의 두려웠던 과거의 고난의 경험으로 보고하고 있는 것이다.[293]

26. "여러 번 여행에 강의 위험과 강도의 위험과 동족의 위험과

---

290) 미쉬나, *Sanhedrin*, 7.56-60; Hughes, 410.

291) Barrett, 298.

292) Martin, 378.

293) Meyer, 449; Bachmann, 384, 주 1; Plummer, 325; Windisch, 357에서 요세푸스도 로마로 가던 중 아드리아 바다에서 유사한 경험이 있었다(Vita 3)는 것을 언급한다(Thrall, 739, 주 587 인용).

이방인의 위험과 도시에서의 (시내의) 위험과 광야의 위험과 바다의 위험과 거짓 형제 중의 위험을 당하고…" (ὁδοιπορίαις πολλάκις, κινδύνοις ποταμῶν, κινδύνοις λῃστῶν, κινδύνοις ἐκ γένους, κινδύνοις ἐξ ἐθνῶν, κινδύνοις ἐν πόλει, κινδύνοις ἐν ἐρημίᾳ, κινδύνοις ἐν θαλάσσῃ, κινδύνοις ἐν ψευδαδέλφοις,). "여러 번 여행에"는 여기에 나오는 8번의 위험은 여러 차례의 선교 여행에서 발생한 것들이라는 것을 먼저 밝히는 것이다. 여기서의 바울의 여행은 사도로서의 전도 여행을 말하고 있으므로 이 모든 위험은 사도로서 사역 중에 당한 위험들이다. 크게 자연으로부터 오는 위험과 사람으로부터 오는 위험으로 나누어져 있다. 부분적으로는 유사한 위험이나 대조적 위험끼리 짝을 이루고 있으면서도 다 그렇지는 않다. 예로, "강의 위험"은 "시내의 위험"과 같이 짝을 이룰 수 있었으나 가장 먼저 언급되었고, "거짓 형제의 위험"은 앞에 언급되는 일련의 사람으로부터 오는 위험과 짝을 맞추어 쓸 수 있었다.

"강의 위험"은 홍수로 여행이 어려웠던 경험을 말한다.[294] 이 위험이 가장 먼저 쓰인 것은 25절에서 바다에서의 고난을 언급하였기 때문에 물과 관련된 사항으로 보아 여기서 먼저 언급했을 것이다.[295] "강도의 위험"은 바울 같이 여러 지방을 여행하는 이들이 늘 조심해야할 위험이었을 것이다. 강도는 단순히 물건을 절취할 뿐 아니라 목숨까지도 빼앗을 수 있었기 때문이다. "동족의 위

294) Furnish, 517; Barrett, 299; Martin, 378.

295) Thrall, 743.

험"은 같은 유대인이지만 다른 종교적 가르침을 전하는 바울에게 실제로 큰 위협이 아닐 수 없었다. 비시디아 안디옥, 이고니온, 루스드라, 데살로니가, 고린도 등에서와 같이 유대인들이 이방인들을 선동하여 바울을 위협하기도 했다(행 9:23, 29; 13:8, 45; 14:2, 19; 17:5; 18:6; 12; 20:3, 19; 21:11, 27). 그러나 바울은 동족에 대한 사랑을 가지고 위험을 무릅쓰고 그들에게 복음을 전했다(롬 9:1-5; 11:1). 이에 비해 이와 대칭을 이루는 "이방인의 위험"은 오히려 그 위험성이 약한 것으로 보인다. 바울이 로마 시민권을 가졌고, 이방 세계에서 태어났기 때문인지도 모른다. 더구나 그 자신이 이방인의 사도로 부르심을 받았다(롬 15:16; 참조, 엡 3:1, 6). 그러나 바울은 여전히 유대인으로서, 새로운 이질적 종교, 그것도 절대적 구원의 도리로서 복음을 전하였기 때문에 이방인들로부터 오는 위험은 심각한 것일 수밖에 없었을 것이다(행 16:21; 19:23; 고후 1:8-11).

"시내(市內)의 위험"(κινδύνοις ἐν πόλει)은 "도시에서의 위험"으로 고쳐 읽어야 오해가 없을 것이다. 뒤에 나오는 "광야의 위험"이나 "바다의 위험"과 대조적으로 썼다. 즉 "도시에서의 위험"은 "사람이 사는 곳"에서의 위험이고 뒤에 나오는 위험은 모두 사람이 없는 곳에서의 위험이다. 트롤은 이 세 개의 위험이 앞에 나오는 위험들을 모두 포함하는 위험으로서 수사학적으로 반복하여 쓴 것으로 본다.[296] 즉 도시는 유대인과 이방인이 함께 거주하는 곳이며, 광야나 바다는 강도나 자연적 피해를 입을 수 있는 곳으로서 이미 앞서 언급한 내용을 반복하고 있다고 본다.

296) Thrall, 743.

"거짓 형제 중의 위험"(κινδύνοις ἐν ψευδαδέλφοις)을 모든 위험 중 가장 어려운 위험으로 간주하여 마지막에 썼다고 본다. 또한 바로 앞에 언급된 "바다의 위험"과 함께 "가장 어려운 위험"으로 여겨서 대조적으로 함께 썼다고 보기도 한다.[297] 또는 앞서 말한 불신 유대인들과 이방인들의 위험과 대조하여 여기서는 믿는 형제들의 위험을 말하고 있다고 도 본다.[298] 이들의 정체에 대해서 "거짓 형제들"(ψευδαδέλφοις)을 바울이 앞서 13절에서 말한 "거짓 사도들"(ψευδαπόστολοι)과 관련 시켜서, 고린도 교인들이 거짓 사도들을 분별하지 않고 용인하여서 바울을 대적하게 만드는 일이 얼마나 위험한 것인가를 다시 경고하려는 의도가 있다고 보는 이들이 많다(11:4, 13-15, 19).[299] "거짓 형제"나 "거짓 사도"은 대개 유대인 그리스도인들로 본다(갈 2:4, 5, 11-14). 그들은 율법 준수를 강요하면서, 이방인들에게 그리스도 안에서 율법으로부터의 자유를 선언하는 바울의 복음을 반대하였을 것이다. 그러나 "거짓 형제의 위협"과 "거짓 사도의 위협"을 구별하는 것이 필요하다고 본다. "거짓 사도들"이 바울의 사역을 방해한 것과 같이 "거짓 형제들(일반 평신도들)"도 바울의 사역을 방해했을 것이다(딤전 1:19-20). 그러므로 우리는 이 모든 가능성을 함께 생각하여 바울은 여기서 자신의 사역을 방해한 "거짓 형제들의 위험"을 언급하면서 "거짓 사도들의 위험"도 함께 암시하고 있다고 본다.

27. "또 수고하며 애쓰고 여러 번 자지 못하고 주리며 목마르고

297) Lieztmann, 151; Wendland, 242.

298) Barrett, 299.

299) Barrett, 299; Hughes, 412-13; Zmijewski, 259; Martin, 379; Thrall, 744; Barnett, 546.

여러 번 굶고 춥고 헐벗었노라"(κόπῳ καὶ μόχθῳ, ἐν ἀγρυπνίαις πολλάκις, ἐν λιμῷ καὶ δίψει, ἐν νηστείαις πολλάκις, ἐν ψύχει καὶ γυμνότητι·). 바울은 계속하여 그의 신교사역의 시련들을 열거한다. 26절은 선교사역 중의 위험들이며, 여기서는 그 위험들의 결과나 그 외의 일들로 겪은 육체적 궁핍함을 말한다. 본문의 희랍어 문장은 네 개의 ἐν으로 이루어진 정황을 나타내는 말들이 나타나는데, 수고와 애씀, 추위와 헐벗음 같은 유사한 내용으로 짝을 이루고 반복된다. "여러 번"(πολλάκις)이란 말을 26절에 이어 두 번 언급하면서 고난의 중함을 나타낸다.[300] 이런 모든 말들은 그리스도의 사도로서 교인들을 위해 희생하는 바울의 모습을 잘 나타내면서 고린도 독자들의 사도의 진정성에 대한 합리적 판단을 하게할 뿐만 아니라 인간적인 동정심을 일으킬 수도 있었을 것이다.

"수고하며"(κόπῳ)는 실제로는 수단을 나타내는 여격 명사형으로 나온 것을 동사적 의미로 바꿔 번역한 것이다. 이 말은 23절에도 나왔고, 6장 5절에서도 언급되었다(참조, 고전 15:10, 58). "애쓰고"(μόχθῳ)도 마찬가지로 여격 명사형이며, 동의어이다. 이 두 말이 데살로니가전서 2장 9절과 데살로니가후서 3장 8절에서도 함께 나타난다. 구태여 그 의미를 구분하면, "수고하며"(κόπῳ)는 보다 수동적 의미이고, "애쓰고"(μόχθῳ)는 능동적이라고 한다.[301] 우리 말 번역도 이런 의미를 각기 나타내고 있다. 이 두 말

300) Zmijewski, 261.

301) Allo, 297.

이 뒤에 나오는 시련들에 대한 제목의 역할을 한다고 본다.[302] 이 말들이 바울의 설교, 가르침 등 일반 사역과 함께 천막 만들기도 포함한다고 보는 이들도 있다.[303]

"자지 못하고"(ἀγρυπνίαις)는 야간에 일하는 것이나 여행하는 것(시락서 38:26-30; 마카비 2서 2:26), 또는 염려로 잠자지 못하는 것(시락서 34:2), 나아가 영적인 훈련을 가리킬 수 있다(고후6:5). 한 마디로 고린도 인들이 잠잘 때나, 혹은 그의 반대자들이 쉴 때에도 바울은 쉬지 않고 일했다는 것이다. 더구나 28절을 고려할 때 바울은 고린도 교회 문제로 고민하며 잠을 이루지 못했다고 볼 수도 있다.[304] 또 1세기 스토익 철학자들에게 않자는 것을 정신적 훈련의 하나로 보았으며, 시세로는 잠을 자지 않고 깨어 있는 것을 행동을 위한 철저한 준비와 강인한 자세를 보여주는 지도자의 덕목으로 보았다.[305]

"주리며 목마르고"(ἐν λιμῷ καὶ δίψει)는 바울의 가난함을 나타낼 수도 있으나, 문맥에서는 실제 여행 중 겪은 굶주림과 목마름을 가리킨다.[306] 만일 전자의 경우라면, 그가 자비량 선교를 고집하였기 때문일 수도 있다(11:7; 12:13-15; 참조, 행 18:2; 20:33-35).[307] 바울의 가난함은 독자들에게 그의 사도직의 진정성을 잘

302) Martin, 380.

303) Filson, 402; Thrall, 745-46.

304) 참조, Thrall, 746.

305) Ebner, *Leidenslisten*, 143; Epictetus, *The Discourses*, I 7.30; III 15.11; 22.95.

306) Héring, 90; Martin, 380.

307) Thrall, 747.

보여 줄 것이다.

"여러 번 굶고"(ἐν νηστείαις πολλάκις)를 앞의 "주리며"(ἐν λιμῷ)와 구별하여 의도적인 종교적인 금식을 나타낸다고 보는 이들이 있다.[308] 그러나 구별하지 않고 사역 중에 먹을 것이 없거나 잦은 투옥 등으로 인한 비자발적인 굶주림으로 보는 이도 있다.[309] 이 경우 앞의 "주리며"(ἐν λιμῷ)와 구별하기가 어렵다. 한편 이 말을 위에서와 같이 철학자의 인내를 위한 극기 훈련과 관련하여 바울의 사도적 인격 형성을 위한 훈련으로 보는 경우도 있다.[310] "주리며"(ἐν λιμῷ)와 결국 같은 의미이지만, 여러 정황에서의 연유된 굶주림을 가리키는 것이라고 본다.

"춥고 헐벗었노라"(ἐν ψύχει καὶ γυμνότητι)는 인간 생존에 있어서 가장 낮은 상태를 보여 준다. 이 말은 육체적으로 낮은 단계에서 인간의 존엄성이 완전히 상실된 부끄러운 상태를 가리킨다(고전 4:11; 롬 8:35; 참조, 고후 5:3). "벌거벗음"은 수취를 나타내는 말이다(창 2:25; 3:7, 10, 11; 겔 16:8; 나 3:5; 미 1:11; 계 3:18). 이런 극도의 불쌍한 모습이 홀로 먼 선교 여행길에서 음식을 구할 수 없을 때, 잦은 투옥 생활에서, 그리고 천막 만드는 일을 할 때에 바울의 실제 모습이었다고 생각된다. 한편 당시에 철학자들은 춥고 배고픔을 견디는 극기 훈련을 통해서 수양을 쌓았다.[311] 여기

308) Allo, 298; Barrett, 300; Thrall, 747.

309) Windisch, 359.

310) Zmijewski, 263.

311) Furnish, 518; Dio Chrysostom, *Or.* VIII 16.

서 바울이 자발적으로 수양을 위한 금식을 했다고 할 수는 없고, 그의 여행 중에 어쩔 수 없이 당한 고통을 말하고 있다. 어쩌면 바울은 헬라문화에 젖은 고린도 교인들이 그의 이런 모습을 존경스럽게 여기리라고 기대했을지도 모른다. 그럼에도 불구하고 바울이 진정으로 원한 것은 모범적인 도덕적 스승으로서의 모습으로서 보다 자기 십자가를 지고 가는 그리스도의 진정한 제자로서 인식되기를 바랐을 것이다. 바울은 그리스도와 고린도 교인들에 대한 지극한 사랑이 있었기 때문에 온갖 고난도 불사했다. 그런 의미에서 바울은 진정한 사도다.

이렇게 23절부터 시작한 바울의 육체적 시련의 목록은 여기서 끝내고 28절부터는 정서적 스트레스를 말한다.

c. 나는 교회를 위해 늘 염려한다 (11:28-29).

28. "이외의 일은 고사하고 오히려 날마다 내 속에 눌리는 일이 있으니 곧 모든 교회를 위하여 염려하는 것이라" (χωρὶς τῶν παρεκτὸς ἡ ἐπίστασίς μοι ἡ καθ᾿ ἡμέραν, ἡ μέριμνα πασῶν τῶν ἐκκλησιῶν). "이외의 일은 고사하고" (χωρὶ τῶν παρεκτὸς)의 "이외의 일" (παρεκτὸς)에 대해서 두 가지 번역이 있다. 하나는 "이외의 일" 이며, 다른 하나는 "외적인 일들" 이다. 첫 번째 번역은 아직 바울이 말하지 않고 마음속에 남겨둔 일들을 가리키고, 두 번째는 앞에서 열거한 고통들을 말한다. 그 고통들은 지금 말하는 염려가 내적인 데 반해서 외적인 것들이기 때문이다.[312] 개역한글

312) KJV, NEB, REB, Barrett, 288.

성경을 포함한 대다수가 첫째 번역을 지지한다. 바울이 "외적인 일들"을 의미하려 했다면 παρεκτὸς 대신 τὰ ἔξω 또는 τὰ ἔξωθεν을 썼을 것이라고 한다.[313] 그렇다면 "이 외의 일들"은 무엇인가? 곧 말하는 교회를 위한 염려라고 볼 수 있으나, 그보다 바울이 채 말하지 않은 유사한 다른 종류의 고통들을 말한다고 본다.[314] 바울은 그가 말하려는 더 중요한 고통을 말하기 위해서 유사한 다른 외적 고통들을 더 말하지 않고 지나쳐 가는 것이다.

"날마다 내 속에 눌리는 일이 있으니"(ἡ ἐπίστασίς μοι ἡ καθ' ἡμέραν)에서 "눌리는 일"로 번역된 희랍어 ἐπίστασίς는 "압력"이란 말 이외에도, "주의," "감시," "장애," 등의 의미가 있다.[315] 모두 그런대로 문맥과 통하는 의미이지만, 대부분의 주석가들이 내적 고통이라는 의미의 "압력," 즉 "눌린다"는 말이 가장 적절하다고 본다.[316] 이런 번역이 이어서 동격으로 나오는 "염려"(ἡ μέριμνα)와 잘 조화된다.

바울의 마음을 날마다 누르고 있는 "염려"(ἡ μέριμνα)는 고린도 교회뿐만이 아니라 모든 교회를 위한 것이다. 실제로 그의 거의 모든 서신들이 각 교회에 대한 그의 염려를 반영하고 있다. 이런 염려는 고린도후서에서 바울이 성난 자녀를 달래는 부모의 심

---

313) Plummer, 329.

314) Allo, 298; Windisch, 360; Tasker, 164; Martin, 381; 참조, Héring, 90; Filson, 402; Zmijewski, 268-9; Thrall, 749.

315) Thrall, 749.

316) Bachmann, 385; Plummer, 329-30; Windisch, 360; Barrett, 288; Bultmann, 218; Furnish, 512; Thrall, 749

정을 가지고서 고린도 교인들을 설득하는 자세에서 나타난다 (6:11; 7:3; 12:14-15; 참조, 11:2-3). 이런 내적 고민은 바울이 언급한 외적 고통보다 더 클 수 있다. 왜냐하면 외적 고통은 주로 과거의 고통으로 언급되었으나 내적 고통은 "날마다" 계속 되기 때문이다. 더구나 갈라디아서 끝에서 바울은 그의 심적 괴로움이 육체적 상처로 나타났다고 토로한다: "이 후로는 누구든지 나를 더 괴롭게 말라. 내가 내 몸에 예수의 흔적을 가졌노라" (갈 6:17). 고린도후서 12장 7절에서 말하는 "육체의 가시"가 이렇게 생긴 병을 가리킬 수도 있을 것이다. 교회를 위해 겪는 이런 내외적 고통을 견디며 사역한 것이 바울의 "육체적 자랑" 임과 동시에 역설적으로 그의 "약함의 자랑" 도 되며, 또한 그에게 내재하는 그리스도의 능력이 된다(12:10). 그래서 바울은 그의 고난에 대해서 보다 긍정적 평가를 내린다. 골로새서 1:24에서도 "내가 이제 너희를 위하여 받는 괴로움을 기뻐하고 그리스도의 남은 고난을 그의 몸된 교회를 위하여 내 육체에 채우노라" 라고 말한다. 여기서도 그의 심적인 고난을 사도직의 진정성의 증거로 제시하고 있다.[317)]

29. "누가 약하면 내가 약하지 아니하며 누가 실족하게 되면 내가 애타하지 않더냐?" (τίς ἀσθενεῖ καὶ οὐκ ἀσθενῶ; τίς σκανδαλίζεται καὶ οὐκ ἐγὼ πυροῦμαι;) 바울은 앞에서 말한 교회를 위한 목회적인 염려를 예를 들어 설명한다. "누가 약하면

---

317) M. M. DiCicco, 87, 91: 스토익 철학에서 "역경은 사람의 인격을 가장 잘 나타내주며, 고난의 시간이 사람의 가치의 진정성을 가장 잘 시험한다" 라는 말이 있다. 이런 당시 철학적 사고에 의해서 바울은 모든 역경을 잘 견디었으므로 그리스도의 사도임이 입증된다는 암시를 줄 수 있다.

내가 약하지 아니하며" 에서 "약함의 주제" 가 언급되었다고 할 수 있다. 여기서 언변이나 외양 같은 바울 자신의 약함을 가리키는 것이 아니라 고린도 교인들의 약함을 동정하며 나누는 바울의 목회적 자세를 말하려는 것이지만, 바울이 자신의 약함을 자랑하는 전체 문맥에서 볼 때 "바울의 전인적(全人的) 약함" 을 가리킨다고 보는 것이 옳다.[318] 바울은 그리스도의 사도로서 그의 모든 육체적이고 영적인 약함을 통해서 고린도 교인들의 모든 종류의 약함을 이해하고 동정하고 나눈다는 뜻이다.[319] 고린도전서와 로마서에서 "약함" 은 음식 규정에 관련하여 나타나기도 했다(롬 14:1, 2; 15:1; 고전 8:7-12). 또 유사하게 율법에 관한 논쟁이 있는 갈라디아 교회에서도 "약함" 이 문제가 되었을 것이다(갈 2:11-13). 자기가 세운 이 모든 교회 교인들의 "약함의 일들" 로 말미암아 바울은 염려할 수밖에 없었을 것이다. 한편, 교인들의 바울에 대한 무례하고 거친 공격이 성숙하지 못한 그리스도인들의 "약함" 으로 간주되는지에 대해서는 알 수 없다. 그러나 그들의 공격을 받아서 바울이 심적으로 크게 타격을 받은 것은 사실이다(2:1; 12:21). 그들의 공격으로 바울은 그의 "약함" 을 경험하였을 것이다. 폴론(F. T. Fallon)은 바울은 그를 구하는 기적적인 능력이 없어서 "약하나" 그의 마음은 안타까운 사랑의 정으로 찼다고 주석한다.[320] 그러나 12장 1-4절에서 바울이 그의 영적 경험을 말하고 있고, 또 12

318) Martin은 바울의 약함의 주제를 언급하나, Thrall은 이를 반대하면서 여기서의 약함은 고통을 나누는 목회적 자세를 가리킨다고 지적한다(Martin, 382; Thrall, 751). Barrett는 바울의 약함의 주제가 언급되었음을 인정한다(301-2).

319) Thrall, 751.

320) F. T. Fallon, *2 Corinthians*, New Testament Message 11 (Willmington, Del.: M. G;lazier/Dublin: Veritas, 1980), 102, 103.

장 12절에서 자신의 "표적과 기사"를 사도적 증거로 제시함을 고려할 때, 여기서 바울의 "약함"의 의미를 "기적의 능력의 부족함"과 관련하여 추론하는 것은 무리라고 본다.

"누가 실족하게 되면 내가 애타하지 않더냐"에서 "실족하다"(σκανδαλίζεται)는 "악이나 거짓에로 유혹하다"는 뜻이다.[321) 한 신자라도 잘 못되면 바울은 안타까운 마음으로 그를 구하기 원한다(2:4-8; 4:12; 11:2, 3). 이런 바울의 목회적 자세는 선한 목자는 잃은 양을 찾고 또 자신의 양을 위해서 목숨을 버린다는 예수님의 가르침과 일치한다(요 10:15; 눅 15:4). 그는 고린도 교인들을 자식처럼 생각하는 부모의 마음을 가지고 그들과 생사고락을 함께하는 진정한 사도이다(1:6; 6:13; 7:3; 12:14). 이런 바울의 마음(pathos)은 동시에 바울이 건전한 이성적 판단력(ethos)을 소유하고 있음을 반증한다. 즉 교인들의 실족에 대해서 동정적인 바울은 무엇이 실족인지를 알 수 있는 분명한 판단 능력도 함께 소유하고 있다. 반대자들의 가르침은 단순히 다른 견해가 아니라 근본적으로 잘못된 가르침으로서, "다른 예수, 다른 영, 다른 복음"이다. 더구나 그들은 "거짓 사도들"이며 "사단의 일꾼들"이므로 그들로부터 고린도 교인들을 반드시 구해야 한다는 확고한 사도적 책임 의식을 가지고 있다(11:13-15). 바울 사도는 이러한 영적 예지력과 통찰력이 있으므로 진정한 그리스도의 사도이다.

---

321) Bultmann, 219; Stählin, *TDNT* 7:356.

d. 나는 나의 약점을 자랑한다(11:30-33).

30 "내가 부득불 자랑할진대 나의 약한 것을 자랑하리라"(Εἰ καυχᾶσθαι δεῖ, τὰ τῆς ἀσθενείας μου καυχήσομαι.). 여기서 바울은 지금까지 열거한 그의 "육체적 자랑" 속에 감추어 두었던 진정한 주제가 바로 "약함의 자랑"이란 것을 비로소 밝힌다. 바울의 적들이 그의 육체적 "약함"-자천서가 없음, 외양과 언변이 부족함, 이방인을 위한 사도로서 말씀의 목격자가 아님, 몸의 질병, 물질 착취 등-을 들어 그의 사도적 능력을 비하하였으나, 바울은 그의 고난의 사역을 예로 들면서 오히려 약함이 진정한 사도적 증거가 될 수 있음을 반증한다. 그러나 그의 약함의 자랑도 결국 반대자들의 "육체적 자랑"과 같은 것임을 인정하면서 부질없는 "어리석은 자랑"이라고 연설 시작 전과 마친 후에 스스로 비하시켰다(11:16-21; 12:11).[322] 이렇게 바울은 "바보의 연설" 초두에는 육체적 정신적 고난의 경험을 가지고 그의 적들의 "육체적 자랑"에 맞서지만, 연설 마지막에서는 그의 고난에 대한 "육체적 자랑"을 "약함의 자랑"이라고 역으로 해석함으로서 반대자들의 "육체적 자랑"과는 정반대되는 측면이 있음을 강조하는 것이다. 즉 반대자들의 자랑은 철저히 인간적인 오만함을 나타내지만 바울의 자랑은 그리스도의 겸비함을 나타내어 그리스도의 몸 된 교회를 세우기 위한 것이기 때문이다(5:15; 10:8; 12:19). 이런 겸비는 단순한 도덕적인 겸비 이상의 겸비로서 거룩한 신적 겸비이다. 하나님의

322) S. H. Travis, "Paul's Boasting in 2 Corinthians 10-12," *Texte Untersuchgen* 112(1973) 530: "바울은 모든 그레꼬 로만인들의 자랑에 대한 자세를 부질없는 일로 낮추어 버리고 말았다."

아들 그리스도가 십자가에서 보여준 겸비를 따르는 겸비이며, 전능하신 하나님 앞에서 아무것도 아닌 "나" 자신을 철저히 인식하는 겸비이다(12:11). 그러므로 바울은 앞의 고난의 경험보다 더 분명하게 그의 약함을 나타내는 "다메섹 성에서의 탈출 이야기"와 "몸의 가시"라는 이야기들을 계속하여 약함의 주제를 한층 강화시킨다. 그리고 약함의 자랑 조차도 자신의 오랜 경험의 결과라거나 전통적인 격언이 아니라 바로 주님의 계시에 의한 것임을 밝힌다(12:9). 주님의 계시는 객관적 원칙이다. "계시로 진리를 받았다는 것" 조차도 자랑이라고 할 수 있으나, 바울의 자랑은 반대자들의 자랑과 차원이 다르다. 그들의 자랑은 사욕적이며, 바울의 자랑은 하나님의 뜻에 순종하는 자세가 있다.

이렇게 보면 이 진술은 그의 바보의 연설의 클라이맥스인 "약함의 자랑" (12:9-10)을 하기 위한 예비적 진술도 되고 바로 다음에 나오는 다메섹에서의 탈출 이야기의 의미를 미리 설명한다고도 볼 수 있다.[323] 즉 앞에서의 고난의 경험 진술과 그 보다 더 분명히 약함의 자랑을 나타내는 진술들(다메섹에서의 도피와 "몸의 가시" 이야기)을 연결시켜서 "약함의 진술"이라는 주제로 분명하게 이끌어가는 중간 고리 역할을 하는 것이다.

31. "주 예수의 아버지 영원히 찬송할 하나님이 나의 거짓말 아니하는 줄을 아시느니라" (ὁ θεὸς καὶ πατὴρ τοῦ κυρίου Ἰησοῦ οἶδεν, ὁ ὢν εὐλογητὸς εἰς τοὺς αἰῶνας, ὅτι οὐ ψεύδομαι). 바

323) Thrall, 758-61; Hughes, 418; Zmijewsiki, 278-9; Furnish, 539; Allo, 30-31

울은 하나님을 찬양하는 말로 시작되는 맹세문의 형식으로 자신의 정직성을 나타낸다(1:3; 11:11; 롬 1:25; 9:1; 갈 1:20). "참말을 하고 거짓말을 아니하노라"는 바울의 양심선언 양식구이다(롬 9:1; 딤전 2:7). 여기서와 12장 6절에는 뒷부분과 앞부분이 나누어져 나온다. 여기서 바울은 지금까지의 진술과 앞으로 할 진술의 내용이 진실함을 재확인함으로서 독자들이 믿기 어려운 시련들과 이제 말하려는 놀라운 영적 체험담(12:1-4)과 또 하나님의 계시가 바울의 주관적 주장이 아니라 객관적 증거임을 나타내는 것이다.[324] 더구나 그의 고난이 "육체적 자랑"도 되고 "약함의 자랑"도 되는 역설적 논리는 독자들에게 논리적 혼돈을 줄 수도 있으므로 그의 증거가 모두 인위적인 것이 아니라 실제적 사실에 기초한 것이며 또한 하나님의 계시임을 천명한다. 한편, 이러한 사실 증명에 대한 바울의 심각한 노력은 바울이 그의 진실성을 의심하는 고린도교인들이 상당수 있다는 것을 알고 있음을 보여준다(13:3). 또한 그의 정직함을 앞서 정죄한 거짓 사도들과 대조시키려는 의도가 있다고 보기도 한다.[325] "거짓말한다"란 희랍어 ψεύδομαι(프슈도마이)와 13절의 거짓 사도란 희랍어 ψευδαπόστολοι(프슈드아포스토로이)가 모두 같은 접두사(ψευδ)로 시작된다는 것을 중시하기 때문이다.

"주 예수의 아버지 하나님"(ὁ θεὸς καὶ πατὴρ τοῦ κυρίου Ἰησοῦ)은 로마서 15장 6절과 에베소서 1장 17절에도 같은 표현이

324) 앞의 23-27절에서 말한 것에 대한 증거라는 의견과(Hughes, 419; Tasker, 167; Martin, 384), 뒤에서 말할 내용에 대한 것이라는 의견이 있다(Calvin, 153; Strachan, 28).
325) Martin, 384.

나온다(엡 1:3; 벧전 1:3). "주 예수"란 칭호는 초대 교회에서 이미 굳어진 표현이었으며(롬 10:9; 고전 12:3; 빌 2:11), "아버지 하나님"(또는 순서대로, 하나님 아버지)은 복음서에 있는 대로 예수님이 하나님을 아버지로 호칭한 사실을 바울이 잘 알고 있다는 증거이다.

32. "다메섹에서 아레다 왕의 방백이 나를 잡으려고 다메섹 성을 지킬새 33. 내가 광주리를 타고 들창문으로 성벽을 내려가 그 손에서 벗어났노라"(ἐν Δαμασκῷ ὁ ἐθνάρχης Ἁρέτα τοῦ βασιλέως ἐφρούρει τὴν πόλιν Δαμασκηνῶν πιάσαι με, καὶ διὰ θυρίδος ἐν σαργάνῃ ἐχαλάσθην διὰ τοῦ τείχους καὶ ἐξέφυγον τὰς χεῖρας αὐτοῦ). 바울은 그의 "약함을 자랑"하기를 천명하고(30절), 그의 진술의 진실성을 공포한 후(32절)에 앞서 언급한 고난의 목록(23-29)과 관련되면서도 보다 약함의 성격이 뚜렷한 구체적인 고난의 경험을 계속 진술함으로써 "약함의 자랑"의 주제를 더욱 강화시킨다. 앞에서의 고난의 이야기는 영웅적 측면이 있으나, 다메섹 성에서 바구니를 타고 도망한 이야기는 영웅적 모습이 아니라 사도로서 부끄럽고 나약한 모습이다.[326] 바울이 "약함의 자랑"을 선언한 뒤에 이런 자신의 약한 모습을 분명하게 보여주는 이야기를 하는 것은 당연하게도 보이지만, 앞에서 말한 영웅적 제자도에 비해서, 너무나 무능하고 약한 바보 같은 모습을 보여 준다. 그래서 어떤 이들은 바울이 고난의 경험을 모두 말한 후에, 그의 약함을 자랑하겠다고 말하고, 끝으로 맹세로

326) K. Prümm, Diakonia , 657; Schlatter, *Paulus, der Bote Jesu*, 657, 주, 1; Windisch, 365..

마무리까지 하고 난 뒤에 불현듯이 이 사건이 생각이 나서 디모데에게 부가적으로 쓰게 한 말이라고 본다.[327] 학자들은 이 이야기의 위치가 어색하다고 보면서 바울이 여기서 이 이야기를 하게 된 더 자세한 연유를 나름대로 추정한다.

첫째, 이 사건과 12장 1-4절의 삼층천 경험이 거의 같은 시기에 일어났기 때문이다.[328] 그러나 이에 대한 확실한 증거는 없다. 둘째, 바울이 회개하고 처음 당한 일이어서 잊지 않고 기억하고 있었다. 이런 견해는 수긍이 가지만, 여전히 하필 여기서 그 경험을 말해야하는 이유가 확실하지 않다. 셋째, 바울의 겸비함을 나타내는 이야기로서 이 부분의 전체 주제와 일치된다.[329] 그러나 오히려 이를 바울의 담대한 영웅적 사건으로 생각한다면 이 문맥에 맞지 않는다고 볼 수 있다.[330] 그러나 이 이야기를 위의 고난의 사건과 구별하여 기록한 것은 분명히 이 이야기가 위의 고난의 사역 이야기에 비해서 바울의 부끄럽고 우스꽝스런 모습을 보여주기 위해서 따로 기록했다고 본다. 넷째, 바울의 반대자들이 이 사건을 들어서 바울의 약함을 비난했기 때문에 바울은 그들이 아는 사건을 들어 약한데서 강해진다는 논지를 펴나가는 것이다.[331]그러나 반대자들이 이 이야기를 알고 있다는 증거가 없다.[332] 다섯째, 앞의 고난의 이야기에 이어서 다메섹 성에서 내려와 도망하는 비

327) Windisch, 364; Héring, 82.

328) Osiander, 447.

329) Furnish, 541-2.

330) Windisch, 363.

331) Bousset, 209; Plummer, 332-3; Strachan, 28.

332) Bultmann, 220.

천한 모습을 다음에 나오는 삼층천에 오르는 고상한 이야기와 대조적으로 쓴 것이다.[333] 매우 수긍이 가는 제안이다. 그러나 바울은 이런 대조를 통해서 약함의 주제를 일관되게 유지하고 있다고 본다.[334] 즉 다메섹에서의 도피 이야기는 물론, 12장 1-4절의 삼층천 경험도 결국은 역설적으로 약함의 논리를 강조하는 역할을 하고 있다. 즉 "자고하지 않게 하기 위해 주신 몸의 가시"를 위한 예비적 이야기라고 본다. 여섯째, 당시 로마 시대 전쟁 시에 적의 성벽을 먼저 오르는 병사를 영웅으로 추대하던 전통을 바울은 자신의 반대되는 경험(성벽을 타고 내려 오는 경험)을 들어 비웃는 패러디로 나타내고 있다. 즉 "육체적 자랑" 을 버리고 대신에 "약함의 자랑"을 하는 것이다.[335] 일곱째, 바울은 잠언 21장 22절의 "지혜로운 자는 용사의 성에 올라가서 그 성의 견고히 의뢰하는 것을 파하느니라"를 염두에 두고서 그의 적들이 성에 올라간 지혜로운 자들로 자처하는 것에 견주어 자신은 성을 도망해 나온 비천한 처지임을 말하고 있다고 본다.[336] 바울은 이런 비교를 통해서 자신이 하나님을 의지하여 구원 얻었고 적들은 자신들의 지혜만 의지하고 있음을 암시한다고 한다.[337] 그러나 독자들이 이런 바울의 암시적 의미를 알았을지는 의문이다.[338] 여덟째, 위에서 우리가

333) Hughes, 422.

334) 참조, Thrall, 764.

335) Furnish, 542; Martin, 384; 두 사람 모두 다음의 두 자료를 사용한다: E. A. Judge, "The Conflict of Educational Aims in New Testament Thought", *Journal of Christian Education* 9 (1966), 32-45, 44-45; Travis, 530.

336) Martin, 384-5.

337) Martin, 385.

338) Thrall, 756.

지적한 바와 같이 이 이야기는 위치와 성격상 앞의 고난의 이야기와 뒤에 나오는 삼층천 경험을 연결해주는 고리 역할을 한다.[339] 앞의 고난의 목록이 약함과 영웅적 담대함("육체적 자랑")을 동시에 나타낸다면, 이 이야기는 같은 고난 이야기 이지만 순수하게 약함만을 나타내는 이야기로서 아래에 나오는 "몸의 가시"와 함께 강조되는 "약함 가운데 강해짐"의 주제와 잘 연결된다고 본다. 바울은 앞의 고난의 이야기가 이중적 성격을 가졌다고 본다. 즉 그의 "약함"을 나타내는 증거도 되지만, 육체적 자랑에 해당된다고 보고 언급하기를 주저했다(11:16-18). 그래서 30절에 "내가 부득불 자랑할진대 나의 약한 것을 자랑하리라"라고 말한 뒤에 순수하게 자신의 약함을 나타내는 일례를 들고 있는 것이다.[340] 바울은 그리스도의 사도로서 고난당하는 것은 자랑에 해당되고, 순수한 약함을 나타내는 증거가 될 수 없으므로 다메섹에서 도망한 이야기로써 사도라는 자신의 약하고 무능했던 이야기를 솔직하게 공개하는 것이다. 이 사건은 기적도 아니고, 고난을 견디는 이야기도 아닌, 고난을 피해 도망했던 이야기로서 바울의 사역 가운데 창피하고 부끄러운 예로서 그의 약함의 주제를 잘 나타내는 것이다. 다음에 나오는 삼층천의 이야기는 이 이야기와 뒤에 나오는 "약한 가운데서 강해진다는 계시"와 함께 약함에 대한 전체적 주제를 강조하기 위해서 역설적이고 대조적인 역할을 하고 있다고 본다. 즉 이런 영적 체험은 자고하게 하는 위험성이 있어서 나를 약하게 만드는 경험들을 하나님께서 주셨다는 것이다. 실제로 위

339) Zmijewski, 288-9.

340) 참조, Thrall, 765.

에서 지적하였듯이 바울은 고린도후서에서 자신의 약함을 의도적으로 나타내어서 같은 약한 경험을 가진 독자들에게 호소하고 그로 인해서 서로 친밀하게 되려는 증거들이 있다. 1장에서 바울은 아시아에서 당한 고난을 말하면서 죽음에 직면하여 두려웠던 감정을 솔직히 말하고 있고, 4장 7절에서도 바울은 자신을 질그릇같이 약한 것으로 나타내면서 자신의 약한 모습을 그린다. 본문도 이런 입장에서 사도와 교인이라는 형식적인 관계를 넘어서서 진솔하고 평범한 인간관계 가운데서 일어나는 깊은 내면적 형제의식을 가지려고 하는 듯하다. 이런 겸비한 자세는 거룩하고 오만한 자랑으로 자신들을 높이려는 반대자들과 대조를 이루는 것이다. 위의 학자들의 추정들 가운데 셋째(바울의 약함)와 다섯째(삼층천 경험과 대조적 이야기) 그리고 여덟째가 우리의 견해와 보조를 같이 한다.

이 사건은 약간의 기록의 차이는 있으나 사도행전 9장 23-25절에 언급된 사건과 대체로 일치한다.[341)] 이 사건은 바울 회심 후 주후 39년경에 일어난 것으로 본다.[342)] 바울은 회심 후에 2년간 다메

341) Thrall은 두 기록을 비교하면서 몇 가지 차이점들을 지적하나 한 사건임이 분명함을 말한다(770-1).

342) J. Taylor, "The Ethnarch of King Aretas at Damascus: A Note on 2 Cor 11.32-33," *Revue Biblique* 99 (1992), 727; Murphy-O'Connor, *Paul: A Critical Life* (Oxford: University Press, 1996) 82; 이들 모두 이 사건을 주후 39 년으로 보는 C. Saulnier를 따른다. C. Saulnier, "Hérode Antipas et Jean le Baptiste. Quelques remarques sur les confusions chronologiques de Flavius Josèphe," *Revue Biblique* 91 (1984), 362-76; Strachan, 28; Denney, 345; Wendland, 243, 등도 바울의 회심을 37년으로 보고 2년 뒤 39년에 일어난 사건으로 본다.

섹에 체류하면서 복음을 전했고, 그곳 주민은 나바타인(Nabataean)이지만 바울은 그곳에 거주하는 유대인들의 미움을 받아서 유대인들이 소동을 일으키자 헤롯 안티바스의 장인이며 로마의 분봉왕 아레다4세(Aretas IV, 9 B.C. 39/40 A.D.)의 방백(ἐθνάρχης, 시장)이 민심 수습을 위해서 바울을 잡으려고 한 것으로 본다.[343)]

e. 나도 영적 체험을 했다 (12:1-4).

12:1. "무익하나마 내가 부득불 자랑하노니 주의 환상과 계시를 말하리라"(Καυχᾶσθαι δεῖ, οὐ συμφέρον μέν, ἐλεύσομαι δὲ εἰς ὀπτασίας καὶ ἀποκαλύψεις κυρίου). "무익하나마 내가 부득불 자랑하노니"는 이미 앞서 11장 16, 17절에서 독자들의 양해를 구하며 한말이 여기서 다시 되풀이 된다. 이것은 바울이 11장 16절에서 시작한 "육체적 자랑"의 주제를 계속해서 이어간다는 증거다. 실제로 바울은 10장부터 "육체적 자랑"을 논하기 시작했다(10:8, 13, 15-17; 11:10, 12). 그러나 자신의 "육체적 자랑"을 집중적으로 열거한 것은 11장 15절 부터이다. 11장 22절에서 33절까지는 바울의 고난의 사역을 자랑하였으나, 12장 1-4절의 삼층천 경험은 이와 달리 영적으로 고양된 경험이다. 그러나 앞서 지적한 바와 같이 이 경험에 이어서 다시 "육체의 가시"라는 고난을 언급하므로, 바울은 "육체적 자랑"을 통해서 "약함을 자랑"하고 있다.

343) Thrall, 766-771에서 이 사건의 역사적 배경과 나바타 왕에 대한 더 자세한 설명을 보라.

영적 체험담은 그의 약함을 강조하려는 예비적 이야기에 불과하다는 것을 계속 주지해야 한다. 바울은 영적 체험을 자랑하는 것도 결국은 "육체적 자랑"이라고 본다. 영적 체험은 하나님의 선물인데 그것을 사람들에게 자랑하여 자신을 높이려는 것은 오만한 것이며 결국은 "육체적 자랑"에 해당되는 것이다.[344] 어쩌면 영적 체험에 따라서 객관성이 없는 당사자의 주관적 환상으로 판명이 되는 경우도 있을 수 있으므로 신뢰성 문제도 있다. 그러므로 이런 자랑은 "무익하다"고 한다. 그럼에도 바울은 그의 대적자들이 영적 체험 자랑을 하면서 바울은 그런 경험이 없다고 멸시함으로 그들의 육체적 자랑의 어리석음을 밝히기 위해서 자신도 그들이 자랑하는 영적 체험에 못지않은 영적 체험이 있었으나 여태껏 그들처럼 자랑하지는 않았다고 밝혀야 할 때라고 생각하는 것이다.[345] 학자들은 바울의 적들이 자신들의 영적 체험을 자랑하며 사도의 중요한 표로 제시하였다고 본다.[346]이에 대해서 바울은 영

---

344) Martin, 398.

345) Martin, 398.

346) A. Schlatter, *Paulus, der Bote Jesu* (Stuttgart: Calwer Verlag, 1969), 658; J. Baumgarten, *Paulus und die Apokalyptik, Die Auslegund apokalyptischer Überlieferung in den echten Paulusbriefen,* WMANT 44 (Neukirchen-Vluyn: Neukirchener Verlag, 1975), 145, 146; A. T. Lincoln, *Paradise Now and Not Yet*, SNTS 43 (Cambridge: University Press, 1981), 72; "Paul the Visionary: the Setting and Significance of the Rapture to Paradise in 2 Corinthians 12:1-10," *NTS* 25 (1979), 204-20; Schmithals, *Gnosticism*, 209; Barrett, 307; Plummer, 338; Wolff, 242. 한편, Windisch는 대부분의 학자들과 달리, 본문에서 반대자들이 영적 자랑을 하였다는 증거가 없다고 한다(368). 그러나 11:22, 23절에서 바울이 적들과 자신을 비교하였고, 또 12:9에서 주님으로부터 받은 계시의 말씀(환상이 아닌)을 중시하는 것으로 보아서 반대자들의 영적 체험 자랑을 경계한다고 보는 것이 옳다고 본다.

적 체험의 자랑이 하나님의 영광을 막고 사람의 영광을 나타내는 것이라면 그것은 무익할 뿐만 아니라 오만한 죄가 된다고 본다(12:7). 영적인 체험을 자주 말하면 말하는 사람에게 관심이 집중되고 그를 필요 이상으로 거룩한 사람으로 오해하게 만들어 하나님의 영광을 가릴 수 있다는 것을 바울은 알고 있다.[347] 바울은 그리스도의 사도로서 자신의 진정한 자랑은 영적 체험의 자랑이 아니라 죄인을 깊이 사랑하는 그리스도의 마음으로 그리스도의 고난에 동참하는 것임을 고린도 교인들에게 알려서 그들이 진정으로 바른 믿음을 가지는 것을 간절히 원한다(13:4; 7). 바울의 목적은 그의 대적자들처럼 영적 체험의 자랑을 통한 사도권 확립이 아니라 고린도 교인들이 그리스도를 충심으로 사랑하는 바른 믿음을 가져서 그리스도의 왕권이 온전히 확립되는 것이다(13:10). 다시 말해서 반대자들의 영적 체험 자랑을 남용하는 것을 막기 위해서 바울 자신의 영적 체험을 자랑할 수밖에 없었다. 그것은 일종의 "필요 악"이었다.[348] 자랑하는 것이 상책은 아니지만 자랑하지 않는 것이 더 부적절하다고 보았다.[349]

거듭 말하지만, 바울이 영적 체험을 말하는 목적은 역시 전체 고난의 주제를 강조하기 위한 예비적인 것이다. 즉 바울이 이런 영적 체험도 가지고 있으나, 그 보다 더 중요한 것은 자신이 그리

---

347) Martin, 396.

348) Martin, 396.

349) Barrett, 306; Demetrios Trakatellis, "Power in Weakness: Exegesis of 2 Corinthians 12, 1-13" in *Verteidigung und Begründung des Apostolischen Amtes(2Kor 10-13)*, ed., Eduard Lohse, Monographische Reihe von Benedictina (Roma: Abtei St. Paul vor den Maurn, 1992), 68.

스도의 고난에 참여하고 있다는 것이다. 그런데 진정한 그리스도의 사도의 표가 고난이란 사실도 바울 자신이 생각해 낸 것이 아니라, 그리스도의 계시에 의한 객관적인 것임을 알리는 것도 이 부분의 중요한 목적이다(12:9). 바울의 그리스도 중심 신학은 자신의 추론이 아니라 그리스도의 계시에 근거한 것이다. 바울은 대적자들 보다 고난도 많이 받았고, 또 그들에게 못지않게 영적 체험에 있어서도 대단하다는 포괄적인 자랑을 하고 있을 뿐만 아니라, 그가 주장 하는 고난의 의미와 효능도 사실은 그리스도로부터 직접 받은 계시임을 밝힘으로써, 그의 사도로서의 권위에 대한 신뢰성을 한층 더 높이려는 것이다.

"주의 환상과 계시를 말하리라"에서 ὀπτασίας(환상)과 ἀποκαλύψεις(계시)가 각기 복수인데도 바울은 실제로 한 가지 영적 체험만을 말하고 있다. 이것은 바울이 7절에서도 밝히는 대로 자신은 실제로 여러 영적 체험을 가졌으나, 여기서는 한 가지만 말하는 것이 대적자들의 영적 체험의 남용의 부당함을 지적하는 자신의 입장에 적절하다고 생각한듯하다. 바울의 여러 환상에 대한 언급의 예는 사도행전 9장 3-7절, 18장 9-11절, 22장 17-21절, 23장 11절, 27장 23, 24절에 있고, 고린도전서 9장 1절, 15장 8절에서 부활한 주님을 만난 것을 언급한다. 또 고린도후서 4장 6절도 다메섹 경험을 가리킨다고 볼 수 있다. 바울의 말하려는 삼층천 경험은 분명히 "환상과 계시"의 이중적인 경험이었다. 바울은 그곳이 삼층천임을 알았고(2), 또 "말할 수 없는 말"도 들었기 때문이다(4).

ὀπτασίας(환상)과 ἀποκαλύψεις(계시)는 특별한 차이가 없는 동의어 이다.[350] 바울 서신에서 ὀπτασίας(환상)보다 ἀποκαλύψεις(계시)가 더 많이 쓰였으므로 중요한 개념이라고 볼 수도 있으나[351] 모든 환상이 계시를 말하고, 모든 계시가 환상을 수반하는 것은 아니다.[352] 여기서는 환상이 계시를 수반한 경우이며, 12장 9절은 환상이 없는 직접 계시로 보인다.[353]

한편 "주님의 환상과 계시"에서 κυρίου(주님의)의 제 2격을 소유격(환상과 계시를 한정하는 의미, 즉 "주님의")으로 보고 번역할 것인가 인가 아니면 기원의 주격으로 볼 것인가를 두고 이견이 있다. 대부분은 기원의 주격으로 보고 "주님이 주신 환상과 계시"로 보며, "주님의 환상과 계시"("주님을 보는 환상과 계시")로 보는 이는 적다.[354] 그러나 환상과 계시를 주신 주님이 결국 모든 진정한 환상과 계시의 목적임을 주지할 때 지나친 구별은 피해야 한다.[355]

2. "내가 그리스도의 안에 있는 한 사람을 아노니 십 사년 전에 그가 세째 하늘에 이끌려 간 자라(그가 몸 안에 있었는지 몸 밖에

---

350) Windisch, 368; Furnish, 524.

351) 롬 2:5; 8:19; 고전 1:7; 갈 1:12; 2:28; 참조, 살후 1:7.

352) Plummer, 338; Tasker, 170.

353) 12:2-4를 실제 체험이 아니라 반대자들의 영적 체험을 비웃기 위한 패러디로 보는 Furnish, (533)과 H. D. Betz, *Der Apostel Paulus und die sokratische Tradition*, 84-93을 보라. 이를 비판한 Thrall(777-8)을 보라.

354) Bultmann, 220; Furnish, 524.

355) Zmijewski, 330-1; Lincoln, 205, 205; Hughes, 428, 주 97; J. Dunn, *Jesus and the Spirit* (Philadelphia: Westminster Press, 1975), 414, 주, 88.

있었는지 나는 모르거니와 하나님은 아시느니라)" (οἶδα ἄνθρωπον ἐν Χριστῷ πρὸ ἐτῶν δεκατεσσάρων, εἴτε ἐν σώματι οὐκ οἶδα, εἴτε ἐκτὸς τοῦ σώματος οὐκ οἶδα, ὁ θεὸς οἶδεν, ἁρπαγέντα τὸν τοιοῦτον ἕως τρίτου οὐρανοῦ). 바울은 벌써 14년 전 일이지만 잊지 못할 놀라운 그의 영적 체험을 술회한다. "내가 그리스도의 안에 있는 한 사람을 아노니" 에서 바울이 그의 영적 경험을 말하면서 자신을 3인칭으로 나타낸 것에 대해 여러 의견이 있다.[356] 첫째, 바울은 랍비들이 자신을 가리킬 때 "본인" 으로 말하는 예를 따르는 것으로 보는 견해가 있다.[357] 그러나 왜 여기에서 이렇게 말하느냐가 문제다. 둘째, 바울은 그의 반대자들이 그들의 영적 경험으로 자신들의 현재적 신분을 자랑하는 데 대하여 자신을 제3자로 표시하여 그의 영적 경험은 자신의 장래의 영광된 존재의 예비적 모습일 뿐이며 자신의 현실적 존재는 아니라고 반박하고 있다고 본다.[358] 그러나 여기서 현재와 미래의 존재 형식이 주제가 아니며, 반대자들이 영지주의자라는 견해는 다수의 학자들이 반대하고 있다.[359] 셋째, 바울은 영적 경험을 개인의 신앙문제로 간주하고, 자신의 공적 사역에서는 거리를 두려는 뜻에서 3인칭으로 썼다.[360] 그러나 바울은 주저하면서

---

356) 어떤 학자들은 3인칭으로 표현된 것을 중시하여 바울이 아닌 다른 사람에 대한 경험을 쓴 것이라고 하나, 전체 문맥에서 바울이 자신을 향해 말하는 것이 자명하다. 이에 대한 학자들의 다양한 견해를, Thrall, 778-780에서 보라.

357) Str-B 3:531.

358) Schmithals, 212-13.

359) Thrall, 781.

360) Käsemann, "Legitimität," 64, 66-7; Baumgarten, *Apocalyptik*, 143-44; Spittler, "Limits," 261; Furnish, 544; Lincoln, "Visionary," 210.

도 이 영적 체험을 자랑하기 위해 언급한다고 한다(12:1). 넷째, 세 번째와 유사하게 바울은 자신의 영적 경험을 자랑을 하는 것을 주저하면서 겸손히 말하기 위해서 3인칭을 쓰고 있다.[361]이 견해를 주장하는 벧츠(H. D. Betz)가 말하는 대로 바울의 겸비한 자세를 소크라테스같은 헬레니즘 철학자들의 덕의 전통을 따르는 것이라는 견해는 받아들일 수 없으나,[362] 초두에서 바울이 이런 자랑을 꺼리고 있는 것은 분명하다.[363] 카슨(D. A. Carson)도 바울이 자신을 보통 사람으로 낮추는 표현이라고 생각한다.[364] 바울이 서두에서 자신을 낮추고 있으나 동시에 여러 큰 계시의 경험을 "자랑하고" 있으므로(7) 이 구절을 겸손한 표현이라고만 보기도 어렵다. 다섯째, 바울의 경험은 그리스도 안(ἐν Χριστῷ)에서 자신이 배재된 철저히 수동적 체험이었으므로 3인칭을 썼다.[365] 이 견해는 다음 견해와 거의 일치한다. 여섯째, 바울은 영적 경험 중 몸과 자아가 분리된 것을 말하고 있다.[366]이런 견해에 대하여 환상 속에서 자신이 몸과 분리되었다면 이 환상 경험은 어떻게 기억하였겠느냐고 반박하는 견해가 있다.[367]그러나 이런 반박은 단순히 환상이 아닌 입신 같은 깊은 영적 경험에서 일어 날 수 있는 가능한 사실

361) Furnish, 542-44; H. D. Betz, *Der Apostel Paulus und die sokratische Tradition*, 84-92.

362) H. D. Betz, *Der Apostel Paulus und die sokratische Tradition*, 84-93.

363) Furnish, 542-44; Martin, 398.

364) Carson, 64.

365) Martin, 398-99.

366) Furnish, 69; J. D. G. Dunn, *Jesus and the Spirit*, 214-15; Wendland, 219; R. Reizenstein, *Hellenistic Mystery Religions*, tr. J. E. Steely (Pittsburgh: Pickwick, 1978), 82, 83.

367) Windisch, 369; Héring, 90.

을 도외시하는 순전히 논리적인 반박일 뿐이다. 바울은 자신이 몸 안에 있었는지 몸 밖에 있었는지를 느끼지 못했다고 한다. 그런데도 이런 영적 경험에 대한 두뇌의 기억 능력이 작용한 것이다. 다니엘이 계시를 받았을 때의 경험과 유사한 것이라고 볼 수 있다(단 8:18; 10:8, 9). 다니엘은 영과 육의 분리의 경험을 했다는 말은 없으나 잠들거나 정신을 잃은 상태가 같은 경험을 나타낸 것이라고 말할 수 있고, 잠이 깬 후에 그가 본 이상을 그대로 기억하여 기록할 수 있었다. 우리는 이런 설명과 함께 다섯째 견해와, 그리고 바울이 그의 경험을 겸손하게 말하려는 의도라는 네 번째의 견해를 받아들인다.[368]

"그리스도 안"(ἐν Χριστῷ)은 다른 데서와 같이 "예수 믿고 구원받은 사람이 갖는 그리스도의 능력과 권세의 영역"을 나타내는 의미로 볼 수 있다(2:17; 5:17; 12:2).[369] 그러나 여기서는 다른 데서와 달리 신비한 영적 경험을 말하고 있으므로 "그리스도와의 깊은 영적 교제"의 의미가 전제되어 있다고 보아야 한다. 바울은 자신이 그리스도의 사도로서 오직 주되신 그리스도의 능력과 권세로 말미암은 진정한 영적 경험을 하였음을 강조한다. 그의 영적 체험은 그리스도와 영적 교제 가운데 그의 능력과 권세로 일어난 그리스도 중심적 진정한 경험이다. 이런 영적 체험의 그리스도 중심적 성격에 대한 강조는 다른 데서 이 구절이 사용된 바와 같이 그의 영적 경험을 그의 대적자들의 것과 차별하려는 뜻이 있다. 그들은

368) Thrall, 782; Martin, 398.

369) J. A. Ziesler, *Pauline Christianity* (Oxford: University Press), 63.

"육체를 따라서 그리스도를 아는 이들"이며(5:17), "육체를 따라 자랑하기를 좋아하는 이들"이며(10:7, 10; 11:18), 거짓 사도들이며, 사단의 역군들로서(11:13, 15), 그리스도와 상관이 없는 "그리스도 밖"에 있는 이들이다. 그러므로 그들이 자랑하는 영적 체험도 진정한 체험이 아니라는 암시가 있다. 바울은 영과 육이 분리되는 신비한 체험을 하는 경우에도 "그리스도 안"에서 떠나지 않았음을 강조하고 있다. 흔히 말하는 자기도취나 어떤 보편적이고 자유로운 종교적 체험이 아니라, 그리스도의 영적 능력과 권세에 복종하는 경험이었다는 것이다. 5장 18절에서 원하는 대로 몸을 떠나 온전히 그리스도와 함께 있는 경험을 한 것이다. 그러나 5장 19절에서 말하는 대로 바울은 사나 죽으나 그리스도를 중심으로 살고 그를 기쁘시게 하는 자가 되는 것이 삶의 목적이라는 의미가 들어 있다.

"십 사년 전에"(πρὸ ἐτῶν δεκατεσσάρων)에서 바울이 이런 오랜 세월을 언급하는 특별한 의도에 대해 이견이 있다. 첫째, 바울은 이런 경험을 당시에 말할 수도 있었으나 자랑이 될 수 있으므로 오래 동안 일부로 말하지 않다가 대적자들의 오만한 자랑을 막기 위해서 이제야 말한다는 뜻이다.[370] 고린도 교회의 반대파들이 영적 경험의 자랑을 하고 있지만 바울 자신은 같은 경험을 이미 14년이란 오랜 세월 전에 했다는 뜻도 있을 것이다. 다만 반대자들의 의심을 피하기 위해서 "14년 전"이란 말로 그 경험의 실제성을 밝힐 필요는 있었다고 생각했을 것이다. 둘째, 첫 번째 견

370) Chrysostom, *PG* 61 cols. 575-6; *NPNF*, XII, 398.

해와 유사하게, 바울이 오래 동안 이 경험을 말하지 않은 것은 그것이 사도직의 정당성에 관련된다고 보지 않기 때문이었고, 지금도 그렇다는 뜻이다.[371] 그러나 지금은 주저하면서도 그 경험을 말할 수밖에 없는 상황이라는 것이다. 셋째, 바울은 자신의 경험의 사실성을 밝히려는 것이다. 즉 바울은 예언자들이 소명을 받을 때 경험한 체험을 말하면서 정확한 날짜를 언급하여 그 환상이 실제로 일어난 역사적인 사건임을 밝히는 전통을 따라서 14년이란 세월을 언급한 것이다. 바울이 자신의 체험의 사실성을 강조한다는 것을 대부분의 학자들이 지지한다.[372] 넷째, 오랜 세월 동안 바울이 이 체험을 기억한 것은 그 체험이 바울에게 가장 깊고 소중한 경험이었고 또 희귀한 것이었음을 가리킨다. 이런 귀한 경험은 함부로 쉽게 말해서는 안 되는 특별한 내적 경험으로 보고 간직하여 왔던 것임을 밝힌다.[373] 그러나 바울은 7절에서 이 경험이 독특한 경험이긴 하였으나 결코 이와 유사한 경험이 적었던 것이 아니라 많았던 것이라고 말하여 대적자들이 자신들은 바울 보다 더 많은 경험을 가졌다고 자랑하지 못하게 예방한다. 이 경험은 많은 계시들의 경험 가운데 대표적 경험이다. 끝으로, 넷째와 유사하게, 이 경험을 사람들에게 공개하지 않도록 하나님께 지시를 받았을 것이다(4절). 그 경험의 내용이 장래의 비밀을 말한 것이라면 정한 시일까지 인봉하였다가 그 후에야 공개할 수 있다는 것은 묵시의 경험이나 종말에 대한 교훈에서 흔히 있는 일이다(사 29:11;

---

371) U. Heckel, *Kraft in Schwachheit. Untersuchungen zu 2. Kor10-13*, WUNT 2, Reihe 56 (Tübingen: Mohr, 1993), 59.

372) Baumgarten, 143; Zmijewski, 334; Thrall, 782, 83.

373) Thrall, 783; Hughes, 428; Trakatellis, 70.

단 12:4, 9; 마 24:36; 막 13:32; 행 1:7; 계 5:1; 6:1; 10:4; 22:10). 그렇다고 지금에 와서 이 경험을 공개하라는 특별 지시를 받은 것은 아니지만 14년이란 긴 시간이 지나고 이 경험과 거의 동시에 "육체의 가시"가 생겼기 때문에 이 경험을 여기서 예로 드는 것이 적절한 것으로 보았다. 실제로 바울은 그 내용을 공개한 것은 아니다. 경험 사실만을 공개한 것이므로 비공개의 원칙을 지키고 있다. 본문에서 4절의 "말 할 수없는 말"이 "말해서는 안 되는 말"의 뜻이라면 바울은 여전히 그 내용에 대해서는 비공개 지시사항을 지키고 있는 것이다. 이런 여러 가지 추정이 모두 가능하다.

물론 바울이 14년 전의 계시의 경험을 여기서 말하는 분명한 이유는 반대자들의 영적 체험 자랑에 대하여 자신도 같은 경험이 있음을 말하여 그들의 오만함을 지적하기 위한 것이다. 바울 자신은 이 경험과 다른 계시의 경험이 많았다고 밝히면서 이내 자신의 "몸의 가시"에 대해 말한다. 그 "몸의 가시"는 "하나님께서 나를 자고케 하지 않게 하시려고 주셨다"고 말한다(12:7). 고린도 교인들은 아마도 바울의 이 몸의 가시의 약점을 오랫동안 알았을 것이고 그의 반대자들도 이를 알았을 것이다. 그들은 바울이 자신의 병도 못 고치는 무능한 사도라고 비판하였을 것이다. 바울은 이를 알고 자신의 영적 체험을 몸의 병과 함께 말하여 영적 체험의 부작용(즉 남들이 그 경험을 지나치게 확대하여 생각할 수 있는 문제와 자신이 스스로 오만해 질 수 있는 문제)을 예방하고(6, 7), 자신이 깨달은 하나님의 뜻을 말하려는 것이다. 즉 영적 체험보다 더 중요한 것은 약한 데서 강하게 하시는 하나님의 능력이라는 것이다(9). 그는 솔직하게 자신의 병을 들어 내놓고 역설적으로 나타나는 하나님의 은혜를 말하지만, 그의 반대자들은 영적 체험담으로 자신들을 거룩하게 가장하는 오만한 거짓 사도들임을 암시하는 것이다(11:13).

이 경험을 바울의 생애의 특정한 사건과 관련시켜 언제 일어 난 일인가에 대해 논의하기도 한다. 바울이 고린도후서를 쓴 해가 주후 55년이라고 보면, 바울은 주후 41년에 이 경험을 했다.[374] 이 경험이 다른 데서 언급한 바울의 다른 경험을 가리키는 것이 아닌지에 대해서 몇 가지 제안이 있다. 첫째로, 이 경험은 갈라디아서 2장 2절에 바울이 이방선교를 논의하기 위해서 예루살렘에 올라갈 때 받았다는 계시를 가리킨다.[375] 더구나 이 계시도 "14"년 전에 받았다고 회상한다. 그러나 그 계시가 여기의 체험과 성격 상 같지 않다고 본다.[376] "14"년 이란 숫자도 우연한 일치일 뿐이라고 한다.[377] 둘째, 바울은 다메섹 경험을 말하고 있다고 본다. 바울은 그의 사도직의 정당성을 밝혀야하는 입장에서 그의 소명시의 초월적인 경험을 말하여 자신의 사도직의 정당성을 방어한다는 것이다.[378] 그러나 본문 4절에서 "말할 수 없는 말을 들었다"는 것은 그의 소명 경험과는 다른 체험으로 보인다. 소명 체험에서 바울은

---

374) 다른 여러 견해를 Martin, 399에서 보라.

375) J. E. Belser, *Der zweite Brief des Apostels Paulus an die Korinther* (Freiburg im Breisgau: Herder, 1910), 346; Bruce, 246.

376) Windisch, 373.

377) Martin, 399; J. Knox, *Chapters in the Life of Paul* (New York: Abingdon Press, 1950) 78, 주3.

378) 행9:3-19; 22:6-10; 26:12-18; C. H. Buck and G. Taylor, *Saint Paul: A Study of the Development of His Thought* (New York: Scribner, 1969), 222-4; 정규남, 182.

그리스도를 보았고, 그는 그의 말을 알아들었고 되풀이하여 말할 수 있었다(행22:7-8; 26:14-18). 셋째, 이 경험은 바울이 사도행전 22장 17-21절에서 말하는 예루살렘 성전에서 주의 말씀을 직접 들은 경험과 같은 것이다.[379] 그러나 여기서도 본문의 4절에서 주님을 만났다는 말이 없이 "말할 수 없는 말을 들었다"고 하나 사도행전 22장 18절에서는 바울이 주를 만나서 구체적으로 지시하는 말을 들었으므로 상충된다. 이상과 같이 여기서의 경험과 제대로 맞는 기록된 경험들이 없다. 또한 실제로 일어난 시기도 추정할 수밖에 없다. 바울이 바나바와 함께 안디옥에서 사역하는 기간 중일 수도 있다(행 11:26).[380] 또 본문과 갈라디아서 2장 1절에 있는 "14년"이란 말과 관련하여 바울이 예루살렘 방문 전 길리기아 다소에서 머무는 동안에 있었다고 추정하기도 한다(주후41년).[381] 또 좀 지나친 추정이지만 바울이 사도행전 14장 19절에서 루스드라에서 유대인들에게 돌 맞고 기절했을 때 경험한 것이라고 추정하기도 한다.[382] 결국 본문의 경험과 일치된 경험을 알 수 없고, 언제 일어났는지에 대해서도 바울이 말하는 대로 "14년 전"이라는 말 외에 아는 바가 없다. 바울이 더 분명히 그 경험의 역사적 정황을 말하지 않은 것은 아마도 이런 경험 자체를 언급하는 것조차 꺼리는 입장에서 자세히 말하기를 원치 않았을 것이다.

---

379) J. E. Osiander, *Commentar über den zweiten Brief Pauli an die Korinther* (Stuttgart: Calwer Verlag, 1858), 453; Denney, 347-48.

380) Hughes, 430, 31; Denney, 347.

381) Bruce, 246.

382) Martin, 399.

“그가 세째 하늘에 이끌려 간 자라” (ἁρπαγέντα τὸν τοιοῦτον ἕω τρίτου οὐρανοῦ). 이 말은 우선 히브리어의 하늘(שָׁמַיִם 샤마임)이 복수라는 사실을 생각나게 한다. 구약에서 3층 구조로 하늘을 나타내는 곳이 있다.[383] 느헤미야 9장 6절, 열왕기상 8장 27절, 역대하 2장 6절, 6장 18절에서는 “하늘과 하늘들의 하늘” (הַשָּׁמַיִם וּשְׁמֵי הַשָּׁמַיִם)이란 표현이 나온다(참조, 신 10:15; 시 68:33; 시 148:4). 첫째 하늘은 공기층을 가리키고, 둘째 하늘(“하늘들의 하늘”)은 그 위의 별들이 있는 궁창을 가리키고, 그 위에 보이지 않는 하나님이 계시는 곳이 있는 것으로 나타난다.[384] 첫째와 둘째 하늘은 가시적인 하늘이지만 둘째 위에 있는 하나님이 계신 셋째 하늘은 보이지 않는 세계로 추정된다. 특히 시편 68편 33절은 하나님이 “하늘들의 하늘을 타신” 것으로 말한다. 즉 하나님이 둘째 하늘 위, 즉 보이지 않는 3층천에 계신 것으로 말한다. 마치 하나님이 영으로 보이지 않으나 영적 실재인 것과 같이 그가 계시는 세계도 영적 실재(spiritual reality)이다. 히브리서 기자도 4장 14절에서 우리의 큰 대세자장 예수님께서 “승천하셨다” (개역 한글)고 했는데, 문자적으로 번역하여 “하늘들을 통과하여 지나 가셨다” (διεληλυθότα τοὺς οὐρανούς)라고 해야 옳다. 계속해서 히브리서 7장 26절에는 같은 대제사장 예수님이 “하늘들보다 더 높이 되신 자라” (ὑψηλότερος τῶν οὐρανῶν γενόμενος)고 한다. 이것을 피조 세계에 높이 군림하는 그리스도의 승귀의 의미로 해석할 수도 있으나, 히브리서의 모형론에 근거한 더 좋은 영원한 본향에

383) Hughes, 432-34.

384) 참조, Lincoln, 77, 78; Hughes, 432-34.

대한 일관되고 확고한 논리에 비추어 볼 때 여기서 삼층천의 개념을 배제한다고 보기 어렵다(11:10, 14, 40). 더구나 에베소서 4장 10절에도 예수님이 "모든 하늘들 위에 오르신 자"(ὁ ἀναβὰς υπεράνω πάντων τῶν οὐρανῶν)라는 말이 나온다. 즉 이두 경우 모두 위의 시편 68편 33절과 일치되게 둘째 하늘 위에 보이지 않는 셋째 하늘을 가리키고 있다.[385] 물론 신약에 그리스도께서 천국 위에 계신다는 말 대신 "천국으로 들어가셨다"라고 언급하는 곳이 있다.[386] 이 말도 그리스도께서 하나님이 계신 보이지 않는 삼층천에 가신 것을 의미한다고 생각된다.

칼빈은 3이란 숫자는 가장 높고 가장 완전함을 나타내는 숫자로서 천국의 지극히 귀한 곳들을 가리키기 위해 상징적 의미로 사용되었다고 본다.[387] 칼빈은 삼층천은 천상이 여러 층들로 이루어졌음을 가리키는 것이 아니라 천국 내에 있는 가장 높은 곳과 은밀한 밀실(密室)들을 가리킨다고 한다. (이와 유사하게 유대 랍비 전통에서는 낙원은 가장 높은 천국 안에 있는 지성소를 가리킨다고 보았다.)[388] 칼빈이 삼층천을 천국 내에서의 보다 높고 은밀한 부분을 가리키는 것으로 해석하지만 구체적인 층이 아니라 천국을 가리킨다는 점에서 우리의 견해와 일치한다. 그리고 칼빈은 성경에서 우리에게 알려준 지식 이상에 대하여 호기심을 갖는 것을

385) Hughes, 434.

386) 막 14:19; 눅 24:51; 행 1:10; 3:21; 벧전 3:22; 엡 5:9.

387) Calvin, 156, 157.

388) Morray-Jones, "Paradise Revisited," 268.

경계한다.[389] 휴즈도 칼빈과 같이 삼층천이란 말이 보이지 않는 영적 실재의 영역을 나타내기 위해 사용되었으나, 인간의 제한적인 용어로 보면서 다음과 같이 말한다.[390] "루돌프 불트만과 다른 많은 현대 학자들이 생각하는 바와 같이, 우리가 본문에서 당면한 문제는 과학이전시대의 유치한 삼층 구조의 우주에 대한 단순한 문제가 아니다. 그것은 초월성과 가장 탁월함을 어떻게 표현하는가의 문제다. 이런 것은 다만 "위," "저편," "더 높은 곳," 등의 지역을 나타내는 언어를 사용하여 암유적으로만 표현할 수 있다. 현대가 과학시대라고 하지만 이런 지역을 나타내는 언어들을 암유적 의미를 나타내기 위해서 일상생활에서 필수적으로 사용하고 있고, 심지어 과학적인 용어에서도, 등급, 비교, 권위 등의 (막연한)개념들을 사용하고 있는 것과 같다."[391] 휴즈는 다른 많은 학자들과 같이 3층천을 4절의 낙원과 같은 곳으로 보면서, 칼빈의 의견처럼 고난 받는 바울에게 하나님께서 주신 특별한 경험으로서 온전한 나라가 오기 전에, 영혼과 부활한 육체가 결합하기 전에, 미리 장래의 영광을 맛보는 특권을 주어서 그가 더욱 담대하게 사역할 수 있게 하기 위한 것이라고 한다.[392] 그러나 이 구절이 논쟁적인 문맥에 위치하고 있음을 고려할 때, 바울은 그의 반대자들의 영적 체험의 자랑에 맞서서 자신도 그들과 같은 영적 체험을 가졌음을 자랑을 하고 있음을 주지해야 한다. 더구나 바울이 이런 특별한 환상이나 계시를 받았다는 것은 그가 신적 계시의 매개자로

389) Calvin, 157.

390) Hughes, 438.

391) Hughes, 434.

392) Hughes, 435, 438; Calvin, 157.

서 하나님께 인정받았음을 증명하므로 고린도 교인들에게 그의 사도권을 인식시키는 데 도움이 되었을 것이다(12:11). 그러나 바울은 그의 대적자들과 달리 이런 체험의 부작용이나 위험성을 알고 있다(12:6, 7). 즉 경험자가 교만해지거나, 듣는 자가 들은 것을 부연 확대시키거나 경험자를 신성시하는 위험성이다. 아바 반대자들은 그들의 경험을 말하면서 이미 이런 경험자의 교만의 오류에 빠져있고 또 듣는 사람들을 미혹하였을 것이다. 그러므로 바울의 궁극적 목적은 이런 "육체적 자랑"을 넘어서 그의 약함을 자랑하고 그 가운데 그리스도의 능력이 있음을 가르쳐서 그의 사도권의 진정성을 나타내는 데 있다.

한편 유대교 문서에서는 7층천 구조를 자주 언급한다. 에녹2서(2 Enoch) 3-22장에서 에녹은 6층천을 지나서 7층천에서 주님을 만났다는 기록이 있다(*OTP* I, 111-39). 에녹서에는 하나님의 처소는 분명히 7천층이다(20-22; *OTP* I, 115; 135; 137). 많은 랍비문서에도 7층천이 언급된다(미쉬나, *Hagiga* 11b). 교부들도 이를 받아들였다.[393] 이외에 5층천이나 10층천에 대한 기록들도 있다.[394] 또 삼층천에 대한 언급이 유대교 묵시문학인 모세의 묵시(*Apocalyse of Moses*) 37장 5절과, 에녹 2서 8장 1절에 나온다.[395] 당시 사람들

---

393) Irenaeus(130?-202 A.D.), *Against Heresies*, Book I, ch. v, 2(*ANF*, vol. I, 322); Tertullian(160-220 A.D.), *Against the Valentinians*, xx(*ANF*, vol. III, 514); Clement of Alexandria(150-215 A.D.), *The Stromata*, Book IV, ch. xxv(*ANF*, vol. II, 438); Origen(185-254 A.D.), *De Principiis*, Book II, ch. xi, 6, 7(*ANF*, vol. IV, 299); *Against Celsus*, Book VI, ch. xxi(*ANF*, vol. IV, 582-83); Epiphanius(298-403 A.D.), *Haereses.*, Book XXVI, ch. x; Augustine(354-430 A.D.), *De Haer.*, 1, 4.

394) Lincoln, 212-3; *Apocalypse of Baruch* 11:1; *2 Enoch* 20:3b.

이 하나님의 세계를 더욱 높게 보면서 점차 천국 층을 증가시키는 경향이 있었다고 본다.[396] 삼층천은 7층천보다 아래인 낙원(paradise, 파라다이스)을 가리키는 것으로 보인다.[397] 바울은 본문에서 3층천에 갔다고 말하지만, 그렇다고 그가 일반적으로 알려진 7층천 구조를 몰랐다고는 볼 수 없다. 그런 말을 알고 있었으나 평소에 바울은 위의 구약 성경 구절들의 해석에 근거하여 7층천 설 보다 3층천 설을 따르고 있었다고 볼 수 있다.[398] 즉 본문에서 바울이 ἕως(…에까지)라는 특정한 장소에 이르는 전치사를 쓴 것은 3층천이 제일 높은 곳을 의미하는 곳으로 보면 더욱 그렇다.[399] 만일 7층천이 있는데도 3층천밖에 올라가지 못했다면 바울의 반대자들의 비웃음을 받을 수도 있었을 것이고, 바울이 그런 예상을 하면서 3층천까지만 올라간 경험을 여기서 구태여 말할 필요는 없었을 것이다.[400] 바울은 위의 성경구절들이 3층천을 나타낸다고 보고 3층천이 7층천 보다 신빙성이 있다고 보았을 것이다. 설령 바울이 당시 유행하던 묵시문학의 7층천에 대한 견해를 알고 있었다고 해도 3층천의 견해를 보다 성경적인 견해로 보고 받아들인 것으로 생각할 수 있다. 그러나 4절에서 3층천을 다시 낙원으로 고쳐서 말한 것을 보면, 바울 자신이 3층천을 문자적으로 믿었다기보다 당시 사람들의 용어를 빌려 쓰는 것에 불과하며,

---

395) 알파 사본의 *The Testament of Levi* 2-3장에 3층천에 대한 언급이 나오지만, 원래는 7층천으로 기록 된 것을 후대에 고친 것으로 본다(Thrall, 118, 주 118).

396) Thrall, 790.

397) Thrall, 789.

398) Barrett, 310; Martin, 402; Thrall, 789.

399) Hughes, 433; Tasker, 171; Martin, 402; Plummer, 343-4; Lincoln, 212.

400) Irenaeus, *Against Heresies,* Book II, ch. xxx, 7 (*ANF*, vol. I, 405); Lincoln, 212.

하나님이 계신 낙원의 세계에 이르는 영적 극치의 신비한 경험을 나타내는 말로 쓰였을 것이다. 사실 3층천이라고 하지만 1층천과 2층천은 결국 천국이 아닌 가시적인 물질세계에 속한 것이기 때문에, 이런 가시적인 물질세계와 대조적인 보이지 않는 영적세계를 가리키는 말이다. 그렇다면, 바울이 말하는 3층천은 신약의 다른 기자들이 말하는 천국과 같은 곳이며, 위의 칼빈이나 휴즈가 3층천을 "'영적 실체의 영역'에 대한 상징적인 표현"으로 보는 해석에 가깝다고 본다. 결론적으로, 바울은 그의 영혼이 본 곳이 이 세상과 구별될 뿐만 아니라 구약 성경의 가시적인 "하늘과 하늘들의 하늘"의 위에 있는 보이지 않는 지고의 영적 세계로서 하나님과 구원받은 성도들의 영혼이 거하는 세계임을 나타내기 위하여 그 당시 잘 알려진 3층천이란 말을 쓰고 있다.

"이끌려 간자라"(ἁρπαγέντα τὸν τοιοῦτον)에서 "이끌려"(ἁρπαγέντα)란 말은 마치 "휴거" 가운데 "환상 체험"을 한 것과 같다.[401] 여기서는 휴거가 아니라 입신 경험이라고 본다. "이끌려 갔다"(ἁρπαγέντα)는 말은 데살로니가전서 4장 17절에서 성도들이 주를 만나기 위해 공중으로 들림 받는 것을 가르칠 때 다시 나온다. 바울 당시 공중으로 들림 받는 종말론적 기대는 잘 알려진 일이었다.[402] 그렇다고 아무에게나 흔한 경험은 아니며, 그런 경

---

401) Martin, 401; Lincoln, 81; *Apocalypse of Moses* 37:5; *Wisdom of Solomon* 4:11; 행8:39; 계12:5.

402) Barrett, "New Testament Eschatology," *SJT* 6 (1953), 138, 139; 2 Enoch 7:1; 3 Apocalypse of Baruch 2:2; 랍비들의 영적 경험에 대해서, J. W. Bowker, "'Merkabah' Visions and Visions of Paul," *JJS* 16 (1971), 157-73; P. Schäfer, "New Testament and

험을 가진 사람을 특별히 존경하는 것은 자연스럽다. 그러나 우리는 이 전체 문맥("바보의 연설")에서 바울의 중심 주제를 늘 염두에 두어야 한다. 바울은 그의 약한 데서 강해지는 계시의 중요함을 가르치기 위해서 이런 영적 체험 이야기를 보조적으로 하고 있음을 주지해야 한다. 즉 이런 일시적이고 현상적인 영적 체험보다 더 중요한 것은 약한 가운데서 온전해지는 그리스도의 능력을 소유하고 나타내는 것이다(12:9).

"그가 몸 안에 있었는지 몸 밖에 있었는지 나는 모르거니와 하나님은 아시느니라"는 삽입된 진술이다. 바울이 이 말을 특별히 부가적으로 말하는 이유는 무엇인가? 그리고 이와 함께 바울이 그가 몸 안에 있었는지 몸 밖에 있었는지를 분명히 의식하지 못했다는 것을 말하는 뜻은 무엇인가? 첫째, 바울은 육체와 영혼이 분리된 무아지경 상태를 자신도 경험했다고 말하면서 고린도 교회 반대자들의 자랑에 정면 대응하는 것이라고 볼 수 있다. 바울은 그의 독자들이 헬라인들이든, 유대인들이든, 이런 진술을 잘 이해했으리라고 보고 말한 것이다. 헬라인들에게 영혼이 육체를 떠났다가 돌아온다는 이야기는 잘 알려진 것이다.[403] 또 유대인 독자들에게는 에녹이나 엘리야의 승천 이야기와 함께 에녹 2서에 나오는

Hekhalot Literature: The Journey into Heaven in Paul and Merkavah Mysticism," *JJS* 35 (1984), 19-35; 헬레니즘의 신비적 경험에 대해서, Plato, *Republic* 10:614-21; Philo, *The Migration of Abraham*, 34-35; *The Special Laws*, 3:1-2.

403) Plato, *Republic* X 614B-621B; Windisch, 374; Furnish, 525; Wolff, 243; Loncoln, 216; Plummer, 342; C F. G. Heinrici, *Das zweite Sendschreiben des Apostel Paulus an die Korinther* (Berlin: de Gruyter, 1887), 490.

이야기, 또 "아브라함의 약속"같은 위경(僞經)에 나오는 유사한 이야기들과 같이 익숙하게 들릴 것이다.[404] 당시 유대인들은 이런 묵시문헌을 통해서 희랍인들과 마찬가지로 영혼이 육체를 떠나는 경험에 익숙했다. 바울은 반대자들이 유대인이든, 헬라인이든, 그들의 영적 체험 자랑을 염두에 두고 너희들이 자랑하는 영혼과 육체가 분리되는 신비한 영적 경험을 나도 오래 전에 이미 했다는 사실을 강조하기 위해서 이 말을 삽입하고 있다. 실제로 바울 자신의 인간구조에 대한 생각도 대체로 2분법으로 육체(σώμα)와 영(πνεύμα)으로 나누어 생각하고 있다.[405] 둘째, 첫째 견해와는 대조적으로, 고린도 교회의 반대자들이, 영지주의적 황홀경의 체험을 자랑하는 이들이라면, 영혼이 몸 밖에 있었다는 경험을 말했을 것이고, 유대인들이라면 몸이 움직이는 경험을 말했을 터이지만 바울은 어느 쪽도 아니라는 뜻으로 이렇게 말한 것이다.[406] 바울은 반대자들의 경험과 자신의 경험을 차별화하기를 원했다. 이런 견해의 정당성은 고린도 교회 반대자들이 어떤 부류의 사람들인지가 제대로 파악되느냐에 달려 있다.[407] 또한 당시 유대인들이

---

404) 창5:24; 왕하2:11; *2 Enoch*, 1:6-10; 3:1(*OTP* I, 106, 108, 110); 22:8, 11(*OTP* I, 138, 140; *The Testament of Abraham*, 8:1-3; 12:12-14(*OTP* I, 899, 901); C. R. A. Morray-Jones, "Paradise Revisited (2 Cor 12:1-12): The Jewish Mystical Backgrounbd of Paul's Apostolate. Part 1: the Jewish Sources: Part 2: Paul's Heavenly Ascent and its Significance, " *HTR* 86 (1993), 268.

405) 롬 8:10, 16; 고전 2:5, 11; 5:4, 5; 6:17; 고후 7:1; 참조, 살전 5:23.

406) R. Jewett, *Paul's Anthropological Terms: A Study of their Use in Conflict Settings*, AGJU 10 (Leiden: Brill, 1971), 278; H. Saake, "Paulus als Ekstatiker. Pneumatologische Beobachtungen zu 2 Kor 12, 1-10," *Biblica* 53 (1972), 405; also in *NovT* 15 (1973), 154.

407) Thrall, 787.

영혼과 육체가 분리하는 것을 모른다고 가정하는 것도 무리다. 위에서 본 바와 같이 묵시문헌에서 그런 사례가 많이 나타나기 때문이다. 무엇보다 바울 자신의 인간론도 영혼과 육체의 2중 구조를 인정한다(고후 4:16; 5:1; 고전 15:51-53; 빌 1:23). 물론 희랍 인간론과 다른 점은 마지막 때에 일어날 육체의 부활이다. 셋째로, 앞의 적극적인 견해들과 달리, 바울은 여기서 3인칭을 사용하고, 무의식적 자아망각 상태를 말하면서 그의 대적자들의 자랑에 반대하여 이런 개인적이고 주관적인 영적 체험을 사도직의 증거로 내세우는 것이 부당함을 암시하고 있다고 본다.[408] 그러나 앞서 지적했듯이, 바울이 영적 체험 자랑을 육체적 자랑으로 보고 자랑하기를 주저하는 것은 사실이며, 이런 영적 체험 자랑도 결국 그의 약함을 자랑한다는 주제를 위해 보조적 목적으로 제시되고 있지만, 일단 자랑을 하는 이상, 지금은 그의 경험의 깊이와 진실성을 충분히 알리는 데 관심이 있다고 본다. 그래서 같은 말을 3절에서 되풀이 하고 있으며, 6절에서는 그는 그의 경험의 진실성을 다시 강조한다. 넷째, 바울의 경험에 있어서 몸과 영혼이 분리된 상태에서도 의식을 가지고 몸의 감각을 느끼는 경험을 그대로 말한 것이다. 뿐만 아니라 바울은 이러한 신비한 체험에서 느끼는 반의식적 무아지경 상태에 대해서 이미 알고 있었다고 본다. 에녹 1서 71장 1-5절에서도 같은 영적 체험에 대해 말하면서, 1, 5절에서는 영혼이 몸을 떠난 것으로 말하고 있으나, 3절에서는 미가엘 천사가 에녹의 오른 손을 잡아 올리는 것으로 표현된다.[409] 더구나 5장 8절

408) Martin, 403.

409) Lincoln, 216 재인용.

에서 바울이 "우리가 담대하여 원하는 바는 차라리 몸을 떠나 주와 함께 거하는 그것이라"고 말하는 것은 이런 과거의 황홀한 영적 경험을 회상하면서 말하는 것일 수도 있다. 그러나 이런 육체적 표현은 단순히 영적 경험에 대한 표현이거나 꿈을 꿀 때 몸이 움직이는 정도의 입신 상태에서의 부분적인 육체적 움직임을 말하는 것이며 몸 전체가 실제로 다른 세계로 간 것을 말하는 것은 아닐 것이다. 바울이 "몸 안에 있었는지"라는 말을 근거로 몸을 가진 채로 3층천으로 갔다고 보는 것은 무리한 문자적 해석이다.[410] 본문에서 바울은 의식과 감각이 있는 상태에서 입신한 경험을 말한다.[411]하나님의 계시를 받을 때의 인간의 상태가 이런 애매모호한 상태라는 것은 흔하다(단 10:8, 9). 이와 유사하게 누가는 바울과 베드로의 환상 경험을 비몽사몽이란 말로 썼다(행 10:10; 11:5; 22:17). 인간이 하나님과의 깊은 영적 교통을 할 때 인간 존재는 거의 무의식적이 된다. 그러나 "하나님은 아시느니라"는 말은 그 신비한 존재 상태가 바울의 육체적인 비정상적인 원인 때문이거나 또는 마술 같은 속임수도 아니며, 인간의 영적 훈련으로 도달한 상태도 아니며, 악령 같은 외적 요인에 의한 것이 아니라, 순전히 하나님께서 바울과 교통하기 위해서 만드신 특별한 존재 상태였음을 강조하는 것이다. 또한 바울의 경험이 단순한 영적 체험이 아니라 하나님이 주신 매우 중요하고 진정한 경험이라는 뜻도 있다. 바울은 아마 여기서 5장 1-10절에서 말하는 죽음으로 영혼과 육체가 분리가 되었다가 마지막 때 다시 재결합하는 신비

410) Plummer, 342; Martin, 400.

411) Thrall, 787; Cf. C. Rowland, *The Open Heaven: A Study of Apocalyptic in Judaism and Early Christianity* (London: SPCK, 1982), 384.

한 인간 존재의 변화에 대한 소망이 그의 14년 전 경험에서 현실적으로 이루어지는 것을 확인하고 크게 놀라워했음을 회상하는 것이다.[412]이 경험이 매우 놀라운 경험이었으므로 그는 거의 같은 말을 다시 3절에서 반복하고 있다.

3. "내가 이런 사람을 아노니 (그가 몸 안에 있었는지 몸 밖에 있었는지 나는 모르거니와 하나님은 아시느니라)" (**καὶ οἶδα τὸν τοιοῦτον ἄνθρωπον, εἴτε ἐν σώματι εἴτε χωρὶς τοῦ σώματος οὐκ οἶδα, ὁ θεὸς οἶδεν,**). 2절과 14년이란 말을 제외하고는 내용상 차이가 없으므로 반복적 진술이다.[413] 그러나 **καί**(그리고)란 접속사가 있고, 4절에는 3층천과 다른 낙원이란 말이 나오므로 바울이 다른 두 가지의 경험을 말한다고 보는 학자들도 고대로부터 있다.[414] 그러나 3층천의 경험이 너무나 고귀하고 거룩하고 말로는 형용할 수 없는 가슴이 벅찬 경험이었으므로 같은 말로 반복하고 있다고 보는 것이 더 자연스럽다.[415] 두 번 같은 말을 반복하고 나서 그는 겨우 그의 경험을 보다 자세히 진술할 수 있었다(4절).

412) Hughes, 431; Tasker, 171; Martin, 400.

413) Hodge, 283; Windisch, 371; 372; Tasker, 171; Barrett, 310; Hughes, 435; Zmijewski, 335; Martin, 403; Thrall, 791.

414) Irenaeus, *Against Heresies,* Book I, ch. v, 2(*ANF*, vol. I, 322); Tertullian(160-220 A.D.), *Against the Valentinians*, xx(*ANF*, vol. III, 514); Clement of Alexandria(150-215 A.D.), *The Stromata*, Book IV, ch. xxv(*ANF*, vol. II, 438); Denney, 349; Plummer, 344; Filson, 406; Schlatter, Paulus, 663, 663; J. D. Tabor, *Things Unutterable; Paul's Ascent to Paradise in its Greco-Roman, Judaic, and Early Christian Contexts*, Studies in Judaism (Lanham and London: University Press of America, 1986), 115; Meyer, 469; Heckel, *Schwachheit*, 57, 주. 17.

415) Windisch, 371.

또 4절에서 말하는 낙원에 대한 언급이 3층천에 대한 보다 자세한 추가적인 언급이라고 보면 3절이 καί로 시작되는 것은 자연스럽다.[416] 즉 3절에서 시작하여 4절에서 끝나는 낙원에 대한 내용이 2절에 있는 3층천에 대한 추가적 내용이다. 만일 3층천과 낙원이 두 가지의 독립된 경험들을 가리키거나 한 경험의 두 가지 다른 단계들이라면, 2절에서 14년이란 시간을 밝히고 듯이, 변화된 시간을 나타내는 말이 있어야 한다.[417]

"그가 몸 안에 있었는지 몸 밖에 있었는지 나는 모르거니와 하나님은 아시느니라"(**εἴτε ἐν σώματι εἴτε χωρὶς τοῦ σώματος οὐκ οἶδα, ὁ θεὸς οἶδεν,**). 2절에서 언급한 이 독립된 삽입절이 다시 반복되는 것은 바울의 경험이 너무나 거룩하고 감격적인 것이었음을 나타낸다.[418] 앞의 진술과 비교할 때, "나는 모르거니와"(**οὐκ οἶδα**)가 한번만 나오고, 몸 "밖"이라고 할 때, 앞에서는 **ἐκτὸς**를 썼으나 여기서는 **χωρὶς**를 쓰고 있다. 그러나 전체 의미에 있어서 모두 일치한다. 위에서 말했듯이 신령한 하나님이 인간과 영적 교통을 할 때 인간 존재 상태를 적절하게 변화시키는 것이다. 인간존재는 전능하신 하나님의 완전한 손에 사로 잡혀서 무아지경으로 들어가고 영혼이 육체를 떠나서 거의 죽은 자와 같이 되게 하는 것이다. 마틴은 이런 자아망각적인 표현이 반대자들이 유

---

416) Hughes, 437.

417) Bachmann, 391; Allo, 305; Hughes, 435; Wolff, 244; Lincoln, 211; Barnett, 560, 주, 21; Bultmann, 223; Barrett, 310; Morray-Jones, "Paradise Revisited," 278: 유대교 묵시 문학에서 두 단계 영적 체험의 예가 없다 고함.

418) Windisch, 371.

사한 영적 체험을 자신들의 사역의 타당성으로 내세우는 것을 책망하기 위한 부정적 의미가 있다고 한다.[419] 자신도 모르는 무의식적 경험을 가지고 사도직의 정당성의 증거로 삼는 것은 타당하지 않다는 것이다. 그러나 앞에서 지적한 바와 같이 바울이 영적 경험을 자랑하는 것을 반대하고 그 자랑의 위험성을 경계하는 것은 사실이지만, 그렇다고 그의 영적 경험의 가치나, 개인에게 미치는 내적 효과조차 무시하는 것은 아니다. 그는 또한 하나님의 모든 계시가 이런 특별한 상태를 통해서만 온다고 믿지도 않을 것이다. 그는 꿈을 통하여서도 계시를 받았고, 기도 중에서도 계시를 받았다. 그는 자연 계시도 믿었다(롬1:20). 그러나 바울은 이 독특한 "환상과 계시"의 경험을 매우 소중히 생각하고 14년 동안 간직해 왔다. 그리고 여기서 그 체험이 매우 감격적이었음을 반복적으로 진술하여 나타내고 있으며, "하나님은 아시느니라"는 말로 그 경험의 진정성을 누차 강조하고 있으며, 다시 6절에서 그 진정성을 강조하고 있다. 물론 문맥에서 바울은 이런 영적 체험의 자랑이 궁극적 목적이 아니고, 그의 반대자들과 전혀 다른 차원에서, 자신의 모든 약함 가운데서 그리스도의 능력을 가지고 있다는 것을 밝히는 것을 그의 궁극적 목적으로 삼고 있다. 바울은 영적 체험으로 오만해지는 위험도 알고 있다. 바울은 반대자들의 영적 체험의 남용을 지적하면서 자신의 영적 체험의 선용을 보여 주는 것이 목적이다. 그러나 우선은 반대자들의 자랑에 맞서서 그의 영적 경험의 감격과 진실성을 충분히 밝혀야 할 필요가 있다고 보는 것이다(1절).

---

419) Martin, 403.

4. "그가 낙원으로 이끌려가서 말할 수 없는 말을 들었으니 사람이 가히 이르지 못할 말이로라"(ὅτι ἡρπάγη εἰς τὸν παράδεισον καὶ ἤκουσεν ἄρρητα ῥήματα ἃ οὐκ ἐξὸν ἀνθρώπῳ λαλῆσαι.). 바울은 낙원으로 이끌려갔다고 한다. 여기에 나오는 "이끌다"(ἁπάζειν)는 동사는 수동태(ἡρπάγη)로 나와 있다. 신적수동태(神的受動態, *passvum divinum*)라고 하나님에 의해서 이루어지는 동작을 나타낸다. 이 신비스런 경험에서 바울은 영적으로나 육적으로 자신의 의지와는 상관없이 완전히 하나님의 인도와 능력으로 움직였다는 것이다. 바울은 하나님의 사람으로서 이런 체험을 전능하신 하나님께서 하게하신 것이었다. 이런 경험에 대한 증거는 바울이 영적 경험에 있어서 약하다고 비난하는 반대자들에게 반증 자료가 되는 것이다(4:6; 13:3).

낙원(παράδεισος)은 아마도 페르샤에서 기원한 것으로 보며, 일반인들이 다닐 수 없는 특별한 경내(境內), 또는 귀족의 정원을 가리킨다.[420] 희랍어로는 제노폰(Xenophon)이 처음으로 페르샤 왕이나 귀족의 정원을 가리키는 말로 썼다.[421] 70인역에서는 창세기 2장 8절과 3장 1, 23절에서 에덴동산(גן עדן, 간 에덴)을 가리키는 말로 나오며 전도서 2장 5절(פרדס, 파르데스), 에스겔 28장 13절, 31장 8절에도 나온다. 후기 유대교 묵시 문학에서는 이사야의

420) Hughes, 436.

421) J. Jeremias, on παράδεισος in *TDNT*, 5:765-73; Xenophon, *Anabasis*, I 2:7; II 4:14; *Cyropaedia*, I 3:14.

승천 9장 7절, 에녹2서 8장과 모세의 묵시 37장 5절에 나온다.[422] 신약에서는 본문과 누가복음 23장 43절, 요한계시록 2장 7절에 모두 3번 나온다. 요한계시록 2장 7절의 낙원은 에덴동산과 같은 모습으로 묘사되어 천국의 정원을 가리키며, 누가복음 23장 43절의 낙원은 "의로운 자"가 죽음 후에 가서 쉬는 곳으로 나타난다. 그러나 결국 모두 믿는 자가 죽은 후에 가서 쉬는 곳을 가리킨다. 바울은 그리스도의 사도로서 살아 생전에 장래의 영광스런 삶을 미리 맛보도록 초청받은 것이었다. 이 사실이 그의 사도직의 진정성을 증거하는 데 일조하기를 바울은 바라고 있을 것이다(13:3).

위에서 지적한 바와 같이 낙원은 2절의 3층천을 반복하여 설명하는 것이라고 본다. 차이가 있다면 3층천은 이 세상과 구별되는 하나님의 지고(至高)한 영역을 가리킨다면, 낙원은 그 같은 영역에서 성도의 교제가운데 평안과 즐거움이 있는 곳이라는 의미가 있다고 본다. 낙원은 유대교 묵시 문학에서 노아, 에녹, 아브라함, 모세, 엘리야, 이사야, 예레미야, 에스겔, 같은 인물들이 함께 거주하는 곳으로 나타난다.[423] 신약 시대 이후부터 낙원은 믿는 자들이 사망 후에 그들의 영혼이 쉬는 곳으로 나타난다. 공관 복음서의 변화산 경험에서 예수의 모습이 변하고 그가 모세와 엘리야와 교제할 때, 제자들은 두려워 아무 말도 하지 못했으나, 베드로가 "여기가 좋사오니 장막을 짓고 머물자"라는 제안을 했다는 것을 본문의 바울의 낙원의 경험과 비교해 볼 때에 유사한 점들이 있음

---

422) 후기 유대교 묵시문헌에서의 이 말의 발전에 관해서는 Windisch, 372, 373을 보라.

423) Hughes, 437.

을 본다(막 9:2-8; 마 17:1-8; 눅 9:28-36). 아마도 본문의 낙원에서도 바울은 이런 성도들과 교제하는 가운데 "말할 수 없는 말"을 들었을 것이다.

그러나 바울이 낙원에서 "말 할 수 없는 말을 들었다"는 사실은 장래에 대한 지식이 믿는 자에게 비밀로 제한되었음을 뜻한다.[424] 그러나 이 말이 바울이 들은 말을 공개하지 못하도록 지시 받았다는 뜻인지 자신도 무슨 말인지 이해하지 못하여 말할 수 없다는 뜻인지 알 수 없다.[425] 유대교 전통에서 장래에 대한 계시가 하나님이 정한 시간에 이루어 질 때까지 비밀로 지켜지는 사례가 있음을 생각할 때 전자가 후자보다 더 가능한 뜻으로 보인다.[426] 또 "사람이 가히 이르지 못할"(οὐκ ἐξὸν ἀνθρώπῳ λαλῆσαι)에서 ἔξεστι(에크세스티)는 신약에서 31번 나오는데, 모두 "그것이 옳다"는 뜻으로 쓰였다. 그러나 "그것이 가능하다"는 뜻도 있다. 앞에서 "말할 수 없는"(ἄρρητα, "말로 표현할 수 없는")이란 말이 있고, 여기서는 "말하는 것이 옳지 않다"고 금지하는 뜻이 분명하므로, "말로 표현이 불가능한" 계시는 공개해서는 안 된다는 하나

---

424) Calvin, 157; Martin, 405.

425) 전자로 보는 견해: Calvin, 157; Meyer, 470; Bultmann, 224; Zmijewski, 339; Barnet, 561, 주, 23; Martin, 405; Lincoln, 216; 후자로 보는 견해:J. D. G. Dunn, *Jesus and the Spirit*, 215; 두 견해를 종합한 견해: Hughes, 439; Thrall, 794.

426) 사 8:16; 단 12:4; 계 14:3; 에녹2서 17; J. Jeremias, *Jerusalem in the Time of Jesus*, tr. F. H. and C. H. Cave (London: SCM Press, 1969) 237-41; R. P. Spittler, "The Limits of Ecstasy: An Exegesis of 2 Corinthians 12:1-10," in *Current Issues in Biblical and Patristic Interpretation, in honor of Merril C. Tenney*, ed. G. F. Hawthorne, 259-66(Grand Rapids: Eerdmans, 1975) 263, 264.

님의 뜻을 전제하고 있다고 볼 수 있다.[427] 하나님의 신성한 계시의 비밀성과 비공개 지시도 하나님의 주권에 속하는 사안이라는 것이다. 아마도 바울의 대적자들은 영적 계시를 받았다고 자랑하면서 그 내용을 공개했을 것이다. 그러나 바울은 자신의 경우에는 "말할 수 없는" 내용이므로, 말하지 말도록 지시 받은 것으로 알고서 침묵한다. 반대자들은 이런 바울의 계시의 비공개를 비난하면서 그 진정성 문제를 제기할 수 있을 것이다. 바울도 이를 염려하면서 그 계시의 내용을 하나님이 금하시므로 공개하지 못하지만 그 경험의 진정성을 강조한다(6).

한편, 이런 특별한 하나님의 금지의 지시가 없었다 하더라도, 바울은 그의 경험의 의미를 더 깊이 생각하고 그 영향을 가늠하기 위해서 그 경험을 공개하지 않았을 수도 있다. 랍비 유대교의 전통은 기적이나 개인 체험을 언제나 성경의 가르침에 비추어 보아서 그 합당성을 평가했다.[428] 물론, 그러나 후자의 가능성, 즉 바울이 전혀 말을 이해하지 못했다는 가능성도 무시할 수 없다. 바울이 거의 무의식적 신비한 상태에서 계시를 받았음으로 계시의 불가해성은 납득 할만하다. 바울은 반대자들이 어떻게 말하든지 그의 경험을 그대로 말할 수 밖에 없다고 생각했을 것이다. 어떤 경우든지, 그 경험은 바울 개인에게 대단한 감동을 주었고, 바울 자신의 사역과 가르침에 크게 도움이 되었을 것이 확실하다.[429] 바울은 이

---

427) Hughes, 439; Thrall, 794: 은 "말로 형용할 수 없는" 이란 뜻이 지만, "말을 해서는 안되는" 이란 뜻도 있다고 함. 그러나 신비한 경험을 말하는 가운데 "말로 표현 할 수 없는" 의 의미가 들어 있다고 본다.

428) Eduard Lohse, 『신약성서배경사』, 박창건 역, (서울:대한기독교출판사, 1984), 209.

429) Calvin, 157.

후에 더욱 큰 확신과 열심을 가지고 사도직을 수행했었을 것이다.[430] 이런 점이 영적 체험의 긍정적 영향이다. 하지만 여기서 바울은 그 부정적 영향을 심각하게 생각하면서 이를 경계한다(7).

"말할 수 없는 말"(ἄρρητα ῥήματα)이 실제로 무엇을 가리키는 가에 대해 논의가 있다. 첫째는 유대인의 관점에서 보아서, 천사들의 노래아니면 하나님의 이름의 지칭이라고 한다. 에녹 2서 17장에서 에녹이 천사들의 노래를 들었는데 표현하기가 불가능한 노래였다고 한다.[431]또 2세기 랍비 아키바(Aquiba)는 말로 표현할 수 없고 해서도 않되는 하나님의 존재의 깊은 비밀들과 관련된 말들을 들었다고 한다.[432] 퍼쉬와 트롤은 바울이 들은 "말할 수 없는 말"이 아마 "하나님의 칭호"와 관련된 내용 일 것이라고 추정한다.[433] 그러나 이런 견해들은 유사한 사례에 근거한 추정들일 뿐이다. 둘째로, 바울은 당시 헬라시대의 밀의(密議) 종교의 예배 용어를 빌어서 그의 경험을 나타내고 있다고 보는 견해가 있다.[434] 밀의 종교의 의식적 용어는 외부인들에게는 이해할 수 없는 교리, 어귀, 환상의 표현들이라고 한다. 그 예로 헤로도터스(Herodotus)에서 종교 의식을 "말할 수 없는 말들"(ἄρρητοι)이라고 말 한

430) Calvin, 157; Hughes, 439; Martin, 406.

431) *OTP* I, 130.

432) Morray-Jones, "Paradise Revisited," 281.

433) Furnish, 545; J. W. Bowker, "'Merkabah' Visions and the Visions of Paul,' *Journal of Semitic Studies* 16 (1971), 157-73; Thrall, 795.

434) Windisch, 377-8; Georgi, *Opponents*, 282.

435) Herodotus, V 83; BAGD, ἄρρητος를 보라; Windisch, 377; Lincoln, 216; Thrall, 796, 재인용.

다.[435] 또 유리피데스(Euripides)의 바케(*Bacchae*)에도 바케 밀의(密儀) 종교에 입단하지 않은 사람들에게 그 종교 의식을 알리지 말라는 경고가 있다.[436] 이외에도 푸르타크(Plutarch)도 ἄρρητα를 다른 이들에게 알리지 말라고 명하고, 또 필로(Philo)도 유사하게 말한다.[437] 그러나 이런 용례가 바울의 경우와 일치하지는 않으나, 적어도 바울이 당시 헬라 인들이 알고 있는 유사한 용어와 경험을 쓰고 있다고 보아야 할 것이다.[438] 바울은 그의 무의식적 상태를 언급하였으므로 그의 계시의 비밀성이 하나님의 주권에 의한 것이며, 자의적인 결정이 아님을 암시한다. 바울은 그런 식으로 반대자들의 경험에 대하여 자신의 영적 우월성을 나타내려는 의도가 있었을 것이다(7). 다만 하나님이 바울에게만 알린 어떤 비밀이 바울의 가르침 속에 어떻게 나타났는지는 의문이다. 어쩌면 바울은 요한 계시록에 나타난 장래 세계에 대한 묵시적이고 상징적인 말들을 들었는지도 모른다. 그러나 그 내용은 보다 구체적인 종말론적 시간 계획일 가능성이 높다. 그런 상세한 계획은 하나님의 아들이 지상에 있을 때에도 알려 주지 않았다(마 24:36; 행 1:7). 사실 그런 세부 계획은 하나님의 백성들의 유익을 위하여서도 알리지 않는 것이 좋다. 사람들이 그런 계획을 알게 되면 하나님 노릇하듯이 교만 해질 수 있을 뿐만 아니라, 꾀를 피우거나 게을러질 수 있다. 하나님은 그의 백성들이 진지하게 종말을 기다리기를 원한다. 예수님도 종말을 기리리되 늘 깨어서 기도하며, 부지런히

---

436) *Bacchae* II. 471-2; Windisch, 377; Furnish, 527; Lincoln, 216; Thrall, 796 재인용.

437) Plutarch, *The Moralia*, 360; Windisch, 377; Furnish, 527; Philo, *De Somniis*(*Dreams*), I 191; Furnish, 527, Thrall, 796 재인용.

438) Thrall, 796-797.

일하는 착하고 신실한 종이 되도록 가르쳤다(마 24:36-44; 25:1-30; 행 1:7, 8). 휴즈는 바울이 낙원에서 들은 말들을 담은 진리는 바울의 종말론적 가르침 가운데 은연중에 간접적으로나마 나타났을 것이라고 생각한다.[439]

f. "몸의 가시"와 나의 약함 자랑(12:5-10)

5. "내가 이런 사람을 위하여 자랑하겠으나 나를 위하여는 약한 것들 외에 자랑치 아니하리라" (ὑπὲρ τοῦ τοιούτου καυχήσομαι, ὑπὲρ δὲ ἐμαυτοῦ οὐ καυχήσομαι εἰ μὴ ἐν ταῖς ἀσθενείαις.). "이런 사람"이란 앞서 2절에서 말한 "그리스도 안에 있는 한 사람"을 가리키는 것이다. 바울은 영혼이 육신에서 분리되어 낙원에 들어 간 입신 체험을 말하면서, 그의 영혼을 제3자로 객관화하여 의식 중에 있는 "나" 또는 육체를 가진 "나"와 분리하여 표현하는 것이다.[440] 그 특별한 체험을 가진 존재를 바울의 영혼이라고 보고, 그런 경험의 자랑을 그의 영혼의 자랑거리로 돌리는 것이다. 그리고 육신을 가진 자신을 위하여는 약한 것들 외에는 자랑치 않겠다고 하는 것이다. 이 말은 결국 바울은 12장 1절에서 말하듯이 그의 영적 체험에 대해 자랑하는 것을 사욕에서 나오는 어리석은 육체적 자랑으로 보고 꺼리고 있음을 나타내는 것이다. 그런 특별한 경험으로 초월적이고 미래적인 영광을 본 것을 자랑하는 것은 비현실적이며 땅에서 고난 받는 현재의 바울 자신

439) Hughes, 439; 고후 5:1-10; 고전 15:50 이하; 롬 8:38이하; 빌 1:21, 23; 살전 4:13 이하; 딤후 4:8, 재인용. 여기에 살후 2:2, 3도 추가될 수 있을 것이다.

440) Lietzmann, 155; Barrett, 312.

의 형편과는 동 떨어진 것이기 때문이다. 그가 진정 자랑하기 원하는 것은 "낙원에 갔던 영광의 존재"가 아니라 현재 이 땅 위에서 그리스도의 사도로서 사역하면서 받는 모든 실제적인 고난과 수고이다. 이런 의미에서 "낙원에서의 경험" 이야기를 넘어서 11장 23-33절에서 말하는 고난 받는 사역의 주제를 계속 이어가려는 것이다. 반대자들은 자신들의 신비한 경험을 가지고 자신들의 사도직의 정당성을 증거하려 하지만, 바울은 반대로 그런 경험이 아니라 고난의 경험을 진정한 사도직의 증거로 삼는 것이다. 바울은 평소에 장래의 영광은 현재의 고난 없이 이루어 질 수 없다는 것을 굳게 믿는다(고후 4:17; 고전 15:19, 58; 롬 5:3-4; 8:17). 현재의 고난 없는 장래의 영광은 진정한 그리스도인의 증표가 될 수 없다(고후 1:7; 빌 1:29; 3:10; 골 1:24; 살후 1:5; 딤후 1:8, 12; 2:3; 4:5). 다시 말하면, 신비한 경험 보다는 복음 사역을 위하여 수고하는 것이 진정한 사도의 마땅한 도리다(11:23; 12:12; 고전 15:10; 참조, 벧후 1:16-17; 3:15-16). 신비한 체험은 하나님의 선물이지만, 그에 대한 보상은 없다. 그러나 고난과 수고는 영적 성장과 장래의 보상이 약속된다(롬 5:4; 딤후 4:5-8). 더구나 바울이 12장 7절에서 지적하듯이 신비한 체험은 하나님의 은혜와 영광을 나타내는 대신에, 경험한 사람의 영광을 나타내어 오만하게 하는 위험도 있다. 그러므로 바울은 실제로 이런 영적 체험을 자랑하는 것이 아니라, 반대자들이 바울이 영적 경험이 부족하다는 비난에 대하여 자신도 과거에 놀라운 경험이 있음을 밝히는 것이다. 그러나 그 특별한 경험의 효능에 대해서는 소극적인 자세를 견지한다. 도리어 고난과 약함의 효능에 대해서는 적극적으로 말하는 것이다. 어떻게 그리스도의 유형을 따라서 사역하였느냐가 사도의 진정성 문제를 위한 가장 확실한 판단기준이 되는 것이다(10:13-16; 11:23-33). 또한 이런 영적 체험이 복음의 핵심이 아니라 그리스도의 십자가와 부활이 핵심이기 때문이다. 영적 체험도 6, 7절에서 말하는 부정적인 면이 있다.

6. "내가 만일 자랑하고자 하여도 어리석은 자가 되지 아니 할 것은 내가 참말을 함이라 그러나 누가 나를 보는 바와 내게 듣는 바에 지나치게 생각할까 두려워하여 그만 두노라"(Ἐὰν γὰρ θελήσω καυχήσασθαι, οὐκ ἔσομαι ἄφρων, ἀλήθειαν γὰρ ἐρῶ· φείδομαι δέ, μή τις εἰς ἐμὲ λογίσηται ὑπὲρ ὃ βλέπει με ἢ ἀκούει [τι] ἐξ ἐμοῦ). 5절에서 바울은 영적 체험의 자랑의 주제에서 고난의 주제로 화제를 돌리기 시작했다. 그리고 여기서는 화제를 돌리는 이유를 영적 체험의 효능의 한계 또는 부정적 면이 있기 때문이라고 지적한다. 5절에서 바울은 영적 경험을 자랑하는 것에 대하여 소극적이었다. 아마도 그 유익과 효능에 있어서 고난(약함)보다 못하기 때문이었다고 보았기 때문일 것이다. 그러나 여기서 그 영적 경험이 진실한 것임을 재확인한다. 그리고 그것은 단순한 자랑이 아니라 실제로 바울의 개인적 영적 성장을 위해 도움이 되었을 것이다. 그러나 바울은 곧 그 영적 체험의 부정적 효능 때문에 계속 자랑하기를 그친다고 말한다. 첫째, 고린도 교인들이 바울이 말하는 환상("나를 보는 바")과 계시("내게 듣는 바")를 듣고, 바울을 지나치게 하나님의 거룩한 사람, 또는 신인(神人, θεῖος ἀνήρ)으로 보고 영광을 하나님께 돌리지 않고 바울에게 돌리게 되는 위험성이 있음을 보는 것이다. 바울은 고린도 교인들이 자신이 그리스도를 위하고 그들을 위해 평소에 진실하

게 봉사하는 사도로서 이해하기를 원하는 것이다(5:15; 7:2-3; 11:9). 둘째, 고린도 교인들이 바울을 "육체를 따라" 알고 "주를 따라" 알지 못하는 것을 원치 않았다(11:17, 18). 바울은 외적인 증거보다는 그리스도의 사신으로서 그의 연약함 가운데 그리스도의 능력이 나타남을 증거하기를 원했다. 실로, 바울은 그의 다른 많은 경험들을 말할 수도 있었으나, 영적으로 미숙한 고린도 교인들이 잘못된 길로 빠지게 되기를 원치 않았기 때문에 그만 두기로 했다. 그의 반대자들은 이런 영적 체험의 부정적 효능의 위험성을 모르고 그들의 영적 체험을 자랑삼는 것과는 대조적이다. 어쩌면 여기서 "내가 만일 자랑하고자 하여도 어리석은 자가 되지 아니할 것은 내가 참말을 함이라"라는 말은 상대적으로 그 반대자들이 자랑하는 영적 체험의 진실성을 증명하기가 어렵다는 뜻도 내포되어 있을 지도 모른다(13:8).[441] 적어도 이런 이유들로 바울은 영적 체험의 자랑의 주제에서 떠나 고난의 주제로 돌아온다. 환상적인 "천상의 바울"에서 고난 받는 "지상의 바울"로 다시 돌아온다. 바울은 고린도 교인들과 반대자들이 그가 그리고 있는 그의 그리스도의 사도직에 대한 자화상의 전체 윤곽을 점차 파악하기를 원한다. 바울의 자화상은 하나님의 사람으로서의 거룩한 모습도 있으나, 그보다 온갖 고난으로 점철된 진실한 모습이며, 어둠 가운데 영광이 비치는 주님의 형상을 닮은 감동적인 모습으로 점차 드러나고 있는 것이다.

여기서 "내가 만일 자랑하고자 하여도 어리석은 자가 되지 아니할 것은 내가 참말을 함이라"라는 말은 방금 말한 영적 체험의

441) Barrett, 312.

부정적 의미와 달리 자신의 체험의 진실성, 사실성을 강조하고, 또한 앞서 지적한 육체적 자랑의 어리석음에도 불구하고(12:1; 11:16-18), 적어도 자신의 자랑의 진실성을 밝혀야 한다고 생각하는 것이다. "내가 참말을 함이라"는 말은 앞의 11장 31절에서의 "거짓말을 아니한다"는 말과 함께 바울의 양심선언 양식구이다(롬 9:1; 딤전 2:7). 바울은 여기서 먼저 한 말을 수정하여 거짓된 자랑이 아닌 진실한 자랑은 어리석지 않다고 말하고 있는가? 그러나 바울이 앞서 자신이 실제로 겪은 고난 목록을 말할 때도 어리석은 자랑이라고 말한 것으로 미루어 보아서 "거짓이 아닌 진실한 자랑"은 괜찮다는 뜻으로 말하는 것은 아니다(11:16-17). 모든 인본주의적인 육체적 자랑을 어리석은 자랑이라고 보는 것이 문맥에서 분명하다.[442] 바울이 다른 곳에서도 이런 인본주의적 자랑을 금하고 있다(참조, 롬 15:17). 그럼에도 불구하고 반대자들에게 미혹 받는 고린도 교인들을 위해서 잠시 어리석은 자로서 자신의 자랑을 할 수 밖에 없다는 것을 누차 말하고 있다(11:16-17; 12:1; 12:11). 여기서는 단순히 바울의 자랑의 내용의 진실성을 강조하는 말이라고 본다. 모든 육체적 자랑이 어리석지만, 사실이 아닌 거짓된 자랑은 더욱 어리석은 것이다. 육체를 따라서 자랑하는 일은 모두 어리석은 일이지만, 바울의 자랑은 적어도 실제로 일어난 것임을 강조하는 것이다. 자랑하는 것이 어리석은 줄 모르고 절제

---

442) 바울은 다른 곳에서도 이런 인본주의적 자랑을 금한다: 롬 1:30; 2:17; 3:27; 4:2; 고전 1:29; 3:21; 4:7; 5:6; 갈 6:4, 13. 다른 곳에서 바울은 그리스도로 말미암은 자신의 사역의 자랑을 하고 있으나 자의에 의한 것이 아니라 그리스도의 은혜로 말미암은 것임이 전제되어 있거나 이를 강조한다: 고전 9:15, 16; 15:31; 고후 1:14; 갈 6:14; 엡 2:9; 빌 1:26; 2:16; 3:3; 살전 2:19; 살후 1:4.

할 줄 모르는 반대자들만큼 어리석지는 않다는 뜻이다. 아마도 바울은 반대파들이 그의 영적 경험에 대해서 아예 회의적이거나 부정적으로 반응을 보일 것을 미리 예상하고 이를 차단하는 말이라고 본다.[443]

7. "여러 계시를 받은 것이 지극히 크므로 너무 자고하지 않게 하시려고 내 육체에 가시 곧 사단의 사자를 주셨으니 이는 나를 쳐서 너무 자고하지 않게 하려 하심이니라"(καὶ τῇ ὑπερβολῇ τῶν ἀποκαλύψεων. διὸ ἵνα μὴ ὑπεραίρωμαι, ἐδόθη μοι σκόλοψ τῇ σαρκί, ἄγγελος σατανᾶ, ἵνα με κολαφίζῃ, ἵνα μὴ ὑπεραίρωμαι.). 희랍어 διό(그러므로)가 어떤 사본에는 없으나 대부분의 학자들이 원래 있는 것으로 본다는 것을 본문비평에서 이미 거론하였다. 또 διό가 접속사로서 문장의 초두에 있어야 한다고 보면서 7절의 뒷부분을 이끄는 말로보고, 앞부분인 "여러 계시를 받은 것이 지극히 크므로"를 6절에 부쳐서 바울이 신비한 체험에 대해서 더 말하기를 피하는 이유를 더 강화시키는 말로 보는 이들이 있다.[444]이 경우 "누가 나를 보는 바와 내게 듣는 바에 지나치게 생각할까 두려워하고 그리고 여러 계시를 받은 것이 지극히 크기도 해서"라고 읽게 된다. 이 경우 접속사 καί의 해석이 어색하게 될 뿐만 아니라 "여러 계시를 받은 것이 지극히 크므로"가 "자고하지 않게 하시려고"의 이유로서 자연스럽게 연결되는 것을 무시하고 6절의 이유를 강화시키는 단순한 삽입구로 보게

443) Windisch, 381; Lietzmann, 155; 참조, Thrall, 802.

444) Zmijewski, 354; Furnish, 528; Martin, 389; 412.

된다.[445]다시 말하면 "여러 계시를 받은 것이 지극히 크므로"가 διό를 뒤에 따라 나오는 "너무 자고하지 않게 하시려고"라는 이유절(또는 목적절)을 강화시키는 말로 보면 의미가 잘 통한다. 그러므로 우리는 더 많은 학자들의 번역과 그리고 한글 개역을 따라서 모두 7절에 부쳐서 읽는다.

바울은 그의 계시를 복수로 말하면서 계시의 경험이 많았음을 말한다. 또 "크다"는 뜻의 명사 의 ὑπερβολῇ(후페르볼레)의미가 양적인 뜻과 함께 질적인 뜻을 다 함께 갖고 있으므로 그 계시의 경험이 매우 경이로웠다는 의미도 된다.[446] 바울은 그의 서신에서 그의 복음이나 교훈, 그리고 결정의 근거가 자신의 주관적 사상이나, 복음 전승이나, 사도적 전승과 구별되는, 주님으로부터 직접 받은 계시나 환상임을 자주 천명한다(롬 16:26; 고전 7:25, 40; 11:23; 갈 1:12; 2:2; 3:23; 엡 3:3; 참조, 행 16:9-10; 18:9, 10; 27:23, 24; 엡 1:17). 이런 사실은 바울의 복음의 계시적 기원과 성격을 보여주어 신적 권위를 나타낸다. 바울이 앞에서 말하는 3층천의 경험도 바울의 복음의 권위와 사도적 권위를 강조하는 효과를 기대하고 있다. 더구나 본문에서 계시를 복수로 나타내고, "지극히 크다"는 말로 표현한 것은 이런 기대를 나타내는 것이라고 본다. 또한 6절에서 강조하는 바와 같이 이런 계시는 허황된 것이 아니라 진정한 것이다. 그러나 바울은 이런 계시나 환상에 대한 언급이 정당한 것이고 필요한 것이지만, 반대파의 영적 체험 자랑을 경계

445) Lincoln, 218; Barrett, 313; Hughes, 449, 주, 138; Thrall, 805; 참조, Martin, 412.
446) Martin, 410.

해야하는 현재의 문맥에서는 이런 언급도 "육체적 자랑"에 해당되므로 주저하면서 말한다(12:1). 더구나 이런 경험을 계속 말하는 것은 결국 반대자들과 다를 바 없이 "육체적 자랑"에 빠지는 결과가 된다는 것을 알고 있다. 그러므로 바울은 이제 이 여러 놀라운 계시의 경험의 주제를 떠나서 고난의 주제로 바꾼다. 전체의 주제가 바울의 고난과 약함을 나타내고 있으므로 이 놀라운 경험을 오히려 고난의 의미를 강조하기 위한 예비적이고 보조적인 의사소통의 수단으로 삼고 있는 것이다. 즉 이런 놀랍고 신비한 경험도 많지만, 바울이 진정으로 자랑하려는 것은 그런 것보다는 지금까지 말해왔듯이 자신이 겪는 고난과 약함이라는 것이다. 그 고난과 수고의 경험이 신비한 경험 보다 진정한 사도직을 평가하는 데 더 정확한 지표가 되기 때문이다. 바울이 그런 고난을 겪었다는 사실은 그가 아무런 사욕 없이 오로지 그리스도의 교회의 유익을 위해 애썼다는 것이 증명이 된다(4:15; 5:15; 6:3; 7:2-3; 11:10). 더구나 이런 사역의 자세가 주님이신 그리스도의 고난의 사역의 유형에 맞는 것이기 때문이다. 이와는 반대로, 바울의 반대자들은 신비한 경험을 가지고 스스로 교만하고 있다.

그러므로 바울은 "너무 자고하지 않게 하시려고 내 육체에 가시 곧 사단의 사자를 주셨으니 이는 나를 쳐서 너무 자고하지 않게 하려 하심이니라"고 말한다. "내가 자고하지 않게 하시려고"(ἵνα μὴ ὑπεραίρωμαι)라는 같은 어귀를 두 번 연거푸 되풀이하면서 이런 자세를 경계하는 것이다(참조, 살후 2:4). 영적인 경험이라도 얼마든지 사욕적인 자랑으로 변질될 수 있으며, 그런 자랑은 결국 외모나 육체의 자랑과 같은 것이다(5:12; 10:7; 11:18). (사실 바울도 이런 영적 경험을 가지고 육체적 자랑을 한다고 자인했다[12:1]. 그러나 바울은 그 경험을 반대자들과 달리 고난을 강조하기 위한 예비적인 이야기로써 사용하고 있음을 알게 된다). 여기서 바울은 사도인 자신도 자고할 수 있는 연약한 인간 존재라는 것을 인정하며 자신을 한껏 낮추고 있다. 롬 7장 후반부의 고민과 또 과거에 교회를 핍박한 경력을 회상하는 것을 제외하면, 바울 서신에서 사도 바울이 이렇게 자신의 연약함을 솔직히 인정하는 것은 드문 일이다. 바울의 인간적인 솔직함이 잘 들어난 부분이라고 할 수 있다. 더구나 바울에게 "몸의 가시"가 주어졌다. 여기서 수동태("주어졌다," ἐδόθη)가 쓰인 것을 주목할 필요가 있다. 이 동사는 12장 2절에서 "이끌려"(ἁρπαγέντα)란 말과 같이 신적수동태(*passivum divinum*)이다. 하나님의 은혜가 베풀어진다는 뜻으로 쓰였다(갈 3:21; 엡 3:8; 5:19; 딤전 4:14). 여기서 문법적으로는 "가시"가 주어이지만 하나님이 의미상의 주어이다. 선하신 하나님께서 가시를 계시로 말미암아 "자고하지 않게 하시려고 나에게" 주셨다는 뜻이다. 바울은 이런 신적 수동태를 써서 그의 계시와 가시가 모두 하나님이 주신 것으로 본다. 환상과 계시같이 좋은 선물은 물론 가시 같은 악한 것도 선하신 하나님의 섭리 가운데 바울에게 주어진 것이다. 신적 수동태는 이 "가시"가 하나님에게서 온 것임을 직접 말하지 않고 암시적으로 나타내는 것이다.[447] 욥기를 비롯한 성경에서 유일하시고 의로우신 하나님이 악도 주관하신다는 사실을 나타낼 때, 하나님이 직접 악을 관장하신다고 말하지 않고, 사단을 통해서 간접적으로 허락하신다고 말한

447) Prümm, *Diakonia*, I:657.

다. 선하신 하나님이 직접 악을 관장한다는 표현을 피한다. 여기에 물론 선신(善神), 악신(惡神) 같은 이방적인 이원론적 신학의 자리는 전혀 없다. 이사야 선지자도 유일하신 하나님이 선과 악을 지배한다는 신정론(神正論)을 단지 선과 악을 암시하는 표현으로 나타낸다. "나는 빛도 짓고 어두움도 창조하며 나는 편안도 짓고 환난도 창조하니 나는 여호와라 이모든 일을 행하는 자니라"(사 45:7). 유일신 하나님의 지혜와 예정이 확고하게 자리 잡고 있어서 자연발생적인 사고의 자리는 없다. "몸의 가시"는 그 수많은 놀라운 계시의 경험들의 결과로 생긴 것이라거나, 반대로 많은 계시의 경험들 때문에 "몸의 가시"가 생긴 것이라고 말하지 않는다.[448] 다름 아닌 하나님께서 선하신 뜻 가운데서 친히 그렇게 주관하신 것이다. 이것은 바울의 사사로운 경험적이거나 주관적인 판단이 아니다(12:9). 아래에서 바울은 이 가시와 관련하여 하나님의 계시의 말씀을 직접 들었기 때문이다. 이렇게 "가시"가 바울에게 주어졌다는 신적 수동태에는 역설적으로 나타나는 하나님의 지혜로운 섭리가 암시되어 있다. 하나님은 악을 허락하실 때 자신의 깊은 뜻을 인간에게 알리지 않으시고 감추신다(창 22:2; 욥 1:12; 2:6). 그러나 그가 사랑하는 자녀들에게는 모든 것이 합력하여 선이 되도록 역사하시면서 그의 영광과 능력을 더 크게 나타내시는 것이다(창 22:12-18; 욥 42:10, 12-17). 고난이 하나님의 영광과 능력이 나타나는 은혜의 통로가 되게 하시는 것이다. 이런 사실이 바울의 "가시"에 대한 적극적 의미에서 나타난다. 즉 그를 자고케하지 않게 하시고(7), 약한데서 강하게 하시는 하나님의 능력을 주신 것이

448) 참조, Thrall, 806.

다(9). 바울의 이런 믿음은 근본적으로 죽으시고 부활하신 그리스도 안에서 형성된 것이다.

"가시"(σκόλοψ)라는 말의 어원에 대해서는 두 가지 제안이 있다. 첫째는 끝이 뾰죽한 말뚝으로서 전쟁 시 군대를 보호하는 담으로 사용하거나 또는 처형 도구로 쓰였다.[449] 바울이 현재 당하는 괴로움을 처형당하는 죄수의 모습으로 보는 것은 과장된 느낌을 받는다.[450] 둘째는 식물의 가시이다. 구약(LXX)에서 이 말은 이스라엘을 괴롭히는 이방나라를 가리킨다(민 33:55; 겔 28:24; 호 2:8). 구약에서와 같이 본문에서도 이 말이 암유적으로 쓰였으므로 구약을 따라 가시라고 보는 이들이 많다.[451] 이 가시가 "몸"(τῇ σαρκί)에 있다. 칼빈은 여기서 몸을 부패한 인간성으로 보지만, 단순히 육체를 가리키는 것이라고 보는 것이 지배적이다.[452] 바울은 고린도전서 5장 5절에서 사단으로 하여금 치리 받는 자의 "육신을 멸하도록 하게 한다"는 말이 있고 그 음행한 자의 부패한 육적인 행위를 가리키는 것으로 보이지만, 여기서는 실제로 바울의 육체적인 병을 가리킨다고 보는 것이 일반적이다. 바울은 가시를 또한 "사단의 사자"(ἄγγελος σατανᾶ)로 표현하고 있다. 사단이 그의 천사들을 가지고 있다는 생각은 마태복음 25장 41절이 요한

---

449) G. Delling, on in *TDNT* 7:411, 412; Schlatter, *Paulus*, 666; D. M. Park, "Paul's σκόλοψ τῇ σαρκί: Thorn or Stake?(2 Cor. xii 7)," *NovT* 22(1980), 179-83.

450) Martin, 412.

451) Meyer, 475; Martin, 412; Windisch, 384; Tasker, 173-4; Barrett, 305; Zmijewski, 370; Thrall, 807.

452) Calvin, 159; Tasker, 174-6; Barrett, 305; Furnish, 513; Martin, 388; Thrall, 807.

계시록 17장 9절에도 있다.[453] 여기서 사단의 사자가 하는 일은 바울을 계속해서 (특히, 머리를) 치는 일이다(ἵνα με κολαφίζη).[454] 가시가 질병이라면 그로 인한 고통을 수반한다. 그 가시로 인한 고통은 하나님이 허락하신 것이며 동시에 사단이 주는 것이다. 이런 하나님과 사단의 병행적 역사는 마태복음 4장 1절에서 성령에 이끌리어 마귀의 시험을 받은 예수님의 광야 시험 이야기와 욥기 1장 8-12절, 2장 3-6절에서도 나타난다. "몸의 가시"가 바울의 질병이라면 바울은 그의 병에 대한 공식적 해명을 해야 하는 입장일 것이다. 어쩌면 이미 반대자들이나 일반 고린도 교인들이 모두 바울의 질병을 바울의 약함, 또는 사단의 역사로 보았을 수 있기 때문이다.[455] 이에 대해서 바울은 그의 질병은 약한 가운데서 온전케 하시는 하나님의 은혜의 도구라고 역설적으로 해명한다고 볼 수 있다. 물론 이 해명은 바울이 만든 것이 아니라 하나님의 계시에 의한 것임을 강조한다(9절). 그러나 반대자들이 바울의 질병을 실제로 사단의 역사로 보았는지는 알 수 없다. 다만 여기서 바울이 그렇게 언급하는 것은 사실이다.

"가시"가 실제로 무엇을 가리키는가에 대한 오랜 논란은 아직 아무런 결론에 이르지 못했다. 이 논란은 세 가지로 요약된다. (1) 시험이나 근심 같은 내적 심리적 상태; (2)외부적 반대; (3) 육체의 병이나 신체장애.

---

453) *Epistle of Barnabas* 18:1; *T. Asher* 6:4; *OT Pseudepigrapha* , I, 818.

454) K. L. Schmidt, *TDNT* 3:819-21; Martin, 414.

455) E. Güttgemannes, *Der leidende Apostel und sein Herr* (Göttingen: Vandenhoeck & Ruprecht, 1966), 164-5; Heckel, *Schwachheit*, 80.

(1) 심리적 상태: 이 부분은 대개 3가지로 나누어서 논란되어 왔다.

(a) 성적 유혹: 중세의 그레고리 대제로부터 토마스 아퀴나스, 그리고 17세기 초 라피데(Cornelius a Lapide)에 이르기 까지 가시를 성적 유혹을 가리키는 것으로 보았다.[456] 라피데는 로마서 7장 23절에 언급된 지체의 갈등과 고린도전서 9장 25-27절에 언급된 몸의 절제에 대한 말들을 근거로 바울의 성적 유혹을 가리키는 것으로 보았다. 만일 다른 문제 이었다면 분명하게 밝혔을 것이라고 한다.[457] 에스티우수(Estius)도 이 같은 성경 구절들과 같이 본문에서도 사단이 시험을 하는 것으로 나타남으로 성적 시험을 가리키는 것으로 보았다.[458] 칼빈과 루터는 이런 견해를 반대하고 "가시"는 여러 가지 시험이라고 보았다.[459] 이런 견해에 대해서 반대하는 근거들은 다음과 같다. 첫째, 로마서 7장 23절과 고린도전서 9장 25-27절에서 성적 시험이 아닌 일반적인 시험을 나타내는 것이며, 특히 고린도전서 7장 7-9절에서 바울은 독신생활을 장려하면서 절제를 권하고 있다.[460] 그러나 이런 사례들이 여기서의 문

---

456) J. B. Lightfoot, *The Epistle of St. Paul to the Galatians* (London: Macmillan, 1865; reprint, Grand Rapids: Zondervan, 1962), 188; Allo, 313, 주, 1..

457) Cornelius a Lapide, "Commentarius in Secundam Epistolam ad Corinthos," in *Commentaria in Scripturam Sanctam* XVIII (Paris: L. Vives, 1866), (C. van den Steen, *Commentaria in omnes Divi Pauli Epistolas* [Antverpiae: apud Henricum et Cornelium Verdussen, 1705]), 503-4.

458) G. Estius, *Omnes Divi Pauli Apostoli epistolas commentariorum Tomus Prior* (Douaci: Balthagar Bellerus, 1614), 649-50.

459) Hughes, 444.

460) Meyer, 478; Osiander, 473; Heinrici(1883), 372; Plummer, 350; Windisch, 385; Lightfoot, *Galatians*, 188.

제가 성적 시험이 아니라는 증거로 사용될 수 없다. 둘째, 바울은 성적 시험을 그가 자랑하는 약함으로 말하지 않았을 것이다.[461] 셋째, 고린도 같이 음행이 보편적인 도시에서 이런 정도의 성적 시험을 가지고 고백하는 것을 고린도 독자들이 대수롭지 않게 생각했을 것이므로 별 큰 의미도 없었을 것이라고 한다.[462] 넷째, 이런 성적인 시험이 선교 사역 중에 있는 바울에게 없다가 갑자기 닥쳐서 기도하게 되었다고 보기가 어렵다.[463]

(b) 바울이 과거 기독교인들을 핍박한 데 대한 양심적 고통: "사단의 사자" 에서 사단은 "고소자" 라는 뜻이다. 사단은 바울이 기독교인들을 핍박한 것을 가지고 계속해서 그를 고소하여 양심적 교통을 느끼게 하는 것이다.[464] 그러나 바울이 다른 데서 그가 교회를 핍박한 사실을 그대로 말하는 데 왜 여기서는 암시적인 말로 했어야 하는가에 대한 마땅한 답이 없다(고전 15:9; 딤전 1:13). 더구나 교회를 핍박한 데서 오는 고통은 바울의 회심 직후에 있었을 것이며, 지금은 "가시" 를 그 후에 일어난 "환상과 계시" 의 경험과 관련하여 말하고 있다.[465]

(c) 바울의 유대인 동족들이 복음을 받지 않는 것: 바울은 로마서 9장에서 복음을 거절하는 유대인들에 대한 바울의 안타까운

---

461) Lightfoot, 188; Plummer, 350; Beet, 459.

462) Allo, 310; 참조, Osiander, 473.

463) P. H. Menoud, "L'écharde det l'age satanique (2 Cor 12,7)," in *Studia Paulina*, FS. de Zwaan, ed. J. N. Sevenster and W. C. van Unnik (Haarlem: Erven F. Bohn, 1953), 163-4.

464) Schlatter, 666-7.

465) Thrall, 811.

심정을 토로했다.[466] 유대인들이 복음을 믿지 않는 것이 이방인들에게 복음을 전하는 데도 방해가 되었다. 이런 유대인들의 불신의 배후에는 사단의 역사가 있다고 본다(고후 4:4). 그러나 이런 것을 가지고 10절에서 말하는 바울의 약함을 가리킨다는 것은 어색하다. 더구나 유대인들의 복음을 받지 않은 것이 그의 영적 유익이 되었다고 말하는 것은 더욱 이상하다.[467] 이외에 루터는 바울의 낙심과 사도직 수행을 태만하게 하는 것이라고 보았고, 칼빈은 인간의 부패한 본성이라고 했다.[468] 그러나 휴즈는 "몸"을 신학적 의미가 아닌 단순한 의미로 본다.[469] 보다 최근에 캄라(Kamlah)는 바울의 급한 성격을 가시로 보았다.[470]

이상의 심리적 제안들의 공통적 문제는 바울이 12장 1절에서 자랑한다고 한 것이 과연 이런 종류의 심리적 시험들을 가지고 자랑한다고 하였겠느냐라는 것이다. 더구나 이런 해석은 이런 심리적 고통은 바울이 "가시"(σκόλοψ)와 "사자"(ἄγγελος)같은 구체적인 단수 명사로 나타내는 사실과 잘 맞지 않고, 문맥에서 가리키는 대로 "가시"가 어떤 특별한 시점에서부터 문제가 되기 시작했다는 사실과도 맞지 않는다.[471] 무엇보다 심리적 고통이라면 바울이 "몸의 가시"라고 하지 않고 "마음의 가시"라고 했어야 옳다(11:28).

---

466) Menoud, 169-71.

467) Thrall, 811.

468) Lightfoot, *Galatians*, 188-9, 재인용; Calvin, 159.

469) Hughes, 448.

470) Kamlah, "Leiden," 218-19.

471) Thrall, 811.

(2) 외부적 반대: 바울이 당하는 외부적 압력과 위협으로서 고대 교부시대로부터 현대 학자들에게 이르기 까지 지지를 받고 있다. 다만 교부들은 일반적인 압력으로 보는 반면에, 현대 학자들은 보다 구체적인 사안들을 찾는다.

(a) 크리소스톰(Chrysostom)은 사단은 "반대자"란 뜻이라는 데 착안하여, "사단의 사자" 즉 "가시"는 디모데후서 2장 17절과 4장 14절에 각기 언급된 바울을 반대하는 후메내오, 빌레도와 구리장색 알렉산더, 그리고 나아가 모든 복음의 적들을 가리킨다고 했다.[472] 어거스틴을 비롯한 대부분의 후기 교부들이 이 견해를 따른다. 그러나 이런 구체적인 인물들이 그렇게 심각하게 계속해서 바울을 괴롭혔다고 보기 어렵다. 이런 견해를 다른 견해보다 낫다고 보고 따르는 타스커는 "가시"는 무엇보다 바울에 대한 반대자들의 "반대"를 가리키며, 이런 반대가 그의 영적 경험의 자만심을 가장 잘 굴복시킬 수 있다고 했다.[473] 그러나 바울의 사역에 있어서 그에 대한 반대는 필연적으로 늘 있어 왔던 것이고, 이런 것을 떠나게 해 달라고 기도했을 것 같지 않다.[474] "몸의 가시"는 이런 사람들의 반대로 인한 정신적 고통보다 육체적인 고통을 가리킨다고 본다.[475]

---

472) Chrysostom, *NPNF*, XII, 400); Hughes, 443: Augustine, Theodore of Mopsuestia, Theodoret, Photius, Theophylact 등이 이에 동의한다. Augustine은 시편 99주석에서는 "아마 육체적 질병일 것"으로 추정한다.

473) Tasker, 176.

474) Meyer, 478; Heinrici (1883), 372.

475) Thrall, 812.

(b) 고린도 교회의 반대자들의 핍박을 가리킨다. 멀린스(Mullins)는 "가시"는 고린도의 바울의 반대자들 중에서 바울을 괴롭히는 특정한 인물을 가리킨다고 한다.[476] "사자"라는 말과, "친다"(κολαφίζη)는 말이 사람과 그 행위를 가리키는 것으로 보이기 때문이다. 더구나 11장 14-15절에서 바울은 사단을 "빛의 천사"로, 그의 반대자들을 "사단의 일꾼들"로 지칭하고 있다. 또 민수기 33장 55절과 에스겔 28장 24절에서 "가시"는 대적자를 가리키는 말로 쓰였다.[477] 이런 견해에 대해서 트롤은 바울이 어떤 특정한 인물로 인해서 오랫동안 고통당했다는 증거가 바울 서신이나 사도행전에서 찾을 수가 없다고 한다.[478] 그리고 이 고난이 바울의 사역 기간 중에서 어떤 시점, 특별히 14년 전의 "환상과 계시"의 경험과 거의 동시에 시작된 것이라고 본다면, 특정한 반대자 이론은 타당치가 않다.

비더(Bieder)와 티리(Thierry)도 "가시"는 10-13장에서의 바울의 대적자들을 가리킨다고 본다. 비더는 "가시"를 4장 10절에서 바울이 그리스도의 십자가의 죽음을 짊어진다는 언급과 관련하여 보면서 "가시"는 반대자들이 주는 고통을 가리킨다고 한다.[479] 티리는 "가시"는 바울의 적들이 그를 "사단의 사자"라고 비난한 것을 바울이 되받아 공격하는 것이라고 본다.[480] 그러나 이런 이론은

476) T. Y. Mullins, "Paul's Thorn in the Flesh", *JBL* 76 (1957), 302.
477) Mullins, 302.
478) Thrall, 812.
479) W. Bieder, "Paulus und seine Gegner in Korinth", *TZ* 17 (1961), 319-33.
480) J. J. Thierry, "Der Dorn im Fleische", *NovT* 5 (1962), 301-10.

본문에서 말하는 대로 "가시"의 고난이 특정한 때부터 시작되었다는 사실을 설명하기 어렵다. 대적자들로 인한 고난은 바울의 모든 다른 교회 사역에서도 늘 있어 온 문제였다. 바레(Barre)는 쿰란문서 1QH 2장 22절의 "하나님께서 그의 능력을 나타내기 위하여 쿰란 저자에 대항하는 '벨리알(마귀)의 회중'의 적대적 활동을 허락하시고 일으키신다"는 어귀를 본문과 관련하여 보고 바울의 "가시"와 "사단의 사자" 그리고 "친다"는 말은 모두 바울의 적대적 사람들로 말미암은 고통을 가리킨다고 보았다.[481] 그는 바울의 "약함"은 종말론적 투쟁 가운데서 사단의 사자들로 말미암은 것이라고 한다. 본문과 쿰란의 찬양 시에 표현된 사상의 유사성에도 불구하고, 차이도 있다. 그 1QH 2장 22절에는 "약함"이란 말이 없고, 또 "몸의 가시"이라는 말도 없다.

이렇게 바울의 "가시"를 적대적인 사람들이나 특정 인물을 가리키는 것으로 보는 견해의 공통적 문제는 앞서 심리적 고통으로 보는 견해의 문제점과 같이 바울이 "가시"를 "마음의 가시"라고 하지 않고, "몸의 가시"라고 표현한 것을 등한히 여기는 것이다. "몸의 가시"라는 표현을 중시할 때 바울의 고난은 심리적 고통이나 사람으로 말미암은 고통이라기보다는 육체적 고통과 관련이 있어 보인다. 더구나 이런 대적자들로 말미암는 고통은 모든 복음 사역에서 거의 필연적으로 따라 다닐 수밖에 없는 보편적인 문제임을 바울 자신도 잘 알고 있었을 것이다. 그런데도 대적자들로 인한 고난을 떠나게 해달라고 특별히 세 번 기도를 했다고 보는

481) M. L. Barré "Qumran and the 'Weakness' of Paul," *CBQ* 42 (1980), 216-27.

것은 적절치 않다(8절).

(3) 육체적인 병이나 신체장애: 터툴리안(Tertullian) 이후 "가시"를 바울의 어떤 질병을 가리킨다고 보는 견해가 있다.[482]우선 "몸의 가시"라는 암유적 표현이 육체적인 병을 가리킨다. "사단의 사자"라는 표현도 질병을 가리킬 수 있다(눅 13:16). "친다"(κολαφίζῃ)는 말은 그 고통이 계속되는 "신체적 장애"라는 뜻으로 본다. 그러나 그것이 실제로 어떤 질병이냐에 대한 제안은 다양하다.

(a) 두통: 터툴리안은 "가시"를 두통이나 귓병으로 보았다: "dolorem, ut aiunt, auriculae vel capitis."[483] 제롬(Jerome)도 이를 따라서 같은 견해를 가졌고[484] 크리소스톰(Chrysostom)도 이를 확인했다(동의 한 것은 아니다).[485]이런 견해는 "친다"(κολαφίζῃ)는 말이 원래 "귀에 올려놓은 상자"라는 의미라는 데서 기인한 것이다.[486]즉 그 상자가 귀나 머리를 눌러 통증을 일으킨다는 것이다. 두통이라는 견해에 대하여 빈디쉬와 트롤이 동의한다.[487]

---

482) Tertullian, *PL* 2 col. 1004: "그들이 말하는 대로, 귀나 머리의 고통이다." Lightfoot, *Galatians*, 186, 재인용.

483) Tertullian, *PL* 2 col. 1004.

484) Jerome, *PL* 26 col. 381: "Nam tradunt eum gravissimum capitis dolorem saepe perpessum"(그들은 그가 극심한 두통으로 자주 고생했다고 말한다).

485) Chrysostom, *NPNF*, XII, 400.

486) K. L. Schmidt, on κολαφίζῃ, in *TDNT* III, 819.

487) Windisch, 387-8; Thrall, 814, 818.

(b) 눈병(안질): 갈라디아서 4장 14, 15절에서 바울이 갈라디아에서 처음 설교 하였을 때 "육체의 약함이 있었으나", 갈라디아 교인들이 바울을 극진히 영접하여서 눈이라도 빼어 줄 수 있었다고 회상하는 데서 기인한다. 그러나 갈라디아서 4장 15절의 말은 보통 갈라디아 교인들이 실제로 그들의 눈을 준다는 말이라기보다, 가장 귀한 것도 줄 정도로 바울을 사랑하였다는 말로 해석한다.[488] 또 6장 11절에서 바울이 "내 손으로 이렇게 큰 글자로 쓴 것을 보라" 고 하는 데 이것을 바울의 눈이 좋지 않았기 때문에 특별히 "큰 글자로 썼다" 고 말했다는 것이다. 휴즈는 결정적이지는 않지만 이 견해에 가장 높은 가능성을 준다.[489] 그러나 갈라디아서 6장 11절의 말은 바울이 대필로 쓰게 하다가 끝부분에서 자신의 친필로 써서 독자들에게 친밀감을 주면서 내용을 인증하는 방식으로 본다.[490] 또 우리는 사도행전 9장 8-18절에서 바울이 다메섹 도상에서 강한 빛으로 눈이 사흘 동안 손상되었다가 아나니아의 안수로 다시 보게 되었다는 기사를 읽고, 어쩌면 그 일 이후 눈병이 도졌다고 추정할 수도 있다. 사실 사도행전 23장 5절에서 바울은 대제사장을 제대로 알아보지 못했다. 그러나 사도행전 9장 18절에서 바울이 다시 보게 되었다는 말과 함께 강건하여졌다는 말이 있으므로 본문의 "약함" 의 주제와는 맞지 않는다. 그렇다면 "가시" 가 안질이라는 주장은 결국 약한 추정에 불과하다.

---

488) Lightfoot, *Galatians*, 191, 주, 1.

489) Hughes, 444.

490) 참조, Thrall, 814.

(c) 간질: 크렝캘(Krenkel)은 이 견해를 지지하면서 이 견해를 처음 제안한 사람은 지글러(Ziegler)라고 한다.[491] 크렝캘은 유대인이나 헬라인, 그리고 로마인들이 모두 간질환을 귀신들이 일으키는 것으로 보았다고 한다.[492] 마태복음 17장 15절에도 간질 걸린 아이를 예수님이 귀신을 쫓아내어 고치셨다고 한다(참조, 막 9:17, 18). 그리고 "친다"는 말을 간질이 발작하여 뇌경련을 일으키는 것을 가리킨다고 본다. 크렝캘은 갈라디아서 4장 14절에서 갈라디아인들이 바울을 "버리지도 아니하고"(οὐδέ ἐξεπτύσατε) 라는 말이 원래 "침을 뱉어서 악귀를 예방하는 것"을 의미하고, 특별히 간질환과 관련 있다고 해석 했다.[493] 또한 본문의 바울의 환상의 경험과 관련하여, 간질은 흔히 환상을 수반한다고 했다.[494] 그리고 사도행전 9장 4절에 바울이 다메섹으로 가다가 갑자기 쓰러진 경험도 간질의 발작으로 본다.[495] 크렝캘은 줄리어스 시저나, 모하멧, 크롬웰, 나폴레옹도 간질을 앓고 있으면서도 큰 일을 했으므로 바울도 같은 경우라고 한다.[496] 물론 이런 인물들이 실제로 간질을 앓았는지는 알 수 없다. 그러나 간질이 육체적

491) Krenkel, *Beiträge*, 66-7; K. L. Ziegler, *Theologische Abhandlungen* 2 (Göttingen: Die Terich, 1804), 128; 이들의 견해를 따르는 이들은, P. W. Schmiedel, *Die Briefe an die Thessaloniker und an die Korinther*, Hand-Commentar zum Neuen Testament, vol. 2 (Freiburg: J. C. B. Mohr, 1891), 294; W. Bousset, *Kyrios Christos*, ETr, J. E. Steely (Nashville and New York: Abingdon, 1970), 211-12.

492) Krenkel, 49, 58-9.

493) Krenkel, 98; 여기서 Krenkel은 Plautus, *Captiviti* 18, 이 간질을 "morbus qui sputatur," 즉 "사람이 그 앞에서 침을 뱉는 질병"이라고 했음을 인용한다.

494) Krenkel, 103.

495) Krenkel, 111.

496) Krenkel, 117-24; Hughes, 445..

이고 정신 적인 병이므로 본문의 "가시"와 "사단의 사자"라는 이중적 표현에 맞는 설득력이 있는 견해라고 본다. 크랭캘이 하나님의 환상과 계시의 경험을 간질의 발작으로 보는 것을 문제로 삼을 수 있으나, 하나님이 그런 "약함"을 통해서 놀라운 환상과 계시의 은혜를 주시는 기회로 삼으신다는 것이 바로 본문에서 바울이 말하려는 주제라고 보면 크게 문제 될 것이 없다. 또한 본문에서는 바울이 환상의 경험 후에 "가시"가 발생한 것으로 말하므로, 크랭캘이 바울의 환상과 계시의 경험을 간질발작과 동일시하는 것을 비판할 수 있다.[497] 그러나 간질 증세가 환상의 경험과 구별되어 그 후에 발생되었다고 볼 수도 있다. 트롤은 알로(Allo)를 인용하면서 "가시"는 극심한 고통을 말하는 데, 간질의 발작은 무의식 상태로 일어나는 것으로 맞지 않는다고 한다.[498] 그러나 실제로 간질은 제대로 호흡을 할 수 없고, 온 몸이 경련을 일으키는 등 심한 육체적 통증을 수반한다. 간질 환자는 발작 후에는 장시간의 휴식이 필요하다. 그러나 크랭크가 갈라디아서 4장 14절의 "버리지도 아니하고"(οὐδέ ἐξεπτύσατε)라는 말을 간질과 관련시키는 것은 무리라고 본다. 고대인들은 거의 모든 질병이 귀신과 관련되어 있다고 보았고, 이에 대해서 침을 뱉어 귀신을 쫓아내는 축사(逐邪)관습(apostropaic gesture)이 있었다.[499] 마가복음 7장 33절에서 예수님이 침을 뱉어서 귀먹고 벙어리 된 사람을 고쳤고, 8장 23절에서도 소경의 눈에 침을 뱉어서 소경을 고치셨다. 또 요한복

---

497) Thrall, 815.

498) Thrall, 815; Allo, 317, 18.

499) Lietzmann, 156-7.

음 9장 6절에서 예수님께서 소경을 고치실 때 침을 뱉어서 진흙을 만들어 그의 눈에 발라서 고치신 것도 이런 관습과 무관하지 않다고 본다. 그러므로 갈라디아서 4장 14절이 특별히 간질을 가리킨다는 증거는 없다. 그러나 "가시"라는 표현은 간질의 심한 육체적 고통은 가리키고, "사단의 사자"라는 말은 다른 어떤 질병의 증세보다도 간질의 갑작스런 발작 증세를 잘 가리킨다고 본다. 다시 말하면 간질이란 질병이 다른 어떤 질병보다도 육체적 고통과 정신적 충격을 모두 가진 독특한 병이고, 본문에 나타난 "가시"라는 물질적인 말과, "사단의 사자"라는 초월적인 표현이 간질 증세를 적절히 나타낸다고 한다. 그러나 이런 주장의 가장 큰 약점은 간질 같은 병은 갑자기 생길 수가 없고 바울의 회심 이전에도 있었을, 어쩌면 출생 이후에 계속됐을 오래 된 병일 가능성이 있는데, 본문에서는 "가시"가 환상의 경험 이후에 "바울의 영적 자고 함을 막기 위해서" 시작되었다고 하기 때문이다. 바울이 이를 떠나도록 특별히 세 번 기도했다는 말도 간질 같은 오랜 병이 아니라 갑자기 생긴 어떤 병이라는 추측을 하게 한다. 정말 간질이라면 회심 이전에도 계속 기도했을 것이 분명하다. 그러므로 간질이라는 견해도 여전히 추정에 불과하다.

(d) 학질(말라리아): 램지 경(Sir William Ramsay)은 동부 지중해, 특히 밤빌리아(Pamphylia) 지방의 학질은 병자로 하여금 완전히 기력을 잃게 하고 심한 두통도 수반하고 같은 증세가 반복되므로 본문에서 말하는 바울의 증세와 닮았다고 한다.[500] 램지 경은

500) William. M. Ramsay, *St. Paul and the Traveller and Roman Citizen* (London: Hodder

바울이 1차 전도 여행 시에 밤빌리아의 버가에 들린 사실을 중시하면서 바울이 이 때 말라리아 병에 전염되었다고 보면서 이 병을 본문의 "가시"로 확신한다. 알렉산더(W. M. Alexander)는 램지 경의 학질을 더 자세하게 몰타열(Malta Fever)이라고 본다.[501] 이병은 심한 통증, 정신 착란, 발진, 탈모, 등을 수반하는 목숨까지 잃게 되는 질병이라고 한다. 아마도 이병이 지중해의 바울이 파선중에 들였던 몰타섬(멜리데, Malta)의 이름에서 유래한 것으로 짐작된다. 그러나 바울이 이 섬에 들린 것이 고린도후서 쓰고 난 뒤의 일이므로 이 섬의 병에서 전염되었다고 보기는 어렵다. 다만 그런 병에 누구나 어느 때든지 걸릴 수 있다고 볼 수 있다. 알로(Allo)는 이 몰타 열병이야 말로 한 치의 의심도 없이 바울이 말하는 병에 일치한다고 주장한다.[502] 이 병의 반복되는 증세가 바울이 세 차례 기도하였다는 부분과 부합되고, 이 병이 일어나는 지역이 바울의 선교지역과 일치하는 점 등으로 가능성도 있으나, 확실한 증거는 없다.

(e) 기타 제안들: 어떤 이는 바울이 황홀한 종교적 체험 후에 일어난 우울증이나 신경반응증세라고 한다.[503] 그러나 위에서 말했듯이 "몸의 가시"라는 말은 바울의 고통은 정신적 고통이라기

& Stoughton, 1935), 94-97; 갈 4:13의 바울의 "육체의 약함"에 대해 학질로 설명한다. 이 견해를 따르는 이들은, Gouge, 121; Allo, 320-1; Prümm, *Diakonia* I, 665.

501) W. M. Alexander, "St. Paul's Infirmity," *The Expository Times* 10 (1904), 469-73; 545-48.

502) Hughes, 445, 재인용.

503) Clavier, "Santé," 77-82.

보다는 육체적 고통인 듯하다. 바레트는 고린도후서 1장 1, 9-11절, 11장 6절과 갈라디아서 4장 13-15절에 근거해서 바울의 언어 장애를 "가시"라고 보았다.[504] 그러나 이런 증세가 신비한 경험 이후에 갑자기 나타나서 바울을 괴롭게 해서 세 번씩 기도하게 했다고 보기 어렵다. 그리고 "가시"가 암시하는 것 같은 육체적 고통이라고 보기 어렵다.[505] 트롤은 단순히 열병이라고 추정한다.[506] 프라이스(R. M. Price)는 바울의 낙원 환상 경험을 유대인의 메르카바(merkabah) 신비주의와 관련시켜서 환상가가 신비한 경험 중에 있을 때 자주 귀신의 공격을 받는다는 것을 지적하면서, 본문의 환상과 "사단의 사자"라는 말의 관련성을 추정한다. 다시 말하면 12장 1-10절 전체를 일련의 환상 체험으로 보는 것이다. 그러나 트롤이 지적하는 대로 환상의 경험에서 바울은 "말 할 수 없는 말"을 들었으나, 계시의 경험에서 바울은 "내 은혜가 네게 족하도다. 이는 내 능력이 약한 데서 온전하여짐이라"는 분명한 계시의 말씀을 들었다. 문장적으로도 두 자료는 5절과 6절로 나누어져 있다. 그리고 주어도 3인칭에서 일인칭으로 바뀌고 있다. 또한 고난은 "친다"(κολαφίζη)라는 현재 동사로 계속되는 의미인데 반하여, 환상의 경험은 일회적이다.[507] 그러므로 같은 경험으로 볼 수 없다.

---

504) Barrett, 315; W. K. Lowther Clarke, *New Testament Problems* (London: SPCK, 1929), 136-40; Martin, 416.

505) Thrall, 816; Martin, 416.

506) Thrall, 817.

507) Thrall, 817.

학자들은 이런 견해들을 제안하면서도 모두 추정일 뿐이라고 결론 짓는다.[508] 그러나 다수의 학자들이 어떤 육체적인 병을 가리킨다는 데 동의 한다.[509] 성적 유혹이란 견해는 바울이 그런 것으로 자랑한다고 볼 수 없기 때문에 받아들이기 어렵다. 심리적인 고통이라고 보는 견해는 본문의 "몸의 가시"라는 말이 육체적인 병을 강력하게 암시하므로 받아들이기 어렵다. 대적자들의 반대로 보는 견해도 마찬가지 이유로 받아들이기 어렵다. 다만 육체적인 병일 가능성이 높으나 어떤 병인지는 알 수 없다. 트롤은 바울서신과 사도행전의 기록으로 미루어 볼 때, 바울은 대체로 어려움을 잘 견디는 매우 건강한 남자라고 본다.[510] 그리고 갈라디아서 4장 13절의 "육체의 약함" 도 약함(ἀσθένειαν)이란 말에 관사가 없기 때문에 특정한 병이 아닌 부족함이라고 한다. 그러나 트롤은 본문에서의 "가시"는 분명히 심각한 육체적인 병이라는 사실에 동의 한다.[511] 어쩌면 이 병 때문에 바울이 갈라디아서 교인들에게 처음 설교 할 때에 그들을 실망시켰다(갈 4:13). 바울은 갈라디아 교인들이 그를 천사같이 영접할 때에 이 병이 재발한 것을 기억하고, 본문에서 같은 병을 "사단의 사자"로 명명하는 것인가?[512] 어쩌면 이 병이 바울로 하여금 데살로니가 교회를 방문하지 못하게 방해했을 것이다. 그래서 바울은 그 병의 배후에 사단이 있어서 그를 방문하지 못하도록 막았다고 하는가?(살전 2:18)

---

508) Hughes, 446; Martin, 416.

509) Thrall, 817-180; Martin, 416.

510) Thrall, 816; Tasker, 175; Martin 415.

511) Thrall, 817.

512) Hughes, 448.

아마 바울 자신이 "가시"라고 할 때 고린도 교인들이 이 "가시"가 무엇인지 알고 있었을 것을 짐작하였을 것이다. 그러나 우리의 호기심으로 말미암은 추정은 한계가 있다. 휴즈가 지적한대로 우리는 "가시"가 무엇인지 알려고 하기 보다는 하나님의 은혜가 우리의 약함과 함께 나타난다는 바울의 가르침에 귀를 기우려야 할 것이다.[513] 본문에서 "가시" 자체가 선한 것이란 생각은 없다. 그것이 비록 하나님의 은혜의 도구가 되었으나 그것은 하나님의 능력으로 말미암은 것이며, 그것 자체가 선한 것은 아니고, "사단의 사자"라고 말한다. 다시 말하면 여기서 고행주의적 증거를 찾을 수 없다. 악을 이기는 하나님의 능력과 영광을 가르치는 것이다. 고난을 통해서 사람의 영광이 아닌 하나님의 영광을 극대화시키는 것이다. 이것이 그리스도의 부활의 신학이며, 고난을 통한 사도직 변명의 배경이 되는 신학이다. 하나님은 고난을 통해서 그의 능력과 영광을 나타내신다. 하나님은 그의 사랑하는 사도 바울에게 신비한 경험도 주시지만 고난을 더 많이 주신다. 하나님을 믿는 자는 신비한 경험뿐만이 아니라 고난을 통해서 하나님의 영광과 능력을 보게 된다는 것을 안다. 그것은 빛의 창조 이전에 세상이 혼동과 암흑 가운데 있었던 것과 같은 원리이다. 이런 원칙은 병 주고 약 주는 것과는 다르다. 하나님은 그의 사랑하는 자녀들을 고난을 통해 믿음을 자라게 하시고, 훈련시키신다. 그들이 그의 궁극적인 영광과 구원의 세계에 이르기 까지 고난을 은혜의 도구로 삼으시는 구원 역사를 통해서 그의 영광과 구원의 능력을 증거하시는 것이다. 단순히 고난을 악한 것으로만 보고 이를 떠나기만

---

513) Hughes, 443.

간구하는 사람들은 고난을 은혜의 도구로 바꾸시는 십자가에서 나타난 하나님의 크고 놀라운 능력을 증거하지 못한다.

"내 육체에 가시 곧 사단의 사자"(σκόλοψ τῇ σαρκί, ἄγγελος σατανᾶ)에서 두 말이 동격관계의 주격으로 되어서 그 의미를 강화시키고 있다. 우선 바울의 병은 사단이 일으킨 나쁜 것이다. 그러나 이런 동격 관계만 보고 위에서 지적한 신적 수동태(ἐδόθη)의 의미를 무시해서는 안 된다. 본문에서와 같이 고난은 하나님이 주실 수 있다(창 22:2; 욥 1:12; 2:6; 마 4:1; 26:39). "가시"의 의미상의 주어가 하나님인 것이다. 그런데도 두말의 동격 관계만을 보고 "모든 고난(가시)은 마귀가 일으킨 것이므로 나쁜 것이다"라는 귀신론은 단순한 원시적 신앙을 반영한다. 본문에는 "가시"는 분명히 하나님께서 허락하신 것이다. 여기에는 하나님께서 고난을 허락하신다는 신학이 있다. 비록 개역한글판에는 우리말로 수동태로 번역하는 것이 어색해서 "주셨다"라고 능동태로 번역했으나 고난에 감추어진 선하신 하나님의 깊은 지혜와 의도가 있음을 감안하여, "허락하셨다"는 말이 원래의 의미를 보다 정확히 나타나는 것이다. 성경에서 우리는 오직 선하시고 의로우신 하나님의 사랑과 구원 심판의 말씀과 역사에 초점을 맞추어야 하며, 귀신론 같은 사상을 찾으려는 것은 옳지 않다. 그런 생각이나 해석 자체가 "말씀을 혼잡케 하는" 마귀의 미혹을 받은 것이다(2:17; 3:15; 4:4). 성경은 의도적으로 마귀에 대한 언급을 되도록 피하여 오로지 하나님의 역사에 초점을 맞추는 것이다. 악한 존재에 대한 언급을 하면 할수록 결국 그의 존재를 인식하고 그의 세력을 두려워하는 셈이 되므로 의식적으로 이의 언급을 피하는 것이다. 물론 이 말은 성경이 그의 존재를 부인하거나 그 세력을 전혀 무시한다는 말이 아니라, 그것이 성경의 중심 주제가 아니라는 것이다. 성경의 중심 주제는 하나님의 구원의 역사이다.

바울은 고행주의를 믿는 것은 아니다. 그는 고난을 피할 수 있으면 피하여야 한다고 믿는다(고후 1:10; 12:8). 그러나 동시에 고난이 그리스도를 위한 고난이라면 피하지 않고 달게 받아야 함을 알고 있다(고후 1:5, 7; 빌 1:29; 3:10; 골 1:24; 딤후 1:8). 바울은 "가시"를 허락하신 하나님의 깊으신 뜻을 9절에서 설명한다.

8. "이것이 내게서 떠나기 위하여 내가 세 번 주께 간구하였더니"(ὑπὲρ τούτου τρὶς τὸν κύριον παρεκάλεσα ἵνα ἀποστῇ ἀπ᾽ ἐμοῦ). 바울은 애초에 그의 병이 발발하였을 때 그 병의 의미를 알지 못하고 다만 그 병이 낫기만을 기도했다. 하나님은 그의 깊은 지혜를 인간에게 감추시다가, 그의 섭리 가운데 어느 시점에서 그의 깊으신 지혜와 구원을 베푸시어 인간으로 감탄하게 하시고 그에게 영광을 돌리게 하신다(욥 42:3). 바울은 9절에 주님의 계시의 말씀을 듣고 기뻐할 때까지 그의 "몸의 가시"를 떠나게 해 달라고만 기도했다고 회상한다. 바울은 고행주의자는 아니다. 바울은 앞서 1장 10절에서도 아시아에서 당한 환난 중에서 건지신 하나님을 찬양하며, 장래에도 어려움에서 하나님이 건져 주실 것을 바란다고 했다. 바울은 모든 사람들처럼 고난을 원치 않는다. 하기야 예수님도 고행주의적 자세로 고난을 받으신 것은 아니다(마 26:39). 그러나 바울은 그리스도의 사도로서 "몸의 가시"는 부끄러울 뿐만 아니라 복음사역에 방해가 된다. 그리고 세 번씩이나

떠나도록 간구하였던 것은 그만큼 심각했던 문제로 보인다. 어쩌면 "몸의 가시"는 바울 개인의 생명을 위협하는 절박한 상황을 초래했는지도 모른다.

"이것"(τούτου)은 "몸의 가시", 또는 "사단의 사자"를 가리킨다. 이 두 개가 모두 남성 명사이므로 "이것"은 희랍어로 남성 2격으로 되어있다. 인격화된 지시대명사이다. 그러나 여러 번역에서 의미상으로 중성 대명사(it)로 번역되었다. 바레트는 "그이"(he)로 주장한다.[514]바울이 "사단의 사자"를 인격체로 인식한다는 것을 유의해야 한다. 그는 인격체로서 우리 인간을 쉽게 유혹할 수 있는 충분한 능력과 지혜를 소유하고 있음을 암시하는 것이다.[515]

3번 기도했다는 말에 대해서 학자들은 실제로 3번 기도했다는 말인지 아니면 상징적 의미인지에 대해서 논쟁해왔다. 크리소스톰(Chrysostom)은 여러 번 기도한 것을 상징적으로 3번 했다고 표현했다고 한다.[516] 바레트도 진정으로 반복하여 기도한 것을 나타낸다고 본다.[517]헤켈(Heckel)과 트롤도 여러 차례 반복된 기도를 세 번으로 표현하였다고 한다. 즉 여러 차례 기도한 것을 처음, 중간, 나중으로 대체로 나누어 말한 것이라고 한다.[518] 마틴은 세 차례란 말은 기도의 긴박성을 나타낸다고 본다.[519] 그러나 3이란 숫

514) Barrett, 316.

515) Hughes, 441, 주, 1; Zmijewski, 375.

516) Chrysostom, *PG* 61 col.. 578(*NPNF,* XII, 400); Calvin, 160.

517) Barrett, 316.

518) Heckel, Schwachheit, 84-5; Delling, τρεῖς, *TDNT* VIII, 222: "어떤 행동이나 사건이 3번 반복되었다는 것은 그 것이 완전하게 끝나고, 단정적이라는 의미이다."

자가 유대교나 헬라문화에서 실제로 기도와 관련하여 자주 쓰인 경우가 있다. 아론의 축복이 3부분으로 나누어져있고(민 6:24-26; 행 10:16; 요 21:17; *Midrash Tehumna* 22:2), 엘리야도 과부의 아들을 위해서 몸을 3번 펴서 엎드리며 기도했다(왕상 17:21). 예수님도 겟세마네에서 3번 "이 잔을 내게서 지나가게 하옵소서"라고 기도했다(마 26:39-44). 유대인들은 하루에 3번씩 기도했다(시 55:16-17; 단 6:10, 13; 1QS 10:1-7; 1QH 12:3-9).[520] 헬라 종교에서도 3번씩 기도하는 관습이 있었다.[521] 이런 문화 영역에서 세 번의 기도가 장려된 것이 분명하다.[522] 이런 헬라 사회에서의 기도의 예는 바울의 헬라 독자들이 바울의 기도에 대한 진술을 어떻게 이해할 수 있는가를 가늠하게 할 뿐이다. 바울 자신은 복음 전승이나 유대교적 배경에 보다 친숙하였을 것이다. 그러나 쉬지 말고 기도하라고 가르치는 바울이 세 번 기도해야한다는 율법적이고 관습적인 전통을 따라서 세 번 기도했다고는 볼 수는 없다. 바울은 특별히 숫자에 매이지 않았으나 실제로 3번 기도한 것으로 본다. 바울이 2절에서 14년이란 햇수를 말한 것으로 보아 실제로 3번에 걸쳐 심각한 기도를 하였다고 본다. 한편, 이 3번 기도했다는 말이 처음

519) Martin, 418.

520) Windisch, 389; Furnish, 529.

521) Windisch, 389; Euripides, *Hipp.* 46; Furnish, 527; H. -D. Betz, "Aretalogie," 293; A. Deissmann, *Light from the Ancient East*, tr. R. M. Strachan, (London: Hodder & Stoughton, 1927), 153, 308: 그는 여기서 어떤 쥴리어스 아펠라스(M. Julius Appellas)는 사람이 에피다우로스(Epidauros)에 있는 아스클레피오스(Asklepios)신전에서 치료받았다는 기록을 인용한다.

522) Windisch, 389; Zmijewski, 377, 주, 386; Thrall, 819; Martin, 418.

병이 난 후에 연이어 3번 기도했다는 말인지,[523] 아니면 병이 3번에 걸쳐 재발할 때마다 모두 3번 기도 했는가에 대한 것인지도 분명하지 않다.[524] "몸의 가시"라는 표현은 일회적인 고통보다는 계속적인 고통을 가리킨다. 어떤 병인지는 알 수 없으나 재발하여 바울을 괴롭혔다고 보고, 그럴 때마다 세 차례에 걸쳐서 심각한 기도를 하였던 것 같다.

여기서 기도의 대상이 주님(κύριον)이란 것도 특이하다. 9절의 기도의 응답에서 "나의 능력"은 그 다음에 나오는 "그리스도의 능력"과 같은 말이기 때문이다.[525] 바울이 하나님이 아닌 그리스도에게 직접 기도한 경우가 몇 번 있다(살전 3:12-13; 고전 1:2; 16:22).[526] 플러머는 여기서 바울이 예수께 직접 기도한 이유는 그리스도가 지상에 계실 때 병도 고치시고, 귀신도 쫓아내신 분이라는 복음 전승을 따르는 것이라고 한다.[527] 실제로 바울이 본문에서 쓰는 "간구하였다"(παρεκάλεσα)는 동사가 복음서에서도 발견되는 동사이다(막 1:40; 5:23; 6:56; 7:32; 8:22).[528]

523) Bruce, 249; Martin, 418; Heckel, 84-5; Thrall, 819.

524) Hughes, 449; Bachmann, 441.

525) Martin, 417; Bultmann, 227; 프러머, 353; Windisch, 388; Zmijewski, 380; Thrall, 819.

526) Filson, 409; R. J. Bauckham, "The Worship of Jesus in Apocalyptic Christianity," *NTS* 27 (1980-18), 322-41; P. F. Bradshaw, *Daily Prayer in the Early Church* (London: SPCK, 1981), 36; R. T. France, "The Worship of Jesus" in *Christ the Lord*, FS D. Guthrie, ed., H. H. Rowdon (Leicester: IVP, 1982), 17-36.

527) Plummer, 353-4.

528) Plummer, 353-4.

어쨌든 바울은 우리 보통 사람들처럼 고통에 직면하여 고통이 떠나도록 기도하였다. 그러나 그 의 기도에 대한 주님의 반응은 바울이 바라는 것과 일치하지 않았으나, 매우 놀라운 응답이었다.

9. "내게 이르시기를 내 은혜가 네게 족하도다 이는 내 능력이 약한데서 온전하여짐이라 하신지라 이러므로 도리어 크게 기뻐함으로 나의 여러 약한 것들에 대하여 자랑하리니 이는 그리스도의 능력으로 내게 머물게 하려함이라"(**καὶ εἴρηκέν μοι· ἀρκεῖ σοι ἡ χάρις μου, ἡ γὰρ δύναμις ἐν ἀσθενείᾳ τελεῖται. ἥδιστα οὖν μᾶλλον καυχήσομαι ἐν ταῖς ἀσθενείαις μου, ἵνα ἐπισκηνώσῃ ἐπ᾽ ἐμὲ ἡ δύναμις τοῦ Χριστοῦ**). 바울의 3번째 기도에 대한 주님의 응답은 "몸의 가시"(**σκόλοψ τῇ σαρκί**)가 그리스도의 힘이 주어지는 통로가 된다는 기이하고 놀라운 것이었다. 그래서 바울은 고난 중에도 기뻐하게 되었다. 과연 하나님을 사랑하는 자에게는 모든 것이 합력하여 선을 이루게 하시는 것임을 알게 된 것이다(롬 8:28). 여기서 바울이 "약한데서 온전케 되는 능력"의 진리가 자신의 오랜 경험이나, 전통적 지혜의 말에서 온 것이 아니라 주님의 계시임을 밝히는 것은 중요한 의미가 있다. 아무리 사실이라 해도 그의 고난을 자신의 공로로 말하면서 고린도 교인들의 공감이나 동정을 바라는 것은 여전히 육체적 범주에 속하는 자랑이다. 그렇다면 바울의 자랑이 반대자들의 자랑과 차별화가 될 수 없다. 그러므로 바울은 "이 약함 중에 강해지는 진리"가 고난을 통해 스스로 터득한 진리가 아니라 순전히 계시로 받은 것임을 밝히는 것이다. 또한 "몸의 가시"는 물론 앞에서 말한 고난의 사역도 모두 주님의 섭리 가운데 주님께서 주신 것이

다. 그러므로 바울은 그의 수고에도 불구하고 전혀 자랑할 여지가 없는 것이다. 그의 계시도 주님께서 주신 것이다. 그의 사역에서 나타난 모든 역사는 전적으로 주님에게서 나온 것이고 바울에게서 나온 것은 없다. 바울은 그야말로 주님의 종일뿐이며 자랑할 것이 하나도 없다. 자랑할 것이 있다면 주님의 은혜의 통로가 된 사실뿐이다. 모든 것이 주님의 은혜로 말미암음이라는 것이 바울의 중심 사상이다. 그의 사도로 부르심도 은혜이며(고전 15:10), 구원도 은혜로 말미암은 것이다. 주님의 뜻은 바울이 "몸의 가시"를 지닌 채 약한 상태에서 사역하시기를 원하신다. 주님은 그런 약한 가운데서 그의 능력을 나타내시기를 원하신다.

"이르시되"(εἴρηκέν)의 동사 εἰρηκέναι(에레케나이)는 하나님의 말씀을 가리키는 말로 쓰인다.[529] 마틴은 여기서 바울의 간구는 과거형(παρεκάλεσα)으로 되어있고 주님의 응답은 과거분사(εἴρηκέν)로 되어 있다는 점을 중시한다.[530] 바울의 간구는 단순한 과거의 사실이지만, 주님의 응답은 단호한 거절을 의미한다.[531] 같은 기도를 해도 절대로 들어 주지 않는다는 의미이다. 더구나 이 기도의 응답이 바울의 뇌리 속에서 계속 메아리 쳐왔을 것이다.[532]그러나 기이하게도 주님의 부정적인 응답은 긍정적인 의미

529) Plummer, 354; 행 13:34; 히 1:13; 4:3; 4; 10:9; 13:5. 이 구절들은 구약 인용구들이다.

530) Martin, 418.

531) Meyer, 480; Bachmann, 401; Barrett, 316; Plummer, 354; Zmijewski, 378; Furnish, 530; Martin, 418; Thrall, 821. 한편 Windisch는 여기서 과거분사(εἴρηκέν)는 과거와 같은 의미라고 한다(319). 그러나 Moule은 이것이 헬라어 과거분사의 좋은 예라고 한다(15).

532) Hodge, 286.

를 담고 있었다. 그것은 고난을 통해서 힘을 준다는 기이한 응답이었다. 그리고 그 응답은 바울의 삶 가운데서 위로와 능력으로 나타났다.[533] 바울의 기도는 과거의 사실로 끝났으나, 주님의 응답은 계속해서 바울의 능력의 원천으로 나타나고 있는 것이다. 바울의 기도는 "가시"가 고통스러워 사역에 방해가 되니 없애 달라는 것이었으나, 전능하신 주님은 그 "가시"를 바울에게 능력을 주는 도구로 삼았던 것이다. 바울은 고통을 통해서 그리스도의 능력을 나타냈던 것이다.

한편, 바울이 주님으로부터 기도의 응답을 들었다는 것 자체가 바울의 사도권의 정당성을 증명하고 있다. "내게 이르시기를"에서 주님이 바울에게 직접 말씀하셨음을 알 수 있다. 바울은 주님과 깊은 교제를 통해서 주님의 뜻을 잘 아는 신뢰할 수 있는 사도라는 것이 입증되는 것이다. 비록 바울의 기도가 거절로 나타났으나, 그 거절에 대한 의미까지 주께서 친히 말씀하여 주셨다는 것은 바울에 대한 주님의 신뢰가 매우 높다는 것을 보여 준다.[534]

"내 은혜가 네게 족하도다 이는 내 능력이 약한데서 온전하여짐이라 하신지라"(ἀρκεῖ σοι ἡ χάρις μου, ἡ γὰρ δύναμις ἐν ἀσθενείᾳ τελεῖται). 바울의 기도에 대한 주님의 응답은 휴즈가 말하듯이 "바울의 사도직의 전체 범위를 한 눈으로 볼 수 있는 바

533) Bruce, 249.

534) Betz, "Aretalogie," 292-301: Betz는 디오카시우스(Dio Cassius)의 안토니누스(Antoninus)가 모든 치료의 신들로부터 치료받음을 거절당했다는 기록을 본문과 유사한 경우로 들지만 이런 기록들은 기도가 주제가 아님으로 거리가 있다.

울의 서신의 정점에 해당된다."[535]바울이 원하는 응답을 받지 못했으나, 주님의 확실한 응답을 얻었다. "주님의 은혜"는 곧 주님의 능력"을 가리킨다.[536] 이 능력은 일회적인 것이 아니고, 고난받을 때나, 약할 때면 언제나 효력이 나타나는 능력이다(12:10).[537] 이 능력은 "기(氣)"같은 자연적이거나 인위적 힘이 아닌 죄인을 사랑하여 대신 죽으신 하나님의 아들 그리스도의 은혜와 사랑에 근거하는 초월적인 힘이다.[538] 이 능력은 그리스도 안에 있는 사람에게 어떤 고난도 이길 수 있게 하는 능력이다(6:4-10; 11:23-28; 12:10; 롬 8:38, 39). 바울이 받은 약함 가운데 강해지는 그리스도의 은혜와 능력은 바울에게만이 아니라, 약함 중에 있는 모든 그리스도인에게도 주시는 것이다. 실로 그것은 하나님의 세상 경륜의 특징이기도 하다.

한편 본문의 주님의 응답은 신명기 3장 23-26절의 모세의 기도에 대한 하나님의 응답과 유사하다. 모세는 약속의 땅에 들어가기를 기도했지만 하나님은 "그만해도 족하니 이 일로 다시 내게 말하지 말라"고 냉정히 거절했다. 트롤은 3장에서 모세와의 대조를 생각하면 혹 이런 모세의 기도를 심중에 두었는지도 모른다고 생각한다.[539] 그러나 이런 추정은 본문에서 바울이 분명히 자신의 생각이 아닌 주님의 계시의 말씀으로 보도하는 사실을 부정하는 것이므로 받아들일 수 없다. 본문과 비교할 때 동사도 다르고,

535) Hughes, 451.
536) Windisch, 391; Bultmann, 229; Furnish, 530.
537) Bultmann, 229; Héring, 93.
538) Barrett, 316.
539) Thrall, 822.

"약함 가운데 강함"의 주제도 없다. 모세의 경우는 리더십 사임이라는 피할 수 없는 필연적 성격이 지배적이지만, 바울의 경우는 "그리스도의 능력"이라는 고무적인 성격이 강하다. 한편 "족하다(ἀρκεῖ)"는 말이 스토익 철학에서의 "자족(自足)함"과 같다고 보기도 한다.[540] 그러나 본문의 "족함"은 오랜 수양과 훈련을 통해 터득한 내적 도덕적 자족함과는 다르다. 본문의 "족함"은 주님 안에서 주님과의 인격적 교제와 사랑을 통해서 주님으로부터 선물로 받는 자족이기 때문이다(빌 4:11). 그리스도 안에 있는 바울에게 "가시"나 "사단의 사자"나 다른 아무 피조물이라도 그리스도의 사랑으로부터 그를 끊을 수가 없는 것이다(롬 8:38, 39).

"이는 내 능력이 약한데서 온전하여짐이라 하신지라"는 말은 "내 은혜가 네게 족하도다"라는 말을 설명하는 말이다. 위에서 지적하였듯이, "내 은혜"와 "내 능력"은 같은 의미라고 본다.[541] 자기에게 있는 능력을 그리스도의 능력이라고 말함으로써 바울은 그리스도의 사도임을 나타내기를 원한다(갈 2:20). 그러나 동시에 그리스도 안에 있는 모든 믿는 자도 같은 능력을 가지고 있음을 의미한다.[542] 이 진리는 특별히 죽으시고 부활하신 그리스도를 믿는 이들에게 분명한 진리이다. 그러나 본문에서는 역시 바울의 특별한 고난의 사역과, 특별히, "몸의 가시"를 극복하는 원동력이 인간의 의지나 자연적 힘이 아닌 바로 "그리스도의 은혜와 능력"이었음을 나타낸다. 그 능력이 하나님에게서 오기 때문에 인간이

---

540) Furnish, 530; Epictetus, *Discourses*, I.1, 7-13, IV.10, 14-16..

541) O'Collins, 522; Bultmann, 229.

542) C. F. D. Moule, *The Phenomenon of the New Testament*, SBT 2d ser. 1 (Naperville: Allenson, 1967) 21-42; Martin, 420.

일반적으로 예상할 수 없는 방식으로 나타난다. 일반적으로 힘은 주로 강한 것에서 나타나지만 그리스도를 통한 하나님의 능력은 오히려 약한 데서 나타나는 것이다. 이에 대해서 빈디쉬(Windisch)와 헥켈(Heckel)은 이 진리가 격언같이 세상 경험이 많은 사람들이라면(고린도 교인들을 포함해서) 수긍할 수 있는 보편적인 진리라고 한다.[543] 사실 세상에도 "궁즉통"(窮卽通)이나, "새옹지마"(塞翁之馬)같은 인간 경험에 근거한 예상 밖의 행운을 가리키는 말도 있다. 이런 세상 진리는 인간의 의지나 소원과는 상관없는 자연주의 사상에 기초하고 있다. 그러나 바울이 여기서 말하려는 것은 이런 좋은 행운이 자신에게 절로 나타났다는 것이 아니라, 하나님이 초월적으로 그리스도의 능력을 연약한 자신에게 특별히 은혜로 주셨다는 것이다. 이 형통함을 하나님의 구원의 역사하심으로 믿고 그에게 감사와 영광을 돌리는 것이다. 그러나 반대자들은 "외모"를 자랑하고 "육체"를 따라 자랑한다(5:12, 16; 10:7; 11:18). 즉 그들의 언변, 예루살렘 사도들의 추천, 그들의 영적체험과 능력 등이다. 물론 그들은 그들의 "외모"나 "육체"도 하나님의 선물이라고 자랑할 수 있을 것이다. 이에 대해 바울은 그런 정도의 육체적 자랑은 자신도 할 수 있다고 하면서 자랑한다. 그러나 바울의 자랑은 주로 사역 가운데 고난 받은 일들에 대한 것이다(11:23-28). 고난 받은 것도 분명히 육체적 자랑 거리이지만, 반대자들의 육체적 자랑과는 차이가 있다. 바울에게서 고난은 바울의 약함을 나타내는 것이 되기도 한다. 또 고난은 바울의 인내 덕을 나타내는 것도 된다(12:12; 롬 3:4). 그래서 바울은 다른 자

543) Windisch, 391; Heckel, 91.

랑 보다는 자신의 약한 것들을 오히려 자랑하겠다고 한다(11:30). 약함으로 십자가에서 죽으신 그리스도처럼 그의 약함을 자랑하기를 원한다. 그리고 그의 약함의 자랑이 주님께로부터 받은 계시의 말씀으로 그 타당성이 확증되었다(11:30; 12:9, 10). 즉 약하게 죽으셨으나 부활하신 주 안에 있는 자에게는 약한 가운데서 그리스도의 능력이 나타나서 강해진다는 것이다(13:4). 이것이 바울의 기독론 중심 신학이다. 하나님의 아들 예수의 죽음을 구원의 방법이 되게 하신 전능하신 하나님은 인간의 약함을 이용하여서 그의 능력을 나타낸다. 그는 죽음을 생명으로 바꾸시는 능력의 하나님이시다(2:14-17; 4:7-15; 6:4-10; 13:4, 9). 인간의 예상을 뛰어 넘는 그의 역사로 그의 능력과 영광을 극대화 시킨다. 이 역설적인 고난과 영광의 신학 사상이 바울의 중심 신학 사상이다. 자신의 입장을 지지하기 위해서 자신이 만든 신학이 아니라 주님께로부터 직접 받은 계시의 말씀에 근거한 신학이다. 바울은 그리스도의 능력이 고난을 통해서 온전하게 된 것 같이 자신도 약함을 통해서 온전하게 된다는 말씀을 고난을 당하시고 지금은 영광중에 계신 주님으로부터 직접 들은 것이다. 더구나 바울이 자신의 병을 고치지 못하면서도 남을 고치는 사도라고 할 수 있느냐고 반대자들에게 비판받았다면,[544] 이런 계시의 말씀을 통해서 바울은 자신 같이 외모나 육체는 약한 사도를 통해서도 그리스도의 능력이 얼마든지 나타날 수 있다고 증거 하게 된 것이다. 하나님의 생각은 인간의 생각과 다르며, 그의 길은 인간의 길과 다르기 때문이다(사 55:8, 9). 어쨌든지 바울은 고린도후서 전체에서 그의 사역의 진정

544) Jervell, "Charismatiker," 191-5.

성을 반대자들의 영광의 사역과 구별하여 그리스도의 십자가의 죽음과 부활에 근거하여 이해하고 있다(1:10; 4:7-15; 5:15; 6:4-10; 11:23-12:11; 13:4). "바울은 그의 연약함을 기독론적으로 승화시키고 있다."[545] 바울이 평소에 가지고 있던 그리스도 중심 신학 사상이 이 계시로 말미암아 더욱 확고하게 되었을 것이다. 그래서 바울은 그의 연약함을 원망하지 않고, 오히려 기쁘게 받아들이게 되었고, 그의 "몸의 가시"와 같이 약한 것들을 자랑하게 되었다.

한 가지 강조할 것은, 바울이 그의 고난과 영광의 신학이 자신의 추론적 결과나 경험의 소산이 아니고 그리스도로부터 직접 받은 계시에 의한 것임을 밝히는 것도 중요한 본문의 목적이라는 것이다. 물론 평소에 바울이 하나님의 은혜로 말미암는 구원 진리를 가르쳐 왔다. 그러나 그것도 하나님의 계시에 의한 것이다(갈 1:12). 이런 계시는 대적자들로 하여금 바울이 자신의 연약함을 가지고 스스로 미화시키고 있다는 비난을 할 수 없게 만드는 것이다. 동시에 바울은 고린도 교인들에게 그가 이 모든 육체적 정신적 고난을 받으며 복음을 전하는 진정한 사도일 뿐만 아니라 깊은 영적 체험도 가지고 있으며, 무엇보다 그의 고난의 복음이 그리스도의 계시에 근거한 것임을 밝힘으로써 그의 사도적 권위와 신뢰성을 증대시키는 효과를 기대하고 있을 것이다.

한편 여기서 바울이 결국 계시를 받은 사실을 가지고 자신의 사도적 권위를 자랑하는 것이라고도 볼 수 있으나, 위에서 지적하였듯이, 바울이 진심으로 원하는 것은 이런 자랑이 아니라 그의 사역 가운데 하나님께서 자신을 약하게 만드시고 하나님께서 역사하셔

---

545) O'Collins, 532; 이에 동의하는, Güttgemanns, 169, 170.

서 모든 구원 사역을 이루신다는 것이다. 12장 11절에서 바울은 자신은 "아무것도 아니다"라고 낮춘다. 바울은 하나님께만 모든 영광을 돌리는 데 관심이 있다. 본문의 계시의 성격 자체가 하나님의 절대적 주권과 은혜를 암시하는 것이다. 바울은 그의 부르심과 그의 구원론을 하나님의 은혜 중심으로 설명한다. 그렇다면 본문에서의 바울의 관심도 약한 자신을 통해 역사하시는 하나님을 높이는 것이 주된 관심이며, 모든 믿는 사람들이 그렇게 자신을 낮추고 하나님을 높이면서 살아야 함을 가르치고 있는 것이다. 이렇게 자신을 낮추는 것은 단순히 도덕적인 겸비가 아니라 그리스도 안에서 그리스도의 십자가의 사랑과 은혜와 능력을 믿는 사람의 겸비이다.

"이러므로 도리어 크게 기뻐함으로 나의 여러 약한 것들에 대하여 자랑하리니 이는 그리스도의 능력으로 내게 머물게 하려함이라"(ἥδιστα οὖν μᾶλλον καυχήσομαι ἐν ταῖς ἀσθενείαις μου, ἵνα ἐπισκηνώσῃ ἐπ' ἐμὲ ἡ δύναμις τοῦ Χριστοῦ). 그리스도의 능력이 약함을 통해서 온전하여 짐을 알게 되고서, 바울은 그의 여러 약한 것들을 부끄러워하지 않고 오히려 기뻐하며, 자랑하게 되었다. "그러므로"(οὖν)는 결론적 진술을 이끄는 접속사이다. 그의 약함이 도리어 그리스도의 능력이 온전하게 된다는 계시를 받고서 그의 약함의 적극적인 유익을 알고서 오히려 기뻐하게 된 것이다. "도리어"(μᾶλλον)라는 부사가 무엇보다 "도리어" 약함을 자랑한다는 말인가? 8-9절의 기도인가?[546] 아니면, 2-4절의 "환상"인가?[547] 이 부사가 바로 앞의 기도를 가리킨다고 볼 수 있으나, 5절과 9절 상반절에서 "약한 것들을 자랑하겠다"는 말이

546) Bachmann, 402; Plummer, 355; Zmijewski, 387; Furnish, 531; Keckel, 101-2.
547) Barrett, 317; Martin, 421; Thrall, 826.

거듭 나왔으므로 그 앞에서 언급한 "환상"을 가리킨다고 볼 수도 있다. 어느 쪽이라도 의미가 통하지만, 바울이 대적자들의 환상의 자랑에 맞서고 있는 정황을 고려 할 때, "기도"보다는 "환상"이 비교 대상이 된다고 본다.[548] 그러므로 여기서 바울이 말하는 것은 "환상" 보다 도리어(μᾶλλον) 약함을 자랑한다는 것으로 풀이된다. 그러나 여기서 바울의 가장 큰 관심은, 11장 15절 이후부터 말하는 고난의 주제와 관련하여서, 고난이 그리스도의 사도의 가장 중요한 표라는 것은 자신이 스스로 주장하는 것이 아니라 그리스도가 직접 자신에게 계시한 것임을 알리는 데 있다. 그렇게 함으로써 반대자들의 어떤 반론도 막고, 한편으로는 고린도 교인들에게 그의 신뢰성을 높이는 이중적 효과를 기대하였을 것이다(13:2). 동시에 "나의 여러 가지 약한 것들"(ταῖς ἀσθενείαις μου)은 고린도후서 전체에서 바울과 그의 반대자들이 지적하는 바울의 약한 것들을 일 수도 있다. 즉 신뢰성 결여(1:15-2:1), 말씀의 목격자가 아니라는 것(3:1; 5:16), 언변부족(10:10), 외모부족(10:10), 신령한 체험 부족(12:1-7), 신령한 능력 부족(12:12), 질병(12:6-9), 재물 갈취(7:2; 12:16-18), 고난의 사역(11:23-33) 등이다. 반대자들은 바울의 고난의 사역이 하나님이 바울과 함께하지 않는 증거로 역공할 수도 있다. 그러나 이런 모든 약함들이 그리스도 안에서 하나님의 능력으로 바뀌는 역사가 일어나게 되는 것이다. 바로 이런 역사가 바울의 사역 가운데 계속해서 나타나고 있음을 바울이 증명하였다(2:14-17; 3:18; 4:6-15; 6:4-10; 7:6). 이런 바울의 사역은 진정한 그리스도의 사도임을 증거하는 것이다.

---

548) Plummer, 355; Martin, 421; Thrall, 826.

"크게 기뻐함"(ἥδιστα)이 희랍어 본문에는 처음 나오는 말이다. 이 말은 ἡδέως(헤데오스)의 최상급으로 "매우 기뻐하였다"는 뜻이다. 주님의 계시에 대한 바울의 반응은 기쁨이었다. 그의 기도대로 응답이 되지 않았으나 기도를 통해서 "몸의 가시"를 허락하신 주님의 은혜롭고 호의적인 뜻을 알게 되었기 때문이다. 불치의 병이라고 낙담하였는데, 주께서 그의 능력을 나타내시겠다고 약속하시니 크게 기뻐하게 된 것이다. 더구나 주님이 그를 그의 귀한 계시의 통로로 쓰셨다는 사실이 그 기쁨을 더하게 하였을 것이다(6:4-10). 무엇보다 이런 기쁨의 저변에는 모든 어려움 중에서도 전능하신 하나님을 전적으로 신뢰하면 결국 승리한다는 바울의 믿음이 있다(1:9, 10; 2:14; 3:4; 4:10; 6:4-10; 11:11; 13:4). 하나님은 인간의 연약함을 통해서 오히려 그의 기이한 은혜의 역사를 베푸시는 놀라우신 분이시라는 것이다(출 15:11; 욥 5:9; 10:16; 시 107:8; 139:14; 사 29:14; 눅 1:52-55; 롬 11:33-35; 계 15:3).

여기서 한 가지 문법적인 문제는 ἵνα가 이끄는 목적절을 그대로 번역하면 바울이 마치 그리스도의 능력을 가지기 위하여 약한 것들에 대하여 자랑하는 것으로 나타나는 것이다. 다시 말하면, 약한 것들의 자랑의 결과로 그리스도의 능력이 나타난다는 의미가 되어 이해하기 어렵다. 그러나 10절에서는 기뻐함(자랑함)이 약함에서 강함을 경험한 결과로 발생하는 것으로 말한다. 10절의 의미를 따라서 이 부분을 번역하면, "나의 여러 약한 것들에 대하여 자랑하리니, 그 결과(그것으로 말미암아, δι ὧν)로 그리스도의 능력이 내게 머물게 하려 함이라"라고 번역할 수 있다.[549] 한편,

549) Thrall, 827.

본문의 ἵνα은 바울의 목적이 아니라 하나님의 목적을 나타낸다고 볼 수 있다. 즉 "나의 여러 약한 것들에 대하여 자랑하리니, 하나님의 목적은 그리스도의 능력이 내게 머물게 하려 함이라"고 번역할 수도 있다. 두 가지 모두 가능하나, 후자가 전자보다 문법적으로나 의미상으로 적합하다.

"나의 약한 것들(ταῖς ἀσθενείαις μου)"에서 바울의 "약한 것들"은 육체적 약함만을 말한 것은 아니다. 비록 "몸의 가시"라는 육체적 약함에서 시작된 말이지만 "나의 약한 것들(ταῖς ἀσθενείαις μου)"이란 보편적인 말로 표현되었으므로 바울의 모든 약함을 나타낸다고 보아야 한다. 바울의 육체와, 능력의 약함뿐만이 아니라 모든 존재론적, 심리적 약함도 가리킨다. 바울은 고린도 교회 문제로 근심하는 중에 있었다(2:1; 11:28). 4장 7절에서 바울은 자신의 존재를 질그릇으로 말하였다. 그리스도의 약한 가운데서 강해지는 능력이 자신의 존재와 사역에서도 작용한다고 믿는 것이다. 더구나 여기서는 그 사실이 계시의 말씀으로써 객관적으로 확인되었음을 알리는 것이다. 바울은 평소에 그가 그리스도와 존재론적으로 연합되고 실존론적으로 본받는다고 하였으므로 여기서도 그리스도의 죽음과 부활의 유형에 따라서 그의 존재와 사역을 이해한다고 본다. 그러나 이런 존재론적 의미 외에도 그의 육체적 약한 것들도 포함한다고 보아야 한다. 즉 언변의 부족함(10:10; 11:6), 외모의 부족함(10:1, 7, 10), 사도적 권세 행사 부족(10:8; 13:2; 10), 고난(11:23-33), "몸의 가시"(12:7), 그리고 역사적 예수와의 접촉 결핍(5:12, 16), 교회를 핍박한 과거(고전 15:9) 등이다. 바울은 이런 약한 자신의 부족함이나 어려움들 가운데서 오히려 그리스도의 능력이 나타난다고 증거한다. 예로 1장과 7장에서 말하는 환난 후에 받는 위로와 감사함, 그리고 2장 14-17절에서 말하는 그리스도의 향기로서의 승리이다. 바로 그런 약함의 사역 자체가 그리스도의 진정한 사도적 증거라고 말한다(13:4).

"그리스도의 능력"(ἡ δύναμις τοῦ Χριστοῦ)이란 무엇인가? 희랍어 명사의 2격이 기원(起源)을 나타낼 수 있으므로 그리스도에게서 오는 능력이란 뜻도 되고 그리스도가 가지고 있는 능력도 된다. "그리스도의 능력"은 로마서 8장 35-39절에서 말한 대로 모든 피조 세계의 공간적 시간적 위협과 고통에서 인간을 구원하는 능력이다. "그리스도의 능력"은 과거의 그리스도의 부활 사건에서 실제로 증명되었고, 그를 믿는 사람 가운데 계속 역사하는 능력이다. 4장 7-15절에서 바울은 자신의 계속되는 고난의 사역을 통해서 그리스도의 부활의 능력이 나타났다고 한다. 바울 자신이 고난의 목회 현실 가운데서 그리스도의 죽음을 체험하며, 동시에 그의 생명도 나타낸다고 믿었다(4:10, 11). 문제는 바울의 대적자들은 그리스도의 능력을 외적인 능력으로 국한시켜서 자랑하는 것이다. 바울은 외적인 능력도 인정하지만 보다 내적인 능력을 강조한다. 그래서 육체를 따라 고난의 사역을 자랑도 하고(11:18), 영적 체험도 자랑하지만(12:1-4), 그 보다 고난 받는 사역자로서의 약한 면을 자랑한다고 한다(11:30; 12:9). 무엇보다 "몸의 가시"의 경험을 통해서 하나님만을 온전히 의지하게 하고(1:9), 내적 성숙과 영적 단련, 그리고 믿음과 영원한 소망을 굳게 가지게 하는 그리스도의 능력이 나타남을 알고 기뻐하는 것이다(4:16-5:10; 12:10; 롬 5:3, 4). 이런 그리스도의 능력은 인간이 매일 당면하는 일상적인 문제들은 물론 인간의 궁극적인 존재론적 문제와 존재 이유를 확고하게 세워주어 모든 문제들을 이기고 날마다 새로운 힘으로 살게 하고 영원히 살게 하는 능력이다. 이런 사상은 결국 하나님의 은혜로 구원 얻는 바울의 구원론 사상의 현실적 적용과 같은 것이다.

"머물게 하려 함이라"의 희랍어 επισκηνώση는 "거주한다", "머문다"의 뜻도 있으나 "비친다"는 뜻도 있다. 즉 그리스도의 임재와 영광을 동시에 가리키는 말로 볼 수 있다. 출애굽기 40장 34-35절에서 구름이 회막 위에 덮이고(ἐπεσκίαζεν), 여호와의 영광이 충만하여 모세가 그리로 들어 갈 수가 없었다고 한다. 바울이 이런 구절을 마음에 두고 썼을까? 3장에서도 모세의 얼굴에 비친 일시적 영광을 새 언약의 일꾼의 영원한 영광과 비교하여 논한 바 있기 때문에 이런 가능성을 무시할 수 없다. 그러므로 본문의 ἐπισκηνώση(에피세키노세, "머물게 하려 함이라")가 출애굽기 40장 34-35절에서의 "하나님의 영광의 임재"(세키나, שׁכינה)의 배경을 가지고 있다고 볼 수 있을 것이다. 이 희랍어의 접두어(ἐπι)를 뺀 줄기어(σκηνή="천막")의 세 개의 자음(s, k, n)이 히브리어 세키나(שׁכינה)의 세 자음과 일치하는 것과 본문의 ἐπισκηνώση(에피스키노세)가 출애굽기 본문의 ἐπεσκίαζεν(에페스키아젠, LXX)과 유사한 글자로 구성된 사실도 그냥 넘길 수 없다.[550] 그리스도의 영광의 임재가 그의 능력과 함께 나타난다는 것이다. 그리스도의 능력이 바울의 사역에 계속 머문다는 사실은 바울의 사도권의 진정성을 더욱 강화시켜 줄 것이다.

---

550) Plummer, 355; Strachan, 33; Héring, 94; Tasker, 179; Hughes, 452; Barrett, 367; Schlatter, 669; Hodge, 287; Göttgemanns, 169; Bultmann, 230; Martin, 421.

"내 능력이 약한데서 온전하여짐이라"는 말에 관한 한 가지 질문은 바울의 약함이 바울에게 이미 있어왔던 그리스도의 능력을 나타내는 수단이 된다는 의미인가 아니면,[551] 지금까지 없던 새로운 그리스도의 능력이 들어오는 통로가 된다는 말인가?[552] "몸의 가시"가 있기 전부터, 바울에게 그리스도의 능력이 있었던 것이 분명하다. 그가 사도로서 부르심을 받았을 때부터 그는 고난을 받았고, 그런 가운데 나타나는 그리스도의 능력을 경험 하였을 것이다(행 9:16; 18, 22). 십자가와 부활에서 나타난 그리스도의 구원 능력이 바울의 근본 사상이라면, 이 사상과 함께 그의 삶에서도 약함을 통해 그리스도의 능력이 나타남을 평소에 경험하였을 것이다(고전 1:27-29; 15:9-10; 고후 4:7-15; 6:4-10; 13:3, 4). 4장 7-15절에서 바울은 자신의 고난의 사역 가운데서 그리스도의 부활의 능력이 나타났다고 말한다. 11장 23절 이하에서 그는 많은 고생 가운데 약함을 경험하였음을 말한 후에, 30절에서 나의 약한 것을 자랑할 것이라 말할 때, 이미 그 이유, 즉 그리스도의 능력이 나타나기 때문이라는 이유를 암시했다고 봐야 한다. 그러나 모든 약함 가운데서도 "몸의 가시"로 말미암아 고통당하며 기도할 때, 특별히 받은 계시로 말미암아 그 진리를 확실하게 더욱 깨달았다는 것이다. 더구나 그 가시로 인한 큰 고통 중에서 받은 계시에서 나타난 주님의 사랑과 지혜를 깨닫고 크게 기뻐하였던 것이다. 다시 말하면, 바울의 "몸의 가시"가 바울에게 이미 현존하는 그리스도의 능력을 분명하게 나타내는 수단이 되었다. 그러므로 여기서 바

---

551) Bultmann, 228-30; *NT Theology* 1:285, 349, 351; Plummer, 354; Betz, *2Corinthians 8 and 9*, 303; O'Collins, "Power" 537.

552) Käsemann, *Legitimität*, 39; Windisch, 391, 392; Strachan, 530.

울이 전에 몰랐던 새로운 그리스도의 능력을 받았다고 볼 수 없고, 계시를 통해서 "몸의 가시"가 그에게 이미 현존하는 그리스도의 능력을 나타내는 수단이 된다는 진리를 분명히 재확인하였다고 보아야 한다.

그러나 여기서 바울은 이런 "약함 가운데 강해지는 진리"는 모두 계시에 의한 것이며, 자신의 경험이나 추론 또는 남의 생각에 의한 것이 아님을 분명히 밝혀서 반대자들이 바울이 그의 약함이나 고난에 대해서 인위적으로 의미를 부가하는 것이라고 반박하는 것을 아예 차단하려는 의도가 있다고 본다(참조, 갈 1:12). 또한 바울이 그의 신학과 사역의 중심 사상인 "약함의 능력"은 바울의 자신의 약함이나 약점들에 대한 인위적 구실이나 변명이 아니라 주님으로부터 받은 계시에 의해 받은 객관적이고 타당한 진리라는 것을 보여주는 것이다(11:10; 13:8).

한편, 바울 자신이 깨달은 이 보편적 진리를 자기의 경우에만 적용한다고 볼 수 없다. 바울은 고린도후서 전체에서 이런 영적 엘리트 의식을 반대한다(1:24; 3:3, 18; 6:3; 7:3; 10:13; 11:21; 12:19; 13:9).[553] 자신이 깨달은 진리는 보편적 진리로서 그리스도 안에 있는 모든 사람들에게 균등하게 적용되는 하나님의 은혜의 진리로 선포하고 있다(참조, 딤후4:8).[554] 이런 하나님의 능력은 사도에게만 나타나는 것이 아니라 모든 그리스도인들에게도 나타난다. 1장과 7장에서 모든 환난 가운데서 위로하시고 감사하게하시는 하나님의 능력이나, 모든 것을 합력하여 선을 이루시게하시는

553) Martin, 422.

554) Bultmann, 230; Martin, 422, 423; 이에 반대하는 G. G. O'Collins, 528-37; Thrall, 831.

하나님의 능력도 약함 가운데 처한 모든 그리스도인들에게 일어나는 같은 하나님의 능력을 가리킨다(롬8:28).[555] 특히 12장 19절에서 바울은 그가 지금까지 한 말이 자신의 개인적 변명이 아니라 고린도 교인들의 덕을 세우기 위함이라고 말하면서 사도로서 자신의 경험을 통해서 고린도 교인들을 가르치는 것이 서신의 목적임을 분명히 밝히고 있다.

10. "그러므로 내가 그리스도를 위하여 약한 것들과 능욕과 궁핍과 핍박과 곤란을 기뻐하노니 이는 내가 약할 그 때에 곧 강함이니라"(**διὸ εὐδοκῶ ἐν ἀσθενείαις, ἐν ὕβρεσιν, ἐν ἀνάγκαις, ἐν διωγμοῖς καὶ στενοχωρίαις, ὑπὲρ Χριστοῦ· ὅταν γὰρ ἀσθενῶ, τότε δυνατός εἰμι.**). 이 말은 직접적으로는 9절에서 받은 계시의 말씀에 대한 바울의 기쁜 반응을 확대하는 말이다. 즉 "몸의 가시" 뿐만이 아니라 바울이 사역 가운데 겪는 온갖 고통을 오히려 기쁘게 받아들이게 되었다는 것이다. 보다 구체적으로 11장 23절 이후에서 지금까지 말하는 모든 내용과 그 의미를 요약하고 결론내리는 진술이다.[556] 나아가 바울의 전체 사역의 본질적 성격에 대한 요약이라고 할 수도 있다. 특별히 4장 7-15절의 "질그릇과 보배" 의 역설적인 대조와, 6장 4-10절의 죽고 사는 사역에서 이미 언급되었던 것이다. 한마디로 외적으로는 고난과 죽음이 점철되어 있으나 내적으로는 기쁨과 생명이 넘치는 역설적인 사역이다. 여기서 바울의 약한 것들과 모든 고난은 바울 자신이나 다

555) Martin, 서론, lx, lxi.

556) Barrett, 317, 18; Zmijewski, 395; Martin, 423.

른 그 무엇을 위한 것이 아닌 "그리스도를 위한(ὑπὲρ Χριστοῦ)" 것임을 분명히 말하고 있다.[557] 이 점에서 바울의 고난은 다른 여러 가지 일반적인 고난과 구별된다. 다른 세상의 고난과 구별되는 것은 물론, 다른 거짓 사도들의 고난과도 구별될 것이다. 아마 대적자들도 바울과 유사한 고난들을 어느 정도 겪었다고 대응 할 수 있을 것이다. 그러나 그 고난의 목적이 과연 진정으로 그리스도를 위한 것이었는가는 바울의 대적자들에 대한 단호한 정죄적 발언(11:13-15)과 의심(11:23)에서 볼 때 부정적이다. 그들은 가장(假裝)하기 잘 하는 거짓 사도들로서 그들의 고난조차도 가장된 고난일 수 있다. 바울의 고난의 진정성, 즉 다름 아닌 그리스도를 위한 고난이란 사실은 9절의 계시의 말씀에서 전제되어 있는 의미이며, 주님의 계시로서 객관적 사실임이 확인된 것이다.

한편, 여기서 어떤 스토익 철학에 영향 받은 고대 기독교의 고행주의적 고난 사상도 배제되어야 한다.[558] 이런 사상은 심리적 불안을 인위적 고행으로 타개하려는 인본주의적 신학이다. 바울의 고난의 신학은 결국 기쁨의 신학이기 때문이다. 희랍어 원문에서 이 부분의 결론에 해당하는 이 진술의 첫 말을 접속사 "그러므로"(διό)와 함께 "기뻐한다"(εὐδοκῶ)는 말로 쓴 것은 지금까

557) Barrett, 306; Tasker, 179; Martin, 423. 그러나 "그리스도를 위한"을 고난 받은 사실 대신에 "기뻐한다"와 연결하는 주석가들도 있다: Meyer, 482; Bachmann, 402; Plummer, 355; Windisch, 393; Furnish, 531. 즉 바울이 고통 중에 기뻐하는 것은 그리스도를 위함이다. 그러나 이런 번역은 고난이 주제인 문맥에서 어색하다. 고난 받은 것이 "그리스도를 위한"(ὑπέρ Χριστοῦ)이란 구절과 가까이 있으므로 "그리스도를 위해 받은 고난"으로 보는 것이 무난하다고 본다. 그리스도를 위한 고난이란 말이 바울 서신에 자주 나타난다(롬 8:17; 고후 1:5, 7; 빌 1:29; 3:10; 골 1:24).

558) Tasker, 179; Hughes, 452: "a joyless theology of insecurity"; Martin, 423.

지 말한 모든 고난을 주님 안에서 기쁨으로 바꾸어 주시는 하나님의 은혜를 강조하려는 뜻이 있다. 바울은 자신의 경험이나 노력으로 "약함 가운데서 강함의 진리"를 깨달은 것이 아니라 순전히 계시에 의한 것이며 이 놀라운 계시적 진리에 대하여 자신은 기뻐할 뿐이라는 것이다. 그리고 이런 역설적인 은혜의 진리가 바울 자신에게만이 아니라 그와 같이 그리스도의 고난에 참여하는 모든 사람들에게도 일어나는 것으로 말한다. 그리스도 안에 있는 이들에게는 그리스도의 죽음의 고난과 부활의 능력이 동시에 작용하기 때문이다. "몸의 가시"는 그리스도 안에 있는 누구에게나 있을 수 있는 것이며, 하나님은 그 "가시"를 그리스도 안에 있는 모든 사람들에게 그리스도의 능력을 공급하는 통로가 되도록 바꾸어 주시는 것이다. 이런 하나님의 능력은 이상한 것이 아니라 바로 복음의 능력의 특성이다. 한 마디로 하나님의 은혜에 절대적으로 의지하여 구원받는다는 바울의 구원론과 다를 바 없다. 그러므로 본문에서의 바울의 약함의 자랑은 결국 "내가 복음을 부끄러워하지 아니하노니 이 복음은 모든 믿는 자에게 구원을 주시는 하나님의 능력이 됨이라"(롬1:16)에서도 반복되어 나타나는 것이다.

이 구절에서 11장 23절 이하의 긴 고난 목록에 비해서 짧은 고난 목록이 나온다. "약한 것들"(ἀσθενείαις)은 모든 고난의 일반적인 성격이고 그에 대한 자세한 고난의 종류가 4개가 짝을 이루어 나타난다. 첫째는 "능욕"(ὕβρεσιν)이다. 이 말이 다른 서신에서는 나타나지 않고 여기에만 나타나는 것은 그 만큼 바울이 반대자들로부터 중상모략을 심하게 받았기 때문인지도 모른다(11:19-

21).[559] "궁핍"(ἀνάγκαις)은 6장 4절에서도 언급된 바와 같이 "필요한 것" 또는 "환난"(고전 7:26)을 가리킨다.[560] 그러나 필요한 것이 부족함을 의미한다고 보고 "궁핍"으로 번역하기도 한다(6:4; 12:10; 살전 3:7). 그 궁핍은 무슨 운명적인 것이 아니라 그리스도를 위한 헌신의 결과로 자초한 것이다.[561] "핍박"(διωγμοῖς)은 종교적 이유로 받는 고난을 가리킨다(롬 8:35; 참조, 살후 1:4; 딤후 3:11).[562] "곤란"(στενοχωρίαις)은 6장 4절에도 나오고, 4장 8절에는 동사형이 나온다(롬 8:35). 이 말은 좁은 틈을 가리키며, 거기서 끼어있어서 헤어나기 어려운 상태를 나타낸다.[563] 한 마디로 이런 고난 목록은 바울의 약함의 이력서이다.

이렇게 약함을 자랑하는 바울의 관심은 보다 복합적이다. 자신을 고난 받는 주님의 종으로 나타내고, 또한 주님의 계시의 도구로 증명하려는 의도가 분명하고(12:11), 또 오만한 반대자들을 경계하려는 뜻도 보이지만, 한편으로는 자신의 연약함을 그대로 나타내어 "약한 고린도 교인들"과 친숙한 관계를 형성하려는 의도도 있다고 본다. 바울은 초인이 아니라 독자들과 같이 보통 사람임을 나타낸다. 그는 1장에서도 아시아에서 죽을 뻔한 경험과 두려움을 그대로 말하면서 우리 모두가 환난 중에 위로받는 불쌍한 처지에 있음을 말하고 있다(1:10). 그는 고린도 인들과 함께 살고 함께 죽는 동지 의식을 가지고서 진정한 인간관계를 이루기를 원

---

559) Furnish, 551; Zmijewski, 393; P. Marshall, *Enmity in Corinth: Social Conventions in Paul's Relations with the Corinthians,* WUNT 2, Reiche (Tübingen: Mohr, 1987), 202.

560) Tasker, 93,

561) Martin, 173.

562) BAGD, 201.

563) Filson, 347.

하는 것이다(1:12; 7:3; 11:11; 12:15). 그러므로 본문에서 사도로서의 계시와 환상의 경험에도 불구하고 약한 인간으로서 당하는 고난과 "다메섹에서의 탈출," 그리고 "몸의 가시" 같은 그의 약점들을 솔직히 나타내는 것이다. 바울이나 고린도 교인들이나 모두 하나님의 은혜와 능력으로 살아가야 하는 약한 존재들이라는 의미를 나타내면서 고린도 교인들과의 우의를 다지려는 측면도 있다.

주 해(11:16–12:10):

11장 16절-12장 10절의 "바보의 연설" 의 주제는 "주안에서의 약함의 능력" 이다. 실제로 이 주제가 고린도후서 전체의 주제라고 할 수 있다. 바울의 변명이 이 주제를 중심으로 형성되기 때문이다. 그것은 곧 서신 초두에서 밝힌 "거룩함과 진실함" 으로 행하는 바울의 사역을 통해서 나타나는 하나님의 은혜와 지혜를 가리킨다(1:12). 즉 세상의 지혜를 따라서 행하지 않고 하나님의 은혜와 지혜를 따라서 사역하는 가운데 많은 어려움이 따르지만 결국 하나님의 능력이 나타나서 승리한다는 것이다(2:14-17). 이것은 다름 아닌 바로 그리스도의 십자가의 능력과 지혜이다(고전 1:23-25). 이 주제는 바울의 이신득의 구원론과도 직결된다. 바울은 4장 7-15절과 6장 4-10절에서 자신의 그리스도 중심의 사역을 논할 때도 같은 주제를 언급하면서 자신의 사도직을 변명하였다. 여기서도 바울은 자신의 "몸의 가시" 라는 특별한 경험 가운데서 주님으로부터 직접 들은 계시의 말씀으로서 그 주제의 신적 권위와 함께 계시의 통로서의 바울의 사도적 권위를 확고히 하려는 것이다. 이런 주제 아래서 바울은 자신의 고난의 사역을 중심으로 육체적 자랑을 하였다(11:16-33). 그러나 한편으로 그의 고난을 자랑하는 것은 곧 그의 약함을 자랑하는 것이라고 생각하기도 한다(11:30). 그리고 3층천에 올라간 영적 체험을 육체적 자랑의 범주에 포함하여 자랑한다(12:1-4). 그러나 이와는 대조적으로 "몸의 가시"는 육체적 수치로 말하지만, 그런 약함이야말로 주안에서 진정한 자랑이 될 수 있음을 알게 되었다고 한다. 사람의 자랑하는 것이 자신의 영광을 위한 것이라면 무슨 자랑이든지 어리석은 것이다. 그러나 그 자랑이 진정 하나님의 영광을 나타내는 자랑이라면 그것은 지혜로운 것이다. 바울은 그의 대적자들을 따라서 어리석은 육체적 자랑도 하였으나, 그의 진정한 자랑은 그의 약한 것이다. 그는 그의 "몸의 가시" 경험을 통해서 그리스도의 능력이 자신의 연약함을 통해서 나타난다는 것을 주님으로부터 들었기 때문이다(12:9). 그래서 그는 오히려 그의 약함을 부끄러움 없이 자랑하면서 하나님의 영광과 능력이 자신의 사역 가운데 넘치기를 바라는 것이다. 사실 약함 가운데서 나타나는 그리스도의 능력에 대해서 "질그릇과 보배"의 비유로 고난의 사역을 말하는 4장 7-15절과 역시 고난의 사역을 말하는 6장 4-10절 등에서 이미 구체적으로 말하였다. 그리스도의 능력은 어려운 사역에서 힘을 주시고 이기게 하시는 신적 능력이다. "몸의 가시"는 바울의 모든 역경 중의 하나의 사례일 뿐이다. 그러나 그 사례가 다른 사례보다 중요한 것은 고난의 의미를 계시로 받아 확실히 깨닫는 계기가 되었기 때문이다. 이런 바울의 연설은 분명히 그의 반대자들의 육체적 가치를 따라하는 세상적이고 사욕적인 자랑과는 대조적이다. 고린도 교인들이 그들의 이런 자랑에 의해서 바울을 떠났다면, 바울의 그리스도의 고난과 부활에 근거한 목회신학과 그의 계시로 받은 "약함 가운데서 강함"의 진리를 듣고 다시 돌아오기를 바라는 것이다.

한 가지 기억할 것은 바울의 "약함"은 육체적 약함만을 말한 것은 아니다. 비록 "몸의 가시"라는 육체적 약함에서 시작된 말이지만 "나의 약한 것들(ἀσθενείαις μου)"이란 보편적인 말로 표현되었으므로 바울의 전 인간적 약함을 나타낸다고 보아야 한다. 모든 외적 능력과 함께 존재론적, 실존론적 약함을 가리킨다(4:7-15). 그러나 바울은 그리스도와 존재론적으로 일치되고(존재적 일치가 아님) 또 실존론적으로 본받는다고 하였으므로 여기서도 그리스도의 죽음과 부활의 유형에 따라서 바울의 존재와 사역을 이해한다고 본다. 또한 바울의 약함은 고린도후서에서 바울이 언급하는 구체적인 그의 모든 약함들을 포함한다(언변의 부족함[10:10; 11:6]; 외모의 부족함[10:1, 7, 10]; 역사적 예수에 대한 지식 부족함[5:16], 고난[11:23-33], "몸의 가시"[12:7], 사도적 권세 행사 부족[10:8; 13:2; 10] 등). 바울은 이런 역경 가운데서 하나님께서 그의 사역을 승리로 이끌어 주시는 것이 바로 그의 사도직의 진정성으로 증거한다. 즉 1장과 7장에서 고린도 교회의 어려움이 해소 되었다는 기쁜 소식을 디도를 통해서 듣고서 환난 중에서 위로하시는 하나님께 감사한다. 어려운 일의 추이를 인내로 지켜보면서 그 일이 해결될 때 하나님의 은혜로 믿고 감사하는 것이다. 또 2장 14-17절에서 도처에서 이김을 주시는 하나님께 감사한다는 말도 이런 맥락에서 이해할 수 있다.

한편, 블랙(D. A. Black)에 의하면 바울서신에서 약함(ἀσθένεια)이란 말이 모두 44번 나오는데, 고린도전서에 29번 나오고, 고린도후서에 14번 나온다고 한다. 14번 모두 10-13장에 나온다. 블랙(Black)은 바울이 이 단어의 잦은 사용으로 "약함의 신학"을 형성하였다고 한다.[564] 마틴은 불랙의 연구에서 더 나아가 바울의 예루살렘 사도회의 이후 예루살렘 사도들과의 소원한 관계가 이 신학의 배경이라고 본다. 고린도 교회에서 예루살렘 사도들의 추천장을 가지고 온 선교사들의 바울 반대 운동이 고린도후서에서 바울의 위기감을 더 고조시켰다고 본다.[565]

바울의 연설은 그 역설적인 주제와 함께 역설적인 설명으로 넘친다. 이런 역설적 특성은 반대파들의 공격에 대한 반격을 위해 바울이 사용한 수사학적 특성이라고도 할 수 있으나, 평소 바울의 그리스도의 십자가 중심의 신학과 그의 계시의 경험이 고린도 교회의 대립적 정황에서 필연적으로 이런 연설의 역설적인 성격을 형성한 것이다. 성경에 나타난 하나님의 구원 역사를 전체적으로 볼 때 본문에 있는 역설적인 진술들은 이상한 것이 아니라 정상적인 것이며, 예수의 복음 전승의 성격을 그대로 반영하는 것이다. 하나님은 가난한 자를 진토에서 일으키시며, 궁핍한 자를 거름 무더기에서 드셔서 방백들과 함께 세우신다(시 113:7-9). 그는 낮은 자를 높이시고 슬픈 자를 흥기시켜 안전하게 있게 하신다(욥 5:11). 그는 그리스도의 죽음을 구원의 역사로 바꾸시고, 바울 같이 교회를 핍박하던 사람을 불러서 구원의 복음을 선포케 하시는 전능하신 하나님이시며, 영광과 찬양을 받으시기에 합당하신 분이다.

무엇보다 본문에서 바울의 모든 역경을 그리스도의 능력이 나타나는 기회가 된다는 가르침은 바울 스스로가 주장하는 것이 아니라, 주님이 친히 바울에게 말씀하신 계시임을 밝혀서 바울의 사

564) David Alan Black, *Paul, Apostle of Weakness. Astheneia and Its Cognates in the Pauline Literature* (New York: Lang, 1984), 85.

565) Martin, 서론, liii-lxi, 특히, 1vi, lix.

역과 가르침의 신적 기원과 권위를 확고하게 세우고 있는 것이다. 그러나 우리가 계속 지적해 왔듯이 바울의 사도권 확립을 위한 노력은 바울의 이기적 사욕에서 나온 것이 아니라(7:2, 3; 11:2-10; 12:14-18; 13:9), 그리스도의 종으로서 그의 지시에 따라서 그리스도의 왕권을 고린도 교회에 세우려는 것이다(4:5; 10:5-6, 8; 13:10; 참조, 빌 2:6-11).

이런 목적을 위해서 바울은 무엇보다 고린도 교인들이 진정한 그리스도의 십자가 중심적 신앙을 갖는 것이 절실하다고 말한다(12:19; 13:5). 그러므로 약한 가운데서 강해지는 진리는 바울 자신의 사도적 특권이 아니라 그리스도를 믿는 모든 사람에게 주어지는 혜택이다. 사람들은 세상의 힘을 믿고 산다. 지식, 건강, 재물, 영향력, 직업, 인적 관계, 사회적 위치 등에 의존한다. 바울에 의하면 이런 것은 거짓 선지자들이 의지하는 외모나 육체적인 것이다(5:12; 10:7; 11:18, 22). 그러나 이런 것은 불안한 가치들이며, 잠시 있다가 우리를 떠나게 되는 것이다. 세상 모든 사람들에게 언젠가는 아무 힘도 없고 연약해 질 때가 온다. 그들의 육체적 정신적 건강, 인간관계의 힘, 재정적 힘, 사회 구조적 위치 등을 잃게 될 때가 온다.[566] 그들의 연약함 가운데서 주님을 찾을 때, 주님은 그들을 물리치지 않으시고, 받으시며, 말씀하신다. "내 은혜가 네게 족하다. 이는 내 능력은 약한 데서 온전하여 짐이라." 진정한 믿음은 모든 것을 버리고 주님만을 의지하는 데서 출발한다.

그렇다면 주님의 십자가의 능력은 무엇인가? 한마디로 그 힘은 우리를 죄에서 구원하는 힘이며(13:4), 또 현실의 모든 어려움에서

566) Barnett, 574.

우리를 구원하는 힘이다. 그 힘은 우리의 죽을 영혼을 구원하는 힘이며 이 현상 세계에서 당면하는 모든 어려움에서 우리를 구원하는 초월적인 힘이다. 이 세상 저편의 영원하고 신비한 하나님의 세계를 보여 주는 힘도 되고(12:2-4), 고통 중에 우리를 위로하는 힘도 되고(1:4), 고통을 제거해 주는 힘도 되고(12:8), 고통을 그냥 두면서 그 고통을 이기는 힘도 된다(12:9). 바울의 "몸의 가시"의 경우는 후자의 경우다. 주의 능력은 고통 중에서도 주님께 의지하여 사랑, 믿음, 소망을 가지고 싸워 이기게 하며, 성령의 좋은 영적 열매들을 맺게 하여 주신다(12:10; 롬 5:3, 4; 갈 5:22). 그러므로 바울은 "몸의 가시"를 지니고서도 이런 놀라운 주님의 능력을 자신이 소유하였음을 알고서 기뻐했다. 바울의 대적자들을 포함해서 많은 믿는 사람들은 주님의 능력을 외적으로 나타나는 능력으로만 생각하고 그런 능력을 자랑하고 그런 능력이 나타나기를 바란다. 주님의 능력을 신비한 체험을 하게하고, 병을 고치고, 고난을 제거하는 능력으로만 안다. 그러나 주님의 능력은 내적으로도 나타나는 것이다. 사랑의 능력 같이 모든 것을 참으며, 모든 것을 믿으며, 모든 것을 바라면서, 모든 것을 견디면서 사는 능력을 주시는 것이다. 우리가 세상에 사는 날 동안 고통이 떠나지 않는다면, 이런 저런 고통을 떠나게 해달라는 기도보다는 그 모든 고통을 이기는 사랑과, 믿음과 소망 같은 본질적인 내적 능력을 구하는 기도가 더 필요하다. 그러나 이런 내적 능력은 세상의 도덕적이고 의지적인 능력과는 다르다. 도덕적 능력은 어디까지나 인간의 힘이며 인간관계에 국한된다. 그리스도의 능력은 인간 존재가 필요한 현재와 장래의 모든 육적, 지적, 정서적, 영적, 문제들을 이기게 하는 궁극적이고 초월적인 십자가의 능력이다(롬 8:32-39). 이 능력은 그리스도의 십자가를 믿는 모든 사람에게 언제나 얼마든지 주시는 능력이다(고전 1:23, 24; 롬 8:31-34). 문제는 사람들이 외적인 능력만을 추구하면서 이런 내적인 능력을 등한히 하거나 무시하는 것이다. 그래서 바울은 고린도 교인들이 잘못된 육체적 자랑을 그치고 모두 이런 그의 믿음의 자리에 함께 오도록 초청하는 것이다(7:3; 12:19; 13:5, 7, 11).

한편 위에서도 지적하였듯이 바울은 사도로서 고린도 교인들과의 원만하고 진실한 관계를 원하지만, 그것은 사도와 교인이라는 형식적인 관계가 아니라 보다 내면적이고 진실한 사랑의 관계를 원한다. 그래서 여기서도 그는 사도로서의 권위를 말하기도 하지만, 그보다 그의 약하고 부끄러운 모습을 솔직히 보여 준다(11:33, 12:5). 1장에서도 아시아에서 자신이 죽을 뻔한 경험과 두려움을 솔직히 그대로 나타냄으로서 그의 약한 모습을 보여준다. 4장 7절에서도 자신을 질그릇으로 나타낸다. 7장 3절에서 함께 죽고 사는 운명적 공동체로서 그와 고린도 교인들과의 관계를 말한다. 11장 12장에서의 "약한 것들에 대한 자랑" 은 사도로서의 특별한 권위를 나타내려는 것으로만 볼 것이 아니라 바울이 사도라는 높은 위치에서 자신을 여러 약점을 가진 인간 바울로서 자신을 일부로 낮추어서 고린도 교인들과 진정한 사랑의 관계를 이루려는 의도도 담겨 있다고 본다. 그렇게 함으로 반대자들의 위선적이고 오만한 모습과는 다른 그리스도의 종으로서의 진솔한 모습을 보여 주려고 하는 것이다. 바울은 그리스도의 사도이지만 군림하는 권위적 자세를 버리고 피차 약한 인간들임을 알고 같은 마음으로 서로 위로하는 그런 인간적인 진실한 관계를 원했던 것이다(1:4-6). 하나님께서는 이런 약한 존재들에게 그의 은혜를 베푸신다는 믿음이 그 배경을 이루고 있다. 그것은 그리스도께서 하나님의 아들이시만 높은 보좌에서 나은 종의 신분으로 내려와서 사람들을 구하시는 큰 구원의 역사를 바울이 모본하는데서 기인하는 것이다(5:14, 15; 빌 2:4-11).

마틴은 바울이 특별히 고린도후서에서 십자가 신학을 그의 사역의 중심적 사상으로 삼게 된 것은 바울이 예루살렘 사도회의 이후 유대주의자들과 할례문제와 관련한 이방 선교에 대한 시각차로 인해서 유대주의자들로부터 배척당하고 주후 50년 경 예루살렘 교회의 신앙 노선을 따르려는 안디옥 교회로부터 선교지원을 상실하게 된 사실에서 기인한다고 본다(행 15:1, 2, 24; 21:21; 갈 2:11-12).[567] 이 견해를 더 발전시켜 생각하면, 바울이 마가 문제로 바나바와 헤어지고 나서(행 15:39), 고린도에 가서 천막을 만들며 자비량 선교를 하게 된 것도(행 18:3) 안디옥 교회의 지원이 끊겼기 때문이라고 볼 수 있다. "바울이 이 선교 시점에서 얻은 십자가의 교훈은 십자가란 영광으로 이르는 길의 과정도 아니고, 그리스도의 이야기 가운데 지나가는 일시적 외도(外道)가 아니다. 십자가는 그리스도인의 존재의 본질(esse)이며, 10장 7절에서 바울이 말하는 '그리스도인이 되기' (Χριστοῦ εἶναι) 위한 결정적인 판단기준이다. 예수의 죽으심은 지나간 과거의 단순한 사건으로만 보아서는 안 되고, 부활의 영광 가운데 사라지는 마지막 이야기가 되어서도 안 된다. 십자가는 예수를 역사적 인물로서 특징짓는 모든 것들의 증표이며, 그를 전파하는 것은 곧 십자가를 전파하는

567) Martin, 서론, lx, lxi.

568) Martin, 서론, lx, lxi.

것이다(고전 1:18)."[568] 계속해서 마틴은 바울이 십자가의 교훈을 그의 사역에 적용시켜서 자신이 그리스도와 함께 죽는 것으로 말한다(4::10). 역설적으로 "약함"을 사도적 권세의 자리로 여긴다(12:9, 10). 그 사도적 권세는 파괴하는 세상적인 힘을 내는 권세가 아니라 약함으로 세우는 십자가의 권세이다(10:8; 13:10).

3. 바울의 마지막 사도직 변명(12:11-18).

본문:

> 11. 내가 어리석은 자가 되었으나 너희가 억지로 시킨 것이니 내가 너희에게 칭찬을 받아야 마땅하도다 내가 아무것도 아니나 지극히 큰 사도들보다 조금도 부족하지 아니하니라 12. 사도의 표 된 것은 내가 너희 가운데서 모든 인내로(참음과) 표적과 기사와 능력을 행한 것이라 13. 내 자신이 너희에게 폐를 끼치지 아니한 일 밖에 다른 교회보다 부족하게 한 것이 무엇이 있느냐 너희는 나의 이 공평치 못한 것을 용서하라 14. 보라 이제 세 번째 너희에게 가기를 예비하였으나 너희에게 폐를 끼치지 아니하리라 나의 구하는 것은 너희 재물이 아니요 오직 너희니라 어린 아이가 부모를 위하여 재물을 저축하는 것이 아니요 이에 부모가 어린 아이를 위하여 하느니라 15. 내가 너희 영혼을 위하여 크게 기뻐함으로 재물을 허비하고 또 내 자신까지 허비하리니 너희를 더욱 사랑할수록 나는 덜 사랑을 받겠느냐 16. 하여간 어떤 이의 말이 내가 너희에게 짐을 지우지는 아니하였을지라도 공교한 자가 되어 궤계로 너희를 취하였다 하니 17. 내가 너희에게 보낸 자 중에 누구로 너희의 이를 취하더냐 18.내가 디도를 권하고 함께 한 형제를 보내었으니 디도가 너희의 이를 취하더냐 우리가 동일한 성령으로 행하지 아니하더냐 동일한 보조로 행하지 아니하더냐

본문 비평:

1. 11절에서 소문자 사본(MSS) 가운데 καυχώμενος를 더하여,

"내가 *자랑을 하여* 어리석은 자가 되었으나"라고 읽기도 한다(ψ 0243 syr). 그러나 이 말이 없는 사본이 더 많다(p^{46} α A B D* F G K 33 81 1175 1736). 타스커는 이 말이 없어야 문장이 더 활력이 있다고 한다.[569]

2. 12절에서 "표"(σημεῖα)는 두 번째 나오는 "표적"(σημείοις)과 같은 말이지만 구별하여 번역하는 한글 개역을 따른다(NEB, NIV[marks]). 두 번째 **σημείοις** 는 p^{46} ℵ B 0243 33 81 1175 1739 에 그대로 나오고, A D* Ambrosiaster에는 **τε**없이 **σημείοις**로 나오고, ℵ² D² 에는 **ἐν σημείοις**로 나온다.

3. 14절에서 "이제"라고 번역된 지시대명사 **τοῦτο**("이")는 ℵ A B F G 에는 있지만, K L P 614 629 945 1241에는 없다.

4. 15절 하반절에서("너희를 사랑할 수록 …") ℵ² D¹ K L P vg syr goth arm eth 에는 **καί**가 **εἰ** 뒤에 나온다. D* it$^{d, g, r}$ Ambroiaster 같은 소문자 사본(MSS)에는 아예 **εἰ**가 없다. 우리의 본문은 p^{46} ℵ*** A B F G 33 cop를 따르는 것이다.

5. 15절 하반절에서 ℵ* A 33 104* 에서는 **ἀγαπῶ**(동사형)가 나오고, p^{46} ℵ² ψ B D F G 0243에서는 **ἀγαπῶν**(분사형)으로 나온다. 그래서 대개 학자들이 이를 다음과 같이 표기한다: **ἀγαπῶ[ν]**.[570]

569) Tasker, 179.

570) Metzger, *Textual Commentary*, 586, 587; Thrall, 848-849.

6. 15절 하반절("너희를 사랑할수록 나는 덜 사랑을 받겠느냐?")이 p[46] ℵ[c] ψ B D 0243 81 1739 1881 it vg goth Chrys에는 마침표(.)로 끝나고, ℵ* A 33 syr cop에는 희랍어 의문부호(;)가 있다. 문맥이 의문문임을 지지한다.[571)]

7. 본문의 **οὐ κατεβάρησα**("짐을 지우지는 아니하였을지라도")는 A B D[2] ψ 0243에 나오고, 두 가지 다른 모양으로써 **οὐκ εβάρησα**가 P[46] D*에 나오며, **οὐ κατενάρκησα ὑμῶν**이 ℵ F 81 104 1881에 나온다.

내용개요:

바울은 12장 11-18절에서 "바보의 연설"을 그치고 다시 사도직의 변명의 주제를 시작한다. 학자들은 바울이 본문에서 자랑의 주제를 떠났다고 하지만 실제로 12장 12절에서 끝난다. 11절에서 바울은 자신이 "지극히 큰 사도들" 보다 조금도 부족하지 않다고 결론을 내리고 12절에서 지금까지 말한 사도로서의 역량을 요약하면서 이 결론을 뒷받침한다. 그리고 바울은 12장 13절에서부터 18절까지 재물에 대한 오해에 대하여 변명한다.

13-16a절에는 바울이 다른 교회로부터는 재정 지원을 받으면서, 유독하게 고린도 교회로부터는 재정적 지원을 받지 않는 것을 고린도 교회를 무시하는 처사라고 비난받은 것에 대해 변명한다. 이 문제는 앞서 11장 7-12절에서도 언급한 문제지만, 여기서 다시 다루고 있다. 다시 다루는 이유는 12절에서 말하는 사도의 신뢰성

571) Tasker, 182.

문제와 관련하여 이 문제에 대해서 다시 분명히 짚고 가야한다는 필요성을 느꼈던 것 같다. 바울은 고린도 교회로부터 재정 지원을 받는 것은 그들을 결코 무시하기 때문이 아니라 진정으로 사랑하기 때문이라고 한다(14, 15). 그는 고린도전서에서 결코 재정 지원을 받지 않겠다고 선언하였다(고전 9:15; 11:10). 이제 그 말을 바꾼다면 반대파들의 또 하나의 비난거리가 될 것이다. 더구나 바울이 반대파들이 재정 지원을 받는 것을 비난하였으므로, 이제 다시 재정지원을 받는다면 그들의 행위를 인정하는 셈이 된다고 보는 것이다.[572] 바울은 결코 재물을 탐내는 사람이 아니라 오히려 자신을 희생까지 하면서 고린도 교인들을 사랑한다고 한다(15).

16b-18절에서는 바울이 겉으로는 재정지원을 받지 않는다고 하면서, 뒤로는 헌금을 거두어 가로챈다는 비난에 대해서 변명한다(8:20-21). 실제로 재물을 약탈하였다는 것은 모두 거짓 증거이며 자신과 디도, 그리고 다른 형제 모두 재물에 대해서 깨끗하다고 밝힌다(18; 참조, 8:16-24). 바울은 3번째 방문을 앞두고 고린도 교인들 가운데 바울이 과거에도 교묘히 재물을 빼앗더니 이 제 다시 같은 목적으로 온다고 선동할 사람들이 있을 것으로 알고 자신의 결백함에 대한 예방적 진술을 하는 것이다. 더구나 8, 9장에서 헌금을 준비하도록 이미 말했기 때문에 반대파들이 고린도후서를 읽은 후에 바울의 재정문제에 대한 공격을 다시 시작될 수 있음을 예측하고 경계하는 것이다.

본문은 실제로 10-13장의 바울의 논쟁을 마치고 있다. 나머지 부분에서 바울은 그의 사도로서의 권위를 가지고 반대자들을 경

572) Martin, 428.

계하면서 일반 교인들이 보다 확고한 믿음의 자세를 가지고 3차 방문에 잘 대비하라는 권면을 하고 있다.

주석:

a. 이상의 증거들로써 나는 진정한 사도이다(12:11).

11. "내가 어리석은 자가 되었으나 너희가 억지로 시킨 것이니 내가 너희에게 칭찬을 받아야 마땅하도다 내가 아무것도 아니나 지극히 큰 사도들보다 조금도 부족하지 아니하니라" (Γέγονα ἄφρων, ὑμεῖς με ἠναγκάσατε. ἐγὼ γὰρ ὤφειλον ὑφ᾽ ὑμῶν συνίστασθαι· οὐδὲν γὰρ ὑστέρησα τῶν ὑπερλίαν ἀποστόλων εἰ καὶ οὐδέν εἰμι.). 11장 1절 이후에 바울은 자랑하는 것이 어리석은 자의 짓이라고 하면서도 자랑할 수밖에 없었다. 지극히 큰 사도들보다 못하지 않은 것(11:5), 지식이 많은 것(11:6), 고린도 교회로부터 재정 지원을 받지 않고 일한 것(11:7-12), 고난 당한 것(11:23-27), 교회를 위해 염려하는 것(11:28, 29), 낙원에 간 것(12:2-4), 등에 대하여 자랑을 하였다(5:12). 이런 경험들이 진실한 것이므로 거짓 사도들의 자랑과 구별해야 하지만 육체적 자랑인 점은 바울 스스로 인정한다(11:15-18; 12:6). 바울은 거짓 사도들의 자랑과 거짓 선전에 현혹되고 자신을 오해하는 고린도 교인들에게 어쩔 수 없이 원치 않는 자랑을 하여 진실을 밝히고, 자신도 그들에게 못지 않는 사도적 역량을 가졌음을 보여 주어서 고린도 교인들이 미혹받지 않기를 원했다(13:3).

본문에서 바울은 자신이 반대자들에 맞서서 자화자찬(自畵自

讚)하는 어리석은 일을 하기 전에 자신을 통해서 복음을 받아 그리스도인이 된 고린도 교인들이 먼저 사도로서의 자신의 정당성을 지지해주고 성원해주기를 원했다는 것을 밝힌다(3:1, 2). 대다수의 고린도 교인들은 디도가 방문하기 까지는 침묵하거나 반대자들과 동조했던 것이다(7:7, 9). 바울은 이제 3차 방문을 앞두고 반대자들의 선동으로 말미암아 그런 사태가 다시 재발되지 않기를 바라면서 고린도 교인들을 간접적으로 책망하는 것이다(2:1; 12:20,21).

"내가 아무것도 아니나(εἰ καὶ οὐδέν εἰμι)" 의 의미에 대해서 몇 가지 제안이 있다. 첫째, 자신이 앞에서 한말(희랍어 원문 어순에서), 즉 "지극히 큰 사도들보다 조금도 부족하지 아니하니라" 라고 자신을 높이는 말이 지나치게 오만하게 들리는 어감을 조절하기 위한 부가적 진술이며 별 뜻은 없다. 둘째, 반대파들이 바울을 가리켜 "그는 아무것도 아니다" 라고 비난한 말을 그대로 반복하면서 실제로 자신의 사도직을 변호하려는 것이다.[573]바울을 가리켜 아무것도 아니라고 한 이들에게 바울이 적어도 그들과 동등하다고 말하고 있으므로, 그들도 결국 마찬가지로 아무것도 아니라는 논리이다.[574] 셋째, 희랍철학자들의 무지함의 인정을 진정한 지혜로 보는 전통에 비추어 이해해야 한다. 소크라테스의 희랍 철학 전통에서 무지함을 자인하는 것이 궤변가들의 지혜와 대조적으로 진정한 지혜로 인정된다.[575] 여기서 바울의 평소의 겸손함이 나

---

573) Tasker, 180.

574) Windisch, 396; Forbes, 10; Bachmann, 404; Allo, 324; Barrett, 320; Martin, 427, 434.

575) Betz, *Der Apostel Paulus und die sokratische Tradition*, 122, 주, 578: Plato, *Phaedr.* 234E. 여기서 소크라테스는 본문의 ouvde,n이라는 말로 자신의 무지함을 말한다.

576) Martin, 434.

타나는 말이다(10:1, 2; 고전 15:8, 9).[576] 넷째, 바울의 역설적 진술이다. 그는 반대자들이 지적하는 실제로 여러 약점들을 가지고 있고, 그 외에 다른 약점들도 있으나, 바로 그 약점들을 통해서 그리스도의 능력이 나타난다고 말해왔다(12:9). 이런 의미에서 "내가 아무것도 아니다"라는 말은 "내게 그리스도의 능력이 있다"는 뜻이다.[577] 결국 이 말은 "내게 그리스도의 능력이 없으면, 나는 아무 것도 아니다"라는 뜻이다.[578] 이 마지막 뜻이 문맥에 가장 적절한 의미라고 본다. 트롤은 바울이 고린도 교인들에게 자신의 사도직의 역설적인 의미("약함 중에 강함")를 계속 강조하기 위해서 역설적으로 말하고 있다고 한다.[579] 그러나 이 역설적인 의미가 위의 다른 의미들을 포함하고 있다고 본다.

한편, 본문의 "내가 큰 사도들 보다 조금도 부족하지 아니하니라"는 진술이 11:5에서도 언급되었는데 거기서나 여기서 모두 반대자들의 바울의 재정문제에 대한 비난과 관련된 사실이 흥미롭다(11:7-12; 12:13-18). 아마도 반대자들은 큰 사도들의 추천과 인정을 받는 정식 사도들로서 재정지원 받는 것을 타당하게 여기면서, 바울이 재정지원 받지 않는 것을 가지고 바울이 열등한 사도이기 때문에 스스로 사양하는 것이라고 보았을 것이다. 이에 대해서(3:1), 바울은 자신이 결코 큰 사도들보다 못해서 돈을 받지 않는 것이 아니다. 그의 사심없는 희생적인 십자가의 사역원칙을 따르는 것이라고 말하는 것이다.

577) Bultmann, 233; Martin, 427, 434.

578) Thrall, 836.

579) Thrall, 837.

b. 나도 사도직의 일반적인 증거를 가지고 있다(12:12)

12. "사도의 표 된 것은 내가 너희 가운데서 모든 인내로 (참음과) 표적과 기사와 능력을 행한 것이라"(**τὰ μὲν σημεῖα τοῦ ἀποστόλου κατειργάσθη ἐν ὑμῖν ἐν πάσῃ ὑπομονῇ, σημείοις τε καὶ τέρασιν καὶ δυνάμεσιν.**). 고린도 교인들이 바울에게서 사도된 표(σημεῖα τοῦ ἀποστόλου)를 찾고 있는데(13:3), 그 표란 주로 외적인 것들로서 여기서 말하는 표적과 기사와 능력이다. 바울은 실제로 그들에게 그런 표를 그들과 함께 있을 때 모두 나타냈다고 한다. 그러나 고린도 교인들의 입장에서 볼 때 사도들로 자처하는 이들이 다수인 현실에서 누가 진정한 그리스도의 사도인지 판별할 수 있는 기준이 필요했다. 고린도 교인들은 자신들도 여러 사도들의 가르침들로 말미암아 혼돈된 가운데 사도직에 대한 일정한 판단 기준이나 "사도의 표"에 대한 관심이 있었을 것이다(고전 1:11, 12; 2:3-9; 고후 12:3). 그래서 "사도의 표"란 말이 고린도 교회의 반대자들이나 일반 교인들에게서 온 말이라는 견해가 있다.[580] 반대자들은 자신들의 배경이나 능력을 과시하면서 "사도의 표"라고 말하면서 바울에게는 그런 분명한 표가 없다고 말했을 수 있다(3:1-3; 11:18).

바울은 지금까지 자신의 사도직 변명을 하면서 자신이 진정한 사도인 근거들을 제시하여 왔다. 바울은 반대자들의 자랑에 맞서서 그리스도의 사도로서 정직함과 진정한 사랑을 가지고 그리스

580) Bultmann, 233; Barrett, 321.

도의 고난에 동참하는 자신의 사역에 대해서 설명하였다. 바로 앞에서는 자신은 약한 것들을 자랑한다고 하면서 반대자들의 외모나 육체적 조건으로 자랑하는 것을 비그리스도적인 자세로 지목하였다. 그러나 본문에서 바울은 이런 약한 것에 대한 자랑만으로는 고린도 교인들이 원하는 사도직의 외적 증거들로서 부족하다고 보고서 바울은 계시와 환상(12:1-7), "표적과 기사와 능력"을 사도직의 표시로 요약 제시한다. 그러나 여기서도 바울은 여전히 "모든 인내 가운데"(ἐν πάσῃ ὑπομονῇ)라는 자신의 사역 자세를 나타내는 말을 맨 앞에 놓았다. 약함의 주제에 입각하여 자신의 "표적과 기적사와 능력들"은 모두 그리스도적 특성이 있음을 상기시킨다. 물론 로마서 15장 18절에서도 여기서와 같이 "표적과 기사와 능력"이란 말을 포함하여 그의 사도적 증거를 제시하고 있다.[581] 다른 데서도 같은 말이나 유사한 어귀가 나온다(행 2:22; 히 2:4; 살후 2:9; "기사와 이적": 행 2:43; 4:30; 5:12; 7:36; 14:3). 그러나 바울은 여기서 이런 증거들 앞에 "모든 인내 가운데"라는 제한적인 어귀를 부쳐서 이러한 증거들은 무엇보다 "그리스도적 인

581) Martin, 436-438: Martin은 "표적과 기사와 능력"(σημείοις τε καὶ τέρασιν καὶ δυνάμεσιν)이 주격이 아니라 여격으로 되어 있으므로 사도직의 절대적이고 유일한 표가 아닌 단순히 사도직을 수반하는 표라고 보아야 한다면서 그 중요성을 약화시킨다. 이런 표적들은 사도직의 표(the *signa apostolica*)의 부수적인 것이며 십자가의 예수가 사도직의 근본적인 판단 기준이라고 한다(438). 사실 롬 15:18에서도 같은 말들이 여격으로 나온다(참조, 갈 3:5; 살후 2:9). 그러나 주격이 아니고 여격으로 되어 있다고 해서 이런 능력들을 사도들의 중요한 은사가 아니라고 할 수는 없다. 바울이 본문이나 로마서에서 같은 말들로 자신의 사도직의 신빙성을 제시하는 것으로 보아서 이런 능력들이 반대자들이나 거짓 사도들에 의해서 자기 자랑 거리로 오용되었음에도 불구하고 바울 자신이 이를 중요한 사도의 표로 여긴 것이 분명하다. Martin의 견해에 대한 Thrall의 비판을 보라(Thrall, 839-840).

내"를 따라서 나타내어야 진정한 사도적 증거들이 될 수 있다는 점을 강조한다(4:7-15; 5:14, 15; 6:4-10; 11:23-28; 12:7-10). 12장 초두에서 영적 체험을 말하고, 7절에서 지극히 큰 계시들을 받았다고 한 뒤에 즉시 하나님께서 "몸의 가시"를 주어서 자신이 영적 환상과 계시로 자고하지 않게 하셨다고 말하여 이런 초월적 경험과 능력보다 더 본질적인 사도직의 판단 기준을 제시한다. 즉 진정한 그리스도의 사도직의 기준은 그리스도처럼 고난을 받으면서 인내하며 하나님의 능력에 온전히 의존하는 것이다. 그래서 그는 그의 고난을 열거하면서 약한 것을 자랑한다고 한다(11:30; 12:9, 10). 바울은 고린도후서 전체에서 이런 겸비한 자세가 실제로 그의 사역에서 나타나고 있음을 애써 증거한다. 한글 개역의 "모든 참음과"(ἐν πάσῃ ὑπομονῇ)는 문자적으로 "모든 인내 가운데서"로 번역하는 것이 옳다. 우리는 앞에 "너희 가운데서"라는 말과 중복을 피하기 위하여 "모든 인내로"라고 번역한다. 이렇게 번역한다고 해서 인내를 바울의 사도된 표로 보지 않는다는 뜻은 아니다.[582] "인내"란 말이 "표적," "기사," "능력"과 함께 여격으로 되어 있으므로 바울의 사역의 독립된 특성으로 볼 수도 있으나, "인내"는 이 말들의 앞에 위치하며, ἐν πάσῃ···(모든··· 가운데)라는 어귀로 시작하고 있으므로 인내를 하나의 독립된 사도의 표로 보는 것보다는, "표적과 기사와 능력" 같은 사도의 표들을 언제나 "모든 인내"를 가지고 수행했다는 뜻으로 보는 것이다(참조, 롬

582) Héring, 95; Martin, 436.

583) Thrall은 "인내"(ὑπομονῇ)가 πάσῃ라는 말로 다른 "표적과 기사와 능력"과 구별되어 있다고 한다(838); 그러나 Calvin은 "인내"를 "기사와 표적과 능력"과 함께 하나의 사도의 표로 본다(163, 164). Hughes도 이를 따른다(457).

15:18).[583] 바울은 디모데후서 2장 10절에서 "모든 참음"을 사도직의 표로 말한다. 또 계속해서 디모데후서 2장 24절에서 참음을 감독의 품성으로도 말한다. 바울은 그의 모든 사도직 수행을 모든 인내 가운데 수행한 것이 틀림없다. 여기의 "모든 인내"(πάσῃ ὑπομονῇ)이란 말은 모든 경우에 어떤 모욕이나 수취도 참으며 사도의 표를 나타냈다는 것이다(2:1; 11:23-33; 고전 2:3; 4:12; 9:12; 13:7).[584] 이런 사역은 그리스도의 고난에 동참하는 믿음에서 나오는 것이며(6:4-10), 바울의 반대파들이 자신들의 사도적 권위를 자랑하며 자신들이 영광을 받으려는 것과는 대조적이다(10:12, 18; 11:18; 12:1, 7, 9). 바울은 반대파들도 자랑하는 "표적과 기사와 능력"같은 하나님의 신적 능력을 나타낼 때 자신은 하나님께 모든 영광을 돌림으로써 그리스도의 사도의 직을 바르게 수행하였다.

이 "표적과 기사와 이적"은 다른 기적의 형태를 말하지만 특별히 나누어 말하기 어려운 초월적인 기적행위를 나타낸다.[585] 바울의 치유행위를 나타낼 수도 있고, 축사(逐邪)나 성령의 역사를 나타낼 수도 있다(행 13:11; 14:10; 15:12; 16:18; 19:11-12; 28:3-6, 8). 각 의미를 구별한다면, "표적"(σημεῖοιν)은 교훈이 담긴 기적을 가르키며, "기사"(τέρας)는 신기한 놀라움을, "능력"(δύναμις)은

---

584) Martin, 435; Thrall은 이 견해를 반대한다(840). Thrall은 이런 기적들은 바울의 초기 방문 시에 행한 것으로 보고, 당시에는 바울이 특별히 고난을 당하지 않았으므로 "인내"라는 말이 적합지 않기 때문이라고 한다. 그러나 이런 기적을 초기 사역에만 한정시킬 수 없다. 다메섹 성에서의 탈출은 분명히 초기 사역에서의 고난의 사례이다(11:32, 33). 애초부터 유대인들의 미움을 받은 것이다. 또 바울은 초기부터 고린도에서 천막을 만들며, 유대인의 핍박을 받는 등 고생했다(행 18:3-17).

585) Tasker, 180, 181.

586) Calvin, 164; Martin, 437.

하나님의 초월적인 능력을 나타낸다.[586)]

본문에서 언급된 사도의 "표"와 "표적"은 모두 같은 명사이다(σημεῖον). 그러나 앞의 말은 사도의 일반적인 표라는 의미이고, 뒤에 나오는 것은 구체적인 기적행위를 나타낸다.[587)] 앞의 것은 결국 바울이 행한 "표적과 기사와 능력"같은 모든 기적 행위들을 가리킨다. 이런 표적들은 모두 바울이 고린도 교인들 앞에서 직접 행한 것들이다. 그러나 여기서 바울이 이런 기적 행위를 "모든 인내로" 나타낸 것을 강조하고 있음에 유의해야 한다. 바울은 기적을 행할 때 자신은 고난을 받으며 모든 영광을 하나님께 돌린 것을 반대파들과 구별되는 진정한 사도적 증표로 말하고 있기 때문이다. 바로 위에서 그의 3층천 경험을 말하기 전에도 그는 고난 목록을 열거하였고, 3층천 경험 직후에도 하나님께서 자신을 자고하지 않게 하려고 "몸의 가시"를 주었다고 하였는데, 여기서도 "인내로"라는 말에는 반대파들이 결핍한 기적 수행을 위한 요건, 즉 자신은 고난을 받고, 하나님께 모든 영광을 돌려야하는 자세로 기적을 수행하였다는 것이다. 이렇게 바울은 본문에서 단순히 초월적 표적이 사도직의 판단 기준이라고 하지 않고, 먼저 고난 받으시고 죽으신 그리스도의 "인내함"을 사도적 본질로 전제하는 것이다.

그렇다고 자신만이 이런 능력을 가진 사도라고 주장하는 것은 아니다. 누구나 이런 기준에 합당한 사도라면 진정한 사도인 것이다. 비록 여기서 바울이 τοῦ ἀποστόλου(사도의)라고 관사가 함

587) Denney, 361, 362; Hughes, 457; Martin, 434, 437: Martin은 앞의 "표"와 뒤의 "표적"의 의미를 구별하여 앞의 것은 사도의 일반적인 표로서 고난과 희생의 표를 나타내며, 뒤의 것은 구체적으로 기적을 나타낸다고 한다.

께 사용되었으므로 바울 자신에게 한정적 의미로 썼다고 볼 수 있으나, 일반적 의미를 나타낸다고 볼 수도 있다.[588)]

여기서 바울이 "표적과, 기사와 능력"을 중요한 사도직의 기준으로 제시하고 있으나, 이 외에 보다 본질적 사도의 판단 기준은 하나님의 부르심과(1:1; 4:6), 진실한 마음 자세(1:12; 2:17; 3:4, 5; 4:2; 5:11; 6:3; 7:2; 10:13-18; 11:6)와 그리스도의 순수한 복음 증거(2:17; 4:2-5)와, 그리스도의 고난에 동참하는 헌신적 삶 등이 있다(1:1; 4:6; 4:7-15; 5:15; 6:4-10; 11:23-33, 12:9, 10; 13:4). 한편, 기적은 환상이나 계시와 같이 사람을 교만하게 할 수도 있고, 사람을 속일 수도 있으며, 사람들에게 사욕적이고 거짓된 신앙을 가지게 할 수도 있다(12:7; 행 8:13; 고전 1:22; 살후 2:9; 마 7:22; 12:38, 39; 24:24, 막 13:22; 출 7:3, 11, 12).[589)] 그러므로 바울은 그의 진실한 마음과 희생적 사역에서 그의 사도직의 판단기준을 찾기를 원한다. 그럼에도 불구하고 바울은 본문에서 기적을 행하는 것이 중요한 사도직의 증거임을 제시하고 있다.[590)] 실제로 그의 기적들이 그의 반대자들의 기적 보다 더 그리스도의 기적에 가까운 진정한 것임을 말한다. 그것들이 진정한 사도의 요소인 "모든 인내로" 행해 졌기 때문이다.

여기서 "행한 것이라"(κατειργάσθη)는 말이 역시 신적 과거 수동태로 되어 있음을 유의해야 한다. 바울이 과거의 모든 역경

588) Martin, 435.

589) D. E. Aune, "Magic in Early Christianity," in *Aufstieg und Niedergang der roemischen Welt*, 2/26.2, ed. H. Temporini and W. Haase (Berlin & New York: Walter de Gruyter, 1981), 1507-57.

590) Thrall, 840.

가운데 이런 기사들을 자신의 능력이 아닌 하나님의 은혜로 말미암아 행하였음을 보여 준다.[591] 하나님이 이런 초월적 능력은 자신의 능력이 아닌 하나님의 은사이다. 이 은사를 주신 목적은 바울의 복음을 듣는 사람들이 그의 복음을 믿고 순종케 하며(13:3-4; 롬 15:18), 또한 그의 복음 사역을 인정하고 확신케하기 위함이다.[592] 바울은 그의 은사는 하나님이 주신 것으로 그 은사의 행사도 하나님을 가리키고 하나님의 영광을 위한 것이나 반대자들은 자신들의 능력에 초점을 맞추고 있다. 그 반대자들이 예루살렘 사도들과의 연결을 가정한다면(3:1; 10:15-18; 11:22) 반대자들의 기적 행위의 배경을 초기 예루살렘 사도들의 기적 사역에서 유추해 볼 수도 있을 것이다(2:22; 3:6-8; 4:30; 5:5).

c. 삯을 받지 않고 일했다(12:13).

13. "내 자신이 너희에게 폐를 끼치지 아니한 일 밖에 다른 교회보다 부족하게 한 것이 무엇이 있느냐 너희는 나의 이 공평치 못한 것을 용서하라" (**τί γάρ ἐστιν ὃ ἡσσώθητε ὑπὲρ τὰς λοιπὰς ἐκκλησίας, εἰ μὴ ὅτι αὐτὸς ἐγὼ οὐ κατενάρκησα ὑμῶν; χαρίσασθέ μοι τὴν ἀδικίαν ταύτην.**). 바울은 12절에서 사도직의 일반적인 증거를 밝힌 후에, 이제 또 다른 사도적 증거를 제시한다. 즉 11장 7-10절에서 이미 거론했던 바울의 자비량 선교 또는

591) Plummer, 358.

592) Calvin, 164.

593) 바울의 자비량 선교와 관련된 문제들은 앞서 11장 7절 이하에서 더 자세히 논하였다.

재정적 지원을 받지 않는 사실이다.[593] 반대자들이나 고린도 교인들은 바울의 재정의 투명성에 대해서 문제를 제기했지만 바울 자신은 재정문제에 관한한 그는 자신의 사도의 진정성을 분명히 변명할 자신이 있었다. 그는 자비량 선교를 하기 때문이다(11:10).

그러나 바울의 자비량 선교는 다른 사도들의 재정 의존적 선교와 마찰을 일으켰다(고전 9:3-7). 더구나, 앞서 지적했던 바와 같이 바울의 반대자들은 바울이 마게도냐와 같은 다른 교회의 지원은 받으면서 유독 고린도 교회의 재정적 지원을 거절하는 것을 문제 삼아서 이것은 바울이 고린도 교회를 경시하고 무책임하게 사역하는 증거라고 비난했던 것으로 보인다(11:8, 9).[594]고린도 교인들은 재정적 부담을 지지 않음으로 인해서 자신들이 다른 교인들보다 못하다는 열등감을 가졌을 수 있었다.[595] 또한 바울이 성도를 위한 헌금을 거두면서도 재정적 지원을 거절하는 것은 뒤로는 받으면서 겉으로는 안 받는 식으로 교묘하게 물질을 착취하는 행위라고 비난했던 것 같다(12:16). 반대자들을 포함한 다른 사도들도 이런 바울의 자비량 선교로 인해서 교회의 재정에 의존하는 자신들의 입장이 상대적으로 난처했을 것이다. 그러나 바울은 이런 오해와 문제에도 불구하고 그것은 순전히 고린도 교회를 돕기 위한 것이었으며, 복음을 값없이 전하는 자비량 선교가 움직일 수 없는 자신의 소신임을 밝힌 바 있다(고전 9:15; 11:11; 12:14, 15). 실제로 바울은 천막을 만들어 생활하면서, 고린도 교인들에게 더 이상 도움을 받을 필요가 없다고 믿었던 것이다(행 8:2).

594) Tasker, 181.
595) Georgi, 237.

본문에서 바울은 그의 재정 독립형 선교가 고린도 교인들에게 오히려 누가 되었다면 용서하라는 것이다. 물론 진정한 의미의 용서를 구한다기 보다 냉소적인 말이다. 그러나 여기서 "이 공평치 못한 것을 용서하라"는 말을 문자적으로 받아드려야 한다는 주장도 있다. 즉 바울은 고린도 교회에 재정적 짐이 되지 않기 위해 한 일이 오히려 고린도 교인들을 불편하게 했다면 미안하다는 말로 진정한 자세로 용서를 구하는 측면이 있다고 보는 이도 있다.[596] 그러나 14절을 보면 바울이 용서를 구하는 것이 아니라 오히려 질책성 진술이라고 보아야 한다. 바울이 고린도후서에서 이 재정 문제를 적어도 3번 언급하는 것으로 보아서(7:2, 11:7-10), 이 문제가 매우 심각한 문제로서 고린도 교회와 바울의 관계를 어렵게 했던 것으로 보인다.[597]그러므로 마지막 부분에서 다시 이 문제를 거론하는 것이다. 바울의 변은 자신의 독립형 선교가 결코 다른 어떤 사욕적 의도가 있는 것이 아니라 복음을 값없이 전한다는 자신의 기본 선교 정책일 뿐이라는 것이다(고전 9:18). 물론 마게도냐 교회 같은 데서 재정적 지원을 받았으나, 그것은 예외적인 경우이다. 재정적 지원을 받지 않음으로 교회 폐를 끼치지 않는 것을 가지고 문제를 삼는 것이 오히려 문제가 아니냐고 반문하는 것이다. 그러나 이런 기본적 이유 외에도 바울이 유독 고린도 교회의 재정적 지원을 계속 거절하는 특별한 이유는 고린도 교회의 거짓 사도

596) Hughes, 459; Martin, 439: 고린도 교인들이 그들의 사례가 너무 적어서 바울이 거절하였다고 생각한다면 그런 뜻에서 거절한 것이 결코 아니라고 바울이 부인하는 것이라고 볼 수 있다고 한다. 그러나 문맥에서 문책적이고 냉소적인 어조가 지배적이므로 진정하게 용서를 비는 뜻이라고 볼 수 없다.

597) Strachan, 34.

들이 자신들이 재정 지원을 받는 것을 오히려 진정한 사도의 표로 주장하면서 바울은 스스로 무엇인가 부족한 점이 있으므로 재정적 지원을 거절하는 것이라고 바울을 비난하기 때문이다(11:12). 또한 바울이 고린도 사역을 시작했을 때(주후 50년 말) 여러 가지 문제로 안디옥 교회의 지원이 끊긴 상태였다(행 18:2). 그때 바울은 고린도 교회에 재정적으로 의존하지 않는 선교를 하겠다고 다짐한 것으로 보인다(고전 9장). 여하튼 바울은 자신이 재정적 지원을 받지 않음으로 어떤 면으로든지 고린도 교회에 손해를 입혔다는 주장은 억지이며, 자신의 순수하고 진지한 의도를 무시하는 것이라고 반박하고 있다.[598] 이렇게 재정적으로 의존하지 않고 일하는 자신을 고린도 교인들이 진정한 사도로 보고 오히려 칭찬했어야 마땅하다고 한다(12:12).

(i). 3차 방문 시에도 물질적 부담을 주지 않을 것이다(12:14).

14. "보라 이제 세 번째 너희에게 가기를 예비하였으나 너희에게 폐를 끼치지 아니하리라 나의 구하는 것은 너희 재물이 아니요 오직 너희니라 어린 아이가 부모를 위하여 재물을 저축하는 것이 아니요 이에 부모가 어린 아이를 위하여 하느니라"(Ἰδοὺ τρίτον τοῦτο ἑτοίμως ἔχω ἐλθεῖν πρὸς ὑμᾶς, καὶ οὐ καταναρκήσω· οὐ γὰρ ζητῶ τὰ ὑμῶν ἀλλὰ ὑμᾶς. οὐ γὰρ ὀφείλει τὰ τέκνα τοῖς γονεῦσιν θησαυρίζειν ἀλλὰ οἱ γονεῖς τοῖς τέκνοις.). 계속 재정문제를 언급하면서 바울은 임박한 3차 방문 시에도 결코

598) Windisch, 397; Wendland, 252; Lietzmann, 158; Tasker, 181; Martin, 439; Thrall, 842.

재정적인 부담을 지우지 않을 것이라고 한다. 바울은 고린도 교인과의 깊은 교제를 원하고 있다(6:11-13; 7:2; 11:11; 29). 그 관계는 부모와 자녀의 뗄 수 없는 관계와 같은 것이다. 왜냐하면 바울이 고린도 교회의 창립자이며, 고린도 교인들이 그의 사역으로 구원받았기 때문이다(3:1-3; 고전 9:2). 한편 반대자들은 고린도 교회를 침입하여 오만하게 자랑하고 재물을 탐내는 사람들로서 진정한 친교를 원치 않고 사욕만을 채우려는 사람들이다(10:15, 16; 11:3, 13, 15). 반면에 바울은 자식을 위해 희생하는 부모와 같이 고린도 교인들에게 결코 재정적인 짐을 지우지 않는다(행 18:3; 20:33-35).

"보라" (Ἰδοὺ)는 말은 주제를 바꾸면서 독자들의 주의를 환기시키는 말이다.[599] 바울은 3차 방문에서도 고린도 교인들에게 재정적인 짐을 지우지 않을 것임을 공언하는 것이다. 고린도 교인들은 바울의 선교 정책이 변함없이 지속되는 것을 볼 것이다.

"이제 세 번째 너희에게 가기를 예비하였으나" (**τρίτον τοῦτο ἑτοίμως ἔχω ἐλθεῖν πρὸς ὑμᾶς**)에서 "세 번째" 란 말을 "갔다" 는 말과 연결시켜서 보아야 할 것인가 아니면 "예비하였으나" 와 연결하여 볼 것인가가 문법적인 문제가 된다. "예비하였다" 는 말과 연결되었다고 보면 이왕에 두 번 방문을 준비하였으나 실제로는 한번 만 갔던 것으로 해석될 수 있고 이 경우 이번 방문은 세 번째가 아니라 두 번 째 방문이 된다. 이런 해석은 10-13장이 1장에서 말하는 방문이 취소되고 대신 보낸 "눈물의 편지," 또는 "엄격한 편지" (2:4)의 일부라는 주장을 지지하는 해석이 된다.[600]그러나 대

599) Thrall, 843; Martin, 439.

600) R. A. Batey, "Paul's Interaction with the Corinthians," *JBL* 84(1965), 159-46.

601) Allo, 326, 327; Bruce, 250; Hughes, 459-62; Martin, 440.

부분의 학자들은 "세 번째 갔다"로 해석한다.[601] 우선 바울이 재정적인 짐이 되지 않을 것이라고 말하는 것을 보아서 단지 예비하는 것이 아니라 실제 방문을 가리키는 뜻으로 해석되고, 실제 방문이 아니라 방문을 예비한다는 말이면 바울은 항상 방문을 예비하였다가 취소만하는 사람이라는 비난을 1장에서와 같이 다시 들을 수 있기 때문이다(1:15-2:1). 무엇보다 13장 1절에서 바울은 3번째 방문이라고 분명히 말하고 있다(Τρίτον τοῦτο ἔρχομαι πρὸς ὑμᾶς). 첫 번째 방문은 사도행전 18장의 1차 선교 여행에서 교회를 세울 때의 방문이며, 둘 째 방문은 2장 1절에서 말하는 고통스러운 방문이었다. 그 방문은 고린도전서를 쓰고 난 뒤에 고린도교회가 어려워졌다는 소식을 듣고 간 것이며, 성과 없이 돌아 온 후에 2장 4절에서 말하는 "엄격한 편지", 또는 "눈물의 편지"를 써서 보낸 것이다.[602]

"너희에게 폐를 끼치지 아니하리라 나의 구하는 것은 너희 재물이 아니요 오직 너희니라." 이 말은 바울은 오로지 돈만 바란다는 비난을 받았기 때문인지도 모른다. 그러나 바울이 원하는 것은 결코 돈이 아니라 고린도 교인들이다.[603] 바울이 원하는 것은 오로지 고린도 교인들이 온전하게 되고 그와 화목하게 되어 함께 그리스도의 교회를 세우는 것이다(13:10). 재물은 삯군 목자들이나 구하는 것이다. 바울은 또 재물뿐만 아니라 그들의 믿음을 좌지우지 하려는 것도 아니다(1:24). 다만 그들이 온전한 믿음에 이르게

602) Martin, xlvii.

603) Windisch, 399. Windisch는 유사한 Cicero의 말을 인용한다: "여러분은 제 재산이 아니라, 나를 자랑하셔야 합니다. 만일 우리가 진정한 친구들이라면 말입니다"(Cicero, Fin. II 26:85).

되기를 도와 줄 뿐이다(13:5, 9). 한 마디로 바울이 원하는 것은 자신과 고린도 교인들과, 또한 그리스도와 고린도 교인들 간의 신뢰관계를 회복하는 것이다.[604]바울이 재정문제를 가지고 계속 논하는 것을 볼 때 고린도 교회에서 바울의 재정 지원 거절 문제가 매우 심각한 문제였음을 알 수 있다.[605]

"어린 아이가 부모를 위하여 재물을 저축하는 것이 아니요 이에 부모가 어린 아이를 위하여 하느니라." 바울은 자신의 재정관리의 투명성을 자신의 진정한 사랑의 한 가지 증거로 말하고 있다. 바울이 비록 10-13장에서 1-9장에서와 달리 매우 엄격한 어조로 말하고 있으나, 바울이 여전히 깊은 애정을 가지고 있음을 잊어서는 안 된다(11:11; 6:11-13; 7:2-4).[606] 바울은 고린도 교인들의 창립 사도로서, 그리스도의 심정을 가지고서 고린도 교인들을 사랑한다(5:14, 15; 고전 4:15; 참조, 빌 1:8). 이런 교회 설립자로서의 진실한 애정을 부모가 자식을 사랑하는 것으로 표현하는 것보다 적절한 것이 없다(6:13). 부모는 자식을 위하여 모든 것을 기쁘게 희생한다. 이것은 보편적인 자연법이다. 바울에게 고린도 교인들은 그의 자녀들과 같아서 모든 것을 주고 모든 것을 희생해도 좋다(1:23; 2:4; 4:10, 12; 6:4-10; 12:15). 그는 스스로 자신의 생활비를 벌기 위해서 일했다(행 18:3; 20:33-35). 그런데도 고린도 교인들이 바울의 심정을 제대로 이해하지 못하는 것이 몹시 안타깝다(6:11-13; 11:11; 12:11). 그의 진정한 사랑은 재정적 부담을 주지 않는 것에서 뿐만 아니라 그의 전체 사역의 성격에서 나타난다(12:15).

---

604) Barrett, 323; Furnish, 564; Martin, 440, Thrall, 844.

605) Strachan, 34.

606) Hughes, 462; Allo, 326; Martin, 441.

바울의 진정한 사랑의 호소에도 불구하고 고린도 교인들 편에서 볼 때 바울이 마게도냐 교회로부터 보조를 받으면서 유독 고린도 교회의 지원을 거절함으로써 편애나 불공평함을 보였다고 불평할 수 있을 것이다(12:13).[607] 어쩌면 바울이 사역의 댓가를 받지 않는 것이 자신이 다른 사도보다 못하다고 생각하기 때문에 스스로 사양한 것으로 보는 고린도 교인들도 있었을 것이다.[608] 앞서 11절에서 "내가 지극히 큰 사도들보다 조금도 부족하지 아니하니라"는 말은 이런 의구심을 의식하고 한 말이라고 본다(11:5). 그러나 바울은 자신은 어디까지나 부모로서 자식의 형편과 처지에 따라서 적절하게 보살피는 것이라고 대답하고 있다. 비록 바울 자신이 고린도전서 9장 14절에서 동의하듯이 사도들이 재정 지원받는 것이 성경적이고 합법적이라 해도 경우에 따라서 특히 고린도 교회와 같이 문제가 되는 거짓 사도들이 재정 지원 받는 것을 사도의 표로 내세우는 경우에는 재정 지원을 거절하는 것도 필요하다고 보는 것이다. 부모로서 자식을 바르게 훈계하기 위해서는 자식이 원치 않는 말이나 행동도 필요하다고 보는 것이다. 고린도전서 9장에서 바울은 재정적 지원을 받지 않고 사역하는 것을 바울의 독특한 은사로 보는 것이다. 그러나 여기서는 반대자들의 재정 문제에 대한 공격에 맞서서 고린도 교인들을 사랑하고 아끼는 진정한 사도의 하나의 표로 주장하고 있다. 그러나 다음 절에서 말하듯이 바울의 진정한 사랑은 재정의 영역을 초월하여 모든 영역에 미친다.

---

607) Thrall, 845.

608) Martin, 442.

(ii). 내 재물과 내 자신도 희생할 각오가 되어 있다(12:15).

15. "내가 너희 영혼을 위하여 크게 기뻐함으로 재물을 허비하고 또 내 자신까지 허비하리니 너희를 더욱 사랑할수록 나는 덜 사랑을 받겠느냐?" (ἐγὼ δὲ ἥδιστα δαπανήσω καὶ ἐκδαπανηθήσομαι ὑπὲρ τῶν ψυχῶν ὑμῶν. εἰ περισσοτέρως ὑμᾶς ἀγαπῶ[ν], ἧσσον ἀγαπῶμαι;). 바울은 이미 앞에서 고린도 교인들을 위하여 진지한 사랑을 가지고 희생적인 사역을 한다고 말해왔다(1:23; 2:4; 4:7-15; 5:15; 6:4-13; 7:2; 11:11, 23-28). 그러나 고린도 교인들은 그의 변치 않는 진실한 사랑에 대해서 지속적이고 적극적인 반응을 보이지 않았으므로 바울은 이를 촉구해 왔다(6:11-13; 8:8, 24; 11:11). 바울의 사랑은 말로만의 사랑이 아니었다. 그의 진지한 사랑은 부모와 같이 헌신적인 고난의 사역 가운데서 증명되었다(11:23-33). 특히 고린도 교회의 물질적 지원을 철저히 배제한 것도 그의 사역의 동기가 순수함을 증명하는 것이다. 한편, 반대자들은 자신들의 사욕만을 채우는 삯군 목자들이다. 그러면서도 그들은 오히려 바울의 재정 독립형 선교를 비난한다(11:7-9; 12:16).

14절에서 바울은 고린도 교인들에 대한 그의 사랑을 부모의 진지하고 극진한 사랑에 비교하였지만, 여기서는 더 나아가서 사랑의 가장 최고점인 자신의 희생도 불사한다고 한다(참조, 빌 2:17). 바울의 사랑은 이타주의로 가장한 기만적인 이기주의적 사랑이 아니다. 남의 유익을 위해서 기꺼이 자신의 모든 것을 희생하는 순수하면서도 열의가 있는 아가페 사랑이다. "내가 너희 영혼을 위하여"라고 말한 것은 고린도 교인들의 궁극적이고 통전적 유익을 위해서 바울이 힘쓴다는 것을 말한다.[609] 이를 위하여 바울은 그의 물질과, 힘과, 시간과, 자신까지도 모두 기쁘게 희생하기를 원한다(4:10-12; 13:5). 이것이 바로 그리스도의 사역의 특성이었다(5:14, 15). 그러므로 참된 그리스도의 사도로서 바울은 아무런 사욕이 없는 순수한 동기와 열의를 가지고 있음을 천명하는 것이다. 그러나 바울은 이런 그의 순수하고 열의 있는 사랑에 대하여 고린도 교인들의 같은 사랑의 반응을 원한다(8:8, 24; 11:11). 비록 디도를 통하여 고린도 교인들이 회개하고 열심히 사모한다는 소식을 들었으나 바울이 방문할 때까지 같은 사랑과 열의를 가지고 있을지 분명하지 않아서 염려한다(7:11). "너희를 더욱 사랑할수록 나는 덜 사랑을 받겠느냐" 의문문의 형식 가운데 이런 염려가 들어 있다(12:20, 21).[610] 동시에 고린도 교인들이 3차 방문 이전에 회개하고 잘못을 고칠 것을 촉구한다. 15절의 의문문 형식은 직접적인 책망을 피하고 스스로 반성을 촉구하는 효과가 있다.[611]

(iii). 나의 일행도 청렴한 자세로 일해왔다(12:16-18).

16. "하여간 어떤 이의 말이 내가 너희에게 짐을 지우지는 아니하였을지라도 공교한 자가 되어 궤계로 너희를 취하였다 하니" (Ἔστω δέ, ἐγὼ οὐ κατεβάρησα ὑμᾶς· ἀλλὰ ὑπάρχων πανοῦργος δόλῳ ὑμᾶς ἔλαβον). "하여간 어떤 이의 말이"

609) 여기서 "영혼을 위하여"라고 하는 말은 문자적인 의미가 아니라 고린도 교인들을 아끼고 사랑하는 대상으로 여기는 호칭으로 본다. Thrall, 847, 주, 586: 여기서 다음을 인용한다. R. Jewett, *Anthropological Terms: A Study of their Use in Conflict Settings* AGJU 10 (Leiden: Brill, 1971), 346.

('Εστω δέ, "설령 그렇다고 하자"의 의역)라는 말이 어떤 특정 반대자를 가리키는 말로 생각할 수도 있다("Some of you admit." *Life Application Living Bible*). 그러나 이 말이 특정한 개인의 비난이라기보다 바울이 들어 온 그에 대한 하나의 비난을 가리킬 수 있다. 의미상으로는 "이런 말이 들리는 데"이다("Be that as it may." NIV). 문자적으로는 3인칭 명령형이지만 가정적으로 번역해서 "그렇다고 하자"("Let it be")는 말이다.

이렇게 바울이 재정과 관련하여 자신의 진실성을 계속 강변하는 이유는, 반대자들이 바울의 재정문제에 대해 집요하게 공격하기 때문이다. 바울은 여기서 더 심각한 문제 즉 자신의 재정 약취 의심 문제를 언급한다. 바울이 협잡꾼처럼 헌금을 미끼로 고린도 교인들을 취한다(ἔλαβον)는 것이다. 베츠(H. D. Betz)는 πανοῦργος(공교한)라는 말이 당시 궤변철학자들(sophists)과 종교적 미신을 가리키는 말로 썼다고 한다.[612] 그러나 트롤은 여기서 바울이 궤변학자라고 공격당한 증거가 없으므로 적절한 의미라고 볼 수 없다고 하면서 일반적인 의미로서 "공교한," "교활한"의 뜻으로 본다.[613] 8, 9장에서 바울이 디도와 형제를 헌금을 위해 파송한다고 했는데, 이들의 헌금 사역에 대하여서 반대자들이 문제를 삼았던 것으로 보인다. 반대자들은 바울이 겉으로는 재정적 지원받지 않는다고 하면서도 헌금을 거두어(8, 9장) 뒤로 재정을

610) Martin, 444.

611) Thrall, 847.

612) Betz, *Der Apostel Paulus und die sokratische Tradition*, 104, 주 440-1에서 인용하는 관련 희랍문서들을 보라.

613) Thrall, 851.

몰래 빼돌리는 것으로 의심했던 것이 분명하다. 바울이 8장 9장에서 헌금을 독려할 때에는 이런 문제를 언급하지 않다가 여기서 언급하는 것은 무슨 까닭인가?(참조, 8:20, 21). 아마 헌금을 독려하는 8장과 9장에서는 이런 감정적인 문제를 꺼내는 것이 적절치 않다고 보았을 것이다.[614] 끝부분에서 재정 지원 거절 문제를 언급하다가, 헌금과 관련하여 재정을 축낸다는 비난이 생각났을 것이며 이에 대한 대답도 아울러 여기서 함께 해야겠다고 생각하였을 것이다. 어쩌면 바울의 반대자들이나 고린도 교인들이 최근에 바울이 고린도후서를 쓰는 동안에 이 문제를 다시 거론하였다는 소식을 들었는지도 모른다.[615] 17-18절에서 디도와 어떤 형제의 재정문제를 논하는 것도 그들의 헌금 모금 운동에 대하여 고린도 교회가 비난하였기 때문이라고 볼 수도 있다.

반대자들은 바울 자신이 무엇인가 사도로서 부족하기 때문에 스스로 재정 지원을 거절하는 것이라고 부정적인 시각으로 말하지만, 한편으로 어떤 고린도 교인들은 바울이 그들과 달리 재정 지원을 받지 않는다는 사실로 바울을 훌륭한 모범적 사도로 보는 것을 알았을 것이다. 그러므로 그들은 바울이 예루살렘 성도들을 위한 헌금을 거두는 사실을 가지고 바울이 겉으로는 재정지원을 받지 않는다고 자랑하지만, 실제로는 고린도 교인들의 재정 지원을 받는 통로로 사용하는 위선자라고 비난했던 것 같다.[616] 휴즈는 반대자들이 바울이 시작한 예루살렘 헌금 운동을 저지함으로써 자신들에게 더 많은 재정적 지원이 들어오게 하려했다고 추정

614) Thrall, 446.

615) Thrall, 851.

616) Strachan, 35, 주, 1.

한다.[617] 이런 반대자들의 시도를 예루살렘 성도들을 위한 헌금이 지연된 이유로 추정할 수도 있다(8:10, 11; 9:5). 그러나 이들이 예루살렘에서 온 이들이라면 그들의 고향 사람들에게 갈 돈을 가로채어서 그들로부터 비난받는 일을 자초하지는 않았을 것이라고 본다. 반대자들은 모든 악한 생각을 추정하여 바울과 그의 동역자들에게 덮어씌우는 것이다. 칼빈이 말하듯이, "악한 자들은 자기들이 할 수만 있으면 하기 원하는 일들을 염치도 없이 하나님의 일꾼들에게 곧 잘 덮어씌운다."[618]

17. "내가 너희에게 보낸 자 중에 누구로 너희의 이를 취하더냐?" (μή τινα ὧν ἀπέσταλκα πρὸς ὑμᾶς, δι᾽ αὐτοῦ ἐπλεονέκτησα ὑμᾶς;). 반대자들의 바울에 대한 공격은 곧 그의 동역자들에 대한 공격으로도 이어졌을 것이다. 바울은 4개의 연속적 질문을 통해서 자신이 보낸 디도를 비롯한 그의 동역자들이 재정적 문제로 잘못한 문제가 있느냐고 묻는다. 바울은 자신과 동역자들을 나쁜 사람들로 몰지 말고 구체적 증거를 가지고 말하라고 다그친다. 그러나 이런 질문들을 통해서 바울이 원하는 것은 결국 자신의 진실성에 대한 변명이다. 그가 헌금을 위해 파송한 디도나 그의 형제들이 신실한 사람들임을 고린도 교인들이 잘 알고 있듯이 자신도 그런 사람임을 알아 달라는 것이다.

여기서 바울은 문법적으로 일치되는 않는 파격구문(anacoluthon)을 쓰고 있다. 바울이 뒤의 남성 대명사 αὐτοῦ(그

617) Hughes, 465.

618) Hughes, 465. 재인용

의)에 따라서 남성 대명사 τινός(누구)를 써야하는데 대신 중성 대명사 τινα(어떤 것)를 쓰고 있는 것이다. 헤링은 이런 격의 불일치가 당시 일반 희랍어 글에서도 자주 발견된다고 한다.[619)]

18. "내가 디도를 권하고 함께 한 형제를 보내었으니 디도가 너희의 이를 취하더냐 우리가 동일한 성령으로 행하지 아니하더냐 동일한 보조로 행하지 아니하더냐?" (παρεκάλεσα Τίτον καὶ συναπέστειλα τὸν ἀδελφόν· μήτι ἐπλεονέκτησεν ὑμᾶς Τίτος; οὐ τῷ αὐτῷ πνεύματι περιεπατήσαμεν; οὐ τοῖς αὐτοῖς ἴχνεσιν;). 고린도 교인들은 바울이 파송한 디도와 어떤 형제가 바울의 동역자들로서 모두 신실하게 행하였으며 아무런 재정적 문제가 없음을 잘 알 것이다. 이들이 모두 동일한 성령의 인도를 받아서 사욕을 버리고 복음 사역에만 힘쓰며, 바울의 사역의 정신, 즉 재정적 부담을 끼치지 않는 선교정책에 따라서 사역하는 사람들이라는 것을 이들을 지켜 본 고린도 교인들이 누구보다 잘 알고 있을 것이다. 고린도 교인들이 이들을 신뢰할 수 있다면 그들의 동역자인 바울도 신뢰하는 것이 마땅하다고 한다.

"디도를 권하고" (παρεκάλεσα Τίτον)라는 말은 고린도로 가도록 권했다는 말이다.[620)] 디도는 적어도 두 차례 고린도를 방문하여 모금 문제를 담당해왔던 것으로 보인다. 아마 고린도전서를 쓰기 이전에 고린도전서 5장 9절에서 말하는 편지를 가지고 한 번 방문하였을 것이며(고전 16:1), 이때 헌금 문제를 논의했을 것이

619) 96, 주, 32.

620) Martin, 447.

다. 다음으로, 고린도전서, 또는 고린도후서 2장 4절과 7장 8절 이하에서 말하는 "눈물의 편지" 또는 "엄격한 편지"를 가지고 가서 헌금을 독려하였을 것이다. 고린도후서 8장 6절에서도 바울은 디도가 고린도 교회에서 헌금을 과거에 시작하였다고 말한다.[621] 9장 2절에서는 고린도 교회에서 헌금을 1년 전부터 시작하였다고 한다. 본문에서 언급하는 디도의 방문은 8장 6절의 방문과 같은 방문으로 본다. 8장 16-24절의 방문은 두 형제를 보낸다고 말하고 있으므로 한 형제를 말하는 본문의 방문과는 다르다. 8장 16-24절의 방문은 고린도후서를 가지고 방문하는 것으로 아직 이루어 지지 않은 방문이다. 알로(Allo)는 본문의 **παρεκάλεσα**(권했다)는 말과 8장 17절의 "저(디도)가 (너희에게)나아갔다"(ἐξῆλθεν)와, 8장 18절과 22절에 각기 언급된 두 명의 형제들을 "보냈다"(συνεπέμψαμεν)는 말이 과거형으로 되어 있음을 중시하고 바울이 고린도후서를 쓸 때 디도와 다른 두 형제들을 이미 고린도로 보냈다고 한다.[622] 그러나 휴즈는 이 8장 17, 18, 22절의 과거 동사는 수신자들이 서신을 받을 때는 바울이 이들을 보낸 것이 이미 과거의 사실이 된다는 것을 고려하여 서신을 쓸 때에 아예 과거("서신 아오리스트[epistolary aorist]," "예상 아오리스트[anticipatory aorist]")로 쓰는 것이라고 보았고 본문의 과거는 단순과거로 보았다.[623] 그렇다면 본문의 방문과 8장 17절의 방문은 다른 것이다. 본문은 고린도후서 이전에 있었던 과거의 어떤 방문을 언급하는 것이며, 8장 17절은 고린도후서를 가지고 갈 때의 아직

621) Hughes, 293-294, 466.

622) Allo, 329.

623) Hughes, 468; Tasker, 119.

일어나지 않은 방문을 예상된 과거형으로 쓴 것이다. 그러므로 디도와 형제들은 고린도후서를 다 쓸 때까지 기다렸다가 편지를 가지고 고린도로 갔다고 본다. 본문의 "한 형제"가 8장 18절의 "한 형제"와 같은 인물인지는 알 수 없다.[624]

디도와 한 형제의 헌금 사역에 대해서 반대자들이 바울이 헌금을 유용할 것이라고 의심하였을 가능성이 있고 이에 대하여 바울은 아무 증거도 없는 일로 문제 삼지 말도록 말하는 것이라고 볼 수도 있으나, 그보다 디도와 그 형제들이 지금껏 아무런 문제없이 헌금 사역을 잘 담당하여 왔으니 만큼 그들을 보낸 나의 청렴성도 인정해달라는 뜻이라고 본다. "동일한 성령으로"(τῷ αὐτῷ πνεύματι)를 성령으로 해석하지 않고 "같은 정신으로" 또는 "동일한 보조로"라고 해석하기도 한다.[625] 그러나 곧 이어서 "동일한 보조로"(τοῖς αὐτοῖς ἴχνεσιν)라는 말이 병행되어 따라 나오므로 중복적으로 말하였을 가능성 보다 "동일한 성령으로"라는 뜻으로 다르게 말하였을 가능성이 더 높다.[626]

주해(12:11-18):

12장 11-18절에서 바울은 최종적으로 자신의 사도직에 대한 변명을 요약하여 말한다. 다른 사도들보다 바울이 열등한 사도라는

---

624) Hughes, 468: Hughes는 12:18에는 한 형제가 언급되는 반면에 8:16-24에는 두형제가 언급되므로 서로 다른 방문이라고 본다. 8:16-24은 고린도후서 이전의 다른 과거의 방문을 가리킨다. Martin도 이에 동의 한다(448); 참조, Furnish, 38..

625) Barrett, 326; Hughes, 465; Héring, 97; Martin, 449.

626) Tasker, 184.

비판에 대하여 자신은 다른 사도들과 같이 분명히 그리스도의 사도로서 부르심을 받았고 이에 따르는 사도적 증거들이 있다고 한다(12:12). 또 바울이 재정적 보조를 받지 않은 것은 스스로 무엇인가 부족하다고 느끼거나 또는 헌금을 가로채어 썼기 때문에 양심상 받지 않은 것으로 의심하는 데 대하여 바울은 오히려 고린도 교인들을 위하여 돈은 물론 모든 것을 바쳐서 희생할 각오가 되어 있다고 반박한다. 바울 자신을 믿지 못하겠으면, 그가 보낸 동역자들이 지금까지 문제없이 일해 온 것을 보라고 한다. 모든 같은 성령으로 정직하게 일하는 그리스도의 일꾼들이라는 것이다.

바울은 이런 자랑을 스스로 하는 것이 어리석다고 하면서 자신을 잘아는 고린도 교인들이 자신을 위해 대신 변명했어야 했다고 책임을 묻는다(12:11). 이렇게 바울은 그의 긴 "바보의 연설"(11:1-12:10)을 마친 후에 마지막으로 반대자들의 비난을 의식하고 그의 사도직의 진정성과 청렴성을 요약적으로 변명하면서 그의 3차 방문이 은혜롭고 성공적인 방문이 되기를 소망한다.

바울은 하나님 앞에서와 자신의 양심에 비추어서 조금도 부끄러움이 없는 삶을 살았다. 그의 메시지가 이천년이 지난 오늘 까지도 살아 있는 말씀으로 들리는 것은 성령의 역사하심과 함께 그의 말이 곧 그의 삶으로 나타나는 진실성이 때문이다.

E. 3차 방문 약속과 경고(12:19-13:10)

본문:

19. 이때까지 우리가 우리를 너희에게 변명하는 줄로 생각하는구나 우리가 그리스도 안에서 하나님 앞에 말하노라 사랑하는 자들아 이 모든 것

은 너희의 덕을 세우기 위함이니라 20. 내가 갈 때에 너희를 나의 원하는 것과 같이 보지 못하고·또 내가 너희에게 너희의 원치 않는 것과 같이 보일까 두려워하며 또 다툼과 시기와 분냄과 당짓는 것과 중상함과 수군수군 하는 것과 거만함과 어지러운 것이 있을까 두려워하고 21. 또 내가 다시 갈 때에 내 하나님이 나를 너희 앞에서 낮추실까 두려워하고 또 내가 전에 죄를 지은 여러 사람의 그 행한 바 더러움과 음란함과 호색함을 회개치 아니함을 인하여 근심할까 두려워하노라. (고린도후서 13장) 1. 내가 이제 세 번째 너희에게 갈 터이니 두 세 증인의 입으로 말마다 확정하리라 2. 내가 이미 말하였거니와 지금 떠나 있으나 두 번째 대면하였을 때와 같이 전에 죄 지은 자들과 그 남은 모든 사람에게 미리 말하노니 내가 다시 가면 용서하지 아니하리라 3. 이는 그리스도께서 내 안에서 말씀하시는 증거를 너희가 구함이니 저가 너희를 향하여 약하지 않고 도리어 너희 안에시 강하시니라 4. 그리스도께서 약하심으로 십자가에 못 박히셨으나 오직 하나님의 능력으로 살으셨으니 우리도 저의 안에서 약하나 너희를 향하여 하나님의 능력으로 저와 함께 살리라 5. 너희가 믿음에 있는가 너희 자신을 시험하고 너희 자신을 확증하라 예수 그리스도께서 너희 안에 계신 줄을 너희가 스스로 알지 못하느냐 그렇지 않으면 너희가 실격한 것이라(버리운 자니라) 6. 우리가 실격하지 (버리운 자 되지) 아니한 것을 너희가 알기를 내가 바라고 7. 우리가 하나님께 너희들이 악을 행하지 않도록 (우리가 하나님께서 너희로 악을 조금도 행치 않게 하시기를) 구하노니 이는 우리가 (그리스도의 사도로) 인증 받았음(옳은 자임)을 나타내고자 함이 아니라 오직 우리는 실격한 것과(버리운 자) 같을지라도 너희로 선을 행하게 하고자 함이라 8. 우리는 진리를 거스려 아무것도 할 수 없고 오직 진리를 위할 뿐이니 9. 우리가 약할 때에 너희의 강한 것을 기뻐하고 또 이것을 위하여 구하니 곧 너희의 온전하게 되는 것이라 10. 이를 인하여 내가 떠나 있을 때에 이렇게 쓰는 것은 대면할 때에 주께서 너희를 파하려 하지 않고 세우려 하여 내게 주신 그 권세를 따라 엄하지 않게 하려 함이니라

본문비평:

1. 19절에서 p^{46}에는 부정사 οὐ(아니다)가 나타나는데 19절 상반절이 긍정적인 대답을 예상하는 의문문이 되게 한다.[627] 이것은

같은 οὐ로 시작되는 12장 18절 하반절에 영향 받았다고 할 수 있다. TR은 Πάλιν(다시) 나타나는데, 이것은 3장 1절과 5장 12절의 영향이라고 생각된다. 그러나 Πάλαι(이미)가 문맥에 잘 맞지 않는 더 어려운 말로서 א* A B F G 33 330 1175 1739 1881 lat에 나타나므로 일반적으로 어려운 말을 더 신빙성이 있다고 보는 원칙(*difficilior lectio potior*)에 따라 원형으로 본다.

2. 19절에서 κατέναντι("앞에")가 D ψ에 나오고, κανέναντι가 p46 א B F G 33 81 7775 1739 1881에 나타난다.

3. 12장 19절 상반절을 의문문으로 볼 것인가(개역한글성경, KJV/AV, RSV, NIV, ESV, Philips) 아니면 서술문으로 볼 것인가(RV, ASV, NEB, TEV/GNB)로 의견이 나뉜다. 어느 쪽이든지 의미상의 차이는 없다.[628]

4. 20절에서 단수형 ἔρις("다툼")가 p46 א A 0243 33 1739 1881에 나타나고, 복수형 ἔρεις가 B D F G y syrh에 나타난다. 단수형이 원형이며, 복수형은 복사자가 다른 명사들이 복수로 된 것을 보고 맞추려고 변경한 결과로 본다.

5. 20절에서 단수형 ζῆλος("시기")가 p46 A B D* F G 33 syrp boms에 나타나고, 복수형 ζῆλοι가 א D1 ψ 0134 syrh에 나타난다. 이것도 복사자가 다른 복수 명사와 맞추려고 수정한 듯이 보인다.

---

627) Hughes, 460, 주, 156.

628) Tasker, 184.

6. 21절의 첫 문장 ἐλθόντος μου ταπεινώσῃ με ὁ θεός μου πρός ὑμᾶς("[또] 내가 [다시] 갈 때에 내 하나님이 나를 너희 앞에서 낮추실까 두려워하고")는 p46 ℵ* A B F G 33 81 1175에 나타나는 것이며, 두 개의 다른 모양으로서 ἐλθόντα με ταπεινώσῃ με ὁ θεός μου πρὸς ὑμᾶς로 ℵ ψ 0243에, ἐλθόντα με πρὸς ὑμᾶς ταπεινώσῃ με ὁ θεός μου로 D1 syrp Tert에 나타난다. 두 개의 다른 모양은 원형의 어려운 문법 문제를 고친 것으로 보인다.

7. 21절의 가정형 ταπεινώσῃ("낮추실까")가 미래형 ταπεινώσει로 p46 D F G L P 1175에 나타난다. 이 경우 문법적으로 부정사 μὴ대신에 부정사 οὐ가되어야 하는데, μὴ가 미래형과 함께 그대로 나타나므로 문제가 된다. 그래서 플러머는 오히려 가정형 ταπεινώσῃ가 수정된 것이라고 하나 설득력이 없다.

8. 3장 2절에서 γράφω가 νῦν뒤에 D1 vgms syrsa에서 나타나는데 삽입된 것으로 본다.[629] 그러나 본문이 p46 ℵ A B D* F G 0243 1175 1739 1881의 지지를 받는다.

9. 3장 3절에서 ἐπεὶ앞에 ὅτι가 있는 경우가 있다(F G Ambrosiaster). 마틴은 이유를 강조하기 위한 것이라고 한다.[630]

10. 13장 4절에서 καὶ γὰρ뒤에 εἰ있는 소문자사본들(MSS)이 있

629) Hughes, 476, 주, 169; Metzger, *Textual Commentary*, 587.
630) Martin, 452.

다(א² A D¹ ψ lat syr Ambrosiaster). 분문은(ἐι 없는) p^{46} א* B D¹ F G 0243 33 81의 지지를 받는다. 바레트는 가 있는 경우에 "약함"과 "강함"의 강조의 균형이 깨져서 바울의 의도를 벗어난다고 본다.[631]

11. 3장 4절에서 ἐξ(ἐκ)는 보통 장소를 나타내어 "…에서부터"라는 뜻이지만 여기서는 이유를 나타내어 "…로(말미암아)"라고 번역한다.[632] 하기야 "…에서부터"라는 말을 "…을 근거로"라고 생각하면 이유를 나타내는 의미가 원래 들어 있다.

12. 3장 4절에서 많은 소문자 사본들(MSS)이 본문의 ἐν αὐτῷ(저의 안에)대신에 σὺν αὐτῷ(저와 함께)를 쓴다(א A F G syr^{p} bo). 뒤에 나오는 다른 σὺν αὐτῷ를 따라 수정한 것으로 본다. 반대로 뒤의 σὺν αὐτῷ을 앞의 ἐν αὐτῷ을 따라서 통일하여 쓰는 경우도 있다(p^{46vid} D* 33). 본문은 B D ψ 0243 vg syr^{h} sa의 지지를 받는다. 위의 변형은 다수 학자들의 지지를 받지 못한다.[633]

13. 13장 4절의 끝에 있는 εἰς ὑμᾶς(너희를 위하여)가 B D²에는 없다. 휴즈에 의하면 복사자가 이 말을 "하나님의 능력"과 관련하여 보고 어색하다고 생각하여 제거한 듯 하다고 한다. 그러나 "살리라"는 말과 연결하여 "너희를 위하여 살리라"로 번역하면 이 말

631) Barrett, 327; Martin이 Barrett에 동의한다(452).

632) BAGD, 235.

633) Metzger, *Textual Commentary*, 587, 588; Barrett, 327, 337; Martin, 452.

이 이 위치에 필요하다고 한다(참조, NIV).[634] 그러나 본문에서 바울이 문제가 된 고린도 교인들을 책벌하는 의미로 해석하여 "너희를 향하여"라는 한글 개역이 타당하다.

14. 13장 5절의 'Ἰησοῦς Χριστὸς는 B D ψ vg^{ms} syr에 나타나고, Χριστὸς 'Ἰησοῦς는 ℵ A F G P 0243 1175 1739 1881 Ambrosiaster에 나타난다.[635]

15. 13장 5절은 전체를 하나의 의문문으로 보거나 몇 개의 작은 의문문으로 나누어 볼 수 있다. 또는 서술문으로 보기도 한다.[636]

16. 13장 7절에서 본문의 εὐχόμεθα("우리가 구하노니")는 p^{46} ℵ B D* F G K P 33 81 1175 lat에 나오고, εὐχόμαι("내가 구하노니")는 D^{2} ψ 0243 vg^{mss} syr^{p} sa^{ms}에 나온다.[637]

내용개요:

이 부분은 고린도후서의 마지막 부분이다. 바울은 이제 고린도 교회 3차 방문을 앞두고 고린도 교인들이 회개하고 자신들을 돌아 볼 것을 권면한다. 그들이 바울에게서 사도적 증거를 찾으려고 하지만, 바울은 오히려 그들이 스스로 자신들을 돌아보며 진정한 그리스도인의 증거가 있는지를 살피라고 반문한다(12:3, 5). 바울

634) Hughes, 479, 주, 175; Martin, 452..

635) Plummer, 376.

636) Martin, 452.

637) Plummer, 337.

은 편지의 진정한 목적이 사도직 변명이 아니고, 고린도 교인들의 믿음과 삶을 바르게 인도하여 그리스도의 교회를 세우려는 것임을 거듭 밝힌다(12:19; 13:10; 참조, 10:2, 8).[638] 이를 위하여 필요한 경우 사도의 권세로 문제된 자들을 징벌할 수밖에 없음을 경고한다(참조, 10:6). 그러나 바울은 그의 방문 전에 고린도 교인들이 스스로 자신들의 믿음을 점검하고 문제들을 해결하여, 바울을 진정한 사도로서 영접하는 화해의 방문이 되기를 바란다(12: 20-21).

12장 20-21절에서 바울은 고린도 교인들의 죄를 교회를 분열시키는 죄와 성적인 죄로 나누어 열거하고 방문 전에 이들을 제거하라고 명한다. 이 죄들이 두 그룹의 죄들을 나타내는지 또는 같은 한 그룹의 죄들인지에 대한 논쟁이 있다.

13장 1-4절에서 바울은 이 방문이 3번째 방문임을 밝히면서(첫 번째는 행 18장의 고린도 교회를 세운 방문, 두 번째는 2:1의 "고통의 방문"), 12장 19-21절에 이어서 방문 주제가 계속된다. 특히 바울은 그의 사도권 행사를 통해서 고린도 교회에서 문제가 된 이들을 용서하지 않고 치리할 것이라고 경고한다. 여기서도 바울이 현재의 두 종류의 그룹을 말하고 있는지, 한 그룹의 과거와 현재의 행위에 대해 논하는지가 분명하지 않다. 이들이 바울에게서 "표적과 기사와 능력" 같은 사도된 표를 나타낼 것을 원하지만(12:12; 13:3), 바울은 대신 그의 사도권으로 이들을 치리할 것이라고 경고한다.[639] 그의 사도권은 세상의 권세와 달리 그리스도의 죽음과 부활같이 역설적인 권세이다(13:4). 3절에서 그리스도의

638) Bultmann, 239; Strachan, 36.

639) Martin, 455.

약함과 능력이 교차 구문으로 나타나고(Chiasmus), 4절에서는 καί(그리고) ἀλλά(그러나)가 연속 되는 문장에서 그리스도의 "약함과 능력"이 바울의 "약함과 능력"과 대조되고 병행되는 구조가 나타난다.[640] 바울은 반대자들에게 업신여김 당하며 약한 가운데 있지만 방문 시에 그의 사도권을 사용하여 이들을 치리할 것이다(13:2). 그러나 그리스도의 약함을 따르는 자신의 약함을 언급하면서 여전히 이들 또는 이들에게 동조한 일반 교인들이 회개하면 그리스도의 사랑으로 용서할 것이라는 암시도 한다(13:7, 9, 10). 즉 바울이 진정으로 원하는 것은 징계가 아니라 고린도 교인들이 회개하고 고쳐서 바른 믿음을 회복하는 것이다.

마지막 부분인 13장 5-10절도 여전히 방문과 관련하여 약함과 강함의 주제를 가지고 논한다. 또 다른 공통 주제는 "누가(바울과 고린도 교인들) 자격이 미달인가?"의 주제다(13:3, 5, 6, 7). 즉 고린도 교인들이 바울이 자격미달의 열등한 사도라는 반대자들의 말을 더 이상 듣지 말고, 오히려 자신들의 믿음이 바른 믿음 인지를 스스로 점검하여 주님 앞에서 회개하고 바로 서야 모든 사태가 정리되고 바르게 잡힐 수 있다는 주제이다. 고린도 교인들이 바른 믿음을 가지고 주되신 그리스도 안에 바로 자리 잡고 서게 되는 것이 바울의 소원이다(13:5). 이렇게 말하는 것은 바울이 고린도 교인들을 자신의 편으로 끌어드리려는 사욕 때문이 아니라 고린도 교인들이 진정으로 그리스도를 바로 믿고 구원받아야 한다는 사도적 확신과 책임 때문이다. 바울은 고린도 교인들의 믿음을 자기의 마음대로 좌지우지하려는 것이 아니라 도우려한다고 이미

640) Martin, 456.

밝혔다(1:24). 그는 고린도 교인들이 스스로 그들의 믿음을 점검하기를 원한다. 그는 자신이 주님에게 버림을 받을 지라도 고린도 교인들이 주 안에 있게 되기를 원한다(13:7). 이런 말도 바울이 진정한 그리스도의 사도임을 나타내는 말이다.

주석:

1. 세 번째 방문이 원만히 되도록 회개를 촉구함(12:19-21)

19. "이 때까지 우리가 우리를 너희에게 변명하는 줄로 생각하는구나 우리가 그리스도 안에서 하나님 앞에 말하노라 사랑하는 자들아 이 모든 것은 너희의 덕을 세우기 위함이니라" (Πάλαι δοκεῖτε ὅτι ὑμῖν ἀπολογούμεθα. κατέναντι θεοῦ ἐν Χριστῷ λαλοῦμεν· τὰ δὲ πάντα, ἀγαπητοί, ὑπὲρ τῆς ὑμῶν οἰκοδομῆς). 지금까지 바울은 자신의 사도직을 위해 변명하였다. 그러나 그가 변명의 진의는 단순히 자신의 유익을 위한 것이 아니었다. 오히려 편지의 중심 목적은 고린도 교인들의 믿음이 바르게 확립 되게 하는 것이었다(12:5). 바울은 희생되더라도 고린도 교인들이 온전히 바르게 되는 것이다(13:9; 4:12). "이 때까지 우리가 우리를 너희에게 변명하는 줄로 생각 하는구나"라는 의문문으로 번역되었으나 어떤 이들은 이를 서술문으로 번역하는 이들도 있다.[641]그러나 대부분의 학자들은 이를 의문문으로 본다.[642] 휴즈

641) Furnish, 560; Barrett, 326; NEB; REB: JB.

642) Hughes, 460, 주, 156; Plummer, 367; KJV; RSV; NRSV.

는 초기 사본인 P46에 부정사 οὐ(아니다) 나타나는데 이것은 19절 상반절이 긍정적인 대답을 예상하는 의문문이 되게 한다고 지적했다.[643] 트롤은 만일 19절 상반절이 서술문이라면, 뒤의 내용과 상반되는 내용으로서 뒤에 나오는 문장이 대조를 나타내는 ἀλλά(그러나)같은 접속사로 시작되어야 하는데 그런 접속사가 없으므로 의문문으로 보아야 한다고 한다.[644] 물론 의문문이든, 서술문이든, 그 의미는 같다. 바울은 지금까지 자신이 말한 것에 대하여 고린도 교인들이 잘못 생각하고 있을 것이라고 추정하는 것이다. 바울이 추정하는 고린도 교인들의 잘못은 무엇인가? 첫째, 바울이 그들에게 자신을 변명하고 있다고 생각하는 것이다. 그러나 바울이 변명한다면 그것은 하나님께 자신을 변명하는 것이라고 한다.[645] 실제로 바울은 "우리가 그리스도 안에서 하나님 앞에서 말하노라"고 말한다(2:17; 5:10). 바울은 하나님이나 그리스도의 심판대 앞에서 말하듯이 정직하게 말한다. 즉 거짓 자랑을 하지 않는다(10:17, 18; 11:31; 12:6). 둘째, 바울은 자신을 변명하는 것이 아니라 교회를 세우기 위해서 말하였다고 한다. 바울이 "이 모든 것은 너희의 덕을 세우기 위함이라"고 말하고 있다.[646] 교회를 세우는 것이나 덕을 세우는 것이 바울의 사도적 임무이다(고전 3:9; 8:1, 10; 10:23; 14:3, 4, 5, 12, 17, 26; 고후 10:8; 13:10).[647] 그렇다면 지금까지 바울이 고린도 교인들에게 말 한 것이 자신의 사도

643) Hughes, 460.

644) Thrall, 859.

645) Wendland, 253; Windisch, 407-7; Barrett, 328.

646) Bachmann, 409.

647) Barrett, 328.

직 변명을 한 것이 아니란 말인가? 변명(*apologia*)이란 원래 자신을 상대방에게 더 잘 보이게 하기 위해 자신을 자랑하는 논쟁이다.[648] 우리가 서론에서 본 바와 같이 바울의 진술은 다분히 당시 재판소에서의 변명과 같은 문학형식을 취하는 것으로 나타났다. 혐의를 받은 사람이 여러 증거를 가지고 자신의 잘못이나 오해를 벗어나기 위해서 변명하는 헬라시대의 재판의 진술과 고린도후서의 구조가 흡사한 것이다.[649] 그러나 바울은 누차 자신이 자신의 유익을 구하지 않고 고린도 교인들을 위한다고 말해왔으므로 고린도후서가 이런 일반적 변명의 목적과는 일치한다고 할 수 없다.[650] 베츠도 여기서 바울이 일반적인 수사학적 변명을 부정하는 것이라고 했다.[651] 바울은 일반적 변명의 이기적인 측면이 없는 특별한 "변명"을 한 것이다. 바울의 변명은 고린도 교인들이 생각하는 통속적인 변명은 아니라는 것이다. 바울이 개인적인 유익을 위해서 말한 것도 있으나 그런 것도 결국은 사도적 책임이나 목회적 책무와 관련된 것이었지 자신의 사욕적인 것이라고는 할 수 없다고 한다. 그는 항상 양심대로 순전하게 일해 왔다(1:12, 18, 23; 4:2; 5:11; 7:12; 11:11, 13; 롬 1:9; 9:1; 빌 1:8; 살전 2:5, 19). 여기서도 바울은 모든 것을 고린도 교인들의 덕을 위해서 말했다고 한다. 그런 뜻에서 바울은 그들을 "사랑하는 자들아"라고 부르고 있다.[652] 그는 자신을 허물어서 교회를 세우기 위해 힘써왔다. 즉 바

648) Barrett, 665.

649) Harris, 46.

650) Schlatter, *Paulus*, 672; Windisch, 406; Héring, 99; Furnish, 567.

651) Betz, *Der Apostel Paulus und die sokratische Tradition*, 39.

652) Sunderman, *Kraft der Rede*, 208, 211: Sudermann은 바울은 고린도 교인들이 그의 서신을 러브 레터로 생각하기를 바라고 있다고 말한다.

울의 헌신적인 사역을 통해서 고린도 교인들의 믿음을 세우려고 했다. 그러나 문제는 고린도 교인들이 이런 순전한 사도 바울의 심정을 몰라주는 것이다. 그래서 바울은 그들에 대한 의구심과 불안을 떨쳐버릴 수가 없다. 어쩌면 "변명" 이란 말 가운데 "단순히 말뿐인 바울" 이라고 고린도 교인들이 대단치 않게 생각하리라는 의미가 담겨 있는 지도 모른다. 가까이 있지도 않고 멀리 떠나 있으면서 동역자들을 통해서 편지로나 사역하는 바울을 겁낼 필요가 없다는 이들에 대해서 바울은 이번 3차 방문은 결코 그렇게 쉽지 않을 것임을 계속 말한다(10:1, 10).

20. "내가 갈 때에 너희를 나의 원하는 것과 같이 보지 못하고 또 내가 너희에게 너희의 원치 않는 것과 같이 보일까 두려워하며 또 다툼과 시기와 분냄과 당짓는 것과 중상함과 수군수군 하는 것과 거만함과 어지러운 것이 있을까 두려워하고" (φοβοῦμαι γὰρ μή πως ἐλθὼν οὐχ οἵους θέλω εὕρω ὑμᾶς καγὼ εὑρεθῶ ὑμῖν οἷον οὐ θέλετε· μή πως ἔρις, ζῆλος, θυμοί, ἐριθείαι, καταλαλιαί, ψιθυρισμοί, φυσιώσεις, ἀκαταστασίαι·). 19절에서 바울은 그의 서신 집필의 목적이 사도로서 고린도 교인들의 덕을 세우기 위함인 것을 밝힌 뒤에 여기서는 지금까지 보다 구체적인 서신의 목적을 요약하여 말한다. 20절은 19절과 γὰρ(이는)로 연결되어 이유를 나타낸다. 바울은 편지를 쓰는 이유를 말한다. 이번 3차 방문 시에("내가 갈 때에") 교회를 세우는 권세를 쓸 수 밖에 없는 이유를 말한다. 교회를 세우는 권세란 그리스도의 교회를 세우는데 방해되는 것들을 척결하는 일을 의미한다(6:14-7:1). 바울이 편지를 쓰는 목적은 임박한 그의 3차 방문이 진정으로 자

신과 고린도 교인들이 하나가 되어 새로운 출발을 하는 장(場)이 되게 하기 위해 아직 남아 있는 화해에 방해되는 모든 요소를 과감히 척결하도록 권면하기 위한 것이다. 바울은 그리스도의 사도로서 그리스도의 몸 된 교회가 그리스도의 평강 가운데 온전하게 서도록 하는 책임이 있다(10:5-8; 13:10). 그는 화해의 사도로서 복음의 화해 정신에 따라서 고린도 교인들과 화해와 평강을 위해 일해야 함을 잘 알고 있다(5:19-21). 그러기 위해서는 화해에 방해되는 모든 요소들을 제거해야 하는 것을 잘 알고 있다. 더구나 바울은 과거에 실패한 방문의 경험들이 있었으므로 3차 방문이 성공적이 되도록 준비하는 것이 필요함을 잘 알고 있었다(고전 2:3; 고후 2:1). 바울은 앞서 6장 14절-7장 1절에서도 화해의 장애가 되는 세상적인 것들을 제거할 것을 권면하였듯이 10장 이후 자신과 고린도 교인들 사이에 남아 있는 진정한 화해에 장애되는 요소들을 지적하여 버리고 진정한 관계 개선을 위한 은혜로운 방문이 되도록 준비할 것을 당부 해 온 것이라고 밝힌다. 지금까지는 주로 편지로 권면하였으나 이번 3차 방문은 직접 대면하는 방문이므로 보다 철저한 대비를 당부하는 것이다. 사실 "혹독한 편지" 의 좋은 결과가 얼마 가지 못해 바뀔 것을 두려워하고 있는 것이다(7:8-18). 더구나 지금은 거짓 사도들이 들어와 그 세력을 확장하려는 상황이다(11:4, 19). 그러나 두 번째의 "고통의 방문" 시에 어려웠던 것을 회상하면서 이번 방문은 단순히 수동적인 자세만으로 일관하지 않을 것임을 경고하고 있다.

그러나 바울은 이런 징계 사역을 하게 되지 않기를 바라지만, 이런 경고를 통해서 고린도 교인들이 정신 차리고 자체 정화 노력을 시작하기를 원하는 것이다. 바울은 모든 인내로 그의 사역을 감당해 왔다(12:12). 지금도 고린도 교인들이 그의 방문 전 까지 그들의 문제를 스스로 해결하기를 촉구한다. 이 구절은 고린도전서 4장 21절의 말을 상기 시킨다: "너희가 무엇을 원하느냐 내가 매를 가지고 너희에게 나아가랴? 사랑과 온유한 마음으로 나아가랴?" 바울의 자세는 순전히 고린도 교인들의 자세에 달려 있다.

"또 다툼과 시기와 분냄과 당 짓는 것과, 중상함과 수군수군하는 것과 거만함과 어지러운 것이 있을 까 두려워하고"는 바울이 열거하는 8개의 원치 않는 고린도 교인들의 죄목들이다. "두려워하고"는 원래 없는 말이지만 앞 문장에 있는 같은 말(φοβοῦμαι)이 생략된 것으로 보고 보충하여 번역한 것이다. 이런 죄의 항목들은 교회의 분열을 조장하는 죄들이며 21절의 죄의 항목들은 성적인 것들이다.[653] 이런 두 개의 죄의 항목을 두고 바레트는 바울이 고린도 교회를 두 그룹으로 나누어서 말한다고 본다.[654] 즉 20절의 죄들은 교회분열을 조장하는 반대파를 가리키고(11:4), 21절의 성적인 죄들은 이방 습관을 버리지 못한 교인들을 가리키는 것이라고 한다(6:14). 이에 대해서 마틴은 여기서 바울이 특별히 교인들을 나누고 있다는 증거는 없고 모든 교인들에게 말하고 있다고 본다.[655] 고린도전서 1장에서 말하는 분파들이 어떤 모양으로든지 남아 있다하더라도, 그 분파들을 반드시 바울의 반대파로 볼 필요는 없다는 것이다. 오히려 모든 교인들이 여러 분파와 관련되

653) Martin, 453, 462.

654) Barrett, "Paul's Opponents in 2 Corinthians," in *Essays on Paul*, 233-54.

655) Martin, 462.

어 있다고 봐야 할 것이며 바울은 고린도전서에서와 같이 이에 대해서 우려하고 있는 것이라고 본다. 마찬가지로 성적 죄악에 대한 경고는 이방 습관을 버리지 못하는 다수의 고린도 교인들에게 대한 것이라고 한다. 그러나 13장 2절에서 "전에 죄 지은 자들과 그 남은 모든 자들"이라고 지칭하는 말에서 바울이 여기서 특정한 분파를 지목하고 있다고 볼 수 있다.

"다툼"(ἔρις)은 고린도전서 3장 3절, 로마서 1장 29절, 13장 13절, 빌립보서 1장 15절에 있는 "악의 목록"에 나타난다. 고린도 교인들은 이제 하나님의 성숙한 백성으로서 자신들을 세워야할 책임이 있다. 이 말은 다시 바울의 책임인 사도적 교회를 세우는 것과 관련된다. 하나님은 교회를 세우는 최고의 건축자이시고, 바울은 하나님의 종으로서의 건축가이다(고전 3:9, 10). 바울이 세우는 것은 곧 하나님이 세우시는 것이다. 고린도 교회의 다툼은 바울이 그리스도의 화해의 사신으로 임명받은 사실을 다시 상기 시킨다(5:19-21). 바울은 모든 분쟁의 궁극적 해결은 모든 사람들이 자신들의 주장을 버리고 그리스도 안에서 그리스도의 권위에 복종할 때 가능한 것이라고 말한다.

"시기"(ζῆλος)는 히브리어 (קנא[카나] "질투," "열심")와 같이 "열심"이라는 적극적 의미(고후 7:7; 11:2; 참조, 출 20:5; 왕상 19:10; 왕하 19:31)와 "시기," "질투"라는 부정적 의미도 있다(고전 3:3; 롬 13:13; 갈 5:20; 약 3:14, 16). 그러나 "질투하는 하나님"(출 34:14; 신 6:15; 참조, 출 20:5 등)의 경우에는 그 의미를 예외로 보아야 할 것이다. 하나님은 그가 택하신 백성만을 사랑하므로 그의 백성이 다른 신을 섬길 때에 질투하시는 것은 그가 참된 신이시라는 증거이다. 고린도 교인들의 경우에는 질투는 나쁜 의미에 해당된다. 위의 "다툼"(ἔρις)이란 말과 짝을 지어 나타나기도 한다(롬 13:13). 시기는 분쟁의 요소로서 그리스도의 몸을 와해시키는 작용을 한다. 바울은 그리스도의 사도로서 그의 몸된 교회를 세워야하고 이에 방해되는 이런 요소를 제거해야 하는 책임을 가지고 있다.

"분냄"(θυμοί)도 갈라디아서 5장 20절, 골로새서 3장 8절, 에베소서 4장 31절의 "악의 목록"에 나타난다. 이것은 인간의 감정의 폭발로서 하나님을 두려워하는 사람이 취할 마땅한 태도가 아니다. 분노는 사람 앞에서 내어도 결국 하나님이 주되심을 잊고 자신이 주인이 되어 하나님을 무시하는 오만한 태도라고 할 수 있다. 이것도 그리스도의 몸을 무너뜨리는 악한 요소이다.

"당짓는 것"(ἐριθεῖαι)도 갈라디아서 5장 20절의 "악의 목록"에 나타나고, 로마서 2장 8절, 빌립보서 1장 17절, 2장 3절, 야고보서 3장 14, 16절에서도 나타난다(빌립서와 야고보서 개역한글판에는 "다툼"으로 번역되었음). 이 말은 "대적하는 것"(rivalry), 또는 "이기적 야심"(selfish ambition)으로 번역되기도 한다.[656] 그러나 "파벌을 조장하는 것"이 가장 적절하다고 본다.[657] 여하튼 "당파"도 그리스도의 몸을 무너뜨리는 분쟁적 요소로서 제거되어야 한다.

"중상함"(καταλαλιαί)은 복수형으로서 중상하는 사례가 흔한 것을 나타낸다고 할 수 있다.[658] 베드로전서 2장 11절에 명사형이 나오고, 형용사형은 로마서 1장 30절에, 동사형은 야고보서 4장

656) E. de W. Burton, *A Critical Exegetical Commentary on the Epistle to the Galatians*, ICC (Edinburgh: T&T Clark, 1921), 308; Martin, 463; Thrall, 865.

657) Thrall, 865.

658) Martin, 463.

11절에 나온다. 중상도 교회를 분열시키는 요소로서 마땅히 제거되어야 한다. 바울도 그의 대적자들을 정죄하였으나 이것을 중상이라고 할 수는 없다(11:13-15). 바울은 그리스도의 사도로서 진실을 밝혀야 하고 또 참말을 하기 때문이다(4:2; 11:31; 12:6). 잘못된 것을 제거하라는 말과 거짓을 퍼뜨리는 것을 구별해야 한다. 그러나 바울의 반대파는 이런 말을 가지고 오히려 바울을 역공할 수 있을 것이다. 바울도 같은 잘못을 하고 있다고 반발할 수 있다. 그러나 바울은 고린도 교회의 설립자로서 자신의 교회의 일치를 위해 일하지만, 다른 거짓 사도들은 침입자들로서 결국 바울의 교회를 분열시키는 일을 한다는 비난을 받아 마땅하다(10:16).

"수군수군하는 것"(ψιθυρισμοί)은 문자적으로 "수군거리는 자들"이라고 번역해야 한다. 그러나 그런 행동을 나타낸다고 볼 수도 있다. 이 말이 복수로 쓰인 것은 아마도 이것이 고린도 교회에서 흔하게 있는 일임을 나타내는지도 모른다.[659] 신약에는 여기서만 나타난다(시 40:8; 시락서 5:14; 21:48; 크레멘1서 30:3, 35:5).[660] 그러나 동의어로서 "수군수군하는 자"(ψιθυριστής)가 로마서 1장 29절의 "악의 목록"에 나타난다. 이것도 진실하지 못한 행동으로서 그리스도의 교회를 어지럽게 하는 것으로 제거되어야 한다.

"거만함"(φυσιώσεις)은 명사형은 신약에서 여기서만 나오고 동사형은 고린도전서 4장 6, 18, 19절, 5장 2절, 8장 1절, 13장 4절에 집중되어 나온다. 이 자세가 반대파들의 자랑과 관련되었을 수도 있으나 하나님을 모르는 모든 이들의 공통된 자세라고도 볼 수

659) Barrett, 329.

660) Windisch, 409.

있다(5:12; 10:17, 18; 11:18). 창조주 하나님 앞에서 피조물임을 인정하는 사람이나, 겸비함으로 죽으신 그리스도를 믿는 사람은 거만할 수 없다. 거만함은 그리스도의 교회에서 마땅히 제거되어야 한다.

"어지러운 것"(ἀκαταστασίαι)은 다른 말로 무질서이다. 바울은 고린도전서 14장 33절에서 "하나님은 어지러움의 하나님이 아니시오 오직 화평의 하나님이시니라"라고 말하였다(참조, 약 3:16). 이 말도 역시 교회의 분열을 나타내는 말이다.

바울이 이런 분열의 증상들을 일일이 열거한 것은 고린도 교회 상태가 매우 심각한 것으로 진단하였기 때문이라고 본다.[661] 바울이 왜 그토록 자신의 사도직을 강변할 수밖에 없었는지를 잘 보여 준다.[662] 바울이 다른 데서 잘 쓰지 않는 말들을 여기서 쓰는 것을 보아도 고린도 교회의 사태가 매우 심각하다는 것을 보여 준다. 이것은 그리스도의 교회의 증상이라기보다 세상 집단의 증상이라고 해야 옳을 정도다. 이런 증상은 조속히 그리고 철저히 치료받지 않으면 안 된다. 심각한 위기에 빠진 고린도 교회를 사도 바울이 직접 방문해서 문제를 해결해야한다는 당위성이 한층 높아진다. 그러나 여전히 바울이 원하는 것은 방문 전에 고린도 교회가 스스로 회개하여 온전하게 되는 것이다(13:5, 10). 그렇지 않을 경우 바울은 어려운 징벌문제를 다루어야 할 것이며, 그럴 경우 진정한 화해를 이루는 원만한 방문을 기대하기 어려울 것이기 때문이다.

21. "또 내가 다시 갈 때에 내 하나님이 나를 너희 앞에서 낮추

---

661) Meyer, 492; Bultmann, 239-40; Martin, 464; Thrall, 862.

662) Thrall, 862.

실까 두려워하고 또 내가 전에 죄를 지은 여러 사람의 그 행한 바 더러움과 음란함과 호색함을 회개치 아니함을 인하여 근심할까 두려워하노라"(μὴ πάλιν ἐλθόντος μου ταπεινώσῃ με ὁ θεός μου πρὸς ὑμᾶς καὶ πενθήσω πολλοὺς τῶν προημαρτηκότων καὶ μὴ μετανοησάντων ἐπὶ τῇ ἀκαθαρσίᾳ καὶ πορνείᾳ καὶ ἀσελγείᾳ ᾗ ἔπραξαν). 바울은 이번 3차 방문이("내가 갈 때에") 지난번 2차방문과 같은 고통스런 방문과 같이 되기를 원치 않는다(2:1). 고린도 교인들의 죄가 그냥 있는 상태에서 방문하면 지난번 방문 처럼 어려운 방문이 될 수밖에 없음을 잘 알고 있다. 그래서 바울은 그의 방문 이전에 그들이 죄를 회개하고 스스로 문제를 척결하여 원만한 방문이 되도록 준비하기를 권하는 것이다. 여기서의 죄는 성적인 죄를 가리킨다. 세 개의 죄의 내용이 같고, 문법적으로 같은 하나의 관사만 있다(τῇ).[663]그러므로 20절의 분파적 죄와는 다르다. 죄의 유형이 다르게 보이는 문제와 관련하여 어쩌면 바울이 두 개의 다른 분파를 상대로 말하는 것이라는 의견이 있다. 즉 20절의 분열을 조장하는 죄는 바울의 반대파, 거짓 사도들을 가리키고, 21절의 성적 죄는 이방적 행위를 아직 버리지 못한 고린도 교회의 다른 그룹을 가리킨다는 것이다.[664] 바레트는 고린도전서와 달리 고린도후서에서 영지주의적 문제는 사라졌으나, 영지주의적 자유주의적 영향은 아직 남아있어서 성적 남용이 용인되고 있었다는 것이다. 즉 그들은 순전히 영적인 존재들로서 육체적 제약을 받지 않기 때문에 어떤 성적인 행위도 자신들의 영

663) Martin, 468.

664) Barrett, "Paul's Opponents," 75, 76.

적 존재에 어떤 영향도 줄 수 없다고 믿고 성적으로 문란했다는 것이다. 그래서 바울은 21절에서 이들을 책망하는 것이라고 본다. 마틴은 13절에서 바울은 이 두 가지 문제를 두 개의 분파의 개별적 문제로 보지 않고 고린도 교회 전체의 문제로 본다. 그러므로 마틴은 바울이 여기서 두 개의 분파를 염두에 두고 말한다고 보는 바레트의 견해에 대해 회의적이다.[665] 마틴은 로마서 13장 13절의 "죄의 목록"에서 "호색함"(ἀσελγείᾳ)이 "쟁투"와 "시기"와 함께 언급되고 있음을 지적한다. 그러므로 이 문제들이 개별적인 어떤 특정 분파의 문제들로 나누어 볼 것이 아니라, 어떤 한 분파가 가지고 있는 문제들로 보아야 한다는 것이다. 그러나 위에서 지적하였듯이 13장 2절에서 "전에 죄 지은 자들과 그 남은 모든 자들"이라고 지칭하는 말에서 바울이 여기서 특정한 분파를 지목하고 있다고 볼 수 있다.

21절의 문법적인 문제로서 "다시"(πάλιν)를 "간다"(ἐλθόντος)는 말을 수식하는 부사로 보아야 하는지, 아니면 "낮추실까"(ταπεινώσῃ)라는 동사에 부쳐서 해석해야 하는지를 두고 이견이 있다. 어느 쪽으로 해도 문법적으로 가능하고 문맥에서 그 의미가 통한다. 우선 이를 "간다"는 말과 관련시켜 "다시 간다"로 번역하는 것이 가능하다(개역한글판, NIV). "간다"가 위치상 가까운 말이고, 또 14절과 20절에서 방문을 언급하기 때문이다. 그러나 "간다"(ἐλθόντος μου)는 말이 여기서 희랍어의 독립 분사구문(genetive absolute)로 되어 있어서 부가적인 문장으로서 오히려 주동사인 "낮추실까"(ταπεινώσῃ)라는 동사를 가리키고 있을 가

665) Martin, 468.

능성이 있다는 것이다.[666] 플러머는 고린도전후서에서 바울이 "다시 간다"는 말을 할 때 "다시"(πάλιν)라는 부사를 사용하지 않는다는 사실을 지적하면서 여기서도 이 말이 "간다" 보다는 "낮추실까"를 수식한다고 말했다(고전 4:18; 19; 11:34; 14:6; 16:2, 5, 10, 11, 12, 고후 1:15, 23; 2:3; 8:17; 12:20). 이 경우 바울은 이전의 고통의 방문 경험(2차방문)을 상기하면서 다시는 그런 방문을 하지 않겠다는 뜻이 된다. 그러나 이 번역 문제가 전체의미에 주는 영향이 미미하다. 다만 "다시"가 어느 동사에 관련되느냐의 문제는 어느 동사에 강조를 두느냐의 문제 일뿐이다. "다시 가든지"라고 하면 그의 방문을 강조하는 것이며, "다시 낮추시든지"라고 하면 그의 두려움을 강조하는 것이 된다. 그러나 어느 해석도 결국 "간다는 말"과 "낮추신다는 말"이 다 들어있으므로 강조의 문제이지 의미상 차이는 없다.

"낮추실까"(ταπεινώσῃ)라는 말이 어떤 의미인가에 대한 논쟁이 있다. 다수의 학자들이 바울이 사도로서 고린도 교인들을 잘 가르쳐서 죄를 짓지 않도록 해야 하는데 고린도 교인들이 죄를 계속 짓는 경우 그가 사도로서 실패하였다는 평가를 받으므로 하나님께서 그를 부끄럽게 하실 것이라는 의미로 본다.[667] 다른 해석은 고린도 교인들이 죄를 회개하지 않을 경우에 바울이 그의 사도권을 억지로 행사해야한다는 두려움으로 보기도 한다.[668] 그러나 이런 해석은 단호하게 징계를 다짐하는 문맥에 맞지 않는다. 첫번째 견해, 즉 바울이 두려워하는 것은 고린도 교인들이 회개하지

666) Martin, 464, 465; Bultmann, 240.

667) Windisch, 410; Furnish, 567; Filson, 416; Martin, 465; Thrall, 866, 867.

668) Bultmann, 241; Martin, 466..

않음으로 자신이 사도로서 실패하였다는 하나님의 평가를 받는 것이라는 것은 본문을 지나치게 액면 그대로 읽는 결과라고 본다. 바울의 솔직한 심정은 지난 2차 방문 때 처럼 고린도 교인들에게 모욕당하는 것이 싫다는 것이다(2:1). 그러나 그렇게 말하면 이기적으로 들릴 수 있으므로, "하나님께서 자기를 낮추신까 두려워 한다"는 우회적인 말로 표현한 것이라고 본다. 20절에서 바울은 고린도 교회의 분쟁적인 상태를 지적했다. 이런 상태에서 바울이 방문하면 전에 경험한 고통을 다시 경험 할 것이 분명하다. 바울은 다시 많은 호전적인 사람들에게 공격당하는 모욕을 원치 않는 것이다(고전 2:3; 고후 2:1). 물론 여기서 "낮추실까"의 실제적인 주어가 하나님이다. 바레트가 지적한 대로, 하나님이 "몸의 가시"나 "사단의 사자"를 사용하신 것과 같이, 고린도 교회의 문제 되는 이들을 통해서, 바울을 다시 낮추시는 것을 20절에 이어 계속 두려워하는 것이라고 말한다.[669] 그러나 바울은 내심 고린도 교인들에게 받는 모욕이나 괴로움을 원치 않는 것이다. 1장 초두에서도 환난에서 구해주신 것을 감사하고 아시아에서 죽을 뻔한 경험을 말하면서 하나님께서 구해주신 것을 감사하고 있다(1:8-10). 무엇보다 2장 1절에서도 "내가 다시 근심으로 너희에게 나아가지 않기로 스스로 결단하였노니"라고 말하면서, 자신의 근심으로 고린도 교인들도 근심하게되는 방문은 애초에 피하는 것이 옳다고 보고 방문하지 않았다고 변명한다. 여기서도 바울은 이 전의 쓰라린 경험을 되풀이하고 싶지 않으니 이번에는 20절에서 지적한 분쟁의 요인들을 미리 회개하고 청산하여 좋은 만남이 되도록 하자는

669) Barrett, 331.

것을 계속 말하는 것이다. 이런 모욕이나 멸시도 고린도 교인들을 위한 희생이므로 달게 받아야 하는가? 그러나 바울은 피할 수 있는 고난이나 희생은 피해야 한다고 생각한다. 바울은 고행주의자가 아니다. 여기서 바울의 권면의 초점은 고린도 교인들이 회개하지 않음으로 해서 일어날 자신의 피해(모욕)를 포함한 고린도 교회와의 불화같은 총체적 어려움을 미리 말하여 그들이 속히 잘못을 뉘우쳐서 3차 방문이 정말로 좋은 만남이 되도록 하자는 데 있다. 그러므로 여기서 바울이 모욕적인 방문을 원치 않는다고 말하는 것을 이기적이거나 사욕적 자세라고 비난하는 것은 바울의 진의를 무시하는 것이다.

바울이 두 번째로 두려워하는 것은 고린도 교인들의 성적인 죄로 말미암아 슬퍼하게 되는 두려움이다. 물론 바울은 그의 사도권으로 이들을 치리할 수 있으나, 그렇게 하기 이전에 이들이 스스로 변화되기를 원하는 것이다. 자식의 징벌을 위하여 강권을 쓰는 것은 모든 사랑하는 부모들이 원치 않는 것이다. 바울도 그와 같은 부모의 심정으로 이들에게 사도권을 사용하여 징벌하기를 원치 않는 것이다(12:16). 마틴은 그의 강권적 징벌은 바울을 비난하는 율법주의자들에게 바울의 은혜의 복음을 비난하는 기회를 줄 것이기 때문에 바울이 더욱 이를 사용하기를 원치 않고 있다고 한다.[670] 바울의 은혜의 복음이나 성령의 역사에 맡기는 가르침이 결국 고린도 교회의 성적 문란에 기여했다는 반대자들의 비난에 대한 두려움이라는 것이다. 그것은 실로 바울의 복음 전체에 대한 도전이 될 것이므로 바울은 매우 큰 위기의식에 사로잡혀서 "두려

670) Martin, 467.

워한다"는 말을 하고 있다는 것이다.[671] 그러나 이것은 지나치게 문제를 확대하는 해석이다. 바울이 이렇게 까지 복잡한 정황을 염두에 두고 "두려워한다"고 말한다고 보기 어렵다. 여기서 20, 21절에서 바울이 "두려워한다"는 말은 실제적인 공포보다는 단순히 "염려한다"는 뜻으로서 불순종하는 자녀와 같은 고린도 교인들을 대하여 걱정하는 부모의 심정을 가지고 말하는 것으로 보아야 한다. 바울은 12장 14절 이후 계속하여 부모 된 심정을 가지고 자식에게 책망도하고 타이르듯이 말한다고 보아야 한다(12:17). 또한 고린도 교인들이 변화되지 않을 경우 어쩔 수 없이 사도적 권세를 사용하게 되는 것을 두려워한다는 해석은 지나치게 과장하는 해석이다.[672] 바울은 아래에서 사도권 사용 가능성을 언급하지만 그것을 사용하는 것을 두려워한다고 말하지는 않는다(13:1, 2, 10). 오히려 필요하면 담대하게 사용할 것이라고 말하면서, 동시에, 그렇게 사용하여 문제를 해결하기 보다는 고린도 교인들이 스스로 먼저 해결하기를 바란다고 말한다.

여기서 바울이 슬퍼하게 될 이유는 "전에 죄를 지은 여러 사람의 행하 바와 회개치 아니함"(πολλοὺς τῶν προημαρτηκότων καὶ μὴ μετανοησάντων) 때문이다. 이 "죄를 지었다"(προημαρτηκότων)와 "회개하다"(μετανοησάντων)는 두 동사(독립 분사형)가 각기 과거완료와 과거로 쓰인 것은 "고린도 교인들이 죄를 계속 지어왔고, 죄를 회개할 기회가 있었으나 놓쳤다"는 뜻으로 말하는 것이다.[673]그 기회란 바울의 "고통의 방문"

671) Bruce, 252; Thrall, 866.

672) Martin, 466.

(2:1)이나 "눈물의 편지"(2:4)를 가리킬 수 있다. 바울은 3차 방문 시에도 그들이 여전히 죄를 지으면서 회개하지 않았을 경우에 (그들이 그리스도로부터 버리움을 당할 것을[13:5, 7]) 슬퍼하게 될 것을 염려한다. 죄를 회개하지 않으므로 멸망당하는 이들에 대한 슬픔은 고린도 교인들의 영혼 구원을 위해 전력을 다하는 사도 바울에게 당연한 감정이다(11:2; 12:15). 그러므로 "두려워한다"는 말은 속히 죄를 회개하라고 촉구하는 말과 마찬가지다. 물론 사도적 권세로 이들을 징벌할 수도 있다. 그러나 위에서 지적하였듯이 그 권세를 사용하는 것을 지금 두려워한다고 볼 수는 없다. 오히려 13:1, 2에서 바울은 그의 권세를 사용할 것이라고 경고하고 있다.

바울이 열거하는 이들의 회개치 아니한 성적인 죄는 "더러움"(ἀκαθαρσίᾳ), "음란함"(πορνειᾳ), "호색함"(ἀσελγείᾳ)이다. 위에서 지적하였듯이 모두 하나의 관사(τῇ)아래 있는 같은 종류의 죄이다. 갈라디아서 5장 19절에서도 이 세 개의 죄가 함께 나타나고, 골로새서 3장 5절과 에베소서 5장 3절에는 앞의 두 죄가 언급되었다. "호색함"은 에베소서 4장 19절, 베드로전서 4장 3절, 마가복음 7장 22절에도 나타난다(참조, 유다 4; 벧후 2:2, 7, 18). 타스커는 "더러움"은 정욕에 젖은 삶을 나타내고, "음란함"은 성관계나 음행을 가리키고, "호색함"은 성적 비행을 가리킨다고 보았다.[674] 바울은 고린도전서 6장 9-10절에서 이런 죄를 지은 자는 하나님의 나라에서 제외 된다고 가르쳤다. 이런 심각한 죄를 계속 지으면서

673) Plummer, 370; Martin, 467.

674) Tasker, 185, 186.

도 회개치 아니함을 가서 볼 때 그들이 멸망당할 것을 알고 사도 바울은 애통할 것이다. "슬퍼한다"(πενθήσω)는 말이 본문과 같이 성적 죄를 지적하면서 그런 자를 교회에서 추방하라는 고린도전서 5장 2절("통한히 여기고", ἐπενθήσατε)에서도 나타나는 것을 특기할만하다.

이런 음행의 죄를 계속 지어온 사람들은 여러 사람들(πολλοὺς)이다. 이들은 고린도 교인들의 일부 무리로서 바울의 "고통의 방문"이나(2:1), "눈물의 편지"(2:4)를 통해서도 회개하지 않았다. 물론 고린도후서 2장 4절 이하에서 이 무리 중 한 사람이 책벌 받았다고 보이지만, 아직도 여러 사람들이 그들의 죄를 부끄러운 줄 모르고 계속 짓고 있다고 본다. 바울은 6장 14절 이하에서도 이런 무리들의 죄를 언급했다고 본다. 그리고 아래 13장 1, 2절에서 이들을 용서하지 않을 것이라고 한다.

위에서 지적하였듯이 20절의 분열을 조장하는 사람들이나 본문에서의 이방인의 습관에 젖어서 성적 죄를 짓는 이들을 엄격히 구별하기보다는 모두 바울이 함께 경계하는 무리들로 본다.[675]

2. 반대자들에 대한 경고(13:1-2)

13:1. "내가 이제 세 번째 너희에게 갈 터이니 두 세 증인의 입으로 말마다 확정하리라"(Τρίτον τοῦτο ἔρχομαι πρὸς ὑμᾶς· ἐπὶ στόματος δύο μαρτύρων καὶ τριῶν σταθήσεται πᾶν ῥῆμα). 바울은 이제 3차 방문을 준비하면서, 고린도 교인들에게 이에 대

675) Martin, 468-469; Thrall, 869-870.

비하여 회개하고 새롭게 될 것을 촉구하였다. 특히 본문에서는 3차 방문 시에 문제가 되는 사람들을 불러서 치리할 계획임을 밝힌다. 이것이 실제 계획이지만, 바울은 이런 계획을 밝히면서 3차 방문 이전에 고린도 교인들이 문제가 되는 사람들 또는 그의 반대자들에 대한 자신의 단호한 입장을 알고 이들에 대해 보다 분명한 자세를 취하고 자신의 지지를 보다 분명하게 하기를 촉구하는 것이라고 볼 수 있다. 반대자들은 바울이 지난번 방문도 취소한 것을 비난하였으니 만큼, 바울의 방문도 여차하면 또 취소할 것이라고 대수롭지 않게 받아들일 수 있음을 바울은 알고 있다. 그러므로 보다 구체적으로 그의 방문 계획을 밝혀서 반대자들의 냉소적 반응을 차단하는 것이다. 그러나 바울이 진정으로 원하는 것은 3차 방문 시에 반대자들을 자신이 치리하는 것이 아니라 반대하는 자들과 동조하는 세력이 바울의 단호한 자세와 경고로 말미암아 스스로 회개하든지 아니면, 다수의 고린도 교인들의 그들의 세력을 완전히 척결하기를 원하는 것이다. 그렇게 되어야 3차 방문이 원만한 성공적인 방문이 될 것이기 때문이다(13:10). 그러나 본문에서 적어도 겉으로 바울은 매우 엄격한 자세로 청문회를 통한 징벌 계획까지 구체적으로 밝혀서 그의 방문이 예전의 약하고 두려워 떤 방문과는 달리 매우 강경할 것임을 나타낸다(2:1; 고전 2:3).

"세 번째 갈 터 이니"에서 단순히 방문을 예정만 하는 것이 아니라 간다는 뜻이 분명히 나타난다. 바울은 4번씩 계속하여 3차 방문을 언급했다(12:14, 20, 21, 13:1). 바울은 처음 고린도 교회를 세울 때 방문하였고(행 18장), 두 번째로 고린 전서를 쓴 이후 "혹독한 편지"를 쓰기 전에 고린도 교회가 어렵다는 말을 듣고 "고통의 방문"을 했다(2:1).[676] 그러므로 이번이 세 번째가 된다.[677]

"두 세 증인의 입으로 말마다 확정하리라"는 신명기 19장 15절(LXX)에서 온 것이다. 혐의를 확정하기 위해서 한 명 이상의 증인들을 요구하는 것이다. 마태복음 18장 16절, 디모데전서 5장 19절, 히브리서 10장 28절에 교회 치리 문제와 관련하여 같은 말이 나온다. 이런 규정이 랍비 문헌에서도 나타나지만 헬라법이나 로마법에는 없다.[678] 이 두 세 증인이 누구를 가리키는가에 대한 논란이 있다.

문자적으로 바울이 고린도 교회 방문 시에 실제 법적 증언을 할 사람들을 가리킨다. 바울이 고린도전서 6장에서 믿는 이들이 세상 법정에서 서로 송사하는 것을 금하면서 실제로 교회의 법정을 구상하였다고 보는 견해도 있다.[679] 그러나 바울이 실제로 법적인 징계에 대해서 말하고 있다는 견해에 대해 반대하는 견해도 있다. (1) 신명기 19장 15절은 원래 피고인을 보호하려는 규정이며, 본문은 법적인 의미라기보다 경고성 진술이다.[680] 그러나 바울은 랍비 전통과 초대 교회 전통으로 이미 이 규정을 잘 알고 있었으므로 이 규정을 교회 책벌에 그대로 적용할 수 있었을 것이다. (2) 바울이 언급한 죄들은 이미 다 알려진 죄들이므로 실제 증인들이 필

676) Martin, xlvii.

677) Meyer, 499; Plummer, 371; Windisch, 412-413; Allo, 335.

678) H. van Vliet, *No Single Testimony. A Study on the Adoption of the Law of Deut. 19:15 par. into the New Testament*, Studia Theologica Rheno-Traiectina 4 (Utrecht: Kemink & Zoon, 1958), 11-25; 50-53; 60-62; 58-59에서 CD 9:17-23; 1QS 5:25-26을 언급함, 또 Furnish, 569를 보라.

679) M. Delco, "The Courts of the Church of Corinth and the Courts of Qumran," in *Paul and Qumran*, ed. J. Murphy-O'Connor, *Paul and Qumran*, 69-70, 75-76; Filson, 417; Tasker, 188; Hughes, 475; Allo, 335; Schlatter, *Paulus*, 675..

680) Bachmann, 412.

요하지 않았을 것이다.[681] 그러나 여기서는 이단 문제 같이 특별히 문제가 된 이들의 재판을 가리킨다고 볼 수 있다(11:13-15). (3) "두 세 증인들"이란 실제 증인들을 가리키는 것이 아니라 바울의 방문 횟수를 가리킨다.[682] 즉 과거의 두 번과 지금하려는 3차 방문을 의미한다. 바울은 방문을 통해서 고린도 교인들의 신앙을 점검하였다는 뜻이라고 한다. 그러나 방문을 증인으로 보는 예가 어디 있는가? 문맥에서 바울이 암시적으로 말하고 있다는 증거는 없고 오히려 구체적으로 분명히 말하고 있다.[683] 더구나 첫 번째 방문은 교회를 창립하는 방문이었으므로, "증인"이란 암시적 의미를 적용할 수 없다. (4) 바울이 20절에서는 분쟁을 종식하도록 권면하고서 다시 분쟁을 조장시키는 법적 증언을 계획한다는 것은 이상하다.[684] 그러나 고린도 교인들의 분쟁과 바울이 말하는 재판의 성격을 구별해야 한다. 바울이 말하는 재판은 분쟁을 종식시키기 위한 공식적인 재판이며, 교인들은 사욕적인 문제로 인한 분쟁이다. 이렇게 "두 세 증인이" 실제적 법적 증인이 아니며 바울의 방문이나 "혹독한 편지"를 가리키는 것이라고 주장하는 견해는 근거가 약하다. 마틴은 구체적인 "두 세 증인"이란 뜻이거나 다른 상징적인 의미가 아니라 3차 방문 시 문제된 사람들에 대해서 바울이 분명하게 최종적 판단을 하겠다는 의지를 나타낸다고 본다.[685] 그러나 바울은 이렇게 애매모호하게 말하여 그의 반대자들

---

681) Bachmann, 412; Lietzmann, 160; Windisch, 414; Bultmann, 243 Martin, 469.

682) Chrysostom, *PG* 61, col. 596(*NPNF*, XII, 411); Calvin, 169; Bachmann, 412; Plummer, 372; Bruce, 253; Strachan, 38; Windisch, 413; Thrall, 875.

683) Héring, 99.

684) Plummer, 372.

685) Martin, 470.

을 경고할 수 있다고 보지 않았을 것이다. 상징적인 빈 말은 오히려 그들의 빈축만 살 것임을 알고서 보다 구체적인 계획까지 밝혀서 그들에게 경고하고 있다고 본다. 그러므로 우리는 문자적으로 바울은 3차 방문 시 교회 재판을 열어서 문제가 된 이들을 실제로 책벌할 것이라는 뜻으로 본다. 한 가지 문제는 바울이 6장 14절 이하에서 세속적인 고린도 인들에게 이방적인 생활을 버리고 거룩한 그리스도인의 생활을 촉구할 때, "보라 지금은 은혜 받을 만한 때요 보라 지금은 구원의 날이로다"라고 사뭇 화해적인 어조로 권면하는데 반해서 여기서는 매우 단호한 자세를 보이는 것이다. 이에 대해서 10-13장을 "혹독한 편지"로 보거나, 9장까지 쓰고 난 뒤에 교회의 형편이 또 다시 악화되었다는 소식을 받았기 때문이라고 보는 견해가 있다고 했다. 그러나 고린도 교인들의 입장이 다양했기 때문에 6장에서는 바울에게 우호적인 다수의 교인들에게 보다 유화적으로 말한 것이고, 여기서는 반대자들과 그에 동조하는 적대적인 교인들에게 경고하는 말로 볼 수 있을 것이다(13:2).

2. "내가 이미 말하였거니와 지금 떠나 있으나 두 번째 대면하였을 때와 같이 전에 죄 지은 자들과 그 남은 모든 사람에게 미리 말하노니 내가 다시 가면 용서하지 아니하리라"(προείρηκα καὶ προλέγω, ὡς παρὼν τὸ δεύτερον καὶ ἀπὼν νῦν, τοῖς προημαρτηκόσιν καὶ τοῖς λοιποῖς πᾶσιν, ὅτι ἐὰν ἔλθω εἰς τὸ πάλιν οὐ φείσομαι,). 바울은 이번 방문이 지난 2차 방문 때 처럼 자신이 약하고 떠는 방문이 될 것이 아니라, 또 말뿐인 방문이 아니라, "문제 가된 이들"에 대한 단호한 조치가 실제로 있을 방문이 될 것임을 계속 경고한다. 바울은 2차 방문시에 반대자들에게

모욕을 당하면서도 그들을 경고하였다. 또 10장 이후에도 계속하여 그들을 경고해 왔다. 바울은 방문 이전에 이들에 대한 정죄의 사를 분명히 밝힘으로써 반대자들과의 일전을 불사할 것임을 밝히고, 중립적 입장에 있는 다수의 고린도 교인들에게 반대자들에 대한 보다 분명한 처리와 자신에 대한 지지를 촉구하는 것이다. 바울은 2장에서 문제가 된 어떤 이에 대한 책벌을 "눈물의 편지"에서 지시했고 고린도 교인들이 이 지시를 따라서 그를 치리하였음을 칭찬하면서, 이제는 다시 그 징계를 해제해야 할 것을 지시하였다(2:5-10). 본문에서 바울이 책벌을 하겠다는 말을 하고 있고, 2장 6절에는 이미 어떤 사람을 책벌한 것이 나타남으로, 10-13장을 2장 4절에서 말하는 "눈물의 편지"로 보는 이들은 본문을 10-13장이 1-9장보다 먼저 보낸 편지라는 증거로 본다. 그러나 본문에서 바울이 이들을 심문하고 치리하겠다는 계획을 말하는 것이며, 치리를 지시하는 것은 아니라고 보면, 2장 4절의 편지와는 구별할 수 있다.[686]

본문에서 "전에 죄 지은 자들과 그 남은 자들"이라고 지목되는 "문제가 된 인물들"이 실제로 어떤 이들을 가리키는지 잘 알 수 없다. 다만 "전에 죄 지은 자들"은 2차 방문 시에 바울이 문책했던 이들인 것 같고, "그 남은 사람들"(τοῖς λοιποῖς πᾶσιν)은 어떤 바울을 반대하는 무리들이라고 볼 수밖에 없다. 이런 사람들이 아직 남아 있다는 사실은 우리가 주장해 온 바와 같이 10-13장이 독립된 편지라기보다 바울이 자신을 지지한 이들을 반대하는 이들을 염두에 두고 9장에 이어 쓴 글임을 지지해준다. 바넷은 "전에 죄

686) Martin, 470-471.

지은 자들"(τοῖς προημαρτηκόσιν)은 21절에서 언급한 성적 죄를 회개하지 않는 "전에 죄 지은 여러 사람들"(πολλοὺς τῶν προημαρτηκότων)과 같은 사람들로 보고 "그 남은 사람들"은 이들을 암암리에 후원하고 동조하던 무리라고 본다.[687] 퍼니쉬는 "그 남은 사람들"을 다른 모든 고린도 교인들을 가리킨다고 하나, 이 경우 그냥 "너희들"로 말했을 것이다.[688] 마틴은 "전에 죄지은 사람들"은 20절의 성적 죄인들 뿐만 아니라 21절의 분열을 조장하는 이들도 포함된 것으로 본다. 그리고 "그 남은 사람들"은 이 모든 죄인들과 동조하는 무리로서 바울을 모르는, 바울이 떠난 이후에 바울의 반대자들이 들어 온 이후에 그들의 감화로 새로 믿기로 작정 한 이들로서 바울의 반대자들을 따르는 이들이라고 한다.[689] 본문에서 바울은 어떤 죄를 지은 사람들(분열 조장하는 죄인들, 성적인 죄인들)이냐로 구별하지 않고, 바울을 아는 기존 교인들("전에 죄지은 사람들")과 이들과 동조하는, 바울을 모르는, 새 교인들("그 남은 사람들")로 구별하고 있다는 것이다. 20절과 21절에 차례로 언급한 고린도 교회에서 분열의 죄와 성적인 죄를 지은 모든 사람들("[바울을 아는] 전에 죄 지은 이들")과 이에 동조하는 모든 이들("[바울을 모르는] 그 남은 사람들")을 모두 바울의 반대파로 보고 그들에게 경고하고 있다고 보는 것이다. 이런 견해도 가능하나 20, 21절은 각기 다른 죄를 지은 이들을 나누어 말하고 있는 것이 사실이다. "전에 죄지은 사람들"이 어떤 죄인들인지

687) Barnett, 600.

688) Barnett., 600, 주, 36, 재인용, Furnish, 570.

689) Martin, 471.

를 분명히 알 수는 없으나 20, 21절에서 말하는 분열을 조장하고 성적인 죄를 지은 회개할 줄 모르는 모든 죄인들로서 바울을 반대하는 이들이라고 본다.

그러나 여전히 바울은 목회자로서 내심으로는 3차 방문 이전에 이들이 회개하고 그의 방문 시에 화해를 하기 원하는 것이 분명하다. 바울은 "파하는 권세" 보다 "세우는 권세" 를 원하고 있기 때문이다(13:10). 그러나 여기서 바울은 "죄 지은 자들" 뿐만 아니라 이들에 대해 우유부단한 자세를 취하고 있는 다수의 고린도 교인들을 염두에 두고 있는 것이다. 즉 바울은 2장 6절에서 바울의 지시에 따라 문제가 된 사람을 치리한 것처럼 다수의 고린도 교인들이 믿음과 진리에 서서(13:5-9) 바울의 방문 이전에 보다 명확하게 바울을 반대하는 이들을 반대하고 바울에 대한 지지를 분명히 하게 되기를 바라는 것이다. 그러나 2장 6절의 경우와 달리 이들에 대해 직접 치리를 지시하지 않는 것으로 보아서 어쩌면 그 때보다 사태가 더 심각한 것으로 보고 바울 자신이 이들에 대한 징계를 직접 계획하고 있다고 보아야 할 것이다.

"내가 다시 가면" (ὅτι ἐὰν ἔλθω)을 번역할 때 ἐάν을 "만일…면" (if)으로 번역하지 않고 "…때" 로 번역하는 이들이 있다(NEB). 즉 "내가 다시 갈 때" 로 번역해야 한다는 것이다.[690] 방문을 단순히 가정이나 예정으로 말하는 경우, 독자들의 편에서 볼 때, 1장에서 말하는 바울의 변덕스런 방문 습관이 다시 재현될 수 있다는 느낌을 가질 수 있다는 것이다. 바울이 이런 오해를 원치 않았을 것이고, 또 본문의 문맥에서 바울의 책벌 의지가 강조되고 있으므

690) Tasker, 186, 187; Bruce, 253; Hughes, 476.

로, "내가 다시 가면" 보다는 "내가 갈 때"가 적절히 바울의 의중을 나타내는 번역이라고 한다. 또 실제로 ἐάν이 요한복음 16장 7절과 요한일서 3장 2절에서 "때"의 의미가 있다(요 13:2: NIV).[691] 그러나 본문의 "내가 다시 가면"이란 번역도 여전히 가능하다(NIV). ἐάν의 의미와 상관없이 바울의 방문 의지와 책벌 계획은 분명하다.

3. 바울의 진정성을 묻는 대신 고린도 교인들 자신들의 진정성을 확인할 것(13:3-10)

3. "이는 그리스도께서 내 안에서 말씀하시는 증거를 너희가 구함이니 저가 너희를 향하여 약하지 않고 도리어 너희 안에서 강하시니라" (ἐπεὶ δοκιμὴν ζητεῖτε τοῦ ἐν ἐμοὶ λαλοῦντος Χριστοῦ, ὃς εἰς ὑμᾶς οὐκ ἀσθενεῖ ἀλλὰ δυνατεῖ ἐν ὑμῖν). 중립적인 다수의 고린도 교인들은 바울이든 누구든지 분명하게 사도적 증거를 보이는 사람을 그들의 사도로 따르기를 원하고 있을 것이다. 고린도전서에서 나타난 바와 같이, 고린도 교회는 초기부터 바울파, 게바파, 아볼로파, 그리스도파로 나뉘어져 갈등이 증폭되어 왔다(고전 1:12; 3:3-4). 바울은 이에 대해서 교회의 일치를 중시하면서 모두 같은 그리스도의 동역자들로서 각자가 맡은 사역을 하고 있다는 관용적인 자세를 보였다(1:13-17; 3:5-9). 아마 바울의 관용적인 자세가 다수의 고린도 교인들에게는 바울만을 절

---

691) Tasker, 186.

692) Thrall, 834.

대적으로 지지할 수 없는 원인을 제공했는지도 모른다.[692] 물론 지금의 거짓 사도들이 바울이 언급한 게바나 아볼로와 같은 이들과는 달랐다고 하더라도, 초신자들이 대부분인 고린도 교인들은 이들에 대한 바울의 분명한 정죄가 있기 전에 큰 사도들의 추천장을 가지고 나타난 거짓 사도들을 다른 사도들과 구별하기 어려웠을 것이다. 고린도 교인들의 바울의 사도직에 대한 의문은 고린도전서를 쓸 당시에도 제기되었다(고전 9:1-2; 15:8-10). 바울은 이제 보다 분명한 자세를 취하여 반대자들을 정죄하고, 자신이 "큰 사도들 보다 조금도 부족함이 없음"을 밝혀서 고린도 교인들이 보다 분명한 자세를 가지도록 촉구하는 것이다.

고린도후서에서 바울은 고린도 교인들이 진정한 사도들을 판단하는 기준이 잘못되었음을 지적해왔다. 그들은 바울의 반대자들이 제시하는 추천장이나 외모나 "육체의 자랑"(유대인, 예수와의 접촉, 말씀의 목격자, 카리스마 리더십, 웅변, 외적인 영적 은사, 등)을 진정한 사도의 판단 기준으로 중시해왔기 때문이다(3:1; 5:12; 10:, 7, 10, 12; 11:6, 12, 18, 22-23; 12:11-18). 바울은 이런 판단 기준에 의해서 반대자들에게 열등한 사도로 멸시를 받았다(10:10). 이에 대해서 바울은 자신도 그런 사도적 증거들이 있다고 하였다(11:22-28; 12:1-4; 12:11, 12). 그러나 바울은 진정한 사도직의 증거를 외적으로 나타나는 증거에서 찾기 보다는(12:12), 하나님의 진실한 영에게 사로 잡혀(고전 7:40; 참조, 고전 14:37), 그리스도의 마음을 회중들에게 가르쳐서(고전 2:16;참조, 빌 2:5), 그들을 그리스도 안에 온전하게 세우는 데서 찾는다(3:1; 10:8; 12:19;

---

692) Thrall, 834.

13:5-10). 바울은 그리스도의 진리를 제대로 전파하고 실제로 그렇게 사는 것이 진정한 사도직 판단 기준이라고 보았다(2:17; 4:2-15, 5:14, 15; 6:4-10; 11:4-6, 23-28; 12:9, 10; 15). 실제로 바울의 복음 전파 사역을 통해서 고린도 인들이 변화되었다(3:2; 고전 2:4; 4:15; 15:11). 바울은 하나님의 말씀을 능력으로 나타나는 통로가 되었다. 이렇게 바울은 외적인 능력과 내적인 증거를 나타내었으나, 고린도 교인들은 계속해서 바울에게서 그리스도가 말하는 증거(δοκιμὴν)가 무엇이냐를 묻고 있다. 다시 말하면 바울의 복음 사역이 진정한 판단 기준이라면 당신의 복음 사역을 어떻게 그리스도의 사역으로 신뢰할 수 있느냐라는 것이다. 이에 대해서 바울은 "저가 너희를 향하여 약하지 않고 도리어 너희 안에서 강하시니라" 고 대답한다. 즉 지금까지는 내가 약한 자세로 너희들을 대했으나 3차 방문 시에는 그리스도가 주신 엄격한 사도권으로, 너희들, 특히 문제가 된 이들을 엄하게 다룰 것이라는 것이다(10;7; 13:10). 바울은 1, 2절에서 이미 엄한 사도권 발동으로 문제가 된 이들을 용서하지 않고 정죄할 것이라고 대답하였다. 3절은 이에 대한 이유절로 시작되었다(ἐπεί). 즉 엄한 사도권을 발동할 밖에 없는 이유는 고린도 교인들이 회개하지 않고 바울을 열등하고 무능한 약한 사도로 보기 때문이다. 그러므로 바울은 그리스도께서 주신 엄한 사도권을 나타내어 문제가 된 이들을 심판하여 "그리스도가 내안에서 말씀하신다는 증거" 를 보여 주겠다는 것이다. 그리스도께서 바울에게 주신 권세는 교회를 세우는 것인데, 이 권세는 교회를 세우는 일에 방해되는 요소들을 척결하는 권세를 포함하는 것이다(10:8, 13:10).

물론 고린도 교인들이 바울이 사도권 발동으로 그리스도의 사도임을 증명하겠다는 반응에 대해서 대부분 만족하지 않았을 것이다. 트롤에 의하면 고린도 교인들이 바울 안에서 그리스도가 말씀하시는 표로 원하는 것은 바울이 말이나 통상적인 징계조치로 반대자들이나 문제가 된 이들을 위협할 것이 아니라, 한번 초월적 능력을 발휘하여 이들을 벌하는 것이 가장 효과적인 방법이라고 생각했을 것이라고 한다. 즉 사도행전 13장 8-11절에서와 같이 복음의 원수로 행동하는 박수 엘루마를 눈이 멀게 한 것과 같은 초월적인 능력으로 벌하는 것이라고 한다.[693] 재물을 감추고 거짓말한 아나니아와 삽비라도 베드로의 저주로 죽었다(행 5:1). 고린도 교인들은 사도들의 이런 초월적 능력을 이미 직접 보았거나 들어서 알고 있었을 것이다. 그리고 이같이 어려운 난국을 타개하기 위해서는 어떤 큰 초월적 능력으로 반대자들을 복종시키는 것이 교회를 안정시키고 바울의 사도권을 확립하기 위하여 가장 효과적인 조치일 것이라고 믿고 있었을 것이다(10:5, 6). 그러나 이런 초월적 능력에 대한 기대가 언제나 복음 정신에 일치되는 것은 아니다. (1). 그런 기대가 단순히 초월적 행사를 보고 즐기려는 일반적인 종교적 호기심에서 나온 것일 수 있기 때문이다(마 12:38, 39; 병행, 눅 11:29; 눅 23:8). (2). 복음 정신은 사람들을 위협하여 믿게 하는 것이 아니라, 참고 설득하고 사랑으로 감동시키는 데 있다(고전 12:28-31; 참조, 마 26:52-54). 그래서 바울은 12장 12절에서 자신의 사도된 표는 "모든 참는 가운데서 표적과 기사와 능력을 행한 것" 이라고 말한다. (3) 이런 외적 초월적 능력은 자의적으로 가능한 것이 아니라 그 시에 도우시는 성령의 동의와 역사가 없이

---

693) Thrall, 880.

는 불가능한 것이다(13:9). 바울이 자의로 고린도 교인들에게 3차 방문 시에 반대자들에게 이런 능력을 발휘하겠다고 미리 약속할 수 없는 것이다. (4) 무엇보다 고린도후서에서 바울은 고린도의 거짓 사도들이 이런 외적 초월적 능력을 자랑하는 것을 경계하여 왔다(12:1-6; 10-12). 바울은 그리스도의 진정한 능력은 약한 가운데서 강하게 되는 것이라고 믿는다(12:9, 10). 그러므로 고린도 교인들이 초월적 능력을 발휘할 것을 원했다하여도 바울이 그런 소원을 쉽게 받아들일 것이라고 기대할 수는 없다.

유사하게 불트만과 바레트는 바울이 생각하는 "그리스도 가 내 안에서 말씀하시는 증거"를 하나님의 심판과 그리스도의 능력으로 반대자들을 정죄하는 것이라고 본다.[694] 그러나 13장 1, 2절에서 바울은 보다 구체적인 교회 재판이나 청문회를 통한 징계를 구상하는 것이 분명하다. 이런 구체적인 법적 제재가 막연한 "하나님의 심판" 의 경고보다 효과적인 반응을 일으킬 것이기 때문이다.

그러므로 바울이 선택한 "그리스도가 내 안에서 말씀하시는 증거"는 "주께서 주신 파하는 권세"를 사용하여 반대자들을 징계하는 것이다. 물론 거듭 지적한 바와 같이 바울은 내심으로는 문제가 된 이들이 스스로 죄 회개하거나 고린도 교인들이 솔선수범하여 이 죄악을 척결하여 그가 방문 할 때는 그의 파괴적인 권세를 쓰지 않아도 되기를 바라고 있다(12:20. 21, 13:5-10). 그러나 그들의 반응에 따라서 바울은 단호한 척결 의지를 가지고 있는 것이다.

"저가 너희를 향하여 약하지 않고 도리어 너희 안에서 강하시

694) Bultmann, 244-5; Barrett, 334-5.

니라"는 말은 바울의 징계 결의의 타당성을 고린도 교인들을 향하여 그리스도께서 강하게 역사하심에서 찾는 것이다. 그리스도께서 지금까지 너희를 위한 나의 사역가운데 약하게 계셨으나 이제부터는 그렇지 않을 것이라는 것이다. 그리스도께서 바울 사도를 통하여 반대자들을 벌하게 하심으로써 그의 강하심을 나타낼 것이라고 경고하는 것이다.

한편, 이런 어귀에는 바울이 그리스도의 사도로서 그리스도의 사역의 유형의 선택에 대한 예지가 있다는 암시가 있다. 바울은 성령의 뜻과 그리스도의 마음을 아는 통찰력을 가졌다(고전 2:10-16).

바울의 이런 사도권을 통한 징계 조치가 고린도 교인들에게 얼마나 효과적 반응을 일으킬 수 있을 런지는 알 수 없다. 이미 고린도전서 5장 3-5절에서 바울은 음행한 자를 책벌하도록 지시한 적이 있었고, "엄한 편지"에서도 "근심하게 한자"를 징벌하도록 명하여, 고린도 교인들이 징벌한 예가 있다(고후 2:6). 그러나 계속된 징벌에도 불구하고 문제가 되는 이들이 그치지 않음으로 인해서 고린도 교인들이 바울의 이 같은 징계의 경고에 대하여 크게 동요할 것이라고 보기는 어렵다. 그러나 고린도 교인들의 반응과 상관없이 바울은 이런 경우 사도로서 마땅히 해야 할 일은 결국 징계조치에 대해 미리 경고하여 이들을 회개에 이르도록 최선의 노력을 다하는 것이라고 결론 내린 것이다.

4. "그리스도께서 약하심으로 십자가에 못 박히셨으나 오직 하나님의 능력으로 살으셨으니 우리도 저의 안에서 약하나 너희를 향하여 하나님의 능력으로 저와 함께 살리라"(καὶ γὰρ

ἐσταυρώθη ἐξ ἀσθενείας, ἀλλὰ ζῇ ἐκ δυνάμεως θεοῦ. καὶ γὰρ ἡμεῖς ἀσθενοῦμεν ἐν αὐτῷ, ἀλλὰ ζήσομεν σὺν αὐτῷ ἐκ δυνάμεως θεοῦ εἰς ὑμᾶς.). 바울은 13장 1-3절에서 고린도 인들이 자신이 사도된 표를 구하는 것에 대하여 "문제가 된 죄인들에게 징계조치를 할 것으로" 대답한 후에 이런 엄한 조치의 타당성을 그리스도의 죽으심과 부활의 유형에 의거하여 설명한다.[695] 지금까지 바울은 "그리스도 안"에서 그리스도의 약하심을 따라서 고린도 교회에서 사역해왔다(4:7-15; 6:4-10; 10:1a). 바울은 온갖 고난을 받으며 사역에 충실해왔다(11:23-33). 그리고 온갖 수모를 겪으면서 약한 것을 자랑해왔다(10:7; 10; 11:6; 11:30; 12:10, 9). 그러나 고린도 교회가 아직도 심각한 국면이 있음을 보면서 이제는 약한 자세에서 담대한 자세로 문제를 해결해야 할 때가 되었다는 것이다. 즉 13장 1, 2절에서 말하는 징계 계획의 타당성을 설명하는 것이다.

이 구절은 두 개의 대조구문이 병행되어 나타난다. 그리스도의 약하심과 강하심이 바울의 약함과 강함으로 나타난다. 이런 대조구문과 또 "저의 안"(ἐν αὐτῷ), 즉 "그리스도 안"이란 어귀는 다시 한 번 바울이 그의 존재와 사역에 있어서 그리스도와 매우 일치하고 있음을 나타낸다. 물론 바울이 그리스도와 같은 존재라는 의미가 아니지만 그와 같은 마음으로 일치되게 행동한다는 뜻이

695) 여기서 그리스도의 부활에 대한 언급에 대하여 대다수의 학자들은 바울의 징계 조치와 관련된 것으로 본다. Meyer, 506-7; Bachmann, 415; Allo, 338; Strachan, 38; Hughes, 479-80; Plummer, 375; Héring, 100, 주, 3; Tasker, 188; Furnish, 571; Barnett, 605; Martin, 477; Thrall, 887. 그러나 Heckel, *Schwachheit*, 133에서 종말론적 해석을 보라.

다(고전2:16; 빌 1:21). 바울은 그리스도의 권위를 받아서 그의 능력으로 행한다. 바울의 반대자들은 바울이 외적으로 들어나는 능력이 없는 열등한 사도로 비하시켜왔다. 바울은 지금까지 그리스도의 약함 가운데 모든 수모를 참아왔다(1:8-11; 4:7-15; 6:4-10; 11:23-33; 12:5-10). 그것은 오로지 하나님만 의지하는 고난 받는 모든 의인의 존재 형태이기도 하다(1:9; 욥 1:21, 22; 시 69:29; 70:5; 마 10:38; 26:39). 더구나 다음 5절에서 바울은 고린도 인들에게 "그리스도가 그들 안에 있는지 그들의 믿음을 확증하라"고 권하면서, 4절에서는 바울이 그리스도 안에 있다고 말한다. 이것은 바울은 자신이 이미 그리스도 안에 있으므로 그리스도에게 인정받는 사도라는 것이다. 그러나 고린도 교인들은 그것이 분명하지 않으므로 스스로 점검하고 분명한 믿음을 가지라는 것이다. 그리고 그들이 회개하지 못하고 믿음을 회복하지 못하면 사도권을 쓸 수 밖에 없다는 것이다. 즉 3절 하반절에서 말한 반대자들에게 대한 징계 계획의 타당성을 재확인하는 말이다.

십자가와 부활은 과거의 역사적 사건으로 끝난 것이 아니라 현재의 그리스도의 사역 가운데서 계속 재현되는 것이다. 그리스도 안에 있는 사람들에게 고난과 승리는 계속 나타나는 것이다. 그러나 그것은 자연주의적 순환 사상과는 다른 것이다(고전 1:5-7; 3:15). 하나님의 선하심과 의로우심을 향한 현재의 고난은 결국 영광스런 승리를 보장하며, 그런 의미에서 그리스도인의 현재의 고난은 최후의 승리를 향한 예비적 단계와 같은 것이다(고후 4:17; 롬 8:17, 18). 그러나 그 고난이 너무나 보편적이고 지속적이므로 바울과 같이 그리스도 안에 거하는 사람들에게는 그리스도의 약함 가운데서 일하는 것이 그들의 일상적인 존재 유형 자체가 되어

버린 것이다. 부활하신 그리스도는 외적인 능력과 영광의 그리스도로만 나타나는 것이 아니라 여전히 십자가에 달리신 약하신 그리스도로 나타나는 것이다.[696] 그러므로 그리스도인을 핍박하던 사울에게 나타난 예수님은, "나는 네가 핍박하는 예수라"고 말씀하셨다(행 9:5). 그러나 바로 그 약하신 그리스도가 강한 사울을 회개시켜 그리스도의 사도로 만든 것이었다. 그것이 바울이 말한 바로 약한 데서 강하게 되는 그리스도의 신비한 능력이다. 아무런 예수에 대한 믿음이 없을 뿐만 아니라 오히려 적그리스도이었던 사울을 그리스도를 위한 사도로 변화시킨 힘은 약함으로 핍박받는 예수 그리스도의 능력이었다. 이것이 바울을 그 많은 고난 중에서 승리하게 하시는 그리스도의 능력이다. 이것이 바울이 진정한 그리스도의 사도된 증표였던 것이다(11:12). 그러므로 그는 그의 약한 것을 자랑하게 되었다(12:9, 10). 바울은 아마 이런 진리를 이전에도 알고 있었을 것이다. 그러나 계시로 말미암아 더욱 확고하게 되었다.

외적 능력을 자랑하는 바울의 반대자들도 나름대로 그들의 사역에서의 고난을 경험하였을 것이다. 그러나 그들은 그런 고난이나 약함을 감추고 외적 영광과 능력을 나타내어 자랑하였던 것이다. 그들에게는 약한데서 강하게 하시는 그리스도의 능력이 없고, 십자가의 그리스도의 증표가 없다. 그들은 십자가 없는 영광의 그리스도만을 믿을 뿐이었다.[697] 그러나 그것은 "다른 예수"이다. 그러므로 그들은 사도들로 가장한 거짓 사도들인 것이다

696) Martin, 475.

697) Martin, 475: 바울은 여기서 *theologia gloriae*(영광의 신학)을 반대하고 대신 *theologia crucis*(십자가의 신학)을 견지하고 있다.

(11:13-15).

그러나 본문에서 바울은 문제된 이들의 징계 계획을 밝히면서 이제 강할 때가 되었다고 말한다. 문제가 된 이들에 대한 강경한 조치로서의 자신의 징계 계획의 법적 신학적 근거를 약한 가운데서 강하신 그리스도라는 기독론에서 찾는 것이다. 동시에 바울은 자신을 열등한 사도로 간주해온 고린도 교인들을 책망하고 있는 것이다. 고린도 교인들이 진정한 사도를 열등한 사도로 오해하는 것은 매우 심각한 문제로 보는 것이다. 그것은 오해를 당하는 바울 자신의 괴로움이 문제가 아니라 사랑하는 고린도 교인들이 반대자들의 잘못된 선전에 속아서 악을 행하게 되고 바른 믿음을 잃게 되기 때문이다(12:19; 13:7). 그 결과 고린도 교회가 비사도적이고 비복음적인 교회로 전락될 수 있기 때문이다.

그러나 바울은 여전히 그의 3차 방문 전에 문제가 된 고린도 교인들이 죄를 회개하고 바른 믿음을 회복하기를 원한다. 그래서 자신이 다시 온유함으로 그들에게 나타나서 화해하며 기쁘게 지낼 것을 원한다(5:18-21; 7:15, 16; 10:1; 13:9, 10). 다만 그들이 3차 방문 이전에 회개하지 않는다면 강경책을 쓸 수밖에 없다는 것을 경고하는 것이다. 바울은 지금 강경책을 말하지만 어디까지나 그리스도의 겸비함 가운데 그의 사도권을 쓰기를 원치 않을 것이다. 바울은 고린도 교인들이 회개하고 바른 믿음을 회복하여 징계할 필요가 없게 되어 온유하고 겸비하게 만나기를 원한다(10:1). 그러나 고린도 교인들이 회개를 하지 않았을 경우 겸비함으로 이들을 대할 수 없을 것이다. 본문에서 바울이 어떤 경우든지 그들을 반드시 겸비함으로 대할 것이라고 말하는 것은 아니다. 오히려 12장 21절에서는 3차 방문에서는 전과 같은 부끄러움을 당하지 않을 것이라는 암시적 의미가 강하다. 또 13장 1절 이후 바울은 문제가 된 이들을 징계하는 강경조치 계획을 계속 밝히면서 그 근거를 그리스도의 강하심에서 찾고 있다.[698]그러나 13장 7-10절에서의 마지막 권면에서 바울은 다시 그리스도의 겸비함으로 고린도 인들을 만날 수 있도록 고린도 인들이 바른 믿음에 서게 되기를 바라고 있다. 그 결과 자신은 사도적 권세를 쓰지 못하는 별수 없이 약하고 무능한 사도라는 말을 반대자들로부터 들어도 상관없다는 것이다(7).

"그리스도께서 약하심으로"(ἐξ ἀσθενείας)에서 ἐξ는 보통 "…에서 부터"라고 번역되나 여기서는 이유를 나타내는 전치사로 보아서 "…로 말미암아"로 번역해야 한다. 사실 "…에서"라는 지역의 의미가 논리적 근거를 나타내는 이유의 의미로 전환될 수 있기 때문이다.[699] 그래서 "그리스도께서 약하심으로 말미암아"로 번역해야 한다.[700] 그러나 한글 개역의 "그리스도께서 약하심으로"라는 번역에서 "말미암아"가 생략되었다고 보고 그대로 받아들일 수 있다. 또한 "약하심으로"(ἐξ ἀσθενείας)는 뒤에 나오는 "하나님의 능력으로"(ἐκ δυνάμεως θεοῦ)와 대칭을 이룬다.[701]

한글 본문의 "오직 하나님의 능력으로"에서 "오직"은 의미를 강조하기 위한 번역자의 추가이며 희랍어 원문에는 없다.

희랍어 본문의 끝에 있는 "너희를 향하여"(εἰς ὑμᾶς)라는 구절은 원래 "…에 대하여," 또는 "…에 관하여"라는 뜻으로 그대로 번

698) Martin, 476-77.

699) Barnett, 603, 주, 57.

700) Heckel, *Schwachheit*, 129; Martin, 452; Thrall, 884.

701) Heckel, 129.

역하면 어색하다.[702] 위에서 지적한 바와 같이 이 말은 어떤 희랍어 사본에는 아예 없다(B D[2]). 복사자가 4절 하반절이 장래 부활을 의미한다고 보고서 이 어귀가 어색하다고 보고 지운 것이라고 본다.[703] 그러나 대부분의 학자들이 말하는 것처럼 본문의 부활을 바울의 사도권 행사로 해석하는 경우, 한글 개역과 같이. "너희를 향하여," 또는 "너희 앞에서"라는 뜻으로 번역할 수 있다.[704]

5. "너희가 믿음에 있는가 너희 자신을 시험하고 너희 자신을 확증하라 예수 그리스도께서 너희 안에 계신 줄을 너희가 스스로 알지 못하느냐 그렇지 않으면 너희가 실격한 것이라(버리운 자니라)"(Ἑαυτοὺς πειράζετε εἰ ἐστὲ ἐν τῇ πίστει, ἑαυτοὺς δοκιμάζετε· ἢ οὐκ ἐπιγινώσκετε ἑαυτοὺς ὅτι Ἰησοῦς Χριστὸς ἐν ὑμῖν; εἰ μήτι ἀδόκιμοί ἐστε). 바울은 지금까지의 강경한 자세에서 한결 온건한 어조로 돌아온다. 징계의 문제를 떠나서 다시 회개를 권면하고 있다. 바울은 앞 절에서 자신은 분명히 그리스도 안에 있는 그리스도의 사도임을 확인하였다. 바울은 비록 약한 모습으로 사역하나 도리어 그것이 그리스도의 능력이 나타나는 진정한 그리스도의 사도의 사역인 것이다. 그러므로 바울은 이제 고린도 교인들이 자신의 그리스도의 사도된 증거를 요구하기보다는(13:3), 그들이 4절에서 언급한 약함 가운데 죽으시고 부활하신 그리스도를 진정으로 믿는지를 먼저 점검하라고 권면한다. "너희 자신을 시험하라"는 말에서 강조형(Ἑαυτοὺς)이 본문

---

702) BAGD, eivj 5.

703) Thrall, 887, 주, 125.

704) Martin, 477.

을 시작하고 있고, 또 "시험하라"(πειράζετε)는 말이 중심 주제로 나타난다. 이와 관련된 말로 본문에서와 6, 7절에서 "(시험에) 실패한," 또는 "낙제한"("버리운 자," ἀδόκιμοι)이라는 부정형 형용사와 "인증된,"" 또는 "합격한"(δόκιμοι)이라는 긍정형 형용사가 동사형과 함께 반복되어 나타나는 것에 유의해야 한다.[705] 이런 동족어가 반복되는 것으로 보아서 이 부분에서의 중심 주제로서 진정한 그리스도의 사도로서의 증거와 또한 진정한 그리스도인으로서의 증거가 함께 거론된다는 것을 알 수 있다. 다른 표현들도 이 주제 말("너희 자신을 시험하라")을 중심으로 해석해야 함을 보여 준다.

"너희가 믿음에 있는가 너희 자신을 시험하라"(εἰ ἐστὲ ἐν τῇ πίστει, ἑαυτοὺς δοκιμάζετε)는 말에서 바울은 자신에게 사도적 증거를 찾는 고린도 교인들에게(13:3) 그들에게 진정한 그리스도인 된 믿음의 증거가 있느냐고 반문한다.[706] 고린도전서 16장 13

---

705) 이 말의 긍정적 의미가 3절에서 처음 "합격한," "인증된," (δόκιμος)이란 형용사형으로 나오고("그리스도께서 내 안에서 말씀하시는 증거"), 본문에서 첫 번째는 동사형("[시험에] 합격하다," "인증하다"(δοκιμαζειν)로, 두 번째는 부정형 형용사형("실패한," 또는 "낙제한", ἀδόκιμος)으로 나온다. 이 동사는 원래 어떤 자격이나 인정을 위한 시험에 통과하다는 뜻이다(8:22; 고전11:28; 롬1:18; 14:22; 엡5:10; 살전 2:4). 한글 개역은 3절의 명사형(δοκιμὴν)을 "증거"로 번역하고, 5절의 첫 번째 동사형은 "확증하라"(δοκιμάζετε)로 적절하게 번역했으나, 두 번째 부정적 형용사형(ἀδόκιμοι)을 "버리운 자"로 명사화하여 번역했다. 그러나 여기서는 "실격하였다"라고 번역하는 것이 더 적절하다. 2001년 표준 새번역 개정판도 유사하게 "실격자"라고 해석한다. 마찬가지로 6, 7절의 같은 부정형 형용사형(ἀδόκιμοι)을 명사화하여 "버리운 자"로 번역했으나 거기서도 "실격하였다"로 번역하는 것이 우리 말 어감에 적절하다. 7절에는 한글개역은 δόκιμοι를 "옳은 자"라고 번역하나 "인증 받았음"이라고 번역하는 것이 더 분명하다. 2001년 표준 새번역 개정판은 "합격자"라고 번역한다,

절에서도 바울은 "믿음에(ἐν τῇ πίστει) 굳게 설 것"을 권면한다. "믿음 안에"(ἐν τῇ πίστει)는 문형에 있어서 본문의 중반절의 "너희 안에 그리스도"('Ιησοῦς Χριστὸς ἐν ὑμῖν)와 병행을 이룬다. 그러므로 그리스도에 대한 바른 믿음이 없이는 진정한 사도직에 대한 증거가 무엇인지 알 수 없다. 바른 믿음이란 이미 4절에서 지적한 대로, 약함으로 십자가에서 죽으셨으나 하나님의 능력으로 부활하신 그리스도를 믿는 믿음이다. 고린도 교인들이 믿는 그리스도가 실제로 이런 그리스도인지를 스스로 점검하라는 것이다. 지금까지 거짓 사도들에게 미혹을 받아 육체를 따라서 외적인 조건과 초월적 능력으로 사도직을 평가하는 고린도 교인들의 자세는 그들의 신앙이 과연 십자가에서 약함으로 죽으신 그리스도를 믿는 신앙인가를 의심케 하기 때문이다(5:12; 10:7; 11:4; 19).[707] 영광의 그리스도만을 알고 고난 받으신 그리스도를 모르면 진정한 그리스도를 아는 신앙이 아니다. 고린도 교인들이 약함으로 십자가에서 죽으셨으나 능력으로 다시 사신 그리스도를 믿는 대신 영광의 그리스도만을 믿는다면 온전한 믿음을 가진 것이 아니다. 그

706) Héring(100)은 5절의 질문을 고린도 교인들의 양심을 점검하라는 뜻으로 해석하나, 여기서는 고린도 교인들의 신앙이 문제이지 도덕적인 순결성이 문제가된다고 볼 수 없다. Héring의 견해를 수용하는 마틴(478, 480)을 보라.

707) Martin, 478; 참조, Bultmann, 247; Furnish, 577: 이들은 여기서 믿음이란 복종이라고 한다. 10:6에서 바울이 그리스도께 복종케 한다는 말이 있고, 현재 문맥에서 바울의 사도직의 책임으로써 고린도 교인들을 그리스도께 복종케 한다는 의미가 가능하지만, 그리스도에 대한 바른 이해가 더 가까운 의미라고 본다. 트롤은 1:24에서와 같이 넓은 의미로서 신뢰, 복종을 가리킨다고 본다(889). 그러나 본문에서 그리스도에 대한 바른 믿음이 바울의 사도직 이해와 반대자들의 사도직 이해와 직접 관련되어 있다고 본다. 5절 중반절에서의 바울의 질문도 역시 그리스도가 너희 안에 있느냐란 것임을 볼 때 더욱 그렇다. 이런 견해를 다음에서 보라. Barrett, 338; Wendland, 257.

러므로 그들은 "다른 예수," "다른 영," "다른 복음"을 용납한 것이다(11:4). 이것은 그들의 순수한 믿음이 오염된 증거이다. 20, 21절에서 지적된 고린도 교인들의 분열의 죄와, 성적인 죄도 결국 그리스도를 잘못 믿은 결과라고 볼 수 있다. 약함으로 죽으시고 부활하신 그리스도를 믿는 것이 온전한 신앙이다. 그렇지 않을 때, 그리스도와 상관이 없고 그리스도의 사도인 바울과도 상관이 없다. 바울은 그리스도의 약함을 따라 사역해 왔기 때문이다. 바울이 고린도 교인들에게 그들의 믿음을 점검하도록 요구하는 것은 그들이 바울의 사도직을 의심하면서 "바울 안에서 그리스도가 말씀하시는 증거"를 찾기 때문이다. 그러나 바울은 고린도 교인들이 먼저 진정한 그리스도에 대한 믿음이 있는지 점검하라는 것이다. 그리고 나서 그 믿음에 의해서 바울이 진정으로 그리스도의 사도인지를 점검하라는 것이다. 고린도 교인들의 그리스도에 대한 믿음이 바르게 나타나면, 그로 인해서 바울의 사도직에 대한 판단도 바르게 나타날 것이기 때문이다.

"예수 그리스도께서 너희 안에 계신 줄을 너희가 스스로 알지 못하느냐 그렇지 않으면 너희가 실격하였느니라." 바울은 믿음을 점검하라고 말하면서 고린도 교인들이 진정으로 그리스도를 믿는지를 점검하라고 한다. 즉 "약함으로 죽으셨으나 하나님의 능력으로 부활하신 그리스도"가 그들이 믿는 그리스도 인지를 확인해보라는 것이다. 그렇지 않을 경우 그들은 그리스도인 확인 시험에 낙제한 자들로서 그리스도는 물론 바울과도 상관이 없는 이들이다. 고린도 교회는 진정한 사도적 교회가 될 수 없다. 진정한 그리스도를 모르면, 바울이 진정한 그리스도의 사도인지를 알 수 없기 때문이다. "약함으로 죽으시고 부활하신 그리스도"를 믿는 믿음이 진정한 그리스도인임을 확인하는 리트머스 시험지이며, 동시에 바울이 그리스도의 진정한 사도인지를 판단하는 기준이다.[708] 바울은 언제나 약함으로 십자가에서 죽으셨으나 오직 하나님의 능력으로 다시 사신 그리스도의 사도를 따라서 약함 가운데서 온전해 지는 그리스도의 능력을 증거하며 사역해왔다(2:13-17; 4:7-15; 11:23-33; 12:9, 10). 특히 2차 방문 이후(2:1) 지금까지, 바울은 고린도 교인들에게 무능하고 열등한 사도로 업신여김을 당해왔다. 이는 고린도 교인들이 그리스도에 대한 바른 믿음을 가지지 못했기 때문이다. 고린도 교인들은 거짓 사도들이 제시하는 외적이고 육적인 가치 판단 기준에 의하여 "다른 예수," "다른 영," "다른 복음"을 받았던 것이다(5:16; 11:4). 또한 같은 가치 판단 기준으로 바울을 열등한 사도로 평가절하 했던 것이다. 바울은 거짓 사도들의 사도직 평가 기준을 한 마디로 "육체를 따르는 자랑"이라고 비판했다(11:18). 바울 자신은 육체적으로 부족한 점은 있으나, 자신도 육체적 자랑을 할 수 있다고 하면서 실제로 그 예를 들었다(10:8-15; 11:1-12:6). 그는 언변은 부족하나, 지식은 부족하지 않고(10:10; 11:6), 주께서 주신 사도권(10:8)과, 자신의 이방 선교 지역을 지키는 것(10:13, 15, 16), 순전한 복음 전파(11:4), 교회의 재정적 부담을 주지 않는 사역(11:7-12), 하나님의 선민 이스라엘 사람(11:22), 많은 고난의 사역(11:23-33), 많은 환상과 계시(12:1-7), "모든 참은 가운데 나타낸 표적과 기사와 능력"(12:12) 등이다. 그러나 바울은 이런 자랑은 어리석고 무익한 자랑이라고 했다(11:1; 16, 17, 12:1, 11). 이런 육체적 능력은 오만케하여 약함 가운

708) Chrysostom, PG 61 col. 601(*NPNF*, XII, 414); Hughes, 480-1.

데서 나타나는 그리스도의 능력이 나타나지 못하게 한다(12:10). 약함 가운데서 오직 하나님만을 의지함으로 그리스도의 능력이 나타난다(1:9). 그것이 진정한 하나님의 능력이다. 바울은 이러한 자신을 잘 알고 자신의 사역을 통해서 은혜를 받고 변화된 고린도 교인들이 반대자들의 비난에 맞서서 바울을 변호하여 주기를 원했으나, 그들이 침묵함으로 바울은 원치 않는 자찬(自讚)을 할 수 밖에 없었던 것이다(12:11). 바울은 그의 반대자들에게 근본적 문제가 있으나, 고린도 교인들도 문제가 있다고 지적한다. 그들이 바른 믿음을 스스로 지켜야할 책임을 등한히 한 것이다. 바른 믿음을 가지고서 바른 사도를 따라야할 책임을 다하지 못한 것을 지적하는 것이다. 약함으로 십자가에서 죽으시고 부활하신 그리스도를 믿는다면, 광명의 천사로 가장하여, 영광의 신학을 가르치는, 거짓 사도들의 복음을 애초에 거절했어야 했다. 그러나 그들은 이들을 받아들여 그들의 종노릇을 했다(11:20). 이제 바울의 3차 방문을 앞두고 그들이 회개하고 진정한 그리스도의 신앙을 회복하기를 바란다. 바울이 진정한 그리스도의 사도라는 증거는 바로 고린도인들이 진정한 믿음을 가지고 있느냐의 여부에 달려 있기 때문이다.

바울은 고린도 교인들이 스스로 자신들의 믿음을 점검하기를 원한다. 그들이 "그리스도 안"에서 그리스도의 죽음과 부활에 나타난 그리스도의 인격과 능력을 알고 그에게 순종하며 새로운 피조물로 긴밀한 교제를 하고 있는지, 아니면 그리스도를 "육체를 따라서" 외적인 증거와 "비본질적인 것을 본질"로 믿는 비복음적인 믿음을 가지고 있는지를 점검하라고 한다(5:12; 10:7). 바울이 아무리 믿음에 대해서 가르쳐도 결국은 당사자인 고린도 교인들이 스스로 그들의 믿음에 대해서 책임을 지게 되는 것이다. 믿음은 결코 인위적으로 생기게 할 수는 없는 것이다. 그래서 바울은 고린도 교인들의 믿음을 주관하려하지 않고 다만 도울 뿐이라고 말했다(1:24). 또한 믿음은 항상 유동적인 것으로 내외적 요인들로 말미암아 강화되거나 약화될 수 있다. 한 때 바울을 사도로 믿고 따르던 고린도 교인들이 바울을 반대하는 사도들을 따르게 된 것이다(11:20). 이런 유동적인 약한 믿음을 가진 고린도 교인들은 계속하여 자신들의 믿음을 스스로 점검하여 그 진정성을 확인해야 한다. 결국 믿음의 주체자는 믿는자 자신이기 때문이다. 더구나 바울의 3차 방문을 앞둔 시점에서 원만한 방문이 되기 위해서는 화해의 장애가 되는 불신앙적 요소들을 버리고 그리스도의 죽음과 부활을 중심으로 통일된 신앙을 가졌는지를 확인해야 하는 것이다. 바울은 그리스도 중심 신앙을 분명히 가졌다(13:3-4). 그러나 고린도 교인들의 신앙은 그들의 바울에 대한 불신적인 태도로 미루어 볼 때 의심스럽다. 그러므로 그들 스스로 그들이 그리스도의 죽음과 부활의 핵심적 신앙을 가지고 있는지를 점검해야 할 것이다(13:5).

5절에서 바울은 4절에서 말한 "그리스도의 약함의 능력"을 모든 그리스도인의 사상과 삶의 근본적 자세로 제시하고 있다. 약함으로 십자가에 달리신 그리스도가 고린도 그리스도인들의 존재의 주인으로서 그들의 마음과 생각을 지키시기를 바라는 것이다. 물론, 바울 자신은 이런 원칙으로 일관된 사역을 해오고 있다(1:23, 24; 2:4; 4:5, 7-15; 6:4-10; 7:3; 8:9; 12:15; 빌1:21). 특히 그의 서신의 마지막 부분에서(13:4-10) 바울은 이러한 원칙을 다시 적용하여 그의 사도권을 강제로 사용하여 자신을 나타내기를 원하지 않고, 고린도 교인들이 스스로 믿음에 서기를 바라고 있다.

6. "우리가 실격하지 (버리운 자가 되지) 아니한 것을 너희가 알기를 내가 바라고" (ἐλπίζω δὲ ὅτι γνώσεσθε ὅτι ἡμεῖς οὐκ ἐσμὲν ἀδόκιμοι). 바울은 5절에서 바울의 사도직에 대한 증거는 고린도 교인들의 진정한 믿음에 달려 있다고 말했다. 만일 고린도 교인들이 그리스도에 대한 진정한 믿음을 가지고 있다면, 모든 약함 중에서 사역하는 바울이 진정한 그리스도의 사도임을 알게 될 것이다. 바울은 그가 약함에서 사역해왔으나, 사도로서 실패한 것이 아니라 오히려 합격한 것이라는 것을 알게 될 것이다. 그의 약함 가운데서의 사역이 그리스도의 약함을 본받는 것이기 때문이다.[709] 그러나 반대로 그들이 잘못된 믿음을 가지고 있다면 그들이 바울을 그리스도의 사도로 인정하지 않을 것이며, 그들은 진정한 사도적 교회가 될 수 없을 것이다. 그리스도의 신앙 전통을 바르게 이어나가는 사도적 교회가 되어야 진정한 그리스도의 교회가 될 수 있다. 그러므로 바울은 그들이 자신들의 믿음을 검증하여 바른 믿음을 가지는 것이 무엇보다 중요하다고 보는 것이다. 그리스도에 대한 바른 믿음을 가지고 바울을 적합한 사도로 판정하기를 바라는 것이다. 그리스도에 대한 바른 믿음이란 인간을 구원하시기 위해서 약함으로 죽으시고 부활하신 하나님의 아들이시란 것이다. 그리스도를 진정으로 믿는 이들은 온갖 약함 가운데서 그리스도의 사도로 수고하는 바울을 진정한 그리스도의

709) Martin, 480.

사도로 인정할 것이다.

한편 이 구절에서 바울이 실격한 사도가 아니라는 사실을 고린도 교인들이 알기를 원한다는 말의 뜻이 무엇을 의미하는가에 대한 논쟁이 있다. 첫째로, 바울이 문제가 되는 고린도 교인들을 바울이 사도권을 사용하여 징계하겠다고 위협하는 의미로 보는 부정적인 견해가 있다.[710] 즉 3차 방문 시에 고린도 교인들이 회개하지 않을 경우 바울이 약함으로서가 아니라 강함으로서 문제가 된 이들을 정죄하여 그에게 요구하는 "그리스도가 말하는 증거"를 보이겠다고 말하는 것이라고 한다(13:3). 바울이 "인정받지 못한 것," 또는 "실격하지 않았다는 것"은 그리스도의 사도권을 여전히 가졌다는 뜻이라고 한다. 그리고 "너희가 알기를"(γνώσεσθε)이 미래형이므로 바울이 3차 방문 시에 고린도 교인들에게 그의 사도권을 가지고 문제 된 이들을 징벌하여 그들이 요구하는 "그리스도께서 바울 사도 안에서 말하는 증거"를 보이겠다고 엄하게 경고하는 것이라고 한다(13:3).

둘째로, 대부분의 학자들은 이런 위협적인 의미를 반대하고 오히려 바울의 적극적인 소망을 나타낸다고 본다. 즉 바울의 권고를 따라서 고린도 교인들이 자신들의 믿음을 점검하여 그리스도에 대한 바른 믿음을 가진 것으로 확증이 되면(13:5), 그들이 저절로 바울이 실격한 사도가 아니라, 진정한 그리스도의 사도로 인정하게 될 것이라는 것이다. 불트만이 지적하는 대로, 만일 바울이 이들을 위협하려고 했다면, "바란다"(ἐλπίζω)라는 말 대신 20절에서와 같이 "두려워한다"(φοβοῦμαι)는 말을 썼을 것이라고 한

710) Chrysostom, *PG* 61 col. 601(*NPNF*, XII, 415); Meyer, 508.

다.[711] 바울은 고린도 교인들이 그리스도에 대한 바른 믿음을 회복하게 되면 그들이 바울을 그리스도의 약함 가운데 그리스도의 참된 메시지를 전하는 진정한 그리스도의 사도로 인정할 것이라고 기대한다고 본다(고전 2:3; 고후 4:5, 7-15; 6:4-10; 11:7; 12:14, 15). 반대로 그들이 외적이고 육적인 가치관을 가진 사욕적인 반대자들이 거짓 사도들임을 알게 되기를 바라는 것이 암시되어 있다(10:10, 12, 15; 11:18, 22; 12:16).

"바울이 실격한 사도가 아니라는 사실을 고린도 교인들이 알기를 원한다"는 말의 뜻이 부정적인지(바울의 사도권을 사용하겠다는 위협), 긍정적인지(고린도 교인들의 바울사도 인정) 문맥을 보아도 판단하기 어렵다. 문맥에서 바울이 부정적이고 적극적인 자세를 함께 보이기 때문이다. 어느 의미든지 바울은 고린도 교회가 바울의 사도권을 존중하여 바른 관계를 갖자는 뜻이다.

7. "우리가 하나님께 너희들이 악을 행하지 않도록 (우리가 하나님께서 너희로 악을 조금도 행치 않게 하시기를) 구하노니 이는 우리가 (그리스도의 사도로) 인증 받았음(옳은 자임)을 나타내고자 함이 아니라 오직 우리는 실격한 것과(버리운 자) 같을지라도 너희로 선을 행하게 하고자 함이라" (**εὐχόμεθα δὲ πρὸς τὸν θεὸν μὴ ποιῆσαι ὑμᾶς κακὸν μηδέν, οὐχ ἵνα ἡμεῖς δόκιμοι φανῶμεν, ἀλλ' ἵνα ὑμεῖς τὸ καλὸν ποιῆτε, ἡμεῖς δὲ ὡς ἀδόκιμοι ὦμεν**).[712] 계속해서 바울은 자신의 사도직 문제를 중심 주제로 삼고서 고린도 교인들을 격려한다. 바울은 자신의 사도직

---

711) Bultmann, 249.

문제를 논하고 있으나 그가 실제로 원하는 것은 자기 유익이 아니라, 고린도 교인들의 유익이 최우선적 관심임을 밝힌다. 즉 그들이 회개하고 악을 버리고 선을 행하는 것이다. 여기서 "악"과 "선"은 일반적인 도덕적 개념과 함께 문맥에서 바울의 사도직에 대한 고린도 교인들의 바울 사도에 대한 판단과 관련되어 있다. 즉 바울을 진정한 그리스도의 사도로 인정하는 것은 선이며, 배척하는 것은 악이라는 의미가 있다.

---

712) 개역한글성경의 "하나님께서"는 문자적으로 "하나님께"라고 해야 옳다. 희랍어 원문에는 하나님이 주어가 아니라 기도의 대상이다. "…에게 기도한다"(εὐχόμεθα πρός)는 형식은 흔하게 발견된다(LXX:민 11:2; 21:7; 왕하 10:2; 또 외경, 주빌리서 22:27; 마카비2서 15:27). 즉 "우리가 너희들이 악을 행하지 않도록 하나님께 기도한다"로 해야 한다. 그러나 개역한글성경은 하나님을 의미상의 주어로 보고, "너희"를 목적으로 보았다. 그러나 사역적인 의미로 보아서 "너희"가 부정사("행하다," ποιῆσαι)의 주어도 되는 것으로 나타난다. 즉 "하나님께서 너희로 악을 조금도 행하지 않게 하시기를 기도하노라"이다. 이런 번역은 문법적으로 틀린 해석일 뿐만 아니라 의미도 어색하다. 우선 부정사("행하다," ποιῆσαι)의 주어는 대개 우리(ὑμᾶς)로 본다. 그래서 "우리가 하나님께 너희들이 악을 행하지 않도록 기도한다"로 번역한다(NEB[1970]; 휴즈, 480; Bultmann, 247; Furnish, 572; Héring, 101; 바레트, 339; Martin, 481; Thrall, 894; Barnett, 610.). 그러나 우리(ὑμᾶς)를 목적으로 보고 번역하면, 부정사의 의미상의 주어를 하나님, 또는 "우리"로 보아서 번역한다. "우리가 하나님께 하나님께서 너희를 벌하시지 않도록(너희에게 아무런 해를 주시지 않도록) 기도한다(NEB[1961]; Lietzmann, 160-162; Kümmel, 214)." 또는, "우리가 하나님께, 우리가 너희를 벌하지 않도록(너희에게 악을 행하지 않도록) 기도한다"고 번역한다. 괄호속의 말들은 주어가 하나님이냐 우리냐에 따라서 적절히 개조한 것이을 행하게 하고자 함이라"는 말에서 "너희"가 주어로 된 사실과 일치되지 않는다(Bultmann, 247). 그리고 "선"과 "악"을 모두 인간의 도덕적인 개념으로 볼 때 하나님이나 우리를 주어로 삼아서 "벌한다"는 뜻으로 번역하는 것이 맞지 않는다. 그러므로 "너희"를 주어로 보는 것이 옳다. 개역한글판의 "조금도"란 말도 원문에는 없는 의미를 강조하기 위한 추가된 번역이다. 표준 새번역은, "우리는 여러분이 악을 저지르지 않게 되기를 하나님께 기도합니다"라고 번역한다.

"우리가 하나님께 너희들이 악을 행하지 않도록 (너희로 악을 조금도 행하지 않게 하시기를) 구하노니" 에서 바울은 목회자로서 고린도 교인들이 악을 버리도록 기도한다. 또 하반절에서는 그의 기도가 고린도 교인들이 선을 행하게 하기 위함이라고 한다. 바울은 이런 말로 바울 자신의 사도직 문제에만 집착하는 것 같은 인상을 피하려는 것이다. 그러나 악을 버리고 선을 행하라는 일반적인 가르침을 말하면서 여전히 진정한 그리스도의 사도직에 대한 바른 판단을 종용하고 있다. 고린도 교인들의 바울의 사도직에 대한 판단은 바울 자신의 사사로운 문제나 지엽적인 문제가 아니라 그리스도인의 근본적인 선과 악의 판단에 속하는 중요한 문제가 되기 때문이다. 그것은 최종적 그리스도의 심판대 앞에서 책임 져야 할 선과 악의 중대한 문제로 암시하고 있는 것이다(5:10). 그러므로 바울은 고린도 교인들이 바울의 사도직 문제를 하나님의 뜻대로 바르게 판단할 수 있도록 기도하고 있다.

"오직 우리는 실격한 것과(버리운 자) 같을지라도 너희로 선을 행하게 하고자 함이라." 여기서는 "실격한 것" (ἀδόκιμοι)이란 말은 문자적으로 "시험에 낙방한," "자격 미달의" 라는 형용사이다. 사도로서의 자격을 갖추지 못해서 사도로 인정받지 못한 것을 가리킨다. 반대되는 의미는 사도권을 가지고 필요할 때(징계 시) 사용하여 사도의 권위를 보여서 그 권위를 인정 받는 것을 말한다. 바울은 전체 문맥에서 이 말의 부정적의미를 나타내기도 하고(6절) 긍정적 의미를 나타내기도 한다(7절). 본문에서는 고린도 교인들이 회개하고 선하게되어 3차 방문 시에 자신이 사도권을 써서 징계할 필요가 없게 되어 반대자들이 보기에 그를 무능한 "자격 미달" 의 사도로 보더라도 고린도 교인들이 회개하여 선하게 되면 상관이 없다는 것이다. 바울이 원하는 것은 3차 방문 이전에 고린도 교인들이 회개하고 바르게 판단하여 바른 믿음을 가지게 되는 것이다. 바울은 고린도 교인들이 회개하지 않음으로써 자신이 방문 시에 사도권을 가지고 그들을 정죄함으로써 사도로서의 권위를 인증 받기를 원하지 않는다("우리가 [그리스도의 사도로서] 인증 받았음을 나타내고자 함이 아니라"). 고린도 교인들이 회개하는 경우에 바울이 더 이상 엄한 사도권 행사를 할 필요가 없어져서, 반대자들에게 바울은 역시 무능하고 약한 사도라고 무시당하고 인증 받지 못하더라도("우리는 실격한 것과[버리운 자] 같을지라도"), 다수의 고린도 교인들이 바른 믿음을 가지게 되어 바른 판단기준을 가지고 바울을 바르게 판단하게 되는 것을 원한다("선을 행하게 하고자 함이라")(12:19; 13:9).[713] 다수의 고린도 교인들이 회개하고 바울을 인증하여 다시 그리스도의 약함으로 교제하게 되면, 반대자들은 바울은 떠나 있으면 (편지로) 큰 소리치고, 실제로 만나면 아무것도 못하는 약한 사람이라고 비난할 것이다(10:1, 10).[714] 그리고 그들은 계속 그의 사도적 권세를 징계로 증명해보이라고 요구할 것이다. 그러나 바울은 아무런 사도권을

713) Martin(481-2)과 Thrall(895)은 7절에서의 "실격한 것(버리운 자)" (ἀδόκιμοι)이 6절에서의 그것과 의미가 다르다고 하나 모두 "약함으로 말미암아 사도로서 인증 받지 못하는 것"이라는 공통된 뜻이 있다. 다만 긍정적 의미와 부정적 의미로 달리 쓰인다. 6절에서는 믿음을 회복한 고린도 교인들에게 바울이 그리스도의 약함의 능력을 본받는 사도로서 인증 받게 되는 긍정적 의미로 쓰이고, 7절에서는 고린도 교인들이 믿음을 회복하는 경우, 바울이 사도권을 쓰지 않게 됨으로써, 사도적 증거를 요구하는 반대자들에게(13:3), 약한 사도로 무시당하게 되고, 그들의 판단 기준에 의해서, 그리스도의 능력 있는 사도로 인증을 받지 못하게 되는 부정적 의미로 쓰이고 있다. 결국 바울은 같은 말로 6, 7절에서 각기 긍정적, 부정적인 뜻을 나타내고 있는 것이다.

714) Hughes, 482; Martin, 481.

쓰지 못하는 무능한 사도로 배척을 받아도, 그의 약함의 진리를 끈질기게 지키면서, 고린도 교인들이 믿음에 바로 서게 되는 것을 원한다는 것이다(13:8, "우리는 진리를 거스려 아무것도 할 수 없고 오직 진리를 위할 뿐이니"). 바울은 자신은 희생되더라도 고린도 교인들이 바로 서는 되는 것이 그의 목회 소신임을 누차 밝혔다(2:4; 4:7-15; 5:14, 15; 6:5-10; 7:2; 11:11; 12:14, 15, 19). 특히 12장 19절에서 바울은 자신의 사도직 변명이 고린도후서의 주된 목적이 아니라, "너희의 덕을 세우는 것" 이 그 진정한 목적이라고 했다. 물론 바울의 사도직 확립과 고린도 교회를 세우는 것은 직결된 문제이다(10:8; 13:10). 그러나 바울의 사도직 확립의 동기는 자신의 유익이 아니라 고린도 교인들의 유익임을 다시 밝히는 것이다. 이런 희생적 자세가 죄인을 사랑하여 죽으신 그리스도가 보내신 진정한 그리스도의 사도의 마땅한 자세라고 일관되게 믿기 때문이다. 이렇게 그리스도의 십자가의 약함을 따라 교회를 세워야 진정한 사도적 교회가 되고 온전한 그리스도의 교회가 되기 때문이다. 마귀는 그리스도의 교회가 비복음적인 율법적 권세가 주장하는 인위적이고 세속적인 조직으로 되게 하기 위해서 애쓴다. 바울이 2장 7절에서 "눈물의 편지" 에서 징계를 지시하여 징계 받은 이를 이제는 용서하라고 한 것은 복음의 교회를 유대교 회당의 율법주의와 혼동케 하려는 마귀의 궤계를 알았기 때문이라고 했다(2:11). 그러므로 여기서도 바울은 고린도 교회가 진정한 복음적 그리스도적 사도적 교회되게 하기 위해서 자신의 사도권을 써서 반대자들을 정리하라는 주장을 쉽게 받아들이지 않는 것이다.

두 개의 ἵνα절은 바울의 기도의 목적 보다 기도의 내용을 나누어 말하는 것으로 본다.[715] ἵνα절로 나오는 말들이 바울이 기도의 결과로 이루어지기를 바라는 것이라기보다는 기도의 내용으로 보는 것이다.[716] 즉, 바울은 고린도 교인들이 회개를 하지 않아서 자신이 사도권을 발동하여 이들을 정죄함으로써 반대자들에게 사도로 인증 받는 것을 원치 않고, 고린도 교인들이 회개하고 바른 믿음을 가지게 되는 것이 그의 기도임을 밝힌다. 그러나 그 내용을 기도의 목적으로 보아도 전체 의미에 별 영향을 주지는 않는다.

여기서 "악을 행하지 않도록"에서 "악"(κακόν)은 12장 20, 21절에 나오는 분열과 성적인 죄를 가리킬 수 있고, 또 그들의 믿음을 점검하라는 명령을 듣지 않고 거역하면서 바울의 사도적 증거를 계속 요구하는 것이라고 볼 수 있다. 이와 대조적으로 "너희가 선을 행하게 하고자 함이라"에서 "선"(καλόν)이라는 말은 12장 20, 21절의 악을 다 버리고 회개하고, 그들이 스스로의 믿음을 점검하여(13:5) 진정한 그리스도인이 되어서, 바울을 진정한 사도로 믿고 받아들이는 것이다. 바울은 고린도 교인들이 회개하지 않아서 그들을 징계함으로써 사도로 인증 받는 것은 원치 않으나, 그들이 회개하여 사도 바울을 진정한 그리스도의 사도로 인증 하는 것은 원한다(13:6). 바울은 그 자신이 진정한 그리스도의 사도임을 굳게 믿기 때문에 자신을 받아들이는 것이 곧 바른 그리스도의 믿음을 가지는 것이고 또 그것이 하나님 앞에서 선한 행위라고 생각하기 때문이다.

---

715) Plummer는 목적절로 본다(377).

716) G. P. Wiles, *Paul's Intercessory Prayers*, SNTSMS 24 (Cambridge: University Press, 1974), 244; Martin, 481; Thrall, 894-5.

8. "우리는 진리를 거스려 아무것도 할 수 없고 오직 진리를 위할 뿐이니…"(οὐ γὰρ δυνάμεθά τι κατὰ τῆς ἀληθείας ἀλλὰ ὑπὲρ τῆς ἀληθείας.). 여기서 "진리"를 복음으로 보기도 하고, 또는 도덕적 진리로 보기도 한다.[717] 또 다른 견해는 7절과 관련 시켜서 고린도 교회 사태의 진전 상황을 나타낸다고 본다. 즉 바울은 고린도 교인들이 바르게 되면 사도권을 쓰지 않을 것이며("우리는 진리를 거스려 아무 것도 할 수 없고"), 사태의 추이를 따라서 일할 수밖에 없다는 뜻으로 본다.[718] 그러나 불트만이 지적한 것과 같이, 진리(ἀλήθεια)라는 말이 "일의 실제 정황"을 나타내는 예가 없다는 것이다.[719] 또 진리를 복음으로 보는 견해는 너무 막연하고, 본문의 문맥에 적절한 것 같지 않다. 우리는 여기서 진리란 그리스도께서 약한 가운데 죽으셨으나 하나님의 능력으로 다시 사신 것과 같이(13:5), 그리스도를 진정으로 믿는 이들에게 그리스도의 능력이 약한 가운데 나타나는 진리를 가리킨다. 바울은 이 진리를 따라서 그리스도의 사도로서 자신의 유익을 돌보지 않고 교인들의 유익을 위해 헌신적으로 봉사한다. 바울은 자신은 약하고 열등한 사도로 여김을 받더라도, 고린도 교인들이 바른 믿음

---

717) Denney, 381; Furnish, 573; 579; Filson, 421; Tasker, 189; Martin, 483. 4:2; 6:7; 11:10; 참조, 갈2:14. 다른 구절은 복음 진리를 나타내는 것이 분명하나, 11:10의 "진리"는 문맥에서 그리스도의 "약함의 능력"을 가리키는 진리로 본다. 바울은 이 원칙에 의해서 재정적으로 하나님에게만 전적으로 의지하는 사역을 한다. 한편 Barnett은 진리를 복음 진리와 함께 도덕적 진리로 본다(7:14; 11:31; 12:6).

718) Chrysostom, *PG* 61 cols., 602-3(*NPNF*, XII, 415-16); Meyer, 511; Plummer, 378; Hughes, 483; Bruce, 254.

719) Bultmann, 250.

을 가지고 바로 서는 것을 원한다. 바로 이런 자세를 가진 바울이야 말로 그리스도가 그의 안에서 말씀하시는 사도로서 검증되는 것이다. 또 "진리"가 실제로 이와 유사하게 쓰인 경우가 있다고 본다. 11장 11절에서 바울이 "그리스도의 진리가 내 속에 있으니"라고 말한 것은 그리스도의 겸비 또는 약함을 가리키며, 그 문맥에서는 바울이 스스로를 낮추어서 교회에 재정적 누를 끼치지 않으려는 자세를 가리킨다. 바울은 십자가의 그리스도의 겸비를 진리로 삼아서 그리스도의 희생과 약함을 본받는 사역을 해왔다(1:24; 4:5, 7-15; 6:4-10; 11:7; 12:9, 10, 14, 15; 13:5). 이런 해석이 문맥의 의미와도 맞는다. 7절의 "우리는 실격한 것과 같을지라도 너희로 선을 행하게 하고자 함이라"는 말과 9절의 "우리가 약할 때에 너희의 강한 것을 기뻐하고 또 이것을 위하여 구하니 곧 너희의 온전하게 되는 것이라"의 배경이 되는 바울의 "약함"의 목회 원칙을 말하는 것이다. 특히 9절은 "왜냐하면," "이는…"(γὰρ)로 시작하여 앞의 진술과 연결하여 말한다. 즉, 9절에서 바울이 약함 가운데 사역하면서 고린도 교인들이 강한 것을 기뻐하는 것은 그들이 온전해 지기를 원하기 때문이라고 말하는 것은 8절의 "약함의 진리"를 그의 사역과 관련하여 설명하는 것이라고 본다. 바울의 모든 사역이 "그리스도의 약함"을 본받아 자신은 희생하고 남에게 유익을 주는 사역이다. 이런 사역은 고린도 교회의 거짓 사도들이 사욕적인 사역과 대조된다(11:20). 그리스도의 교회는 외적 권세가 아니라 그리스도의 십자가의 약함을 따라 세워야 온전하게 되기 때문이다(2:11).

9. "우리가 약할 때에 너희의 강한 것을 기뻐하고 또 이것을 위

하여 구하니 곧 너희의 온전하게 되는 것이라"(χαίρομεν γὰρ ὅταν ἡμεῖς ἀσθενῶμεν, ὑμεῖς δὲ δυνατοὶ ἦτε· τοῦτο καὶ εὐχόμεθα, τὴν ὑμῶν κατάρτισιν.). 편지의 마지막으로 접어들면서 지금까지의 엄한 어조가 보다 부드럽고 따뜻한 어조로 나타난다. 이 구절은 한글개역에는 분명하게 나타나지 않으나 "왜냐하면," "이는…"(γὰρ)이란 말로 시작해야 한다. 앞의 진술에 대한 이유를 나타내는 것이다. 바울은 4절 이후 8절까지 거듭 주장해온 "약함의 진리"를 다시 자신의 사역에 적용하며 말한다.[720] 고린도 교인들이 바른 믿음을 가져서 그가 사도권을 사용하지 않게 되어 무능한 사도라는 평가를 받아도 바울은 기뻐할 것이다. 바울이 원하는 진정한 사도의 표는 강권을 쓰는 것보다도 그리스도의 약함에 따라서 다수의 교인들의 유익("온전하게 되는 것"-회개와 바른 믿음 회복)을 위해서 라면 자신의 명예(사도권 사용) 같은 것을 기쁘게 희생하는 것이다(2:4; 4:5, 7-15, 5:14; 6:6-10; 11:11; 12:9, 10, 15; 13:3-4). 그것이 그리스도의 사역의 핵심적 특징이기 때문이다. 복음 사역은 외적인 능력보다 죄인을 구원하시기 위해 죽으신 그리스도의 사랑을 나타내는 것이다(2:4, 8; 5:14-15; 12:14-15; 고전 16:14; 갈 5:13; 엡 5:2; 빌 2:2).

"너희의 강한 것"은 믿음이 강해지는 것을 의미한다.[721] 그리스도를 믿는 믿음이 강해지면 결국 "온전하게 되는 것이다." 바울은 그의 약함의 사역의 목적을 고린도 교인들이 믿음과 삶에서 영적으로 온전하게 되는 데 두고 있다(12:19).

---

720) Barrett, 340; Furnish, 57-80.

721) Meyer, 511; Thrall, 898.

"온전하게 되는 것"(κατάρτισιν)은 희귀 명사이지만, 동사형 "온전하게 되다"(καταρτίζω)의 뜻은 도덕적, 종교적 온전함에 이르는 것을 말한다(참조, 엡 4:12).[722] 또한 "잘못된 것이 바르게 회복되는 것"이란 뜻도 있다.[723] 잘못된 믿음에서 온전한 믿음의 회복, 또는 그리스도와의 소원한 관계에서 바른 관계로 회복, 바울과의 불화의 관계에서 화해의 관계로의 회복을 뜻한다고 볼 수 있다.[724] 그러나 문맥에서 온전한 믿음에 이르는 것이 곧 그리스도와 또 바울과의 온전한 교제를 의미함으로 상호 관련이 된다(13:4, 5, 6). 그러므로 12장 19절에서 바울은 고린도 교인들의 덕을 세우기 위해서 고린도후서를 썼다고 했다. 13장 10절에서는 그의 사도적 권세는 파하는 것이 아니라 세우는 것이라고 했다(13:10). 고린도 교인들의 신앙회복이 곧 고린도 교회가 사도적 교회로 온전하게 되는 것과 직결된다. 그들이 온전한 믿음에 굳게 서서 바울이 아무런 사도권을 발동할 필요가 없게 되어 다시 무능하고 약한 사도로 보이게 되어도, 바울은 기뻐할 것이다. 혹 고린도 교인들이 자신이 방문 할 때까지 회개하지 않아서 온전하지 못하므로 그들을 징계한다 해도 바울은 징계로 말미암아 그들이 악을 버리고 선을 행하여 온전하게 되기를 기도할 것이다(13:7; 고전 5:5). 여기서 바울은 다시 그의 "약함의 능력"의 사역을 그리스도의 사도된 증표로 제시한다. 그리스도의 사도의 진정한 본질적인 권세는 외적인 권세가 아니라 그리스도께서 사랑과 인내로 죽으신 십자가의 약함 가운데 나타나는 권세이다(1:12; 12:12). 이 권세는 종으로서

722) Filson, 421; Hughes, 484; Thrall, 898.

723) Barrett, 430; Plummer, 378; Allo, 340; Martin, 484.

724) Martin, 484; Thrall, 899.

의 지도자의 리더십이다(the Servant Leadership). 바울의 반대자들은 이런 권세가 아니라 세속적이고 인위적인 외적 육체적 모양을 자랑하는 권세이며, 권위주의적 횡포를 부리는 권세이다(3:1; 5:12; 10:7, 12, 15; 11:18). 문제는 고린도 교인들이 이런 잘못된 비사도적인 권세를 진정한 사도적 권세로 미혹 받아 복종하는 것이다(11:20). 그리고 바울 사도의 "약함"의 권세를 비사도적 권세로 의심하는 것이다(13:3). 바울은 이런 고린도 교인들에게 계속해서 진정한 사도적 권세는 약함 가운데서 그리스도의 능력을 나타내는 것이라고 가르치고 있다. 물론 바울은 필요하면 법적 사도권을 사용하는 수밖에 없음을 앞서서 말했다(13:1-2). 그러나 그것은 비본질적인 사도적 권세이다. 본질적 사도적 권세는 그리스도의 십자가의 약함을 통해서 나타나는 하나님의 능력으로 말미암는 권세이다. 그의 진정한 소원은 언제나 그리스도의 약함으로 사역하기를 원한다. 그러므로 그의 강한 사도적 권세를 한번 증명해 보라는 반대자들의 요구에 굴복하기를 원치 않는다(13:3, 7, 10). 그가 원하는 것은 고린도 교인들이 온전케 되는 것이며, 고린도 교회를 그리스도의 약함을 따라서 세우는 것이다. 그리스도의 약함을 따라서 세운 교회라야 온전하고 진정한 그리스도의 교회가 될 수 있기 때문이다(2:11).

10. "이를 인하여 내가 떠나 있을 때에 이렇게 쓰는 것은 대면할 때에 주께서 너희를 파하려 하지 않고 세우려 하여 내게 주신 그 권세를 따라 엄하지 않게 하려 함이니라"(Διὰ τοῦτο ταῦτα ἀπὼν γράφω, ἵνα παρὼν μὴ ἀποτόμως χρήσωμαι κατὰ τὴν ἐξουσίαν ἣν ὁ κύριος ἔδωκέν μοι εἰς οἰκοδομὴν καὶ οὐκ εἰς

καθαίρεσιν). 10장에서 시작된 엄격한 경고의 메시지를 마친다. "떠나 있을 때"(ἀπὼν)는 1절에서 도 나타난다. "대면할 때"(παρὼν)는 1절에서 다른 말(κατὰ πρόσωπον)로 나타나지만, 10장 11절과 13장 2절에서 나타난다. 바울은 가다듬은 자세로 지금까지 솔직하고 담대하게 한 말들로 시험받지 않도록 양해를 구한다. 바울이 엄한 말로 편지를 쓴 것은 3차 방문 이전에 모든 일이 원만하게 이루어져 정작 방문 시에는 사도권을 발동하는 일이 없게 되기를 원하기 때문이다(13:7).[725] 앞서 1, 2절에서 말한 "문제가 된 이들"에 대한 치리 계획이 단순히 경고가 아니라 실제 계획이지만 바울이 진정으로 원하는 것은 방문 이전에 이들의 문제가 자체적으로 해결되기를 촉구하는 것이다. 설령 사도적 권세를 부득불 써야하는 경우에도 그는 파괴적이 아닌 건설적인 방향으로 쓸 것이다. "파하려 하지 않고 세우려고 내게 주신 권세"는 10장 8절에서 언급한 말과 매우 유사하다. 바울이 지금까지 한 모든 말은 고린도 교인들을 세우기 위함이다(12:19). 그의 반대자들이 바울에게 원하는 사도적 권세의 사용은 자칫하면 교회를 건설하기 보다는 파괴할 수 있다(2:4-11). 사실 2차 방문 이후 "엄한 편지"로 이런 강력한 사도권이 여러 번 사용되었으나 별 효과가 없었다. 지금도 같은 엄한 말로 썼다. 그러나 이런 엄격한 자세는 바울이 지금까지 견지해온 약함의 신학에 맞지 않는다. 바울은 끝까지 사도권의 파괴적 사용 가능성을 주저하면서 자신의 약함의 사역 가운데 "그리스도의 능력"이 나타나기를 소망한다. 즉 고린도 교인들이 스스로 회개하고 믿음을 회복하는 것이다. 설령 그의 권

725) Barrett, 327.

세를 써야 한다 해도 고린도 교회를 세우기 위해 건설적으로 쓸 것이다.

바울의 3차 방문이 성공적 이었는지는 분명히 알 수 없으나, 성공적일 수 있었다는 가능성은 있다. 해리스(Harris)는 바울이 로마서를 고린도에서 썼는데, 만일 고린도 교회가 지금처럼 어려웠다면 로마서에서 기도 부탁을 했을 수 있으나 아무런 문제를 제시하지 않는다는 것을 지적한다.[726] 15장 30, 31절에 "유대에 순종치 않는 자들"을 위한 기도를 부탁하지만 그것은 미래를 위한 염려를 반영한 것이다. 대신 거기서 예루살렘 성도를 위한 헌금을 예루살렘 성도들이 받아 주도록 기도를 부탁 하고 있고, 15장 28절에서는 고린도 교회(마게도냐와 아가야)에서 예루살렘 성도들을 위한 헌금을 모두 마쳤다는 말도 있다. 고린도 교회 문제가 어느 정도 해결이 되지 않았다면 생각하기 어려운 일이다(8, 9장). 그러나 물론 바울의 방문이 성공적 화해의 방문이 되었다 해도 고린도 교회의 문제가 영구적으로 해결된 것 같지는 않다. 클레멘트 1서(주후 96년)는 고린도 교인들이 다시 옛날 방식으로 되돌아갔고 바울의 영향력이 약화되었다고 말하고 있다.

주해(12:19–13:10):

바울은 12장 19절-13장 10절에서 고린도 교인들에게 3차 방문 이전에 그들의 죄를 회개하고 개혁하여 방문이 원만하게 되기를 바란다. 이런 논조는 6장 14절-7장 3절에서 세속적 생활을 청산하고 거룩한 생활을 촉구한 것과 유사하다. 거기서도 여기서와 같이

---

726) Harris, 404-405.

바울은 고린도 교인들에게 그들의 죄와 바울의 사도직에 대한 의구심을 버리고 화해할 것을 촉구한다(7:2, 3). 그러나 여기서 바울은 보다 구체적으로 그들의 죄를 분열의 죄와 성적 죄들을 열거하고(12: 20, 21), 그에 대한 실제적인 징벌을 계획하고, 고린도 교인들이 그들의 믿음을 스스로 점검하기를 원한다(13:5). 그들이 그리스도 중심의 믿음, 특히 "약함" 으로 죽으셨으나 하나님의 능력으로 부활하신 그리스도를 믿을 때, 바울을 진정한 사도로 인정하고 영접할 수 있기 때문이다(13:4-6). 바울은 고린도 교인들이 요구하는 사도권 사용으로 문제가 된 이들을 징벌할 수도 있으나, 그런 것은 그의 "약함의 능력" 의 목회 원칙에 맞지도 않고 이전의 경험으로 미루어 보아 후유증도 심하다(2:4-11; 고전 5:5). 그가 진정으로 원하는 것은 그런 강제적 사도권을 쓰는 대신에 고린도 교인들이 회개하고 죄를 척결하는 것이다(13:7, 10). 바울은 고린도 교인들의 죄와 바울 사도에 대한 배척을 매우 심각한 문제로 본다. 그것은 궁극적인 선과 악의 문제로서 마지막 날에 그리스도의 심판대 앞에서 판단 받아야 할 문제라고 암시한다. 그래서 바울은 편지를 마치기 전에 고린도 교인들이 악을 버리고 선을 행하도록 기도한다(13:7). 바울은 이런 심각한 문제의 가장 좋은 해결은 강권이 아니라 여전히 약함과 사랑의 힘, 곧 십자가의 능력이라고 보는 것이다(13:8, 9). 여기서 바울은 그리스도교 지도자들의 본보기를 보여 주고 있다. 즉 종으로서의 지도자(the Servant Leadership)이다. 이런 지도자 상은 권세로 사람들을 휘어잡는 세상의 잘못된 지도자상이나, 특히 고린도 교회의 거짓 사도들이 고린도 교인들을 종으로 삼아 함부로 대하는 권위주의적 지도자 상과 대조된다(11:20). 4장 5절에서 바울은 그가 고린도 교인들에게 그리스도의 주되심과 고린도 교인들의 종 된 것을 전했다고 했는데, 그의 반대자들의 행태는 이와는 대조적이다. 모든 그리스도 교회의 지도자들은 이런 외적, 법적 권세를 어쩔 수 없이 써야 할 때가 있으나, 또 이를 쓰고 싶은 유혹도 있으나, 이를 최대로 억제하고, 그리스도의 은혜와 약함의 지혜로 사역해야 할 것을 보여준다. 모든 그리스도교 지도자는 "그리스도의 사랑이 강권하시는 도다"라는 말씀대로 그리스도의 사랑의 힘으로 사역해야 한다(5:14). 그것은 단순한 패배주의적 변명이나 유약함이 아니라, 하나님의 사람으로써 하나님께 전적으로 의지하는 것이기 때문이다. 또한 약함을 통해 진정한 그리스도의 능력이 나타나기 때문이다(12:10, 9). 그 약함의 능력조차도 인위적 물리적 능력이 아니라 하나님의 은혜와 사랑의 능력이다. 그리고 그 사랑의 능력은 모든 피조물의 능력을 능가한다(10:4; 롬 8:39). 끝으로 바울은 그의 모든 권면은 오로지 고린도 교인들을 위한 바울의 깊은 사랑에서 나온 것임을 말한다(13:9-10). 모든 경과와 질책 가운데서도 그리스도의 화해의 사도로서의 본분을 지키고 있다. 고린도 교회를 그리스도 중심의 사도적 교회로 세우는 것이 그의 궁극적인 목적이기 때문이다(10:8; 12:19; 13:10). 이렇게 보면 바울은 고린도 후서에서 처음부터 끝까지 그리스도의 사도로서 고린도 교인들과의 진정한 화해를 위해 편지를 쓰고 있다.

VI. 결 론－인사와 축복기도 (13:11-13)

본문:

11. 마지막으로 말하노니 형제들아 기뻐하라 온전케 되며 위로를 받으며 마음을 같이 하며 평안 할지어다. 또 사랑과 평강의 하나님이 너희와 함께 계시리라. 거룩하게 입맞춤으로 서로 문안하라. 12. 모든 성도가 너희에게 문안하느니라. 13. 주 예수 그리스도의 은혜와 하나님의 사랑과 성령의 교통하심이 너희 무리와 함께 있을지어다.

본문비평:

1. 11절의 χαίρειν(기뻐하라)을 goodbye나 "안녕"이라는 말로 보는 번역들이 많지만[1] 원래의 의미대로 보는 이들도 많다(살전 5:16).[2] 계속되는 다른 세 개의 명령형 동사들 앞에 있어서 원래의 의미로 보아야 한다는 것이다.[3] 우리는 개역한글성경을 그대로 따른다.

2. 11절의 καταρτίζεσθε("온전케 되며")가 수동태로 보면, 개역한글성경처럼 "온전케 되다"가되고(살전 3:10),[4] 중간태이면, "온전케 되기를 되기를 힘쓰라"로 번역된다.[5] 개역한글성경은

---

1) Plummer, 380; Denney, 384; Bultmann, 252; Barrett, 342; "farewell": KJV, RSV, NEV; "good-bye": NIV.

2) Furnish, 581; Hughes, 486; Moule, *Idiom Book*, 161; Martin, 490; Thrall, 906.

3) Thrall, 906.

4) Windisch, 426; Allo, 342; Furnish, 581, 582.

5) NIV; Hughes, 486; Harris, 405; "고쳐라," "회복하라" RSV, NEB; Barrett, 342; Filson, 423; Martin, 491..

문자적으로는 수동태이지만, 결국 능동적(중간태적) 의미를 갖고 있다. 여기서 우리는 다른 학자들을 따라서 중간태의 의미를 따른다.

3. 11절의 παρακαλεῖσθε("위로를 받으며")은 축약동사(παρακαλέω)로서 수동태이면, "나의 호소를 들으라"는 뜻이 되고,[6]중간태라면, "서로 격려하라"는 뜻이 된다.[7] 문맥에서 모두 적절하다고 볼 수 있다. 그리고 개역한글성경의 번역("위로를 받으며")도 가능하다(1:6).

4. 11절의 φρονεῖτε("마음을 같이 하며")도 축약동사(φρονέω)로서 직설법 2인칭 복수이거나 명령형 2인칭 복수가 된다. 다른 명령형 복수와 함께 있으므로 당연히 복수 명사로 보아야 한다.

5. 11절의 'Ασπάσασθε("문안하라")는 과거명령형이다. 다른 동사는 현재 명령이나 이동사만 과거 명령인 특별한 이유는 없다. 단지 일상적 권면을 나타내기 때문이다.[8]

6. 11절의 ἐν ἁγίῳ φιλήματι("거룩하게 입맞춤으로")는 ℵ B D K에 ἐν φιλήματι ἁγίῳ은 A F G L에 나타난다. 후자가 다른 데 나

---

6) RSV, NIV("take our appeal to heart"); NEV("accept my appeal"); Hughes, 487; Furnish, 582; Plummer, 380.

7) Barrett, 342; Bultmann, 252; 참조, Windisch, 426; Martin, 491.

8) Martin, 491.

9) Plummer, 381.

타난 유형을 따르는 것으로 보인다(고전16:20; 롬16:16; 살전5:26).[9)]

7. 대부분의 영어 번역본들이 14절도 되어 있다(KJV, RSV, NEB, ESV, NIV). 이렇게 나누어 진 것은 1572년 출판된 Bishop's Bible부터이다.[10)]

8. 13절의 Χριστοῦ(그리스도)가 B ψ 1881에는 없다.

9. 13절의 "성령의 교통하심"(ἡ κοινωνία τοῦ ἁγίου πνεύματος)은 성령을 주격 2격으로 볼 때의 해석이고[11)] "성령을 나눔"은 목적격 2격으로 볼 때의 번역이다.[12)] 어느 쪽도 가하나, 앞의 그리스도(Χριστοῦ)가 주격 2격이므로 이를 따라서 "성령의 교통하심"으로 본다. 두 의미를 함께 보아서 "성령의 함께 나눔의 교제"로 번역하기 한다.[13)]

10. ἀμήν("아멘")이 $\aleph^{c}$ ψ k it^{d} vg syr cop goth 에는 나오고, p^{46} $\aleph^{*}$ A B F G 33 it^{g} vg^{mss} arm^{mss} ετη에 는 없다.[14)]

---

10) Furnish, 583.

11) Plummer, 383; Bruce, 255; Tasker, 191; Hughes, 488; Harris, 406; A. Schlatter, *Paulus, der Bote Jesu: Eine Deutung seiner Briefe an die Korinther* (Stutgart: Calwer Verlag, 1969), 62; Wendland, 234; Martin, 491;

12) Barrett, 344; Hauck, *TDNT* 3:807; Furnish, 584; Windisch, 428; Lietzmann, 162; Bultmann, 253; J. Hainz, "Koinonia: Kirche als Geneischaft bei Paulus," *Biblische Untersuchungen* 16 (1972), 47-51.

13) Martin, 491; Denney, 388..

14) Metzger, *Textual Commentary*, 588.

11. 모든 바울 서신은 바울의 마지막 말이 끝에 각 서신의 명칭이 기재되어 있듯이 고린도후서 끝에도 πρὸς Κορινθίους β(고린도후서)라는 말이 기재되어 있다.[15)]

내용개요:

이 부분은 고린도후서를 끝맺는 말이다. 바울은 "마지막으로"라는 말로 시작한다. 대체로 바울의 서신들의 끝맺는 말과 같이, 인사, 찬양, 축도로 되어 있다(고전16:19-24; 빌4:21-23).[16)] 이런 끝맺는 말은 편지가 예배 중에 읽혀지기 때문에 예배를 고려한 인사라고 본다(고전16:20-24).[17)] 10-13절의 편집설을 주장하는 이들 가운데, 이 부분이 원래 9장의 끝에 있었는데, 10-13절을 편집할 때 13장 뒤에 부친 것이라는 이들이 있다.[18)] 이를 반대하여 원래부터 13장 끝에 있었다고 보는 이들도 있다.[19)] 그러나 바울 당시 헬라세계에서 두 서신을 편집할 때는 두서신의 처음과 마지막

---

15) Metzger, *The Text of the New Testament*, 205, 206.

16) R. P. Martin, *New Testament Foundations* 2 (Grand Rapids: Eerdmans, 1978), 246, 247; L. G. Champion, *Benedictions and Doxologies in the Epistles of Paul* (Oxford: Published privately, 1934), 20, 25-37; B. Rigaux, *The Letters of St. Paul*, ed. and tr. S. Yonich (Chicago: Franciscan Herald Press, 1968), 131-33; W. Doty, *Letters in Primitive Christianity* (Philadelphia: Fortress, 1973), 39-43; T. Y. Mullins, "Benedictions as a New Testament Form," *AUS* 15(1977), 59-64.

17) C. F. D. Moule, "A Reconstruction of the Context of Maranatha Invocation and Jude 14, 15(I Enoch 1:9)," in *Christ and Spirit in the New Testament*, FS C. F. D. Moule, ed. B. Londars and S. S. Smalley (Cambridge: University Press, 1973), 189-96; Martin, 492.

18) Strachan, 145.

19) Plummer, 379, 380; Windisch, 426.

을 모두 그대로 함께 썼다. 특별한 경우에만 편집자가 조정 하였다.[20] 또 13장 11-13절은 그 앞의 13장 9절과 잘 연결된다. 기뻐하라는 말이 13장 9절과 11절에 다 들어 있다. 마찬가지로 "온전하게 된다"는 말이 양쪽에 모두 있다. 그리고 13장 11-13절을 9장 끝에 부쳐보면 어색한 것이 금새 들어난다. 9장은 낙관적이나 10장과 13장에는 모두 경고와 불안함이 지배적이다.

바울은 11절에서 4개의 명령형 동사로 권면한다. "기뻐하라," "온전케 되라," "위로를 받으라," 그리고 "마음을 같이하여 평안할 지어다." 바울은 "형제들아"라고 사랑의 어조로 고린도 교인들을 부르면서 이들이 믿는 자들로서 그리스도 안에서 마땅히 해야 할 일들을 이런 말로 요약하고 있다고 볼 수 있다. 이 모든 말들은 고린도 교회의 어려운 사태를 고려할 때 단순한 겉치레 권면이 아닌 의미심장한 사도적 당부인 것이다. 특별히 사랑과 평강의 하나님의 임재를 약속하는 것도 고린도 교회에게는 단순한 형식적 의미 이상일 것이다(고전 14:33; 롬 15:33; 16:20; 살전 5:23; 빌 4:9). 사실 앞의 4개의 동사는 바울이 고린도후서에서 가르친 말들이다. "기뻐한다"는 동사는 7장 9, 13, 16절, 12장 9, 10, 15절, 13장 9절에 비교적 많이 언급된다. "온전케 되라"는 말은 13장 9절에 나오고(참조, 7:1; 12:9), 위로는 1장에서 7장에서 자주 언급되었다. 고린도 교인들이 바울의 권면의 말씀들을 잘 지키면 그 결과로 사랑과 평강의 하나님이 함께 계실 것이다. 사랑과 평강을 선물로 주실 것이다.[21]

---

20) Furnish, 585.

21) Martin, 494.

바울은 계속해서 거룩한 입맞춤을 권한다. 이것도 바울의 서신에 나오는 공통적인 가르침이다(고전 16:20; 롬 16:16; 살전 5:26; 참조, 벧전 5:14). 이것이 기독교인들만의 전통은 아닌 것 같으나 유대교 회당 전통이라는 증거도 없다. 사랑하는 형제들 사이의 입맞춤으로 교회의 사랑과 평강을 유지하고 확인하는 중요한 의례가 된 것이라고 본다.

문안의 인사도 바울 서신의 마지막 부분에서 나오는 것이다(빌 4:22; 고전 16:20; 딛 3:15). 그리고 삼위일체 하나님의 축도로 끝맺는다. 여기 나오는 축도가 가장 잘 정리된 축도라고 한다.[22] 바울은 고린도 교회에서 "다른 예수"와 "거짓 영"을 전하는 거짓 사도들의 잘못된 가르침과 영향력으로 부터 삼위일체 하나님의 이름과 역할로 고린도 교회를 사도적 교회로 보호하고 막아주는 사도로서 축복한다(11:4). 바울은 모든 경고와 질책 후에도 사랑과 기대의 축복으로 그리스도의 화해의 사도로서의 품위를 끝까지 지키고 있다.

주석:

11. "마지막으로 말하노니 형제들아 기뻐하라 온전케 되며 위로를 받으며 마음을 같이 하며 평안할지어다 또 사랑과 평강의 하나님이 너희와 함께 계시리라 거룩하게 입맞춤으로 서로 문안하라" (Λοιπόν, ἀδελφοί, χαίρετε, καταρτίζεσθε, παρακαλεῖσθε,

---

22) 롬 16:20; 고전 16:23; 갈 6:18; 빌 4:16; 살전 5:28; 살후 3:18; 빌 25; 골 4:18; 딤전 6:21; 딤후 4:22; 딛 3:15; Filson, 424; Martin, 495..

τὸ αὐτὸ φρονεῖτε, εἰρηνεύετε, καὶ ὁ θεὸς τῆς ἀγάπης καὶ εἰρήνης ἔσται μεθ᾽ ὑμῶν Ἀσπάσασθε ἀλλήλους ἐν ἁγίῳ φιλήματι). "마지막으로 형제들아"는 두 말이 함께 또는 따로 바울 서신에서 서신의 말미를 나타내는 말로 쓰인다(롬 16:17-18, 19b; 고전 16:13-22; 갈 6:17; 빌 4:8-9a; 살전 5:25, 27; 몬 20-22). "형제"라는 말은 동질성과 동등성을 나타낸다.[23] 같은 믿음을 가지고 같은 신분을 가진 절친한 인간관계를 나타내는 것이다. 이 말은 초대교회 성도들 간에 자주 통용되는 칭호였다(마 23:8; 참조, 12:50).[24] 또 여자들도 포함된 말이다.[25] 바울은 고린도 교인들을 믿음의 형제들로 다정히 부르면서 그리스도를 중심으로 그들의 문제에도 불구하고 그의 사랑과 믿음으로 일치된 신앙공동체의 일원임을 상기시킨다. 바울은 고린도 교인들이 거짓사도들을 따르면서 그를 진정한 그리스도의 사도로서 의심하면서 여러 가지 죄를 짓고 있으므로, 그들을 징계하기로 계획하고 있으나(13:1-2), 그들을 여전히 믿음의 형제로 생각하고 있다. 어쩌면 바울이 이 칭호를 아직도 자신을 따르는 고린도 교인들만을 염두에 두고서 이렇게 불렀다고 볼 수도 있다. 그러나 바울이 고린도 교인들 전체를 대상으로 이렇게 불렀다고 보는 것이 더 타당하다.[26] 지금까지 바울은 고린도 교회에 대한 넘치는 사랑과 열의를 가지고 그들을 바른 믿음을 가지고 다시 자신에게 돌아오도록 권면하여 왔기 때문이다. 이러한 바울의 고린도 교회에 대한 끈질긴 사랑과 관심

---

23) Furnish, 581; Thrall, 905.

24) Deissmann, *Bible Studies*, 87, 88.

25) Barrett, *1 Corinthians*, 31; 참조, 갈 3:28; 골 4:15.

26) Furnish, 581; 112, 113.

에서, 바울은 그들이 진정한 믿음의 형제로서의 의리와 도리를 많이 상실했으나 형제라는 호칭으로 불러줌으로써 그들로 하여금 그들에 대한 바울의 신뢰와 사랑올 재확인시키고, 그들이 바울로 말미암아 믿음을 가지게 된 것을 다시 상기 시키려는 것이라고 볼 수 있다(3:2). 또 사실 바울이 고린도전서에서는 19번씩이나 고린도 교인들을 형제라고 부르지만, 고린도후서에서는 1장 8절, 8장 1절 그리고 여기에서만 그렇게 부른다. 이런 사실로 트롤은 바울이 고린도 교인들을 "형제"로 부르는 것은 소원해진 고린도 교인들에게 편지 말미에서 화해의 제스추어를 보이는 것이라고 그 의미를 약화시키고 있다.[27] 그러나 바울은 고린도 교인들에 대해 끈질긴 애정을 간직하고 있다고 생각할 때 단순한 제스추어라고만 할 수는 없다(2:4; 4:5, 7-15; 7:3; 11:2-4, 11; 12:15; 13:7). 바울이 그들을 포기하려고 했다면 벌써 했을 것이다. 이렇게 편지로 그들을 설득하는 것 자체가 그들에 대한 바울의 변함없는 애정을 증거한다. 트롤이 인정하듯이 고린도전서에서 "형제"라는 칭호가 많이 쓰인 것은 바울이 주로 윤리적 교훈을 고린도 교인들에게 직접 말하고 있기 때문이며, 고린도후서에서 형제라고 부르는 빈도가 적은 것은 바울이 주로 자신에 대한 변명을 하고 있기 때문이다.[28]

"기뻐하라"(χαίρετε)를 위에서 단순히 인사로 보는 견해가 있음을 지적했다. 실제로 사도행전 15장 23절, 야고보서 1장 1절, 빌립보서 3장 1절, 4장 4절에 같은 예가 있다. 그러나 앞의 13장 9절

27) Thrall, 906.

28) Thrall, 906.

에서 기뻐한다는 말이 나왔고, 또 다른 명령형 동사들과 함께 있으므로 문자적으로 기뻐하라는 뜻이라고 본다.[29)] 데살로니가전서 5장 16절의 "항상 기뻐하라"는 권면도 다른 여러 개의 명령형 동사들로 된 권면들 앞에 나와 있다. 그러나 이 말은 10장 이후 지금까지 바울이 말하는 엄격한 내용에 전혀 부합되지 않는 것 같다.[30)] 고린도 교인들이 기뻐할 이유가 무엇인가? 그들은 바울의 질책을 받고 일부는 징계 대상으로 지목되지 않았는가?(13:1-2). 이 말도 결국은 겉치레로 하는 마지막 인사말 인가? 그러나 "형제"라고 부르는 것이 겉 치례가 아니라 바울의 진정한 애정의 표현이라면, "기뻐하라"는 말도 같은 맥락에서 이해해야 할 것이다. 12장 9, 10절에서 바울은 그리스도의 능력이 약함 가운데 온전하게 된다는 계시의 말씀을 듣고 기뻐한다고 했다. 그리고 13장 4절 이후에 약함 중에 부활의 능력이 나타남을 말하면서 바울의 약함 가운데 그리스도의 능력이 나타날 것을 말하고 있다. 그리고 바울은 고린도 교인들이 악을 버리고 선을 행할 것과 바른 믿음을 가지고 온전케 될 것을 기도한다(12:7). 그들이 온전케 되어서 바울 자신은 아무런 권세를 쓰지 못하는 약한 사도로 인정받아도 상관없다고 말한다(13:9). 고린도 교인들이 기뻐해야할 이유는 바로 그들을 사랑하는 바울이 아직도 이렇게 그들에 대한 애정과 믿음 회복의 기대를 가지고 그들을 위해서 기쁘게 사역하며 그들의 신앙회복을 위해 기도하고 있다는 것이다. 3차 방문 까지 아직 고린도 교인들의 신앙 회복의 기회가 있는 것이다. 바울의 기도가 응답될 수 있는 여

---

29) Hughes, 486; Furnish, 581; Moule, *Idiom Book*, 161; Martin, 498.

30) Plummer, 380.

지가 있는 것이다. 믿음이 약한 고린도 교인들이 다시 재기할 수 있는 시간이 있는 것이다. 그렇게 되면 그들은 여전히 약함 중에 온전케 하시는 하나님의 은혜를 증거 할 수 있을 것이다. 그들이 결단하고 스스로 문제를 해결하면 그들은 진실로 기뻐할 수 있다.

"온전케 된다"(καταρτίζεσθε)는 위에서 지적했듯이 이 동사를 수동태로 보면 "온전케 된다"는 뜻이고, 중간태로 보면 "온전히 되기를 힘쓰라"라고 본다.[31] 그러나 개역한글성경과 같이 수동태로 변역해도 의미에 있어서 큰 차이는 없다. 많은 학자들이 이 말을 "회복한다"는 뜻으로 본다.[32] 위의 9절에서 같은 말을 주석할 때 두 가지 의미가 유사하므로 모두 수용한다고 했다. 이 경우 고린도 교인들이 9절에서 온전케 되도록 비는 바울의 기도에 의해서 회복된다(수동태)로 번역하기도 하고,[33] 스스로 온전케 되기를 힘쓴다고 보고 중간태로 번역 하기도 한다.[34]

"위로를 받으며"(παρακαλεῖσθε)라는 말도 위와 같이, 수동태로 보면, "나의 호소를 들으라"의 뜻이 되고, 중간태로 보면, "서로 격려하라"는 뜻이 된다.[35] 수동태로 보는 경우 바울의 호소에 반응을 보이라는 뜻으로 번역하기도 한다.[36] 그러나 이 말

31) Plummer, 380; Filson, 423.

32) Tasker, 190; Furnish, 581; Barrett, 341-2; Martin, 490; Thrall, 906.

33) Furnish, 581.

34) Martin, 499.

35) Barrett, 276; Martin, 499.

36) Hughes, 487; Prümm, *Diakonia Pnuematos* I, 728; Furnish, 581-2.

이 1장 6절에서는 "위로 받는다"로 번역되었으므로, 여기서도 같은 뜻으로 번역할 수 있다고 본다.[37] 그러나 "위로 받으라" 말이 1장에서는 적절한 뜻이지만, 10-13장의 엄한 내용과는 대조적인 어조가 된다. 그러나 1장에서도 환난 중에 위로받았음을 말하고 있듯이, 여기서도 고린도 교인들이 거짓 사도들로 말미암은 믿음의 시련 가운데서 바울의 말로 위로를 받으라는 뜻으로 볼 수 있다.

"마음을 같이하여"(τὸ αὐτὸ φρονεῖτε)는 12장 20절의 분열된 모습에 대해서 하나가 되기를 힘쓰라는 권면일 것이다(롬 12:16; 15:5; 빌 2:2; 4:2). 특히 그리스도 안에서 하나의 통일된 믿음을 가지도록 권면하는 것으로 본다(10:5, 6; 13:5; 참조, 엡 4:5).[38]

"평안할지어다"(εἰρηνεύετε)도 12장 20절의 분열에 대한 경고를 상기시킨다. 평화는 한 마음이 되는 결과를 가리킨다.[39] 논쟁과 분쟁이 이는 곳이면 반드시 마귀가 역사한다.[40] 바울은 고린도 교인들이 속히 분쟁을 그치고 그리스도께 온전히 복종하여 서로 화목하게 되기를 원한다(5:19-21; 10:6). 이 동사는 현재형 명령형으로서 평화를 계속 이루어 가는 것을 의미한다.

"또 사랑과 평강의 하나님이 너희와 함께 계시리라"에 대하여 이 말이 약속이냐 조건이냐에 대한 논쟁이 있다. 즉 하나님이 바울의 권면을 따르는 이들에게 사랑과 평강을 그 권면들을 성취할

---

37) Plummer, 380; Hughes, 487; Tasker, 191; Thrall, 907.

38) Hughes, 487; Tasker, 191; Martin, 499.

39) Calvin, 170; Plummer, 380.

40) Calvin, 170.

수 있도록 지원해 주신다는 것인가? 아니면 권면을 따르면, 그 결과로 사랑과 평강의 선물을 주신다는 것인가?[41] 이 문제는 결국 하나님의 은혜 대 인간의 노력이라는 펠라기우스 논쟁과 관련된다. 바레트는 약속도 되고 조건도 된다고 본다.[42] 휴즈도 하나님께서 바울의 요구를 성취할 수 있는 은혜를 주신다고 말한다.[43] 그러나 이런 은혜를 받는 것은 각 교인들이 사랑과 평화를 위한 부단한 노력의 결과라고 한다. 이런 하나님의 은혜와 인간의 노력의 갈등 문제에 대한 설명은 양자를 함께 인정하는 것이다. 그러나 하나님의 은혜(약속)가 논리상 인간의 노력(조건) 보다 앞서는 것이 당연하다. 그래서 우리는 이 말을 평강을 위한 인간의 노력을 지원한다는 약속이 아니라 은혜로 평강을 주신다는 약속으로 본다. 고린도 교인들이 바울의 권면들을 실행할 때에 사랑과 평강의 하나님의 임재를 경험하게 된다는 약속이다.[44] 사랑과 평강은 "마음을 같이 하여 평안할 지어다"라는 권면을 따를 때 주시는 것이다. 이렇게 평강을 은혜의 약속이라고 보는 것이 하나님의 축복을 말하는 전체 문맥에도 맞는다. 축복은 인간의 노력이 아니라 하나님의 은혜이기 때문이다. 마귀는 분쟁을 일으키고, 하나님은 평강을 주신다(롬 15:33; 16:20; 살전 5:23; 빌 4:9; 고전 14:33; 살후 3:16). 평화는 또한 성령의 열매이다(갈 5:22). 마귀는 또한 미움을

41) Windisch, 426; Tasker, 191; G. P. Wiles, *Paul's Intercessory Prayers: The Significance of the Intercessory Prayer Passages in the Letters of St. Paul*, SNTSMS 24 (Cambridge: University Press, 1974), 33-34.

42) Barrett, 343.

43) Hughes, 488.

44) Martin, 501; Thrall, 911.

일으키나, 하나님은 사랑을 주신다. 미움과 분쟁, 사랑과 평화는 같이 있게 마련이다. 평강은 랍비들의 편지와 헬라 편지에 모두 나타나는 마지막 인사말이다.[45] 사랑과 평강의 하나님의 임재의 약속은 우리가 부단히 사랑과 평강을 위해 노력할 때 주시는 은혜의 선물이다.

"계시리라"(ἔσται)가 기도인가 또는 축복인가에 대한 견해가 있다. 이 동사가 미래형이고 희구법이 아니지만, 바울 서신에서 미래형이 기원과 축복을 모두 나타낼 수 있다(롬 16:20a; 빌 4:19; 살전 5:24b). 또 시편 20편 9-11절(LXX)에서도 그렇게 나타난다.[46] 그러나 편지 끝에서 보다 축복의 성격이 강하다고 본다.[47] 한편, 이 축복 형식은 바울의 은혜 축복 형식과 달리 동사(ἔσται)가 있다는 것이다. 은혜 축복은 동사가 없다(13:13).

"거룩하게 입맞춤으로 서로 문안하라"(Ἀσπάσασθε ἀλλήλους ἐν ἁγίῳ φιλήματι)는 말로 바울은 계속하여 화해와 사랑의 인사말로 편지를 맺고 있는 것이다. 모든 영어 번역에서는 이 구절이 12절 상반절로 되어 있거나 12절로 되어 있다. 또 12절 하반절("모든 성도가 너희에게 문안 하느니라")이 13절로, 13절의 축도가 14절로 나눈 곳도 있다(KJV, RV, NEV, REV; 1572년 *Bishop's Bible*의 제2판에서 기원함).[48]

"거룩하게 입맞춤"은 헬라 서신들의 마지막 인사말에서 흔히

---

45) J. A. D. Weima, *Neglected Endings: The Significance of the Pauline Letter Closings*, JSNTSS 101 (Sheffield: Sheffield University, 1994), 65-66; 99.

46) Weima, 33-34.

47) Thrall, 911.

48) Furnish, 583.

발견된다.[49)]바울 서신 가운데 "거룩한 입맞춤"이 서신낭독(살전 5:26)이나, 성도의 문안인사(고전 16:20; 고후 13:12; 롬 16:16) 이전에 언급되었다. 물론 기독교적 특징은 "거룩한"이라는 형용사가 붙은 것이다. 입맞춤은 유대를 포함한 고대 중동지방과 헬라사회의 여러 정황에서 여러 가지 목적으로 행해지던 관습이다.[50)]친척과 친구 사이에 인사와 사랑과 화해의 표시로 행해졌다. 유다도 예수에게 입 맞추었다(마 26:49). 또 종교적인 집단에 입단할 때 신앙의 우의적 교제로 행해졌다. 바울이 말하는 "거룩한 입맞춤"이란 믿는 사람 상호 간에 신뢰와 존경을 나타내는 교제의 방법으로 제시된 것이다. 그러나 믿는 남, 녀 간에는 이런 인사방법이 허용되지 않은 것 같다.[51)] "거룩한 입맞춤"은 믿는 자의 성령 안에서의 교제이므로 세상 사람들의 입맞춤과 구별된다.[52)] 초대교회와 속사도교회에서 "거룩한 입맞춤"은 서신과 교제에서 뿐만이 아니라, 성찬, 세례 의식과 관련된 예배에서도 사용되었다(참조, 고전 6:20, 22; *Didache* 10:6).[53)] 교회의 이런 "거룩한 입맞춤"의 관행이 바울 서신에서 기원한 것인지 교회의 의식에서 먼저 기원한 것인지에 대해서 논쟁이 있다. 교회의 의식에서 기원하였다는 견해의 강점은 "입맞춤"이 복음 이전의 오랜 문화 관습이라는 것이다. 그러나 약점은 속사도 시대의 교부들은 이런 "입맞춤"에 대한 언급

49) Weima, 39-45, 105.

50) G. Säetlin, on φιλέω in *TDNT* IX, 119-24.

51) Hering, 103.

52) Thrall, 912.

53) H. Lietzmann, *Mass and Lord's Supper*, ETr. D. H. G. Reeve (Leiden: Brill, 1979), 186; Martin, 501-502; Thrall, 913.

을 전혀 하지 않았다는 것이다. 2세기 중엽 저스틴이 처음으로 성만찬 의식 직전에 하는 "입맞춤"의 교제에 대한 언급을 했다.[54] 동시대의 터툴리안도 기도 이후에 기도의 인증으로 "입맞춤"을 언급했다(*de Orat.* 18 [On Prayer]). 이런 시대적 공백은 속사도시대의 예배 의식에서의 입맞춤이 초대 교회의 예배 의식 전통의 계승이라기보다, 바울 서신을 근거로 후대 교회에서 시작한 것이라고 보게 하는 것이다. 다시 말하면 "거룩한 입맞춤"이 초대교회 예배 의식에서 시행되었다는 증거가 없으며, 교부시대부터 바울 서신의 언급에 따라 예배의식에서 사용되기 시작한 것으로 본다는 것이다. 그러나 바울 서신에서 이 관행이 서신낭독(살전 5:26)이나, 문안인사(고전 16:20; 고후 13:12; 롬 16:16)에 나타나고, 특히 고린도전서 16장 19-24절에는 개인적인 문안 인사 이후에 언급되고(20), 그 후 바울의 사인(21), "마라나타"("주님의 강림하심")(22), 그 다음 축복이 나타나므로 "입맞춤"의 예배 의식을 반영하는 것으로 생각할 수도 있다. 그러나 고린도전서 16장 19-24절이 초대교회에서 예배로 성도들이 모였을 때 "거룩한 입맞춤"으로 교제한 것은 증거하지만, 예배 의식에서 직접 행해졌다는 분명한 증거는 될 수 없다.[55] 결론적으로 "거룩한 입맞춤"이 초대교회에서 예배를 위해 모였을 때에 성도 간에 사랑과 존경의 표시로 행해진 것은 분명하나, 성만찬, 서신 읽은 후 등 예배 의식에서 시행된 것인지는 분명하지 않다.

---

54) Justin, *Apology*, I 65; 재인용, Windisch, 427; Stäelin, 140,

55) Thrall, 914; 그러나 Martin은 "거룩한 입맞춤"이 예배의식에서 행해졌다고 한다. Martin, 501-502, 506.

12. "모든 성도가 너희에게 문안하느니라"(Ἀσπάζονται ὑμᾶς οἱ ἅγιοι πάντες.). 이와 같은 문안 인사가 바울의 서신에 흔히 나타난다(롬 16:16, 고전 16:19, 빌 4:21; 골 4:10-15; 딛 3:15; 빌 4:21; 참조, 딤후 4:19-21). 이 말은 고린도 교회가 모든 사도적 교회의 일원임을 인식하게 하는 것이다. 그리고 그리스도를 머리로 하는 하나의 믿음을 가진 공동체임을 나타내는 것이다. 그들의 많은 문제에도 불구하고 바울은 그들을 그리스도의 몸으로 인정하고 있다는 증거이다.[56] 또한 이런 많은 성도들의 문안을 언급하는 것은 바울의 사도적 권위를 나타내는 말로 볼 수 있다. 바울은 그를 지지하고 존경하는 이들에게 싸여있는 모습을 보여 주는 것이다.[57] 본문의 "모든 성도들"은 바울이 고린도후서를 쓰는 빌립보나 그 부근 마게도냐 지방의 성도들일 것이다.[58]

13. "주 예수 그리스도의 은혜와 하나님의 사랑과 성령의 교통하심이 너희 무리와 함께 있을지어다"(Ἡ χάρις τοῦ κυρίου Ἰησοῦ Χριστοῦ καὶ ἡ ἀγάπη τοῦ θεοῦ καὶ ἡ κοινωνία τοῦ ἁγίου πνεύματος μετὰ πάντων ὑμῶν). 삼위일체 하나님으로 축도하는 양식은 바울 서신의 특징이다. 다른 초대교회 예배의식에서 이런 축도 양식이 있었다는 증거는 없다.[59] 그러나 이런 언급이 초기 삼위일체 신론이 점차 형성되는 증거로 보기도 한다.[60]

---

56) Hughes, 488; Martin, 503.

57) Weima, 339.

58) Bruce, 343; Martin, 503.

59) Plummer, 382, 383.

60) Barrett, 345; Thrall, 915.

주로 세례 양식 어귀로 쓰인 것이라는 견해도 있다.[61] 또는 하나님의 종말론적 사역에 대한 바울의 신앙고백이라는 견해도 있다.[62]

이 축복 양식과 내용이 고린도후서 초두의 문안 양식과 유사하다. 모두 하나님과 그리스도를 언급하는데, 문안 양식에서는 하나님이 그리스도 앞에 언급되고 축복 양식에서는 그리스도 다음에 언급된다. 아마도 서두에서는 창조자 되신 하나님을 먼저 언급하고 후미에서는 구원 역사의 마침이 되신 그리스도의 은혜를 강조하는 것을 복음신앙에 비추어 의미 있게 보았을 것이다.

다른 축도의 예에서는 단순히 그리스도의 은혜만을 언급하는데, 여기서는 하나님의 사랑과 성령의 교제를 모두 언급하므로 후대의 삽입으로 보기도 하지만 추정일 뿐이다.[63] 이 축도에서 그리스도가 가장 먼저 언급된 것은 바울의 복음의 중심이 그리스도이기 때문이다(롬 1:9; 15:19; 고전 9:12; 고후 4:4; 9:13; 10:14; 갈 1:7; 빌 1:27; 살전 3:2; 살후 1:8). 그리스도의 십자가로 구원의 새로운 역사가 시작되었기 때문이다.[64] 성부, 성자, 성신의 순서는 후기 교회가 삼위일체론을 형성하면서 생긴 것이다.[65] 바울은 각 삼위

61) J. Jeremias, *Jerusalem zur Zeit Jesu* (Göttingen: Vandenhoeck & Ruprecht, 1958), II, 109; Didache, 7; Justin 1 *Apology*, 46; cf. 6:2; 65:3; 67:2, 13; Irenaeus, *Epideixis*, 7; Hippolutus, *Apostolic Tradition*, esc. 21.

62) Kümmel, 214.

63) Barth, 343.

64) Strachan, 145; Denney, 358; Martin, 496.

65) Tertullian, "*trinitas*" : *de Pudicitia* 21; von Dobschütz "Zwei-und dreiliedrige Formeln," 141ff.; J. N. D. Kelly, *Early Christian Doctrines* (London: A & C. Black, 1958), 109-37; idem, *Early Christian Creeds* (London: Longman, 1960), chaps. 1-3.

에 대한 역할을, 은혜, 사랑, 교제로 나누었다. 이런 요소들이 그리스도교 신앙의 근본적 요소로 보았을 것이다. 특히 11장 4절에서 거짓 사도들이 가르치는 "다른 예수," "다른 영"은 자신이 가르치는 그리스도와 성령과는 다르다는 것을 알고 경계하였던 것이다.[66]

이 축복 기도에 대한 문제들을 몇 가지로 정리하면 다음과 같다. 첫째, 바울의 확장된 삼위일체 축복에 영향을 준 배경이 있는가? 둘째, 삼위일체 축복에서 각 삼위의 역할은 무엇인가? 셋째, 어떻게 그리고 왜 일반적으로 쓰이던 그리스도 중심 축원에 성령이 추가되어 삼위일체 축원으로 되었는가?

첫째로, 이 확장된 삼위일체 축복에 영향을 준 배경이 있는가? 빈디쉬는 이 삼위일체 축복의 양식은 1세기 당시 헬라 종교의 관심인 기도할 때 삼신(三神)을 부르던 관습이나, 1세기 유대인 학자 필로가 하나님, 지혜, 로고스를 자주 함께 언급하던 전통이 반영된 것이라고 한다.[67] 또 원래 사도적 축복 양식은 하나님과 그리스도, 또는 아버지나 아들의 양식이었는데 여기에 바울이 성령을 추가 한 것이라고 한다. 그러나 불트만이 지적하듯이, 바울이 이런 외부의 영향을 그대로 받았다면, 여기서 하나님이나 아버지를 먼저 언급했었어야 하는데, 그리스도를 먼저 언급하고 있다는 점을 고려해야 한다. 오히려 마태복음 28장 19절에 나오는 "아버지와 아들과 성령의 이름으로 세례를 주고"라는 어귀와도 삼위에 대한 언급과 유사하다. 그러나 여기서도 그 칭호와 순서가 다르다.

---

66) Martin, 497; 이 견해에 대한 Thrall의 비판을 보라(920).

67) Windisch, 429-30.

이렇게 보아서 바울의 삼위일체 축도는 초대교회의 축도의 전통을 반영하고 있으나, 특히 순서에 있어서 그리스도의 은혜를 강조하는 바울 자신의 신학이 반영되었다고 볼 수 있다.[68]

둘째로, 각 삼위의 역할의 의미는 무엇인가? 먼저, 이 양식이 축복인가 아니면, 선언인가? 삼위 하나님의 은혜와, 사랑과, 교제가 성도들과 함께 있기를 기도하는 것인가 아니면 이런 것들이 성도들이 가지고 있다는 사실, 또는 가지게 될 것이라는 사실을 말하는 것인가? 이런 질문은 있어야할 εἰμί동사("…이다"; 영어의 be 동사)가 빠져 있기 때문에 가능한 εἰμί동사의 형태를 추측하면서 생기는 질문이다. 즉 기도에 나타나는 희구법으로서 εἴη 또는 명령형으로서 ἔστω 인가 아니면, 직설법으로서 ἐστίν("있다")이거나 ἔσται("있을 것이다")인가? 만일 희구법이나 명령형이라면, 삼위 하나님의 은혜와 사랑과 교제가 성도들과 함께 있기를 기도하는 것이 되고, 직설법이라면, 이런 것들이 성도들과 함께 있다는 것, 또는 있을 것이라는 의미가 된다. 희구법에 의한 축복의 예는 로마서 15장 5, 13절, 데살로니가전서 3장 11-13절, 5장 23절에 나타난다. 명령법은 다른 헬라 서신에 나타난다.[69] 이렇게 보면 바울은 여기서 희구법이나 명령법에 의하여 축복을 하는 것이라고 볼 수 있다.

또 한 가지 다른 문법적 문제는 각 삼위의 제2격(genetive)을 주격 2격, 즉 기원(起源)의 의미로 볼 것인가 아니면 목적격 2격으로 볼 것인가의 문제다. 우선 "그리스도의 은혜"(Ἡ χάρὶ τοῦ

---

68) Thrall은 외부의 영향을 배제하고 바울이 스스로 만든 양식이라고 한다(916).

69) Weima, 83-84.

κυρίου 'Ιησοῦ Χριστοῦ)와 "하나님의 사랑"(ἡ ἀγάπη τοῦ θεοῦ)이 주격 2격으로 보는 것은 모두 동의한다. 즉 그리스도의 은혜가(주격) 우리들에게 미치는 것이고, 하나님의 사랑이(주격) 우리에게 오는 것이다. 반대로, 우리가 그리스도의 은혜를(목적격) 가지거나 하나님의 사랑을(목적격) 얻는다는 뜻과는 다른 것이다. 위로부터 오는 것이냐 아래에서 위로 향하는 것이냐의 차이는 신학적으로 크게 차이가 나는 것이다. 즉 하나님의 은혜냐 인간의 노력이냐의 구원론적 문제와도 관련되는 것이다. 그러나 세 번째 "성령의 교통하심"(ἡ κοινωνία τοῦ ἁγίου πνεύματος)을 주격 2격으로 보는데 대해서 이견이 있다. 주격 2격으로 보면 성령이 성도간의 교제를 베풀어 주신다는 뜻이다. 앞의 두 개의 구가 모두 주격 2격으로 번역했고, 또 문맥에서 분열된 고린도 교인들을 교제로 이끄시는 성령의 역할이라고 볼 때 문제가 없어 보인다.[70] 개역한글성경의 "성령의 교통하심" 이나 2001년 표준 새번역 개정판의 "성령의 사귐"은 모두 주격 2격으로 보는 번역이다(NIV). 성령이 베푸시는 성도 상호간의 교제로 본다. 그러나 이런 번역에 반대하는 이견도 있다.[71] 신약에서 "교제"(ἡ κοινωνία)란 말을 따라 나오는 2격은 모두 목적격의 의미로 성도들 상호간이 아닌 성도와 성령과의 교제를 나타나는 점이다(고전 1:9; 10:16; 빌 2:1; 3:10).[72] 또 데살로니가후서 2장 13절에서 주격 2격이 목적격 2격과 함께 나오는 경우가 있으므로("성령의[주격 2격] 거룩하게

70) Plummer, 383, 384; Bruce, 255; Tasker, 191, 192; Harris, 406; Schlatter, *Paulus*, 682; Wendland, 234; Schweitzer, *TDNT* 6:434.

71) Thrall, 919.

72) Martin, 505.

하심과 진리를[목적격 2격] 믿음으로") 여기서도 "성령의 교통하심"을 앞의 "그리스도의 은혜," "하나님의 사랑"의 주격 2격과 함께 반드시 주격 2격으로 볼 필요가 없고, 목적 2격으로 볼 수 있다는 것이다. 이렇게 "성령의 교통하심"을 목적 2격으로 볼 때에 성도들의 상호간의 교제가 아니라 성도와 성령과의 교제가 된다.[73] 의미상으로도 목적격으로 번역하여 "성령과의 교제"(the fellowship in *or* with the Holy Spirit)라고 할 때 성령 하나님과 성도들의 친밀한 관계를 나타내는 것으로 문제가 없다. 그러나 목적격으로 보고 "성령과의 교제"로 번역할 때의 가장 큰 약점은 사람이 주도가 되어 성령과 교제하는 것을 격려하는 것이 축복의 내용으로 부적절하다는 것이다. 축복의 특성은 사람에게 권면하는 것이 아니라 하나님께서 사람에게 베푸시는 것이다. 그리스도께서 성도들에게 은혜를 베푸시고, 하나님께서 사랑을 베푸시는 것이다. 그렇다면 여기서의 "성령의 교제"도 성령과의 교제를 사람들에게 권면하는 것으로 보아서는 안 되고 성령이 성도들 상호간의 교제를 베풀어 주시기를 축원하는 것으로 보는 것이 옳다.

한편, 두 번역이 문법적으로 모두 가능하다는 견해도 있다. 여기서의 2격이 이중 2격으로서 주격도 되고 목적격도 된다는 것이다.[74] 즉 성도간의 교제는 성령이 주신 것이며, 성령과의 교제라는 것이다. 그러나 문법적으로 가능하다고해서 주어진 문맥에서

---

73) Barrett, 344; Hauck, *TDNT* 3:807; Moule, *Idiom Book*, 41; Furnish, 584; Windisch, 428; Lietzmann, 214; H. Seesemann, *Der Begriff KOINONIA im Neuen Testament*, BZNW 14 (Giessen: Töpelmann, 1933), 62-72; J. Hainz, Koinonia: Kirche als Gemeinschaft bei Paulus, *BU* 16 (1979), 48; Thrall, 919.

74) Filson, 425; Denney, 386; Prümm, *Diakonia Pnümatos* I, 732.

두 가지 번역이 가능하다고 보는 것은 무리다.[75] 우리는 하나를 선택해야 한다. 우리는 위에서 말한 대로 축복의 특성을 고려하여 "성령의 교제"를 목적격 2격으로 보고 성령이 주도하시고 베푸시는 성도 상호간의 교제로 본다. 이렇게 보아서 "성령의 교통"이라고 번역하는 한글개역과 "성령의 사귐"이라는 표준 새번역, 그리고 *the fellowship of the Holy Spirit*로 번역하는 NIV를 비롯한 영어 번역본들의 번역이 옳다.

셋째로, 어떻게 그리고 왜 일반적으로 쓰던 그리스도 중심의 축원에 성령이 추가되어 삼위일체 축원으로 되었는가? 학자들은 바울은 처음에는 그리스도의 은혜만을 언급하는 축원을 쓴 것으로 본다(고전 16:23; 갈 6:18; 엡 6:24; 빌 4:23; 살전 5:28; 살후 3:18; 몬 25).[76] 그 다음에 하나님의 사랑을 언급했는데, 이것은 서신 초두에 그리스도와 하나님을 함께 말하기 때문이다. 마지막으로 성령의 교통하심이 언급되었을 것이라는 것이다.[77] 그러나 왜 본문에서 이런 종합적이고 확대된 삼위일체 축복을 했느냐가 논쟁의 초점이다. 어쩌면 플러머가 지적하듯이 분열된 교회에서 화해의 정신이 필요하다고 판단하고 성령의 교제를 언급했을 수도 있다.[78] 이와 관련하여 12절에서 "너희 모두"(πάντων ὑμῶν, 개역한글판은 "너희 무리," 2001년 표준 새번역판은 "여러분 모두")라는 말에서도 이런 화해의 의미를 엿볼 수 있을 것이다. 고린도 교회에 문제가 되는 이들도 있으나 바울은 이런 말로 그들 모두를

75) Thrall, 919.

76) Furnish, 383.

77) Thrall, 919.

78) Plummer, 383;

품으려는 의도를 보여 준다고 볼 수 있다. 마틴은 "성령의 교통"은 11장 4절의 이단적인 영을 경계하면서 한 말이라고 제안한다.[79]이런 견해는 고린도 전서에서 보듯이 고린도 교회에 영적 은사의 문제로 인해 적지 않은 논쟁이 있었다는 사실로 볼 때 타당해 보인다. 또 이런 경향을 영지주의와 관련하여 논하는 견해도 있었다.[80] 그러나 고린도전서 축복 어귀에는 그리스도만 언급되고 성령이 언급되지 않는 것은 이상하다. 트롤은 바울이 10장 16절에서 고린도 지방을 넘어 다른 이방지역으로 선교지를 확대한다고 말했고, 고린도후서를 보내고 3차 방문 시에 고린도에서 쓴 로마서 15장 22-24절에서 로마와 서바나로 간다고 말한 것으로 보아서 어차피 떠날 고린도 교회에게 공식적인 이별의 기록으로서 온전한 축복의 양식으로 삼위일체의 축원을 하였을 것이라고 한다. 그러나 이런 견해는 너무 장황한 견해라고 본다.

우리는 마틴의 견해대로 어느 교회보다 거짓 사도들이 이단적 교훈으로 바울의 복음과 사도직에 도전하는 고린도 교회에서 보다 확실한 사도적 교회로서의 인장을 찍는다는 뜻으로 삼위일체 축원을 한 것으로 본다. 너무나 많은 문제가 있고 바울의 혼자 힘으로는 다루기 어려운 고린도 교회를 능력의 삼위일체 하나님에게 맡기는 것이다. 그리고 약함 중에 나타나는 그리스도의 능력이 자신과 고린도 교회에 나타나기를 소망하며 기다리는 것이다.

---

79) Martin, 497.

80) Windisch, 328; Bultmann, 205; W. Schmithals, *Gnosticism in Corinth*, 117-285; U. Wilckens, Weisheit und Torheit (Tübingen: J. C. B. Mohr, 1959); E. Göttgemanns, Der leidende Apostel, 168; U. Wilckens, Weisheit, 218, 주, 2.

주해(13:11-13):

11-13절은 바울의 마지막 인사말이다. 다른 서신에 비해 잘 정돈된 인사말에서 바울은 고린도 교인들을 권면하고(11b), 문안하고(12), 축복한다(11b, 13).[81] 10장 이후 바울은 거의 엄한 말로 일관하였으나 마지막에서는 바울은 목회자로서 부드러운 말로 이들을 격려하고 축복하는 것이다. 이런 부드러운 말을 겉으로만 들으면 지금까지의 반대자들에 대한 경계심도 나타나지 않고 고린도 교인들의 배반으로 인한 고난의 흔적도 찾을 수 없다. 그러나 우리는 이모든 부드럽고 다정한 인사 말 속에는 지금까지 말한 바울의 고린도 교회를 향한 열정적인 사랑과 안타까운 심정이 모두 숨어 있다고 보아야 한다. 모든 강력한 책망을 끝내면서 바울은 다시 약한 자세로 "그리스도의 약함의 능력"을 믿고 그의 승리를 믿으며 그들을 축복한다. 전능하신 삼위일체 하나님께 그들을 맡기는 것이다. 고린도 교인들이 고린도후서를 보고 다시 바울에게로 돌아 왔다면, 이런 마지막 인사말에서 고린도 교인들이 사도 바울의 진정한 그리스도의 사도로서의 인내와 권위를 보고 바울에게 돌이켰을 수도 있었을 것이다. 그렇게 고린도 교인들을 질책하고서도 바울은 사사로운 감정이나 증오에 사로잡히지 않고 이들을 타이르고 문안하고 축복하는 바울에게서 그리스도의 화해의 사도로서의 모습을 발견할 수 있었을 것이다(5:19-21). 거기에는 부활 후 에 디베랴 바다에서 고기를 잡는 제자들에게 나타나셔서 책망 대신에 "와서 조반을 먹으라"고 말씀하신 예수 그리스도의 변함 없는 사랑과 축복이 조합되어 있다(요21:12).

---

81) Weima, 209.

고린도후서(한국성경주석총서)

2007년 5월 30일 초판 발행

지은이 · 강창희
발행인 · 이형자
발행처 · 도서출판 횃불
등록일 · 1992년 6월 10일 제21-355호
등록주소 · 서울시 서초구 양재동 55번지
횃불선교센타

전화 : 02-570-7030
팩스 : 02-570-7011

ISBN 978-89-5546-050-6 03230

총판 : 두란노서원
주문처 : 두란노서원 영업부 02)749-1059